THEATER

WARNING!
SPOILERS AHEAD!

NOW SHOWING

NOW SHOWING

TICKET

IN

OUT

OPEN

This book belongs to:

Rating Icon Summary

Movies are rated on a 1 to 5 scale for Fidelity to Text and Quality of Movie. An example of a movie where the weapon is used is given below. Some movies, like *And Then There Were None*, will use more than one weapon icon. In stories where no violence occurs, the icon depicts the theme.

You can find more details in the introduction.

BLUNT INSTRUMENTS

Candlestick: *Witness for the Prosecution*, 2016

Chair: Deadly when your head hits one made of marble. *King of Clubs* (1989)

Club: Including any solid weapon that doesn't have its own icon. *The ABC Murders* (1992)

Cosh: *The Mystery of the Blue Train* (2006)

Decanter: *Ordeal by Innocence* (2018)

Fireplace tongs: *The Spider's Web* (1960)

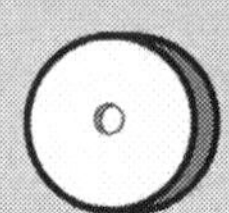

Quern: *Murder in Mesopotamia* (2002)

Statue: *The Adventure of the Italian Nobleman* (1993)

Sugar hammer: *Mrs. McGinty's Dead* (2008)

Wrench: *The Pale Horse* (1997)

CUTTING WEAPONS

Axe-hatchet job: Not a physical attack, but how the movie depicted Agatha Christie as a character. *Agatha*, (1979)

Straight razor: *Hercule Poirot's Christmas* (1995)

Corn knife: *Lord Edgware Dies* (1934)

Knife: *The Murder of Roger Ackroyd* (2000)

FALLING

Cliff: *Why Didn't They Ask Evans?* (1980)

Stairs: *Four and Twenty Blackbirds* (1989)

THRUSTING WEAPONS

Dart: *Death in the Clouds* (1992)

Hatpin: *The Sunningdale Mystery* (1983)

Javelin: *Cat Among the Pigeons* (2008)

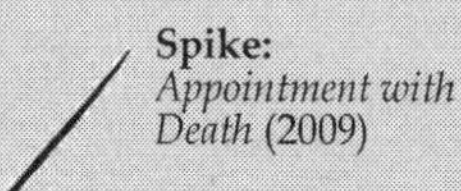

Spike: *Appointment with Death* (2009)

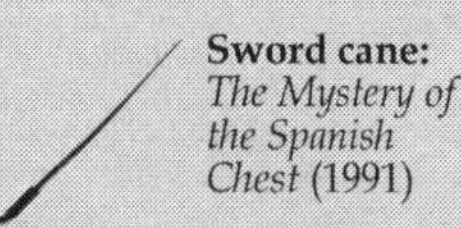

Sword cane: *The Mystery of the Spanish Chest* (1991)

POISONS

Beer: *Five Little Pigs* (2003)

Candy: *The Chocolate Box* (1993)

Cocktail: *The Mirror Crack'd* (1980)

Cocoa: *Nemesis* (2009)

Mushrooms: *Murder Is Easy* (2009)

Poison: *The Mysterious Affair at Styles* (1990)

Tea sandwich: *The House of Lurking Death* (1983)

Spray: *Murder Is Easy* (2009)

Syringe: *Promise of Death* (J-2021)

SUFFOCATING

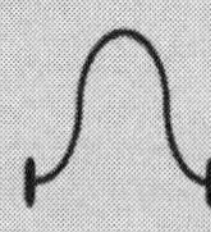

Garrote: *Nemesis* (1987)

Hanging: *Dead Man's Folly* (2013)

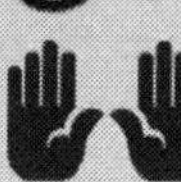

Strangling: *Murder, She Said* (1961)

OTHER WEAPONS

Auto: Struck by vehicle. *Murder Is Easy*, 1982

Bomb: Blown up through an explosion, a timed device, or tampering with a natural gas line. *After the Flood*, 2006

Cat: An obstacle tripped over or used to frighten those with a weak heart. *Murder at the Gallop* (1963)

Chess piece, electrified: *The Big Four* (2013)

Drowning: *Hallowe'en Party* (2010)

Handgun: *A Murder Is Announced* (1985)

Infrared heater: *The Big Four* (2013)

Pharoah's curse: *The Adventure of the Egyptian Tomb* (1993)

Rook rifle: *The Tragedy at Marsdon Manor* (1991).

NON-VIOLENT ICONS

Counterfeit money: *The Crackler* (1983)

Damsel in distress: *The Case of the Missing Lady* (1983)

Ghost: *The Clergyman's Daughter* (1983)

Gigolo: *The Case of the Middle-Aged Wife* (1982)

Mouse: An in-joke you'll understand if you've seen *Hickory Dickory Dock* (2008)

Ransom note: *The Adventure of Johnnie Waverly* (1989)

Spy: *The Incredible Theft* (1989)

Theft: *The Million Dollar Bond Robbery* (1991)

Treasure map: *The Case of the Discontented Soldier* (1982)

Agatha Christie,

She Watched

From left: Vanessa Redgrave in *Agatha* (1979), Fenella Woolgar in *Doctor Who: The Unicorn and the Wasp* (2008), and Ruth Bradley in *Agatha and the Truth of Murder* (2018)

BOOKS FROM PESCHEL PRESS

To keep up with our appearance schedule and new books,
visit www.peschelpress.com and sign up for our monthly newsletter,
or follow us on Instagram (https://www.instagram.com/peschel_press/).

Career Indie Author Series

Career Indie Author by Bill Peschel and Teresa Peschel
Career Indie Author Quote Book by Bill Peschel

The 223B Casebook Series, Notes and Annotations by Bill Peschel

The Best Sherlock Holmes Parodies and Pastiches: 1888-1930
Sherlock Holmes Victorian Parodies and Pastiches: 1888-1899
Sherlock Holmes Edwardian Parodies and Pastiches I: 1900-1904
Sherlock Holmes Edwardian Parodies and Pastiches II: 1905-1909
Sherlock Holmes Great War Parodies and Pastiches I: 1910-1914
Sherlock Holmes Great War Parodies and Pastiches II: 1915-1919
Sherlock Holmes Jazz Age Parodies and Pastiches I: 1920-1924
Sherlock Holmes Jazz Age Parodies and Pastiches II: 1925-1930
The Early Punch Parodies of Sherlock Holmes
The Cases of Blue Ploermell by James Thurber

Annotated Classic Mystery Novels by Bill Peschel

The Complete, Annotated Whose Body? By Dorothy L. Sayers
The Complete, Annotated Mysterious Affair at Styles By Agatha Christie
The Complete, Annotated Secret Adversary By Agatha Christie
The Complete, Annotated Murder on the Links By Agatha Christie
The Complete, Annotated Secret of Chimneys By Agatha Christie
The Complete, Annotated Man in the Brown Suit By Agatha Christie
The Complete, Annotated Murder of Roger Ackroyd By Agatha Christie

The Steppes of Mars Series by Odessa Moon

The Bride from Dairapaska
The White Elephant of Panschin
The Vanished Pearls of Orlov
Escape to HighTower

The Rugeley Poisoner Series, Notes and Annotations by Bill Peschel

The Illustrated Life and Career of William Palmer
The Times Report of the Trial of William Palmer
The Life and Career of Dr. William Palmer of Rugeley

Other Books

Fed, Safe, and Sheltered by Teresa Peschel
Sew Cloth Grocery Bags by Teresa Peschel
A Dictionary of Flowers and Gems by Skye Kingsbury
Hell's Casino by Bill Peschel
Writers Gone Wild by Bill Peschel
The Casebook of Twain and Holmes by Bill Peschel
An English Reporter in Gilded Age New York by Harry H. Marks

Agatha Christie, She Watched

One Woman's Plot
to Watch 201 Christie Adaptations
Without Murdering the Director,
Screenwriter, Cast,
or Her Husband

Teresa Peschel

Peschel Press ~ Hershey, Pa.

Visit Teresa at www.peschelpress.com
Cover design by Bill Peschel. Curtain photo: DepositPhoto. Movie and cast photos: Bill Peschel's collection.

ISBN-13: 978-1-950347-39-1
Library of Congress Control Number: 2023906190
First printing: April 2023

To the directors, writers, crew,
and casts who brought
Agatha Christie's works to the screen.
You don't just keep her alive,
you reintroduce her to new audiences.

Agatha Christie's writer characters on the screen include three versions of Ariadne Oliver — Lally Bowers in *The Case of the Discontented Soldier* (1982), Jean Stapleton in *Dead Man's Folly* (1986); and Zoë Wanamaker in *Cards on the Table* (2006) — while mystery novelist Daniel Clancy, played by Roger Heathcott, appeared in *Death in the Clouds* (1992)

People tell me, don't you care
what they've done to your book?
I tell them, they haven't done anything
to my book. It's right there on the shelf.

— James M. Cain

No writer wants to see his ox
turned into a bouillon cube.

— John le Carré

Romance writer Salome Otterbourne was played by Angela Lansbury in 1978's *Death on the Nile* and Frances de la Tour in the 2004 David Suchet version (she was transformed into a blues guitarist in the 2022 version). Miss Marple's author nephew Raymond West was played by Fumiko Orikasa in *Sleeping Murder* (2005), and Richard E. Grant in *Nemesis* (2009)

Table of Contents

Movies are listed in chronological order. Years with letters in front of them represent non-UK, US adaptations from these nations: C: China, F: France; G: Germany, I: India, J: Japan, R: Soviet Union/Russia.

Introduction

I've always been a fan of Agatha Christie, but not an obsessive one. I didn't read and reread the novels. I didn't go looking for obscure short stories. I didn't read (and still haven't) her Mary Westmacott novels. I treated her like most people did: She wrote good mysteries, and if they were handy, I read them.

Then Bill began the Complete, Annotated project by publishing Dorothy L. Sayers' *Whose Body?*, followed by Agatha's *The Mysterious Affair at Styles*. Over the years, as he annotated the next five of Agatha's early novels, I read them carefully for possible footnotes. As I did, I paid more attention to her writing, her deft plotting, her sly sense of humor, and her ability to describe a character with a few sentences.

As I became more familiar with her novels, I realized that she's underrated, probably because she was categorized as a genre writer. Some even consider her works cozies. Clearly, they never read *Appointment with Death* (1938), *And Then There Were None* (1939), or *Endless Night* (1967). I suspect that her Mary Westmacotts — which are described as romances — are anything but.

The publishing world applies labels to make it easier for bookshops to shelve their books in the store, not because they're accurate.

In July 2020, as the world began opening up from the Covid-19 shutdowns, I was at the library, looking for a DVD to borrow. I spotted *Crooked House* (2017). I liked the novel, so I thought, "Why not?"

Crooked House was the second Agatha Christie film adaptation I had seen. Sir Kenneth Branagh's *Murder on the Orient Express* (2017) was the first.

We needed fodder for the website (peschelpress.com) and I'd already been reviewing books, so I wrote a review of *Crooked House*. This reminded me that Bill was working on an annotated edition of *The Secret of Chimneys*. Was there a movie version? A review for the book would be nice. There was. It was an episode in a box set from ITV's *Marple*.

Oookaaaay.

Having become overly familiar with *Chimneys*, I knew Agatha wrote it years before Miss Marple was a twinkle in her eye. But we watched it anyway. It was terrible. Bill wrote his review for *The Complete, Annotated Secret of Chimneys*, and I wrote mine for the website.

Since the library's *Marple* DVD set included three more episodes, we watched them and I reviewed them for the website.

That's when Bill said the fateful words that brought us here: "Let's watch more Agatha films. You write the reviews. I'll post them on the website, and we'll publish them as a book."

So here we are nearly three years later. We had no idea how big the Agatha project would become or how many films have been made for cinema and TV. Bill and I have watched more than 200 adaptations. This includes all the English-language ones we could find beginning with *Adventures, Inc.* (a 1929 silent movie), and many of the foreign versions too. For those, we were limited by availability and whether or not they had English subtitles. It's criminal neglect that some of the finest Agatha Christie film adaptations in the world are from Japan, yet they're unavailable in the West.

To my knowledge, we are the only people who've watched all the films. I'm definitely the only person who's written and posted reviews for all those forgotten TV shows and kinescopes.

Along the way, I became much, much more familiar with Agatha's writing as I had to read the novels and short stories to compare them to the films. She was cutting edge from the beginning. She invented what we call The Poirot, the practice of bringing together the suspects, explaining the clues, and fingering the criminal. It was a trope born of necessity, when her first attempt — Poirot testifying at the trial — didn't fly with her publisher.

She began experimenting with narrative structure in 1924 with *The Man in the Brown Suit*. That novel has two narrators, one of them unreliable. *Brown Suit* is also a romantic thriller disguised as a mystery. Read the passage where Anne Beddingfeld administers to a mysterious, half-naked, sexy stranger's wounds. This scene could be ripped from any romance novel of today (the sweet kind, not the spicy which would include far more detail). As a side note, the 1989 TV movie is very true to the text despite being turned into a contemporary.

Agatha was an innovative writer throughout her career. Her *The Seven Dials Mystery* (1929) is a mash-up of P. G. Wodehouse and John Buchan thrillers. *Partners in Crime* (1929) is a loose cycle of 16 short stories starring Tommy and Tuppence. Each short story is also a parody of a famous mystery writer, including herself! And unlike Miss Marple and Hercule Poirot, Tommy and Tuppence aged in real time, from the young, eager lovers in *The Secret Adversary* (1922) to retired grandparents in *Postern of Fate* (1973).

And what's *And Then There Were None* (1939), in which 10 characters are dispatched in an entertaining manner for their sins, but a PG-rated slasher flick? As a sign of its influence, the basic plot has been lifted, the serial numbers filed off, and rewritten in dozens more novels and movies. *The A.B.C. Murders* (1936) is a prototypical serial killer novel.

Agatha's innovations could fill a book and go a long way to explaining why she's still read today.

The other reason is more subtle.

Whatever you can say about the quality of the adaptations (like *The Secret of Chimneys*, bleah), they keep Agatha in the public eye. Never underestimate the importance of TV shows and movies on an author's reputation. For each person who reads, 100 people go to the movies, and a 1,000 people watch TV. Every time an Agatha Christie film is shown, people who've never heard of her learn she exists. Some of them search out her books and discover how good her writing is.

When a writer dies, they can vanish under the constant tsunami of books being written and published daily. Dorothy L. Sayers is a prime example. Sayers wrote at the same time as Agatha. She's highly regarded and her books are great. But her estate, unlike Agatha's, shows no interest in licensing her stories and novels for TV or movies. Say the phrase: "Murder at *Downton Abbey*," then ask why her literary estate isn't capitalizing on Lord Peter Wimsey, detective in the peerage and a duke's brother.

The Agatha Christie estate does not want her writing to suffer that fate, so they license her short stories and novels. Some adaptations are excellent; some are dreadful. For a few, the only commonality between novel and film is the name. Most range in between but all have something to offer, even if it's only great period clothes, quality acting, or English Country House Porn. Linenfold paneling! Crenelated ceilings! Parquet floors as elaborate as the finest Persian carpet!

Excuse me while I stop and fan myself.

Watching 200+ Agatha adaptations also taught me plenty about filmmaking, pacing, and soundtracks. I can now, sometimes, recognize an actor from another adaptation. I've enjoyed seeing how one novel can be interpreted multiple ways, resulting in wildly different films. *The Pale Horse* (1961) is a good example. The three films (including Miss Marple in one!) are recognizably the same story, yet they've nothing to do with each other. The emphasis is different, the characters different, the tone is different.

I've watched 13 different Poirots (including an anime version). Seven different Marples (including an anime version). Multiple Tommy and Tuppences. Each actor or actress brings something new to the character.

The foreign films demonstrate how universal she is. She wrote about dysfunctional families, mapped the class divide, noticed the lengths we go to for status and security, and found reasons for murder ranging from money to passion to safety.

Ironically, foreign filmmakers respect Agatha more than she is at home. *Appointment with Death* (1938) has been filmed three times, but the Japanese version is the only one that captures the novel's cruelty and horror. The two English language versions fail, one moderately and one spectacularly. Of the four versions of *The Mirror Crack'd From Side to Side* (1962), only the Japanese version gives a voice to Margo Bence, one of Agatha's most abused secondary characters. The other three versions ignore her because to face Margo Bence's pain would mean admitting that the film business cares nothing for children unless they can be sold to make money.

We did not watch every single foreign TV episode even when they were readily available. There just wasn't enough time. The best we could do was see enough to convey the flavor of a given series. If you want to see them, enjoy yourself! They provide very different views of Agatha and can be rewarding.

The novel that's been adapted the most is *And Then There Were None* (1939). We saw ten versions, ranging from a blurry kinescope to slick studio productions with an all-star cast, so it merits its own chapter. Some versions hew to the stage play with its radically rewritten ending. Others stick to the novel, nihilism intact. Some combine the stage play and the novel, so Vera Claythorne learns who the puppet master was, begs for her life, and receives rough justice.

One final warning before you go: spoilers abound, so beware! Unlike Agatha, I don't play fair with my reviews and hide whodunnit. Where I play fair is in telling you what I thought of them. I liked films that critics panned, and I disliked films others loved. I say why. I go down sidetracks. I enjoyed myself and I hope you will too.

So won't you join me for an Agatha Christie Movie Marathon? You've got hundreds of hours of viewing pleasure ahead of you. Just remember to never accept a cup of tea you didn't make, or take trips to lonely islands (or châteaus, or country houses) with strangers.

How to use this book

The films are organized by the starring detective. Miss Marple comes first, followed by Poirot, and Tommy and Tuppence. Next, a chapter is devoted exclusively to *And Then There Were None*, followed by the rest of the adaptations, and the final chapter is movies in which Agatha herself is the star.

Each chapter opens with a photo gallery showing the actors and actresses who played her detectives and characters.

There's also an index, which is more important than it appears.

Seems logical, yes? Except that some adaptations removed Agatha's chosen detective, turning the novel into a police procedural. When that happens, the movie is not included in the detective's chapter. It's included in "The Rest of the Christies". Many of the foreign adaptations fall into this category.

Other adaptations (cough, ITV's *Marple*, cough) insert a detective who didn't exist in the novel. That's why many standalone novels appear in the Miss Marple chapter. She's now the star of *The Sittaford Mystery, Murder Is Easy, The Pale Horse*, and others. She also appears in a Tommy and Tuppence novel, *By the Pricking of My Thumbs*. Similarly, Margaret Rutherford snatched two Poirot novels and made them her own, so they appear in the Miss Marple chapter.

The chapters dedicated to *And Then There Were None* and the movies not part of a detective series are self-evident. "Agatha the Star," however, deserves an explanation. In addition to her stories, Agatha's life has become fodder for Hollywood. This includes the dreadful Vanessa Redgrave/Dustin Hoffman biopic *Agatha* (1979), a documentary that quotes from her and her work, a *Doctor Who* episode, and three movies that show Agatha's exciting life investigating mysteries in a parallel universe. It focuses on Agatha, not her writing. Any relationship to Agatha's real life should be considered coincidental. Even the documentary in this chapter is not entirely reliable.

Within each chapter, the films are organized chronologically. As you move forward in time, you'll see changes in how a character was depicted and movie-making styles. *Adventures, Inc.* (1929) sets the stage. It's the earliest Agatha film and the scriptwriter, Jane Bess, played fast and loose with the text. She led the way for hack screenwriters everywhere to rewrite Agatha's prose.

Each review gets two pages. We chose a banner image and six photos of important cast members. I rate films by fidelity to text (or life in "Agatha the Star," and either the play or the novel in *And Then There Were None*) and by the quality of the movie overall. The two ratings are separate, but they complement each other and give you a clearer understanding of what to expect.

The cast lists place detectives and police at the top. Everyone else follows in rough order of importance. We group families together to make it easier to work out relationships. Our cast lists are not comprehensive but the main characters are there.

Also note that for those foreign films which don't name their characters from the novel, we provide that information. This was omitted when they rewrote them so much (such as *Unknown* (1965), the Indian version of *And Then There Were None*) that it would not be helpful.

At the end of the list come the film locations, or (in a couple episodes) a song list. Internet Movie Database and Agatha Christie Wiki provided most of the locations, but Bill added to that from other sources (see the bibliography). Knowing the film locations means you, dear reader, can visit the same castle as Poirot or Miss Marple.

Subtitles matter to me. We always looked for versions with subtitles as so many actors mumble or the sound quality is bad. If I can't understand the dialog, I miss important points. Not every DVD was released with subtitles.

Fortunately, some of the older films like the Joan Hickson *Miss Marples* are being cleaned up for streaming. They get subtitles. But they aren't being released as new DVDs so, no subtitles. If you can watch a streamed version, no problem. If you must use your TV and DVD player, you're out of luck.

We had to have subtitles for the foreign films. We couldn't see some films we wanted to (we especially regret passing up the Japanese *Murder on the Orient Express*) because they either weren't available with subtitles or they weren't available at all.

The index will help you find a specific film. This isn't just because some novels got Miss Marple inserted, putting them into the Miss Marple chapter. Agatha's novels were often released under different names. For example, the novel *Lord Edgware Dies* (1933) was released in the U.S. as *Thirteen At Dinner*. It's been filmed three times, twice as *Lord Edgware Dies* and once as *Thirteen At Dinner*. But they're all based on the same novel and the index connects them.

I list all the names, with a note as to which film it applies to. Or, as with Margaret Rutherford, the film's name doesn't correspond to any edition of the novel but I tell you what to look for.

The bibliography provides further reading and shows where some of my information came from.

Enjoy the book. We enjoyed watching the movies, podcasting about many of them, and writing the reviews. We want it to be used, encouraging you to watch Agatha Christie on the screen, always different but always her.

How the movies are rated

Each movie is given two ratings. *Fidelity of text* is exactly what it sounds. How close is the film to the original text? Sometimes, only the names match. Other films are so faithful, they're lifeless.

Quality of movie is about the movie itself. Did everything together work as a film? Often, a very good movie isn't faithful to the text at all (see Miss Marple in *Ordeal By Innocence* (2007)). If something jars about the movie, I'll indicate it here.

The rating icons demonstrate Agatha's many, many ways of killing. Blunt objects, poisoned cocktails, garrotes, knives, guns, stranglers, being pushed down a flight of stairs. They usually reflect the first murder in the film.

A few films, such as *And Then There Were None*, get five different symbols to reflect all the ways those nasty people got iced.

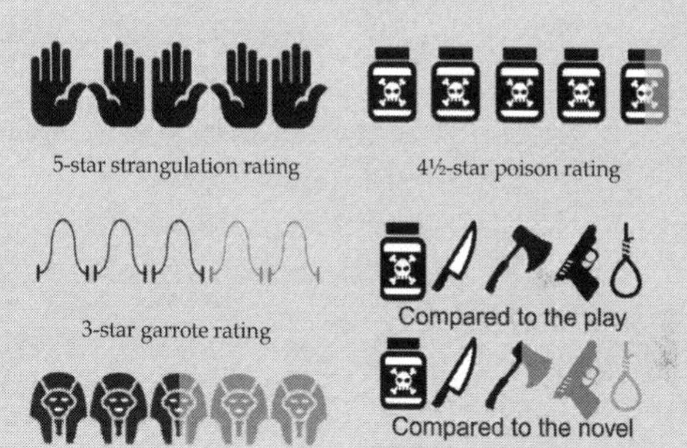

How to find the movies

We watched the vast majority of the films on DVD on our TV set, the one our neighbors were throwing away. You're correct that we count our pennies.

That's why we use our public library. If yours is like ours, it contains a surprisingly large collection of Agatha Christie films. All you have to do is get a library card to borrow them.

You may, like us, have access to more than one library. It's worth learning what's available in your area. We belong to our local library (the Hershey Public Library) and to our county library (the much larger Dauphin County Public Library). They often carry different titles so I always check both before moving on to the next step.

Your library is bigger than your municipality, your county, or even your state. Ask for the interlibrary loan librarian. For us, it's Denise Philips. Denise got us all kinds of DVDs from libraries across the country. This service is usually free, as libraries are tax-supported. Ask and you may be very pleased. The interlibrary loan may take a few weeks for the requested movie to arrive, but it nearly always will.

If Denise could not get us a title, Bill would search eBay and Amazon. We bought a universal DVD player so we could play DVDs from Europe.

There were obscure kinescopes that were on YouTube, so we watched them on the computer.

There are streaming services, including Amazon which gave us access to Britbox. Dailymotion let us watch the Japanese films.

We don't recommend skeevy pirate sites. They're illegal, don't pay royalties to the creators, and whatever you get will be loaded with viruses and malware and the film may be incomplete or damaged.

I. Miss Marple

Miss Jane Marple was born Caroline Sheppard in *The Murder of Roger Ackroyd* (1926). Recalling the aunts and grandmothers she knew as a child, Agatha created a smart, inquisitive, and imaginative middle-aged spinster who knew everyone in the village. Caroline could make great leaps of intuition. She was often wrong, but never in doubt. But beneath her brusque exterior, she cared deeply.

The next year, Agatha wrote "The Tuesday Night Club" in 1927 and Jane Marple became a tribute to all the ignored old ladies she knew and loved.

The first Miss Marple, Margaret Rutherford, was in her late 60s when she played the role, but subsequent actresses ranged widely in age. At 54, Angela Lansbury looked too youthful and full of beans, and you keep seeing Jessica Fletcher of *Murder, She Wrote* fame. Helen Hayes and Joan Hickson reached their late 80s when they made their last Agatha film appearance.

But no matter what age, the flock of Marples share a dogged desire to know the truth. Knitting in hand, she'll talk to anyone and everyone until she grasps the thread that unravels the snarl of lies. She can be brisk, efficient, dithery, batty, or easily flustered. Sometimes, she uses her age as a disguise to conceal a sharp intellect. She even gains the respect of the local law, partly because she doesn't want the credit.

From left: Angela Lansbury in *The Mirror Crack'd* (1980), Helen Hayes in *Murder With Mirrors* (1985), and Kaoru Yachigusa in *Sleeping Murder* (J-2005)

Geraldine McEwan with Timothy Dalton in *The Sittaford Mystery* (2006)

Joan Hickson in *The Moving Finger* (1985)

Margaret Rutherford in *Murder at the Gallop* (1963)

Julia McKenzie, left, with Joanna Lumley in *The Mirror Crack'd from Side to Side* (2010)

"A policeman asking questions is open to the gravest suspicion. But an old lady asking questions, is just an old lady asking questions." Possessing "a mind like a bacon slicer," Miss Marple is underestimated by everyone until it is too late … for the murderer.

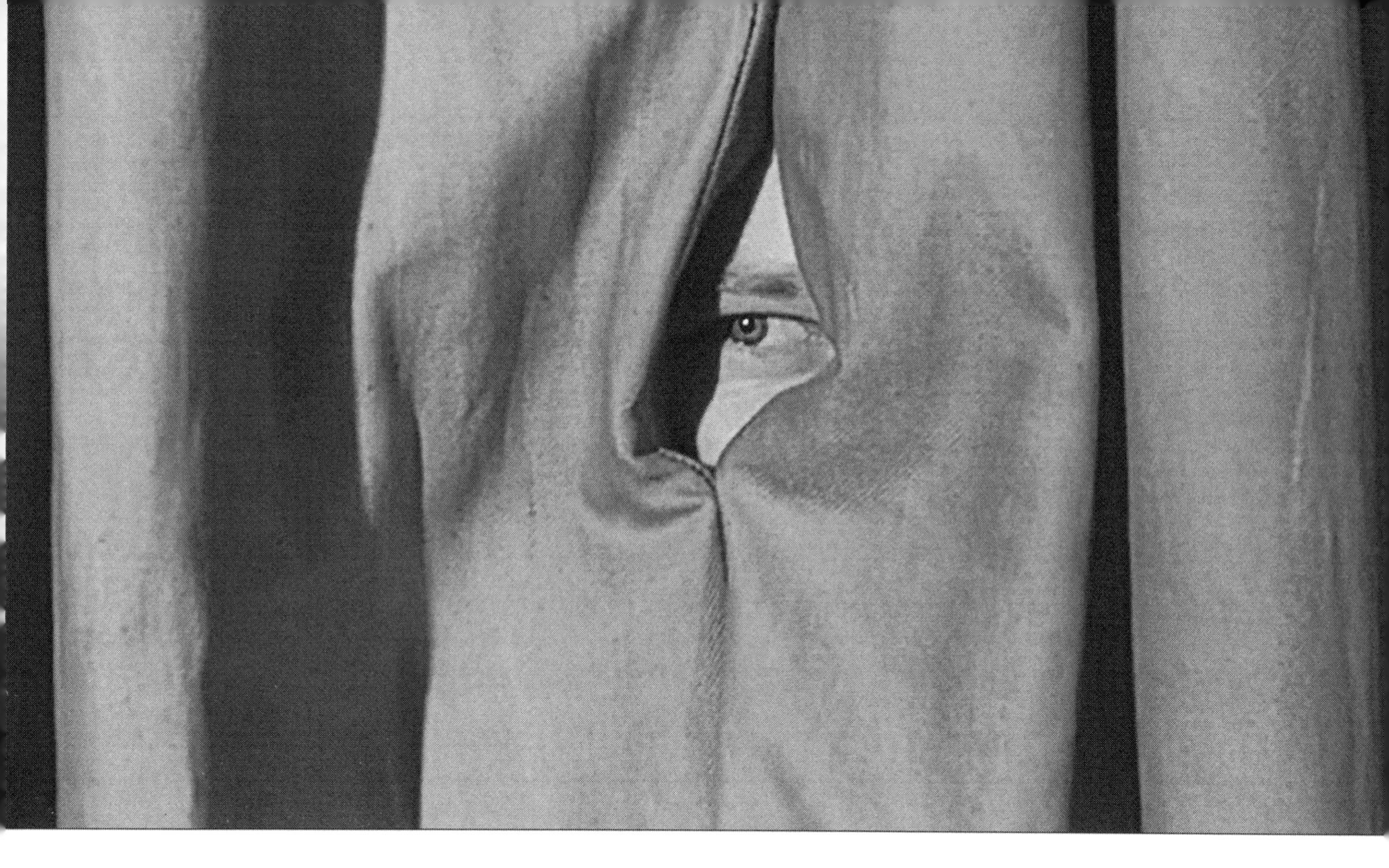

Murder, She Said (1961)

Miss Marple's an energetic, no-nonsense spinster who goes undercover to solve a mysterious woman's death on a train

You know you're in for something completely different the minute the music starts to play. It's a bright, bouncy, harpsichord and violin score, wildly at odds with the British railway system or Agatha Christie murder mysteries. Yet there it is, accompanying a formidable old lady as she settles into the train compartment for the ride home. She passes the time by reading a tawdry murder mystery when she isn't watching the passengers on a train gliding alongside her own.

Then, the shade snaps up and our formidable old lady witnesses a man strangling a blonde. But not like the movie poster implies; this blonde's slip is concealed by her clothing.

Then the film diverges from the source material. The formidable old lady is not Elspeth McGillicuddy. It's Miss Marple herself who witnesses the crime. Since she does the sleuthing, there's no need for Lucy Eyelesbarrow, the novel's other important character. She disappears and Miss Marple puts on cap, apron, and uniform and gets hired at Ackenthorpe Hall as the new maid.

But first, listen closely to Miss Marple's conversation with the clerk at the servants' employment agency. At first, the clerk thinks she is looking for a maid for her household. Once he learns differently, his entire attitude changes from dismissive to obsequious. The scene is a witty parody of how desperate the upper class was to hire someone, anyone, to clean up after them and what they were willing to pay.

Fidelity to text

The film closely follows the murder plot in *The 4.50 From Paddington* but changes everything else. Several major characters are dispensed with while a new one is added: Mr. Stringer, librarian/accomplice (played by Margaret Rutherford's real-life husband, Stringer Davis).

Quality of movie

If you can overlook how the scriptwriter played fast and loose with Agatha's characterization of Miss Marple, you'll love this film. It's fast-paced and funny, has real moments of suspense, and you get to see two Miss Marples at once!

Once at Ackenthorpe Hall, a character you expect from the novel pops up: Alexander. He's a sharp lad who gives as good as he gets. He's also bored, since his friend from the novel, James, was written out of the story and his father, Brian Eastley, also lost most of his scenes. Alexander spars with Miss Marple and plans to get rid of her, like he got rid of other servants. But she's onto him and turns him into an unreliable ally.

Because James got written out of the plot, so did his family, including the mysterious Martine connection. Retained, however, is Mr. Ackenthorpe's daughter Emma, along with her three brothers: Albert, Harold, and Cedric. They remain true to form and two of the

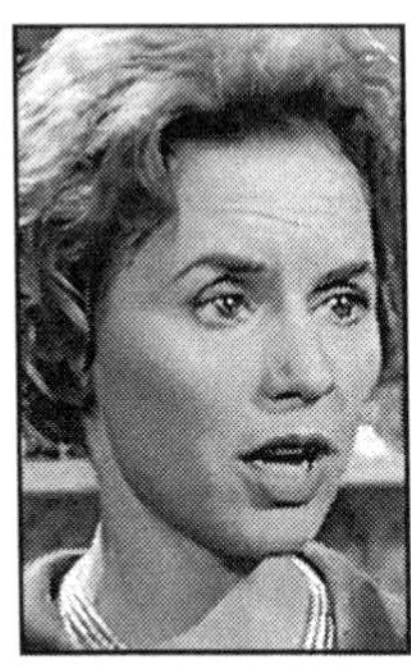

Emma Ackenthorpe (*Muriel Pavlow*), the trapped ingenue

Dr. Paul Quimper (*Arthur Kennedy*), the dedicated beau

Cedric Ackenthorpe (*Thorley Walters*), the sleazey artist

Alexander Eastley (*Ronnie Raymond*), the incorrigible scamp

Jim Stringer (*Stringer Davis*), the loyal Watson

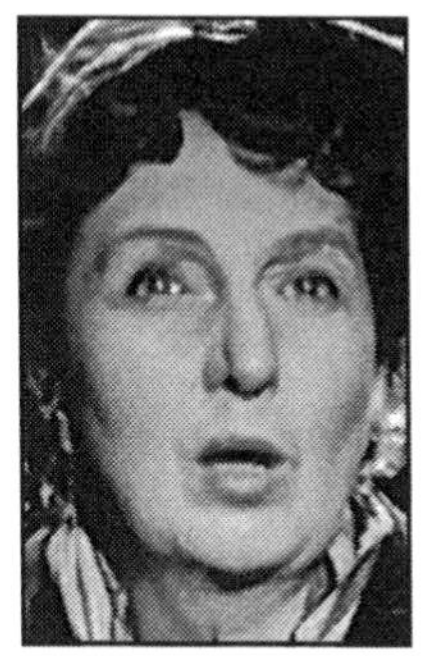

Mrs. Kidder (*Joan Hickson*), the acidic maid

three are murdered. Albert dies of poisoning (as in the book) whereas Harold dies of a supposed suicide by shotgun (a la the Joan Hickson adaptation; it was poison in the novel). Cedric, the louche painter, survives. So does Brian Eastley, Alexander's father. Cedric gets more to do than Brian Eastley does. Dr. Quimper is also present to treat the survivors and court Emma.

Two servants are present: Hillman the gardener and Mrs. Kidder, the village char. Hillman gets a major rewrite, turning him into a more sinister figure. Mr. Ackenthorpe relies on him for both obvious and nefarious but implied reasons. Those reasons are never clarified, an omission that the scriptwriter could have done something interesting with. Mrs. Kidder is played by our own Joan Hickson. It's odd and amusing to see her facing off with Margaret Rutherford; two Miss Marples at different stages in their lives.

Since Miss Marple is the new maid and housekeeper, she's the one who goes golfing and discovers the body in the barn. Not wanting to blow her cover, she gets her accomplice, Mr. Stringer, to call the police.

Inspector Craddock is very surprised when he arrives at Ackenthorpe Hall to discover the dotty old spinster who reported the murder on the train is proved right. And worse, she's on the spot, working undercover to find the killer. No matter who plays Miss Marple, one trope holds true: Her relationship with the local constabulary can be fraught for her and entertaining for us.

Finally, Miss Marple takes matters in her hands. She has the musical compact, discovered earlier in the barn, stolen and then returned by Alexander. It's the key to the killer who recognizes its song, *Frère Jacques*.

Unlike the novel or the other adaptations, this film doesn't provide any motive or backstory for the murders, other than a desire to inherit more of the Ackenthorpe estate. Every bit of complexity is removed, and you're left wondering how Miss Marple is going to solve the murder. Unlike the other two versions, she does it without a trap involving fish paste sandwiches. Instead, she has Alexander play with the compact in front of the suspects, then take it back to her room.

General Information

Based on: *4.50 from Paddington / What Mrs. McGillicuddy Saw* in U.S. (novel, 1957)
Run time: 1 hr., 27 min. **Subtitles:** Yes

Writers: David D. Osborn (adaptation), David Pursall, Jack Seddon
Director: George Pollock

Cast

Margaret Rutherford as Miss Marple
Stringer Davis as Jim Stringer
Charles "Bud" Tingwell as Inspector Craddock
Gordon Harris as Sergeant Bacon

Muriel Pavlow as Emma Ackenthorpe
James Robertson Justice as Luther Ackenthorpe
Thorley Walters as Cedric Ackenthorpe
Conrad Phillips as Harold Ackenthorpe
Gerald Cross as Albert Ackenthorpe
Arthur Kennedy as Dr. Paul Quimper
Ronald Howard as Brian Eastley
Ronnie Raymond as Alexander Eastley
Joan Hickson as Mrs. Kidder
Michael Golden as Hillman
Barbara Leake as Mrs. Helen Stainton
Richard Briers as "Mrs. Binster"
Lucy Griffiths as Lucy
Olive Gregg as Alexander (voice)

Film Locations

Euston Station, London (Paddington Station)
Misbourne Cottage, Denham, Buckinghamshire (Miss Marple's home)
Denham (Miss Marple and Stringer walk along the railway line)
Gerrard's Cross, Buckinghamshire (rail embankment)
Amerden Lane, Taplow, Buckinghamshire (Ackenthorpe Hall entrance gates and road under railway bridge)
Radnor Hall, Elstree, Hertfordshire (Ackenthorpe Hall)

In due course, Dr. Quimper arrives. After some byplay where Miss Marple confirms his identity, he tries to murder her too, only to be stopped by the police. It was a great scene, full of sharp dialog and suspense.

Sadly, the movie ends shortly thereafter. Much too shortly. We never see Emma again so we never see her reaction to discovering that Dr. Quimper murdered some strange woman plus two of her brothers. We're also not given a reason why Dr. Quimper murdered the woman on the train. We must assume it's for the same reason as in the novel: She was his Catholic wife who wouldn't give him a divorce so he could marry Emma. The reason for the other deaths is the usual one. Emma would be a much richer woman if the Ackenthorpe estate didn't get divvied up among the five heirs.

Even with the inadequate ending, there's plenty to love about this adaptation. There are little shoutouts to the novel here and there. Miss Marple's maid is named Lucy, possibly after Lucy Eyelesbarrow. Miss Marple deduces, based on the dead woman's hands, that she's not Martine, a Normandy peasant. It isn't spelled out that her hands are soft and clean, well-manicured, and unacquainted with scrub-brushes and mops, but that's the implication when they show the camera moving up her body and stopping at her hands. In the novel, it's the condition of the dead woman's feet, beaten up from years of ballet, that helps identify her.

Then there's Dame Margaret Rutherford, whose performance polarizes Miss Marple fans. Agatha didn't like her portrayal. You either enjoy her unique spin on Agatha's spinster sleuth or retreat to your collection of Joan Hickson DVDs. Margaret is pushy, bossy, obstinate, plus-size, very funny, and far more of an action girl than any other Miss Marple. Julia McKenzie's interpretation probably comes closest to Rutherford's but she's not nearly as full of beans.

Murder She Said is a lively, comic, well-acted and well-paced movie. As long as you don't insist on a faithful adaptation of the novel or the standard interpretation of Miss Marple, you'll have fun.

Murder at the Gallop (1963)

With Miss Marple back in the saddle, a combo hotel and riding academy becomes the home for fatal horseplay

After the Funeral (*Funerals Are Fatal* in the U.S. editions) was a Hercule Poirot novel published in 1953. It is outstanding, one of Agatha's best, and would have made a terrific film. This version isn't it.

Even though the scriptwriter slashed apart the novel, you need to be familiar with the storyline in order to follow the film's plot. Too much material was skipped or glided over. Motivations in particular were decidedly unclear, other than greed. That one's easy, but it's not the motivation for murder in the novel, and it's not the motivation here either. Sort of, but again, it's hard to tell. The script was that muddy.

Murder at the Gallop was one of the many reasons why Agatha Christie became so reluctant to agree to more movie or television contracts. Hollywood took a perfectly good plot involving Poirot and reworked it into an almost unrecognizable Margaret Rutherford vehicle. Metro-Goldwyn-Mayer owned the rights and they galloped into the sunset with them.

I know the James M. Cain quote about how Hollywood doesn't ruin books: the book is still up there on the shelf. That's true, but let's be honest. For every person who reads a novel, one hundred people watch a movie. How many of them read the novel a movie is based on? Quite a few, based on the paperbacks I see at the grocery store book rack with an image from the film as the new cover. Then comes the more important question. How many of those readers are aghast when they read the original story? It's not like the movie at all! If they preferred the movie (which does happen because some movies are far better than their source novel) they'll never pick up another book by the author again.

Or worse, they'll have a completely wrong interpretation of what Author writes. If Movie Viewer never again reads a book by Author, Author loses. The Hollywood money was nice, sometimes very nice, but Author lost a potential reader along with Reader's book-loving friends. That's the effect *Murder at the Gallop* would have. You can see the original story

Fidelity to text

Yes, cats. A cat serves as the first murder weapon followed by a hatpin in this extremely loose interpretation of *After the Funeral*, a Hercule Poirot novel. What's that you shrieked? Margaret Rutherford is portraying Miss Marple in a Poirot novel!? Yes, and that's just the beginning.

Quality of movie

It should have been better. Margaret Rutherford is always fun to watch, she's got great costars, and the original story is complex and satisfying. Too bad the film didn't hold together. The scriptwriter cut out everything that explained motivation while adding plenty of loose ends that never got tied up.

Hector Enderby (*Robert Morley*), the nephew

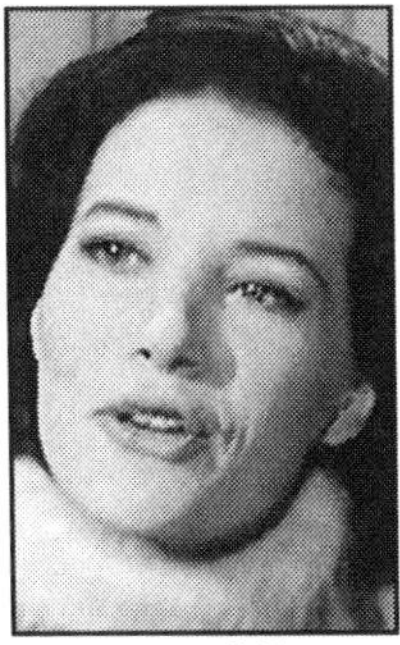
Rosamund Shane (*Katya Douglas*), the niece

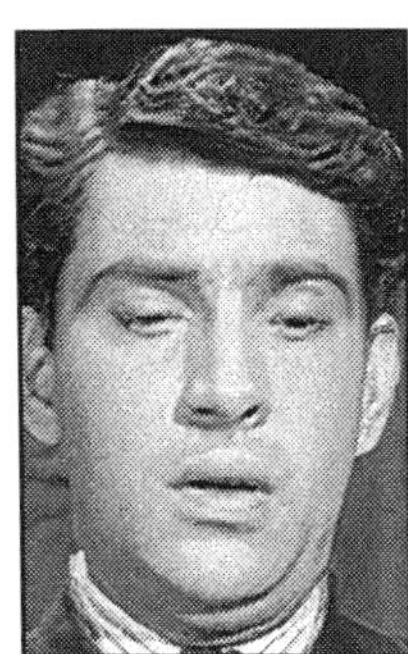
Michael Shane (*James Villiers*), her husband

George Crossfield (*Robert Urquhart*), the cousin

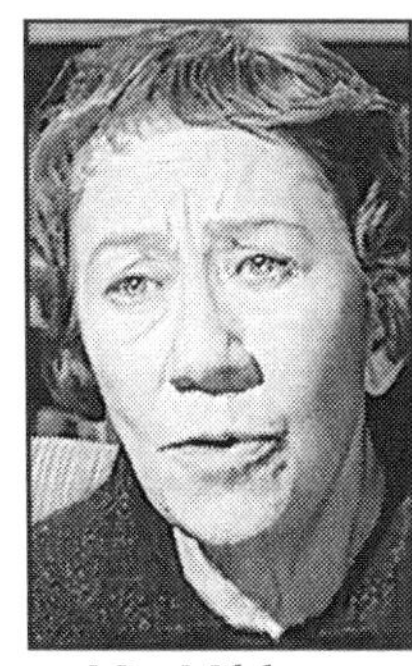
Miss Milchrest (*Flora Robson*), the mousy companion

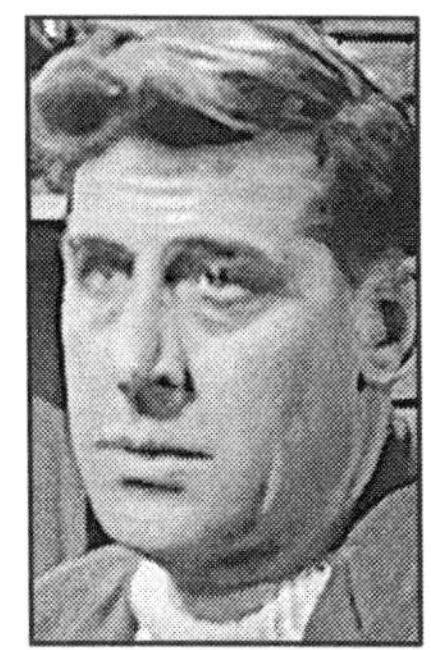
Hillman (*Duncan Lamont*), the miffed stableman

writhing underneath, trying to break free and failing, and confusing potential readers.

So if you blank out memories of Hercule Poirot and tea shops does the movie work? Mostly, it does. It opens with a bang. Miss Marple and Mr. Stringer are soliciting door-to-door for a criminal rehabilitation charity. They come darn close to breaking into the Enderby mansion looking for donations. But they manage, and witness terrified, elderly, reclusive and rich Mr. Enderby stagger to the top of the stairs and fall down them.

Enderby is pathologically afraid of cats. He'd never permit one in his house. It's a tidy method for murdering an old man: scare him into a heart attack, he'll die, and no one suspects the cat hiding under the bed. The murderer won't be anywhere near the place when the crime happens. All he had to do was slip the cat inside the house and wait.

Miss Marple notifies the police. Inspector Craddock ignores her. She and Mr. Stringer listen in on the reading of the will (an amusing scene; make sure you pay attention to how the bequests were written so you can modify your will accordingly) and then they hear sister Cora, heavily veiled and estranged from the family, ask if Enderby was murdered.

Miss Marple, taking the law into her own hands like always, visits Cora to investigate and discovers her dead, with another cat in her lap. Cora was murdered with a hatpin. If you've never seen one, a hatpin is sharp-tipped and as long as a knitting needle. You can do serious damage to a masher with a hatpin and ladies did just that back in ye olden days. But even so, killing someone with one was harder. You'd have to go through the eye or ear into the brain, not some random place in the ribs.

Cora's companion, the timid and mousy Miss Milchrest, is aghast. She's also no help.

The action moves to Hector Enderby's conveniently nearby hotel for equestrians. Miss Marple checks in and sleuths around. She is unable to prevent another murder. The method is also strange: a victim is trapped in a horse's stall and the animal tramples him, terrified by a car's racing engine outside, its accelerator pressed down by a boulder. Again, very tidy and hands-free for the cautious murderer, as long as no one sees them driving the car and abandoning it in the stable yard.

General Information

Based on: *After the Funeral / Funerals Are Fatal* in U.S. (novel, 1953)
Run time: 1 hr., 21 min. **Subtitles:** Yes

Writer: James P. Cavanagh
Director: George Pollock

Cast

Margaret Rutherford as Miss Marple
Stringer Davis as Mr. Stringer
Charles "Bud" Tingwell as Inspector Craddock
Gordon Harris as Sergeant Bacon

Robert Morley as Hector Enderby
Robert Urquhart as George Crossfield
Katya Douglas as Rosamund Shane
James Villiers as Michael Shane
Flora Robson as Miss Milchrest
Finlay Currie as Old Enderby
Duncan Lamont as Hillman
Noel Howlett as Mr. Trundell
Kevin Stoney as Dr. Markwell
Frank Atkinson as Hotel Night Porter
Fred Griffiths as Fred the Deliveryman
Roger Avon as Forensic Photographer
Guy Standeven as Forensic Photographer
Tony Castleton as Hotel Guest

Film Locations

Village Road, Denham, Buckinghamshire (opening titles)
Church of St. John The Baptist, Little Marlow, Buckinghamshire (opening titles)
Hilfield Castle Bushey Heath, Hertfordshire (Old Enderby's house)
Piers Place, Amersham, Buckinghamshire (Milchester police station)
High Street, Amersham
The Kings Arms, Amersham (will reading)
Misbourne Cottage, Denham (Miss Marple's home)
Corners Cottage, Little Marlow, Buckinghamshire (Cora Lansquenet's home)
Church Farm, Aldenham, Hertfordshire (The Gallop Hotel)
Winchbottom Farm, Little Marlow (sports car roaring by horses)

Eventually Miss Marple solves the murders but how is a darned good question. We never watch her making logical deductions from clues the audience could pick up on. Nor does she prove whydunnit. There's the mysterious painting, supposedly worth £50,000. This is separate from the £25,000 each of the heirs will receive. That's a lot of money but I wasn't sure why the murderer cared. I understood why the rest of the family cared, even the ones who wanted the painting only to hang on their wall.

The novel has a rational and sad motivation for the crime; not one bit made it into the film unless you count Hector Enderby wanting to keep his hotel going. Compared to the novel, the movie's ending did not make sense. Mysteries are supposed to be solvable by the reader or audience. The clues uncovered by the detective should be equally available to the audience. Not here.

That's not to say the film is bad. The acting is great. Robert Morley in particular has a wonderful time, although how he got thrown from his fractious horse without breaking every bone in his body is another good question. There are wonderful set pieces, from Miss Marple climbing up stacks of barrels to spy on legal proceedings to her dancing the twist and faking a heart attack to unmask the villain. You even hear of a non-existent Agatha Christie: Miss Marple is reading *The Ninth Life*. She recommends to Inspector Craddock that Christie novels should be required reading for policemen.

You'll probably enjoy *Murder at the Gallop*, as long as you pretend it has nothing to do with Agatha's novel. But only once. The second time around, you won't be able to ignore the plot holes big enough to ride a horse through.

Murder Most Foul (1964)

Miss Marple steps to the footlights to join a backwater acting troupe as an old sin leaves a woman hanging

We open with one of the few surviving bits from *Mrs. McGinty's Dead.* A hapless lodger is arrested. He murdered his landlady after stealing her savings. By the time the hanging judge gives a masterly summation against the defendant, everyone knows the verdict will be guilty.

Except Miss Marple is on the jury, and she knows he's innocent. The case is declared a mistrial, giving Miss Marple time to prove that someone else murdered the landlady, ex-actress, barmaid, and good-time girl known as Mrs. McGinty. Her own sister calls her a slut so you know she was no good.

Yes, Mrs. McGinty had a checkered past, and Miss Marple a checkered present, when we see her trouncing the constable several times at the game. Are they connected? It's possible the scriptwriter is making a subtle joke in multiple directions. The Margaret Rutherford Miss Marple series refers to her dramatic past as a championship golfer (*Murder, She Said*), equestrienne (*Murder at the Gallop*), and here, lady's pistol champion. Why not also the local checkers champion?

As further proof of her extensive talents, after she deduces that the solution to the murder lies with the Cosgood Players, she auditions for them with a fiery rendition of Robert W. Service's (1874-1958) great narrative poem, "The Shooting of Dan McGrew."

Fidelity to text

The film is based on a Hercule Poirot novel, *Mrs. McGinty's Dead*. Miss Marple takes over, Poirot's gone, Ariadne Oliver is gone, everyone else is gone, and virtually all of the plot is gone.

Quality of movie

Nonetheless, it works and quite well too. Margaret Rutherford is a force to be reckoned with, and she gets a much better script than in *Murder at the Gallop*. She shines and so does the rest of the cast.

Margaret Rutherford's Miss Marple is a true renaissance woman, although her past is not as checkered as Mrs. McGinty's.

More inside jokes are hiding in the dialog. It's laced with Shakespearean references, the most obvious being the title, followed by the reference to a Rose by any other name. Pay attention for more literary references: a play called *Murder, She Said*, supposedly written by Agatha, and Cosgood claiming his play will run longer than *The Mousetrap*.

Ron Moody is worth singling out. He plays Driffold Cosgood, a would-be playwright, theater impresario, and ham actor. He's trying his best to keep his little troupe going while dealing with murder. Watch him complain to Inspector Craddock when he postpones their performance merely because one of his actors is poisoned! Then one of his actresses

H. Driffold Cosgood (*Ron Moody*), the troupe's director

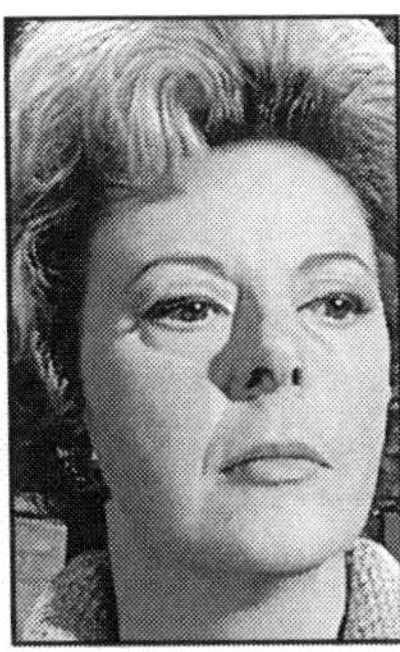
Maureen Summers (*Pauline Jameson*), the scorned wife

Ralph Summers (Ralph Michael), the philanderer

Bill Hanson (*James Bolam*), the ambitious lad

Sheila Upward (*Francesca Annis*), the posh fiancée

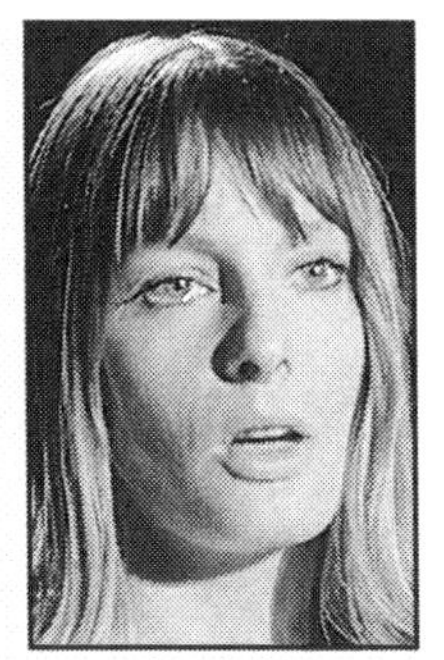
Eva McGonigall (*Alison Seebohm*), the would-be psychic

dies, leaving him even more short-handed. But the show must go on and lurid stories about murder make for boffo box office receipts. Or so he hopes. That's also why he suddenly changed his mind about accepting Miss Marple into his theater troupe. It's not her stalwart rendition of "Dan McGrew." It's that she's a single lady of independent means which implies plenty of money for his theater and no annoying husband checking up on her spending.

It's always amusing to watch a film involving the theater because the actors playing actors get to ham it up in ways they'd never be allowed to do otherwise. Don't miss our weird, witchy sleepwalking actress, Eva (Alison Seebohm). She knows something is wrong and tells everyone all about it. Or does she just want attention? Then there's Arthur (Neil Stacy), who goes out of his way to make rude remarks about his rival leading man in the heartthrob division, Bill (James Bolam). Arthur's got reason to be jealous of Bill and not merely because they compete for roles.

Bill is Sheila's fiancé. Sheila Upward (Francesca Annis) is not just another ingenue. She's an heiress! Sheila is sure that daddy won't be upset when she marries a third-rate actor in a fourth-rate touring theater company. She doesn't see anything odd about Bill's unusual intensity or how he tries to strangle Arthur and then pass it off as a joke. That's just Bill being amusing.

There's also Cosgood's mysterious play called *Remember September*. Miss Marple deciphers a clue leading to the play's opening night in 1951. She joins the troupe and moves into their boarding house, where the script is left on her pillow. She reads it and is unimpressed. The play was performed only once, and it was so bad that it was booed offstage by the audience halfway through the second act. This is also the play Mrs. McGinty starred in, long ago on that terrible opening night.

That terrible night, full of terrible actors, also turned into terrible tragedy, although the tragedy was presumably unrelated to the play. One of the actresses on that long ago opening night, Rose Kane, murdered her cheating husband with weedkiller, purchased at her behest by their ten-year-old son. The Crown executed Rose Kane, but what happened to the son?

Miss Marple finds out, eventually, leading to the other surviving bit of the novel. The innocent child of a murderer grows up and must face the deadly past.

Along the way, Miss Marple faces off with Inspector Craddock. He's not thrilled about dealing with that dotty old lady again. He knows it always ends in tears for someone. Him, in this case, when he ends up in the hospital.

Other characters fare better with Miss Marple. Mr. Stringer aids and abets her, whether it's pretending to be a Lothario insurance agent or doing the legwork needed to decipher clues from the past. There's also the boarding house landlady for the acting troupe. She's used to dealing with actors. She lectures Miss Marple against bringing gentlemen callers upstairs and prefers the company of her six cats. Despite not paying rent, cats are more reliable and less self-centered than actors.

This is an amusing and enjoyable outing. Why didn't I give this film that all-important fifth garrote? It needed to be longer, at least a little bit, to tie up loose ends. What happened to the hapless lodger, the one who didn't murder Mrs. McGinty? He never shows up again. There's also the murderer's friends and relatives. There's never a scene where a friend says "I knew it!" or "You had a close call." I like seeing at least a little bit of the aftermath of murder because the crime doesn't stop reverberating in people's lives for months or even years.

Even so, despite its checkered antecedents, don't miss this film. Despite what Agatha thought about the movie, you won't miss Hercule Poirot. Margaret Rutherford admirably fills his patent-leather shoes.

General Information

Based on: *Mrs. McGinty's Dead* (novel, 1952)
Run time: 1 hr., 30 min. **Subtitles:** Yes

Writers: David Pursall and Jack Seddon
Director: George Pollock

Cast

Margaret Rutherford as Miss Marple
Stringer Davis as Jim Stringer
Charles Tingwell as Inspector Craddock
Windsor Davies as Sergeant Brick

Ron Moody as H. Driffold Cosgood
Ralph Michael as Ralph Summers
Pauline Jameson as Maureen Summers
James Bolam as Bill Hanson
Alison Seebohm as Eva McGonigall
Francesca Annis as Sheila Upward
Annette Kerr as Dorothy
Maurice Good as George Rowton
Neil Stacy as Arthur
Andrew Cruickshank as Justice Crosby
Megs Jenkins as Mrs. Gladys Thomas
Stella Tanner as Mrs. Florrie Harris
Dennis Price as Harris Tumbrill
Terry Scott as Police Constable Wells
John Wilder as Chief Constable
John Adams as Constable
Edwin Apps as Constable Carrying Tea Tray
Fred Davis as Constable
Arthur Howell as Constable in Theatre Box
Ross Parker as Mr. Swanbridge
Sydney Arnold as Vicar
Eric Francis as Stage Manager
Garard Green as Doctor

Film Locations

Aylesbury Crown Court, Aylesbury, Buckinghamshire (opening titles)
Sarratt, Hertfordshire (village scenes)
The Boot, Sarratt (constable drinks a beer)
Sarratt Sub Post Office (pub)
Palace Theatre, Watford, Hertfordshire (theatre exterior)
Shady Lane, Watford (police station)
West House and Pinner Memorial Park, London (Y.M.C.A. and park)
62 The Parade, Watford (theatrical agency)

Murder Ahoy! (1964)

A trustee's poisoning derails his inquiry into a shipboard reform school's finances and Miss Marple is asked to find out why

Fidelity to text

There are scraps of plot from *They Do It With Mirrors* lurking under the waves surrounding the H.M.S. *Battledore*. But other than Miss Marple, nothing remains of Agatha Christie.

Quality of movie

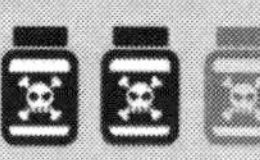

Murky and muddy, dragging when it should be sailing along. This is as anchor-bound as the ship most of the action takes place on.

This movie will make a lot more sense if you've read *They Do It With Mirrors*, a genuine Miss Marple property unlike the two previous Margaret Rutherford outings. The underlying plot (stolen from the novel) is simple. The trust benefitting a home for wayward boys is being embezzled. At the same time, the wayward boys are being trained, a la Fagin, as burglars. Here, the two crimes are unrelated. The embezzler is unaware of the thieves' ring, and the person running the theft scheme doesn't know about the embezzling.

We set sail in a promising fashion. Miss Marple gets fitted for a quasi-Royal Navy uniform and joins the board of a trust dedicated to rehabilitating misguided youth. Why the naval uniform? Because the facility is the H.M.S. *Battledore*, a tall sailing ship operated by a crew charged with installing backbones into young jellyfish.

During her first trustee's board meeting, a member dies suddenly before he can reveal the dreadful truth about the H.M.S *Battledore*. His death is diagnosed as a heart attack by the brisk country doctor, but Miss Marple is suspicious. She deduces poisoned snuff, based on her close reading of the mystery *The Doom Box* by J. Plantagenet Corby. It's no wonder Inspector Craddock thinks Miss Marple is unhinged.

But it turns out Miss Marple is correct when she discovers traces of strychnine in the remaining snuff. How does she do this? By turning into Sherlock Holmes and using her girl's junior chemistry set and analyzing the snuff. Never forget that the Margaret Rutherford version of Miss Marple comes loaded with hidden talents.

She and her friend Mr. Stringer investigate. Miss Marple insists on moving on board the *Battledore*, and as the senior person on board, displaces Captain Rhumstone from his stateroom. Since rank has its privileges, Captain Rhumstone evicts Commander Breeze-Connington from his quarters, who moves out Lieutenant Commander Dimchurch, and on down the line until Sub-Lieutenant Humbert ends up sleeping in a hammock in a corner of the hold.

Miss Marple outmaneuvers the captain again, getting him to ask her to stay longer than one night to inspect the ship. This gives her time to investigate and pass information via Morse code to Mr. Stringer, snug in a hotel room overlooking the bay where the *Battledore* rides at anchor.

Sydney Rhumstone (*Lionel Jeffries*), the brave captain

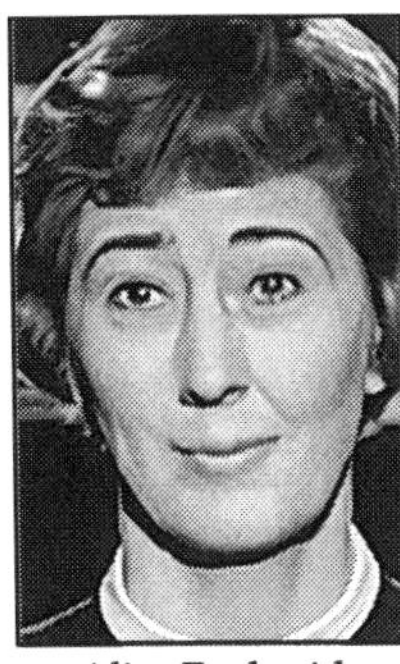

Alice Fanbraid (*Joan Benham*), the lonely matron

Breeze-Connington (*William Mervyn*), the ambitious officer

Lt. Compton (*Francis Matthews*), the arriviste officer

Shirley Boston (*Norma Foster*), the assistant matron

Eric Humbert (*Derek Nimmo*), the sub-lieutenant

There's a whole lot of running around at night on board the *Battledore*, with Miss Marple and the cast skulking around. It threatens at times to turn into a fun French bedroom farce, but the action stalls and nothing funny happens.

Meanwhile, Mr. Stringer follows the boys on shore leave (looking crackerjack in their flap-collared jumpers and white anklets) and discovers they're burglarizing houses. He rows between the hotel's quay and the ship to tell Miss Marple, unnoticed by the ship's watch.

The next morning, Miss Marple discovers the second body. Lieutenant Compton has been run through with a sword and hung from the yardarm. How no one, even the captain who was on deck for his morning shower, noticed the body swinging freely is more evidence of how badly the ship is run.

The plot is complicated further by the death of Assistant Matron Shirley Boston by a poisoned mousetrap. Miss Marple recognizes the murder method because it, like the death of Lieutenant Compton, is right out of *The Doom Box*. Coincidentally, there's a copy in the ship's library. The collection of expensive jewelry found near her body is not, however, from the book. Miss Marple deduces this is the action of a second criminal aboard the *Battledore*.

Shirley's story — involving her two junior officer swains — was particularly murky. She was leading on the socially well-connected Sub-Lieutenant Humbert because he got her into posh country houses for posh parties. She'd case the joint, then tell Lieutenant Compton — with whom she was also carrying on — where to send the wayward boys to break in and steal the jewelry. She's a hot brunette, so it's plausible. Sailors turn off their brains when faced with hot brunettes. There's a scene where Shirley is seated between the two junior officers, holding hands with one and stroking the back of the other. But I couldn't tell who was who.

Another red herring involves Lieutenant Commander Dimchurch, but it is so poorly developed it shouldn't be there at all. Captain Rhumstone and Matron Fanbraid have a romance arc of their own that should have been on full, glorious display during the sneaking-around-the-ship-at-midnight scenes but it wasn't. I would have also liked to have seen more scenes with the wayward boys being taught seamanship and thievery.

At last, after still more wasted chances at quality writing, Miss Marple uncovers the murderer. I could buy the murderer's motivation: If you're ambitious, being passed over for promotion is difficult to swallow. It was harder to buy Chief Inspector Craddock and Sergeant Bacon being unable to figure out another way out of the hold. It's true that ships are built like three-dimensional mazes but once they realized they were stuck, they should have gone deeper into the hold and found another way up topside.

But I really couldn't buy Miss Marple holding her own in a sword duel. Sure, she was the ladies' fencing champion in 1931. But this is 33 years later! Has she been practicing her fencing for the last 33 years? And she's fit enough to not fall prostrate to the deck within minutes of whipping out a saber? Both her and the murderer should have had heart attacks. I'll admit Margaret Rutherford could handle a sword. She practiced for a month for the scene but she was still 70 years old. Even Rocky Balboa knew when to stop fighting. I suppose this is part and parcel of her retaining her golf talents, horsemanship skills, and marksmanship abilities, each showcased in the climax of the three previous movies.

Is there anything to like about *Murder Ahoy*? The ship is nice. Very nice. It's Training Ship *Arethusa*, built in 1911. She was in service with the Royal Navy, then — in a case of art imitating life — repurposed as a home for wayward boys. Only the stern, where Captain Rhumstone's cabin is located, is pure Hollywood magic. Even with that enhancement, I would have liked to have seen more of the *Arethusa*.

There are good moments. It's a pleasure to watch Mr. Stringer and Miss Marple together. Their affection for each other is palpable (they were married in real life). Lionel Jeffries as Captain Rhumstone shamelessly overacts. He'd fit right in with the Cosgood Players in *Murder Most Foul*. But this movie just didn't jell. It should have sparkled like sunlight on breaking waves. Instead, it's becalmed.

General Information

Based on: Original script
Run time: 1 hr., 33 min. **Subtitles:** Yes

Writers: David Pursall and Jack Seddon
Director: George Pollock

Cast

Margaret Rutherford as Miss Marple
Stringer Davis as Jim Stringer
Charles Tingwell as Chief Inspector Craddock
Terence Edmond as Sergeant Bacon
Nicholas Parsons as Dr. Crump

Lionel Jeffries as Capt. Sydney Rhumstone
William Mervyn as Commander Breeze-Connington
Gerald Cross as Lt. Comm. Dimchurch
Francis Matthews as Lt. Compton
Derek Nimmo as Sub-Lt. Eric Humbert
Joan Benham as Matron Alice Fanbraid
Norma Foster as Asst. Matron Shirley Boston
Paddy Smith as Steward
Miles Malleson as Bishop Faulkner
Henry B. Longhurst as Cecil Ffolly-Hardwicke
Henry Oscar as Lord Rudkin
Tony Quinn as Kelly
Lucy Griffiths as Millie
Bernard Adams as Dusty Miller

Film Locations

Village Road, Denham (Milchester)
Piers Place, Amersham (Milchester House)
Misbourne Cottage, Denham (Marple's home)
Training Ship *Arethusa* (H.M.S. *Battledore*)
The Ship and Castle Hotel, St. Mawes (hotel)
Aldenham Grange, Letchmore Heath, Hertfordshire (patrol burgles house)

The Mirror Crack'd (1980)

Elizabeth Taylor leads an all-star cast in this lighthearted adaptation that features Angela Lansbury as a smoking Miss Marple

This is the second version of *The Mirror Crack'd* we watched. I had minor issues with version #1 (ITV's *Agatha Christie's Marple*). After seeing this version — an actual theatrical movie with an all-star cast — the ITV television version looks like Proust. The production values are not nearly as good. The DVD we saw looked like the movie had been shot on videotape.

The main reason to see this is to watch Elizabeth Taylor (as Marina Gregg) and Kim Novak (as Lola Brewster) spar. Both were nearing the end of long careers, and they had a wonderful time playing catty, aging, at-each-other's-throat divas. Great costumes too, including in the movie–within-the-movie when they played Mary, Queen of Scots (Elizabeth) and Queen Elizabeth I (Kim).

As a side note, the filmmakers mysteriously changed Marina Gregg's last name to that of her husband, Jason Rudd! There's no reason for that decision because actresses don't change their professional names when they marry. Or divorce. Or remarry. Or divorce again and take up with husband number three. It confuses the fans. At most, you'll get a hyphenation such as Farrah Fawcett becoming Farrah Fawcett-Majors when she married Lee Majors. After the divorce, she went back to Farrah Fawcett.

Another drawback, I'm sorry to report, was Angela Lansbury as Miss Marple. This is not her fault. I just couldn't get past my mental image of Jessica Fletcher. *The Mirror Crack'd* was released in 1980 and *Murder, She Wrote* still lay four years in the future. I wouldn't have had a problem in 1980 but today? I kept seeing Jessica Fletcher. It's hard not to! The two sleuths have so much in common, although Jessica Fletcher was a far snappier dresser than Miss Marple.

Fidelity to text

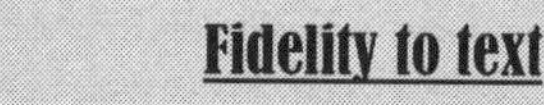

The producers played fast and loose with Agatha's story.

Quality of movie

Problems, problems, problems. So why should you bother with this version? To watch Elizabeth Taylor and Kim Novak chew up the scenery and each other, naturally. They are a hoot.

This doesn't always happen: In *Knives Out* (2019), Chris Evans played Hugh Ransom Drysdale, and after about fifteen minutes, I stopped looking for his Captain America shield. What allowed me was that role was radically different from Captain America. There's not nearly as big a difference between Miss Marple and Jessica Fletcher, other than nationality. They're both crime-solving older spinsters and always the smartest people in the room.

In addition to dowdying up Ms. Lansbury, the filmmakers did a bad job artificially aging her and it shows. She was fifty-five when she made this picture. They would have been better off rewriting Miss Marple as a fifty-five-year-old woman. Another questionable

Marina Rudd (*Elizabeth Taylor*), the fragile star

Jason Rudd (*Rock Hudson*), the suffering director

Lola Brewster (*Kim Novak*), the taunting rival

Martin N. Fenn (*Tony Curtis*), the smarmy producer

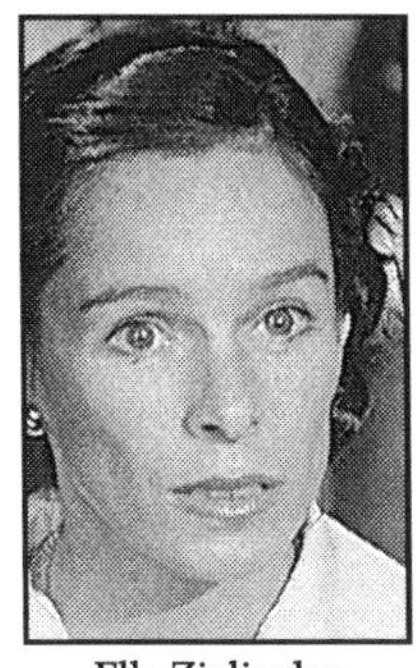

Ella Zielinsky (*Geraldine Chaplin*), the loyal assistant

Heather Babcock (*Maureen Bennett*), the fanatic fan

choice was having Miss Marple smoke cigarettes! I've read almost all of Agatha Christie's oeuvre and Miss Marple never, ever smoked.

It was jarring.

You also never, ever saw Miss Marple in bed in her nightie in any of the books. You do here. She's wearing a discreet, tasteful nightgown but it still felt wrong to see Miss Marple in her bedroom.

The filmmakers changed the setting of the film to 1953. There was no reason for this decision that I could see. The novel was published in 1962 and it would have been perfectly acceptable to keep the setting as it was. Agatha did not write historicals. She wrote contemporaries and her characters moved with the times.

But time shifts can be justified. The ITV series *Agatha Christie's Marple* all had their time adjusted to the 1950s. This was a stylistic and continuity choice by the producers and it permitted a more uniform tone to the series as a whole and let them keep using the same wardrobes, cars, accessories and so forth.

This film did not have that constraint.

Another area where the movie failed was in rewriting Agatha's story. A big part of Marina Gregg's backstory involves her children. A major plot point is the discovery that the attractive young photographer is actually Marina Gregg's estranged adopted daughter. That's gone. Vanished. And yet, according to Internet Movie Database, Margot Bence (played by Marella Oppenheim) gets a credit. She never speaks. We never even see her face as she's always seen behind a camera, taking pictures. I can only assume that Marella Oppenheim filmed scenes that were left on the cutting room floor.

Here's another major mistake: Ella Zelinsky (Jason Rudd's faithful assistant) was murdered, but it's never revealed who did it! Miss Marple does not ignore bodies. She knows who the killer was. But in this film? Crickets. The audience is left hanging.

Then there's the weird pacing. The camera lingers on bucolic landscapes, tours of Miss Marple's cottage at various times of the day, birdwatching far in excess of what the plot demands and so on. I have no idea why. Those choices didn't add one iota to the film, slowed it down, and made sure that there was no time for important plot points. It's not like the novel didn't provide plenty of material to work with.

Dolly Bantry got rewritten entirely. She's no longer Jane Marple's friend. Worse, her most important scene in the novel is assigned to Jane! This is where Dolly is an eyewitness to Marina Gregg's blank, frozen stare at the party when she's introduced to Heather Babcock. Dolly quotes Tennyson's *The Lady of Shallot* to explain what she saw. Not in this movie.

The ending was all wrong. The novel is ambiguous as to Jason Rudd's culpability. In the film, he's guilty until he's not. Wrong, wrong, wrong. The filmmakers also excised everything about Marina Gregg's traumatic life and how her entourage excused everything about her behavior because of said trauma. Marina Gregg lost a lot of depth due to that decision.

By now you may be asking what the filmmakers did right. This is easy: They cast Elizabeth Taylor as Marina Gregg. She's having fun in the role and it shows. Kim Novak plays her arch-rival, Lola Brewster. Kim's having a ball. They snipe and snap at each other and the film springs to life. These ladies make the film worth watching. Too bad the DVD isn't subtitled because you miss a lot of zingers.

You also get Tony Curtis as Martin N. Fenn, long-suffering producer of the movie-within-a-movie and Lola Brewster's current paramour. Tony Curtis enjoys himself hugely as he plays the archetypal Hollywood producer. He chews the scenery with gusto.

I can't say the same for Rock Hudson. He's quite subdued as Marina Gregg's husband and director. He's great to look at but he doesn't dominate the screen like Tony Curtis does. I don't know why because normally I can't take my eyes off him.

You also get — a bonus today although it wasn't in 1980 — about thirty seconds of a very young Pierce Brosnan playing an extra in the movie-within-a-movie. He's the one Elizabeth Taylor as Mary, Queen of Scots, is cuddling to her bosom.

Overall, I was disappointed in *The Mirror Crack'd*. It has plenty to like, particularly Elizabeth Taylor, Kim Novak, and Tony Curtis. If you're going to watch all the Agatha Christie-based films, you'll want to see this one too. But if you want a better version, stick to ITV's film. It's much, much truer to the original novel.

General Information

Based on: *The Mirror Crack'd from Side to Side* (novel, 1962)
Run time: 1 hr., 45 min. **Subtitles:** No

Writers: Jonathan Hales and Barry Sandler
Director: Guy Hamilton

Cast

Angela Lansbury as Miss Marple
Edward Fox as Inspector Craddock

Elizabeth Taylor as Marina Rudd
Rock Hudson as Jason Rudd
Tony Curtis as Martin N. Fenn
Kim Novak as Lola Brewster
Geraldine Chaplin as Ella Zielinsky
Marella Oppenheim as Margot Bence
Charles Gray as Bates
Wendy Morgan as Cherry
Margaret Courtenay as Mrs. Bantry
Maureen Bennett as Heather Babcock
Carolyn Pickles as Miss Giles
Eric Dodson as The Major
Charles Lloyd Pack as Vicar
Richard Pearson as Doctor Haydock

Film Locations

St. Clere Estate, Heaverham, Kent (Gossington Hall)
Compton Wynyates, Warwickshire
"The Thatched House," Smarden, Kent (Miss Marple's cottage)
Shoreham, West Sussex (St. Mary Mead)

A Caribbean Mystery (1983)

Hayes comes closest to Miss Marple of the novels in this Americanized tale of gaslighting and murder

This first adaptation of *A Caribbean Mystery* set the stage for the next two, as they also made the same change to a major character.

In the novel, Esther Walters is Mr. Rafiel's secretary. Mysteriously, although no other names were changed, in this version Esther became Ruth so we'll stick with her new name. Ruth's a good employee. She's also got very poor taste in men. Her ne'er-do-well, wastrel husband died in a drunken accident and left her penniless. Getting widowed was a blessing in disguise. She had to start working for Mr. Rafiel to support herself and her child. Unbeknownst to her, she's also going to be a rich woman when Mr. Rafiel dies.

Jackson, Mr. Rafiel's manservant, masseuse, and dogsbody, is a snoop. He discovers Ruth's potential windfall and tells the wrong person. The wrong person is Tim Kendall.

In the novel, Ruth knows Tim Kendall but she doesn't flirt with him. At the climax, you, dear reader, discover that she's in love with Tim, but until that moment, there's no sign they've been conducting an affair under his wife's and her boss' respective noses. They're friendly — guest to innkeeper — and that's all.

This film changed that, a change repeated in the two subsequent adaptations. Ruth is clearly on Tim Kendall's side. She disparages his wife, Molly. She repeats rumors about Molly being mentally unbalanced and unfaithful. She, believing anything a bad boy tells her, is sure that poor Tim is trapped in a loveless marriage to a cheating, crazy wife.

Fidelity to text

Some minor characters disappear and everyone turned into Americans, but it's all here, setting the template for subsequent adaptations.

Quality of movie

It's a little slow; slow enough that some dropped plot elements could have been worked into the script.

Ruth does not know that Tim is a murderer, and he's very careful to make sure that she, potential heiress, never finds out. His plan is to marry her after Molly's supposed suicide when a decent interval has passed. Later, following the path laid down with Molly and at least one other former wife, maybe two, Ruth will die tragically and poor Tim will look for another stupid, naïve rich woman who believes what a charming wastrel tells her.

Having her character rewritten means you, dear viewer, aren't surprised when Ruth defends Tim and blames the murders on crazy Molly. I can't decide if this rewrite is a flaw or not, but movies are a different medium from text, and they've got to compress motivation and add action.

Molly Kendall
(*Season Hubley*),
the stressed wife

Tim Kendall
(*Jameson Parker*),
the besieged husband

Lucky Dyson
(*Cassie Yates*),
the saucy wife

Dr. Graham
(*Brock Peters*),
the curious physician

Mr. Rafiel
(*Barnard Hughes*),
the wealthy man

Ruth Walter
(*Swoosie Kurtz*),
the loyal assistant

The variation from here on in the *Caribbean* adaptations is how complicit Ruth (or Esther) is with Tim Kendall's plans. I've always wondered what happened to Ruth afterwards, when she realized what a lovestruck fool she'd been. We don't get a hint here. The Joan Hickson version (1989) doesn't cover it. It's only in the 2013 Julia McKenzie film where Ruth/ Esther sits at the bar with newly widowed Greg Dyson and they stare moodily into their drinks.

Another change is the removal of Major Palgrave's glass eye (his right). Screenwriter Sue Grafton decided he didn't need it for her plot, I guess. That's a flaw because misunderstanding his vision defects slowed Miss Marple down, giving her a valid reason for making a mistake about who Major Palgrave was looking at when he was about to show her the photograph of a murderer.

Grafton — the future best-selling mystery novelist — also remade everyone into an American. As Miss Marple, Helen Hayes may have come from St. Mary Mead in Merrie Olde England, but she doesn't sound like it. None of the other guests did either, so it worked out.

Helen Hayes may not be the definitive Miss Marple, but she performed admirably. She played Miss Marple truer to the novel than some of her counterparts. You'd never believe that Julia McKenzie or Joan Hickson would be seen as dithery or dotty. Their eyes gleam with intelligence, Julia McKenzie especially. Julia's also much spryer.

Helen Hayes, however, played a foolish old woman to a tee. Watch her manipulate Dr. Graham into accepting her point of view, smoothly persuading him that it's his idea to investigate Major Palgrave's death. Similarly, when she discusses the case with Captain Daventry, she leads him gently down the garden path until he comes around unwittingly to her way of thinking.

Helen also has wonderful scenes with Bernard Hughes, playing Mr. Rafiel. Believe it or not, they have chemistry. Sexual chemistry. Yes, yes, I know that we live in a sex-saturated world but not really. Sex is only acceptable between young and gorgeous people, not when you're old and gray. But watch them together. Watch Mr. Rafiel watching her, looking wistful. As if he's seeing a different life, a life he could have had with this charming, witty, sharp, canny woman who gives as good as she gets. If only he had met her decades ago.

But they never met, until they ended up together at the resort hotel solving a murder and that life together is no longer possible. Those scenes are wonderful and all done with longing glances. This is what great actors can do with a good script.

In addition to making everyone American, Sue Grafton put serious effort into showing the power of rumor and gossip. Throughout the film, characters discuss what they've heard. Sometimes the gossip is true and sometimes not, but everyone assumes that what they're told is true even though no one remembers where the story originally came from. How does everyone know that their hostess, Molly, is mentally unbalanced? That she had an unsavory boyfriend before meeting the eminently suitable Tim Kendall? That Major Palgrave suffers from high blood pressure? That Lucky Dyson and George Hillingdon are having an affair?

That last one was easy, because Lucky made it obvious. But the other rumors are harder to pin down. Miss Marple works at finding out, but even she, super-sleuth, can't quite find the source.

It is, of course, Tim Kendall, setting the stage for his nefarious plans. As the resort's innkeeper, he's in and out of everyone's rooms, talking to the guests, overseeing the staff, and being friendly and chatty. With the right word in the right ear, like, say Ruth Walter, who laps up everything he tells her, the narrative he wants everyone to know rapidly spreads all over the resort. It's really well done. The guests are regulars, coming back year after year for their holiday and when the Kendalls bought the resort, the guests remained loyal. They're primed to believe what they're told.

Although it drags at times, it's an interesting film. Unlike the later adaptations, there's no voodoo and little about the lives of the staff. But it's worth watching Miss Marple and Mr. Rafiel flirt while solving a mystery.

General Information

Based on: *A Caribbean Mystery* (novel, 1964)
Run time: 1 hr., 32 min. **Subtitles:** Yes

Writers: Sue Grafton and Steve Humphrey
Director: Robert Michael Lewis

Cast

Helen Hayes as Miss Jane Marple
Barnard Hughes as Mr. Rafiel
Swoosie Kurtz as Ruth Walter
Michael Preston as Arthur Jackson
Zakes Mokae as Captain Daventry
Brock Peters as Dr. Graham

Jameson Parker as Tim Kendall
Season Hubley as Molly Kendall
Cassie Yates as Lucky Dyson
Stephen Macht as Greg Dyson
Beth Howland as Evelyn Hillingdon
George Innes as Edward Hillingdon
Maurice Evans as Maj. Geoffrey Palgrave
Lynne Moody as Victoria Johnson
Bernard McDonald as The Minister
Santos Morales as Miguel
Sam Scarber as Sergeant
Cecil Smith as Hotel Guest

Film Location

El Encanto Hotel and Garden Villas, Santa Barbara, California

The Body in the Library (1984)

A trespassing corpse lures Miss Marple to a seaside resort and into a wealthy family's secrets

> **Fidelity to text**
>
> So close it uses Agatha's own dialog. Minor changes, such as adding the village idiot who discovers the burned-out car with the body in it. They also moved the time period from 1942 to the 1950s.
>
> **Quality of movie**
>
> Splendid; messier and closer to real life. The characters look like you'd meet them in real life and the locations are equally authentic. Docked the last half-garrote for skimping on subtitles.

Watching the BBC *Miss Marple* series (1984-1992) alternating with the ITV *Agatha Christie's Marple* series (2004-2013) revealed the enormous contrasts between the two. They can be jarring.

Miss Marple was filmed on 16mm film, resulting in softer images that added a tinge of nostalgia. For *Agatha Christie's Marple*, a better grade of film stock was used, resulting in crisper-looking images that, combined with the neatly manicured grounds and magazine-perfect settings (as well as neatly manicured and magazine-perfect actors and actresses), lend an air of unreality to the stories.

Agatha Christie's Marple regularly played fast and loose with the text. You never knew what you'd get, up to and including changing the identity of the murderer! With *Miss Marple*, there'd be changes but this series was far more faithful to the novels.

The third huge difference is Joan Hickson. Joan *is* Miss Marple. She was 78 when she filmed *The Body in the Library* and nearing 90 when the series ended with *The Mirror Crack'd from Side to Side*, and it shows. She wasn't a woman in her sixties made up to look like an octogenarian. You can feel her age in the way she moves and holds herself. She realistically struggles with not being able to remember her lines perfectly. As in the novels, Ms. Hickson's Marple doesn't go racing after criminals. She lets the police and her companions do that, while she sits quietly and thinks.

By contrast, Geraldine McEwan was 72 when she first played Miss Marple. Six years doesn't seem like a lot. If you're 22 and your friend is 28, it isn't. When you're 72 and they're 78, it's as big a gap as the span between ages 2 and 8. Your body changes rapidly at both ends of your lifespan. Even younger and more jarring, Julia McKenzie was 66 when she began playing the role.

To acquire the rights to Agatha's novels, the BBC promised her daughter Rosalind (who controlled the estate after her mother's death) that the series would be faithful to the source material, and, other than setting the episodes in the 1950s, they succeeded.

They stayed faithful to the historical times as well. The English countryside looks naturally overgrown

Conway Jefferson (*Andrew Cruickshank*), the lonely tycoon

Adelaide Jefferson (*Ciaran Madden*), the solicitous widow

Josie Turner (*Trudie Styler*), the injured dancer

Mark Gaskell (*Keith Drinkel*), the caring widower

Basil Blake (*Anthony Smee*), the louche artist

Malcolm (*Colin Higgins*), the looney local

and unkempt, in contrast to the neatly manicured aristocratic homes. The people look like they belong there. The villagers and country folk appear worn with age and manual labor, and not like they stepped out of central casting.

T.R. Bowen, who wrote eight of the series' twelve episodes including this one, made one major change that would spark outrage today. He added Malcolm, a village idiot who discovers the burned-out car with a body in it. You could never do this trick nowadays. Too many people would complain that it was anti-village idiot although every village had one. Or more. Those folks have families, too, and their families have to cope, and the village as a whole gets to deal with these challenging people. If you don't have a village to care for you, you can end up in a snake-pit of an institution. The village of St. Mary Mead is caring and tolerant of "our Malcolm," even if they do not take him or his wild stories seriously.

Another evocative addition involved the disappearance of 16-year-old Pamela Reed, who vanished during a Girl Guide event. Her father's behavior during his interview with the police contrasts nicely with Josie Turner's behavior on discovering that her cousin, Ruby Keene, was dead. It parallels nicely with Conway Jefferson's loss of his legs, his wife, his son, and his daughter in a plane crash. That's why he is still keeping close company with his son-in-law (Mark Gaskell) and his daughter-in-law (Adelaide Jefferson). They are bound together by mutually shared grief.

Another thing that struck me about this adaptation is the class divide, depicted in the sheer disdain everyone other than Conway Jefferson held for Ruby Keene. Her appeal to Jefferson is obvious. There's no fool like an old fool. What could a rich, lonely, disabled old fool like better than a sweet-natured, cheerful blonde who resembles his long-lost daughter?

Everyone else, including her cousin, Josie, suspects she has ulterior motives and despises her for this. Yet everything we see of Ruby shows she's exactly what Conway thinks she is. Raymond Starr, the hotel's tennis pro, admits he thinks Ruby is dim and not smart enough to be a gold-digger. She doesn't even have a boyfriend. This is a telling point because if there's one thing that staff in a large, luxury hotel knows, it's everyone else's personal lives.

Everyone goes into great detail about how Ruby is rising above her station in life to take advantage of an old man, who everyone describes as strong-willed and intelligent. Clearly, Ruby is no better than she should be, manipulating poor Conway Jefferson. Telling Miss Marple and the police that Ruby is also vapid and naïve is a contradiction they can't see. Vapid, naïve 18-year-olds don't make effective gold-diggers.

Ruby Keene did nothing wrong, other than have a lonely old man pay attention to her. He liked her youth and beauty, and she liked him back. You can see why. Conway Jefferson was safe. He didn't paw at her like the male hotel guests undoubtedly did while dancing with her. He treated her well. Like a daughter, in fact. It must have been a relief. She could relax and let down her guard because an old man in a wheelchair didn't want that one thing from her that every other man around her probably did.

It was fascinating to watch the well-bred, well-educated, upper-class people and their servants despise Ruby Keene for doing what they, themselves, did: Marry for money and status. Even Miss Marple fell into the trap of disregarding Ruby's humanity. She's ever so slightly dismissive.

Class differences also show up in the relations between the village constable, Inspector Slack, Colonel Melchett, and Sir Henry Clithering. They know their places in the hierarchy. It affects the investigation and who gets to question who and how aggressively. I didn't see this depicted nearly as much in ITV's version.

I'd definitely watch this version of *The Body in the Library* again. It is far superior to the ITV *Marple* production with Geraldine McEwan and its radical reworking of the murderer.

General Information

Based on: *The Body in the Library* (novel, 1942)
Run time: 2 hr., 36 min. **Subtitles:** No

Writer: T.R. Bowen **Director:** Silvio Narizzano

Cast

Joan Hickson as Miss Marple
Raymond Francis as Sir Henry Clithering
David Horovitch as Det. Inspector Slack
Frederick Jaeger as Col. Melchett
Ian Brimble as Detective Constable Lake
John Bardon as PC Palk
Sarah Whitlock as WPC

Andrew Cruickshank as Conway Jefferson
Keith Drinkel as Mark Gaskell
Ciaran Madden as Adelaide Jefferson
Andrew Downer as Peter Carmody
Jess Conrad as Raymond Starr
Trudie Styler as Josie Turner
Sally Jane Jackson as Ruby Keene
Arthur Bostrom as George Bartlett
Gwen Watford as Dolly Bantry
Moray Watson as Col. Bantry
Anthony Smee as Basil Blake
Debbie Arnold as Dinah Lee
Colin Higgins as Malcolm
Valentine Dyall as Lorrimer
Hugh Walters as Mr. Prescott
John Moffatt as Edwards
Stephen Churchett as Major Reeve
Astra Sheridan as Pamela Reeve
Jacqui Munro as the body

Film Localtions

Bournemouth, Dorset (Danemouth)
Nether Wallop, Hampshire (St. Mary Mead)
Wherwell Priory, Hampshire (Gossington Hall)
Bournemouth Highcliff Marriott Hotel, Dorset (The Majestic)
Carlton Hotel, Bournemouth, Dorset (The Majestic)
Royal Bath Hotel, Bournemouth, Dorset (Majestic interior)

Murder With Mirrors (1985)

A country manor turned reformatory is not what it seems as Miss Marple helps her friend discover the truth

Fidelity to text

I expect characters in adaptations to disappear and be combined, plots to be simpler, and names to be changed. I don't expect fiery deaths of nonentity characters who suddenly turn into criminal-minded zealots.

Quality of movie

It's a pleasure watching old pros like Helen Hayes, Bette Davis, and Leo McKern strut their stuff and show the kids how it's done. But there were other questionable choices.

This film is — in some ways — the best of the three adaptations of *They Do It With Mirrors*. Most of the simplifications worked to the point that if you don't know the novel, you won't notice the changes.

The first major change was to Carrie Louise's sister and, my, did Joan Collins chew the scenery with gusto in the 2009 version. She's gone, so Christian Gulbrandsen, Carrie Louise's stepson, urges Miss Marple to investigate what's brewing at Stonygates.

Carrie Louise's family menagerie was vastly simplified. Former husbands vanished and stepsons disappeared, taking their fates to be murdered with them. That reduces Gina's love quadrangle with the Restarick boys (Alexis and Stephen) to a triangle, and they're no longer unrelated kids raised as brothers and sister so it's less creepy.

That is, as long as Gina's husband Wally doesn't care. In this version, he does and he expresses it early when he punches Stephen's lights out for hitting on his wife. Wally's no longer a cowboy from out west, but he's still an American fish out of water. He's also still the only practical, capable-with-his-hands male at Stonygates.

Gina is made even more of a flighty, self-centered, high-maintenance princess, and if she does go back to the U.S. with Wally, she'll make him earn that happy ending. Liane Langland plays Gina as needing desperately to be under some man's thumb and fighting him every step of the way until she submits for the moment. There will be fireworks.

The story got modernized to 1985, with '80s hair, clothes, cars, recording equipment, and so on. Thus, Gina and Wally's backstory got altered. Instead of meeting during a quickie WWII romance, they met while she was at school in the U.S. and he was a medical student.

Since Alexis Restarick's gone, Miss Marple is the one who nearly gets killed by stage lights being dropped on her head. The Shakespeare play the delinquents put on is a better choice but not the best. Stephen Restarick chooses *The Taming of the Shrew* instead of *Romeo and Juliet*. It's clear that the people producing these films (all of them) have no idea which Shakespeare teenage boys would choose: something bloody like *Richard III* rather than a play involving dressing up in women's clothing.

The financial shenanigans and embezzlement plot

Carrie Louise Serrocold (*Bette Davis*), the wealthy victim

Lewis Serrocold (*John Mills*), the visionary husband

Gina Markham (*Liane Langland*), the untamed wife

Wally Markham (*John Laughlin*), the unsettled spouse

Edgar Lawson (*Tim Roth*), the unstable inmate

Dr. Max Hargrove (*Anton Rodgers*), the utopian medico

involving former delinquent students placed into respectable banking positions got disappeared, but then, it always does.

The other embezzlement plot was changed as well. Dr. Hargrove (the creepy shrink in charge of the juvenile delinquents) gained a new name, a motivation for murder, an assault on Miss Marple, and a fiery death while trying to escape in a Ford Pinto Pony.

For you kids who don't read fifty-year-old car litigation reports, Pinto Ponies became notorious for exploding gas tanks resulting in lawsuits and recalls. The car Dr. Hargrove roared off in didn't look like a Pinto Pony (I used to own one and never had a problem) but it sure acted like the ones you saw in cartoons. When he rammed through a barrier and into a closed gate, the car exploded in a fireball that only happens when a gasoline tanker is set on fire.

The ending changed too. Lewis Serrocold didn't bother rescuing Edgar from drowning. He stood idly by and watched. Lewis is only a father-figure to Edgar, not a biological father. Since he doesn't drown rescuing his illegitimate son, he gets to die dramatically offscreen. It was … okay, I guess. The plot made it clear that he was using Edgar and had no paternal feelings.

The name of the film is taken from the novel's American title. *Murder With Mirrors* is a bad name compared to *They Do It With Mirrors*. No actual mirrors are involved like the first title states; the second title implies stagecraft and sleight-of-hand.

But the murder of Christian Gilbranson worked. I know the novel well and Agatha does a good job of concealing what's in plain sight. The 1991 Joan Hickson version of the murder is so obvious, it's painful. If you think for thirty seconds, you'll see what happened. The 2009 Julia McKenzie version is better, but it's still clear whodunnit because they're the only suspects out of eyeshot.

I didn't notice that with this version. It worked and, mind you, I've read the novel and seen the other films.

Where this film shines is in the three leads. Helen Hayes was wonderful in this, her last film. Bette Davis (ten years younger than Helen despite looking ten years older due to a recent stroke) was terrific. She only made a few films afterward, dying in 1989.

General Information

Based on: *They Do It With Mirrors* (novel, 1952)
Run time: 1 hr., 40 min. **Subtitles:** Yes

Writer: George Eckstein **Director:** Dick Lowry

Cast

Helen Hayes as Miss Jane Marple
Leo McKern as Inspector Curry
Christopher Fairbank as Sergeant Lake

Bette Davis as Carrie Louise Serrocold
John Mills as Lewis Serrocold
Tim Roth as Edgar Lawson
John Woodvine as Christian Gilbranson
Liane Langland as Gina Markham
John Laughlin as Wally Markham
Dorothy Tutin as Mildred Strete
Anton Rodgers as Dr. Max Hargrove
Frances de la Tour as Miss Bellaver
James Coombes as Steven Restarick
Amanda Maynard as Miss Valentine

Film Locations

Trafalgar Square, London
Carlton House Terrace, London (Gilbranson's office)
Westminster Bridge, London
Seer Green and Jordans railway station, Seer Green, Buckinghamshire
Beaconsfield Golf Club, Buckinghamshire (station parking lot)
Turville, Buckinghamshire (drive to Stonygates)
Skirmett, Buckinghamshire (drive to Stonygates)
Brocket Hall, Hertfordshire (Stonygates)

Leo McKern was outstanding. McKern's opening scene as Inspector Curry with Miss Marple is a marvel. After he arrives at Stonygate, he demands to interview Miss Marple first, not any of the other, far more likely suspects. Behind closed doors, Miss Marple dithers and flutters. She's the picture of an overwhelmed and shocked old lady who cannot even *begin* to cope with murder and can't *imagine* how anyone would do such a *dreadful* thing and why on *earth* does the inspector want to speak to *her*, when there are other, more *likely* suspects waiting.

Inspector Curry tells her to quit the act. He *knows* who she is, and he goes into detail about what other police inspectors think of her, both good and bad.

It's funny watching Miss Marple regroup when her cover's blown. She and Inspector Curry snipe at each other during the inquiry until they develop a grudging respect for each other's brains and professionalism. They're terrific, and the reason to watch the movie.

And Bette Davis. She's got a difficult role, but luckily the script-writer didn't rewrite her into some-thing she wasn't. Carrie Louise is otherworldly, naïve, and not paying much attention to reality. Yet she's the reason for Stonygate, why the family clusters around her, and the source of love and tension. Her relationship with her daughter, Mildred, was well-handled, something that doesn't happen in the other films. So is her relationship with Miss Bellaver, who's her companion, housekeeper, nurse, and tolerates no interference from well-meaning daughters.

In her usual fashion, Miss Marple tells Carrie Louise a story about someone like Mildred, and it's enough to open her eyes to someone who needs her, but whom she doesn't see.

The three versions of *They Do It With Mirrors* are so different. Each highlights different parts of the novel, or rewrites it into something that Agatha never envisioned. Of them all, this version is the closest to the original text. As a class in film studies, it's worth watching all three to see how one novel can be interpreted into three very different films.

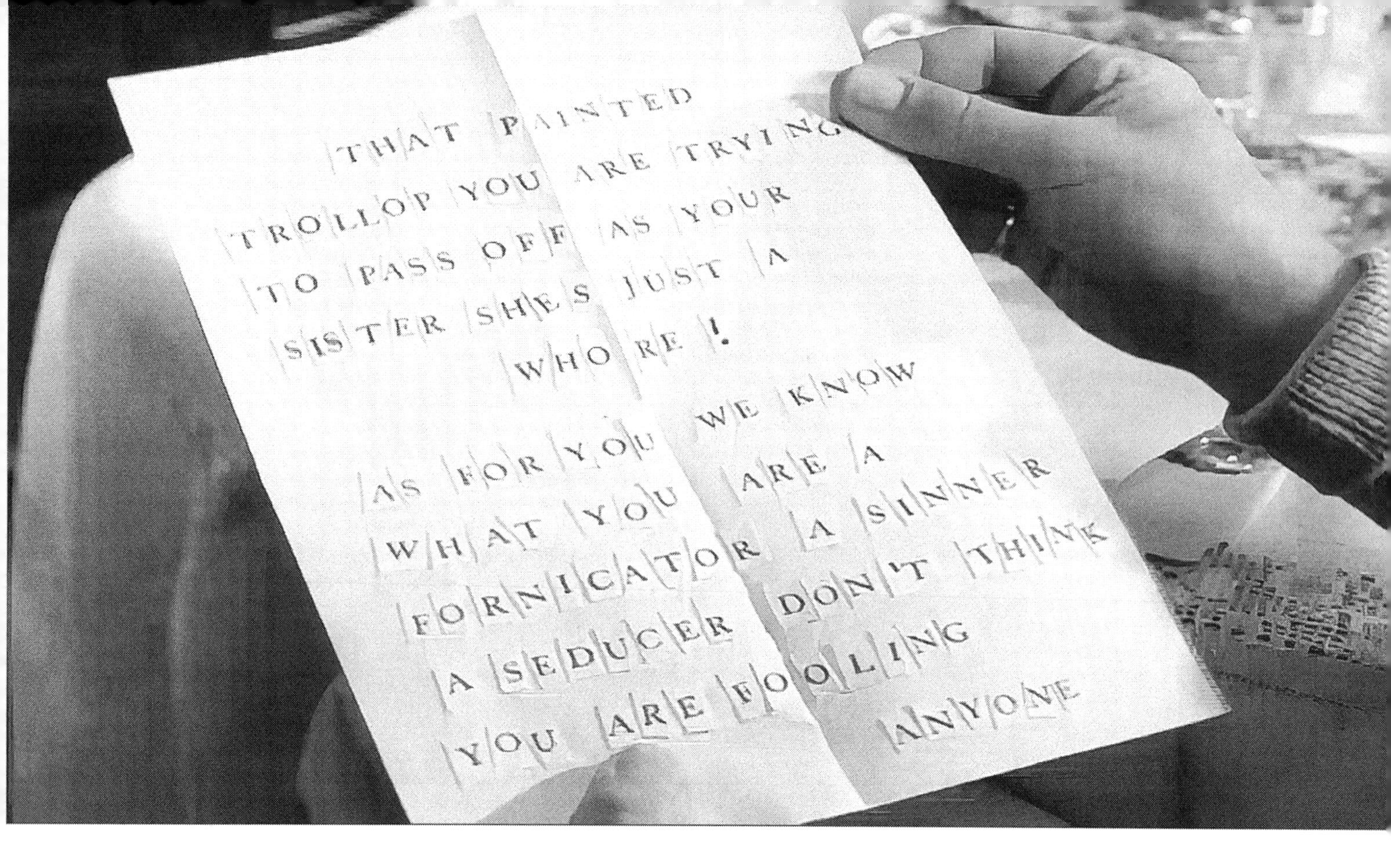

The Moving Finger (1985)

Where there's smoke, there's fire but it's up to Miss Marple to find the mysterious source of the tinder

Fidelity to text

Miss Marple shows up soon after Gerry Burton gets a poison pen letter and she gets much of his role. In the novel, she's offstage until the last quarter.

Quality of movie

Overly truncated and too many wonderful characters got short shrift. But it's still fun to watch, other than Megan who was a black hole on the screen.

If you're not up on your Bible stories or your Omar Khayyám, the title comes from quatrain 51 of the *Rubáiyát*, which he based on the Book of Daniel. Daniel correctly interpreted the message written on the wall of Belshazzar's palace. The idea here is that the anonymous letters shift the blame from one villager to another but in the end, someone's doomed.

The most famous (and first English) translation is by Edward FitzGerald (1809-1883):

"The Moving Finger writes; and, having writ,
Moves on: not all thy Piety nor Wit
Shall lure it back to cancel half a Line,
Nor all thy Tears wash out a Word of it."

Think about that quatrain when the end credits roll and consider what's going to happen to the Symmington boys. Their world has been shattered.

The Moving Finger is Agatha's third Miss Marple outing and she was already experimenting, using what she learned with her Poirot novels. In this case, Miss Marple doesn't show up until the last quarter when she, like an emergency quarterback, arrives to win the game and save the day. Mrs. Calthrop, the vicar's wife, needs an expert in evil. Naturally, her thoughts turned to Jane. But while the village suffers and waits, Jerry Burton (his first name changed to Gerry for this episode) narrates the novel and if he doesn't know something, neither does the reader.

But Jane can't show up in the last fifteen minutes of her own show so she's conveniently onstage, visiting the vicarage, when the poisoned pen letters arrive. She is concerned that one of the letters will strike home. In the novel, she notices what Mrs. Calthrop spots. The letters are vile but they don't seem to be explicitly tied to village life, something they would be if they were written by a longtime resident who knew where all the bodies were buried. It's surmised that an older woman wrote them but, again, the mystery woman doesn't seem to be tied into the gossip chain.

I know what Miss Marple and Mrs. Calthrop mean. If you're part of an isolated social group (and nothing is more isolated than a tucked-away English village) you already know or can easily learn the nasty gossip about who's cheating, who's a drunkard, who's

Joanna Burton
(*Sabina Franklyn*),
the loyal sister

Gerry Burton
(*Andrew Bicknell*),
the wounded veteran

Megan Hunter
(*Deborah Appleby*),
the blossoming girl

Edward Symmington
(*Michael Culver*),
the patient attorney

Owen Griffith
(*Martin Fisk*),
the foreign doctor

Eryl Griffith
(*Sandra Payne*),
the lovelorn sec'y

stealing from the poor box, who's poaching, and who's trying to get above her station in life by stealing the master from his harridan wife.

The letters are … not quite accurate. They're also not being sent to the right people. The gorgeous blonde nursery governess in the Symmington household, who might be expected to catch the eye of Mr. Symmington, especially when compared to his high-maintenance, difficult wife, did not receive one. She's such an obvious target that it's suspicious when she doesn't receive one.

The film should have made more of this fact instead of wasting time on Jerry's plot-demanded pursuit of Megan. Much of the novel is devoted to their love story but here, you'll wonder what on earth he sees in her. She's whiny, childish, has a very '80s haircut in the early '50s, poorly educated (a girl of her class would have learned about Pygmalion at school, either via Greek mythology or George Bernard Shaw's play), self-centered, and has no discernible sense of humor or personality.

The part's underwritten but a different actress — one with charisma — might have made something of the role. As it is, she has all the appeal of under-salted porridge. Her makeover scenes in London are blue-tinged still photos rather than actual footage of her and Jerry getting to know each other, in keeping with her non-personality. Her blackmail of her stepfather, when she's made no secret of disliking her mother, is equally out of the blue. True, it's to reveal him as the murderer and mastermind behind the letters, but why would she care? Other than to see justice done, I mean, but that would demand thinking about something beside her own woes.

That's time that could have been spent with Mr. Pye, who lights up the screen every time he appears. He's criminally under-used, disappearing completely in the second half. He should have been commenting acidly and amusingly about Megan's makeover, the budding relationship, the Women's Institute show within a show, and ferreting out clues with Miss Marple.

We should have also seen far more of Jerry's sister, Joanna, and her romance with Owen Griffith, foreign doctor. He's foreign because he's Welsh. They were both far more interesting; him because he's an outsider yet a trusted doctor and her because she's a sophisticated city girl trapped in the country. In the novel, Dr. Griffith introduces Joanna to the real world when she's forced to assist him with a village woman's difficult and dangerous labor and delivery. Here, we barely get longing glances despite these two actors having more chemistry in a few seconds than entire scenes with Jerry and Megan.

We also don't get an answer as to what happens to Dr. Griffith's sister, Eryl (Aimée in the novel). She pines for Mr. Symmington but he, married to the harridan and ensnared by blonde, capable Elsie, ignores her. Eryl writes the poison pen letter to Elsie, gets arrested for murder, and then … vanishes. She must be off in a pub with Mr. Pye, comparing notes about where their story arcs went.

I'd have liked to see more of Cleat, the gardener, and Mrs. Cleat, the village hedge witch. They act as a Greek chorus, commenting on the action in many scenes, and then … they disappear too, joining Eryl and Mr. Pye for a pint. They both should have gotten poison pen letters; him for not double-digging the flower beds when he claims he did and her for potions gone wrong.

We also didn't get to see Miss Marple make comparisons between Lymston (Lymstock in the novel) and St. Mary Mead. She should have! She always says one village is much like another so I'd expect parallels.

But there's plenty to like. Joan Hickson is always wonderful to watch. She spars ever so gently with Superintendent Nash. He's not about to listen to a twittering old lady and you can see why. She's obviously daft and he didn't get the memo from Scotland Yard that she's not to be ignored. There are other great moments: Beatrice and George, Jerry and Joanna being put in their place by Partridge, the housekeeper, Mr. Pye, Reverend Calthrop.

Watch this and then watch ITV's version from 2006 with Geraldine McEwan. They're the same novel, same plot, same characters, yet so different. They complement each other like Mr. Pye compliments the people around him: with a touch of amusing acid.

General Information

Based on: *The Moving Finger* (novel, 1942)
Run time: 1 hr., 42 min. **Subtitles:** No

Writer: Julia Jones **Director:** Roy Boulting

Cast

Joan Hickson as Miss Marple
Geoffrey Davion as Superintendent Nash
Roger Ostime as Inspector Crawford
Victor Maddern as P.C. Johnson
Gerald Sim as Coroner

Andrew Bicknell as Gerry Burton
Sabina Franklyn as Joanna Burton
Martin Fisk as Owen Griffith
Sandra Payne as Eryl Griffith
Michael Culver as Edward Symmington
Elizabeth Counsell as Angela Symmington
Deborah Appleby as Megan Hunter
Lucy Gleeson as Robert Symmington
Stuart Mansfield as James Symmington
Imogen Bickford-Smith as Elsie Holland
Ninka Scott as Miss Ginch
Dilys Hamlett as Maud Calthrop
John Arnatt as Rev. Guy Calthrop
Penelope Lee as Partridge Couls
Hilary Mason as Emily Barton
Richard Pearson as Mr. Pye
Juliet Waley as Beatrice Dunn
Michael Waterman as George Ellis

Film Locations

Hoxne, Suffolk (Lymston)
Elm House, Green Street, Hoxne (The Furze)
St. Peter and St. Paul Church, Hoxne
Goldbrook Bridge, Hoxne
Village Hall, Hoxne (Women's Institute)
Monks Hall, Syleham, Suffolk (Symington home exteriors, Pye's drawing room)
Weybourne Station, North Norfolk (train station)

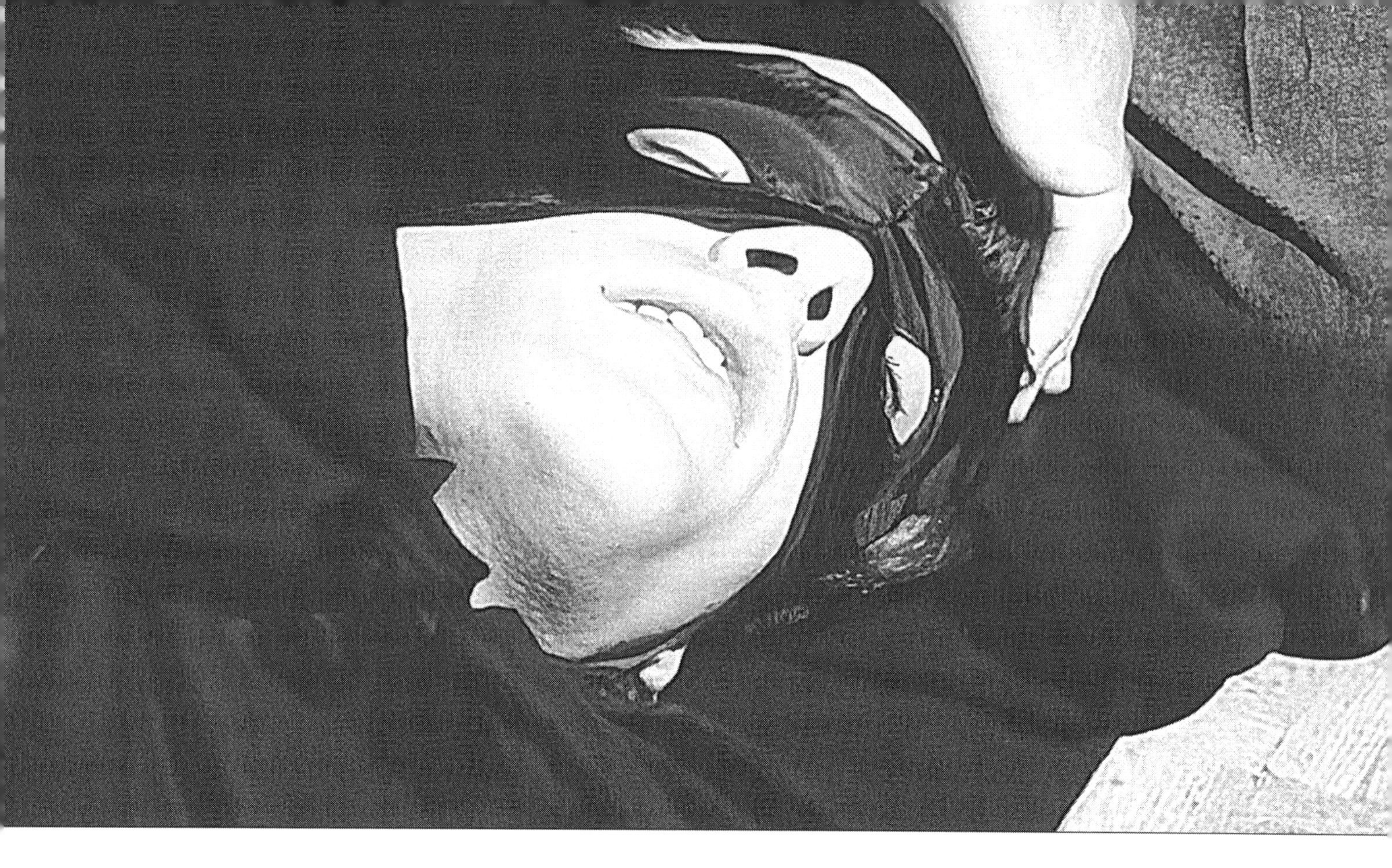

A Murder Is Announced (1985)

Not everyone is who they seem in this isolated village, and someone is willing to kill to keep their secrets

I dislike name changes in Agatha adaptations. She always chose her names for a reason. The sole reason for some hack scriptwriter changing them is to justify their salary.

Exhibit A is the vicar's cat who provides Miss Marple with a vital clue. In the novel, the cat's name is Tiglath Pileser. In the film, he becomes a she and is renamed Delilah, permitting the vicar to make a sex joke. For those of you not up on your ancient history like the vicar, Tiglath Pileser was the name of a series of Assyrian kings (I, II, and III) who ruled more than 3,000 years ago. While Tiglath Pileser is a very good name for a well-educated vicar's cat, so is Delilah.

The refugee cook's name changes from Mitzi to Hannah. That shouldn't have happened. Hannah is a very English name and Mitzi is not. Tiglath Pileser would confuse the overwhelming majority of modern viewers and Delilah would not. But Mitzi to Hannah? The scriptwriter must not have wanted confusion with Mitzi Gaynor and who's going to do that these days?

Phillipa Haymes loses her awful boss, Mrs. Lucas (and my, but Agatha had fun with her), so Inspector Craddock doesn't get to interview that self-satisfied harridan. Mrs. Lucas exemplifies why Miss Blacklock gets that particular group of visitors when the *Chipping Cleghorn Gazette* publishes the murder party announcement. Despite all the changes in English village life that Miss Marple alludes to, Chipping Cleghorn is still a tiny village with residents descended from the days of William the Conqueror. Mrs. Lucas, an important person in the village, is too important to socialize with Miss Blacklock, an outsider in the social hierarchy.

The novel and the film imply that Miss Blacklock's circle are all outsiders, who moved to the middle of nowhere for their own reasons. In case you wondered, that's why she didn't have everyone in the village at her door. It's not just to keep the cast manageable.

Moving to a village in the middle of nowhere and having to assert your bona fides is also why Miss Blacklock took Patrick and Julia Simmons into her home. They were distant enough relatives that they didn't know each other on sight, *but* they vouched for each other if anyone asked prying questions. This was especially important for Miss Blacklock in case anyone

Fidelity to text

The usual minor changes. The black-market activities between the neighbors are almost gone. That's the real reason they left their backdoors unlocked, not because the village is boringly safe.

Quality of movie

But only because I couldn't always understand the dialog. The story is allowed to unfold as it needed to; no frenetic jump cuts or annoyingly truncated storylines where you ask "what just happened?"

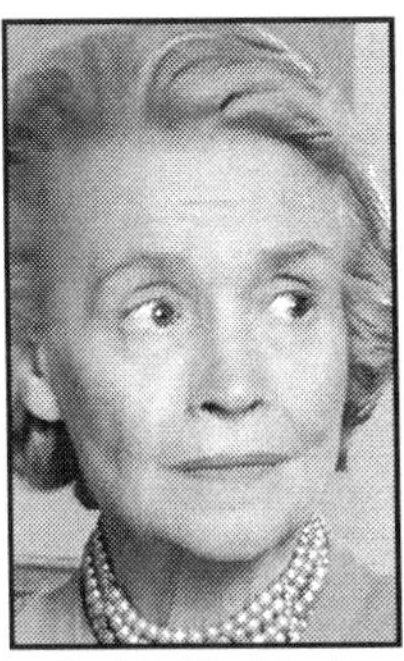

Letitia Blacklock (*Ursula Howells*), the secretive heiress

Dora Bunner (*Renée Asherson*), the longtime friend

Julia Simmons (*Samantha Bond*), the distant cousin

Phillipa Haymes (*Nicola King*), the war widow

Amy Murgatroyd (*Joan Sims*), the dotty farmer

Miss Hinchcliffe (*Paola Dionisotti*), the farmer's partner

asked why she didn't return to the part of England where she grew up.

The vicar and his wife are a special case. They're outside the village hierarchy because they have to minister to the needs of everyone in the congregation, high or low. They can attend the murder party because it's fun and they won't lose status by doing so, whereas Mrs. Lucas would.

This adaptation was wonderful. I admit the story took its time, but it's darned hard to compress a complex story into 90 minutes.

In this case, we got time (2 hours, 33 minutes). But it wasn't wasted as I've already observed in other Agatha adaptations where I'm left wondering why the camera focused on a bird in a tree or a lingering panoramic view of a lake and wishing they'd just get on with the story, dammit.

There are scenes of Inspector Craddock driving from one place to another but those one-lane-wide English backcountry roads between fields and pastures were oddly compelling. They were one step above gravel. They point out how isolated Chipping Cleghorn is, as does the presence of meandering cows in the village lanes. I believe these conscious choices were made not to pad out the film but to make the viewer wonder why Letitia Blacklock, an obviously well-educated, well-traveled lady of means, chose to bury herself in a tiny village in the middle of nowhere.

Miss Marple comments that everyone in a village used to know each other going back for generations. The locals knew each other's grandmothers' scandals. Someone from the outside would have to be vetted by a respected resident but they would always remain an outsider. Grandchildren might — might! — become insiders instead of being the grandchildren of the Blacklocks who moved in fifty years ago.

But change comes to us all, including backward little villages. Entire households of people arrive and we have to accept on faith what they claim about their background and identity. They have to do the same with us. Miss Marple, being the astute judge of human nature that she is, recognizes the golden opportunity to lie about one's personal history.

As always, she's proved correct: she never trusts what anyone says because her lack of faith in humanity is regularly justified by events. Look at the facts and deduce from them. Listen to what everyone says but don't believe them. Work out how a pile of statements from different suspects align with each other and, more importantly, where they differ. The truth lies somewhere in that tangle.

Each of our possible suspects notices the same thing — the central heating is on. They also can't quite believe what they are seeing and hearing and being told, but, because no one knows each other well, they have to accept what they are told.

There was one change the scriptwriters could have made to the text that I would have appreciated. We never find out what Colonel Easterbrook's wife is up to. She's much younger than her elderly husband. In a village packed with dowdy, real-looking people, Mrs. Easterbrook is glamorous. Old Colonels don't get to marry hot blonde vixens unless they've got something (usually money) that the vixen wants enough to go to bed with a doddering geezer. Agatha doesn't tell us what Mrs. Easterbrook is hiding. I would like to know.

What a great film. It played fair with the text, it didn't skip any of the clues, the actors and actresses were uniformly terrific and I could tell them apart.

Aha!

I know why the cat's name was changed from Tiglath Pileser to Delilah. The scriptwriter didn't want the audience thinking of any cats from T. S. Eliot's *Old Possum's Book of Practical Cats*. If you know your Broadway shows, Eliot's little book of poems became the worldwide phenomenon called *Cats* in 1980. Those cats had exotic, complex, made-up names like Munkustrap, Jennyanydots, and Rum Tum Tugger. Tiglath Pileser would have fit right in with that bunch. When *A Murder Is Announced* was aired in February of 1985, the audience might have thought of those singing, dancing cats instead of the vicar's cat who gave Miss Marple her vital, crime-solving clue.

General Information

Based on: *A Murder Is Announced* (novel, 1950)
Run time: 2 hr., 33 min. **Subtitles:** No

Writer: Alan Plater **Director:** David Giles

Cast

Joan Hickson as Miss Marple
John Castle as Detective Inspector Craddock
Kevin Whately as Detective Sergeant Fletcher
Richard Bebb as Chief Constable George Rydesdale

Ursula Howells as Letitia Blacklock
Renée Asherson as Dora Bunner
Samantha Bond as Julia Simmons
Simon Shepherd as Patrick Simmons
Nicola King as Phillipa Haymes
Elaine Ives-Cameron as Hannah
Joan Sims as Amy Murgatroyd
Paola Dionisotti as Miss Hinchcliffe
Matthew Solon as Edmund Swettenham
Mary Kerridge as Mrs. Swettenham
Ralph Michael as Colonel Easterbrook
Sylvia Syms as Mrs. Easterbrook
Vivienne Moore as Mrs. Harmon
David Collings as Reverend Harmon
David Pinner as Rowlandson
Liz Crowther as Myrna Harris
Victoria Williams as Bluebird Cafe Waitress
Tim Charrington as Rudi Scherz
Joyce Carey as Belle Goedler
Kay Gallie as Sister McClelland

Film Locations

Powerstock, Dorset (Chipping Cleghorn)
Ardverikie House, Newtonmore, Scotland (Belle Goedler's home)

A Pocketful of Rye (1985)

This tragedy about a discarded maid is undone by loose plot threads and a contrived, unsatisfying ending

A Pocketful of Rye makes promises to the viewer it has no intention of fulfilling, and it starts with the opening scene.

We see businessman Rex Fortescue skipping giddily along the London street, spontaneously buying flowers for his hot executive secretary, and chortling over reports in a very unbusinesslike manner. We are never given a reason for this behavior. Is it normal? His staff takes him in stride, so maybe it is. Or is their fabled English reserve combined with the staff knowing who's paying them so they shut up? Or is this an indication that this just-this-side-of-legal businessman is losing his marbles? Percival, his oldest son and heir, doesn't get scenes showing him cleaning up after his father's shenanigans. We never learn anything. It's possible these scenes were designed to tell us that Rex Fortescue is an unpleasant human being, but that's not what came across to us. Rex is a happy, spontaneous, giddy adulterer!

Anyway, Rex dies in his office, and rye is found in his coat pocket. The police investigate, and we're taken into his home to meet the family and staff, especially Gladys, the housemaid. She's pudgy, shy, awkward, and mistake-prone. It's unusual to have a housemaid as a major character, especially if she isn't a raving beauty destined to marry the lord's handsome son. Girls like Gladys exist in stories to dust in the background. If they're lucky, they move the plot forward by giving the detective a vital clue. And if the gods smile on them, they'll help solve the case, like Mitzi in *A Murder Is Announced*.

Gladys' fate is to be used and strangled very nastily when she's no longer of use. Her body is left with the laundry in the mansion's back garden, with a clothespin on her nose. Before she goes out to meet her fate at the clothesline, she leaves behind cryptic clues. She makes and takes anxious phone calls. We see her sad little garret bedroom and — another unfilled promise — we see her address a letter to Miss Marple, the old lady who took her from the orphanage and trained her to be a housemaid. In the novel, the letter provides (in the last two pages) critical evidence about the guilt of the murderer. In the movie, it simply vanishes.

Fidelity to text

Plenty of minor irritating changes like the title from *A Pocket Full of Rye* and Miss Ramsbottom becoming Miss Henderson. More serious changes were confusing, altered the tenor of the film, and rescued the villain from justice.

Quality of movie

One of the worst of the Hickson adaptations. Large chunks of the dialog were garbled. If you're familiar with the novel, the ending fell apart completely. If you're not, you may not notice.

Adele Fortescue (*Stacy Dorning*), the young widow

Lance Fortescue (*Peter Davison*), the black sheep

Patricia Fortescue (*Frances Low*), the obtuse wife

Percival Fortescue (*Clive Merrison*), the good brother

Jennifer Fortescue (*Rachel Bell*), the bored wife

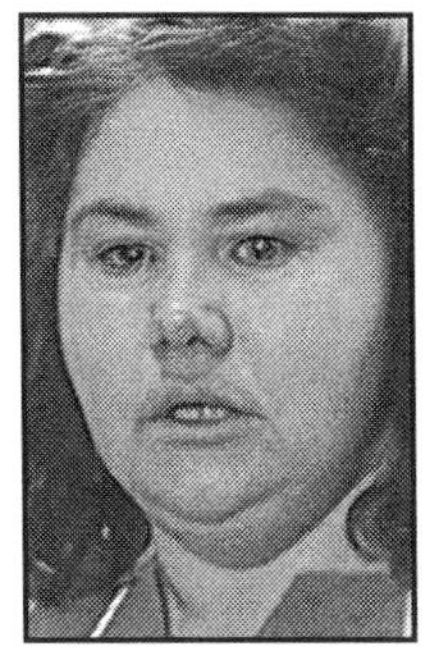

Gladys Martin (*Annette Badland*), the suspicious servant

Also gone are Elaine Fortescue, the youngest daughter, and her socialist schoolteacher boyfriend. I understand this choice because 103-minute-long films don't have time for every red herring. What I do not understand is eliminating Inspector Neele's interview with Mrs. Mackenzie, the widow of the man Rex stole the Blackbird Mine from and possibly murdered. She's critical to a major red herring, and she's dispensed with in a few mumbled sentences from Miss Marple about her mind being too far gone to be questioned. As if that ever stopped Miss Marple before!

It was also never made clear that our hyper-competent housekeeper, Miss Dove, apparently leads a gang of thieves. After she works in a wealthy house for a year or so, she leaves and a few months later, thieves break in. The thieves know the location of the silver, the jewelry, the fur coats, and anything else worth stealing. We also lose the scenes with the Inspector and Miss Dove discussing her blackmail attempts and shady past.

The truncated script also reduced Vivian Edward Dubois' role as Adele Fortescue's fancy bit on the side (and here's the one case in the story where a name change would be worthwhile; no one uses Vivian as a man's name anymore). As the much younger, glamorous second wife to Rex Fortescue, Adele does not get along with her stepchildren. It's hard for Percival Fortescue to look at dad's new cookie who's younger than he is and hotter than his own wife, Jennifer. Vivian has a darn good reason to murder Rex and then to murder Adele, but he vanishes from the scene far too quickly.

Another change that you won't notice if you haven't read the book is that Jennifer Fortescue is in a bad marriage. The bigger change is that she apparently got Rex Fortescue to will her £40,000 just by asking, because Percival was mean to her. Not in the book, folks, but I suppose it let the scriptwriter avoid adding Mrs. Mackenzie to the cast, even though she should have been included.

General Information

Based on: *A Pocket Full of Rye* (novel, 1953)
Run time: 1 hr., 43 min. **Subtitles:** No

Writer: T.R. Bowen **Director:** Guy Slater

Cast

Joan Hickson as Miss Jane Marple
Tom Wilkinson as Detective Inspector Neele
Jon Glover as Detective Sergeant Hay
Charles Pemberton as Sergeant Rose
Laurin Kaski as Police Constable White

Timothy West as Rex Fortescue
Fabia Drake as Miss Henderson
Clive Merrison as Percival Fortescue
Rachel Bell as Jennifer Fortescue
Peter Davison as Lance Fortescue
Frances Low as Patricia Fortescue
Stacy Dorning as Adele Fortescue
Martyn Stanbridge as Vivian Dubois
Selina Cadell as Mary Dove
Annette Badland as Gladys Martin
Merelina Kendall as Mrs. Crump
Frank Mills as Mr. Crump
Susan Gilmore as Miss Grosvenor
Nancie Herrod as Miss Griffith
Rhoda Lewis as Mrs. Brogan
Suzie Cerys as Daisy
Louis Mahoney as Dr. French
Beau Daniels as Ellen

Film Locations

Thelveton Hall, Diss, Norfolk (Yew Tree Lodge)
Nether Wallop, Hampshire (St. Mary Mead)
The Old Chapel, Nether Wallop (infants school)
Dane Cottage, Nether Wallop (Miss Marple's cottage)

> *All businessmen are the victims of greed, some way to another, I fear.*
> Miss Marple

The biggest change was to the ending. I won't spoil it for you (assuming again that you haven't read the novel). No. Just no. It felt so *deus ex machina*. To make that contrivance even more unconvincing, the killer revealed that his emotionally abusive upbringing justified the deaths. This violates Agatha's belief that the killer was a bad seed from day one.

I agree that an ending that works in a book doesn't necessarily translate to the screen and should be changed. In the novel, we know that a certain someone will meet the hangman, but we don't see it. Instead, we see Miss Marple receiving proof in the mail. Remember the letter that is noticed — by Miss Marple and ignored! — in Gladys' room? This is the letter, and it never plays a role in the story again.

In the novel, after she reads the letter and looks at the enclosed photograph, you get this passage:

> *The tears rose in Miss Marple's eyes. Succeeding pity, there came anger — anger at a heartless killer.*
> *And then, displacing both these emotions, there came a surge of triumph — the triumph some specialist might feel who has successfully reconstructed an extinct animal from a fragment of jawbone and couple of teeth.*

The murderer will swing, but we don't see it. This is where the scriptwriter could have made a change similar to the end of *Crooked House*. We could have seen the murderer confronted with the evidence that was mailed to Miss Marple. But we don't. Instead, we get this ridiculous scene where the killer is accidentally run over by a random lorry. It's like the universe forgave him for his murders, letting him escape justice, and denying Gladys and the other victims justice because they weren't as special.

There's a saying at Pixar, who know a thing or two about storytelling: "Coincidences to get characters into trouble are great; coincidences to get them out of it are cheating." The same rule applies to screenwriters.

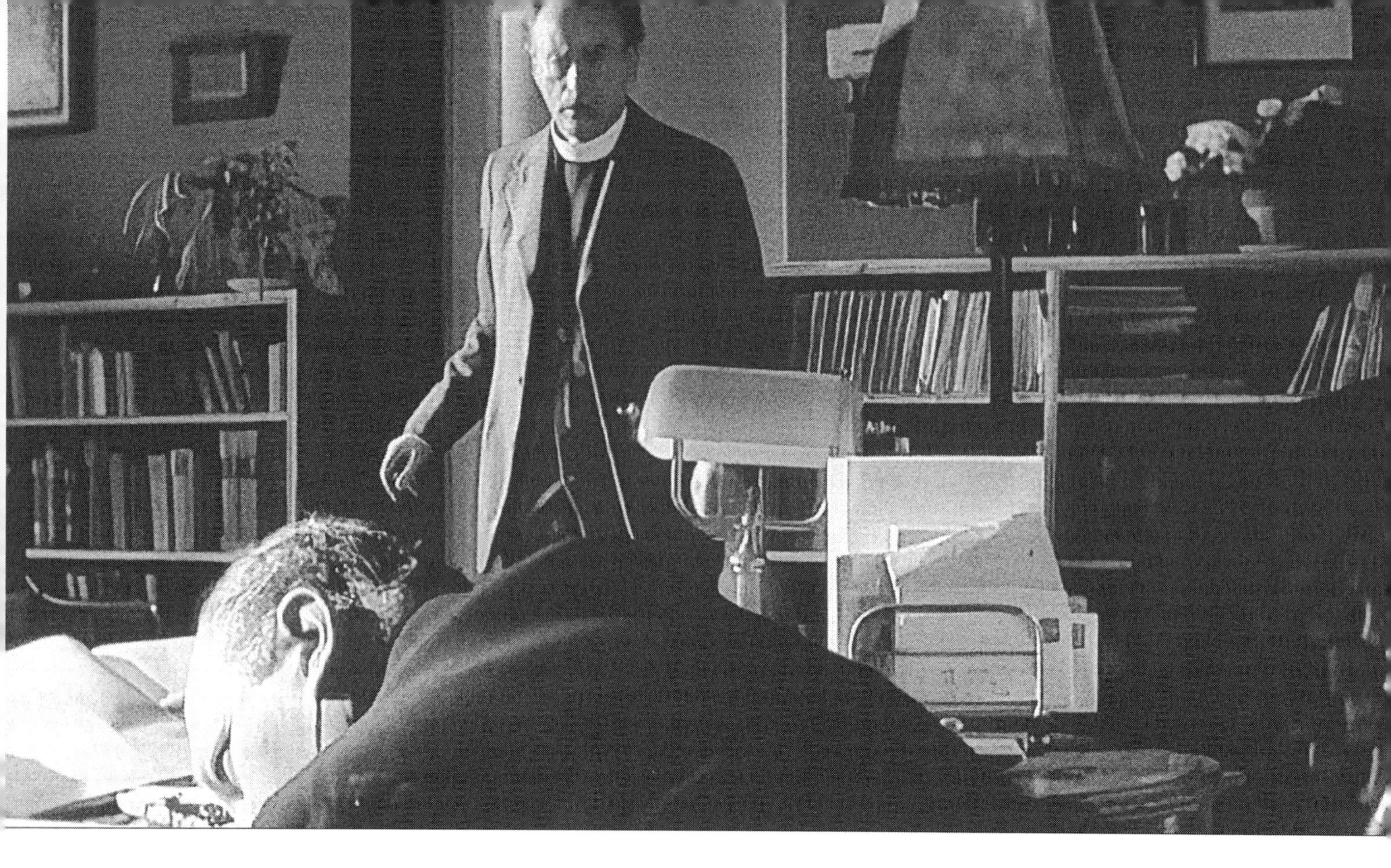

The Murder at the Vicarage (1986)

Poor lighting and a needless rewrite leaves viewers in the dark in this tale of adultery, artistry, and angsty teens

Fidelity to text

Condensing or removing characters, some of whom were important (Dr. Stone and his hapless assistant). The plan to trap the murderer is radically different. Worst of all, one of the murderers commits suicide out of remorse.

Quality of movie

The pacing was off, the dialog was murky in the extreme, large sections were shot in the dark, and the lead characters had zero chemistry.

Miss Marple made her debut in the short story collection, *The Thirteen Problems* (retitled *The Tuesday Club Murders* in the United States). She then went on to star in her first novel, *The Murder at the Vicarage* (1930). If they know Miss Marple at all, this novel is probably the one most people are familiar with.

Thus, it behooves the BBC to produce an adaptation that is true to the text, since far more people watch TV than read. If you're showcasing a major fictional character, why not tell the story the way the author intended? Allowing for the differences between film and text, the BBC generally does it up fine, as demonstrated by Joan Hickson's four previous outings as Miss Marple.

Except, on reconsideration, the major and dreadful rewrite of Lance Fortescue's character in *A Pocketful of Rye*. The same proved true for *The Murder at the Vicarage*. I can accept characters being disappeared because 102 minutes doesn't allow for a lot of leisurely complex plot development. But rewriting Miss Marple's plot to trap the murderer by having him murder an almost entirely new, made-up-from-whole-cloth character didn't play well with me, particularly since much of it was shot in the dark. The cat was a nice touch, though. The murderer was very careful about not harming the cat while trying to gas the victim.

I really didn't like the other murderer's suicide. Oh, oh, oh, oh, the guilt, the shame, the agony of knowing they'd killed another person. Well, no. That murderer was quite clear: He had it coming and there wasn't so much as a snip of guilt. I suppose the reasoning behind this was to make for more drama for the film. Or, the screenplay wasn't properly developed and so the scriptwriter had to come up with something dramatic.

In the novel, although the crimes are solved, we do not see what happens next. We assume that arrests are made, the case is brought to trial, and the murderers convicted (since Miss Marple deduced the motives and methods, this is a foregone conclusion) and then hung by the Crown. The scriptwriter must have decided to finesse this ending with one of their own. That still leaves the other murderer, the instigator of the plot, hanging freely and offscreen.

Another thing I didn't like about this adaptation

Col. Lucius Protheroe (*Robert Lang*), the tough nut

Ann Protheroe (*Polly Adams*), the wife/stepmother

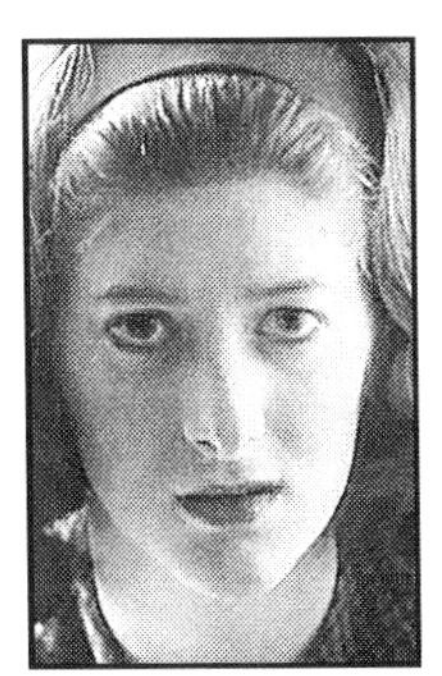
Lettice Protheroe (*Tara MacGowran*), the wild child

Mrs. Lestrange (*Norma West*), the concerned mother

Lawrence Redding (*James Hazeldine*), the louche artist

Rev. Leonard Clement (*Paul Eddington*), the moral force

was it didn't spell out the reasons for the murders. There's always a reason, usually money, sex, or fear. In *The Murder at the Vicarage*, money and sex feature prominently, but you'd never know it from this adaptation.

It's so bloodless. Agatha is never bloodless. Her novels seethe with passion requited and unrequited. The desperate need for money runs a close second. Sometimes it's needed to save the estate from ruin, other times it is the dire need to escape poverty.

In this case, our villains want to run away and live in sin, and be comfortable while doing so. Yet that is never made clear. Part of this is due to the actor playing Lawrence Redding. He's got all the liveliness and charisma of a Ken doll.

One thing I did like was seeing a lot more of Mary, the vicar's insolent and incompetent maid, and her young man, Bill Archer. Archer is the local poacher. He has regular run-ins with Col. Protheroe. He's also, like Mary, a representative of the lower, working-class villagers who normally only show up to add background color despite doing all the work. The same is true of the villagers that the vicar visits only to discover that he's been fooled in order to get him far away from the scene of the crime. These two sturdy farmers make jokes at the vicar's expense and it's a funny scene.

So is the scene involving Griselda, the vicar's wife, and the group of old ladies she is having tea with, including Miss Marple. I would have enjoyed this part even more if I could have understood better what everyone was saying.

Too much of this movie was shot in the dark. There are long, long moments when you'll have no idea what is going on. Characters are creeping around in the dark, but you're not sure why. At times, I wasn't sure who was creeping around. This includes a lengthy sequence when Anne Protheroe — who is checking the house for prowlers — could have turned on the darned lights! Nobody investigates mysterious noises in the attic without turning on the lights. These folks have electricity. We see properly lit rooms everywhere.

The poor lighting does help conceal the lack of English Country House porn. Other episodes in this series have been better, especially *The 4.50 From Paddington* episode with (oh-my-God look at that fantastic fill-in-the-blank!) Rutherford Hall.

The Protheroes supposedly live in a grand house, but it didn't look that grand to me. It may have been completely authentic down to the baseboards but it didn't make me drool with envy and dream of redecorating. On the other hand, the church in St. Mary Mead was gorgeous.

Then there's the scene that made no sense at all. It wasn't part of the novel. It didn't solve the crime. It didn't advance the plot. It's Mary taking a basket lunch to church and then tucking it away between a pair of flying buttresses at the side of the church so her poacher boyfriend can find the basket.

Why do this? If the producers were looking to fill airtime, they could have shown Anne Protheroe and Lawrence Redding's torrid affair. Or how awful Col. Protheroe was. Or Lettice's distaste for her stepmother *and* her father. Or more about Mrs. Lestrange. Or why Dr. Haydock was so emotionally involved with Mrs. Lestrange. Or why that painting in the Prothereoe's attic was slashed. Or how Miss Marple deduced the solution. Anything! If you've read the novel, you can add more examples to the list.

I still think this episode of *Miss Marple* is worth watching simply because Joan Hickson is worth watching. She is Miss Marple. Just don't expect the sumptuous feast of *The Body in the Library* or *A Murder Is Announced*. I can't believe I'm going to make this recommendation, but here it is: the 2004 version of *The Murder at the Vicarage* with Geraldine McEwan — despite its many flaws — is a better adaptation of the novel. If you can only spare the time for one adaptation, choose that one.

General Information

Based on: *The Murder at the Vicarage* (novel, 1930)
Run time: 1 hr., 34 min. **Subtitles:** No

Writer: T.R. Bowen **Director:** Julian Amyes

Cast

Joan Hickson as Miss Marple
David Horovitch as Det. Inspector Slack
Ian Brimble as Det. Sergeant Lake

Paul Eddington as Rev. Leonard Clement
Cheryl Campbell as Griselda Clement
Rachel Weaver as Mary Wright
Jack Galloway as Bill Archer
Christopher Good as Christopher Hawes
Robert Lang as Col. Lucius Protheroe
Polly Adams as Ann Protheroe
Tara MacGowran as Lettice Protheroe
James Hazeldine as Lawrence Redding
Norma West as Mrs. Lestrange
Michael Browning as Dr. Haydock
Rosalie Crutchley as Mrs. Price-Ridley
Barbara Hicks as Miss Hartnell
Deddie Davies as Mrs. Salisbury

Film Location

Nether Wallop, Hampshire (St. Mary Mead)

"

I first came across Inspector Slack over that dreadful business at Gossington Hall. He is rather like these diesel engines that are now appearing all over our railways: most unappealing, but, I am told, efficient.
Miss Marple

Sleeping Murder (1987)

This tale of repressed memories and thwarted love entertains despite the victim's murky motivation

Fidelity to text

It's close; mainly shifting the film's date to the early 1950s and compressing and removing minor characters.

Quality of movie

The usual problems of film quality (16 mm doesn't age well) and lack of subtitles. Otherwise, this version was well-paced and atmospheric, but unanswered questions remain.

Sleeping Murder was a treat after sitting through *Murder at the Vicarage* (1986). The producers got a clue and shot the film so you could see what was going on rather than watching dark shapes move against a darker background. It was sunny, a nice contrast to the very unsunny subject matter.

It always amazes me that people think Agatha wrote cozies. That she doesn't is proved again here. The implications of the murderer and his motives are unsettling. If he can't have the object of his unnatural obsession, no one can. This is one of the very few Agatha Christie stories that don't involve money as a major motive. It's passion and obsession here; wanting what you can't and shouldn't have.

This story also plays into the theme of old sins casting long shadows, and how those sins can be remembered in strange, unexpected ways.

Which is why we get the stunning coincidence of Gwenda Reed, newlywed expat returning from New Zealand and finding the perfect house in a quaint village on the English coast. It's a house that feels strangely and startlingly familiar in odd ways. The musical score, something I don't normally notice, played this up nicely without being over the top.

My only criticism is that it's too short. There were all kinds of motivations and reasons that went missing. Agatha wrote *Sleeping Murder* during the London Blitz and placed it in a vault along with *Curtain*, Hercule Poirot's last case. She was at the height of her powers, writing complex, well-plotted, and detailed mysteries. She didn't slow down until the late 1960s.

So why then do we not get more of an explanation of Helen Spenlove Kennedy Halliday's motives? That's Gwenda's mysteriously vanished stepmother. Everyone says she ran off with another man. Everyone implied that she was crazy about men and loose with her affections.

Miss Marple would tell you to never believe what anyone says. She never does. She expects people to misremember, shade the truth, and outright lie, and she's right.

I could figure out (especially after the big reveal) why Helen ran away from the quaint village all the way to India intending to marry Walter Fane, boring

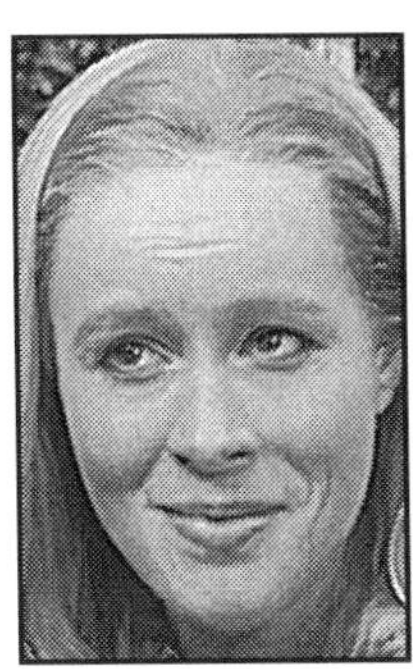
Gwenda Reed (*Geraldine Alexander*), the haunted

Giles Reed (*John Moulder-Brown*), the homeowner

Dr. James Kennedy (*Frederick Treves*), Helen's half-brother

Walter Fane (*Terrence Hardiman*), the jilted attorney

Richard Erskine (*John Bennett*), the tempted husband

Jackie Afflick (*Kenneth Cope*), the coach owner

solicitor, who'd relocated to India himself. She was desperate to leave. Why didn't she marry Walter? Maybe because she'd had a torrid affair with a married man on the ship to India and discovered she didn't want to settle?

Well, okay. Even so, while marrying Walter Fane might not have been the best choice, it was far better than remaining in that quaint little village. She escaped an obsessed man in that village.

But Helen said no to Walter Fane on the dock in some port in India. She boarded a ship and sailed back to England, which made no sense. It was there that Helen met Gwenda's father, Kelvin Halliday, a widower with a little girl. They fall in love (those shipboard romances! Someone should write a novel) and marry. Okay.

Except they return to England, the place that Helen wanted to escape. Still okay. England's a big place. Not as big as the United States but large enough that there were plenty of counties, cities, towns, and villages to choose from.

Yet Helen agrees to return to the quaint little English seaside village that she couldn't run away from fast enough and for very good reasons. Was this her new husband's decision and she went along? We don't know.

This is really important to me, because Helen's motivations drive the plot. Why did she flee the village? Why did she return? Why did she — apparently — flee again with some other man in the dead of night?

We are not given an explanation for Helen's motives. Yet if she had not returned to the quaint English seaside village, life would have been different for her, her husband, and her little stepdaughter. For one thing, she might not have vanished in the night, leaving behind a husband who thinks he strangled her and dies a suicide, and a traumatized stepdaughter who gets shipped off to relatives in New Zealand.

I don't have a problem with the unlikeliness of this plot mechanism. I swallowed whole the set of books about four midgets trekking across a wilderness to throw a ring into a volcano. But I expect reasonably plausible, internally consistent explanations for why the characters do what they do.

General Information

Based on: *Sleeping Murder* (novel, 1976)
Run time: 1 hr., 42 min. **Subtitles:** No

Writer: Ken Taylor **Director:** John Davies

Cast

Joan Hickson as Miss Marple
Peter Spraggon as Detective Inspector Last
Geraldine Alexander as Gwenda Reed
John Moulder-Brown as Giles Reed

Gary Watson as Kelvin Halliday
Frederick Treves as Dr. James Kennedy
Terrence Hardiman as Walter Fane
Jean Anderson as Mrs. Fane
John Bennett as Richard Erskine
Geraldine Newman as Janet Erskine
Kenneth Cope as Jackie Afflick
Jack Watson as Mr. Foster
Joan Scott as Mrs. Cocker
Eryl Maynard as Lily Kimble
Ken Kitson as Jim Kimble
Jean Heywood as Edith Paget
John Ringham as Dr. Penrose
Georgine Anderson as Mrs. Hengrave
Edward Jewesbury as Mr. Sims
David McAlister as Raymond West
Amanda Boxer as Joan West
Esmond Knight as Mr. Galbraith

Film Locations

Otterton, Budleigh Salterton, Devon (opening scene cottage)
Watch Hill, Budleigh Salterton, Devon (Hillside)
Lympstone, Devon
Cadhay House, Ottery St. Mary, Devon (Anstell Manor)
Sidmouth, Devon (Dillmouth)
Starcross, Devon (Starcross Hospital)

At least Gwenda's motivations were understandable. She wanted to find out what happened and why this mysterious house that she was sure she'd never seen before triggered intense memories. She had a chance to learn secrets hidden from her for her entire life. I understood her husband's motivations. He wanted his wife to be happy, and he was curious, too.

I understood everyone else's motivations, from gardeners to former housemaids to lawyers to shop assistants to former friends and lovers. They all made sense.

Miss Marple's motivations made sense. She knew to let sleeping dogs lie and what would come of disturbing them. Since no one took her good advice and those dogs got roused, she wanted to solve the crime and prevent another crime from happening to Gwenda and Giles.

But we were not told Helen's motivations. This is one of those opportunities that a good scriptwriter can take and run with. If it's not spelled out in the book or glossed over or omitted entirely, the adaptation can tell the full story. This is why sometimes (but not always) the movie can be better than the book.

We've seen this successfully done in other adaptations. The 2011 version of *The Blue Geranium* — a very early Miss Marple short story — was far superior to the source material. It can be done.

Sadly, it wasn't done here. I can't blame it on time limitations either because the BBC presents longer adaptations when they want to. *Sleeping Murder* was 102 minutes long. That's not a lot of time to fully flesh out everyone's motivations and yet, other than Helen's, they managed.

Despite that issue, *Sleeping Murder* still worked. I didn't question Helen's motivations while watching the film. This came afterwards, while Bill and I were walking around the block on our nightly constitutional. It's a reminder that Alfred Hitchcock, who knew a thing or two about successful movies, was right. As long as the audience doesn't say "wait a minute!" during the movie and wait until they get into the lobby to start dissecting the flaws, the film succeeded.

By this standard, so did *Sleeping Murder*.

At Bertram's Hotel (1987)

Agatha's musings on growing old, set in a London hotel frozen in time, get lost in the condensed story

At Bertram's Hotel (1965) was Agatha's next-to-last Miss Marple novel. The final Miss Marple was *Nemesis*, published in 1971. *Sleeping Murder*, while published in 1976, was written in the early 1940's. Does this matter? Yes, it does, because Miss Marple has been slowly and subtly aging. She hasn't lost any of her mental sharpness but her body is getting older.

She can still eavesdrop with the best of them, but she can no longer go after a murderer with weedkiller like she did in *Sleeping Murder*. She's also acutely aware of the passage of time.

The extensive changes wrought in England during her lifetime are on her mind when she arrives at Bertram's Hotel. She's enjoying a two-week vacation courtesy of nephew, Raymond. She'd stayed at Bertram's as a young girl and is astonished at how unreal it seems; almost a caricature of an Edwardian-era hotel right down to the uniformed and capped chambermaids. Bertram's Hotel chambermaids even curtsey like an Edwardian-era servant would and a modern chambermaid would not.

There's a reason for that behavior but since the movie compressed so much of the text into 110 minutes, it's almost completely lost. It needed another ten minutes or more to explain the criminal activity that Miss Marple detects in the background.

Fidelity to text

Most things are present and accounted for until the overly compressed ending. Moving the date from the early 1960s to about 1953 loses Agatha's comments on the era via Miss Marple.

Quality of movie

The compressed plot made it hard to follow the complicated storyline. The unintelligible dialog didn't help; we had to replay a scene four times and I still think Miss Marple said "spoon" and not "policeman."

At Bertram's Hotel contains a great movie struggling to break free. The culture clash alone was worth more time. The hotel installed a television room, because the American guests like it! The handsome Irish groom who didn't know his place! Absentminded Canon Pennyfather stumbles into the crime, yet the action is so truncated, we get cryptic, unintelligible telephone calls that are supposed to explain and only muddy the waters still further.

At times, I thought there were two totally unrelated plots competing for screen space. We have Elvira Blake and her very unsuitable boyfriend and her estranged adventuress of a mother. We also have a mysterious string of high-stakes robberies involving famous people who couldn't have done it. Finally, we have a murder. Are the stories related?

Bess Sedgwick (*Caroline Blakiston*), the adventuress

Elvira Blake (*Helena Michell*), the heiress

Col. Derek Luscombe (*James Cossins*), the guardian

Ladislaus Malinowski (*Robert Reynolds*), the racecar driver

Canon Pennyfather (*Preston Lockwood*), the absent-minded

Michael Gorman (*Brian McGrath*), the commissionaire

Yes, except there's not enough onscreen evidence. We got significant glances and lingering camera shots of Bertram's exquisite high tea dessert tray and quick shots of newspaper headlines that we couldn't read. This shouldn't have happened. The BBC could have filmed another ten minutes; a minute here, thirty seconds there, to show us better how the two stories intertwined. Rationing doesn't exist anymore. They could have bought more film stock.

As I stated in my review of *Nemesis* (1987), filmmakers should never, ever, ever assume the audience read the book. I'd bet that at least half the audience for *Miss Marple* have never cracked open a Miss Marple novel. And this is in Great Britain, a literate, reading culture that adores Agatha Christie.

If you haven't already read *At Bertram's Hotel*, you'll be lost. I know the storyline and *I* was lost.

Excising most of the gang of thieves plot also ruined what could have been a very tense movie. Bertram's Hotel is so nostalgic as to be unreal. That's because it is. A gang of thieves uses it to cover their crimes. They're running a real hotel, with real guests camouflaging the presence of fake guests transporting stolen goods.

But what if a real guest is a sharp-eyed, snoopy old lady? She behaves suspiciously, asks prying questions, lurks in odd corners, and openly eavesdrops. That old lady is in for a world of hurt. She could easily slip and fall down a flight of stairs. An attending doctor's first thought would not be "she was pushed." It would be "we need better handrails and how about an elevator to prevent these tragic yet completely normal accidents?" That should have been played up considerably. I would think that a criminal syndicate operating out of a hotel would be wary about what the guests saw. Not this bunch.

I also could not figure out how Miss Marple was able to follow Elvira and the Italian boyfriend to the seedy diner. I really couldn't figure out how Elvira and her adventuress mother were able to reconcile the Italian boyfriend since he was carrying on with both of them. I know Elvira narrowly escaped murder at gunpoint but even so. Most daughters and mothers I know don't share their lover and a near-death experience won't reconcile them to doing so.

General Information

Based on: *At Bertram's Hotel* (novel, 1965)
Run time: 1 hr., 50 min. **Subtitles:** No

Writer: Jill Hyem **Director:** Mary McMurray

Cast

Joan Hickson as Miss Marple
Joan Greenwood as Selina Hazy
George Baker as Chief Inspector Fred Davy
Philip Bretherton as Detective Inspector Campbell
Douglas Milvain as Sir Ronald Graves

Caroline Blakiston as Bess Sedgwick
Helena Michell as Elvira Blake
James Cossins as Col. Derek Luscombe
Preston Lockwood as Canon Pennyfather
Robert Reynolds as Ladislaus Malinowski
Helen Horton as Mrs. Cabot
Peter Baldwin as Mr. Humfries
Brian McGrath as Michael Gorman
Irene Sutcliffe as Miss Gorringe
Neville Phillips as Henry
Henrietta Voigts as Alice
Kate Duchêne as Rose Sheldon
Randal Herley as Richard Egerton
Charlotte Barker as Bridget Sotheby
Edward Burnham as Dr. Whittaker

Film Location

Brown's Hotel, Mayfair, London

The film's ending was changed. In the book, Miss Marple and the inspector deduce who did it but they have no proof. The inspector assures Miss Marple that the murderer won't get away with it but we don't know how he'll prove his case. Movies need a dramatic moment when the murderer is confronted with evidence of their guilt, so we get a scene involving a handkerchief sachet. This is a folded-over pair of satin pockets that you stuff with your fancy, embroidered handkerchiefs. It keeps them clean and flat. It's also perfect, according to Miss Marple, for stashing illicit love letters and anything else you don't want seen and she proves it by discovering the murderer's diary.

This seemed weak. If a handkerchief sachet is a common place to hide things, then don't you think that's the first place an inspector (or a nosy old lady) will look?

I did like Bess Sedgwick very much, right up to the ending. Jumping into her sports car and fleeing the police was accurate to the book, but it didn't feel right. She'd have run over that peddler on a bicycle instead of crashing. And even though Bess wasn't wearing a seatbelt (they didn't have them in 1953) it's hard to believe she would have died. Badly injured? Sure. Got away with it? Quite possible. Killed instantly? I doubt it.

Elvira Blake was interesting; living proof that the apple doesn't fall far from the tree. Again, the novel gave us far more material about her adventuress-in-training ways. The movie only gave us hints.

I wanted more of that Irish groom who became a doorman for Bertram's Hotel. He had a complex relationship with Bess. Was that why he ran to Elvira Blake's rescue? Or was he was the heroic type as well as it being his job to rescue guests? We don't get those answers. I don't believe he was part of the criminal gang running the hotel but the movie was poorly written so I'm not quite sure.

I don't always want my movies to be longer. This time, I did. I'll have to watch *At Bertram's Hotel* a second time to see if I can catch what I missed the first time. Subtitles would have helped, no doubt, but so would have a better, more comprehensive script and better enunciation.

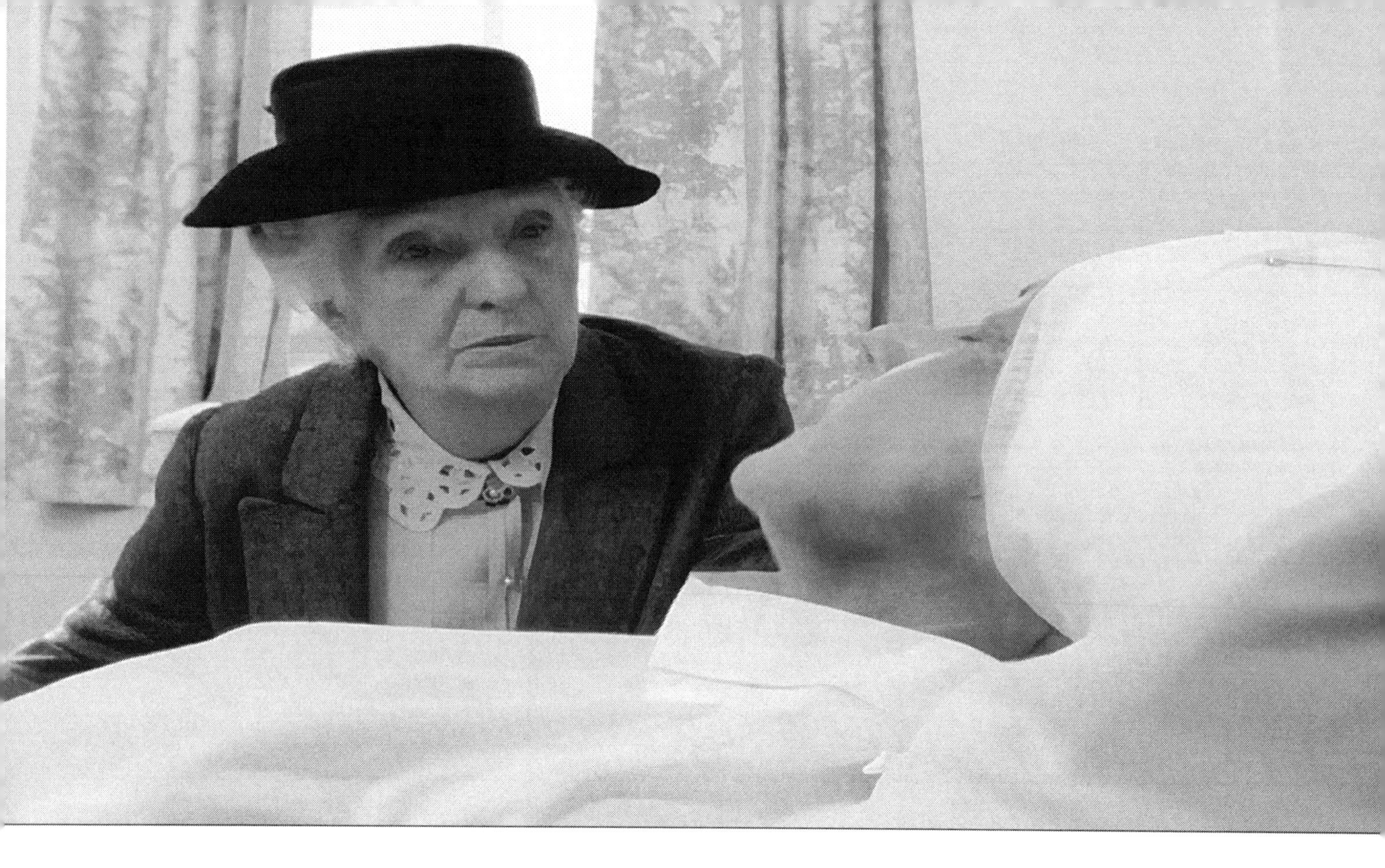

Nemesis (1987)

A too-short script drops some plot, but buy a ticket for this mystery tour of great English country mansions

Fidelity to text

Many, many changes, new characters were added (which worked) and Michael Rafiel got a major rewrite (which didn't).

Quality of movie

I liked it, but I already knew the plot. At 102 minutes, the movie omitted critical information making it hard for Bill to know what the heck was going on.

Movie producers adapting a novel should never assume everyone in the audience read the book. The number of readers is vastly smaller than the number of TV watchers. If critical plot points are elided over, the nonreading audience will not understand, will switch to something less challenging and more viewer-friendly, and will not tell their friends to watch this must-see TV.

This problem can be solved by adding new characters, such as Miss Marple's godson, Lionel Peel. Thrown out of his house by his wife, he visits Miss Marple and ends up joining the bus tour. He acts as Miss Marple's legs, travels to London to run down a lead at her request, and takes over some tasks that Professor Wanstead performed in the novel.

Lionel was added to give Miss Marple a Watson to talk to and allow the audience to follow her thinking. He got kind of short shrift there at the end. It felt to me that the tour guide, Madge, (Mrs. Sandbourne in the novel) might be flirting with Lionel but that came to nothing. Pity, since I enjoyed watching Madge in her perky uniform trying her darnedest to shepherd the tour group into keeping on track and on schedule. Lionel and Madge seemed made for each other.

Another new character was Mrs. Brent, Nora Brent's mother. Nora was a Broad in the novel. You can guess why the scriptwriter changed her last name and I won't argue. The scene where Professor Wanstead interviews Mrs. Brent about her missing daughter was deeply moving. It's been almost a decade since her Nora vanished and she's still grieving. She's sure her daughter is dead since there's been no contact for all those years but she doesn't *know*.

Like the Joan Hickson version of *The Body in the Library*, the scriptwriter emphasized what we so often don't see in mysteries: the devastated family left behind. And they are devastated. When consuming entertainment, we should be reminded to pay as much attention to the people as to the puzzle the murder presents.

Michael Rafiel is devastated too and in more ways than one. He's Jason Rafiel's ne'er-do-well son and Verity Hunt's lover. A problem I had with the novel and again with this adaptation is the age difference between the Rafiels. Mr. Rafiel looks to be at least 80 when he dies. Michael, on the other hand, is in his early thirties. So Jason Rafiel fathered a son at age 50? This is

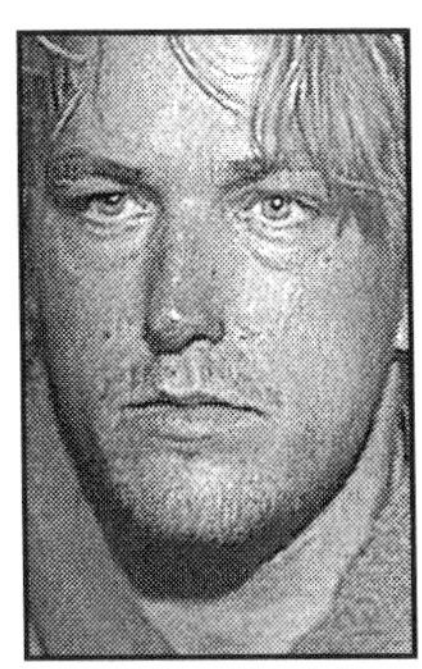

Michael Rafiel
(*Bruce Payne*),
the charitable heir

Clothilde Bradbury-Scott
(*Margaret Tyzack*),
the handsome sister

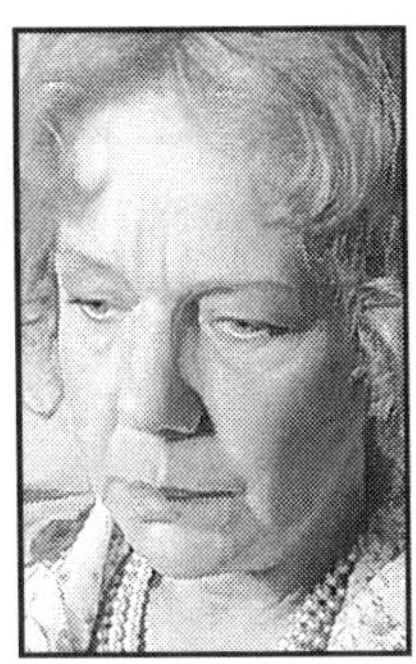

Anthea Bradbury-Scott
(*Anna Cropper*),
the scatty sister

Lavinia Glynne
(*Valerie Lush*),
the plain sister

Professor Wanstead
(*John Horsley*),
the criminal doctor

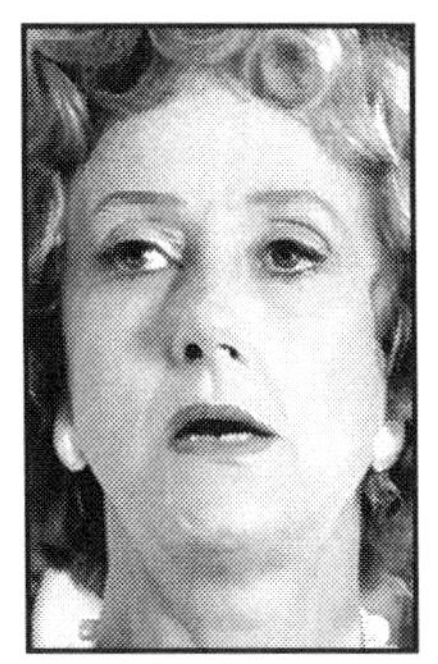

Mrs. Brent
(*Liz Fraser*),
the supportive mother

certainly possible with a hot young wife, a business tycoon's typical accessory. But we're never given details, either in the novel or in the adaptation about Mr. Rafiel's wife. She's dead and that's all there is to it.

Most people won't mind, but I get hung up on what I think of as bus schedules, whether they're time tables or age discrepancies. This is one of those cases where an astute scriptwriter can make changes I would agree with: they have the chance to clarify or fix a discrepancy in the original text.

Michael is suspected of beating and strangling Verity Hunt. In the novel, he's imprisoned in a mental institution. In this adaptation, he's a homeless bum, living on the street. We are shown what a nice guy he really is by the close relationship he has with his mongrel dog and by testimony from other homeless men about how Michael stands up for them.

Okay. Sure. I can buy that.

What I can't buy was watching homeless, sleeping-on-the-streets Michael in 1954 or thereabouts looking like he'd just shaved the night before. He was extremely attractive and well-groomed for a bum, with a very fashionable stubble. Nobody wrinkled their nose at his body odor. The shaving was particularly noticeable since any man who doesn't shave on a regular basis is going to grow a beard pretty darn quick. I watch my husband and our son go days or weeks without shaving and the beard and mustache show up promptly. More time away from a razor and the beard and mustache get longer. And longer. And longer. That attractive, fashionable stubble requires regular maintenance with a razor.

Hollywood strikes again.

Our leading man's fashionable stubble was even more in your face when all the other homeless bums had straggly, arrest-me-now thatches of facial hair cascading down their chests. Not our Michael. A shave, a wash, and a new suit will transform him into a gentleman and that is indeed what happens. This did not ring true to me, although everything else in *Nemesis* did.

I really enjoyed our tour guide, Madge. I enjoyed even more following their tour of England's historic homes and gardens. Wow. Castles, stately manors, libraries several stories high, abbeys, huge gardens. Wow. Just wow. No wonder Miss Marple said yes to Mr. Rafiel's crazy request to solve an unstated crime. She didn't just earn £20,000 pounds and bring more justice into the world. She got an all-expenses-paid tour of England!

I also liked the three sisters, living in their slowly decaying manor. This building would never be included in an English historic homes and gardens tour. Not enough history and too much dry rot and leaky roofs. The rundown house perfectly reflects Clothilde Bradbury-Scott, Lavinia Bradbury-Scott Glynne, and Anthea Bradbury-Scott. If you're up on your Greek mythology, you may notice certain similarities between the three sisters' names and those of the Fates: Clotho, Lachesis, and Atropos. Their companion in mythology is, naturally, Nemesis, who delivers justice and exacts retribution for sin and crime.

There was so much to like about this film. The lawyers trying to administer Mr. Rafiel's will. The mysterious young women on the tour who kept showing up at odd moments. The other tour members. The scenery. My God but the scenery. Wow.

There are also things to dislike. The movie was difficult to understand at times. Some of the actors couldn't enunciate worth a damn or their quaint regional accent was thick enough to spread with a knife on toast.

What would have really helped was about ten more minutes to better explain why Verity Hunt was living with the weird sisters. The relationship between Miss Temple and Verity Hunt. Why Michael Rafiel, whom everyone in town was convinced was a murderer, was a homeless bum and not in jail. Why Mr. Rafiel waited until he was at death's door to hire Miss Marple.

Heck, why did Mr. Rafiel give such cryptic instructions to Miss Marple? We're told he liked puzzles and games and manipulating people, but even so. If you want justice done, you don't make the challenge deliberately difficult.

But those are minor points. *Nemesis* is a worthy addition to Agatha Christie film adaptations.

General Information

Based on: *Nemesis* (novel, 1971)
Run time: 1 hr., 42 min. **Subtitles:** No

Writer: T.R. Bowen **Director:** David Tucker

Cast

Joan Hickson as Miss Jane Marple
Peter Tilbury as Lionel Peel
Joanna Hole as Madge

Frank Gatliff as Jason Rafiel
Bruce Payne as Michael Rafiel
Barbara Franceschi as Miss Kurnowitz
Roger Hammond as Mr. Broadribb
Patrick Godfrey as Mr. Schuster
Ann Queensberry as Miss Wimpole
Helen Cherry as Miss Elizabeth Temple
John Horsley as Professor Wanstead
Peter Copley as Archdeacon Brabazon
Jane Booker as Miss Cooke
Alison Skilbeck as Miss Barrow
Valerie Lush as Lavinia Glynne
Margaret Tyzack as Clothilde Bradbury-Scott
Anna Cropper as Anthea Bradbury-Scott
Liz Fraser as Mrs. Brent
Roger Booth as Mr. Pelham
Reginald Stewart as Mr. Hallowes

Film Locations

Chipping Campden, Gloucestershire
Burgh Island, Devon (La Rocheverte)
Berkeley Castle, Gloucestershire (Kingminster Castle)
Blenheim Palace, West Oxfordshire, Oxfordshire
Dyers Hill, Charlebury, Oxfordshire (Mrs. Brent's home)
Stourhead Garden, Warminster, Wiltshire
Chipping Campden, Gloucestershire (Abbey Ducis, church, tea room, graveyard)

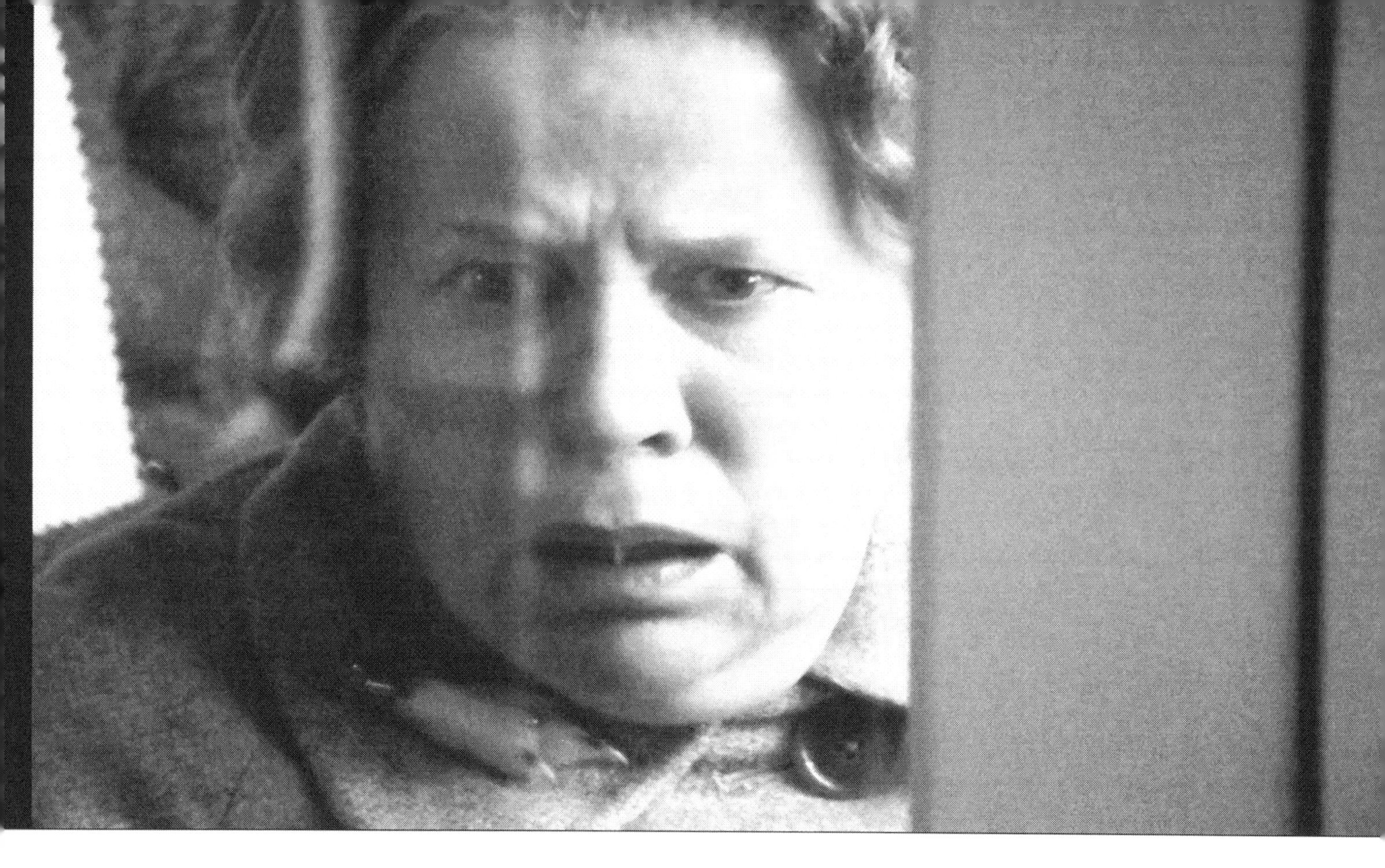

4.50 from Paddington (1987)

A strangler on a train sends a woman to a mansion where she encounters a family's secrets and romance

Fidelity to text

The Martine "girlfriend or wife of Edmund" subplot is simplified. One murder doesn't occur, although medical malpractice does. Another is radically changed. The ending is far more dramatic.

Quality of movie

Pretty good, although Lucy Eyelesbarrow was miscast, everyone mumbled, and Miss Marple pulled the solution from her knitting bag.

This version of *The 4.50 from Paddington* follows the urtext fairly closely at the beginning, other than excising minor characters. As the movie progresses, fidelity to text decreases. Even so, the story made sense as a movie. In some ways, it made more sense than the novel did.

I'm referring to the added scenes of police legwork needed to identify the first murder victim. They made the story work: the autopsy said the body Lucy found had an athlete's musculature. This allowed Miss Marple to make — based on the condition of the victim's feet — the mental leap to dancer. Miss Marple acts on intuition, but intuition isn't accepted in court. Courts demand verifiable facts, or they should.

Miss Marple then makes the second leap. Based on the victim's clothes (a mix of old but good-quality, and new but cheap and flashy) she deduces that the victim didn't have a reliable income. She postulates a traveling dance troupe with unstable bookings and thus unstable revenue.

Chief Inspector Duckham of Scotland Yard knows her reputation, accepts her logic, and searches for verifiable facts. He interviews owners of dance troupes (instead of farming out the legwork to constables as would be normal) to see if anyone is missing and lo and behold, Anna Stravinska of the Ballet Maritska has gone off with a man. Her real name is Martine Isabelle Perrault. Suspiciously, she's missing and her cheap flat was tossed, with every scrap of identification removed.

This version made Miss Marple's hidden logic clearer because it didn't waste time on extra subplots and extraneous characters. Since Martine was discovered inside an abandoned sarcophagus located inside a locked barn crammed with dubious-quality antiquities *and* her body was tossed out of a train onto a particular steep slope overlooking said barn, her initial conclusion as to the killer's identity follows easily.

The murderer had to be someone intimately familiar with the Crackenthorpe estate who could come and go without raising eyebrows. This wasn't spelled out in the novel and fixing this omission would have let the scriptwriter shine, but it wasn't.

This leads Miss Marple to the next question, also not spelled out in either novel or film. Why would any member of the Crackenthorpe family murder some

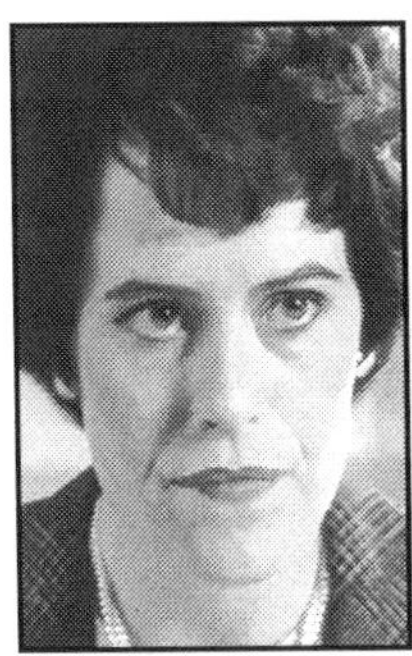
Lucy Eyelesbarrow (*Jill Meager*), the spying servant

Luther Crackenthorpe (*Maurice Denham*), the cranky old man

Emma Crackenthorpe (*Joanna David*), the dutiful daughter

Cedric Crackenthorpe (*John Hallam*), the amoral artist

Bryan Eastley (*David Beames*), the steadfast pilot

John Quimper (*Andrew Burt*), the devoted doctor

third-rate dancer? Unless the dancer married a Crackenthorpe *and* bore a Crackenthorpe heir, she meant nothing to the disposition of the estate. Showing a conversation between Lucy and the invisible staff would have revealed that other than the mysterious Martine, the deceased Edmund's French fling, the Crackenthorpe family's marriages and children were public record. No one ran off with a chorus girl.

The interview with the lawyer further clarifies why Josiah Crackenthorpe's will was such an obstacle to the Crackenthorpe grandchildren. This is a weird concept for American audiences where the estate is split up equally among the surviving heirs unless other provisions are spelled out in full. The Crackenthorpe estate, being English, probably fell under the rule of primogeniture where the oldest surviving male heir inherits everything other than small bequests to sisters, no matter what their birth ranking, or younger brothers.

Just like a tontine, the winner takes it all.

Miss Marple noticed (but didn't state, which she should have) that murdering a chorus girl made no sense. Arranging convenient accidents for other family members does because the inheritance can be divided among fewer heirs.

Harold dies in a very suspicious hunting accident. Miss Marple visits his widow (offscreen) and informs the police that Harold was a huge ballet fan. Their flat was filled with posters and memorabilia, including some from the Ballet Maritska. If Harold was connected to the mysterious Anna Stavinska, he'd be murdering other people to inherit more, not getting killed himself.

Miss Marple would ask herself why Harold died and the answer is clear (to her). Because Harold might be able to identify a connection between the family and the dead dancer.

Thus, we arrive at Miss Marple's logical deduction that's never spelled out in the novel and poorly spelled out here. It's backed up by police legwork, what the lawyer revealed, and a visit to Somerset House to look up marriage certificates.

Somerset House, in case you wondered (I did!), is the repository for birth, marriage, and death certificates for all of England and Wales going back to 1837 and only ending in 1970 when those records got moved to St. Catherine's House at Aldwych. Somerset House shows up frequently in Agatha's novels. Characters are always visiting to check for secret or bigamous marriages.

General Information

Based on: *4.50 from Paddington* / U.S. title: *What Mrs. McGillicuddy Saw* (novel, 1957)
Run time: 1 hr., 50 min. **Subtitles:** No

Writer: T.R. Bowen **Director:** Martyn Friend

Cast

Joan Hickson as Miss Jane Marple
Jill Meager as Lucy Eyelesbarrow
David Horovitch as Detective Inspector Slack
Ian Brimble as Detective Sergeant Lake
David Waller as Chief Inspector Duckham
Alan Penn as Patmore

Juliette Mole as Anna Stravinska
Mona Bruce as Mrs. McGillicuddy
Maurice Denham as Luther Crackenthorpe
Joanna David as Emma Crackenthorpe
Bernard Brown as Harold Crackenthorpe
Robert East as Alfred Crackenthorpe
John Hallam as Cedric Crackenthorpe
Andrew Burt as Dr. John Quimper
David Beames as Bryan Eastley
Christopher Haley as Alexander Eastley
Daniele Stroppa as James Stoddart-West
Pamela Pitchford as Mrs. Kidder
Jean Boht as Madame Joliet

Film Locations

Marylebone Station, London (Paddington station)
Wiltshire Constabulary Divisional Police Headquarters, Salisbury (county constabulary)
Orchardleigh House, Frome, Somerset (Rutherford Hall)

Only one person meets Miss Marple's requirements and has the brains to plan. It's Doctor Quimper. He's courting Emma (rich heiress, but richer if her brothers died), he's local, he knows the area, and he's at Rutherford Hall on a near-daily basis.

Dr. Quimper is a subtle man. He took advantage of names to sow confusion. He arranged for Alfred to die by not diagnosing a medical condition that, if caught early, could be cured. He makes Luther think he's sicker than he is, so when it's Luther's time to go, no one will be surprised.

You wonder what he would have done with Cedric, who inconveniently lives on Ibiza. Or how he'd remove Alexander Eastley, the only Crackenthorpe great-grandchild.

Would he let Emma live? She adores him and everything we saw says he loves her and he'd have married her if only his Catholic dancer wife would have divorced him. But as Miss Marple and Poirot always say, one murder leads to another. Each subsequent killing gets easier. Since a bigger inheritance is always nice, he might have still murdered Emma's brothers. And maybe Emma, if he got tired of her and met another dancer.

The character who didn't work for me was Lucy Eyelesbarrow. She was, as expected, hypercompetent. She got things done. She brooked no nonsense from anyone unless she chose to. But I could not envision any of the Crackenthorpe males or Brian Eastley getting lathered up about her. She was too practical and too much like a bossy governess to be alluring and delicious.

I can see why she chose Brian Eastley over Cedric. He's the common-sense choice. He won't cheat like Cedric would. She can make him into his best self and he'll like it. As Miss Marple says, by the time Lucy's had her third child with Brian, she'll be madly in love with him.

Dr. Quimper's scheme came undone because he didn't know Lucy better. He would have realized, as Miss Marple feigned choking at tea before a witness to the murder, that Lucy would *never* leave bones in the fish paste sandwiches.

A Caribbean Mystery (1989)

When evil checks into a island resort, Miss Marple discovers similarities between Barbados and St. Mary Mead

The movie opens with Miss Marple's empty, dark house, with the mail piling up. It's a good opening, moving from dreary, rainy, gloomy England to the vivid sunshine and palm trees of the Caribbean island of Barbados. To recover from bronchitis, Miss Marple is enjoying an all-expenses paid vacation in exotic surroundings and plenty of fresh tropical air courtesy of nephew Raymond West.

To further emphasize the change from England, the soundtrack changes too. I noticed those steel drums at once and the brighter, bouncier music. We also see far more of the locals than appeared in the novel. Inspector Weston gets far more scenes demonstrating his quiet competence. And, remarkably, he knows who Miss Marple is!

The scriptwriters took the trouble of fleshing out Victoria the maid as well, adding a charming scene in which Miss Marple visits Victoria's Aunty Johnson for tea. They hit it off right away as they both understand the true nature and power of gossip: It lets you understand human nature and what people do versus what they say. Aunty Johnson and Miss Marple recognize that people are much the same the world around. We also get a sadly true-to-life scene afterwards when Molly, our hotel owner, tells Victoria to remember her place and not take the paying guests off hotel grounds to meet the real residents of the

Fidelity to text

The island was changed and a character's motive altered. Otherwise, changes were in line with the film's needs: minor characters dropped, island citizens added, and scenes added and cut.

Quality of movie

A half-poison bottle deducted for lack of subtitles as actors, even English ones, mumble. We see more of the island, especially the local police force and residents. Loved Aunty Johnson who recognizes Miss Marple as a kindred soul.

island. It spoils the fantasy of visiting paradise when you see worker housing, transportation, and poverty.

Another very atmospheric addition was the exhumation of Major Palgrave, overseen by Inspector Weston. We watch the coffin being dug up and hauled out. It's done late at night, I assume, to slow down the gossip and appropriate music matches the scene.

Another change was to Inspector Weston, who gets many more scenes interrogating the suspects. He knows his business and the contrast between him and the island governor couldn't be stronger. The governor is more interested in his stamp collection and not being bothered. He definitely doesn't want to bother those higher up the food chain, even if that means justice won't be done. Inspector Weston, competent and caring, is forced to work around his chain of command

Molly Kendal
(*Sophie Ward*),
the troubled hostess

Tim Kendal
(*Adrian Lukis*),
the worried husband

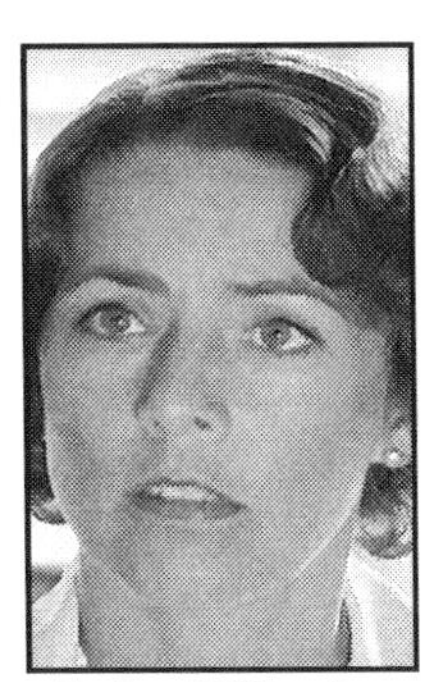
Evelyn Hillingdon
(*Sheila Ruskin*),
the loveless upstart

Edward Hillingdon
(*Michael Feast*),
the lying naturalist

Lucky Dyson
(*Sue Lloyd*),
the good luck charm

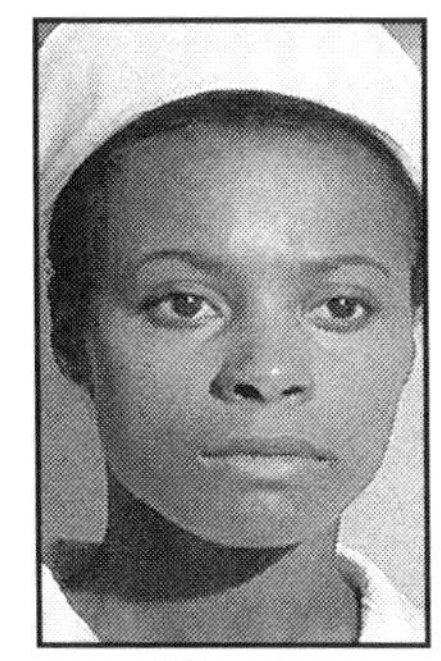
Victoria
(*Valerie Buchanan*),
the nosy maid

to see justice carried out.

We lose a few characters but they aren't missed. The biggest character change is to Lucky Dyson. She's still married to Greg Dyson while carrying on an affair with Edward Hillington. She gets a scene with Inspector Weston where she clarifies her motivation in helping Greg Dyson's first wife, Mary, along to her death. It was a mercy killing because Mary (named Gail in the novel) was suffering horribly as she died by inches from cancer and Lucky, the nurse, couldn't stand to see her dear friend suffer any longer. In the novel, Lucky is far more unpleasant. She fooled her lover Edward into getting the drugs needed to murder Mary. She then married the grieving widower about a month later, and is blackmailing Edward over helping her in her crimes. In the film, she's toying with him because it's fun but it didn't seem like Edward helped overdose Mary with morphine.

This motivational improvement does not save Lucky from her fate. The actress playing Lucky was perfect. A loud, brassy, bottle blonde, she stole every scene. Supposedly she slightly resembles Molly Kendal but only if you aren't paying attention, you're seeing her from the back, and if it's dark.

Molly, I'm sad to say, was a tepid drip of water compared to Lucky.

I'll be charitable and say the actress playing her was showcasing a overburdened woman being driven insane by her gaslighting husband. Belladonna poisoning with its hallucinations and blackouts would make anyone nuts.

But my God was she bland. Nice looking, but there wasn't any spark in her. It's like her only function in life was to marry the wrong bad boy so he could mooch off her and when he was done mooching, trade what was left of her in for a richer, stupider model.

This being an Agatha mystery, that richer, stupider model was already waiting in the wings.

The other interesting character was Edward Hillington, but not interesting in that I couldn't tear my eyes away from the screen. Oh, no. I could not for the life of me see why a live wire like Lucky Dyson wasted time on a tepid, reserved man whose sole purpose in life was capturing, torturing, and killing butterflies followed by sketching their remains. A different actor might have livened up Edward Hillington. I understand why his wife might have married him; boy next door, family approval, there wasn't much to choose from, but Lucky Dyson? Remove her motive for amusing herself with Edward Hillington and you're left with, with, well, I don't know what you're left with. She can't be *that* bored.

General Information

Based on: *A Caribbean Mystery* (novel, 1964)
Run time: 1 hr., 44 min. **Subtitles:** No

Writer: T.R. Bowen
Director: Christopher Petit

Cast

Joan Hickson as Miss Marple
Joseph Mydell as Inspector Weston

Donald Pleasence as Jason Rafiel
Barbara Barnes as Esther Walters
Stephen Bent as Jackson
Sophie Ward as Molly Kendal
Adrian Lukis as Tim Kendal
Robert Swann as Greg Dyson
Sue Lloyd as Lucky Dyson
Michael Feast as Edward Hillingdon
Sheila Ruskin as Evelyn Hillingdon
Shaughan Seymour as Napier
Frank Middlemass as Major Palgrave
Valerie Buchanan as Victoria
Isabelle Lucas as Aunty Johnson
T.P. McKenna as Dr. Grahame
James Curran as Piers Musgrave
T.R. Bowen as Raymond West

Film Location

Coral Reef Hotel, Barbados

Joan Hickson was wonderful as always. She expresses her boredom listening to Major Palgrave so well and her sparring with Mr. Rafiel is a pleasure to watch. And yes, at the climax, you get to see her (in Mr. Rafiel's words) as nemesis, wrapped in a fluffy pink shawl.

The climax was enhanced by the scriptwriter's choice to emphasize another tidbit of island culture. Aunty Johnson tells the murderer that it's been nine days since Victoria was murdered. Victoria was buried with a whip in each hand and she came back to see justice done. Was that a hint of voodoo? It could be. I know that in the Episcopal church, you don't get buried with a whip in each hand if you were murdered. I have no idea if the scriptwriter made that tidbit up out of whole cloth but it helped demonstrate again that Miss Marple was alone on an island, not her own. Understanding the motivation behind the whips and the effect it would have on the murderer she took in stride.

I've heard her called the best personality analyst in the world, a ruthless forensic brain – a mind like a bacon slicer would do very well.

INSPECTOR WESTON

She does return to St. Mary Mead and it is, naturally, gloomy and raining. Oh to be in England instead of a tropical island in the Caribbean. Not that she minded. She was home, surrounded by villagers whose behavior Aunty Johnson would recognize even if she didn't know their names, faces, and family connections.

Add *A Caribbean Mystery* with Joan Hickson to your must-be-watched pile. You'll enjoy your tropical vacation with a side of murder.

They Do It With Mirrors (1991)

Turning a good novel into a bad film doesn't take magic, it just takes weak acting and a script full of holes

Fidelity to text

Name changes and minor character removal, and Inspector Slack replaces Inspector Curry. The ending was far more dramatic than the novel but badly thought out. Plus: modern dance.

Quality of movie

One flat film. It gave me plenty of time to ask why this murder was so hard to solve. It was obvious, and not just because I read the book!

Up till now, the Joan Hickson adaptations have been average to excellent. This film is fair, at best. It was flat, flat, flat; flat like the surface of the pond at the climax but without the sparkle.

Was it the added scene where Miss Marple and her old friend Ruth van Rydock watch a bizarre performance of modern dance set to a modernistic, challenging, and virtually atonal score? The three dancers wear what looks like body paint (one rather Satanic) and enthusiastically roll around on the stage. I'm not sure what it was, except it wasn't *Swan Lake*. I must assume the film needed padding, the director's friends needed jobs, or it portrayed Alex Restarick as an avant-garde theatrical type.

Could the problem lay with Walter Hudd's purchase of a horse for his wife, Gina? We weren't given a reason why Walter buys the horse. Gina doesn't ask for one. We don't see Gina pining over horse paintings or wearing clothing suitable for riding. But suddenly, Walter buys Gina a horse with … money from some unknown source. By the movie's end, they agree to relocate to the United States and … leave the horse behind?

Maybe it was Walter's accent? He's supposed to be an American G.I. from Iowa who Gina met, fell madly in love with, and married after a three-week courtship. His accent was all over the map. Deep South? Yep. Texas twang? Heard that too. Midwestern nasal? You betcha. Middle-of-the-road Mid-Atlantic like a TV reporter? Well, sure. Todd Boyce, the actor playing Walter, was born in Ohio and raised in upstate New York, Germany, Chicago, Brazil, and Australia. He couldn't decide which accent to use, so he used them all.

How about Inspector Slack bringing a suitcase of magic tricks into the office? Perhaps he was preparing an act for a charity function or holiday pantomime. We're never given an onscreen payoff, so it's just a guess. The sole reason Inspector Slack displayed his collapsing top hat, brilliant artificial flowers, and magic wand was to provide Miss Marple a clue.

Why did Gina decide to relocate to Iowa with her hubby Walter? She was clearly more interested in the Restarick brothers despite her husband being the only man on the estate who knows how to fix something or

Carrie Louise Serrocold (*Jean Simmons*), the wealthy victim

Lewis Serrocold (*Joss Ackland*), the visionary husband

Edgar Lawson (*Neal Swettenham*), the unstable inmate

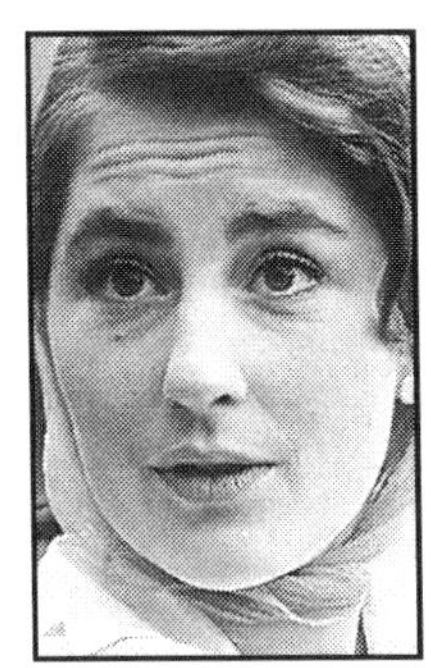

Gina Hudd (*Holly Aird*), the untamed wife

Walter Hudd (*Todd Boyce*), the unsettled spouse

Alex Restarick (*Christopher Villiers*), the adoring sibling

do anything practical. But he buys her a horse and suddenly — against every bit of evidence we see on screen — she's madly in love with him all over again?

What was the relationship between Carrie Louise, her three husbands, her daughters (one by birth and one adopted), multiple stepsons by two marriages, and granddaughter? A scoresheet would have been handy. I had to return to the novel to figure out the relationships since the movie didn't bother to clarify the connections.

Why is a school full of delinquent, socially maladjusted boys who must have at least one 1952-equivalent of an ASBO (Anti-Social Behavior Order) apiece putting on *Romeo and Juliet*? I understand theater as therapy. I do not understand any sane director choosing a play where whoever is forced to play Juliet or her nurse is going to be teased to the point of suicide. Or homicide.

Why was the pond so small? In the novel, Edgar Lawson runs for the lake (not a pond!), steals a boat to row across the lake and escape. The boat's bottom is rotted, and he falls into the lake and drowns. Dear old dad dives in after him and drowns too. A lake can be much too big to swim across for an average swimmer and far too large for pursuers to run around it and meet the escapee on the other side. A boat makes sense. However, every time we see *this* body of water, including when we see delinquent students cleaning out water weeds as a bit of foreshadowing, it's small. Like small enough to run around it easily and meet an escapee on the other side. Like small enough to swim across.

In the novel, Edgar Lawson's death is related in a letter. That won't work for TV. It lacks drama. It's replaced with a hot pursuit of Edgar fleeing through the woods of the estate and up to the edge of the pond, where he plunges in despite not knowing how to swim. At the water's edge, the police round up the boat and go after him. He still drowns as does dear old dad.

Of all the ridiculous scenes in the film, this one was the most ridiculous. We watch young and agile Edgar run through the woods pursued by old and fat Lewis Serrocold and Lewis can keep up! Yet the police, presumably fit even if not young, are unable to keep pace with old, fat Lewis. When they reach the shore, they behave like Keystone Kops, getting in each other's way and giving Edgar time to escape and drown. I can't believe the local constabulary would be this incompetent. Nor can I believe that they'd stand idly by on the shores of the pond and watch a fleeing murder suspect and his dad drown without someone diving in to save them.

The novel's climax made more sense. Edgar escaped in the only boat and the bottom fell out in the middle of the lake, too far away for anyone to quickly mount a rescue. Here, the pond was small and the police had the boat.

Then there's the first murder. Anyone who thinks about the crime for thirty seconds could solve it. It takes place while everyone else is watching an antique film dating back to 1905 or so. Two people are out of the room, not counting the victim. It's a locked house. The delinquents are in their supervised and locked dormitory. Who kills victim number one? It can't be anyone watching the vintage film footage, so that leaves the two people out of sight since the mansion has no servants that I saw, other than the housekeeper who was watching the film.

When the screenwriters added bizarre modern dancing, Walter's soon-to-be abandoned horse for Gina, and the extended chase scene at the climax, we lost details about Gina and Walter and how most of the family would have been happy to have Walter be the murderer. More importantly, we lost the complex backstory of what Lewis Serrocold was really up to with his delinquent students and his accounting background. He was robbing the trust blind and, thanks to placing his graduates in various positions in London, robbing other firms blind too. All that detail gone to watch dancers in striped tights roll around on a stage.

General Information

Based on: *They Do It With Mirrors* (*Murder With Mirrors* in U.S.) (novel, 1952)
Run time: 1 hr., 40 min. **Subtitles:** No

Writer: Kevin Elyot
Director: Tom Shankland

Cast

Joan Hickson as Miss Marple
David Horovitch as Chief Inspector Slack
Ian Brimble as Sergeant Lake
Anne Atkins as W.P.C.
Tony Red Richards as Police Sergeant

Faith Brook as Ruth van Rydock
Jean Simmons as Carrie Louise Serrocold
Joss Ackland as Lewis Serrocold
John Bott as Christian Gulbrandsen
Holly Aird as Gina Hudd
Todd Boyce as Walter Hudd
Gillian Barge as Mildred Strete
Christopher Villiers as Alex Restarick
Jay Villiers as Stephen Restarick
Saul Reichlin as Dr. Maseryk
Brenda Cowling as Mrs. Rodgers
Neal Swettenham as Edgar Lawson
Matthew Cottle as Ernie Gregg
David Doyle as Neville
Jake Wood as Bert
Tom Kerridge as Keithie
Stee Billingsley as Dancer
Rachel Bond as Dancer
Bryn Walters as Dancer
Roger Low as Dr. Rosenbloom
David Coatsworth as The Hand Loading the Murder Weapon

Film Locations

Little College Street, Westminster, London
St. Edward Street, Leek, Staffordshire (street scene)
Bowcock & Pursaill Solicitors, Leek, Staffordshire (solicitors office exteriors)
The Heath House, Stoke-on-Trent, Staffordshire (lodge, stables, house and garden, lawn orangery)
Bewdley Station, Worcestershire (railway station, signal box)
Former Police Station, Leonard Street, Leek, Staffordshire (police station exteriors)

The Mirror Crack'd from Side to Side (1992)

Hickson's swan song peters out when it protects a lackluster Gregg from the consequences of her sins

Fidelity to text

Adopted daughter Margot Bence was shortchanged, particularly when she was such a strong presence at the opening and in the novel. Otherwise, the usual changes especially to Arthur Badcock.

Quality of movie

Competently made, acted, and shot, and that's all. ITV's version with Julia McKenzie is better, but watch the 1980 Angela Lansbury version for the Elizabeth Taylor / Kim Novak fireworks.

Joan Hickson was 86 when she filmed this movie. I wish I could say she left the stage in a blaze of glory. This film was not a suitable swan song for her talented portrayal of Miss Marple. It never came to life; a sad verdict when a film is about a fading movie star pitted against her past and the younger, hotter future star getting ready to displace her.

Miss Marple knows all about getting old, change, and the indignity of being treated like a child (like Miss Knight does to her). Her mind is as sharp as ever even as her body grows frail.

As I watched, I kept thinking about karma and old sins casting long shadows. *The Mirror Crack'd* is loaded with examples. Heather Badcock dies because of the choice she made as a starstruck fan. She probably didn't understand the risk she was taking; not to herself but to her idol. Did she even know that Marina Gregg was pregnant? Or that her quarantine for rubella was not to keep her safe but to ensure the safety of the community at large?

Whatever else you can say about Heather Badcock, she would have been horrified if she'd learned the truth. This is a woman who lives to help other people, even when they don't want or need her help. She died, not knowing why, and I suppose you can say she might have deserved it.

Except being thoughtless and self-centered isn't a crime.

Ella Zeilinsky, secretary to Jason Rudd, died too. In her case she was blackmailing people, which is a crime. She was also besotted with her boss and the boss' wife didn't like it. Since no adultery was committed, only one-sided wishful thinking, was that a crime? No, it was not. We shouldn't police thought crimes.

Then we come to Marina Gregg. She's endured plenty of tragedy, much of it self-inflicted. Marrying five husbands goes well beyond the triumph of hope over experience. But she was a movie star and rational thought doesn't play much part in the acting profession.

Rationality must not have been behind the casting of Claire Bloom as Marina Gregg. She is an accomplished actress but she didn't make me believe that she was a glamorous movie star that eager fans like Heather Badcock idolized and movie magazines swooned over.

Marina Gregg
(*Claire Bloom*),
the movie star

Jason Rudd
(*Barry Newman*),
the director

Lola Brewster
(*Glynis Barber*),
the rival star

Dolly Bantry
(*Gwen Watford*),
the concerned friend

Ella Zeilinsky
(*Elizabeth Garvie*),
the assistant

Heather Badcock
(*Judy Cornwell*),
the rabid fan

Elizabeth Taylor did. So, for that matter, did Lindsay Duncan in ITV's version of *The Mirror Crack'd*, although she didn't have nearly as much star wattage as Elizabeth Taylor. Bloom was competent, but she is not and never has been a movie star.

Did Marina Gregg deserve to meet Heather Badcock, eager fan girl, and get exposed to rubella, ensuring her fetus would be born with severe birth defects? Well, let's see. Marina was desperate for children. When she could bear none of her own, she adopted three kids. She rescued them from penury, opened up her home, gave them the chance at a new life. And then, when she became pregnant several years later, she dumped those kids as fast as she could because she didn't need them anymore.

How do you think those kids felt? Agatha tells us via Margot Bence, photographer, who was one of those abandoned kids. Margot loathed Marina Gregg for what she did to her and her adopted brothers. All of them struggled emotionally after being dumped. Margot had a lot to say in the novel, very little of which made it into the film. This was a pity because it shows us much, much better what kind of person Marina Gregg was. Let's quote Margot:

> *"Why shouldn't I hate her? She did the worst thing to me that anyone can do to anyone else. Let them believe that they're loved and wanted and then show them that it's all a sham."*

The other two versions of *The Mirror Crack'd* didn't spend much time with Margot Bence. In the 1980 version, Margot didn't get a single line of dialog. In the 2011 film, Margot got a few lines but nothing like her scene in the novel. I expected to see much more of Margot here because the opening showed Margot snooping around, shooting photographs, and praying in church before she ever made it to the village fête. It even showed her taking off the wig she used for her disguise! We never get an explanation for why she disguised herself.

But the scriptwriter chickened out. Margot's role in Marina Gregg's life was again glossed over, despite what it did to her and her brothers. The only reason for this is that once again, Marina Gregg, movie star, is excused for truly awful behavior by everyone around her. She's Marina Gregg and she should not be judged by normal standards of human decency. We don't get the scene in the novel where Margot tells us that Marina Gregg didn't recognize her, despite having raised her! Instead, Margot once again gets disappeared.

The karma wrapping around the film was fascinating. Marina Gregg harmed children through her own selfishness and she didn't care one damned bit. Heather Badcock harmed a child through her own selfishness and if she'd known, she'd have been devastated. When Marina Gregg's compromised baby was born, did she do what most mothers do and do her damnedest to take care of that child? No. She abandoned that baby (he wasn't perfect thus fulfilling her need for perfection) to caregivers in an asylum. I'm sure they were competent caregivers, but she wasn't there. She didn't even visit her child. It was too emotionally distressing for her, according to her enabling husband, Jason Rudd.

And there we are again, making excuses for Marina Gregg, movie star. What happens to everyone on that film set whose livelihood depends on Marina Gregg showing up to do her job? Nobody cares because they're just spear carriers in Marina Gregg's life.

This film could have been richer and deeper if the scriptwriters had mined the undercurrents that Agatha layered in. Instead, it was flat and lifeless. Chances that could have been taken, i.e., more time with Margot Bence, were ignored. Discussions of what kind of person Marina Gregg was, what pursuing fame and then catching it did to her. Not there. Disappeared from view like those children.

This version of *The Mirror Crack'd* was competent, but it could have been so much more. We're still waiting on an adaptation that does full justice to the tragedy of Margot Bence and her brothers, abandoned by Marina Gregg when they became an unwanted stage prop.

General Information

Based on: *The Mirror Crack'd from Side to Side* (novel, 1962)
Run time: 1 hr., 46 min. **Subtitles:** No

Writer: T.R. Bowen **Director:** Norman Stone

Cast

Joan Hickson as Miss Jane Marple
David Horovitch as Superintendent Slack
John Castle as Detective Inspector Craddock
Ian Brimble as Sergeant Lake

Claire Bloom as Marina Gregg
Barry Newman as Jason Rudd
Norman Rodway as Dr. Gilchrist
Elizabeth Garvie as Ella Zeilinsky
John Cassady as Giuseppe Murano
Constantine Gregory as Ardwyck Fenn
Glynis Barber as Lola Brewster
Michael Stroud as Delancey
Gwen Watford as Dolly Bantry
Judy Cornwell as Heather Badcock
Christopher Hancock as Arthur Badcock
Amanda Elwes as Margot Bence
Margaret Courtenay as Miss Knight
Anna Niland as Cherry Baker
Rose Keegan as Gladys Dixon
Rhoda Lewis as Mrs. Brogan
Christopher Good as Rev. Christopher Hawes
Barbara Hicks as Miss Hartnell
Celia Ryder as Mrs. Hopkins
Reggie Oliver as Chris
T.R. Bowen as Raymond West

Film Locations

The Street, Smarden, Kent (St. Mary Mead)
Bishops Lydeard station, West Somerset Railway, Somerset
Burgh Island, Bigbury-on-Sea, Devon
Ealing Studios, Ealing, London
Paignton & Dartmouth Steam Railway, Devon
Somerley Estate, Hampshire (Gossington Hall)
East Lodge, Amport House, Amport, Hampshire (Gossington Hall lodge)

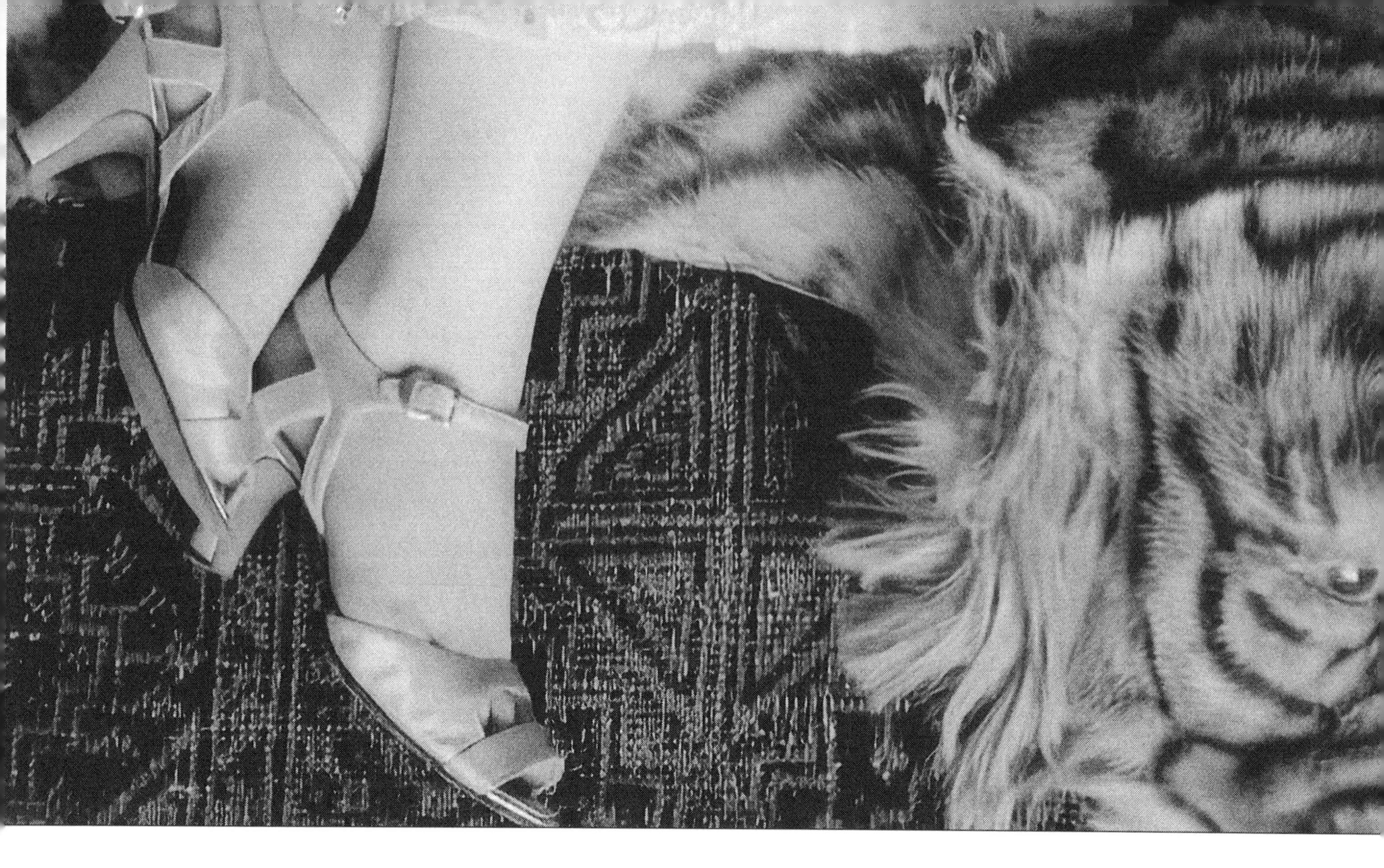

The Body in the Library (2004)

Faithful adaptation puts a fun spin on the story of a dancer's fatal end but crashes at the unexpected climax

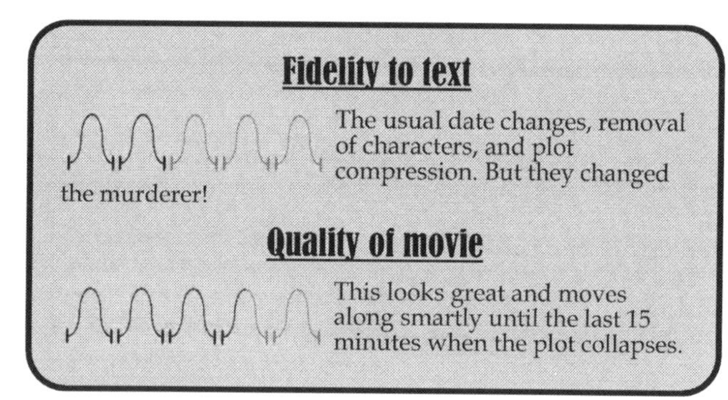

The Body in the Library (1942) is not the first Miss Marple novel; that honor goes to *The Murder at the Vicarage* (1930). When ITV's *Marple* series began filming, they discarded any internal chronology. This opening episode demonstrates what you'll get from the series. It looks great, it's loaded with actors you've seen in other English TV productions, the costuming is top-notch, the soundtrack works reasonably well (I didn't notice it too much so it wasn't terrible), flashbacks reveal the past, and most of all, the scriptwriter felt the need to put his own stamp upon Agatha.

It's a time-honored tradition, too, dating back to *Adventures, Inc.* (1929) when Jane Bess rewrote Agatha. Except the vast majority of adaptations don't change whodunnit. They alter all kinds of stuff, but not the identity or motives of the murderer.

ITV's *Marple* feels no such compunctions. They adapted the twelve novels, two short stories, and then, needing more material, seized other novels and had their way with them. They left Poirot alone, for which we should all be grateful, but grabbed plenty of standalone novels.

In addition to the major change of rewriting the identity of the murderous couple in *Body*, ITV also decided to give Miss Marple a tragic, completely unbelievable, and unacceptable backstory. You'll catch a hint of it in the young officer's picture that Miss Marple gazes at wistfully, wishing for what might have been. You'll be spared *that* reveal, but only because it's reserved for ITV's *Murder at the Vicarage* (2004).

When Agatha wrote *The Body in the Library*, she wanted to play with the time-honored trope in the title. The library belongs to Colonel Bantry. He's stuffy, elderly, and married to Dolly, an avid gardener who runs the village fêtes. They live in a magnificent mansion with a gigantic, stuffy library packed with unread books. It's even got a tiger skin rug, of the sort that English visitors to India shot and brought back home as trophies.

The body is as unlikely as possible for the setting. The victim (alive or dead) is not the sort of person who frequents the homes of English gentry. She's a heavily-made-up teenager, her hair is bleached platinum blonde, and she's wearing a cheap, old, spangled cocktail dress and tawdry, impractical shoes. Not our kind, dear. And, shades of Elinor Glyn, she's discovered sprawled upon the tiger skin rug.

With the discovery of the body, we're off to the races.

Ruby Keene
(*Emma Williams*),
the innocent dancer

Conway Jefferson
(*Ian Richardson*),
the wealthy adoptee

Adelaide Jefferson
(*Tara Fitzgerald*),
the lonely in-law

Mark Gaskell
(*Jamie Theakston*),
the despairing in-law

Basil Blake
(*Ben Miller*),
the louche director

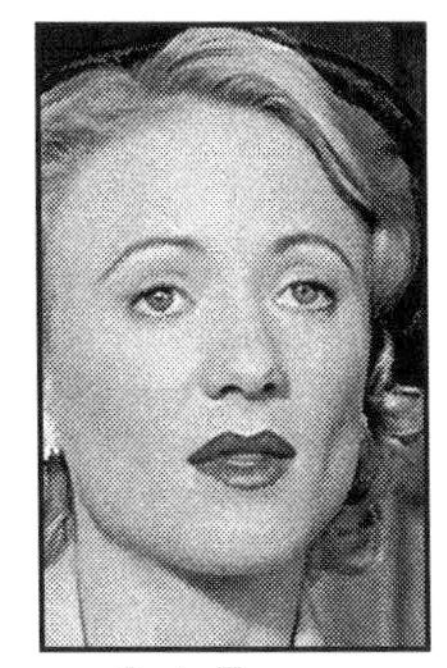

Josie Turner
(*Mary Stockley*),
the damaged dancer

Col. Bantry swiftly learns what's in store for him when Col. Melchett asks him, man to man, what his relationship was with the victim. This version didn't spend much time on it — wasting precious moments on waves washing ashore on the pebble beach — but the Bantrys must cope with a vicious whispering campaign because the colonel must have known the hot blonde teenager, because why else would she be dead in his library on his tiger skin rug?

Why else indeed.

Dolly calls in Miss Marple. Col. Melchett is nonplussed. They learn that the body might be that of Ruby Keene, teenaged dancer at the nearby Hotel Majestic. But the person who reported her missing was not her cousin, Josie Turner. It was Conway Jefferson, an elderly disabled hotel guest who'd taken a shine to Ruby. She reminded him of his daughter, according to Mark Gaskell, the son-in-law who sponges off him.

The relationship between Ruby and Conway Jefferson is interesting. Everyone agrees that Ruby's young and pretty, but not that bright. They all assume she's a gold-digger, yet at the same time, cousin Josie, the hotel's dance host, Raymond Starr, and the hotel's manager agree. She has always behaved well. In a hotel like the Majestic, if Ruby was stepping out, someone would have noticed and the gossip would have spread everywhere.

So why was Ruby being so friendly with Conway Jefferson? Besides it being her job to be friendly with guests, especially on the dance floor? My guess is that she liked the attention from a father figure who didn't want to stick his hand down her dress and his tongue down her throat. Watch the scene with Ruby dancing with Basil Blake and you'll see what I mean. That's what she contended with daily. Being with Jefferson, despite how his family despised her, must have been a relief.

Jefferson's in-laws stay with him at The Majestic. His daughter-in-law, Adelaide, was a widow with a baby son who married his son, Frank. Son-in-law Mark Gaskell married his daughter. Son and daughter were killed during a bombing attack on London and what's left of the family clings together. Partly because of grief, partly because they have nowhere else to go, and partly because he's the one with the money.

General Information

Based on: *The Body in the Library* (novel, 1942)
Run time: 1 hr., 34 min. **Subtitles:** No

Writer: Kevin Elyot **Director:** Andy Wilson

Cast

Geraldine McEwan as Miss Marple
Joanna Lumley as Dolly Bantry
James Fox as Col. Arthur Bantry
Jack Davenport as Superintendent Harper
Simon Callow as Colonel Melchett

Ian Richardson as Conway Jefferson
Tara Fitzgerald as Adelaide Jefferson
Steven Williams as Peter Carmody
Jamie Theakston as Mark Gaskell
Ben Miller as Basil Blake
Emma Cooke as Dinah Lee
Mary Stockley as Josie Turner
Emma Williams as Ruby Keene
Adam Garcia as Raymond Starr
David Walliams as George Bartlett
Richard Durden as Mr. Prestcott
Florence Hoath as Pamela Reeves
Zoe Thorne as Florence
Anna Rawlins as Beatrice
Robin Soans as Dr. Haydock

Film Locations

Dorney Court, Buckinghamshire (Gossington Hall)
Shrubs Wood, Chalfont St. Giles (Blake's house)
Eastbourne, East Sussex
Grand Hotel, Eastbourne (Majestic Hotel)

Mark and Adelaide don't appreciate Jefferson's plans to adopt Ruby. They *really* don't like him settling a vast sum of money on her in his will.

Miss Marple and Dolly investigate people at the hotel, while the police investigate everything else. Another girl goes missing, about Ruby's age, but a respectable Girl Guide won't have connections to louche film producers or hotel dancers. Except her body turns up in a burned car belonging to a hotel guest.

Very soon thereafter, the plot goes off the rails. Remember that the story takes place in about 1950. England's still under wartime rationing. Times were considerably more straightlaced. Alternative lifestyles were virtually unheard of. But, like always, people commit murder for money, for passion, for status.

It made sense in the novel that Mark Gaskell would secretly marry Josie. She's pretty, smart, and capable. She's also socially one step above a taxi dancer. Since he's much higher up, their relationship has to remain secret. Jefferson would be furious. He'd cut off the money. There are subtle hints in the novel that they know each other better than would be expected between hotel guest and hostess. They murder Ruby because of money. And maybe she saw something she shouldn't have, after Josie sprained her ankle.

But here! Aargh. Miss Marple reveals the awful secret to the gang of investigators. Josie had been carrying on surreptitiously not with Mark, but with Adelaide! There was nothing to set this up. Nothing. Not even the normal expectation that lonely widowers would develop illicit feelings for hot, friendly blondes. Not one longing glance. Not one scene where Adelaide and Josie stand too close together. Nothing. There was zero chemistry between the actresses.

The lesbian relationship comes out of left field. The scriptwriter must have thought they were being edgy, updating Agatha for the modern era.

Even stupider was seeing Adelaide dragged down the prison hallway while Josie, in her cell, screams out to her, "I love you! I love you!" If you're feeling sorry for them, recall that they murdered two teenage girls and planned to murder the old man. Why? So they wouldn't have to be poor.

The Murder at the Vicarage (2004)

A young Miss Marple committing adultery was not the worst crime committed in this messy episode

Fidelity to text

The story remains, but the scriptwriters inserted an unnecessary, egregious backstory for Miss Marple. Changing the date from 1930 to 1951 caused problems too.

Quality of movie

Well done, but the script shoved in unneeded things, ensuring that solving the murder got short shrift.

The Murder at the Vicarage was published in 1930. This ITV production is set in 1951 (the camera pans across a calendar, although the prop person got the days of the week wrong. August 1, 1951, is Wednesday, not Tuesday.)

I understand ITV's rationale to set the series in the 1950s. It's easier to film a TV series if you can keep using the same costumes, cars, accessories, etc., rather than needing a warehouse stocked with 40 years of material (1930-1971). You also needn't worry about your star never aging despite the passage of decades.

But novels set in 1930 reflect different cultural issues than novels set in 1951. Agatha wrote contemporaries. Divorce was a major scandal in 1930, but much less so in 1951. In 1930, virtually every man had served in the Great War. In 1951, it was World War II. Some men (and women) served in both wars. WWII was a different war, a bigger war, a war in which British civilians suffered directly and heavily. In 1951, they were still suffering under wartime rationing. The upheaval during those decades changed Britain radically.

So as a modern viewer, I'm asking myself: Why didn't Anne Protheroe get a divorce? I could understand why not if the film took place in 1930. Divorce was socially ruinous. However, the script didn't give us a good reason for murder.

Except there *was* a perfectly good reason that would explain the murderer's rationale. Instead, vast swathes of time were wasted on an egregious subplot inventing an unconvincing past for Miss Marple.

Miss Marple did not, as a hot young woman, have a torrid affair with a married man.

To compound the stupidity, we watch young Jane see her married lover off to war while his wife is nowhere in sight. Young Jane kisses him in public in the train station in front of a crowd including men from his village (who would serve in the same unit) who know he's an adulterous cad and she's a hussy! If my husband was going off to risk death in battle, you can bet I'd be at the train station noticing if some hussy was kissing my husband goodbye. I was in the Navy. Families don't ignore their spouse's deployments. If they can possibly be there to wave goodbye one last time, they are.

Proof again that far too many Hollywood types have

Colonel Protheroe (*Derek Jacobi*), the tough nut

Anne Protheroe (*Janet McTeer*), the wife/stepmother

Lettice Protheroe (*Christina Cole*), the wild child

Mrs. Sylvia Lester (*Jane Asher*), the concerned mother

Lawrence Redding (*Jason Flemyng*), the louche artist

Ronald Hawes (*Mark Gatiss*), the suspicious curate

zero real-world experience with the military.

It was also stupid to make Anne Protheroe best buddies with Miss Marple. She was not. I suppose this was to make us feel sympathy for Anne, because she and Miss Marple had something in common: adultery. Gag me. This change culminated in Miss Marple praying in church while the murderers are hanged, again to show (I guess) her difficult choice. She could further the case for true love or she could choose justice.

Except that Miss Marple, like Hercule Poirot, seriously disapproves of murder, no matter how much the deceased deserved it.

So what reason could the screenwriters have given to justify murder instead of divorce? Money, naturally. If divorce throws you into poverty, then a .38-calibre divorce makes sense.

But we don't get this explanation stating why our murderers choose murder and not, say, running off together to Argentina where no one would know they were living in sin.

What's ironic is that Agatha provides this very justification in the novel! A legal divorce meant the murderer and his paramour would live in poverty. A lead divorce ensured inheriting a huge estate. This motivation was right there in the text, yet the scriptwriter ignored it in favor of making up an adulterous affair for Miss Marple.

Maybe they thought this would make Miss Marple more interesting, relevant, and human. Our culture teaches us to indulge our animal instincts at every opportunity. Why deny yourself an adulterous affair if that's what you want? Who cares what his tedious wife thinks? She doesn't matter. Honoring vows is for boring, bourgeois commoners following outmoded modes of behavior; not for special people like us.

Another time-wasting change swapped a silver-stealing burglar and his hapless assistant for a French professor and his granddaughter who claimed to be researching Colonel Protheroe's historic mansion. Why? The logical conclusion is it further demonstrated Colonel Protheroe's evil nature; apparently Agatha's own words were inadequate. No, you have to drag in French resistance fighters, betrayal to the Nazis, and embezzling to justify his murder.

General Information

Based on: *The Murder at the Vicarage* (novel, 1930)
Run time: 1 hr., 34 min. **Subtitles:** No

Writer: Stephen Churchett
Director: Charles Palmer

Cast

Geraldine McEwan as Miss Marple
Stephen Tompkinson as D.I. Slack
Stephen Churchett as Coroner
Martin Heathcote as PC Hurst

Tim McInnerny as Rev. Leonard Clement
Rachael Stirling as Griselda Clement
Julian Morris as Dennis Clement
Mark Gatiss as Ronald Hawes
Derek Jacobi as Colonel Protheroe
Janet McTeer as Anne Protheroe
Christina Cole as Lettice Protheroe
Herbert Lom as Ausgustin Dufosse
Emily Bruni as Helene Dufosse
Jason Flemyng as Lawrence Redding
Jane Asher as Mrs. Sylvia Lester
Robert Powell as Dr. Haydock
Miriam Margolyes as Mrs. Price-Ridley
Angela Pleasence as Miss Hartnell
Siobhan Hayes as Mary Hill
Paul Hawkyard as Frank Tarrant
Ruth Sheen as Mrs. Tarrant
Julie Cox as Young Miss Marple

Film Locations

Hambleden, Buckinghamshire (Street scenes, church exterior)
Hambleden Village Hall, Hambleden (village hall exterior)
Hambleden Manor, Hambleden (Protheroe home)
Church Cottage, Turville, Buckinghamshire (Miss Marple's cottage)
St John the Baptist, Little Marlow, Buckinghamshire (church interior)
Horsted Keynes Railway Station, Haywards Heath, West Sussex (train station)
The Old Vicarage, Turville (vicarage)
Church Lane, Windsor, Berkshire (Melchester High Street)

There are things to like. The scenery and sets are gorgeous as always. The clothes are to die for. The ladies wear the most wonderful, stylish clothes including gloves and hats. The gentlemen look great too. We really lost a lot when our culture decided it was socially acceptable to walk around in ratty T-shirts, yoga pants, and pajama bottoms.

One thing I didn't like about the scenery is a personal quirk: every expanse of grass looked freshly mowed and with a gasoline-powered rotary mower, too. A manual reel mower clips the grass and scatters the clippings where they lay in clumps. They (dear son mows our lawn with one) do not provide sleek, carpet-like grass unless you like shag carpets. This isn't period-correct as everyone in 1951 used a manual reel mower, assuming they weren't using sheep or scythes. Gas-powered mowers wouldn't become common until the 1960s. Also, remember that wartime rationing was still ongoing in 1951. No one wasted gasoline on an expensive gasoline-powered rotary mower when a reel mower cost nothing but muscle and there was already one in the shed. Gasoline was saved for cars.

In addition, every single garden had been meticulously weeded prior to the camera coming near it. Real gardens have weeds. You can mow, edge, weed, rake, and trim in preparation for the Queen's visit and while you're waiting for her motorcade to arrive, weeds will sprout. Leaves will skitter across your newly mowed grass. Someone will throw a soda can in the middle of your herbaceous border. Guaranteed. But not here in pristine St. Mary Mead.

Another amusement — when you're not trying to work out how Miss Marple solved the mystery without real clues — is playing spot the character actor. Be sure to look for Mark Gatiss (Mycroft Holmes) as the thieving curate and Miriam Margolyes (Miss Phryne Fisher's Aunt Prudence) as a neighborhood busybody.

Should you watch this? Yes. After the first viewing, watch it again to dissect the flaws in the script.

4.50 from Paddington (2004)

Clever changes (Noël Coward!) keep the story chugging along until it derails with its impossible climax

ITV has never felt the need to slavishly follow Agatha's plots and they remain true to form, playing fast and loose with *4.50 from Paddington*. Characters vanish, not surprising since a 94-minute movie doesn't have a lot of time for quaint villagers, faithful servants, and local color. Mysteriously, 94 minutes did give Miss Marple time to interrupt Noël Coward's song routine with Lucy Eyelesbarrow in the middle of a cocktail party to ask for her assistance in locating a body. That was not in the text, but it worked in the film. Those few minutes showed how incredibly well-connected Lucy is: she was Noël Coward's temporary housekeeper and he was pathetically grateful to have her services. Thus, Lucy arriving at Rutherford Hall and offering her services to the hard-up Crackenthorpe family and having them eagerly say yes was easy to accept.

Since it has been decades since I read *Paddington*, I didn't notice that the railway clerk was rude and officious instead of being Miss Marple's helpful great-nephew. Yet it worked. Two daft old ladies claiming they'd seen a murder and the body had been thrown from the train? That's exactly the response they'd get.

John Hannah (Dr. Gerrard in 2009's *Appointment with Death*) showed up as the local police inspector. He conveniently rents rooms to boarders. Miss Marple moves in to enjoy the quaint village, a fact he has a hard time believing. Unless you watch a lot of TV, you might remember Hannah best as Jonathan Carnahan in *The Mummy* (the 1999 Brendan Frasier version, not the Tom Cruise debacle). He was just as fun to watch here wilting under Miss Marple's interrogations, since she remembered him as a naughty, apple-stealing lad from St. Mary Mead and here he is, all grown up and a police inspector, no less.

Hannah's character becomes more important at the end of the movie because the screenwriter decided that Lucy shouldn't choose between Cedric Crackenthorpe and Bryan Eastley as in the novel. No, this completely made-up character steals her heart and there's no guessing about it, unlike the novel where Miss Marple knows who Lucy will choose but she refuses to say.

Other changes were made. Some were minor and unnoticeable, like moving the date from 1957 in the

Fidelity to text

A *lot* of changes. The largest is reworking the murderer's motivation to make us ooze with sympathy for the trap he's in. He also murders one less person than in the novel, because he's doing it for love and not for love of money. Plus, there's Noël Coward.

Quality of movie

I got caught up in the story — despite serious rewriting, it fired on all cylinders — until the awful, out-of-character ending.

Luther Crackenthorpe
(*David Warner*),
the disappointed dad

Emma Crackenthorpe
(*Niamh Cusack*),
the harried daughter

Cedric Crackenthorpe
(*Ciarán McMenamin*),
the family artist

Alfred Crackenthorpe
(*Ben Daniels*),
the family wastrel

Harold Crackenthorpe
(*Charlie Creed-Miles*),
the family masher

Dr. Quimper
(*Griff Rhys Jones*),
the family medico

novel to the end of 1951. But there were more substantial changes. Harold Crackenthorpe's wife becomes a character. Harold doesn't get murdered. He becomes far more of a rotter than in the novel; he's not just a shady financier, he's a lecher and a rapist as well. I believe Harold didn't get murdered in the film as it demonstrated what a big-hearted guy our murderer was, not offing an obvious cad who deserved it.

A *very* noticeable change was having the murderer's motivations become almost noble. He murders only two people instead of three and he does it all for love. Well, no. Not really. He does it because of the money. He wants to marry money and if members of the Crackenthorpe family die (as in the novel), there's more money left to be divided between the survivors.

We actually have to witness Miss Marple tell Emma Crackenthorpe that it was love on the murderer's part causing him to strangle a woman in cold blood. Gag. I have no idea where the scriptwriter's head was because Miss Marple has never excused murder before. Miss Marple's statement echoes various characters telling each other that love is all that matters. I can't agree because behavior matters, too, and the Crackenthorpe family may believe in love, and blather on about love, but they sure don't act like they love each other.

Something else that threw me out of the film was the scene when the murderer is identified. Miss Marple was eating fish paste sandwiches (sounds disgusting, doesn't it: pureed tuna) in the train compartment with five other people. She pretends to choke on a fish bone, the murderer leans over to help her, the shade whips up, and Mrs. McGillicuddy in the car on the parallel track recognizes him as the murderer (similar to her original sighting of a murder being committed). Then people in both train compartments pull some sort of magic chain that make both trains stop!

Really? Really? I don't know which element seemed more unrealistic. That they could successfully reenact the strangulation scene for Mrs. McGillicuddy using trains that pass in the night with split-second timing or that any railway in the entire world would allow the passengers anywhere near the brakes for the whole train. Other trains run on the same tracks, too, you know, and if passengers start pulling the magic chain emergency brake, you're going to get trains rear-ending each other, accompanied by trainloads of costly damage, injuries, death, and lawsuits.

Agatha did not write anything so foolish as trains that pass in the night and magic chain emergency brakes. One train was enough for the novel to get the story in motion. Instead, the identification of the murderer takes place over tea in the dining room and it's far, far more realistic (as things go in the mystery genre).

What finally killed the movie for me, besides Miss Marple saying that it was all for lurve, was I could not tell how she knew. Subtitles would have definitely helped here as I couldn't always understand what everyone was saying. But I don't think so. The novel isn't clear how Miss Marple worked out the identity of the murderer, either. It's like it came to her in a dream and she ran with it and got lucky.

I can't accept that copout. Not all of Agatha's efforts were stellar and this lack of explanation isn't typical. Even Homer nods on occasion. This moment was the scriptwriter's chance to shine. They could have added a scene or two showing us how Miss Marple solved the crime. They could have come up with something clever that would fit into the text and wouldn't be as egregious and flat-out wrong as making Miss Marple a party to adultery when she was young and pretty.

Luckily, we did not get subjected to that little bit of whimsy again; Miss Marple staring longingly at a sepia-toned photograph of a handsome young soldier to inform the audience that's why she remained a spinster.

What can you do? If ITV Productions ever releases this episode with subtitles, I'll probably watch it again to see if I'm wrong about the scriptwriter. I'd like to be because I'd like to believe that Miss Marple doesn't rely on dreams to direct her sleuthing.

General Information

Based on: *4.50 from Paddington / What Mrs. McGillicuddy Saw* in U.S. (novel, 1957)
Run time: 1 hr., 34 min. **Subtitles:** No

Writer: T.R. Bowen **Director:** Martyn Friend

Cast

Geraldine McEwan as Miss Jane Marple
Amanda Holden as Lucy Eyelesbarrow
John Hannah as Inspector Tom Campbell

Niamh Cusack as Emma Crackenthorpe
David Warner as Luther Crackenthorpe
Ciarán McMenamin as Cedric Crackenthorpe
Ben Daniels as Alfred Crackenthorpe
Charlie Creed-Miles as Harold Crackenthorpe
Rose Keegan as Lady Alice Crackenthorpe
Jenny Agutter as Agnes Crackenthorpe
Michael Landes as Bryan Eastley
Kurtis O'Brien as Alexander Eastley
Griff Rhys Jones as Dr. Quimper
Rob Brydon as Inspector Awdry
Pam Ferris as Elspeth McGillicuddy
Celia Imrie as Madame Joliet
Tim Stern as Attendant
Toby Marlow as James Stoddard-West
Pip Torrens as Noël Coward

Film Locations

Highclere Castle, Highclere, Hampshire (Rutherford Hall great hall)
Knebworth House, Stevenage, Hertfordshire (Rutherford Hall exterior)
Eltham Palace, London (Noel Coward's house)
Rothley station, Leicester, Leicestershire (Paddington Station)
Loseley Park, Guildford, Surrey (Rutherford Hall library, dining room)
Chiswick House, London (exterior scenes)

A Murder Is Announced (2005)

Chipping Cleghorn undergoes many changes, not all for the better, in this tale of shifting identities

Fidelity to text

Complete rewrites of three relationships. Say goodbye to the vicar, his wife, and their cat, while Miss Marple gains yet another distant relative.

Quality of movie

Docked a half-gun for the scriptwriter rewriting Agatha's better, more plausible, and more dramatic reveal of the murderer. It wasn't an improvement.

I never know what I'm going to get with ITV's *Miss Marple* adaptations. Their desire to be cutting edge and different leads sometimes to regrettable scripting decisions. *A Murder Is Announced* is an example of an episode where they should have left perfect alone.

As always, it looks gorgeous. That spa Miss Marple stays at is astounding with stunning blue tile everywhere. We visit a castle in Scotland and the charming village of Chipping Cleghorn.

But Chipping Cleghorn is where we start having problems. It's so clean! So manicured! Every building looks freshly pressure-washed.

That house where Miss Hinchcliffe and Miss Murgatroyd live is a *palace*. Their cobblestone drive must have been weeded mere moments before filming began. I have never seen such immaculate cobblestones. There wasn't even any moss on them and considering England's climate, that's impossible. God only knows how two women, running a farm on their own, managed to do all that work without servants or farmhands.

The novel makes it clear that while Miss Hinchcliffe and Miss Murgatroyd are managing, they aren't rich. They'd be able to afford the English cottage equivalent of a doublewide. Not this estate.

Miss Hinchcliffe and Miss Murgatroyd are the first of the major relationship changes. In the novel, their relationship is implied. Here, watching them hold hands and kiss, you know they're sharing a bed. Since the vicar, his wife, and their cat, Tiglath Pileser (but more about the cat later) were written out of the script, Miss Murgatroyd is drafted to be Miss Marple's distant relative. This explains why Miss Marple is invited to stay and — gasp! — possibly notice the illicit relationship between the two women.

Even in 1951 or so, I doubt Miss Marple would care. She's seen every aspect of human nature. Since the two ladies are well-behaved, discreet, take good care of their farm, and are not murderers, she won't gossip. It's not as if she's unfamiliar with the concept of a Boston marriage. Those go back a long way. Plenty of women have lived together to save money and provide companionship. It's only tacky moderns like us who won't leave the implication alone and ask prying questions about bedpartners.

Letitia Blacklock (*Zoë Wanamaker*), the secretive heiress

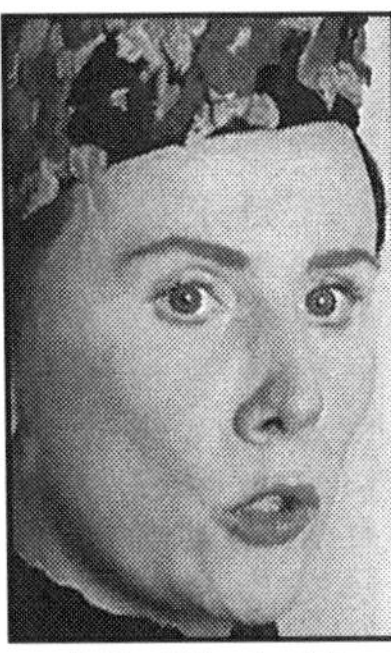

Mitzi Kosinski (*Catherine Tate*), the fearful refugee

Patrick Simmons (*Matthew Goode*), the lighthearted kin

Archie Easterbrook (*Robert Pugh*), the cashiered colonel

Amy Murgatroyd (*Claire Skinner*), the dotty farmer

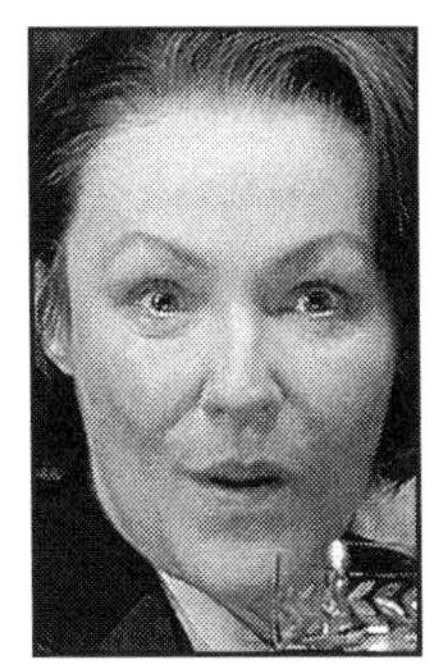

Lizzie Hinchcliffe (*Frances Barber*), the farmer's partner

Colonel Easterbrook morphed into someone unrecognizable. He lost his wife, Laura, along with her glamorous and possibly criminal past. Instead, we get a story about his being drummed out of the army in disgrace, his drunkenness, and his estrangement from his daughter. He gets a new relationship with Mrs. Swettenham, which did not exist in the novel. Mrs. Swettenham is revealed to be a single mother — gasp! — whose son, Edmund, heartily disapproves of their relationship because he's a selfish, grasping toad.

Edmund, in turn, loses his chance at happiness with Philippa since in this version no relationship exists at all. In the novel, they flirt and eventually marry. Not here, even though they appear to be the only unattached people under the age of thirty for miles around. They ignore each other. He's too busy prying into his mother's love life to have one of his own. Philippa has too much to hide.

The contentious triangle of Colonel Easterbrook, Mrs. Swettenham, and Edmund is complicated by the presence of his faithful black dog. The dog was written into the script to show that Colonel Easterbrook isn't married and has only a dog to talk to, poor soul. That duty done, the dog disappears even though as a good and loyal dog, he would have been glued to his master's side. The screenwriter had no idea how close a lonely man can get to his dog. The poor dog must've spent the rest of the show crated in a back bedroom. England being a nation of dog-lovers, Colonel Easterbrook's neighbors would have complained and he'd end up on charges of dog abuse long before he becomes a murder suspect.

The dog also did not help Miss Marple solve the mystery, unlike the Vicar's cat, Tiglath Pileser. The cat served a real purpose in the novel, adding that random element of serendipity. Miss Marple would have worked out the crime on her own, but the cat made sure of it.

The third relationship change ensured the viewer and Miss Blacklock were suspicious about the openly icky relationship between Patrick and Julia, her visiting, distant cousins. They're brother and sister but they sure don't act like it.

You may ask if this adaptation did anything right besides gorgeous settings and costumes. It did. Mitzi, the refugee servant, was much closer to the novel, even retaining her name and gaining a Swiss nationality. Her treatment by Patrick was suitably horrible; he harassed and teased her and she had to endure it because she was a foreigner, refugee, and servant. He, the scion of a good family, could be nasty to a helpless and trapped woman and get away with it.

Zoë Wanamaker made an outstanding Letitia Blacklock. In fact, the entire cast was very good other than the casting director showing a decided taste for prettier than normal. If you watch the Joan Hickson version of *A Murder Is Announced*, you'll see what I mean. *Those* actors and actresses looked like real people you could meet on the street in your hometown. *These* actors and actresses look like actors and actresses pretending to look like common people. Kind of the same way the village of Chipping Cleghorn is an idealized vision of a tiny village out in the middle of nowhere rather than the isolated, dirty, messy reality complete with weeds and cow manure in the streets. Even the pigsties were neat.

ITV was reasonably successful compressing a complex novel down to 94 minutes of screen time. If you aren't familiar with the novel, you won't even notice the changes until you get to the end. I could not accept how the murderer figures out that Miss Murgatroyd is a danger. It wasn't set up properly. Then Mitzi (a wasted Catherine Tate) bursts onto the scene screaming about who the murderer is! In the novel, you get Mitzi being very brave and risking death to unmask the killer. Here, you get a temper tantrum from a difficult servant.

You do get to see the Easterbrook/Swettenham triangle resolved but in the most cursory way. I suppose the participants realized, after numerous murders, that life is short and decided to bury the hatchet somewhere other than in each other's skulls. But it felt forced, as if the screenwriter needed a happy ending after three people were shot, poisoned, and strangled, and couldn't write anything better.

Watch this version of *A Murder Is Announced* for completeness' sake, but unless you really want to see that spa again, there's no need to revisit Chipping Cleghorn.

General Information

Based on: *A Murder Is Announced* (novel, 1950)
Run time: 1 hr., 43 min. **Subtitles:** No

Writer: Stewart Harcourt **Director:** John Strickland

Cast

Geraldine McEwan as Miss Marple
Alexander Armstrong as D.I. Dermot Craddock
Gerard Horan as D.S. Fletcher

Zoë Wanamaker as Letitia Blacklock
Elaine Paige as Dora Bunner
Keeley Hawes as Phillipa Haymes
Matthew Goode as Patrick Simmons
Sienna Guillory as Julia Simmons
Catherine Tate as Mitzi Kosinski
Christian Coulson as Edmund Swettenham
Cherie Lunghi as Sadie Swettenham
Robert Pugh as Col. Archie Easterbrook
Claire Skinner as Amy Murgatroyd
Frances Barber as Lizzie Hinchcliffe
Christian Rubeck as Rudi Schertz
Richard Dixon as Rowlandson
Nicole Lewis as Myrna Harris
Lesley Nicol as Nurse McClelland
Virginia McKenna as Belle Goedler

Film Locations

Debenham House, London (Royal Spa Hotel interiors)
Eilean Donan Castle, Kyle of Lochalsh, Scotland (Belle Goedler's home)
Dorchester Abbey, Oxfordshire (church)
Chilworth Manor, Surrey (Little Paddocks interiors)

Sleeping Murder (J-2005)

(*Suripingu Mada*)

A line from a play triggers painful recollections, opening a door into a woman's traumatic past

There are 39 episodes in *Agatha Christie's Great Detectives Poirot and Marple*. We've watched two novel adaptations; one featuring Poirot and one Miss Marple. For Poirot, I chose *Mystery at End House* because that novel had only been adapted once, for the TV series with David Suchet.

For the Miss Marple episode, the choice was more limited. Agatha wrote twelve Marple novels. All have been adapted at least twice; once for the Joan Hickson series (1984-1992) and again by ITV's *Marple* (2004-2013). In addition, a few of those novels have been filmed with other actresses.

The anime series filmed eight Miss Marple tales in all, six short stories and two novels. One of the two novels was *4.50 From Paddington*. That's been filmed three other times, beginning with Margaret Rutherford's version in 1961, renamed *Murder, She Said*.

The other novel in the anime series was *Sleeping Murder*. That's only been filmed twice and so here we are.

What's interesting about *Sleeping Murder* is that it's so heavily influenced by the Jacobean tragedy *The Duchess of Malfi* by John Webster (1580-1632). First performed in 1613, it echoes down the ages. It is still performed today and influencing authors.

It was also based on real events. Italian noblewoman Giovanna d'Aragona, Duchess of Amalfi (1478-1510) was married off at age 12 and widowed by age 20. Her two brothers, Luigi d'Aragona (who was Cardinal of Aragón) and Carlo, Marquis of Gerace didn't want her to remarry or have children because they'd lose control of her estates and her money. They also didn't want the stain on the family by her marrying a commoner. But Giovanna remarried in secret for love and she chose a man of good character but multiple steps lower on the social scale, Antonio Beccadelli of Bologna (1475-1513).

Her brothers conspired to have Giovanna and her children disappeared and most likely murdered. There's no proof, you understand, but there's plenty of evidence to say Giovanna and her kids didn't live long after they were captured. Antonio died a few years later when the brothers caught up with him and had him assassinated.

Gwenda Reed (*Misato Tanaka*), the haunted

Captain Erskine (*Leo Morimoto*), the tempted husband

Helen Halliday (*uncredited*), the murder victim

Dr. James Kennedy (*uncredited*), the half-brother

Edith Paget (*uncredited*), the family cook

Lily Kimble (*uncredited*), the observant maid

A friend of Antonio's, Matteo Bandello (1480-1562), turned the tragedy into a novella which John Webster adapted for the stage. At its heart is a woman trying to chose her own path in life against the wishes of her controlling brothers. The play doesn't end well for anyone. By the last act, the stage is littered with bodies, although not with too much blood because most of the victims were strangled. The rest were poisoned and stabbed.

Jacobean tragedies, named for King James I, who ruled Britain from 1603 to 1625, were the slasher flicks of their time. They were hugely popular and free from censorship because amid the soapy gore, there was a moral about not slaughtering family and friends for money, power, and status because catastrophe would follow.

General Information

Based on: *Sleeping Murder* (novel, 1976)
Run time: 1 hr., 40 min. **Subtitles:** Yes

Writer: Shôji Yonemura
Director: Naohito Takahashi

Cast

Kaoru Yachigusa as Miss Marple
Fumiko Orikasa as Maybelle West
Masaya Katô as Raymond West
Masako Joh as Oliver

Misato Tanaka as Gwenda Reed
Leo Morimoto as Captain Erskine
Li Lixian as Mrs. Eleanor Fane

Fun stuff for the whole family! Take the kids! It's okay because it's culture.

But back to Miss Marple, who says at the conclusion: "We were all stupid. We should have seen at once. Those lines from *The Duchess of Malfi* were really the clue to the whole thing."

Helen Kennedy's life mimicked the Duchess. Her half-brother, Dr. Kennedy, is older and so hyper-controlling he cut up her tennis net so she couldn't play with friends. He's the one who spreads rumors about her being a man-crazy slut. He's probably the one who framed Helen's boyfriend, Jackie Afflick, and got him fired. He's the reason she fled to India to marry Walter Fane.

But Helen, like the Duchess of Malfi, had good character. She met Captain Erskine during the sea voyage and fell in love (which was glossed over in this film) but refused to break up his marriage. She went on to India and broke it off with Walter Fane because she didn't love him.

On the voyage back to England, she met the recently widowed Kelvin Halliday and little Gwenda and fell in love. Notice that Helen and Kelvin married quietly in London, presenting a *fait accompli* to her half-brother.

Which, like the Duchess' brothers, he did not accept. He pretended to, and Helen tentatively believed him. But he couldn't control himself, and she became fearful; fearful enough that she persuaded Kelvin they had to leave Dillmouth. Unfortunately, she didn't tell hubby the extent of her fears, leading to his being poisoned with hallucinogens by Dr. Kennedy and convinced that he became insane and strangled Helen.

Like the Duchess' brothers, Dr. Kennedy didn't just murder Helen and frame someone else. He told everyone she disappeared because she was a whore who'd run off with another man and abandoned Gwenda.

Gwenda was too young at the time to know any of this, naturally. But she was uneasy about the house in Dillmouth that she recently bought. Strange memories kept surfacing.

Then she attends a production of *The Duchess of Malfi* with Maybelle, Raymond West, and Miss Marple and she hears the fateful lines:

> *Cover her face,*
> *Mine eyes dazzle,*
> *She died young.*

She remembers seeing someone strangling a blonde woman and saying those lines. She cries out, and flees the theater.

Sleeping Murder is a great story, a tragedy for the ages, but this version is considerably cleaned up and simplified for the kiddies. Jackie Afflick becomes a nonentity, Captain Erskine's jealous wife loses her lines, and Walter Fane disappears into the background.

The novel never addressed it and none of the adaptations have either, but I always felt that Walter fell madly in love with Helen. When she dumped him, he never got over her. It says something about how she drew people to her that none of the men she'd been involved with twenty years ago ever forgot her.

Neither did her half-brother. Most of the creepy, repressed urges that Dr. Kennedy had for his sister vanished. The novel never states that he laid a hand on his much-younger half-sister and he probably didn't. Agatha didn't write that kind of book.

For a novel loaded with drama, this adaptation is flat and without savor. Maybelle takes all of Giles Reed's lines — he doesn't show up until the last few minutes — and some of Miss Marple's, yet she never quite comes to life. Oliver the duck (possibly named after Ariadne Oliver?) was surprisingly muted for a cute animal sidekick. Unlike *Mystery at End House*, you could remove Oliver from this film and never miss him.

Also flat is the overarching storyline begun in episode one when Maybelle insists on becoming a detective. She's coming to a better understanding with her father and will write home more often. But I don't know if her story is resolved in episode 39. I'm not watching all 39 episodes to find out, and unless you're introducing young kids to Agatha Christie, I recommend you don't bother, either.

Sleeping Murder (2006)

Adding a seaside music hall troupe deepens the story of a woman gone missing during a memorable summer

Fidelity to text

The producers made dozens of changes, from irritating but minor to wholesale rewrites. The Funnybones theatrical troupe is completely new.

Quality of movie

It's lively and fun to watch. I would have given it a higher score except Miss Marple's solution was so truncated as to have been pulled out of her knitting bag.

This version of *Sleeping Murder* is very, very different from Joan Hickson's 1987 opus. The main beats of the text are there: orphaned young woman arrives in England after growing up overseas and by astounding coincidence buys the house she lived in as a toddler. This is the house where, as a toddler, she witnessed her stepmother being strangled. Miss Marple shows up to solve the case. A few characters remain in their original form, notably Dr. Kennedy, Walter Fane, his mother Mrs. Fane, a former parlormaid, the former cook, and a clerk in a yarn shop.

After that, the script veers off into dramatic and exciting new territory. We begin in India, with Bollywood style color and drama. Kelvin Halliday is notified that his wife died tragically in a car accident, yet oddly, there's no mention of why the Indian police couldn't retrieve her body. Too deep in the tiger-infested gorge? Or too deep in the gorge and the car's on fire? This fact will become important.

The grieving widower and his toddler daughter sail off to England, don't meet anyone onboard ship, land in Dillmouth, and he meets the hot redheaded actress, Helen Marsden. She's the star of a small theatrical troupe called the Funnybones. Sparks fly. To the consternation of their servants and the villagers, they don't wait for the quickie wedding to move in together.

Then Helen Marsden vanishes the night before the wedding.

In the current day, we meet Gwenda Halliday, fiancée of an older businessman whose face we never see. He stays in India because his job is more important than the hot, much younger blonde he's marrying. Instead, he assigns a young, male employee to escort Gwenda around England. Not surprisingly, Hugh Hornbeam does a lot more than help Gwenda buy and rehab a house. It's always a bad idea to outsource your husbandly duties to a younger man and we get to watch the proof.

Within days of arriving in England, Gwenda purchases the mysteriously familiar house in Dillmouth, a nondescript seaside town at the edge of nowhere. Strange memories surface. Hugh turns out to have a dear friend (or distant relative, the film wasn't clear) named Miss Marple. She arrives and Gwenda's vivid, complicated past is uncovered in record time, all except for the completely missing past belonging to

Helen Marsden (*Anna-Louise Plowman*), the missing fiancée

Gwenda Halliday (*Sophia Myles*), the haunted fiancée

Hugh Hornbeam (*Aidan McArdle*), the able assistant

Dr. James Kennedy (*Phil Davis*), the mourning kin

Dickie Erskine (*Paul McGann*), the mourning manager

Walter Fane (*Peter Serafinowicz*), the mourning solicitor

Helen Marsden, who appears to have arisen from the sea foam off Dillmouth like Botticelli's Venus. She's even a redhead.

And that was a flaw in the mystery. Twist endings are fine, but the audience shouldn't be completely blindsided. At no point did anyone mention that Helen *never* talked about her past, including where she learned to perform. Nor, when investigating everything else, did Gwenda investigate Helen's past prior to Dillmouth.

The novel was almost completely rewritten to incorporate Helen and the Funnybones. As a result, we get to enjoy period music hall song and dance routines, with comedy thrown in. The Funnybones interact with major and minor characters in the past and in the present. I didn't mind at all. We even get an interesting subplot involving Walter Fane, his mother, and Janet and Dickie Erskine that lets the gentlemen demonstrate their character.

What I did mind, and the reason for not awarding the fifth strangler, was the film was too short. Ninety-three minutes was not enough time for Miss Marple to convincingly solve Helen's disappearance. She pulled that solution out of her knitting bag. At best, you could say she's naturally suspicious of whatever she's told. Being handed a conveniently saved postcard along with a creepy epigram on the back of an old photograph (so the handwriting can be matched up) makes her wary. So does Dr. Kennedy's name confusion between Kelvin Halliday's dead wife from India and potential wife #2, Helen Marsden. I'm guessing here because even though Miss Marple witnessed Dr. Kenney's mix-up, we don't see her react.

A minute of added film would have made her deductions plausible.

A few more added minutes of film would have made clear how plot-critical information would have magically arrived from India. Supposedly the film takes place in 1951. I know they had telephones and telegraphs way back then, but you couldn't get instant information from the Indian bureaucracy that was exactly what was needed to solve the murder. I don't believe you could get instant information from today's Indian bureaucracy. Or from any bureaucracy. Bureaucracies don't work that way. It takes time for clerks to go digging through dusty filing cabinets crammed with decades-old records.

There was also the question of Indian police work and forensics in 1934. A tragic auto accident generally leaves enough remains that the body can be identified, but apparently not in India which I find hard to believe. Are we supposed to believe tigers dragged Clare Halliday's body from the car and ate it? No police force anywhere likes loose ends and missing bodies are a major loose end. If the Indian police force can send an officer to Dillmouth, England, looking for a jewel thief, they'll search the wrecked car for the body of that suspected jewel thief.

We also didn't spend nearly enough time with Dr. Kennedy. He's the reason his sister Clare fled to India, became a nursery maid, got fired for theft, became a taxi dancer at a nightclub, and met Kelvin Halliday. That was a touch difficult to accept (I had to don my romance writer's hat) because promising young under-secretaries as a rule don't marry taxi dancers. Without the time spent watching Dr. Kennedy and Clare, the solution to the mystery arises because the script said so and not because the crime grew organically from the characters.

The plot holes and missed opportunities made the connection between Gwenda's mother and stepmother feel forced. It wasn't just out of left field. That ball park was in India.

Part of this was caused by the Funnybones, whose shenanigans used up plot space that could have been used to weave a tighter plot. I liked them very much and would have liked more screen time with them, but not at the expense of seeing Miss Marple uncover clues and solve the mystery in a fashion that I could follow.

ITV Productions should have splurged on another ten minutes of film stock. Maybe fifteen.

You can always count on ITV to take artistic risks and sometimes, like mostly here, they pay off. Understand when you watch their *Sleeping Murder* that it's not true to the text other than at the most basic level. If you can suspend your critical judgment of hack screenwriters "improving" Agatha Christie, you'll enjoy this movie.

If you can't, stick with Joan Hickson's version, which follows the text about as closely as a movie can follow a novel.

General Information

Based on: *Sleeping Murder* (novel, 1976)
Run time: 1 hr., 42 min. **Subtitles:** No

Writer: Stephen Churchett
Director: Edward Hall

Cast

Geraldine McEwan as Jane Marple
Russ Abbot as Chief Inspector Arthur Primer
Emilio Doorgasingh as Sergeant Desai
Sophia Myles as Gwenda Halliday
Aidan McArdle as Hugh Hornbeam

Anna-Louise Plowman as Helen Marsden
Julian Wadham as Kelvin Halliday
Peter Serafinowicz as Walter Fane
Geraldine Chaplin as Mrs. Fane
Phil Davis as Dr. James Alfred Kennedy
Dawn French as Janet Erskine
Paul McGann as Dickie Erskine
Harry Treadaway as George Erskine
Martin Kemp as Jackie Afflick
Sarah Parish as Evie Ballantine
Nickolas Grace as Lionel Luff
Una Stubbs as Edith Pagett

Film Locations

Sidmouth, Devon (Dillmouth)
Kit's Close, Fawley, Buckinghamshire (Dr. Kennedy's home)
Hampton Court House (Afflick's house)

The Moving Finger (2006)

A hurt, suicidal veteran and his sister move to a quiet village complete with murder, and poison-pen letters

Fidelity to text

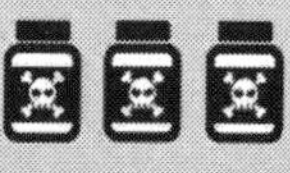
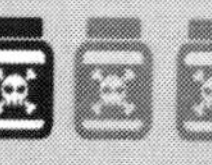

All the usual condensing and removal of minor characters, plus Miss Marple shows up at the very start and Jerry Burton becomes a damaged, alcoholic vet who tried to kill himself in a motorcycle accident.

Quality of movie

Mr. Pye was a hoot and his English Country House Porn is to die for. The actors chewed the scenery with gusto. Great costumes too, especially Megan's transformation into Audrey Hepburn.

ITV's *Marple* episodes have been hit or miss. Their screenwriters like mucking about with Agatha's text in order to justify their salaries. The results are not always golden.

In this case? *The Moving Finger* was a hit. I got everything I wanted to see more of, like Mr. Pye and his gilded porcelain in his gilded dining room. Even better, I got to see why Miss Marple was able to solve the crime. There were actual, interpretable clues. These were clues that even doofus audience members like me — always fooled by the red herrings — could grasp.

Jerry Burton, our narrator, was less of wet blanket than he was in the 1987 version. His injury was handled much more realistically, something I, as a sometimes cane user, appreciated. He started out with two canes, slowly moved down to one and then, sometimes, none. He never turned into an athlete. He limped and not just when the plot called for it. It was also much clearer in this version why he fell in love with Megan Symmington.

I had hopes for how the script handled his relationship with the governess, Elsie Holland. In the novel, Elsie is a stunner. Jerry crushes hard on her until the moment she opens her mouth and he hears her flat, competent voice. The magic flees and she becomes part of the charming and bucolic scenery of Lymstock, permitting him to better see Megan Symmington.

But Hollywood must be Hollywood, even in British television. Elsie had to have a lovely voice to match her lovely exterior. And that sundress! My God, she stops traffic with her cleavage and probably threw the Symmington boys into early puberty. So we're forced to accept watching a red-blooded young man kiss the most ravishing woman around for miles and say meh.

Yeah. Sure. I could believe that a man would fall out of a dazed crush when he hears the screechy voice of this glorious-in-every-other way version of Elsie Holland. But without that spur, Jerry would be dragging Elsie into the shrubbery surrounding Mr. Pye's lovely terrace to closely and intimately inspect the flowerbeds. Repeatedly.

This version of *The Moving Finger* also gave a better picture of upper-class life in Lymstock. In pre-

Jerry Burton
(*James D'Arcy*),
the broken veteran

Joanna Burton
(*Emilia Fox*),
the spritely sister

Megan Hunter
(*Talulah Riley*),
the lonely girl

Cardew Pye
(*John Sessions*),
the confirmed bachelor

Rev. Caleb Calthrop
(*Ken Russell*),
the elderly minister

Elsie Holland
(*Kelly Brook*),
the beautiful governess

television days, in little villages out in the middle of nowhere, everyone knows each other well enough that they're comfortable making their own entertainment. It's not like there's much else to choose from. The Symmingtons throw dinner parties with sparkling dialog interspersed with bitchy banter about the neighbors. The artistic confirmed bachelor — read gay — Mr. Pye holds musical evenings, complete with badly sung duets, and the vicar — eccentrically played by director Ken Russell — reciting Horace in the original Latin.

I would have given this version of *The Moving Finger* a higher rating, except I couldn't always understand the sparkling dinner table conversation. Not every conversation mattered to solving the murder but enough did that it was annoying when the actors mumbled.

Overall, each of the main characters got some screen time, giving me a better feel for their relationships. But the 93-minute run time still felt much too short. In the novel, Dr. Owen Griffith enjoyed charming scenes with Joanna Burton, Jerry's sister. Most of them were axed, including the vital one where Dr. Griffith introduces Joanna to the real world by dragooning her into helping him with a difficult and challenging childbirth. Instead, in the film, he gives her a picture he took of a diseased spleen. For some mysterious reason, Dr. Griffith also displays a stutter which I do not recall from the novel.

Another mid-sized change was having Jerry's sister, Joanna, do Megan Symmington's makeover in Lymstock. In the novel and the Joan Hickson version, Jerry sweeps her off to London where a modiste and hairdresser turn the ugly duckling (by Hollywood beauty standards) into a swan. Having Joanna clean up and transform Megan into Audrey Hepburn worked very well, as did Megan's uncomfortable feelings about her transformation.

I would have liked this version to be longer. I enjoyed spending time with the characters and visiting Lymstock. I wanted more.

There were moments when I wanted to better understand what was going on. Did Mr. Pye imply an illicit relationship with the colonel who shot himself in the opening scene? I wasn't sure. Did the colonel shoot himself? Or was he helped? A few more minutes and a rewrite would have added so much. If the script sets up questions like this, they should be answered.

It was also unclear if Miss Marple was referring to her adulterous relationship mentioned in previous episodes of the ITV series. The gentleman in question had a war to fight and "other commitments." You mean the commitment he made to his wife on their wedding day? That's a commitment. Adultery is a sin, folks. It's hard for me to buy Miss Marple having a torrid affair with a married man even when she was young and hot. She has too much moral fiber.

Would I watch this version of *The Moving Finger* again? Absolutely. Is it better than the 1987 Joan Hickson version? Yes, it is, even though the 1987 version is truer to the original text than this 2006 version. Watching the two episodes is instructive. You can see where the screenwriters differed. What they thought needed to be emphasized. What they jettisoned. What they changed wholesale or invented. As a writer watching two adaptations of the same novel, I enjoyed seeing the differing interpretations and working out why the scriptwriters did what they did.

Scripts matter as much as — or sometimes more — than the actors being cast. Two versions of the same novel show why.

General Information

Based on: *The Moving Finger* (novel, 1942)
Run time: 1 hr., 33 min. **Subtitles:** No

Writer: Kevin Elyot
Director: Tom Shankland

Cast

Geraldine McEwan as Miss Marple
Keith Allen as Inspector Graves
Stephen Churchett as Coroner

James D'Arcy as Jerry Burton
Emilia Fox as Joanna Burton
Rosalind Knight as Partridge
Imogen Stubbs as Mona Symmington
Harry Enfield as Richard Symmington
Talulah Riley as Megan Hunter
Angela Curran as Miss Ginch
Kelly Brook as Elsie Holland
Ellen Capron as Agnes Brown
Sean Pertwee as Dr. Owen Griffith
Jessica Hynes as Aimee Griffith
John Sessions as Cardew Pye
Ken Russell as the Rev. Caleb Dane Calthrop
Frances de la Tour as Maud Dane Calthrop
Thelma Barlow as Emily Barton

Film Locations

Chilham, Kent (Lymstock)
Chilham Castle (Cardew Pye's House)
St. Mary's Church, Chilham (Lymstock Church)

Miss Marple: *I sometimes wonder if the tale bearer is as guilty as the tale maker.*

Cardew Pye: *Oops, my dear Miss Marple! You're being moral and forget that you're among friends.*

By the Pricking of My Thumbs (2006)

Miss Marple helps a lush Tuppence navigate loneliness with the help of child murder and a sinister village

Fidelity to text

Miss Marple joins a Tommy and Tuppence novel. The story arc remains, but there are numerous changes to time period, main plot, subplots, minor characters, names, locations ... it's a long list.

Quality of movie

Miss Marple fits in beautifully, taking the place of Tommy, who's off doing spy stuff and appears only when needed. The film moved along smartly. Great clothes, locations, and most of all, atmosphere.

ITV *Marple* productions are hit or miss. *By the Pricking of My Thumbs*, despite Miss Marple never coming anywhere near the original novel, was a hit. She fitted in surprisingly well.

We meet Tommy and Tuppence visiting an elderly, unpleasant aunt in a high-end rest home and who else is there visiting?

Miss Marple, naturally. You would expect to meet Miss Marple visiting an elderly friend of hers at a rest home. It felt natural that they meet this way, unlike claiming that somehow Jane Marple is related to Tommy, Tuppence, or anyone they know. She's not. Miss Marple is who she is: a nosy, perennially curious old lady with a taste for mysterious death. So when Tommy doesn't listen to Tuppence's anxiety over overhearing something, eagle-eared Miss Marple does and away we go. She's thrilled to go haring off with a total stranger based on disquieting feelings of creepiness and wrongness.

The overall arc of the story remains: a child's murder under mysterious circumstances and the disappearance of an old lady. You still get creepy villagers, loquacious villagers, friendly villagers, hostile villagers, and the new lord of the manor. You lose Tommy and his co-worker, Ivor Smith, and their investigation into a gang of thieves. You lose the gang of thieves. You also lose the numerous child murders that took place over the years along with ancillary murders of people who look suspiciously at our murderer, wondering what he's getting up to when no one's looking. There were plenty of child murders in the novel; so many that the actual count is never given. It's implied that there were at least five. Or more.

And people say Agatha writes cozies.

There was also the comment from a loquacious villager to Tuppence about how Sir Phillip loved children but not in the normal way. That didn't quite make it into the film, although Sir Philip did.

To substitute for the thieves subplot, we get young love in the form of a village lass, an American soldier stationed nearby, and the local bobby. We also get a nod to Sir Phillip's interest in children with an even weirder subplot about filming *Jane Eyre* and having a

Tuppence Beresford (*Greta Scacchi*), the lonely wife

Tommy Beresford (*Anthony Andrews*), the traveling agent

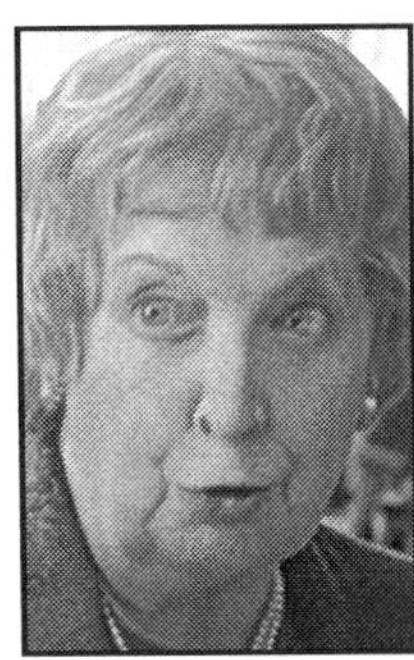
Mrs. Lancaster (*June Whitfield*), the caring mother

Sir Philip Starke (*Leslie Phillips*), the local lord

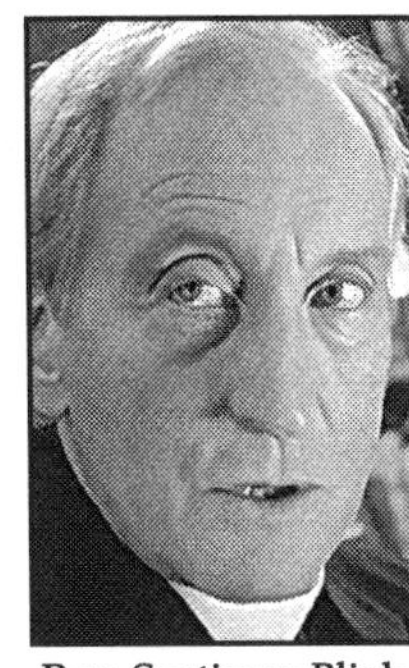
Rev. Septimus Bligh (*Charles Dance*), the despondent vicar

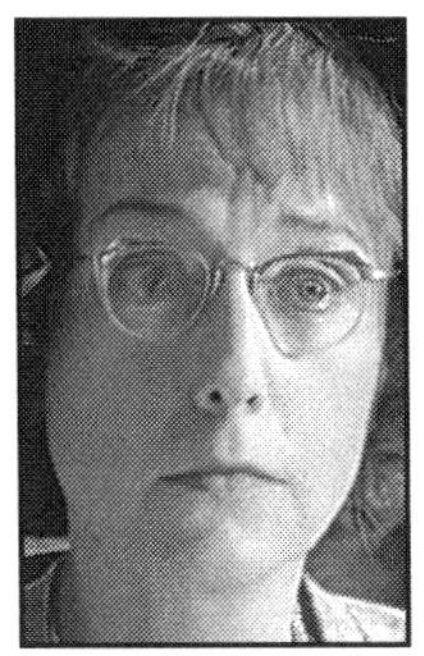
Nellie Bligh (*Lia Williams*), the helpful wife

young village lass portray Jane Eyre's dying friend. She would give Veruca Salt a run for her money. She proves useful when she tells Tuppence the location of the mysterious house in the painting Mrs. Lancaster gives to Aunt Ada.

General Information

Based on: *By the Pricking of My Thumbs* (novel, 1968)
Run time: 1 hr., 42 min. **Subtitles:** No

Writer: Stewart Harcourt
Director: Peter Medak

Cast

Geraldine McEwan as Miss Marple
Anthony Andrews as Tommy Beresford
Greta Scacchi as Tuppence Beresford
Josie Lawrence as Hannah Beresford

Clare Holman as Miss Packard
Miriam Karlin as Marjorie Moody
June Whitfield as Mrs. Lancaster
Claire Bloom as Aunt Ada
Leslie Phillips as Sir Philip Starke
Michael Maloney as Dr. Joshua Waters
Michelle Ryan as Rose Waters
O.T. Fagbenle as Chris Murphy
Michael Begley as Ethan Maxwell
Charles Dance as Rev. Septimus Bligh
Lia Williams as Nellie Bligh
Jody Halse as Amos Perry
Bonnie Langford as Betty Johnson
Brian Conley as Eric Johnson
Eliza Bennett as Nora Johnson
Steven Berkoff as Mr. Eccles
Patrick Barlow as Mr. Timothy
Chloe Pennington as Young Hannah
Oliver Jordan as Young Ethan
Sid Strickland as Jane Eyre

Film Locations

Turville, Buckinghamshire
Loseley Park, Guildford (Sir Philip Starke's manor house)

Oh, and Nellie Bligh? She's not just Sir Phillip's long-suffering and devoted secretary, she's also the vicar's wife. She and the vicar keep plenty of secrets they'd like to stay buried. Or in the vicar's case, drowned.

Another major change was making Tuppence into an alcoholic. I'm ambivalent about this. It worked, but I can't see Tuppence ever falling inside a bottle. She's too practical and too imaginative. She'd be off doing good works in the local parish. Writing racy novels. Running her own detective agency. Becoming a lush because she doesn't know what to do with herself, and she resents not being a spy like Tommy? I dunno.

I suppose the scriptwriter couldn't conceive of a strong, intelligent, older woman who doesn't end up with the life she dreamed of as a young woman but remains sober. Imagine that. Coping with disappointment with grace instead of addiction. How very old-fashioned.

Despite dipping into a bottle of scotch at every opportunity, Tuppence looked great. She reminded me of an observation from *The Lost Art of Dress* (2014) by Linda Przybyszewski. Ms. Przybyszewski devotes many pages to discussing how before the early '60s, adult women did not dress like teenagers, or worse, like toddlers. Teenage girls dressed for their age and planned for when they got enough years under their belts to dress in a more … mature way.

Tuppence's wardrobe in *By the Pricking of My Thumbs* is a perfect example of this dictate. Her clothes are perfectly fitted and designed for an older, sophisticated, worldly woman, comfortable with displaying her cleavage and handling men's responses to said cleavage.

You've heard of mutton dressed like lamb? The reverse is true: Lambs shouldn't dress like mutton. Sophisticated, classy, experienced ladies of a certain age and experience dress more dramatically. That's Tuppence, who always dresses to impress while remaining appropriate at all times. Our young love interest for the G.I.? She wears pretty sundresses and youthful cardigans. Our Veruca Salt clone dresses still younger. They don't wear each other's clothes.

Similarly, Miss Marple dresses for her age. She's moved past fascinating men and making their IQs drop as their sap rises. Her clothes are practical and hard-wearing.

As in the novel, Tuppence confronts the murderer. It is, however, Miss Marple (since it's her show) who deduces the plot behind the plot. I thought she was very clever and it made sense. She perceives the village's underlying reality instead of the concealing quaintness. It's tiny, isolated, suspiciously clean, and ruled since time immemorial by the Warrender family. They had long since died out, although the local church was filled with centuries of memorial plaques dedicated to various family members. So why is a plaque dedicated to Julia Starke smack in the middle of the Warrender family plaques? No one in this inbred, hidebound village with not a blade of grass out of place complains about the desecration?

No, the villagers take it in stride. There's a reason and not just because Sir Phillip Starke bought the old Warrender estate and moved in, filling the role in the village once filled by the Warrenders. The Warrenders, like the villagers, are described as being inbred.

Inbreeding leads to craziness as well as to birth defects and so it proves here too.

I'll be honest. I did not expect to like this movie. I like Tommy and Tuppence and wish that their novels would be filmed accurately. They are that rarity in Agatha Christie's oeuvre: they age, they have a family, and they live in the real world. As the world changes, their novels change, reflecting the era in which they were written. The idea of shoehorning Miss Marple into one of their stories felt ill-conceived at best.

However, it worked. It was fun, well-plotted with lots of twists and turns, and yet despite all the changes, it still played true to the novel. Give this one a try with an open mind.

The Sittaford Mystery (2006)

Epic expansion of Trevelyan's life leaves little room for a coherent mystery for Miss Marple to sort out

Fidelity to text

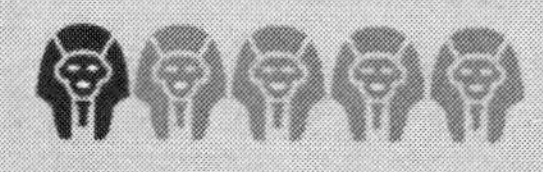

The novel was eviscerated. The murder, séance, escaped prisoner, and a few names remain. Everything else, including the murderer, were altered beyond recognition. Miss Marple resented being shoved in; she stayed defiantly offstage for long stretches.

Quality of movie

The scriptwriter shoved ten pounds of plot into a five-pound running length and the result is incoherence with snow.

Queue up Sir Mix-a-Lot and "Baby Got Back" and recite along with me:

Oh. My. God.
Look at that plot!

You'll have to sit through this episode twice (at least) to understand what's going on. This film is 93 minutes long, not long enough for all the disparate plot threads to be woven in a cohesive fashion. The film needed a minimum of another twenty minutes running time to do it justice.

But since ITV didn't do that, you, dear viewer, will be left asking what just happened? Rewind, dammit! That's what we did. Repeatedly. Yet there were many moments when I still can't tell you what was going on.

The trouble starts with forcing Miss Marple into a property that was never written for her. This can work: see ITV's *By the Pricking of My Thumbs*, a Tommy and Tuppence novel.

Not here. In fact, Miss Marple disappeared for long stretches of the film, doing heaven only knows what in Sittaford House while sitting out the blizzard. Maybe she was questioning the staff (we only see one servant in the mansion but there must be more), knitting, and speed-reading Captain Trevelyan's memoirs. She certainly wasn't at the Three Crowns Inn, inspecting the body and questioning the guests, even though most of the action takes place there.

An entirely new plot is shoehorned in, vastly expanding Captain Trevelyan's character and backstory. Suddenly, he's a war hero (WWI), a suspected war profiteer (WWII), an Olympic skater in between (I think; the dialog was incomprehensible at many key points), a major candidate to be the next prime minister (Winston Churchill (!) has a scene with Captain Trevelyan), *and* he's a noted archeologist having discovered a major tomb in Egypt back in 1927 that made his fortune! Compared with Capt. Trevelyan, Indiana Jones was a lazy amateur.

But all this rewriting was necessary to give Timothy Dalton scenery to chew to earn his paycheck. In the novel, Captain Trevelyan exists to be swiftly murdered. He doesn't even get one line. In the movie

Clive Trevelyan
(*Timothy Dalton*),
the captain of all

Ahmed Ghali
(*Jeffery Kissoon*),
the questing servant

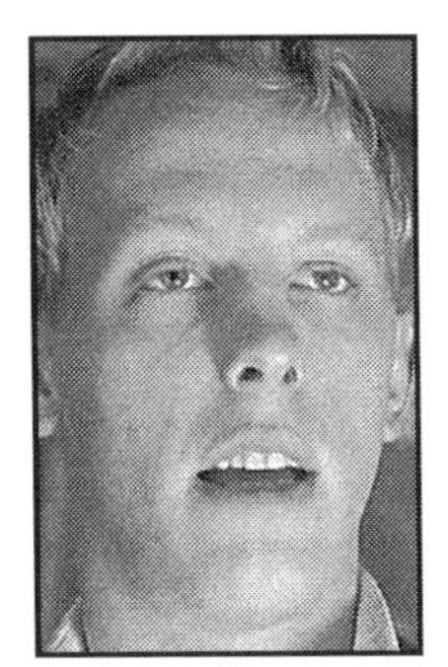

James Pearson
(*Laurence Fox*),
the playboy ward

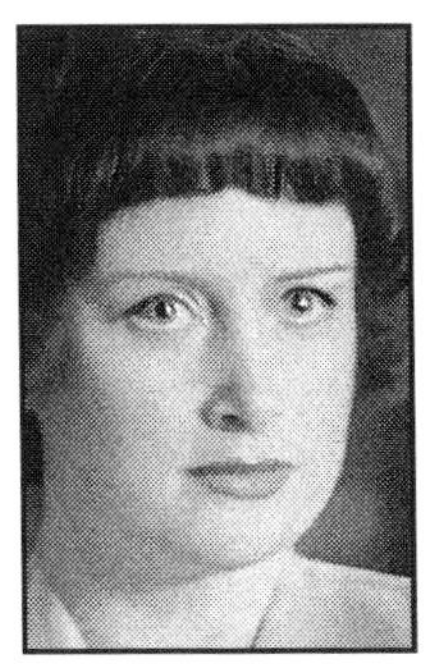

Emily Trefusis
(*Zoe Telford*),
the fickle fiancé

Charles Burnaby
(*James Murray*),
the devious reporter

Violet Willett
(*Carey Mulligan*),
the daddy's girl

— since he's Timothy Dalton — when he's not emoting in front of us, he's the topic of conversation by the other characters.

Which I can understand. It's Timothy Dalton, and my goodness does he look yummy. Some men age very well and he belongs to that lucky cohort. He's also got to be expensive so the producers made sure to get their money's worth. Pity they didn't spend some of their money on a better script or more film stock.

But he didn't age *that* well. I had a hard time believing that virginal, lovely, dewy, eighteen-year-old Violet Willets (Carey Mulligan) fell madly in love with a man old enough to be her grandfather. I know why *he* did, and it's not just because Violet resembles the woman he callously abandoned twenty-five years prior in Egypt. Violet is delicious, naïve, and believes every word he says and what man doesn't want that? As for Violet, she didn't come across as a gold-digger, which is the usual reason sweet 18-year-olds marry men old enough to be their grandfather. Or maybe she was one and the tacked-on ending where Violet runs off to Argentina with Emily Trefusis proves it.

Violet certainly wasn't broken up about her husband being murdered on their wedding night. If anything, she seemed relieved. She got it all. The Trevelyan name, the inheritance, two tickets to Buenos Aires, and she didn't have to sacrifice her sweet toothsome body to some old man, even if he was Timothy Dalton.

The Egyptian subplot was of major importance yet it didn't make any sense. There was the paranormal aspect too, with a ghostly maiden showing up in Captain Trevelyan's visions. Was there a curse on the gold scorpion? Was he going crazy? We're never told. The ghost follows a different movie's script when it appears and vanishes.

This script also doesn't tell us how an Egyptian servant can show up in isolated Sittaford in 1949 and get hired on, no questions asked. I understand that the servant problem was bad enough that the upper crust didn't ask as many questions as they could. But here? Really?

We know Captain Trevelyan did potentially bad things in Egypt. Yet he wasn't suspicious when this mysterious Egyptian showed up at his door? He'd been having weird dreams about his past. He's got a burgeoning political career which means close scrutiny of his private life. He's supposed to be a smart man.

Add in the even more incoherent subplot about the escaped prisoner from Dartmoor prison. None of that made sense; not the purchase of the inn a year prior to the events of the story, not the backstory of how the star-crossed lovers met, not how the prisoner escaped from Dartmoor prison and found his way across the moors to be reunited with his paramour and cousin and their eventual escape to freedom.

There's also the American war profiteer who helped Captain Trevelyan make a fortune manufacturing substandard munitions that killed more American sailors than the enemy. The American war profiteer's personal aide-de-camp and quack doctor made even less sense. Why did the war profiteer need him around, other than as a dogsbody? There was mumbled dialog that sounded like they were both in the mafia, but it was unclear.

We also meet the incompetent government clerk who's looking into Captain Trevelyan's background to ensure nothing questionable is revealed to the press, thus discrediting the party. He's not doing a very good job if Captain Trevelyan was a known associate of American war profiteers and he doesn't know.

Then there's Charles Burnaby. In the novel, he's boy-reporter Charles Enderby. The name change was the first step in his complete reworking of motives and backstory. Yet we get no foreshadowing of his dramatic personal life or of his connections to the Trevelyan family.

We get almost nothing of James Pearson's connection to Captain Trevelyan either. We get even less of a reason for Emily Trefusis to be engaged to James Pearson, boy alcoholic, other than that old standby: He'll inherit big when Captain Trevelyan dies. Maybe that's why Emily runs off to Argentina with Violet. She gets the money and the girl and doesn't have to marry the boy alcoholic.

I could rant on, but you get the picture: This movie was a mess, barely suitable for Timothy Dalton fans. ITV could have saved the cost of his salary and paid for a better script. Or, they could have capitalized on Timothy Dalton and added another twenty minutes of movie, explaining all the subplots and how they connected.

General Information

Based on: *The Sittaford Mystery*
(U.S. title: *The Murder at Hazelmoor*; novel, 1931)
Run time: 1 hr., 40 min. **Subtitles:** No

Writer: Stephen Churchett
Director: Paul Unwin

Cast

Geraldine McEwan as Miss Marple

Timothy Dalton as Clive Trevelyan
Mel Smith as John Enderby
Jeffery Kissoon as Ahmed Ghali
Laurence Fox as James Pearson
Zoe Telford as Emily Trefusis
James Murray as Charles Burnaby
Rita Tushingham as Miss Elizabeth Percehouse
Michael Brandon as Martin Zimmerman
Paul Kaye as Dr. Ambrose Burt
Patricia Hodge as Mrs. Evadne Willett
Carey Mulligan as Violet Willett
Matthew Kelly as Donald Garfield
James Wilby as Stanley Kirkwood
Robert Hardy as Winston Churchill

Film Locations

The Flower Pot Pub, Henley-on-Thames, Oxfordshire (pub exterior)
Dorney Court, Dorney, Buckinghamshire (Sittaford House interiors)

At Bertram's Hotel (2007)

Big rewrite adds Louis Armstrong, stolen art, a missing millionaire, and Nazis, and makes a hash of it

Fidelity to text

Mickey Gorman's murder and motive for his death remain. Otherwise, ch-ch-ch-changes galore. Characters vanish while new ones take their roles, motivations change, and the art theft subplot is replaced with fleeing Nazis.

Quality of movie

It looks great, but ITV skimped on rewrites. They had far too much script crammed into 93 minutes so portions of the film blurred into incomprehensibility.

At Bertram's Hotel was always a Miss Marple novel, so some genius at ITV decided that if one Miss Marple was good, then two must be better!

Thus, we get the added character of Jane Cooper, chambermaid, following in Miss Marple's wake and snooping in places where Miss Marple can't go.

In other words, Scrappy-Doo tags along after Scooby-Doo.

It makes sense in a hotel setting because while staff are ignored, they see everything. Jane Cooper spies on the guests, deduces, and reports her findings to Miss Marple. She also shows off her deducting chops to the nice police inspector, Larry Bird.

This leads to a truly idiotic scene at the finale demonstrating how little the screenwriter knew about the 1950s or the history of policing in England. As part of the happy ending, Inspector Bird tells Jane that the force is getting ready to open its doors to women officers.

Except the British police didn't wait until the 1950s. There were female prison matrons as early as 1883. By the turn of the century, socially prominent women had pointed out for years that women criminals needed women arresting them for propriety's sake. And so, in 1915, Edith Smith became Britain's first female constable. More women police officers followed. Moving up the hierarchy was glacial and the women were kept separate, but English policewomen existed decades before Inspector Bird told Jane about the possibility.

Then, to compound this historical inaccuracy, Jane joyously tells Miss Marple that she and Inspector Bird were going to live together without benefit of marriage! In the early 1950s?

Well, no. They would not have done this. Inspector Bird, who comes across as a sharp cookie, would not willingly jeopardize his career. Not if he wanted one, and not if she wanted to join the force either. Living in sin was not acceptable for police officers. They were supposed to be moral exemplars for the community. He and Jane would date and marry in the socially and culturally approved fashion of the times. The wedding might be sudden if she became pregnant, but they wouldn't move in together without being married.

The Nazi subplot replaces the novel's gang of super-

Mickey Gorman (*Vincent Regan*), the old flame

Bess Sedgwick (*Polly Walker*), the longtime daredevil

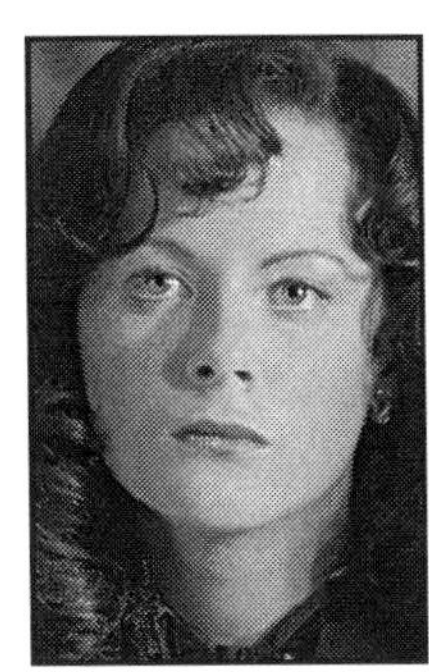

Elvira Blake (*Emily Beecham*), the madcap heiress

Ladislaus Malinowski (*Ed Stoppard*), the mysterious racer

Brigit Milford (*Mary Nighy*), the damaged friend

Mutti (*Danny Webb*), the fad hatter

thieves operating out of Bertram's Hotel and using doppelgangers of famous people to defray suspicion. The time period is correct for Nazis fleeing Europe for South America, so okay.

Apart from that, the plot has more holes than Swiss cheese. First, Jane, girl detective, is aware of the weirdness of guests hiding in suite 123 for weeks on end, checking in and out in the dead of night. Yet despite the torrent of news, books, and movies raving about escaping Nazis, she doesn't question it. Miss Marple would have noticed but lets give Jane the benefit of the doubt. She doesn't know that she can be more than a mere chambermaid, not yet.

Then there's the Blake family. This gets convoluted so bear with me.

Bess Sedgwick, adventuress, was married to Lord Blake. She dumped him and their daughter, Elvira, years before. She fought in the French Resistance. I think she's hunting Nazis but the dialog was so unclear, I can't be sure. But Bess Sedgwick, adventuress, should recognize when something's out of kilter. She's stayed at Bertram's Hotel before. Yet she remains oblivious.

Her former husband is Lord Blake, millionaire and owner of Blake Airlines. He's been missing for seven years and has been declared legally dead. Bess and Elvira are at Bertram's for the reading of the will. Ready? The mystery hotel guests are referred to as Blake guests, brought in from Europe on Blake Airlines! Yet Bess Sedgwick — adventuress, French Resistance fighter, and regular guest of the hotel — doesn't make the connection.

These mystery guests arrive at Bertram's Hotel via Blake Airlines and pay their tab with stolen art. No one notices large wooden crates coming into and out of the hotel either. Even a small painting, if it's valuable, isn't going to be moved across continents wrapped in a sheet. It travels cushioned inside a custom-built wooden crate with plenty of protective padding. No one notices. No one notices the rotating art on the walls either as paintings arrive, are sold, and get replaced.

We are told that Lord Blake disappeared at sea in a plane crash. Maybe he's enjoying his ill-gotten gains in Argentina but that loose end is left a-dangling for someone writing Miss Marple fanfiction.

I could not wrap my head around this subplot. We've got Herr Mutti, elderly Jewish victim of the Nazis, and Ladislaus Malinowski, much younger concentration camp survivor and racecar driver — and sometime lover of Bess Sedgwick; it was unclear — working with Bess to capture escaped Nazis, yet the Blake connection entirely passes them by. Why did the scriptwriter use the same name for the fleeing Nazi guests and Elvira Blake's dad if there's no connection? This is a basic writing rule: Don't use confusing or similar names if characters or events aren't connected.

Elvira Blake gets radically rewritten, over and above her blonde hair dyed brunette. She's sort of carrying on with Ladislaus, but not really. Her real interest is dear, dear friend, Brigit Milford, whom she feels deeply, deeply guilty over. Elvira's desire to swim in polluted water exposed Brigit to polio, crippling her right hand. Then, after practically shoving Brigit into the dirty Italian river, our Elvira refuses to follow her in. She's guilty and she knows it, which is supposed to explain her motivations.

None of this explains Brigit's motivations. She's a gold-digger, a very smart girl with a long-range and far-fetched revenge plan, or a total doormat. Pick the option you like.

I got the distinct impression our Elvira takes after both her parents: mum who does whatever she wants and damn the consequences and dad who provides sanctuary for fleeing war criminals in exchange for stolen fine art.

Throw in blackmailing chambermaids (not our Jane), matching hats, lying solicitors, Lady Selena Hazy's own troubles, and twin safecrackers and you've got a script that needs more than 93 minutes.

Oh, and did I mention Louis Armstrong showing up with his band to play jazz for the guests? He brings along jazz singer, Amelia Walker (very good by the way). Ms. Walker has her own troubles. Bess Sedgwick stole her husband and then Ms. Walker buys fine art stolen by the Nazis.

This is a jam-packed movie. It's much faster paced than the Joan Hickson version but it doesn't make as much sense. If you must watch, enjoy the sets, the jazz band, and the clothes. Don't watch if you skip reading *At Bertram's Hotel* but still plan to discuss the novel at a dinner party. You'll be socially embarrassed.

General Information

Based on: *At Bertram's Hotel* (novel, 1965)
Run time: 1 hr., 24 min. **Subtitles:** No

Writer: Tom MacRae **Director:** Dan Zeff

Cast

Geraldine McEwan as Miss Marple
Martine McCutcheon as Jane Cooper
Stephen Mangan as Inspector Larry Bird

Mark Heap as Mr. Humfries
Vincent Regan as Mickey Gorman
Hannah Spearritt as Tilly Rice
Francesca Annis as Lady Selina Hazy
Charles Kay as Canon Pennyfather
Ed Stoppard as Ladislaus Malinowski
Polly Walker as Bess Sedgwick
Emily Beecham as Elvira Blake
Mary Nighy as Brigit Milford
Nicholas Burns as Jack Britten/Joel Britten
Danny Webb as Mutti
Mica Paris as Amelia Walker

Film Locations

Polesden Lacey, Dorking, Surrey (hotel interiors)
Oriental Club, Stratford Place (hotel exteriors)
Osterley Park palm court, Isleworth (dénouement)
Claremont Fan Court School, Surrey (rooftop chase)

Ordeal by Innocence (2007)

Highlighting Gwenda's story adds another layer of tragedy for a family doomed to be destroyed by the truth

Fidelity to text

In addition to adding Miss Marple, changes were made to the murder victims, characters were added and dropped, and the house relocated to an island in a lake. Despite all that, this adaptation was faithful to the spirit of the novel.

Quality of movie

There were a few unclear patches, due mostly to mumbling. Otherwise, what a great film. We were riveted. The changes enhanced the story and elevated it to Shakespearean tragedy.

Ordeal By Innocence could have been ruined by adding Miss Marple (see my review of *The Secret of Chimneys*). Here, it was enhanced because we got the tragic story of Gwenda Vaughn, devoted secretary to Leo Argyle.

In the novel, Gwenda had little backstory. Here, she was an orphan whom Miss Marple trained up as a housemaid. Miss Marple encouraged her to strive for something more out of life, to learn, to grow, to reach her full potential. Thus, Gwenda Vaughn, orphan from the working class, becomes a private secretary to a man of letters.

Two years after the murder of the man's wife, Gwenda, who has been quietly in love with her boss all along, is on the verge of marrying him. She's alone in the world so her sole wedding invitation goes to Miss Marple, the only family she has. It was the happiest moment of her life; the eve of her wedding to a man she loved and becoming part of the Argyle family, like she had always longed to do and Miss Marple was there to share in her joy.

That very night, tragedy arrives in the form of Arthur Calgary, scientist. He tells them that Jacko Argyle didn't murder his mother, for which he was executed. His alibi that he was riding in a stranger's car was true all along. That means, if you've read the novel, someone else in the family bashed Rachel in the head.

She had it coming, by the way. Several flashbacks proved she was a vicious, controlling harridan. One of the daughters even admits to Miss Marple they were all better off with Rachel dead and the disreputable Jacko hanged by the Crown.

The family that Gwenda thought loved and accepted her instantly condemns her, starting with her not-so-devoted-after-all fiancé, Leo Argyle. She must have murdered Rachel because she wanted to marry her boss and needed to remove her rival and anyway, she's not one of us. Notice Leo's name? There was nothing manly or virtuous about Leo's behavior, despite his insistence on the importance of character. He tosses Gwenda to the wolves without a flicker of hesitation on the day before their wedding! He's a louse, not a lion.

Gwenda Vaughn (*Juliet Stevenson*), the poor nobody

Leo Argyle (*Denis Lawson*), the feckless stepfather

Rachel Argyle (*Jane Seymour*), the wicked stepmother

Kirsten Lindstrom (*Alison Steadman*), the loyal housekeeper

Micky Argyle (*Bryan Dick*), the resentful child

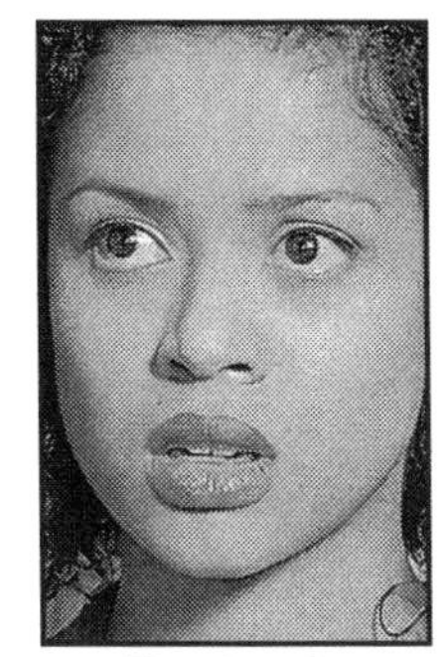

Tina Argyle (*Gugu Mbatha-Raw*), the independent child

Poor Gwenda. The Argyles turn on her, every last one of them, despite claiming previously that they welcomed her into their family. We see her trying on her wedding veil and staring at herself in the mirror, knowing everything she'd hoped for had turned to ashes in her mouth.

The family continues to tear itself apart, trying to work out which of them did it. Yet, everyone agrees, the most likely person remains Jacko. The Crown hung him (an improvement over the novel where he died in prison of pneumonia) and he went to his grave without fingering anyone else. He even told his twin brother, Bobby, that he was doing what was right for perhaps the first time in his life.

Bobby was an added character and a good one. He's bent like Jacko but in a different way. Even if Arthur Calgary never showed up on the Argyle's doorstep, his actions would have torn the family to shreds when revealed.

Philip and Mary Argyle Durant changed too. In the novel, he's the investigator, not Gwenda. Like Gwenda, he's an outsider who married in. Here, Philip and Mary have an unhappy marriage because he's a philandering dog, even indulging in an affair with his wife's younger sister. But it worked better to have Gwenda doing the investigation rather than Philip; it helped highlight how dysfunctional this supposed happy family truly was.

One piece of weirdness for me was discovering Richard Armitage, the actor playing Philip, was also Thorin Smokenshield from *The Hobbit* films. Yep, that's Thorin but without the impressive weapons, even more impressive musculature, and thickets of hair. I did not recognize him at all. But he was beautifully cast.

In fact, all the actors felt correctly cast, not something I can normally say. They looked like real people you could meet in the real world as opposed to Hollywood glamour. Every one of them lit up when they were onscreen, even in minor parts like the car salesman's wife who told Arthur Calgary how much of a lying cad Jacko was and how, even after everything that happened, she'd still give the charming Jacko anything he wanted.

Another thing ITV did right with this adaptation was focusing tightly on what was, at heart, a closed circle murder. Changing the location of the house was another touch of genius. Sunny Point (terrific name because life inside that house was anything but) is now on an island and everyone has to row across the lake in the family's collection of row boats. The isolation is intense. You can see why, despite knowing Rachel kept wads of cash on hand, a burglar was never really suspected of her murder.

We're told everyone — including in the community at large — knows about the money but to get to it, you've got to row across a lake in the dark. Most burglars won't work that hard and the police know it. So does the family, meaning they know it's one of them. One of them bashed Rachel's head in with a blunt instrument; furiously, angrily, to the point of smearing her brains across the desk. That's a lot of anger. Burglars tend to be professionals. A burglar would wait in the shrubbery until Rachel left the office and then they'd rob the place in peace and quiet.

No, this was an inside job and everyone knew it.

The ending worked too. Miss Marple was emotionally involved in Gwenda's fate, and it drives her to discover the murderer. She takes full advantage of gossipy staff (Kirsten the housekeeper), distraught family members desperate to unburden themselves, and Arthur Calgary, who's struggling with his own guilt. He thought he was the hero, riding to the rescue of an innocent man, and discovered he was wrong, wrong, wrong.

Miss Marple unraveled the clues provided by personality, character, and circumstances. And when she leaves Sunny Point, the family is left to face what they did to themselves and to Gwenda. Leo, in particular, can't avoid facing his weak character and utter spinelessness. He'll never be able to look at himself in the mirror again. *Ordeal by Innocence* is a tragedy that will take a few more generations to fade.

General Information

Based on: *Ordeal by Innocence* (novel, 1958)
Run time: 1 hr., 33 min. **Subtitles:** No

Writer: Stewart Harcourt
Director: Moira Armstrong

Cast

Geraldine McEwan as Miss Marple
Julian Rhind-Tutt as Dr. Arthur Calgary
Reece Shearsmith as Inspector Huish

Juliet Stevenson as Gwenda Vaughn
Denis Lawson as Leo Argyle
Jane Seymour as Rachel Argyle
Alison Steadman as Kirsten Lindstrom
Richard Armitage as Philip Durrant
Lisa Stansfield as Mary Argyle Durrant
Stephanie Leonidas as Hester Argyle
Tom Riley as Bobby Argyle
Gugu Mbatha-Raw as Tina Argyle
Bryan Dick as Micky Argyle
Burn Gorman as Jacko Argyle
Andrea Lowe as Maureen Clegg
Camille Coduri as Mrs. Lindsay
Michael Feast as John Croker
James Hurran as Cyril Price
Pippa Haywood as Mrs. Price
Greg Bennett as Police Constable
Leighton Haberfield as Prison Warden
Carl Isherwood as Scientist
Steve Munroe as Desk Sergeant

Film Location

Nether Winchendon House, Nether Winchendon, Buckinghamshire

Towards Zero (2007)

Miss Marple is added to the cast to investigate an abused ex-wife being gaslit into a fatal confession

Fidelity to text

Yet another non-Miss Marple property that ITV reconfigured to suit their needs. Inspector Battle is replaced and Angus MacWhirter vanished; their roles were given to Miss Marple. Otherwise, it's surprisingly close, right down to dialog lifted from the novel.

Quality of movie

Far better than the atrocious hack-job that was *Zero Hour* (F-2019). ITV did Agatha proud with this adaptation. Miss Marple fit into *Towards Zero* surprisingly well.

ITV always delivers on the eye-candy and *Towards Zero* is no exception. The action takes place at a stately mansion overlooking a cove on the Devon coast. This area has been called the English Riviera based on its warm weather (thanks to the Gulf Stream), scenic beauty, and stunning ocean views. It's gorgeous. The location was properly chosen because the cove looks to be swimmable, a key plot point. I could conceive of the murderer swimming across this cove at night whereas there are other English coves where that would be impossible. Too wide, too rough, too cold so the swimmer dies of hypothermia, too full of sharks and jellyfish so he either gets eaten or stung to death. This cove is sheltered enough that not only is it lined with resort hotels, but the ferry is both small and open at all hours.

Tourists (or locals) wouldn't ride that little boat across rough, choppy waters in the North Sea. Too dangerous. Here? It's perfect.

So is the house, Gull Point. Besides getting to ogle the lavish, luxurious house, we even get to see — another key plot point — how it's wired for servants' bells. We see the wires connecting Lady Tressilian's bedroom to her maid's room. If Lady Tressilian were to ring in the middle of the night, Barrett could respond promptly since the bell would jangle right over her head, waking her up. I always wondered how that worked. I knew servant bells rang below stairs, when everyone was up and about, but not in the servants' attic bedrooms. No wonder girls chose factory work over going into service.

Since both Inspector Battle and Angus MacWhirter were done away with, Miss Marple gets many of their lines and observations. Where she doesn't, Inspector Mallard, a new character, does. He's the local inspector for Lady Tressilian's district and eventually becomes Miss Marple's able support, after initially resisting the intrusions of a nosy busybody.

Removing and reworking a major character is a risky move that could cause the plot to fall apart. In the novel, Angus MacWhirter plays a crucial role. He rescues Audrey from suicide. Here, we see her ex-husband, Neville Strange, pulling her back from the

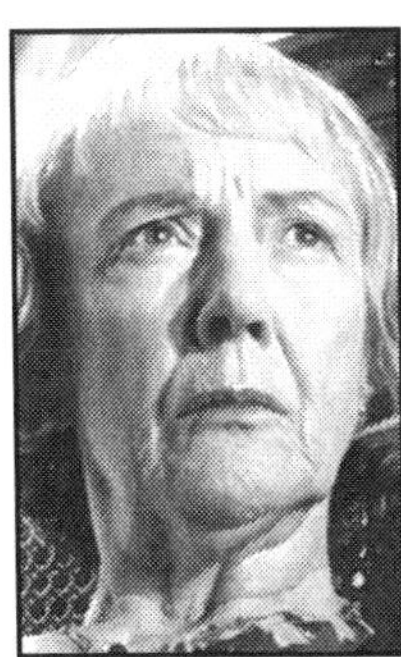

Camilla Tressilian
(*Eileen Atkins*),
the grand dame

Mary Aldin
(*Julie Graham*),
the spinster cousin

Nevile Strange
(*Greg Wise*),
the brave sportsman

Kay Strange
(*Zoë Tapper*),
the trophy wife

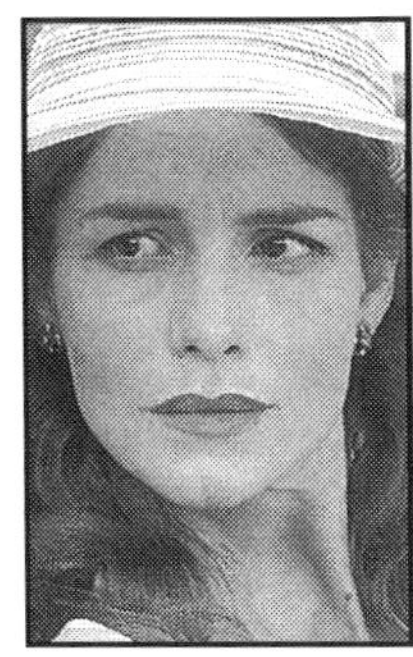

Audrey Strange
(*Saffron Burrows*),
the former wife

Thomas Royde
(*Julian Sands*),
the would-be beau

cliff and professing his undying love. It was a creepy scene, no question. It would have been better if the script sent Thomas Royde rushing out to save her. After all, he ends up marrying Audrey, not Neville. It would also have made the ending plausible, because I could not see why Audrey chose Thomas for her happy ending other than because the script made her do it.

Angus MacWhirter's other major role was to figure out how the crime was committed. He lies to Inspector Battle about what he saw, albeit with the same explanation Miss Marple gives. Deductions are all very well, but the police must have facts to work with. Angus consistently demonstrates to Audrey what a competent, caring man is like and so at the end of the novel, you can understand why she runs off to Chile with him. She doesn't run off to Malaya with Thomas Royde, who's a cipher.

In the novel, Inspector Battle recognizes Audrey as an abused, gaslit woman who doesn't actually confess to the crime but she doesn't proclaim her innocence either. It's a relief to her when she is arrested. It ends the overwhelming pressure she's under and wherever she'll end up, it won't be with her psycho ex-husband. Inspector Battle's got a valid reason to believe her, since his own daughter was trapped in a similar situation. Inspector Mallard does not.

This was my major complaint about the movie. We don't see Miss Marple talking to servants or Thomas Royde, Lady Tressilian, or Mary Aldin about the relationship between Audrey and Neville the way Inspector Battle and Angus MacWhirter do in the novel. Instead, she leaps across the cove to make her deductions and pulls part of the solution out of her knitting bag. A few more minutes of film devoted to Miss Marple gossiping with the cook would have more than repaid losing a few minutes of Devon's coastal scenery. We don't even get a village parallel explaining why she recognized what Audrey was enduring!

I also wanted a resolution of why no one noticed that Neville Strange was wearing a soaking wet suit. In the novel, this is finessed with raincoats. We don't get that here (despite the pouring rain), leading one to wonder why no one said anything. This is England! It rains so much every infant is assigned an umbrella, raincoat, and galoshes at birth. Yet no one notices when Neville shows up at the hotel to play billiards soaking wet and reeking of dead fish. Ted Latimer should have and if he was too drunk to notice, the script should have said so.

Then there's the dénouement, where Miss Marple sketches Audrey with Thomas Royde. Really? He's a poor substitute for his brother, Adrian, with whom Audrey was going to run away with, abandoning her husband to a life of sin. Thomas Royde has all the personality of a pine cupboard. It's possible there's treasure within, but it's more likely that the cupboard is bare of life and humor.

But these are quibbles. Overall, everything worked. The confrontation scene at the end, where Inspector Mallard and Miss Marple force a confession was masterful. It was funny too, watching Miss Marple accidentally on purpose shove Ted Latimer overboard. We get to watch the murderer break down when his scheme is revealed and that works too.

There are so many good moments.

I really enjoyed watching Kay Strange (wife #2) squabble with Audrey Strange (wife #1). This was played up considerably more than in the novel where everyone was boringly civilized. Lady Tressilian gets several scenes dissecting that scarlet-toed, husband-stealing hussy but even here, we get more complexity. Lady Tressilian also tells Neville that he married Kay and he's got to stick with her. He made his bed and he's got to lie in it. Kay was hot, hot, hot; a redhead in a red dress she spilled out of. You can see why poor Ted Latimer carries a torch for her.

This adaptation of *Towards Zero* is well worth watching, even with the rewrites. It works. It would have been better if they'd kept Angus MacWhirter, but considering ITV Production's track record of inserting Miss Marple where she never appeared, it's darn good.

General Information

Based on: *Towards Zero* (novel, 1944)
Run time: 1 hr., 25 min. **Subtitles:** No

Writer: Kevin Elyot
Directors: David Grindley & Nicolas Winding Refn

Cast

Geraldine McEwan as Miss Marple
Alan Davies as Superintendent Mallard
Ben Meyjes as Inspector Tipping
Thomas Arnold as Detective Sergeant Jones
Stewart Bewley as PC Williams

Eileen Atkins as Lady Camilla Tressilian
Julie Graham as Mary Aldin
Greg Wise as Nevile Strange
Zoë Tapper as Kay Strange
Saffron Burrows as Audrey Strange
Julian Sands as Thomas Royde
Tom Baker as Frederick Treves
Paul Nicholls as Ted Latimer
Amelda Brown as Barrett
Peter Symonds as Hurstall
Jo Woodcock as Alice
Eleanor Turner-Moss as Diana Brinton
Guy Williams as Dr. Lazenby
Wendy Nottingham as Mrs. Rogers
Mike Burnside as George
Greg Rusedski as Merrick

Film Locations

Salcombe, Devon (outdoor, beach scenes, tractor ferry)
Tides Reach Hotel, South Sands, Salcombe, Devon (Easterhead Bay Hotel)
Danes Berkhamsted, Hertford, Hertfordshire (Balmoral Court Hotel)

Nemesis (2009)

Despite some marvelous changes, Geraldine McEwan's swan song flounders in its chaotic third act

Fidelity to text

You'll be aghast at what ITV Productions did to the story. About all that remains is Verity, her tragic life, Jason Rafiel's enjoyment of manipulating people, and the coach tour of the great houses of England.

Quality of movie

Excellent and terrible in equal measures. Despite the screenwriter playing fast and loose, the movie worked up until the third act when it fell apart into an incoherent, illogical mess. The final scene was the rotten cherry atop the rancid sundae.

I liked the first two-thirds of this film. I really did. Introducing a '50s version of the *Mission: Impossible* opening was a nifty touch. The late Jason Rafiel, who befriended Miss Marple in *A Caribbean Mystery*, sends his last request to her via a gramophone record. If she cooperates, she'll win the £500 bequest. In the novel, the bequest is considerably larger but Jason Rafiel was considerably richer. Here, he was a "man of letters" and noted philanthropist. As a "man of letters," he must not be very rich or else he spent all his wealth arranging the tour.

The tour had a definite *And Then There Were None* vibe. In the novel, some members of the tour group were sent by Jason Rafiel, but not all. Here, every single person including the tour guide is in on the plot. As you would expect, the bodies start to pile up with the least guilty dying first while Miss Marple unravels the clues about the long-ago vanished Verity along with figuring out how everyone is related to everyone else.

We'll start with Michael Rafiel. He's still Jason Rafiel's son but with a different last name. He's also a Luftwaffe pilot, shot down over England after Dunkirk, which is how he meets Verity, then a novice nun. She nurses him back to health and naturally, they fall in love. The sisters of St. Elspeth, Clothilde in particular, are not happy about Verity running off to Ireland with an enemy combatant and tell her so. Verity disappears under mysterious circumstances and Michael gets picked up by the police and spends the rest of the war in a POW camp. He begs his father (a resident alien living in London) to find Verity. Dear old dad refuses and the estrangement begins.

Verity's caretaker Clothilde is still present in vastly different form. She's a nun at the St. Elspeth convent. We meet her and her mother superior, Sister Agnes. A generous, anonymous benefactor provides them with two tickets for the all-expense tour. Naturally, they put their religious duties in London on hold and race off to the worldly pleasures of visiting England's great houses.

No one else from the novel remains. Even the tour guide gets a character revamp. In addition, Raymond

Georgina Barrow (*Ruth Wilson*), the tour guide

Margaret Lumley (*Laura Michelle Kelly*), the passenger

Michael Faber (*Dan Stevens*), the Luftwaffe pilot

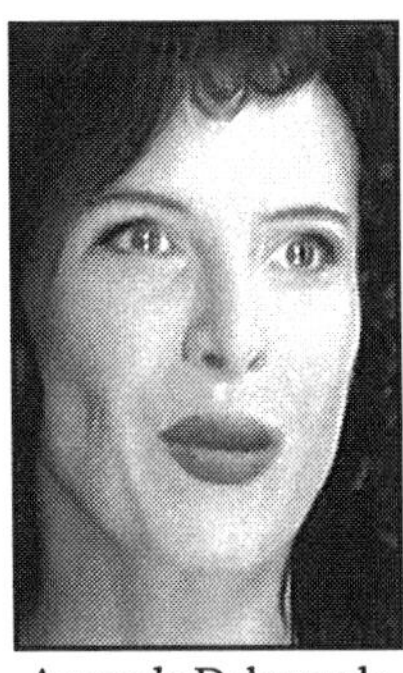
Amanda Dalrymple (*Ronni Ancona*), the heiress

Martin Waddy (*Will Mellor*), the wounded vet

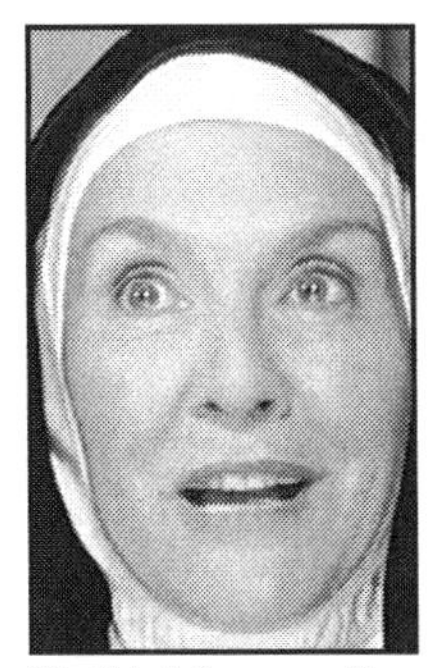
Clotilde Merryweather (*Amanda Burton*), the loving sister

West (Richard E. Grant) appears from out of thin air. He's Miss Marple's author nephew, so when Jason Rafiel tells Miss Marple she needs a companion, she chooses him. We get some great scenes with Grant chewing the scenery and chasing after everyone in a skirt. I don't remember that predilection from the novels but here we are.

But these changes worked, until they didn't. The tour group members were distinctive, interesting, and had logical if sometimes far-fetched ties to Verity.

Then we encounter the implausible. We discover multiple cases of mistaken identities, misidentified wounded soldiers with apparently blind wives, lying lawyers, and tour guides who were intelligence operatives during the war despite not looking nearly old enough.

That was something else I kept noticing. The ages of the actors were wrong. At twenty-two, you have a dewiness about you that isn't present when you're thirty-two. The action takes place both in 1940 and in 1951, yet none of the protagonists have aged a day. They looked either too young for their part or too old.

But back to the story. The tour bus gets sabotaged and the passengers are forced to spend the night in the abandoned St. Elspeth convent. An awful lot of furniture and religious statuary were left behind when the nuns moved. I had a hard time accepting that all those icons would be left to rot, or that the nuns would abandon hundreds of useful candles and lanterns, saving them money that could be spent on the poor. Stretching credulity further, there's a scene where, despite no one having been inside the convent in years, all those abandoned candles are strategically placed and lit, lighting the convent so our heroes can dash about in the semidarkness. Who did that? No explanation.

The climax arrives and it's one ridiculous scene after another. Verity reappears in her nun's habit. Where did those clothes come from? The stocks of poisoned cocoa are found when the convent kitchen has been left empty for years. Why does anyone cart poisons around with them? Yet apparently, one of the characters does just that. And how about impaling yourself on a spear? No one dies that quick. Poisoned cocoa would kill much faster. A spear, plunged through the abdomen, would take hours unless you hit a major artery and even then it takes minutes to bleed out. Since amateurs are not surgeons, the odds are much better that the victim will die of sepsis after hours to days of agony. That's certainly enough time to get the victim to a doctor.

And of course, our wounded soldier discovers his true identity, recovers some of his lost memory, and meets his grieving — for eleven years — widow. But we don't get any dialog! Nothing. Not a faint, not a scream, not even, "I never forgot you even when I thought I was someone else." The screen fades to black as though the scriptwriter had used up all his imagination in adding gramophones with the voice of Jason Rafiel directing the action from beyond the grave.

Worse, the realization dawns that Jason Rafiel was one manipulative jerk, pulling everyone's strings like a master puppeteer. He had zero empathy for anyone else — including his son — so it's not a surprise that he doesn't care what his little plot does to the unfortunate puppets. I suppose that's what comes of being a "man of letters." You stop thinking of people as people. They turn into characters that you manipulate to suit the needs of your plot. If they die, they die.

Then we come to the final scene. *Nemesis* was Geraldine McEwan's final turn as Miss Marple for ITV Productions. Future episodes would have Julia McKenzie in the role, so one would assume ITV wanted to give McEwan a proper sendoff.

Here's what we got: We see Miss Marple cutting a rose and pricking her finger and bleeding. She stares at her hand and then at the camera. Her expression suggests she's just realized what a terrible, awful mistake she made. Was she wrong about who murdered Verity and two other people? That she was wrong about who the true murderer was in all the other cases she solved? Or that she should have signed the contract for another season? We'll never know.

What I do know is if you like a coherent plot that's truer to the novel than this mess, watch Joan Hickson's version of *Nemesis* (1987) instead.

General Information

Based on: *Nemesis* (novel, 1971)
Run time: 1 hr., 23 min. **Subtitles:** No

Writer: Stephen Churchett
Director: Nicolas Winding Refn

Cast

Geraldine McEwan as Miss Marple
Richard E. Grant as Raymond West
Lee Ingleby as Det. Constable Colin Hards

Ruth Wilson as Georgina Barrow
Laura Michelle Kelly as Verity Hunt / Margaret Lumley
Johnny Briggs as Sydney Lumley
Dan Stevens as Michael Faber
George Cole as Laurence Raeburn
Ronni Ancona as Amanda Dalrymple
Adrian Rawlins as Derek Turnbull
Will Mellor as Martin Waddy
Emily Woof as Rowena Waddy
Anne Reid as Sister Agnes Carson
Amanda Burton as Sister Clotilde Merryweather
Herbert Lom as Jason Rafiel's voice
Graeme Garden as Matthew Broadribb

Film Locations

Kenilworth Court, London (West office)
Syon House, Brentford, Middlesex (Forrester Grange)
Norney Grange, Guildford, Surrey (Flying Horse Hotel)
Waverley Abbey, Farnham, Surrey (scarecrow, cemetery)
St. Mary Magdalene Church, Paddington, London (interior, St. Elspeth's Church)
Harpsden Court, Harpsden, Oxfordshire (distant view, St. Elspeth's)

A Pocket Full of Rye (2009)

Sex scenes and tone-deaf casting don't distract from this improved tale of a business, a mine, and poison

ITV Productions veer all over the map when it comes to adapting Agatha's novels. In this case, every minor deletion contributed to a better movie. It tightened the plot, keeping it focused on the Fortescue family and their circle. Unlike other ITV films, it didn't "improve" Agatha's text by making up complications out of whole cloth.

What works in a novel doesn't generate the drama that a film needs. In *A Pocket Full of Rye*, Miss Marple deduces the crime like a paleontologist working out the body and attributes of a dinosaur based on a few teeth and toe bones. The Joan Hickson version cheated on the ending to add drama and turned Lance Fortescue into an entirely different character. Here, despite the lack of drama (Miss Marple reads a letter) you get a subtle reward, true to the text.

The murderer will not just get arrested. He'll suffer mentally and emotionally until the moment the Crown hangs him, as he realizes that he's not nearly as clever as he thinks he is. No escape for him, courtesy of a convenient lorry driver.

I'm less sure about the need for the three gratuitous sex scenes. Agatha wrote very passionate novels but she kept the bedroom shenanigans offstage. She's an adult, she wrote for adults, and adults already know what goes on behind closed doors. We don't need instruction manuals. Perhaps because ITV didn't rev up the drama for the climax, we get not just a scene of adulterous action in a storage closet, but two more with Lance and Pat Fortescue.

I can grasp Adele's scene. It's easy shorthand to make sure the audience knows she's cheating on her much older husband and with whom. It's sordid, too. A closet? When he's working at a nice hotel? Tacky, tacky, tacky, but a manicurist from Brighton might not expect better. Adele holds the upper hand in the relationship but she's too dumb to realize it. She also isn't smart enough to demand better accommodations, or maybe she prefers being bent over a table.

But Lance and Pat? Was this to demonstrate they adore each other? To show that even though they have a luxurious bed handy, they use the back of the hallway door because they're free-spirited? I dunno.

Fidelity to text

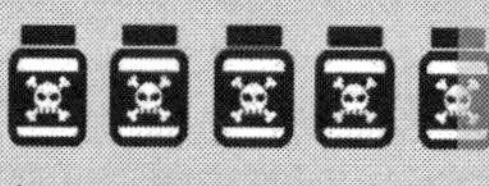

ITV Productions is unreliable in this area but here they were virtually letter-perfect. Miss Ramsbottom was cut, as were a few minor housemaids and secretaries. Miss Marple gets one of Inspector Neele's scenes.

Quality of movie

I enjoyed Julia McKenzie's first outing as Miss Marple. The ending was spot-on when the Joan Hickson version cheated on this point. But in Julia, I kept seeing Jessica Fletcher and not Miss Marple!

Adele Fortescue (*Anna Madeley*), the cheating wife

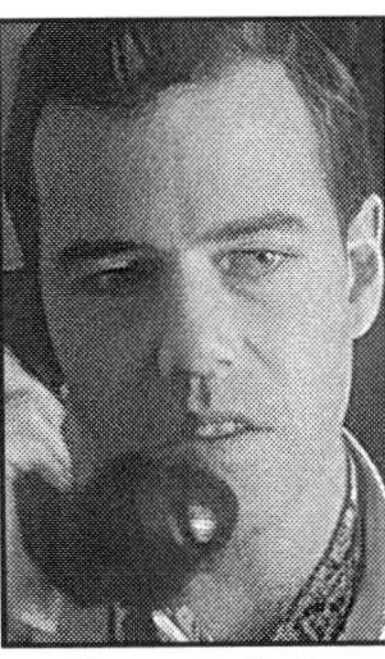
Vivian Dubois (*Joseph Beattie*), the professional lover

Percival Fortescue (*Ben Miles*), the good son

Jennifer Fortescue (*Liz White*), the lucky nurse/wife

Lance Fortescue (*Rupert Graves*), the bad son

Pat Fortescue (*Lucy Cohu*), the charming wife

My back hurt watching that scene, along with thinking the actors cheated because Pat's skirt was clearly in the way, as were Lance's pants. Miss Dove, the housekeeper, must have felt her ears burning as well as her opinion of Lance and Pat declining sharply.

I appreciated the scenes showing why Percival Fortescue was fighting with his father. They made it clear that dear old dad was losing his mind. The business was suffering, bankruptcy loomed, and Percival knew he'd have to pick up the pieces. Dad marrying a sexpot manicurist from Brighton was the least of his worries. Lance's untimely return and demands were a much bigger problem.

Overall, the casting was excellent other than Elaine Fortescue and worse, Gladys, the housemaid. The film industry does this all the time. They show us an actress whom all the characters claim is plain, even ugly, and we, the audience, ask "on what planet?" I suppose the Planet of the Beauty Queens.

Elaine is supposed to be plain enough that only her money will attract a boyfriend. In this case, it's Gerald Wright, school teacher and Communist. You know he's only marrying Elaine for her money but she seems happy enough. But Elaine Fortescue is not plain. She can do far better than Gerald Wright, C0mmunist, and no amount of Hollywood foolishness will make me say otherwise. Miss Marple would agree.

Gladys was much worse cast and, in this case, the Joan Hickson version did better. This actress was not plain. She wasn't a raving beauty queen, but most of us aren't. She was pretty in a normal way. Joan Hickson's Gladys Martin, by comparison, was dumpy, lumpy, frumpy, and the sort of girl who's so desperate to be noticed by a boy that she'll do or say anything he wants to keep him happy and around. ITV Productions did a better job of showing us the relationship between Miss Marple and Gladys and was far better at demonstrating how credulous and gullible Gladys was.

Poor Gladys Martin. Destined to be used by the people around her because she's not smart enough to understand what's happening to her. Neither does she have Adele's beauty to cushion her life. As an orphan, she's got no family to protect her. Only Miss Marple.

Another character to watch is Jennifer Fortescue, whom Percival married after she nursed him through pneumonia. She's so ambivalent about him you wonder why she married him. Her nefarious purpose is revealed, but what happens next? The huge secret she's hiding has come between them since the day they met. Will they remain married? Get divorced? Jennifer is unhappy, lonely, and bored. She won't be in the future; her destiny is left ambiguous as is Percival's. I spent some time speculating what they would do, because it's clear that he still cares about her, even if he's clumsy in how he expresses himself.

I would have liked to see more of golf and tennis pro Vivian Dubois. We never find out what happens to him — not even a paragraph — in the novel. Similarly, he gets short shrift in both adaptations. Agatha sometimes gives us an ending for a minor character, such as Raymond Starr, the Majestic Hotel dancer in *The Body in the Library*. He loses his bid to escape the hospitality industry via an advantageous marriage but we're still given a snapshot of his future. With Vivian, we get nothing. ITV could also have changed his name and I wouldn't carp. Vivian is no longer a man's name anywhere in the world.

This film worked so much better than the 1985 BBC production with Joan Hickson. It was true to the text while still being well-paced, well-acted, and fun to watch. Great English country house porn, too. Wow. What a house. It needed a lot more maids than Gladys to keep it spic and span.

Stick with this version. You won't be disappointed.

General Information

Based on: *A Pocket Full of Rye* (novel, 1953)
Run time: 1 hr., 33 min. **Subtitles:** Yes

Writer: Kevin Elyot
Director: Charlie Palmer

Cast

Julia McKenzie as Miss Marple
Matthew Macfadyen as Inspector Neele
Ralf Little as Sergeant Pickford
Greg Bennett as Police Constable

Kenneth Cranham as Rex Fortescue
Anna Madeley as Adele Fortescue
Ben Miles as Percival Fortescue
Liz White as Jennifer Fortescue
Hattie Morahan as Elaine Fortescue
Chris Larkin as Gerald Wright
Rupert Graves as Lance Fortescue
Lucy Cohu as Pat Fortescue
Joseph Beattie as Vivian Dubois
Rose Heiney as Gladys
Helen Baxendale as Mary Dove
Wendy Richard as Mrs. Crump
Ken Campbell as Crump
Laura Haddock as Miss Grosvenor
Paul Brooke as Billingsley
Prunella Scales as Mrs. Mackenzie
Rachel Atkins as Sanatorium Sister
Andrew Care as Doctor
Edward Tudor-Pole as Professor Bernsdorff
Thea Collings as Tilly

Film Locations

Englefield House, Theale, Reading, Berkshire (Yew Tree Lodge)
Victoria House, Bloomsbury London
15 Pl. du Tertre, Montmartre, Paris (exterior Fortescue's lodgings)
West Wycombe Park, Buckinghamshire (Pinewood Sanatorium)

But you can see [in photo to Miss Marple], what a nice boy he is.

Gladys Martin in her last letter

Murder Is Easy (2009)

Watching pre-*Sherlock* Cumberbatch is the sole reason to watch this film that dispensed with most of the novel

Murder Is Easy is one of my favorite Christie novels. It has creepy villagers playing at witchcraft, press magnates who believe their own press, an expat from Malaya, a daring rescue where the damsel rescues herself, even a great murderer who justifies her many crimes. It was all done for love, you know; sour, curdled, unrequited, I'll-get-my–revenge-for-being-spurned obsessive love, but still love of a twisted sort.

All that's gone the way of all flesh, with only a few bones to litter the scene. The press magnate and the witchcraft wannabes gone. The murderer is still there, but they radically changed her motivation, along with some of her crimes. Benedict Cumberbatch shows up as Luke Fitzwilliam, late of the Malayan police force, and he doesn't even get to rescue the damsel. The damsel, Bridget Conway, underwent a body-and-soul makeover until she's unrecognizable to anyone who's read the novel.

Viewers will also experience a frisson watching Benedict Cumberbatch emote. This film was released in 2009, a year before he burst onto the world's stage with *Sherlock*. He was just another up and coming character actor then, not leading man material. His scenes were so truncated compared to his counterpart in the novel that he could have been dropped and his scenes handed over to Police Constable Reed, who is a more logical person to investigate suspicious doings with Miss Marple. They already had the seed of a character arc with PC Reed learning how to ask questions from the mistress of leading questions, and it would have been fun watching her train him up like one of her maids. The film also would have been a lot less confusing without Benedict co-sleuthing with Miss Marple. She worked hand-in-glove with PC Reed and didn't need help from some flatfoot from Malaya.

The other reason for removing Benedict was Bridget Conway's character. In the novel, they solve the murders and fall in love while doing so. In the film?

Fidelity to text

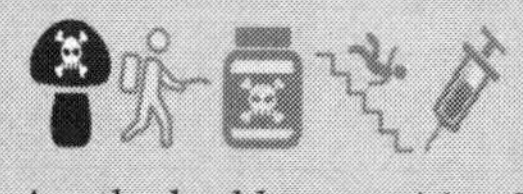

Where to start, where to start. There are so many choices. This novel (a personal favorite) never starred Miss Marple. Agatha had been writing Miss Marple novels and short stories for over a decade by the time she wrote *Murder Is Easy* (1939). If she'd wanted this to be a Miss Marple story, she'd have made it one. ITV's scriptwriter got out the knives and slashed away. About all that remains from the text after they ran it through a woodchipper are the names and some methods of death.

Quality of movie

An overcrowded mess rescued by good performances. Sometimes the movie took flight, such as watching PC Reed learning his trade. But there was too much going on in 93 minutes to keep track of who was who and why it mattered.

Luke Fitzwilliam
(*Benedict Cumberbatch*),
the bad ex-policeman

Bridget Conway
(*Margo Stilley*),
the mad Yank

Honoria Waynflete
(*Shirley Henderson*),
the caring spinster

Maj. Hugh Horton
(*David Haig*),
the guilty pol

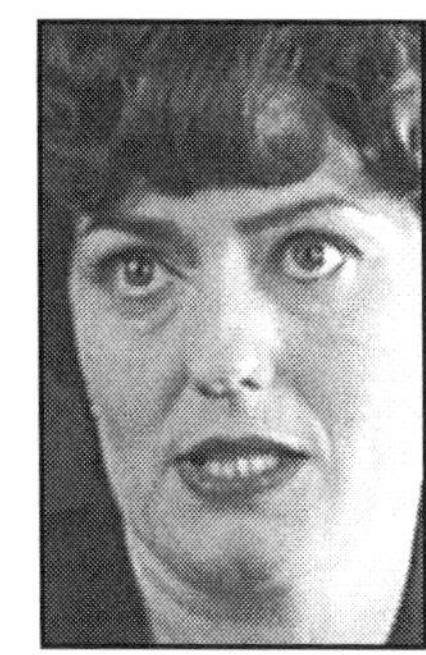

Lydia Horton
(*Anna Chancellor*),
the politician's wife

Jessie Humbleby
(*Jemma Redgrave*),
the cheerful widow

Bridget is not only an American snooping around alone; she displays the type of crazy that's best to back away from. This version of Bridget has zero need for a charming young man like Benedict Cumberbatch, so his other reason for appearing vanishes.

Even with the romance arc removed, there's so much extraneous plot larded into the story. Political campaigning? Check. Infighting and betrayal in said political campaign? Check. Crazy, grieving widow? Check. Potential affair between married politician and grieving widow? Check. Socialist doctor eyeing his elderly partner's daughter? Check. Vicar with beekeeping hobby? Check. Unpleasant, snobby spinster with simpleton brother? Check. Librarian with missing books? Check. Lingering gratuitous near-nudity? Check. Hedge-witch granny? Check. Herbal abortion potions being passed around like cups of tea? Check. Secret babies? Check. Studly gardener in a torrid affair? Check. Incest and rape? Check.

There's even a Persian cat who plays a critical role in the murder, but at least Mr. Wonky was in the novel. Besides, every TV mystery needs a cat.

There was just too much going on. ITV would have done better by sticking with the original text which had plenty of action. How could the scriptwriter add incest, affairs, and secret babies and omit the witchcraft rituals run by the local antiques dealer? That wasn't exciting enough? Perhaps they're saving it to add to a novel where no witchcraft appears.

Adding Miss Marple wasn't as terrible as it could have been (*cough* *The Secret of Chimneys*). She replaces Luke Fitzwilliam in the opening scene, meeting Lavinia Pinkerton on the train. This was plausible. Miss Marple, known busybody, would listen to another old lady's story of murder and not discount it. It was equally plausible that when Miss Marple read about Lavinia's sudden death (murder that doesn't look like murder) she would rush off to investigate. We all have to have a hobby, and seeing justice done is hers.

Weirdly, no one in Wychwood under Ash thinks it strange when the stranger at the funeral stays. And stays. And stays. Maybe it's the power of old ladies to become invisible. Maybe after multiple sudden deaths and far too many characters running around, everyone's too exhausted emotionally to comment. At least they have distinctive features so I could tell them apart. I just didn't get enough time with most of them to care.

Another problem is that too many subplots never got an ending. Why was Dr. Humbleby's wife so glad about his death? We're never given a reason. Why was the poisons book missing from the library for five years and not just the two weeks needed to look something up? Did Major Horton quit drinking after that dreadful drunken incident led directly to someone's death? It was implied but never stated. And, why oh why did Bridget Conway carry a postcard of the Empire State Building in her purse? She didn't know she was going to give it to Luke Fitzwilliam and reenact *An Affair to Remember* (1957). She didn't even set a date and time. "Soon" does provide one important clue which Luke will ignore because the script tells him to. It's screaming don't meet the crazy American. Remember, he's supposed to be a policeman. It's clear he's a bad one.

I suppose the reason for watching this film is to see Benedict Cumberbatch before he became Sherlock. Give this one a pass if you aren't a Cumberbitch. Otherwise, to figure out the convoluted subplots, you'll have to force yourself to watch it twice.

General Information

Based on: *Murder Is Easy* (novel, 1939)
Run time: 1 hr., 33 min. **Subtitles:** No

Writer: Stephen Churchett
Director: Hettie Macdonald

Cast

Julia McKenzie as Miss Marple
Benedict Cumberbatch as Luke Fitzwilliam
Russell Tovey as Police Constable Terence Reed

Margo Stilley as Bridget Conway
Steve Pemberton as Vicar Henry Wake
Shirley Henderson as Honoria Waynflete
Julian Lightwing as Leonard Waynflete
Lyndsey Marshal as Amy Gibbs
Tim Brooke-Taylor as Dr. Edward Humbleby
Jemma Redgrave as Jessie Humbleby
Camilla Arfwedson as Rose Humbleby
James Lance as Dr. Geoffrey Thomas
David Haig as Maj. Hugh Horton
Anna Chancellor as Lydia Horton
Hugo Speer as James Abbot
Sylvia Syms as Lavinia Pinkerton
Steven Hartley as George Rogers
Stephen Churchett as Coroner

Film locations

Southgate Underground Station, London (Lavinia Pinkerton's escalator fall)
Church of St. Michael, Blewbury, Oxfordshire (church)
William Malthus Charity School, Blewbury, Oxfordshire (Humbleby home and clinic)
Church Road, Blewbury, Oxfordshire (Miss Marple asks Luke about lunch with Bridget Conway)
Church End, Blewbury, Oxfordshire (Honoria Waynflete's house)

Florrie Gibson knew her onions as far as mushrooms were concerned. And the vicar would hardly forget to wear his mask with his Wellington boots. … Murder is easy, as long as nobody thinks it's murder.

LAVINIA PINKERTON

They Do It With Mirrors (2009)

Making Carrie drive the reforms weakens the couple's dynamics, but this still beats the Hickson version

Fidelity to text

Plenty of changes, the most egregious being rewriting Carrie Louise's personality and altruism and changing Lewis Serrocold's motives. Characters vanish, get combined, or are raised from the dead (Carrie Louise's husband #2).

Quality of movie

The murderer's motivation was unacceptable. Wally and Gina's reunion was poorly handled. At least there weren't five minutes of avant-garde modern dance with accompanying atonal music like the 1991 version.

Let's start with the actress you all want to read about. I loved Joan Collins as Ruth van Rydock, Carrie Louise's sister. She gets top billing although she doesn't have, sadly, much screen time. When she's on the screen, you can tell who the star is. You can also understand why, as Miss Marple says, Ruth and Carrie Louise have a great relationship as sisters as long as there's an ocean between them. Joan is perfect as the glamour queen whereas Penelope Wilton is equally perfect as her dowdy younger sister.

Carrie Louise is the focus of the movie, as she is in the novel. In the novel, she's more acted upon. Here, she's the one who wants to reform criminals and spends her wealth to do so. It's not husband #3, Lewis Serrocold. He morphs into the ever-supportive, adoring spouse who wants everything to be perfect for his beloved. And I do mean everything with a capital E. He's also jealous of husband #2 (Johnny Restarick) who shows up unannounced and expects to move in. There are some funny scenes between the two husbands.

Carrie Louise comes across as the kind of altruistic do-gooder that you want to avoid. She is so sure she's right that she doesn't care or even notice when her beliefs hurt the people around her or don't work period. In the case of the convicts she's reforming, well, some of them might benefit. At a minimum, they're getting a second chance out in the sunshine and fresh air. Stonygates is far more pleasant than Dartmoor prison although the food may not be.

Make sure you notice the reworking of Dante (1265-1321) over Stonygates' main entrance: *Recover Hope All Ye Who Enter Here*. It's a very nice rephrasing but the gate with its sign kept making me think of the sign at Auschwitz. You know: *Work Makes You Free*.

Where Carrie Louise's blindness really shows is in how she treats her daughters.

Adopted daughter Gina is lovely, vivacious, fun, and, based on the flashback, she's always been that way. Natural daughter Mildred, a few years younger than Gina, is seen in the same flashback as plain, shy, wearing glasses — dowdy alert! — and nowhere near as sparkling. What mother wouldn't be more invested in the livelier, more charming daughter?

Carrie Louise Serrocold (*Penelope Wilton*), the loaded reformist

Lewis Serrocold (*Brian Cox*), the altruistic spouse

Gina Hudd (*Emma Griffiths Malin*), the divided wife

Wally Hudd (*Elliot Cowan*), the unhappy husband

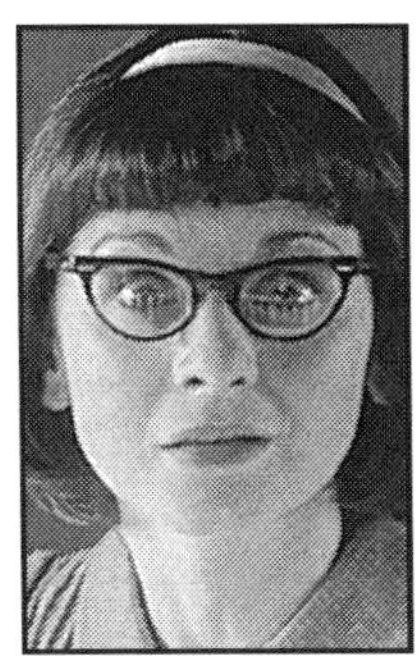

Mildred Strete (*Sarah Smart*), the resentful sister

Edgar Lawson (*Tom Payne*), the erratic inmate

Even better, Carrie Louise has the perfect reason to openly and obviously favor Gina. Since Gina's adopted, she needs more love and attention. Mildred, nerdy and dull, can be ignored. It's a very sharp observation of the flaws in Carrie Louise's worldview. She doesn't pay much attention to reality and the real needs of messy people unless it suits her. If it doesn't suit her, she'll find a reason to discount them.

You'll observe the same dynamic between Carrie Louise and Wally, Gina's husband. He doesn't fit in either, he's openly unhappy, but since he's not a project like one of her convicts, he doesn't matter.

Nor does Carrie Louise notice the weird and creepy byplay between Gina and Stephen Restarick. Stephen is Carrie Louise's stepson from husband #2. Since Gina's adopted and Stephen has a different mother and father, they're completely unrelated genetically. Nonetheless, the implication is that they've grown up together as brother and sister, even if only part-time. It's off-putting how they flirt and right in front of Gina's husband, Wally, too. Yet since Carrie Louise doesn't see anything wrong with this picture, neither does anyone else.

The novel handles Gina and Wally much better than either adaptation. I could not understand why Gina chose Wally when it's so obvious she's no longer attracted to him. And why should she be? He's sullen, sulky, ignores her, and doesn't punch out Stephen Restarick's lights for pawing at his wife.

Because Carrie Louise takes over the running of the reform school, all of Lewis Serrocold's motivations get twisted beyond recognition. It doesn't work nearly as well as in the novel. Altruistic reasons for what he did? Really? This would make things better for Carrie Louise and her convict rehabilitation project? For a supposedly intelligent man, he's stupid. Thirty seconds of thought would demonstrate the flaws in his plan.

It sounds like I didn't like the film, but I did. It was well-paced, well-acted, looked fabulous (that house!) and showed a very good understanding of the dynamics between sisters. Mildred is very jealous of Gina and it's understandable. She's spent her entire life in the shadow of her older, more glamorous sister. That's why Mildred makes sure Gina sees the old newspaper with the story of her birth mother's execution for arsenic poisoning. What I would have liked was an explanation for where Gina got the wig and dress. Did Mildred supply them?

There were so many great scenes, many of them quite funny. I was really enjoying the movie. Then the ending fell apart. Edgar Lawson's dramatic flight into the lake didn't make sense. We needed more screen time to explain why he thought that was a good idea. We needed more screen time to explain why Lewis Serrocold panicked and ran after Edgar. Remember, the convict rehabilitation scheme wasn't his idea. It was Carrie Louise's. His single goal in life was to support her in whatever she chose to do. Then he abandons her to the long arm of the law to chase after some psycho teenager who threatened him with a pistol?

It made even less sense when Gina decided to choose the man she married and then ignored over the stepbrother she'd been hanging off of (to his great enjoyment) throughout the entire movie. There was also a sort of reconciliation between Mildred and Carrie Louise but it was so truncated, it might as well have not been there. It should have been. Carrie Louise needed to have the scales fall from her eyes but it didn't quite happen. I didn't get the reconciliation I would have liked between Mildred and Gina either. It wasn't either girl's fault that mom played favorites.

A tighter ending would have made this a far better film. Even so, despite the changes the scriptwriter inflicted on the novel, it's pretty good. It's much better than the Joan Hickson version. I'm looking forward even more now to watching Helen Hayes' 1985 version *Murder With Mirrors*. The same novel, filmed three different ways. It will be fascinating to see what gets changed and whether or not the changes succeed.

General Information

Based on: *They Do It With Mirrors* (*Murder with Mirrors* in U.S.), 1952
Run time: 1 hr., 33 min. **Subtitles:** No

Writer: Paul Rutman **Director:** Andy Wilson

Cast

Julia McKenzie as Miss Marple
Alex Jennings as Inspector Curry
Sean Hughes as Sergeant Lake

Penelope Wilton as Carrie Louise Serrocold
Brian Cox as Lewis Serrocold
Joan Collins as Ruth Van Rydock
Maxine Peake as Juliet "Jolly" Bellever
Nigel Terry as Christian Gulbrandsen
Elliot Cowan as Wally Hudd
Emma Griffiths Malin as Gina Hudd
Sarah Smart as Mildred Strete
Liam Garrigan as Stephen Restarick
Ian Ogilvy as Johnny Restarick
Alexei Sayle as Dr. Maverick
Tom Payne as Edgar Lawson

Film Location

Fawley Court, Fawley, Buckinghamshire

"

[Carrie Louise] surpassed herself with her latest cause. Criminals. *She imagines she can* do *something with them. So there they all are, living it up in some so-called reform facility at the bottom of her garden.*

RUTH VAN RYDOCK

Why Didn't They Ask Evans? (2009)

Frankie and Bobby still investigate the mad Savages, but the subplot involving China will test your sanity

As with the novel, we open with our hero, Bobby, out on the picturesque cliffs overlooking the sea. But he's no longer golfing. To the amusement of local girls, he's goofing off.

If you think the opening was designed to demonstrate Bobby's fecklessness, you're right. By contrast, our heroine, Frankie, is so assertive she comes across as a pushy, don't-confuse-me-with-facts harridan in training. If they get together, as the movie implies in the badly underwritten conclusion, they'll both be miserable. Frankie will wipe her feet on Bobby, he'll let her, and she'll despise him for it.

Anyway, Bobby discovers the dying man whose last words are "Why didn't they ask Evans?" and we're off. Sort of. Bobby refuses the hero's call, despite the urgings from Frankie (young and pretty, so it's incomprehensible that he says no) and Miss Marple (sharp-tongued old lady, routinely ignored division). But his mini adventure in London helps him grow a spine.

Frankie, in the meantime, joyfully accepted the hero's call. She learns the dead man is somehow connected to the Savage family. Frankie infiltrates their castle by deliberately wrecking her car outside its gate. And it is a castle. All it needed was a moat to contain the people wandering about, including the family, hired pianists, loony friends, and the headshrinker next door operating his sanitarium full of crazy patients, including his wife.

Fidelity to text

Miss Marple's here as a friend of the family who pretends to be Frankie's governess. Names changed, characters deleted, combined or made up, backstories altered, motivations radically changed. Only the centerpiece murder remains the same.

Quality of movie

I'd have given it four but that ending was incomprehensible. Sylvia Savage's two children from marriage #1 were teleported in from China. Miss Marple pulled the solution from her knitting bag because she sure didn't find any clues.

What the castle is missing is servants. We see the butler, Wilson, and the lazy, newly hired gardeners who never say a word. Sylvia, matriarch of the family, bemoans the lack of servants. This is a clue, but a bad one, because it wasn't followed up on properly. Where's the cook who would reveal family secrets to Miss Marple? Where are the housemaids who know all the dirt? Or daily chars from the village who'd know the family history going back five generations? It is impossible for the cook to keep that pile clean when she's cooking from scratch for a minimum of eight people three times a day plus tea followed by the washing up. There must be servants other than Wilson, but he's the only one we see other than the two

Frankie Derwent (*Georgia Tennant*), the vivacious golfer

Bobby Attfield (*Sean Biggerstaff*), the daring sleuth

Alec Nicholson (*Rik Mayall*), the dedicated shrink

Moira Nicholson (*Natalie Dormer*), the insane wife

Claude Evans (*Mark Williams*), the orchid fancier

Sylvia Savage (*Samantha Bond*), the caring matriarch

gardeners lazing about.

Wilson does hint to Miss Marple about Sylvia's tragic history and the even more Shakespearean history of her two husbands, George (#1) and Jack (#2 and George's younger brother). But he doesn't hint enough to Miss Marple to make her solution plausible.

It's a pity too, because up until the ending, the movie zipped along. We even get deadly orchids to go with the venomous snakes. Check out Tom, Sylvia's younger son, dangling mice over the snake tanks. Snakes got to eat too and if they're encased in glass boxes, they can't go out and hunt on their own.

Sylvia Savage is the heart of the mystery. Once you've seen the ending, you understand how she brought her dreadful fate on herself. Marrying the older brother and then carrying on a torrid affair with the younger brother? Vulgar. Watching younger brother have older brother murdered in China? Vile. Marrying younger brother? Insane, even if it does get her out of prewar China and lets her remain in the castle. Not fighting husband #2 over abandoning husband #1's children? Unconscionable and a darned good reason for her guilt. Having children with husband #2 despite knowing what kind of man he is? Dreadful, especially when she deliberately neglects these kids because of her guilt over her first set of children.

She deserves to feel guilty! That woman brought misery upon herself because she refused to control her appetites. She wanted what she wanted, damn the consequences, and now she whines.

In case you're wondering why Jack Savage (hubby #2) had his brother George's (hubby #1) kids removed, it was to inherit the estates. George's son would be the next peer, not him. If the peer dies while his wife is pregnant with his son, the boy becomes a peer the moment he's born, with mom or an uncle acting in his name. Younger brothers don't inherit the estate unless older brother has zero male issue.

This raises the question of why didn't Jack have the kids murdered along with their father. They were all in China, with no oversight from the British government, snooping servants, or nosy villagers. If Jack could get his brother murdered (thereby also removing an obstacle to the Japanese invasion), slaughtering the kids should have been easy.

Let this be a reminder, folks. If you murder your older sibling to inherit, make sure you kill older sibling's kids too. They'll come back and haunt you if you don't.

There was so much to like about this movie. Watching mad women wander about the grounds in diaphanous white negligees is so Gothic and perfectly in keeping with the castle's appearance and the sanitarium next door. Listening to Claude Evans talk about poisonous orchids and then watching him have sex with his flowers. (He was hand-pollinating them. What, you think an orchid collector also raises the specialized insects needed to pollinate every variety of orchid he owns, including those from different continents? All flower breeders have sex with their flowers. They do it with paintbrushes and cotton swabs. Evans has more fun with his flowers than Frankie and Bobby ever will.)

Then there's the shrink, who's as loony as his patients, and the officious stuffed shirt, Commander Peters, who comes across as incompetent but probably isn't. We get the louche pianist who flatters Sylvia, ignores her daughter, Dottie, whom he's supposed to be teaching piano to, carries on with Moira, the shrink's loony wife, and then chases after Frankie, claiming none of the other ladies mean anything to him.

Well, they don't, or rather they matter very much, but not the way Frankie does. Luckily, she comes to her senses, which leads us to the underwritten and unsatisfying ending. Once again, Frankie is stranded by the side of the road (her wrecked car miraculously restored, including an immaculate paint job). She's got a flat tire. Bobby, driving the limo, stops to rescue her and discovers the spare is also flat. They stare at each other meaningfully. Neither one opens their fool mouth. Did Frankie slash her tires, hoping Bobby would stop? It's not stated, so the audience is left wondering.

Too much of this movie went unstated. Ninety-two minutes was not enough time. Another ten minutes would have filled in the missing bits of plot and this Miss Marple outing would be the movie it was valiantly struggling to become.

General Information

Based on: *Why Didn't They Ask Evans?* (novel, 1934)
Run time: 1 hr., 23 min. **Subtitles:** Yes

Writer: Patrick Barlow
Director: Nicholas Renton

Cast

Julia McKenzie as Miss Marple
Warren Clarke as Commander Peters

Georgia Tennant as Frankie Derwent
Sean Biggerstaff as Bobby Attfield
Helen Lederer as Marjorie Attfield
Samantha Bond as Sylvia Savage
Freddie Fox as Tom Savage
Hannah Murray as Dorothy Savage
Rik Mayall as Alec Nicholson
Natalie Dormer as Moira Nicholson
Rafe Spall as Roger Bassington
Mark Williams as Claude Evans
David Buchanan as John Carstairs
Siwan Morris as Florrie
Richard Briers as Wilson

Film Locations

Loseley Park, Guildford, Surrey (Castle Savage)
Shrubs Wood, Chalfont St. Giles, Buckinghamshire (Nicholson's clinic)

The Pale Horse (2010)

A cryptic list from a murdered minister leads Miss Marple to a village where devilish proceedings are going on

Fidelity to text

The original story is still here: murder for hire, misdirection, witches, and cleverly disguised thallium. Miss Marple replaces Ariadne Oliver and does most of the sleuthing.

Quality of movie

The ITV episodes are terribly inconsistent, but here everything worked. The pace was good, the Pale Horse was an English country inn on steroids, and the actors clearly had a good time.

Miss Marple is forced into action by that oldest of tropes: She receives a letter begging for help from a dear friend (Father Gorman) who is then fatally coshed in a mugging gone wrong. We at home know immediately it was murder because no one gets coincidentally mugged right after mailing incriminating evidence to a super-sleuth. Miss Marple recognizes this but the police, who depend upon evidence and not intuition, take longer.

She asks the landlady the right questions and, since inquisitive old ladies are totally harmless, is even permitted to examine the dead woman's personal effects. The police haven't been there so Miss Marple interferes with a criminal investigation — however badly run — and removes crucial evidence. Thus, she ends up at the Pale Horse Inn in Much Deeping just in time for the annual witch burning.

A movie cannot fail when it's got a witch burning. Add in modern-day witches hovering about in a very unique inn in the middle of nowhere and you've got an exciting story.

Miss Marple discovers that Father Gorman's death is part of a larger string of deaths. But while the other deaths result in heirs getting rich much sooner than they'd hoped, all of them were caused by unusual illnesses. Even Father Gorman's deathbed vigil (prior to his being coshed) was for a woman dying from an unusual illness. Those deaths looked suspicious to non-inheritors, but without a bloody blunt object laying around, a sad illness is not murder.

Except when the sad illness is helped along by the right kind of poison, as Miss Marple knows.

She starts sleuthing in the inn full of suspicious guests and very soon, one of them dies under suspicious circumstances. While napping supposedly; but as Inspector Lejeune tells Miss Marple, Captain Cottam wasn't napping alone.

This was one part of the story I wanted more of. Captain Cottam, his wife, Kanga, and their widowed housekeeper, Lydia Harsnet, are staying at the Pale Horse because their house burned down under suspicious circumstances. The implication (normal enough) is that Captain Cottam is having an affair with

Mark Easterbrook (*Jonathan Cake*), the inquisitive godson

"Ginger" Corrigan (*Amy Manson*), the suspicious ally

Mr. Venables (*Nigel Planer*), the village grouch

Paul Osbourne (*J.J. Feild*), the suspicious lodger

Thyrza Grey (*Pauline Collins*), the pub proprietor

C.R. Bradley (*Bill Paterson*), the turf accountant

his hot blonde housekeeper, his hot blonde wife not being enough to keep him satiated.

But there's more! Captain Cottam needs an aphrodisiac to get it up with his hot blonde housekeeper, an aphrodisiac supplied by one of the Pale Horse's witches. Then, after said aphrodisiac turns out to be poisoned (but not with thallium), we get a scene where the hot blonde wife implies she was okay with the affair!

How could the scriptwriter give me a setup like this and then not follow through with soapy answers? It left so many questions unanswered that are unrelated to Miss Marple's sleuthing or the murder-for-hire plot.

Anyway. Back to murder for hire. The witches were an interesting bunch. By the end, you know who believes, who loses her faith, and who is playacting for the money.

Thyrza Grey owns the Pale Horse. She's suitably witchy in an upper-class crazy aunt way and runs the coven.

Sybil Stamfordis is young and ravishing in an early 1950s Goth manner. She believes. When she sweeps onstage to perform witchery for Mark Easterbrook — swathed in a full-length black cloak — we were hoping she'd be skyclad underneath. And she was, sort of. Sybil dramatically shed her cloak to reveal her gorgeous embroidered azure dress the exact color of a perfectly blue summer sky.

Witch number three was, I thought, the most interesting. This is Bella Webb, the Pale Horse housekeeper and char. She is a sturdy peasant hedge witch, the sort of woman the villagers visit discreetly for love potions, abortifacients, minor curses, and cures for sick sheep. She knows her herbs, our Bella, and she raises chickens for more than just eggs and soup.

Of the three witches, I'd guess that Bella was the only one who had real occult abilities. But because she was working class, did the dirty work, and didn't look hot and sexy, the scriptwriter relegated her to the background. After the hubbub dies down, Bella, I predict, will quietly disappear from the police radar and go back to being the local and anonymous village hedge witch. If you need to know who she is, you will. If you don't, you'll never find out.

The other character to look out for is Mr. Bradley, the disbarred lawyer. What a great criminal. He knows the law well enough that you can't slide a razor blade between him and illegality, yet he remains safely within the law. Watch him explain how to place a bet on some rich relative's early demise and how that bet is perfectly legal. He knows what he's doing, he feels fully justified, and he knows he won't be prosecuted. Other people are taking those risks, not him.

Mr. Venables was fun too. He's a crotchety old man in a wheelchair with no explanation for where his money comes from. Everything about him screams suspicious, but is he really? He denies being involved in burning down the Cottam's house. I know! Perhaps Mr. Venables was the reason why Kanga Cottam didn't mind her husband's affair with their housekeeper. Kanga was having her own affair with Mr. Venables and if Lydia the housekeeper kept her husband busy, she had time for bed sports of her own.

Kanga Cottam having an affair with a crotchety, scarred man in a wheelchair while her husband's having his own affair would be new and different and a blow for disabled rights. But alas, it was not to be.

Instead, we get the usual sweet meeting of young lovers, in this case Mark Easterbrook and Ginger Corrigan. As soon as you see them together, you know how it will end, and it does. The added fillip is having Mark pretend to arrange Ginger's murder but again, that's par for the course. He has to be clever, she has to be brave, and they have to help Miss Marple solve the crime. Which is a good thing because there wasn't enough sleuthing to set up Miss Marple's deductions.

Despite my thwarted hopes, I really enjoyed *The Pale Horse*. It's got everything, including a room designed for witchcraft with the best custom-made rug I've ever seen. Don't miss it and feel free to speculate afterwards on what happens next for Kanga and Mr. Venables. She's a merry widow, and he's single so fanfiction writers, start your laptops.

General Information

Based on: *The Pale Horse* (novel, 1961)
Run time: 1 hr., 29 min. **Subtitles:** Yes

Writer: Russell Lewis **Director:** Andy Hay

Cast

Julia McKenzie as Miss Marple
Jonathan Cake as Mark Easterbrook
Amy Manson as "Ginger" Corrigan
Neil Pearson as Inspector Lejeune
Jason Merrells as Dr. Kerrigan

Pauline Collins as Thyrza Grey
Susan Lynch as Sybil Stamfordis
Jenny Galloway as Bella Webb
Nigel Planer as Mr. Venables
Bill Paterson as C.R. Bradley
Tom Ward as Captain Cottam
Holly Valance as Kanga Cottam
Sarah Alexander as Lydia Harsnet
Lynda Baron as Mrs. Coppins,
Elizabeth Rider as Mrs. Davis
Nicholas Parsons as Father Gorman
J.J. Feild as Paul Osbourne
Mike Shepherd as Chief Mummer
Holly Willoughby as Goody Carne
Julia Molony as Thomasina Tuckerton
Jodie Hay as Bertie

Film Locations

Hughenden Manor, Hughenden, Buckinghamshire (Venables house, street scenes)
Dorney Court, Dorney, Buckinghamshire (The Pale Horse)
St. Michael and All Angels, Hughenden (church)
Church of St. Mary, Denham, Buckinghamshire (churchyard)

The Secret of Chimneys (2010)

Shoehorning in Miss Marple turns this homage to Ruritanian thrillers into a plot-holey murderous mess

Fidelity to text

Some names match. The house is terrific. Miss Marple replaces Inspector Battle.

Quality of movie

Plot holes you could sail battleships through. Incoherent, sloppy, and Miss Marple dredges the solution out of her knitting bag.

What a mess. (Deep sigh). Let's start with the first of a series of egregious changes the producers inflicted on a fast-moving thriller with a studly romantic leading man.

Miss Marple solves the crime.

Miss Marple! I ask you. How could she show up when Agatha published *The Secret of Chimneys* in 1925? Miss Marple was a twinkle in Agatha's eye until 1927. *Chimneys* stars Inspector Battle, criminally underused in both prose and film. This is his case, not some dotty old lady, but he's gone. Perhaps, being an ace detective, he realized he'd be wasting his time serving as the old lady's dogsbody.

After that, it gets worse.

In the novel, our hero is Anthony Cade, an adventurer with a past. He's virility personified, honest when he must be, dashing, daring, and everything you want in your romantic lead. He's asked to return compromising letters to an unknown damsel being blackmailed, so naturally he races to her rescue. You can see why Virginia Revel falls in love with this exciting man of action.

In the film, he's relegated to a supporting player with about fifteen minutes of screen time. He's also been castrated by the film-makers into a whiny, ineffective, dull dweeb who protests his innocence but does nothing to prove it. The actor playing Anthony Cade also looks so much like the actor playing Bill Eversleigh that I had trouble telling them apart. Bill Eversleigh is supposed to be a waste of space and he still is. In the novel, the contrast between the two men is immense. Here, it's not. They're cut from the same limp, wet dishrag.

Virginia Revel, our heroine, is no longer a dashing widow-about-town. Nope, she's Lord Caterham's younger daughter. At least she can't be confused on sight with Bundle, Lord Caterham's other daughter. Bundle was an effervescent flapper; she's turned into a dried-up spinster.

The original story of derring-do, international intrigue, African connections, missing heirs to thrones, secret letters and tell-all memoirs, international jewel thieves, and visiting detectives from France vanishes. Instead, we get a mess that Agatha would have never written. I agree that *Chimneys* can be preposterous at times, but even when far-fetched, her plot held together.

This mess did not. The story has more holes in it

Lord Caterham (*Edward Fox*), the weary lordship

"Bundle" Brent (*Dervla Kirwan*), the dutiful daughter

Virginia Brent (*Charlotte Salt*), the wild daughter

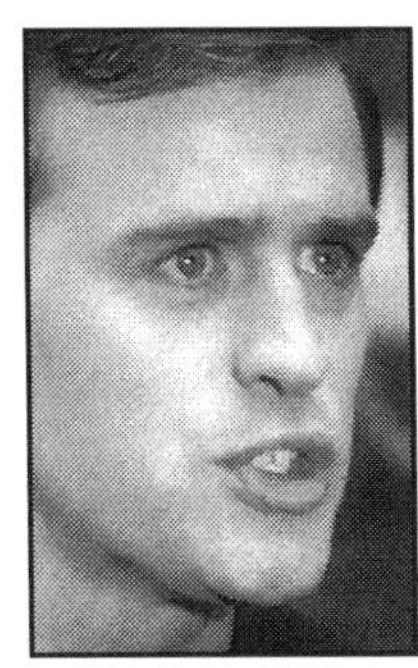
Anthony Cade (*Jonas Armstrong*), the careful adventurer

Ludwig Von Stainach (*Anthony Higgins*), the tender aristocrat

Hilda Blenkinsopp (*Ruth Jones*), the austere official

than the victims.

The other characters are treated equally badly. Lord Caterham? Completely rewritten. Treadwell, the butler, gets a sex-change with no explanation or improvement to the story. Other characters vanish. Totally new characters appear. Some of these characters get murdered too, so the sole reason they're added is to die dramatically.

George Lomax remains as does his secretary, Bill Eversleigh. George Lomax is similar in that he's a bureaucrat trying to solve diplomatic issues for the good of England. He becomes not just irritating, but obviously and openly incompetent, which he is not in the novel.

A huge diamond still disappears. That stays the same. Otherwise, there is virtually nothing left of the original story, other than a few names and a line of dialog here and there.

Why did the producers do this? Were they concerned they'd run out of genuine Miss Marple material? This fiasco appears late in season 5. Since there was money to be made, other Christie stories got Miss Marple shoe-horned into them and so here we are: A Miss Marple mystery that never featured Miss Marple in the first place. Keep in mind that plenty of Miss Marple short stories were ignored.

That brings us to the movie. I should say TV episode but it's about 90 minutes long and feels like a movie rather than a Jessica Fletcher *Murder, She Wrote* episode.

As a film, the action moves along reasonably well. The dialog was clear. The house standing in for Chimneys is fantastic, a premium English country house on steroids. Those floors! That carved paneling! A secret passageway hidden behind a Van Dyck painting of the Duke of Richmond! Balconies and stately grounds and suits of armor!

I have no idea how they keep that house clean and those thousands of acres of gardens manicured and all that stonework repointed when there appeared to be two, count them, two servants. That would be the thieving maid, run off in 1932, and the other maid, elevated to the position of butler. Because she was named Treadwell, like the butler in the novel? That's as good an explanation as any.

The acting was decent, other than the utterly bland Ken doll the casting director brought in to play Anthony Cade. There must be some actor out there who can channel Errol Flynn because that's who should be playing Anthony Cade. Not some piece of carved pine with plastic hair. The young man is probably quite nice in real life but he did not light up the screen and make me *feel* why Virginia fell at his feet, panting to get to know him better.

Some men and women radiate charisma. The rest of us just muddle along.

The mystery plot was rewritten into an atrocity. There were obvious red herrings everywhere. The African connection was a throw-away line. There was no lost heir to the throne. The reason for the theft of the jewel was absurd. No one behaved in character, least of all Lord Caterham. Parts that could have been interesting, like the motivation of the National Trust representative, were given short-shrift. She, by the way, was far more vigorous and manly than Anthony Cade. None of the writers seemed to have any idea what servants do or how they would act in the mid-1950s (when the story takes place). George Lomax was supposed to be capable and yet was unable to conduct the most cursory of background checks. And then, when a character's true identity was revealed, everyone still used his false name and position in life even though he couldn't have possibly been that person!

To add insult to injury, Miss Marple pulled the solution out of her knitting bag.

If you're watching all six seasons of *Agatha Christie's Marple*, there's no reason to skip this episode, even though it's drivel. If you don't know that it's based on a wildly different novel, you'll still notice the plot holes but they won't be as infuriating as if you're expecting a story that is close to the original *Secret of Chimneys*.

Eventually, someone will make a good version of *The Secret of Chimneys*. The novel is very much of its time, written in 1924 and published in 1925, so that time will be far off in the future, when we've gotten over our chronocentrism and quit judging people from the past by the standards of today.

This movie was bad. Knowing what the original story was and what the movie could have been makes it worse.

General Information

Based on: *The Secret of Chimneys* (novel, 1925)
Run time: 1 hr., 29 min. **Subtitles:** Yes

Writer: Paul Rutman **Director:** John Strickland

Cast

Julia McKenzie as Miss Marple
Stephen Dillane as Inspector Finch

Edward Fox as Lord Caterham
Dervla Kirwan as Eileen "Bundle" Brent
Charlotte Salt as Virginia Brent
Jonas Armstrong as Anthony Cade
Adam Godley as George Lomax
Mathew Horne as Bill Eversleigh
Michelle Collins as Treadwell
Anthony Higgins as Count Ludwig Von Stainach
Ruth Jones as Hilda Blenkinsopp
Alex Knight as Jaffers
Laura O'Toole as Agnes
Ian Weichardt as Young Lomax
Robert Dunbar as Young Count
Letty Butler as Young Treadwell
Nicci Brighten as Madeleine

Film Locations

Hatfield House, Hatfield, Hertfordshire (Chimneys, interiors, exteriors)
Knebworth House, Knebworth, Hertfordshire (Chimneys interiors)

The Blue Geranium (2010)

Adding more characters and grafting them into the mystery turned this short story into a flowering drama

Fidelity to text

The original story is there but it's been greatly expanded, especially considering how minimalist the source material is.

Quality of movie

It's good on its own merits *and* it's more interesting than the original short story. Only purists will carp.

One of the pluses of ITV's *Marple* is they take risks. You never know what you'll get. Frequently, the daredevil leap into original fanfiction taking place in a universe parallel to Agatha's own world plummets to earth when the last fifteen minutes of the film collapses into a messy, disjointed heap.

But not always! *The Blue Geranium* demonstrates why ITV should have filmed all the Miss Marple short stories. The original story, while clever, had little else going on. The film is terrific. Let this remind TV producers everywhere that, unlike Poirot, the vast majority of Miss Marple stories remain unfilmed and that those nothing stories can be made into something special.

I was, I admit, apprehensive because of previous failed leaps into the unknown. *The Secret of Chimneys* (see the previous review) was dreadful; a pale, castrated shadow of the novel which never involved Jane Marple and proof that ITV'S wholesale rewrites can fail spectacularly.

"The Blue Geranium" is an actual Miss Marple short story, not another story shoehorned into the series so the TV producers could make more episodes and thus more money. But there's darn little there, after the clever idea. The scriptwriter made the story better. Much, much better.

For those of you who aren't familiar with it, "The Blue Geranium" is one of Agatha's earliest short stories involving Jane Marple. Agatha also used the hackneyed and awkward trope of a group of people sitting around a dinner table telling true crime stories to see if the other dinner guests can figure out whodunnit.

I'm not fond of this trope. There's no tension because the mystery is secondhand. The mysteries are pared down to skeletal remnants, another reason not to care what happens to the participants. In these short stories, Miss Marple is the winner of each competition. She always knows because someone in the village of St. Mary Mead did something similar. She's also twittering and dithery, in her black lace mittens and lacy fichus and fluffy pink wool shawl. As Agatha developed Miss Marple, she became a more active, competent amateur detective and less of a caricature of ye olde Victorian Spinster Lady with a capital L.

The core mystery has been amplified. The original protagonists remain: George Pritchard, his crazy wife,

George Pritchard
(*Toby Stephens*),
the conflicted husband

Mary Pritchard
(*Sharon Small*),
the harridan wife

Philippa Pritchard
(*Claudie Blakley*),
the helpful sister

Lewis Pritchard
(*Paul Rhys*),
the wastrel brother

Hazel Instow
(*Caroline Catz*),
the haunted artist

Caroline Copling
(*Claire Rushbrook*),
the caring nurse

Mary, Nurse Copling, the mysterious psychic, Zarida. The other protagonists, chatting over dinner, vanish with the exception of Miss Marple and Sir Henry Clithering.

An entirely new cast of characters arrived, fleshing out the story from the skeletal remains: George's ne'er-do-well brother, his wife (George's old flame and Mary's sister), their kids, the vicar, the vicar's niece, the doctor, the artist, the mysterious drunk, the golf club set, the list goes on.

And it works! Suddenly, the characters become breathing, living people in terms of motivation, family dynamics, and long-seated resentments instead of paper dolls. The Vicar's painting of the Seven Deadly Sins? That village is rife with examples. An entire school of red herrings swims in, letting Miss Marple make a St. Mary Mead parallel between tangled yarn and tangled motivations.

The blue geranium is still there.

For you non-gardeners, geraniums do not come in blue. Nor do holly-hocks or primroses. Those flowers come in a lot of colors but blue isn't one of them. This is important to the storyline and it provides a clue right in the title to the more scientifically-minded viewer, who remembers basic chemistry class and spots what Nurse Copling is doing with that little strip of paper and Mary's chamber pot.

Very few flowers are blue. Every other color is present in the garden other than blue or true black. There are loads of green flowers; mostly small and on trees which is why you don't notice them. When gardening catalogs claim a flower is blue, they're lying. The flower is actually a shade of purple. If you're an ad copy writer, you describe the blossom in lyrical terms to fool the unwary gardener into believing that yes! This flower will be blue! Blue dahlias! Blue tulips! Blue hyacinths! Blue violets! Blue hydrangeas!

These flowers are not blue.

They are shades of purple and lilac. Hold a blue hyacinth up to the sky on a clear, sunny day and you'll see how purple it really is. If you want actual blue flowers, like an indigo bunting is blue and a bluebird is not, you'll have to grow Himalayan Blue Poppies and good luck with that endeavor since those are one of the fussiest plants in the world.

If, like Nurse Copling, you want to manipulate flower color you can dye them after they've been cut. Or, you can grow hydrangeas. They come in three colors: white, pink, and what gardening catalogs euphemistically label blue. If you manipulate the acidity of your soil, you can magically alter the color of your hydrangeas, turning pink flowers blue-ish and vice versa. The more acidic it gets, the "bluer" your hydrangeas. White flowering hydrangeas remain white. It requires several growing seasons, some knowledge of basic chemistry, and a soil testing kit.

General Information

Based on: *"The Blue Geranium"* (short story, 1929)
Run time: 1 hr., 29 min. **Subtitles:** No

Writer: Stewart Harcourt
Director: David Moore

Cast

Julia McKenzie as Miss Marple
Kevin McNally as Detective Somerset
Donald Sinden as Sir Henry Clithering

Sharon Small as Mary Pritchard
Toby Stephens as George Pritchard
Claudie Blakley as Philippa Pritchard
Paul Rhys as Lewis Pritchard
Benjamin Harcourt as Peter Pritchard
Thomas Harcourt as Michael Pritchard
Molly Harcourt as Susan Pritchard
Claire Rushbrook as Nurse Caroline Copling
Caroline Catz as Hazel Instow
David Calder as Rev. Dermot Milewater
Joanna Page as Hester Milewater
Patrick Baladi as Dr. Jonathan Frayn
Jason Durr as Eddie Seward
Rebekah Manning as Nurse Susan Carstairs

Film Locations

Hatfield House (Clithering's club and reading room)
Hambleden, Buckinghamshire

But back to the film. The added elements held together beautifully, explaining the complex motivations far better. Miss Marple fits in much better too, since she's on the spot during the crimes and not commenting on them from a bloodless remove over dinner. She's involved. She knows these complicated, hurting people. Then, at the last possible moment, she realizes the truth. She makes a daring, last-minute move to save the day, rescue the innocent, and name the true villain.

I did not like how Mary, suitably crazy and antagonistic, is described by the other characters. They imply she's a glutton, ruled by her appetites (which she is). They claim she's fat, even obese. We see Mary out of bed in a fitted blue dress (you'll never see a flower that shade of blue). Yeah, she's no size 6. I'd say about a size 18. She's overweight but the way the other characters talk, she's morbidly obese. She is not. She is the size of a normal woman.

It was jarring and a reminder that Hollywood has no idea what normal people look like. In Hollywood, if you have any body fat at all, you're obese. If you're a normal weight, you're morbidly obese. But if you're actually obese *and* you're the flavor of the month, you're a freedom fighter against unrealistic standards of beauty until you stop being popular. At that point, you become — once again — disgustingly obese *and* you should vanish so decent people don't have to witness your flabby self.

Mary, as it turns out, is really ill and not just a spiritualism-crazed, attention-mad hypochondriac. Nurse Copling figures it out, but Dr. Frayn does not. Eventually, Miss Marple figures it out too.

No matter what you've heard about ITV's *Marple*, don't miss this episode. You'll quickly figure out why it's worth taking the risk of watching.

The Mirror Crack'd from Side to Side (2010)

A few major changes don't affect the story of a monster everyone in Hollywood loves to protect

The film follows the book reasonably closely, allowing for usual condensing needed to turn several hundred pages of novel into a 90-minute movie. The changes include setting the story in the 1950s, minor characters disappear (including Heather Badcock's husband, but he was a nonentity so he didn't matter), and other, more important changes.

There is no Vincent Hogg, gossip columnist to the stars, in the book. He's a maliciously funny replacement for Ardwyck Fenn, big shot Hollywood producer. Vincent loves being in the spotlight and has figured out how to be a successful writer in Hollywood. He's also, as would be expected with Hollywood types, one of Marina Gregg's many ex-husbands. He loathes Marina and vividly recalls their marriage as being hell on earth. His arm candy, Lola Brewster, was in the novel and here, she steals the show every time she sashays onscreen. She's six feet tall, redheaded, and with a va-va-voom figure encased in red satin. Wow.

I noticed. Bill really noticed. Every time Lola came on stage, he noticed. It was hard not to notice when the cameraman noticed, making sure his camera lingered on Lola's phenomenal cleavage. As would be expected with Hollywood types, Lola was Jason Rudd's former lover and a rival to Marina Gregg. She's not any more keen on Marina than Vincent is and makes pointed remarks about aging women panting after men half their age.

Fidelity to text

Minor character removals and alterations and a major character rewrite. Margo Bence is actually allowed to speak.

Quality of movie

Coherent, fast-paced, and Lindsay Duncan made almost as credible a movie star as Elizabeth Taylor did in her version.

Such is Hollywood.

Lindsay Duncan, playing Marina Gregg, was a marvel. Because of her performance, I could really grasp why Agatha named the novel *The Mirror Crack'd*. It had never been clear before.

For those of you not up on your Tennyson (1809-1892), the title refers to this verse in his epic poem, *The Lady of Shalott*.

> *"Out flew the web and floated wide –*
> *The mirror crack'd from side to side;*
> *"The curse is come upon me," cried*
> *The Lady of Shalott."*

What was the point of this title? Agatha Christie always had a reason and this choice of title was important. In this case, Marina Gregg, Hollywood movie star, was suddenly and dramatically confronted with a truth she had not previously known and it

Marina Gregg
(*Lindsay Duncan*),
the overbearing star

Jason Rudd
(*Nigel Harman*),
the protective director

Vincent Hogg
(*Martin Jarvis*),
the malicious gossip

Lola Brewster
(*Hannah Waddingham*),
the malicious rival

Ella Blunt
(*Victoria Smurfit*),
the faithful secretary

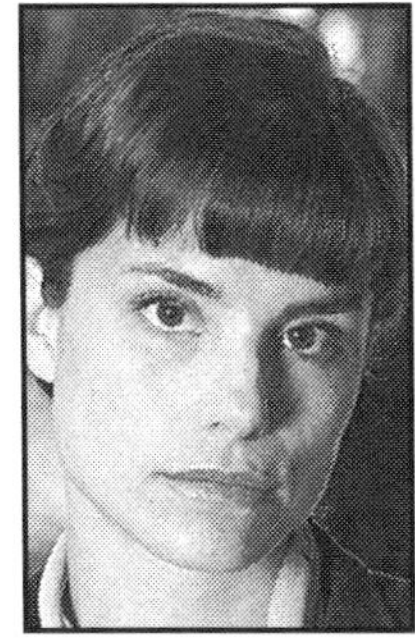

Margot Bence
(*Charlotte Riley*),
the sad photographer

destroyed her. I had never made the connection until I saw this film. When I read it in the novel, it got me to look up Tennyson, but I didn't get it.

Now, I do.

Another change was the movie within a movie that Marina Gregg was filming, with Jason Rudd (hubby #5) directing. She'd already made one comeback film starring as Marie Antionette. This one was to be the follow-on, cementing her return to glory: a biopic of Nefertiti. Other versions of *Mirror* showcase different historical costume epics but they're always about queens and empresses. No factory workers for Marina Gregg!

Miss Marple and her friend, Dolly Bantry, go sleuthing on set to watch and ask questions. Keep an eye on Marina Gregg on set and how for a simple, two-person scene with her costar playing Ramses, they're up to their 19th take. Marina's causing trouble, not learning her lines, and trying to upstage her costar. Her husband, the director, keeps the rest of the set under control, but not her.

What was truly interesting about the film was, for the first time, evaluating the character of Marina Gregg, Hollywood actress, in a way that I had not done when reading the novel. I'm thinking in particular of how everyone around Marina Gregg made excuses for her behavior because she was so beautiful, so talented, so creative, and had suffered so deeply in her art and her life. A careful rereading of pertinent parts of the novel showed that although Agatha didn't make a big deal of it, she didn't excuse Marina Gregg the way her retinue did.

What did Marina Gregg do? Well, she was a movie star, so you can start with that. But what was unforgivable to me, today, was her adopting three young children and then, when she became pregnant with a "real baby of her own," she got rid of those children despite claiming in print that she'd love them like they were her own kids. They *were* her own kids after she adopted them. Dumping them off like an unwanted litter of kittens was intensely cruel and demonstrated her completely selfish character more clearly than anything else ever could.

No one, other than Margo (grown to adulthood in the novel) disapproves of this behavior. If you're a famous, beautiful movie star, it's okay to adopt children and then walk away when they're no longer useful for your self-image. Every version of *Mirror* gives Marina Gregg a pass on treating children like accessories. Margo gets some screen time in this version but she doesn't get to say how cruel Marina was to her and her brother. No one, even Miss Marple, tells Margo that she was treated shabbily and deserved better.

It's always worthwhile to reread a good novel to see what changes as you, the reader, grow and change. When I first read *The Mirror Crack'd* all those years ago, this part didn't bother me. It does now.

Something else I didn't know until after I saw this film and did some research was discovering that Agatha had based the central, inciting incident on a real-world example. Gene Tierney (1920-1991), luminously beautiful movie star was pregnant in 1943. She volunteered at the Hollywood Canteen and a fan, ill with rubella, broke quarantine to see her. As a result, Ms. Tierney gave birth to a severely handicapped daughter who was institutionalized for most of her life. About two years later, according to Ms. Tierney's autobiography, she met the fan again at a garden party and the fan admitted sneaking out of quarantine to meet her.

This is why rubella (aka German measles) is included in the standard MMR (measles, mumps, rubella) vaccine given to every child soon after birth. The vast majority of people who develop rubella get a rash for a few days and make a full recovery. If you're in your first trimester of pregnancy, your baby is doomed to congenital rubella syndrome. You'll either miscarry or the baby will be born with major handicaps. It's heartbreaking and that's why we get a vaccine against a minor disease.

It's not a minor illness if your baby suffers.

Heather Badcock didn't know any better when she broke quarantine to meet Marina Gregg. She'd have been devastated to learn that she'd compromised the health of her idol's baby. Watching everyone onscreen dismiss Heather as an annoying, busybody do-gooder while giving Marina Gregg a pass on far worse behavior proves that power and status matter more than anything.

Famous, beautiful, wealthy stars do whatever they damn well please and get away with it. Rules of behavior only apply to the little people, don't you know.

General Information

Based on: *The Mirror Crack'd from Side to Side* (novel, 1962)
Run time: 1 hr., 286 min. **Subtitles:** Yes

Writer: Kevin Elyot
Director: Tom Shankland

Cast

Julia McKenzie as Miss Marple
Joanna Lumley as Dolly Bantry
Hugh Bonneville as Inspector Hewitt
Samuel Barnett as Sergeant Tiddler

Lindsay Duncan as Marina Gregg
Nigel Harman as Jason Rudd
Martin Jarvis as Vincent Hogg
Hannah Waddingham as Lola Brewster
Charlotte Riley as Margot Bence
Victoria Smurfit as Ella Blunt
Brennan Brown as Hailey Preston
Caroline Quentin as Heather Badcock
Olivia Darnley as Cherry Baker
Lois Jones as Primrose Dixon
Michele Dotrice as Mrs. Hubbard
Don Gallagher as Man in Livery
Neil Stuke as Dr. Haydock
Will Young as Casey Croft
Anna Andresen as Maisie Cooper

Film Location

North Mymms Park, Hatfield, Hertfordshire (Gossington Hall)

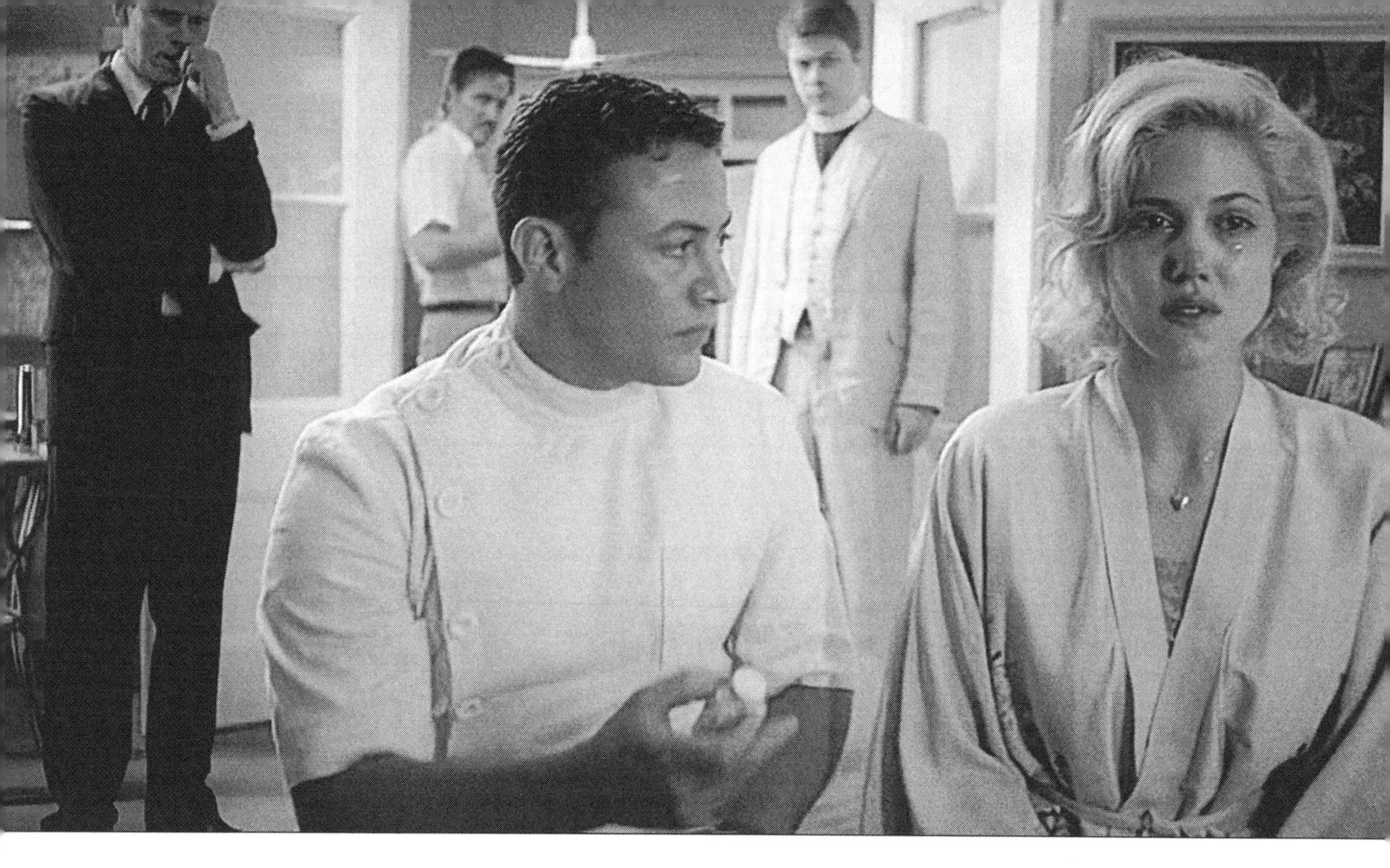

A Caribbean Mystery (2013)

Sun, sand, and surf cannot keep out murder at a resort, but Miss Marple and voodoo help solve the case

Fidelity to text

Unusual for ITV, this follows Agatha's story. Minor characters vanish and Ian Fleming and James Bond (the ornithologist) appear. Mama Zogbe adds a terrific zombie/voodoo element and Canon Prescott grew younger and got a happy ending.

Quality of movie

So much to enjoy: settings, local color, great acting, encounters between staff and guests, and Miss Marple getting a real mystery to chew on. Plus voodoo!

Since Miss Marple gets around, it's no surprise when she arrives in the sunny Caribbean, courtesy of devoted nephew Raymond West and his profitable career as a literary novelist.

Agatha clearly had a lot of fun with Raymond West. Unlike her or her alter-ego, mystery writer Ariadne Oliver, he was respected by the literary establishment. Miss Marple, however, didn't think much of Raymond's novels. More amusingly, Raymond's modernist novel writing paid extremely well, something that might have been marginally possible back in England in the 1950s and impossible today. Today, literary novelists are at the bottom of the heap in terms of earning money at writing, whereas hack genre writers can write full time, pay the bills, and afford luxury vacations in the Caribbean. If they're writing in the "I Was the Alien's Love Slave" subgenre, they can afford their very own Caribbean beach house and not have to stay in a hotel like the rest of us. Their bank respects them even if the literary world does not.

But I digress. I'm still amazed at how well Cape Town, South Africa, stood in for a sunny 1950s Caribbean island. You shouldn't be surprised by the coconut palms. Like successful hack genre writers, they prefer oceanside living. Their coconuts drop into the sea, are carried away by the currents, and thus you can find coconut palms everywhere in the world where the climate is even the slightest bit warm enough. Even so, you would never guess where this movie was filmed if they didn't admit it.

Many of the actors were fresh faces (at least to me) and that was nice too; I didn't get mixed up, confusing who I was watching with a character from another movie.

Meanwhile, at the Golden Palms hotel, Miss Marple becomes moderately bored by her calm and sunny vacation until, as luck would have it, Major Palgrave tells her a boring story about murderers he has known. Unlike most people, Miss Marple is not bored since she's met many murderers. This vacation has suddenly gotten interesting. It gets even more interesting when

Molly Kendall
(*Charity Wakefield*),
the troubled hostess

Tim Kendall
(*Robert Webb*),
the worried husband

Mr. Rafiel
(*Antony Sher*),
the wealthy guest

Maj. Robert Palgrave
(*Oliver Ford Davies*),
the veteran bore

Mama Zogbe
(*Andrea Dondolo*),
the voodoo practitioner

Victoria Johnson
(*Pippa Bennett-Warner*),
the nosy maid

Major Palgrave clams up and hastily changes the subject, followed by him dying that night under suspicious circumstances.

She's off to the races, meeting the wealthy wheelchair-bound guest Mr. Rafiel and persuading him to listen to her when no one else will, including the police.

The situation heats up at the Golden Palms when the hotelkeeper, Molly, shows signs of craziness. The tension rises with the voodoo dance done for the tourists. It reminded me of similar tourist productions in Hawaii, where I was stationed for three years with the U.S. Navy. What tourists pay to see bears little relation to what the natives do in private. The tourist show is flashy, showy, dramatic, and has little to do with local cultural practices or religious beliefs which are not sold for public consumption.

Miss Marple confirms this fact when she visits Mama Zogbe. She found a gris-gris doll in the shrubbery and wanted to know if it meant anything. According to Mama Zogbe, it meant nothing. She showed off a box full of them, made for the tourists to take home and illustrate their stories about their exotic Caribbean vacation.

Later, Mama Zogbe reveals that sometimes voodoo — when not being used to harvest tourist dollars — is real. She sold Canon Prescott a voodoo charm. Despite being an Anglican minister, he was desperate enough to use a heathen religious system to help him stay on the straight and narrow path. As a godly man, Canon Prescott recognizes occult power when he sees it.

Red herrings abound in this adaptation, including the weird dynamics between Lucky and Greg Dyson and Colonel and Evelyn Hillingdon. Watch Evelyn's face. She's saddled with a poor excuse for a husband who's unable to see her value. Her scene with him, when he accuses her of never loving anyone, is priceless. It demonstrates how obtuse he is and makes the viewer wonder if he'll ever recognize he got lucky.

Then there's the weirdness between Esther Walters and Tim Kendall, Molly's oh-so-devoted husband. For a hotel guest, Esther is awfully fond of her hotelkeeper.

General Information

Based on: *A Caribbean Mystery* (novel, 1964)
Run time: 1 hr., 29 min. **Subtitles:** Yes

Writer: Charlie Higson
Director: Charles Palmer

Cast

Julia McKenzie as Miss Marple
Anele Matoti as Inspector Daventry
Joe Vaz as Sergeant Weston

Charity Wakefield as Molly Kendall
Robert Webb as Tim Kendall
Antony Sher as Mr. Rafiel
Montserrat Lombard as Esther Walters
Warren Brown as Arthur Jackson
Pippa Bennett-Warner as Victoria Johnson
Kingsley Ben-Adir as Errol Johnson
Andrea Dondolo as Mama Zogbe
Daniel Rigby as Canon Prescott
Alastair Mackenzie as Colonel Hillingdon
Hermione Norris as Evelyn Hillingdon
Charles Mesure as Greg Dyson
MyAnna Buring as Lucky Dyson
Oliver Ford Davies as Maj. Robert Palgrave
Jeremy Crutchley as Ian Fleming
Charlie Higson as James Bond

Film Location

Cape Town, South Africa

I particularly appreciated the scenes with Victoria and Errol, members of the hotel's staff. You're reminded how much make-believe is involved in tropical resort vacations and how lush vegetation screens third-world poverty from the guests. Victoria needed the money. Don't forget that when you watch and rewatch this episode to catch all the great bits. Remember it when you go on your vacation so you tip your chambermaid. Those women work hard for their money.

I would be remiss in not mentioning Ian Fleming (1908-1964), would-be novelist. He shows up briefly, looking for the blandest name possible for his new spy hero. Inspired by Miss Marple's comment, he finds it in the name of a local ornithologist, James Bond, in town to give a lecture on tropical birds. The inspiration for Bond is true, by the way. Bond specialized in birds of the Caribbean and wrote the definitive book on them: *Birds of the West Indies*. Ian Fleming met him, liked his name, and the rest is spy-novel history. Fleming and Bond play no part in *A Caribbean Mystery*, other than to add an amusing frisson of reality.

The ending pulls everything together very nicely. Just like Agatha wrote it, our hotelkeepers have a more complex background than they admit to. The last few scenes make you wonder what happens next. Not everyone gets their happy ending. Watch Greg Dyson sitting at the bar with Esther Walters. Watch Esther as she realizes what a complete and utter fool she was and how close she came to dying herself a few years later, when Tim found another sucker. Then, watch a flash of a happier future for Canon Prescott and the girl of his dreams.

What a great film. Don't miss it.

One last note: Because ITV filmed the Miss Marple novels out of sequence, *Nemesis* was released in January of 2009, four years prior to this film. In reality, Agatha wrote that novel as a sequel of sorts to *A Caribbean Mystery*. Mr. Rafiel, impressed with her sleuthing and sense of justice in *A Caribbean Mystery*, asks Miss Marple to solve a personal mystery of his own in *Nemesis*. The two ITV productions should be considered as independent films since except for Rafiel they've got nothing to do with each other.

Greenshaw's Folly (2013)

An abused wife and her son hide at a woman's estate that's home to deadly secrets involving orphans

This episode leaps into the story when a blonde damsel bangs on Miss Marple's door one dark and stormy night. She seeks refuge for herself and her son, Archie, from her evil ex-husband. Louisa Oxley also needs work and, naturally, Miss Marple knows a dear friend in need of a secretary.

We're off to Greenshaw's Folly, a castle built in a mishmash of architectural styles. It's owned by Katherine Greenshaw, a dotty lady mad scientist following in her feared and hated father's footsteps. But unlike daddy dearest, she experiments on plants, not orphans. She needs a secretary who doesn't mind living in a spooky castle surrounded by poisonous plants. Nonetheless, there are parts of the castle Louisa's warned not to enter.

Louisa and Archie move in, but they struggle to adjust to an increasingly weird, haunted castle. She finds it queer that our lady scientist brews her atropine eye drops from deadly nightshade (*atropa belladonna* for scientifically-minded gardeners with a taste for home remedies). The household consists of an off-putting housekeeper (Mrs. Cresswell), a ghost-enthusiast butler (Cracken), and a handsome ex-con gardener (Alfred) whose hobby is archery. There's also a creepy houseguest who slinks around, spying and prying, and is clearly up to no good.

Miss Greenshaw also has a strange relationship with the local orphanage run by a drunken, gambling priest (a hackneyed trope).

Fidelity to text

The plot is enhanced with wills, housekeepers, and gardeners with secret pasts. Add a damsel fleeing an abusive husband on a dark and stormy night, nefarious medical experiments on orphans, and Agatha goes Gothic!

Quality of movie

We have a winner! The Miss Marple short stories benefit from scriptwriters running amuck. I wanted more of the crazy house and the medical experiments.

Matters don't improve when they're joined by Miss Greenshaw's smarmy nephew. Nat Fletcher is an aspiring actor and the son of her ostracized sister. It seems dear sister married beneath herself and was ejected from the family by daddy dearest. But where there's a rich estate, poor relations don't hesitate to show up hoping to weasel their way into the will.

Nor is he alone in that quest. The orphanage priest wants a share of the inheritance too, after Miss Greenshaw moves on to her reward. But will the money go to rescue orphans or will he waste it on gambling and drinking? While it's very nice that one of the wealthiest women in the district helps support the orphanage, Louisa gradually uncovers a closer, weirder, many-leveled relationship.

Events take a creepier turn. Flowers arrive for Louisa from a secret admirer. It's a lovely spray of lilies,

Louisa Oxley (*Kimberley Nixon*), the runaway wife

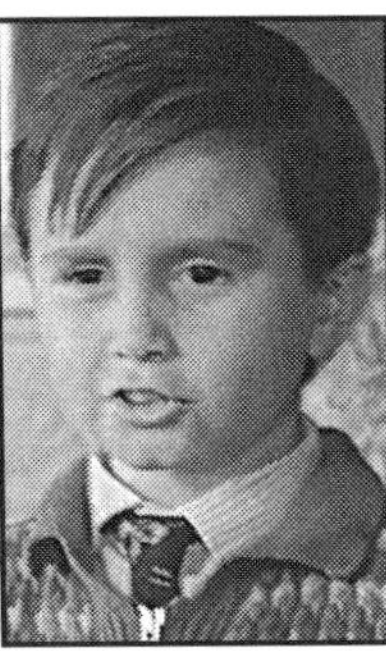

Archie Oxley (*Bobby Smalldridge*), the runaway son

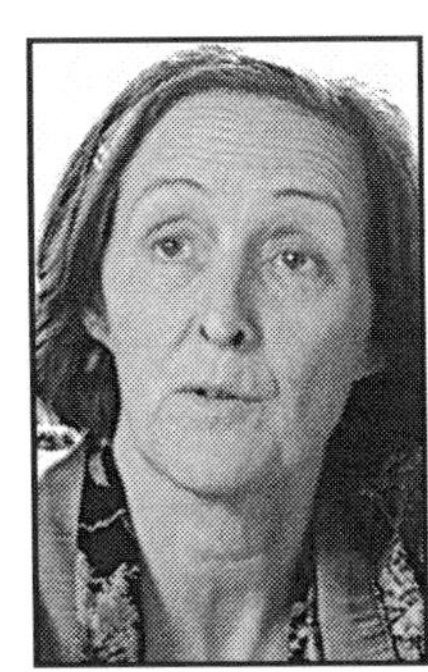

Katherine Greenshaw (*Fiona Shaw*), the scientist's heir

Alfred Pollock (*Martin Compston*), the capable gardener

Nat Fletcher (*Sam Reid*), the hopeful nephew

Father Brophy (*Robert Glenister*), the orphan's friend

suitable for a funeral arrangement on a lady's casket. The butler dies in what looks like an accident, but Miss Marple knows better. The creepy houseguest disappears under mysterious circumstances.

Then, Louisa and Mrs. Cresswell are locked into their rooms while Archie is off somewhere with the gardener. They watch in horror as Miss Greenshaw is shot to death by an arrow while gardening. An archer must have done it and the only one around is Alfred, who's been teaching Archie how to use a bow and arrow.

Panic ensues, ratcheting up to eleven when Louisa's evil ex-husband shows up to kidnap his son.

And we haven't even got to the crazy old lady villager who knows what Miss Greenshaw's evil mad scientist father did. She shows up to rescue Archie, but not from his father. She's trying to save her dead little brother, gone for fifty years or more. She's afraid Archie will be experimented on.

Enough plot for you? No? Good, because there's more. What is the true relationship between Nat Fletcher and the Greenshaw family? How about Alfred the gardener and the Greenshaw family? You'll find out and you'll applaud.

It's a great episode, but not without flaws. Louisa and Alfred are supposed to slowly fall in love but there was no chemistry between them. This was an acting as well as a script problem. Even without dialog, they could have stared longingly at each other whenever they were in the same room. The camera would have picked up on their desire, but no. That didn't happen. I suppose the scriptwriter wanted us to think she was pining after matinee-handsome Nat Fletcher. If so, that wasn't fleshed out either, yet it could have been. It would have demonstrated that our Louisa had a genius for choosing the wrong kind of man. Then, when she noticed the right kind of man, it would have been an even more satisfying happy ending.

I wanted more interactions between the villagers and Greenshaw's Folly. I'd bet a gallon of atropine that they knew plenty about daddy dearest's cruel experiments on innocent orphans. The survivors grew up and did not forget. But other than one crazy old lady, we don't get this subplot fleshed out.

We should have learned more about Horace Bindler, creepy houseguest. No one came looking for him after his disappearance and someone should have. He's not an eight-year-old orphan with no family or coworkers keeping track of his whereabouts. I also wanted to know who tossed his room after he disappeared and why.

It was also strange that a huge castle like Greenshaw's Folly had only three servants: the butler, housekeeper, and gardener. Those gardens alone needed at least three full-time people plus a few part-time locals when the miles of hedges needed pruning. I also can't believe the housekeeper cleaned that entire pile by herself. And then followed up with cooking and washing up for family, guests, and staff? I don't think so. The elderly butler wasn't hoovering those carpets and dusting the chandeliers. This was the chance for a few village chars to show up, bearing gossip about the house's evil history to scare Louisa and Archie thoroughly as well as enlighten Miss Marple.

I also wanted to see more of the house. In the short story, the Greenshaw castle is described as being built by an extremely rich man who wanted every possible architectural feature added to his house. Minarets, towers, arches, flying buttresses, ogees, widow's walks: You name it and it was on the building. But the exteriors we did see, while lovely, didn't say rich man's bizarre fantasy castle.

The mad scientist's laboratory was properly scary and creepy, however. We should have spent more time in there, rescuing terrified children or distressed damsels. Don't miss the examination chair from Satan's dentist, complete with restraints so the patient can't escape.

I enjoyed seeing the abusive ex-husband get his comeuppance at the hands of a man he would sneer at for merely existing. Since the evil ex was a doctor, he should have ended up in the mad scientist's lair and picked up a scalpel or two. Sadly, he didn't, leaving a wonderfully creepy and Gothic plot twist on the operating table.

This is one of ITV's best *Marple* episodes and, like *The Blue Geranium,* demonstrates the heights that scriptwriters running amok with Miss Marple short stories can achieve. Maybe when the remaining short stories are filmed at some future date, the writers will remember these episodes and be inspired.

General Information

Based on: "Greenshaw's Folly" (short story, 1956, and "The Thumb Mark of St. Peter," short story, 1928)
Run time: 1 hr., 29 min. **Subtitles:** Yes

Writer: Tim Whitnall **Director:** Sarah Harding

Cast

Julia McKenzie as Miss Marple
John Gordon Sinclair as Inspector Welch
Matt Willis as Sergeant Cayley

Kimberley Nixon as Louisa Oxley
Bobby Smalldridge as Archie Oxley
Oscar Pearce as Philip Oxley
Fiona Shaw as Miss Katherine Greenshaw
Julia Sawalha as Mrs. Cresswell
Sam Reid as Nat Fletcher
Vic Reeves as Cracken
Martin Compston as Alfred Pollock
Rufus Jones as Horace Bindler
Robert Glenister as Father Brophy
Judy Parfitt as Cicely Beauclerk
Joanna David as Grace Ritchie

Film Locations

Knebworth House, Stevenage, Hertfordshire (Greenshaw's Folly)
St. Joseph's College, London (orphanage)

Endless Night (2013)

Miss Marple haunts Gypsy's Acre in this uneven, illogical adaptation of love and Modernist architecture

Fidelity to text

Miss Marple shows up, trying to dominate a story not her own. The architect gets an unneeded name change, a more dramatic and implausible ending, and a drowned baby brother.

Quality of movie

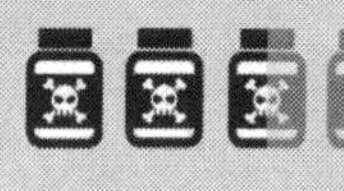

Enjoyable, but only when Miss Marple's not around. It's like a jigsaw puzzle assembled from different boxes. The images clash.

Endless Night is one of Agatha's later novels. It's told in the first person, a technique she didn't often use. The narrator is Mike Rogers, a working-class lad. He's wildly different from most of Agatha's characters who, if they aren't servants, are at least middle-class. It's a stunning novel, an elegy for lost love and lost chances that she burns down around you in the last two chapters and you have to rethink everything you've read up till that point.

One of the oddities about *Endless Night* is that it isn't a mystery until the climax. There's no detective onstage. It's clear from other people's actions (like Ellie's lawyer, Mr. Lippincott, or the local constable) that there's detecting going on, but Mike Rogers remains blissfully unaware it's taking place.

Stuffing Miss Marple into the story felt clumsy and strained at best; ridiculous at worst. One of the issues is why she shows up in Kingston Bishop in the first place. Keep in mind that *Endless Night* takes place over the course of a year at minimum and that's taking into account the very unreliable narrator.

The story opens with Mike drifting aimlessly, working a series of dead-end jobs. He ends up in Kingston Bishop looking at the sale notice about Gypsy's Acre. Who should he meet but Miss Marple? She's visiting a recently widowed friend, Marjory Phillpot. Major Phillpot, an important character in the novel, gets killed off and all of his scenes are assigned to Miss Marple. Mike looks very handsome in his chauffeur's uniform so it's not surprising that Miss Marple chats him up and again later, at the land auction.

Miss Marple keeps visiting Marjory Phillpot, even traveling overseas with her, just so she can keep running into Mike and pontificating about Gypsy's Acre, its curse, and the activities of the resident crazy old gypsy lady, Mrs. Lee.

The plot demands that Miss Marple keep turning up like a bad penny. She shows up when Mike meets Ellie. She runs into him in other villages. She meets him several more times in Kingston Bishop, with or without Marjory in tow since Marjory lives there and why else would Miss Marple be there? She shows up during the quick courtship but missed Mike meeting his childhood friend Robbie, now an architect dying of consumption. But she returns during the construction of the modernistic horror of the house.

Ellie Gutman
(*Joanna Vanderham*),
the kind heiress

Mike Rogers
(*Tom Hughes*),
the aspirational man

Greta Anderson
(*Birgitte Hjort Sørensen*),
the good friend

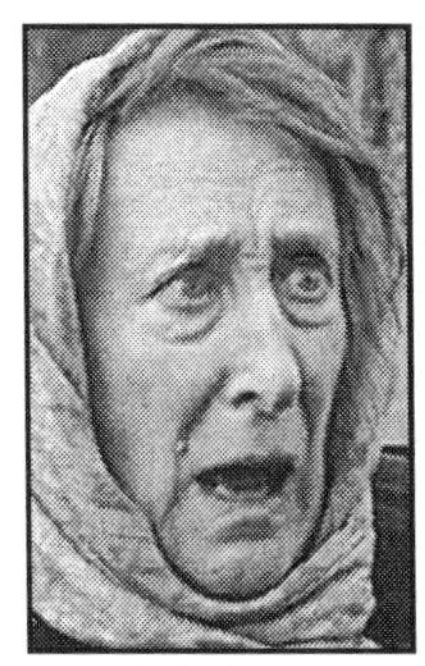

Mrs. Lee
(*Janet Henfrey*),
the vengeful gypsy

Robbie Hayman
(*Aneurin Barnard*),
the ailing architect

Mrs. Rogers
(*Tamzin Outhwaite*),
the knowing mother

General Information

Based on: *Endless Night* (novel, 1967)
Run time: 1 hr., 29 min. **Subtitles:** Yes

Writer: Kevin Elyot **Director:** David Moore

Cast

Julia McKenzie as Miss Marple
Wendy Craig as Marjorie Phillpot
Celyn Jones as Sergeant Keene

Tom Hughes as Mike Rogers
Joanna Vanderham as Ellie Gutman
Birgitte Hjort Sørensen as Greta Anderson
Aneurin Barnard as Robbie Hayman
Janet Henfrey as Mrs. Lee
Tamzin Outhwaite as Mrs. Rogers
Adam Wadsworth as Pete Hayman
Glynis Barber as Cora Van Stuyvesant
William Hope as Lippincott
Michael McKell as Frank Stanford
Rosalind Halstead as Claudia Hardcastle
Hugh Dennis as Dr. Shaw

Film Locations

The Homewood, Esher, Surrey (Gypsy's Acre)
Dorchester on Thames, Oxfordshire (Kingston Bishop)
High Street, Dorchester on Thames (Miss Marple meets Claudia Hardcastle)
Fingest, Buckinghamshire (Gypsy's Acre view)
Carlton Gardens, London (street scene)
Cliveden House, Taplow, Buckinghamshire (London park, interiors)
West Wycombe House, West Wycombe, Buckinghamshire (honeymoon hotel in Rome)
Zoroastrian Burial Ground, Brookwood, Surrey (Green-Wood Cemetery, New York)
The Red Lion, London (pub)
Duke of York Steps, London (street)

That house must have taken years to build after Ellie bought the property. First, The Towers, the original massive heap of crumbling historical stone, had to be demolished. Then the lot had to be cleared. Robbie the Architect had to draw up blueprints, get bids, secure permits, purchase lumber and cement, arrange for subcontractors, and supervise the building of the house. It's a modern pile of concrete slabs with acres of glass windows and flat roofs.

I guarantee the roof leaked within six months of completion, especially in England's rainy climate.

It's got glass curtain walls, ensuring that at night, the outside is a dark force pressing inward and during the day, only the isolation of the place promises any privacy. Being 1955 or so, the glass is single-pane, ensuring the building roasts in the day (greenhouse effect) and freezes at night. Winters would be dreadful, with even worse temperature swings.

Add the decorating, driveways, garages for cars, utility hookups and so forth and we're talking a long time. Yet there's Miss Marple hovering like an avenging Fury as though she moved from St. Mary Mead to Kingston Bishop just so she could spy on Mike and Ellie.

When she's back home, investigating other crimes, the movie works. When she intrudes for another extended visit with Marjory, it's like someone else directed the movie and the tone of wistful creepiness vanishes. That's an odd combination, I know, but it's hard to describe *Endless Night* without sounding wistful or creepy.

Eventually, Greta arrives. Miss Marple notices as does everyone else. Hot blondes in low-cut dresses have this effect. Soon afterwards, Mrs. Lee mysteriously vanishes and who investigates Mrs. Lee's unlocked cottage? Miss Marple, naturally, despite not being a resident of the village. She discovers the wad of cash big enough to choke a horse. Not the police. Not Mrs. Lee's distant relatives either, who pay no attention to a possible inheritance.

Then Ellie dies from a tragic accident. Miss Marple suspects murder because when pretty young women die around her, it's always murder. She snoops around even more, leading to the dramatic confrontation inside the folly between the murderer and Miss Marple. She reveals everything she knows: how, what, why, and when, including the hidden relationship between murderer and companion.

The murderer attempts to strangle Miss Marple. He's young and strong, and she's an old lady. It's not a fair fight. I was actually cheering him on because this wasn't her movie! It was his! She was interfering!

This episode of *Marple* is the last one ITV filmed. It would have made a macabre but appropriate ending to the series if Miss Marple got murdered sticking her nose into someone else's storyline.

But no. She escapes but not because she turns into Wonder Woman and develops the strength of ten because her heart is pure. It was a relief when the *deus ex machina* of Robbie the Architect arrived. He discovers to his shock and horror that his boyhood chum had not struggled to save his drowning little brother as everyone thought.

No, dear friend had murdered little brother over a wristwatch. In anger, Robbie the Architect torches the modernistic heap of glass curtain walls and poured concrete. This distracts the murderer from killing Miss Marple.

I was distracted too, trying to figure out what was burning in that pile because concrete and glass are not flammable like timber. The building had flames shooting out of it, yet from the party scenes it didn't seem like there were enough furnishings and wooden floors to burn with that kind of enthusiasm. Maybe Robbie the Architect lit the gas first. Only a gas explosion would make concrete burn and maybe not then. Arson of this kind, in this sort of structure, requires accelerants.

If you can separate Miss Marple from the rest of the movie, it works quite well. The mood is a nightmare-tinged dream. There are dark settings, modernist architecture, beautiful clothes, and scenery-chewing actors. Mike is compelling and you can see why Ellie fell for him and why his mother knows he can't be trusted.

But unless you're a Miss Marple fan, this *Endless Night* can feel true to its title. Stick with the 1972 adaptation where the scriptwriter didn't "improve" the novel by shoving the old lady where she was never meant to be.

II. Hercule Poirot

When her sister dared her to write a mystery, Agatha drew on her extensive reading and current events to create her detective. The Great War had begun, Germany had overrun Belgium, and refugees flooded her hometown of Torquay. She realized a retired Belgian detective was topical and sympathetic to readers. As a foreigner, he would be underestimated by villains and the police. She also needed a dopey Watson to act as the reader surrogate, so Agatha gave him Captain Hastings, an English partner who introduced Poirot everywhere.

Readers loved Poirot and demanded more of the fastidious little Belgium. But Agatha grew to detest his mannerisms and tics. To amuse herself, she paired him with Ariadne Oliver, her author avatar, who regularly denounced *her* detective, Sven Hjerson, as that manic, vegetable-eating Finn.

Never constrained by past stories, Agatha changed Poirot's habits to suit the plot. He'd crawl on the carpet hunting for clues in one story and scorned clues in favor of using psychology to find the killer in another.

The actors portraying Poirot have varied wildly, too. David Suchet kept Poirot faithful to Agatha's vision. He studied the stories closely and incorporated them into his acting. He remains most fans' favorite Poirot.

But Hollywood does as it pleases. Austin Trevor, the earliest Poirot, was too tall and mustache free. Tony Randall turned Poirot into a parody like Inspector Clouseau.

In others' hands, he'd be stern and unforgiving. He'd be tall and genial but exquisitely turned out. He'd be taller and a rumpled slob. He'd be a despairing ex-priest. He'd be an action hero, chasing suspects on a trestle bridge hundreds of feet above the gorge. He'd develop a sense of humor, growing square, mustachioed pumpkins. He'd solve crimes with a girl and a duck.

No matter the incarnation, he'd always remain the outsider and — as he'll tell you himself — the smartest person in the room.

From top: Austin Trevor, left, in *Lord Edgware Dies* (1934), Tony Randall in *The Alphabet Murders* (1965), Albert Finney in *Murder on the Orient Express* (1974),Kôtarô Satomi in *The Mystery of End House* (J-2002), Konstantin Raikin in *Poirot's Failure* (R-2002), and John Malkovich in *The ABC Murders* (2018)

David Suchet as "Mad Dog" the cat burglar in *The Veiled Lady* (1990)

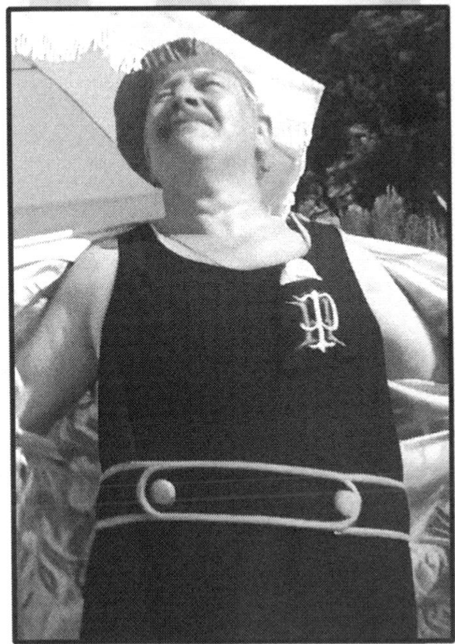
Peter Ustinov in *Evil Under the Sun* (1982)

Sir Kenneth Branagh in *Murder on the Orient Express* (2017)

Like his creator, Hercule Poirot has traveled the world, from his home base in London to Egypt, Iraq, and the Mediterranean. Although he has many acquaintances and a good friend in Hastings, he lives fundamentally alone with his little gray cells.

Mansai Nomura in *The Murder of Kurido* (2018)

Alfred Molina in *Murder on the Orient Express* (2001)

Lord Edgware Dies (1934)

This early Christie was marred by wooden acting, boring direction, and miscasting Poirot and Hastings

This was interesting. Interesting is a good word because it doesn't imply a value of "good." Merely … interesting. It's a curiosity.

This is currently the second-oldest filmed Agatha Christie adaptation, the 1929 German silent, *Adventures, Inc.* being older. All of the others are either lost or buried deep inside a U.S. Army warehouse next to the Ark of the Covenant.

This film demonstrates all of the reasons Agatha didn't care for movie adaptations of her fiction, although she did like movies based on her plays. She wrote plenty of them, after all. However, her plays were written to fit within a set running time and were designed to work on a stage. Everything a novel needs (interior monologues, settings, and character descriptions) is jettisoned by a playwright.

Converting a novel to a movie requires the studio to hack the novel into shreds to make it fit onto a screen. Then the director casts whomever the studio wants to promote, despite having far more capable and appropriate actors available.

Which brings us to Austin Trevor, the actor playing Hercule Poirot. He's too darned tall. He was one of the tallest men on screen. He looked nothing like our image of Poirot, whether it be Peter Ustinov (6 feet but he made it work), Albert Finney, David Suchet, Sir Kenneth Branagh, or even John Malkovich. Many other actors played Poirot over the years but they, too, look more like Poirot than Austin Trevor did. Some of his woodenness was an artifact of moviemaking at the time, but not all of it. He's as thin as a beanpole and, unforgivably, lacks Poirot's signature mustache and intelligence.

Fidelity to text

Two major plot points were skipped but the rest of the plot got crammed into 80 minutes. Austin Trevor must be the worst Poirot ever. The actor playing Hastings — short, round, and with a mustache — fits the Poirot image much better.

Quality of movie

For an 80-minute film, it drags. The pace is glacial. The actors seem made of wood. The action never goes outside of a building. The sets look similar, making sure the audience gets confused as to where the story is taking place.

Richard Cooper, portraying Capt. Arthur Hastings, was equally miscast. He displays Poirot's round, short silhouette and sports a mustache. In fact, I thought he was Poirot until both actors came to life and began acting. Trevor gave us a bad Belgian accent to indicate who he was, but otherwise nothing about him said Poirot.

As Hastings, Cooper played the buffoon in virtually every scene, but alas, he did not steal those scenes. Hastings started as a parody of Watson but Agatha never wrote him as a complete idiot, only a partial one. Her Captain Hastings never walked into walls, while

Lady Edgware
(*Jane Carr*),
the unhappy actress

Lord Edgware
(*C.V. France*),
the unhappy peer

Geraldine Edgware
(*Sophie Stewart*),
the unhappy daughter

Capt. Roland Marsh
(*Michael Shepley*),
the feckless heir

Bryan Martin
(*Leslie Perrins*),
the jealous actor

Inspector Japp
(*John Turnbull*),
the thick investigator

this Hastings does. Of all the adaptations I've seen, this Hastings takes the cake for idiocy, even more than poor Robert Morley in *The Alphabet Murders* (1965).

If you know the plot of *Lord Edgware Dies* (published in America as *Thirteen at Dinner*), you'll see that after making allowances for an extremely short running time much of it made it onscreen. Most of the minor characters, including the Dowager Duchess of Merton, who objected to the Duke's plan to wed Jane Wilkinson (Lady Edgware), vanish without a trace. Oddly, the Covent Garden taxi driver gets several minutes of screen time, allowing the director to make Hastings the butt of another joke.

That was a poor choice because it forced the screenwriter to omit two crucial points. The first was why Lord Edgware had to die. Bill had to ask me and since I'd read the book, I knew. Bad scriptwriter! Bad scriptwriter! We're going to drag you back to scriptwriting school! Learn that some people adhere to their religious values. Merry widows are acceptable, but gay divorcées are not.

The second major omission was how Poirot came to realize who stabbed Lord Edgware in the back of the neck with a corn knife. That entire sequence, involving the Judgment of Paris, was skipped but it's crucial to understanding how Poirot worked out the solution.

The Judgment of Paris is also crucial in understanding why victim number three had to die, stabbed by the same corn knife.

After watching the film, I googled corn knives. A corn knife never shows up in this film, so I kept envisioning a machete used to chop down cornstalks. Back in 1934, movies didn't show murder victims sprawled on the floor in pools of blood with knives sticking out of them. At least the classy movies didn't.

Understanding what a corn knife is helps to understand how the murderer killed the victims. The novel doesn't go into gruesome detail (Agatha never does) but she does explain how the murderer knew how to wield a corn knife effectively and not for its intended purpose. And it fits! It's perfectly in keeping with the murderer's character.

General Information

Based on: *Lord Edgware Dies* (novel, 1933)
Run time: 1 hr., 20 min. **Subtitles:** No

Writer: H. Fowler Mear
Director: Henry Edwards

Cast

Austin Trevor as Hercule Poirot
Richard Cooper as Captain Hastings
John Turnbull as Inspector Japp

Jane Carr as Jane Wilkinson, Lady Edgware
C.V. France as Lord Edgware
Sophie Stewart as Geraldine Edgware
Michael Shepley as Capt. Roland Marsh
Leslie Perrins as Bryan Martin
Esme Percy as Duke of Merton
Phyllis Morris as Alice

A turn-of-the-century corn knife was used to shave corns off the feet. They have a long, narrow, razor-sharp blade, the better to shave off layers of bad skin without removing healthy skin. It's home surgery on your feet. They were common in England so Agatha assumed when she wrote "corn knife," readers would understand her.

Because I had a different knife in mind, I wondered how the murderer smuggled a machete around in 1930s London. The murderer didn't. The passage of decades and medical techniques concealed the past. And, demonstrating poor choices on the director's part, we never see a corn knife so we don't know how easily one can be smuggled inside and wielded at the last moment, surprising the victim.

Agatha also assumes that you, dear reader, recognize the story of the Judgment of Paris. Paris is the handsome young son of Priam of Troy. He has to decide which of the goddesses (Hera, Athena, and Aphrodite) are the most beautiful. The vain goddesses bribe him because each fears being thought less beautiful than the others. Hera offers being king of men, Athena victory in war, and Aphrodite offers Helen of Troy. He likes Aphrodite's bribe the best and from that decision we move on to the *Iliad*, followed by the *Odyssey*, and then the *Aeneid*.

The Judgment of Paris works beautifully in the novel. It demonstrates who studied hard in college and who got her education from *Vogue* magazine. It reveals hidden identities. It's a crime that the scriptwriter omitted it entirely because without this scene, the final murder and the unveiling don't make much sense. Again, Agatha didn't like the movie versions of her novels because she didn't like watching her carefully constructed plots get butchered to suit some director's "vision."

Hercule Poirot: Why are you so anxious to get rid of Lord Edgware?
Lady Edgware: 'Cos I want to get married again.
Captain Hastings: Surely a divorce is the thing to go for. It's as easy as buying a pound of tea nowadays.

Overall, this was … interesting. I wouldn't watch it again. I am much more interested in seeing David Suchet's version. You can bet I'll be looking for the scene with the Judgment of Paris. It will also be refreshing to watch a Poirot who matches my mental image of Poirot instead of a long, lean, rangy, tall man who's been shaved within an inch of his life, being closely shadowed by a clone of Tweedledee.

The Alphabet Murders (1965)

A comedy director turns Poirot into a Belgian version of Clouseau in this murderous misfire of a film

Dear Reader, Bill and I took one for the team, sitting through this turkey so you won't have to endure it.

I wasn't expecting anything stellar like *Witness for the Prosecution* (1957), but I did expect to be entertained. Maybe even laugh. Tony Randall can act, so can Robert Morley, and they have impeccable comic timing. Their talent wasn't on display here.

The director of this travesty is Frank Tashlin. He's a Renaissance man, capable of animating and directing Looney Tunes cartoons as well as writing and directing live-action movies. He made numerous well-regarded comedies, including six movies with Jerry Lewis. Where was that talent? Not here. I'm not sure who thought Tashlin was a good choice for directing a mystery since that's not the kind of movie he made.

Although … oh dear God. The light dawneth. Somebody wanted to turn Hercule Poirot into Inspector Clouseau, who appeared in *The Pink Panther* (1963) and *A Shot in the Dark* (1964). One is Belgian, one is French, but both cultures eat horse meat so they're the same, right? That's an actual joke in the film, by the way. Just in case you were still planning on ignoring my rating and seeing for yourself.

This explains so much! Such as why the film opens with Tony Randall on a movie studio's backlot talking directly to the audience *as himself* and then turning into Hercule Poirot. If you're going to break the fourth wall so brazenly, daring the audience, the movie had better be funny. Which this one is not.

It also explains why Poirot keeps telling everyone the mysterious blonde is six feet tall. That would be Anita Ekberg. She plays Amanda Beatrice Cross (get it? Huh? Huh?), woman of mystery. She's also five foot seven. Other actors tower over her, including her shrink, Duncan Doncaster (Guy Rolfe, six foot four) and paramour, Franklin Clarke (James Villiers, also six foot four). Tony Randall is five foot eight so she's not towering over *him*. Since she regularly wears flats (the better to run away from the terrible dialog she's forced to recite) it's impossible to accept that the brilliant Poirot misjudges her height so badly. But if Randall is playing Poirot as a version of Clouseau — shudder — then his inability to estimate height should come as no surprise.

Except that Poirot is frequently the most competent

Fidelity to text

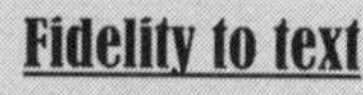

Some plot elements of *The A.B.C. Murders* remain. Otherwise, it's unrecognizable. Even Hastings got a major rewrite, turning him into a bungling Robert Morley.

Quality of movie

Dreadful. Suffer through this, and you'll understand why Agatha refused to sell more film rights for years.

Amanda B. Cross (*Anita Ekberg*), the beautiful lure

Hastings (*Robert Morley*), the hapless helper

Duncan Doncaster (*Guy Rolfe*), the networking shrink

Franklin Clarke (*James Villiers*), the risk-taking scion

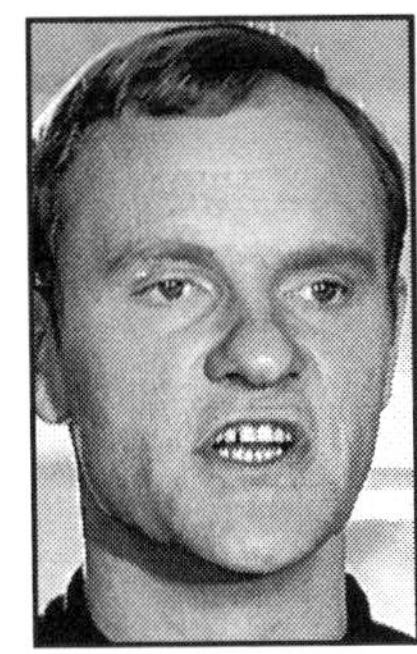
Don Fortune (*Julian Glover*), the angry boyfriend

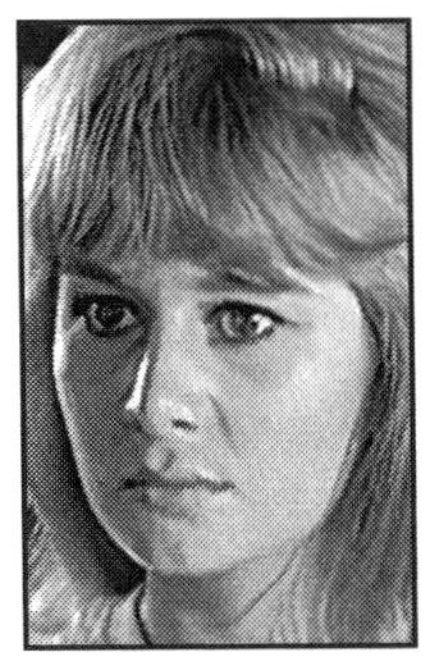
Betty Barnard (*Grazina Frame*), the bowling girlfriend

person in the room. Watch him in the bowling alley throwing strike after strike (you didn't know that Hercule Poirot bowled, did you? Or that he wore casual, long-sleeved pullovers?). Then, after being dared by another bowler, he throws two strikes simultaneously in adjacent lanes!

So why does he keep getting Anita Ekberg's height wrong? Because the script made him stupid when it's necessary for the plot.

Robert Morley is in a similar fix. He plays Captain Hastings. He's never met Poirot before. Instead, his Hastings is an incompetent member of some vague British secret service, trying to get Poirot out of Britain and back to Belgium. His reasoning was illogical, he's an ineffectual buffoon, and his antics are supposed to be funny. Is it funny to watch Robert Morley run out of a spa, wearing only a towel, and meet a marching band playing "Rule, Britannia?" I didn't think so, yet I could see how the scene should have worked. The audience should have been rolling on the floor instead of rooting around in their popcorn. Bob Hope would have made the joke work. So would Jerry Lewis, who was never above making a fool of himself to get a laugh.

Robert Morley, on the other hand, is better served by comedies of the absurd. He's not the slapstick comedian this movie needed.

Randall and Morley's miscasting was made even more obvious by the rest of the cast. The film is loaded with longtime character actors, all of whom performed much better than the stars. Notice in particular Austin Trevor in his last role as Judson, Sir Carmichael Clarke's butler. Trevor played Hercule Poirot in three early films: *Alibi* (1931), *Black Coffee* (1931), and *Lord Edgeware Dies* (1934). The first two are lost, but the third remains and you can see that, like Tony Randall, Austin Trevor was woefully miscast as Poirot. But as an imperturbable butler coping with craziness, he's spot-on.

There's also the leering. Yes, there's male nudity. Both Poirot and Hastings wear nothing more than a towel. They both should wear more. But that's not where the camera lingers. No, it pans slowly across every female bosom within eyeshot. Is some dame showing her décolletage? The cameraman dives in. Is a lady wearing a tight sweater? The camera lingers. As an added bonus, all the art on the sets is of nude women, mostly nude women, or statues of nude women. Because it's culture, it's okay to pan across the bare nipples. Bill didn't have an issue with this artistic choice, but I did. It wasn't necessary! Plus, it made the plodding plot drag even more.

This is a 90-minute film, and you'll count every one of them as they lurch past. If the talented people who made this movie had done a good job, at least 20 minutes of what's onscreen would have been replaced with actual, you know, plot. With explanatory dialog so the audience isn't left guessing why characters show up apparently at random. Maybe they were the producer's friends and needed the money.

I will admit that the camera work is astonishing. One amazingly framed shot after another. Terrific, atmospheric lighting that made the most of the settings. Very dramatic. But I shouldn't be noticing the cinematography! That's not why I go to the movies. I go to be entertained, not ooh and aah over the mise-en-scène. I also shouldn't be paying attention to the bright, bouncy score that made sure — wink, wink, nudge, nudge — I knew when to laugh or gasp. It was yet another irritation.

Thank God Miss Marple and Mr. Stringer showed up. Yep, this film put Miss Marple and Hercule Poirot together, although only for a few minutes and for the purpose of making a joke. Say what you will about Margaret Rutherford as Miss Marple, she's a much better fit with Agatha than Tony Randall is. She wouldn't have taken nearly as long to solve the murder but then, her scriptwriters didn't make her stupid.

There is only one reason to sit through this film and that's for the sake of completeness. Or you could take your cue from Agatha herself on the subject:

"*The A.B.C. Murders* I was not allowed to see. My friends and publishers told me the agony would be too great."

General Information

Based on: *The A.B.C. Murders* (novel, 1936)
Run time: 1 hr., 30 min. **Subtitles:** No

Writers: David Pursall and Jack Seddon
Director: Frank Tashlin

Cast

Tony Randall as Hercule Poirot
Robert Morley as Hastings
Maurice Denham as Japp

Anita Ekberg as Amanda Beatrice Cross
Guy Rolfe as Duncan Doncaster
Grazina Frame as Betty Barnard
Julian Glover as Don Fortune
Sheila Reid as Mrs. Fortune
Cyril Luckham as Sir Carmichael Clarke
Sheila Allen as Lady Diane Clarke
James Villiers as Franklin Clarke
Austin Trevor as Judson
Clive Morton as "X"
Richard Wattis as Wolf
David Lodge as Sergeant
Patrick Newell as Cracknell
Alison Seebohm as Miss Sparks
Windsor Davies as Dragbot
Margaret Rutherford as Miss Jane Marple
Stringer Davis as Mr. Stringer

Film Locations

14 Savile Row, Mayfair, London (Poirot's tailor)
Clifford Street, Westminster, London (Clifford Street Baths)
12-16 Buckingham Palace Road, Westminster (Hastings chases Amanda from the sauna)
Uxbridge Police Station, London (Hastings visits police station)
Wembley Stadium Bowl, London (Poirot bowling)
Hyde Park, London (Poirot on horseback)
Victoria Square, Belgravia, London (Betty Bernard's flat)
Heathrow Airport, London

Murder on the Orient Express (1974)

All aboard as an international cast rides the legendary train in pursuit of a child killer who got away

Fidelity to text

It's just about perfect except for Poirot. This version lets him get persuaded a little too easily. He's normally dedicated to justice, and the film didn't show his crisis of conscience well.

Quality of movie

So many stars! So much talent! They each deserved more screen time with less time devoted to scenes of steam locomotives chugging through the Balkans.

Wow. What a great movie from start to finish. I loved the lengthy opening scene getting the Orient Express ready for its journey from Istanbul to Paris. It's time that could have been spent showing off the stars, but it showed the amount of work involved getting a luxury train ready.

The crowds in the Istanbul train station were equally fascinating. The director, Sidney Lumet, demonstrated that Istanbul is the crossroads between East and West, the center of Eurasia, visited by people from around the world. It sets up why such a wildly disparate group of travelers would be on the train in the first place.

After that, I could have done with fewer scenes of the Orient Express traveling through the Balkans. One wooded, snowy mountainside looks like another. That was time that could have been better spent giving each of the stars room to develop their characters and set the stage for murderous doings.

I could have skipped the sequence in the weirdly empty Istanbul luxury restaurant too, despite the serious eye-candy decor on display, complete with live band. Yes, it sets up Poirot meeting the Orient Express' director, M. Bianchi, and thus getting a seat on a fully-booked train. But it could have been compressed. Worse, I just can't buy Hercule Poirot tearing up a menu and tossing the shreds onto the table and floor. Poirot would not make a mess. Nor would he deliberately make a mess and expect someone else to clean it up.

I suppose what this does is show that Sidney Lumet and Albert Finney's Hercule Poirot is not like the others. Perhaps that's why this Poirot didn't seem too conflicted over which of his two deductions got chosen. Hercule Poirot is not a fan of vigilante justice, no matter how well-motivated or the crime being avenged, yet that disapproval didn't come through as well as it could have.

Fortunately, the other stars were perfect for their roles. Let's begin with Lauren Bacall as Mrs. Hubbard. She gets all the best lines. She's funny, she's sharp, and she doesn't hesitate to snap at anyone, including the Princess Natalia Dragomiroff. The elderly Russian princess should be above sniping at noisy Americans but flamboyant Mrs. Hubbard gets under her skin.

Mrs. Hubbard (*Lauren Bacall*), the ugly American

Col. Arbuthnot (*Sean Connery*), the India hand

Greta (*Ingrid Bergman*), the earnest missionary

McQueen (*Anthony Perkins*), the secretive secretary

Princess Dragomiroff (*Wendy Hiller*), the old-line aristocrat

Ratchett (*Richard Widmark*), the fearful gangster

Mrs. Hubbard is the perfect annoying American tourist; so perfect and so typical that she's outrageous.

Her character was changed from the novel because, hey, it's Lauren Bacall. She's relying on the story spread about that she's ill and in seclusion because of the Armstrong tragedy. That's why she can assume no one will recognize she's the famous actress, Linda Arden. In the novel, Agatha spells out that Mrs. Hubbard wasn't just loud and wearing bedazzled clothes. She put on some serious weight, making it harder for her fans to recognize her. In the movie – it's subtle – it's clear that Poirot does recognize her when he comments on her "playing her part" and asks "Why did you bring the dagger from the place?" Poirot had watched her portray Lady Macbeth – the dagger line is from the Scottish tragedy – and he remembered.

As the Russian Princess Dragomiroff, Wendy Hiller is very much a Grande Dame, and she couldn't possibly be involved in anything as plebeian as the murder of some American gangster. She's accompanied by a German lady's maid, and a pair of Pekinese dogs, beautifully trained. I was impressed with how well her dogs ate in the dining car. They had better manners than most of the passengers, I'm sure.

Oooh, there's Sean Connery as Col. Arbuthnot. Very British, very stiff upper-lip, yet he, like a true gentleman, betrays himself when he leaps to Mary Debenham's rescue. Poirot wasn't surprised; he'd already seen them in a clinch on the ferryboat to Istanbul. As a professional detective and astute observer of human nature, you can trust Poirot to peek into keyholes and eavesdrop on conversations because he never knows when it's going to be useful. And once again, he's right! Spying casually on the British couple pays off when they claim they're complete strangers on the Orient Express. Miss Debenham is played by Vanessa Redgrave, and you can tell she helped plan the sting. She's far too competent and self-contained to stand on the sidelines and wait.

Ingrid Bergman plays Greta the missionary. She won an Oscar for the role. She perfectly embodied a damaged, distraught woman who found God as a result of tragedy. However, I didn't like Poirot's deduction that Greta is lying because she didn't know the word "emolument." That means salary or fee for professional services. I say this because my mother would have done what Greta did: smile tightly because she didn't understand the word and then look it up later in the dictionary. My mother would not have asked what that strange word meant because asking made her look stupid. No heavily accented immigrant trying to fit in is going to make it harder on themselves, so no, I don't accept this clue, either from Agatha or from Poirot.

General Information

Based on: *Murder on the Orient Express* (novel, 1934)
Run time: 2 hr., 8 min. **Subtitles:** Yes

Writer: Paul Dehn **Director:** Sidney Lumet

Cast

Albert Finney as Hercule Poirot
Martin Balsam as Bianchi

Richard Widmark as Ratchett
Anthony Perkins as Hector McQueen
John Gielgud as Beddoes
Sean Connery as Col. Arbuthnot
Vanessa Redgrave as Mary Debenham
Lauren Bacall as Mrs. Hubbard
Ingrid Bergman as Greta
Michael York as Count Andrenyi
Jacqueline Bisset as Countess Andrenyi
Wendy Hiller as Princess Dragomiroff
Rachel Roberts as Hildegarde
Jean-Pierre Cassel as Pierre
Colin Blakely as Hardman
Denis Quilley as Foscarelli
George Coulouris as Doctor
Vernon Dobtcheff as Concierge
Jeremy Lloyd as A.D.C.
John Moffatt as Chief Attendant
David de Keyser as Ticket Collector (voice)
Leon Lissek as Dining Car Steward
Robert Rietty as Loudspeaker
George Silver as Chef
Leslie Soden as Turkish hotel pianist
Vic Tablian as Hawker
Nubar Terziyan as Traveling Salesman

Film Locations

High Canons, Hertfordshire (Armstrong house)
Salacak, Üsküdar, Istanbul (Bosporus ferry)
Gare de l'Est, Paris (railway station)
Montbenoît, France (train bridge)
Maisons-du-Bois-Lièvremont, France (train in snow)

These stars are just the beginning of the all-star cast. Sidney Lumet chose actors and actresses the public already knew to make it easier to tell the story. He understood it would be much easier to keep everyone straight, especially vital if a star only has a few minutes to leave an impression. It's too easy for the audience to get mixed up with a large cast. It worked for me: I was always able to tell everyone apart. I can't say that for many movies that have too many anonymous blondies and Ken doll knock-offs who look alike in their plastic prettiness. I like variety in my casting, and I got it here.

Unfortunately, too many scenes of trains chugging down the tracks meant not enough screen time for the stars, especially Mr. Hardman (Colin Blakely) and Foscarelli (Denis Quilley). They lit up the screen when they appeared. I especially enjoyed Michal York as Count Andrenyi and Jacqueline Bisset as his countess. Between the two of them, York and Bisset got about 10 minutes screen time. I wanted more, but the movie was already two hours and eight minutes long.

Back in 1974, they didn't make these nearly three hour slog-fests that blockbusters all seem to be today. This film could have been longer, and it would have still zipped along. Or Sidney Lumet could have filmed fewer scenes of trains rolling down the track.

No matter, don't miss this version of *Murder on the Orient Express*. Agatha liked it, and you can't get a better recommendation than that.

Death on the Nile (1978)

An all-star sequel to *Orient Express* sends a spurned fiancée after her man during a leisurely voyage up the Nile

I enjoy leisurely movies that don't hit me over the head with explosions and frenetic action. If you insist on a bang a minute, then you might think this version is slow. With one major exception, I did not.

The pacing was calm yet inexorable, giving each member of the big cast time to come to life. The village yokels could comment on Linnet Ridgeway's fabulous wealth and looks. Barnstable, Ridgeway's new butler, learned how demanding the new mistress of the manor would be. The impression — and it's correct — is that Linnet Ridgeway is smart, capable, doesn't suffer fools gladly, demands what she wants out of life, and has little patience for anyone who doesn't dance to her tune.

But Linnet Ridgeway doesn't have anyone who genuinely likes her until we meet her friend Jackie. In the novel, we learn Jackie and Linnet met at school and became dear friends. Money didn't come between them, despite Jackie's poverty and Linnet's wealth.

We think it shows a human side to Linnet, until Jackie asks Linnet to hire her fiancé, Simon Doyle, because he needs a job so they can marry. Then, sadly, Linnet reveals her true nature. She's Linnet Ridgeway, she gets what she wants, and she wants her best friend's man.

There's a beautiful scene in the novel where Linnet, when broken-hearted Jackie is stalking her and Simon, asks Poirot for help. Poirot responds with the parable of Nathan telling King David of the rich man who took the poor man's ewe and slaughtered it to feed his guest. Like King David, Linnet doesn't want to hear that she could have chosen not to steal someone else's true love. She wanted what she wanted and justified it to herself — and Poirot — after the fact.

It's a shame this scene did not make it into the movie. I would have preferred that the director cut a few minutes of leisurely Nile scenery from onboard the paddle ship *Memnon* (starring as the S.S. *Karnak*) and film Poirot's diamond-hard assessment of Linnet's character. It would have gone a long way to explaining more of Jackie's resentment and the plan she concocted. It was also a nice demonstration of the bubble Linnet lived in.

Linnet's lack of empathy shows up in other areas as well. Yes, she does the technically correct thing for Louise, the maid, but Louise didn't think so. Yes,

Fidelity to text

It's very close to the novel, while making allowances for taking a complex story and simplifying it into a coherent movie. The important people remain and a cobra was added, although how the murderer found a cobra on board a ship is a mystery.

Quality of movie

Gorgeous Egyptian settings, an all-star cast, great lines, and a leisurely cruise up the Nile to enjoy them. What more do you need?

Linnet Ridgeway (*Lois Chiles*), the demanding heiress

Simon Doyle (*Simon MacCorkindale*), the fickle husband

Jacqueline De Bellefort (*Mia Farrow*), the jilted girlfriend

Salome Otterbourne (*Angela Lansbury*), the soused novelist

Mrs. Van Schuyler (*Bette Davis*), the acidic socialite

Colonel Race (*David Niven*), the capable detective

Linnet's lawyers are cheating her. Yes, the German doctor might be a quack, based on what he did to a friend of Linnet's and thus her ruining him and his clinic. Yes, Linnet's father ruined Miss Bowers' family, forcing her to act as a dogsbody to the harridan Mrs. Van Schuyler (the two were played by Maggie Smith and Bette Davis and they get some of the best lines in the film). Yes, novelist Salome Otterbourne (a terrific Angela Lansbury) libels Linnet.

Watching Linnet in action made me think "she had it coming," but Poirot would disagree. As he will tell you, he disapproves of murder. People shouldn't be killed for being world-class entitled jerks. But it's equally clear that if Linnet had been a decent friend, she wouldn't have been shot to death at close range. She'd still have to manage her maid, lawyer, assorted lawsuits, libelous novels, and angry relatives but she'd be alive to manage them. She had more than enough money to throw at those problems and make them go away.

Other than that missing scene, everything works. The all-star cast performs at the top of their game.

First and foremost, the paddle ship *Memnon* stars as the Nile cruise ship *Karnak*. What a beautiful, luxuriously appointed ship, although I doubt the crew below decks got gorgeous paneling and plush carpets in their quarters. She was built to sail in calm waters as evidenced by all the glass bric-à-brac on the tables and at the bar. If the Mediterranean Sea is a lake compared to the Atlantic, sailing the Nile must be like riding on well-greased train tracks. Not so much as a ripple disturbs the ship. We even catch glimpses of the staff it takes to run the ship and cater to the luxury tourist trade.

I wasn't sure how I'd feel about Peter Ustinov as Poirot. He doesn't fit the mental image I've developed, particularly after watching David Suchet. But he had to be better than Tony Randall or Austin Trevor.

It turns out that Ustinov makes an admirable Poirot. He was witty, sly, observant, clever, and thought on his feet without ever mugging for the camera. I've got five more Ustinov outings ahead of me so I hope he can keep up his performance.

Ustinov is ably assisted by David Niven as Colonel Race. Agatha never did much with Colonel Race, which was a pity. A dashing adventurer with a hidden past? Give me more! The added scene with the cobra showed a flash of what Colonel Race could have been. He doesn't hesitate to whip out his sword-cane to slay the cobra and save Poirot. Were you surprised Colonel Race carries a sword-cane and knows how to use it? I wasn't. He's a crack shot too, but he knows which is the correct weapon to use. A sword is handier with a cobra than a pistol when everyone on board is already on edge.

Other than Colonel Race and Poirot, this is really an actress' movie. Simon Doyle, commie Ferguson, quack Doctor Bessner, and shyster Pennington paled in comparison to the ladies who chewed the scenery with gusto.

And the clothes! Anthony Powell won a well-deserved Oscar for his designs, and he made sure each actress stood out and their clothes expressed their essential nature. He draped Salome Otterbourne in scarves, a turban, far too much costume jewelry, and capacious handbags in which to stow likker. Mrs. Van Schuyler was swathed in elaborately overdone lace dresses and a black ribbon choker three inches wide to conceal her crepey neck. Miss Bowers, her companion/warden, wore wonderful mannish outfits that perfectly expressed her no-nonsense attitude. The pair of them made me think of Gertrude Stein (1874-1946) and Alice B. Toklas (1877-1967), although I don't think that was intentional. Linnet Ridgeway flashed across the screen in the most expensive clothing — that liquid silver dress! — while Jackie was more subdued and obviously poorer. Rosalie Otterbourne did her best to compensate for her mother's flashiness. Compared to the other women, she approached dowdiness with a hint of genteel poverty. Even the maid, Louise, was well-turned out in a very smart uniform.

The climax was a bit truncated compared to the novel, but everything you needed was there. Motivation, resentment, rationalization, and the willingness to do anything for love all played their part. Wow. Don't miss this one.

General Information

Based on: *Death on the Nile* (novel, 1937)
Run time: 2 hr., 20 min. **Subtitles:** Yes

Writer: Anthony Shaffer
Director: John Guillermin

Cast

Peter Ustinov as Hercule Poirot
David Niven as Colonel Race

Lois Chiles as Linnet Ridgeway
Simon MacCorkindale as Simon Doyle
Mia Farrow as Jacqueline De Bellefort
Jane Birkin as Louise Bourget
Jon Finch as Mr. Ferguson
Angela Lansbury as Mrs. Salome Otterbourne
Olivia Hussey as Rosalie Otterbourne
I.S. Johar as Manager of The Karnak
Bette Davis as Mrs. Van Schuyler
Maggie Smith as Miss Bowers
George Kennedy as Andrew Pennington
Jack Warden as Dr. Bessner
Harry Andrews as Barnstaple
Sam Wanamaker as Rockford

Film Locations

Hambledon, Buckinghamshire (opening village)
Compton Wynyates, Warwickshire (country house)
The Great Pyramids, Giza, Egypt
The Sphinx, Giza Plateau, Giza, Egypt
Nile River, Egypt
Hotel Pullman Cataract, Aswan, Egypt (Old Cataract Hotel)
Abu Simbel Temple, Abu Simbel, Egypt
Karnak Temple, Luxor, Egypt
Sharia Abtal el Tahrir, Aswan, Egypt
Temple of Amun, Karnak Temple, Luxor, Egypt

Evil Under the Sun (1982)

On an island resort, many wanted to do in the Broadway musical star, except everyone also had an alibi

Fidelity to text

The usual condensing of characters, revising the location, plus a sex-change and new occupations to ramp up the show biz aspects. But it's all in service to the story.

Quality of movie

This was a terrific bitch-fest: sharp, witty, and caustic. Everyone got in great lines. Agatha's plot, however, didn't quite work.

Before we dig into the meat of Peter Ustinov's second outing as Hercule Poirot, let me apologize for not figuring out which classic ship appeared as Horace Blatt's yacht. She's a lovely ship with clean lines and just the right size (in 1935 or so) for a cockney millionaire to own and show off. These days, millionaires demand mega-yachts to forcibly demonstrate to us peasants how rich they are. They have no sense of restraint, despite mega-yachts not being able to moor in charming island coves like those in the Balearic Islands and why else would you own a yacht other than to cruise between charming, scenic islands? There are many boats in this movie, all correct for the period, from paddle boats to local ferries to a gorgeous, vintage wooden speedboat to Sir Horace's yacht. Alas, they remain unnamed.

With that out of the way, there's plenty of eye candy to go around. Maggie Smith as Daphne Castle and Diana Rigg as Arlena Marshall are just the beginning and my, how those women despise each other. You can tell they've got a long history between them. Both of them worked their way up from the chorus, using similar methods, but Daphne got the better deal. As the King of Tyrania's mistress, she got his summer palace when he married someone else, for "services rendered." That turned her into an exclusive innkeeper catering to the rich. Hard work to be sure, but better than relying on a string of fickle men as you age and your looks fade.

That appears to be Arlena Stuart Marshall's fate. She's a former Broadway star, married to a man she doesn't love, stepmother to a daughter she despises (the feeling is mutual) and chasing after handsome, younger men. She's not very bright, and she's a bag full of neediness, including the intense desire to be the center of attention at all times. She is — as Poirot observes — the type of woman whom men care for easily and of whom they easily tire. Horace Blatt proves it; he had a brief affair with Arlena and it's not her he wants back; it's the diamond he gave her.

However, Arlena escaped her fate of becoming an aging and embarrassing caricature of herself by getting murdered. She has a torrid affair with the wrong man, he steals from her, and she doesn't realize what happened. But he does.

Arlena Stuart Marshall (*Diana Rigg*), the capricious star

Kenneth Marshall (*Denis Quilley*), the faithful husband

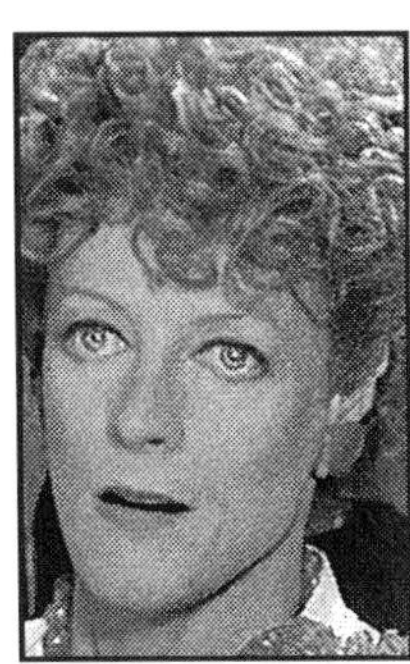

Daphne Castle (*Maggie Smith*), the mistress hotelier

Rex Brewster (*Roddy McDowall*), the gossipy biographer

Patrick Redfern (*Nicholas Clay*), the roving husband

Christine Redfern (*Jane Birkin*), the mousy wife

Since Arlena Marshall is a Broadway singing star, the script ran with that notion and many of the changes to the text reflect Arlena's show business past. Most of the background music was Cole Porter, and Daphne and Arlena sing a show-stopping version of Porter's "You're The Top."

Another change was turning Miss Brewster, spinster, into Rex Brewster, writer, raconteur, and man-about-town. Does he make you think of Noël Coward, getting all the best lines? He should. Like the rest of the cast, it's clear Roddy McDowall had a blast. Arlena left Rex hanging high and dry when she refused to sign the release for the lurid, scandalous, factual tell-all biography he wrote about her.

Similarly, the Gardeners are made over into a pair of Broadway producers, chasing after Arlena to star in their next production. She can open a show like nobody else. They know because Arlena starred in their last show. It opened to rave reviews and boffo box office and then a few weeks later, she walked out, leaving the cast in the lurch and the Gardeners in debt to the rafters. They need Arlena desperately to recoup their losses, but is she interested? Not a chance.

Then there's Patrick Redfern. He's a handsome man and well-aware of it, so Arlena doesn't have to work hard at chasing him. It's a mutual attraction on full, immoral display, much to the dismay of her husband, Kenneth, and his wife Christine and the caustic amusement of the rest of the guests. Is Kenneth happy? Not at all. Is Christine amused? Not one bit. Arlena makes both of them angry and bitter.

Arlena makes an enemy of almost everyone she encounters, so it's no surprise when she is murdered. The question is who did it, when everyone is proved to have an alibi for when the murder must have occurred.

This is where the plot didn't work for me.

The murder takes place on a very tight timetable. The murderers have to work closely together, coordinating their actions along with their unimpeachable and unsuspecting witnesses to make the scheme work. When I read the novel, I didn't have a problem following along and accepting the distances that had to be traversed in order for one person to appear to be in two places at once.

But when I watched the movie, I couldn't buy it. I'm gawking at those cliffs, those steep, narrow paths suitable only for mountain goats, those flights of stairs, that ladder stretching down the side of another cliff, that hotel with still more stairs, the sail around the island to get to the isolated cove at just the right time, and, and, and. You get the picture.

Words can disguise the frantic running around that's required for the plot to work. The more running around needed — with split-second timing — the more chances for the plot to fail.

But a movie is a visual medium. It shows the running around and split-second timing, as the characters race about like gazelles with cheetahs hot on their heels. It has to *look* plausible for the audience to accept it. If the scheme looks like it depends on Olympic-level athleticism to pull off and those are normal people and not superheroes racing about, then — in movie terms — it fails. It's not believable.

This inability to suspend disbelief is not a fault of the director or the cast. They had to work within the constraints of the plot set out by Agatha when she wrote the novel. Some of the changes actually made the plot more plausible than the novel, such as Christine waving to a witness from the edge of the cliff instead of her prancing across a narrow suspension bridge and Christine tossing the bottle into the sea instead of into the garden.

But despite that, I loved this movie. Everything else worked, from the opening murder on the moors to the dénouement when the murderers are hauled off to jail.

This film even supplied a joke reused in the David Suchet *Poirot* episode *The Disappearance of Mr. Davenheim*. Very early on, Poirot arrives at the insurance company to report that they must pay the death benefits to the husband of the murdered woman found on the moors. He's announced by the secretary as Hercules Parrot.

General Information

Based on: *Evil Under the Sun* (novel, 1941)
Run time: 1 hr., 57 min. **Subtitles:** No

Writer: Anthony Shaffer
Director: Guy Hamilton

Cast

Peter Ustinov as Hercule Poirot

Colin Blakely as Sir Horace Blatt
Jane Birkin as Christine Redfern
Nicholas Clay as Patrick Redfern
Maggie Smith as Daphne Castle
Roddy McDowall as Rex Brewster
Sylvia Miles as Myra Gardener
James Mason as Odell Gardener
Denis Quilley as Kenneth Marshall
Diana Rigg as Arlena Stuart Marshall
Emily Hone as Linda Marshall
John Alderson as Police Sergeant
Paul Antrim as Police Inspector
Cyril Conway as Police Surgeon
Barbara Hicks as Flewitt's Secretary
Richard Vernon as Flewitt
Robert Dorning as Concierge
Dimitri Andreas as Gino
Walter Henry as Waiter
Eric Kent as Desk Sergeant
Guy Standeven as Vicar On Train

Film Locations

Yorkshire Dales (moors)
Swaledale, North Yorkshire
Muker, North Yorkshire (police station exterior)
Cala Monjo, Balearic Islands, Spain (hotel, sea front)
Raixa Estate Mallorca, Balearic Islands (hotel, gardens)
Formentor, Balearic Islands (Gull Cove beach)
Cala Blanca, Balearic Islands (Arlena murder scene)
Serra de Tramuntana, Balearic Islands (mountain range)
Bunyola, Balearic Islands (town)

Thirteen at Dinner (1985)

Poirot navigates the movie business with the help of a future Poirot to hunt down a nobleman's killer

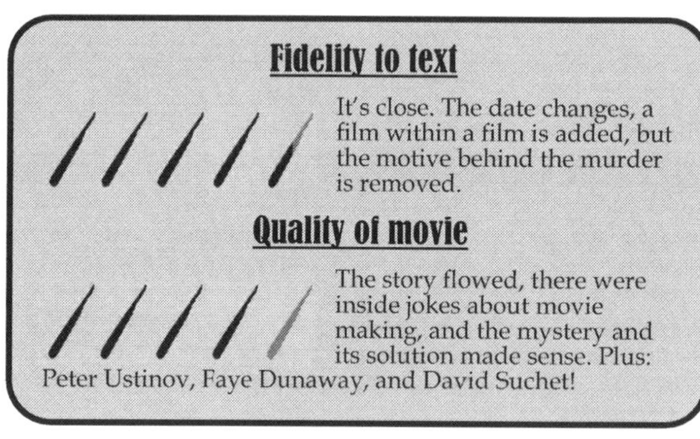

Fidelity to text

It's close. The date changes, a film within a film is added, but the motive behind the murder is removed.

Quality of movie

The story flowed, there were inside jokes about movie making, and the mystery and its solution made sense. Plus: Peter Ustinov, Faye Dunaway, and David Suchet!

I like Peter Ustinov's portrayals of Hercule Poirot. He seems driven by an interest, nay, an obsession with preventing crime, but without the OCD mannerisms in Suchet's portrayal. He's genial, genuinely interested in the people around him, and while he's the smartest person in the room, he doesn't flaunt it more than necessary.

The oddest part of this film is the date change. Ustinov's two previous outings as Poirot were *Death on the Nile* and *Evil Under the Sun*. Both were 1930s period pieces accurate down to the last detail of clothes, hair, and cars. They were also feature films, with feature-film budgets.

Thirteen at Dinner was filmed for television, meaning a much smaller budget. It became a contemporary, and the massive savings on wardrobe and sets paid for an all-star cast and a tour of London.

Poirot's wardrobe is still exquisitely tailored, but it's in keeping with the 1980s. It's a far cry from the flashy bow ties, perfectly cut suits, and patent leather shoes Suchet's Poirot favors.

As if that wasn't modern enough, the film opened with a scene that should have been jarring but instead anchored the film in the modern day.

Poirot is interviewed on a chat show by David Frost. Many of you may not remember Frost (1939–2013). He was a major TV personality and journalist. He hosted a talk show where he interviewed everybody who was anybody— including eight British Prime Ministers and seven U.S. presidents. If you were in the spotlight, you had a good shot at chatting with David Frost. If you were the world's greatest detective, it's guaranteed.

The TV talk show format also neatly introduced Bryan Martin (movie star), Carlotta Adams (impersonator), and Jane Wilkinson (movie star who was watching the show) to Poirot and to the audience.

As a result, Wilkinson meets Poirot and begs him for help. She badly wants a divorce from her husband, Lord Edgware, and he's refusing. She's so furious over his refusal she tells Poirot she could murder him.

Agatha played fast and loose with the mystery conventions in *Thirteen at Dinner* (the U.S. title for the novel; in Britain it was *Lord Edgware Dies*). Watch Jane Wilkinson closely and listen to what everyone says about her.

Faye Dunaway did a great job as Jane and her impersonator, Carlotta Adams. Jane is amoral, selfish,

Jane Wilkinson (*Faye Dunaway*), the glamorous actress

Bryan Martin (*Lee Horsley*), the egotistical actor

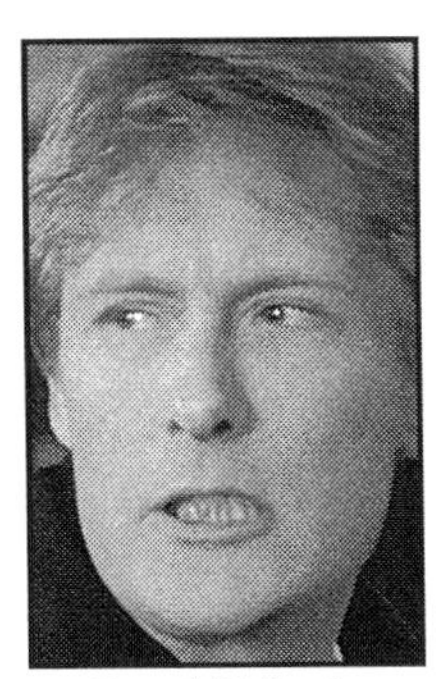

Ronald Marsh (*Bill Nighy*), the soused heir

Geraldine Marsh (*Amanda Pays*), the heir's caretaker

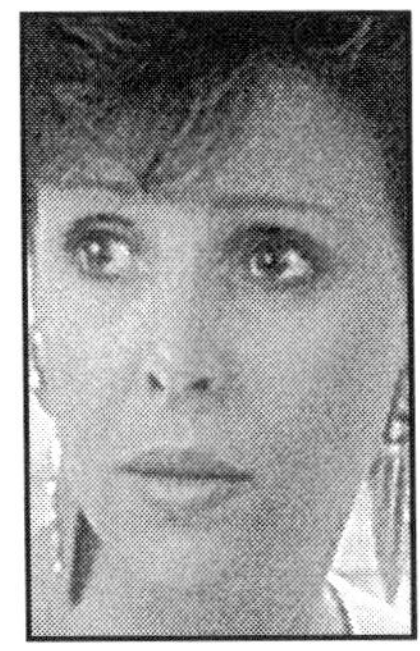

Jenny Driver (*Diane Keen*), the fashion designer

Donald Ross (*Benedict Taylor*), the curious witness

narcissistic, poorly educated, and everyone who knows her agrees that she's definitely capable of murder. Carlotta Adams, by contrast, is funny, friendly, well-educated, and everyone agrees that she's a wonderful person.

Mystery readers know what this setup means. No matter what happens, Jane couldn't possibly knife her hated husband. It's too obvious! It must be Carlotta Adams, because she's so unlikely. Yet at the same time, who is the most likely candidate for murdering a spouse? Every policeman in the universe will tell you.

This is the conundrum at the heart of *Thirteen at Dinner*. Jane visited Lord Edgware the night of the murder, but at the same time she was dining with friends. It's impossible for her to stab her husband, but there's his body.

The film omits the method of murder for no discernible reason. In the novel, it's a corn knife; a specialized, razor-sharp, extremely narrow and thin-bladed folding knife used to slice off dead skin (called corns) from your feet. It's a great murder weapon. It slides so easily and neatly through the back of the neck and into the brain, resulting in instant death. The movie doesn't mention corn knives or indeed much about how the murders were committed. This does keep the gore to a minimum.

The major omission, also ignored by 1934's *Lord Edgware Dies*, was the motive. Hollywood, being a bastion of hardcore atheists with a less-than-zero understanding of religious belief, must be the reason. The producers decided that an audience wouldn't accept or understand the original motive. But why skip it? Audiences aren't stupid. They can understand an explanation delivered through good acting and a well-written script. Agatha provided a very good reason for murder so why not use it?

But they didn't, so I'll clue you in. The Duke of Merton is a devout Anglo-Catholic. He's extremely serious about his faith. He could marry a widow but not a divorcée. If Jane Wilkinson wants to become the Duchess of Merton (over the duke's mother's strenuous objections, another skipped plot point), she needs to do something about her inconvenient husband.

Thirteen at Dinner has several comic high points. The film within a film was amusing, especially as you gradually get the joke: Bryan Martin (Lee Horsley) doesn't do his own stunts. In fact, he doesn't do anything in his own movie other than appear when it's safe or in a closeup and some emoting is needed. He also throws his weight around, ordering the director to reshoot scenes because he didn't like how his stunt double acted. Poirot uses this observation to rule out Martin as a murderer. If he doesn't risk his neck when there's virtually no risk, he certainly won't risk it when it could mean prison.

Jonathan Cecil played a wonderful Hastings, as good as Hugh Fraser in the *Poirot* TV series. He appears in two more of Ustinov's Poirot films, and I'm looking forward to them.

But the actor you're dying to know about is David Suchet. He plays Inspector Japp to Ustinov's Poirot, giving you, dear filmgoer, two Poirots for the price of one.

After seeing many *Poirot* episodes, it felt odd to watch Suchet, sans mustache and smart morning suit, chewing up the scenery and everything edible within range. The investigation into Lord Edgware's murder meant no breakfast for him, so if there's food nearby, he's wolfing it down. This Inspector Japp is a worthy detective. He's a dogged policeman, needing facts, not too keen on working with a theatrical Belgian, but willing to bend in order to solve the crime. Moreover, unlike some of the other Poirot adaptions I've suffered through, this Japp is not an idiot.

Suchet claims he didn't like his performance in this film. However, he did a good enough job that Ustinov told him he'd make a good Poirot.

There's so much to like about this movie. It's an '80s festival of hair and clothes and earrings the size of doorknobs. The producers restrained themselves not just in the gore department. Despite scenes taking place while fashion designer Jenny Driver is getting her models ready for her upcoming show, there's no gratuitous nudity, which I expected. The soundtrack was fine too, skipping the usual annoying excesses of TV movie music.

And there are boats! There's a charming scene where Jane is jogging alongside a narrow canal. Keeping pace with her and asking questions is Poirot in a small, powered dory. Hastings mans the outboard and the tiller, providing stalwart support for the master.

You'll like this film.

General Information

Based on: *Lord Edgware Dies* (UK title) / *Thirteen at Dinner* (US title) (novel, 1933)
Run time: 1 hr., 28 min. **Subtitles:** Yes

Writer: Rod Browning **Director:** Lou Antonio

Cast

Peter Ustinov as Hercule Poirot
Jonathan Cecil as Capt. Arthur Hastings
David Suchet as Inspector Japp

Faye Dunaway as Jane Wilkinson / Carlotta Adams
Lee Horsley as Bryan Martin
John Barron as Lord Edgware
Bill Nighy as Ronald Marsh
Amanda Pays as Geraldine Marsh
Diane Keen as Jenny Driver
Benedict Taylor as Donald Ross
John Stride as Film Director
Allan Cuthbertson as Sir Montague Corner
John Quarmby as Sir Montague's Butler
Glyn Baker as Lord Edgware's Butler
Peter Clapham as Mr. Wildburn
Lesley Dunlop as Alice Bennett
Avril Elgar as Miss Carroll
Oriane Grieve as Serious Actress
Russell Grant as Moxon
Geoffrey Rose as Duke of Merton
David Frost as Self

Dead Man's Folly (1986)

Ariadne Oliver invites Poirot to a party where murder is a game until someone changes the rules

Fidelity to text

Aside from the date change, adding Hastings, and the usual compressions needed for film, it's amazingly close.

Quality of movie

I liked it and not just because there were boats galore. The story flowed, it amused, the acting was first-rate, and it played fair with the audience.

After I watch an Agatha adaptation, I research the film online to see if I missed any interesting tidbits. I can't help but see other opinions. In this case, as with *The Man in the Brown Suit* (another maligned film), I disagree with the consensus.

I liked this movie and not just because I like Peter Ustinov as Poirot. I enjoyed the movie from the opening scene in Harrods food hall with Ariadne Oliver (Jean Stapleton) until the ending when Amy Folliat (Constance Cummings) is confronted with her own negligence and complicity.

A major reason is the movie played fair. This doesn't always happen, either with Agatha adaptations or with mystery movies in general. Movies are art by committee, so it's easy for important points to get skipped because someone else was supposed to make sure they got addressed.

It starts with the script. Despite Hollywood's belief that screenwriters are "schmucks with Underwoods," they play a vital role. If the script doesn't provide the clues, you, dear filmgoer, are left throwing popcorn at the screen and ranting about how a vital clue was hidden on a newspaper artfully folded and left on an end table in the far end of the room and the camera spent less than one second of screen time panning across said room.

That happened in David Suchet's *Peril at End House*. We went frame by frame with that film, looking for that clue. That film was riddled with similar errors where something important was either glossed over (not playing the game) or omitted entirely (unfair to anyone who hadn't read the book). I don't expect to be spoon-fed my clues but if I'm paying attention, I should be able to spot them during the second viewing of the movie.

Dead Man's Folly put in the clues. I didn't shout at the screen and rant afterwards about bad writing and being cheated.

If anything, the film should have been longer, since there's plenty of story to go around. Alec and Sally Legge in particular got short shrift, yet they're a major red herring.

This version also didn't significantly rewrite Agatha, a common flaw. Yes, they added Hastings, yet it worked. He stayed in the background, letting Ariadne Oliver shine. When Poirot needed him, Hastings was there.

And he was needed because the movie compressed the action. In the novel, the fake Hattie Stubbs vanishes.

Amy Folliat
(*Constance Cummings*),
the lonely widow

Sir George Stubbs
(*Tim Pigott-Smith*),
the lord of the manor

Hattie Stubbs
(*Nicollette Sheridan*),
the young wife

Amanda Brewis
(*Susan Wooldridge*),
the secretary

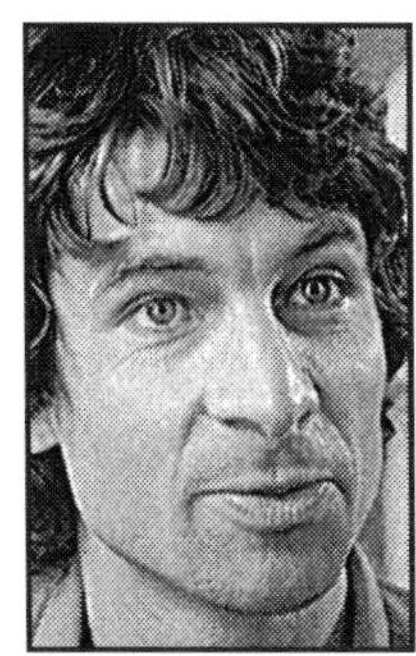

Michael Weyman
(*Ralph Arliss*),
the pet architect

Eddie South
(*Jeff Yagher*),
the record producer

Months later, she's still missing, and her fate is never explained. We assume she got away with murder. Since the film tightened events from several months to a few days, Hastings was available to capture her and drag her back to Nasse to face Poirot, the police, and justice.

The film changed the real and fake Hattie into Americans along with Etienne De Sousa, Hattie's cousin. He's now Eddie South, from her hometown. But, like De Sousa in the novel, Eddie is very much a fish out of water in England. Like De Sousa, he's got the foreign hair, wardrobe, yacht, insouciant attitude, musical tastes, and earring to set Inspector Bland's teeth on edge.

Another American was Jean Stapleton as Ariadne Oliver. Despite her nationality change, she remains Agatha's fictional counterpart. Jean filled the role beautifully, displaying intelligence, intuitiveness, and scatterbrained thinking in equal measures. If you're of a certain age, you *might* hear her voice and think Edith Bunker, her most famous role. I watched *All in the Family* back in the 1970s, and while it didn't bother me, it did bother Bill. If you don't know what I'm talking about, you'll enjoy seeing Ariadne Oliver hold her own with Poirot.

West Wycombe Park played Nasse House. What a stunning mansion with equally stunning grounds. You'll understand why Amy Folliat would do anything to keep Nasse in the family. As Old Merdell tells Poirot (and anyone else who'll listen), there will always be a Folliat at Nasse. Amy Folliat is a Folliat by birth (second cousin) as well as by marriage so she's got many reasons to want to hang onto the property. The fête scenes really showed off the grounds and that house! Wow. You'll get a great tour.

The English class system was on full display. Throughout the movie, you know who's on top, and it's not Inspector Bland investigating Marlene Tucker's murder. Despite onerous death duties and the collapse of the landed gentry, England hasn't changed much.

This was a subtle clue to Sir George Stubbs' true identity. He's a parvenu who's called "Sir" because he demands it (he certainly wasn't knighted). Yet the locals call him "Sir" because Amy Folliat does. If Lady Folliat thinks he's acceptable, then who are they to disagree?

Compare this to other Johnny-Come-Latelies in Agatha's novels, starting with Alfred Inglethorp in *Styles*. The locals never accepted that social climber getting above his station.

Another attraction of this *Folly* are the boats. Lots and lots of boats. I counted at least seven, from a variety of rowboats to a ferry (where Poirot and Hastings meet the foreign girls hiking from youth hostel to youth hostel) to a police boat to Eddie South's yacht to a Zodiac used by police divers to retrieve a body from the river. For added nautical flavor, there were sailboats drifting in the background.

After Poirot and Ariadne Oliver, the most important character in *Dead Man's Folly* is Amy Folliat. She's the dark heart of the novel. She was once the most important and grandest lady in the district. By the time of the murder, she's old, alone, widowed, poor, and renting the lodge from that parvenu, Sir George. Her husband lost most of the family fortune on horses and gambling and died an alcoholic. Her older son died of fever. Her younger son, Jamie, was wild and reckless and disappeared under unpleasant circumstances. Multiple death duties forced her to sell Nasse House. All she has left is her pride. Yet why does she accept Sir George when she accepts so little else? Why did she discard family portraits and mementos, when aristocrats never throw anything away that proves they date back to William the Conqueror?

It's her pride and her unwillingness to recognize her younger son for what he is that led to the multiple tragedies at Nasse House. Poirot confronts her, forcing her to see her guilt. Amy Folliat was unable to accept the world changing around her. She was willing to do almost anything to keep a Folliat at Nasse. Compare her to Dolly Bantry in *The Body in the Library* and *The Mirror Crack'd* who accepted that the world had moved on. Dolly Bantry let go of the past. Amy Folliat could not and paid the price. So did Marlene Tucker, Old Merdell, and Hattie Stubbs.

Give this version of *Dead Man's Folly* a try. You won't regret it.

General Information

Based on: *Dead Man's Folly* (novel, 1956)
Run time: 1 hr., 30 min. **Subtitles:** Yes

Writer: Rod Browning **Director:** Clive Donner

Cast

Peter Ustinov as Hercule Poirot
Jonathan Cecil as Capt. Arthur Hastings
Jean Stapleton as Ariadne Oliver
Kenneth Cranham as Detective Inspector Bland

Constance Cummings as Amy Folliat
Tim Pigott-Smith as Sir George Stubbs
Nicollette Sheridan as Hattie Stubbs
Susan Wooldridge as Amanda Brewis
Christopher Guard as Alec Legge
Caroline Langrishe as Sally Legge
Jeff Yagher as Eddie South
Ralph Arliss as Michael Weyman
Siv Borg as Blond Hostel Girl
Jimmy Gardner as Old Merdell
Pippa Hinchley as Marlene Tucker
Vicky Murdock as Marilyn Tucker
Marjorie Yates as Mrs. Tucker
James Gaddas as Young Foreign Man
Simon Cowell-Parker as Forensic Man
Sandra Dickinson as Marilyn Gale

Film Locations

Harrods, London
Cliveden, Buckinghamshire (Folliat's cottage, Nasse House boathouse)
West Wycombe Park, Buckinghamshire (Nasse House)

Murder in Three Acts (1986)

Under the sunny skies of Acapulco, an aging actor and Poirot investigate a murder without clues or motive

Fidelity to text

Updating to 1986, moving from Cornwall to Acapulco, swapping Hastings for Satterthwaite, name and nationality changes, but the biggest issue is the most subtle.

Quality of movie

Acapulco looks great! Tony Curtis turns in a stellar performance. There are some nifty boats, too. After that, well ...

Updating *Murder in Three Acts* to 1986 is acceptable. The producer saves big bucks on period wardrobe, sets, and cars to pay for Tony Curtis and location shooting in Acapulco. In a contemporary film, the director doesn't fret about anachronisms in language or something modern seen at the edge of the screen. A contemporary, filmed on location in Acapulco, even allows for moments of inadvertent documentary. Enjoy watching Poirot interact with the locals in the street market. If you'd visited Acapulco in 1986 and ventured from the hotel, you'd have seen the same sights.

Similarly, why not film in Acapulco as opposed to Cornwall? The weather's probably better and it's exotic, always nice for the audience. You get dramatic scenery, such as "The Crow's Nest," Charles Cartwright's house built high up on the crags for stunning views while still remaining close to the water.

It's a gorgeous house, too, designed to take advantage of the ridge line. It used to be Lana Turner's Acapulco getaway! Sadly, between then and now, a new owner tore it down and rebuilt so don't bother looking for it the next time you're in Acapulco.

I didn't mind Hastings replacing Mr. Satterthwaite. The novel takes place mainly from his point of view, as he watches Charles Cartwright and Egg investigate. It's a Watson perspective, one step removed, and since he's so unfamiliar to readers (Agatha rarely used Satterthwaite and even more rarely with Poirot), why not go with what's familiar? Thus, Jonathan Cecil reunites with Peter Ustinov.

Except Cecil was given nothing to do other than be the butt of beachcomber jokes, make introductions to the British expat community, and take notes, which Poirot ignored. It was painful to watch. I enjoyed Cecil's performances in *Thirteen at Dinner* (1985) and *Dead Man's Folly* (1986) and looked forward to watching him strut his stuff. He would have had a lot to do, because in the novel, Satterthwaite was in virtually every scene. Poirot shows up at the beginning, has a scene in the middle, and then takes over the last few chapters. Hastings — in place of Satterthwaite — would have been running the investigation and filling in a faraway Poirot. But alas, no. He got shunted off to the side. This was a sad way

Charles Cartwright (*Tony Curtis*), the constant actor

"Egg" Eastman (*Emma Samms*), the innocent admirer

Ricardo Montoya (*Fernando Allende*), the good friend

Angela Stafford (*Diana Muldaur*), the actress ex-wife

Miss Milray (*Frances Lee McCain*), the vigilant secretary

Dr. Strange (*Dana Elcar*), the concerned doctor

for Cecil to end his run as Hastings. I hope he enjoyed his Acapulco vacation and getting to act in sandals and an assortment of guayaberas instead of a suit and tie.

The rest of the cast, apart from Tony Curtis, turned in acceptable performances. They're a wide range of TV actors, nearly always in the second tier other than Emma Samms as Egg. They turn in strong supporting roles but they were capable of doing more. The novel's complex with plenty of red herrings as to who handed a poisoned cocktail to Rev. Babbington and then, later, to Dr. Strange.

But the scriptwriter swept all of those layers away, leaving a group of people standing around while Poirot and Charles Cartwright chewed up the scenery and hogged the limelight. It's a pity because sometimes, one of them got to stand out. It showed how good this movie could have been, with a better script and about ten more minutes of running time.

There were so many questions to be answered that would have added drama to the movie. Why was Freddy Dayton a lush? What was the deal with Miss Milray behaving as much like a wardress as a secretary? Why, in 1986, did Janet Crisp feel the need to write her plays under a man's name? Where did Daisy Eastman's money go, so she encouraged her daughter to chase after Charles Cartwright, aging movie star, instead of Ricardo Montoya, who was young, rich, and obviously well-connected? What was the relationship between Charles Cartwright and Angela Stafford (played by Diana Muldaur in a wasted role)? She didn't like young Egg chasing Charles, but why did she care? Why was Ricardo so passive in his pursuit of Egg? All those hints and possibilities left lying about like pebbles on the beach.

The role of Charles Cartwright needed a big star to fill it. Someone capable of playing a flamboyant actor who's always altering his performance to suit the audience in front of him. Tony Curtis filled that role admirably. From the moment you see Charles Cartwright on his sailboat in the fjord by his home, he's the center of attention. It's a very nice sailboat and he's handling it smoothly in the wind and waves. The more you see of Charles, the more you can understand why he fascinates Egg. It's the allure of a lion just past his prime, but when compared to all the other men around her, very prime indeed. He makes Ricardo, the would-be boyfriend, resemble a neutered tomcat.

General Information

Based on: *Three Act Tragedy* (novel, 1935)
Run time: 1 hr., 34 min. **Subtitles:** Yes

Writer: Scott Swanton **Director:** Gary Nelson

Cast

Peter Ustinov as Hercule Poirot
Jonathan Cecil as Hastings

Tony Curtis as Charles Cartwright
Diana Muldaur as Angela Stafford
Frances Lee McCain as Miss Milray
Emma Samms as "Egg" Eastman
Marian Mercer as Daisy Eastman
Lisa Eichhorn as Cynthia Dayton
Nicholas Pryor as Freddie Dayton
Dana Elcar as Dr. Strange
Concetta Tomei as Janet Crisp
Fernando Allende as Ricardo Montoya
Philip Guilmant as Rev. Babbington
Jacqueline Evans as Mrs. Babbington
Pedro Armendáriz Jr. as Col. Mateo
Ángeles González as Housekeeper
Claudia Guzmán as Rosa
Rodolfo Hernández as Miguel
Martin LaSalle as Doctor
Alma Levy as Nurse
Julio Monterde as Manager
Rene Pereyra as Waiter
José Chávez as Watchman

Film Location

Acapulco, Mexico

Peter Ustinov is Poirot again and he's jokier and more mannered than in previous outings. Not to the OCD-extent that Suchet reaches, but he didn't seem to take it seriously. Some of it comes from the plot. Some of it is Acapulco. Despite being an eyewitness to Reverend Babbington's death, he doesn't believe it's murder. There's no reason to kill him, and murder always has a reason.

The big issue that you'll notice is the ending. This is because there are two versions of the novel; one published in the U.K. and one in the U.S. When Agatha wrote *Three Act Tragedy* (the original title) in 1934, it had a different motive for murder. The motive worked in England because the divorce laws were different. There were very few acceptable reasons for divorce back then, and insanity was not one of them. If your spouse was a lunatic, you were stuck. Remarriage was out of the question. But by 1934, in the United States, twenty states allowed you to divorce your crazy spouse.

So the book's climax got rewritten with a different motive for the U.S. market. The clues remained the same, the plot is the same, the murderer is the same. And thus, here we are today with two rather different endings for the same novel! It depends on which one you read as to whether or not you gasp with horror at how some hack scriptwriter rewrote the climax. If you've read the American version, it's fine. If you've read the English version, you're horrified at how Hollywood once again played fast and loose with Agatha's text.

Except they didn't. Despite the name, setting, and date changes, and radically compressing the script, this version follows the text surprisingly closely. The *American* text.

Which brings us back to Tony Curtis. He was terrific, from start to finish. He's the only reason to watch this film twice. The first time you'll admire Acapulco and learn the plot. The second time you'll reinterpret everything Tony Curtis does as he portrays Charles Cartwright, famous actor, madman, and murderer.

Appointment with Death (1988)

A domineering mother's authority reaches the breaking point during her family's trip to the Holy Land

Peter Ustinov's last Poirot outing should have ended on a high note rather than this sour one. It's the script, not the talent, although the director's choices didn't help. Smacking doors into your star's face like some slapstick clown? Why screenwriters think they can do better than the queen of crime is beyond me.

From the opening credits, you're in for an appointment with mediocrity. The movie begins with our villainous matriarch (an outstanding Piper Laurie) blackmailing her shyster lawyer (David Soul) into burning the true will. Does the weather become psychotropic? Naturally. Evil deeds demand a sudden, torrential thunderstorm.

What made it stranger (for me) was the equally sudden time leap. When Ustinov began making Poirot films, they were set in the mid-1930s. His next three outings leaped forward to contemporary 1980s. I accepted it because the date switch was handled well and the films stayed true to the source material.

Suddenly, we're back in 1937. It was jarring to see everyone in period dress, driving period cars, when I'd gotten used to '80s hair and fashion. To make sure you know it's 1937, the movie's climax includes a coronation ball for George VI as well as an argument about Wallis Simpson.

Unfortunately, they didn't keep the novel's psychologically compelling story. Mrs. Boynton is one of Agatha's best villains. She loves power and mental torture. She's slowly destroying her four children's minds. As a result, they behave much younger than their calendar age. They've never been let off the leash even to attend school. Most of that was swept away, turning Mrs. Boynton — despite Piper Laurie's best efforts — into a TV movie of the week monster. She even gained a first name, Emily. Not having that bit of humanizing effectively emphasized her distance from normality.

With their immaturity gone, her four children lost most of their complexity. In the book, the oldest stepson Lennox is near-catatonic from despair. His wife Nadine is ready to leave him to save her sanity. Ray contemplates murder but doesn't know where to begin. Carol feels equally trapped. Both Ray and Carol are still strong enough to be terrified of what's happening to Ginevra, Mrs. Boynton's natural daughter and youngest child. She escapes her mental torture by sinking into a fantasy world where she's a

Fidelity to text

It's reasonably close if you ignore that ridiculous chase through the souk, cardboard characters, and Agatha's dialog abandoned in favor of the product of a screenwriter's derivative imagination.

Quality of movie

Lethargic pacing, bad music, wasted stars, and plot threads that went nowhere despite the extensive scenery in which they had room to bloom.

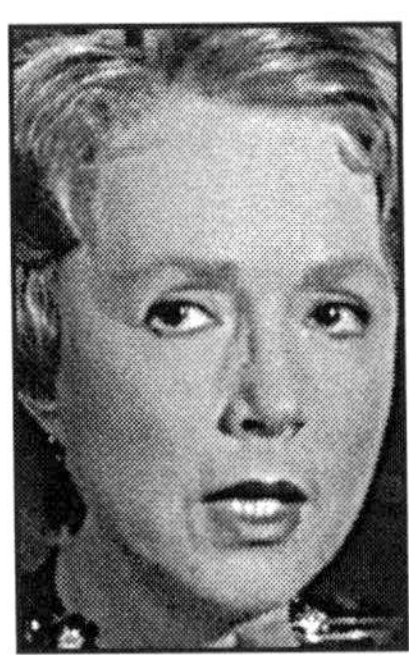

Emily Boynton
(*Piper Laurie*),
the despot mother

Nadine Boynton
(*Carrie Fisher*),
the wayward wife

Lady Westholme
(*Lauren Bacall*),
the outspoken pol

Miss Quinton
(*Hayley Mills*),
the bold archaeologist

Jefferson Cope
(*David Soul*),
the lucky attorney

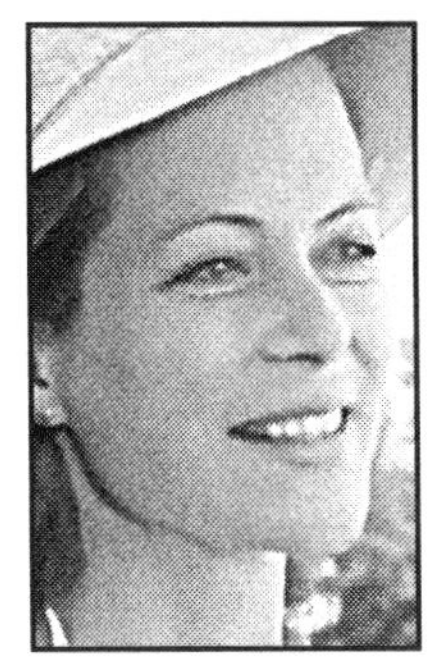

Dr. Sarah King
(*Jenny Seagrove*),
the athletic medico

kidnapped princess. But unless she's rescued, she'll walk through the door into schizophrenia and never return.

Nadine was handled about as badly as it was possible. Carrie Fisher had the thankless task of playing an adulterous woman whose behavior is more schizophrenic than Ginevra's. In the novel, Jefferson Cope is an old and dear friend. Even though she agrees to leave her husband for him, she is not having an affair with him. She's desperate to save Lennox and their marriage, and if jealousy won't rouse him from his torpor and come for her, then nothing will. Either way, Nadine has to leave to save herself.

Movie Nadine is openly cheating with Jefferson. Yet you never see the payoff scene with Lennox where she explains how desperate she was to get him to pay attention and come back to life. Nor do you see Jefferson — when he learns the truth — take it with a good grace because he'd rather see Nadine happy than miserable even if it means they don't marry.

Turning Jefferson Cope into a shyster worked because it gave Mrs. Boynton the leverage to blackmail him. It even worked when Jefferson showed up onboard ship and she tried to poison him. Having Lennox accidentally rescue Jefferson from poisoning by attacking him after discovering the affair, however, did not work. There was no setup showing Lennox as anything other than catatonic and then afterwards he went back to ignoring Nadine!

Worst of all was having Poirot witness Mrs. Boynton bribe an Arab to kidnap Jefferson. He vanishes, only to return to the dig a few days later with Miss Quinton, girl archeologist and Lady Westholme's traveling partner, who had also vanished! They were brought back by a band of Arab horsemen after unlikely adventures we never see, and never receive an explanation for, but which apparently resulted in Jefferson and Miss Quinton getting to know each other extremely well during those chilly desert nights. Except, when the script called for it, they forgot they knew each other and Jefferson was back to panting after Nadine.

Hayley Mills was wasted as Miss Quinton. Hope she enjoyed her tour of Israeli deserts.

This movie's got plenty of travelogue, from the family's tour of London, Florence, Venice, to Syria, but it's dull.

General Information

Based on: *Appointment with Death* (novel, 1938)
Run time: 1 hr., 42 min. **Subtitles:** Yes

Writers: Anthony Shaffer, Peter Buckman, and Michael Winner
Director: Michael Winner

Cast

Peter Ustinov as Hercule Poirot
John Gielgud as Colonel Carbury

Lauren Bacall as Lady Westholme
Hayley Mills as Miss Quinton
Jenny Seagrove as Dr. Sarah King
Piper Laurie as Emily Boynton
Nicholas Guest as Lennox Boynton
Carrie Fisher as Nadine Boynton
John Terlesky as Raymond Boynton
Valerie Richards as Carol Boynton
Amber Bezer as Ginevra Boynton
David Soul as Jefferson Cope
Douglas Sheldon as Captain Rogers
Michael Sarne as Healey
Michael Craig as Lord Peel

Film Locations

Jaffa, Israel (Trieste, Italy; Jaffa, Israel)
London (tour)
St. George's Cathedral, Jerusalem, Israel (Tower of London grounds)
Canal Grande and Rialto Bridge, Venice (tour)
Florence, Italy (Sightseeing)
American Colony Hotel, Jerusalem, Israel
Dead Sea, Israel

Nothing unusual or interesting and filmed awkwardly enough that, cutting from the cast to the scenery, you know it's the second unit doing the work and the stars are nowhere near that extremely well-known landmark. We never learn Emily Boynton's motivation behind giving the family a vacation. Readers know she wanted to open the cage door and give her unhappy prisoners a taste of freedom. Then, when they returned to the family compound, her children and daughter-in-law would be more unhappy than ever, and she could revel in their suffering.

At least we get Lauren Bacall, who was fabulous as Lady Westholme. She's a thinly veiled portrait of Viscountess Nancy Astor (1879-1964), an American who married a British peer and was elected as a member of Parliament in her own right. Lady Astor was the kind of hyper-organized, aggressive, insensitive, humorless do-gooder who makes the unfortunate poor in the pub slug back their drinks and flee when she appears.

Novel Poirot determines who murdered Mrs. Boynton purely on logic. Movie Poirot depends on transatlantic cables to prove his theory. The scriptwriters even gave a villain speech to Lady Westholme so she could justify her (admittedly praiseworthy) murder.

The same scriptwriters decided that there wasn't enough action (ignoring Jefferson Cope, Miss Quinton, and the Arab horsemen after setting up that amazing complication) and added a secret witness to the murder. Thus, after we watch a shadowy figure beg to talk to Poirot but then refuse to — the script needed padding — we have to watch this same lithe, agile young man show up and flee through the souk with Sarah King, girl doctor, in hot pursuit. Yes, folks, a skinny Englishwoman in a dress and heels can chase a young man through a crowded souk he knows like the back of his hand and keep him in sight. Then, when he's shot by a mysterious assailant, she's menaced by the locals and conveniently rescued by the astonishingly well-timed intervention of British military police.

I could go on and on and on. Every time the movie came to life, it fell back into dopiness. It's a meeting with tedium, best avoided unless you're a major fan of one of the stars.

The Adventure of the Clapham Cook (1989)

Exploring the 'trivial' disappearance of a servant unmasks a devious plan leading to a cold-blooded murder

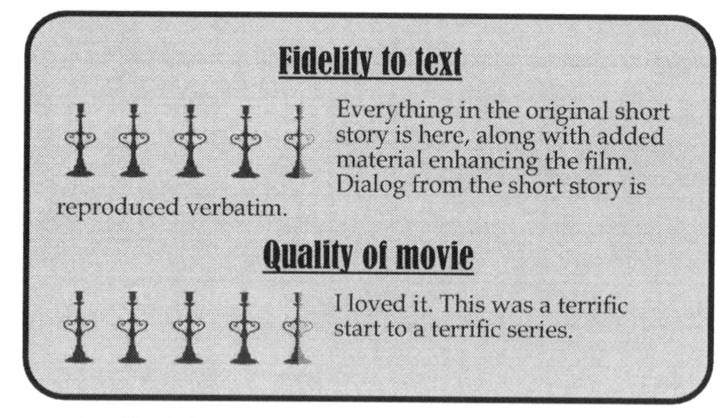

Fidelity to text

Everything in the original short story is here, along with added material enhancing the film. Dialog from the short story is reproduced verbatim.

Quality of movie

I loved it. This was a terrific start to a terrific series.

Hercule Poirot has been filmed many times, both for the movies and for television. He's been onstage too, as well as radio plays. But with this series, ITV — although they didn't know it at the time — made history. They eventually filmed every novel and the vast majority of short stories that Agatha wrote about Poirot. They skipped "The Lemesurier Inheritance" and squeezed the twelve short stories of *The Labours of Hercules* into a single, remarkably good and coherent movie. They didn't miss much. Later on, David Suchet narrated "The Lemesurier Inheritance" as an audio book, so he can legitimately state that he performed every Poirot story Agatha wrote.

Think of that! Starting in 1989 when this first episode aired, and ending in 2013, there were 13 series with 70 episodes, and all performed by Suchet over the course of 24 years. That's a lot of Poirot.

Prior to this episode, I'd watched exactly two *Poirot* episodes and that was a long time ago. So this version of Poirot was relatively new and fresh for me. I didn't have many preconceived notions. Thus, I can answer the most important question: Did *The Adventure of the Clapham Cook* provide a good introduction to David Suchet, Hercule Poirot, and the series as a whole? Yes, it absolutely did.

Start with the setting. Poirot's literary life runs from 1920 to 1975 (55 years!). ITV Productions decided to set nearly all of the episodes in the mid-1930s (say 1934 to 1936). It makes sense to stick to one time period for ease of filming. The 1930s have a wonderful Art Deco look and ITV takes full advantage of the esthetics of the period.

Never going past 1936 also lets ITV Productions avoid getting tangled in World War II. The cast is aware of the slowly escalating troubles in Europe but it's in the background if it comes up at all. Some of the stories involving espionage allude directly to what everyone's afraid off, looming on the horizon. But it's not a major plot point. No one knew what would happen, and many people preferred to believe that there would never be another world war. Remember that Poirot, Belgian refugee from World War I, would not be keen to endure another world war. No one wanted to go through that trauma again. The last terrible war to end all wars was fresh and raw in too many people's memories.

Mrs. Todd
(*Brigit Forsyth*),
the irate wife

Mr. Todd
(*Antony Carrick*),
the snide husband

Arthur Simpson
(*Dermot Crowley*),
the kind lodger

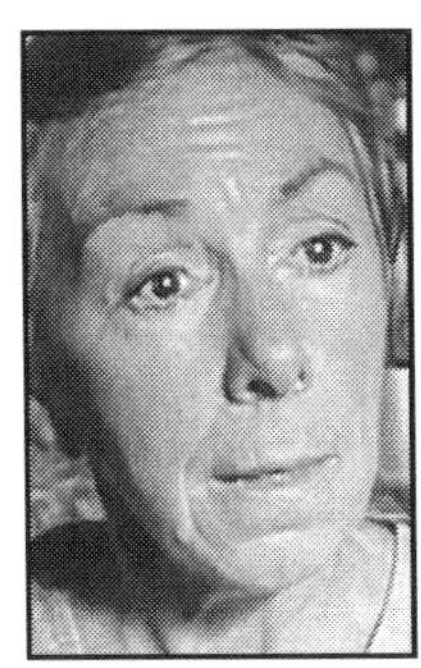

Eliza Dunn
(*Freda Dowie*),
the lucky cook

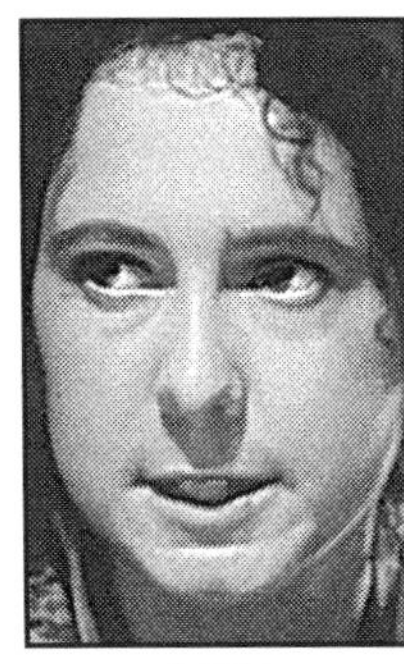

Annie
(*Katy Murphy*),
the suspicious maid

Railway Porter
(*Danny Webb*),
the vital witness

We're introduced to Poirot in a long shot that begins with his immaculately clean shoes and white spats, pauses to watch him brush invisible lint from his pants, and ends with him listening intently to a series of crime stories in the newspaper. He rejects investigating each one, including a bank embezzlement for £90,000: ("But that's a king's ransom!" "When it is used to ransom a king, then it becomes interesting to Poirot."). Immediately we get a feel for his attitudes, mannerisms, obsessiveness over detail, and love for order.

We meet Capt. Arthur Hastings, the sidekick, who was reading the headlines to Poirot. Captain Hastings is bluff and rather stupid, a good foil for Poirot. We meet Poirot's personal secretary and assistant, Miss Lemon. She's much better looking in the TV show than she is in the books, but that's Hollywood for you. We also meet Inspector Japp of Scotland Yard, who'll work with Poirot frequently to solve murders. Inspector Japp develops a deep respect for Poirot's little gray cells.

The other two semi-regulars from the novels don't appear but they will. That would be George, Poirot's valet, and Ariadne Oliver, his mystery writing friend.

The episode is 51 minutes long and uses every one of them to establish England in the early 1930s. Poirot's London apartment building (Whitehaven Mansions) is a model of Art Deco architecture. Mrs. Todd's house is respectable but not rich. She has a cook and at least one maid of all work. She also has a boarder, further demonstrating that she and her husband are not rich. If you're renting out rooms, you need the money.

We see the cars, the bridges, the streets and parks in London bustling with people, most of them on foot. Lots of trains and train stations too. We also see the cook's rural house, inherited from a distant relative way out in Keswick. It's out in the boondocks compared to London. Poirot is unimpressed by the English countryside and his patent leather shoes suffer from the excursion into its muddy fields.

David Suchet was perfect as Poirot. This was his debut outing and it will be fascinating to see if he changes anything in his performance. I can understand why so many people say he's the definitive Hercule Poirot, like Joan Hickson is the definitive Miss Marple. According to Suchet's memoirs, he studied Poirot, carefully absorbing every word Agatha wrote about him and keeping track of every bit of description, personal mannerisms, and little quirks so he could more completely become Poirot. All that effort shows onscreen.

Among those quirks is Poirot being as foreign as he needs to be to ferret out facts. People are more likely to be open (and condescending) to comic foreigners. He flatters maids and railway clerks to get information. He pays close attention to what his eyes tell him. He's willing to admit when he makes a mistake, and then, as he did here, capture the escaping murderer when he realizes the mistake the railway clerk made.

Everything we need to know about Hercule Poirot, right down to his obsession with orderliness when he has Miss Lemon adjust the position of a nail by one centimeter, is on display.

The mystery worked too; a perfect demonstration that something insignificant can be far more important than anyone would guess. A minor incident — a cook disappearing suddenly — points to a much larger crime. It is, as Poirot himself says, a reminder to never disregard the trivial or undignified.

A note about the rating murder weapon: I don't actually know how the victim was killed because it's not shown onscreen. But since the murderer wasn't a professional and we aren't given any details, I'll assume it was a candlestick in the boarding house bedroom. Few of us keep pistols around, apothecaries make you sign the poison book, garroting is up-close and personal and thus not often used by amateurs, and knives tend to leave blood spatters, alerting the landlady and the police to a possible crime.

If ITV Productions can maintain this level of quality, it will be a pleasure to watch the remaining 69 episodes. I can certainly recommend this one.

General Information

Based on: "The Adventure of the Clapham Cook" (short story, 1923)
Run time: 51 min. **Subtitles:** No

Writer: Clive Exton
Director: Edward Bennett

Cast

David Suchet as Hercule Poirot
Hugh Fraser as Captain Hastings
Philip Jackson as Chief Inspector Japp
Pauline Moran as Miss Lemon

Brigit Forsyth as Mrs. Todd
Antony Carrick as Mr. Todd
Dermot Crowley as Arthur Simpson
Freda Dowie as Eliza Dunn
Katy Murphy as Annie
Richard Bebb as Mr. Cameron
Danny Webb as Railway Porter
Frank Vincent as Ship's Purser
Brian Poyser as Salvation Army Speaker
Phillip Manikum as Police Sergeant
Jona Jones as Police Constable
Nicholas Coppin as Police Constable

Film Locations

Florin Court, Charterhouse Square, London (Poirot's apartment)
Battersea Park, London (Clapham Common)
Albert Bridge, London (Poirot and Hastings walk)
The Royal Masonic Hospital (Belgravia and Overseas Bank)
Fell Cottage, Keswick, Cumbria (Dunn's cottage)
Surbiton Station, Surbiton, South West London (Twickenham Station)

Murder in the Mews (1989)

Suicide or murder? Scotland Yard needs Poirot's help when a woman is found shot in her alley apartment

We open with a lovely scene of bygone days that you probably don't experience today in modern London. For you Yanks, it's Guy Fawkes Day, celebrating the man who tried to blow up Parliament and King James I in 1605. There's even a little rhyme to make sure no one in England forgets:

Remember, remember the Fifth of November,
The gunpowder, treason, and plot,
I know of no reason
Why the gunpowder, treason,
Should ever be forgot.
Guy Fawkes, Guy Fawkes, t'was his intent
To blow up the king and Parliament.

I doubt that they let little kids play with those kinds of fireworks today and especially unsupervised. They'll blow their wee hands off or lose an eye, with lawsuits swiftly to follow.

The opening also provides a chance for Hercule Poirot to demonstrate his ignorance of English culture which is forgivable. He didn't grow up burning the Guy in effigy every year in a spasm of culturally approved violence. For Hastings not to know when Poirot asks if blowing up Parliament was a sin or a good deed — "It's no good asking me, old son, I was never much a one for politics" — demonstrates that our captain is an idiot.

Fidelity to text

The story's fleshed out, which is good, but changes to Jane made her decision unbelievable, which is bad.

Quality of movie

I grooved on the mid-1930s vibe until the ending jerked the Art Deco Rug out from under my feet.

The Guy Fawkes celebration provides great cover for murder. All those fireworks and bonfires and screaming make more than enough noise to cover a stray gunshot. It's even commented on, and then, of course, a body is discovered. Lovely, blonde Mrs. Allen is found dead in her simply stunning Art Deco flat; pause frequently to fully appreciate the two-level suite, the décor, and the *objets d'art*. Wow. These ladies were not poor.

Loads of eye candy here, including a bird statue in the flat that reminded me of the Maltese Falcon. It was just sitting there, another knickknack among dozens of decorative objects. Like the tiger skin rug and the harp, it must have served as a prop for Jane Plenderleith's photography business.

A pistol is suspiciously placed in the dead blonde's hand to make murder look like suicide. There are two people's cigarettes in the ashtrays and a man's cufflink on the carpet to further suggest that whatever happened, it wasn't suicide.

Jane Plenderleith (*Juliette Moler*), the icy roommate

Charles Laverton-West (*David Yelland*), the political fiancé

Major Eustace (*James Faulkner*), the suspicious friend

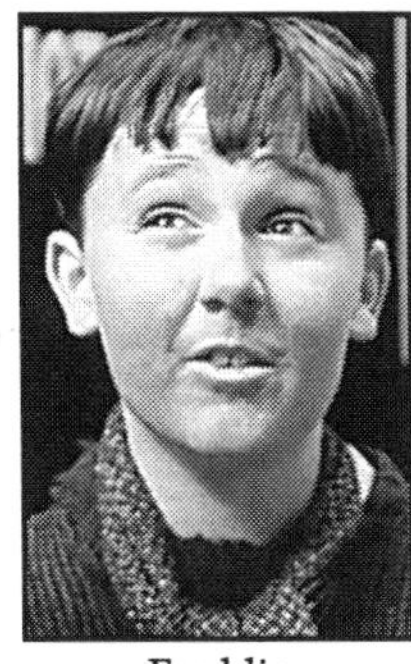

Freddie (*Nicholas Delve*), the boy mechanic

Mrs. Pierce (*Gabrielle Blunt*), the helpful "daily"

Chief Inspector Japp (*Philip Jackson*), the investigator

As the discoverer of the body, Jane Plenderleith is quick to fall under suspicion. She has an alibi, however, and aids Inspector Japp and Poirot in their investigation. She's full of opinions about her dead roommate, Mrs. Allen. She cheerfully points out Mrs. Allen's pompous, stuffed-shirt fiancé, Charles Laverton-West. Laverton-West would make a good villain since he doesn't seem to care about his fiancée's mysterious death other than the harm gossip would cause to his political career.

The other suspect is more intriguing. The scriptwriter outdid himself with Major Eustace, especially when he moved the interview from Major Eustace's flat (boring!) to a quasi-oriental nightclub where in the middle of the day gentlemen are already drinking and being attended to by costumed barmaids. The barmaids — a racially diverse bunch as one would expect down at the docks and near London's Chinatown — are distinguished by their painted-on cheongsams and coolie hats. They hover over the male clientele, providing a distinct strip club vibe to the place. There's even a girl singer in a very revealing costume (Moya Ruskin) serenading the guests. None of the guests pay much attention to the gyrating singer onstage despite her being superhot. They're too busy feeling up the girls in their laps.

It's clear from Major Eustace's occupation (running a questionable bar) and his reaction to the police that he's got something to hide. Quite a lot of somethings, in fact, at least according to the source material. Sadly, Major Eustace's checkered past is completely omitted in favor of the innuendo.

Poirot returns to following Jane Plenderleith, which leads him to a golf course. He discovers many broken golf clubs in the undergrowth, which is to be expected. He does not expect to catch Jane tossing an attaché case into a lake that normally only receives errant golf balls. This is when he works out what she's really trying to hide.

Everything was going great until we reached the ending, where Poirot interrogates Jane again, with Inspector Japp and Hastings looking on. He lectures Jane about what the true murder in this case is: not Mrs. Allen's death by gunshot but the murder of a man by the Crown because he was falsely accused of murdering Mrs. Allen. *Murder in the Mews* is the first time Agatha worked with this trope. Later, she expanded it significantly in *Towards Zero* (1944).

Poirot reprimands Jane about using murder by the Crown to punish a culprit who was guilty of garden-variety criminal behavior. He strongly disapproves of murder and does not believe it can ever be justified. In future episodes, this belief will be challenged.

When he gets Jane to admit she lied, the ending fell apart. Jane was devoted to her friend, Mrs. Allen. She wanted the best for her. She disliked Mrs. Allen's fiancé, recognizing him as an idiot who would fail her friend. She loathed Major Eustace, who was blackmailing Mrs. Allen. She has vengeance in her heart over her friend's dreadful death.

Yet when Poirot lectures her on murder, this woman gives up easily?

I don't think so.

This was the change the screenwriter made that shouldn't have been made. He didn't spell out why she should change her mind. In the short story, Poirot and Inspector Japp tell Jane that Major Eustace is in jail and will stay there for some time. Not because of blackmail; but because of his other criminal activities, nefarious behavior that came to light because of the murder investigation. Jane doesn't need to perjure herself to get revenge for her friend's tragic death. The Crown will take care of it for her. Major Eustace won't dance the hemp fandango, but he'll spend years in jail nonetheless.

I could buy Jane Plenderleith accepting Major Eustace's prosecution as being good enough, especially if she wants to avoid being charged with interfering with a criminal investigation. I cannot accept the ending I watched, where she says "okay" without knowing that Major Eustace would be punished with years in jail. She wanted revenge and punishment and didn't get either. Poirot appealing to her conscience would get her to change her mind just like that? She done Major Eustace wrong because he had it coming. No, just no.

It's still a good episode: well-paced, well-acted, fantastic clothes and plenty to watch. I'll watch it again, even knowing that the scriptwriter pulled his punches at the climax.

General Information

Based on: "Murder in the Mews" (short story, 1937)
Run time: 51 min. **Subtitles:** No

Writer: Clive Exton
Director: Edward Bennett

Cast

David Suchet as Hercule Poirot
Hugh Fraser as Captain Hastings
Pauline Moran as Miss Lemon
Philip Jackson as Chief Inspector Japp
John Cording as Division Inspector Jameson
Barrie Cookson as Dr. Brett

Juliette Mole as Jane Plenderleith
David Yelland as Charles Laverton-West, M.P.
James Faulkner as Major Eustace
Gabrielle Blunt as Mrs. Pierce
Nicholas Delve as Freddie
Christopher Brown as Golfer
Beccy Wright as Maid
Bob Bryan as Barman
Moya Ruskin as Singer

Film Locations

The Royal Society, Carlton House Terrace, London (Laverton-West's office)
Club Athenaeum, Waterloo Place, London (Laverton-West's club)

The Adventure of Johnnie Waverly (1989)

When Poirot can't stop the abduction of a country squire's son, he discovers all is not what it seems in the manor

Fidelity to text

It's close. The major change is Mr. Waverly hiring Poirot before the kidnapping rather than afterwards.

Quality of movie

It looks great, it's well-acted, it's got some great scenes, but it was also a missed opportunity for deeper storytelling.

The Adventure of Johnnie Waverly shows what happens when you must adapt a thin story but still leave room for the stars of the show instead of delving into why the kidnapping happened.

Johnnie is the only child of a country squire who has received threatening notes: pay thousands of pounds or the kid gets snatched. With each succeeding note, the ransom rises until at last the kidnapper specifies that at a certain day and time, Johnnie will vanish from Waverly Hall.

Mr. Waverly visits Chief Inspector Japp, who gives Mr. Waverly a sensible speech about why the police don't have a pre-crime department. People make threats all the time and never follow through. You'd have to, as Poirot tells Mr. Waverly afterwards, hire a policeman to shadow every citizen every day to have an effective pre-crime department. Pre-crime departments have their own problems as shown in *Minority Report* (2002). What if your pre-crime department is wrong? And would you, dear taxpayer, like to pay for this kind of police state?

Since Scotland Yard's no help, the frantic squire turns to Poirot and Hastings, and they rush to Waverly Hall in Hastings' racing car. The change from the short story makes sense because films demand immediate action, and he's a worried father who wants to forestall a terrible crime to his only son and heir.

Waverly Hall is a gorgeous example of what generations of time, tons of money, and exquisite taste can do when building the proper country estate for the family. It's also costly to maintain as evidenced by the abandoned scaffolding right by the front door. It's clear Mrs. Waverly controls the money, not Mr. Waverly. He, as is customary with both gentry and peerage, married Mrs. Waverly for her dowry. He needed the money and she, equally customary with ambitious young women, wanted to marry up in the world.

Yet they don't agree on how to spend the money. Tredwell, the butler, later tells Poirot that Mrs. Waverly doesn't understand how things should be done, such as proper staffing of the mansion. He implies that Mrs. Waverly wasn't brought up properly, like a member of the gentry would have been. She comes from new money. She never learned any better and worse, she doesn't care to learn now.

There are other signs this is true: When Poirot and

Marcus Waverly (*Geoffrey Bateman*), the concerned father

Ada Waverly (*Julia Chambers*), the economical mother

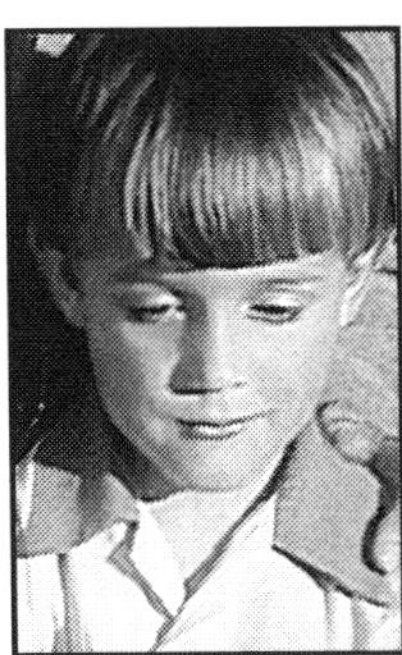

Johnnie Waverly (*Dominic Rougier*), the kidnap target

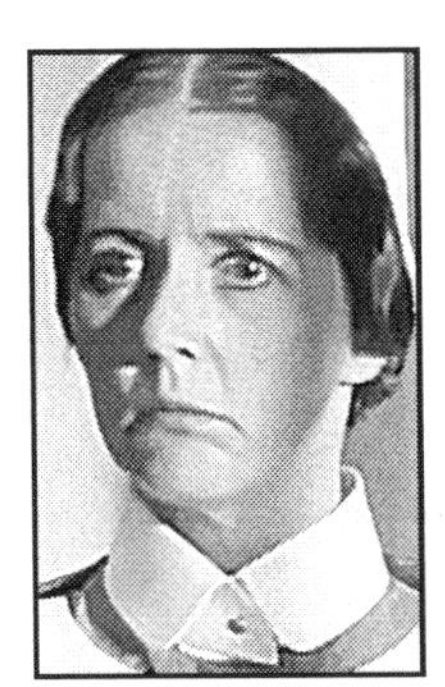

Jessie Withers (*Carol Frazer*), the resentful maid

Tredwell (*Patrick Jordan*), the trustful butler

Miss Collins (*Sandra Freeman*), the loyal secretary

Captain Hastings have dinner, the food is parceled out like it's been counted. If you grew up poor, you know what I mean. Four people for dinner meant four hamburgers, and if you wanted seconds, you ate more of the cheap mashed potatoes or the cheaper soup made from yesterday's leftovers and today's vegetable scraps.

In other words, Mrs. Waverly counted out cheap potatoes! To guests!

Mrs. Waverly's scrimping is even more apparent at breakfast. It's kedgeree, a dish brought to England from India by returning British colonials. It's supposed to be boiled rice mixed with cooked, flaked fish, boiled eggs, butter and cream, parsley, curry powder, and raisins. Yeah, that's for breakfast and so much tastier, I'm sure, than baked beans on cold toast. Classical English cooking, shudder. But Hastings can't find anything in the kedgeree other than rice. Plain boiled rice and for guests! This is serious penny-pinching but we're never told why Mrs. Waverly is so cheap. There must be a reason.

Knowing that reason would have been fascinating. This was the scriptwriter's chance to shine and fill out a very skimpy story. Did Mrs. Waverly resent being married off for her money? She's the reason the mansion is short-staffed according to the butler. According to Hughes, the builder, Mrs. Waverly is the reason the restorations on Waverly Hall were stopped. Did she resent paying for expensive redecorating? Or did she so dislike spending money, she was okay with letting the roof leak and water and mildew destroy her husband's ancestral home? And what does that mean about her feelings for her husband? Is this punishment because she didn't get the social status she wanted?

We aren't told. What makes this weird and obviously wrong is that the Waverlys act like a happy couple. They both love their son. We never see so much as a cross glance between them, despite how poorly they feed guests and how the front of the Hall looks like a construction zone. There must be conflict between them — any marriage counselor will tell you how money issues can tear a couple apart like nothing else — and yet we get nothing.

General Information

Based on: "The Adventure of Johnnie Waverly" (short story, 1923)
Run time: 51 min. **Subtitles:** No

Writer: Kevin Elyot
Director: Tom Shankland

Cast

David Suchet as Hercule Poirot
Hugh Fraser as Captain Hastings
Philip Jackson as Chief Inspector Japp
Pauline Moran as Miss Lemon

Geoffrey Bateman as Marcus Waverly
Julia Chambers as Ada Waverly
Dominic Rougier as Johnnie Waverly
Patrick Jordan as Tredwell
Carol Frazer as Jessie Withers
Sandra Freeman as Miss Collins
Robert Putt as Rogers
Patrick Connor as Hughes

Film Locations

Wrotham Park, South Mimms, Hertfordshire (Marcus Waverly's country home)
The Bull & Butcher, Turville (Hastings and Poirot take breakfast)
Turville Church, Buckinghamshire (background)

It didn't feel right. It felt even less right when Poirot reveals who the kidnapper had to be, since every clue pointed towards the only person capable of this inside job. £70,000 is a pretty darn good motivation. The sudden acquisition of £70,000 being spent on renovations would be deeply suspicious. If Mr. Waverly had to stop renovations because his dear wife wouldn't pay for them and she pays close attention to spending, then wouldn't she notice?

Believe me, I'd notice if my dear husband suddenly began contacting builders to reside the house with cement-fiberboard siding, install new windows, completely gut the kitchen and dining room, and add a fireplace when I know there's no money to do so.

But the title of the show is *Poirot* and not *Waverley*, so we spend time with him, Miss Lemon, and Hastings. It's great fun. Miss Lemon and her miracle filing system was amusing as well as so useful. She demonstrated again why she's the perfect secretary for a man as obsessed with order as Poirot.

We see more of Captain Hastings and his passion for motorcars. We see Poirot interacting with the British countryside in all its messy, weedy, disorganized glory. They even indulge in a sing-along while driving down country lanes! As Hastings, Hugh Fraser does a good job portraying an amiable idiot.

> *Prevention of crime is not what policemen are best at. They would need to have one constable for every citizen and go everywhere with him. But, fortunately for the human race, most of us have our own little policeman, up here.*
>
> HERCULE POIROT

In the end, though, the problem with this episode is the central mystery and it's not Johnnie Waverly's little adventure. It's the fraught relationship between his parents. That part of the story needed far more detail than what we got and was the scriptwriter's chance to shine. It was opaque, opaque enough that Hercule Poirot with his little gray cells could not penetrate the veil of mystery concealing the relationship between Mr. and Mrs. Waverly.

Four and Twenty Blackbirds (1989)

The case of the eccentric artist found dead at the foot of his stairs hinges on a change in eating habits

We open with two minor mysteries: Poirot is dining with his dentist (with whom he has a fraught relationship) and listening to the waitress about a regular who's eating wildly out of his usual routine.

Could these two mysteries be related? You bet they are. The first mystery I'll solve for you. Poirot is eating dinner with his dentist because — other than professionally — he likes the man. Also, Dr. Bonnington likes to see the results of his work in action.

They're enjoying dinner and speculating why a regular customer of extremely regular habits would disrupt his regular routine. Molly, the chatty waitress, is mystified and wants an opinion. She's waited on this man every Wednesday and Saturday for decades and he's never behaved differently before. Poirot, being Poirot, has his curiosity piqued. A few days later, he discovers that the diner has died, supposedly from a fall down the stairs. The nosy neighbor ladies noticed the accumulation of milk bottles although the milkman did not.

That was a mistake, because I would have thought the milkman would leave a note or something and pick up the unopened bottles as they stacked up like dead soldiers. Milkmen, like mailmen, see everything on their route and they know their customers' habits. Like mailmen, they expect notes from their customers about

Fidelity to text

Minor changes of name and character, far more background material and eye candy (including plenty of gratuitous nudity, both painted and real), but the overall arc remains, right down to motive and evidence.

Quality of movie

The changes and additions worked beautifully, enlarging and enhancing a short story into something larger. It could have been longer, though.

changes in delivery. Don't miss how the horse hauling the milk truck is ambling down the street, apparently unattended, while the milkman runs back and forth, delivering fresh, full bottles and picking up the empties. The horse knows the routine as well as his master.

I used to have milk delivered to my home decades ago in Norfolk when a local dairy still did delivery. They collected the empty bottles to reuse them. More importantly, milk left standing out on the stoop goes sour fast so I don't believe they liked leaving them hanging around. Sour milk discourages potential customers from signing up. That milk, by the way, was far better than any supermarket milk I've ever bought. I also purchased (from the dairy) an insulated metal box to sit on my front stoop to keep the milk cold. Sadly, the metal box ensures the neighbors don't see a suspicious accumulation of milk bottles and thus they do not investigate to see if you've fallen down the

George Lorrimer (*Richard Howard*), the artist's nephew

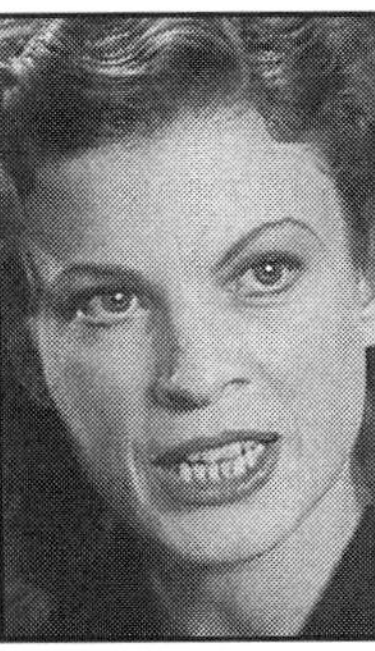

Dulcie Lang (*Holly De Jong*), the artist's model

Peter Makinson (*Clifford Rose*), the artist's agent

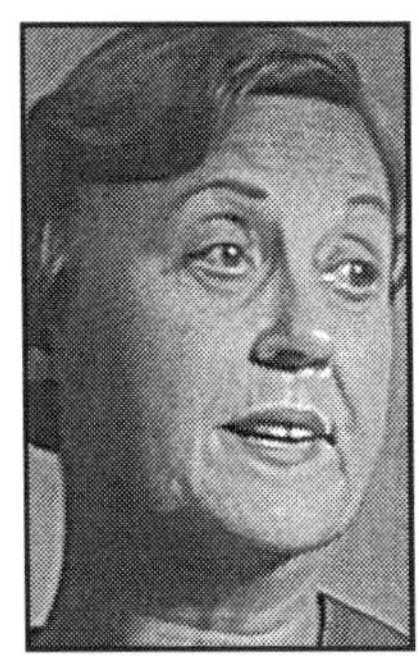

Irene Mullen (*Marjie Lawrence*), the artist's neighbor

Molly (*Cheryl Hall*), the artist's waitress

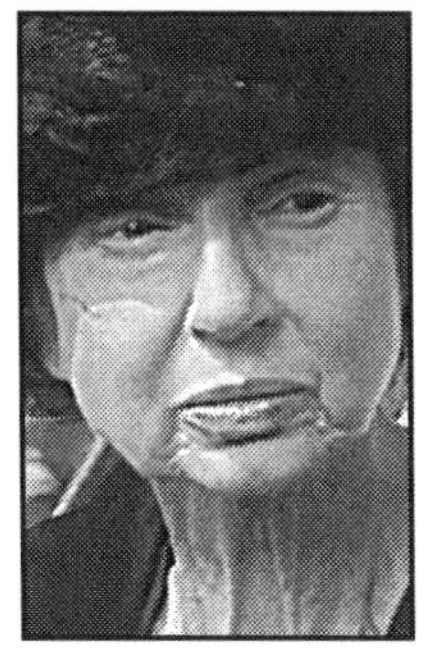

Amelia Hill (*Hilary Mason*), the irate housekeeper

stairs and your cats are snacking on your remains.

Anyway, that's what twigged the neighbors to call the bobby on the beat. They make the dreadful discovery and we're off.

Poirot discovers that the old man, Henry Gascoigne, was a good painter who refused to sell his paintings. This leads to the unspoken conclusion that he had money because if Henry wasn't selling paintings, then he had to be paying his bills some other way. If there's money hanging around unattended, then someone will be looking for it. Further investigation reveals the suspects: the painter's agent; his model, Miss Dulcie Lang; his estranged brother, Anthony Gascoigne; and a nephew, George Lorrimer.

The estrangement between fraternal twin brothers was interesting and more could have been done with it. Henry painted his brother Antony's wife nude. Was that the reason? Or was it something else? Or both? A bit of backstory would be welcome here, just because I'm always curious about these things. This painting added a second nude woman to the episode in addition to Dulcie Lang, nude model.

I always notice when we get nude female models for artists and not nude male models. There's plenty of nudity in this episode, including Miss Lang herself, seen posing from above. In a comic moment, Poirot appreciates the view and moves on about his business. Hastings is conflicted; wanting to gape over the railing with his tongue hanging out and drooling over that hot nekkid redhead while at the same time, remaining a perfect gentleman and pretending he didn't see a thing.

According to the agent and the model, Henry Gascoigne's paintings were valuable but couldn't be sold because he objected. With him dead, they can be. Henry also had a decent-sized estate, so this is evidence that his fall down the stairs might have been helped along.

But the twin brother who hated him is also now dead, and without a will. Mrs. Hill, Anthony Gascoigne's housekeeper, nurse, and companion, is angry and bitter and well she should be. She's an older woman with presumably no family of her own. With her employer dead, she's jobless, homeless, and has no legacy to help her out in her own old age. She tells Poirot all about it and mentions the nephew will inherit everything.

Miss Dulcie Lang, who probably needs the money (how much does nude modeling pay?), is adamant. She won't sell her Gascoigne paintings.

The trail leads to the nephew, George Lorrimer. He's a music hall impresario, so we see vignettes of a rehearsal in progress, complete with nearly nude dancers. They're actually wearing skimpy (for 1934) bathing suits. You'll also enjoy the comedy act being rehearsed.

There's so much to see in this episode. The Art Deco buildings and interior décor alone are worth the price of admission. Then, because the story revolves around an artist and his model, you'll get fine art, including a Miró (1893-1983) that Poirot appreciates but Hastings does not. There's also the latest forensics by Scotland Yard, which permits Inspector Japp to comment on how detective work is changing. Poirot uses the forensics department to trap his murderer, or rather, to prove his theory. He knows whodunnit but knowing isn't proof.

Hastings and Miss Lemon have their moments as well. Hastings gets to blather on about cricket. His speeches on the subject were unintelligible to me, a non-cricket fan. It reminded me that in Douglas Adam's universe, cricket is considered by most sentient galactic beings as being in rather bad taste. Poirot has the last laugh about cricket, astounding Hastings and everyone else with his knowledge of the game.

At the end, we return to the beginning and Poirot and his dentist. Teeth have a lot to do with solving the mystery. Teeth are why, after Poirot examines Henry Gascoigne's body in the morgue, he suspects murder. Teeth are one of the clues used in solving it.

You'll enjoy this episode. David Suchet is in top form as Poirot, the story is tight and well-paced, and the eye candy is top-quality. My only quibble is it could have been longer; more about the brothers' estrangement, more scenes in the music hall, more scenes with Miss Dulcie Lang, hot redhead, and how Hastings didn't know what to do with himself around her.

General Information

Based on: "Four and Twenty Blackbirds" (short story, 1926)
Run time: 50 min. **Subtitles:** No

Writer: Russell Murray
Director: Renny Rye

Cast

David Suchet as Hercule Poirot
Hugh Fraser as Captain Hastings
Philip Jackson as Chief Inspector Japp
Pauline Moran as Miss Lemon

Richard Howard as George Lorrimer
Geoffrey Larder as Harry Clarke
Holly De Jong as Dulcie Lang
Clifford Rose as Peter Makinson
Marjie Lawrence as Irene Mullen
Su Elliot as Edith
Hilary Mason as Amelia Hill
Denys Hawthorne as Bonnington
Cheryl Hall as Molly
Tony Aitken as Tommy Pinner
Charles Pemberton as Stooge
John Bardon as Lavatory Attendant
Philip Locke as Cutter
Peter Waddington as Forensic

Film Locations

Wilkins Building, University College, London (art gallery)
Cumberland Gardens, Clerkenwell (Henry Gascoyne's home)
Brighton Bandstand, West Sussex

The Third Floor Flat (1989)

A late-night rescue is interrupted when a dumbwaiter ride leads to the discovery of a dead tenant

We open with Poirot shrouded under a towel, breathing in steam. He's got a dreadful cold, all's wrong with the world, and he needs stimulation to keep his little gray cells from deteriorating further. Hastings suggests they see a mystery play, *The Deadly Shroud*. Poirot agrees and is rewarded with an idiot playwright who does not play fair with the audience. Poirot guesses wrong (!) as to who the murderer is (because the answer is wildly illogical) and owes 10 quid to Hastings.

We also meet Ernestine Grant, who's just moved into the lovely Art Deco apartment building, Whitehaven Mansions. She takes a flat one floor below Pat's flat and two floors down from Poirot's. She's still unpacking but that doesn't stop her from introducing herself to the neighbors overhead. She doesn't meet Pat and Mildred — they're dancing up a storm to loud music on the gramophone — but it seems she wants to complain about the noise they're making. She slips a letter under their door, demanding a meeting. Ernestine also meets a mysterious stranger wearing very stylish brown wingtips. She knows who he is, even if we do not. Not yet.

The irritating play and the new neighbor do not improve Poirot's cold or his concern about losing his faculties. What he needs is a murder and thanks to the new neighbor, he gets one.

That evening while Poirot and Hastings are watching the badly written play, so are two couples: Pat and Donovan and Mildred and Jimmy. Seeing the same play, unbeknownst to each other, gives them something to discuss later.

Poirot and Hastings come home from the theater, Poirot complaining about idiot playwrights who don't play fair with the audience, and that his cold has grown worse.

Pat and Donovan and Mildred and Jimmy also come home from the theater but their evening doesn't go smoothly either. Pat's key is missing. The building's concierge has gone home for the night. The gentlemen spring into action and decide to break into Pat's fourth-floor flat by smuggling themselves up in the small freight elevator. It was designed to deliver coal to each of the flats, so it can easily support the weight of two adult men.

Fidelity to text

(4 of 5 guns) A fleshed-out story and improved motivations, Miss Lemon as a ministering angel, and a dramatic chase scene.

Quality of movie

(4 of 5 guns) It all worked beautifully, except how shabbily the film and Poirot treated Mildred, Pat's friend.

Donovan Bailey (*Nicholas Pritchard*), the boyfriend

Pat Matthews (*Suzanne Burden*), the girlfriend

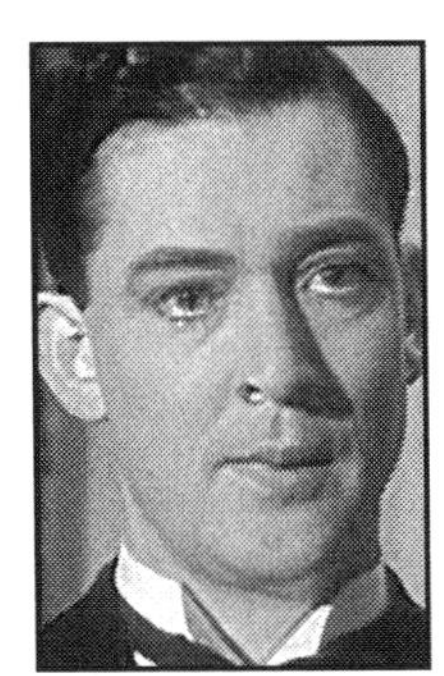

Jimmy Faulkener (*Robert Hines*), the second boyfriend

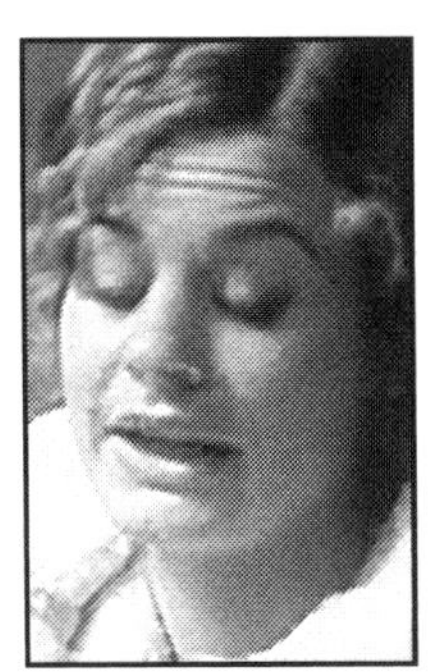

Mildred Hope (*Amanda Elwes*), the second girlfriend

Mrs. Ernestine Grant (*Josie Lawrence*), the upstairs neighbor

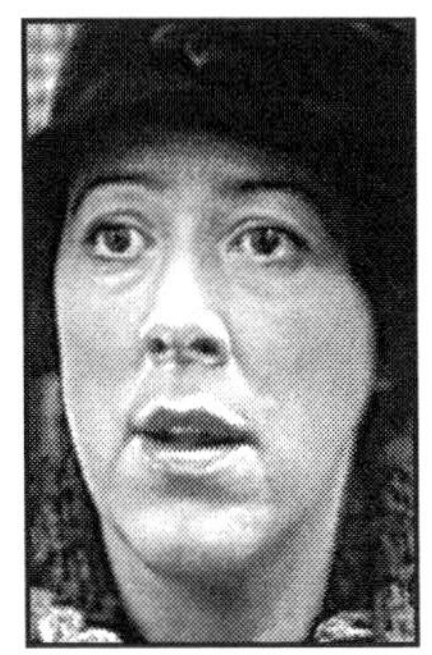

Trotter (*Susan Porrett*), the shocked maid

The gentlemen arrive in Pat's kitchen, but the kitchen light doesn't work. They move into the next room, turn on the light, and make the shocking discovery that they are not in Pat's flat after all. The lads miscounted floors, and they're in the flat below it. More shockingly, they discover the dead, bloody body of Ernestine Grant. The police are called.

Since Poirot lives in Whitehaven Mansions, he naturally steps in to see what's going on. Inspector Japp (replacing Inspector Rice in the short story) finds a letter in the victim's pocket and a handkerchief monogrammed "J.F." and decides the case is cut and dried. Whoever J.F. is, he shot Mrs. Grant at close range. Poirot is more suspicious; not about the shooting but about the identity of the shooter.

It's so convenient when the murderer leaves obvious clues to his identity at the scene of the crime. Almost like a badly written play, one would say.

Looking back on the episode, it's readily apparent that Poirot figured out almost immediately who had done what. Motivations and proof took longer to work out. Watch for his misdirection: It's classic Poirot.

The dénouement includes the villain's extremely self-serving sob story. Keep in mind as you watch that we only have his word for what happened. We have no idea what Ernestine Grant would have done after moving into the flat underneath Pat's flat. We know only one thing for sure: Ernestine Grant moved into the building that day, only to be shot that evening. We have no proof of anything else the murderer claims.

There's plenty of moments to appreciate. The theater scenes are especially engaging, with the hammy acting and beautifully dressed patrons enjoying the scenery chewing. The day Ernestine Grant moves in, there's an old lady operating a tea stand in front of Poirot's building selling tea to the movers. We meet her again when the villain steals Hastings' beloved Lagonda motorcar and crashes it into her tea stand. Miss Lemon, doing her darnedest to get Poirot to breathe in helpful steam. Long-suffering Inspector Japp, managing nosy neighbors, needing proof and not speculation.

What didn't I like? How Mildred, Pat's friend was treated. She's a good friend; that's clear from the opening scenes with Pat. They double-date at the theater. Pat goes with Donovan who wants to marry her, while Mildred's date is Jimmy.

General Information

Based on: "The Third Floor Flat" (short story, 1929)
Run time: 50 min. **Subtitles:** No

Writer: Michael Baker
Director: Edward Bennett

Cast

David Suchet as Hercule Poirot
Hugh Fraser as Captain Hastings
Philip Jackson as Chief Inspector Japp
Pauline Moran as Miss Lemon
Alan Partington as Inspector Flint
Jona Jones as Police Constable

Suzanne Burden as Pat Matthews
Nicholas Pritchard as Donovan Bailey
Robert Hines as Jimmy Faulkener
Amanda Elwes as Mildred Hope
Josie Lawrence as Mrs. Ernestine Grant
Susan Porrett as Trotter
James Aidan as Major Sadler
Gillian Bailey as Mrs. Sadler
Norman Lumsden as Vicar
John Golightly as Removal Man
Peter Aubrey as Removal Man
George Little as Dicker
Helena McCarthy as Tea Stall Owner

Unfortunately, Pat is a hot, vivacious blonde whereas Mildred is an average-looking, sedate brunette. So for that matter is Ernestine Grant. You know what that means in Hollywood. Ernestine Grant's fate is to serve as murder victim. Mildred's fate is to vanish from the second act even though she must be living with Pat! Why isn't she on the scene after the murder, right below Pat's flat, is discovered? Because no matter what Hollywood likes to claim about diversity, sedate, average-looking brunettes don't count.

They count so little that when the murderer's motivation is revealed, Poirot asks Jimmy about his interest in Pat. Not Mildred, the woman he escorted to the theater. No, it's Pat, who was planning to marry Donovan and not Jimmy. But now Pat needs Jimmy's strong, manly support during the upcoming trauma of the police investigation, newspaper coverage, and trial. Mildred doesn't just vanish from the scene. She loses her friend *and* her boyfriend.

Couldn't Mildred help Pat cope with the trauma? Apparently not. She gets disappeared even though it doesn't make any sense. Where did Mildred go? If the scriptwriter had time in 50 minutes to write a completely superfluous scene with the movers asking the tea lady to have a hot cuppa ready for them, the scriptwriter had time to show Mildred onstage with Pat, helping her cope with the shock of discovering who her fiancé truly was.

Or, the scriptwriter could have had Jimmy say he likes Pat well enough, but he's in love with Mildred.

But average-looking brunettes with unattractive names don't earn happy ever afters. Those are reserved for hot, vivacious blondes. Average-looking brunettes remain spinsters and adopt a lot of cats as they age, alone, because they don't rate a husband unless they dye their hair blonde.

If you don't have a problem with this issue, you'll enjoy *The Third Floor Flat*. If you do, brace yourself for what happens to Mildred. It's business as usual for Hollywood.

Triangle at Rhodes (1989)

Poirot's restful vacation gets upended when he's accused of being a spy and a restless woman inspires murder

Fidelity to text

Expected changes to characters and a change you wouldn't expect: The Italian authorities accuse Poirot of espionage.

Quality of movie

Characters yakking away in Greek and Italian — but without subtitles! — added local flavor but they also made it feel like Poirot pulled the solution from his boutonnière vase.

This episode was the first *Poirot* filmed in an exotic location: the island of Rhodes, 11 miles from the Turkish coast, and the crossroads of the Mediterranean since ancient times. It is drop-dead gorgeous. The director took full advantage of the historic buildings and glorious scenery so this movie is worth watching for that alone.

There are plenty of great mid-1930s vintage ladies' fashions too, from swimwear to eveningwear. Check out those beach pajamas! The gentlemen looked even better, particularly Commander Tony Chantry in his vintage one piece. You can see why Pamela discussed his resemblance to a gorilla. That was more polite, I suppose, than calling him Black Irish, which is what he really resembles with plenty of black hair, black eyes, and swarthy skin.

We open at Whitehaven Mansions on a typical English morning: rainy, dreary, dank. From the postman and the porter, we learn no one's home in 56-B. Captain Hastings is off shooting unfortunate animals, and Miss Lemon is communing with her sister. Even the "Frenchman" Poirot is somewhere foreign. The porter admits: "He sent me a postcard with goats on it."

Cut to Rhodes with its brilliant sunshine and blue skies, but dark clouds loom overhead. If you pay attention to what's happening in the background, you'll see plenty of Italian Blackshirts marching around, catcalling the women, and expecting everyone to get out of their way. Italy seized the island in 1912 from the Ottomans and settled down for a long stay. The locals don't like them. There's a huge portrait of Mussolini (1883-1945) in the police department. The newspaper is blaring about unrest in Italian-occupied Abyssinia. People are afraid of what's coming.

The English tourists are oblivious. Well, except the radically youthened Major Barnes, who spends his time annoyingly mooning after Pamela. It turns out he's using his doofus persona to cover up the true reason he's exploring Rhodes. We only get hints, and that's a shame. His greatly expanded story would have benefited from a longer film. When everyone leaves at the finale, he heads off to go ostrich hunting in Abyssinia. Sure. Why not. Perhaps he'll discover interesting things about the Italian invaders that the British government would like to know.

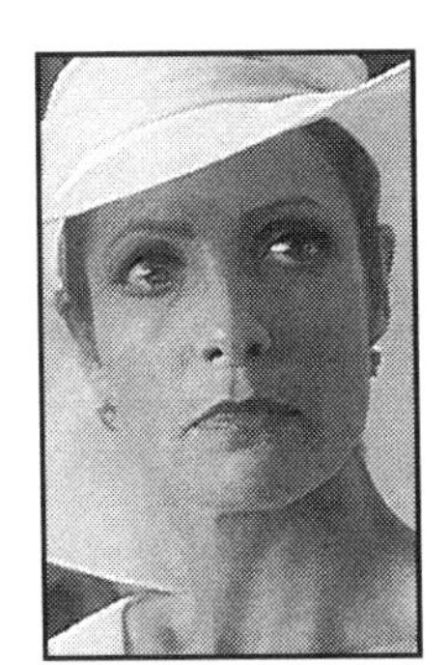

Valentine Chantry (*Annie Lambert*), the heedless temptress

Tony Chantry (*Jon Cartwright*), her fifth husband

Douglas Gold (*Peter Settelen*), the tempted husband

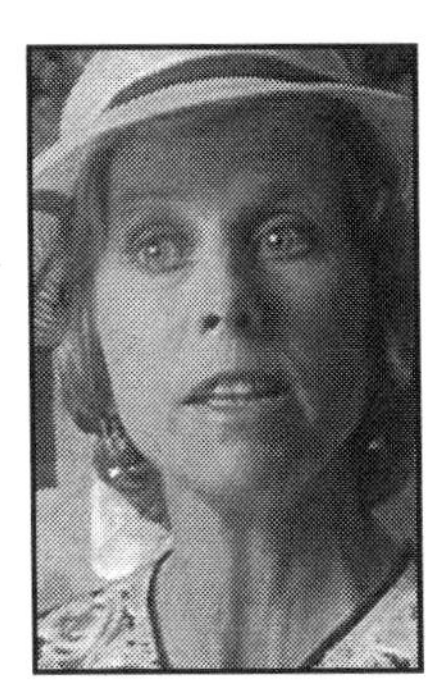

Marjorie Gold (*Angela Down*), the fretful wife

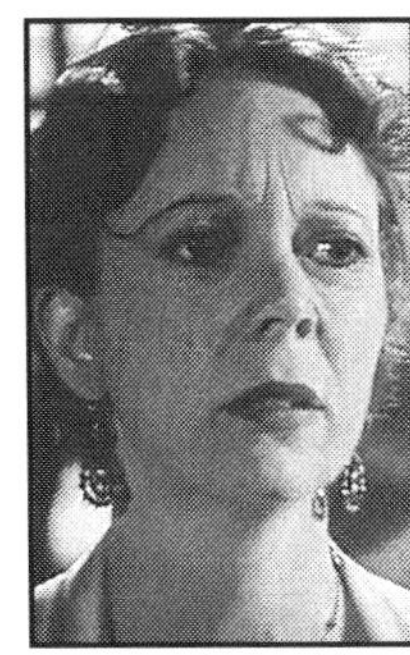

Pamela Lyall (*Frances Low*), the Greek chorus

Greek Girl (*Georgia Dervis*), the helpful local

At the hotel, Poirot overhears Marjorie and Douglas Gold. They had trouble getting to the hotel, and Douglas gripes about coming to Rhodes. Poirot learns Marjorie was the one who insisted they visit Rhodes rather than someplace closer to home. I think this is what happened, but again, poor enunciation and no subtitles.

This scene is important because the next morning, Marjorie tells people that it was Douglas' idea to visit Rhodes, not hers. Marjorie also ruminates about how awful it is when people divorce at the drop of a hat. She is, naturally, referring to the wealthy and glamorous Valentine Chantry. Commander Chantry is Valentine's fifth husband, and it's doubtful that even in 1935 a woman would have been widowed four times.

Pamela, sitting at beachside with Poirot, can't help but notice Valentine. She has a more interesting take: that women like Valentine don't remain married because their *husbands* eventually get sick of their drama. They watch Valentine order Commander Chantry around like a flunky. To Marjorie's distress, Valentine seduces Douglas Gold into becoming another lackey.

It's Pamela who draws the triangle in the sand, illustrating typical human nature. Poirot evaluates what they're seeing and hearing, compares it to what he overhead the previous evening, and silently draws a more subtle conclusion about the mismatch. It even leads him to warn Marjorie Gold, in a classic Agatha bit of misdirection, that if she values her life, she'll leave Rhodes.

A lot of what you should notice about the inconsistencies in Douglas and Marjorie's story — and thus understand Poirot's deduction — was not presented well. Douglas is apparently a devoted Catholic; he crosses himself at an icon-laden altar. Devout Catholics didn't divorce casually in 1935, unlike what Marjorie claims she fears. Poirot comments to Douglas that his faith will sustain him in difficult days to come.

Marjorie isn't afraid of a six-foot long venomous snake, yet later on (I think) she claims to have been frightened by a bug. Again, murky dialog.

All the sideways glances, innuendo, and browbeating of unhappy spouses culminates in Valentine drinking her husband's pink gin cocktail and dying in agony.

I didn't know gin could be pink. I learned that adding a dash of Angostura bitters makes the difference between a gin-swilling low-class sot in the East End and a tuxedo-clad aristocrat in a resort in Rhodes.

Commander Chantry accuses Douglas of trying to poison him, so Douglas can run off with Valentine. Marjorie is even more distraught.

Poirot would have stepped in, but he had already checked out of the hotel and he's arguing with customs over their spy accusation. Unlike in England, he gets no respect from the local law, and this is one of the rare scenes where you'll see Poirot furious. Pamela frantically searches for him and since justice must be done and his boat left without him, Poirot takes the case.

Just like with customs, he gets nowhere with the police. Fortunately, Major Barnes knows the local coroner; an Englishman who's gone native. The coroner tells them that the poison was rare and made locally. With no official help, Poirot and Pamela search the souks of Rhodes looking for the source of the poison.

This is where subtitling the Greek dialog would have saved the episode. We meet the same Greek girl who had helped Pamela avoid Major Barnes at the beginning of the episode. Greek girl speaks a few words of English and leads them to her blind grandmother who doesn't. I couldn't understand what was going on, and I couldn't figure out why the Greek girl helped Pamela at the beginning, just that she did.

Poirot saves the day using the Greek grandmother's information. Sadly, he does not ask why she was selling snake venom to English tourists in the first place. Even more sadly, we don't get a good summation of the case, leaving me to guess how he made his deductions.

It's still a good episode for the scenery, costumes, and the scenery chewing. Listen carefully to the Easter egg concealed in the music: it's the Poirot themes played on Eastern Mediterranean instruments. It only needed more explanation and better enunciation to make it a perfect episode.

General Information

Based on: "Triangle at Rhodes" (short story, 1936)
Run time: 50 min. **Subtitles:** No

Writer: Stephen Wakelam
Director: Renny Rye

Cast

David Suchet as Hercule Poirot
Frances Low as Pamela Lyall

Jon Cartwright as Cmdr. Tony Chantry
Annie Lambert as Valentine Chantry
Peter Settelen as Douglas Gold
Angela Down as Marjorie Gold
Timothy Kightley as Major Barnes
Georgia Dervis as Greek Girl
Sofia Olympiou as Good Woman
Anthony Benson as Skelton
Patrick Monckton as Hotel Manager
Tilemanos Emanuel as Customs Officer
Al Fiorentini as Police Inspector
Stephen Gressieux as Italian Policeman
George Little as Dicker
Martyn Whitby as Postman

Film Locations

Casa del Fascio (police station)
Kallithea Springs (beach scenes, restaurant)
Mandraki Harbour (Chantrys and Golds' arrival)
Monolithos Castle and the Greek church (excursion)
Rhodes old town
Rodiaki Epavli (Palace Hotel exterior)
Temple of Apollo (Valentine's outing with Pamela and Marjorie)

Problem at Sea (1989)

Poirot knows the identity of the killer of a harridan wife on a Mediterranean tour, but can he prove whodunnit?

Fidelity to text

Hastings arrives on board along with more passengers and added subplots. The altered ending, implausible as it is, is far more plausible than the one in the short story.

Quality of movie

An enjoyable cruise on the Mediterranean that should have been much longer. Those added subplots didn't get neatly tied off.

This was a good episode, clearly shot on a real, vintage ship out at sea. The filming took place right after *Triangle at Rhodes* was shot. This allowed the director to transform the island of Rhodes into Alexandria, Egypt. His set designer did a terrific job since I didn't say, "I saw that building last episode!"

This does beg the question of when Captain Hastings joined Poirot since he wasn't present at the last port of call, Rhodes. Nothing is said, so I'm assuming Hastings' trip to shoot animals in northern England (referred to in the opening of *Triangle at Rhodes*) didn't go well. Thus, he joined Poirot at some exotic port of call and is consoling himself by setting up clay pigeon shooting competitions on board the ship. Maybe clay pigeons are easier to shoot, even on board a ship at sea.

I was impressed that such a small ship had the launching apparatus, along with clay pigeons, shotguns, and plenty of ammo. I've no idea where the purser stowed all that gear when he had to find space for the much more important mountain of luggage along with linens and groceries needed by the passengers. Ships don't generally have a lot of room to spare. That was not a roomy, flat-bottomed cruise ship capable of carrying hundreds of passengers. The crew must have hot-racked to make extra space.

The cruise ship is real: she is the Motor Yacht *Madiz*, built in 1902. A ship of her class was likely cruising the Mediterranean in 1935. She's still in service today and still has many of her original fittings, so you aren't seeing a film set. You're seeing the real thing. I would have liked to have seen more of her, especially the bridge, but there's only so much time in a 51-minute episode. When you're watching, notice that, based on the size of the portholes, Kitty and Pamela's stateroom is barely above the waterline. They've also got bunks to conserve space. Poirot paid for a more luxurious, spacious upper cabin as did the Clappertons.

I wanted to see a lot more of Mrs. Adeline Clapperton. She's rich, entitled, sarcastic, and used to having her own way. She's desperately fighting off age and resents her husband's close attention to the much younger, much jollier Kitty and Pamela. You can tell she doesn't consider Ellie Henderson, despite her charming personality, to be a threat. Adeline is an unhappy, bored woman with too much time on her hands. The story implies that she was very happy running her hospital for

Adeline Clapperton (*Sheila Allen*), the harridan wife

Col. John Clapperton (*John Normington*), the harried husband

Ellie Henderson (*Ann Firbank*), the lonely woman

General Forbes (*Roger Hume*), the lonely man

Kitty Mooney (*Melissa Greenwood*), jolly girl #1

Pamela Cregan (*Victoria Hasted*), jolly girl #2

wounded soldiers during World War I. She was married before, widowed, and then met Colonel Clappperton.

It's readily obvious who holds the purse strings, and it's not her husband. We know why he married her. The question is why did she marry him? And why is she still married to him? She snipes at him constantly, reminding him of his lowly status, yet he's still hanging around. She doesn't reserve her vitriol for her husband either. One of the other passengers tells Poirot that it wouldn't be surprising if a woman like Adeline Clapperton got a hatchet smashed through her skull. She doesn't. She gets a knife in her heart.

So why did General Forbes keep the flame burning for Adeline? He tells Poirot that she was a much different woman when she was younger. Disappointed in love, I suppose, and naturally, she pays no attention to the older general pining for her. That's a story that needed telling. Perhaps General Forbes will connect with Ellie Henderson who deserves her own happy ending. They both do.

Adeline loathes and fears the jolly young misses flirting up a storm with her despised husband. Kitty and Pamela lack money, sophistication, high-status connections, and savoir faire, but they have something Adeline no longer enjoys: youth. Watch Adeline singing a popular song of the time to herself in the mirror. No one sings that to her, not anymore. It was a reminder that she used to be a different person when she was young and lovely, before the vicissitudes of life soured her, back when she was the girl General Forbes wistfully remembers.

I'd also like to know what those two jolly sorority sisters, Kitty and Pamela, were doing on a small cruise ship without chaperones or a stated reason like going to visit extended family. Young ladies like them wouldn't have jaunted off into the unknown for no reason, not even in 1935. If they're looking to snag rich husbands by compromising them, Col. Clapperton is the wrong target. If they're looking to amuse themselves by annoying an older woman pining for her lost youth, they're succeeding!

General Information

Based on: "Problem at Sea" (short story, 1936)
Run time: 51 min. **Subtitles:** No

Writer: Clive Exton
Director: Renny Rye

Cast

David Suchet as Hercule Poirot
Hugh Fraser as Captain Hastings

John Normington as Col. John Clapperton
Sheila Allen as Adeline Clapperton
Roger Hume as General Forbes
Ann Firbank as Ellie Henderson
James Ottaway as Mr. Russell
Geoffrey Beevers as Mr. Tolliver
Caroline John as Mrs. Tolliver
Melissa Greenwood as Kitty Mooney
Victoria Hasted as Pamela Cregan
Dorothea Phillips as Nelly Morgan
Sheri Shepstone as Emily Morgan
Louisa Janes as Ismene
Ben Aris as Captain Fowler
Colin Higgins as Skinner

Film Locations

Kolona Harbour, Rhodes (Alexandria dock)
Arionos Square, Rhodes (market scenes)
Theofiliskou Street, Rhodes (police station)

So Adeline dies in a locked cabin but to Poirot, the solution becomes clear once he gives the little gray cells time to work. Who is the most likely suspect? Who had the most motivation built up from swallowing years of contempt while accompanied by a driving desire to remain rich? Divorce doesn't lead to riches, not when one partner used to be a music hall performer who married way above his station in life. Poverty doesn't draw jolly young ladies like moths to a flame, not when significant other assets, like youth and virility, are missing. But wealth does.

The climax is the other major change. In the short story, Poirot manages to locate — on this 187-foot-long cruise ship, the actual length of *Madiz* — a nearly life-sized ventriloquist's dummy. Sure. That's even less likely (unless a ventriloquist is a passenger) than finding a clay pigeon launcher, shotguns, crates of clay pigeons, and cases of ammo stowed in the hold. An average-sized cruise ship is about 1,000 feet long or five times the size of the *Madiz*. Maybe there, but not on board the *Madiz*.

Monsieurs, Madames. What I am about to do might surprise you a little. You'll probably think of me as eccentric – perhaps mad. You might say, "the little Belgian is taking leave from his rocker," hein? *But I must assure you, that behind my madness is, what you English say... method.*

HERCULE POIROT

Instead, we and Poirot are introduced early on to the youngest passenger on board, Ismene. She's the niece of two other passengers, and she plays with dolls. Ismene graciously agrees to lend Papa Poirot both a doll and her voice to capture the murderer. It's plausible, made more plausible by the fact that her two aunts, ladies of a certain age, enjoy entertaining the company with singing and recitations. Ismene is following in their footsteps with her performance; a performance that doesn't just entrap a murderer. It executes him, so the hangman doesn't have to.

You'll enjoy *A Problem at Sea* from stem to stern. It could have been longer to fill out all the subplots but you can't have everything.

The Incredible Theft (1989)

Poirot and a traitor are locked into a cat-and-mouse game over plans for an inventor's revolutionary plane

Fidelity to text

Added car chases because what is a Poirot episode without car chases? Hastings, Japp, and Miss Lemon show up, and the plans alter slightly.

Quality of movie

Funny lines, English country house porn, top-notch fashion, a touch of gratuitous nudity and a vintage fighter plane dive bombing its target!

We open with Poirot demonstrating the proper way to keep a shine on patent leather shoes. Hastings is preoccupied with learning architectural terms to impress his new girlfriend, a student of the subject. He's trying to read a book about Gian Lorenzo Bernini (1598-1680), famous Italian architect and sculptor, but can't make head nor tails of it.

Sadly, Hastings being Hastings, it's wishful thinking on his part, and Poirot knows it. Girls, he tells his friend, do not want to talk about Bernini.

"I don't know that she wants to talk about anything," Hastings replies. "She's never in when I go round to see her. I end up having tea with her mother every day." There are a lot of these jokes embedded in the dialog, and you'll have to pay close attention to catch them all.

Here's another one. This is Tommy Mayfield asking an important question of Sir George Carrington, MP.

"Why do politicians treat everyone else like idiots?"

"Probably because they voted for us in the first place."

Sir George should know, since Tommy Mayfield, wealthy industrial magnate and genius aircraft designer, is an idiot outside of his engineering and business skills. His wife, Lady Mayfield (daddy was an earl so she retains her title despite marrying a commoner) knows her beloved husband is an idiot, which is why she hires Poirot to save him from himself. Poirot wants backup on this mission and plants Hastings in the nearby inn.

Sir George also knows that Tommy Mayfield is an idiot, based on his plan to salvage his reputation. That's why Sir George has Chief Inspector Japp hiding out in the same inn until he's needed. Naturally, being a small establishment, there's not enough room at the inn. Hastings and Japp don't just share a room. They share a bed. Hastings reveals to Poirot that Japp doesn't merely talk in his sleep. He roars.

Meanwhile, everyone other than Hastings and Japp is assembled at a fine English country house for drinks on the terrace, dinner, and cards afterward, and then … espionage courtesy of Mrs. Vanderlyn, American adventuress. She's the hussy Lady Mayfield is fretting over. What will happen to her husband as a result of Mrs. Vanderlyn's machinations? Lady Mayfield knows the gruesome story about the young lord who

Lord Tommy Mayfield (*John Stride*), the industrialist

Margaret Mayfield (*Ciaran Madden*), the worried wife

Sir George Carrington (*John Carson*), the senior civil servant

Isabelle Carrington (*Phyllida Law*), the bridge lover

Mrs. Vanderlyn (*Carmen Du Sautoy*), the charming spy

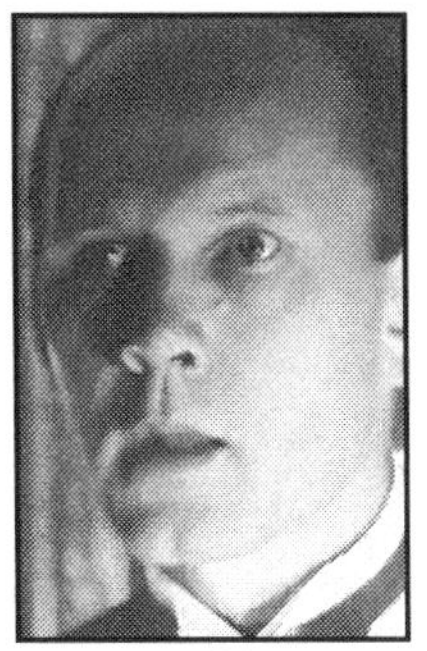
Carlile (*Albert Welling*), his lordship's sec'y

committed suicide after his run-in with Mrs. Vanderlyn and she doesn't want her Tommy to suffer.

Sir George is also worried about Mrs. Vanderlyn, but in a different way. Thanks to a previous scandal involving the Japanese, Tommy's reputation is mud down at Whitehall. As a result, the government is reluctant to back his new bomber design. Tommy decides to invite Mrs. Vanderlyn to the house, catch her in the act of stealing the plans, and show the government and Sir George he's worth trusting. Now the audience is sure he's an idiot.

The stolen plans, a fighter in the story, transform into a bomber. Since most of us can't tell them apart on sight, it doesn't matter. They're airplanes. They fly.

You can immediately tell the difference on sight between Lady Mayfield's upbringing and Mrs. Vanderlyn's more checkered past.

Lady Mayfield wears great clothes with great hats but they're appropriate for whatever situation you see her in, including meeting Poirot at the Penguin Pool at the London Zoo. Insert morning dress versus evening dress jokes here if you like. Poirot is, after all, underdressed compared to the penguins. That's a rare situation for him!

In contrast, Mrs. Vanderlyn wears fabulous clothes, but she's always overdressed. It's part of her image. That slinky silver lamé dress is to die for. Then there are her fitted suits with matching hats and mink stoles. She's got clothing just for the boudoir, a lovely confection of lace and satin. When the plans vanish and she's hauled off to the police station, Mrs. Vanderlyn supplies intimations of gratuitous nudity when she's strip-searched by a female constable behind privacy glass. Watch Inspector Japp trying very hard not to ogle and failing repeatedly.

The female constable doesn't find anything suspicious because Mrs. Vanderlyn doesn't make rookie mistakes. Even her gratuitous namedropping (like her overdressing) isn't a mistake because she's ensuring those English snobs underestimate her.

She escapes with the secret bomber plans, leading to the exciting added chase. Hastings is at the wheel of a stolen police car, following Mrs. Vanderlyn and her chauffeur to the conveniently located English country estate being rented by the ambassador from Germany. She drops off the stolen plans, snaps off a Heil Hitler salute and rides away, satisfied with a job well done.

One has to wonder what her chauffeur thought, watching the lady who employs him dropping off a suspicious suitcase with the German ambassador after being pursued by a police car at high speed through the English countryside. But we aren't told. Similarly, what does Mrs. Vanderlyn's maid think? Mrs. Vanderlyn must have one with that stunning wardrobe to take care of but we never learn what her lady's maid knows. We never see her lady's maid at all.

The espionage case is swiftly solved by Poirot. It's so simple Hastings could have solved it. If only two people have access to the plans, then those are the two people involved. This was not the kind of plot involving *Mission: Impossible* ninjas worming their way in via the skylights and threading through spider webs of laser beams to steal the plans.

Ah, but are those the real plans Mrs. Vanderlyn stole, you ask? Not exactly. They're close though. Close enough that Mrs. Vanderlyn is very pleased with herself. If she had any doubts about the validity of the plans, the strip-search and police chase put them to rest. Close enough, one assumes, to fool the German high command. Close enough that all ends happily for Tommy and Lady Mayfield. Papa Poirot gives them a little lecture on communication skills, and you know they'll live happily ever after.

It's a pity that Captain Hastings doesn't listen to Poirot about communications skills between couples but if he did, he wouldn't be our captain.

For a very simple story, there's plenty to enjoy in *The Incredible Theft*. With incredible clothes, great Art Deco settings, snappy dialog, unexpected humor, and most of all, a vintage fighter plane dive bombing its target! The pilot must have had a blast flying a genuine Supermarine Spitfire IX and demonstrating her maneuverability and firepower although that may have been special effects. This episode has it all.

General Information

Based on: "The Incredible Theft" (novella, 1923)
Run time: 1 hr. **Subtitles:** No

Writers: David Reid and Clive Exton
Director: Edward Bennett

Cast

David Suchet as Hercule Poirot
Hugh Fraser as Captain Hastings
Pauline Moran as Miss Lemon
Philip Jackson as Chief Inspector Japp

John Stride as Lord Tommy Mayfield
Ciaran Madden as Lady Margaret Mayfield
John Carson as Sir George Carrington
Phyllida Law as Lady Isabelle Carrington
Guy Scantlebury as Reggie Carrington
Carmen Du Sautoy as Mrs. Vanderlyn
Albert Welling as Carlile
Dan Hildebrand as Chauffeur
Phillip Manikum as Sergeant
Uncredited actor as Dawson

Film Locations

Chenies Manor House, Chenies, Buckinghamshire (Mayfield residence)
RAF West Malling Airfield, Kent (plane demonstration)

"

Stand back lads, he's got a blancmange!

INSPECTOR JAPP, TALKING IN HIS SLEEP

The King of Clubs (1989)

The turn of a card hints at secret ties to financial chicanery that if played could trump an aristocratic marriage

There were so many missed opportunities and unwelcome changes. They all stem from Valerie Saintclair, our heroine and damsel in distress. In the 1923 short story, she's a dancer in a nightclub run by a very shady man. Can you say organized crime ties? Maybe Agatha didn't write them but readers of the time would have thought of them. Seedy nightclub dancers are the very definition of unsuitable wives for princes like Prince Paul of Maurania, Valerie's lover. They're mistress material, born to be enjoyed and discarded. To respectable people, nightclub dancers were one step above taxi dancers and two steps above prostitutes.

In this episode, Valerie has morphed into a well-regarded actress. That's still not quite respectable, but an actress in the 1930s enjoyed far more cachet than a nightclub dancer did in the 1920s. She could conceivably marry Prince Paul and even — if it's not a morganatic marriage — become his princess consort and watch their children inherit.

That is, if his royal family doesn't find other reasons to object to that blonde hussy who kisses strange men in public because it's her job. And there are reasons, which Valerie and the louche studio head both know. Remember, Valerie is an actress, which makes her a professional liar. If she conceals her secret shame, they'll never learn it from her. If you can fake sincerity, you can get people to believe anything you say.

Fidelity to text

The basic story is intact, but the changes weaken the conflict, motivations, and the mystery. They also weaken the characters because there's no reason to care about Valerie Saintclair's dilemmas.

Quality of movie

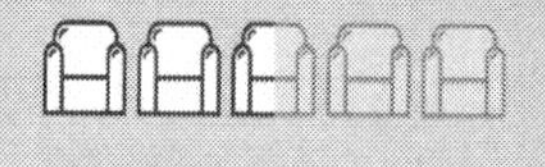

It's entertaining, well-acted, gorgeous eye-candy as usual, yet you won't care about any of the principals. They're forgettable.

We see plenty of evidence that Henry Reedburn is a typical studio head. He's abusive, loud, dictatorial, and a Lothario (watch his interaction with his hot secretary). His manservant admits Reedburn gets routine late-night lady visitors, and he collects blackmail material to keep the talent in line. Quite routine for a studio boss, but so much more could have been done with this goldmine of material.

The mystery is likewise given short shrift. In the short story, Valerie claims she visited a clairvoyant and was warned about the King of Clubs. That fit nicely with a seedy nightclub owner but not so much with a studio head. The visit to the clairvoyant is dropped entirely. Instead, the only King of Clubs we see is the missing card Poirot discovers from observing the bridge hands spread out on the table in the Oglander's parlor.

Henry Reedburn
(*David Swift*),
the studio chief

Valerie Saintclair
(*Niamh Cusack*),
the rising star

Ralph Walton
(*Gawn Grainger*),
the falling star

Bunny Saunders
(*Jonathan Coy*),
the harried director

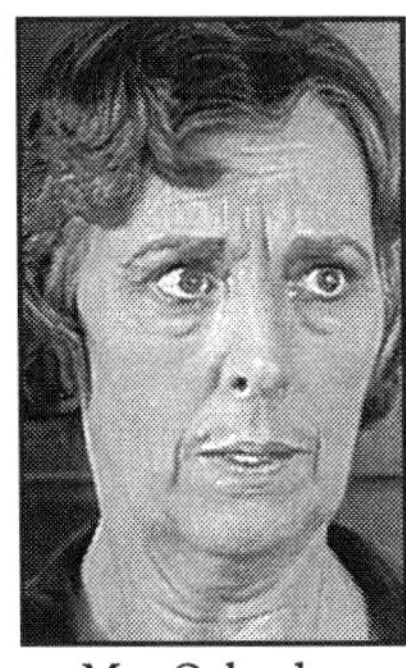

Mrs. Oglander
(*Avril Elgar*),
the good Samaritan

Prince Paul
(*Jack Klaff*),
the royal fiancé

Wait. Who? Why, the Oglanders are the household that Valerie escapes to in her blind panic over discovering Reedburn's murdered body. They live in a nearby house, but not the closest house. Valerie had to find it by running through the tangled woods in the dark in her evening gown and high heels. In the pouring down rain. Sure.

When Poirot investigates, Hastings in tow, the Oglanders are blasé about the famous movie star staying in their house who's escaped from a dreadful crime scene. Drenched movie stars must regularly show up on their doorstep in the middle of the night. They also seem protective of Valerie, despite not knowing her other than watching her kiss strangers at the pictures.

Poirot notices the family portrait from previous years: the Oglanders and their three children, two daughters and a son. He's met the son and one daughter. Where is daughter number three? Dead, Mrs. Oglander says.

Inspector Japp investigates and gets sidetracked from examining the crime scene by discovering a gypsy's boots in the woods. Reedburn had been squabbling with a local band so they make likely suspects, made even more so because Valerie insisted she saw hobnailed boots sticking out from underneath the floor-length draperies in Reedburn's library. Japp focuses on this and ignores other evidence.

I know darn well they had basic forensics in 1935; we saw evidence of this in Four and Twenty Blackbirds. Why wasn't Japp's team examining the library, including the fancy lion-headed chairs? Because they would have discovered that the death didn't happen the way a first glance at the body implied. I can't stand it when otherwise intelligent characters act incompetent because the plot demands that they do.

So Japp and his investigators completely overlook the smear of blood on one of the chairs. They don't bother to follow Valerie's panicked trail through the woods to the Oglander's house. I know gypsies make credible suspects, and maybe the local police would ignore other evidence when dirty, thieving gypsies are hanging about. But Japp's too dogged (as he tells Poirot) and thorough to overlook other possibilities.

By now, an astute viewer will have figured out that Valerie, despite her protests of virtue, had to be involved. So are the Oglanders because of their behavior. Valerie is the missing and estranged Oglander daughter, but it didn't seem like she was estranged from them at all.

General Information

Based on: "The King of Clubs"
(short story, 1923)
Run time: 50 min. **Subtitles:** No

Writer: Michael Bakjer
Director: Renny Rye

Cast

David Suchet as Hercule Poirot
Hugh Fraser as Captain Hastings
Philip Jackson as Chief Inspector Japp

Niamh Cusack as Valerie Saintclair
Gawn Grainger as Ralph Walton
David Swift as Henry Reedburn
Jonathan Coy as Bunny Saunders
Jack Klaff as Prince Paul of Maurania
Rosie Timpson as Miss Deloy
Jeffrey Harmer as Assistant Director
Marc Culwick as Young Man
Vass Anderson as Frampton
Avril Elgar as Mrs. Oglander
Abigail Cruttenden as Geraldine Oglander
Sean Pertwee as Ronnie Oglander
Cathy Murphy as Maid

Film Locations

High and Over, Highover Park, Amersham, Buckinghamshire (Reedburn's house)
Hoover Building, Greenford, Middlesex (studio exterior)

Which brings us to the secret that Reedburn was using to blackmail Valerie with, keeping her tied to his studio with an onerous contract and (hint, hint) performing favors of a personal and intimate nature. It seems that Oglander is not the family's real name. It's Hawtrey. Mr. Hawtrey committed serious fraud, enough to hit the newspapers and be brought up on charges.

We don't know if Hawtrey went to jail for it, but we can guess that Prince Paul doesn't know this sordid story, and if his royal family knew, they'd be livid. Actresses are bad enough, but actresses involved in suspicious deaths and who are related to thieves? *Quelle horreur*.

Thus, using the missing card from the bridge game and the mysterious closeness between Valerie and the Oglanders, Poirot pulls the solution from out of his boutonnière vase. Valerie met Reedburn but she wasn't alone. She went with her brother. An altercation took place resulting in Reedburn's death.

But since Reedburn was a terrible man, Valerie is a desperate and sort-of-innocent woman, and her family reunited to save her, she escapes justice. Her brother isn't charged with manslaughter. She'll marry Prince Paul of Maurania and his family will remain unaware of her tawdry past. Inspector Japp will be left with an unsolved crime, after harassing innocent gypsies who had nothing to do with the case.

This episode was gorgeous to watch, but it felt so bloodless. I didn't care about Valerie's troubles. There should have been lurid scenes set at the studio with other victims of Reedburn's excesses. Or the Oglander family should have been more upset and fearful when Valerie showed up on their doorstep, desperate for help from the people she abandoned when they needed her. Or the clairvoyant who told Valerie to beware the King of Clubs should have been left in, adding an interesting red herring.

Instead, we get serviceable and forgettable. Watch it, enjoy it, and move on to other, better films that are worth rewatching. This one isn't.

The Dream (1989)

Passion, portents, and pies: Poirot is asked to determine the meaning behind a businessman's nightly visions

One side effect of reviewing 200 Agatha Christie adaptations is that you think you're as smart as the old girl in the plotting department. You start thinking about means, motive, and opportunity while normal viewers are content watching the sets, dresses, motorcars, and Poirot getting snippy with Hastings and solving the case.

This reaction showed up in *The Dream* when Benedict Farley appears. In the short story, we never meet him. Here, he looks like he stepped from the pages of Dickens, opening the new wing of his pork pie factory and what a stunning Art Deco building it is. Watch that newsreel footage and see if you envision Mrs. Tweedy from *Chicken Run* (2000) saying, "Chickens go in, pies come out." Farley probably says, "Pigs go in, pies come out." Listen closely to his opening speech to his uniformed workers, the press, and the Lord Mayor. He thinks he's a benevolent owner but his workers may silently disagree.

Later, Farley summons Poirot by mail to his home — located next door to his factory — for a consultation. Here's when I started thinking like Poirot. He instantly knows something is up, because when the appointment was made, Farley instructed Poirot to bring the letter with him. Why?

Next, he's seated in what looks like the interrogation room down at the local precinct with blindingly bright lights trained on him. This is not how a normal consultation goes with an ace detective. When Poirot and Farley finish their discussion of Farley's bizarre suicidal dreams, he asks for the letter. Poirot hands him the wrong letter.

I can't believe Hercule Poirot would make a mistake like that. I can believe that Poirot handed over the wrong letter deliberately because he thought the setup was strange and he came prepared with the real letter and a fake, to be used if needed. But no, apparently, Poirot made a mistake.

Later on, Farley does indeed kill himself exactly as he foretold to Poirot, and the letter is discovered in his

Fidelity to text

Benedict Farley and his business got the most changes, but they enhance the story. The murder is more plausible: no stuffed cats are involved. The police inspector transforms into Japp, and Hastings and Miss Lemon are added. And of course, the scriptwriter provided the obligatory chase scene at the climax.

Quality of movie

I would have added another half-gun, but I couldn't work out why the murderer called in Poirot. It didn't make sense, except you wouldn't have a story. Otherwise, what great eye candy. Don't miss the cameo at the beginning: the band conductor is Christopher Gunning, Poirot's composer.

Benedict Farley
(*Alan Howard*),
the factory owner

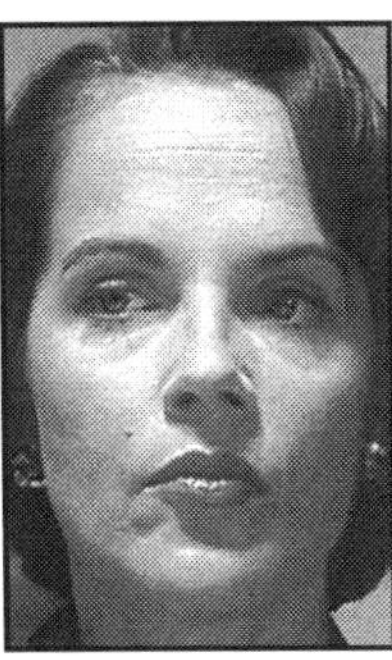

Mrs. Farley
(*Mary Tamm*),
the new wife

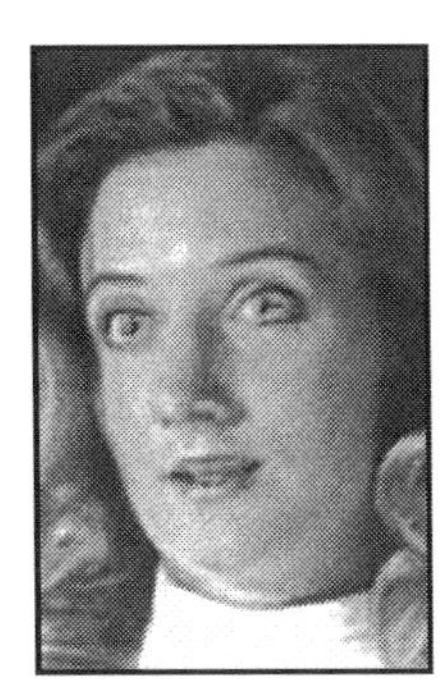

Joanna Farley
(*Joely Richardson*),
the father's daughter

Herbert Chudley
(*Martin Wenner*),
the fired lover

Hugo Cornworthy
(*Alan Howard*),
the busy secretary

Mr. Tremlett
(*Christopher Saul*),
the capable manager

papers. Dr. Stillingfleet and Japp feel this is suspicious and indicative of murder because when Poirot's around, it's always murder. During discussions with Farley's widow (wife #2 and only eight years older than her resentful stepdaughter), she confirms that Farley had been suffering from suicidal nightmares. Dear daughter flatly denies this. Dear daughter also doesn't like or miss her dead father for reasons of her own. The secretary, Cornworthy, knows nothing about the suicidal fixation.

This is the part the scriptwriter could have spelled out better. Why did the murderer involve Poirot? That practically screams hubris as well as "investigate closer." If the murderer had skipped calling in the well-known master detective, Farley's death would have been accepted as suicide. Dr. Stillingfleet even said so and Japp agreed. I know that if the murderer hadn't made such a tomfool move, we wouldn't have a show, but we've seen *Poirot* writers improve Agatha's stories (*cough* "The Lost Mine" *cough*). Give me some vaguely plausible reason for the characters to act like they have more brains than a pig destined to become a pie.

On second thought, make that a chicken. They are far less intelligent than pigs; pigs wouldn't make this mistake.

Poirot investigates but it's Miss Lemon, between wrestling bouts with her recalcitrant typewriter, who provides the clue he needs. Without a clock in the office, she checks the time for Poirot by leaning out the window to look at a nearby church clock. Voila! Poirot knows. Why does Farley keep his office where it is, facing a blank wall? So he can lean out his window and see the factory steam whistle signaling when the ovens are baking. He keeps an eye on his factory, even when he's no longer needed in the day-to-day operations.

By the way, we learn from this episode that Miss Lemon does not swear. When she makes a mistake typing, she says "bother" as she reaches for the eraser. Also, lest you think a highly qualified secretary like Miss Lemon made routine typos, she didn't. It was the typewriter, long past retirement age, that caused her errors by jamming its keys.

Watching the episode, I believe Poirot was suspicious of certain people as soon as he heard of Farley's death. But he needed a method to reach the solution, one the little gray cells did not provide. Miss Lemon saves the day for him, and he duly rewards her with her heart's desire: a clock.

I guess Poirot *can* make mistakes, since Miss Lemon would have much rather had a shiny, new typewriter.

There's a lot to like in this episode. It's amusing, nicely paced, and well-acted. It's packed with lovely period details like the factory women's uniforms, the Lord Mayor's ceremonial garb, and the band in their uniforms. There are plenty of instances of civic pride and not just in the newsreel footage. There are also hints of labor problems with those two unimpeachable witnesses waiting to speak with Mr. Farley. This calls back to his speech when he opens his factory.

The factory scenes are interesting to watch, a reminder that mass-produced food has been with us for decades. There are also plenty of gorgeous Art Deco lobbies, offices, rooms, stone veneers, and ornaments to drool over.

The actors contribute to the fun. Watch Joanna, the daughter, interact with her stepmother. The two women don't like each other. Watch her reaction to stepmom's crocodile tears. Joanna didn't like her father but he's still her father. She's honest with Poirot about her conflicted feelings. There's also Joanna's fiancé, who gets to save the day and foil the villain after Hastings muffs it. He and Joanna were going to elope, but with Farley dead they don't have to.

I enjoyed it all, except for the business with the letters and calling in the detective. I guess the reason — which could have been spelled out better in the script — was that the killer had to be sure the police and the doctor's conclusions were suicide and not murder. With Poirot as an unimpeachable witness, accompanied by a letter to prove the consultation, the verdict would be beyond dispute: Farley was dogged by suicidal thoughts (verified by his wife) and acted upon them.

It's a minor quibble, though. You'll enjoy this episode. It's a strong end to the overall excellent first season of *Poirot*.

General Information

Based on: "The Dream" (short story, 1937)
Run time: 50 min. **Subtitles:** No

Writer: Clive Exton
Director: Edward Bennett

Cast

David Suchet as Hercule Poirot
Hugh Fraser as Captain Hastings
Philip Jackson as Chief Inspector Japp
Pauline Moran as Miss Lemon

Alan Howard as Benedict Farley
Mary Tamm as Mrs. Farley
Joely Richardson as Joanna Farley
Martin Wenner as Herbert Chudley
Paul Lacoux as Dr. Stillingfleet
Alan Howard as Hugo Cornworthy
Neville Phillips as Holmes
Christopher Saul as Mr. Tremlett
Tommy Wright as Workman
Fred Bryant as Workman
Donald Bisset as Mayor
Arthur Howell as Fencing Instructor
George Little as Dicker
Christopher Gunning as Bandmaster
Richard Bebb as Newsreel Voice

Film Locations

Hoover Building, A40, Greenford, Middlesex (Farley's factory)
Wandsworth Town Hall, London (factory offices)

Peril at End House (1990)

While staying at a seaside resort, Poirot must prevent the murder of a woman whom nobody seems to like or trust

Fidelity to text

The obvious change is removing Freddie Rice's worthless husband and adding Miss Lemon. Inspector Japp and Hastings get their roles beefed up too. The concealed change is removing the evidence Poirot used to solve the crime.

Quality of movie

It's gorgeous, fast-paced, beautifully acted, and missing large chunks of vital storyline. Another ten or fifteen minutes of exposition would have prevented the impression that Poirot yanked the solution from his boutonnière vase.

Peril at End House features a classic trope that Agatha used several times (and possibly even invented). It's the unimpeachable witness, in which someone of sterling character is maneuvered into seeing something concocted by the villain to hide the truth. And who could be a more unimpeachable witness than Hercule Poirot?

The film opens with Poirot and Hastings flying across the English countryside to St. Loo (one of Agatha's many *nom de places* for her hometown of Torquay). They're aboard a small plane, the sort that, at the time, only wealthy travelers would have used. Hastings loves the flight; Poirot is not nearly as enamored with flying. This is a genuine vintage plane, by the way. It's also a subtle allusion to Michael Seton, an important character in the story even though we never meet him.

Michael is the famous, daredevil pilot attempting an around-the-world flight. He's also the sole heir of the second-richest man in England as well as Magdala "Nick" Buckley's fiancé. Her happiness is riding on him making it back to England safely and marrying her. Or, since he thoughtfully made a will leaving his millions to her, dying at the hands of cannibals in the Solomon Islands. Either way works.

At the gorgeous Art Deco resort, Poirot is still shaken from his harrowing flight over the green fields of England and is having a hard go of it. Unsteady, he trips and is rescued by Nick. To his dismay, she claims to have never heard of the great detective. She joins him and Hastings, swats away wasps, and tells them that strange things have been happening to her, possibly murderous attempts on her life.

Poirot seizes the lifeline she tosses and away we go, as he tries to solve who could possibly want to murder such a delightful young lady. His first clue is the hat Nick accidentally leaves behind, complete with bullet hole, and an easily found spent bullet. She wasn't swatting at wasps, after all. Except shouldn't someone in the hotel have heard a gunshot?

Conveniently, everyone who could want to murder such a charming lady is at her home, End House. Is it

"Nick" Buckley (*Polly Walker*), the bereft homeowner

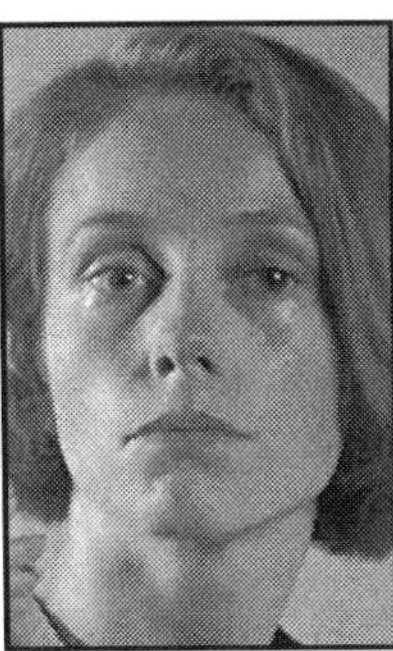
Freddie Rice (*Alison Sterling*), the close friend

Maggie Buckley (*Elizabeth Downes*), the distant cousin

George Challenger (*John Harding*), the poor yachtsman

Bert Croft (*Jeremy Young*), the Aussie lodger

Milly Croft (*Carol MacReady*), the disabled wife

her dearest friend, Freddie Rice, who oh so casually tells them that Nick is a terrible liar? How about Nick's housekeeper who doesn't like her? Or the nice Australian couple renting the lodge who tell Poirot and Hastings that no one in the village likes Nick? Or Nick's cousin who tells Poirot that Nick is obsessed with keeping her mausoleum of a house going? Perhaps it's Nick's sailor friend who has no visible means of support?

If you know Agatha, you know where this is going. If you don't know Agatha or worse, haven't read the novel, you'll feel not only misled at the climax, you'll feel cheated. The novel nicely lays out all the clues, some in plain sight, along with the red herrings, also in plain sight. You can follow Poirot's deductions at the climax; then reread and see what you missed, marveling at Agatha's subtle hand.

The film, however, elides over the clues so much that when Poirot solves the crime, it's with great leaps of fact-free logic, as if he was hopping from one remote South Pacific atoll to another in search of fresh water and fuel. There are no flashbacks showing missed clues or misunderstood connections. None. One of the most vital clues is so subtle that you won't see it, unless you slow down the DVD and move forward frame by frame and then zoom in on the table in the library.

It was maddening. I didn't just rant after the movie was over. I ranted during all four laps of our late evening walk, working out the missed opportunities when, if the scriptwriter had played fair, the clue would have been seen by an observant viewer. I don't expect the solution to be handed to me on a silver platter along with my dry martini. I do expect to have a fighting chance of working out whodunnit.

This was a pity, because there was much to admire about this episode, from the opening scenes of the Devon coast from the air to the vintage sailboats and stunning motorcars that Hastings pants over. The St. Loo harbor is charming. End House is suitably atmospheric, especially the ghoulish gardener's son reveling in watching pigs getting their throats cut. The resort hotel is an Art Deco dream and so is the nursing home.

General Information

Based on: *Peril at End House* (novel, 1932)
Run time: 1 hr., 43 min. **Subtitles:** Yes

Writer: Clive Exton **Director:** Renny Rye

Cast

David Suchet as Hercule Poirot
Hugh Fraser as Captain Hastings
Pauline Moran as Miss Lemon
Philip Jackson as Chief Inspector Japp
Godfrey James as Inspector

Polly Walker as Magdala "Nick" Buckley
John Harding as Cmdr. George Challenger
Paul Geoffrey as Jim Lazarus
Alison Sterling as Freddie Rice
Elizabeth Downes as Maggie Buckley
Christopher Baines as Charles Vyse
Jeremy Young as Bert Croft
Carol MacReady as Milly Croft
John Crocker as Dr. Graham
Geoffrey Greenhill as Wilson
Mary Cunningham as Ellen
Joe Bates as Alfred
Jane Paton as Hotel Receptionist
Fergus McLarnon as Hood
Jenny Funnell as Nurse Andrews
Janice Cramer as Maid
Edward Pinner as Pageboy
Tony Red Richards as Hotel Guest

Film Locations

Salcombe Hotel, South Devon (hotel exterior)
The Moult, South Sands, South Devon (End House exterior)
Salcombe Yacht Club (nursing home exterior)
Kingswear, Devon (station and forecourt)

The fashions are equally eye-catching, whatever the occasion. The stylish black evening gowns with scarlet capes even matter for story purposes and not just as eye candy; one woman is shot instead of the other because their clothing was similar.

The acting is first rate. Polly Walker plays Nick Buckley and she's a marvel; a charming free spirit concealing a core of darkness. Freddie Rice (Alison Sterling) loves her friend but she subtly conveys that something's wrong. The Australian couple, who are always good for a laugh, lay it on thicker than thick and subject Poirot and Hastings to thousands of photographs of Australia.

Then there's Maggie Buckley (Elizabeth Downes). She barely has a line in the movie; her sole purpose is to be mistaken for her cousin, Nick. Watch her scene at the dinner party when Nick discovers that Michael Seton's plane was lost somewhere out in the vast South Pacific. Maggie doesn't say a word. She doesn't have to and she can't. Her parents figure in the novel, but they're excised from the film; a mistake, I thought, because their scene brings home the true cost of murder. The people who die leave grieving relatives behind. A scriptwriter should never forget that.

A bonus is watching Miss Lemon lead a séance, although again, the script fell down here. Poirot uses Miss Lemon to do some detecting in London and she visits End House to report, but he doesn't warn her that she's expected to channel spirits? I couldn't accept it. Poirot knows the séance is critical to revealing the killer, and he wouldn't leave anything to chance.

Should you watch this film? Yes. There's an awful lot to like. But read the novel first. Then you'll know where the scriptwriter skipped important bits and you won't mind when there's so much to enjoy. If you don't read the novel first, you'll feel cheated.

Peril at End House should have been better; the source material is first-rate and by the start of the second season of *Poirot*, the production company and David Suchet knew what they were doing. They're better than this.

The Veiled Lady (1990)

Christie recycles Sherlock Holmes but adds disguises, burglary, capture, and pursuit through a museum

Fidelity to text

It's a faithful adaptation, down to the dialog lifted wholesale from the short story. The additions — a suspicious housekeeper and a chase through a museum — flesh out the story beautifully.

Quality of movie

One of the best episodes in the series; fast-paced and very funny. It's loaded with great lines. It's so good that you won't question the wildly implausible plot hole until afterwards, if then.

The episode opens with a daring daylight robbery of a jewelry store. The story makes it into the newspaper for Hastings to prod Poirot with when he bemoans the lack of crime to stimulate the little gray cells. He admits the bandit handing the jewelry to a confederate as he's being captured is clever, but the case is still beneath his skills. Similarly, he discounts the mysterious death of a British citizen in Holland as due to tinned fish. Ah, if only Poirot had been born without moral scruples! He'd become the genius of crime, a real-life Moriarty, known to police everywhere but invisible and uncaught.

Next, they are summoned by a mysterious veiled lady to the Athena Hotel. There is someone watching her, she explains, hence the disguise. She's Lady Millicent, on the eve of her marriage to a wealthy duke. She tells them a mournful story about being blackmailed over a scandalous letter she wrote years before that will wreck it. The letter is hidden inside a Chinese puzzle box which is concealed in the blackmailer's house where no one can find it. Only the great Poirot can possibly save her from this wicked man.

Of course, Hastings is smitten by Lady Millicent. Such grace! Such charm! Such a lovely flower of the aristocracy, no matter how impoverished! Lady Millicent's face is her fortune, explaining how a destitute Irish peer's fifth daughter managed to snag a duke. Since Hastings reads the society columns, he knows all about Lady Millicent's good fortune in marrying extremely well although he, like Poirot, has never seen her.

If you've read your Conan Doyle (particularly "The Adventure of Charles Augustus Milverton") you think you know where the story is going. Poirot summons the blackmailer, Lavington, to his flat and makes a counteroffer for the letter. Lavington is unmoved. He wants his money, and she can raise it from her friends, "particularly if she went the right way about it."

Hastings explodes at his crude and louche insinuation about such a delightful lady, so much so that Lavington, staring right at him, comments about Poirot's excitable office boy. Poirot, on the other hand, pays close attention to the information Lavington

Lady Millicent
(*Frances Barber*),
the noble blackmailed

Lavington
(*Terence Harvey*),
the jeering blackmailer

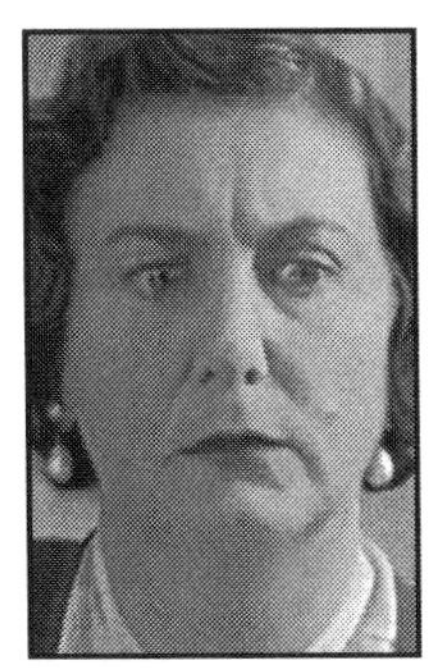

Mrs. Godber
(*Carole Hayman*),
the stern housekeeper

Constable
(*Don Williams*),
the gulpy policeman

"Mad Dog"
(*David Suchet*),
the cat burglar

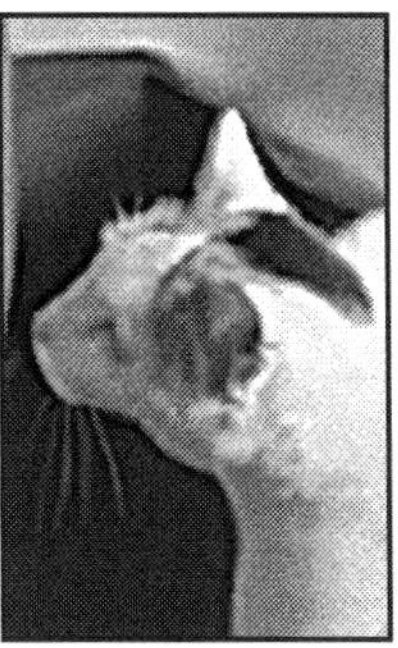

Museum Cat
(*Cat*),
the feline snitch

carelessly reveals: He is leaving for Paris that day. On his return Tuesday, he expects his money.

This sets up a great comic sequence that the short story dispenses with in a couple of sentences. Fastidious Poirot combs out his mustache, changes from his morning suit into workman's clothes, and bicycles to Lavington's house. He informs the housekeeper, Mrs. Godber, that he is a locksmith hired by Lavington to install burglar-proof locks. She is suspicious but lets him work on the locks.

That night, Poirot and Hastings burgle the house. Yes, Poirot emulates a common housebreaker to save Lady Millicent's reputation. They search the house and, as dawn nears, discover the Chinese puzzle box cleverly hidden in the kitchen's wood supply. Poirot points out how safe a location this is in July. But the search takes too long. Mrs. Godber awakes and summons the constable on his beat. In another great scene, the constable confronts these dangerous criminals. Hastings escapes by crashing through the French doors because he can't get them open. Poirot gets frog-marched off to jail.

The comedy ramps up when Inspector Japp arrives to bail out Poirot. Notice how cleverly he never uses Poirot's real name in the police station and how little Poirot appreciates the courtesy. Poirot also doesn't appreciate Hastings making a run for it, but Hastings' hasty exit is why he got bailed out of jail.

Can this episode get better? Yes, it can. Lady Millicent meets Poirot to get back the letter but insists on it taking place at London's Natural History Museum. Wow. What an entry hall, complete with a giant dinosaur skeleton. Along the way, Poirot tells Hastings that Lavington was already dead in Holland (remember the newspaper story?) when he met them. This is where Christie takes the story away from Conan Doyle and makes it her own.

In the museum, Poirot returns the letter, then fences with Lady Millicent over who keeps the Chinese puzzle box as a souvenir (costing all of two pence in Limehouse). She grabs it, her accomplice shows up (it's the fake Lavington!) and you get another great chase scene in the museum, ending in the closed-off Hall of Mammals.

Is it possible to vanish in thin air? Why yes, because the mammals — an astonishing display of the taxidermist's art — are draped in Holland covers. Lady Millicent and Lavington conceal themselves under the drapes, hoping to go unnoticed. Unfortunately for them, the museum's cat notices Lady Millicent's shoes peeping out from under the sheets and decides he needs petting. This is the only reference to the short story's explanation of how Poirot recognized that Lady Millicent was not who she claimed she was. In the story, he spots her shoddy shoes. He knows that a real aristocrat, no matter how impoverished, would never wear dime-store junk.

There's no explanation as to when or how Poirot figures out her deception, other than her insistence on keeping the Chinese puzzle box. Yet he must know, or he wouldn't have arranged to have Inspector Japp on hand to arrest Lady Millicent. Was it Hastings? If Hastings believed her story, then the woman had to be a liar. But if that's true, I would expect Poirot to acknowledge his reliance on Hastings always being wrong.

But that's not the gaping plot hole.

Remember the gun-wielding bandit robbing the jewelry store in a posh shopping arcade? He snatched three ostentatious, gaudy necklaces consisting of what look like hundreds of diamonds strung together. They look like something Marie Antoinette would have worn at Versailles. Subtle, they are not. Some of those diamonds are dime-sized. They glittered like ice, gorgeous and colorless. I did not notice any dime-sized colored gems.

Fast-forward to when Poirot reveals the contents of the Chinese puzzle box. One side contains the letter. The other side contains a handful of gemstones, colored and white. Um, what? Where are the rest of the diamonds? Those necklaces would have filled a jam jar. Plus, they were all diamonds! No rubies or emeralds, just glittery ice. Yet Poirot spills out a small handful of colored gems in various sizes. Who switched out the stones? And when? And most importantly, where are the missing stones? This question remains unanswered, like how Poirot knew Lady Millicent was a fraud.

It's still a great, funny episode. Watch it twice to catch all the snappy dialog. Everyone shines like a diamond.

General Information

Based on: "The Veiled Lady" (short story, 1923)
Run time: 49 min. **Subtitles:** Yes

Writer: Clive Exton
Director: Edward Bennett

Cast

David Suchet as Hercule Poirot
Hugh Fraser as Captain Hastings
Philip Jackson as Chief Inspector Japp
Pauline Moran as Miss Lemon

Frances Barber as Lady Millicent
Terence Harvey as Lavington
Carole Hayman as Mrs. Godber
Tony Stephens as Sergeant
Don Williams as Constable
Lloyd McGuire as Museum Guard
Peter Geddis as Museum Guard

Film Locations

Burlington Arcade, London (robbery)
Garden Lake, Osterley Park (model yacht sailing)
Senate House, University of London (lobby of Athena hotel)
46 Alisa Road, Twickenham, Surrey (modernist house during Poirot's bicycle ride)
Natural History Museum, London (climax)

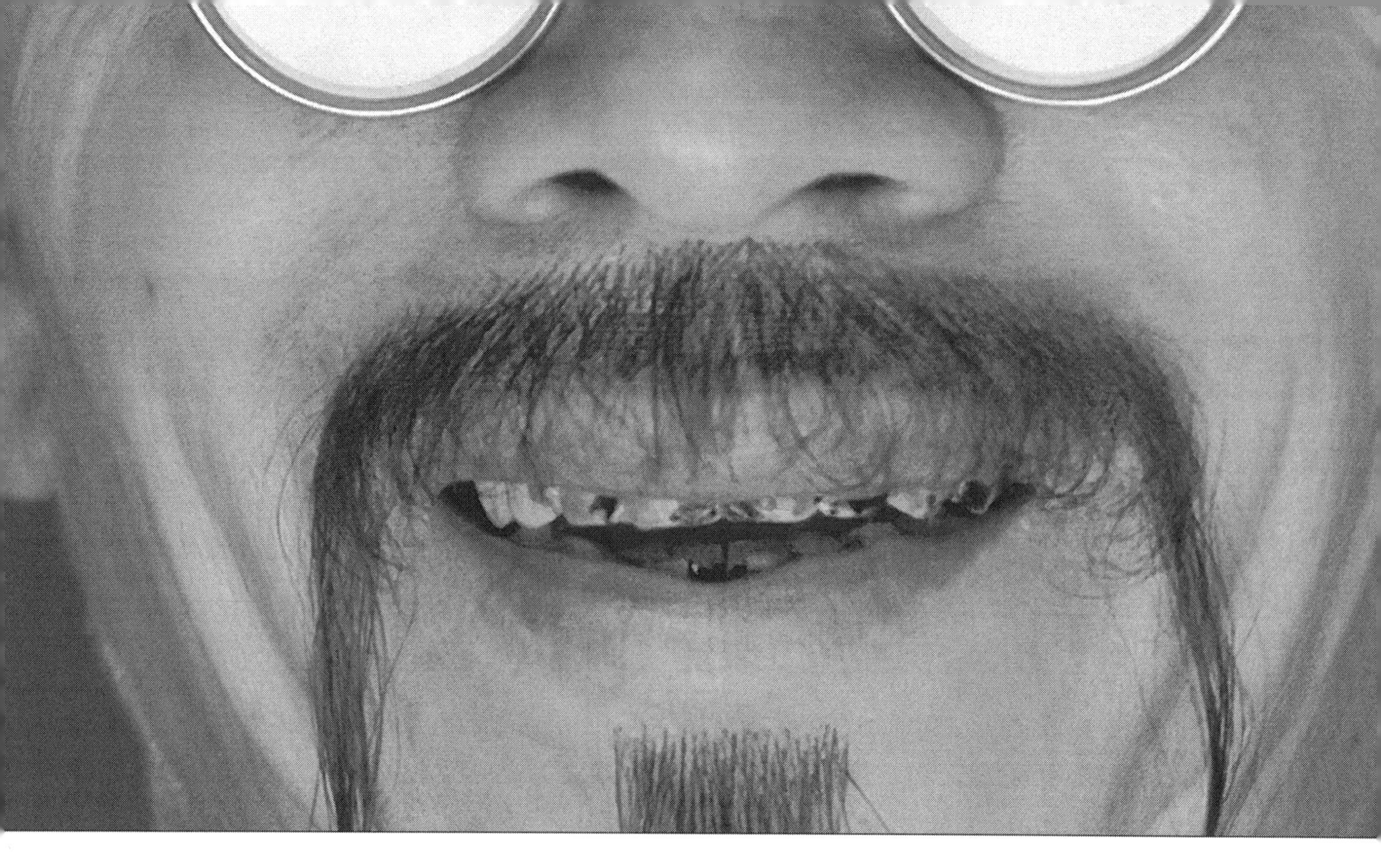

The Lost Mine (1990)

A missing man carrying a map leading to fabulous riches lures Poirot from his Monopoly game into Chinatown

Fidelity to text

Lots of rewriting was needed to turn a nothingburger of a story into something worth watching.

Quality of movie

Most of the time, the rewriting greatly enhanced the plot. This is an action story instead of a remembrance of things past.

The Lost Mine is a very early short story, originally published in 1923. It's dull. It's also clumsily told. Poirot tells Hastings about an earlier case to illustrate his point about not indulging in stock speculation because he — naturally — never does. The only speculative stock Poirot owns are shares in a Burmese silver/lead mine given to him as a reward for services rendered. Since all the action took place in the distant past and we know Poirot succeeded, there's no risk or drama. It's bloodless.

Bloodless won't do for TV. You've got to have action or else you've got a pair of talking heads, making the viewer switch back to Kurt Russell fighting Chinese demons in *Big Trouble in Little China* (1986).

The new and improved plot uses virtually every important element of the short story, other than the adversarial, Poirot-loathing Inspector Miller. Then it adds so much more, beginning with Hastings teaching Poirot to play Monopoly. The game was introduced to Great Britain in 1935 so it stands to reason they'd be playing the exciting new import.

At the same time, Miss Lemon is speculating in stocks, advised by Hastings (wrong as always) and Poirot (not wrong in his advice). A major stock scheme is described in the newspaper as collapsing, bankrupting thousands. A warning sign about the scheme Hastings completely missed but reverently describes is that it would pay investors a 100% return. To give Hastings his due, plenty of savvier investors missed the same red flag.

This episode revolves around money. Poirot and Hastings play Monopoly throughout, providing both a clue to the mystery's solution and an explanation for the bank error that bedevils Poirot. Unlike in the game, the bank error is not in his favor, nor was it the bank that was at fault.

While Poirot is at the bank attempting to resolve the bank error, he gets roped into investigating the disappearance of visiting businessman Mr. Wu Ling. That gentleman, according to Lord Pearson of the bank, carries the long-lost map showing the location of the lost Burmese silver mine. Wu Ling arrived in England, checked into his hotel, and then didn't show up at a scheduled meeting to sell the map to the bank's board of directors. His body turns up in London's Chinatown, stabbed in the back several times. According to Inspector

Han Wu Ling (*Vincent Wong*), the map's owner

Lord Pearson (*Anthony Bate*), the worried banker

Charles Lester (*Colin Stinton*), the druggie investor

Reggie Dyer (*James Saxon*), the roaming smuggler

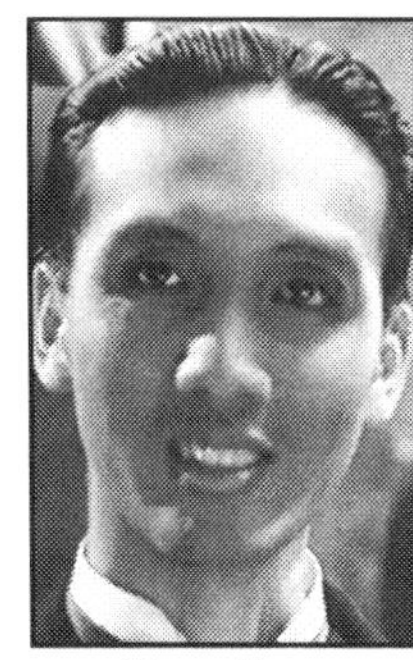
Chow Feng (*Hi Ching*), the casino owner

Mr. Ho (*Ozzie Yue*), the restaurateur

Japp, whoever knifed Wu Ling used an Asian-style blade rather than something you'd find in an English kitchen.

While Inspector Japp is interested in murder, he's more interested in organized crime in Chinatown, involving the Tongs, opium smuggling, illegal gambling, and money laundering. Could Wu Ling have met the wrong person? Is he involved in Japp's other investigation? Does Poirot's investigation intersect with Japp's?

It seems they do, then they don't, but then they do again. Like a Chinese puzzle box, you might say.

Along the way, a stock speculator gets involved. This is Charles Lester, glad-handing American salesman with a dark secret. According to him, he's never met Wu Ling. According to his wife, he's been behaving erratically. According to the hotel clerk, he was the man who met Wu Ling in the lobby shortly before his disappearance.

As the plot threads weave themselves together, you'll get a real treat: a glimpse at cutting-edge police procedures in 1935. It's radio. No, really! Radio transformed law enforcement. Cars can't outrun radio waves.

Japp takes Poirot to the radio room. Policewomen wearing headsets move cars and targets on a huge map of London tracking a criminal, minute by minute, his movements radioed in by watching policemen. The criminal is Reggie Dyer, a man well known to police in many jurisdictions for his underworld dealings. Dyer also apparently met Wu Ling on the boat from China. The hunt for Dyer becomes the now-obligatory chase scene in a *Poirot* episode, effectively managed from afar by Japp.

As Japp pursues the connection between Dyer and Wu Ling, Poirot seeks an explanation for why a traveler would request matches from a hotel clerk when he has plenty in his luggage. Poirot closely examines the cigarette butts cramming the ashtray. There's also a worrying conflict in a key witness' statements.

Eventually, Japp, Poirot, and Hastings end up in London's Chinatown. It's exotic and very different from Poirot's normal haunts but is it really? It looks different, the signs are written in English and Chinese, the citizens look and dress differently, but they're still running small businesses and going about their daily lives like anyone else in London.

And like anywhere else in London there are restaurants, street prostitutes, gambling casinos, and opium dens. Maybe not the opium dens. This illegal den is located in the basement of the quasi-legal casino, accessible via a secret door concealed by a red-eyed dragon.

It's in the opium den that all the threads come together. Charles Lester, stockbroker, is an opium addict, but he's not a murderer. Reggie Dyer is an opium smuggler and a crook, but he's not a murderer either. It's at this point that the story falls apart when Poirot fingers the real murderer of Wu Ling.

Poirot suspected Lord Pearson from the very beginning; Pearson claimed he had never seen Wu Ling but he also claimed that a Chinaman brought into the bank was not Wu Ling. Aha! Pearson must have a reason for lying. Poirot's explanation about investment losses, impersonators, and stolen maps all made sense, as did framing Charles Lester. Lester was in the wrong place at the wrong time and as an opium addict, it was easy to pin blame on him.

But we never see a single scene where Poirot learns that Lord Pearson gambles regularly in the Red Dragon casino, losing heavily. Nor do we ever hear a single person tell Poirot that Lord Pearson invested heavily in the Imperial Trust collapse, losing his shareholders millions of pounds. How could Poirot know these things?

According to what we see on the screen, he can't. I can see why Poirot made the accusation because it fits the facts that he *does* know. But we are never shown a single reason how Poirot could know the motivation behind the murder. It's speculation; exactly what Poirot warned Hastings and Miss Lemon against. It needed a scene or two; just a few minutes to show Poirot talking to distraught relatives, housekeepers, bank clerks, casino dealers, street prostitutes, anyone who knew what Lord Pearson got up to in his spare time.

It's still a good episode and well worth watching. Despite Poirot pulling his solution from his boutonnière vase at the climax, the adaptation is far better than the short story it's based on.

General Information

Based on: "The Lost Mine" (short story, 1923)
Run time: 50 min. **Subtitles:** Yes

Writers: Michael Baker, David Renwick
Director: Edward Bennett

Cast

David Suchet as Hercule Poirot
Hugh Fraser as Captain Hastings
Pauline Moran as Miss Lemon
Philip Jackson as Chief Inspector Japp
John Cording as Inspector Jameson

Anthony Bate as Lord Pearson
Ozzie Yue as Mr. Ho
Gloria Connell as Miss Devenish
Julian Firth as Bank Teller
Peter Barnes as Wilkins
Colin Stinton as Charles Lester
Barbara Barnes as Mrs. Lester
James Saxon as Reggie Dyer
Uncredited actress as Miss Boerum
Vincent Wong as Han Wu Ling
Hi Ching as Chow Feng
Daryl Kwan as Oriental Gentleman
Richard Albrecht as Hotel Clerk

Film Locations

German Historical Institute London, London (St. James Hotel exterior)
Dagenham Civic Centre, London (bank)
Norman Shaw Buildings, London (Scotland Yard)
Gilbert Place, London (sauna exterior)
Columbia Road and Ezra Street, London (Chinatown)
Bloomsbury Square, London (police chase, stockbrokers exterior)

The Cornish Mystery (1990)

A distrustful wife's warning to Poirot spurs him into investigating too late and he vows to uncover the murderer

Fidelity to text

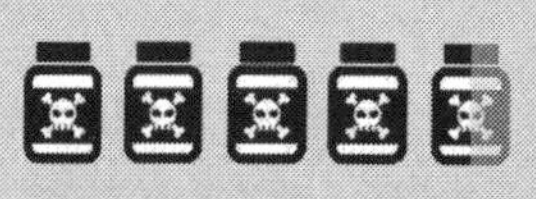

Replace an anonymous landlady with Miss Lemon, an anonymous policeman with Inspector Japp, augment a few scenes alluded to in the text and you've got yourself an enhanced – while still faithful – film.

Quality of movie

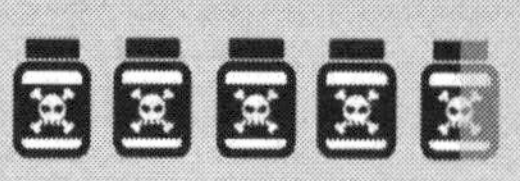

Everything worked, including the weather. For once, it wasn't a sunny day in May. It's raining, far more common in England at any time of the year than the constant sunshine we've seen in the series. I have a few quibbles, but they're minuscule flaws in this gem.

Miss Lemon, we're told, is the perfect secretary. What we didn't know until this episode is her ability to check the windows and spot reluctant clients.

Unlikely, you say? You would be wrong, because on this rainy day Miss Lemon sees a woman loitering in the park in front of Whitehaven Mansions. This apprehensive, drab, middle-aged woman is not the type to loiter in the rain, nervously approaching the building's front door and anxiously retreating. Miss Lemon scents a potential client who's unable to make up her mind about asking Poirot for help.

When she is confronted, Mrs. Pengelley refuses to come inside so Poirot and Hastings meet her in the park under their umbrellas. She's terrified of being noticed since her market town is a hotbed of gossip and someone is always watching, even in London. It's an interesting conversation. When you watch this interview the second time, you'll see how often Mrs. Pengelley lies to Poirot. I didn't catch the subtleties, but Poirot does and they were reason enough for him to take the case. I'll come back to them later.

Poirot doesn't ascribe real urgency to Mrs. Pengelley's problem. It's serious, but not desperate, so he and Hastings don't rush for the next train. The next evening, they arrive in Polgarwith, a market town in Cornwall. They visit the Pengelley home and discover that Mrs. Pengelley, as she feared she would be, is dead. She told Poirot she suspected her husband, Edward, was poisoning her, and it turns out she might be correct.

Why would Edward Pengelley, the town dentist, do such a thing? According to Mrs. Pengelley, her husband hired a hot blonde hussy as his receptionist and hygienist. Miss Marks is a stunner (Hastings is smitten) and you can see why Mr. Pengelley hired her. She'll lure every male client in Cornwall to have her bend over them, even if she is prodding their gums with a dental pick.

The relationship between Mr. Pengelley and Miss Marks is one of the minor changes made. In the short story, Mr. Pengelley may not be conducting a physical

Edward Pengelley (*Jerome Willis*), the stoic dentist

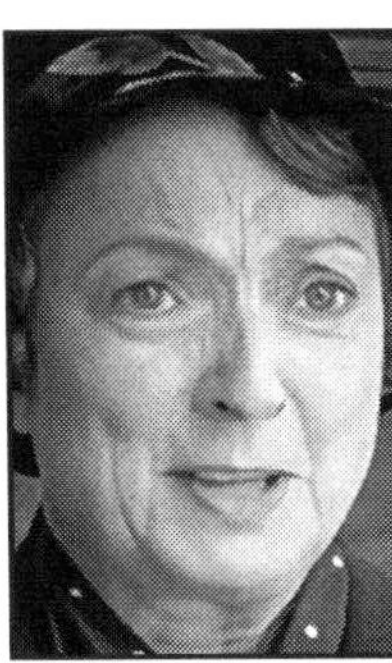
Mrs. Pengelley (*Amanda Walker*), the suspicious wife

Freda Stanton (*Chloe Salaman*), the quarrelsome niece

Jacob Radnor (*John Bowler*), the ambitious fiancé

Edwina Marks (*Laura Girling*), the dentist's assistant

Dr. Adams (*Derek Benfield*), the dubious doctor

affair with Miss Marks, but during the inquest, she admits to an emotional attachment. Mr. Pengelley promised to marry her if he was ever free to do so. In the film, we only see a longing glance between them as they cross paths in the park after Mrs. Pengelley's death.

Poirot is horrified when Jessie, the hysterical maid, tells him about Mrs. Pengelley's sudden death a mere hour before his arrival. Due to his inaction, a client has been murdered! He must investigate at once. Dr. Adams is adamant that Mrs. Pengelley suffered from gastric problems, and it couldn't be poisoning because Edward Pengelley is his good friend and he's not capable of poisoning his grandmother's dog. This is a great scene, watching Poirot get furious with an obstinate country doctor.

Freda, Mrs. Pengelley's niece, is equally shocked and can't conceive of her uncle murdering her aunt. Freda tells Poirot something even more important: the truth about why she moved out in a huff. It was because auntie Pengelley was panting after Freda's fiancé and causing embarrassment all around. Mrs. Pengelley had neglected to tell Poirot this tidbit. Jacob Radner, fiancé and up-and-coming tailor and outfitter, gives Poirot more details about how uncomfortable he was being pursued by Mrs. Pengelley.

Like Jessie the maid, Radner tells Poirot he can't talk dirt about the dead or who he thinks dunnit. He also doesn't want Poirot to pursue Pengelley for murder because of the scandal it would cause. The town thrives on malicious gossip and idle speculation.

Poirot doesn't come to any conclusions, but he agrees to leave. He warns Radner that keeping silent to prevent scandal won't change a thing. *Vox populi* will force the case out into the open. He tells Hastings as they leave that Mr. Pengelley will be in the dock for murder before the August bank holiday.

Weeks later, Edward Pengelley announces his engagement to his hot hygienist. The gossip flares into an inferno, he's roundly denounced as a wife-poisoner, angry letters to Scotland Yard are written, her body is exhumed, and what do you know? The gossips are right: Mrs. Pengelley was poisoned with arsenic in the form of weedkiller.

Poirot and Hastings return to Polgarwith. Poirot watches Mr. Pengelley suffer in the dock as the town turns on him. Cans of weedkiller are waved around in court. Inspector Japp arrives to collect any remaining evidence on this open-and-shut case and enjoy Cornish pasties.

It's then that Poirot confronts the true murderer and extracts a signed confession with the promise of a 24-hour head start. Hastings gets a chance to shine here, proving that he can think on his feet when not blinded by hot blonde hussies. Afterwards, when Poirot lets the murderer leave, Hastings confronts him. Why let the killer go?

Poirot says, "That was not sentiment. That was realism." He had no proof, but now, with a signed confession, he does. As Poirot knows full well, he could testify in court that he knew, courtesy only of the little gray cells, that Mr. Pengelley was innocent and twelve stolid Cornishmen would laugh him out of court and vote to hang.

It was during Poirot's summing up that I felt the scriptwriter missed an opportunity to enlighten us dumber members of the audience. Poirot knew Mrs. Pengelley lied to him. Her niece, Freda, lived with her for eight years by her own admission, yet she didn't know why Freda moved out in a huff? Then, Mrs. Pengelley's manner changed when discussing how the nice Mr. Radnor was merely a pleasant young man. When Poirot interviewed Freda, she was distressed over the murder. She was also open about why she moved out and how awkward and unpleasant it was to watch her 50-something aunt pursue her barely 30-year-old fiancé. At the same time, Freda refused to believe her uncle murdered her aunt.

Who was lying: Mrs. Pengelley or Freda? Poirot used his knowledge of human nature to deduce what happened as opposed to what he was told. Why didn't Poirot rush to Cornwall to save his client? Because he didn't think she was at that great a risk of being poisoned. He knew she lied to him, yet she still died. Just a few sentences of clarification would have been welcome.

The Cornish Mystery is a great episode and worth watching twice. There's so much to enjoy, from I Ching readings and discussions of rice to seeing true English weather: rain, rain, and more rain.

General Information

Based on: "The Cornish Mystery," (short story, 1923)
Run time: 50 min. **Subtitles:** Yes

Writer: Clive Exton
Director: Edward Bennett

Cast

David Suchet as Hercule Poirot
Hugh Fraser as Captain Hastings
Philip Jackson as Chief Inspector Japp
Pauline Moran as Miss Lemon

Chloe Salaman as Freda Stanton
John Bowler as Jacob Radnor
Jerome Willis as Edward Pengelley
Amanda Walker as Mrs. Pengelley
Tilly Vosburgh as Jessie Dawlish
Derek Benfield as Dr. Adams
Laura Girling as Edwina Marks
John Rowe as Prosecutor
Hugh Munro as Judge
Graham Callan as Solicitor
Edwina Day as Landlady
Richard Braine as Shop Assistant
Hugh Sullivan as Vicar
Jonathan Whaley as Policeman
Nick Ryall as Policeman at Gate

Film Locations

Dunster, Somerset
Blue Anchor Railway Station, Blue Anchor, Somerset (Polgarwith Station)

The Disappearance of Mr. Davenheim (1990)

A financier vanishes into the mists like a magic trick, leaving behind a smashed safe and a hated rival

Fidelity to text

Every change enhanced existing story elements, including the parrot. After all, the text references a sparrow in passing. A visiting parrot is funnier.

Quality of movie

Funny, fast-paced, action-filled, and a decent mystery considering the tiny pool of suspects.

A difficulty that all mystery writers experience, and Agatha was no exception, is how to begin a mystery in a way that's new and different. There are only so many ways the detective can be called upon to solve the case.

In this case, the film opens with the mystery. Mr. Davenheim, wealthy financier, discusses the day's plans with his wife. He puts Tchaikovsky's 1812 Overture onto the gramophone. He walks out into the fog to post a letter. His wife seems anxious. She has premonitions. Davenheim's hated business rival, Gerald Lowen, shows up for their scheduled appointment but Davenheim does not return. Lowen storms off in a huff.

Davenheim never returns.

The disappearance of a high-profile, wealthy financier and bank owner is, naturally, investigated. Mysteriously, he vanished into the fog without leaving behind a body or a clue.

Just when you're wondering who will summon Poirot for a routine investigation, the story takes one of Agatha's signature turns.

The scene shifts to Poirot, Hastings, and Japp enjoying a magic act. Or rather, Hastings and Japp are appreciating the show like normal people. They're relishing being fooled. Poirot is working out how the magician did it, especially how the lovely assistant, wearing a large and fetching moth costume, flirts with a flame and then vanishes into thin air.

Over a nightcap in his apartment at Whitehaven Mansions, the conversation turns to disappearances. Where would Poirot go to investigate the disappearing Mr. Davenheim? He states he can do it from home. All he needs are the facts and his little gray cells to solve this case. Inspector Japp bets Poirot a fiver that he can't solve the mystery without leaving his flat. They agree Poirot must solve the crime within seven days, and Hastings may ask questions for him.

Both Japp and Poirot are sure they'll win; it's like taking candy from a baby.

This setup adds a lot of action to an otherwise static plot. Japp and Hastings interview (separately and together) Mrs. Davenheim, the boatman, Gerald Lowen, the household staff, and a thieving tramp. They get in each other's way in amusing fashion. Hastings sometimes manages to keep his mind on his

Mathew Davenheim (*Kenneth Colley*), the forthright banker

Charlotte Davenheim (*Mel Martin*), the worried wife

Gerald Lowen (*Tony Mathews*), the hated rival

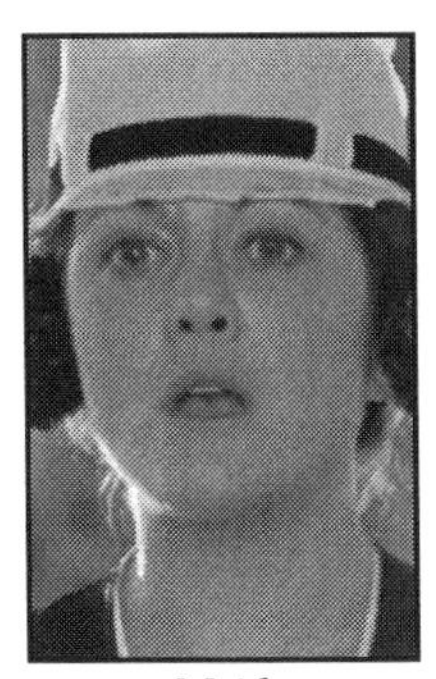
Maid (*Fiona McArthur*), the devoted servant

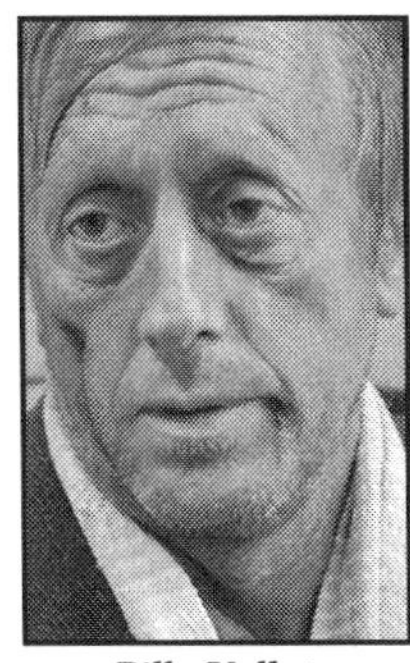
Billy Kellet (*Kenneth Colley*), the passing tramp

Merritt (*Richard Beale*), the salty boatman

work although it can be a near thing. When pursuing Lowen, Hastings discovers they share a common interest: fast cars and racing. There are lovely scenes with vintage Bugattis, even some vintage racing footage. Poor Hastings is doomed to disappointment when he's prevented, at the last moment, from actually driving one of those lovely, sleek racing machines.

At other times, Hastings is forced to embarrass himself, asking impertinent questions and even trying to force open the already robbed safe. Why? Sometime during Davenheim's disappearance, his safe stuffed full of cash, bearer bonds, and high-end jewelry was robbed. Couldn't anyone in the house hear the thief at work?

The nearby lake gets dredged. No body is found, but Davenheim's clothing is hauled up. Later at the racetrack, a thieving tramp tries to pick Japp's pocket. During the arrest, it's discovered that the tramp has Davenheim's signet ring. He claims he found the valuable piece of jewelry.

Meanwhile back at Whitehaven, Poirot keeps busy. He teaches himself magic tricks using *The Boy's Book of Conjuring*. (David Suchet performed all those tricks himself; what you see are not special effects.) Poirot shows off his new skills to Miss Lemon and to her unwanted houseguest: a parrot. The parrot — it's unclear who it belongs to — needed housesitting and entertaining so who else should do this task but the great Poirot? There are some amusing scenes with Poirot, the parrot, the delivery man, and Hastings. I loved the addition of the parrot. It was silly and funny, so trust my judgment and not those reviewers who take a TV show too seriously and disparage the parrot.

Hastings dutifully reports his findings to Poirot. The master entertains the parrot, serves to Hastings and Japp a fine dinner (poultry, a visual joke the parrot does not appreciate), and works out the deception behind the disappearance. Like a magic trick, what you see is designed to fool you into seeing something other than what the magician actually did. The facts are obscured by flash and spectacle.

In this case, the facts are that a wealthy financier disappears at the same time his safe stuffed full of bearer bonds, cash, and expensive jewelry is robbed.

Well within the time limit, Poirot solves the mystery; he links together an extended trip to South Africa, bank failures, razor blades belonging to a man with a bushy beard, the 1812 Overture, and separate bedrooms. He insists that Mrs. Davenheim be brought into the station house to identify the tramp. And what do you know. Mrs. Davenheim is not fooled by the magician's act. She sees through the deception. It was a decent deception too, and if you're not paying close attention, you'll be surprised just like Hastings and Japp were.

It's true that no murder took place, but it could have. If Poirot hadn't solved the crime, the Crown would have hanged an innocent man. Even without officially sanctioned murder, the stakes were high. The bank failure would ruin plenty of small depositors. With the criminal unmasked, at least some of the money was recovered.

I did have a few questions that Poirot did not answer. Who was the tramp's companion? Some random roadside gypsy down on his luck? And who wrote the letters Mr. Davenheim must have mailed home during his trip to South Africa? Did he have an accomplice? There's a strong scent of red herrings with Davenheim's flirtation with a pert housemaid that could have gone somewhere but didn't. That flirtation would have gone a long way to explaining why Mrs. Davenheim was so uneasy. Perhaps the housemaid was more than a flirtation. She might have been his accomplice. We never learn those pesky details.

Despite that, this episode is a winner from start to finish. You'll see the deepening friendship between Poirot, Hastings, and Japp. They are becoming a team. The only loss here was Miss Lemon, who didn't have enough to do other than to feed the parrot.

General Information

Based on: "The Disappearance of Mr. Davenheim" (short story, 1923)
Run time: 52 min. **Subtitles:** Yes

Writer: David Renwick
Director: Andrew Grieve

Cast

David Suchet as Hercule Poirot
Hugh Fraser as Captain Hastings
Philip Jackson as Chief Inspector Japp
Pauline Moran as Miss Lemon

Mel Martin as Charlotte Davenheim
Kenneth Colley as Mathew Davenheim
Tony Mathews as Gerald Lowen
Fiona McArthur as Maid
Richard Beale as Merritt
Kenneth Colley as Billy Kellet
Bob Mason as Sergeant
Peter Doran as Policeman
Stewart Harwood as Delivery Man
Jonty Miller as Mechanic
Malcolm Mudie as Chief Engineer

Film Locations

Joldwynds, Holmbury St. Mary, Surrey (Davenheim house)
Brooklands Museum, Weybridge, Surrey (race track)

"

Miss Lemon, small animals have no part to play in the home life of a private detective from Belgium... Except, of course, as a source of nourishment.

HERCULE POIROT

Double Sin (1990)

Poirot retires! It's up to Hastings to play amateur detective to recover a set of Napoleonic miniatures

Let's start with the title. It's weird. Agatha devised a few good titles (*Why Didn't They Ask Evans?* is perfection) but many of her efforts range from functional to drab. *A Caribbean Mystery? Murder on the Links?* Ho hum. Title writing, like headline writing, demands a unique skill set.

Double Sin however, takes her indifferent title writing to a new low. What does it even mean? Is she referring to the two ladies running the antique shop? The choice of travel style? The sin of deception and the sin of theft? I couldn't figure it out.

When "Double Sin" was published in 1928, the magazine changed the title to "By Road or Rail" which at least tells the reader something about the story's events. Agatha didn't like the magazine's choice and changed it back. But in 1928, there were many readers who didn't know who she was. Yes, this is two years after her famous disappearance, but it's shocking how few people pay attention to current events. A magazine publisher couldn't assume that every reader at the newsstand knew who Agatha Christie was or that they'd buy any issue with her name on the cover.

The original story isn't much. Poirot complains of boredom and wants to retire (again). Hastings persuades him to take a holiday, and since Poirot has to meet a distant friend anyway, off they go. Mystery ensues because Hastings arranges to take a scenic bus tour instead of the train. They meet a charming redhead on the bus whose valuable antique miniatures are stolen. A thief is accused. Poirot deduces the true thief, to Hastings' shock and disbelief. That's it.

The story's okay. There's some very sharp dialog, especially between Poirot and Hastings on the subject of falling for every charming redhead who comes along. But it's not memorable.

The film vastly improves the original story. Sadly, unlike the magazine publisher, the producers couldn't improve the title to go along with the enhanced story, but then we all know who Agatha Christie is today. Her name alone would sell a book of her shopping lists.

We open with Poirot complaining of boredom but this time, he also twits Hastings about needing to develop his own little gray cells. A holiday will do

Fidelity to text

Loads of enhancements, all of which turned a miniature mystery into something far more interesting. Wait till you see Miss Lemon's nightmare, completely made up from whole cloth and completely in character.

Quality of movie

Excellent throughout, but I wanted more explanation from Poirot. I got the distinct impression the thieves' ring had been operating for some time and he did too, but the script refused to spill the beans.

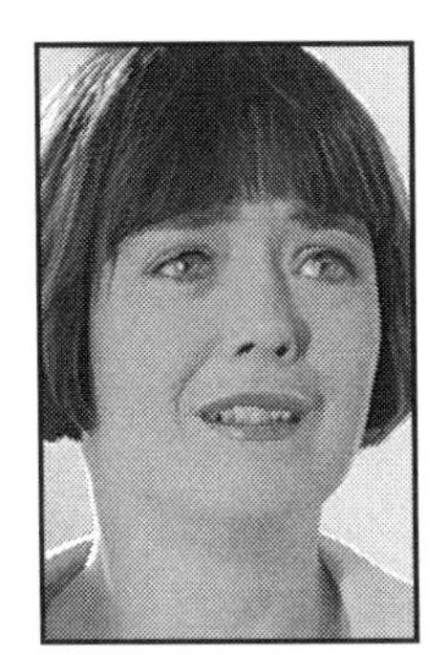

Mary Durrant
(*Caroline Milmoe*),
the eager courier

Miss Penn
(*Elspet Gray*),
the seasoned dealer

Baker Wood
(*Michael Shannon*),
the flush buyer

Amanda Manderley
(*Amanda Garwood*),
the lady on the run

Norton Kane
(*Adam Kotz*),
the man on the run

Sergeant Vinney
(*David Hargreaves*),
Hasting's Watson

them both good, so it is Poirot who makes the arrangements to go to Whitcomb on the coast. Once there, it's Hastings who arranges the scenic, fateful bus tour.

It's on the bus that they meet — several times — a weedy, very rude, agitated young man with a struggling mustache. His behavior is suspicious, no doubt about it.

There's also the charming, delightful, naïve Mary Durrant. A redhead. Hastings is smitten, especially when Miss Durrant gushes about her mission to sell valuable Napoleonic miniatures to a wealthy American collector and make a packet of money. She's learning the antique business from her elderly aunt, Miss Penn, and wants desperately to succeed. The short story notes that Mary Durrant's other career choices are limited to nursery governess or companion; the antique business has got to be more interesting and exciting as well as more lucrative. She's so confiding, so trusting of a strong, noble, stalwart English gentleman, bubbling over with enthusiasm and *joie de vivre*.

This girl won't have trouble selling antiques, or anything else for that matter.

But Miss Durrant does have a problem. She notices a weedy, rude young man with a struggling mustache — the same one Hastings noticed and disliked earlier — trying to steal her suitcase. It turns out she's mistaken. Or so it seems.

When the tour bus arrives at their destination, the miniatures are missing. The dispatch case that held them has been forced open, cleaned out, and tucked back inside Mary Durrant's suitcase.

Poirot tells Hastings that he's retired, so it's up to him to rescue the damsel and save her budding career in the antique business. Poirot hints to Hastings that it's odd someone would take the time to force the lock on the dispatch case, empty it, and put it back, when it would be so much easier to take the case and its contents. Hastings has an explanation, just as he has a suspect: the weedy, rude man with the struggling mustache.

Hastings interviews people, indulges himself in a high-speed chase of a suspect, and learns not to trust giddy damsels on buses. He also gets one of the best lines in the film when Lady Amanda cries: "Why can't you leave me alone! Don't you know what it's like to love a man?"

Hastings' nonplussed reply: "Well, ah, no, ah … not exactly."

While Hastings plays detective, Poirot turns out to have another motive for wanting to take a holiday at this exact time, in this exact location. Chief Inspector Japp is on a speaking tour, discussing his storied career and raising money for the Policeman's Benevolent Association. Why does Japp get a speaking tour and not Poirot? A good question, one that Poirot is interested in. He sneaks off to listen to the speech and learns what Inspector Japp truly thinks of him.

Afterwards, it's back to solving the mystery of who stole the miniatures. A luncheon is arranged, bringing together the local constables, the visiting Inspector Japp, Hastings, Poirot, Mary and her aunt, and the rich, swindled American buyer. The American proves to have a sharp eye. He knows who sold him the miniatures he bought in good faith and it's not Hastings' suspect.

It's someone else entirely.

This is the point where I wanted more of an explanation. If I understood correctly, the rich American would be forced to surrender the stolen miniatures to the police, despite having bought them in good faith. The miniatures would be returned to Mary Durrant and her aunt, Miss Penn, who'd be able to sell them again. Rich American would be out £1,500 but he's rich and he's an American so that's okay! I got the distinct impression that this scheme had been done before. I think Poirot thought so too, but the script didn't go into any detail. I would have liked a bit more.

The other significant addition was Miss Lemon. She has a tiny arc of her own, involving street urchins begging pennies for Guy Fawkes Day. This gives Dicker, Whitehaven Mansions' doorman, a chance to chat her up. She doesn't notice his interest. But the distraction of urchins and Dicker cause her to lose the keys to Poirot's apartment/office. Miss Lemon can't leave the flat unlocked, so she has to spend the night. She dreams (or has a nightmare) in which Poirot and Hastings — who've switched voices — suggest what to do.

Double Sin is a fun episode, fun enough to watch twice.

General Information

Based on: "Double Sin" (short story, 1929)
Run time: 51 min. **Subtitles:** Yes

Writer: Clive Exton **Director:** Richard Spence

Cast

David Suchet as Hercule Poirot
Hugh Fraser as Captain Hastings
Philip Jackson as Chief Inspector Japp
Pauline Moran as Miss Lemon
David Hargreaves as Sergeant Vinney
Gerard Horan as Police Constable Flagg

Caroline Milmoe as Mary Durrant
Elspet Gray as Miss Penn
Michael Shannon as Baker Wood
Adam Kotz as Norton Kane
Amanda Garwood as Lady Amanda Manderley
Paul Gabriel as Speedy Tours Rep.
Harry Goodier as Billy Arkwright
Jeffrey Perry as Hotel Receptionist
Anne Small as Pianist
George Little as Dicker
Ned Williams as First Urchin
Jack Williams as Second Urchin

Film Locations

Holland Park, London
Midland Hotel, Morecambe, Lancashire (Whitcombe Hotel)
Kirkby Lonsdale, Cumbria (Market Square)
Wray Castle, Low Wray, Cumbria (Lake Castle Hotel)
Holme Farm, Cumbria (car chase)

The Adventure of the Cheap Flat (1990)

A couple's huge deal on an apartment conceals a deadly secret in the form of a lethal singer and a resolute killer

Fidelity to text

The main addition is Miss Lemon, undercover agent. Every other story element is from the text; rearranged, expanded upon, or referenced.

Quality of movie

Loved it. Just loved it. My only quibble is that slower, dumber viewers like me need more explanation. I'm not that quick on the uptake.

This episode opens with an appropriate film clip: *"G" Men*, a 1935 Jimmy Cagney flick involving FBI agents battling mobsters with plenty of accompanying gunfire, fast cars, and dangerous molls. Japp and Hastings enjoy the film. Poirot does not.

Soon after, they meet the caricature of an FBI agent (Mr. Burt), come to London in pursuit of stolen submarine plans. He throws his considerable weight around at Scotland Yard, baffling all and sundry with his football references, waving around of guns, and American slang. Inspector Japp tells Poirot there's a technical term for this sort of liaison between law enforcement agencies: disaster.

Later, when Poirot suggests a suspect is connected with the Mafia, Agent Burt insists there is no Mafia, Brotherhood, or Cosa Nostra active in the United States. This is vaguely historically accurate. J. Edgar Hoover, head of the FBI in the 1930s (and decades afterward), never denied the existence of organized crime. It was the Mafia he didn't talk about.

The reason why the Mafia comes into play is thanks to the screenwriter. When Agatha wrote the story in 1923, it was the Japanese government that wanted those stolen top-secret submarine plans. With the *Poirot* series set in the mid-1930s, the scriptwriter saw an opportunity to shift the villain to Italy, creating a cascade of topical references. Italian-born clerk stealing plans? Check. Hot chanteuse with Mafia ties? Check. Mafia assassin chasing the hot chanteuse because she double-crossed them? Check. *Il Duce* needing to upgrade his navy in a hurry because of the looming war? Check. Thus, the Japanese get tossed overboard in favor of Italians, making a more cohesive story.

There's the set of supposedly naïve innocents, Mr. and Mrs. Robinson. Hastings, naturally, is smitten by Mrs. Robinson's beauty. He's puzzled — as is everyone else — as to why the Robinsons got to rent what should have been a £350 per annum flat for a mere £80. It's a Modernist flat with all the conveniences. It even has a little door so the dustbin can be shoved onto the back staircase on trash day. Fully furnished too, and very stylish indeed. Perhaps the couple got the flat so cheap because Mrs. Robinson is such a hot blonde. Or it could have been for a more nefarious reason.

There's the duped low-level clerk in the American

James Robinson (*John Michie*), the gullible husband

Stella Robinson (*Samantha Bond*), the credulous wife

Elsa Hart (*Jenifer Landor*), the temptress singer

Burt (*William Hootkins*), the arrogant FBI agent

Assassin (*Anthony Pedley*), the stolid killer

Bernie Cole (*Nick Maloney*), the slimy club owner

Navy office. He's lured into stealing top-secret submarine plans by a hot, seductive, honeytrap of a nightclub chanteuse. Would he betray his adopted country for a cool half-million and the promise of something even sweeter afterwards? You bet he would.

There's the lurking assassin, hanging around the expensive apartment tower where the Robinsons are so thrilled to find a cheap flat. He's quite noticeable wearing a trench coat and broad-brimmed black hat. Almost a caricature of a man to avoid but hey! it's London in the mid-1930s and there were all kinds of people lurking about in alleys. War was coming so plenty of people were preparing in their own ways.

There's the spectacle of Hercule Poirot setting up the cheap flat for some late-night housebreaking, with Hastings visiting the Robinsons to act as a diversion. Yes, once again, Poirot goes in for burglary but it's okay since it's in the service of justice. He almost gets caught but Hastings, who is capable of thinking on his feet when not distracted by hot women, saves him from discovery. The flat burglary was a reminder to keep those dustbin doors locked at all times. What a potential security breech! The architect should have had his license revoked for that design. I bet his roof leaked too.

There's the seedy nightclub impresario. His nightclub is located on a back street where whores pay off their pimps in the open before soliciting customers inside at the bar (watch carefully for the blonde streetwalker). He's smarmy, undoubtedly cheats on his taxes, uses toothpicks and then puts them back into the dispenser to save money, waters the booze, and probably pays half his staff under the table. His nightclub's name, The Black Cat, is a shoutout to the short story where the stolen plans are sewn into the lining of a black velvet cat being used as a telephone cozy.

The seedy nightclub impresario does one thing right to draw in the crowds. He hires hot, sexy chanteuses with mysterious pasts. In this case, Elsa Hart. She's also known as Carla Romero. Elsa's a spy, adventuress, thief with Mafia connections, married woman who's not above seducing dumb naval clerks, and murderess. Oh, she can sing too! In fact, Elsa Hart has a bona fide singing career and is willing to discuss it with a reporter from the *Lady's Companion* magazine. She sings several songs over the course of the episode, a real treat.

Best of all, Miss Lemon has a chance to shine when she goes undercover for Poirot. She pretends to be a girl reporter for the *Lady's Companion* and interviews Elsa. Why? Because the *Companion's* readers want to read about modern women forging their own path in the modern world and what better exemplar can there be than an internationally known nightclub chanteuse? Elsa Hart is flattered and tells Miss Lemon all sorts of things, permitting Miss Lemon to figure out how much of what she says is a lie.

Finally, in addition to the fabulous clothes, amazing settings, a gloriously stagy New York City nightclub and street scene that you will either love or hate, and a terrific swinging jazz combo, there's the flat Poirot rents to better surveil the Robinson's cheap flat. It's painted almost the same shade as Peschel Press blue! Robin's egg blue or darn close to it. What a wonderful color. I'll bet Poirot paid far more than £80 per annum for a flat with such a meticulous paint job.

Was there anything I didn't like? Well, yes. I had to discuss the film afterwards with Bill to work out that Inspector Japp had briefed Poirot offscreen about Elsa Hart/Carla Romero. Reading the story helped too. It doesn't bother me when a script or a novel is "too on the nose." On the nose means I get it. I understand what's going on. Obscure references and too much subtlety mean I'm left wondering what happened.

But this is a minor quibble over a fantastic entry in the *Poirot* series. You'll love this episode. There is so much to see and enjoy you can watch it several times.

General Information

Based on: "The Adventure of the Cheap Flat" (short story, 1923)
Run time: 51 min. **Subtitles:** Yes

Writer: Richard Spence
Director: Russell Murray

Cast

David Suchet as Hercule Poirot
Hugh Fraser as Captain Hastings
Pauline Moran as Miss Lemon
Philip Jackson as Chief Inspector Japp
William Hootkins as FBI Agent Burt
Gordon Wharmby as Records Agent

Samantha Bond as Stella Robinson
John Michie as James Robinson
Jenifer Landor as Elsa Hart
Luke Hayden as Carla Romero's Husband
Nick Maloney as Bernie Cole
Peter Howell as Mr. Paul
Ian Price as Teddy Parker
Jemma Churchill as Elsie
Nigel Whitmey as Luigi Valdarno
Anthony Pedley as Assassin

Film Location

Campden Hill Gate, London

Japp, I hope you're not so short of manpower you're hiring a shamus. What are they good for, chasing lost dogs? This is a matter of international security we're dealing with here.

FBI Agent Burt

The Kidnapped Prime Minister (1990)

The future of Europe is in the hands of Poirot as he follows his own path to learn the fate of the British leader

Fidelity to text

Plenty of changes, including updating motivation to match shifting the year to the mid-1930s. All of the changes worked to enhance an otherwise slight story.

Quality of movie

I really wanted this to be longer; it needed more detail about motivation. If you're not up on British history, you'll miss the nuances.

This is a complex episode, deeply involved with the sins of the past smacking into the politics of the present-day (about 1935).

If you're not aware of the British and Irish conflicts over Home Rule, much of the story won't make sense. It's too subtle; the film needed to be longer to spell out for us clueless, ahistorical Americans why everyone cared so much. I had to look up Lord Asquith (1852-1928) and the Home Rule bill, and I'm still not sure what happened.

As near as I can figure out, Prime Minister Asquith introduced a bill in 1912 to permit the Irish more self-governing powers. However, some didn't think that bill went far enough. The opposition saw it as a sop to get Irish citizens to shut up and roll over and be grateful to their British masters for allowing them an eighth of an inch of wiggle room. I think. I'm probably wrong. It's a very complex issue. Unless you're really motivated and have plenty of time, I don't recommend you dive into that particular rabbit hole.

Suffice to say, Commander Daniels, the former Mrs. Daniels, and the chauffeur, Egan, had deep-rooted historical and emotional reasons to loathe the prime minister and everything he represented. They believed, with war coming and everyone remembering the catastrophe of WWI, that the enemy of my enemy is my friend. This is a very dubious proposition, on par with making deals with the devil. In the short term, those deals seem to succeed. In the long term, the devil always wins. He's got time on his side, something we mere mortals do not.

Back to *Poirot*. For a serious episode with even more serious undertones, it begins and ends with humor. Poirot, as we know, is a very snappy dresser. He has his suits tailor-made for the perfect fit. So he's arguing with his tailor, Mr. Fingler, about the suit not fitting perfectly. Mr. Fingler tells him that his tape measure did not stretch. No, Poirot's girth stretched so the new suits had to be cut to accommodate his weight gain.

Why does Poirot patronize a Jewish tailor on the less stylish side of London? Because Mr. Fingler trained the boys at Saville Row and Poirot's concern is with acquiring the best suit, not the most fashionable one.

Sir Bernard Dodge (*Ronald Hines*), the irritated official

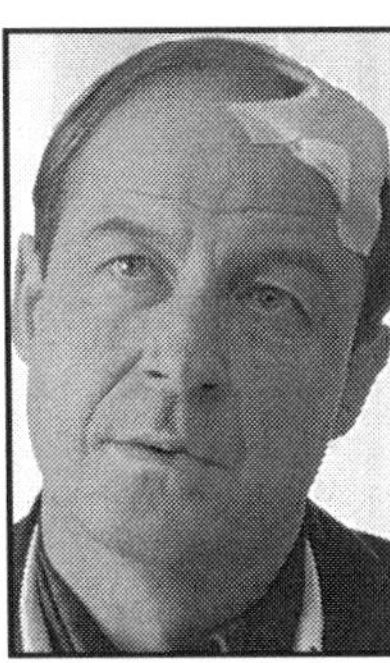

Commander Daniels (*David Horovitch*), the jaded secretary

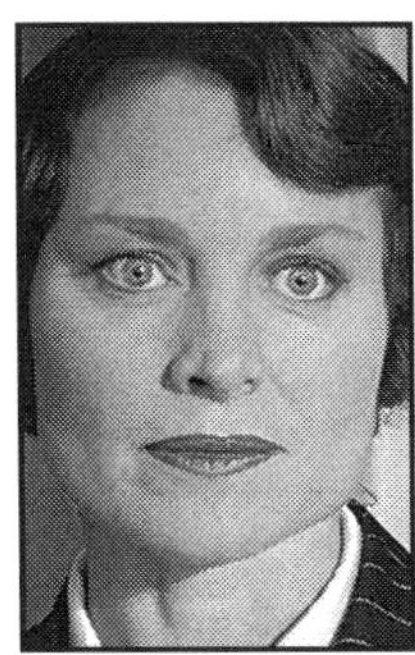

Mrs. Daniels (*Lisa Harrow*), the loyal ex-wife

Egan (*Jack Elliott*), the nimble chauffeur

Major Norman (*Timothy Block*), the annoyed liaison

Mr. Fingler (*Milo Sperber*), the gimlet-eyed tailor

He has his priorities.

Remember this: Poirot always keeps his priorities straight. Whatever sympathy he may feel toward Irish nationalists wanting self-rule, he's Belgian. He was a war refugee who found refuge in England when he had no other place to go. With German militarism on the rise again, he's got a good idea of what the approaching storm will do to Europe and Great Britain.

When he is summoned to investigate the kidnapping of the prime minister, he leaps into action. More specifically, Poirot leaps into mental action. He thinks about what actually happened when the prime minister was kidnapped as opposed to what Lord Estair and Sir Bernard believe happened. Or what Chief Inspector Japp wants. They want, nay, expect him to race around France sniffing for clues. The idea of him sleeping when there is no time to spare (32¼ hours to be precise) is anathema.

But this is a case where thought is demanded and not racing after escaping divorcées in motorcars. Although that does happen because what else is Hastings for if not to race after hot redheads in his Lagonda? He lives for those moments and, God knows, we can't have a Poirot episode without some kind of car chase.

Poirot works out what no one else noticed. If someone wanted to shoot the prime minister, why did they kidnap him after the assassination attempt failed? If the prime minister was kidnapped to assassinate him, why wasn't the body dumped at once? Could the reason be to sow confusion and dissent? That possibility exists. If the prime minister is in the same state as Schrodinger's Cat, then the British government has a serious problem. They're missing an important government official, but he can't be replaced because there is no body laying around proving which state he is in, dead or alive.

General Information

Based on: "The Kidnapped Prime Minister" (short story, 1923)
Run time: 50 min. **Subtitles:** Yes

Writer: Clive Exton **Director:** Andrew Grieve

Cast

David Suchet as Hercule Poirot
Hugh Fraser as Captain Hastings
Philip Jackson as Chief Inspector Japp
Pauline Moran as Miss Lemon

Ronald Hines as Sir Bernard Dodge
Patrick Godfrey as Lord Estair
David Horovitch as Commander Daniels
Lisa Harrow as Mrs. Daniels
Timothy Block as Major Norman
Jack Elliott as Egan
Kate Binchy as Landlady
Milo Sperber as Mr. Fingler
Henry Moxon as Prime Minister
Oliver Beamish as Sergeant Hopper
Anthony Chinn as Shi Mong
Roy Heather as Transport Superintendent
Daniel John as Urchin
Sam Clifton as Urchin

Film Locations

Dover Western Docks railway station, Dover (opening scene)
Quilter Street & Barnet Grove, London (tailor exterior)
Foreign Office, London
Columbia Road, London (Egan's home)
St. Margaret's Bay, Kent (coastal promenade)
Dover Western Docks, Dover (ship for France)
Waterloo Crescent, Dover (Poirot walks)
Dover Harbour Board offices, Dover (seaside hotel exterior)
Finsbury Health Centre, London (Feltham Hospital)
Tower Garage, Egham (phone call scene)
Wells Mews, London (Daniels' flat)
Crescent Grove, London (ex-Mrs. Daniels' home)
Norman Shaw Buildings, London (Scotland Yard)
Ockham Lane, Ockham (car chase)
Ingress Abbey, Kent (Summerscote Hall)

> *Mr. Fingler is an artist, Hastings. And like all artists, he must be treated with a firm hand.*
>
> Hercule Poirot

Poirot also notices that after the near-miss shooting, no one actually sees the prime minister's face. What I find hard to believe is that if the prime minister was shot, followed an hour later by a kidnapping, why didn't Scotland Yard investigate where the prime minister got his face bandaged up? That helps develop the timeline, narrowing down exactly where he was, who he saw, and possibly, unearthing clues to valuable witnesses.

But no, Scotland Yard did not apparently perform this basic task. Poirot must waste his precious time (32¼ hours, remember) interviewing matrons at local hospitals. Chief Inspector Japp *should* be worried about losing his pension and his job!

It was also difficult to believe Poirot could so quickly unearth Egan's address book and turn to the "X" page and discover a clue. But that's fiction for you; compressing a search that would take hours into a single dramatic minute.

The clue does indirectly lead to another clue that ties the case together for Poirot. As he's dialing Commander Daniels' telephone, he sees the photograph of his wife. Estranged wife. Divorced wife after the kind of vicious, no-holds-barred divorce that made all the papers. The kind of divorce that everyone read avidly in all the worst gossip rags.

Why did Commander Daniels keep a picture of his evil ex on his desk? A very good question, Poirot would say. With help from Miss Lemon, he works out where to go to rescue the prime minister. As you would expect, he is correct. Sadly, the rescue still ends in tragedy albeit not for England. The prime minister is proved alive and goes off to the conference as scheduled. Other people, however, will pay and pay and pay.

This is a great episode, subtle and complex. It's a lovely example of old sins casting long shadows.

The Adventure of the Western Star (1990)

Someone's after a hot rock belonging to Belgium's most famous actress, but first they must get past Poirot

Fidelity to text

The movie star changes nationality and a suspicious diamond buyer shows up, as do Japp and Miss Lemon. There are other changes and enhancements, not all of which work.

Quality of movie

They can't all be gems. Murky, overly convoluted, and decidedly unclear motivations.

This episode was beautifully shot, acted, and staged. The individual scenes sparkled. Too bad the story as a whole didn't hold together. Remember, I'm not that bright. I need a clear storyline. We'll start with the first rhinestone in the necklace and work our way to the hen's egg-sized flawed diamond.

Chief Inspector Japp did not appear in the original short story, but he shows up. The scriptwriter devised a clever way of fitting him into the story. Japp is investigating the other added main character, suspicious German arms dealer and diamond collector Henrik Van Braks. Japp has had his eye on this man for some time, along with Hoffberg, the shady gem dealer. Van Braks collects diamonds, and he's not fussy about their provenance. Van Braks also has friends in high places so Japp has to be careful how he treats this suspect.

The movie star becomes Marie Marvelle, Belgian cinema goddess and — my word! — watch Poirot fanboy all over her. It's amusing to watch one of the world's great detectives behave like a teenager meeting his adored idol. The tea he prepares for Miss Marvelle's visit to the office is sumptuous, precisely organized, exquisite; all the better to impress the glamorous diva.

Sadly, no one else is impressed by stars of the Belgian film industry. Even more sadly, Miss Marvelle stands Poirot up, demanding that they meet at her hotel instead. Saddest of all, Miss Lemon's sole role is limited to arranging and then disposing of the sumptuous tea.

(By the way, note the Cubist painting in Poirot's apartment. It is "The Piano (Velazquez)" by Pablo Picasso, and it was painted in 1957, putting Poirot 20 years ahead of his time!)

In her hotel room, Miss Marvelle tells Poirot an absurd story — tosh as he puts it — about mysterious messages from Chinamen seeking the return of her fabulous diamond, the Western Star. Her dear husband, Gregorie Rolf, gave her the hen's egg-sized rock when they married three years previously. He claimed he bought it from a Chinaman in San Francisco who was so desperate to unload the gem that he sold it for a tenth of its value.

The bizarre story prompts Hastings to recall that Lord and Lady Yardly — who are going to host Marie

Marie Marvelle (*Rosalind Bennett*), the Belgian star

Gregorie Rolf (*Oliver Cotton*), her actor-husband

Lady Yardly (*Caroline Goodall*), the worried wife

Lord Yardly (*Alister Cameron*), the doubting husband

Hoffberg (*Bruce Montague*), the go-between

Henrik Van Braks (*Struan Rodger*), the wealthy collector

Marvelle and her hubby at the ancestral castle — met them three years ago in California. According to the gossip, Lady Yardly got exceedingly friendly with Marie Marvelle's hubby.

Soon thereafter, Lady Yardly shows up at Poirot's office. The great man is out, so Hastings takes the opportunity to interview her. He asks leading questions and discovers that Lady Yardly has also received mysterious, threatening letters from Chinamen about her own fabulous, hen's-egg-sized diamond, the Star of the East. Twin diamonds, both stolen from an exotic idol in the mysterious Orient. Hastings is overcome, both by the story and his own cleverness in ferreting out the truth from Lady Yardly.

During Poirot and Hastings' visit to the Yardlys' home, Lady Yardly's diamond is yanked from her neck by a mysterious Chinaman, and the plot begins to founder on the seas of motivation.

I understand why Van Braks wants to add another spectacular diamond to his personal museum. We all need a hobby, and rich arms dealers can afford fabulous diamonds the size of hen's eggs.

I understand why Hoffberg, shady diamond dealer, is willing to work both sides of the street. As long as he doesn't come under Inspector Japp's official scrutiny, he can buy, sell, and get rich. Even better, criminal sales of stolen diamonds don't require paying taxes or fees. Hoffberg gets to keep more money, and he gets rich arms dealers beholden to him. I understand why Hoffberg is afraid of Scotland Yard: He doesn't dare get caught.

I understand why Lord Yardly wants to sell the Star of the East. It's been in the family for generations but he needs the money to keep the estate going. It's not entailed so it can go on the auction block. The Star is a family heirloom and Lady Yardly wants to keep it but he really, really needs the money.

Lord Yardly, by the way, emits distinct Bertie Wooster vibes; he admits he's not that bright especially in financial affairs. Unlike in the story, he seems devoted to Lady Yardly, adores their kids, and there's no gossip about his carrying on with film stars in California.

I also understand why Marie Marvelle is concerned about the Western Star being stolen by Chinamen. It's a big, valuable piece of ice. I understand why she wants to film a movie at the Yardly estate; the set dressing is all done. I even understand why she wanted to keep the Western Star, rather than permitting Poirot to hang onto it for safekeeping. She'd watch that husband-stealing hussy, Lady Yardly, make eyes at Gregorie over dinner. Wearing the Western Star would put that aristocratic slut in her place.

General Information

Based on: "The Adventure of the Western Star" (short story, 1923)
Run time: 50 min. **Subtitles:** Yes

Writer: Clive Exton **Director:** Richard Spence

Cast

David Suchet as Hercule Poirot
Hugh Fraser as Captain Hastings
Philip Jackson as Chief Inspector Japp
Barry Woolgar as Inspector Dougall
Pauline Moran as Miss Lemon
Ian Collier as Sergeant

Struan Rodger as Henrik Van Braks
Rosalind Bennett as Marie Marvelle
Oliver Cotton as Gregorie Rolf
Alister Cameron as Lord Yardly
Caroline Goodall as Lady Yardly
Stephen Hancock as Mullings
Bruce Montague as Hoffberg
Julian Gartside as Hotel Receptionist
Bill Thomas as Steward
Jill Goldston as Street Seller

Film Locations

Widegate Street, London (Van Braks arrested)
Dorney Court, Dorney, Buckinghamshire (Yardley Chase)
Croydon Airport, South London (Shoreham airport / Brighton City Airport)

I even understand why Lady Yardly didn't want to sell the Star of the East. She'd given it to Marie's husband in exchange for incriminating letters she wrote during their affair. Any jeweler would recognize the diamond as being a flashy imitation. Her own dear hubby, sweet but dim, might not forgive her. Divorce and losing her children loom. Of course, so does having the ancestral mansion fall down around their ears due to lack of money for upkeep.

What I did not understand was Gregorie Rolf's motivations. He's the clasp, holding the rhinestones together. He's a lying, cheating, thieving scoundrel in a full-length fur coat, green sharkskin suit, and spectator shoes. Why does he care what happens to Lady Yardly? She can say whatever she wants about his blackmail and his answer is easy: "I don't know what that aristocratic crazy lady is talking about." We are never shown a single reason why he would care what happens to her.

I know why he's selling a real hen's-egg-sized diamond to Van Braks. He wants the money. But why? So he can abandon his gorgeous queen of Belgian cinema? Marie Marvelle adores him or at least that's what we see onscreen. We don't see a single scene showing them fighting over his affairs. He's got no reason to abandon her and fly off to Johannesburg with a suitcase full of money. He's a successful movie star and a producer. Yet there he is, abandoning his career and fleeing Britain for South Africa.

It's as though there's plenty more plot that didn't get filmed; i.e., the plot where Gregorie Rolf meets Lady Yardly at the airport and they run off to Johannesburg together. He abandons his shrewish wife and she dumps her doofus husband and their bratty kids.

Apparently not. As I said at the beginning, I like a crystal-clear plot. This was one flawed diamond. You'll enjoy it as long as you don't look too close.

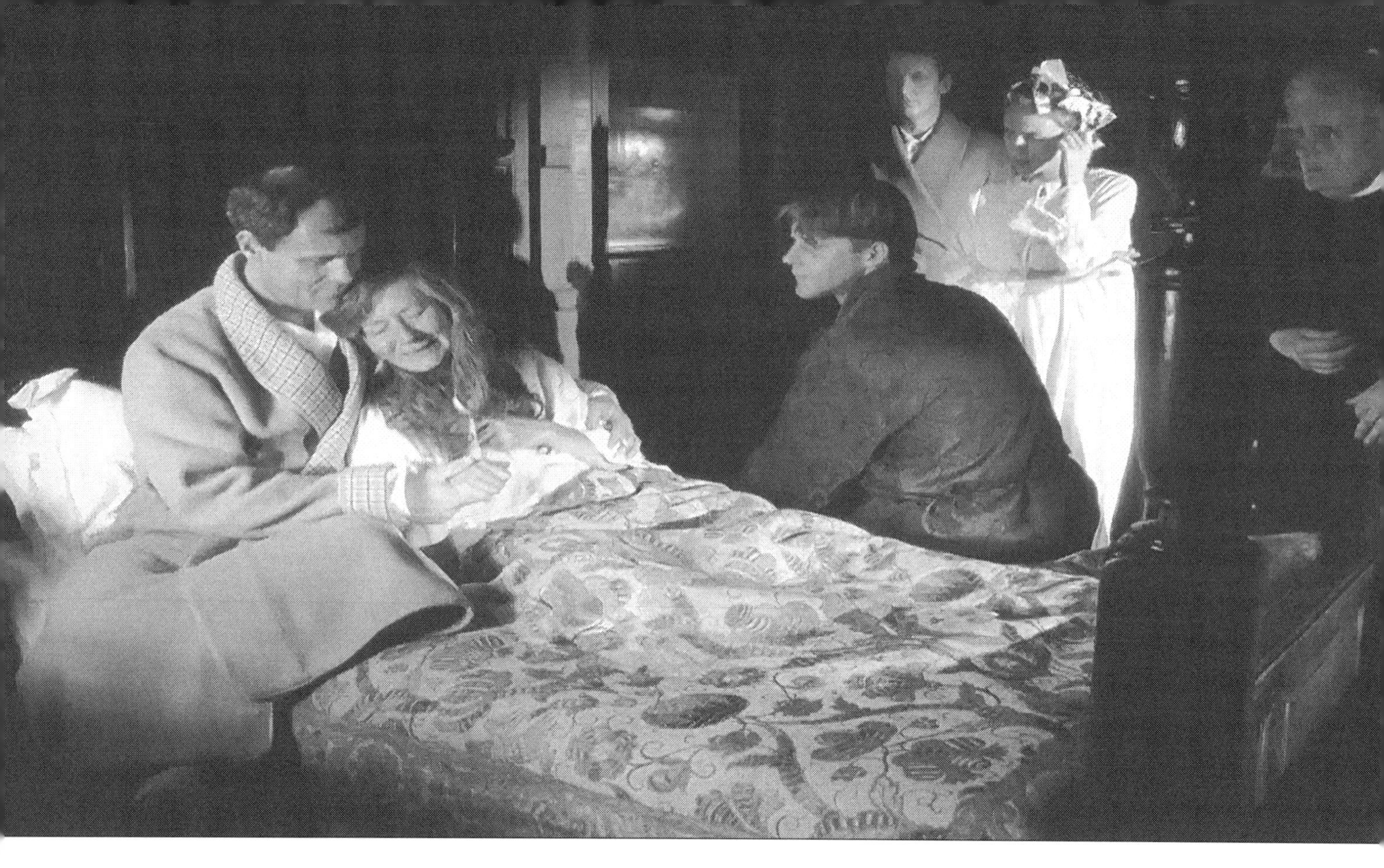

The Mysterious Affair at Styles (1990)

Do the time warp and jump back to WWI, when a recovering Hastings presents murder English style to Poirot

Fidelity to text

Streamlining out characters and adding Poirot and Hastings much earlier.

Quality of movie

Well-paced, well-acted, and well-researched about life in 1917 wartime England. It works very nicely once you adjust to the sudden and unannounced time travel from the 1930s.

If you've been watching *Poirot* in the order in which the films were released, then you might notice that everything suddenly looks different. Cars, trains, clothing, background characters, street vignettes, room lighting, everything.

Where's that 1935 vibe? It's gone because the producers did not film the short stories and the novels in the order in which they were written. They skipped around and finally did the time warp, landing in the past when Poirot arrived in England and solved his first case.

The Mysterious Affair at Styles (1920) was the first novel Agatha published. It could not have its background setting easily rewritten for the mid-1930s. It's very much of its time, taking place in the summer of 1917. The war is in full swing and refugees are flooding England. Thus, we are watching a previous era compared to the rest of the *Poirot* episodes.

This trip back in time should have been announced with a title card to alert the audience, but it wasn't. This is a mistake because you cannot guarantee the audience is familiar with the source material.

We get some backstory about Captain Hastings when he was a mere lieutenant, fighting for the Crown in the war to end all wars. Pay careful attention to the scenes in the convalescent hospital where he's recuperating. Notice the array of injuries in the wounded soldiers. At least one of the background soldiers must have had terrible burns based on the bandages swathing his face. Those lads were tough to have survived that well considering their injuries. In 1917, handwashing was finally becoming recognized as a sensible thing to do and armies no longer lost half their men to poor sanitation.

Pay attention to the film the soldiers are watching. God only knows why someone (I'm assuming the producers paid close attention to convalescent hospital procedures of the time) thought it was a good idea to torture shell shocked veterans with footage of more trench warfare. They'd left body parts and comrades behind in that nightmare. WWI was called the war to end all wars because it was so huge and so dreadful. In addition to the meat grinder the soldiers endured, there were civilian casualties on a massive scale, never seen before. Artillery that would launch shells up to fifteen miles away could be used in barrages on cities

Mrs. Inglethorpe
(*Gillian Barge*),
the Lady Bountiful

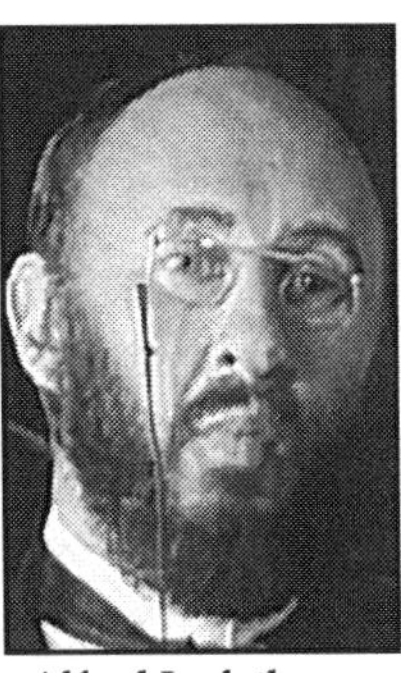

Alfred Inglethorpe
(*Michael Cronin*),
the laconic husband

John Cavendish
(*David Rintoul*),
the angry heir

Mary Cavendish
(*Beatie Edney*),
the suspicious wife

Evie Howard
(*Joanna McCallum*),
the efficient factotum

Cynthia Murdoch
(*Allie Byrne*),
the poor relation

as well as enemy troops. That footage you're watching along with Lt. Hastings looks vintage and real.

In previous wars such as the Civil War, if you were a few miles away from the front lines, you were not directly affected by the fighting unless family members were serving. WWI not only slaughtered civilians and soldiers by their tens of thousands, it forced entire populations to relocate. It's perfectly understandable why Hastings takes up John Cavendish's invitation to Styles, fleeing the hospital to the countryside.

We also meet Hercule Poirot, Belgian refugee, and doing his best to help his fellow refugees and himself adjust to British ways. It's a great introduction. The camera slowly pans from his patent leather shoes and spats as he picks his way through the mud in the English countryside up to his formalwear, so out of place in the woods. Everything is strange, unfamiliar, and disorganized to him.

With this second viewing, I got the impression that Poirot's normal OCD was in hyperdrive because it was the only control he had as a stranger in a strange land. He recognizes one person in this unknown world: Lieutenant Hastings. Poirot is overjoyed to see a familiar face in a foreign land. They had met in Antwerp before the war in a case where Hastings was a suspect.

When murder visits the Styles estate, Lt. Hastings knows who to call. Poirot arrives and begins to immerse himself in English country house living. The Cavendish/Inglethorpe family are still doing very well for themselves despite their straitened circumstances. Admire how badly lit the interior of the house is. The family dines by candlelight because they must. In 1917, even a wealthy family would not have electricity. They're too far away from the big city where electricity arrived first. And of course, there's a war on, as we're reminded throughout the episode.

One part of the plot that was minimized was Mary Cavendish's new job as a Land Girl. Those were the young women, usually upper-class, who went out to the farms to do all the work the men used to do. Great Britain had to eat and despite the industrial revolution, it was still an agrarian nation that fed itself. It's mentioned, but doesn't play the role it did in the novel. That's too bad because it's a fascinating glimpse into culture-clash. The sheltered young women who participated had their lives changed and who knows what came from that experience?

Similarly, watch all the women in the background doing what would have been men's jobs just a few short years before, including several young women straining to move heavy bags of grain that would have been a one-man job. Their understanding of what they could do was abruptly broadened.

We also lost the subplot of Mary Cavendish's (possible) affair with Dr. Bauerstein, conveniently nearby toxicologist. Her husband John's affair with Mrs. Raikes (widowed for the film) remains but it's the barest outline. He claims he's "just helping her out with a loan." The script did a poor job addressing John's relationship with Mrs. Raikes. Why did he loan her £200 to buy a cottage? That was a lot of money back then and an explanation should have been given.

Another piece of lost significance doesn't have anything to do with the producers' choices. Poirot gathers all the suspects together and delivers his summation of the crime. Normal and expected, right? Yet Agatha invented this classic mystery trope and used it for the first time here. She couldn't write the courtroom scene to the publisher's satisfaction, came up with this alternative method, and now, every writer in the world uses her technique where the detective tells everyone whodunnit and why. Real detectives probably daydream of getting this chance to show off.

Watching this scene, I wondered again why Alfred Inglethorpe showed up. He didn't have to. There's more (I think) of a reason given in the novel. Here, he shows up because he's asked. Maybe he thought it was less suspicious. A line of dialog explaining why he agreed would have been helpful.

ITV did a great job. But if you're new to the series or to Agatha's novels, understand that you'll leap back twenty years in time to when Poirot and Hastings met on the grounds of Styles for their first hunt together.

General Information

Based on: *The Mysterious Affair at Styles* (novel, 1920)
Run time: 1 hr., 43 min. **Subtitles:** No

Writer: Clive Exton **Director:** Ross Devenish

Cast

David Suchet as Hercule Poirot
Hugh Fraser as Lieutenant Hastings
Philip Jackson as Chief Inspector Japp

Beatie Edney as Mary Cavendish
David Rintoul as John Cavendish
Gillian Barge as Mrs. Inglethorp
Michael Cronin as Alfred Inglethorp
Joanna McCallum as Evie Howard
Anthony Calf as Lawrence Cavendish
Allie Byrne as Cynthia Murdoch
Lala Lloyd as Dorcas
Michael Godley as Dr. Wilkins
Morris Perry as Mr. Wells
Penelope Beaumont as Mrs. Raikes
David Savile as Summerhaye
Tim Munro as Edwin Mace
Tim Preece as Philips, K.C.
Merelina Kendall as Mrs. Dainty
Bryan Coleman as Vicar
Eric Stovell as Chemist
Donald Pelmear as Judge

Film Locations

Chavenage House, Tetbury, Gloucestershire (Styles)
Easton Grey, Wiltshire (Styles St. Mary)
Horsted Keynes Station, Bluebell Railway, Haywards Heath, Sussex
Central Criminal Court, Old Bailey, London
Lloyd Square, London
Giltspur Street, London
St. Bartholomew's Hospital, London (archway entrance)
Myddelton Square, London

How Does Your Garden Grow? (1991)

Flowers frame a case of murder from the Chelsea Flower Show to a woman's shell-laced garden

Fidelity to text

Extras, surprises, and enhancements galore, all in the service of Miss Lemon and the story.

Quality of movie

A flower-laden episode from Miss Lemon's fabulous grassy outfit to Mrs. Delafontaine's garden to pedigreed roses to the Chelsea Flower Show! There's even a double flower clue. No wonder Hastings gets hay fever.

We open with Poirot getting ready for an important event. He's going to be honored at the Chelsea Flower Show with a new rose variety. It's a hybrid tea rose in pale pink named after him. Not every one gets a rose variety named after them, although I do have to agree with Chief Inspector Japp (an avid gardener) that it should have been a polyantha rose rather than a hybrid tea as they're more highly perfumed. Interestingly, although a named rose was an added incident to the story, it's based on a real event. Agatha Christie was honored in 1988 with a similar pink climbing rose.

Why did Inspector Japp think Poirot should have had a polyantha rose named in his honor? Perhaps he was thinking of how much of a dandy Poirot can be, always impeccably dressed and groomed. Or he knew that polyantha roses date back to 1870s France, where they were first developed. France isn't Belgium, but it's not English either and shouldn't a gentleman from the continent be honored with a continental rose? But I digress.

To make himself perfect for his perfect namesake, Poirot visits George F. Trumper, a gentleman's barber and salon, for the perfect gentleman's cologne. Like the Agatha Christie rose, George F. Trumper exists and you can visit the shop (they have two, Poirot's shop in Mayfair and St. James') the next time you're in London and need gentlemen's grooming accessories. Trumper's also provides one of the ways Miss Lemon assists Poirot in solving the murder *and* the shop gets Hastings in trouble.

Because Poirot is in such a hurry to get to the Chelsea Flower Show, he neglects to open the morning post. Thus, when he's accosted by an old lady in a wheelchair, he doesn't know her or understand why she thinks that he should. But she knows who he is and not just because he's getting a rose named after him according to the posters.

Miss Amelia Barrowby needs professional help, but not in the gardening department. She's overly cautious about talking to him which leads to confusion. Granted, she has her reasons but even so, clearer communication from her to Poirot might have kept her alive. Miss Barrowby is so circumspect in her message that she gives Poirot an empty seed packet, sure he'll

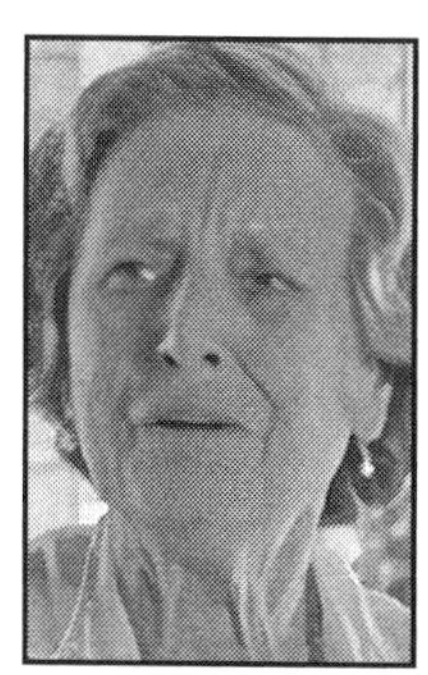
Amelia Barrowby (Margery Mason), the garden enthusiast

Mary Delafontaine (*Anne Stallybrass*), the gardening niece

Henry Delafontaine (*Tim Wylton*), the henpecked hubby

Katrina Reiger (*Catherine Russell*), the Russian companion

Nicholai (*Peter Birch*), the new Soviet man

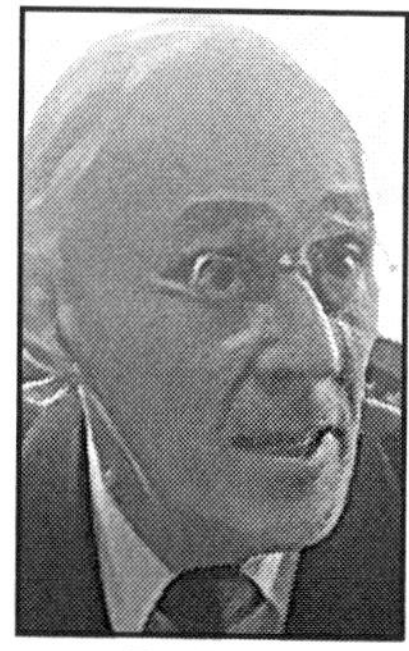
Dr. Sims (*Ralph Nossek*), the local doctor

deduce the hidden message.

This kind of roundabout thinking is why people get themselves poisoned with strychnine. Be clear! Be complete! Don't expect someone to read your mind and decipher your cryptic clues!

When Poirot returns to the office with Miss Lemon and Hastings after his floral triumph, he reads the waiting letter from Miss Barrowby and it doesn't clarify her worries. What is clear is she has a mystery for him to solve that she's afraid to discuss. After all, he spotted her pushy niece and suspicious foreign companion, confirming an underlying problem.

Poirot departs for Miss Barrowby's home (Rosebank in Charman's Green) with Miss Lemon, leaving Hastings in charge. Poor Hastings. He's faced with Mr. Trumper demanding payment for Poirot's purchases and must deal with Miss Lemon's intimidating filing system. He's stymied, can't find the invoice, wrecks her office looking for it, and worst of all, pays up in cash.

Upon their arrival, the parlormaid tells Poirot and Miss Lemon that Miss Barrowby died the previous evening. Shockingly. Suddenly. Under mysterious circumstances. Which is why Inspector Japp turns up next. Miss Barrowby's doctor recognized the symptoms of strychnine poisoning. The question for Japp and the doctor is why, if everyone ate the same dinner, did only Miss Barrowby die? There's also the question of who benefits from the wealthy Miss Barrowby's death.

That's answered in the most charming, roundabout, circumspect, yet very clear manner by Miss Barrowby's solicitor. And, he does it without breeching his client's confidentiality! The solicitor knows his way around words even better than he judges ponies. He also works in what could be a subtle dig against Henry Delafontaine, the pushy niece's husband. The solicitor refers to one of the three ponies as a gelding. Accurate and expected in the horse world, because you get geldings by castrating colts. Charman's Green is a small village and it's a good bet the solicitor has observed Henry Delafontaine and knows whereof he speaks.

Every time we see Henry Delafontaine and his wife, Mary, we know who wears the pants in that family. Mary is also a dedicated gardener. It isn't just her aunt who wanted to attend the Chelsea Flower Show. She did too, as would any gardener. It's the Met Gala for the plant world. Mary's garden is a wonder to behold, she's devoted to it, and based on what's shown, Mary Delafontaine could show her flowers and design ideas at the Chelsea Flower Show. Except, as Poirot and Miss Lemon observe, there's an odd flaw in its perfect symmetry.

Miss Barrowby's Russian companion also attends the flower show. She has to; it's her job. She also wants to because it's a chance to meet her lover who's on the staff at the Soviet Embassy.

This subplot was charming, abounding with red herrings (Commies!) and longing glances. I'm sure flowers were involved, at least when there were no Bolshie spies around to report the embassy staffer and his unacceptable lady-friend to Uncle Josef. Don't miss that giant portrait of Stalin (1878-1953) glowering at his underlings.

Eventually, the loose ends come together and once again, Miss Lemon provides the key. She's horrified at Hastings wrecking her office. She's appalled that he paid in cash because tradesmen conclude your checks are worthless.

Poirot sees his chance, sends Miss Lemon undercover, and they return to Rosebank where Mary and Henry Delafontaine enjoy the gorgeous garden and wait to inherit. Mary's perfect garden with silver bells and cockleshells all in a row proves her undoing. Cockleshells are not oyster shells, so why are oyster shells being used awkwardly, childishly as edging?

That was a flaw, by the way, in Agatha's plotting. Any good gardener needing to hide something organic doesn't leave it where it can be seen. No, that's what compost bins are for. But perhaps Agatha didn't compost and so she had to come up with a solution for getting rid of the evidence. You bury the body (or the oyster shells) in the compost bin and no one will ever know. Not as long as you're the one doing the turning. Two inches of top soil and a bit of mulch and no one would ever know, especially snoopy detectives wearing a pale pink rosebud in their boutonnière vase.

General Information

Based on: "How Does Your Garden Grow?" (short story, 1935)
Run time: 50 min. **Subtitles:** Yes

Writer: Andrew Marshall
Director: Brian Farnham

Cast

David Suchet as Hercule Poirot
Hugh Fraser as Captain Hastings
Philip Jackson as Chief Inspector Japp
Pauline Moran as Miss Lemon

Anne Stallybrass as Mary Delafontaine
Tim Wylton as Henry Delafontaine
Margery Mason as Amelia Barrowby
Catherine Russell as Katrina Reiger
Peter Birch as Nicholai
Ralph Nossek as Dr. Sims
John Burgess as Mr. Harrison
Dorcas Morgan as Lucy
Trevor Danby as Mr. Trumper
John Rogan as Pathologist
Stephen Petcher as Photographer
Philip Praeger as Police Constable

Film Locations

G. F. Trumper, Mayfair, London (perfumery)
Royal Hospital Chelsea, London (Chelsea Flower Show)
Freemasons' Hall, London (Soviet Embassy)
Ham House Stables, London (horse event)
Saint Sophia Cathedral, London (interior)
Dormition Cathedral, London (exterior)

The Million Dollar Bond Robbery (1991)

A threat of robbery on the high seas sends Poirot and Hastings aboard an ocean liner crossing the Atlantic

Fidelity to text

An eight-page story needs embellishment. Each addition deepened and enlarged the scope while remaining true to the text.

Quality of movie

Beautiful fusing of vintage newsreel footage, a locked-room mystery, and classic misdirection Agatha would have approved of.

Wow. We have a winner! But then I do like me some time at sea, and this episode, courtesy of very careful filming and the use of vintage newsreel footage, gives the sensation of being on board the *Queen Mary*.

What a gorgeous ocean liner. Launched in 1936, she dates back to the days when we traveled in a civilized fashion across the globe and never had to deal with jet lag or being crammed into dirty buses in the sky, breathing recirculated air that's been in at least ten other people's lungs.

And yes, I do know what steerage is. Destitute travelers are stuffed into the hold, cheek by jowl, where they endure the journey from port to port. But if you, dear traveler, had some money, you could move up a notch from steerage. You could pay for a bunk you didn't have to share. After that, the sky's the limit when it came to comfort and class.

It's obvious from the accommodations we see on screen that the bank paid for Poirot and Hastings to travel first class on this fabulous ship.

My question throughout the episode was why was Poirot worried about *mal de mer*? In *Problem at Sea*, he sailed aboard the Motor Yacht *Madiz*, a wonderful 1902 small yacht. He made a port of call in Rhodes. He was fine! The Mediterranean is a calm, warm bathtub compared to the North Atlantic, but the *Queen Mary* has a huge draft. She's over 1,000 feet long, compared to *Madiz's* 187 feet. *Madiz* would be rocking and rolling in swells the *Queen Mary* wouldn't notice. So why did Poirot feel he needed to bring an apothecary shop of seasickness meds along with him when it's never been mentioned in the series before?

Perhaps it was the thought of braving the North Atlantic that did him in. Although once aboard, Poirot was fine. Hastings was the sufferer, so much that he couldn't pay proper attention to the hot blonde traveling in the cabin next to them and Ridgeway.

Right. Ridgeway. He's the reason Poirot and Hastings got a cruise on board the *Queen Mary*.

Our episode opens with bankers heading to work on a rainy day. Mr. Shaw, co-general manager of a major bank, is nearly run over by a sporty red car driven by a maniac.

He's shaken but still determined to sail across the Atlantic on the *Queen Mary* to hand-deliver bearer

Mr. Shaw
(*David Quilter*),
the poisoned manager

Mr. Vavasour
(*Ewan Hooper*),
the dim-eyed manager

Philip Ridgeway
(*Oliver Parker*),
the tempted assistant

Esmée Dalgleish
(*Natalie Ogle*),
the worried fiancée

Mr. McNeil
(*Paul Young*),
the strict security chief

Nurse Long
(*Lizzy McInnerny*),
the caregiver

bonds to a bank in New York City. Except he's served poisoned tea by the tea lady so he can't. Instead, the next person in line, Philip Ridgeway, is tapped to sail the high seas with a million dollars in bearer bonds.

This is a position of serious responsibility, not one handed over lightly. Bearer bonds (called Liberty bonds here) are just like cash. The temptation to walk away with a suitcase full of money and quietly disappear must be immense.

The one change to the story that I disapproved of was dropping the mention that Philip Ridgeway was nephew of Mr. Vavasour, the bank's other general manager. It should have been kept, since Ridgeway has a gambling problem. Do you want your bank — holding millions in cash, bearer bonds, jewelry in safety deposit boxes — to hire problem gamblers? I wouldn't. But knowing Ridgeway is related to an important bank executive goes a long way to understanding why he's employed. It makes more sense than keeping him on because he's the sweetie of Mr. Vavasour's personal secretary. It also gives a reason (besides incompetence) for the bank's head of security, Mr. McNeil, to tolerate Ridgeway.

The bank hires Poirot to ensure the bonds make it to New York but they're more worried about the attempts on Mr. Shaw's life, not that his substitute is a gambler with hoods tailing him to grab their money since they don't know this fact. The attempts on Shaw's life prove that something is up; a bad situation when anonymity is what's keeping those bearer bonds safe instead of the ship's safe.

Esmée, the personal secretary, also wants the bonds to arrive safely in New York. She knows about Ridgeway's gambling habit but when she begs Poirot for help, she's too dainty to admit why she's really worried. She's afraid that if anything happens, Ridgeway will be hung out to dry.

Poirot and Hastings set sail with Ridgeway and, alas, when they arrive in New York, the portmanteau has been attacked, then unlocked. The bonds are missing.

Ridgeway claims innocence. He doesn't admit that he ignored his duties in favor of illicit card games where he continued to lose money. He doesn't, in fact, ever admit he has a gambling problem and shouldn't handle his own money or anyone else's. Nor should he marry cute Esmée who obviously adores him. She deserves better. She'll be supporting them both on her salary because he'll lose his at the track or at those illicit Chinese casinos in Limehouse we saw in *The Lost Mine*.

Since the bonds are gone, there's no reason to remain in New York. Poirot, Hastings, and Ridgeway return to England on the next available ship. Muse over that! So many passenger liners crossed the Atlantic on a daily basis that they could buy a ticket and set sail for home right away. Different times …

When they arrive in Southampton, Esmée is waiting for them and so is someone else. Poirot hands Ridgeway over to the waiting bobbies. At the same time, Mr. Vavasour is arrested because his key to the portmanteau of bonds is missing. They share side-by-side cells in a jail familiar to those who've seen *The Veiled Lady*.

Poirot, naturally, has already worked out how the bonds mysteriously disappeared from Ridgeway's stateroom. Granted, Ridgeway made it easier for the criminal by playing cards instead of babysitting his luggage. We don't get an explanation from Poirot about why the criminal hacked at the case, trying to open it, then gave up and simply unlocked it.

Then, in true Agatha tradition, the real culprits are revealed. It's misdirection all the way, including faked illnesses, disguises, and choosing the most likely suspect to be the scapegoat. Hastings is flummoxed but not by the true mastermind. No, it's the mastermind's main henchperson that troubles Hastings. Poirot soothes him with the deeper understanding that he's at the beginning of wisdom.

Sadly, not everyone receives this lesson. I don't believe Ridgeway did. He tells Poirot, Esmée beaming at his side, that he's paid off his debts. Which he has. For now. But I don't buy it. You can bet it won't be smooth sailing for the future Mrs. Ridgeway.

It will be smooth sailing for you, dear reader. You'll love this episode and sleep afterwards dreaming of sailing on the *Queen Mary*, rocked to sleep by the Atlantic Ocean.

General Information

Based on: "The Million Dollar Bond Robbery" (short story, 1923)
Run time: 50 min. **Subtitles:** Yes

Writer: Anthony Horowitz
Director: Andrew Grieve

Cast

David Suchet as Hercule Poirot
Hugh Fraser as Captain Hastings
Pauline Moran as Miss Lemon

David Quilter as Mr. Shaw
Ewan Hooper as Mr. Vavasour
Paul Young as Mr. McNeil
Oliver Parker as Philip Ridgeway
Natalie Ogle as Esmée Dalgleish
Lizzy McInnerny as Nurse Long
Christopher Owen as Chief Purser
Jonathan Stratt as Spivvy Passenger
Dallas Adams as Hood
Kieron Jecchinis as Tom Franklin
Lizzy McInnerny as Miranda Brooks
Richard Bebb as Newsreader (voice)

Film Locations

Bank Subway Station, Threadneedle Street, London
RMS *Queen Mary*, Long Beach, California (ship interiors)
Princes Street, London (Bank of England)
Highpoint 1, London (Dalgleish's apartment)

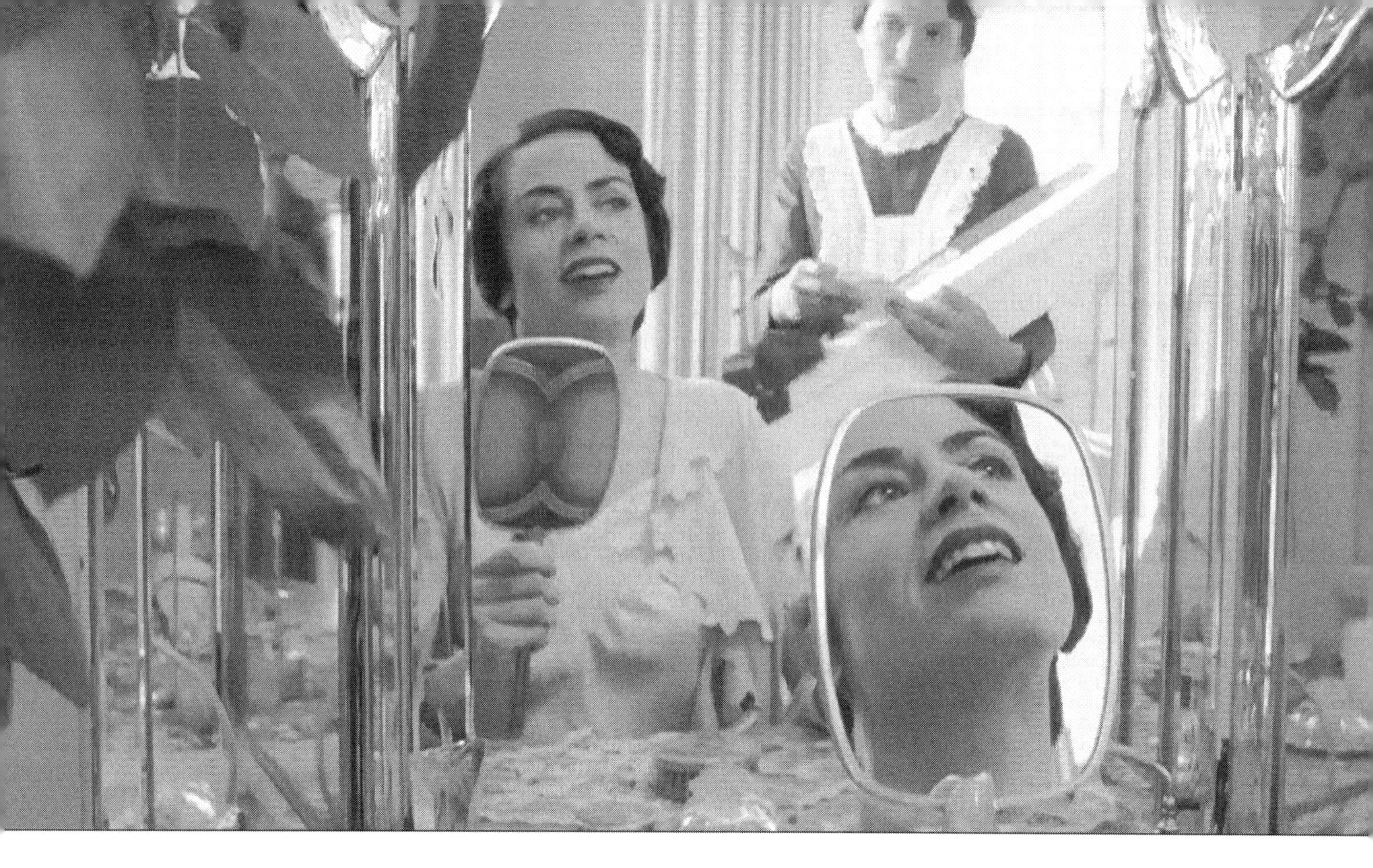

The Plymouth Express (1991)

An heiress found murdered on a train leaves behind an estranged husband and a shady French count as suspects

Fidelity to text

It took lots of changes to turn this slight story into an episode-length *Poirot*. Most importantly, the victim Flossie Carrington is alive at the beginning of the story, radically altering the tone of the ending.

Quality of movie

Sad, moving, emotionally dark, and a reminder that murder isn't fun and games for the victim's family, nor for the detective. Justice may be served, but the victim's still dead.

The short story opens with a naval officer taking the train to Plymouth and discovering a body under his compartment's seat. We never hear from him again. What did he do next after finding the body of a knifed damsel? Did he regret he was too late to save her, even if she was a complete stranger? That's a plot for some Agatha fanfiction because she did nothing with what could have become a thriller. Perhaps that's why, a few years later, she rewrote "The Plymouth Express" into the novel *The Mystery of the Blue Train* (1928).

The naval officer turns up in this episode. As in the short story, he's dispensed with as a mere witness, despite his life being irrevocably divided into two sections: before and after.

A flaw in many mysteries is they rarely acknowledge grief. If you've had someone close to you die, you know what grief is. How much more grief will someone feel when a death is violent and unnatural? You expect your elderly grandfather to die of pneumonia at 96. That's normal. No one lives forever. You do not expect your vivacious, adored daughter to die, stabbed to death in a train compartment over some jewelry.

That's what this episode addresses: grief and loss. It's not a fun, cozy mystery where no one cares someone knifed the victim in a train compartment and shoved her under the seat to bleed out.

Unlike in the short story, we get to know Flossie Halliday Carrington. She's young, she's pretty, she's rich, she's got an adoring father, and her life is on an upswing. She's divorcing her ne'er-do-well husband and a handsome, charming replacement is waiting in the wings, to her father's dismay. He knows le Comte de la Rochefour will not be any better than the boozing gambler she's dumping. Mr. Halliday can hope his daughter will enjoy a flirtation with an unsuitable but charming man, but having learned her lesson with Rupert Carrington, she won't marry him.

Halliday arranges the divorce from Rupert to save his daughter. Hoping to nip her next bad relationship in the bud, he asks Poirot and Hastings to observe le Comte and Flossie at tea at the Adelphi Hotel.

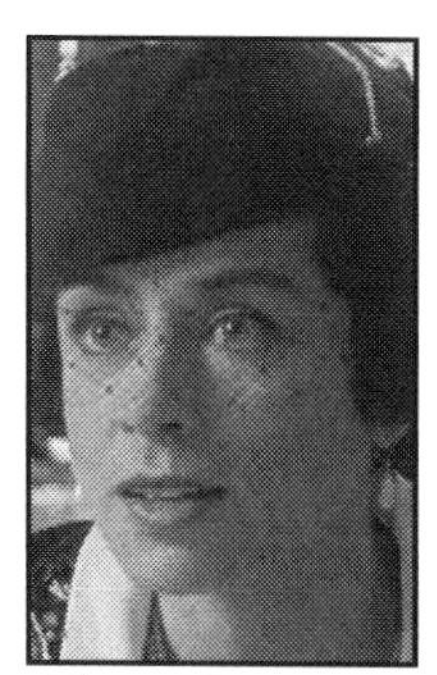

Flossie Carrington
(*Shelagh McLeod*),
the happy heiress

Rupert Carrington
(*Julian Wadham*),
the estranged husband

Comte de la Rochefour
(*Alfredo Michelson*),
the smarmy suitor

Gordon Halliday
(*John Stone*),
the worried father

McKenzie
(*Kenneth Haigh*),
the earnest witness

Jane Mason
(*Marion Bailey*),
the loyal maid

But he can't save her everywhere because she's an independent spirit. She's got a party to go to on the coast, so she's carrying £100,000 in jewelry in a small box. England is a very safe country, so she doesn't think she needs a bodyguard. To protect herself, Flossie is relying on her status and relative anonymity along with the British railway system. She's wrong, of course, but we wouldn't have a mystery if she was right. (See *Agatha and the Truth of Murder* for a similar real-life train murder.)

Published in 1923, "The Plymouth Express" is another example of how Agatha played with reader expectations. From the beginning — at least to Chief Inspector Japp — it's obvious who the murderer must be. Le Comte de la Rochefour is a known swindler, is wanted badly back in Paris by his bank employer, and is carrying £20,000 in bearer bonds for no discernible reason. He loathes Flossie's father because Halliday knows what kind of man he is. Jewelry worth £100,000 would make a delightful addition to his £20,000 in bonds. He could disappear to Argentina and a very plush life.

Hastings, meanwhile, suspects Rupert Carrington. When the divorce is final, Rupert's back to being a penniless ne'er-do-well, the black sheep of the family, and a disappointment to his ancestors going back to the Norman Conquest. To him, £100,000 in stolen jewelry would let him lose more money at the track than he already had and drink what's left over. He certainly won't use it to pay his club fees, his tailor's bills, or re-roof the ancestral mansion.

The scene of Japp and Hastings putting forth their arguments to be quashed by Poirot's logic is amusing. Who does Poirot suspect? An unlikely suspect, one hiding in plain sight. One who required an accomplice, a jewel thief who would kill without remorse. With this scant information, Miss Lemon unearthed a likely candidate from her filing system. "Difficulties," as she tells Poirot, "are made to be overcome." Miss Lemon must have files as comprehensive as the London *Times* or Scotland Yard.

The suspect is a sterling example of why household staff should be thoroughly vetted. Think about it: you've got a poorly paid employee who works essentially every waking moment; who's never noticed as a human being; who doesn't get to be a fun, vivacious, high-spirited party girl; who's expected to be reliable, trustworthy, and to never run off with £100,000 in jewelry. It's surprising how many employees are trustworthy and loyal under trying circumstances.

But being overworked doesn't give you the right to murder your employer, or even work with someone who does the knifing. The murder scene is shockingly graphic for the series. Usually, like grief, the violence done to one human being by another is soft-pedaled. I prefer it this way, as I don't care for the pornography of violence. I prefer to see the ramifications of violence addressed, and in this episode they are.

Mr. Halliday is devastated by his only daughter's death. He has to go back to Australia and rebuild his life. His daughter is gone. Who will inherit his mining company? There's no hope of grandchildren who can learn the trade from him. Unless he remarries and fathers more children (not unheard of for sixtyish men) that part of his life is over.

Surprisingly, someone else is devastated. Rupert Carrington grieves. Watch his scene in the bar with Hastings and wonder why Hastings suspected him in the first place, except that Hastings can be relied upon to be wrong. Rupert is not that good an actor. He grieves. When Halliday tells Rupert that the jewelry has been recovered and that he's Flossie's heir, Rupert refuses to take the precious stones and gold. He'll never be able to reconcile with his wife. That part of his life, that chance, that hope, is gone for good.

Le Comte de la Rochefour doesn't care the same way about Flossie.

Poirot does. He rarely meets the victim before the crime so he's able to remain relatively detached. Not this time. He knows exactly what Gordon Halliday and Rupert Carrington lost and feels their pain. You will too.

General Information

Based on: "The Plymouth Express" (short story, 1923)
Run time: 50 min. **Subtitles:** Yes

Writer: Rod Beacham
Director: Andrew Piddington

Cast

David Suchet as Hercule Poirot
Hugh Fraser as Captain Hastings
Philip Jackson as Chief Inspector Japp
Pauline Moran as Miss Lemon

John Stone as Gordon Halliday
Shelagh McLeod as Flossie Carrington
Julian Wadham as Rupert Carrington
Alfredo Michelson as Le Comte de la Rochefour
Marion Bailey as Jane Mason
Kenneth Haigh as McKenzie
Steven Mackintosh as Newsboy
Leon Eagles as Bank Manager
John Abbott as Detective
Stephen Riddle as Barman
Adrian McLoughlin as Station Official
Nigel Makin as Reception Clerk
Richard Vanstone as Sergeant
Robert Locke as Naval Officer
Duncan Faber as Porter
Reg Thomason as Doorman

Film Locations

Du Cane Court, London (Halliday's home)
Adelphi Building, London (hotel)
Hull Paragon Railway Station, Hull, Yorkshire (Paddington, Bristol and Plymouth stations)
Surrey Steps, Surrey Street, and The Old Watch House, King's College Strand Campus, London (exterior, McKenzie's home)

Wasps' Nest (1991)

Expanding the story of a possible love triangle leading to murder leaves intact its weak moral heart

The original story — all 7½ pages of it — consists almost entirely of dialog: Poirot talks to Harrison, considers his options, then talks to Harrison again, lays out his thoughts, and Harrison listens and accedes to Poirot's suggestions.

That's it. It's bloodless and blah, other than some philosophical musings by Poirot about life, death, and crime.

The film had to be fleshed out to make a compelling story. Sadly, despite some terrific additions, it didn't work nearly as well as it could have.

The major flaw was to make John Harrison a writer of philosophy and ethics. He published three books so he knows something about human behavior, self-control, living a meaningful and virtuous life, and the human condition. That's all well and good, yet at the end, when Poirot speaks to Harrison revealing the murder that almost took place, Poirot doesn't say one word about the hypocrisy of Harrison teaching how to live ethically while ignoring his own misconduct. This was a golden opportunity for Harrison to realize how badly he'd failed at meeting his own standards and resolving to do better, or reveal himself as a churlish hypocrite.

There was plenty of time for this scene to take place. We get lots and lots of footage of wasps buzzing about their nest and the garden. The wasps could have been sprayed into submission, leaving plenty of space for more explanatory dialog. The story would have greatly benefited and the climax would have been a callback to John Harrison's profession.

But no. Instead, we get jokes about how the chemist reads Harrison's tomes and Hastings does not. Since Harrison obviously didn't read his own books (maybe they were ghostwritten by exploited philosophy graduate students), what does it matter if he's a specialist in ethics and philosophy? And it doesn't matter that Hastings didn't doggedly plow through a thousand pages of fine print to learn how to behave better. Whatever else you can say about Arthur Hastings, he's a very decent man. He wouldn't try to murder his rival in love, especially if he's only got a few months left to live. Harrison should enjoy the days he's got left and relish how guilty the survivors will feel when he's moldering in his grave. Instead, he's decided on suicide made to look like murder so the Crown executes his rival.

Fidelity to text

The story isn't much: Poirot talks and John Harrison listens and a murder is prevented.

Quality of movie

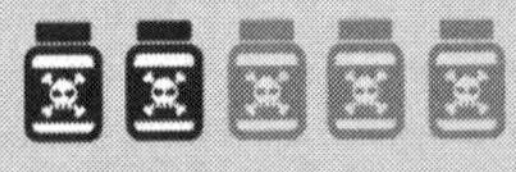

Too many missed opportunities and there's the distinct feeling throughout of the Precrime Department in *Minority Report*. Will they get it right? Do you want to bet your freedom and future on someone's intuition?

John Harrison
(*Martin Turner*),
the moralizing fiancé

Molly Deane
(*Melanie Jessop*),
the dismayed model

Claude Langton
(*Peter Capaldi*),
the genial sculptor

Mrs. Henderson
(*Kate Lynn Evans*),
the watchful chemist

Model Girl
(*Serena Scott Thomas*),
the model witness

Dr. Belvedere
(*John Boswall*),
the mystery man

For a supposedly erudite philosopher, John Harrison doesn't give a damn about everyone he's going to devastate through his selfish behavior. Think of Molly Deane. She'll go to her grave believing her former flame murdered her fiancé. Think of Claude Laughton, sculptor. He'll hang, knowing he's innocent and unable to prove it because, well, there's that adultery charge. Except no one is married yet, so technically, while there's cheating, there's no adultery. Think of their relatives and friends who will have to cope with the unthinkable.

All because John Harrison, erudite and well-regarded elite guide to ethical living standards, chose to behave like some drunken, vindictive low-life from the stews of London.

I get that he's pissed his fiancée, Molly Deane, is starting to love her ex again. Claude Laughton is everything John Harrison is not: loving, funny, and on her level. Even the chemist notices! She tells Hastings that Harrison's affair with Molly Deane, fashion model, is on par with Albert Einstein taking up with Ginger Rogers. John Harrison is out of Molly's league in the brains department. We understand what he sees in her: she's hot and philosopher or not, he's male.

What I can't understand is what she sees in that glowering grump and, in fact, she's returning to her senses and reconnecting with the sculptor and clown. The sculptor is not just more fun. Claude Langton also has the benefit of not lying to Molly about the future, which Harrison is.

Harrison knows he's dying but does he tell Molly? You know, so she can help him or they can make the best plans possible for the time they have left? Why no, why would he do such a ridiculous thing?

Instead, she's apparently supposed to learn via mind reading. What does happen is Harrison's doctor (a very spooky-looking gentleman) tells Molly at the fashion show that her fiancé, a man who promotes better living through Greek ethics, is a liar.

There is plenty to like about the episode. The clothes are to die for. Molly Deane wears one fabulous outfit after another and the fashion show is stunning. The producers must have spent a fortune on wardrobe. There's also the wonderful, subtle clue provided at the fashion show proving to Poirot that Molly and Claude have resumed their affair. Miss Lemon, who's often criminally underused, provides another vital clue to John Harrison's well-being, but it's not clear enough. I had to discuss the episode over four laps around the block with Bill afterwards to work it out.

Miss Lemon is, as always, stunningly dressed. She's not high-fashion like Molly Deane but her clothes are still terrific. I bet she sews them herself because I doubt Poirot pays her well enough to purchase such an extensive wardrobe. Miss Lemon wears three different outfits in this episode; all gorgeous, appropriate, and perfectly fitted. I always notice what Miss Lemon wears. She rarely wears the same outfit twice. Wow.

I also enjoyed Hastings' new hobby of photography. His photographs let Poirot discern subtle clues to the possibility of impending crime while bemoaning how suspicious he is.

Like Miss Marple, Poirot always suspects the worst of people because it so often comes true. Hastings' photograph even allowed Chief Inspector Japp to figure out the identity of the mysterious, grim undertaker figure. And in a logical manner too! Japp doesn't recognize the scary old man from glancing through his rogues' gallery at Scotland Yard. No, the inspector's in the hospital for an emergency appendectomy and — although it takes place offscreen — he fingers the undertaker as a doctor. One of the nurses must have provided the information. This was the only way to insert Japp into the episode that made sense. No crime occurred so how else could Japp show up?

There's also — again subtle and you won't realize it until the climax — the fact that Poirot once again indulges himself in breaking and entering. For a private detective who upholds the law, he often breaks it himself.

Should you watch this episode despite the significant character issues? Maybe. The settings are gorgeous as always. And then there are the clothes. I'll watch something just to see the wardrobe. If I were to watch this episode again, I'd home in on Miss Lemon and the fashion show and endure the rest.

General Information

Based on: "Wasps' Nest" (short story, 1928)
Run time: 50 min. **Subtitles:** Yes

Writer: David Renwick
Director: Brian Farnham

Cast

David Suchet as Hercule Poirot
Hugh Fraser as Captain Hastings
Philip Jackson as Chief Inspector Japp
Pauline Moran as Miss Lemon

Martin Turner as John Harrison
Melanie Jessop as Molly Deane
Peter Capaldi as Claude Langton
John Boswall as Dr. Belvedere
Kate Lynn Evans as Mrs. Henderson
Serena Scott Thomas as Model Girl
Hilary Tindall as Fashion Show *Commère*
Julian Forsyth as Waiter
Mark Chapman as PC Keating
Cole Henderson as Driver

Film Locations

Arnos Grove Underground Station, London (Marble Hill tube station)
The Range, Surrey (Harrison's house)
Royal Masonic Hospital, Hammersmith, London
35 South Street, Mayfair, London
All Saints Weston, London (church in the background)
46 Ailsa Road, London (Langton's house)
Freemasons' Hall, London (fashion show)
Marney's Village Inn, Surrey
43 South Street, Mayfair, London

The Tragedy at Marsdon Manor (1991)

Creatures made of ectoplasm and wax and a mystery-penning hotel owner bedevil Poirot's murder investigation

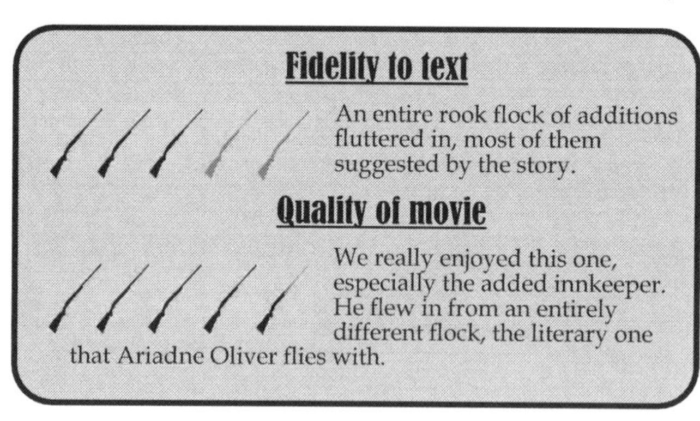

Fidelity to text

An entire rook flock of additions fluttered in, most of them suggested by the story.

Quality of movie

We really enjoyed this one, especially the added innkeeper. He flew in from an entirely different flock, the literary one that Ariadne Oliver flies with.

Let's start with rooks. If your hobby is chess instead of birdwatching, you might wonder what those fluttering black birds are and why the gardener is carrying what looks like a shrunken .22 rifle. Those birds are rooks, a member of the corvid family, similar to crows and ravens. Like crows and ravens, rooks are smart, noisy, flocking birds. You rarely see one rook. If you do, chances are there are plenty more roosting in the tree overhead. The rifle is used to shoot them, one by one, using tiny bullets. Rook shooting is a classic and common British blood-sport that keeps down crop-damaging vermin and — if you're hungry or thrifty — you eat the rooks that were eating your crops.

The tiny caliber makes rook rifles also useful for shooting rabbits. Juvenile rooks and rabbits supposedly make a very nice pie, not that I've ever eaten one. Rabbit can be darn good eating so why not young rooks as well? We forget in these times of splendid largesse available at every supermarket that meat in ye olden days could be hard to come by. It was valued enough to go to the trouble of cleaning birds the size of your hand so you could get the mouthful of delicious protein hidden under all those feathers.

The other point behind the rook rifle, common on every British estate, is the bullet is tiny. I mean pea-sized. It doesn't have a lot of power behind it, which is why the victim can be shot in the mouth, the bullet lodge in the brain, and there's no dramatic, impossible-to-miss exit wound to excite the local police. There's nothing to see but a mouthful of blood.

So when Jonathan Maltravers is found dead under the haunted tree, it's assumed he died of natural causes, despite the mouthful of blood. He's married to a much, much younger hot blonde wife who paints in her copious spare time. Susan Maltravers sure isn't providing him with a much-needed heir to inherit Marsdon Manor which is a primary reason childless old men marry young hotties.

Jonathan Maltravers also has a long-time secretary managing the estate for him. It's implied that Miss Rawlinson has loved Maltravers for decades but alas, she's plain and suffers from resting bitch face so he never noticed her devotion. It's very noticeable that Miss Rawlinson, while remaining polite, does not like

Jonathan Maltravers (*Ian McCulloch*), the old husband

Susan Maltravers (*Geraldine Alexander*), the young wife

Capt. Andrew Black (*Alastair Duncan*), the shunned lover

Miss Rawlinson (*Anita Carey*), the shunned secretary

Geoffrey Bernard (*Edward Jewesbury*), the watchful physician

Samuel Naughton (*Desmond Barrit*), the host-novelist

Mrs. Maltravers.

Under normal circumstances, Poirot would have read about the tragic accidental death of Maltravers in the newspaper and that would have been that. But alas for the murderer, another murder-solver in the village had already written to Poirot, begging for help with serious crimes.

Poirot and Hastings hastily read the letter, skipping the boring parts, and rush down to the quaint village rife with unsolvable murders. They meet Mr. Naughton, innkeeper, who is utterly overjoyed to have the famous Hercule Poirot come in person to his rescue. He's a mystery writer and needs help with his plot. He wrote himself into a corner, all his suspects have unbreakable alibis, and he can't figure out what to do next.

The innkeeper was added to the short story's plot but he fits in perfectly; foreshadowing the later appearance in the series of Ariadne Oliver, mystery novelist.

Poirot is indignant, Hastings is amused, and they're stuck in a town where not much happens until the next train. To fill the time, they tour the spooky yet quaint wax museum. The next morning, as they're leaving for the train station, the road is blocked by local constables investigating the mysterious, tragic, and completely accidental death of Mr. Maltravers. One of the bobbies recognizes the great Hercule Poirot and asks him for assistance.

It's a good thing that he did. Poirot checks the body, speaks with Mrs. Maltravers, meets Miss Rawlinson, and then Captain Black, a visitor from Kenya. He also speaks to Dr. Bernard who was shocked that Maltravers died. He'd had some health issues, it was true, but the good doctor expected him to live for many years to come. Poirot then suggests to Chief Inspector Japp that this body needs an autopsy and surprise, surprise.

The pathologist discovers Mr. Maltravers didn't die from a hemorrhage caused by his ulcer. He died because someone shot him inside his mouth with a small-caliber gun. Could it have been suicide? His estate was in arrears and he'd recently taken out a £50,000 life insurance policy with hot, young, blonde Susan as his beneficiary. Except Susan appears to be a devoted, grieving, superstitious wife. She claims that ghosts haunt the estate and one of them must have scared Maltravers to death. Somehow. Further proving that these are ghosts uniquely able to handle physical objects, Susan is further menaced — in the middle of a crowd — by a poisoned gas mask during an air raid drill.

Who would want to harm lovely, widowed, and potentially very rich Susan? Was it the mysterious Captain Black who tried to flee back to Kenya? He gave Susan a disturbing piece of Kenyan art. Could it be Miss Rawlinson who makes her disapproval very plain? It's probably not the innkeeper; he has enough trouble planning his murders on paper. It wasn't Mr. Maltravers. He's lying on a slab in the morgue and as we all know, ghosts can scare people to death but they can't handle firearms or gas masks.

Poirot knows who did it, but he has no proof. Susan invites him and Hastings to dinner, along with Captain Black because she's too afraid to be left alone in Marsdon Manor. Voices at the windows, faces in the shrubbery, blood smeared across her dressing room table. Someone's got it in for her and she needs help. This leads to an impromptu séance in which, yes, ghosts do come back to confront the guilty party.

Justice triumphs again and all because Poirot didn't carefully read the letter the innkeeper wrote to him, asking for help with his plot. The innkeeper helps solve the murder, and Poirot generously solves his fictional crime in return. In a plot point worthy of Ariadne Oliver, Poirot suggests that the bedridden African explorer shoot a poisoned dart into the fruitcake, thus poisoning the victims.

This is a fun episode. It's got great lines, comeuppances for villains and Poirot alike, lovelorn explorers confronting reality (a scene that should have been longer), high drama, ghosts, and watercolors that serve as clues. Don't miss this one.

General Information

Based on: "The Tragedy of Marsdon Manor" (short story, 1923)
Run time: 50 min. **Subtitles:** Yes

Writer: David Renwick
Director: Renny Rye

Cast

David Suchet as Hercule Poirot
Hugh Fraser as Captain Hastings
Philip Jackson as Chief Inspector Japp

Ian McCulloch as Jonathan Maltravers
Geraldine Alexander as Susan Maltravers
Anita Carey as Miss Rawlinson
Alastair Duncan as Capt. Andrew Black
Desmond Barrit as Samuel Naughton
Edward Jewesbury as Dr. Geoffrey Bernard
Ralph Watson as Danvers
Geoffrey Swann as Police Sergeant
Hilary Sesta as Doctor's Receptionist
David Lloyd as Museum Attendant
Pat Keen as Civil Defence Organiser
Richard Bebb as Newsreader

Film Locations

Reepham, Norfolk (village scenes)
The Dial House, Reepham, Norfolk (The Red Anchor Hotel)
The Bookham Grange Hotel, Leatherhead, Surrey (hotel interiors)
Sennowe Park, Guist, Norfolk (Marsdon Manor)
Normansfield Theatre, Teddington, London (civil defense meeting)

Hercule Poirot; he sees everything and he forgets nothing.

HERCULE POIROT

The Double Clue (1991)

Poirot in love disappoints everyone because his sense of justice vanishes and he abandons his close friends

Fidelity to text

A seven-page story got hugely reworked. Mood, tone, characters all got a make-over, including Poirot. He found a long-lost love and lost his moral compass.

Quality of movie

They can't all be gems. Wholesale changes often improve a nothing story into something suitable for TV, but not this time.

The episode started off so promisingly: a mysterious countess arriving by train in the fog, an ultra-posh evening gala with a star contralto and her Japanese pianist, Hastings asking Poirot (upon seeing a blushing bride and her handsome groom) if he'd ever marry, and Poirot reminiscing about happy husbands murdering their wives and even more devoted wives murdering their husbands. Poirot must have had first-hand knowledge of those murders since he listed exact numbers.

Soon thereafter, Chief Inspector Japp visits Poirot. He's desperate for help. Three jewel thefts have occurred among the high and mighty and he risks losing his job if nothing is done about it.

Five minutes in and the episode falls apart. I can't accept that Scotland Yard would inform the highly respected, capable, and efficient Japp that his job was on the line over a few jewel thefts, even among the toffs. The man clears murder cases on a regular basis — successfully bringing criminals to the Crown's justice — and now his job is at risk? Over theft? Yes, it's felony theft of valuable jewelry worth thousands of pounds, but I couldn't buy it. Maybe if the Crown Jewels had been stolen from the Tower of London, I'd accept Japp losing his job if he doesn't solve the crime and recover the goods, but not over this.

To investigate, Poirot and Hastings visit Marcus Hardiman's Art Deco mansion (I guarantee that not only does the flat roof leak but those windows do nothing to keep out the draft). The safe was broken into and a priceless emerald necklace once owned by Catherine de' Medici (1519-1589) had been stolen. Except the thief is stunningly incompetent. He (or she) leaves behind not only a monogrammed cigarette case but a small white glove.

Huh? The thief put on gloves for the theft — at a time when everyone, male or female, routinely wore them — and then took one off after committing a felony? Plus dropping a cigarette case so it conveniently falls between the cushions of a conveniently placed chair? The thief stopped for a cig during the burglary while magic chemicals ate through the safe's lock? How come they haven't caught him yet?

Sure. Whatever. Worse, despite earlier episodes making much of modern forensics, no one here

Vera Rossakoff (*Kika Markham*), the Russian exile

Marcus Hardman (*David Lyon*), the party thrower

Bernard Parker (*David Bamber*), the go-between

Lady Runcorn (*Charmian May*), the desperate noble

Martin Johnstone (*Nicholas Selby*), the gold collector

Katherine Bird (*Meriel Dickinson*), the singing distraction

behaved as if fingerprints existed. Scotland Yard began using fingerprint evidence in 1901 so they were not ignorant of basic evidence gathering in 1936.

Then, no one at Scotland Yard decides to compare guest lists at the various soirees where the jewel thefts occurred. Who attended each of the parties where a robbery took place? Could it be suspicious that only one person attended all four parties? Why, no, of course not, because that person is a Russian countess and a) aristocrats are above suspicion and b) foreigners are above suspicion. Huh? This is England where we've seen multiple crimes taking place among the upper classes *and* the foreigner is the first person suspected. Poirot himself has commented on this!

Poirot quickly works out that the countess is guilty and then spends the rest of the episode in a flirtatious, wistful *pas de deux* with her because … he's fallen in love with her! Or they were lovers in the past! Or something along those lines because he sure treated Countess Vera Rossakoff differently than he normally treats jewel thieves, particularly jewel thieves who put a colleague's job at risk.

Still worse, the countess stole Bernard Parker's glove and deliberately left it at the scene to implicate him. So, because Countess Vera was an old flame, it was okay for her to implicate Parker, leading to years at Wandsworth Prison for a crime he did not commit?

Unacceptable. Poirot is dedicated to seeing justice done. He doesn't condone theft any more than he condones murder.

While Poirot dallies with Countess Vera at art museums, public gardens, and a lovely picnic lunch, Japp is left hanging out to dry. Hastings and Miss Lemon, visibly distraught at Poirot's behavior, conduct their own investigation, leading to Hastings being shot at by a tramp who drives off in a scarlet MG.

Poirot is concerned enough (finally!) to spring into action. Of a sort. He gathers everyone back at Marcus Hardiman's mansion and proclaims the tramp in the scarlet MG was the thief. What!? Dirty, flea-bitten vagrants — even ones who drive MGs — don't traipse in and out of noble houses unnoticed. Yet, or so Poirot says, this tramp did and the reason he came back was to retrieve the emerald necklace which was caught in the shrubbery just outside the window leading to the room with the safe.

He unlatches the window and easily locates the necklace in the vine. Um, no. Once again, I cannot accept how incompetent this makes Scotland Yard and Inspector Japp look. They would have checked. Poirot's explanation is the tramp was the thief and is now gone and no more jewel thefts at posh parties will occur. And Japp accepts this! And so, apparently, do his superiors at Scotland Yard! Why? Because Poirot said so.

The ending was worst of all. Poirot sees Countess Vera off, first with a charming, wistful luncheon at the train station café and then on the station platform, accompanied by two minders to make sure she stays on the train. They chat about how they are different people treading different paths in life. Countess Vera heads to America to continue her career as a jewel thief and Poirot is okay with this if she doesn't commit crimes in England!

I was appalled. I cannot accept this story line. I don't know what was worse; the complete rewriting of Poirot's character or the fact that Hastings of all people makes a correct deduction. He couldn't understand why Countess Vera thought the contralto was Japanese. If she'd sat through the concerto like she claimed, she would have known it was the pianist who was from Japan. Hastings pointed out the glaring incongruity and Poirot lets it pass without a word.

I was so disappointed. We would finally meet the mysterious Countess Vera Rossakoff, Poirot's old flame. Agatha put her into two short stories; this one and *The Capture of Cerberus*, plus the novel *The Big Four*. That's all. There's plenty of scope for an enterprising screenwriter to develop a complex and heartfelt backstory to flesh out Poirot's younger life and instead, we get this mess.

Was there anything to like? Sure. Beautiful clothes, scenery, acting, set pieces, Miss Lemon and Hastings investigating and you know who was the brains in that duo. Scene after wonderful scene, embedded into a bad script. It mixed emeralds with chips from broken Coke bottles.

General Information

Based on: "Double Clue" (short story, 1923)
Run time: 50 min. **Subtitles:** Yes

Writer: Anthony Horowitz
Director: Andrew Piddington

Cast

David Suchet as Hercule Poirot
Hugh Fraser as Captain Hastings
Philip Jackson as Chief Inspector Japp
Pauline Moran as Miss Lemon

Kika Markham as Countess Vera Rossakoff
David Lyon as Marcus Hardman
David Bamber as Bernard Parker
Charmian May as Lady Runcorn
Nicholas Selby as Martin Johnstone
Michael Packer as Redfern
William Chubb as Blake
Mark Fletcher as Constable
William Osborne as Receptionist
Meriel Dickinson as Katherine Bird

Film Locations

Hull Paragon Railway Station, Hull, Yorkshire (opening scene, end scene)
Myddelton Square, London (Hastings' drive)
Senate House, University of London (art gallery)
Shrub's Wood, Chalfont St. Peter, Buckinghamshire (Marcus Hardman's house)
Norman Shaw Buildings, Westminster, London (Scotland Yard)
Adelphi Building, Strand, London (Johnston office)
Englefield House, Berkshire (Poirot and Countess walk, picnic)

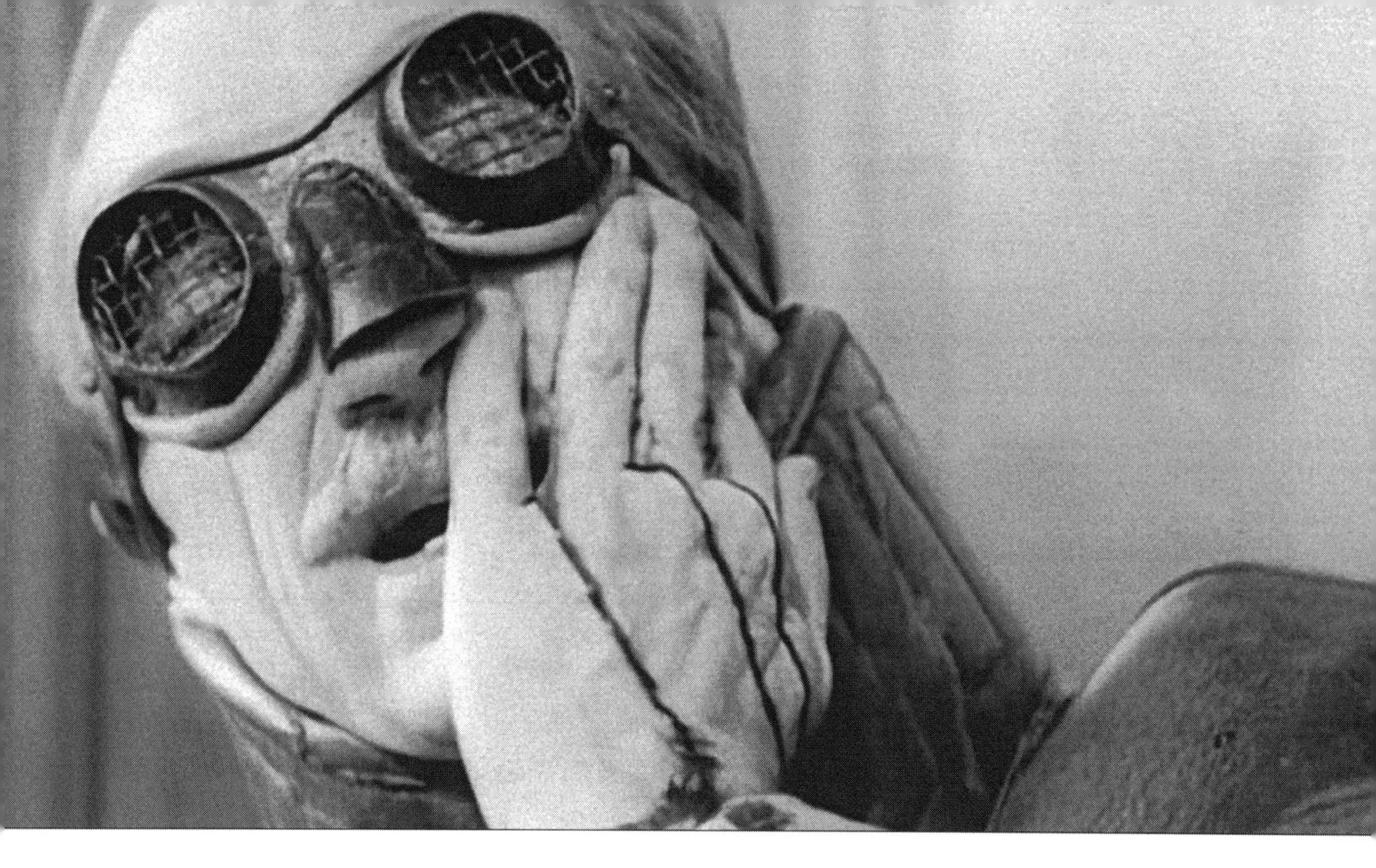

The Mystery of the Spanish Chest (1991)

Sexual jealousy drives a husband to spy on his wife, only to discover death at the point of a sword cane

Fidelity to text

Despite the title, most of the story came from the 1932 short story "The Mystery of the Baghdad Chest," with elements from the 1960 novella rewrite *The Mystery of the Spanish Chest*, plus added plot twists.

Quality of movie

If you're paying attention, you'll figure out who the murderer must be by the halfway point. But there's lots to love, other than the cypher who is Marguerite Clayton.

This episode opens with a terrific, sepia-toned sword fight. Two fencers in full Heidelberg dueling regalia face off inside a little chalk box keeping them toe to toe. The point of the exercise — if you're not familiar with German/Austrian university student dueling — is to prove your courage and ability to bear pain by acquiring facial scars.

Plenty of upper-class young men in Germany and Austria (virtually every university student there was upper-class) were members of dueling societies and regularly dueled. They wore eye protection, a nose-guard, and a high leather collar to limit damage and keep the scars to the face where they could be seen. Because most duelers were right-handed, the scars tend to mark the left side of the face. Many young men who became important politicians and business titans earned multiple scars. Even today, you'll see the scars on some German politicians and industrial magnates. They're a subtle class marker; not nearly as common as they once were, but still around.

After the duel, color returns and we're off to the opera to see *Rigoletto* (1851). Poirot tells Hastings he isn't that interested in opera (Hastings is bored stiff) but he is interested in the psychology of murder.

Why did the script add a reference to *Rigoletto*? I believe it's to better combine the two short stories this episode is based on. The 1932 version was narrated by Hastings and it's short: 7½ pages. Then, in 1960, Agatha rewrote the short piece into a novella *The Mystery of the Spanish Chest*. Hastings is long gone (ranching in Argentina) so Poirot is coping with the hyper-efficient Miss Lemon who does not suffer from Hastings' flights of fancy. A major addition in the novella was Poirot working out that the murderer's methods were similar to Iago's in *Othello*. Iago was a false counselor to Othello, urging the Moor to unwarranted jealousy towards his beautiful wife, Desdemona.

What does that have to do with Giuseppe Verdi's *Rigoletto*? Not as much as it should have, other than *Rigoletto* also involves false counselors, deception, and lies. A quick synopsis: The court jester Rigoletto encourages his master the duke to behave as badly as possible. They're cursed by a courtier the duke ruins.

Edward Clayton (*Malcolm Sinclair*), the jealous husband

Marguerite Clayton (*Caroline Langrishe*), the fretful wife

Maj. Jack Rich (*Pip Torrens*), the wife's friend

Colonel Curtiss (*John McEnery*), the husband's friend

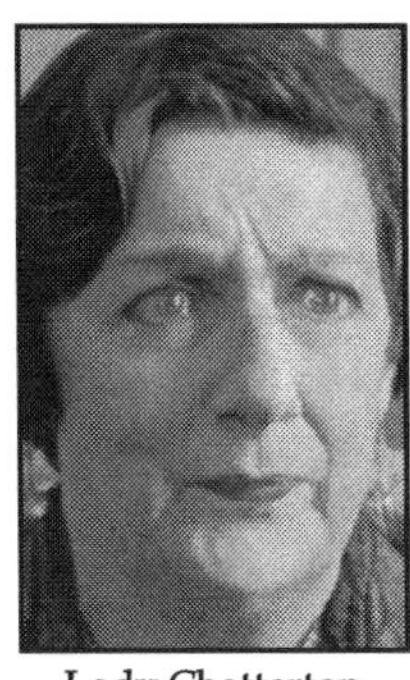
Lady Chatterton (*Antonia Pemberton*), the worried friend

Smithy (*Sam Smart*), the witness

As a result, Rigoletto's beautiful daughter, Gilda, falls in love with the duke (he lies to her) and the opera ends in blood, death, and much lyrical singing.

But it's more important to know that, by being at the opera in a private box, Poirot and Hastings are seen by Lady Chatterton from her private box across the theater. Lady Chatterton tracks down Poirot and asks a favor. She has this lovely young friend, Marguerite Clayton. Every man loves her although she came across to me as a boring cypher.

Poirot and Hastings observe Mrs. Clayton at the intermission being squired about by a man not her husband. He is Major Rich, recent widower and longtime friend. Mr. Clayton was nowhere to be seen. According to Lady Chatterton, he was off glowering and plotting murder against his much younger, much livelier wife.

The question I kept asking was why did Marguerite marry Edward Clayton? No reason like money or status was ever given yet we're constantly told Marguerite could have had any man she wanted. Instead, she chose an unpleasant, older grouch, who, according to Lady Chatterton, is abusive to Marguerite.

Let me be clear: We never see a single moment of Edward Clayton's supposedly violent nature onscreen. He's stiff and surly with Marguerite, but not violent. Lady Chatterton ropes Poirot into attending Major Rich's cocktail party where he can observe the Claytons in action and, presumably, save Marguerite from her husband.

The party is a hoot. Poirot dances a very credible Charleston with Lady Chatterton. He also meets Colonel Curtiss, who stoutly defends Marguerite as the epitome of womanly virtue. Colonel Curtiss also sneers at jazz because it's music enjoyed by second-rate people and written by an inferior race. (I know people talk like that but it's clumsy scriptwriting. You shouldn't telegraph who your suspects are or you should use a stereotype to confound expectations at the story's climax. No such luck here.)

Despite Colonel Curtiss, everyone has a lovely time at the party, other than Edward Clayton. He didn't show up, called away unexpectedly to Scotland on business. Thus, Poirot cannot evaluate Clayton as a wife-beater and potential murderer.

In the morning, Chief Inspector Japp calls on Poirot and informs him he's a witness to a murder. What murder? Why the murder of Edward Clayton in Major Rich's flat the evening before. Rich's manservant discovered the body inside the Spanish chest sitting in the corner behind a screen.

There's nothing minimal about a Spanish chest. They're ornate, heavy, and lavishly decorated with plenty of wood overlays, leather straps, and brass hardware. They're built to store bedding so they're large enough for a man to hide in and spy on his wife to see if she's canoodling with another man at a party.

Poirot swings into action, Hastings at his side. Miss Lemon is nowhere to be seen; like the first version of the story, she's in Frinton visiting her sister. While they're investigating, Marguerite visits Major Rich in jail, weeps and wails, and then returns home. She tries to commit suicide but luckily for her, Poirot and Hastings show up in the nick of time and rescue her from her folly.

The script telegraphing its distaste for Colonel Curtiss was the weakest part of the episode, but how it treated Marguerite was a close second. I have no idea why she was so wonderful, why men fell at her feet, and why Lady Chatterton believed Marguerite was at risk of being murdered by her husband. Her suicide attempt felt like a clumsy plot point written to illustrate her delicate sensibilities. There was no reason for her to do it. Marguerite wasn't a happy wife but with her husband dead through no fault of her own — she's the innocent victim here! — she's free and probably rich. She has no kids to worry about, she's young and lovely, she inherits everything; she's much better off than she was at the beginning of the story.

The climax was suitably dramatic but again, poorly thought out. Poirot would have called in the police as backup when he faced down the murderer. But it's still a good episode. No matter what the era — Shakespeare's or Verdi's or Poirot's — lust, jealousy, and betrayal never go out of style.

General Information

Based on: "The Mystery of the Spanish Chest" (novella, 1960), expanded from "The Mystery of the Baghdad Chest" (short story, 1932)
Run time: 50 min. **Subtitles:** Yes

Writer: Anthony Horowitz
Director: Andrew Grieve

Cast

David Suchet as Hercule Poirot
Hugh Fraser as Captain Hastings
Philip Jackson as Chief Inspector Japp

John McEnery as Colonel Curtiss
Caroline Langrishe as Marguerite Clayton
Malcolm Sinclair as Edward Clayton
Pip Torrens as Maj. Jack Rich
Antonia Pemberton as Lady Chatterton
Peter Copley as Burgoyne
Sam Smart as Smithy
Edward Clayton as Rouse
Metin Yenal as Duel Umpire
Victoria Scarborough as Party Dancer
Christopher Lamb as Party Dancer
Melissa Wilson as Clayton Maid
John Noble as Rigoletto
Catherine Bott as Gilda

Film Locations

Hackney Empire, London (opera)
Walpole House, Chiswick Mall, London (Lady Chatterton's home)
New Square, London (Clayton's office exterior)
Old Palace Terrace, Richmond Green (Claytons' home)
Royal College of Surgeons, London (club)
ACCA Global headquarters, The Adelphi, London (Major Rich's home exterior)
German Gymnasium Pancras Road A5202 / King's Boulevard (Hastings questions Smithy)

The Theft of the Royal Ruby (1991)

Poirot goes undercover in the country to spend Christmas with a family and recover a gem of princely value

Fidelity to text

To which version? The 1923 very short story or the 1960 greatly expanded one? Whichever story you choose, the episode covers most of the bases.

Quality of movie

A charming, clever, good-old-fashioned English Christmas with romance, derring-do, faithful retainers, and kids out of school on holiday who enjoy some murder.

The story has a complex history. Agatha wrote "The Christmas Adventure" in 1923. Poirot had recently lost Hastings to marriage to the hot babe he picked up during *Murder on the Links* so he's all alone. He spends Christmas at King's Lacey, ostensibly to experience a genuine English Christmas. But he's really there to retrieve a prince's priceless stolen ruby. Christmas puddings are involved, as are lovelorn damsels and mischievous schoolkids who see a chance to fool the famous detective.

In 1960, Agatha rewrote and expanded the short story into "The Adventure of the Christmas Pudding," sometimes titled "The Theft of the Royal Ruby." She moved the story to 1960, allowing her to reflect on the passage of time and how much things change such as old-fashioned English Christmases.

But not everything changes, as Mrs. Lacey tells Poirot. Girls are still fascinated by unsuitable young men. Tell them a man is bad for them and they swoon, same as in her day. There's also a lot more backstory about the ruby and the feckless royal who gave it to a tart to wear and got his just desserts. Once again, Christmas puddings are involved as are mischievous schoolkids punking the famous detective.

Then we come to the *Poirot* episode. The date changes to 1935, but there's no snow. The feckless royal gets a major role. Minor characters are deleted. There's the obligatory chase scene, and King's Lacey (the house) turns into a modernist horror. Which was fine! Except a major part of both stories involve Poirot's fear of enduring the winter in a magnificent English mansion built in the 14th century. Drafts and cold and freezing water, you know. He's reassured that King's Lacey has had central heating installed to save guests and family from seeing their breath in the drawing room.

When you see this house, you know central heating was installed when it was built and not retrofitted 600 years later. You can also foresee how the white facades will stain, the roof will leak, the single-pane glass windows with no draperies will be drafty, and thanks to modern construction techniques, the house won't hold up nearly as well as 14th century piles of stone.

The modernist horror creates a very odd backdrop to Colonel Lacey's profession as an Egyptologist. His

Prince Farouk (*Antony Zaki*), the royal heir

Desmond Lee-Wortley (*Nigel Le Vaillant*), the scoundrel lover

Gloria Lee-Wortley (*Robyn Moore*), the alluring sister

David Welwyn (*John Vernon*), the antique lover

Jesmond (*David Howey*), the discreet diplomat

Bridget (*Alessia Gwyther*), the willing victim

collection of artifacts resembles real rubies displayed at Woolworth's. The obelisk in the side garden is an especially odd touch. The house doesn't play well with it, the fabulous sunken gardens, or the charming dowager's house holding more of the collection. At least the modern kitchens are a huge improvement over what Mrs. Ross (the cook) would have endured making Christmas puddings in a 14th century pile of stone.

The episode opens with our feckless royal, Prince Farouk of Egypt, enjoying a drunken dinner with a hot blonde tart. The blonde coaxes him into letting her wear the giant priceless ruby. The inevitable happens: She visits the ladies' room and vanishes, and he's left looking like an idiot.

Meanwhile, Colonel Lacey contemplates which of his wonderful, valuable Egyptian treasures he must sell to keep his estate going. Of course, if he hadn't bulldozed his 14th century pile and built that modernist horror, he wouldn't need the money so badly.

While these men suffer, Poirot prepares for a comfortable, cozy, quiet Christmas at home. It will be just him, his radio, his books, and a demi-kilo (about a pound) of exquisite chocolates. It's time to rest and catch up on his reading.

Alas, he's dragged off, literally, by men in beige to the Foreign Office and coerced into aiding Prince Farouk. News of the gem's disappearance would make the natives restless, and British access to the Suez Canal depends on Prince Farouk recovering the royal ruby.

Thus, Poirot travels to King's Lacey to enjoy an old-fashioned English Christmas. Everyone is excited to meet the famous detective. Within minutes of arrival, he's invited to stir the puddings and bring good luck in the new year. The kids on holiday (Bridget, Colin, and Michael) are particularly enthusiastic and plot how to fool Poirot.

The episode was fun. It was enjoyable. It was a romp. But there were questionable choices by the director and the scriptwriter that keep me from adding that last half thief to the rating:

1) The connection between Prince Farouk and Colonel Lacey was never made clear.

2) I didn't understand why the thieves had to go to King's Lacey, when they had all of England to hide in. Couldn't they have escaped England before the police were alerted about the theft? They could have taken the next ferry across the Channel and disappeared in France. The 1960 short story gave an explanation.

3) Poirot observes a member of the house party dropping something in his coffee cup. To avoid drinking it, he switches cups with Colonel Lacey. How could he be sure it was sleeping powder and not poison?

4) Colonel Lacey was desperate to keep King's Lacey. He was forced to sell some of his treasures to pay the bills and suddenly, he no longer has to. Why? Because he hosted Poirot who retrieved the royal ruby and caught the thieves and Prince Farouk was suitably grateful? Something happened, but it wasn't explained.

5) Annie the maid suspected that someone intended to poison Poirot with an added ingredient in the Christmas pudding. She writes him a warning note, but does nothing else. So it was bad to poison Poirot but okay to poison the family she worked for? She did drop the Christmas pudding but that was because the boys slammed into her while she was getting it down from the shelf. What's particularly irritating was that the solution was already in place: Annie could have said when the boys ran by, she deliberately dropped the pudding to save Poirot and the family.

6) How come Desmond didn't feel the pulse of the body by the obelisk? In the short stories, the victim wore a tourniquet to slow down her blood flow. If she wore a tourniquet in the film, a word or two or rubbing her arm would have sufficed. Or, Poirot could have said he knew Desmond wouldn't bother with her pulse once he noticed the ruby so no tourniquet was needed.

Those are minor points in an otherwise great episode, and I'll leave you with a piece of trivia from David Suchet's memoir. Look for the scene where Poirot demonstrates how to peel a mango. When he was asked how he learned it, he replies, "A duke taught me." That would be Prince Philip, the Duke of Edinburgh. He taught Suchet at a formal dinner in Buckingham Palace and Suchet asked that it be included in a *Poirot* script.

General Information

Based on: "The Adventure of the Christmas Pudding" (short story, 1960), an expanded version of "The Christmas Adventure" (1923)
Run time: 50 min. **Subtitles:** Yes

Writers: Anthony Horowitz and Clive Exton
Director: Anthony Grieve

Cast

David Suchet as Hercule Poirot

Frederick Treves as Colonel Lacey
Stephanie Cole as Mrs. Lacey
Helena Michell as Sarah Lacey
David Howey as Jesmond
Antony Zaki as Prince Farouk
John Vernon as David Welwyn
Nigel Le Vaillant as Desmond Lee-Wortley
Robyn Moore as Gloria Lee-Wortley
John Dunbar as Peverill
Alessia Gwyther as Bridget
Jonathan R. Scott as Colin
Edward Holmes as Michael
Siobhan Garahy as Annie Bates
Susan Field as Mrs. Ross

Film Locations

Freemason's Hall, London (interiors: restaurant, Foreign Office, and art dealer)
36 St. Martins Court, London (chocolatier)
Admiralty Arch, London (drive to Whitehall)
Foreign Office, London (exterior, grand staircase)
Adelphi Building, London (hotel exterior)
Royal Arcade, 28 Old Bond Street, London (arcade outside antiquities dealer)
Ye Olde Bell, Hurley, Berkshire (hotel exterior)
Joldwynds, Holmbury St. Mary, Surrey (King's Lacey)
St. Mary's Church, Hurley, Berkshire (interior)

The Affair at the Victory Ball (1991)

A costume celebration of the end of the Great War is overshadowed when Death crashes the party

Fidelity to text

The major changes made the episode more television-worthy. Sadly, they omitted the doctor's opinion and rigor mortis.

Quality of movie

This is a fun one, with fancy dress, fine porcelain collectibles, baying reporters, and Poirot seeing his name on the front page but not in the way he likes.

The Affair at the Victory Ball was Agatha's first published short story starring Hercule Poirot, written after *The Mysterious Affair at Styles* saw print. Many of her regular tropes appear here. Hastings resides with Poirot and reads the newspaper looking for things to discuss. Poirot expects everyone to know who he is and many people do. Inspector Japp comes calling, asking for help. Poirot stages a theatrical and dramatic unveiling of the murderer.

But it's a rather static story. The show jazzes it up considerably.

It opens with the camera panning across an expensive set of porcelain collectibles (much finer and far rarer than any mass-market collectible of today). Poirot tells us what we're seeing and gives us a bit of history. It's a set of *Commedia dell'arte* characters, a staple of popular theater in Renaissance Italy. The characters are stock, identified by their costumes: Harlequin, Columbine, Punchinello, Pulcinella, Pierrot, and Pierrette. They're comic but also tragic because none of them can escape the roles life sets for them.

From there, we go to Hastings larking about the flat, looking forward to the Victory Ball celebrating the end of WWI. When Agatha wrote the story in 1923, WWI and its jaw-dropping carnage was still fresh in everyone's mind. Despite the producers resetting virtually the entire Poirot canon to the mid-1930s, everyone in England still remembered WWI vividly, either directly (less than 20 years had passed) or from listening to everyone older talking about it. To make the Victory Ball even more poignant, virtually everyone in 1935 was afraid of the war that was coming and hoping to avert it. This is the backdrop to Neville Chamberlain signing the appeasement treaty with Hitler on 30 September 1938, proclaiming "peace in our time." A year later, Hitler and Stalin started World War II.

Hastings is attending, naturally. He begs Poirot to come along, because he's got a friend in BBC radio who wants to meet the great detective. Learning that a major fan is dying to meet him lures Poirot away from his stamp collection. He does not, however, go in costume. He's a famous person and feels no need to dress up. Hastings, for his part, attends as Sir Percival Blakeney. It's perfect for Hastings as Sir Percy is widely known as an idiot whose sole concern is his exquisite tailoring.

You don't remember Sir Percy Blakeney? You should.

Viscount Cronshaw (*Mark Crowdy*), the high-minded toff

Eustace Beltaine (*David Henry*), the greedy uncle

Coco Courtenay (*Haydn Gwynne*), the high-strung actress

Chris Davidson (*Nathaniel Parker*), the louche actor

Mrs. Davidson (*Natalie Slater*), the browbeaten wife

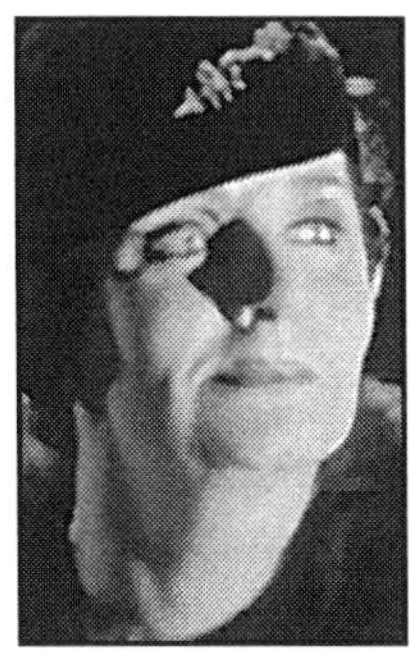

Mrs. Mallaby (*Kate Harper*), the widow on the make

He was also known as the Scarlet Pimpernel (a common and charming European wild flower). Baroness Emma Orczy wrote the play *The Scarlet Pimpernel* in 1903 and it proved so popular she expanded it into a series of novels, starting in 1905. Sir Percy became the model for every foppish aristocrat you've ever heard of who leads a secret double life as a brilliant swordsman, master of disguise, rescuer of damsels, and fighter against crime and evil. Zorro. The Shadow. Dr. Syn. The Phantom. Superman. Batman. You may have heard of them. Sir Percy fought the Jacobins during the Reign of Terror in Revolutionary France, saving aristocrats and other deserving souls from the guillotine.

At the ball, Poirot and Hastings have a grand time with Hastings' radio friend, James Ackerley. The ball becomes even more interesting when Viscount Cronshaw arrives with his party, all in full *Commedia dell'arte* regalia. They're unhappy enough to squabble in public. Poirot witnesses Harlequin bickering with Columbine and then watches the lady leave in a huff with Pierrot. At the unmasking, hours later, Harlequin is seen on the upper balcony. Minutes later, he's found in a supper room, a table knife plunged into his chest. Who could have killed him in a building full of witnesses?

As Chief Inspector Japp says, he'll need to use Albert Hall to have enough room to interview all the potential suspects.

This is where the episode fell down for me. The first is that even though I know Japp regards Poirot as a valued colleague, it's hard to buy that he'd let Poirot (and Hastings!) examine the body before the police arrive. Scotland Yard had a forensics team by then; we've seen it in earlier episodes.

The second issue is the body's stiffness. In the short story, this is spelled out and a logical reason is provided. The doctor comments on the unusual stiffness of the body but he wasn't asked to estimate time of death. Instead, the doctor was told that Viscount Cronshaw had just been knifed mere minutes ago. Thus, it isn't immediately apparent that Viscount Cronshaw had been murdered some time earlier and the body stashed until it was needed. There's also the issue of blood. There wasn't any. There'd be *some* evidence to show that his body had been tucked into the niche behind the curtain, but no. Those issues are glossed over.

Sometimes it seems that Inspector Japp and Scotland Yard get to show off their modern forensics and police procedures only when the plot calls for it and not otherwise. But that's a minor quibble in an otherwise excellent episode.

There's also Mrs. Davidson, who was costumed as Pierrette. She's a cipher. I'm guessing from visual hints that she's probably a downtrodden wife who doesn't dare contradict her actor husband (who dressed as Pierrot). She loves her husband or she's afraid of him or both. When Poirot and Hastings visit her, she lies to cover up what he did, despite the fact that he implicated her in the murder! But we're not given a reason why Mrs. Davidson would do this so, like I said, I'm guessing.

There's also the ending which some reviewers didn't like. It worked for me despite the fact that it wouldn't have held up in court, even in 1935. Poirot likes a dramatic unveiling of the murderer so he gets all the suspects into the radio station studio and brings on actors wearing the costumes worn earlier at the Victory Ball. Looking at the costumes, only one person could have made the quick change necessary to become Harlequin and then vanish. It worked because it referred back to the opening scenes in the radio station and circled back to the fact that because you thought you saw something doesn't mean you actually did.

But watch so you can make the discovery yourself. Along the way, enjoy Eustace Beltaine, hordes of baying reporters, and a loud, brassy, American widow who's on the make for a rich English husband. It looks like she landed one too, courtesy of murder.

General Information

Based on: "The Affair at the Victory Ball" (short story, 1923)
Run time: 51 min. **Subtitles:** Yes

Writer: Andrew Marshall
Director: Rennie Rye

Cast

David Suchet as Hercule Poirot
Hugh Fraser as Captain Hastings
Philip Jackson as Chief Inspector Japp
Pauline Moran as Miss Lemon

Mark Crowdy as Viscount Cronshaw
David Henry as Eustace Beltaine
Haydn Gwynne as Coco Courtenay
Nathaniel Parker as Chris Davidson
Natalie Slater as Mrs. Davidson
Kate Harper as Mrs. Mallaby
Andrew Burt as James Ackerley
Charles Collingwood as BBC Announcer
Brian Mitchell as Second Actor
Sarah Crowden as Receptionist
Bryan Matheson as Butler

Film Locations

30 Ennismore Gardens, London (Viscount Cronshaw's residence)
BBC, Portland Place, London
Ladbroke Hall, Kensington and Chelsea, London (Victory Ball venue)
Highpoint 1, Highgate, London (Coco Courtenay's flat)

Such foolishness! Young people must realize that life is not to be gambled with like the roulette wheel! This is nothing less than poison.

Hercule Poirot, about cocaine

The Mystery of Hunter's Lodge (1991)

A wealthy man is in a killer's sights as Poirot's hunger for *tetras a l'anglois* lures him and Hastings to the moors

Fidelity to text

The murder and plot twist remain but everything else was enhanced, added, omitted, or changed.

Quality of movie

We had to rewatch the opening sequence three times to figure out who was who. After that, it gets better as long as you don't think too closely about timing and identification.

When it comes to adapting a Christie story for television, scriptwriters follow one of two paths. They either expand what's already there (*In a Glass Darkly* or *The Blue Geranium*), or they trash major parts of the story and add their own inventions (*The Sittaford Mystery* or 2009's *Why Didn't They Ask Evans?*).

For this short story, the scriptwriter performed major surgery. Poirot is still sick in bed, while Hastings performs the legwork, but he's sick because he accompanied Hastings to the moors on a grouse-hunting expedition and took a chill. This felt very unlike Poirot (not the getting sick part, but going out into the field) but an explanation was provided. Freshly slaughtered red grouse are a rare gourmet treat, not one found in Belgium. Thus, we are treated to the sight of Poirot, bundled up and wearing earplugs, perched on a folding stool in the frozen wastelands of the Staffordshire moors while perusing what seems to be a pocket guide to cooking game birds.

Hastings always has a friend around. In this case, the friend invited him to a grouse-hunting expedition and Poirot came along to eat the harvest. We're introduced to a host of men in virtually identical overcoats, gumboots, and scarves. There are numerous ladies in fur coats but they soon vanish. Bill and I watched this sequence three times to figure out who was who.

I'll spell out the important people so you don't have to rewind repeatedly.

1) Harrington Pace, also referred to as Harry, Uncle Harry, Mr. Harry, or Mr. Pace. He's rich, obnoxious, and keeps his relatives (legitimate and illegitimate) on a tight leash. He gets murdered. Considering that he's a war profiteer, bad landlord, and cheats his partners, it's a surprise it took this long for someone to murder him.

2) Roger Havering, also referred to as Roger, Mr. Roger, or that worthless nephew. Roger is Harrington's nephew and in line to inherit piles of money. Roger gambles at the track and always loses. Roger does know how to shoot and handle rifles, an important consideration when hunting grouse. Roger is married to Zoe.

3) Archie Havering, also referred to as Archie, Mr. Archie, or that worthless Bolshie nephew. Archie is a destitute schoolteacher living near the lodge. Harrington

Harrington Pace (*Bernard Horsfall*), the hated rich man

Roger Havering (*Jim Norton*), the gambling husband

Zoe Havering (*Diana Kent*), the tempted wife

Archie Havering (*Shaughan Seymour*), the Bolshie teacher

Jack Stoddard (*Roy Boyd*), the bastard relative

Mrs. Middleton (*Denyse Alexander*), the peculiar servant

Pace demands that Archie oversee the hunting box in exchange for a chance at piles of money. Archie doesn't know how to handle firearms, something made plain when he aims his rifle at his uncle while shooting at grouse. Archie never learned that you *never* aim a rifle at someone unless you plan to shoot them. He does shoot Harrington in the hand by accident.

4) Jack Stoddard, also referred to as Jack, Stoddard, or you idiot excuse for a gamekeeper. Jack is Harrington Pace's bastard half-brother. Harrington keeps him on hand because he needs a gamekeeper he can underpay. Among other indignities, Jack wants to marry the housemaid, Joan, and out of sheer nastiness, Harrington won't lend him the money to do so. Jack keeps two hunting dogs.

5) Zoe Havering, Roger's wife. She's a former actress. She also appears to be carrying on an affair with Archie, Roger's cousin. Or not? We see her flirting with Archie — in front of her husband! — yet once the script sets up their liaison, it never does anything with it.

6) Mrs. Middleton, housekeeper. A definite weak point in the film. As soon as you see her coke-bottle glasses and gray bun, you'll think "disguise."

There are also the local bobbies, two housemaids, and a railroad man named Mr. Anstruther. Mr. Anstruther is important because he owns a bicycle, stolen by a mysterious bearded man and then buried.

A lot of the plot made no sense at all. I get adding additional characters to flesh out a very short story with little action. I can understand adding plenty of red herrings. But if you set up what is obviously a torrid affair between two of the principals (Zoe and Archie) then give me a conclusion. He's practically panting whenever he and Zoe are in the same scene, yet nothing happens.

Other plot threads are dropped like shot grouse. Why did Jack Stoddard arm himself and go outside late at night, leaving his faithful dogs behind? Was he planning to shoot Harrington Pace and someone else beat him to it? Was he poaching to supplement his meager salary? Again, a red herring set up with no explanation.

The housemaids Joan and Ellie never noticed that Zoe Havering and Mrs. Middleton were never seen together? Housemaids notice that kind of thing, particularly when the housekeeper insists on leaving pointed notes instead of speaking to the maids in person. That's weird; weird enough for them to comment on it to Poirot. Yet they didn't spot that Zoe — Harrington Pace's hostess — never conferred with the hired housekeeper and neither did Jack Stoddard or Archie Havering.

Why did Hastings question Archie at his school and then leave without an answer as to why Archie loathed his uncle, yet wouldn't kill him?

Roger Havering providing rides to Joan the maid and to Mrs. Middleton was confusing. I watched this scene twice and I'm still not sure what the point was or what they were trying to say. I guess it was to provide alibis? Maybe?

It's also hard to believe the local bobbies and Japp (way out of his jurisdiction) didn't question Mrs. Middleton not using the telephone at the hunting box to summon the police. Instead, she ran out into the night to have Stoddard do it. How she managed to find him when he was lurking in the dark with a rifle is also a good question. She's lucky she didn't get shot.

Every time the episode got moving, something off-key happened, throwing me out of the show and saying "what?" Yet there was plenty to like such as Poirot in his sickbed or his scenes with Mr. Anstruther.

The scenery is spectacular, if you like endless expanses of snow-draped moors. The hunting box is located in desolation central. You can smell the cold and the poverty. A hunting box, by the way, is what normal people call a mansion. It's a large house, full of weaponry, and used only during the hunting season for game animals; grouse in this case. There's a lovely set piece of the beaters driving the grouse before them so the hunters can shoot them from within peat blinds.

Let me add one bit of praise for the true star of the show. This is Stoddard's prize bitch with the best nose in the county. She's some sort of spaniel, a clever girl, and she, alone of everyone in the room other than Poirot, was not fooled by Mrs. Middleton's disguise. Unfortunately, I couldn't identify her breed or even her name. She's a beauty, however, and should have gotten a credit for her role. If you like dogs, you'll watch this episode just for her.

General Information

Based on: "The Mystery of Hunter's Lodge" (short story, 1923)
Run time: 50 min. **Subtitles:** Yes

Writer: T.R. Bowen
Director: Renny Rye

Cast

David Suchet as Hercule Poirot
Hugh Fraser as Captain Hastings
Philip Jackson as Chief Inspector Japp
Christopher Scoular as Sergeant Forgan
Ray Trickitt as Constable Cooke

Diana Kent as Zoe Havering
Jim Norton as Roger Havering
Shaughan Seymour as Archie Havering
Roy Boyd as Jack Stoddard
Bernard Horsfall as Harrington Pace
Victoria Alcock as Ellie
Clare Travers-Deacon as Joan
Arthur Whybrow as Mr. Anstruther
Denyse Alexander as Mrs. Middleton

Film Locations

Castern Hall, Ashbourne, Staffordshire (hunter's lodge)
Haworth Railway Station, Bradford, West Yorkshire (Ashby Pickard station)
Damems Railway Station, Damems, West Yorkshire (Ashby le Walken Halt)

The ABC Murders (1992)

Threatening letters promise murder in alphabetical order unless Poirot can track the bloody trail to the killer

The A.B.C. Murders is regarded as one of Agatha's finest novels. Although she didn't use the phrase "serial killer" in 1936, that's what the murderer appears to be. There's multiple, unconnected murders while a strange, ambivalent character drifts through the novel under very suspicious circumstances. When you're sure that Agatha Christie — groundbreaking as always — has written the proto-serial killer novel, she yanks the rug out from under you. You realize she fed you the biggest red herring ever.

And you swallowed it whole.

I'm amazed that people dismiss her novels as formulaic. They're not. She tried new ideas throughout her career, yet she was very cognizant of the reasons most murders are committed: money, status and/or security, and passion. Insanity is a reason too, but it's not why police investigate the grieving spouse first. Crocodile tears are easily confused with real ones if the grieving spouse is a good-enough actor.

Nor is insanity the reason why police next investigate who benefited financially from someone's death. Money is a huge motivator. Why wait to inherit when you can shove your elderly, annoying, and unsteady older brother down a flight of stairs and cash out sooner? Particularly if your older brother plans to marry his smoking-hot secretary the minute his ailing wife dies and — gasp! — sire an heir? If she produces an heir, your future changed for the worse. The estate, the money, the title? All gone the minute that mewling, puking son is born. Each subsequent son moves you further from the prize.

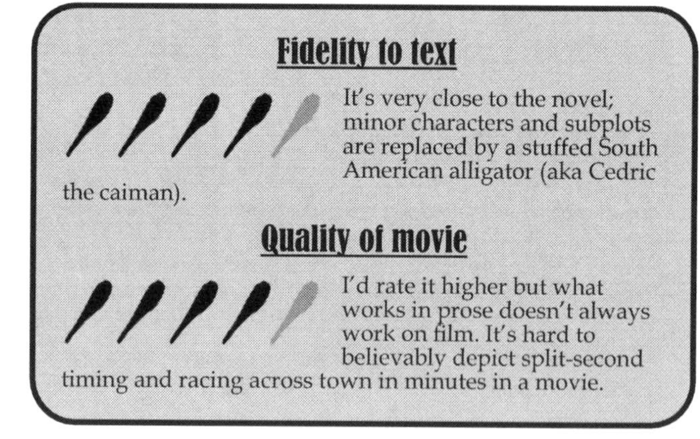

Fidelity to text

It's very close to the novel; minor characters and subplots are replaced by a stuffed South American alligator (aka Cedric the caiman).

Quality of movie

I'd rate it higher but what works in prose doesn't always work on film. It's hard to believably depict split-second timing and racing across town in minutes in a movie.

Look at Princess Margaret (1930-2002). She moved from second in line to the throne of the greatest Empire the world has known to a long shot. Was she ever tempted to push Liz down a flight of stairs? Or King Charles III, who was the world's oldest second banana until his mother died at 93?

You, dear reader, can see why a younger brother might not take any chances. The problem, as Agatha knew, is that the primary beneficiary is also the primary suspect. She knows it, the police know it, we know it, and so does Hercule Poirot. So how can a murder be concealed?

Mary Drower
(*Cathryn Bradshaw*),
the shopkeeper's niece

Donald Fraser
(*Nicholas Farrell*),
the jealous lover

Megan Barnard
(*Pippa Guard*),
the suspicious sister

Franklin Clarke
(*Donald Douglas*),
the would-be heir

Thora Grey
(*Nina Marc*),
the loyal secretary

A. B. Cust
(*Donald Sumpter*),
the stocking salesman

By hiding it within a crowd of murders.

Just like a man can disappear into a crowd at a racetrack, a group of murders can conceal the one that matters by hiding important facts behind flashy distractions. Say, a murder of a woman whose initials are A.A. and she lives in Andover followed by a woman whose initials are B.B. and she lives in Bexhill. A man whose initials are C.C. who lives in Churston is an obvious next victim of a madman. Why, there's nothing special about his death at all. He's the next in the string, soon to be followed by D.D. in Doncaster and E.E in Exeter.

Everyone, police and Poirot included, swallow the red herring.

The episode opens when Hastings returns from an extended vacation in South America. He brings a gift for Poirot: Cedric the stuffed caiman. There is no stuffed caiman (a member of the alligator family) in the novel or anywhere in Agatha's oeuvre. I'm guessing the director or the writer spotted this marvel of taxidermy in a curiosity shop and pounced, knowing that it would be useful in a *Poirot* adaptation.

Poirot is nonplussed until he realizes Cedric is a gift from the heart. Then he has to find room in his flat for the smelly reptile. As comic relief, Cedric works infinitely better than all the supposedly comic scenes combined in the Tony Randall/ Robert Morley version of *The A.B.C. Murders*. Cedric pops up occasionally during the investigation and figures prominently in the dénouement.

Cedric serves as a metaphor that you can't trust what people say: always watch for crocodile tears. The crocodile weeps while eating his prey. He's sad, or pretends to be sad, while getting exactly what he wants.

Our murderer, as you would expect from Agatha, is the most likely suspect. He's Franklin Clarke, Lord Carmichael Clarke's younger brother, and played by Donald Douglas. The other actors were perfect for their roles but not him. He's not the kind of man I could see coaxing Betty Barnard (victim #2) under the pier with him late at night and taking off her belt and presumably her dress. He wasn't charming. In the novel, Franklin Clarke is a bon vivant, the life of the party, the guy you want to dally with under a pier. Douglas' performance as Franklin Clarke is one reason why this film doesn't get five blunt objects.

Contrast him with Donald Sumpter, who was perfect playing Alexander Bonaparte Cust. He looks creepy and played confused and suspicious so well. He's the very image of a disordered man who might be a serial killer in his spare time.

The other reason for this not being a five blunt object film is the unbelievable scenes at the St. Leger Stakes horse race in Doncaster. There's a lot of period stock footage carefully woven into the film. That worked fine. What didn't work was believing Franklin Clarke could work his way out of that packed, jostling mob of humanity, run into the city, track down Cust at his hotel, follow him into a movie theater, stab a random victim (who, unbelievably, did not scream when stabbed in the back!), slide his knife and bloody handkerchiefs into Cust's overcoat pocket, slip out of the theater unnoticed and race back through the St. Leger Stakes mob and return to his seat in time for the rest of the gang to join him.

I couldn't buy it. Horse races last ten minutes, tops. The St. Leger Stakes takes less than four. Plus, it's hard to move through a mob of people, especially in the opposite direction. The mob forces you to move in the direction it's already going. Then to locate Cust in his hotel where he's been sitting and waiting until he hears some magical signal that it's time to go to the movies? No. Just no.

Everything else about this movie worked beautifully. The difference between this version and the Tony Randall atrocity is like night and day. Watch this version. It's terrific, with added period horse racing and stuffed caimans instead of Robert Morley stuffed into a towel.

General Information

Based on: *The A.B.C. Murders* (novel, 1936)
Run time: 1 hr., 43 min. **Subtitles:** Yes

Writer: Clive Exton
Director: Andrew Grieve

Cast

David Suchet as Hercule Poirot
Hugh Fraser as Captain Hastings
Philip Jackson as Chief Inspector Japp
David McAlister as Inspector Glen
Peter Penry-Jones as Superintendent Carter

Donald Sumpter as Alexander Bonaparte Cust
Donald Douglas as Franklin Clarke
Vivienne Burgess as Lady Clarke
Nina Marc as Thora Grey
Ann Windsor as Miss Merrion
Nicholas Farrell as Donald Fraser
Pippa Guard as Megan Barnard
John Breslin as Mr. Barnard
Cathryn Bradshaw as Mary Drower
Michael Mellinger as Franz Ascher
Miranda Forbes as Mrs. Turton
Lucinda Curtis as Mrs. Marbury
Jeremy Hawk as Deveril
Allan Mitchell as Dr. Kerr
Philip Anthony as Doctor
Andrew Williamson as Man in Library
Clifford Milner as Constable
Claude Close as Doncaster Sergeant
Alex Knight as Andover Sergeant
David Fox as Scotland Yard Sergeant
Campbell Graham as Mr. Downes
Gordon Salkilld as Commissionaire
Norman McDonald as Mr. Strange

Film Locations

39 Windsor Street, Uxbridge, West London (exterior Ascher Shop)
The Colonnade, Bexhill-on-Sea, East Sussex (exterior)
St. Leonards-on-Sea, East Sussex (The Royal Victoria Hotel)
De La Warr Pavilion, Bexhill-on-Sea (interior)
The Globe, Doncaster, Yorkshire (Cust's apartment)
Old Regal Cinema Building, Uxbridge, London (Regal Cinema exterior)

Death in the Clouds (1992)

Poirot fights to restore his reputation when gambling and blackmail leads to murder committed while he slept

I would have awarded 3½ darts except tennis bores me. It's period tennis in period tennis-whites played on clay courts, but the time wasted enduring lobs and scoreboard changes could have been better spent filling in plot holes and tying up loose ends. I don't care about the real rivalry in 1935 between British player Fred Perry and German player Gottfried von Cramm or what it said about European rivalries and fear of the upcoming war.

I wanted more action in the casino, in the boulevards and cafés of Paris, a better explanation of where the poison came from, and more of what happened to Lady Cecily Horbury, her husband, and Venetia Kerr. More of Jean Dupont, archeologist, and Daniel Clancy, mystery writer, would have been nice too.

Instead, we got tennis. Worse, we got tennis hooligans but no Hastings to ooh and aah over Fred Perry's smashes and lobs as he creamed von Cramm in the men's singles. No Miss Lemon either, but neither of them appeared in the novel. Other characters who were in the novel got disappeared, but in service of streamlining the story for film.

Death in the Clouds is a classic locked-airplane mystery. Locked rooms always involve substantial amounts of misdirection, particularly when the victim and suspects are 30,000 feet in the air. That is, what did you actually see versus what you thought you saw? Here, Agatha uses one of her frequent tropes: no one sees the staff.

Fidelity to text

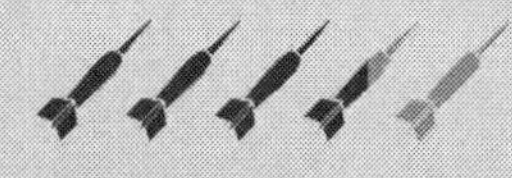

Almost everything important remains except time wasted on tennis that would have been better served filming the baying reporters at the inquest. Agatha was both funny and perceptive about the press.

Quality of movie

The clothes! The scenery of 1935 Paris! The airplane (an anachronistic Douglas C-47B Dakota from 1944 since the plane Agatha described no longer exists)! Japp experiencing Paris!

She also used another favorite trope: the couple who don't appear to be a couple a la *Death on the Nile* or *Evil Under the Sun*. But as she frequently does, she upends it. The wife of the couple is not supposed to be on the plane, but she's a lady's maid so she doesn't get any say in her transportation arrangements. Her boss commands, and she obeys. Although in this case, logic should have prevailed and the lady's maid not risked getting on the plane and disappeared, something she was planning to do anyway.

Quite often today, scriptwriters don't grasp how servants lived and worked in ye olden days. There was no way Lady Horbury would let her maid attend a fancy party in a fancy casino in a fancy dress and chat

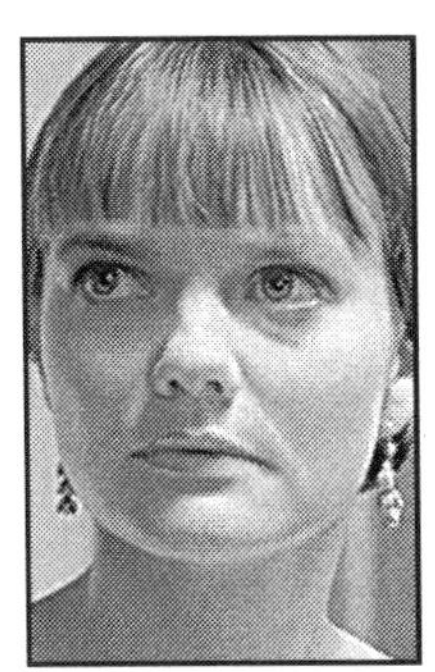

Jane Grey
(*Sarah Woodward*),
the useful stewardess

Norman Gale
(*Shaun Scott*),
the ambitious dentist

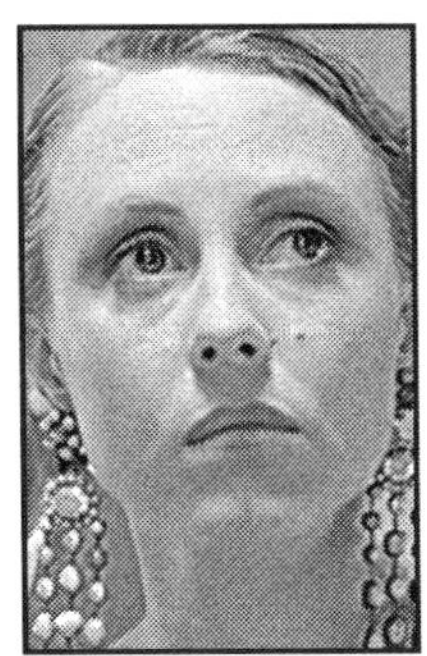

Lady Cecily Horbury
(*Cathryn Harrison*),
the risk-taking wife

Madame Giselle
(*Eve Pearce*),
the moral moneylender

Jean Dupont
(*Guy Manning*),
the wily archaeologist

Daniel Clancy
(*Roger Heathcott*),
the mastered novelist

up the fancy guests. Madeline was a lady's maid. She would have been back at the manor ironing Lady Horbury's gowns, hand-mending split seams, or washing out dainties in the sink. If she was at the party, Madeline the maid would have been serving drinks in her black parlormaid's uniform. She would not have been a guest. The excuse is that the film had to compress 200 pages of exposition into 103 minutes of action, but that doesn't give the writer a pass to make unrealistic choices.

Agatha didn't make that mistake. Agatha also didn't make the mistake of having Lady Horbury not notice when her maid disappeared. In the novel, when Poirot telephones Lady Horbury, she is happy to talk about the base ingratitude of a servant vanishing without a word. In the film? Nothing.

Beside the tennis, the subplot with Lady Horbury, her husband, and Venetia Kerr bothered me the most in this otherwise good adaptation. The script spent plenty of time setting up their love triangle, one that appeared to not be consummated by any of the parties involved. Lady Horbury, former actress, was living a largely separate life from Lord Horbury. He admitted to Poirot to falling madly in love with her — hook, line, and sinker — and marrying in haste to repent at leisure. Yet, when faced with the possibility of the Crown making him a widower, he defended Cecily to Poirot. She, while many things, was not a murderess.

Lord Horbury and Venetia Kerr (a classic horsey member of the peerage) were friendly and companionable but their relationship didn't look like it went past hopeful diary entries and longing but veiled glances. In the novel, Agatha went into detail about how their path to happiness was interrupted by the shooting star that was Cecily. The novel implies that Cecily, following Poirot's suggestion, divorces Lord Horbury. She might or might not run off with an actor she'd been keeping company with (the louche Raymond Barraclough). Lord Horbury and Venetia then do what they should have done all along.

I expected this! We got a huge buildup to Lord Horbury and Venetia's happy ever after or Lord Horbury reconciling with Lady Horbury, which could have worked, and instead … nothing. How disappointing.

Time wasted watching tennis also meant that explanations of the murder were glossed over. I'll admit Agatha thought of wasps on a plane because of meeting Doctor Who and a giant space-alien wasp, causing her eleven-day disappearance (see *The Unicorn and the Wasp*). But professional that she was, she had to come up with a more plausible rationale. In the novel, our villain spent time in South Africa running a snake farm. What was on the poison dart? Snake venom. In the film, there's no explanation for how Norman Gale, everyman dentist, got the venom. There's also no explanation given for why he left the dart to be found or why no one heard anything (psst, the engine noise covered it up).

The film also glossed over what kind of man he was. In the novel, Poirot discovers there was another young lady, similar to Jane Gray, who committed suicide after an affair with Gale. Or did she? Suspicious minds know the answer. Poirot tells us, in film and novel, that Norman Gale fell madly in love — hook, line, and sinker — with Jane Gray. But their relationship wouldn't have ended differently from his previous ones. He'd be rich and alive and she'd be … not.

I would have liked more time with Daniel Clancy, mystery novelist. Think of him as a first draft of Ariadne Oliver, who appeared as a walk-on to Parker Pyne in 1932 and then returned, fully formed, in *Cards on the Table* (1936). In subsequent novels, Ariadne often served as Poirot's foil and companion, but Daniel Clancy came first. He lived at the beck and call of his creation, Wilbraham Rice, banana-eating, nail-biting detective. If you're thinking of Sven Hjerson, vegetarian Finnish detective or a certain famous Belgian sleuth, you've deciphered the clues.

But it's still a good episode and well worth your time. You'll get a fabulous travelogue of Paris, seeing far more than the required views of the Eiffel Tower. The first victim gets a backstory. And, best of all, you'll get to see Chief Inspector Japp in Paris cope with the *Sûreté*! Anglo-French relations will never be the same.

General Information

Based on: *Death in the Clouds* (novel, 1935)
Run time: 1 hr., 46 min. **Subtitles:** Yes

Writer: William Humble
Director: Stephen Whittaker

Cast

David Suchet as Hercule Poirot
Philip Jackson as Chief Inspector Japp
Richard Ireson as Inspector Fournier

Sarah Woodward as Jane Grey
Shaun Scott as Norman Gale
Cathryn Harrison as Lady Cecily Horbury
David Firth as Lord Horbury
Amanda Royle as Venetia Kerr
Harry Audley as Raymond Barraclough
Jenny Downham as Anne Giselle
Eve Pearce as Madame Giselle
Roger Heathcott as Daniel Clancy
Guy Manning as Jean Dupont
Gabrielle Lloyd as Elise
John Bleasdale as Mitchell
Yves Aubert as Airline Clerk
George Rossi as Zeropoulos
Nick Mercer as Policeman
Hilary Waters as Receptionist
Hana Maria Pravda as Concierge
Russell Richardson as French Registrar

Film Locations

Basilica of the Sacred Heart of Paris
Stade Roland-Garros, Paris
Shoreham Airport, Shoreham-by-Sea, West Sussex (Croydon Airport)
French Air and Space Museum, Paris (Le Bourget Airport)
Palais de Tokyo, Paris
Luton Hoo Estate, Bedfordshire & Harpenden counties (Lord Horbury's home)
Théâtre des Champs-Elysées, Paris

One, Two, Buckle My Shoe (1992)

When does the needs of the few outweigh the needs of the many? When murder is in the dentist chair

Fidelity to text

Dropped characters to streamline the novel for film, a minor adjustment in date, and a very different opening that reveals critical aspects of the plot.

Quality of movie

Some of the plot didn't make any sense. I'm also very unsure about that opening sequence: It's atmospheric, creepy, explains the nursery rhyme to everyone who's forgotten it, and reveals too much.

One, Two, Buckle My Shoe is a complex novel, and not merely because of a convoluted plot involving accidents of fate and knowing in advance which dentist a stranger would visit. That plot point, by the way, is never explained in the story, and this mistake is even more glaring in the film.

Where the novel gets really interesting is in the politics. It was published in November of 1940 which means (due to the enormous lag time between writing and publishing) that Agatha wrote it well before the Blitz began. I don't know if she finished writing before 3 September 1939, the day Great Britain and France declared war upon Germany. Traditional publishers can take years between finishing the manuscript, multiple rounds of edits, galleys for one last read through, proofreading, and finally, publication and going on sale at the bookshop around the corner.

Agatha generally didn't tie her books to current events. They're contemporaries but they don't require the reader to peruse the London *Times* from front to back to understand the background. Yet *One, Two* must have already felt dated. Frank Carter is an angry young working-class man and in the film he's a member of the Blackshirts. But the organization (the British Union of Fascists founded by Sir Oswald Mosley in 1932) had been banned by the British government by May of 1940, well before publication. The *Poirot* series sets virtually every episode in the mid-1930s so shifting the date back a few years works perfectly.

This was a period when intellectuals believed democracy would be replaced by fascism or communism, so to reflect that, the novel also features an angry young man from America who's a hardcore Red. That's Howard Raikes, Jane Olivera's boyfriend. Like Frank Carter, Raikes is in favor of burning everything to ash and rubble so a brave new shining city upon the hill can be erected. He tells Poirot that humanity will be perfected and people he considers subhuman exterminated. Perhaps because both philosophies are so similar, he gets dropped from the film.

The central character is Alistair Blunt, supremely important financier, conservative (but not a hardcore right-winger like Frank Carter), thoughtful, cautious, and orderly. Frank and Howard may not agree on much

Alistair Blunt
(*Peter Blythe*),
the patriotic financier

Mabelle Sainsbury Seale
(*Carolyn Colquhoun*),
the chatty missionary

Mr. Amberiotis
(*Kevork Malikyan*),
the slick blackmailer

Frank Carter
(*Christopher Eccleston*),
the moody blackshirt

Gladys Neville
(*Karen Gledhill*),
the tricked girlfriend

Jane Olivera
(*Sara Stewart*),
the poor relation

but they do agree on this: Alistair Blunt is the enemy. He's so much of an enemy that if Frank, Howard, and Alistair met unexpectedly in a dark alley, Frank and Howard would be hard-pressed who to shoot first: their counterpart on the wrong side of the political equation? Or Blunt?

Poirot approves of Blunt. He loathes Frank and Howard, seeing them as opposite sides of the same authoritarian coin. Since the film dispensed with Howard (can't have evil lefties in Hollywood and it simplified the plot), that leaves Poirot with a choice: maintaining the status quo or coming down on the side of innocence, no matter how distasteful that person is.

And make no mistake, Frank Carter is distasteful! Even though he's more sympathetic in the film than the novel, it's obvious what will eventually happen to him and Gladys Neville, Mr. Morley's secretary. Frank's going to beat Gladys on a regular basis, live off her earnings, and eventually, he'll murder her or she'll flee for her life.

Everyone — other than Gladys — agrees that Frank Carter is a wrong 'un. And they're right to do so! But did he murder Mr. Morley, dentist? Did he attempt to murder Alistair Blunt? He doesn't appear to be involved in the deaths of Mr. Amberiotis and Mabelle Sainsbury Seale. Poirot has to make a hard choice. The climax (other than adding the entire cast as witnesses) is remarkably faithful to the final conversation between Poirot and Blunt.

What is the right thing to do? Should the needs of the many outweigh the needs of the few? Should justice prevail? Who will guard the guardians? Agatha rarely gets credit for the subtlety of her writing or thinking. You could say — since dentistry is involved — that like a decayed tooth, corruption from within will eventually undermine and destroy the moral stance you support. And so it proves here.

The film did a good job encapsulating the novel's complexity. But there were poor choices. If you pay attention to the creepy, atmospheric opening, you'll know the dentist was murdered. You won't be thinking suicide like Chief Inspector Japp. You'll know there's a connection between events in India twelve years ago and London, something no one onscreen twigs to until much later on. Watching the scene from *Much Ado About Nothing* should tell you that deception, trickery, and masks are going to figure prominently in the episode.

General Information

Based on: *One, Two, Buckle My Shoe* (novel, 1954)
Run time: 1 hr., 43 min. **Subtitles:** Yes

Writer: Clive Exton **Director:** Ross Devenish

Cast

David Suchet as Hercule Poirot
Philip Jackson as Chief Inspector Japp

Joanna Phillips-Lane as Gerda/Helen Montressor
Peter Blythe as Alistair Blunt
Helen Horton as Julia Olivera
Sara Stewart as Jane Olivera
Carolyn Colquhoun as Mabelle Sainsbury Seale
Christopher Eccleston as Frank Carter
Karen Gledhill as Gladys Neville
Laurence Harrington as Henry Morley
Rosalind Knight as Georgina Morley
Kevork Malikyan as Mr. Amberiotis
Trilby James as Agnes Fletcher
Joe Greco as Alfred Biggs

Film Locations

Harley Street, London (dentist's office)
King William's Block colonnade, Royal Naval College, Dartmouth, Devon (engagement scene)
10 Trinity Square, London (Arnholt's)
Lichfield Court, London (murder scene)
Shrubs Wood, Chalfont St. Giles, Buckinghamshire (Blunt's house)
Bandstand, Battersea Park (British Union rally)
Somerset House, London (marriage records)
Ye Olde Bell, Hurley, Berkshire (Poirot meets maid)

Most of all, you'll wonder why on God's green earth Mr. Amberiotis chose Mr. Morley as his dentist. It was critical for the plot that he do so, but the screenwriter didn't come up with a reason for him choosing Mr. Morley when London is full of dentists.

The novel glosses over this too, but the novel does imply that time passed between the critical chance meeting in the street and murder day at the dentist. This was time used to plan the murder. In the film, it looks like the crime took place on the spur of the moment, right after Mr. Amberiotis began blackmailing Alistair Blunt. Similarly, the novel lets a month elapse before Mabelle Sainsbury Seale's body is discovered. In the film, it's like a day passed.

One, Two is still worth watching, just to see Poirot agonize over saving a worthless example of humanity (delightfully played by a pre-*Doctor Who* Christopher Eccleston). There are unexpected bonuses too. The first (for me) was finally learning courtesy of Chief Inspector Japp clipping his privets why hedge shears are bent. It's so you can lean over the hedge and trim the far side! Decades of gardening and I never knew that. I also caught a gardening mistake. Alistair Blunt lives in a modernistic horror of a house. Based on its design and the time period of the show, the house must have been recently built. Yet that vine covering the sides took decades to grow. I'm guessing the homeowner refused to have his vines stripped off the house for TV verisimilitude.

There's also the lovely, appropriate, vaguely cubist/ Art Deco portrait hanging behind Alistair Blunt in many of the scenes. That's him and his deceased wife, Rebecca, painted in the style of Tamara de Lempicka (1898-1980), a famous society artist of the period. The studio artist combined two of her paintings into this portrait and did a fabulous job.

But before you watch the episode, read the novel. You'll know who did it (which the film opening tells you anyway) but you'll be able to follow the plot.

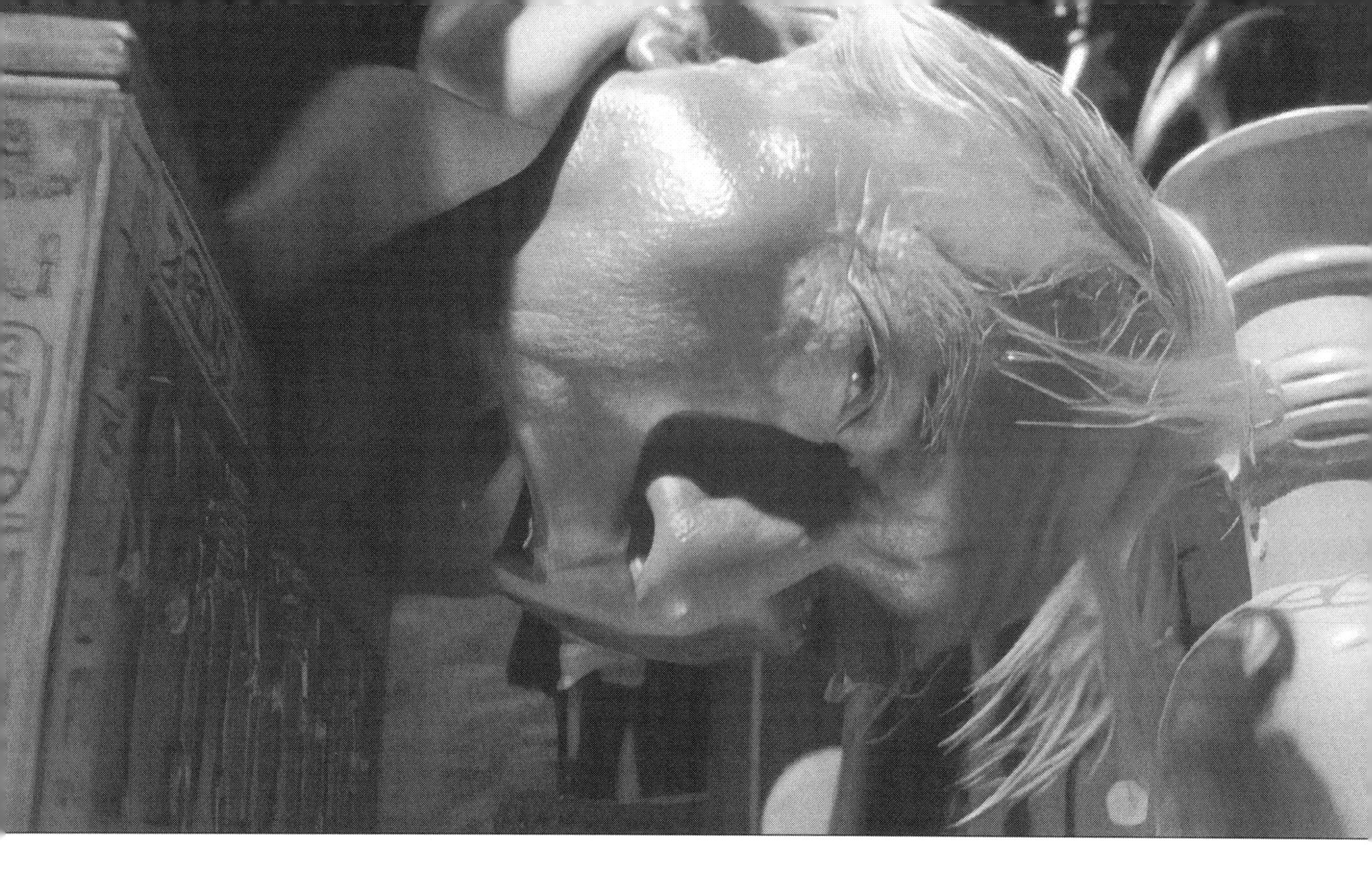

The Adventure of the Egyptian Tomb (1993)

Archeological find sparks tragedies on two continents and Poirot digs up the past to find the cursed connection

Fidelity to text

Miss Lemon shows up to demonstrate her interest in the occult. The timing of events gets seriously messed up and Rupert gets a personality transplant.

Quality of movie

Slow and draggy, with far too many scenes showing off the prop department's expertise and a dig that looked like desert camping and not archeology. The score was good.

The short story starts when Hastings tells us that this was a thrilling and dramatic adventure. It may have been but the film wasn't.

The sad part is how well it opened with a newsreel discussing the discovery and opening of Men-her-Ra's tomb in Egypt's Valley of the Kings. The blend between vintage stock footage and new film was seamless. The narration was perfect, capturing the "Wow! Look at this, folks!" enthusiasm of a 1930s announcer.

Then we jump to the opening of the tomb. Lord Willard, archeologist and noted Egyptologist, discovers the seal locking the doors to the tomb has never been broken. It's 3,000 years old and priceless, like the contents of the tomb. What does he do? He orders the irreplaceable seal smashed so he can reach the treasure quicker. Really? You expect me to believe that an archeologist, even in 1935 when standards were laxer, would smash an artifact when he could spend an hour removing it? Or, he could, I don't know, *cut the ropes* holding the seal to the door knobs.

Lord Willard deserved to die of a heart attack minutes later, after raiding the tomb like grave robbers looking for a big score. Oh wait. That's what archeologists are, only they've got fancy degrees and their loot (usually) ends up in a museum open to the public as opposed to some private collection.

After that, the timing gets very wonky. The short story took place over two months or so. That gave people time to travel from place to place, send and receive cables across oceans, and for the murders to take place. Lord Willard dies. A few weeks later, Felix the financier dies of septicemia, followed shortly by his ne'er-do-well nephew, Rupert, by suicide.

Then, Lady Willard contacts Poirot. She's afraid there really is a curse upon the tomb and her budding archeologist son, Sir Guy Willard, will die at the digs. When Poirot and Hastings arrive at the dig, Professor Schneider has died of tetanus.

The film made it seem like it all happened in about one week, including the time Hastings spends in New York, interviewing Rupert and then discovering his body a day later when he learns about Felix's death. There was no indication that time passed. This is where — since characters wrote reports and read

Sir John Willard (*Peter Reeves*), heart attack

Rupert Bleibner (*Paul Birchard*), suicide

Felix Bleibner (*Bill Bailey*), blood poisoning

Henry Schneider (*Olivier Pierre*), tetanus

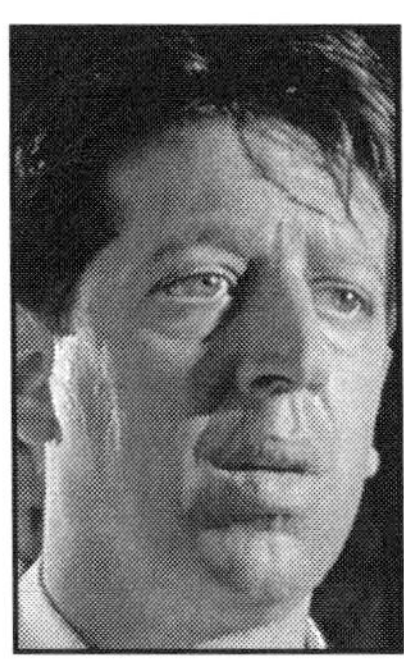

Dr. Ames (*Rolf Saxon*), the quack

Sir Guy Willard (*Grant Thatcher*), the survivor

newspapers — dates could have been provided, showing how events took their time.

Wait. Hastings was in New York? Yes, our man Hastings was mysteriously and providentially in New York, exactly when Poirot needed to learn about Rupert. I had a hard time with this scene because throughout the series, Hastings seems to have no family, no inheritance, and no visible means of support. So what was he doing flying from California to New York? On a business trip? He has no job!

Yet, if Hastings spent time regularly in the United States, he would have known what eggs over easy meant (we're treated to a scene in which he expresses confusion after seeing them in a menu). They're called soft fried eggs in Britain. But I guess if we didn't have the joke, there would be no reason to have the scene at all, since it didn't move the plot forward a jot.

Another irritation is that Rupert got a major personality transplant which eliminated major dramatic possibilities but gave him a better reason for his suicide. In the short story, Rupert was a South Seas beachcomber and a remittance man. That is, he's a ne'er-do-well whose family sends him money regularly to keep him as far away from home as possible. Out there, he can redeem himself or drink himself to death but he won't be around to embarrass his family. Story Rupert has a bad relationship with his uncle. Story Rupert has a friend who paid his way to Egypt. Lots of dramatic possibilities lurk.

Instead, we get Rupert the upstanding nephew, Yale graduate, and anointed heir to Felix the financier. This Rupert has a stunning apartment in New York, a stunning fiancée (who never appears, losing another reason to care about his suicide) and every reason to live. But he doesn't. Hastings, always on the spot, reads his newspaper over eggs over easy and discovers that Felix died in Egypt. He rushes back to Rupert's apartment and discovers the unlocked door and the body.

Wait. Rupert thoughtfully unlocked his door prior to shooting himself so his body could be more easily discovered by passing Englishmen? Apparently so.

Not that it mattered, as both the original Rupert and the improved Rupert got short shrift. Instead, the show wasted valuable time panning slowly over the prop department's fake Egyptian relics that could have been spent on characterization and making us care about the people involved.

General Information

Based on: "The Adventure of the Egyptian Tomb" (short story, 1923)
Run time: 50 min. **Subtitles:** Yes

Writer: Clive Exton
Director: Peter Barber-Fleming

Cast

David Suchet as Hercule Poirot
Hugh Fraser as Captain Hastings
Pauline Moran as Miss Lemon

Rolf Saxon as Dr. Ames
Olivier Pierre as Henry Schneider
Jon Strickland as Dr. Fosswell
Bill Bailey as Felix Bleibner
Paul Birchard as Rupert Bleibner
Simon Cowell-Parker as Nigel Harper
Grant Thatcher as Sir Guy Willard
Anna Cropper as Lady Willard
Peter Reeves as Sir John Willard
Mozaffar Shafeie as Hassan
Robert Wisdom as Waiter
Richard Bebb as Newsreader (voice)

Film Locations

White Gables, Buckinghamshire (Willard House)
Desierto de Tabernas, Andalucía, Spain (desert scenes)
Morocco (desert scenes)
British Museum, London (Poirot visits exhibit)
The Plaza Hotel (Rupert's apartment)

Moving on.

Hastings sails across the Atlantic, picks up Poirot in London, and they travel to Egypt. Hastings enjoys the drive to the archeological site; Poirot does not. But he recovers quickly and expounds on superstition, leading everyone around him to think he believes in that sort of tommyrot.

This is one area the film handled very well. In text and on film, Poirot is firm. He believes in the *power* of superstition. He is not superstitious, but he understands other people are and their beliefs can be used to drive them to do things they otherwise wouldn't or to believe lies told to them by trusted associates. Superstition is very powerful: It makes you believe what isn't real.

This is why added scenes show Miss Lemon dabbling in spiritualism; it shows the power of belief. To discern what happened to her recently deceased cat, she uses tarot cards, followed by using the planchette for a round of automatic writing. She used the planchette correctly although I don't know what she expected her cat to say other than "meow." The tarot card scene proved the scriptwriter didn't know his occult practices. You don't use tarot cards to communicate with the spirit realm. You use them to forecast the future. If Miss Lemon wanted to know if a new cat would show up at her doorstep, the tarot cards might tell her. If she wanted to know what her dead cat thought of the replacement cat, she'd use the planchette.

The show handled superstition poorly in the digs. The crew seemed oblivious to what was going on with their masters. If Men-her-Ra had laid a curse on the tomb raiders, the crew would be nervous, gathering in angry knots, and looking anxious. They'd walk off the site, leaving the archeologists to do the digging. But no. Instead, the native crew ambled out in a picturesque fashion when they could have been used to amplify the suspense.

There were too many missed opportunities here. Maybe the Pharaoh's curse worked!

The Underdog (1993)

Miss Lemon hypnotizing a witness and bloodhounds tracking a suspect add excitement to thin solution

Fidelity to text

The basic plot remains, but characters and settings were changed ranging from a little to a lot.

Quality of movie

It's flawed, but I accepted it until the ending when Poirot pulled his solution out of his boutonnière vase.

The original short story "The Under Dog" (using two words) was published in 1926. Agatha was making forays into longer stories, giving her more room to set up characters and motives. As usual, every character could have offed Sir Reuben Astwell, and the murderer seemed to me to be the least likely suspect. The backstory concerned African gold mine swindles.

The film changes that hoary old chestnut into something more interesting, more modern, more in keeping with the mid-1930s setting, and provides a much better motive.

It's chemical warfare! Specifically, the development and subsequent theft of a marvelous new synthetic rubber astroprene, with more useful properties than real rubber. Synthetic rubber means less reliance on rubber plantations in Malaysia, near a militaristic Japan. That's both useful and strategic. It's always a very bad idea — as any wargamer or supply officer can tell you — to depend on your enemy to produce vital materials for your own industry. Your enemy can cut you off without a second thought and you suddenly can't replace tires, fan belts, or anything else that needs rubber.

Astroprene is a wonderful plot point. It's realistic, because everyone was afraid of the looming war, rubber is vital to the economy, and there were tons of money to be made. Which was why Sir Reuben planned to license the patent to IG Farben, a major German chemical firm.

This horrified Horace Trefusis, head chemist. Because of the looming war? No, it's because if Sir Reuben manufactured the Astroprene, he'd pay Trefusis a big bonus with each ton produced. If Sir Reuben farms out the production of Astroprene, he cheats Trefusis of a big payout.

This is perfectly in keeping with Sir Reuben's nature. He's a bully, a jerk, a swindler, and a cheat. Not that Horace Trefusis was overly concerned with how Sir Reuben acquired the Astroprene formula in the first place. Sir Reuben stole it from an outsider, Humphrey Naylor, and Trefusis, as the head chemist, helped Sir Reuben make the formula work.

We even meet Humphrey Naylor very briefly. He's rifling through Trefusis' files, looking for proof of the theft. Trefusis catches him in the act, a fire starts accidentally, and Naylor flees, disappearing from the story until the climax. This is despite Trefusis seeing him and reporting his presence to Sir Reuben. Naylor's

Sir Reuben Astwell (*Denis Lill*), the loathed patriarch

Lady Astwell (*Ann Bell*), the cheating wife

Victor Astwell (*Ian Gelder*), the scorned brother

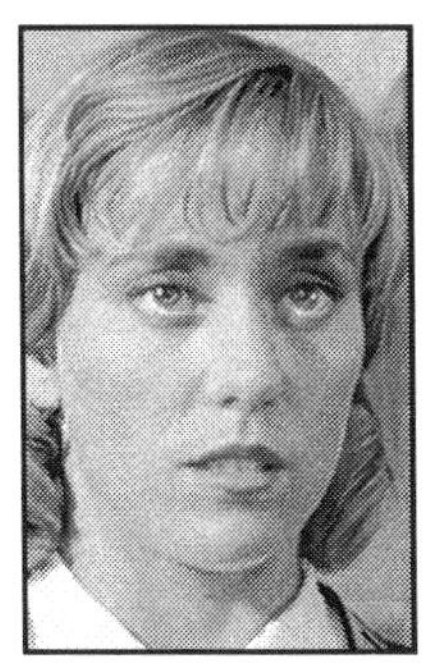

Lily Margrave (*Adie Allen*), the spying companion

Horace Trefusis (*Bill Wallis*), the swindled chemist

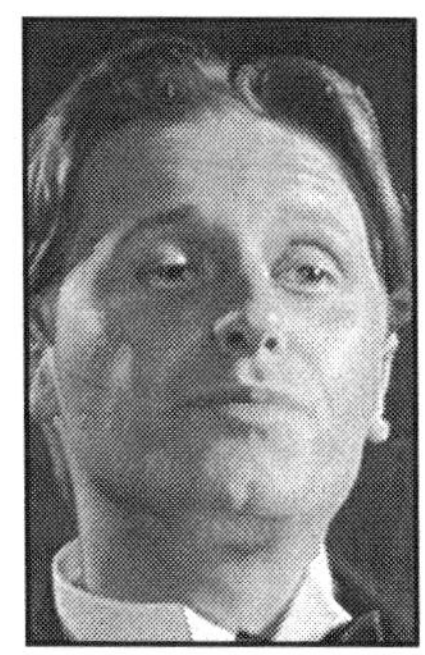

Charles (*Jonny Phillips*), the wastrel nephew

accidental arson wasn't followed up for no reason I could tell. We didn't get to watch Sir Reuben tell Trefusis to keep it quiet since they couldn't afford bad publicity. It should have been mentioned.

Another problem was the actors playing Humphrey Naylor (boy scientist) and Charles Leverson (ne'er-do-well nephew) looked so much alike that I thought *Charles* was rifling through Trefusis' files. It took me most of the episode to realize my mistake. This is why casting matters so much: the audience needs to distinguish one character from another at first sight. It's vitally important when there's not much time to develop characters and you've got seven or eight people running around onscreen.

Poirot and Hastings are conveniently on the scene. Hastings, who's got friends everywhere, is friends with Charles Leverson, ne'er-do-well nephew and wannabe golf pro. He's participating in a golf tournament (check out his plus fours!) with Leverson and staying at the Astwell's Art Deco mansion. Poirot is along for the ride because Sir Reuben has a spectacular collection of Belgian miniature bronzes. Sir Reuben does not appreciate his bronzes like Poirot does, another fine example of why everyone around him wants him dead.

Very oddly, the person who is not on the scene is Inspector Japp. Since there's murder afoot and Japp's jurisdiction seems to encompass all of England, you'd expect him to show up. The only plausible reason is to explain the investigation conducted by the local police of Sir Reuben's murder. He's coshed in the head with a Belgian miniature bronze and — utterly unbelievable since Japp wouldn't have made this mistake and it's 1935 — no one checks the Belgian miniature for fingerprints. No one. Of course, if the local bobby had, then we wouldn't have a mystery.

Sir Reuben's brother, Victor, gets promoted from the short story to his junior partner in the chemical business. He doesn't like his brother, he disapproves of selling Astroprene to IG Farben because of the looming war and not because Trefusis gets cheated, he doesn't seem to disapprove of cheating Humphrey Naylor out of his rights, and he's carrying on an emotional affair with Sir Reuben's wife, Lady Astwell. He also inherits half the business if Sir Reuben dies. Lady Astwell gets the other half so he'll end up with it all. He's an ideal candidate for murder.

General Information

Based on: "The Under Dog" (short story, 1926)
Run time: 50 min. **Subtitles:** Yes

Writer: Bill Craig **Director:** John Bruce

Cast

David Suchet as Hercule Poirot
Hugh Fraser as Captain Hastings
Pauline Moran as Miss Lemon

Ann Bell as Lady Astwell
Adie Allen as Lily Margrave
Jonny Phillips as Charles
Andrew Seear as Humphrey Naylor
Ian Gelder as Victor Astwell
Denis Lill as Sir Reuben Astwell
Bill Wallis as Horace Trefusis
Lucy Davidson as Gladys
John Evitts as Parsons
Michael Vaughan as Sergeant
Charles Armstrong as Receptionist

Film Locations

Boots D6 building, Beeston, Nottingham (factory)
Florin Court, Charterhouse Square, London (Whitehaven Mansions)
St George's Hill Golf Club, Weybridge, Surrey
The Uplands, Blythe Bridge, Staffordshire (Sir Reuben Astwell's house)
Norman Shaw Buildings, Westminster, London (Scotland Yard)
Hull Paragon Interchange, Hull (station)
Royal Albert Hall, Kensington Gore, South Kensington, London
Royal School of Mines, Imperial College London, London

Lady Astwell remains much the same. She was an actress in her youth, she's devoted to her young companion, Lily Margrave, and she's convinced that ne'er-do-well nephew Charles couldn't have coshed Sir Reuben because her intuition tells her so. She and Sir Reuben argue over Lily Margrave rifling through his papers. Say what you will about Sir Reuben's ethics, companions rifling through secret papers should get fired on the spot.

Lily Margrave is apparently carrying a torch for Charles (and not Victor as in the short story but then Victor's busy canoodling with Lady Astwell). Or is she? This was one of those plot threads that got set up and then ignored. You could make a very good case that Lily Margrave was toying with Charles' affections to conceal her own interests in spying on Sir Reuben's chemical contracts. Yet by the end of the episode, the plot thread vanished as if it had never existed.

I did not like the ending. Enough of the short story got rewritten that Poirot could have given a better explanation of the motive and means other than "the little gray cells tell me so." That's right up there with Lady Astwell's intuition; interesting and a possible lead but not admissible in court. The police have standards. Proof must be provided because without proof, anyone could be convicted of anything when someone more important says their intuition tells them who's guilty.

But here, Poirot magically pulls the solution from his boutonnière vase. Somewhere offscreen, he read Trefusis' correspondence (in German!) and worked out the motive. Means and opportunity were provided by process of elimination, despite the entire household being a seething mass of people who hated Sir Reuben and had good reason to murder him.

Still, watch the episode. There's lots to like, such as the period golf tournament and bloodhounds pursuing a fleeing suspect. Miss Lemon even gets a rare chance to shine. In addition to her other spiritualism pursuits, Miss Lemon is a budding hypnotist. She can't hypnotize Poirot but she easily mesmerizes Lady Astwell.

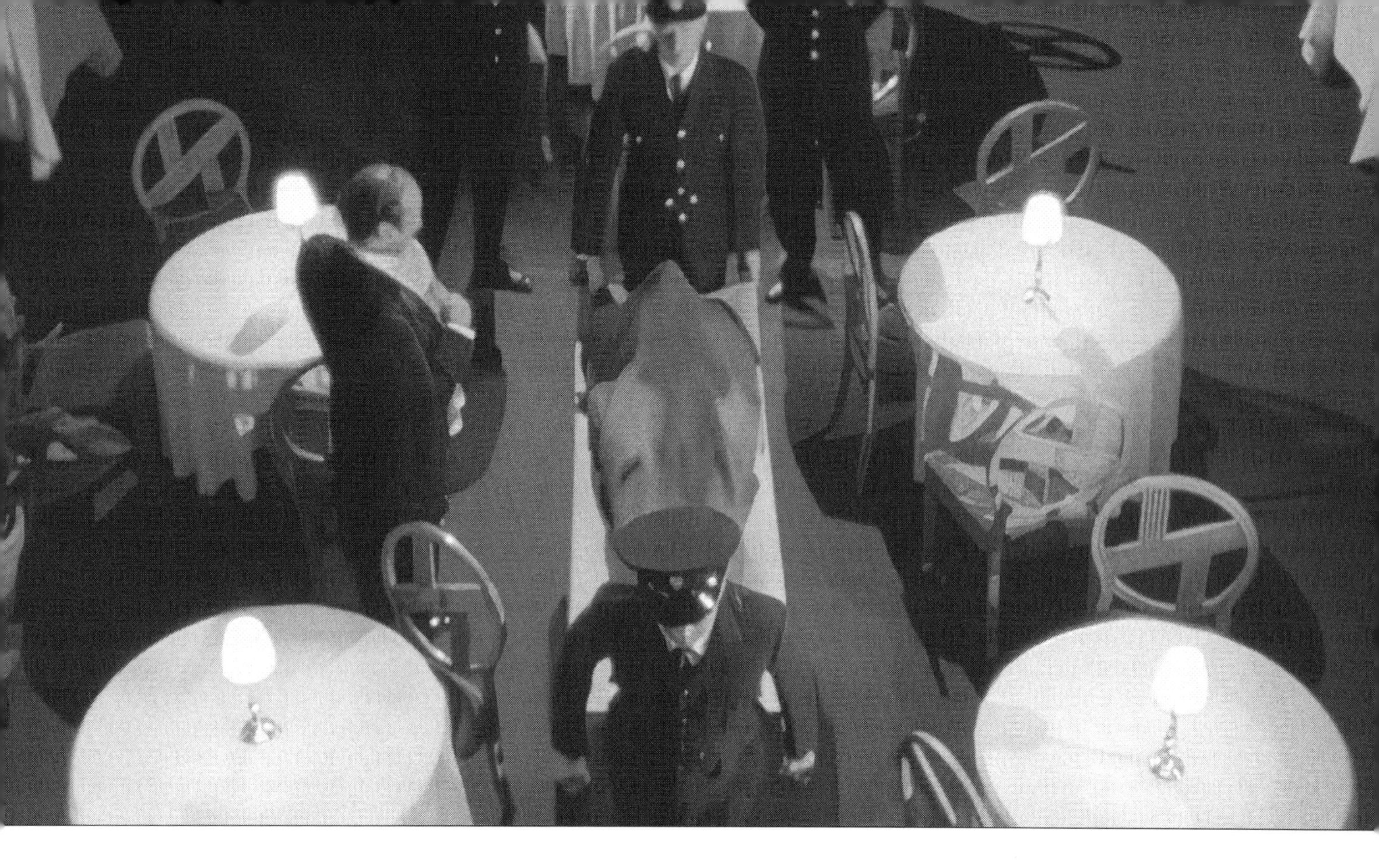

The Yellow Iris (1993)

A revolution in Argentina prevents Poirot from solving a poisoning, but fate hands him a second chance

Fidelity to text

While the core of the story remains, the screenwriter made up the other two-thirds of what you see onscreen.

Quality of movie

This episode has everything: firing squads, bribery, government coups, Latin dancing, cabaret chanteuses, and remembrances of things past.

Agatha wrote *Yellow Iris* in 1937. It's interesting for two reasons. She reworked it extensively, first as a radio play and then, in 1945, as the novel *Sparkling Cyanide*. Among the many, many changes, the criminally underused Colonel Race did the honors of solving the murder.

The other reason is that Agatha wrote song lyrics for the story. She wrote two sets, one for the beginning of the fateful dinner and one for after dinner. The film uses the first set of lyrics twice; first in the Jardin des Cygnes restaurant in Buenos Aires and second in the Jardin des Cygnes restaurant-clone in London.

Wait. What? Buenos Aires? As in Argentina? Since when did Poirot travel to South America?

Since scriptwriter Anthony Horowitz needed to pad out a very short story, that's when. This leads to — if you care about this sort of thing — real issues with timing. The Argentinian president mentioned in the film, Hipólito Yrigoyen, was actually deposed in 1930. He died while under house-arrest in 1933. Not 1934 as the episode claims. That time period was known in Argentina as the Infamous Decade. It was packed with one damn thing after another — civil unrest, military coups, massive economic turmoil, starvation in the streets, you name it — leading to the second issue.

What the heck was Hastings doing running a ranch in La Pampa during this period? And inviting Poirot to visit him when there was rioting in the streets? How could Hastings not have known what the political situation was? Is he truly that oblivious to his surroundings? And if he's running a ranch in La Pampa, what's he doing back in London? With what money? More than ever, it seems as if Hastings has no visible means of support, no job that demands he stick around and do it, and exists solely because the plot demands it.

But if you can get past those real-world continuity issues, it's a darned fine episode.

We begin with a mystery. Two people stare at a grave pinpointing the story's date and argue over what to do next. Then, it's off to Whitehaven Mansions. Poirot receives one shock after another reminding him of unfinished business from his past. Miss Lemon and Hastings demand the truth so we flash back to the hotel in Buenos Aires when Poirot was going to visit Hastings. Social unrest delayed Poirot's train.

Barton Russell
(*David Troughton*),
the man of business

Stephen Carter
(*Hugh Ross*),
the junior partner

Iris Russell
(*Robin McCaffrey*),
the objecting wife

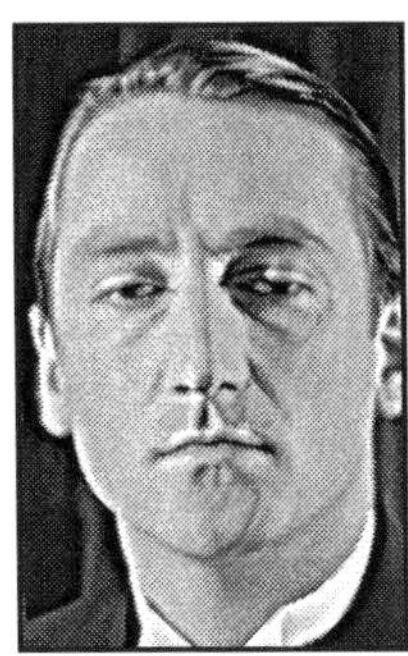
Anthony Chapell
(*Dorian Healy*),
the nosy reporter

Lola Valdez
(*Yolanda Vazquez*),
the fiery dancer

Pauline Wetherby
(*Geraldine Somerville*),
the dewy heiress

Apparently, it also delayed telegraph service to La Pampa so he couldn't inform Hastings he was trapped in the city. While stuck at the hotel, Poirot spies on the other guests and ends up at the fateful dinner party hosted by Barton and Iris Russell.

We know Barton Russell is involved in nefarious doings including bribing government officials. The dinner takes place at a happening supper club and cabaret named Jardin des Cygnes. It's a French restaurant run by an Italian named Luigi in Argentina. Argentina, or at least Buenos Aires, was obviously far more cosmopolitan than I knew. The dance band is terrific and so is the girl singer (Carol Kenyon) dressed all in yellow, matching the yellow irises on the table. She sings the song that Agatha wrote for the short story, "Now I've Forgotten You," most likely set to music by Neil Richardson who did much of the orchestrations for the show's first six seasons.

The song ends with

I've forgotten you
I never think of you
Oh, what a lie
I shall think of you, think of you, think of you
Till I die

I wonder if Agatha was thinking of Archie when she wrote those lines. They'd been divorced for years, and she was happily married to Max Mallowan. Enough time had passed that she could use remembered agony to enhance a story. Whether she did or not, the song works perfectly both as a song that could be sung by a nightclub chanteuse in 1934 and as amplification of the theme that memories never die.

Iris dies of cyanide poisoning at the table, in front of Poirot. He would have investigated her murder, except the revolution arrives and he's arrested, narrowly misses a date with the firing squad, and deported. Although it's not stated at the time, careful reflection leads one to believe that Barton Russell's connections with the new junta might have been behind Poirot's arrest.

Two years later, those events return with a vengeance. This time, however, Poirot is determined to solve the crime. He sends Hastings off to further investigate, and he ends up at Luigi's new version of Jardin les Cygnes in London.

General Information

Based on: "Yellow Iris" (short story, 1937)
Run time: 50 min. **Subtitles:** Yes

Writer: Anthony Horowitz
Director: Peter Barber-Fleming

Cast

David Suchet as Hercule Poirot
Hugh Fraser as Captain Hastings
Pauline Moran as Miss Lemon

David Troughton as Barton Russell
Robin McCaffrey as Iris Russell
Geraldine Somerville as Pauline Wetherby
Dorian Healy as Anthony Chapell
Yolanda Vazquez as Lola Valdez
Hugh Ross as Stephen Carter
Joseph Long as Luigi
Stefan Gryff as General Pereira
Arturo Venegas as Hotel Receptionist
Leonard Maguire as Mr. Grove
Carol Kenyon as Buenos Aires Singer
Tracy Miller as London Singer

Film Locations

Almería, Andalucía, Spain
Florin Court, Charterhouse Square, London (Whitehaven Mansions)

Music

"Now I've Forgotten You," words by Agatha Christie, music by Neil Richardson

Barton Russell has arranged an anniversary dinner to remember his dead wife, Iris. He's convinced it was murder committed by one of the guests back in Buenos Aires. All of them are present again, including Lola the Argentine dancer, conveniently touring in London. Or perhaps she's reuniting with Barton Russell to resume their hinted-at affair. What was weird about the dinner is no one seemed uneasy about the other guests, the yellow irises on the table, or even seemed to note the date. It's as though they'd forgotten what happened the last time this group was together.

I don't know about you, but if *my* hostess dropped dead of cyanide poisoning in a happening nightclub right in front of me after the champagne toast, I'd remember every detail. You wouldn't be able to shut me up. Maybe English citizens in 1936 were more discreet.

The night moves on and things get weirder and weirder. The same song is sung but the London singer (Tracy Miller) isn't nearly as good as the Buenos Aires songstress. Then the past repeats itself and Pauline, Iris' younger sister, dies after the champagne toast.

Poirot performs a fingertip drug analysis and detects cyanide. Who could have done this? Pauline's body is removed and the shocked group retires to a storage room, complete with a parrot in a cage which was weird because parrots aren't normally kept in storage rooms. They don't like it. Poor Luigi. He's probably wondering if his restaurant is doomed because of a murder on opening night.

But as you would expect, Papa Poirot solves the mystery, redeems his honor, rescues the damsel, and true love is allowed to triumph. The solution is clever as long as you don't think too hard about how unlikely it was for the murderer's plan to succeed. He expected to not be noticed but that's asking for a lot, even in the dark with a great, spotlighted singer backed up by a great band drawing all the attention in the room. Asking for that situation to work twice was too much.

You, however, should watch the film twice. It's worth your time.

The Case of the Missing Will (1993)

A wealthy man's attempt to write a new will runs into deadly trouble in this pretty but inconsistent story

Fidelity to text

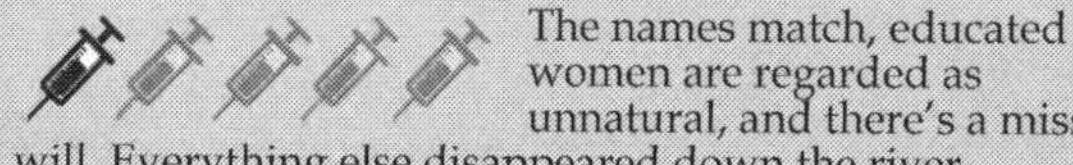

The names match, educated women are regarded as unnatural, and there's a missing will. Everything else disappeared down the river.

Quality of movie

Only because the recreation of 1936 Cambridge was gorgeous. You could pole fleets of punts through the plot holes.

If you're unfamiliar with a punt, you won't thrill to the sight of them being poled beneath Cambridge's Bridge of Sighs. A punt is the bastard offspring of a raft and a canoe. Someone gets to stand up — careful! — and push the light boat along the calm river using a long pole reaching into the river's bed. Punting works best on placid, shallow water, with perhaps just a little current to add speed. Boats of any kind are always a plus in an Agatha Christie adaptation. Sadly, no action takes place on a punt.

Jerome K. Jerome (1859-1927) famously sent his three men in a boat (to say nothing of the dog) punting up the Thames. Their journey was adventurous, comedic, classic, and any lapses in plot were forgivable because there was so much to love.

Not here. There was no comedy or adventure or dogs. The plot didn't make any sense. The more Bill and I discussed it that night while walking in 30° weather with snow on the ground, the less sense it made. I would have welcomed a chase scene involving punts as a nice change from Hastings' usual hot pursuit in a fast motorcar. I would have welcomed a change in weather! Once again, the weather was sunny and warm. With very few exceptions, *Poirot* episodes always take place on sunny June days, despite how few of them there actually are in the English calendar.

If you're familiar with Agatha's version of the story, erase it from your mind. Thus, you won't be startled when Andrew Marsh hosts a gala New Year's Eve party in 1926. At midnight, he announces that he's finally made a will. Apart from a few small bequests, the bulk of the estate goes to a medical charity. And what of Violet, his dear ward whom he's raised since she was a babe in arms? She gets nothing, because girls should be provided for of by their husbands.

I found his notion about women hard to swallow because traditionally, young women were provided dowries. The dowry is supposed to help the woman set up her new household, give some protection against a negligent husband, provide for her widowhood, and take care of any children, even be passed down to them. Dowries are common worldwide. A dowry might be tiny or it might be huge, but it's expected. Andrew Marsh couldn't possibly be ignorant of this fact. He is a Cambridge Don, a career steeped in tradition.

Then there's the ridiculous event Poirot and Hastings

Violet Wilson (*Beth Goddard*), the by-blow

Phyllida Campion (*Susan Tracy*), the old flame

Robert Siddaway (*Edward Atterton*), the by-blow

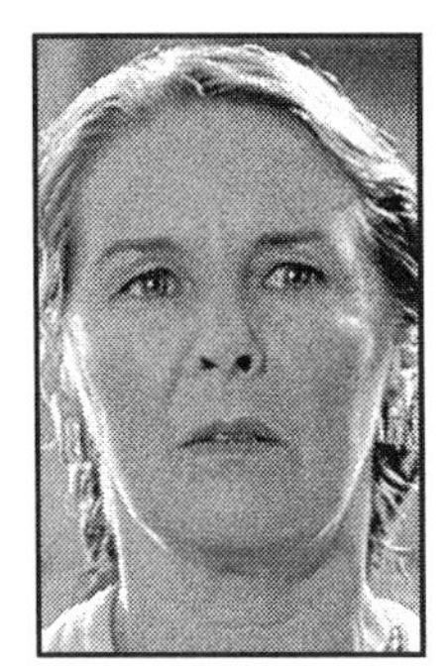

Sarah Siddaway (*Rowena Cooper*), the old flame

Peter Baker (*Neil Stuke*), the by-blow

Margaret Baker (*Gillian Hanna*), the old flame

attend at Cambridge, when the date springs forward to 1936. A student debate is going on about the rights of women. Cambridge was backwards. They didn't permit women to be fully fledged members until 1948, despite the presence of women-only colleges dating back to 1869 when Emily Davies founded Girton College.

But this is 1936! The debater rattles on about the horrors of women working in the fields and the munitions factories as if that had never happened before. What bridge was he living under? The Great War (1914-1918) forced millions of women into the factories and onto the land to take the place of men fighting and dying in the trenches. Every person in England participated in the war effort (if they were old enough) or heard endless stories from their elders about participating in the war effort (if they weren't). This is Cambridge, famous for its rigorous and historically based education.

I guess that debater spent all his time punting and not studying and none of his instructors cared. Worse, Andrew Marsh chimed in as though he — old enough to fight! — had had his memory wiped slick. These fine gentlemen also don't notice the women laboring around them: parlormaids, housekeepers, cooks, laundresses, innkeepers, store clerks, etc. At least that could be attributed to class blindness at its finest.

After the debate, Poirot and Hastings arrive at Crabtree Manor, Andrew Marsh's palatial home, the home he's not bequeathing to Violet. Andrew has a health crisis so Dr. Pritchard springs into action. Pay close attention to the lady assisting Dr. Pritchard. Have a drink every time you see her talk. Later that night, Andrew tells Poirot he's revising his will in Violet's favor.

You know what that means. Seconds — and I do mean seconds — after Andrew says he'll meet his solicitor in the morning, he receives a mysterious phone call arranging a late-night rendezvous in the folly. Off he goes, to meet someone he is clearly comfortable seeing by himself in the dark. Okay, but how did this mysterious phone caller know that Andrew was on the verge of revising his will? At no point are we given the tiniest hint.

In the morning, Hastings and Violet are out riding. It's before breakfast since they don't comment on Andrew not appearing for his morning kippers and cold toast. Hastings spots Andrew in the folly. Slumped over. Not acknowledging them. Our man Hastings may be a fool in a thousand ways but when needs must, he springs into action. He sends Violet for help and waits for the cavalry to arrive.

Poirot is instantly suspicious of the locals. They don't seem to care that Andrew died suddenly in the folly after a mysterious late-night rendezvous. It's heart failure. Well, hearts do fail when their owner is injected with a huge quantity of insulin.

Soon after that, Miss Campion, Violet's main sponsor at Cambridge and a close friend of Andrew, gets shoved down the escalator in London.

At this point, the plot falls apart completely. The dénouement demonstrates how little thought the scriptwriter put into his plot and how much Agatha put into hers. Poirot pulls the solution from his boutonnière vase, leaving you, dear reader, to say "What? Who did this? That person? But that person had like three lines of dialog in the entire 51-minute episode! That person thought they'd get a huge inheritance for their son on the basis of, of, of claiming something that couldn't be proved?"

How did the murderer follow Miss Campion successfully to London and push her down the escalator? How did the murderer even know Miss Campion went to London? How could the murderer think anyone would believe their ridiculous story other than that Andrew Marsh was well known for having an eye for the ladies?

The last scene compounded the tragedies. Violet walks with Miss Campion in a Cambridge courtyard. Neither of them care about Andrew's death. They care even less about the murderer, rending the murderer's family into shreds, or the loss of Violet's potential future family with Robert. Nothing.

Should you watch this? The Cambridge scenery is glorious. Miss Lemon's dress magically changes colors. Those are your reasons.

General Information

Based on: "The Case of the Missing Will" (short story, 1923)
Run time: 51 min. **Subtitles:** No

Writer: Douglas Watkinson
Director: John Bruce

Cast

David Suchet as Hercule Poirot
Hugh Fraser as Captain Hastings
Philip Jackson as Chief Inspector Japp
Pauline Moran as Miss Lemon

Beth Goddard as Violet Wilson
Susan Tracy as Phyllida Campion
Edward Atterton as Robert Siddaway
Rowena Cooper as Sarah Siddaway
Terrence Hardiman as John Siddaway
Mark Kingston as Andrew Marsh
Richard Durden as Dr. Pritchard
Neil Stuke as Peter Baker
Gillian Hanna as Margaret Baker
Jon Laurimore as Walter Baker
Stephanie Thwaites as Violet as a child
Simon Owen as Robert as a child
Glen Mead as Peter as a child

Film Locations

Little Thakeham, Thakeham, West Sussex (Crabtree)
Cambridge Union Building, Cambridge (debate)
St. John's Meadow, Cambridge (drive to debate)
All Saints Passage, Cambridge (Poirot arrives)
Temple of the Four Winds, West Wycombe Park (folly)
56 Trumpington Street, Cambridge (solicitor's office)
New Court, St. John's College, Cambridge (cloister)
First Court, St. John's College, Cambridge (funeral procession)
Florin Court, Charterhouse Square, London (Poirot's flat)
Smithfield Market, London (Liverpool Street Station)
Bridge of Sighs, St. John's College, Cambridge
Normansfield Theatre, London (degree ceremony)

The Adventure of the Italian Nobleman (1993)

Miss Lemon's courtship mixes with murder at a full-service apartment, classic sports cars, chases, and a cat

Why didn't I give this episode 5 statues? Because there were no subtitles, which I could have lived with except there were no subtitles for the Italian dialog. I can approximate what English speakers are saying. If the characters are yakking away in Italian? I have no clue. But that's a minor quibble in a fun-packed episode. It's so fun you'll not care why the murderer chose to directly involve Poirot.

I'll start with the boat. Graves, Count Foscatini's valet, tells Poirot and the gang over tea that he was an ex-navy man. His heart must still be with the sea because he shows off a picture of his boat, *Fantasia Felice*, moored in Chichester. It's a very nice boat, but we didn't see much of it. It looks to be just big enough for two to live on board. It's got a motor and sails.

Pay close attention to the gorgeous Italian racing car Hastings drools over, getting the episode off to a roaring start. The brand (Eliso Freccia) is fake but the car is real. It's a vintage Alfa Romeo 2900A manufactured in 1936. Hugh Fraser (Hastings) enjoyed the privilege of driving it but only for closeups. Most of the driving was done by the car's owner, costumed to look like Hastings.

Similarly, when the Italian car saleslady, Miss Fabbri, was driving, it was really the Alfa's owner's wife disguised as Miss Fabbri. They weren't about to let their precious, jaw-droppingly expensive car get taken out joyriding by actors. And that scene where Hastings rams the escaping murderer's car with the Alfa? Movie magic. No Alfas were harmed during production.

The series likes its car chases, but this was the best one to date by far. It wasn't just stylish vintage cars in the English countryside. This car chase was funny. The drivers careen through the increasingly narrow streets of Chichester, involving bicyclists falling into streams, flocks of geese, open-top tourist buses, and broken crockery. Alas, all car chases must come to an end but this one ended not just with Hastings ramming his Italian speedster into the villain's jalopy. He rammed his fist into the villain's jaw as payback for his betrayal of Miss Lemon.

Every time you admire that sleek motorcar, you'll wonder how on God's green earth Hastings was able to afford it. Maybe he sold the Lagonda along with his ranch in Argentina.

But I digress. The plot is convoluted. As Hastings

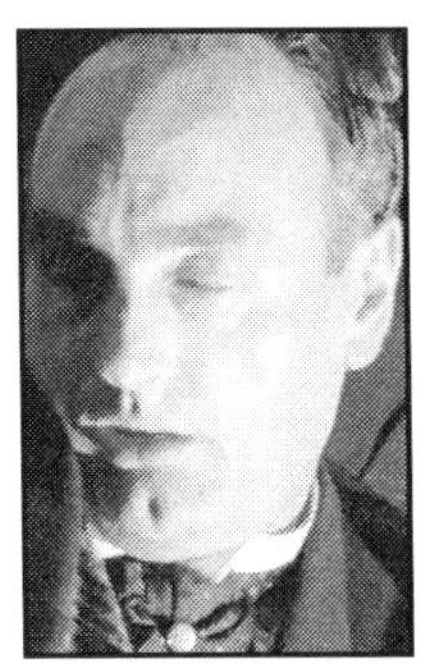

Count Foscatini (*Sidney Kean*), the suspect nobleman

Edwin Graves (*Leonard Preston*), the loyal servant

Bruno Vizzini (*David Neal*), the patriotic car dealer

Margherita Fabbri (*Anna Mazzotti*), the wise saleswoman

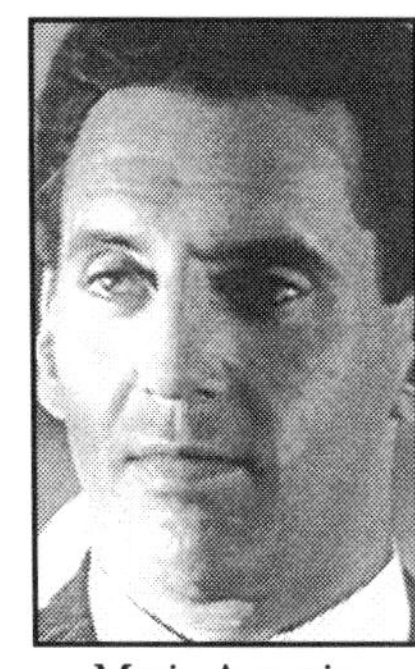

Mario Ascanio (*Vincent Riotta*), the enterprising crook

Darida (*Alberto Janelli*), the loyal secretary

negotiates with the car saleslady (who knows her camshafts), he witnesses an argument between the head car salesman and a visitor. He thinks nothing of it. That evening, Poirot and Hastings dine with a doctor friend. A mysterious phone call later, they're breaking into Count Foscatini's flat and discovering a dead man, a bloody nude marble torso, and a live Siamese cat. There's also a table set for two. A lovely scene follows where Poirot interviews the chef. Count Foscatini lived in a full-service residential hotel, with concierge service, elevator operators, porters, maid service, and a chef who takes orders, cooks gourmet meals, delivers them via the dumbwaiter, and then the dirty dishes are sent back for washing.

Why can't I live in a flat with maid service and a chef?

Inspector Japp arrives promptly and the investigation grinds on. When not investigating, Poirot and Hastings grill Edwin Graves, Count Foscatini's valet, over tea. He's dating Miss Lemon. Our gentlemen are Miss Lemon's family and they're concerned. What are this man's intentions?

It's from Graves they learn details about Count Foscatini's lifestyle, apparently funded by blackmail. As they learn more about Foscatini (Miss Lemon discovers he's not a real Italian count), they find the connection between the Italian car dealer, the Italian embassy, and blackmail. If you've been paying attention, you'll know who one blackmailer is as soon as he steps into view. He's wearing a very sharp suit, normal at the time. He's also wearing spectator shoes, those jazzy two-tone affairs that only lounge lizards and gangsters wore. No true gentleman ever wore spectator shoes, not in *Poirot*. They're too flamboyant.

The action moves to a full-blown rooftop Italian wedding reminiscent of the one you saw in *The Godfather* (1972). It's very un-English, a reminder that even in 1936, England was far more cosmopolitan than cozy mysteries and BBC TV series lead you to believe. A visit to the Italian Embassy follows along with hints of mobsters who are more dangerous than the Mafia. More dangerous and feared than the Mafia? Apparently so.

General Information

Based on: "The Adventure of the Italian Nobleman" (short story, 1923)
Run time: 51 min. **Subtitles:** No

Writer: Clive Exton
Director: Brian Farnham

Cast

David Suchet as Hercule Poirot
Hugh Fraser as Captain Hastings
Philip Jackson as Chief Inspector Japp
Pauline Moran as Miss Lemon

Leonard Preston as Edwin Graves
Anna Mazzotti as Margherita Fabbri
David Neal as Bruno Vizzini
Vincent Riotta as Mario Ascanio
Sidney Kean as Count Foscatini
Alberto Janelli as Darida
Arthur Cox as Dr. Hawker
Vittorio Amandola as 1st Secretary
Ben Bazell as Sergeant Beddoes

Film Locations

Beaumont Hotel, 8 Balderton Street, Mayfair, London (Eliso Freccia showroom)
Brown Hart Gardens, Mayfair, London
Florin Court, Charterhouse Square (Whitehaven Mansions)
Addisland Court, Holland Villas Road, London (Foscatini's apartment)
Kensington Roof Gardens, Kensington High Street, London (wedding)
Rosewood London, 252 High Holborn, London (Italian Embassy)
Jenkins Hotel, 45 Cartwright Gardens, Bloomsbury, London (hotel)
Norman Shaw Buildings, Westminster, London (Scotland Yard)
Bosham, West Sussex (chase)

The spectator-shod blackmailer is hunted down and captured, but not before he burns the evidence. Subtitles would have helped because I'm still not 100% sure this man was a criminal like Count Foscatini.

Poirot solves the murder, undeterred by the flamboyant distractions of mobsters, blackmail, diplomats, and Italian sportscars. He focuses on important clues such as undrawn draperies and the contents of the victim's stomach. Thus, our heroes end up in Chichester where they capture not just the murderer but learn the true extent of his perfidy towards Miss Lemon.

It's always a pleasure to see Miss Lemon get some screen time. She should have gotten a 1930s detective show of her own. She's sharp, canny, well-organized, and she can go undercover. She might be taken in — for a short time — by a villain but she'll always ferret out the truth and so it proves here.

Miss Lemon is also a cat lover. If you recall *The Adventure of the Egyptian Tomb*, she's been grieving over her dead cat. Her suitor reveals his true nature to Miss Lemon. He's tasked with cleaning up Count Foscatini's flat. He'll have to move somewhere else. Count Foscatini had an adored Siamese cat who appears in several scenes. The cat has a speaking part as all Siamese cats do. Will Graves find this charming, affectionate, mouthy cat a new home? No, he'll destroy it. Miss Lemon is livid.

So she isn't upset when Poirot tells her the sordid truth about Edwin Graves. On the contrary. He deserves everything he gets. He was going to kill the cat! He didn't save the cat! But Miss Lemon does, as Poirot discovers.

Yes, the cat has the last word. You know he'll be a very happy cat, living with Miss Lemon. The cat statue Poirot bought at the airport gift shop in Cairo (what, you thought he looted it?) after his Egyptian tomb adventure finally worked its magic. The meaning of Miss Lemon's planchette's automatic writing becomes clear. A blackmailer had to die, but Miss Lemon has a new cat, and balance is restored to her universe.

The Chocolate Box (1993)

Remembrance of sweeties past infuse this tale of murder by poisoning and romantic longing from Poirot

Fidelity to text

A lot was added to sweeten this confection. One possibility was missed, adding an off-taste.

Quality of movie

I loved it. Frothy, delicious, with undertones of grief, loss, and sadness creating a bittersweet finish.

I love chocolate, all kinds, even white chocolate as long as it's well made and not — gag — fake-vanilla-flavored shortening. I live next door to a chocolate factory (Reese's) and can see another chocolate factory (Hershey's) from my upstairs window. Our streetlights are Hershey's kisses, wrapped and unwrapped. Hershey really is the sweetest place on earth and the air really does smell like chocolate. If you crave something different, down the road in Elizabethtown is an M&M Mars factory churning out Dove chocolates. Not far away is Lititz, home of Wilbur Chocolates.

Thus, with a *Poirot* episode named *The Chocolate Box*, I hoped for great things and expected middle-of-the-road. Luckily, *The Chocolate Box* delivered more than that.

It is a gorgeous episode, weaving seamlessly between the last days of La Belle Époque before WWI wiped it away and Belgium of 1936 when the scent of war is in the air, darkening everyone's thoughts.

Chief Inspector Japp has been invited to Belgium to be honored with a prestigious award. Since Mrs. Japp was unable to go with him (she remains an unseen presence in the series), Poirot is invited to join him.

They disembark at the stunning train station (in Antwerp if you want to visit) and meet Claude Chantalier, a dear friend of Poirot's from the old days, when they were young officers in the Brussels police force. Luncheon leads to remembrances of days past when Poirot's little gray cells failed him.

Is that possible? Not according to Poirot. "It was not I who made the mistakes in that case; it was everyone else." At Japp's prompting, he tells the story, and we fade into 1913 Belgium when he was a young up and comer.

Middle-aged and healthy Paul Delourard, an important and wealthy politician, died suddenly after a contentious family dinner. Among other endeavors, Paul's been trying to reduce the power of the Catholic church in Belgium. His mother disapproves, as does an older friend, le Comte St. Alard, who supplies Paul with fine Belgian chocolates. Another family friend, Gaston Beaujeu, tries to make peace as does Virginie, the cousin of Paul's tragically dead wife.

Virginie is suspicious of Paul's death and she begs the young Poirot to investigate. Who could resist a lady like this one? Not Poirot.

The case should hinge on a simple question: Who

Paul Déroulard
(*James Coombes*),
the anti-Catholic pol

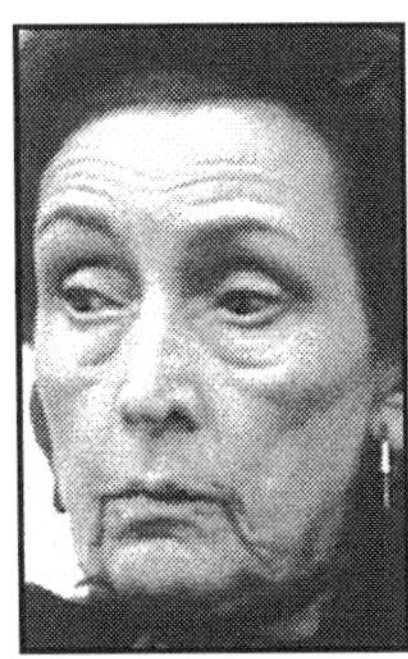

Madame Déroulard
(*Rosalie Crutchley*),
the pious mother

Virginie Mesnard
(*Anna Chancellor*),
the alluring cousin

Xavier St. Alard
(*Geoffrey Whitehead*),
the loyal friend

Gaston Beaujeu
(*David de Keyser*),
the ill confidant

Supt. Boucher
(*Mark Eden*),
the supportive boss

benefits by Paul's death? Except it turns out to not be so simple. Everyone important insists he died of heart failure. Even le Comte St. Alard believes he did, despite stating near an eavesdropping Poirot that he might just as well have shot Paul. Why did le Comte say this? Because, good Catholic that he is, he believed their argument brought on Paul's heart failure. If only he had been kinder and less contentious.

Despite official disapproval, Poirot continues to investigate. Not only does he not wish to disappoint the lovely Virginie, he's curious. Something doesn't fit. He notices in passing the mismatched lids on two chocolate boxes, but focuses more on the chocolate crumbs the fatal box contained. One chemical analysis later, the answer arrives: poisoned chocolate!

The story might have been inspired by a true crime. Agatha may have known about the notorious poisoning case in Delaware in 1898, when Cordelia Botkin, a jilted woman in San Francisco, mailed her lover's wife and family a box of arsenic-laced chocolates that killed two people.

Toxic chocolate and the U.S. Postal System serving as the murder delivery device seized the nation's attention. A sensational trial involving two jurisdictions ensued. Botkin was found guilty and her lover's life and career were destroyed.

In Poirot's case, the chocolates were laced with trinitrin, a heart drug derived from nitroglycerin and renamed to avoid the public associating heart medication with high explosives. The pills were coated in chocolate to disguise their intensely bitter taste.

Poirot quickly discovers who, among the tiny group of suspects, uses trinitrin. It's Gaston Beaujeu, who has his own reasons for staying out of the case. He's fine with Paul's death, by the way, even though he insists he's not involved although his pills were.

Poirot is left with a puzzle. St. Alard had motive but no means. Beaujeu had means but no motive. He does some housebreaking (this is obviously where his burglar skills in *The Veiled Lady* came from) and finds the trinitrin bottle in le Comte's pocket.

Once Poirot accuses le Comte St. Alard, the police superintendent is *really* incensed. Poirot, being Poirot, is convinced he's right.

But he's wrong. He missed a crucial and obvious clue. The two boxes of chocolate had mismatched lids. Why would anyone exchange the lids? Because they're nearly blind. Madame Déroulard demands an interview and tells the truth to Poirot, as she does not wish to see an innocent man hang.

She murdered her son. But not because of his anti-Catholicism! No, that was a side benefit. Madame murdered Paul because she was an eyewitness when he murdered his first wife. The short story gives some detail about Paul's taste for the ladies, something the film ignored.

This was a problem because it provided additional reasons for why a devout mother would kill her only child. If the film had added Madame's other concern, her motives would have been even plainer. In the short story, Madame worried that Paul was chasing after sweet, innocent Virginie, his dead wife's young cousin. If he didn't marry Virginie, he would have left her ruined and unmarriageable (recall this is 1913). If he married Virginie, he wouldn't just cheat on her. There was the chance he might murder her if she disagreed with him.

Murder is always easier the second time around. The horror of taking someone's life wears off.

So why give this film five poison bottles when a critical piece of motivation was lacking? Because everything else worked so well. I loved how well the film slid between the current day and the past. I loved Brussels. What a stunning city; all government buildings should be so grand instead of today's grim, brutal, gray concrete bunkers. The clothes, the vehicles, the meals, the manners, the fine Belgian chocolates. It's a feast for the eyes and the music enhances it.

The ending is perfect. Watch Poirot when he meets Virginie again. She gave him his boutonnière vase, a charming accessory he wears every day. But she married someone else, giving someone else her love and their sons. Not him. Poirot remains alone for life, and he knows what he lost. It's a bittersweet moment and how well it was portrayed with a mixture of public pleasure and private melancholy is a tribute to David Suchet's acting skills.

General Information

Based on: "The Chocolate Box" (short story, 1923)
Run time: 51 min. **Subtitles:** No

Writer: Douglas Watkinson
Director: Ken Grieve

Cast

David Suchet as Hercule Poirot
Philip Jackson as Chief Inspector Japp
Mark Eden as Superintendent Boucher
Jonathan Hackett as Claude Chantalier

Rosalie Crutchley as Madame Déroulard
James Coombes as Paul Déroulard
Lucy Cohu as Marianne Déroulard
Anna Chancellor as Virginie Mesnard
David de Keyser as Gaston Beaujeu
Geoffrey Whitehead as Xavier St. Alard
Jonathan Barlow as Jean-Louis Ferraud
Preston Lockwood as Francois
Linda Broughton as Denise
Kirsten Clark as Jeanette
Richard Derrington as Henri

Film Locations

Cogels Osylei 41, Antwerp (Déroulard House)
Station Antwerpen-Centraal, Antwerp (Gare de Bruxelles)
Hotel Métropole, Place Brouckère, Brussels
Palais de Justice, Brussels
Parc du Cinquantenaire, Brussels
Pharmacie Botanique, Brussels (pharmacy)
Brussels Tram Museum, Avenue de Tervueren 364, Woluwe-Saint-Pierre
Galeries Royales Saint-Hubert, Brussels (cafe)
Rue des Minimes 54, Brussels (Poirot's apartment)
Brussels Town Hall, Brussels (award ceremony)
Groot-Bijgaarden Castle, Dilbeek (Count St. Alard's castle)

Dead Man's Mirror (1993)

Dropping the aristocratic motive and making Japp doubt Poirot turns this story slow, stodgy, and stupid

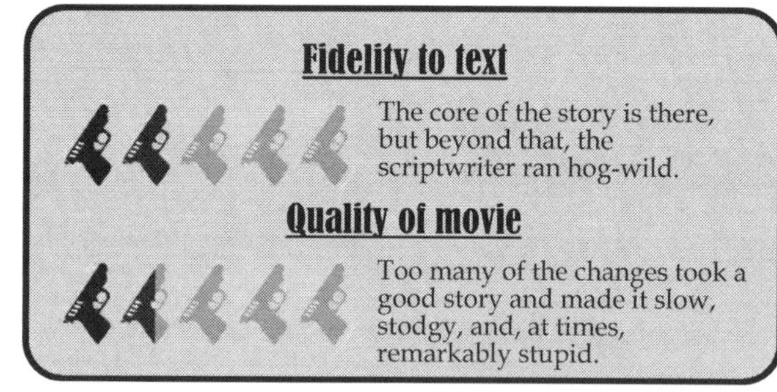

Fidelity to text

The core of the story is there, but beyond that, the scriptwriter ran hog-wild.

Quality of movie

Too many of the changes took a good story and made it slow, stodgy, and, at times, remarkably stupid.

Did you know that "Dead Man's Mirror" (1937) was a completely rewritten version of "The Second Gong," published in 1932? I didn't either. It's not contained in my supposedly complete-in-every-respect tome of short stories, *Hercule Poirot's Casebook*.

When Agatha rewrote "The Second Gong," she added, enhanced, lengthened, and changed it; all the usual things a writer does when they file off the serial numbers and rewrite a story to sell it again.

The core means and method remain and so does Poirot.

The scriptwriter for this episode did much the same, except he didn't spend nearly as much time thinking through the mechanics of means, method, and motive as he should have. Agatha did. Her plot made sense. This one didn't.

Changing Gervase Chevenix from an aristocrat with no son desperate to preserve his family's name to a wealthy art dealer was remarkably stupid. His motivation and behavior stem directly from the security of 400 years of history proving he's better than you and everyone else under the sun.

In the short story, Poirot reads the Debrett's entry and learns the Chevenix baronetcy was granted in 1694. 1694! That means King William III awarded the Chevenix founder with a title. It's not as grand as your title coming over with William the Conqueror in 1066, but a family name like Chevenix implies Gervase's ancestors were part of that invading army. It took them another 600-some years to earn the title, but earn it they did.

This kind of background is unfathomable to most of us. Unless you're a genealogist, I doubt you know any family stories about your ancestors and what they did in 1694.

Without that motivation of continuing the family lineage above all, it doesn't make sense for Gervase to insist that Ruth (adopted daughter) marry Hugo (his sister's son) and adopt the family name.

The hidden reason — despite the fact Hugo can't inherit the title since he's not in the male line of succession — is that Ruth isn't merely just another orphaned baby. While her mama was some low-rent typist, daddy was Gervase's younger brother and that makes Ruth special to Chevenix. That also makes Ruth and Hugo first cousins, even though they think the genetic relationship is further apart. Thus, Gervase keeps the family bloodline going and on both sides! The title will be lost to some extremely distant collateral male relative, but since the property isn't entailed, Ruth and Hugo would inherit everything else.

Gervase Chevenix (*Iain Cuthbertson*), the nasty victim

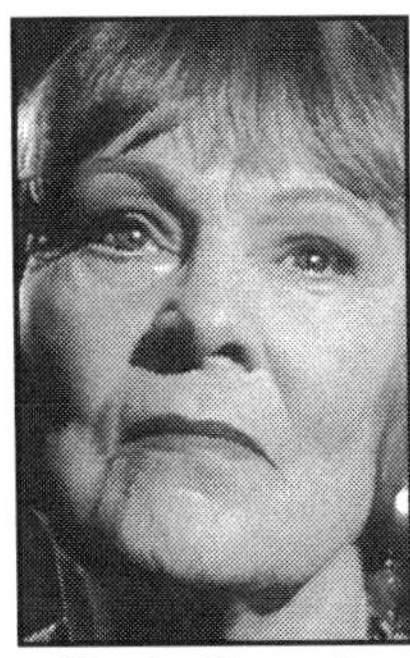

Vanda Chevenix (*Zena Walker*), the psychic wife

Ruth Chevenix (*Emma Fielding*), the resentful adoptee

Hugo Trent (*Jeremy Northam*), the ungrateful nephew

John Lake (*Richard Lintern*), the gullible partner

Miss Lingard (*Fiona Walker*), the research assistant

He could even dream that someday, possibly, they could persuade the crown to award them another baronetcy.

Aristocrats are bred to want this. It's one of the reasons they're able to cling to power. If you aren't indoctrinated while still in the womb and build the appropriate social structures to make it happen, you'll watch your family go through the three-generation cycle of shirtsleeves to shirtsleeves over and over. Assuming of course that you know what your great-great-grandparents were up to and you have a plan for your great-great-grandchildren.

Abandoning the succession crisis drained a source of energy from the story. Another bad change was made to Vanda, Gervase's wife. In the short story, she's batty for the occult, but the local police inspector and Poirot both know that while she seems nuts, she can be surprisingly observant.

Not here. No, we get Vanda gone round the bend, channeling the spirit of an Egyptian queen and spouting ominous premonitions. Vanda's preoccupation with ancient Egypt also let the set designer reuse the warehouse of Egyptian gimcrack they built for *The Adventure of the Egyptian Tomb*. That stuff is everywhere in the house. The Cairo airport gift shop doesn't contain as many cheap knockoffs.

There's also a problem with the casting choices for Hugo Trent (the nephew) and John Lake (the architect). They looked so much alike I had trouble telling them apart.

Their characters, too, got rewritten. Hugo became a modern furniture designer, constructing uncomfortable tubular steel chairs and benches suitable for airport passenger lounges. At least this is historically accurate. The Bauhaus School began designing those unpleasant chairs in the 1920s (i.e., sculpture that shouldn't be sat on) and manufacturing them for waiting rooms soon followed.

John Lake also got a makeover. He's still Ruth's boyfriend, but instead of working as Gervase's land agent, he's an architect who designed the family home and is working on a huge mixed development project funded by Gervase. The fraud plot thread originally assigned to Gervase's secretary (disappeared from the TV episode) is handed to him. Lake comes off as a dumb and trusting idiot, used by his partners to defraud Gervase. Demonstrating his incompetence, when he sets fire to incriminating files, the incendiary device goes off early, he's caught in the flames, and Poirot, Japp, and Hastings (on the spot because the plot decreed it) rescue him from certain death.

It *is* a change from Hastings' usual car chase.

Then there's Chief Inspector Japp. I understand the series is named *Poirot* and not *Japp*, but this episode went out of its way to make Japp stupid by automatically dismissing Poirot's suggestions that Gervase's death was not a suicide.

Japp's not a stupid man. He's worked with Poirot for years, and this reflexive dismissal is inconsistent with how he's treated Poirot in the past.

Contrast this with the short story. Chief Constable Riddle examines the locked room evidence indicating suicide, looks at Poirot, and says, "If you're here, it could be murder." At least one other character says the same thing.

Yet Japp — whom we've seen investigate dozens of murders with Poirot — instantly discounts everything Poirot says as though the great detective is a local loon and not the man who's made sure Japp has a perfect conviction record with Scotland Yard. Oh, and stacking stupidity upon stupidity, Poirot *deliberately* conceals evidence from Japp that would prove it was murder!

As if the scriptwriter accepted a dare to make the story even more stupid, he made Miss Lingard extra evil in a totally unbelievable scene near the end. In the short story, Agatha made Miss Lingard a sympathetic killer. She loathed Gervase Chevenix for what he'd done to her. A lot of her plot was spur of the moment as she dug her hole deeper and deeper. Miss Lingard knew what she'd done, she was glad she'd done it, but she didn't try to save her own neck by incriminating anyone else.

So, in one of the stupidest scenes I've seen in a *Poirot*, Miss Lingard uses Vanda's superstitions to cajole her into writing a confession and hanging herself. Really. She manages to throw her voice into Vanda's bedroom, down the halls, and in the drawing room too! All from inside some sort of cupboard. No house has acoustics like that, especially a huge pile of stone with surprisingly fragile doors installed in those foot-thick walls.

I couldn't buy this episode and you won't either. Watch it for completeness' sake.

General Information

Based on: "Dead Man's Mirror" (novella, 1937)
Run time: 50 min. **Subtitles:** No

Writer: Anthony Horowitz
Director: Brian Farnham

Cast

David Suchet as Hercule Poirot
Hugh Fraser as Captain Hastings
Philip Jackson as Chief Inspector Japp

Iain Cuthbertson as Gervase Chevenix
Zena Walker as Vanda Chevenix
Emma Fielding as Ruth Chevenix
Jeremy Northam as Hugo Trent
Richard Lintern as John Lake
Fiona Walker as Miss Lingard
Tushka Bergen as Susan Cardwell
James Greene as Snell
Jon Croft as Lawrence

Film Locations

Hornsey Town Hall, Hornsey, London (civil marriage)
Horsted Keynes station, Bluebell Railway, West Sussex (Whimperley station)
Marylands, Ewhurst, Surrey (Chevenix's house)
Florin Court, Charterhouse Square, London (Whitehaven Mansions)
Highpoint I, London (Museum of Modern Art)
Norman Shaw Buildings, Westminster, London (Scotland Yard)

Jewel Robbery at the Grand Metropolitan (1993)

It's a murderous seaside rendezvous as a vacationing Poirot matches wits against a thief with a taste for pearls

Fidelity to text

The screenwriter added plenty, but most of the additions were based on hints in the text or accurate — but weird! — period details.

Quality of movie

I'd have given it another half-thief but the solution is wildly implausible. Sadly, it's Agatha's solution so I can't blame the script.

This was a nice finish to the fifth season of *Poirot*, particularly after disappointments like *The Case of the Missing Will* and *Dead Man's Mirror*.

The episode was fun and frothy. There's a play within the play, a Brighton Beach-style brass band playing the soundtrack, and period horse racing scenes. There's even silent movie footage referencing *Salome*, a 1922 flick based on the play by Oscar Wilde (1854-1900). Oscar gets namechecked twice more, when Hastings asks if the play where Celestine and Andrew Hall met was *Lady Windermere's Fan*. It was not, they said. It was *The Importance of Being Earnest*, which gave Poirot's memory a jog and let him make an important correlation. He recalled seeing Worthing, the limping man with the elephant-headed cane at the front desk of the Grand Metropolitan Hotel.

This was part of a lovely rewrite of a scene in the short story in which Poirot observes the hotel staff's changed behavior and deduces that Mrs. Opalsen's pearls were stolen. In the film, he notes Worthing's limp, then how he climbs the stairs instead of taking the lift. Something's off-kilter but it wasn't until later that Poirot saw the connection.

What was Poirot doing at a hotel in Brighton? Taking a much-needed two weeks rest so he could fully recover from his detecting labors. He'd overworked and taken ill.

But Brighton turns into a busman's holiday — you expected otherwise? — which was good for Poirot. He got to exercise his intellect rather than waste time wondering why he was staying at a cold seaside resort, sitting in a deck chair in what looked like 45° F. weather. He's bundled up with a blanket over his clothing, muffler, and overcoat. Even Hastings, made of hardier stuff, looks chilled. The weather remains indifferent, with actual rain, a rarity in *Poirot* episodes where it's normally sunny and warm.

When the weather isn't being typically English, Poirot endures one annoyance after another. He closely resembles Lucky Len, a man in a local newspaper publicity stunt. If a citizen identifies Lucky Len and says the special phrase, Lucky Len is supposed to award his finder with money. Think of it as *Where's Waldo?* with a financial reward.

This is based on a real contest. Back in 1927, the *Westminster Gazette* invented Lobby Lud. If a citizen

Ed Opalsen
(*Trevor Cooper*),
the flashy impresario

Margaret Opalsen
(*Sorcha Cusack*),
the grand actress

Celestine
(*Hermione Norris*),
the lucky maid

Andrew Hall
(*Simon Shepherd*),
the broke playwright

Saunders
(*Karl Johnson*),
the clever chauffeur

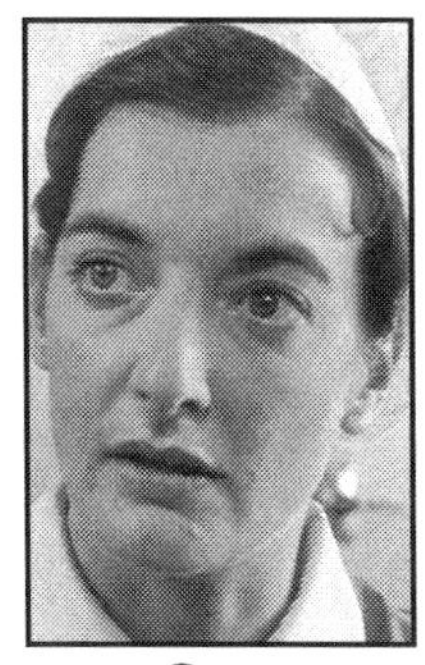

Grace
(*Elizabeth Rider*),
the fast chambermaid

correctly identified Lobby he earned a quick 5 quid, worth about £300 today. With that kind of money at stake, it's no wonder the locals harass Poirot whenever he steps outside the hotel's central heating to take the sea air and endure the cold.

That's when he's not being harassed by theater entrepreneur Ed Opalsen who understands that no publicity is bad publicity. Opalsen is producing a new play called *Pearls Before Swine* starring his wife, Margaret Opalsen, and a priceless necklace of pearls once given to *Salome's* actress by the tsar. Margaret is draped with what appears to be several pounds of pearls.

You may wonder why the audience is gasping at those pearls. Today, pearls are cheap and readily available, but that wasn't true in 1936. The cultured pearl industry was in its infancy. Virtually every pearl anyone saw was natural, born from an oyster and plucked from the bottom of the sea by a pearl diver. Natural pearls are anything but standardized. They're rarely perfectly spherical nor are their colors uniform. Some are positively baroque; misshapen lumps of nacre.

A string of pearls, especially if they're large, perfect orbs with the same hue and luminosity, was worth hundreds of thousands of dollars. A quantity of pearls — all large, and perfectly matched in color, shape, and size — could be worth millions. Margaret Opalsen wore a king's ransom around her neck and an audience in 1936 knew it.

They were literally pearls of great price, equaled in value only by the kingdom of heaven. It makes you wonder about Ed Opalsen's choice of names for his play. He's displaying his pearls before his piggy audiences and praying they'll grunt with applause and ticket dollars.

Naturally, pearls like this would be a prime target for thieves. Yet they're only guarded by a lady's maid, which is right out of the text. There's nothing to stop a thief from barging into the hotel room, overpowering Celestine, and stealing the jewel box so he can open it later at his leisure, but then we wouldn't have a locked jewel box mystery.

It's a nifty little mystery too, since there are only two suspects. There's Celestine, the overworked and underpaid lady's maid with a gambling playwright boyfriend who's in hock to suspicious thugs. She's desperate for money. There's also Grace, the overworked and underpaid chambermaid at the Grand Metropolitan. We don't know anything else about her travails but she's probably desperate for money, too, since chambermaiding doesn't pay well.

If Celestine didn't steal the pearls, then it had to be Grace. Except the two women, strangers to each other, are each other's alibis. Neither left the room long enough for the other to remove the pearls from the locked box. As grand as the Grand Metropolitan hotel is, it apparently isn't grand enough to have a hotel safe. But again, if the Opalsens used the hotel safe, we'd have a very different story.

The solution is clever but it's also wildly implausible. It depended on not only split-second timing, but *also* Celestine leaving the suite twice to get sewing supplies from her adjacent room. There's no way the thieves would know she'd be conscientious enough to get her mending done while the Opalsens were at a party.

The other issue is the room next door to the Opalsen's suite. The rooms have a connecting door, an invention of the hotel industry allowing guests to rent the rooms they need instead of putting up with a suite that's too large or too small. They let suites expand and contract as required. Connecting doors have deadbolt locks on both sides so guests are guaranteed privacy, a must if strangers are renting the adjoining rooms. Connecting doors figure prominently in bedroom farces, where the scantily clad mistress enters through one door while the wife enters from another. They allow discreet passage between bedrooms without having to go out into the hallway and risk being seen by staff or other guests.

How did the thieves ensure they booked the adjoining room? In the short story, the villain was Opalsen's valet. Agatha's choice was plausible since a valet could act as his employer's personal secretary, making hotel arrangements. In the film, the villain is the chauffeur. Chauffeurs take care of the limousine, not the hotel.

But if you can stomach that unlikelihood, you'll enjoy everything else from start to finish.

General Information

Based on: "The Jewel Robbery at the Grand Metropolitan" (short story, 1923)
Run time: 51 min. **Subtitles:** No

Writer: Ken Grieve **Director:** Anthony Horowitz

Cast

David Suchet as Hercule Poirot
Hugh Fraser as Captain Hastings
Philip Jackson as Chief Inspector Japp
Pauline Moran as Miss Lemon

Trevor Cooper as Ed Opalsen
Sorcha Cusack as Margaret Opalsen
Hermione Norris as Celestine
Simon Shepherd as Andrew Hall
Karl Johnson as Saunders
Elizabeth Rider as Grace
Tim Stern as Bell Boy
Andrew Carr as Hubert Devine
Arthur Cox as Dr. Hawker
Peter Kelly as Lucky Len

Film Locations

Florin Court, Charterhouse Square, London (Whitehaven Mansions)
Marylebone Station, London (Eastbourne railway station)
Eastbourne Seafront, Eastbourne, East Sussex
Grand Ocean, Saltdean, East Sussex (Grand Metropolitan Hotel)
Devonshire Park Theatre, Eastbourne
Staines Town Hall, Staines-upon-Thames, Surrey (party venue)
Plumpton Racecourse, Lewes, East Sussex (Windsor Race Course)

Hercule Poirot's Christmas (1995)

Everyone hated the wealthy old man, but only one relative slit his throat, giving everyone a Merry Christmas

Fidelity to text

The usual character deletions and one major addition, but there's also two major unforced errors and no, I'm not including the prologue.

Quality of movie

Darned good right up until the moment Poirot pulled the solution out of his boutonnière vase and you realize the murderer wouldn't have been that stupid.

The next time the holidays roll around, and you're tired of watching Scrooge get scared straight, try *Hercule Poirot's Christmas*. It's Christmas-themed. It's got a large, dysfunctional family gathered for the holidays. There's gorgeous settings and classic Christmas carols. There's also a considerably smaller body count than another traditional Christmas movie: *Die Hard* (1988). They even share this similarity: In both movies, the big villain deserved his gruesome end.

Ambrose Bierce (1842-1914) famously divided murder into four categories: felonious, excusable, justifiable, and praiseworthy (he added that which category makes no great difference to the person slain). In this case, the murder of wealthy family patriarch Simeon Lee is justifiable. It would have been the fourth kind, except the murderer tried to frame innocent people — who also wanted the vicious old sod dead — and that's neither justifiable or praiseworthy.

The film opens with a young Simeon Lee prospecting in the wilds of South Africa. Agatha was very fond of Africa as a result of her round-the-world trip in 1922, and references to the continent pop up often in her stories. The prologue documented Simeon Lee's complete lack of character and humanity. He murders his partner, beds and abandons the woman who rescues him, and becomes a wealthy man who tortures his family. While the prologue was necessary and useful, as we'll see, the scenario it set up fell apart at the dénouement.

We then see Poirot getting ready for a cozy, quiet Christmas at his cozy London flat. He's looking forward to the Christmas he didn't enjoy the previous year when he had to rescue a feckless Egyptian princeling from his folly in *The Theft of the Royal Ruby*. He's all set with his Belgian chocolates, music on the radio, his books, and a fine gourmet dinner. Inspector Japp, on the other hand, is not looking forward to his Christmas holiday. He'll spend it freezing in Wales with his wife's family, and listening to them sing Christmas carols around the piano until they're hoarse.

Neither of them get the Christmas celebration they expected. In Poirot's case, he's settling down to dinner in Whitehaven Mansions when the building's boiler fails. No heat for the tenants until after the holidays. He gets a phone call from Lee demanding he come to his

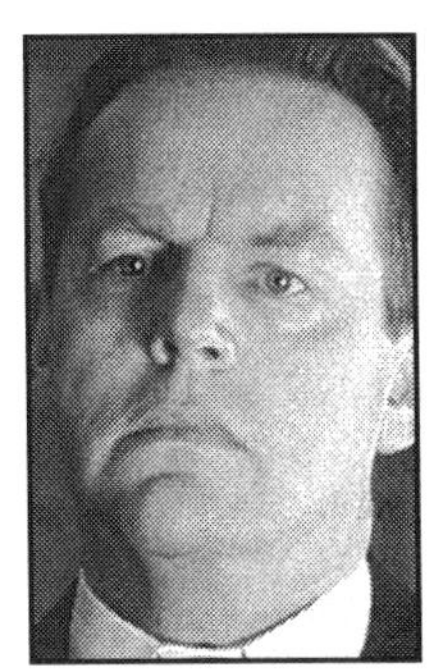

George Lee
(*Eric Carte*),
the political son

Magdalene Lee
(*Andrée Bernard*),
the shady wife

Harry Lee
(*Brian Gwaspari*),
the prodigal son

Pilar Estravados
(*Sasha Behar*),
the lost relative

Alfred Lee
(*Simon Roberts*),
the good son

Superintendent Sugden
(*Mark Tandy*),
the steady investigator

house immediately. Instead of being offended, Poirot has one question: Does Gorston Hall have central heating? Yes, it does, so off he goes.

There, Poirot meets the dysfunctional Lee family and its disagreeable patriarch, Simeon. Simeon wanted him there for … reasons which weren't entirely clear to me. This was a change the scriptwriter made, and it's a bad one. In the novel, Poirot is summoned for the usual reason. Simeon Lee's body was found and he happened to be nearby spending the holiday at the home of a local police inspector (not Japp!). So why not enjoy a busman's holiday? The film could have kept this scenario, and it would have made far more sense than what we saw.

I cannot believe the murderer — a canny, experienced man — would have persuaded Simeon Lee to invite one of the greatest detectives in the world to the scene of the planned crime. No, no, no.

The murder of Simeon Lee is one of Agatha's great *tour-de-forces*. He's a completely despicable man who, even as an old man in a wheelchair, enjoys baiting his relatives. He cuts off one son's allowance and creeps on his granddaughter. The more you find out about him, the more you dislike him.

As for the mystery, it's a locked room, which she didn't do much of. Where she excelled — stretching the boundaries of what was normal (recall that the novel was published in 1938!) —was in the setup and the murderer.

First, Simeon Lee makes no bones about his army of illegitimate sons. He's got so many he brags to Pilar (his granddaughter) that he could field a cohort as his bodyguards. This wasn't typical of cozy mysteries written 83 years ago. Unlike today, fiction used to gloss over this kind of immoral behavior. It was implied, but it wasn't spelled out.

Second, Agatha went a step further and did what she had only done once before: She made a policeman the murderer. Murderous cops are commonplace today, but in 1938? There aren't many examples. Even more unusual, the murderous policeman is the investigating officer and a trusted authority figure.

She also used a motive rare for her. It's not money. It's not passion. It's not status or fear. It's not one spouse killing the other to avoid a ruinous divorce or being exposed for bigamy.

It's rage and revenge for old sins.

General Information

Based on: *Hercule Poirot's Christmas* (novel, 1938)
Run time: 1 hr., 40 min. **Subtitles:** No

Writer: Clive Exton
Director: Edward Bennett

Cast

David Suchet as Hercule Poirot
Philip Jackson as Chief Inspector Japp
Mark Tandy as Superintendent Sugden

Vernon Dobtcheff as Simeon Lee
Simon Roberts as Alfred Lee
Catherine Rabett as Lydia Lee
Eric Carte as George Lee
Andrée Bernard as Magdalene Lee
Brian Gwaspari as Harry Lee
Sasha Behar as Pilar Estravados
Olga Lowe as Stella de Zuigder
Ayub Khan-Din as Horbury
John Horsley as Tressilian
Scott Handy as Young Simeon
Liese Benjamin as Young Stella
Oscar Pearce as Gerrit
Steve Delaney as Sgt. Coombes
Colin Meredith as Shopkeeper
Peter Hughes as Mr Charlton
Joanna Dickens as Cook
George Little as Dicker (voice)
Tony Red Richards as Mrs. Japp's Relative

Film Locations

46 Hertford Street, Mayfair, London (Poirot and Japp shopping)
Chilham Castle, Chilham, Kent (Lee's home)
The Tudor Peacock, Chilham (Stella arrives)
Horsted Keynes Station, Sussex (Poirot, Harry and Pilar arrive)
St. Mary's Church, Chilham (church services)

Think about it. The murderer gains nothing by his crime other than satisfaction. No money, no status, no freedom from fear, no gorgeous wife while keeping the approval of the community.

The film presents this situation beautifully except at the end. I mentioned the first unforced error above. What was the second? Remember the prologue, when young Simeon Lee betrayed the woman who rescued him and left her pregnant and alone? She raised the child to hate the father who abandoned them, and even appeared in the village to watch the revenge carried out.

How Poirot connected the old lady with the port wine stain staying at the inn with Inspector Sugden we never learn. There was no reason whatsoever for Poirot to connect them. There was no way he could have known the old lady was visiting from South Africa. We didn't see a single scene showing him or the police investigating Sugden's background unlike Horbury's, Magdalene Lee's, or Pilar's. No South African souvenirs, war records, gossip from neighbors, or furtive but overheard lunches in the pub between mother and son.

So how did Poirot know? The plot implied he just did, that's how.

I can't stand that kind of sloppy writing, especially when the source material didn't make this mistake. Film is a different medium than print, so we've got to be shown where the answer comes from, even if only for 30 seconds.

But otherwise, this was a great episode and worth watching more than once. There are so many great moments between Poirot and Japp, Poirot and Simeon Lee, and most of all there's Simeon Lee himself. For him, getting murdered meant a quick death and a bonus round of torture and agonizing memories for his family. Wherever he ended up, you can imagine him evilly chuckling knowing that you couldn't tear your eyes away from him. He likes it like that.

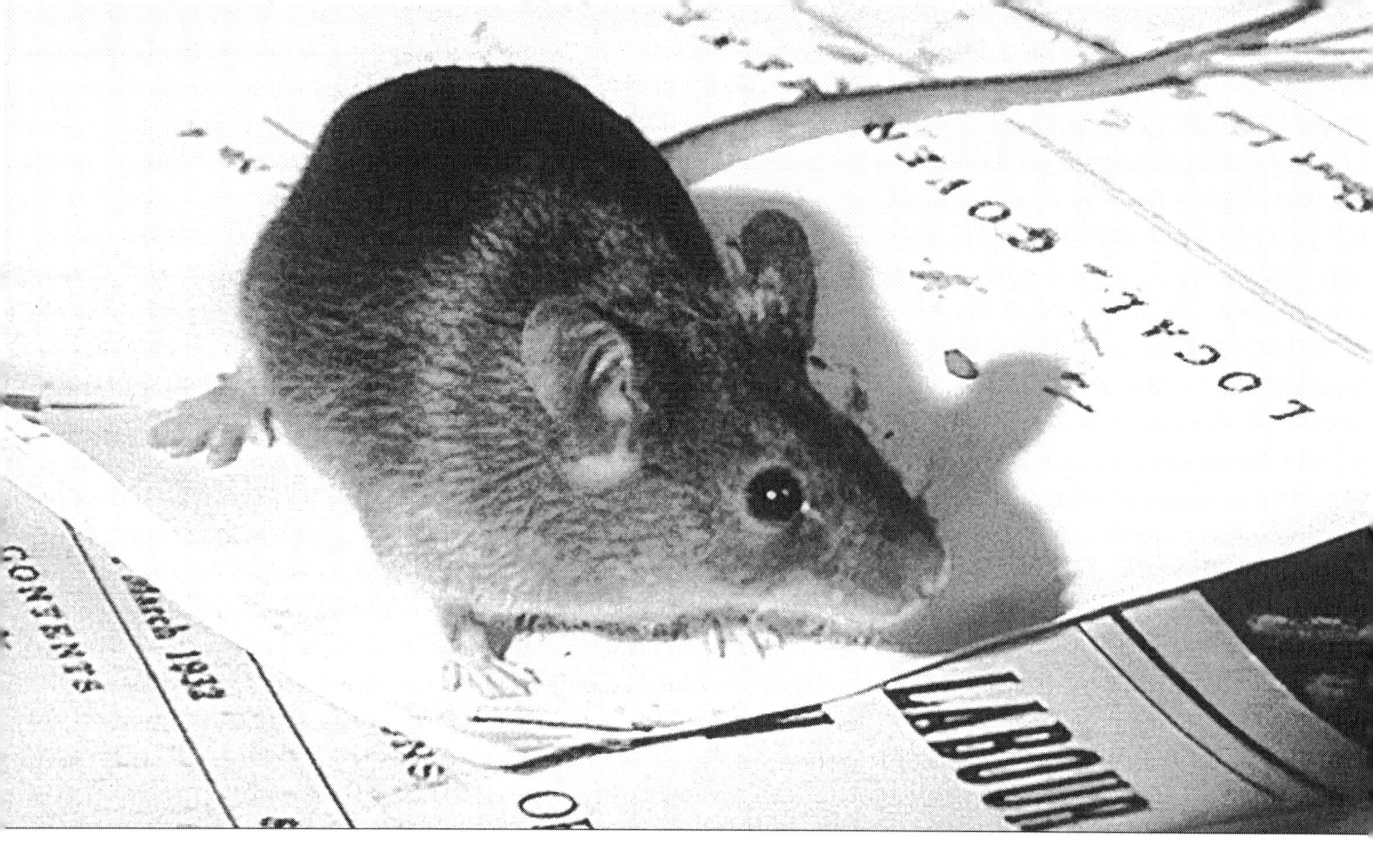

Hickory Dickory Dock (1995)

Dropping the foreign students and focusing too much on mice drains tension from this hostile hostel

Fidelity to text

Ch-ch-ch-changes galore: the plot, characters, subplots, motivations, relationships, and how one of the murders is committed. Plus mice.

Quality of movie

It looks good but feels wrong, like eating vegan "cheese" when you could be enjoying a nice slab of Stinking Bishop. Also, mice everywhere!

All the previous episodes of *Poirot* adapted stories and novels written prior to or during WWII. Changing the setting to the 1930s didn't matter much.

Hickory Dickory Dock, however, was published in 1955. It mirrors the times. One student, a Communist, refers to the American witch hunts. Since that wasn't an issue in 1935, the subplot was dropped without causing a problem.

The problem was the student hostel, providing housing for international students from around the world. They vanished in the adaptation, whitewashed out of existence.

You can complain about Agatha's characterizations of Mr. Akibombo, West African student, and the other diverse students from Jamaica, India, Egypt, France, and so on. But she didn't pretend they didn't exist or deny them a right to an education.

This film does. Cambridge and Oxford were admitting students from India before 1900. By 1930, at least 1,800 Indian students alone attended universities in Britain, including many in London. It was a requirement if they wanted to enter the Indian civil service, or professions back home such as the law, police, engineering, and medicine. Britain was ambivalent about educating non-British citizens of the Empire, but not to the degree this episode implies.

When Mr. Akibombo got disappeared along with the other foreign students (except Sally Finch, hot American brunette), so did many of the novel's plot points.

At least they kept Miss Lemon's sister, Mrs. Hubbard. She's still a widow from Singapore. I'd have liked to have seen more of her and less of mice running rampant in the hostel. I can't believe any sister of Miss Lemon would permit free-ranging vermin.

Mrs. Nikoletis, the Greek owner of the youth hostel, gets a major rewrite. She's much more active in the smuggling business, giving away the major subplot within the first ten minutes. Instead of apparently dying from a fall due to drunkenness (which kept motivations unclear), she's stabbed. This wouldn't normally be a problem (so much more dramatic!) except that she loses her secret daughter in the rewrite.

The daughter is Valerie Hobhouse. She was turned into a fashion student instead of a buyer for a beauty

Sally Finch
(*Paris Jefferson*),
the American student

(*Jonathan Firth*),
the history student

Leonard Bateson
(*Damian Lewis*),
the medical student

Valerie Hobhouse
(*Elinor Morriston*),
the fashion student

Florence Hubbard
(*Sarah Badel*),
the hostel warden

Mrs. Nicoletis
(*Rachel Bell*),
the hostel owner

salon and accessory boutique. As a buyer, she traveled around the continent, easily concealing her smuggling activities. Living in the hostel overseen by her mother (no one knew their relationship) meant she could supervise the operation.

Another major issue is that in the novel, Valerie knew her mother was a lush. It wasn't exactly a surprise when her mother fell in the gutter, hit her head, and died. But when she learned her mother fell as a result of morphine-laced brandy, Valerie got angry. She knew she was going to jail for smuggling. She no longer cared, not as long as she could ensure her mother's murderer went to the gallows.

That vanished in the adaptation. Valerie has no reason to care about Mrs. Nikoletis so why should she care about the murderer's fate? She doesn't and we lose a heartbreaking scene.

Patricia got rewritten. She's a few years older than Nigel Chapman and crazy about him in a maternal, motherly way. In the book, she's constantly after him to reconcile with his father and straighten up his act. She makes excuses about him to anyone who'll listen. Here, she turns into a same-age political junkie who discovers by accident Nigel's hidden past.

Nigel lost most of his complexity. He stopped being the smartest person in the room (in his own mind). Nigel should be superior, overconfident, annoying, smug, and too clever for his own good. He became just another student. It was Nigel who stole the morphine — and two other drugs — to prove he could, not Colin.

The sole reason to make Colin steal the drugs was to tart up the plot. He's a psychology student, not a psychology patient. I couldn't buy him stealing drugs from the pharmacy where Celia works. He's presumably smart enough to know that she, the junior person on staff, would get blamed when the morphine went missing.

Sally Finch transformed from an American student into a junior spy working for the excise and customs bureau as an undercover agent. She claims to be studying (on a Fulbright scholarship, which didn't exist in 1935) English poetry. Poirot quickly figures out she's lying when he quotes Shelley, and she thinks it's Keats.

Replacing Inspector Sharpe with Chief Inspector Japp made sense. He's part of the show's ensemble. I could accept Mrs. Japp being away so he's on his own, leaving dirty dishes in the sink and (badly) ironing his shirts.

I couldn't accept how his relationship with Poirot was handled. Once again, Japp became stupid because the plot demanded it. He and Poirot have known each other for years. So why did Japp not know that Poirot overheated his flat? Why did he have problems with Poirot's cooking? Poirot's cooked for him plenty of times. They've even dined together in restaurants. We get a scene in the fancy butcher where Japp's horrified by the cost of meat and asks for scrag ends. That's the cheapest part of a lamb or sheep's neck. A man who's poor enough to eat that cut isn't going to turn his nose up at meaty pig trotters, as prepared by Poirot, gourmet chef. Japp would cheerfully eat them.

To add insult on insult, we're forced to watch Japp misunderstand the function of Poirot's bidet and use it to wash his face. Again, he's a longtime friend of Poirot and a frequent visitor. This was idiotic.

The entire Japp-as-a-hapless-bachelor scenario set us up for a tasteless closing scene involving faggots (British meatballs made from pork offal, similar to scrapple) and spotted dick (steamed pudding with raisins).

Then there were the mice. Everywhere. The hostel is infested. Scene after scene of circus-quality trained mice scampering through specially-built mouse-sized sets. Why mice? Because the scriptwriter fixated on the nursery rhyme. In the novel, it's minimal. The hostel is on Hickory Street and Nigel twists the rhyme to

Hickory, Dickory Dock
The mouse ran up the clock
The police said "boo"
I wonder who
Will eventually stand in the dock?

Time that could have been spent on characterization and plot was wasted watching mice run along drain pipes and under floorboards. The mouse makes a final appearance, running up the grandfather clock, while Poirot is summing up the case with the aid of Miss Lemon. Where is Miss Lemon's Siamese cat when you need him? Snap, snap! Yum, yum!

General Information

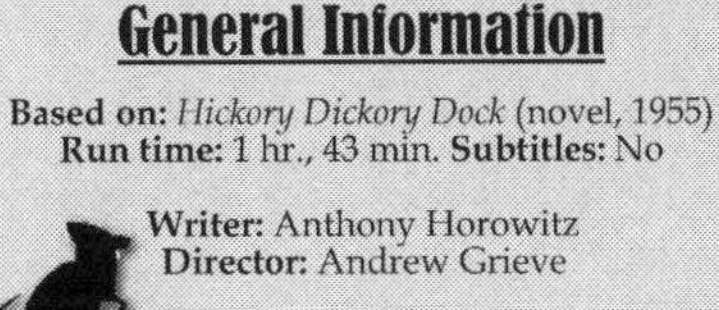

Based on: *Hickory Dickory Dock* (novel, 1955)
Run time: 1 hr., 43 min. **Subtitles:** No

Writer: Anthony Horowitz
Director: Andrew Grieve

Cast

David Suchet as Hercule Poirot
Philip Jackson as Chief Inspector Japp
Pauline Moran as Miss Lemon
Sarah Badel as Florence Hubbard

Paris Jefferson as Sally Finch
Jonathan Firth as Nigel Chapman
Damian Lewis as Leonard Bateson
Gilbert Martin as Colin McNabb
Elinor Morriston as Valerie Hobhouse
Polly Kemp as Patricia Lane
Jessica Lloyd as Celia Austin
Rachel Bell as Mrs. Nicoletis
Granville Saxton as Mr. Casterman

Film Locations

Morden Underground Station, Morden, Surrey (Hickory Road Underground Station)
Former St Paul's Choir School, Carter Lane, London (Hickory Road hostel exterior)
Brushfield Street, Spitalfields, London (Georgis Nicolets' shop)
Charterhouse Square, Clerkenwell, London (Whitehaven Mansions)
University College London, Bloomsbury, London (library)
Brompton Cemetery, London (funeral)

Murder on the Links (1996)

A fearful man seeking help vanishes and Poirot risks his mustache to solve the case while Hastings falls in love

There's plenty to enjoy here as long as you don't believe golf is a good walk spoiled *and* you can accept characters being idiots because the script tells them to. Otherwise, you'll be trapped in one of those sandy bunkers.

The Murder on the Links (1923) was Agatha's second Poirot novel and her third book. She's growing as a writer, working out the tropes, and you can see her evolve a steadily surer hand in planting clues. This novel was also one of two directly inspired by a real crime (the other was *Murder on the Orient Express* which took its inspiration from the kidnapping of the Lindbergh baby). In this case, it was a French crime of the century involving Marguerite Steinheil, adventuress, and my word did that woman live a life of high drama. She got away with murder too, maybe because she had lovers in high places who fixed the trial.

The film opens with newsreel footage of a dramatic murder. If you're paying close attention, this scene may give the game away early. Ten years later, we're in a French train station. Poirot looks around and deduces exactly what kind of holiday Hastings has arranged. It's clear from the crowds around them that Deauville in 1936 is not the place Poirot would have ever chosen. His idea of exercise is a stroll along the boulevard while putting his little gray cells through their paces. Deauville is — based on the numerous tennis rackets, golf club bags, and bicycles — dedicated to *lé sport*. There's also serious swimming (marvel at that swimming facility; my local YMCA never looked that good) both in pools and in the frigid English Channel (in May!). Since plenty of English citizens roam the streets of Deauville, expect equestrian activities and cricket in the surrounding countryside. Sweat will be involved, something Poirot abhors. Watch Hastings dissemble about his ulterior motives and be easily seen through by the master.

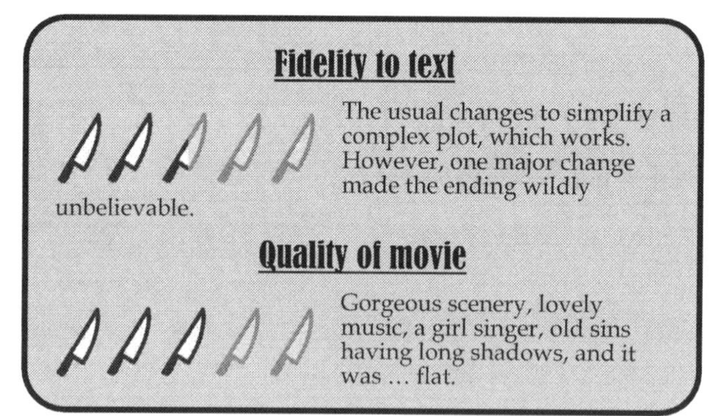

Fidelity to text

The usual changes to simplify a complex plot, which works. However, one major change made the ending wildly unbelievable.

Quality of movie

Gorgeous scenery, lovely music, a girl singer, old sins having long shadows, and it was ... flat.

We meet the Renauld family. Paul, the patriarch, is in danger and asks Poirot for help. We, the audience, saw that newsreel but Poirot has not, so we already know Paul has a criminal past. I'm still undecided if this change helped the film or not. Screenwriter Anthony Horowitz couldn't assume the audience read the book and he had a lot of material to condense and cram into an hour and thirty-four minutes.

The script follows the novel again until we meet

Paul Renauld (*Damien Thomas*), the fearful man

Eloise Renauld (*Diane Fletcher*), the distraught wife

Jack Renauld (*Ben Pullen*), the resentful stepson

Marthe Daubreuil (*Sophie Linfield*), the anxious fiancée

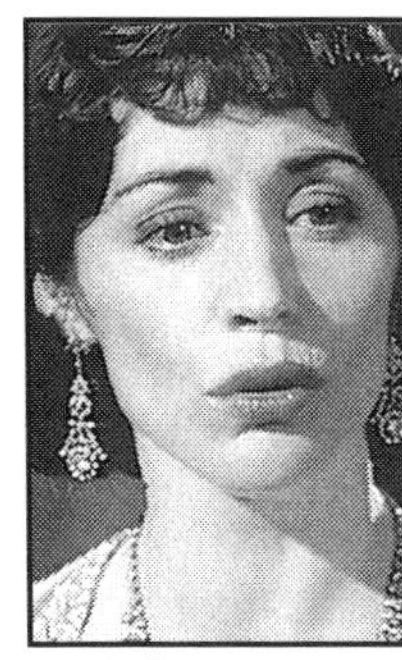

Bella Duveen (*Jacinta Mulcahy*), the torch singer

Giraud (*Bill Moody*), Poirot's arrogant rival

Isabel (Bella) Duveen. In the novel, Captain Hastings meets this self-named Cinderella on the train. She's a flapper (the novel is set in 1923), mouthy, forward, a showgirl (she's an acrobat); everything the good captain finds shocking. She's also a pretty redhead, which he adores. Hastings is deeply conflicted. Cinderella's real name is Dulcie Duveen and, in the novel, she's Bella Duveen's identical twin sister.

In the film, Dulcie is dispensed with altogether, along with her auburn hair and acrobatic skills. Her dramatic scene at the climax unmasking the murderer gets dropped; this despite Deauville being a hotbed of athleticism where she'd fit right in.

Instead, Hastings watches Isabel Duveen sing sad songs on the hotel stage. He's smitten, despite her not being a redhead. Isabel discovers Hastings is involved in investigating the murder of Paul Renauld and she pumps him for clues, which he, overwhelmed, eagerly provides despite how it might contaminate the investigation and he has to lie to Poirot to do it. Why does she take full advantage of Hastings' obsession? In the novel, Isabel (or Bella) has been carrying on an on-off affair with Paul's stepson Jack Renauld. There's confusion over who actually murdered Paul Renauld (who was Paul's father in the novel but there was a lot of time shifting so we'll let that pass).

Why does this matter? Because in the novel, Bella and Jack are still in love despite his affair with Marthé Daubreuil. They're both ready to face the guillotine in order to save the other. Poirot solves the case, true love triumphs and the estranged lovers, having proved their devotion to each other, are reunited. Our Man Hastings, after various travails, runs off to Argentina with Bella's twin sister, Dulcie Duveen, redheaded acrobat. He makes a few more appearances in future Poirot novels but Agatha got what she wanted: a legitimate reason to make Hastings disappear until she needed him for plot purposes.

General Information

Based on: *The Murder on the Links* (novel, 1923)
Run time: 1 hr., 34 min. **Subtitles:** No

Writer: Anthony Horowitz
Director: Andrew Grieve

Cast

David Suchet as Hercule Poirot
Hugh Fraser as Hastings
Bill Moody as Giraud
Bernard Latham as Bex

Diane Fletcher as Eloise Renauld
Damien Thomas as Paul Renauld
Ben Pullen as Jack Renauld
Kate Fahy as Bernadette Daubreuil
Sophie Linfield as Marthe Daubreuil
Jacinta Mulcahy as Bella Duveen
Terence Beesley as Stonor
Andrew Melville as Dr. Hautet
Henrietta Voigts as Leonie
James Vaughan as Adam Letts
Richard Bebb as News Commentator
Belinda Stewart-Wilson as Dubbing Secretary
Simon Holmes as Projectionist
Ray Gatenby as Station Master
Randal Herley as Judge
Peter Yapp as Lawyer
Terry Raven as Tramp
Margaret Clifton as Concierge
Tim Berrington as Golfer
Howard Lee as Golfer
Christopher Hammond as Policeman

Film Location

Hôtel Barrière Le Normandy, Deauville, France (hotel golf exterior)

In the film, there's only Bella Duveen. She's estranged from Jack (sensible girl) but she's still got strong feelings for him. They are strong enough that she's ready to meet the guillotine to save him. He, in turn, is ready to die to save her. This is despite the fact that Jack's carrying on with the girl next door, Marthé Daubreuil, to the point of marriage. And, at the same time Bella's trying to save that cad Jack, she is falling in love with Hastings!

I can accept Hastings falling madly in love with Bella Duveen, despite her not being a redhead. I cannot accept that Bella, estranged from Jack for what seem to be very good reasons, is willing to die to save him and then, when he's saved, she runs off to Argentina with another man. I could accept her leading Hastings on in order to save Jack, but if she's going to do that, she also needs to reconcile with Jack.

This did not make any sense. Jack wants to marry Marthé yet Bella's still carrying enough of a torch to save him by lying about a murder she did not commit but then she turns around and spurns him? Really? Really? This is characters behaving stupidly because the plot demands it. I expect better from a writer of Anthony Horowitz's stature. He knows how to plot.

Other than not acknowledging how many servants — including a cook — it takes to run a mansion like the Renauld's, everything else worked pretty well. The verbal sparring between Poirot and the French detective, M. Giraud, was sharp and funny. M. Giraud is no Poirot fan, and he can't understand why he should let some foreign amateur mess up his crime scene. They make a bet as to who will solve the crime, followed by a lovely scene when you're sure Poirot has conceded victory to his rival.

The time changes, location changes, even the addition of the bicycle race are all competently handled. M. Giraud, despite bad dubbing, steals every scene. But in the end, the film remains … a bit flat.

Maybe more sparkle would have let me accept Bella Duveen acting like an idiot. No, probably not. If you don't know the novel, you may be able to swallow Bella Duveen's self-sacrifice followed immediately by her choosing another man. I couldn't.

Dumb Witness (1996)

In this improved version of the novel, nemesis on four legs shows Poirot the truth behind a woman's death

I like boats, I like dogs, I like snappy dialog, I like seeing fine, upstanding Englishmen and women parade their xenophobia while congratulating themselves on being open-minded, and I like loopy spiritualists. *Dumb Witness* has them all.

Bob became a major character. In the novel, Bob thinks and acts within the constraints of his doggy nature. As the narrator, Hastings interprets for him.

In the film, Bob doesn't need an interpreter. He tells Poirot exactly what's going on. He shows Poirot how he plays with his ball on the stairs and then — what a good dog — puts it away afterwards. He doesn't leave his toys lying around as tripping hazards. Bob shows Poirot how mirrors work, helping him realize the truth of what Wilhelmina saw. Bob's in almost every scene, and with a cock of his ear, the cute furball steals the show.

And, as a reward for being such a good dog, he gets a new furever home with the loopy Tripp sisters. Their beloved Springer Spaniel who'd crossed the rainbow bridge years before recommends Bob to them. Or so says Poirot.

Bob's fate is why I can't get worked up about Dr. Grainger's murder (which wasn't in the novel). His role in the adaptation was substantially beefed up, including turning him into Wilhelmina's suitor. It's always pleasant to see that people over the age of 30 can be permitted to love. However, Dr. Grainger

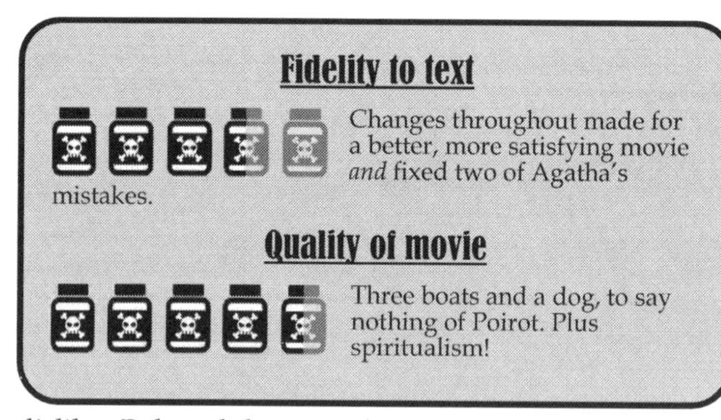

Fidelity to text

Changes throughout made for a better, more satisfying movie *and* fixed two of Agatha's mistakes.

Quality of movie

Three boats and a dog, to say nothing of Poirot. Plus spiritualism!

dislikes Bob and threatens him with death if Poirot doesn't take him in. Bad doctor! He deserved being gassed in Bob's place.

The script fixed two of — dare I say it? — Agatha's errors. Error #1 was her idea that someone can hammer a nail into the baseboard in the middle of the night, unheard by anyone other than Wilhelmina, followed by a quick coat of varnish to disguise the shiny metal. Um, no. A hammer on a nail will wake everyone up, including Bob, and the pungent odor of varnish will irritate them.

The solution here, and it was almost perfect, was to use a screwdriver to start a hole and then screw in a pre-painted screw-eye. Quiet and unobtrusive. Except that the scriptwriter is unfamiliar with home repairs or carpentry. A screwdriver would have twisted the wood. The murderer should have used a gimlet to bore the starter hole. They're silent, fast, and every hardware store carries them. They come in sizes, to match the screw sizes. Every toolbox had a set and still should today.

Wilhemina Lawson (*Norma West*), the browbeaten friend

Emily Arundell (*Ann Morrish*), the rich matriarch

Charles Arundell (*Patrick Ryecart*), the wastrel nephew

Theresa Arundell (*Kate Buffery*), the greedy niece

Dr. Jacob Tanios (*Paul Herzberg*), the foreign husband

Bella Tanios (*Julia St. John*), the downtrodden wife

Error #2 concerns the brooch with the incriminating initials. No one wears a brooch on their dressing gown. It would feel like putting on a tiara for bed. A monogrammed dressing gown, however, is exactly what the well-dressed midnight stalker would wear. It says, "I can afford something fashionable and personalized." Like gimlets, they're sold everywhere.

Charles Arundell evolved from a wastrel with no visible means of support to a wastrel with a very expensive and dangerous hobby, supported by his rich Aunt Emily. He attempts to set water speed records in a powerboat. His latest record-setting try opens the movie and ends when his engine catches fire, forcing him to swim for it. I wondered if the dripping fuel line was a plot point, but it was only poor maintenance. Giving Charles a watery grave to pour money into made him a more interesting, desperate character than just another cad.

The story is rich in boats. In addition to Charles' vintage speedboat, there's the pace boat with timing officials and a rescue team on board and a handsome wooden rowboat for Charles and his sister, Theresa, to row across the lake to break into Aunt Emily's house.

Astonishingly, despite the presence of speedboats, Hastings doesn't get a chase scene across the lake. It seems like every *Poirot* episode involving modes of transportation ends in one. But he still plays a role because Charles turns out to be yet another of his friends. Hastings and Poirot attend the speed trial and meet Emily before she falls down the stairs. Fearing for her life, she asks Poirot for advice. He suggests she rewrite her will and tell the family they're not getting a penny. Her murder gives Poirot an additional reason to find the killer. He feels guilty.

Dr. Jacob Tanios gets his character beefed up into exactly the kind of foreigner good Englishmen and women distrust. Despite being a doctor, he can't practice in England. Worse, according to his wife Bella, he's abusive. She's afraid of him. It's Jacob who gives Emily a bottle of his family's secret, medicinal tonic which she dutifully drinks. Soon thereafter, she dies of poison.

The Tripp sisters are a trip. They're hardcore, loopy spiritualists. They indulge in seances, automatic writing, and channeling spirits from beyond. They're positive they're reaching deep into that undiscovered country and equally sure they know what they're doing, to the point of contacting Emily after her death to find out who killed her. They learn it's Robert Arundell. They decide she meant Bob the dog. Except Bob always puts his toys away and did not cause Emily to fall. Which leads to the question: Who did the Tripp sisters contact?

It's not mentioned in the story, but contacting spirits on the astral plane is a chancy business. The Tripp sisters don't grasp this most basic understanding of the occult. You have no idea who's responding to your call or the accuracy of their answers. A spirit or demon can say whatever they damn well please. They formed their beliefs according to whatever made them happy. They're cheerful, eager to help, and easily convinced, seeing omens and portents everywhere.

The other major change to the story was to Bella. She's an unhappy woman, married to Jacob, a man she is … afraid for? Afraid of? Would like to get rid of? She vacillates and if you're paying attention, you'll notice. In the novel, she's never directly accused of Emily's murder. We never learn what Poirot wrote to her, when he sent her off to hide from Jacob.

That won't work for film. A visual medium requires visual fireworks. Poirot assembles the suspects minus Jacob in Emily Arundell's home. He reviews the evidence and is interrupted by a very angry Jacob. He sees his wife but where are his children? Poirot verbally restrains him, lays out the facts, and it slowly becomes clear who the real villain of the piece was. Bella wanted that money to free herself from an unwanted husband but she was too clever by half. Poisoning a random capsule in the box of liver pills meant she had no control over when Emily swallowed it. Before the new will disinheriting the relatives? Or after? Watch Bella's face. She lost her chance at the money, a relationship with her cousins, her children, and her husband. She lost.

But you won't! Settle in with your good doggy and enjoy the show.

General Information

Based on: *Dumb Witness* (novel, 1937)
Run time: 1 hr., 43 min. **Subtitles:** No

Writer: Douglas Watkinson
Director: Edward Bennett

Cast

David Suchet as Hercule Poirot
Hugh Fraser as Hastings
Geoffrey Freshwater as Sgt. Keeley
Snubby as Bob

Norma West as Wilhemina Lawson
Ann Morrish as Emily Arundell
Patrick Ryecart as Charles Arundell
Kate Buffery as Theresa Arundell
Paul Herzberg as Dr. Jacob Tanios
Julia St. John as Bella Tanios
Tobias Saunders as Alexis Tanios
Layla Harrison as Katya Tanios
Jonathan Newth as Dr. Grainger
Pauline Jameson as Isabel Tripp
Muriel Pavlow as Julia Tripp

Film Locations

Windermere Lakeside station, Lakeside, Cumbria
Broad Leys Lodge, Windermere, Cumbria (racing scenes and boathouse)
Keswick, Cumbria (town)
The Old Police Station, Hawkshead (police station)
St. John's Church, Keswick, Cumbria (funeral)
Bishop's House, Keswick (Dr. Tanio's home)
Tarn Hows Cottage (Theresa's home)
Hammerhole, Graythwaite Estate (Tripps' home)

The Murder of Roger Ackroyd (2000)

Poirot returns from cancellation, but in an episode that altered Christie's great work for the worse

Fidelity to text

The overall arc remains but oh, my God! Losing minor characters is understandable but adding a murder and completely rewriting the ending is not.

Quality of movie

The ending was ridiculous. Characters did things for no reason other than because the plot said so. But the scenery, settings, and costumes look great.

In 1996, Poirot solved his last case. After *Dumb Witness*, London Weekend Television canceled the series due to declining ratings. But that wasn't Poirot's last case. In 1999, the American A&E network put up the money for more *Poirots*.

But which one should they start with? Three years had passed. Audiences needed to be reintroduced to Poirot as — gasp! — they'd moved on to watching other must-see TV *and* they needed an explanation for the gap in time.

Roger Ackroyd filled both needs. It was a blockbuster novel everyone had heard of *and* it began with Poirot's retirement to the village of King's Abbot to grow vegetable marrows.

So far, so good.

But *The Murder of Roger Ackroyd* was going to be a tough novel to film. Its groundbreaking solution made Agatha's reputation and still stuns readers today. When Dear Daughter read *Roger* for our annotation project, she screamed when she read the last page. She'd been completely fooled, just like Agatha intended. She ranted for days about how she'd been bamboozled. When she went back to the text for proof, she saw how she'd swallowed every red herring and overlooked the real clues.

So many people have read *Roger* and so many mysteries have been written since its publication that it's hard to grasp how genre-shattering it was. These days, an unreliable narrator is as common as zucchinis in August. But in 1926? Not so much.

How do you film a novel that depends on you, dear reader, believing everything the narrator (Dr. Sheppard) tells you in his own voice? We only know what Dr. Sheppard tells us. He's genuinely puzzled by some of the events surrounding Roger Ackroyd's murder. He knows some witnesses are lying, but he doesn't know why. He never lies. He's Hercule Poirot's sidekick in the investigation and so must be trustworthy.

But dear Dr. Sheppard is far more than he seems.

The filmmakers had a choice. They could run with the text, knowing that most of the audience already knew whodunnit. Or, they could rewrite the story for the few viewers who — like Dear Daughter — had *not* read the book and so would not rage at the TV when a classic mystery got tossed into a chemical vat, altering the very structure of its DNA.

Roger Ackroyd (*Malcolm Terris*), the rich industrialist

Dr. Sheppard (*Oliver Ford Davies*), the tinkering doctor

Caroline Sheppard (*Selina Cadell*), the snoopy sister

Flora Ackroyd (*Flora Montgomery*), the poor relation

Ralph Paton (*Jamie Bamber*), the wastral stepson

Ursula Bourne (*Daisy Beaumont*), the secretive maid

Unfortunately, the producers chose option two. They did not trust Agatha's text nor did they trust the audience. They went with the safe choice of removing Dr. Shepherd's first-person narration and had Poirot provide it by entering a locked bank vault, retrieving a journal, and reading from it. They added Chief Inspector Japp to a story that did not need him, thus negating the local constables. Worse, Japp took Dr. Sheppard's place.

It's vital to the story that Dr. Sheppard be Poirot's trusted sidekick. Poirot's trust makes the ending all the more striking.

Adding Japp reduced Dr. Sheppard to just another suspect instead of Poirot's right-hand man.

Diminishing Dr. Sheppard also meant downsizing another major character: his sister, Caroline, who was a proto-Miss Marple. She's a spinster who runs his household, provides him with village gossip, is an acute observer of human nature, and is fascinated by Poirot and the murder. Caroline also has a strong moral code, something that proves vital to the ending.

She's mostly gone, popping up only when the plot demands her presence. Her character is so rewritten that she becomes someone else. Thus, when she drives her brother to the meeting at Ackroyd's chemical factory where Poirot is going to reveal the murder, she waits outside in the car (at Poirot's request) and conveniently discovers Dr. Sheppard's journal and his old service revolver in the glove compartment. She reads the journal, is horrified, and then takes it and the gun inside to her brother.

What? Why does she need the revolver? And why is there a gun in a story that had none?

You may not recall a chemical factory in the novel. That was another addition since some producer decided the script needed a climactic chase scene. The Kempton Waterworks and Steam Museum provides wonderful eye-candy in early scenes with Roger, his secretary, Geoffrey Raymond, and Roger's ne'er-do-well stepson, Ralph Paton. It looks exactly like the kind of dark, satanic mill William Blake (1757-1827) railed against. Dr. Sheppard disapproves of it too.

Naturally, they wanted to use the factory as much as possible. Thus, we get the completely rewritten ending that tossed every remaining shred of the novel into one of those giant chemical vats. Poirot assembles everyone in Roger's office and lectures them. He then states that Japp will be arresting the suspect … the next day!

What? Japp would refuse. Scotland Yard doesn't give suspects a head-start to escape justice. They arrest the suspect on the spot.

The other suspects file out of the room but Dr. Shepherd remains to verbally spar with Poirot. Caroline comes charging in and shows him the contents of her bag, containing his journal and his revolver.

Why does she do this? Does she want him to shoot Poirot and Japp? Does she want him to shoot himself? Or does she want him to take hostages so he can flee the country? We are given no reason other than she's his sister. Meaningful glances don't mean a thing when you know nothing about that person or their motivation.

Dr. Sheppard delivers his villain's monologue (bwa ha ha ha!), seizes the revolver from Caroline's bag, flees the room, and shoots at Poirot and Japp as they follow. He flees into the chemical factory, presumably filled with workers and volatile chemicals (although we don't see them).

Poirot and Japp pursue and Caroline is once again disappeared. Japp counts shots, knowing Dr. Sheppard will run out of bullets. He's a lousy shot, somehow not only missing Poirot and Japp every time, but also managing to miss any of the unlucky workers and the huge vats of highly explosive chemicals that should never be mixed.

It's a wonder the factory didn't blow up and kill them all and put the audience out of its misery.

Then we're back at the beginning. Poirot is at his bank, storing Dr. Sheppard's journal and observing how his retirement showed him the countryside is just as steeped in murder as the city.

What? Considering how many murders Poirot solved in quaint country villages, this observation shows growing vegetable marrows turned his brain into squash. Worse, he tells us the case will be marked unsolved as a favor to his friend.

Um, no. We know Dr. Sheppard did it. We've got his journal telling us. He confessed his crimes to Poirot, Japp, and his sister, all of whom are unimpeachable witnesses. How will they explain Sheppard's death, in front of witnesses, to the residents of King's Abbot? An industrial accident?

The film is a great-looking mess and maybe that's enough for you. It wasn't for me.

General Information

Based on: *The Murder of Roger Ackroyd* (novel, 1926)
Run time: 1 hr., 39 min. **Subtitles:** No

Writer: Clive Exton **Director:** Andrew Grieve

Cast

David Suchet as Hercule Poirot
Philip Jackson as Chief Inspector Japp
Gregor Truter as Inspector Davis

Oliver Ford Davies as Dr. Sheppard
Selina Cadell as Caroline Sheppard
Vivien Heilbron as Mrs. Cecil Ackroyd
Malcolm Terris as Roger Ackroyd
Flora Montgomery as Flora Ackroyd
Jamie Bamber as Ralph Paton
Daisy Beaumont as Ursula Bourne
Nigel Cooke as Geoffrey Raymond
Roger Frost as Parker
Rosalind Bailey as Mrs. Ferrars

Film Locations

Castle Combe, Wiltshire (village)
Engine House, Kempton Waterworks (factory)
Kit's Close, Fawley, Buckinghamshire (Ackroyd's home)
Victoria House, Bloomsbury, London (newspaper)

Lord Edgware Dies (2000)

The *Poirot* gang reunites in this masterful adaptation of disguises, divorce, detectives, and dukes

Fidelity to text

Events are rearranged, Jane Wilkinson impersonates Lady Macbeth, and a thieving butler leads our gang on a fatal chase, but almost everything important is there.

Quality of movie

I'd have given it another half-dagger but with no subtitles, I couldn't understand some of the witty banter. Otherwise, this movie fired on all cylinders with very few missteps.

Despite the lengthy hiatus between the end of the *Poirot* TV series in 1996 and the start of sporadic movies in 2000, cast, script, director, settings, and music all came together here as though they'd never been separated by the vagaries of TV ratings and running out of money. Ignore the travesty of the first movie bringing back Poirot in 2000: *The Murder of Roger Ackroyd*. Pretend it doesn't exist and watch the stellar Japanese or Russian versions.

After rebooting the series with *Roger Ackroyd*, the producers next chose to film — for mysterious reasons — *Lord Edgware Dies*. With a thoughtful script, any of the remaining, unfilmed novels (or the criminally neglected short story "The Lemesurier Inheritance") would have sufficed. The various production companies never followed Agatha's own timeline. Lucky for us, unlike *Roger Ackroyd*, *Edgware's* script by Anthony Horowitz was excellent.

One of the additions to Agatha's plot showed Poirot moving back into Whitehaven Mansions. He'd previously reunited — in idiotic fashion — with Chief Inspector Japp in *Roger Ackroyd*. Hastings and Miss Lemon were handled far more skillfully.

Our man Hastings returned to England because he lost his ranch in Argentina due to his incompetent financial management. Are you surprised? It's perfectly in keeping with his nature. Sadly, we don't get to meet Bella again, the woman he met and suspected of murder in *Murder on the Links* and then married. She's back in Argentina trying to sell the ranch.

During Poirot's retirement, Miss Lemon apparently did not open either a secretarial and filing school or a detective agency, both of which she would run efficiently. That's a pity because Miss Lemon (Pauline Moran) has the wattage and acting chops to headline a great TV series about a lady detective in the 1930s. Instead, she stayed home with her adopted Siamese cat she rescued in *The Adventure of the Italian Nobleman*.

The scenes showing the gang settling back together demonstrated genuine warmth, culminating in Japp at the welcome home dinner saying all they needed was a body.

Which showed up the next morning right on schedule. Lord Edgware's body, to be precise.

Because Horowitz restructured Agatha's novel, we

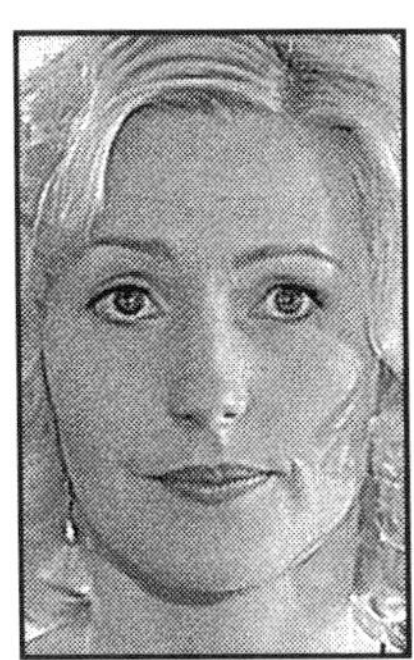
Jane Wilkinson (*Helen Grace*), the ambitious wife

Lord Edgware (*John Castle*), the unhappy peer

Carlotta Adams (*Fiona Allen*), the impersonator

Bryan Martin (*Dominic Guard*), the jealous lover

Geraldine Marsh (*Hannah Yelland*), the hateful daughter

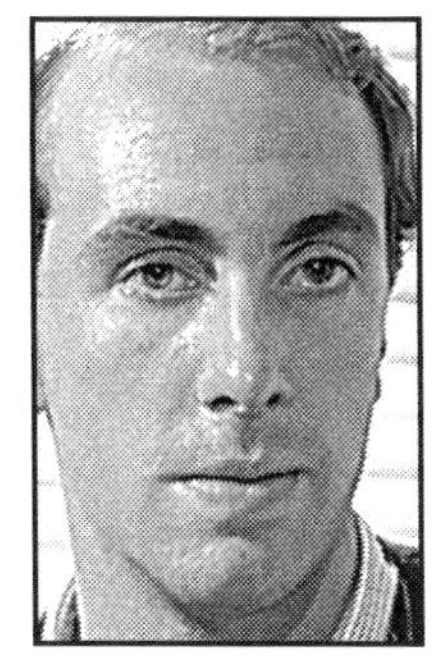
Ronald Marsh (*Tim Steed*), the inheriting nephew

had already met and disliked Lord Edgware. He sat in his private theater box, watching his estranged wife, Jane Wilkinson, perform as Lady Macbeth. According to everyone who knows Edgware, he's a nasty piece of work.

It was an interesting choice to open with *Macbeth*. If you made it through English class in high school, you know that Lady Macbeth is a nasty piece of work herself. Was Horowitz's choice too on the nose?

I'd say no, because every character who knows Jane Wilkinson tells Poirot that she's a nasty piece of work. And, who's the most likely person to murder a man? His wife, especially if she's estranged from him, desperate to get single, and marry her newly found true love.

Yet poor, maligned, obvious suspect Jane Wilkinson couldn't have murdered hubby because a dozen unimpeachable witnesses say she was nowhere near the scene of the crime. Agatha threw down that gauntlet for the reader and Horowitz ran with it.

Where the script fell down was in building up motivations. Not enough time was spent deciphering the relationships between Carlotta Adams (professional impersonator), Bryan Martin (Jane's costar and former lover), Penny Driver (millinery genius and Bryan's second chance at love), Ronald Marsh (deeply-in-debt theater impresario and Lord Edgware's drunken nephew and heir), Geraldine Marsh (Edgware's only child and my but she hated daddy but she's got eyes for her alcoholic cousin, Ronald, proving daddy was right that she didn't inherit any brains), Alton the butler (who's a thief), Miss Carroll (Edgware's adoring secretary for no discernible reason), and Donald Ross (Irish playwright and aficionado of ancient Troy).

These people's lives are intertwined in the novel but how isn't made clear in the film. I could have cheerfully dispensed with the unnecessary chase of a minor red herring through the airport if I learned how everyone knew everyone else. There's clearly bad blood between Jane, Bryan Martin, and Penny Driver.

There's also the Duke of Merton. He needed expanding. This version briefly touched on why Jane needed to be a widow and not a divorcée. The Duke mentions them marrying in Westminster Cathedral (which is Catholic) and not Westminster Abbey (which is Church of England). Poirot picks up on that tidbit immediately. For you non-theology students reading this, devout, practicing Catholics aren't supposed to marry divorcées. Widows are fine.

Yet this script, like the novel and the other two films, never addressed *why* a devout Catholic and defender of the faith like the Duke of Merton is chasing after a married actress. Granted, she's hot and blonde, but she's an actress! She publicly kisses other men for money! By definition, actresses live dissipated lifestyles and even by the 1930s when *Lord Edgware Dies* was written, actresses were not respectable. If the Duke of Merton is serious about his faith, he'd have already married a nice Catholic girl of good family and started fathering lots and lots of children.

Yet he hasn't. Is it because he doesn't actually want to marry and father lots and lots of children? If so, another man's wife — especially another peer like Lord Edgware — is the perfect choice. The Duke of Merton can't marry Jane. She's already got a husband. Thus, he can pursue her (chastely because he's a good Catholic) while at the same time, remain a happy bachelor free from matchmakers. There's a lot to unpack in the Duke of Merton's motivations but alas, they remain obscure. He should count himself lucky Poirot solved the murder, keeping him from making a huge mistake on multiple levels.

The murder weapon got changed too. In the novel, it's a corn knife, used for home surgery on the feet by someone with steady hands and nerves of steel. Instead, Jane uses a run-of-the-mill dagger. In the novel, she knows exactly where to insert the corn knife for nearly instant death. We're not told how Jane learned the correct angle of approach. I wanted to see an actual corn knife in use.

There are great scenes. You'll love watching Lord and Lady Corner arguing about having thirteen at dinner. Jane's the unlucky thirteenth diner, so if superstition is correct, she'll be the next dinner guest to die. There's Carlotta's impersonations, including Poirot! An impeccably clad Miss Lemon gets to go detecting!

You'll thoroughly enjoy this episode. You'll enjoy it enough to watch it twice, which will clarify the snappy dialog you missed the first time around.

General Information

Based on: *Lord Edgware Dies* (novel, 1933)
Run time: 1 hr., 39 min. **Subtitles:** No

Writer: Anthony Horowitz
Director: Brian Farnham

Cast

David Suchet as Hercule Poirot
Hugh Fraser as Hastings
Philip Jackson as Chief Inspector Japp
Pauline Moran as Miss Lemon

Helen Grace as Jane Wilkinson
John Castle as Lord Edgware
Hannah Yelland as Geraldine Marsh
Tim Steed as Ronald Marsh
Fiona Allen as Carlotta Adams
Dominic Guard as Bryan Martin
Deborah Cornelius as Penny Driver
Lesley Nightingale as Miss Carroll
Christopher Guard as Alton
Iain Fraser as Donald Ross
Tom Beard as Duke of Merton

Film Locations

Shoreham Airport, Lancing, West Sussex
The Peacock House, Holland Park, London (Edgware's house exterior)
Two Temple Place, London (Edgware's house interior)
Highpoint I, Highgate, London (Wilkinson's apartment)
Duke's Road, Bloomsbury, London (Driver's shop)
Mount Street Gardens, London (Poirot, Jane in park)
Burlington Arcade, London (jeweler's store)

Evil Under the Sun (2001)

Miscasting and a needless subplot results in a beige adaptation set at Christie's favorite writing retreat

Fidelity to text

Along with the usual changes, Hastings, Miss Lemon, and Japp show up. Miss Lemon works the best, Japp's way out of his jurisdiction, and Hastings sort of works.

Quality of movie

This dragged. Where was the glamour? The witty repartee? The Cole Porter soundtrack? The great boats? Not here.

This version of *Evil* was flat. It dragged. It had no sparkle. Am I saying the Peter Ustinov extravaganza clocking in at one hour and fifty-seven minutes moved faster than this one hour and thirty-eight minutes long slog? Yes, I am. Twenty minutes longer, yet it was better paced and more engaging. It was funnier, it had singing, it had Cole Porter in the background, and most of all, it had serious star power.

Depending on who the character is supposed to be, star power can matter quite a lot. If your central character is an aging, needy movie star who must be in the spotlight, having Diana Rigg play that character adds layers of complexity. You stare at Arlena Stuart Marshall — which she craves! You sense she's not that bright, although she doesn't know it. She's always relied on her looks and sex appeal to get by, but she's getting older. You cringe at the famous, aging movie star foolishly chasing after a younger, married man; oblivious to the presence of her husband and his wife. Diana Rigg was famous, so it's easy to believe Arlena Stuart Marshall was famous.

The actress playing Arlena Stuart here (Louise Delamere) isn't famous. She's pretty enough but she doesn't carry the cultural weight that Diana "Emma Peel" Rigg does, nor does she have the wattage to light up the screen.

Similarly, when you watch *The Mirror Crack'd* (which also centers around a famous, aging movie star), you should watch the 1980 Angela Lansbury version. Elizabeth Taylor plays the aging movie star, and you can absolutely believe a true fan would get out of her sickbed, slap on makeup, and break quarantine to fangirl all over her idol. The actresses in the other two adaptations? Well, no, because they're not Elizabeth Taylor.

But I digress.

This film opens in England with a cyclist discovering a strangled woman in the woods. While she's making her gruesome discovery, the camera keeps cutting back to a sweaty vicar intoning about evil Jezebels. Is there a link? Sort of, but it was badly handled, and we don't find out why until two years later. That's when the sweaty vicar, Rev. Stephen Lane, shows up at the island resort and mutters portentously about evil Jezebels who should get what's coming to

Arlena Stuart Marshall (*Louise Delamere*), the flighty actress

Kenneth Marshall (*David Mallinson*), the cuckolded spouse

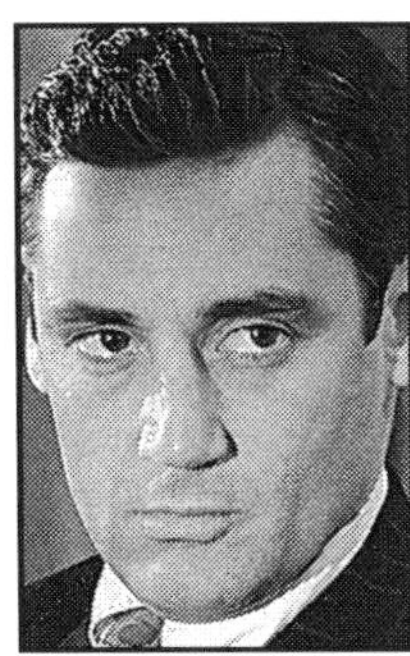
Patrick Redfern (*Michael Higgs*), the straying spouse

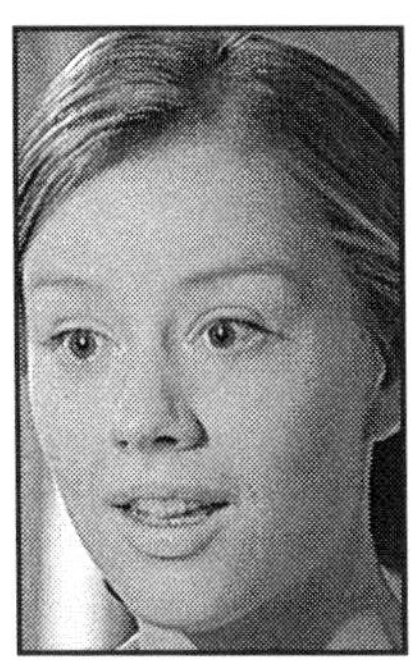
Christine Redfern (*Tamzin Malleson*), the jealous wife

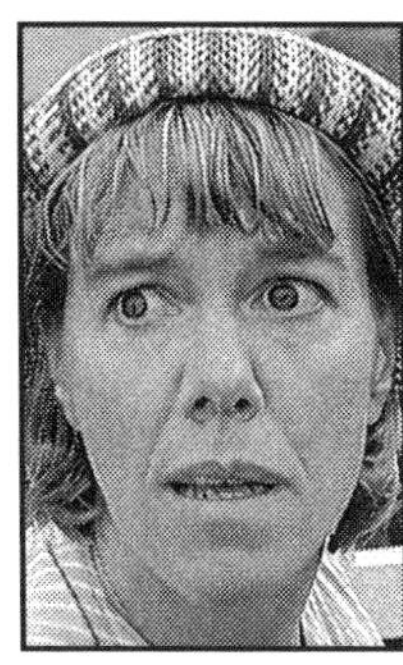
Emily Brewster (*Carolyn Pickles*), the nosy guest

Horace Blatt (*David Timson*), the bluff sailor

them whenever he sees Arlena.

Why does he do this? In a few mumbled sentences he reveals his wife left him for another man. That colored his views so much the vicar can't recognize Arlena's tragedy. Two years have passed since the body in the woods, yet when Poirot and the plot demands it, the vicar is suddenly able to recognize the villain despite seeing him during meals at the resort ever since arriving and *not* recognizing him. The vicar never — because of plot requirements — feels any sympathy for Arlena despite her being strangled.

Hollywood hates Christianity. I understand that many religious leaders, being human, don't live up to what a priest should be. But they are not, by definition, evil and small-minded by virtue of being ministers. Yet here we go again. This was more clumsy writing in a clumsy script. Agatha was never clumsy. Her Rev. Lane showed nuance.

I said two years later? Yep, two years after the body in the woods, Hastings returns to London from Argentina to open a restaurant. Why would he do that? As an investment? There are no cities in Argentina that can support fine dining? This was a clumsy attempt to bring Hastings back from the ranch, yet no mention is made of his wife. I guess she's running the ranch while Hastings loses their life's savings.

Poirot becomes deathly ill at Hastings' restaurant and must retire to the island resort to regain his health. The resort was far more interesting than the plot. It's Burgh Island in the southwest of England. It's an unusual piece of real estate since it's an island only at high tide and connected to the mainland by a causeway at low tide. It uses a sea tractor to transport guests over the water. It's a bizarre contraption Wiley E. Coyote would devise. Think of an open-sided wagon on stilts atop enormous wheels. Agatha stayed at the resort and used the setting for *And Then There Were None* and *Evil Under the Sun*. Seeing the resort she used for the novel was a treat.

Since it's an island, there are a few boats playing important roles in the story. Horace Blatt has a small sailboat. Sometimes his two sails are red and sometimes white. There are also nice plank-built rowboats, suitable for oars or for an outboard motor. That's it for boats.

Poirot and Hastings arrive on the island via the sea tractor and meet the Rev. Lane, Arlena Stuart, and the other suspects. Miss Lemon stays behind to catch up on her filing. There are some amusing scenes of Poirot enduring the doctor-ordered health treatments and suffering through dietary restrictions including drinking glasses of pureed grass clippings. He needs something to enliven his days. Fortunately for Poirot (although not for her) Arlena Stuart gets strangled on the beach of the remote and difficult-to-access Pixie Cove.

A reprieve! Poirot springs into action. Japp arrives too, although he must have flown from London since he arrived so quick. During their investigation, Poirot sends Miss Lemon off to do some sleuthing, unearthing valuable information. Those scenes were excellent. Miss Lemon deserved her own series, where she set up shop as a detective, capturing criminals with the help of her filing system.

Eventually, we reach the explanation of how Arlena was strangled, and it suffers from the same problem as the 1982 film. What's believable in a book isn't believable onscreen. The timing has to be split-second. The villains race around the island like Olympic-level athletes, unnoticed by any of the other hotel guests as they sprint from place to place. I couldn't accept it. It wasn't physically possible to commit murder this way.

Worse, it's not possible that there was no evidence for Japp to find. If Poirot found a small piece of a glass bottle, then where's the rest of it? If Horace Blatt could leave recognizable footprints in the sand at Pixie Cove, then why didn't Arlena's strangulation leave signs of a struggle? Yet the sand was smooth and undisturbed.

I couldn't believe it, and the bland characters didn't get me to care. Stick with the Ustinov film. Despite needing superhero levels of athleticism, it's more plausible and much more fun than this version.

General Information

Based on: *Evil Under the Sun* (novel, 1941)
Run time: 1 hr., 38 min. **Subtitles:** No

Writer: Anthony Horowitz
Director: Brian Farnham

Cast

David Suchet as Hercule Poirot
Hugh Fraser as Hastings
Philip Jackson as Chief Inspector Japp
Pauline Moran as Miss Lemon

Michael Higgs as Patrick Redfern
Tamzin Malleson as Christine Redfern
Louise Delamere as Arlena Stuart Marshall
David Mallinson as Kenneth Marshall
Russell Tovey as Lionel Marshall
Tim Meats as Stephen Lane
Marsha Fitzalan as Rosamund Darnley
Carolyn Pickles as Emily Brewster
Ian Thompson as Major Barry
David Timson as Horace Blatt
Rosalind March as Mrs. Castle
Paul Ready as William
Rebecca Johnson as Gladys Narracott
Roger Alborough as Chief Constable Weston
Jason Davies as Nathan Lloyd
Kenneth Gilbert as Mr. Applegood
Lawrence McGrandles Jr. as Simon Kelso
Grant Gillespie as Jack Lovett
Harriet Eastcott as Librarian

Film Locations

Hambleden Church, Hambleden, Buckinghamshire
St. Mary the Virgin, Hambleden, Buckinghamshire
Frieth Village Hall, Frieth, Buckinghamshire (coroner's court)
Burgh Island, Bigbury-on-Sea, Devon

Murder on the Orient Express (2001)

Agatha's classic retains its power in this updated version that cuts down on the suspects and rumples Poirot

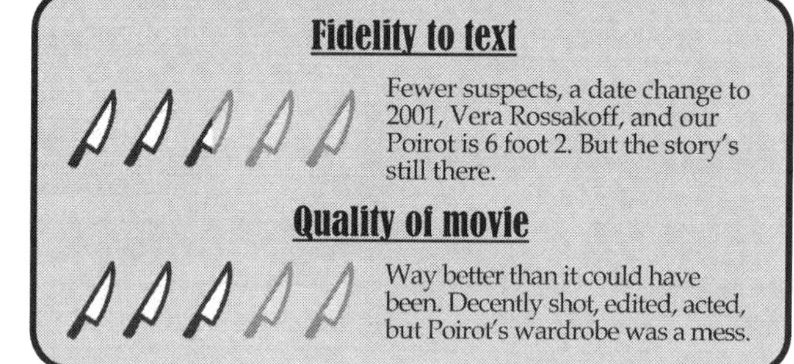

Fidelity to text

Fewer suspects, a date change to 2001, Vera Rossakoff, and our Poirot is 6 foot 2. But the story's still there.

Quality of movie

Way better than it could have been. Decently shot, edited, acted, but Poirot's wardrobe was a mess.

Like Austin Trevor and Peter Ustinov — two other Poirot portrayers — Alfred Molina is a big man. Unlike Trevor and Ustinov, Molina was poorly served by the wardrobe department. Poirot is supposed to be dapper and well-groomed. His shoes are shined, his tie's never askew, his shirts crackle with starch, and there's nary a wrinkle in sight. He's the most formally dressed man around. When the rest of the world gave up waistcoats and pocket watches with fobs, Poirot remained impeccable. This is true whether the movie is set in the 1930s or the 1980s.

Not here. The costumer updated Poirot into a cleaned-up Columbo. From the opening scene with Poirot's tie askew to the sports jacket and ill-fitting pants, the baggy trench-coat, and those lavender socks, Molina's Poirot needed a makeover and an iron.

This had to be a deliberate costume choice. Compare him to Pierre Michel, the conductor, or Herr Bouc, a director of the Orient Express. They're immaculate. When David Suchet took on the role of Poirot, he demanded that wardrobe make him look the part. He turned down a baggy brown suit and got his morning clothes. I don't know why Alfred Molina didn't follow suit.

Does this matter? Yes, it does. When the audience expects a detective renowned for his compulsive fastidiousness and sees someone who's almost a slob, it affects their critical judgment. Molina got marked down in the Poirot rankings because of how he looked. This is a shame, because he made a good Poirot. His acting was fine. He's a head taller than Agatha's description but so were Trevor and Ustinov. Molina's Poirot was observant, willing to badger suspects into revealing vital clues (watch him goad Arbuthnot about Mary Debenham; the man might as well have worn a sign saying "she's mine"), dogged, clever, thorough, patient, and able to reach a conclusion covering all the facts.

But he looked like he dressed in the dark. Even Tony Randall in the dreadful *Alphabet Murders* was perfectly turned out, even in the bowling alley and the steam bath.

This version bookended the plot with Poirot solving a case involving Countess Vera Rossakoff. I didn't have a problem with it. She's not in the novel but she's part of the canon. She's Poirot's Irene Adler, the woman he can't forget despite her being bad for him. She allows the film to introduce Poirot to an unfamiliar

Caroline Hubbard
(*Meredith Baxter*),
the egotist actress

Senora Alvarado
(*Leslie Caron*),
the dictator's widow

Mary Debenham
(*Natasha Wightman*),
the relief worker

Bob Arbuthnot
(*David Hunt*),
the software designer

Tony Foscarelli
(*Dylan Smith*),
the fitness guru

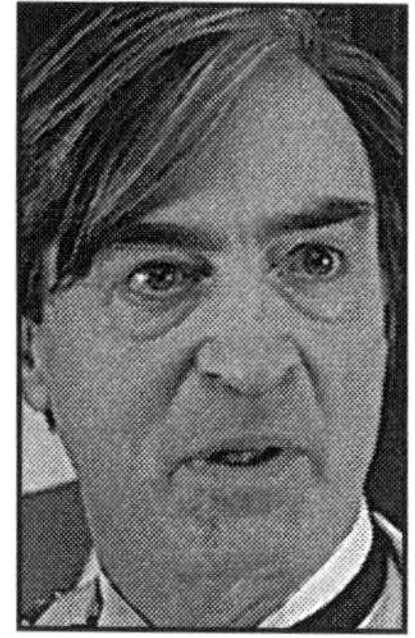

Pierre Michel
(*Nicolas Chagrin*),
the conductor

audience, show off his detecting skills, and set up an ending that permits a sequel.

Poirot's scene with Vera also demonstrates a critical aspect of his character. When Vera's not skirting the law, she oversteps it into full-on criminal behavior. Poirot stands for justice, law and order. He's a policeman. She's a thief and associates with very unsavory people. Her existence in his life tests Poirot's moral code.

This is important because the ending of *Orient Express* requires Poirot to make a critical and difficult decision: Should he let the strictest interpretation of justice prevail? Ratchett was an evil man who directly or indirectly caused the death of four people and devastated the lives of everyone who knew the victims. But he was still murdered in cold blood for revenge. Should his murderers face the justice he escaped? Or should they be permitted to escape justice, since they did what the courts could not do: execute a man who deserved it but got off on a technicality.

In the novel, Poirot must choose between two evils. Letting murderers go free — even praiseworthy ones! — chafes every fiber of his being. Yet that's what he chooses to do. It was not an easy decision. It shouldn't be, because it's the first step down the swift road to vigilante justice.

That's the other reason this movie doesn't succeed. Poirot's scene with Vera sets us up for his agonized decision. Yet when decision-making time comes, there's not a whisper of his concerns about the morality of letting killers go. There should have been, especially since Poirot lectured Vera about adhering to principle. But there was nothing. It weakened the ending. Viewers came away remembering a slob with no moral fiber.

No wonder people don't regard this Poirot outing with kindness.

Yet it's not a bad movie. It's much better than it could have been. The setting was changed from winter to summer but that's because a rock slide is cheaper than filming snow. The updating to 2001 worked surprisingly well. It let the script make jokes about Ross Perot, Brad Pitt, Ron Popeil, and third-tier actresses who portray recurring characters on soap operas. When the VCR ate the tape, Bill was reminded about cleaning tangles of tape out of ours. Instead of knowing every fact about a kidnapping taking place several years before on another continent, this Poirot had to do some research online. Even so, he still depended on his little gray cells to follow the facts to the logical conclusion. What is the difference between reading a story online and reading it in the newspaper? Not much.

The characters were also updated. Instead of being aviators, Armstrong and Arbuthnot are brilliant software designers. Mary Debenham becomes Daisy's tutor. Foscarelli becomes Armstrong's personal trainer. McQueen met Sonia Armstrong through his work at the museum; she's on the board. Probably the least plausible change was making Princess Dragomiroff into a South American dictator's widow.

The script also worked in Agatha Christie references. A character gushes to Poirot about his expert solving of Roger Ackroyd's murder and asks how he realized how the strychnine was administered at Styles. In the epilog, the actress is at a dinner theater in Salt Lake City performing in *The Mousetrap*.

The cast turned in performances ranging from workmanlike to excellent. The critical one is, of course, Mrs. Hubbard. If you can't believe her, it's hard to believe the story. Mrs. Hubbard is Sonia Armstrong's mother and Daisy Armstrong's grandmother in disguise. Meredith Baxter has a grand time playing her as a third-tier celebrity and soap opera actress. She puts Poirot in his place! She doesn't have to listen to *him* just because he's been on TV. She's been there herself! Why is she on the Orient Express? Because she'd been in Istanbul on the set of a new movie about Samson and Delilah. She'd been all set to play the evil high priestess until the producer decided his boyfriend needed the part more. Traveling back to Europe on the Orient Express let her experience the glamour of being a movie star. So there!

Leslie Caron turned in another standout performance as the South American dictator's widow. She's autocratic, disdainful, and like Mrs. Hubbard, won't let some Belgian detective push her around.

This version of *Orient Express* is engaging and often funny. It would have been better with another pass at the script, less Vera, and a finer wardrobe for Poirot. But it's still good enough.

General Information

Based on: *Murder on the Orient Express* (novel, 1934)
Run time: 1 hr., 40 min. **Subtitles:** No

Writer: Stephen Harrigan
Director: Carl Schenkel

Cast

Alfred Molina as Hercule Poirot
Fritz Wepper as Wolfgang Bouc

Peter Strauss as Samuel Ratchett
Meredith Baxter as Mrs. Caroline Hubbard
Leslie Caron as Senora Nina Alvarado
Natasha Wightman as Mary Debenham
Amira Casar as Helena von Strauss
Kai Wiesinger as Philip von Strauss
David Hunt as Bob Arbuthnot
Adam James as William MacQueen
Dylan Smith as Tony Foscarelli
Nicolas Chagrin as Pierre Michel
Tasha de Vasconcelos as Vera Rossakoff
Louis Chamoun as Turk
Jason Croot as Train Guard

Film Locations

Istanbul, Turkey
Leeds, West Yorkshire
Bury, Greater Manchester
Kingston upon Hull, East Riding of Yorkshire

Murder in Mesopotamia (2002)

Poirot chases his Russian countess leaving us less time to explore the mystery of Lovely Louise

Fidelity to text

Hastings stole Amy Leatheran's lines. Countess Vera Rossakoff arose from the sand but for no discernible reason.

Quality of movie

A fascinating archeological dig overshadows what should have been a fascinating excavation of Louise Leidner's personality.

This should have been great. Instead, it was a mess o' pottage, the unsalted kind.

One challenge Agatha routinely faced was how to plot a wife's murder when the most likely suspect is her husband. Her answer here was to postulate two husbands.

Lovely Louise (as she was routinely referred to) was widowed long ago. But did husband Frederick Bosner truly die? Perhaps not. And if he didn't die in that train-wreck, then he must be menacing Louise. It couldn't be her nebbishy, nerdy, nice archeologist second husband. There's also the possibility Bosner's younger brother wants revenge and is behind the threatening letters.

But why should Frederick Bosner (or his brother) be so angry? Bosner was a German spy when he enthralled and married Louise, twenty-year-old daughter of an important American diplomat. The film glosses over who turned him in, but it was Louise. They'd only been married a few months, too, so presumably they were still in the newlywed billing and cooing stage.

Was she that much of a patriot? Maybe not. One of the many, many places where the film failed was in Poirot's reconstruction of Louise Leidner. Her personality — a manipulative charmer who stirs up people so she can enjoy the fireworks — is key to her murder. According to Poirot, Louise married Frederick in haste and repented immediately. He fascinated her, she definitely fascinated him and not just because as an important diplomat's daughter, she got him access to high places. Except marriage involves more than going to parties with a handsome escort. Louise quickly discovered she didn't like being under any man's thumb.

In the novel, but not in the film, Poirot examined her room at the dig and deduced she was an egoist but not a sensualist. That is, pleasure for its own sake didn't ring her bells. It was power; the power to make people jump through hoops for her own cold amusement. Sex was just the tool.

So how to remove an unwanted husband in 1919 without social approbation? By ratting him out as an enemy spy. Louise got what she wanted: her freedom and being adored even more for her selfless patriotism and bravery.

But she quickly learned that she wasn't as free as she thought she was. Whenever she became close to another man, threatening letters arrived. In a way, they became her get-out-of-jail-free card. She could charm

Dr. Leidner (*Ron Berglas*), the archeologist

Louise Leidner (*Barbara Barnes*), the troublesome wife

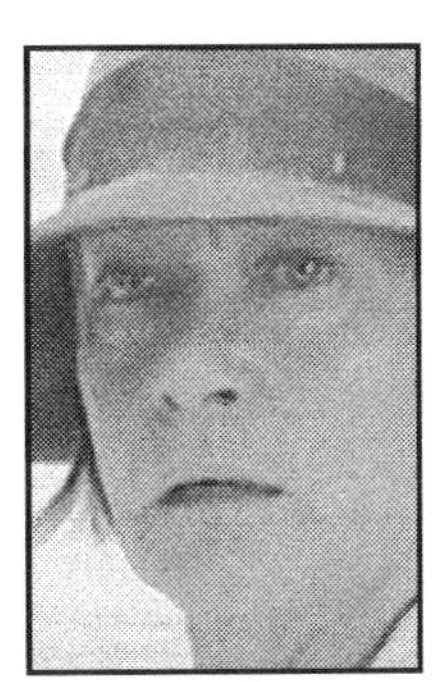

Anne Johnson (*Dinah Stabb*), the loyal assistant

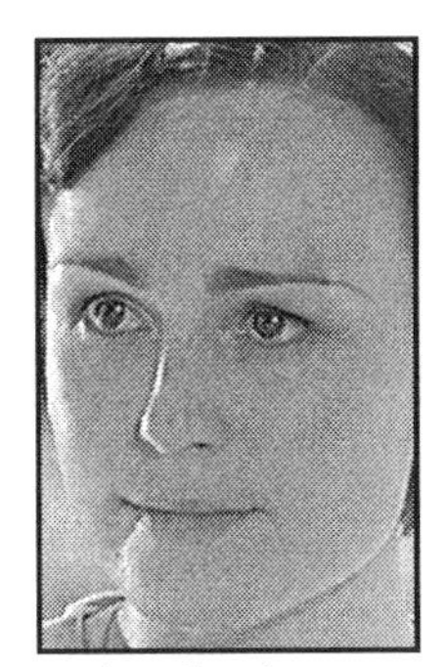

Amy Leatheran (*Georgina Sowerby*), the inquisitive nurse

Father Lavigny (*Christopher Hunter*), the camp priest

Richard Carey (*Christopher Bowen*), the longtime colleague

and seduce and get engaged. A threatening letter would arrive promptly and she'd be able to break off the betrothal.

Then she met Dr. Eric Leidner, Swedish archeologist. Mysteriously, no threatening letters arrived. But after the wedding, she decided Dr. Leidner's best friend and fellow archeologist, Richard Carey, needed to adore her as much as Leidner did. She wasn't planning to seduce him, just enchant him until he couldn't think straight. But she fell in love with him, began the affair, and the threatening letters returned.

That's the setup Poirot and Hastings walk into. Hastings, you say? Why yes. Our man Hastings suddenly – when there had never previously been so much as a rumor of one – has a sister with an adopted nephew the right age as Frederick Bosner's younger brother. Nephew William Coleman is very proud of his Uncle Arthur and has told everyone at the dig all about Uncle Arthur and his dear friend, Poirot.

Almost everything Nurse Amy Leatheran does in the novel is done in the film by Hastings. It's sad. Amy was a fascinating narrator. She's opinionated, professional, doesn't take anyone's guff, becomes Poirot's right hand like a good nurse to a surgeon, and inadvertently reveals her prejudices and misunderstandings. She also falls under Lovely Louise's spell. All gone.

Countess Vera Rossakoff shows up too, wasting valuable screen time Poirot could have spent interviewing witnesses and examining the wreckage surrounding Lovely Louise. Instead, we're forced to watch him quiz the hotel concierge repeatedly: "Do I have a message?" "Did the countess call?" "Has the countess arrived?" What was the point of wasting precious time that could have been spent on the plot? So Poirot could get stuck with Rossakoff's hotel tab.

Admittedly, the novel would be difficult to adapt. Poirot doesn't show up until halfway through, after Lovely Louise gets her head bashed in. It's Nurse Amy's show. But this could have been finessed. Instead of having Hastings drag Poirot to the dig to meet his dear nephew, use the plot but reshuffle the scenes!

Open with the murder. Then have Superintendent Maitland call in Poirot, conveniently in Baghdad on his way someplace else, to solve the murder. Have Poirot interview the witnesses and tell their stories in flashbacks. That way, he learns Lovely Louise's habit of stage-managing the people around her into live entertainment for her own amusement. At the same time, the audience understands Louise and learns why the Baghdad expat community call her an *allumeuse* (or tease).

General Information

Based on: *Murder in Mesopotamia* (novel, 1936)
Run time: 1 hr., 38 min. **Subtitles:** No

Writer: Clive Exton **Director:** Tom Clegg

Cast

David Suchet as Hercule Poirot
Hugh Fraser as Hastings
Iain Mitchell as Superintendent Maitland

Ron Berglas as Dr. Leidner
Barbara Barnes as Louise Leidner
Christopher Bowen as Richard Carey
Dinah Stabb as Anne Johnson
Georgina Sowerby as Amy Leatheran
Pandora Clifford as Sheila Maitland
Christopher Hunter as Father Lavigny
Alexi Kaye Campbell as Joseph Mercado
Deborah Poplett as Mrs. Mercado
Jeremy Turner-Welch as Bill Coleman

Film Location

Oudhna, Tunisia

Since no time is wasted on Rossakoff, time could be spent explaining how Louise could marry a man and not realize – despite the intimacies implied in marriage – that's she's been with this man before. Remember, she was only married to Frederick for a few months. She's not a sensualist. She likes slavish adoration but she doesn't want to get hot and sweaty with her admirers. This implies that while she and Frederick may have been having sex, she was — as a twenty-year-old bride in 1919 — probably laying in the dark and thinking of America. Fast forward fifteen years and she meets Dr. Eric Leidner, well-known Swedish archeologist. He's older, bearded, stooped, a different nationality and skill set, and nothing like the dynamic Frederick.

It's a stretch but considering how idiotic people can be, especially when they're completely self-absorbed, not impossible.

In my scenario, each flashback would reveal another layer of Louise's cruelty and manipulation as well as explain how she ensnared everyone around her. It would have explained why Mrs. Mercado hated Louise. Making Mr. Mercado into a murderer added nothing to the plot and the solution was mishandled. He'd have been better left as a mere drug addict, terrified that Louise would reveal his addiction.

There's also the subplot involving Father Lavigny. It was set up in the movie but then dropped. Hastings asks about plasticine and notices wax adhering to a solid gold drinking cup. And then nothing. Rewriting the script to more closely adhere to the novel — where he was casting fake artifacts to sell — would have fixed the issue. Similarly, Miss Johnson got short shrift as did Richard Carey. They both adored Dr. Leidner for different reasons but not enough of their devotion and guilt showed up.

Murder in Mesopotamia deserved better. This *would* have been better if only the script paid more attention to the novel and its psychological examination of Lovely Louise and less to Hastings and Russian countesses.

Poirot's Failure (R-2002)

(*Neudacha Puaro*)

This Russian adaptation of *Ackroyd* leisurely sets up the surprise climax, while keeping your attention riveted

I've watched three film versions of *The Murder of Roger Ackroyd*, Agatha's groundbreaking novel where she subverts the trusted narrator trope. Like Hastings narrates so many Poirot stories, Dr. Sheppard tells the story in the first person. Like Hastings, Dr. Sheppard acts as Poirot's Watson. We readers believe every word he says because Poirot does too, or so it appears.

How do you film a novel in which the narrator is a liar and has been from the first sentence? Do you trust the audience or do you fall back on rewriting the plot into something conventional? It's bizarre that the production you'd expect to get it right (*Poirot* with David Suchet, written and filmed in English) would be terrible to the point of parody.

Yet the Japanese production, transported to a strange land with an alien culture, did full justice to the novel.

And here we are with the Russian version, transporting Roger and company to another strange land with an alien culture, and they did an even better job.

You won't believe you're in an English village in the late 1920s (houses, clothes, and vegetation all look subtly wrong), yet every aspect of the plot remains. Where it was changed — Dr. Sheppard daydreaming of escape on a cruise ship to nowhere — fits his personality.

Fidelity to text

Virtually every scene is on the screen, down to the dialog. No last-minute changes to motivation either.

Quality of movie

Despite being faithful to the novel, it's never boring or draggy.

I must point out one bit of media that, like the film itself, probably didn't get properly licensed. Each episode opens and closes with the announcement from Orson Welles in the Campbell Playhouse radio version of *Roger Ackroyd* in 1939. I have no idea why the Russian filmmakers did this, other than as a nod to Agatha. That might be why Caroline is seen reading an Agatha Christie novel. Maybe it's an in-joke, a piece of Russian weirdness, but it's distracting in an otherwise flawless film.

Like the novel, the film opens with Dr. Sheppard. He's sitting in his workshop in the wee hours of the night. He looks tired and defeated, as he writes down the events of the day. His thoughts drift back and forth as he decides in what order to tell the tragic story of his friend Roger's murder, then settles on the suicide of Mrs. Ferrars as a suitable starting point. He remembers seeing her speak to Ralph Paton, his friend and Roger's adopted stepson. Mrs. Ferrars is obviously upset and soon, the doctor is called to her bed, where she lies dead from a Veronal overdose.

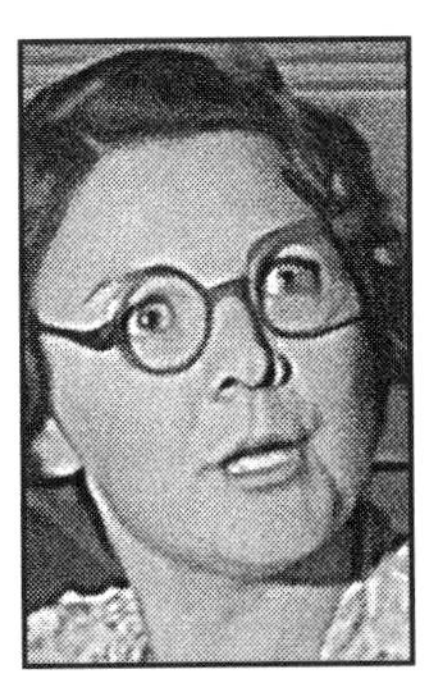
Caroline Sheppard (*Lika Nifontova*), the proto Marple

Roger Ackroyd (*Vyacheslav Zholobov*), the uncertain avenger

Flora Ackroyd (*Olga Krasko*), the poor relation

Ralph Paton (*Roman Romantsov*), the missing heir

Ursula Bourne (*Elena Podkaminskaya*), the secretive maid

Major Blunt (*Alexander Lazarev Jr.*), the laconic hunter

Why did Mrs. Ferrars do this? She's a rich, attractive widow. Her hated, abusive husband has been dead for a year. She's being courted by the richest man in town, Roger Ackroyd. But secrets have a way of coming out. Ackroyd tells Dr. Sheppard that Mrs. Ferrars confessed why she couldn't marry him. She was being blackmailed because she'd poisoned her husband. Ackroyd is taken aback, then horrified when a day later, she's found dead by her own hand.

Dr. Sheppard is equally shocked and insists Ferrars died of gastric issues. He'd never considered that his wife poisoned him. And oh, by the way, did Mrs. Ferrars reveal who the blackmailer was?

She did not, Ackroyd says, but he expects a letter from her revealing the answer.

Events follow the text closely, other than the complete removal of everyone else in the village. There's almost never *anyone* in the background, walking down the street, or working in the garden. That directorial choice makes Dr. Sheppard seem isolated from the rest of humanity, alluding to his aloofness in the novel. It makes Caroline's ability to remain connected even more of a feat.

Caroline was perfect. She's Dr. Sheppard's older spinster sister. She runs his household and his life and has looked after him since he was very young. She considers him weak, something she admits to Poirot, an outsider. Caroline isn't wrong. Dr. Sheppard resents her, but at the same time, she makes him comfortable. The novel and the film hint that he considers himself to be her superior in intellect and ability. He, after all, went to medical school while she never left the village.

But Caroline cares more than him about people. She sees them as real. Think of Caroline as a prototype for Miss Marple. She's a sharp observer of village life, tied into a complex web of relationships and obligations. She's imaginative and can speculate at complete odds to the facts, making her sometimes wrong. But she knew Mr. Ferrars abused his wife and didn't condemn Mrs. Ferrars when she speculated that she'd poisoned her husband. When Ursula Bourne needed her, Caroline plied her with tea and sympathy while her brother did nothing.

Caroline's tragedy is she couldn't save her brother from his weakness. Who knows how many other chances he might have taken, lives he might have ruined, had it not been for his fear of Caroline finding out? Dr. Sheppard's weakness showed when he realized, probably at once, that Mr. Ferrars' gastric upset was caused by arsenic. He could have shown mercy to the abused wife, diagnosed death by gastric issues, and said nothing. He could have granted justice to the murdered man and told the police his suspicions. But he did neither. While congratulating himself on his cleverness, he blackmailed Mrs. Ferrars, hounding her until she killed herself.

And did Dr. Sheppard take the longed-for trip with the money he got? He did not. He lost it in speculations. Was Caroline suspicious of this sudden legacy of £20,000? She probably was, as she probably knew every possible relative they had who could leave her brother money. But she didn't *know* the truth.

Poirot respects Caroline, her hidden kindnesses, her place in the village, and her place shepherding her brother. That's why he arranged that she be absent when he summed up the case to the suspects. He wanted to spare her from learning her failure to keep her brother decent. His plan was that Dr. Sheppard write a confession, exonerating Ralph Paton, and take the decent way out. The police would know, Ralph would go free, the village would speculate, and some unknown tramp would probably get the blame, encouraging the villagers to lock their doors.

This version made a sinister addition with Dr. Sheppard playing with the revolver as he decided on his suicide method. He resents his sister; it shows when he speaks to and about her. Making Caroline find his gunshot body, bloody brains splattered everywhere, would be cruel. The film pulls away, the thunder crashes, and you, dear audience, are left unsure of his choice.

I think he chose the revolver. He was weak in a village full of weak men. Ralph Paton might be redeemed by Ursula Bourne. Ackroyd deliberately kept his family on a tight leash and wouldn't have accepted why Mrs. Ferrars poisoned her husband. Geoffrey Raymond was a gambler. Parker was a blackmailer. Only laconic Hector Blunt has any strength of character. And Poirot, of course, with his ability to combine mercy and justice.

General Information

Based on: *The Murder of Roger Ackroyd* (novel, 1926)
Run time: 4 hr., 20 min. **Subtitles:** Yes

Writer and Director: Sergey Ursulyak

Cast

Konstantin Raikin as Hercule Poirot
Sergey Stepanchenko as Inspector

Sergey Makovetsky as Dr. Sheppard
Lika Nifontova as Caroline Sheppard
Svetlana Nemolyaeva as Mrs. Cecil Ackroyd
Vyacheslav Zholobov as Roger Ackroyd
Olga Krasko as Flora Ackroyd
Roman Romantsov as Ralph Paton
Alexander Lazarev Jr. as Major Blunt
Elena Podkaminskaya as Ursula Bourne
Yuri Chursin as Geoffrey Raymond
Konstantin Zheldin as Parker
Olga Barnet as Mrs. Ferrars
Natalia Vdovina as Mrs. Folliot
Alexander Sirin as Hammond
Elena Kozelkova as Miss Russell
Andrey Shchennikov as Charles Kent

Film Locations

Hall Barn, Beaconsfield, Buckinghamshire (Ackroyd house)
Horsted Keynes Station, Sussex (railroad station)
Van der Hulst House, 6 Starokirpichny Lane, Moscow (Three Boar's Inn)

Five Little Pigs (2003)

Passion, painting, and the past lure Poirot into investigating a summer haunted by melancholy and tragedy

Fidelity to text

A more tragic death for Caroline, Philip Blake is gay, we don't see the painting, and added drama at the climax.

Quality of movie

Gorgeous. Simply gorgeous. Perfectly cast, wonderful music, and the story unfolds through flashbacks that visually reflect their era.

Five Little Pigs is a stunning novel. Very little happens in the present day, other than Poirot interviewing witnesses to the sixteen-year-old crime. No new murders occur despite the truth being revealed and old sins casting long shadows. Yet every page is riveting, as characters reveal themselves to Poirot through conversation and written recollections. How do you film something that's almost entirely recalled memories?

They did it with flashbacks. There are two sets, interwoven with the present. The older set shows Amyas, Caroline, Philip, and Meredith as children. That film is blurry, almost black and white, and usually shot at a distance, like far-off memories. The newer set is sepia-toned and charming, shading into melancholy as characters recall that fateful summer when Amyas died while painting his masterpiece. They're jittery and shot from the point of view of the speaker.

The flashbacks are framed by Poirot's meeting with Lucy Crale, Amyas and Caroline's adult daughter seeking the truth, and his interviews with the survivors. The modern scenes look harsh and color-drained, particularly compared to the sepia-toned memories.

Despite the murder taking place outdoors, this is a closed circle mystery. Other than Amyas and Caroline, only five people were involved. Poirot interviews each person who's left alive. The script did a good job condensing the solicitors, barristers, and inspectors he interviewed in the novel. They all agreed: Caroline was the obvious suspect. As Amyas' wife, she had cause. He was an egotistical serial cheat. He did not, despite what the defense claimed, commit suicide.

Next came interviewing the five pigs of the title. They are Philip Blake (the stockbroker who went to market), Meredith Blake (his older brother who inherited and thus stayed home), Elsa Greer (rich girl who got richer when she married a title so she's eating roast beef), Cecilia Williams (the poverty-stricken governess who has none), and Angela Warren (Caroline's injured half-sister who cried). Each has different memories of that fateful summer. Each is still bound by the past, unable to forget.

There is one subtle reference to pigs. In one of the recollections, you'll see young Lucy with the housekeeper, Mrs. Spriggs. They're playing with origami pigs folded from sheets of pink paper.

Philip and Meredith grew up with Amyas and

Philip Blake (*Toby Stephens*), the piggy who went to market

Meredith Blake (*Marc Warren*), the piggy who stayed home

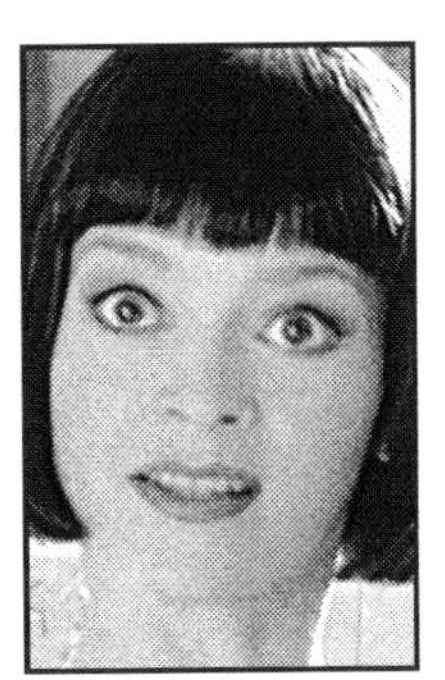
Elsa Greer (*Julie Cox*), the piggy who ate roast beef

Miss Williams (*Gemma Jones*), the piggy who had none

Angela Warren (*Sophie Winkleman*), the piggy who cried "wee, wee, wee"

Caroline Crale (*Rachael Stirling*), the convicted husband poisoner

Caroline. All three boys adored her but she only had eyes for Amyas. The film made Philip gay. There's a plausible explanation if you want to go digging. Philip loved Amyas and claimed he loathed Caroline. But did he loathe her because she captured Amyas' heart and he didn't? (The gay interpretation). Or, did he loathe her because of his internal conflict over loving his best friend's wife *and* she rejected him out of hand.

The script changed Philip into a heavy drinker, on the verge of being a functioning alcoholic. That worked because he was devastated by his best friend's murder.

Meredith was equally devastated. He loved Amyas and Caroline and lost them both. He was always shy and retiring. The murder made him sink into himself, becoming more and more isolated. Like Philip, he never married.

Elsa Greer was the muse for the painting. She's vividly drawn, angry, and sharp. She loved Amyas with a mad passion, despite him being older, married, and a father. She didn't care who she hurt; Elsa got what she wanted. She tells Poirot she enjoyed the trial. It was exciting! She turned down Meredith when he asked her to marry him after the trial. Meredith wanted to rescue her, but she wasn't interested in a boring, stodgy stick like him.

Cecilia Williams, the governess, liked Caroline, liked Angela (her charge), and loathed Amyas. She knew Caroline murdered Amyas but since she wasn't asked, she didn't reveal what she saw until Poirot interviewed her. Ironically, it was her testimony that proved to him Caroline *didn't* poison her husband and was, in fact, protecting someone else.

That someone was Angela, Caroline's younger half-sister. In a fit of temper, Caroline threw a paperweight at her as a baby, disfiguring her and blinding her in one eye. Angela forgave Caroline long ago, but Caroline never forgave herself. Watch carefully when Angela throws a paperweight at Amyas. It brings back terrible memories to Caroline.

I had two issues. I never understood why Caroline stole the coniine from Meredith's laboratory. The novel wasn't clear and the film didn't do much better. The plot needed her to do it, but I wish there'd been some explanation. Perhaps she feared that maybe this time, Amyas would run off with the current mistress?

General Information

Based on: *Five Little Pigs* (novel, 1942)
Run time: 1 hr., 33 min. **Subtitles:** Yes

Writer: Kevin Elyot **Director:** Paul Unwin

Cast

David Suchet as Hercule Poirot

Rachael Stirling as Caroline Crale
Aidan Gillen as Amyas Crale
Aimee Mullins as Lucy Crale
Sophie Winkleman as Angela Warren
Toby Stephens as Philip Blake
Marc Warren as Meredith Blake
Julie Cox as Elsa Greer
Gemma Jones as Miss Williams
Patrick Malahide as Depleach
Annette Badland as Mrs. Spriggs

Film Locations

Benington Lordship Gardens, Stevenage, Hertfordshire (Alderbury)
British Library, London (Poirot research)
Royal Masonic Hospital, Hammersmith, London (Philip Blake's club)
Wonwell Beach, Erme Mouth, Devon

My other problem was the painting. In the novel, Poirot studies Amyas' last painting, a portrait of Elsa. It's his masterpiece. She's vibrantly alive, young and beautiful with the world hers to command. Although he was feeling ill, in reality slowly dying from coniine poisoning, he finished the painting because he was determined to capture her on canvas forever. After the murder, Meredith took the painting, determined that it would never be seen. Poirot realizes the painting is also a clue.

> *"I should have known when I first saw that picture. For it is a very remarkable picture. It is the picture of a murderess painted by her victim – it is the picture of a girl watching her lover die."*

But we never see the painting! We get glimpses, but it's never displayed, Poirot never studies it, and never delivers his judgment of what it shows. The *Poirot* series has gotten bespoke art before. In *One, Two, Buckle My Shoe*, the studio artist produced a very fine Tamara de Lempicka homage showing the main character and his wife. It's not as if they couldn't find an artist to create an appropriate painting. I wanted to see that painting. I was disappointed when I did not, the only disappointment in an otherwise outstanding film.

The ending was enhanced, but it was in keeping with a movie's dramatic requirements. Like the other four pigs, Elsa was devastated by Amyas' death. She, the murderess, had to live with killing her lover because she'd realized he didn't love her. He used her, stringing her along because painting her was more important than loving her. He never had any intention of leaving Caroline, and it drove her mad.

That's why, when Lucy pulls out a pistol (shiny, gold, smuggled in from Canada), Elsa tells her to shoot. She's already dead. She died when she poisoned Amyas. He escaped her. So did Caroline. They're together, where Elsa can't reach them. She would welcome death as long as someone else pulled the trigger.

But Lucy doesn't, evoking a flashback where Lucy and Angela are playing Cowboys and Indians. Lucy refused to shoot Angela then and she refuses to shoot Elsa now. Unlike Elsa – who destroyed a family out of passionate spite – Lucy is not a murderess.

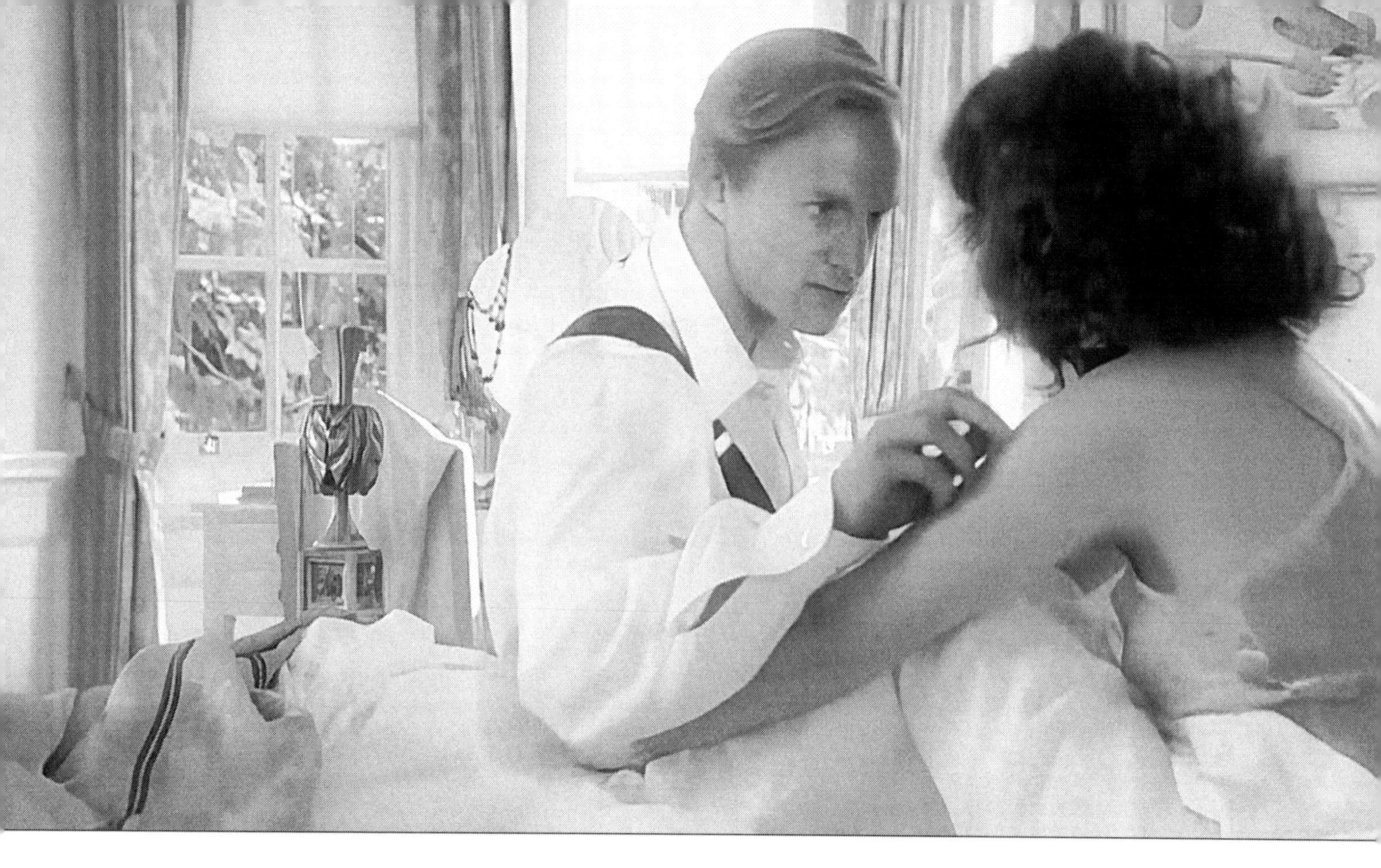

Sad Cypress (2003)

Poirot races the executioner's clock to discover why an innocent woman is determined to punish herself

Fidelity to text

Elinor's not standing trial; convicted of murder, she's waiting for the hangman so Poirot's racing the clock.

Quality of movie

Gorgeous. Everything ties together beautifully, including a sumptuous, haunting score.

> *"Come away, come away, death,*
> *And in sad cypress let me be laid;*
> *Fly away, fly away breath;*
> *I am slain by a fair cruel maid.*
> *My shroud of white, stuck all with yew,*
> *O, prepare it!*
> *My part of death, no one so true*
> *Did share it."*
>
> Feste, Act II, Scene 4 of *Twelfth Night* by William Shakespeare.

If you wondered where the title came from, wonder no more. Why did Agatha choose this verse as the novel's epigram? Because it's about unrequited love.

Elinor is passionately in love with Roddy (appropriately renamed Winter in the film) but while he's fine with marrying her, he's not nearly as devoted. The novel goes into detail about how Elinor keeps her passion under wraps, keeping Roddy guessing as to the true extent of her feelings. She intuitively understands that if he knew how deeply she adores him, he'd reject her.

"Some women are so – oh, I don't know – so damned possessive – so – so dog-like and devoted – their emotions slopping all over the place! I'd hate that."

That's Roddy (Rupert Penry-Jones) confirming her suspicions. He's tall, blond, fastidious, and bloodless. Think of a scentless white rose: beautiful but without fragrance, it's not sensuous.

Elinor appears to be equally cool. It's a façade, her way of controlling what must be disconcertingly unruly, un-British emotions.

Unusual for Agatha, *Sad Cypress* is a "damsel in the dock" novel. The film ran with the concept, making the stakes much higher and the ending far more dramatic. This change worked beautifully. It reinforces how intensely Elinor feels. Her emotions are so strong and her sensibilities so refined that she comes to believe she caused Mary Gerrard's death.

She didn't. She desperately wanted Mary Gerrard dead. She'd even joked with the shopkeeper about the fish paste being poisonous. She prepares salmon sandwiches just for Mary, Mary eats them, and dies. Elinor's guilt is overwhelming. Her conscience goes into overdrive and she doesn't fight to prove her innocence.

Roddy could have done more to fight for Elinor, standing in the dock, but he's in shock too. He'd have been happy enough with Elinor. They were engaged

Elinor Carlisle
(*Elisabeth Dermot Walsh*),
the jilted fiancée

Roddy Winter
(*Rupert Penry-Jones*),
the fallen fiancé

Mary Gerrard
(*Kelly Reilly*),
the lost daughter

Dr. Peter Lord
(*Paul McGann*),
the infatuated

Jesse Hopkins
(*Phyllis Logan*),
the district nurse

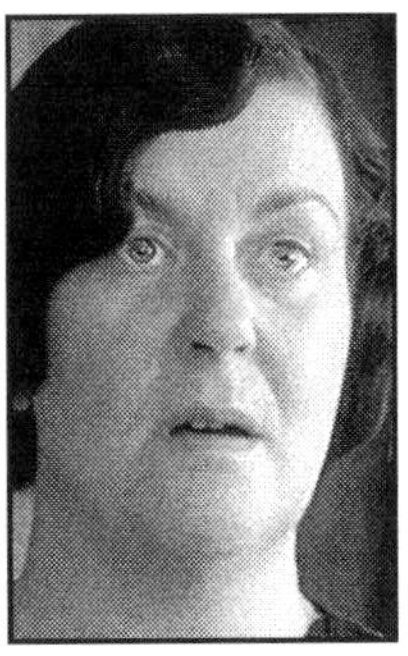

Eileen O'Brien
(*Marion O'Dwyer*),
the Irish nurse

and would marry soon. The film implies they're already intimate. In the same scene, it suggests that while Roddy is ready to get on with the day, Elinor — lounging fetchingly in bed — wants more. Elinor behaves coolly in public but she burns hotter than he does.

Their future is foreordained. Then they traveled to Hunterbury because their wealthy aunt, Laura Welman, had a stroke. Elinor and Roddy were her only living relatives (not related by blood to each other). They expected to split the inheritance because that's what they'd been told. Elinor receives a nasty anonymous letter insinuating Aunt Laura had been swayed by another heir. Inheriting the estate was no longer a foregone conclusion.

That other heir turned out to be Mary Gerrard. Mary, the gardener's daughter, had grown up with Elinor and Roddy. She'd been in Germany for several years working as an au pair and it had been a decade since she and Roddy last met. But when they met this time, Roddy fell head over heels in love with Mary. All his cold ice melted, because of Mary.

Not Elinor, his fiancée. She realizes almost at once that something's up, a suspicion confirmed when she catches Roddy in the library, putting the moves on Mary. If you're paying attention, you can see Mary isn't enthusiastic. She's already got a boyfriend, although Ted loves her more than she loves him.

There's also Dr. Peter Lord. He's got it bad for Elinor, adoring her from a distance; his face full of longing and his heart full of yearning. To Elinor, Peter's an acquaintance in the village her aunt lives in. Nothing more.

Aunt Laura has her own troubles. She's ready to die, pleading with Dr. Lord for a drug to let her slip away. She's pleased Elinor and Roddy will marry soon but she takes the trouble to confirm Elinor doesn't love Roddy too much. It's bad to give your heart completely to some man. Laura's been widowed for decades. As a wealthy woman, she could have easily remarried but never did. The reason is never spelled out but the film does a good job implying why. Long ago, she'd enjoyed a love affair with a married man. His wife was in an insane asylum so divorce was impossible. He died fighting in the Great War, never knowing Laura bore him a daughter. That daughter was Mary Gerrard.

General Information

Based on: *Sad Cypress* (novel, 1940)
Run time: 1 hr., 33 min. **Subtitles:** Yes

Writer: David Pirie **Director:** David Moore

Cast

David Suchet as Hercule Poirot
Alistair Findlay as Prosecuting Counsel

Elisabeth Dermot Walsh as Elinor Carlisle
Rupert Penry-Jones as Roddy Winter
Diana Quick as Mrs. Laura Welman
Kelly Reilly as Mary Gerrard
Paul McGann as Dr. Peter Lord
Phyllis Logan as Nurse Jesse Hopkins
Marion O'Dwyer as Nurse Eileen O'Brien
Stuart Laing as Ted Horlick
Jack Galloway as Marsden
Geoffrey Beevers as Seddon
Louise Callaghan as Hunterbury Maid
Linda Spurrier as Mrs. Bishop
Timothy Carlton as Judge

Film Locations

Hambleden village, Buckinghamshire (Maidensford)
Joyce Grove, Nettlebed, Oxfordshire (Hunterbury externals)
The Charterhouse, London
Freemason's Hall, London (Majestic Hotel)
Dorney Court, Dorney, Buckinghamshire (Hunterbury Arms)

Aunt Laura's pride in her social standing prevents her from acknowledging Mary publicly. She always took an interest in Mary, educating her far beyond her station in life and, unlike typical village girls, inviting her protégé into the manor on a regular basis. She didn't make a will because making one would be tantamount to admitting she would die. No will, no provision for Mary, despite how much Laura must have loved her. As Laura's next of kin, conscientious Elinor inherits everything. *She* makes provisions for Mary, despite knowing Roddy adores Mary in a way he never adored her.

But when Mary dies of poisoning, Laura's body is exhumed and it turns out she'd been poisoned too. Who would want to murder a woman with one foot already deep in the grave and the other foot slipping? Elinor hated Mary for innocently capturing Roddy's heart, but she had no reason to poison her aunt unless it was to prevent her leaving all the money to Mary.

Elinor's arrested and the case against her grows increasingly black. She had the opportunity to steal the morphine, she's cold and collected, she questions the grocer about poisoned fish paste, and Mary stole her fiancé.

The film opens with Elinor in the dock, listening to the charges brought against her. As the prosecuting barrister presents the case, the film slips seamlessly into the past. Poirot's brought in early but it fit. He was already in the village testifying in another case. When Dr. Lord and Elinor tell him about the anonymous letter warning that someone was "sucking up" to her wealthy aunt, he's more concerned than either of them. As the case moves forward, he investigates, thinks, questions, and eventually discovers the truth.

Elinor's convicted and sentenced to death. While waiting for execution, she tells Poirot when she stopped hating Mary Gerrard. She saw the roses on the trellis (Zephirine Drouhin, a classic climbing rose) while speaking to Nurse Hopkins after lunch. They sparked a vivid memory. Roddy favored unscented white roses while she preferred the full-bodied red roses that smelled of summer. The roses give Poirot the final clue.

The ending implies Elinor won't want for love. Her champion, Dr. Lord, is waiting for her. Roddy, on the other hand, is alone. No Elinor, no Mary, and no one else to come along and unthaw his heart.

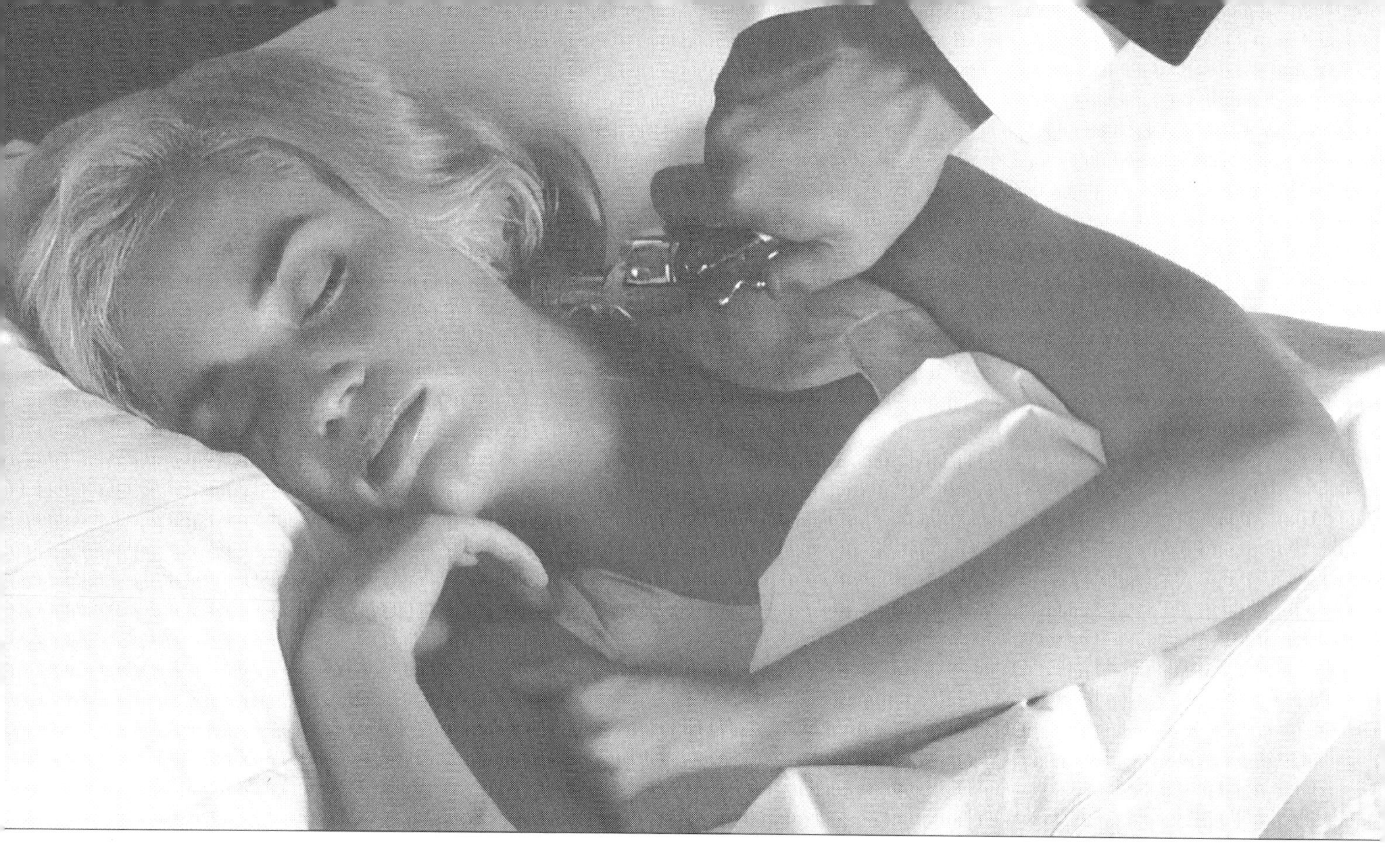

Death on the Nile (2004)

Under this slow boat to Luxor, the Nile's waters flow smoothly, the rocks and shoals are on board

Fidelity to text

4 of 5

It's very close despite choosing different parts of the novel to keep as opposed to the 1978 version.

Quality of movie

3 of 5

Good, fast-moving, keeps one important character analysis scene dropped from the 1978 version, but there were errors.

Let's get the most important point addressed first. The S.S. *Karnak* is portrayed by the Steamship *Sudan*. *Sudan* was built in 1921 as a luxury vessel for the Thomas Cook and Son travel company. She's still in service today, gliding graciously up and down the Nile. You can even book its Agatha Christie suite!

The photographs of the staterooms prove she's even more luxurious a ship than the movie shows. Those staterooms also imply that — despite Salome Otterbourne's complaints — this is one ship that will never experience a wave bigger than a ripple. Those staterooms would get too knocked about. Her wake leaves bigger ripples than what the local waters generate. The S.S. *Sudan* was not built to navigate any body of water more agitated than a bathtub. She'd flounder in the Mediterranean. She'd capsize in the Atlantic. But what a stunner.

Another important point is the film opens with gratuitous nudity. This was an extremely poor choice. We get to watch Jackie and Simon frolicking in some garret bedroom. Except they aren't frolicking. Nudity is very rarely required for artistic purposes; it certainly wasn't needed here. We know Jackie and Simon adore each other, or at least they do before he meets Linnet Ridgeway, beautiful millionairess and Jackie's best friend. So there they are, both in their very early twenties and, and … How can I say this? He's a hunk, she's hot, and he's so upset about their impending poverty preventing them from marrying that he can't perform.

Really? Really? The director expects me to believe that a healthy, virile young man can't get it up when he's on top of a hot naked babe while they're in private? That he's *impotent*? No, absolutely not. This kind of scene exists only to show skin. If the writer and director had paid attention to business — instead of indulging their prurience — we could have watched Jackie and Simon agonize over their future poverty while sitting on a cold park bench and eating fish and chips from newspaper cones. That would have defined their unpleasant reality far more realistically *and* it wouldn't have led me to imagine an impotent Simon Doyle.

You don't start a film with the audience suspecting the leading man is less than a man. It was bad enough Tim Allerton got emasculated. At least there were hints in the text that he wasn't a hot-blooded, action-hero he-

Linnet Ridgeway (*Emily Blunt*), the greedy heiress

Simon Doyle (*J.J. Feild*), the weak husband

Jacqueline De Bellefort (*Emma Griffiths Malin*), the jilted lover

Colonel Race (*James Fox*), the suave spy

Cornelia Robson (*Daisy Donovan*), the poor relation

Salome Otterbourne (*Frances de la Tour*), the racy novelist

man. He was more the intellectual, refined type of man, capable of planning risky, devious and foolproof robberies while diverting suspicions away from himself. You could say Tim Allerton employed the Scarlet Pimpernel school of camouflage, which does not make him any less of a man. In the novel, he and Rosalie Otterbourne get their happy-ever-after and he decides to come clean. In this film, he tells Rosalie she's barking up the wrong tree. Aargh.

I suppose the director decided Rosalie didn't deserve happiness since she wasn't a conventionally hot babe willing to take her clothes off for the camera. As if she hadn't suffered enough as the daughter of Salome Otterbourne. I should be grateful Cornelia did get her happy ending with Dr. Bessner, despite also not being a conventionally hot babe willing to take her clothes off for the camera. As in the text, she recognized the Commie aristocrat Ferguson as an arrogant jerk, which was also nice.

I didn't like James Fox as Colonel Race. Colonel Race is supposed to be dashing, unflappable, a man of action. He rode in on a camel and then slowly departed the film, bit by bit, becoming increasingly inconsequential until he vanished into the Nile, unmissed and unwanted. I can't see him wielding a sword-cane to dispatch a cobra like David Niven, who did a much better job in 1978 of retaining his masculinity while acting as Poirot's sidekick.

Was there anything to like? Plenty. This version made it clearer that if Linnet Ridgeway hadn't decided to steal her best friend's fiancé, she would be alive to cope with her thieving lawyer. Poirot tells a very truncated version of Nathan's speech to King David to Linnet (with, might I add, all biblical references removed despite Poirot being Catholic). She made her choice, reached out her hand, and took what she wanted. That is not to say he condones murder. Poirot never does.

I loved the scene in the luxury hotel in Cairo, where the principals (except Colonel Race) are introduced and gossip about each other. Retaining Tim Allerton, his mother, and Joanna Southwood gave a taste of the larger world Linnet Ridgeway lived in and how people of her class thought. Joanna Southwood wouldn't have thought stealing some poor friend's fiancé was wrong. If you're poor, you deserve what you get. It was a good idea to ditch the Richetti subplot, the one that got Colonel Race on board the S.S. *Karnak* in the first place. That was a complication too far. I liked seeing Cornelia Robson struggle with Miss Van Schuyler, even though it meant dropping Miss Bowers and her contentious relationship as Miss Van Schuyler's companion.

General Information

Based on: *Death on the Nile* (novel, 1937)
Run time: 1 hr., 37 min. **Subtitles:** Yes

Writer: Kevin Elyot **Director:** Andy Wilson

Cast

David Suchet as Hercule Poirot
James Fox as Colonel Race

Emma Griffiths Malin as Jacqueline De Bellefort
J.J. Feild as Simon Doyle
Emily Blunt as Linnet Ridgeway
Judy Parfitt as Miss Van Schuyler
Daisy Donovan as Cornelia Robson
Barbara Flynn as Mrs. Allerton
Daniel Lapaine as Tim Allerton
David Soul as Andrew Pennington
Frances de la Tour as Salome Otterbourne
Zoe Telford as Rosalie Otterbourne
Alastair Mackenzie as Ferguson
Steve Pemberton as Dr. Bessner

Film Locations

Eltham Palace, Court Road, Eltham, London (Wode Hall)
Old Winter Palace Hotel, Luxor, Egypt (Luxor hotel)
Sofitel Winter Palace Hotel, Luxor
S. S. *Sudan* (Nile cruise ship *Karnak*)
Karnak Temple, Luxor, Egypt
Dendarra Temple Complex, Aswan, Egypt

Salome Otterbourne is fun as always. She's so sure of herself, so flamboyant, so obsessed with sex and animal passions. I didn't realize until researching *Death on the Nile* that Salome — exotic wardrobe and all — was based on Elinor Glyn (1864-1943), a flamboyant, confident, obsessed with sex and animal passions writer. Mark Twain (1835-1910), who didn't hold much back, met Elinor Glyn but he didn't write about what they discussed in his *Autobiography*. It was too salacious. Salome Otterbourne would revel in having a poem like this written about her:

Would you like to sin
With Elinor Glyn
On a tiger skin?
Or would you prefer
To err with her
On some other fur?

That's Salome Otterbourne, or at least it was until her books stopped selling because they became too tame for the modern market. Getting murdered on a Nile cruise ship was a great career move. Getting shot probably boosted her sales enormously and got her daughter out of debt. Salome was one of Agatha's many sharp-edged portraits of writers tucked into her novels. She and Agatha even share a novel title. Agatha's first, unpublished romance was titled *Snow Upon the Desert*. Salome's planned novel she was researching during the Nile cruise was *Snow On the Desert's Face*.

Should you watch this version of *Death on the Nile*? Absolutely. In some scenes, it's truer to the novel than the Ustinov film and much more so than the Branagh version. It certainly moves quicker. Watch the three versions, preferably within the same week. They complement each other beautifully, particularly when it comes to seeing murder done, clues ferreted out, and explanations made. Then you can ponder the choices, good and bad, that directors make.

The Hollow (2004)

Murder is no game when Poirot encounters obstacles when a family closes ranks to protect a killer

Fidelity to text

Simplified, sometimes improved, an altered clue, and a badly rewritten climax.

Quality of movie

Everything worked right up to the ending which didn't.

Sadly, *The Hollow* isn't well-known. Agatha really plays with the tropes, stretching the boundaries of what a mystery can achieve. There's only one murder and it doesn't occur until about one-third of the way through. The second, near-murder takes place at the climax when Poirot's on the scene to foil the villain.

The novel is a study of how tangled love can be, how we make our own problems, and how blind adoration can turn toxic. *The Hollow* seethes with emotion. It showcases the class divide, including expectations and entitlements. The value of art is compared to the value of human connections. Everyone is a fully-rounded human being, even the essentially hollow artist Henrietta. Most of all, it shows how a family can compromise their ethics and rally around a murderous relative because "the police won't understand" and "he had it coming."

Which he did! John Christow is the center of the story. Not all his complexity made it to the screen. He's a famous doctor and researcher, adored by his patients. He's enjoyed numerous affairs, none of which his wife knows about, although other people do.

But now he's nearing forty and reevaluating past decisions. One of them was refusing Veronica Cray. They'd met years ago and enjoyed a torrid affair. But Veronica wanted John to abandon his dream of saving lives and follow her to Hollywood to be Mr. Cray, holding her coat at the stage door. He balked and they parted, yet she's still occupying mental space in his head. She hasn't gotten over him either.

John married Gerda because she was the opposite of Veronica. Gerda's slow, quiet, not very bright, and she adores John with every fiber of her being. Henrietta tells Poirot Gerda belongs to John and he likes it like that. The novel was unclear on why Lucy Angkatell invited John and Gerda to her home. Sensibly, the film made Gerda a relative of Lucy.

Meanwhile, John's been carrying on with Henrietta. Henrietta likes Gerda, but she won't give up being John's cookie. Edward Angkatell is madly in love with Henrietta and has been since they were kids playing together at Ainsworth (the ancestral Angkatell estate). Lucy Angkatell adores Ainsworth, but as a daughter, she couldn't inherit. Her husband, Henry, has the Angkatell name but he's further away in succession from Ainsworth than Edward is. Henry loves Lucy but is ambivalent about the importance of Ainsworth. Lucy wants Edward to marry Henrietta and produce heirs to

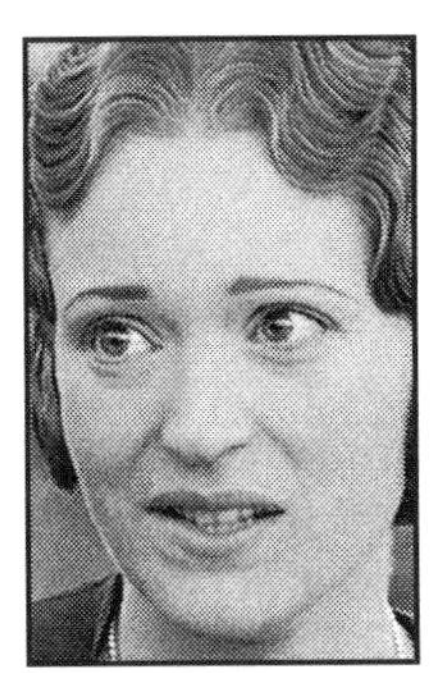

Gerda Christow (*Claire Price*), the timid wife

Henrietta Savernake (*Megan Dodds*), the passionate artist

Lucy Angkatell (*Sarah Miles*), the lady of the manor

Henry Angkatell (*Edward Hardwicke*), the lord of the manor

Gudgeon (*Edward Fox*), the loyal servant

Veronica Cray (*Lysette Anthony*), the movie star

protect Ainsworth and keep it in the family. Henrietta likes Edward as a friend but he's an inadequate dweeb compared to John. The tiny bit of John she's able to enjoy far outmatches having all of Edward. Midge, a poor relation, loves Ainsworth and loves Edward but as long as Henrietta's around, Edward will never notice her.

The film grossly simplified the Midge and Edward story. They argued about her need for a job to pay her bills, something Edward couldn't understand. When Henrietta rejected him after John's murder, he saw Midge as a kindred spirit and rescued her from her awful job. They became engaged, but Midge broke the engagement because she realized Edward still pined for Henrietta and his happiness was more important than hers. In despair over losing both women, Edward puts his head in the gas oven, but he's rescued by Midge.

This entire subplot is reduced to a few lines of dialog in the movie, with no mention of broken engagements and suicide by gas.

So, this is a murder mystery?

Well, yes.

John and Gerda arrive at the Hollow for the weekend. At dinner, they're introduced to Poirot, spending his weekends in a nearby cottage to see if he likes the country. (He doesn't.) After dinner, Poirot leaves, having refused to play Lucy's party game of "Pretend Murder." A few hours later, as the evening's winding down, Veronica Cray sweeps in through the French doors, all platinum blonde hair, evening gown, and platinum fox cape. She claims she needed to borrow matches and then, very showily, suddenly notices her old flame, John Christow!

Veronica sweeps back into the night, trailed by John carrying six boxes of matches. Lucy says what everyone other than Gerda is thinking: "What a performance!" Gerda's not sure what to think but she's not happy. Henrietta's not happy either, but she can't publicly complain.

When Poirot returns the next day for lunch at the pool pavilion, he sees what he thinks is Lucy forcing him to play her "Pretend Murder" game. A body's next to the pool's edge, a woman's standing over him, revolver in hand, and the rest of the house party's standing around in poses of shock and horror. Ever polite, Poirot applauds. But this isn't staged. This is real.

John is dying, but he revives long enough to say, "Henrietta." Not Gerda. His wife doesn't rush to his side; she's holding the revolver. Henrietta takes it from Gerda and clumsily drops it into the pool.

What happens next shows Agatha's mastery of the mystery story. Poirot and Inspector Grange investigate but they're thwarted at every turn by the Angkatell family and servants, closing ranks around Gerda. She couldn't possibly have shot her adored husband. Someone else did it and left her holding the revolver. It's Henry's revolver, part of his extensive gun collection. Does Henry inventory his guns to see if anything else is missing? Why, no, he does not. Does Lucy care who shot John? No, she does not. With John dead, Henrietta might marry Edward, produce an heir and a spare, and save Ainsworth. The butler finds a gun and returns it, taking care to wipe it clean because it was dusty. Does he tell the police? Why should he?

After this wonderful buildup, the ending was a disappointment. Poirot knows he's being led down the primrose path to one dead end after another. Despite being lied to by everyone, including Veronica Cray in a performance that Lana Turner in the dock would have been proud of, he unsnarls the web of lies.

When Lucy warns Henrietta they forgot the holster, she confronts Gerda. Calmly, Gerda provides tea, the holster, and her explanation of why she shot John. Left alone in bed after the party, she went for a walk. In the pool pavilion, she spotted John and Veronica in a position so compromising that it broke her adoration for him. It's heartrending.

But then, instead of letting Gerda attempt to poison Henrietta to protect herself as she did in the novel, the film has Gerda poison herself offscreen to avoid prosecution.

The sign of a great story is that you can contemplate it afterwards. Although it's not stated in either novel or film, I wonder if Gerda had a motivation for murdering Henrietta beyond self-preservation. She realized in the pavilion that John was cheating on her with Veronica. Were her eyes opened to John's relationship with Henrietta too? I think so.

General Information

Based on: *The Hollows* (novel, 1946)
Run time: 1 hr., 34 min. **Subtitles:** Yes

Writer: Nick Dear **Director:** Simon Langton

Cast

David Suchet as Hercule Poirot
Tom Georgeson as Inspector Grange
Dale Rapley as Sergeant Coombes

Jonathan Cake as John Christow
Claire Price as Gerda Christow
Megan Dodds as Henrietta Savernake
Edward Hardwicke as Sir Henry Angkatell
Sarah Miles as Lucy Angkatell
Jamie de Courcey as Edward Angkatell
Caroline Martin as Midge Hardcastle
Edward Fox as Gudgeon
Lysette Anthony as Veronica Cray
Ian Talbot as Victor Simms
Angela Curran as Frances Simms
Lucy Briers as Beryl Collins
Teresa Churcher as Elsie Patterson

Film Locations

Devonshire Close, London (Henrietta's studio exterior)
82 Harley Street, London (Christow home)
Mansfield Street and Duchess Street, London (Gerda stalls the car)
Hampton Estate, Surrey (The Hollow)
Baynards Station, Horsham, West Sussex (Poirot arrives)
Vann Garden, Hambledon, Surrey (Dovecotes, Resthaven)
Queen Mary House, Wormley, Surrey (Coroners Court)

The Mystery of End House (J-2004)

(*Endo Hausu Kai Jiken*)

Japanese anime series for children simplifies novel's dark themes of thwarted love, revenge, and greed

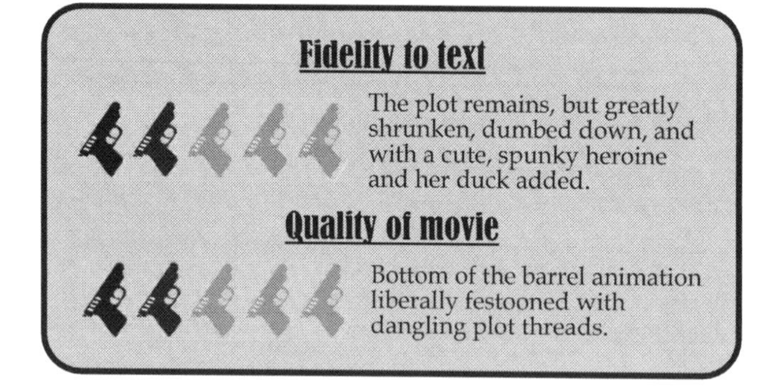
Fidelity to text

The plot remains, but greatly shrunken, dumbed down, and with a cute, spunky heroine and her duck added.

Quality of movie

Bottom of the barrel animation liberally festooned with dangling plot threads.

OLM, Inc. (formerly Oriental Light and Magic) is a Japanese animation and film studio. They've made dozens and dozens of animated shows, some lasting only a few seasons and others running for decades. Their anime covers a wide, wide range of subjects, and they're always looking for new possibilities.

There are many, many Japanese fans of Agatha Christie. Her books are very popular. There's even an annual literary contest called the Agatha Christie Award, given to the best unpublished mystery. The winner gets published by the Hayakawa Publishing Corp.

And thus, the stars aligned and here we are. OLM, Inc., decided to capitalize on the fondness for Agatha and make an anime series based on her stories and novels.

It's called *Agatha Christie's Great Detectives Poirot and Marple*. The show ran for 39 episodes (2004-2005) and lives on in reruns. Manga versions of those episodes were also published. The 39 episodes ranged from short stories covered in one episode to novels that spanned three or four shows.

The unifying conceit is Maybelle (sometimes spelled Mabel) West. She's Raymond West's daughter. In case you forgot, he's Jane Marple's writer nephew. Maybelle wants to be a detective but she's not content to take lessons from her great aunt, Jane. She apprentices herself to Hercule Poirot.

Yes, Hercule Poirot and Jane Marple live in the same universe, at least in this series. Sometimes Maybelle solves crimes with Poirot and sometimes, when she's home, she solves them with Miss Marple. Poirot and Miss Marple never meet although it's a certainty that Maybelle regales her aunt with Poirot stories and vice-versa.

Maybelle does not work alone. She has a duck, Oliver, who while he can't speak, is the model of cute animal sidekicks. He's brilliant, devoted, makes friends with everyone, only makes a mess when it's funny, and brings the detectives' attention to important clues to further the plot.

This three-episode arc is based on *Peril At End*

Nick Buckley
(*Misaki Itô*),
the threatened target

Frederica Rice
(*Shinobu Nakayama*),
the concerned friend

George Challenger
(*uncredited*),
the naval officer

Charles Vyse
(*uncredited*),
the cousin to Nick

Dr. Graham
(*uncredited*),
the physician

Maggie Buckley
(*uncredited*),
the distant relative

House, retitled for no discernible reason. Captain Hastings, Poirot's assistant in the novel, gets relegated to the background. Virtually his entire part was handed over either to Maybelle or the duck. Inspector Japp was replaced by Inspector Sharpe (you can guess why) but otherwise remains much as he did in the novel. Miss Lemon stays in the office.

General Information

Based on: *Peril at End House* (novel, 1932)
Run time: 1 hr., 14 min. **Subtitles:** Yes

Writer: Hiroshi Shimokawa
Director: Naohito Takahashi

Cast

Kôtarô Satomi as Hercule Poirot
Hirofumi Nojima as Hastings
Atsuko Tanaka as Miss Lemon
Fumiko Orikasa as Maybelle West
Masako Jô as Oliver
Yûsaku Yara as Inspector Sharpe

Misaki Itô as Nick Buckley
Shinobu Nakayama as Frederica Rice
Yuichiro Yamaguchi as Mr. Whitfield

The storyline follows the general outline of the novel, but it is grossly simplified. The Australian lodgers and forgers, Bert and Mildred Croft, disappear entirely which was fine. I'd expect to see them go because there's only so much time available and this is a series developed for kids. So does Ellen the parlormaid, who fades into the background and loses her hubby and son.

I wasn't entirely surprised to see Frederica Rice's storyline get simplified; she may still be a cocaine addict but her struggles got lightened. The backstory relating to her abusive ex-husband was reduced to the point where it was never concluded. Her redemption and new love both vanished.

George Challenger, Nick Buckley's would-be fiancé, is no longer a secret drug-dealer working in cahoots with his Harley Street uncle and supplying cocaine to Frederica. He's become a naval commander whose sole purpose is to look manly in the background. Likewise, Nick's cousin and lawyer, Charles Vyse, becomes a background decoration.

At least Dr. Graham and the nursing staff remain.

The plot revolving around Nick got simplified to the point of incoherence. Nick Buckley had many reasons for murdering her cousin, Maggie. The money to save End House was a major part of it, but she also resented the fact that Michael Seton, aviation hero, dumped her and fell in love with her cousin. It was Nick who shot a bullet through her own hat, Nick who sabotaged the picture to make it fall, Nick who damaged the stairs to make it look like someone or something was targeting her.

It was Nick who gave her scarlet shawl to Maggie to keep her warm so when Maggie was shot, everyone assumed Nick had been the target all along.

All well and good and all those scenes were set up in the film and then they went nowhere! Oliver the duck delivers the bullet to Poirot and Maybelle (and Hastings). Poirot confronts Nick about the hole in her hat, she admits to having accidents but denies that anything is wrong. They discuss whether or not ghosts in her ancestral home are to blame and then nothing. Who shot through Nick's hat? Who caused the huge painting to fall onto her bed? Who loosened the step in the cliff staircase?

You'll never learn from Poirot.

Similarly, you'll never learn how much cocaine is floating around or Nick's complex reasons for choosing Frederica, her best friend, to be her patsy. It wasn't merely because Frederica was a viable suspect. It was that Frederica could find love and she couldn't. A point the novel makes is Nick Buckley, despite her superficial charm and vivacity, couldn't sustain a relationship. As a man got to know her better, he'd become uneasy and leave. Why? Because, as Ellen her parlormaid said, there was an evil strain in this branch of the Buckley family and in End House.

The skeleton remains but the heart of the story is gone. Nick's complexity and tragedy is gone. What's also gone is Nick knew who Poirot was. She needed an unimpeachable witness to the murder attempts on her life so the police would believe her story and Poirot was conveniently available. That's glossed over too.

It's a strange little movie in a strange series. Each episode opens with a romantic song while the camera focuses on Maybelle dancing through a flowery meadow and closes with another romantic ballad. You'd think you were watching a romance about a budding young girl finding love for the first time except Maybelle looks like she's thirteen (apparently, she's sixteen). It was creepy.

The animation is very bad. It's stiff. Characters don't react and their mouths barely move. There are long, static pans over watercolor backgrounds. It's not quite Flintstones level where Maybelle (or the duck) race along in front of a repeating background, but it's off-putting. Yet at the same time, there are some lovely bits where feathers drift in front of Nick when she's telling the story of how the painting fell on her or when the fireworks are going off, concealing the sound of gunshots.

The point of watching the series is to introduce kids to Agatha Christie. They won't see anything too unsettling or objectionable and there is a mystery to be solved. For adults, it's got all the savor of unsalted, boiled rice.

The Mystery of the Blue Train (2006)

Agatha hated this novel, but this proto-*Orient Express* will transport you to the sunny south of France

Fidelity to text

Add attempted murder, jewel theft, mysterious nuns, creative backstories, and personality transplants.

Quality of movie

On its own terms, this film works. For a vicious murder story, it's bright, bubbly fun.

Agatha disliked *The Mystery of the Blue Train*. She thought less of readers who gushed that it was their favorite Christie. Why did she disparage her eighth novel? Because she wrote it under extreme duress. She was still recovering from the death of her mother, the fallout from her eleven-day disappearance, and the collapse of her marriage. She didn't want to write anything but she didn't have a choice. She was desperate for money, divorced, had a child to support, and contractual obligations.

In her autobiography, Agatha wrote *Blue Train* was the book that proved to her that she was a professional writer. She could produce a coherent novel despite being over-stressed, uninspired, and unwilling to write a word.

What made the difference? Having to earn her living. Previously, despite seven novels and innumerable short stories, she could tell herself she was a housewife who wrote. Now, she supported her household by herself.

She took a shortcut, reusing the plot of "The Plymouth Express," a short story she'd written several years before. She altered names, added international gem dealers, crowds of extras, and a more complicated plot.

But the short story's core remains: A self-centered, unhappily married heiress takes the train to meet her lover and during the journey, she's murdered and her priceless jewels stolen. Ruth's caddish husband and louche lover remain the major suspects. As before, the murderer turns out to be someone unexpected. In "The Plymouth Express," a naval officer discovers Ruth's body and disappears from the story. In *Blue Train*, Katherine Grey, former companion and unexpected heiress, is involved from beginning to end.

I believe the plot similarities between short story and novel are why so much of the novel was rewritten for the film. The producers, knowing that *The Plymouth Express* appeared during the show's third series in 1991, needed to clearly differentiate between the two *Poirot* episodes. They didn't want viewers saying, "I already saw this."

Like the novel, this film opens with a shady Bolshevik and his henchwoman selling the Heart of Fire ruby to a mysterious buyer. He's U.S. millionaire Rufus Van Aldin (played by Elliott Gould, who was a fan of the series). The Bolshevik and the henchwoman never appear again.

Derek Kettering, Ruth's husband, became a drunk gambler, losing much of his snark and suaveness. He

Katherine Grey (*Georgina Rylance*), the once-poor relation

Lady Tamplin (*Lindsay Duncan*), the welcoming relation

Rufus Van Aldin (*Elliott Gould*), the millionaire dad

Knighton (*Nicholas Farrell*), the efficient assistant

Derek Kettering (*James D'Arcy*), the wayward husband

Ada Mason (*Bronagh Gallagher*), the uncertain servant

lost his love affair with Katherine as he's still – for no good reason – in love with Ruth. He also lost his mistress, the dancer Mirelle. She's now Van Aldin's mistress. Mirelle (Josette Simon) should have had more scenes to explain how Poirot managed to deduce that relationship. As it is, he pulled it out of his boutonnière vase.

Everyone shows up on the Blue Train for the trip to Nice, including Lady Tamplin, Corky (hubby #4), and her daughter, Lenox Tamplin. It does make for an Orient Express feel. The characters race about the train, engineer chance meetings in the dining car, switch compartments, indulge in drunken, high-stakes gambling, and arrange trysts.

Corky became far more fun in the film. He's clearly a member in good standing with the Drones Club a la P. G. Wodehouse. He's also delighted to be what Derek Kettering couldn't stand: a kept man keeping his mistress /owner happy. It's a good bet Corky is Lady Tamplin's favorite husband by miles.

Lady Tamplin became more important. She's a force of nature, coaxing a reluctant Poirot into becoming her houseguest in Nice and demanding Van Aldin and Knighton show up for her lively house party a day after Van Aldin's daughter was beaten to death. Her daughter Lenox isn't as snarky as she is in the novel but she gets to rescue Katherine from a midnight murderer in a furious struggle in which she bites the intruder's neck.

For a film that centers around a brutal death, it's fun. It's got a swinging, jazzy soundtrack. Throw in mysterious nuns, create a new and terrible connection between Katherine and the Van Aldins, give Ruth a crazy mother who turns out to not be dead, and viewers won't confuse the two adaptations.

However, the film ignored a major clue in the novel. Poirot couldn't understand why Ruth had her face bashed in. The killer had no reason to smash her head into jam. Everyone knew who she was. It did allow him to speculate that – due to switching compartments – Katherine might have been the target. Poirot eventually worked out the reason for the disfigurement: It kept the conductor from realizing the woman he delivered dinner to at 10 p.m. was not Ruth Kettering.

The ending was radically different from the novel's static climax. There, Katherine's nowhere to be seen because she's back in St. Mary Mead, taking care of another cantankerous old lady. Accused of murdering his estranged wife, Derek's cooling his heels in a French jail. The rest of the crowd are back at Lady Tamplin's villa. Poirot provides the solution on board the train back to Paris only to Van Aldin and Knighton. The Sûreté are waiting in the next compartment to arrest Knighton and he goes quietly. His accomplice, Ada Mason, is arrested somewhere else.

The film's climax should remind you of *Orient Express*. Everyone's on board, waiting in the club car, including Derek and La Roche, sprung from jail for the occasion. Poirot accuses various people in turn, at last revealing Mason as Katherine's midnight attacker (Lenox's bite mark on her neck proves it) and Major Knighton as Mason's lover, international jewel thief, and murderer.

Knighton isn't a mild-mannered secretary by day and criminal mastermind by night for nothing. He reacts instantly; leaping to his feet, dragging Katherine with him and holding a razor blade to her throat. He drags her down the train's corridor, followed by Poirot and French policemen but they don't dare attack lest he slash Katherine's jugular vein. As Poirot had told everyone, Knighton enjoys killing people. He won't hesitate to kill Katherine, just as he instantly abandoned Mason to save his own skin.

Knighton and Katherine hover in the train door. The platform on the station side of the tracks is aswarm with Sûreté, waiting to arrest him. If he cuts Katherine's throat, he'll definitely be arrested and hung. There's an oncoming train in the next track. He makes his choice, frees Katherine, and leaves her with the razor blade in her hand.

It is, of course, the Heart of Fire ruby.

When you sit down to watch the movie (and you should!), let yourself go and enjoy the ride. It is its own thing. It's not the novel, not the short story, and not the Orient Express. It's the Calais-Mediterranée Express or Le Train Bleu and that's a different rail line altogether.

General Information

Based on: *The Mystery of the Blue Train* (novel, 1928)
Run time: 1 hr., 34 min. **Subtitles:** Yes

Writer: Guy Andrews
Director: Hettie Macdonald

Cast

David Suchet as Hercule Poirot
Roger Lloyd Pack as Inspector Caux

Georgina Rylance as Katherine Grey
Lindsay Duncan as Lady Tamplin
Alice Eve as Lenox Tamplin
Tom Harper as Corky
Jaime Murray as Ruth Kettering
James D'Arcy as Derek Kettering
Elliott Gould as Rufus Van Aldin
Nicholas Farrell as Knighton
Bronagh Gallagher as Ada Mason
Josette Simon as Mirelle Milesi
Oliver Milburn as La Roche

Film Locations

Sheraton Grand London Park Lane Hotel, Piccadilly, London
Nene Valley Railway, Cambridgeshire (Nice and Paris railway stations)
Villa Maria Serena, Menton, France
Fine Arts Museum / Carnolès Palace, Menton, France
Rue de Bréa, Menton, France
Basilica of St. Michael Archangel, Menton, France
Circe Restaurant Beaulieu-sur-Mer, Beaulieu-sur-Mer, France
Mill Road Bridge, Nene Valley Railway
Paris-Gare-de-Lyon, Paris

Cards on the Table (2006)

You'll throw your hand in when you see the changes made to the story of the sinister collector of murderers

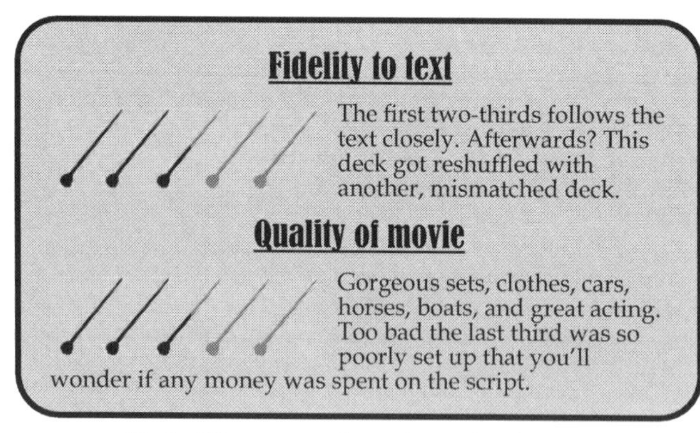

Fidelity to text

The first two-thirds follows the text closely. Afterwards? This deck got reshuffled with another, mismatched deck.

Quality of movie

Gorgeous sets, clothes, cars, horses, boats, and great acting. Too bad the last third was so poorly set up that you'll wonder if any money was spent on the script.

Cards on the Table is a classic closed-circle mystery. Each of the four bridge-playing suspects had the same opportunity and ran the same risk to knife Mr. Shaitana, snoozing in an armchair in front of the fire. Those five people were alone in the room while the Fantastic Four, er, Poirot, Superintendent Battle, Colonel Race, and Ariadne Oliver play bridge in the next room, safely out of view and earshot.

When he discovers Shaitana's murder, Superintendent Battle enlists Poirot, Colonel Race, and more grudgingly, Ariadne Oliver's assistance to solve the mystery. No fingerprints, no witnesses, but each of the suspects had a shady past. Poirot uses psychology and a close evaluation of the bridge scores to deduce whodunnit.

With two exceptions, the first two-thirds of the film follows the novel, allowing for the usual compression of plot and removal of minor characters.

First, Superintendent Battle deduced what was in store for him in the adaptation so he retreated back into obscurity in Scotland Yard, forcing Superintendent Wheeler to take his place. Wheeler is revealed at the climax as not just a typical superintendent. Despite mentioning several times he's a family man, he's been carrying on a clandestine gay love affair with Mr. Shaitana and, maybe, other men. He's also remarkably stupid: he let Shaitana photograph the trysts. I couldn't accept that a supposedly brilliant member of Scotland Yard would be idiotic enough to allow blackmailing pictures taken. Doesn't he read his own case studies?

Next, Colonel Hughes replaced Colonel Race, apparently because the actor who previously played Race in *Death on the Nile* (2004) was unavailable. The producers could have recast the part; it's done all the time. But they didn't, demonstrating that verisimilitude to plot was unimportant. It's a warning for what's to come.

The beginning is promising. Poirot and Ariadne are discussing modern sculpture at the art exhibit when they encounter Mr. Shaitana. Agatha chose his name very carefully. In Hindi, *shaitan* means devil. Mr. Shaitana dresses to accentuate his resemblance to Mephistopheles. Like his namesake, Mr. Shaitana collects murderers who think they got away with it. Not for him the common Black Museum object such as a killer's dagger or the hangman's noose. Mr. Shaitana enjoys toying with people, divining their secrets, and

Shaitana (*Alexander Siddig*), the collector

Major Despard (*Tristan Gemmill*), the hunter

Dr. John Roberts (*Alex Jennings*), the physician

Anne Meredith (*Lyndsey Marshal*), the companion

Rhoda Dawes (*Honeysuckle Weeks*), the best friend

Mrs. Lorrimer (*Lesley Manville*), the bridge expert

watching them squirm.

He mentions his hobby to Poirot and invites him to dinner. Poirot disapproves as it's dangerous to poke tigers with sharp sticks but he attends anyway. At dinner, Poirot discovers the other guests can be divided into two categories. Representatives of law and justice (himself, Ariadne representing mystery writers, Superintendent Wheeler, and Colonel Hughes) and upstanding citizens with shady pasts. Shaitana prods his guests with pointed remarks about poisonings, accidental deaths, and the like. It's an uncomfortable meal, particularly for Anne Meredith. She's a mousy brunette, dressed in virginal white. The other three suspects — Dr. Roberts, Major Despard, and Mrs. Lorrimer — take it in stride.

Dinner over, Shaitana deliberately separates his guests to play bridge. He seats himself in the roomful of murderers, his chair turned away from the table and facing the fireplace. As Poirot feared, murder ensues. Shaitana's been stabbed, the stiletto buried in his chest. It's a charming, almost toylike weapon: an elaborate jeweled hatpin masquerading as a dagger. Shaitana had several daggers on display along with other expensive collectables, just waiting to be picked up and used on an annoying host.

The plot soon goes off the rails, first in small ways and then in large. Poirot, Wheeler, and company begin by interviewing everyone. How each suspect met Shaitana is shown as evocative flashbacks.

Despard's murder turns out to not be murder. He shoots Mr. Luxmore, not to save him from drowning, but to keep him from killing Mrs. Luxmore in a drug-induced psychotic frenzy. A tiny change.

Dr. Roberts murders Mrs. Craddock, but not her husband (who never appears onscreen). She had to die but Roberts isn't covering up loose ends from their torrid affair. Here, Dr. Roberts was conducting an affair with *Mr.* Craddock, infuriating Mrs. Craddock. She'd reveal all and ruin him. This was a much bigger change. Homosexuality was illegal. Mrs. Craddock would have destroyed Roberts' career and probably earned him jail time.

Mrs. Lorrimer is gradually revealed to have murdered her husband by shoving him down a flight of stairs in front of their horrified daughter. The novel tells us nothing about Mrs. Lorrimer's past, only that she poisoned her husband. A minor change.

The major change is that the horrified daughter turns out to be Anne Meredith! That gives Mrs. Lorrimer a plausible reason to insist she stabbed Shaitana. Why? She's protecting Anne from prosecution and making amends to her daughter for killing her father. Mrs. Lorrimer saw Anne bending over Shaitana.

Anne Meredith got dramatic changes. She's still an awkward, nervous damsel with a shady past, earning her living as a mother's helper and companion. Her roommate - who's paying the bills - is Rhoda Dawes. Rhoda wants Anne to admit an accidental poisoning took place where Anne used to work. The old lady drank silver polish by mistake. Anne was an innocent bystander. Wasn't she?

Major, major change. Not only was Anne innocent, it was Rhoda's crime! Rhoda knew Anne would be sacked for thieving (Anne's still a petty thief), so she substituted the bottle and poisoned her aunt. Why? So she and Anne could continue carrying on their torrid lesbian affair!

Every negative aspect of Anne's character in the novel was transferred to Rhoda in the film. Rhoda's jealous when Despard pays attention to Anne, so *she* shoves Anne out the rowboat to drown instead of the other way around, like in the book. Despard heroically rescues *Anne*. Rhoda comes second and conveniently drowns. That sets up the happy ending for Despard and Anne the petty thief. Yes, Anne still steals the silk stockings in the trap Poirot laid for her. That character trait remains.

Meanwhile, Mr. Shaitana's home is burglarized. Poirot discovers the burglar was Superintendent Wheeler! Trying to locate the compromising photographs he starred in with Mr. Shaitana!

Who didn't merely arrange a dinner party of murderers and sleuths. Oh no. Mr. Shaitana drugged his own drink so he'd fall asleep in a roomful of murderers, hoping one of them would take the bait and kill him. He set everyone up so he could commit suicide yet have someone else do the dirty work.

You'll throw your popcorn at the screen. Bleah.

General Information

Based on: *Cards on the Table* (novel, 1936)
Run time: 1 hr., 32 min. **Subtitles:** Yes

Writer: Nick Dear **Director:** Sarah Harding

Cast

David Suchet as Hercule Poirot
Zoë Wanamaker as Ariadne Oliver
Robert Pugh as Colonel Hughes
David Westhead as Supt. Jim Wheeler

Alexander Siddig as Shaitana
Lyndsey Marshal as Anne Meredith
Tristan Gemmill as Major Despard
Alex Jennings as Dr. John Roberts
Lesley Manville as Mrs. Lorrimer
Honeysuckle Weeks as Rhoda Dawes
Philip Bowen as Mr. Luxmore
Cordelia Bugeja as Lily Luxmore
Zigi Ellison as Dorothy Craddock

Film Locations

The Peacock House, Holland Park, London (Shaitana's home)
Leighton House, London (Shaitana's home interior)
Spring Cottage, Cliveden House, Berkshire (Rhoda and Anne's cottage)
Ham House, Richmond-upon-Thames (Despard interview)
Alexandra Court, London (Oliver's home)
Albert Memorial, Kensington (sleuth meetings)
Neal and Palmer, Piccadilly Arcade (stocking shop)

After the Funeral (2006)

Poirot takes a knife to a painting while the script takes a knife to Agatha's most sympathetic villain

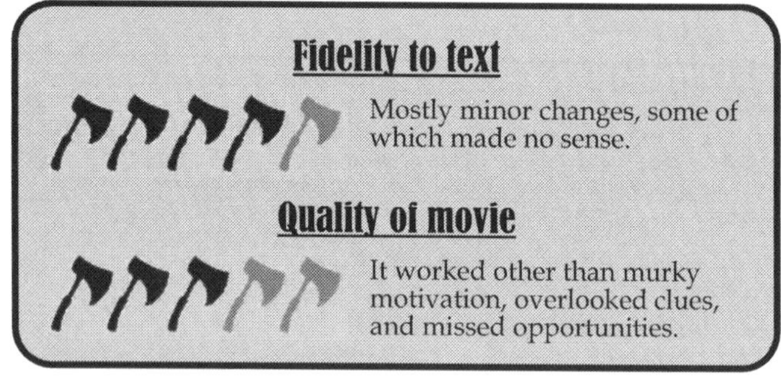

This is not the first film of *After the Funeral*. Back in 1963, Margaret Rutherford starred in *Murder at the Gallop*, a retitled adaptation. She did the sleuthing as Miss Marple (!). To say that it loosely followed the text is being kind. This kind of hatchet-work is why Agatha became increasingly gun-shy about selling her works to Hollywood.

This version — far more acceptable — made its own changes, some of which improved on Agatha's story. Yet like Margaret Rutherford's version, it made its share of nonsensical changes too. Worse, it didn't do justice to Miss Gilchrist, a wonderful character in the Agatha pantheon. She is Everywoman, struggling gamely against the slings and arrows of outrageous fortune. The owner of a tea shop, she used to be a respected member of the local business community. She had some status and her own money.

But she lost her tea shop through no fault of her own, had no family, training, or money to fall back on, and so, in late middle-age, was forced to work as a companion and lackey to Cora Gallaccio, a woman she's come to loathe.

Imagine how you'd feel if you'd poured your heart, soul, and life's savings into a tiny, local coffee shop in your hometown. You're scraping by. With no family to fall back on, your coffee shop is all you have. Starbucks opens across the street and obliterates you. That's Miss Gilchrist's situation.

If she wants a roof over her head and regular meals, Miss Gilchrist must swallow her pride.

The film nicely demonstrates the callousness of the Abernethie family, particularly Susannah. Susannah got a romantic new name (she used to be Susan), lost a worthless husband, and gained a vocation as a missionary doing God's work in South Africa. Yet Susannah, who should know better, treats Miss Gilchrist with the empathy of a queen ordering a peasant to scrub a floor.

Watch her meet Miss Gilchrist for the first time. Susannah's come to inspect the cottage that Gilchrist shared with Aunt Cora. Cora was brutally murdered in bed with seven hatchet blows to the face. Although it's not shown, Miss Gilchrist cleaned up the murder scene, scrubbing brains, bone fragments, flesh and blood from the room. With Cora dead, she's got no place to go. When they meet, Miss Gilchrist has her hands full with mail and full milk bottles. Does Susannah notice or care? No, she promptly hands her suitcase over to be carried upstairs.

George Abernethie
(*Michael Fassbender*),
the reluctant heir

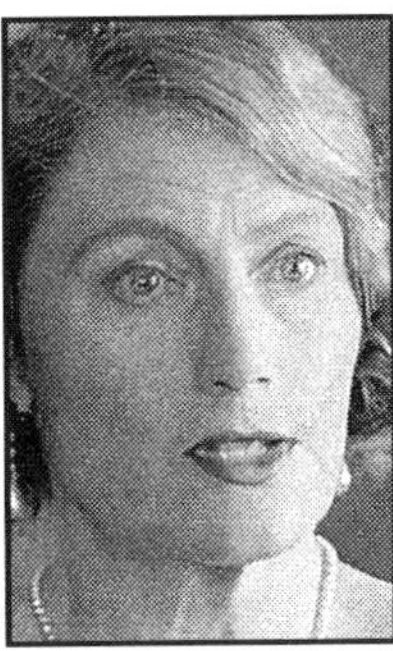

Helen Abernethie
(*Geraldine James*),
the secretive widow

Maude Abernethie
(*Anna Calder-Marshall*),
the helpful wife

Miss Gilchrist
(*Monica Dolan*),
the sad companion

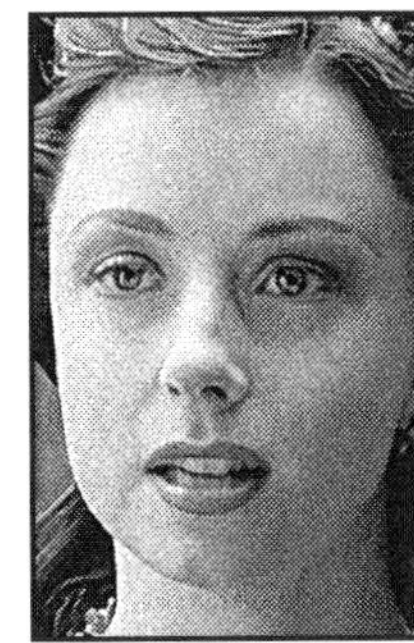

Rosamund Shane
(*Fiona Glascott*),
the upset actress

Susannah Henderson
(*Lucy Punch*),
the driven heiress

She's not a servant, you see. It made me wonder why Susannah was so hot to help unfortunate African children when English slums were crammed with needy, hungry, equally deserving children. Those children don't count any more than Miss Gilchrist does.

The other Abernethies weren't any kinder. As a family, they're uncaring.

Cora was the youngest of the siblings, Richard the oldest. Timothy's somewhere in between. Richard, Timothy, and the other family members ignored Cora after she married an Italian painter and later divorced him. They don't like Cora. She's socially challenged, prone to blurting out what everyone else is pretending not to notice. She's not quite simple-minded because she's often, to everyone's dismay, correct.

Thus, when Cora announces after the funeral that Richard, the wealthy head of the family, was murdered, the family must take notice. They're already shaken up by the reading of the new will. George, the favored nephew and only member of the next generation with the Abernethie name, has been disinherited. The money is being divided up amongst the surviving family.

They're stunned, but happy. George (Michael Fassbender) takes it hard, spending virtually every moment onscreen snapping at his mother (who married Richard's brother) or drunk or both.

That was another change. George discovers his mother and uncle were lovers so his adored father wasn't his father. The night before he dies, Richard tells him, "George, I am your father." It's not quite the same as learning Darth Vader is your father, but George doesn't handle it as well as Luke Skywalker did.

I understand the film didn't want to reveal secrets until the climax, but we needed to see more than George drunk and maudlin. His setup was inadequate.

A totally unneeded change was having Timothy (Richard's younger brother) and Maude steal the deed to Enderby from the lawyer. That made no sense at the time, it made no sense when Bill and I walked around the block discussing the film, it didn't make sense when we hashed it over during our podcast, and it doesn't make sense now. No explanation was given, other than the plot needed a red herring.

General Information

Based on: *After the Funeral / Funerals Are Fatal* (novel, 1953)
Run time: 1 hr., 33 min. **Subtitles:** Yes

Writer: Philomena McDonagh
Director: Maurice Phillips

Cast

David Suchet as Hercule Poirot
Kevin Doyle as Inspector Morton

John Carson as Richard Abernethie
Benjamin Whitrow as Timothy Abernethie
Anna Calder-Marshall as Maude Abernethie
Geraldine James as Helen Abernethie
Michael Fassbender as George Abernethie
Lucy Punch as Susannah Henderson
Fiona Glascott as Rosamund Shane
Julian Ovenden as Michael Shane
Monica Dolan as Miss Gilchrist
Robert Bathurst as Gilbert Entwhistle
Anthony Valentine as Giovanni Gallaccio

Film Locations

Putney Vale Crematorium (funeral)
Horsted Keynes train station, West Sussex
Sharpthorne Tunnel (train trip)
Rotherfield Park Hampshire (Enderby)
Vann, Hambledon, Surrey (Cora's house)
Byfleet Manor, Surrey (Timothy's house)
The Old School House, Beaconsfield (police station, hospital)
Normansfield Theatre and Langdon Down Museum (Susannah's lecture)
Royal College of Surgeons of England, London (London Academy of Arts)

There were other unneeded changes. The painting Cora bought at a yard sale transforms from a Vermeer to a Rembrandt. I dunno. It's true that Rembrandt would be more familiar to an audience, especially the painting they showed (remarkably similar to *Man with a Golden Helmet*). But it was hard for me to believe that even someone as batty as Cora wouldn't recognize it. The producer should have stuck with Vermeer.

What was really irksome was Poirot's reveal of the Rembrandt. The painting was hidden under an indifferent seascape. The film expects you to believe that the art authenticator removed the seascape, examined the painting, then restapled the bad canvas *over* the Rembrandt. He then allowed Poirot *to cut the canvas off* for the big reveal.

Really? Really? Poirot is allowed to slide a pocket knife right next to a priceless painting? He might have nicked the paint!

Were there good changes? Yes; why Rosamund kept her baby. As an actress with an unfaithful husband, the last thing she needs is getting fat and sloppy with pregnancy and then having to cope with an infant. Seeing the abortionist with her tools of her trade, washing bloody cloths in the sink, would make anyone uneasy.

Simplifying the Abernethie family tree was very worthwhile. Any book needing a genealogy chart is too complicated to film.

But there should have been more emotion and better set ups. Poirot revealed too much at the climax, as though he pulled the solution out of his boutonnière vase. He says how he knew Susannah lied but not how he knew George lied, an equally important point. He knew Timothy lied, but the audience didn't. We never learned why Timothy decided to be a professional invalid (in the book it was the only way he could compete with Richard). And why did Helen have the affair with Richard?

But most of all, we didn't get enough of Miss Gilchrist. She was trapped. But when she saw her path to freedom, she took a hatchet to Cora and let loose all her rage and fury at her hated employer and her ruined life. Miss Gilchrist is not a typical villain. She's Everywoman, enjoying some independence and a little business of her own until fate stole it all away. She could be you and me.

Taken at the Flood (2006)

Shifting story to pre-WWII weakens our sympathy for family damaged by guilt, drugs, abuse, and blackmail

Fidelity to text

The plot remains but changing the date completely alters the characters and their motivations for the worse.

Quality of movie

Great looking and well cast, but it's not long enough. How did Poirot know the solution?

Agatha wrote contemporaries but she normally avoided tying them to specific dates. She tucked in cultural references but if you don't know a bit of trivia, it doesn't affect your enjoyment.

This is not true of *Taken at the Flood*.

Like *N or M?*, the date is critical to understanding why the characters behave the way they do. Published in November 1941, *N or M?* was written during the early days of World War II. No one knew what was going to happen. Great Britain declared war in September 1939, followed by Dunkirk eight months later, and then the horrors of the blitz. The U. S. didn't enter the war until 7 December 1941, when the Japanese bombed Pearl Harbor. Until that day, there was a very real chance Britain would lose the war, and that knowledge colored *N or M?*

Taken at the Flood deals with WWII's aftermath. The war's over but England's been shaken up like a snow globe in a mixer; shaken until it shattered into jagged glass confetti. Veterans who found an honored role during wartime no longer had one in peacetime. Survivors had to come to terms with what they did, mourn their dead, and rebuild. Taxes, rationing, and death duties were destroying what was left of the economy. The empire on which the sun never set was collapsing (the British pulled out of India in 1947).

At the same time, the upheavals and disruptions meant someone fast and ruthless could radically change their life for the better.

This is reflected in the title, taken from *Julius Caesar*, Act 4, Scene 3. Brutus is speaking:

> *There is a tide in the affairs of men.*
> *Which, taken at the flood, leads on to fortune;*
> *Omitted, all the voyage of their life*
> *Is bound in shallows and in miseries.*
> *On such a full sea are we now afloat,*
> *And we must take the current when it serves,*
> *Or lose our ventures.*

In simpler words, seize the chance you've been given and don't look back.

The story centers around David Hunter and his sister Rosaleen. She's a young, pretty widow when she meets the much older Gordon Cloade. They fall in love and after a whirlwind shipboard romance, marry in 1944. They arrive in London and two days later, before his family can

Rosaleen
(*Eva Birthistle*),
the widowed heiress

David Hunter
(*Elliot Cowan*),
the resolute protector

Rowley Cloade
(*Patrick Baladi*),
the weak farmer

Lynn Marchmont
(*Amanda Douge*),
the antsy missionary

Frances Cloade
(*Penny Downie*),
the poor relation

Kathy Cloade
(*Celia Imrie*),
the eccentric relation

meet her and he can rewrite his will, his mansion is blown apart in a bombing raid. The only survivors of the blast are Rosaleen and her brother, David.

David, former commando, was very happy when his sister married a rich old man. But when the bombs tore apart his new brother-in-law's mansion, he was faced with a dilemma. Rosaleen didn't survive the blast, but a young Irish housemaid named Eileen did. If he could coax Eileen, concussed and in the hospital, to pretend to be Rosaleen, they were rich. Rosaleen inherited Gordon's millions and Gordon's family – since he hadn't updated his will – were out in the cold.

Meanwhile, the Cloade family struggled. The war disrupted every aspect of their lives. Men who stayed behind like Rowley wrestled with survivor's guilt. He didn't fight, but his farming partner and best friend did and died. His fiancée, Lynn, went to war as a Wren and saw the world. Gordon's brothers, too old to fight other than in the home guard, did all the work and then some. Lionel, a doctor, suffered from neuralgia from exhaustion and overwork and became addicted to morphine.

Like everyone else, the Cloades saw their incomes halved, their investments vanish, and their bills double.

Change the setting from 1947 to 1937 and all that underlying stress and motivation go away. The family still wants its promised inheritance but it's greed, not desperation driving them. The script changes make them even less sympathetic. Dr. Lionel becomes a feckless drug addict. His wife, Kathy, is no longer merely a loony spiritualist. She makes vicious, obscene phone calls to Rosaleen for no discernible reason. Lynn returns from medical missionary work in Africa; she went to escape boring Rowley and her dull future, not because she was patriotic.

The entire family shows zero compassion to Rosaleen, widowed after Gordon's death when their mansion explodes because of a gas leak.

A gas leak? Yes, that's how Gordon dies right after his marriage to Rosaleen and before the family can meet her. David, of course, is responsible. To make it more plausible, he transforms into a road engineer, used to handling explosives to build tunnels. Except! Somehow, despite the "gas leak" killing at least ten people, including millionaire Gordon, the examination doesn't reveal the presence of explosives until Poirot needs to prove his case and then – suddenly! The forensic evidence appears.

General Information

Based on: *Taken at the Flood* (novel, 1948)
Run time: 1 hr., 33 min. **Subtitles:** Yes

Writer: Guy Andrews **Director:** Andy Wilson

Cast

David Suchet as Hercule Poirot
Richard Hope as Supt. Harold Spence

Eva Birthistle as Rosaleen / Eileen
Elliot Cowan as David Hunter
Patrick Baladi as Rowley Cloade
Amanda Douge as Lynn Marchmont
Jenny Agutter as Adela Marchmont
Pip Torrens as Jeremy Cloade
Penny Downie as Frances Cloade
Tim Pigott-Smith as Dr. Lionel Woodward
Celia Imrie as "Aunt" Kathy Cloade
Tim Woodward as "Enoch Arden" / Charles

Film Locations

Englefield House, Berkshire (Furrowbank)
The George Hotel, Dorchester-on-Thames, Oxfordshire (The Stag Inn)
Chilworth Manor, Surrey (Adela's house)
Dorchester Abbey, Oxfordshire (funeral)
Rotten Row, Oxfordshire (flashback)

David Hunter goes out of his way to attack and humiliate the Cloade family, to the point that I couldn't understand why Lynn falls madly in love with him. Remember, she's been getting letters from home. All her relatives tell her he's a nasty piece of work. She watches him mistreat Rosaleen. So naturally, since Lynn doesn't want a hardworking, stable, decent man like Rowley, she falls hard for David seconds after they meet.

She knows David will make her miserable. She informs Rowley that happiness doesn't matter as much as love. David will hurt her but he loves her so it's okay. This is the voice of a woman who'll soon crawl to the battered women's shelter. David even *tells* her that he defiles and desecrates whatever he loves.

Since David's not psychotic enough, despite blowing up a crowded mansion, the script makes him crazier. He makes sure Rosaleen's caught in the blast. He's furious his sister married Gordon, because she's his first and only true love. Never mind that Rosaleen had already married Robert Underhay and been widowed when he disappeared while on a jungle expedition.

Throughout the episode, nagging, distracting questions surfaced.

If Robert Underhay was famous enough to get written about in the newspaper (Poirot shows us the headline), how come no one has a photograph when it comes time to identify the body?

If Lionel substituted castor oil for morphine, why didn't Rosaleen taste it when she sucked down the ampoules in a suicide attempt?

And how did Poirot know David not only got poor, fake Rosaleen pregnant, he forced her to have an abortion? The only clue is when she sings her husband's favorite song at the inquest:

"Your baby has gone down the plughole
Your baby has gone down the plug."

Throughout the film, Poirot's angry at the Cloades and David. He should have been angry at the script.

Mrs. McGinty's Dead (2008)

Ariadne Oliver resists a playwright sexing up her Finnish detective while Poirot reopens a murder case

Fidelity to text

The usual compression bashing a novel into a movie. The bigger change was amping up the character's miserable personal lives.

Quality of movie

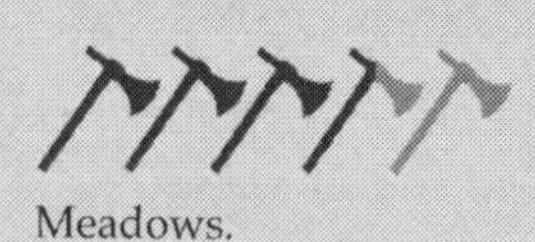

Interesting cinematography – which not everyone will like – emphasizes how poorly Poirot fits into Broadhinny and Long Meadows.

Mrs. McGinty's Dead was filmed once before. Sort of. Margaret Rutherford turned the Poirot novel into a Miss Marple vehicle titled *Murder Most Foul* (1964). If you've seen that film, have no fear. You won't know whodunnit when you watch this.

They are that different.

This adaptation follows the novel closely. You won't notice the missing characters. What you will notice is how unpleasant everyone remaining is, including characters who didn't have contentious private lives in the novel. In particular, it bothered me that Major Johnnie and Maureen Summerhayes turned into English country village versions of George and Martha from *Who's Afraid of Virginia Woolf?* (1962). They're both heavy drinkers, they fight where other people can hear them, and they lost the children the novel gave them.

They're also almost destitute, forced to take in paying guests (PG's in the episode) to make ends meet. No wonder they fight. Still, Poirot's scenes in their once-grand mansion, Long Meadows, are always amusing. The food's terrible, the house is a demolition zone, Maureen is chronically disorganized, Johnnie's trying to write a memoir that will never sell when he's not failing at market gardening, every window leaks (since it's autumn, that means icy drafts), and the Summerhayes dogs are openly hostile to Poirot.

Poor Poirot. He's stuck in Broadhinny for one vital reason. He's doing a favor for Superintendent Spence, discovering if James Bentley is really guilty of Mrs. McGinty's murder or is an innocent man going to be hung. Spence did his damnedest to discover the truth, but Bentley's guilt doesn't sit well with him. He knows criminals and Bentley, with the personality of a moldy dishrag, isn't a murderer.

Unfortunately, other than Maude Williams (who's in love with the boy for plot reasons), the residents of Broadhinny don't understand why Poirot's nosing about when Bentley is so obviously guilty. What they're really afraid of is revealing their own guilty secrets. Since it's obvious Bentley coshed Mrs. McGinty, a private detective in Broadhinny must be investigating someone else. After all, who cares that some char got killed?

Dr. and Mrs. Rendell needed more screen time. Why did he shoot her up with a hypodermic needle? Why did she push Poirot into an oncoming train? Why were they afraid of nasty, anonymous letters? Poirot pulls

James Bentley
(*Joe Absolom*),
the unlucky lodger

Maude Williams
(*Sarah Smart*),
the faithful friend

Eve Carpenter
(*Mary Stockley*),
the scathing spouse

Maureen Summerhayes
(*Raquel Cassidy*),
the slatternly lady

Mrs. Upward
(*Siân Phillips*),
the wealthy widow

Robin Upward
(*Paul Rhys*),
the pushy playwright

the answer from his boutonnière vase.

Eve and Guy Carpenter needed more screen time too, starting with why an aspiring politician married a stripper and why, if she was worried about her past being revealed, she kept her old programs touting her assets lying around.

Robin and Mrs. Upward needed more backstory. They have a very odd relationship. Why did Mrs. Upward adopt Robin as her son? Did she really or do they just say this? There's a lot of money at stake, money he could inherit if he's legally adopted. In the novel, Mrs. Upward is a rich widow whose only son died as a child. Ever since, Mrs. Upward has kept a protégé around as a companion and lackey. But, if she discovers said protégé lied to her about his low-class background, Mrs. Upward tosses him out on his ear.

Mrs. Upward prefers to keep her protégés on a short leash. She also prefers a mother/son relationship to the distasteful cougar/boy-toy scenario. It's so much classier to have a son who's a successful playwright than an unemployed actor whose sole purpose (as far as the neighbors can tell) is bed-warming.

This plot point didn't get a coherent explanation. In the novel, Ariadne discovers Robin's true relationship with Mrs. Upward by accident. Poirot calls it a *polichinelle* secret. The term comes from a 1903 French farce of the same name. It means that if everyone in a group knows the secret, it's not considered a secret but at the same time, the group doesn't discuss the secret because everyone already knows the facts. To an outsider, however, the secret remains a secret not because it's hidden but because no one talks about it.

What is Robin Upward's *polichinelle* secret that everyone in the repertory theater company knows but no one else does? That he's not Mrs. Upward's natural son. This is another tidbit Poirot pulls out of his boutonnière vase. It would have been better to have seen Ariadne learn the secret and tell Poirot.

Ariadne was great fun. She drives up in her dashing motorcar, tosses an apple core, and scores a direct hit on Poirot. Accidental, of course. What is she doing in Broadhinny? She's working with Robin, trying to turn a Sven Hjerson story into a successful play. Ariadne reflects Agatha's own theatrical experiences and frustrations. Ariadne wrestles with Robin over Sven's age, nationality, physical fitness, sexual attractiveness, and eating habits, all of which Robin wants to "improve."

Solving Mrs. McGinty's murder comes as a welcome relief, saving Ariadne from having to rewrite Sven into something he's emphatically not. Her travails felt realistic. Think of what she'd say if a Sven Hjerson novel got turned into a movie with a completely different detective as the star (i.e., Margaret Rutherford).

The sugar hammer features prominently. It was nice to see a real one and, even better, the one Poirot found in Maureen Summerhayes' messy parlor matched the description in the text. If you're unfamiliar with antique kitchen utensils, sugar used to come in big, hard loafs. Think of a five-pound block of rock-hard sugar. To get usable sugar, the cook needed a sugar hammer. Sugar hammers have a hammer on one side of the head, an axe-blade on the other, and a long haft. You break off a chunk of sugar with the blade, then pound the chunk into granules. It's a terrific murder weapon.

That brings up another unclear point in the film. It bothered Superintendent Spence very much that whoever killed Mrs. McGinty left her lying there in the parlor, making no effort to conceal the crime. The same murderer left the stolen money where it could be easily discovered. Yet this careless killer very carefully concealed the murder weapon. Why would a killer be suddenly so cautious? Like Bentley's non-murderous personality, it didn't make sense to Spence. But this critical point wasn't well brought out.

Equally concealed was the tepid relationship between Maude Williams and Bentley. I couldn't see why she liked him, other than the plot told her to. As it turns out, she had a very good reason for showing up in Broadhinny and a good reason for believing Bentley didn't do it. But she needed more time too.

Despite these points, *Mrs. McGinty's Dead* is still a worthwhile movie. It could have been better. It should have been better. But it's the best we'll get and, unlike *Murder Most Foul*, it follows the novel.

General Information

Based on: *Mrs. McGinty's Dead* (novel, 1952)
Run time: 1 hr., 33 min. **Subtitles:** Yes

Writer: Nick Dear **Director:** Ashley Pearce

Cast

David Suchet as Hercule Poirot
Zoë Wanamaker as Ariadne Oliver
Richard Hope as Superintendent Spence

Joe Absolom as James Bentley
Sarah Smart as Maude Williams
Raquel Cassidy as Maureen Summerhayes
Richard Dillane as Major Summerhayes
Simon Shepherd as Dr. Rendell
Amanda Root as Mrs. Rendell
Emma Amos as Bessie Burch
Billy Geraghty as Joe Burch
Ruth Gemmell as Miss Sweetiman
Mary Stockley as Eve Carpenter
Richard Lintern as Guy Carpenter
Paul Rhys as Robin Upward
Siân Phillips as Mrs. Upward

Film Locations

Horsted Keynes Railway Station, West Sussex (Broadhinny Station)
Richmond Theatre, Greater London (theatre)
Hambleden, Buckinghamshire (Broadhinny)
St. Anne's Court, Chertsey, Surrey (Carpenter's house)
The Green, Richmond (Breather & Scuttle)
Freemasons' Hall, London (*The Sunday Comet*)
Harpsden Court, Henley-on-Thames (Long Meadows)
Hertfordshire House (Crossways)

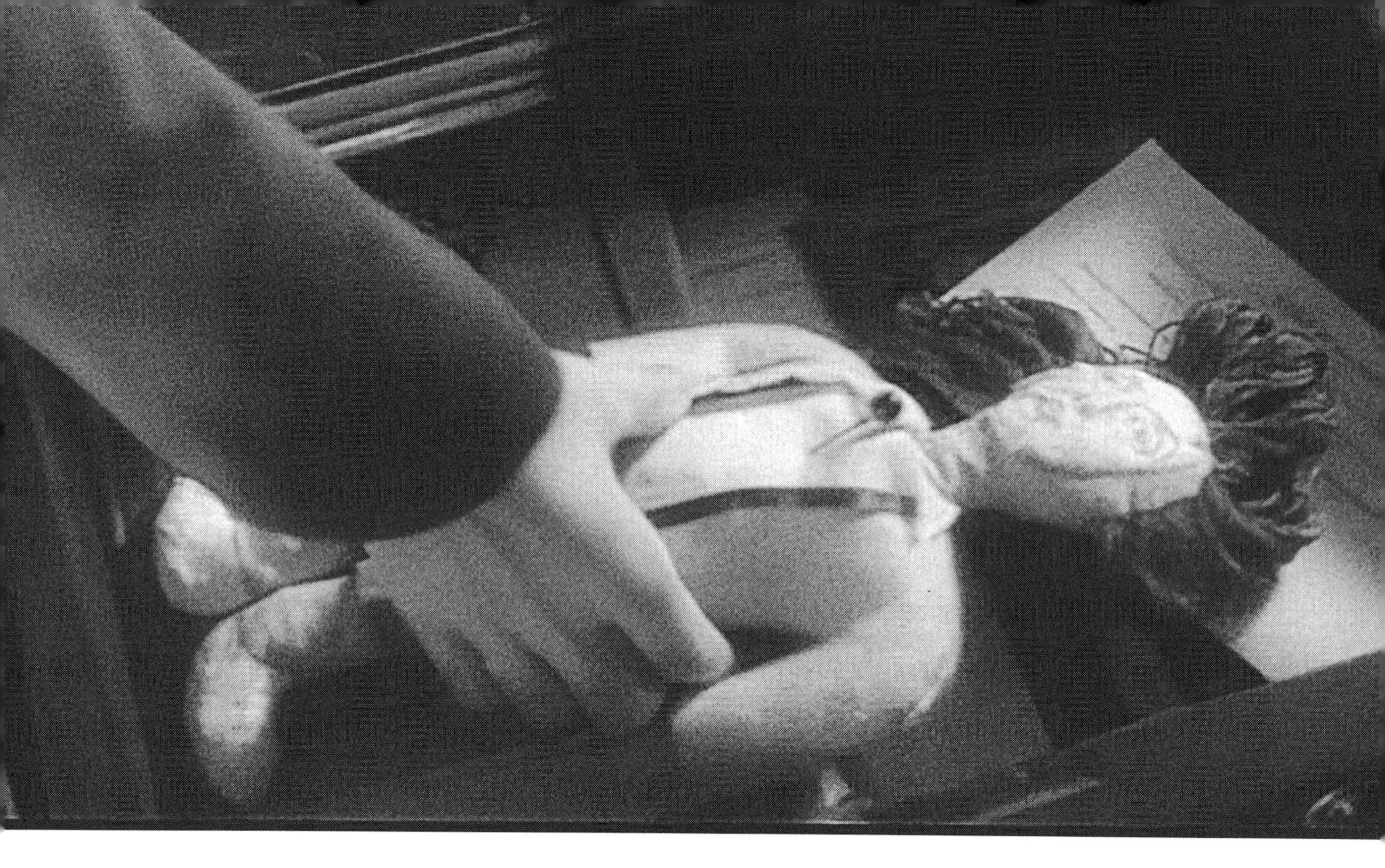

Cat Among the Pigeons (2008)

Stolen rubies lead the chase from revolutionary Ramat to stodgy Meadowbanks school

The film has an intriguing opening. Scenes of the first day of term at a posh British girls' boarding school are intercut with the most unlikely-to-be-connected event possible: a violent revolution in a Middle East kingdom where two men fight to their deaths, the bodies stacking up like cordwood.

What does a coup d'état have to do with a posh girl's school, you ask? Plenty. This is one of the more interesting points of the film, one many viewers missed. Events happen in faraway places you barely knew existed and have zero control over, yet those events directly affect your life. You can't avoid the avalanche bearing down on you. That lack of control, of being the pawn of fate, is terrifying and pretending it's not real doesn't change a thing. We all have more control over our fate than we think we do, but only on the small, day-to-day stuff. The larger world does as it will, and we have to struggle with the aftershocks.

And so it proves here inside the golden bubble of Meadowbanks. The staff and students cannot escape the larger, more dangerous world. The coup so far away dramatically alters lives and forces staff and students to make sometimes very poor choices.

The Forbes family shows the coup's effects in microcosm. Despite the cost, Mrs. Forbes wants Patricia in Meadowbanks because of the social status

and connections. Her husband disagrees. Patricia doesn't get a vote. She's struggling in a situation not of her choice. She's the butt of jokes and the target of Miss Springer's sadism. For Patricia, the coup means rescue.

Princess Shaista is directly affected. That was her cousin, Prince Ali, being murdered by brave rebels in the first scene. Since he's dead, she won't be marrying him. She inherits the throne of Ramat, assuming she can remain alive to claim it. She's a prime kidnapping target. And in fact, she is kidnapped, presumably by the same brave rebels who murdered her betrothed.

Jennifer Sutcliffe's a student who visited Ramat with her mother. That was her Uncle Bob, fighting alongside Prince Ali in the royal palace. Her uncle's dead and Jennifer and mom fled Ramat, just ahead of the brave rebels intent on slaughter and mayhem. What Jennifer doesn't know is Uncle Bob left her a dangerous gift. That's why her house was burglarized soon after she and mom arrived safely home. His little gift is drawing plenty of unwanted and dangerous attention.

Miss Bulstrode (*Harriet Walter*), the idle headmistress

Miss Chadwick (*Susan Wooldridge*), the loyal partner

Miss Rich (*Claire Skinner*), the quiet teacher

Ann Shapland (*Natasha Little*), the new secretary

Princess Shaista (*Amara Karan*), the foreign student

Julia Upjohn (*Lois Edmett*), the new Nancy Drew

Julia Upjohn is another student and Jennifer's best friend. They trade tennis rackets because Jennifer's tennis-mad and Julia's not. The wonky balance doesn't bother Julia. It does bother her when someone tries to break into her room at night. Who would break into a posh girls' school? Good thing Julia's a budding Nancy Drew. She's observant and able to think on her feet. That's why, hearing sinister footsteps in the hall one night, she barricaded her door rather than shivering in fear and praying for rescue.

Miss Bulstrode, headmistress, is considering retirement because running a posh school no longer presents a challenge. She triumphantly conquered *that* mountain years ago and needs something new to occupy her time. Her hardest task in the new term involves choosing a successor who'll keep Meadowbanks as a wonderful, changing school instead of leaving it trapped in aspic to rot. The coup's repercussions throw a monkey wrench into her plans.

Another potential wrench comes from Miss Chadwick. She partnered with Miss Bulstrode to found the school. She adores Meadowbanks, it's her entire life, and she feels that she's the best possible candidate to run it after Miss Bulstrode retires. Who else would maintain the school exactly as it is? When Miss Springer's murdered, her world is turned upside down. When she discovers she's not going to be Miss Bulstrode's replacement, she runs mad and does something she never dreamed she would do.

Miss Springer is the archetype of a sadistic gym teacher. She's sure she's right, she's a snoop, and she adores unearthing dirty secrets so she can torture her victim with her knowledge. She smokes too. Under normal circumstances, she'd bounce from job to job, moving down the food chain of girls' schools from posh Meadowbanks to one that must beg for students. But since Miss Bulstrode hasn't fired her yet, she spots the late-night light in the sports pavilion and investigates. She's confident she can handle whoever is there. She's wrong.

Mlle. Blanche is the French teacher. Miss Springer, with a nose for secrets, senses Mlle. Blanche has something to hide. In the novel, it's that Mlle. Blanche isn't a French teacher; she's taken over her dead sister's identity who *is* a teacher. In the film, it's her greed and lack of character. Like Miss Springer, Mlle. Blanche thinks she can control her situation. She's wrong.

General Information

Based on: *Cat Among the Pigeons* (novel, 1959)
Run time: 1 hr., 23 min. **Subtitles:** Yes

Writer: Mark Gatiss **Director:** James Kent

Cast

David Suchet as Hercule Poirot
Anton Lesser as Inspector Kelsey

Harriet Walter as Miss Honoria Bulstrode
Susan Wooldridge as Miss Chadwick
Carol MacReady as Matron Elspeth Johnson
Claire Skinner as Miss Rich
Natasha Little as Ann Shapland
Amanda Abbington as Miss Blake
Miranda Raison as Mlle. Angèle Blanche
Elizabeth Berrington as Miss Springer
Adam Croasdell as Adam Goodman
Amara Karan as Princess Shaista
Lois Edmett as Julia Upjohn
Pippa Haywood as Mrs. Upjohn
Jo Woodcock as Jennifer Sutcliffe
Adam De Ville as Bob Rawlinson
Raji James as Prince Ali
Don Gallagher as Mr. Forbes
Georgie Glen as Mrs. Forbes
Georgia Cornick as Patricia Forbes
Jane How as Lady Veronica
Katie Leung as Hsui Tai

Film Locations

Joyce Grove, Nettlebed, Oxfordshire (Meadowbank school)
Former Carmel College, Wallingford, Oxfordshire (boathouse)

Miss Rich is another teacher, the one who Miss Bulstrode thinks might be her best replacement. She's got a hidden past too; a love affair that resulted in pregnancy and a still-born child. Miss Springer discovered this so when she gets javelined, Miss Rich doesn't mourn too much.

A poorly handled clue in the film shows how Poirot discovers Miss Rich's secret. She's reading Christina Rosetti's poem, "Goblin Market," to the pupils. Published in 1862, it's about two sisters, Laura and Lizzie. Laura is overwhelmed by the delicious, enticing fruit the goblins sell. She buys some with a lock of her hair and a teardrop and begins wasting away. Lizzie must save her.

Supposedly, the poem's really about the sexual awakening of teenage girls and the wages of sin and sex. I dunno. Reading over the list of fruit the goblins are selling, I didn't think sex. I thought about the availability of fruit in a town in 1862. If it wasn't locally grown and in season, it wasn't available. No wonder Laura was overwhelmed.

I'm just not a romantic. Or I've spent too much time actually growing a food garden.

Then there's the cat among the pigeons, the wolf in sheep's clothing. She's a freelance secret agent living a double life. She was in Ramat on assignment and, quite by accident, saw Uncle Bob hide the rubies inside his niece's tennis racket. Stealing the tennis racket and retiring to a safe life of luxurious anonymity looked to be the easiest thing in the world. No need to burgle Jennifer's house. She merely needed to take a job at Jennifer's posh school, slip into the sports pavilion, and steal her tennis racket.

Murder and kidnapping, fear and terror, at the cosseted environment of an upper-class girls' boarding school and why? Because a handful of rubies were thrown into a metaphorical pond, sending ripples from the Middle East all the way to Meadowbanks.

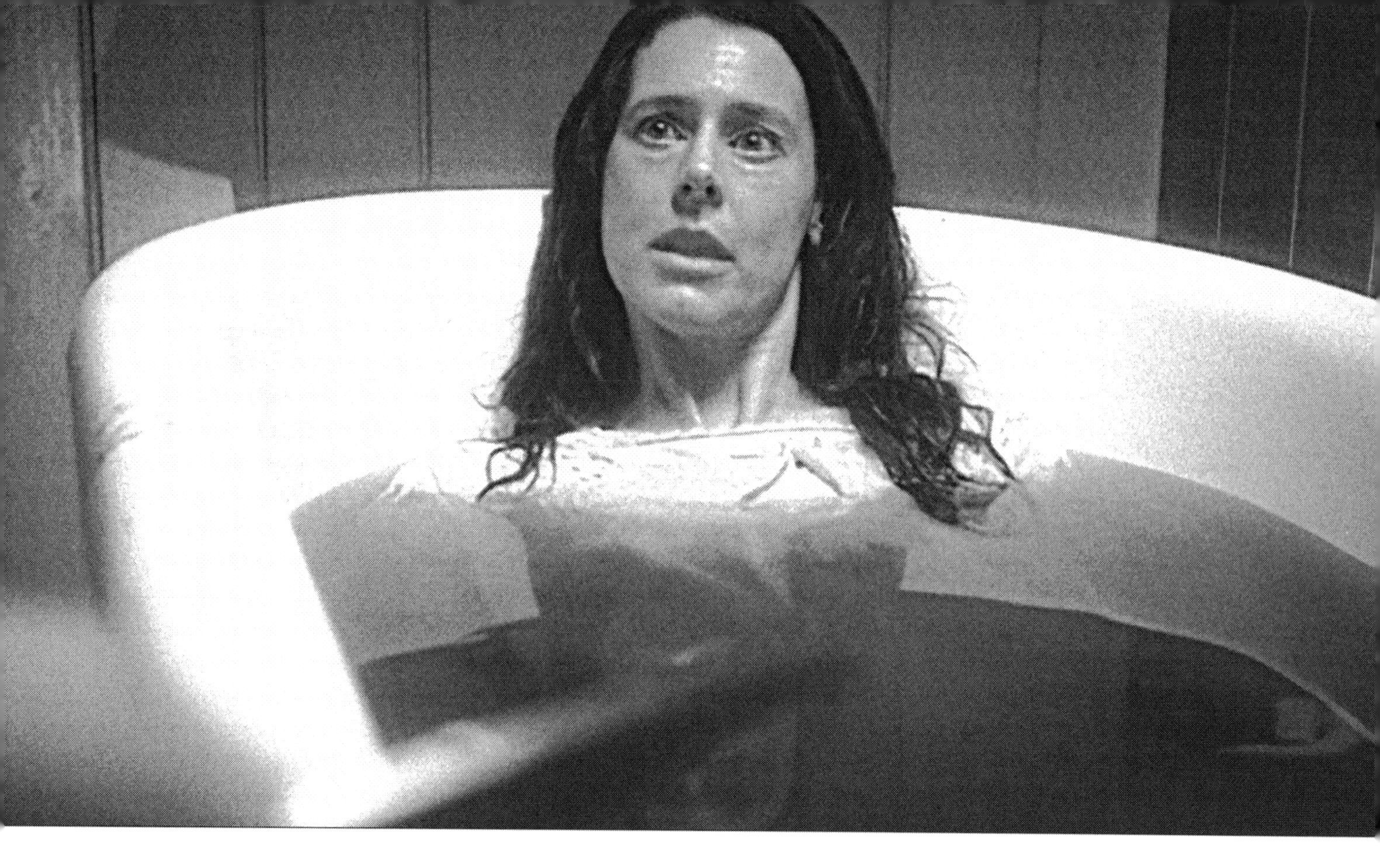

Third Girl (2008)

A young woman's childhood trauma leads her to believe she's heading for dark madness or bloody murder

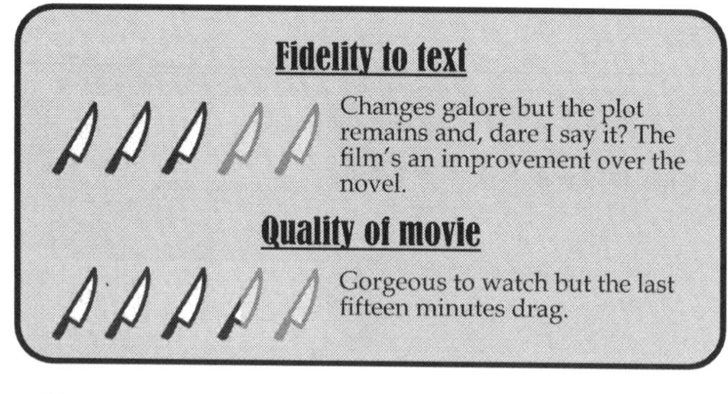

Agatha published *Third Girl* in 1966 when she was 74. When she was born in 1890, Victoria was still queen and the sun never set on the British empire. She died on 12 January 1976 at 85, having lived long enough to see horses give way to cars, the evolution of airplanes, two world wars, and men walk on the moon. As she grew older, she became acutely aware of the passage of time and how it swept away everything familiar.

So did her detectives. Poirot (who should have been about 130 years old in *Third Girl*) is confronted by the fate of irrelevance when Norma Restarick marches into his flat, begs for help, and then, seeing him, pronounces him to be "too old" to help her. London was deep in the swinging '60s, and anyone over thirty was too old. To Norma, Poirot must have seemed like one of Jonathan Swift's (1667-1745) eternally-aging Struldbruggs. He'd lived decades too long and needed to make way for a new generation.

Unfortunately, *Third Girl* is one of Agatha's decidedly lesser novels. It's poorly thought out and needed an editor very badly. But it also accurately reflected the times, including copious drug use.

I was apprehensive, because mod London had to morph into 1937, when Great Britain still had an empire and no one had ever heard of Mary Quant.

And it worked! The script and director pulled a rabbit out of a hat. Not a perfect rabbit, but a much livelier, healthier rabbit than I'd have thought possible. The ending fell apart, but you can't have everything.

At the heart of the story is a flat and the three girls who share it. Claudia is the first girl. She rented the flat and needed roomies to pay the rent. As in the novel, she's Andrew Restarick's secretary and developing a suspiciously close relationship with him. Poirot notices when he's in Andrew's office that Claudia's got a suspiciously empty desk, leading him to wonder how much secretarial work she does. Claudia doesn't like Norma but she tolerates her as a roommate because Andrew wanted it that way.

The second girl is Frances. Claudia found her through an advert asking for a roomie. Frances is hot, buxom, uninhibited (she poses nude for David Baker), and would fit right into the Sixties. She claims to like Norma but she's the one who brought the ice cream to the party, triggering Norma. Frances looks suspiciously like Norma, if Norma were a wild and

Norma Restarick (*Jemima Rooper*), the haunted girl

Andrew Restarick (*James Wilby*), the worried father

Frances Cary (*Matilda Sturridge*), the uninhibited girl

Claudia Reece-Holland (*Clemency Burton-Hill*), the working girl

Sir Roderick Horsfield (*Peter Bowles*), the rich memoirist

David Baker (*Tom Mison*), the peacock painter

free spirit, untouched by trauma.

The third girl is Norma. She's falling apart, traumatized by her father's abandonment at age five, and her mother's suicide at age seven. Despite everyone knowing dear old dad's purpose in life was to set a bad example, Norma's pined for him for nearly twenty years. She accepts him completely, desperate to have a father who loves her. An oddity in both novel and film is that Norma is rich yet as the third girl, she rents the smallest bedroom in the flat. She could afford an entire flat of her own.

The film's first major flaw was removing the main way Norma was gaslit. Frances and Robert Orwell rely on suggestion, innuendo, and well-placed knives to make Norma think she's a crazy murderess. Norma is mentally fragile, but that's not enough. Hallucinogens have been used since biblical times. The 1920s and '30s saw plenty of cocaine usage, along with opium and hashish. Frances could have easily dosed Norma with stimulants to keep her from sleeping, opiates to alter her sense of time, and hallucinogens so she didn't know what was real. There was no reason to drop this plot point and every reason to keep it. The stimulants alone would explain why Norma slept for fourteen hours in Poirot's flat. Once off the drugs, she crashed.

The second major flaw was Robert Orwell. From out of the blue, he usurped Andrew Restarick's place in the sun. We needed to see more scenes showing how Andrew was an irresponsible ne'er-do-well who got up to no good in Africa. How did he meet Robert Orwell? Did they run cons together? How well did they know each other so that Robert could pass as Andrew? A single line of dialog from an expat visiting England would have sufficed. Then, when Orwell's con to swindle Norma out of her fortune was revealed, he went quietly! A man like that would have denied, argued, and then leaped for a window, allowing Hastings to chase him down to face justice. Wait. No Hastings in this film.

The third major flaw was Poirot's summation at the climax. It was murky and went on far too long. Much of it could have been shown during earlier scenes with only a few seconds of flashback to explain to the audience what had actually happened versus what they thought they saw.

A major plus in the film was Ariadne. She lit up the screen. She out-Hastings Hastings, other than in that needed chase scene at the climax. I can't see Ariadne leaping over furniture to tackle the villain. She did have the wonderful chance to tail David Baker, doing something every mystery writer dreams of. Getting coshed on the head will let her write authentic scenes of mayhem, so she benefited there too.

Ariadne also stands in for the audience when she cajoles Poirot into telling us something instead of being mysterious.

A second plus in the film was making the deaths more thematically similar. Norma's mother slashed her wrists, so Norma (at age seven) found her laying in a bathtub of blood. Then she found Nanny Seagram laying in a blood-soaked bed, her wrists slashed. That's enough to make anyone crazy. When Norma kills herself, she slashes her wrists in the tub, just like mom. The scene was gruesome enough to make Frances back away and not waste time smothering Norma with a pillow.

Another plus was how the film was shot. When it focused on Norma, it was a bit askew, the music more jangly, reflecting her mental deterioration. She was always isolated, especially during the wild party that made Ariadne come upstairs to find out what all the ruckus was about.

I liked David Baker, bohemian artist. He got a major character overhaul, turning him from a heartless user into someone who genuinely cared for Norma. Sadly, wardrobe didn't dress him like a peacock. He should have been channeling Oscar Wilde, in rose-colored velvet with lace cuffs. Poirot looked more like a peacock. Where was David Baker's sharkskin suit and spectator shoes? Thirties gentlemen could be flamboyant and he wasn't.

Most of all, Jemima Rooper was great as Norma. She showed us Norma's mental fragility, her need to be believed and cared about. She's the heart of the movie. She becomes the main girl, the first girl, the girl who makes it out alive.

General Information

Based on: *Third Girl* (novel, 1966)
Run time: 1 hr., 33 min. **Subtitles:** Yes

Writer: Peter Flannery **Director:** Dan Reed

Cast

David Suchet as Hercule Poirot
Zoë Wanamaker as Ariadne Oliver
John Warnaby as Inspector Nelson
David Yelland as George

Jemima Rooper as Norma Restarick
James Wilby as Andrew Restarick
Clemency Burton-Hill as Claudia Reece-Holland
Matilda Sturridge as Frances Cary
Tom Mison as David Baker
Caroline O'Neill as Nanny Lavinia Seagram
Peter Bowles as Sir Roderick Horsfield
Lucy Liemann as Sonia
Haydn Gwynne as Miss Battersby
Tim Stern as Alf Renny
Tessa Bell-Briggs as Daphne the Waitress
Jade Longley as Young Norma Restarick
Juliet Howland as Mary Restarick

Film Locations

Alexandra Court, London (Ariadne Oliver's home, death of Nanny Lavinia Seagram)
All Saint's Church, Watlington
Wrotham Park, Hertfordshire (Crosshedges)
Shirburn Castle Gatehouse, Shirburn (Crosshedges driveway)
The Edgar Wallace, London (The Merry Shamrock)
Temple Church, London
Holland Park, London
Witanhurst, London (Meadowfield School)
Alexandra Park, Kensington (Borodene Court)

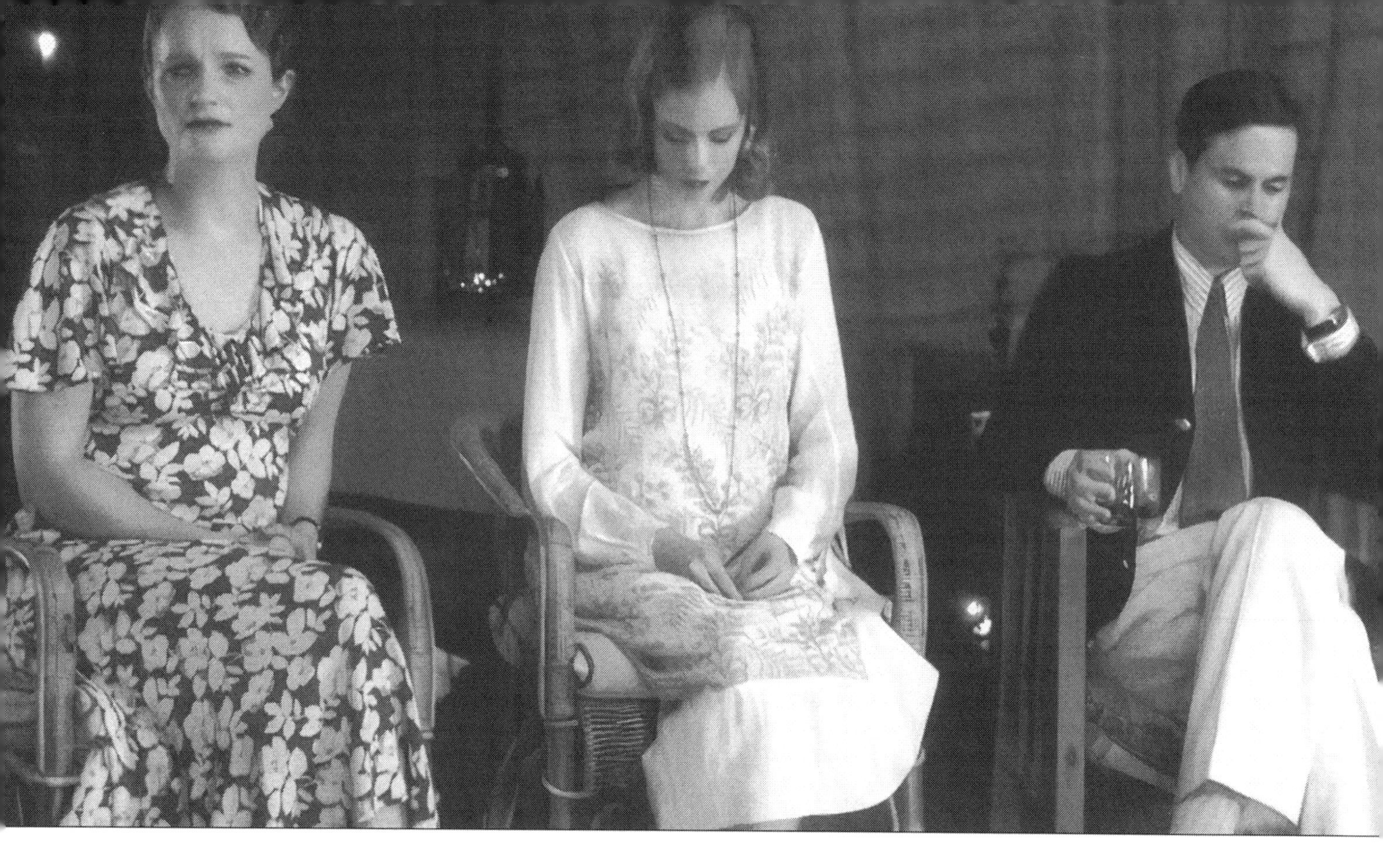

Appointment with Death (2009)

An appointment with drivel drives a slave-trading nun into the sands while despair grips the family

Fidelity to text

You know it's bad when a series known for faithful adaptations opens with a title card saying "based upon." More accurate to say "nodding acquaintance with" or "at least the names match."

Quality of movie

Morocco (standing in for Syria) looks fabulous! The actors emote with the best of them. Nice music (most of the time), too, except when it falls into B-movie clichés.

I was disappointed with Peter Ustinov's version of *Appointment with Death*. It was an appointment with tedium. But this adaptation is worse. It's an appointment with rubbish and absurd hack screenwriting using clichés that Agatha herself disparaged. I'm referring, specifically, to white slavers kidnapping gorgeous auburn-haired teenage girls to sell into the sex trade.

You say there were no white slavers in *Appointment with Death*? You're right! There were also no nuns who were — wait for it — white slavers in disguise! Even more weirdly, Sister Agnieszka is not just a Polish white slaver, but she prays when no one's around. Um, sure. Murderous slavers pray for … forgiveness of sins? Not getting caught? If Sister Agnieszka was truly devout, she'd either not be a slaver and thus could escape this movie or — and I'm just spitballing a reason here — she's under duress and kidnapping Jinny is the only way she can ransom hundreds of other innocent girls being held captive in caves along the Moroccan coast and destined for sex slavery.

Sister Agnieszka's plot gets stupider. Someone attempts to kidnap her tent-mate Jinny in the middle of camp, while they're surrounded by dozens of eyes and ears. Jinny attacks the person who was trying to shove a hood over her head with a rock. Who gets injured by having a sharp rock bashed into their head? Sister Agnieszka. Is Sister Agnieszka outed as being the criminal, since there's no evidence anyone sneaked into the crowded, busy camp? No, everyone swallows the wildly unlikely story.

Eventually, she's unmasked by Poirot (How did he know? He read the script.) But when he turns to unmasking the murderers, Sister Agnieszka steals a truck and vanishes into the desert. You can guess her fate, except you'll wonder why, despite spending much of her time in deserts, she forgot to bring water.

The entire 80-minute movie consists of more of the same idiocy. Every time it gets clever or interesting, it spins on a dime and sinks to a new low. The plot is horribly convoluted with no clear motivations or backstories and unfinished plot points strewn about, yet the producers couldn't spend an additional 10 minutes to a) make this a feature-length film and b) explain what's going on. Is a 90-minute movie too

Celia Westholme (*Elizabeth McGovern*), the vengeful explorer

Lady Boynton (*Cheryl Campbell*), the feared financer

Lord Boynton (*Tim Curry*), the blind archeologist

Jinny Boynton (*Zoe Boyle*), the adopted daughter

Leonard Boynton (*Mark Gattis*), the beset stepson

Dr. Gerard (*John Hannah*), the secretive doctor

much to ask for?

What else was wrong, you ask? Lots.

How do you feel about gruesome child abuse scenes? We get several flashbacks of Lady Boynton's children being punished. This, despite the fact that Lady Boynton was a psychological sadist, not a physical one. But wait! It *was* psychological. She sat and listened while Nanny Taylor administered the beatings and waterboardings. Except why did Nanny hang around that house of horrors? What hold did Lady Boynton have over her? She didn't seem to enjoy torturing children but she didn't flee either. Why was she afraid when Lady Boynton died? No explanation.

Lady Boynton got seriously rewritten. She's no longer a former prison matron and widow with three stepchildren and one natural daughter. Here, she adopted those three kids to have torture subjects. She's also a brilliant and wealthy financial investor who can cower Wall Street titans with a frown. She married Lord Boynton, an archeologist fixated with finding the head of John the Baptist. Lord Boynton may be a dedicated archeologist but he doesn't unearth how Lady Boynton treats everyone else around her. The fourth child, Lennox, becomes Leonard, and he's Lord Boynton's son and heir to the title. He's got to keep things running while dad chases around the Syrian desert looking for a single, special skull in a landscape that must be littered with them. Good thing his wife, Nadine, was written out.

Jefferson Cope gets a radical rewrite and then his story vanishes, despite how much he has in common with Lady Boynton's punching bags and Leonard Boynton. Did we get a scene where these people, all severely damaged by Lady Boynton, connect? No, we did not. Eighty-minute running time, remember, those precious minutes wasted on slave-trading nuns.

Sarah King, girl doctor, does show up. She falls madly in love with Raymond Boynton within seconds after meeting him. He's a sullen lump who ignores her and they have zero chemistry. The script also demanded that her competence as a doctor come and go. Sometimes, she knows what she's doing. When she doesn't, she completely misses the curious presence of wax smeared across Lady Boynton's bloody clothes and body.

General Information

Based on: *Appointment with Death* (novel, 1938)
Run time: 1 hr., 20 min. **Subtitles:** Yes

Writer: Guy Andrews
Director: Ashley Pearce

Cast

David Suchet as Hercule Poirot
Paul Freeman as Colonel Carbury

Elizabeth McGovern as Dame Celia Westholme
Cheryl Campbell as Lady Boynton
Tim Curry as Lord Boynton
Tom Riley as Raymond Boynton
Zoe Boyle as Jinny Boynton
Emma Cunniffe as Carol Boynton
Mark Gatiss as Leonard Boynton
Angela Pleasence as Nanny Taylor
Christian McKay as Jefferson Cope
Beth Goddard as Sister Agnieszka
John Hannah as Dr. Gerard
Christina Cole as Sarah King
Zakaria Atifi as Mahmoud

Film Locations

Mahkama al-Pasha, Casablanca (Hotel Constantine)
Kasbah Boulaouane, Boulaouane, Morocco (Boynton's HQ at Ain Musa)
Boulaouane, Morocco (outdoor scenes)

As for Dame Westholme, member of Parliament and former prisoner of Mrs. Boynton? She morphed into Celia Westholme, well-known travel writer and former housemaid to Lady Boynton. While working for Lady Boynton (then Mrs. Pierce) our Celia had a fling with a guest, got pregnant, had her baby (Jinny) stolen by Lady Boynton, and was shipped off to a convent in Ireland. Twenty years later, she's out for revenge, which is why she rides dramatically into the episode on a camel like Omar Sharif in *Lawrence of Arabia* (1962).

Why'd she wait so long? Because the plot insisted. Did she keep in touch with her lover? No, apparently not, until suddenly Celia learned Jinny was being abused and then equally suddenly, spotted her lover in Vienna. Together, they hatched the plot to murder Lady Boynton and I won't say that Lady Boynton didn't deserve it. But it was ridiculously complex.

The ending was terrible. Poirot reveals the absurdly complicated plot and backstory (pulling them out of a box of archeological relics) that connected everyone, including Dr. Gerard. He's still a shrink, but he's no longer French. He's Scottish. He's also Celia's long-ago lover and Jinny's secret father! Which is why when she comes on to him (because the plot demanded she behave like a slut), he pushes her away.

Poirot lectures everyone in the tent about their sins and then, in front of Jinny and her siblings, pushes Celia and Dr. Gerard into confessing and committing suicide. Yep, Jinny meets her birth parents for the first time and watches them die within a span of three minutes. And Poirot is fine with this, despite the fact that if anyone deserved death, it's Lady Boynton. He let the Orient Express crew off for that reason. Not these two. I guess Jinny deserved more punishment for existing.

The actors worked hard, but the casting didn't always help. Every time John Hannah (Dr. Gerard) came onscreen, I thought of *The Mummy* (1999). Every time Paul Freeman (Colonel Carbury) came onscreen, I saw Belloc in *Indiana Jones and the Raiders of the Lost Ark* (1981). Every time Tim Curry (Lord Boynton) came onscreen, I thought of *Muppet Treasure Island* (1996).

All those movies had sand, fun, and treasure. Here, there's only sand.

Three Act Tragedy (2010)

A lion of the British theatre persuades Poirot to investigate poisonings with the help of an attractive girl

If you think the film is melodramatic and contrived, you're right! Which is just how it should be. The novel (not all editions do this) comes with a frontispiece:

Directed by
Sir Charles Cartwright
Assistant Directors
Mr. Satterthwaite
Miss Hermione (Egg) Lytton Gore
Clothes by Ambrosine, Ltd
Illumination by Hercule Poirot

The novel is broken into three sections, like a stage play.
Act One: *Suspicion*
Rev. Babbington dies under strange circumstances
Act Two: *Certainty*
Dr. Strange dies but this time, it's murder
Act Three: *Discovery*
Poirot connects the crimes and solves the case.

The producers did some rewriting. The obvious bit is removing Mr. Satterthwaite. The novel is mainly told from his point of view as he interacts with Sir Charles and Egg to solve a death that no one else, including Poirot, believes was murder. Sir Charles is adamant from the first day that it had to be murder and he — enjoying the chance to be a real detective instead of pretending — slowly persuades everyone else to his point of view.

Fidelity to text

Be forewarned: This movie follows the British text with a different motivation than the U.S. version. Mr. Satterthwaite gets disappeared, and Poirot's part is beefed up.

Quality of movie

It's theatrical, showy, and deliberately stagy like a play. Go with the flow and you'll enjoy it. If you don't, the artificiality will make you crazy.

With Mr. Satterthwaite gone, Poirot takes center stage as he didn't in the book. He's in most of the scenes, including one where it's hard to believe he'd be Johnny-on-the-spot, following Miss Milray from busy, bustling London all the way to Cornwall to an ivy-shrouded tower to keep her from destroying the mad scientist laboratory used to distill nicotine from rose spray.

So, three acts. We open with Sir Charles on a lovely sailboat in the waters off Cornwall. He's dressed in a movie version of a yachtsman's outfit, much too clean and well-dressed to be handling the rigging. He's probably playacting so it's a good thing he's got Egg, local girl, along to manage the lines and navigate the choppy waters. This sets us up for his sad, unrequited longing for Egg, a luscious damsel young enough to be his daughter, or granddaughter if you're feeling mean.

I could buy Sir Charles panting after Egg, but not him

Sir Charles Cartwright (*Martin Shaw*), the retired stage star

"Egg" Lytton Gore (*Kimberley Nixon*), the sweet ingénue

Bartholomew Strange (*Art Malik*), the nerve specialist

Miss Milray (*Suzanne Bertish*), the star's secretary

Miss Wills (*Kate Ashfield*), the playwright

Oliver Manders (*Tom Wisdom*), the wannabe lover

acting as though it's impossible to win her love. Powerful men always lust after sweet young things, particularly as they get older. Snagging her demonstrates he's still got it. Wealth, status, and power are time-tested aphrodisiacs.

Agatha didn't write this ridiculous bit of Hollywood glurge; she got rewritten. In the novel, Mr. Satterthwaite and later on, Poirot, don't buy Sir Charles' act. He's a theatrical lion, adored by millions and able to have any woman he wants. This is why Angela Sutcliffe, fellow thespian, former lover, and his age, got disappeared. She was probably one of hundreds of his lovers and removing her made him look lonely and forlorn.

So as you're watching, remember Sir Charles knows he's manipulating pretty, naïve Egg. Don't make the mistake of thinking he expects to be rejected. It's part of his script. He'll get his happy ever after with the wife he's been postponing for decades and the charming family to bless his old age.

After a day of sailing, Sir Charles hosts a gathering of friends plus Poirot. The party ends tragically when Rev. Babbington dies after sipping a cocktail identical to everyone else's. Sir Charles springs into action, following a script that says a sudden death at a dinner party must be murder. Poirot, an old hand at this business, demurs.

Act two begins. Dr. Strange is hosting a fancy dinner at his estate. He runs a sanatorium for nerve cases and wealthy lunatics. It's right next door so he's got an easy commute. The guests include almost everyone who was at the fatal dinner in Cornwall. The guest count ticks up when Oliver, also longing for Egg, has a suspiciously convenient accident outside the estate and seeks refuge. Only Poirot, Miss Milray, and Sir Charles don't attend. Dr. Strange drinks his port, chokes, and dies. The temporary butler disappears. This time, an autopsy is performed. It's murder by nicotine poisoning but once again, the fateful glass is untainted.

Sir Charles has been languishing in Monte Carlo, unwilling to return to deadly and lonely Cornwall. He reads about Dr. Strange's mysterious death in the newspaper. Conveniently, he runs into Poirot and persuades him that he was right all along. Poirot agrees and it's back to England, Egg, and investigating the crimes.

General Information

Based on: *Three Act Tragedy* (novel, 1934)
Run time: 1 hr., 34 min. **Subtitles:** Yes

Writer: Nick Dear **Director:** Ashley Pearce

Cast

David Suchet as Hercule Poirot
Tony Maudsley as Supt. Crossfield

Martin Shaw as Sir Charles Cartwright
Suzanne Bertish as Miss Milray
Kate Ashfield as Miss Wills
Kimberley Nixon as "Egg" Lytton Gore
Jane Asher as Lady Mary Lytton Gore
Tom Wisdom as Oliver Manders
Art Malik as Sir Bartholomew Strange
Anastasia Hille as Cynthia Dacres
Ronan Vibert as Captain Dacres
Anna Carteret as Mrs. Babbington
Nigel Pegram as Rev. Babbington

Film Locations

St. Anne's Court, Chertsey (Cartwright home's exterior)
Eltham Palace (Cartwright home's interior)
Novello Theatre, London
Knebworth House, Hertfordshire (Dr. Strange's house)
Villa Maria Serena, Menton, France (hotel)
Wandsworth Town Hall (Majestic interior)
Claridge's Hotel, London (Ambrose store)
Paddington train station
Bluebell Railway Pullman carriages
Wansford Station, Peterborough (station)
Little Marlow St John the Baptist Church (exhumation scene)

On to act three. Poirot can't figure out why and how Rev. Babbington was poisoned. There's no connection between the good reverend and Dr. Strange. As Captain Dacres tells Egg, nobody poisons saintly country vicars. They're harmless. Doctors, on the other hand, know harmful secrets. They do terrible things. They have victims. There's always a reason to kill a doctor.

Poirot races about down England. Sometimes he's with Sir Charles, languishing after Egg, sometimes not. There's an interesting scene with Miss Wills, the playwright. She writes under a man's name, not uncommon in 1935. She's very observant. She points out to Oliver, Charles' rival for Egg, that he should be more active in his pursuit of the damsel. After all, Oliver is young and handsome with his life before him. Sir Charles is a "has-been, a wash-out, a flop."

This is the only hint we get explaining why Sir Charles, theatrical lion, left the stage. My guess is he grew too old for leading man roles and didn't want to play what was left: the old man in the corner. It must be much worse on stage than in movies. Decrepitude is harder to hide when you don't have magical camera tricks, heavy concealing makeup, and the energy to perform six shows a week plus matinees. Sir Charles' dilemma was a choice between retiring at the top to an empty existence (if he doesn't snag Egg) or dwindling into grandfather roles in the provinces.

Then, dénouement. A very theatrical one, taking place on stage at the dress rehearsal for Miss Will's new play. Poirot takes center stage and reveals all.

If you've read the American version of the novel or seen the Peter Ustinov film, know this: the ending was not rewritten. There are two versions of this novel. The American version (Ustinov's film) has one motive. The British version here has a different reason for murder.

You could make the case that Sir Charles was just as crazy in the British version as in the American. After all, he's a famous actor i.e., a professional liar. He fakes sincerity all the time. If he believes something is true, then so will the audience. So why not believe he can get away with murder and bigamy and win sweet, naïve Egg and his happy ever after? But the Crown has other plans for him. Oh well, that's show biz.

Hallowe'en Party (2010)

Snip! Snap! Obsession grasps all in the terrible dragon's flaming jaws in this spooky tale of child murder

Fidelity to text

The plot's simplified, but also improved. No loose ends here!

Quality of movie

Creepy, atmospheric, wonderfully acted, but a few minutes too short.

Agatha was 78 when she published *Hallowe'en Party* in 1969 and it shows. It's got a wonderfully clever setup. She even tells you who the murderer has got to be (if you consider the ramifications of shoving a 12-year-old face-first into a bucket of water) yet it also needed at least one more rewrite along with some serious editing. Too many plot threads are brought out and then left dangling free. There are too many duplicate phrases where you can see she was trying to decide which was the better way to express her thought.

Mark Gatiss did a wonderful rewrite. He wove in loose plot threads, deleted extra characters, added some with better motivations, and turned what could have been a mess into an excellent movie.

He was ably assisted by stellar performances, great music, atmospheric set dressing, and a fabulous, wonderful, glorious garden portraying Michael Garfield's quarry garden suitable for gods to walk through.

The garden, a private one, is Beckley Park. It's not a quarry garden, stepping down into what was once a vast, industrial stone pit. It's beautifully clipped topiary. You should especially notice the dragon teeth hedge, echoing the snap-dragon the kids carefully but eagerly devour at the fateful Halloween party.

If you're unfamiliar with topiary, it's the art of pruning yew or boxwood into shapes and then – this is the hard part – maintaining those shapes while the shrubs continue to grow. Topiary needs to be clipped faithfully while not killing the shrubs. Think of it as English tree-torture, like bonsai is Japanese tree-torture, and espalier is French tree-torture. Nothing in nature will grow into these shapes but a skilled and patient gardener can bend nature to his will.

Gardening at this level is art. Unlike a painting or a symphony, this art exists in four dimensions, in time as well as space. A painting is finished. Having a mind of its own, a garden never finishes. It's always growing and changing. It always needs maintenance. It transforms from season to season so what you see in May is not what you see in October; July is not January. A gardener must accommodate the location, the planting zone, sun, prevailing winds, and expected rainfall. The gardener *must* cope with insects, blight, animals, and homeowners' associations who don't appreciate what the gardener is trying to do.

Topiary gardens add an additional layer of complexity. Annuals are replanted each year. Perennial flowers and grasses take a few years to reach maturity.

Judith Butler
(*Amelia Bullmore*),
the secretive widow

Miranda Butler
(*Mary Higgins*),
the fey daughter

Michael Garfield
(*Julian Rhind-Tutt*),
the tempting gardener

Rowena Drake
(*Deborah Findlay*),
the besotted mother

Reverend Cottrell
(*Timothy West*),
the good Samaritan

Mrs. Goodbody
(*Paola Dionisotti*),
the hedge witch

Topiary takes decades to reach the point the artist envisioned (if it ever does). Once reached, expect faithful, dedicated, highly-skilled trimming to keep the shrubs at their peak.

Do you wonder why Michael Garfield is obsessed? He has to be obsessed with beauty and control just to keep up with those recalcitrant, demanding plants! Most gardeners have some obsession because only our obsession keeps us going; reading deceitful nursery catalogs, dreaming and planning and weeding, instead of turning the entire garden over to grass which is, frankly, much easier.

But a lawn isn't beautiful like a garden filled with beautifully shaped hedges and spilling over with flowers, transforming with the seasons. A mowed lawn's purpose is to serve as a backdrop to the perennial border and the spring bulbs.

I'm not saying I approve of Michael Garfield's behavior. Murder, even when you compost the bodies afterwards to feed the soil to make the best, most ethereal garden soil possible that will grow anything you want, even Himalayan Blue Poppies, is still murder.

But I can understand the obsession of the true artist who sublimates everything to his art, who willingly sacrifices his own flesh and blood because what else matters but the garden?

Miranda is an interesting character. She's fey and lives in a world of her own imagination. Perhaps too subtly, film and novel showed that she's credulous. She believes what she wants to believe and since she doesn't lie or have ulterior motives, she doesn't think other people lie or have ulterior motives. I base this on her reaction to Joyce. Everyone else rolls their eyes at Joyce's wild stories. No one believes Joyce because she's been proved a liar too many times. Even the vicar dismisses Joyce, particularly her story about discovering the wonders of India.

In novel and film, Miranda believes Joyce.

She and Joyce are friends. They tell each other their secrets. I'll agree Miranda should have showed more emotion about Joyce's tragic death. On the other hand, Michael Garfield's been feeding her lies for years. Who's to say Miranda doesn't believe that Joyce has passed into a far more exciting, magical, and wonderful world? The same world Miranda wants so badly to join; the world where the plants and birds talk to her and she's more than a passive observer.

Would Miranda have drunk the poison to atone for Joyce's death and enter that magical realm on the other side of the garden? You bet she would.

I don't expect a girl on the cusp of adolescence to be wary or smart. Miranda's mother, Judith, should have known better but then we wouldn't have a plot. She had the affair with Michael, then fled, hoping to never see him again. She realized he was a dangerous, obsessive, fallen archangel. So why, when Michael Garfield showed up in her safely anonymous village where no one she knew would ever find her, didn't she leave?

This is where a few extra minutes of dialog would have explained why Judith didn't pack up her daughter and head for the hills. It would have especially explained why Judith didn't warn Miranda away from Michael. Judith didn't think Michael could count? That he'd believe her story about love at first sight, quickie wedding, and sudden widowhood? Maybe mom's where Miranda gets her credulousness from.

I also wanted a few extra minutes with Rowena Drake, to see why she was so obsessed with Michael Garfield.

Another fascination with the film was the snap-dragon. Letting your kids play with alcohol-soaked, blazing raisins went out of fashion decades ago. Imagine the lawsuits over burned mouths and fingers if you served up a snap-dragon at your kid's birthday party. Mark Gatiss didn't make up the chant. He cribbed it from Robert Chambers' *Book of Days* (1879):

Here he comes with flaming bowl,
Don't he mean to take his toll,
Snip! Snap! Dragon!
Take care you don't take too much,
Be not greedy in your clutch,
Snip! Snap! Dragon!
With his blue and lapping tongue
Many of you will be stung,
Snip! Snap! Dragon!

Words of wisdom for us to heed. Michael the Archangel slew the dragon. Michael Garfield was a dragon in human form: obsessive, a slave to beauty, and beyond petty mortal concerns.

General Information

Based on: *Hallowe'en Party* (novel, 1969)
Run time: 1 hr., 29 min. **Subtitles:** Yes

Writer: Mark Gatiss **Director:** Charlie Palmer

Cast

David Suchet as Hercule Poirot
Zoë Wanamaker as Ariadne Oliver
Paul Thornley as Inspector Raglan
David Yelland as George

Amelia Bullmore as Judith Butler
Mary Higgins as Miranda Butler
Julian Rhind-Tutt as Michael Garfield
Deborah Findlay as Rowena Drake
Georgia King as Frances Drake
Ian Hallard as Edmund Drake
Sophie Thompson as Mrs. Reynolds
Macy Nyman as Joyce Reynolds
Richard Breislin as Leopold Reynolds
Timothy West as Reverend Cottrell
Paola Dionisotti as Mrs. Goodbody

Film Locations

Beckley Park, Oxfordshire (topiary garden)
St. Ethelreda's Church, Old Hatfield, Hertfordshire (church)
Fore Street, Hatfield, Hertfordshire (solicitor's office)

Murder on the Orient Express (2010)

Poirot rages against vigilante justice but comes off as more pissy about cold and hunger aboard the train

Fidelity to text

Add a suicide (caused by Poirot), a stoning (which he disregards), Ratchett supposedly repenting, and Col. Arbuthnot taking justice into his own hands.

Quality of movie

Beautifully filmed, dressed, acted, and a terrific score. The train looks great! It's nice to see stokers too, showing how trains are powered. But I didn't like *this* Poirot.

David Suchet does a wonderful job playing Poirot. His portrayal is definitive and it's hard to think of anyone else being Poirot. I've seen them all so, yes, Suchet is Poirot.

Here, however, he's not just grumpy over human foibles. He's angry. He's got reason to be, but at the same time, I couldn't accept the climax in the bar car where he rants about individuals taking justice into their own hands. I believe we're watching Poirot being forced to see the limitations of human justice systems and that humans are inherently messy and flawed. Expecting the perfectibility of humanity "if only everyone followed this set of rules" is an idiot's game.

Poirot is a well-dressed ball of rage from the start. The film opens with him solving a murder in Palestine involving a British officer. He proves the woman's death was accidental but the officer with whom she'd been having an affair lied, thus complicating his investigation. Poirot confronts the young, adulterous officer about his failings. The officer replies by snatching a guard's pistol and blowing his brains out, splattering blood and brains on Poirot. If Poirot had been less harsh, would that have happened? Would the officer's wife have become a penniless widow? He'll never know, and that eats at him.

In an Istanbul souk, Poirot eavesdrops on Mary Debenham and John Arbuthnot. They watch a native woman being pursued by an angry mob led by her husband, intent on vigilante justice. She's carrying another man's child. An adulteress! The horror. Mary and John are appalled. Poirot is more sanguine because hey, it's another culture and that woman knew the rules and transgressed anyway. Except the Poirot *we* know would have added that we don't know that woman was an adulteress. People lie all the time. Maybe a jealous rival accused her. Maybe the woman's husband was tired of her and wanted a younger, hotter replacement. Maybe both. We only know what the angry mob is screaming. We watch a woman, in accordance with her culture's rules, get stoned to death.

At the hotel, Poirot can't relax. A telegram from Scotland Yard summons him back to London ASAP. He meets M. Bouc, an acquaintance who's high up in the Wagon-Lit food chain. M. Bouc gets Poirot a berth on the fully-booked Orient Express by having him take

Mary Debenham
(*Jessica Chastain*),
the lame governess

John Arbuthnot
(*David Morrissey*),
the longtime officer

Princess Dragomiroff
(*Eileen Atkins*),
the posh aristocrat

Pierre Michel
(*Denis Ménochet*),
the sole conductor

Caroline Hubbard
(*Barbara Hershey*),
the brusque American

Greta Ohlsson
(*Marie-Josée Croze*),
the godly missionary

the bed belonging to someone who hasn't arrived. Poirot boards and meets his new and unpleasant roommate.

He's pissier than ever, drinking alone in the bar. Ratchett approaches like so many clients do, begging for help. Poirot doesn't like him and turns him down. Much noise and shenanigans all night long, preventing him from sleeping, culminating in the train meeting an avalanche and losing power so everyone's shivering in the dark and eating cold food. Ratchett's body is found.

Poirot's livid. He's always angry when he's cold and damp, but a man he could have saved is dead because he refused his help. After all, murder is always wrong.

Isn't it?

Except that in this case, Ratchett is really Cassetti, a notorious kidnapper and murderer.

I want to be very clear because virtually every review of *Orient Express* gets this wrong.

Ratchett didn't only murder Daisy Armstrong! He kidnapped her and killed her within the hour. He had no intention of returning her in exchange for the ransom. But she wasn't the only victim. Indirectly, he murdered *five other people*. Daisy's unborn sibling. We're never told whether Sonia (mom) was carrying Daisy's brother or sister, but believe me, the obstetrician who delivered the grossly premature, guaranteed-to-die baby knew. So did Sonia and Colonel Armstrong. That baby counts. Sonia died soon thereafter. She counts. Grief and horror overwhelm Colonel Armstrong and he shoots himself. He counts. The French nursery maid is accused by the local police of aiding and abetting the kidnapper. She hangs herself in her cell. She counts. Her mother dies of grief. She counts. Those people shouldn't be forgotten.

Ratchett didn't shoot them down in cold blood, but he murdered them just the same.

He destroyed the lives of everyone connected to the Armstrong family. Grandma. Godmother. Sister. Brother-in-law. Best friend. Valet. Governess. Cook. Chauffeur (and lover of French nursery maid). French nursery maid's father. Obstetrician. Son of bought-off prosecuting attorney. And these are just the people whose stories we're told! Any murder victim's family will tell you how far out the grief spreads, how it never dies, and how often the justice system punishes them more than the guilty.

General Information

Based on: *Murder on the Orient Express* (novel, 1934)
Run time: 1 hr., 29 min. **Subtitles:** Yes

Writer: Stewart Harcourt
Director: Philip Martin

Cast

David Suchet as Hercule Poirot
Serge Hazanavicius as Xavier Bouc

Toby Jones as Samuel Ratchett
Brian J. Smith as Hector MacQueen
Hugh Bonneville as Edward Masterman
David Morrissey as John Arbuthnot
Jessica Chastain as Mary Debenham
Eileen Atkins as Princess Dragomiroff
Susanne Lothar as Hildegarde Schmidt
Barbara Hershey as Caroline Hubbard
Marie-Josée Croze as Greta Ohlsson
Stanley Weber as Count Andrenyi
Elena Satine as Countess Andrenyi
Joseph Mawle as Antonio Foscarelli
Denis Ménochet as Pierre Michel
Samuel West as Dr. Constantine

Film Location

Malta

It's perfectly understandable why these twelve people plot Ratchett's execution. The state, which they relied on, found him innocent of kidnapping and murder. We're told the prosecutor mishandled the case. I'd suggest that the judge and the jury were also either bought off or intimidated into letting Ratchett go free.

The Armstrong family and friends were denied justice. As though they didn't matter. What are they supposed to do?

I understand Poirot complaining about vigilante justice, especially after seeing that woman stoned. He's always been on the side of the law. Except when he's not. Take *Dead Man's Folly*. He lets abettor Amy Folliat and her murdering son take the easy way out. They aren't hauled off to face the Crown. Did the Tucker family get justice for Marlene and Old Merdell? No, they did not. They're peasants and that implies they don't matter.

I can accept Poirot having a crisis of conscience. I can't accept his open cruelty to people who've suffered terribly and who will continue to suffer terribly until the day they die. Clearly, compared to crystal pure, abstract justice, they don't matter.

And for those who claim Ratchett was repenting? Because you saw him on his knees in prayer? Um, no. This is where atheist Hollywood gets Christianity wrong. First, he asks for protection, not forgiveness. Nor does he atone for his sins. Second, many people go through the motions of praying (it looks the same) but they behave as though a prayer is like dropping a coin into a vending machine. Put in the coin, get the candy bar. Say the prayer, get forgiven. As though repentance, atonement, and changed behavior aren't required!

Nothing in Ratchett's behavior showed that he'd gotten religion. He creeps on Mary Debenham. He's rude to his secretary and valet. Oh, he *was* sorry. Sorry he was recognized and sorry he was being threatened. But sorry over murdering Daisy and five other people? You didn't hear a single word about *them* in his prayer. They didn't matter.

They do matter. And so do the Armstrong family and friends, something this Poirot seems to have forgotten.

The Clocks (2011)

A typist is suspected of murder when she finds a stranger's body in a living room full of timepieces

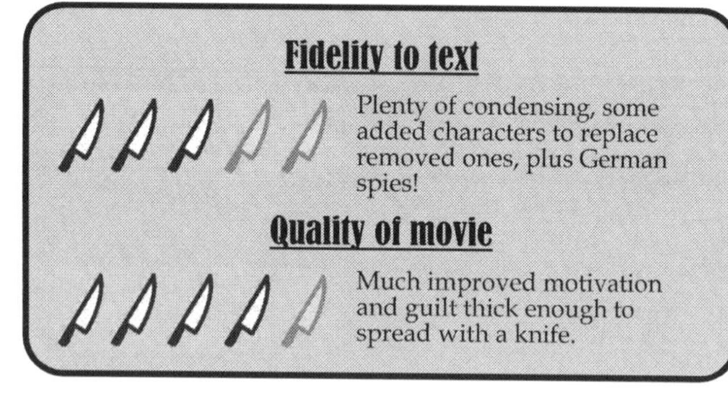

The *Poirot* series lives in a timeless world where it's almost always a sunny day in early June of 1935. There's rarely a mention of what everyone in England is afraid of: the next European war.

It's easy these days to think that Europe has always been at peace or at least the citizens haven't been trying to slaughter each other. Not true. Prior to the Great War, the 43 years between 1871 and 1914 had been the longest interlude without continent-wide warfare. That's only been surpassed by the post-WWII period. Seventy years with nothing more major than the Balkan civil wars and now, Ukraine. Hope you enjoyed it while it lasted.

Historically, the natural state for Europeans is to be up to their eyebrows in blood. Which is why it's a bit odd the *Poirot* series ignores the events of the time. It's true no one *knew* what would happen, but they could guess. The citizens dreaded the coming war but they thought, as everyone always does, that it would be a repeat of the last one. The Great War - vividly within living memory — was a gruesome, drawn-out slugfest. Men died by the tens of thousands in muddy trenches to gain a few feet of ground. If you were a civilian living well away from the battlefields, you'd probably be safe enough.

So it was really nice to watch a *Poirot* where actual concern is shown about what's lurking in the shadowy future. Citizens spying for Nazi Germany was a good updating of the novel's citizens spying for the Soviet Union. The rationale was much the same. The brave new world is inevitable so why not get out in front of it?

Thus, Miss Pebmarsh transforms from a fanatic who abandons her daughter and is devoted to Lenin to a fanatic devoted to preventing any mother's sons from dying as hers did. She refuses to believe her desired future might be the worse choice. I did wonder why she remained Miss Pebmarsh when she had two sons who died in the Great War. Very few cultures at that time celebrated single motherhood. But she was Miss instead of Mrs. A minor point, but an odd one.

Similarly, Mr. Ramsey transforms into Mr. Mabbut. Ramsey loathed England and loved Communism enough to cheerfully betray England and abandon his wife and kids. Jew-loathing Mabbut's so afraid of the Russians that he's happy to betray England no matter how it imperils his kids. Different motivation, same result in the end.

The story opens in the lower levels of Dover Castle,

Sheila Webb (*Jaime Winstone*), the lonely typist

Nora Brent (*Sinéad Keenan*), the watchful typist

Miss Martindale (*Lesley Sharp*), the boss typist

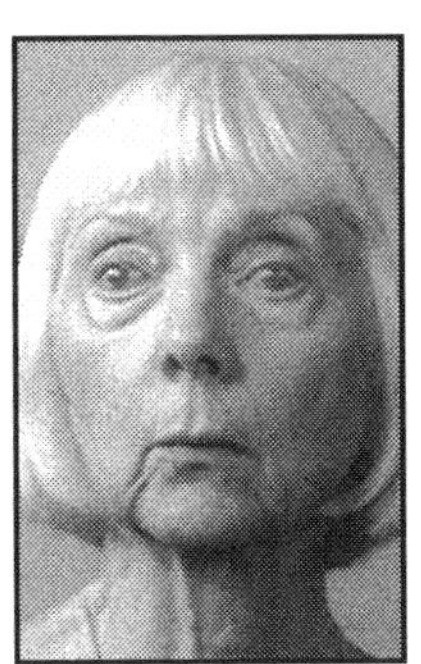
Miss Pebmarsh (*Anna Massey*), the blind developer

Val Bland (*Tessa Peake-Jones*), the hopeful heiress

Joe Bland (*Jason Watkins*), the greedy husband

where Naval Intelligence is keeping an eye on England's borders. But there's a mole in the agency sending critical documents to the Germans. Lt. Colin Race, Col. Race's son, is tasked to find the mole. Sadly, he's too busy winning money at poker to listen to his girlfriend Fiona, who called him to say she's watching the spy steal papers. Fiona and the spy die tragically. Like Miss Pebmarsh, Colin's eaten up with guilt for something he might have prevented.

He's not alone. Plenty of people fail to pay attention and are punished for it. Inspector Hardcastle and the constable ignore flighty Nora Brendt, and she's murdered because she knows something. Hardcastle has a hard time paying attention to Poirot, despite his being vouched for by Scotland Yard and Naval Intelligence. Hardcastle and his constable aren't paying attention when they tail Merlina Rival by car, and she gets murdered practically in front of them.

It's easy to ignore unimportant people when you've got more important things to do. It's easy to use unimportant people. They don't count. That's why Miss Martindale (who'd be mortally offended if you told her she had the same lack of morals as a treasonous spy) could set up her employee Sheila Webb as the patsy in the scheme to steal an inheritance. Sheila's a nobody from nowhere, with no family or friends to help her. She's also a tart, conducting a lonely affair with a client on company time. She doesn't deserve a moment of consideration.

But when you think that way, soon everyone who isn't a close friend, cherished relative, or a high-status person who can help you up the ladder becomes a worthless nonentity who can be sacrificed for the greater good. This thinking is how you end up with heaps of corpses: sacrifices are necessary to bring about the shining city upon the hill.

Not *your* sacrifice, naturally. Someone else, who is unimportant.

This is also why I didn't object to Colin's infatuation with Sheila. Yeah, his girlfriend just died tragically and he should have spent more time grieving, rather than falling for the next damsel who needed his attention. But he did grieve, to the point where he hallucinates Fiona's presence. He's guilt-ridden because he ignored Fiona when she needed him. Having a terrified damsel run into him, begging for help with a murdered man, was a way to atone. If he helps this girl, it might, in some small measure, expiate his guilt. She needs him! He won't ignore her, like he ignored Fiona.

Sheila does need Colin's help. The typist found the dead body in Miss Pebmarsh's clock-filled house. Every policeman knows the person who finds the body is often the cause of that person's death. Hardcastle thinks so, especially after Miss Pebmarsh denies making the phone call requesting Sheila Webb's services. Other citizens tell Hardcastle that they've seen the dead man in Sheila's company. According to her employer, Sheila's got loose morals and shouldn't be trusted.

The conclusion is obvious. Knifing a man isn't something a respectable, important citizen would do. She must be guilty. Sheila's guilt is made more obvious when Colin discovers the stolen clock and the bloody knife in her handbag.

Lucky for her, Poirot is suspicious. Unlike Hardcastle, Poirot pays attention. He listens to what people say to him, drawing them into disarming conversations as though they actually mattered. He makes the people around him feel important and valued and, as a result, he gets information that Hardcastle misses.

The neighboring Mabbutt girls search the garden for Poirot and provide evidence of spying. The crazy cat lady doesn't just supply a critical piece of evidence (a mysterious laundry van), but she also, a la Hastings, says the mystery man went to Miss Pebmarsh's home to be murdered. This clarifies the situation, turning it on its head so it can be viewed in the correct orientation. Most of all, Valerie Bland (Miss Martindale's co-conspirator in the inheritance scheme) admits something that directly contradicts what she'd claimed earlier about her background. She lives in Dover to be near her sister, who Poirot discovers is Miss Martindale.

Poirot succeeds because he recognizes that Sheila Webb matters. If she doesn't, then no one matters. In Pebmarsh and Mabbut's brave new world, innocence or guilt can be assigned as needed to get things done, to make things work, and to build the shining city upon the hill of bones.

General Information

Based on: *The Clocks* (novel, 1963)
Run time: 1 hr., 29 min. **Subtitles:** Yes

Writer: Stewart Harcourt
Director: Charlie Palmer

Cast

David Suchet as Hercule Poirot
Phil Daniels as Inspector Hardcastle
Tom Burke as Lt. Colin Race
Ben Righton as Constable Jenkins

Jaime Winstone as Sheila Webb
Lesley Sharp as Miss Martindale
Sinéad Keenan as Nora Brent
Anna Massey as Miss Pebmarsh
Tessa Peake-Jones as Val Bland
Jason Watkins as Joe Bland
Stephen Boxer as Christopher Mabbutt
Phoebe Strickland as May Mabbutt
Isabella Parriss as Jenny Mabbutt
Beatie Edney as Mrs. Hemmings
Abigail Thaw as Rachel Waterhouse
Guy Henry as Matthew Waterhouse
Frances Barber as Merlina Rival

Film Locations

Waterloo Crescent, Dover, Kent (hotel exterior)
Woburn Walk, Bloomsbury, London (Cavendish Secretarial Bureau)
St Margaret's Bay, Kent (beach and seafront)
Thornhill Crescent, London (Wilbraham Crescent)
Dover Castle, Kent (castle scenes)

Elephants Can Remember (2013)

Horrific psychiatric treatments and a daughter's backstory turn middling novel into compelling film

Elephants Can Remember (1972) is the next-to-last book Agatha wrote, followed by the worse and sadder *Postern of Fate* in 1973. *Curtain* and *Sleeping Murder*, although published afterwards, were written during WWII to provide a nest egg for her family in case she died during the German bombing of London.

The final novels demonstrate Agatha's writing abilities were failing. The seed of a good novel is buried inside *Elephants* but even the best editing — which it didn't receive — wouldn't have made it bloom. It's repetitious, with plot threads dangling everywhere. Ariadne interviews elderly people, then repeats the conversation to Poirot. Not much happens and you won't care about any of the people involved.

A faithful retelling on film would have been dire; an exercise in stasis and tedium. Lucky for us, Nick Dear's script fixed the faults and wove in some of those dangling threads.

The major change is adding the fate of Dorothea Preston-Gray Jarrow's daughter. Dorothea is Margaret's twin sister. The novel calls them Dolly and Molly, something the film dispensed with although that added to the confusion as to who an elephant was remembering. The novel mentions Dorothea's daughter and son. She murdered the son, a toddler, and blamed the killing on her daughter. Dorothea also murdered at least one other child, and injured or tried to injure several other children, including those of her twin sister, Margaret. Dorothea was always jealous of Margaret.

Fidelity to text

They added a loony head-shrinker, his murder, and the daughter of one of his victims, but they slotted in nicely.

Quality of movie

The two separate plots were tied up effectively, although a few more clues along the way would have helped.

But what happened to Dorothea's vanished, unnamed daughter? The film tells her story. She was a child accused of murder, the accusation hushed up when horrified family members and authorities learned it was mom all along. The child was hustled off to boarding schools, rarely seeing her mother and never learning the truth about what she said and did. Dad's dead, so is baby brother, and the rest of the relatives turn their back on her. Sometimes, daughter is reunited with mom, when she's well enough to leave the snake pit asylums she's trapped in. When mom's in the snake pit, enduring horror after horror, she writes to her daughter. The letters are filled with dreadful stories of torture disguised as therapy and the staff telling her how it's all for her own good despite her agonized protests and asking why did her sister abandon her.

Then it happens. A reunion between daughter and mom, at mom's sister's home. Except the day daughter

Celia Ravenscroft
(*Vanessa Kirby*),
the suspect girlfriend

Desmond Burton-Cox
(*Ferdinand Kingsley*),
the artistic heir

Mrs. Burton-Cox
(*Greta Scacchi*),
the concerned mother

Dr. Willoughby
(*Iain Glen*),
the psychiatrist

Marie McDermott
(*Alexandra Dowling*),
the helpful assistant

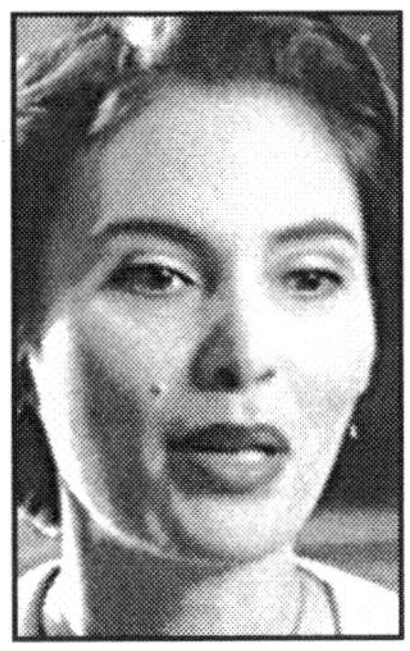

Zelie Rouxelle
(*Elsa Mollien*),
the haunted au pair

arrives, tragedy happens again. Mom shoves twin sister over the cliff. The child overhears only part of an agonized conversation afterwards, where uncle plots with the au pair to murder mom. The daughter is hustled off to Canada on the very next transport, never to learn anything further, including the truth of what happened.

What is that girl, all growed up now, to think? No one — to spare her feelings no doubt — sat her down and told her the despairing truth, unsparing of the gruesome details. Instead, she had to come up with a story of her own.

Which brings me to the film. Films need action, so why not play up the agonized journey of Dorothea's lost daughter, desperate to avenge mom? And here we are. Daughter gets a name, Mary Jarrow, and a mission to exact retribution on everyone who wronged mom, starting with the sadistic alienist who waterboarded her and claimed it was for her own good.

She'll need to earn enough money to come to England, portable job skills, an alias (Marie McDermott) so she can wreak vengeance on all and sundry without interference, and a destination. The logical place is the Willoughby Institute. That's where mom was waterboarded.

Dr. Willoughby, the son of Professor Willoughby and current head of the Institute, no longer uses hydrotherapy on his loony patients. He doesn't believe forcibly submerging patients for hours or days in a bathtub or spraying them with a fire hose works. Hot or cold, water treatment doesn't treat mental illness. Making the water colder or hotter to discipline unruly patients doesn't help.

Mary was probably relieved the younger Willoughby doesn't follow his father's treatment schedules. She must have been equally relieved to learn the old hydrotherapy room in the basement of the institute is still fully functional as if waiting for her revenge.

For his part, Dr. Willoughby was thrilled to hire a young woman from Canada who was not only a good office worker (willing to work cheap!), but willing to be his mistress. This is, after all, why he maintains an apartment at the institute. Yes, it's convenient when he works late and can't go home to the wife and kiddies but that's not all the flat is useful for. Pay close attention when Dr. Willoughby admits to Poirot that he doesn't have patient records for Desmond Burton-Cox. Why doesn't he? Because Mrs. Burton-Cox was poor (or so she claimed) and paid with sex. She probably stared at the same bedroom ceiling that Mary did.

Just like Mary Jarrow might have a touch of her mother's madness, Dr. Willoughby has his father's lack of ethics and morals.

You can almost grasp Mary's point of view, looking at the story from her side of the looking glass. Since her hated aunt and uncle — who could have saved mom — are dead, she's forced to wreak her vengeance on the survivors: Celia and her fiancé, Desmond. Why should they get their happy ending? Mary the innocent victim didn't get hers.

That's where your sympathy will end. You might make a case for Mary murdering Dr. Willoughby and escaping the hangman afterwards to spend the rest of her life at Broadmoor Asylum, but trying to strangle Desmond? That's a bathtub too far. It's also idiotic, because he's far stronger than she is, even when taken by surprise. She was lucky to escape. Her attempted murder of Celia suggests that Mary inherited at least some of her mother's murderous tendencies. Celia never harmed her. She was as innocent as the children her mom murdered.

Like Celia, Mary deserved the truth. But unlike Celia, who apparently was not ostracized by relatives and exiled to Canada, no one took in poor Mary and told her what really happened.

This added backstory hugely enhanced the film. Motivation, tension, drama, high stakes, and misguided revenge. They're all here, turning a short story padded into a novel into a worthwhile movie.

And there's still more! Ariadne interviewing elephants and proving to Poirot why he should pay attention to her intuition. Mrs. Burton-Cox buttonholing Ariadne to ask impertinent questions, showing the perils to authors who appear before the public. The backstage world of concert pianists, the horrors of the past, and, most of all, how old sins cast long shadows.

The past is never past, not as long as someone remembers. And people, as Ariadne noted, have as good a memory as elephants.

General Information

Based on: *Elephants Can Remember* (novel, 1972)
Run time: 1 hr., 29 min. **Subtitles:** Yes

Writer: Nick Dear **Director:** John Strickland

Cast

David Suchet as Hercule Poirot
Zoë Wanamaker as Ariadne Oliver
Vincent Regan as Detective Inspector Beale
Danny Webb as Superintendent Garroway

Adrian Lukis as General Ravenscroft
Annabel Mullion as Lady Ravenscroft
Vanessa Kirby as Celia Ravenscroft
Greta Scacchi as Mrs. Burton-Cox
Ferdinand Kingsley as Desmond Burton-Cox
Iain Glen as Dr. Willoughby
Jo-Anne Stockham as Mrs. Willoughby
Alexandra Dowling as Marie McDermott
Elsa Mollien as Zelie Rouxelle
Caroline Blakiston as Julia Carstairs
Hazel Douglas as Mrs. Matcham
Maxine Evans as Mrs. Buckle
Ruth Sheen as Madame Rosentelle
Claire Cox as Dorothea Jarrow

Film Locations

Longcross Manor, Lyne, Surrey (Overcliffe)
Seven Sisters, East Sussex (chalk sea cliffs)
Sheraton Grand London Park Lane Hotel, London (book awards)
Florin Court, Charterhouse Square, London (Poirot's apartment)
Dean Rees House, London (Willoughby Institute)
Greys Court, Henley-on-Thames, Oxfordshire (Carstairs' house)
Netherwylde Farm House, Aldenham, Hertfordshire (Matcham's house)

The Big Four (2013)

Christie's worst novel is turned into one of the best Christie films thanks to a script that rebuilt the story

Fidelity to text

Mark Gatiss completely re-arranged and recast the novel into something where, at best, the names and situations match.

Quality of movie

Gatiss made it a much better movie than it should have been! Cohesive, internally consistent, and reasonably plausible.

I was dreading *The Big Four*. Agatha "wrote" the novel at the worst time in her life. Her mother was dead, her marriage was over, she was enduring the public humiliation from her eleven-day disappearance (even today, still white-hot in everyone's minds), and her publisher was demanding she fulfill her contract like right now. Like today. Like we don't care that your life has been ruined as long as you produce something we can print and sell.

They're a publishing house. You expected better?

Anyway, Campbell Christie, Archie's brother, found a solution. He suggested that she take twelve Poirot short stories previously published in *Sketch* magazine in 1924 and string them together into a novel. He helped by revising the beginning and ending of each short story, making them flow together into a more coherent narrative.

To my knowledge, they haven't been republished in their original form. They're certainly not in *Hercule Poirot's Casebook*, which contains fifty stories and claims to be the definitive collection. I'd have remembered reading the death by chessboard or the murder by leg of mutton. So, unless you've got the pertinent issues of *Sketch* handy, reading *The Big Four* is the only way you'll read these very early Poirot tales.

Considering Agatha's stress levels, she (and Campbell) performed a fairly good Frankenstein surgery, stitching the stories together into a novel that was never meant to be.

The Big Four is a ridiculous, over-the-top, round-the-world thriller involving an evil Chinese mastermind (a la Fu Manchu), a mad French lady scientist, Poirot's secret twin brother, an American soap millionaire, and a plot to rule the world. It almost reads as a parody of that era's Bulldog Drummond novels. Bulldog is patriotic, loyal, physically and morally intrepid. He's got money, brains, and friends. He predates Doc Savage and The Executioner, but enjoys similar, wildly implausible, globe-spanning thrilling adventures.

Read *The Big Four*, keeping Bulldog and Doc Savage in mind, and you can see what Agatha (and Campbell) had in mind. It didn't have much to do with Poirot. The book met her deadline and gave her enough breathing space to write *The Mystery of the Blue Train*. But it still isn't a very good book. It reads like a badly composed, over elaborate Cobb salad. Individual elements are tasty but there's just too much going on.

That's the novel Mark Gatiss had to adapt. He seized

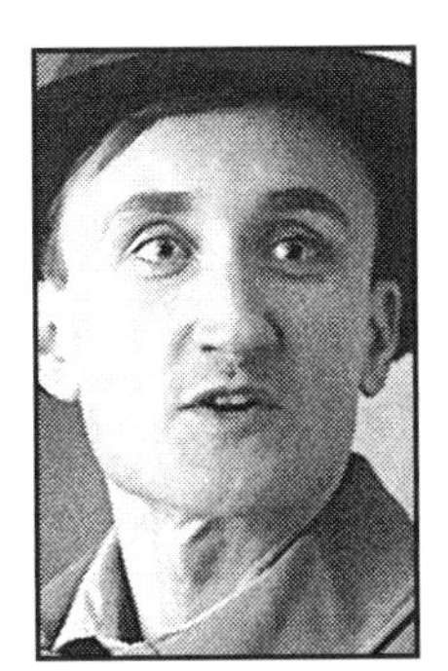

Tysoe
(*Tom Brooke*),
the driven reporter

Flossie Monro
(*Sarah Parish*),
the alluring actress

Abe Ryland
(*James Carroll Jordan*),
the mystery man

Madame Olivier
(*Patricia Hodge*),
the tart scientist

Dr. Quentin
(*Simon Lowe*),
the obscure physician

Diana Paynter
(*Teresa Banham*),
the jilted wife

upon names, plots, and scenarios. He rewrote, rearranged, and turned situations topsy-turvy. He addressed the central issue head-on: Is it possible, even plausible, for a small cabal of evil, international geniuses to take over the world and run it from their evil villain lair in the Swiss Alps?

Heck, could a cabal of egotistical, international evil geniuses even get along long enough to not kill each other within a few hours?

You're told the answer in one of the earliest scenes, soon after the series' gang of four (Japp, Hastings, Miss Lemon, and valet George) assemble for Poirot's funeral. Intrepid reporter Tysoe confronts Ingles, an important man in the foreign service. Tysoe claims he's got information about The Big Four. They're causing riots and mayhem all around the world, destabilizing it so they can seize control. Ingles eyes him, recognizes the credulous, tinfoil-hatted idiot he's dealing with, and dismisses Tysoe's story as Bulldog Drummond claptrap.

There are other little clues to Gatiss' intentions scattered throughout. How could an aging, has-been actress be involved with the Big Four? Could Diana Paynter be correct that her husband's not a secret mastermind, merely a commonplace adulterer? Why would the anonymous, murdered informant be wearing decades-out-of-date formalwear with the remains of a costumer's label inside? Why would the estranged nephew of the murdered Sinophile keep a trunkful of theatrical souvenirs? And why would said nephew not show up to collect his inheritance? The Sinophile had a very nice collection of Chinese antiquities stored inside a very nice manor. An heir with sense would have shown up promptly to rake in the loot from the estate sale. Unless that heir had other roles to play.

And so he does.

There is no complicated plot involving criminal masterminds and world domination. The world is busy preparing to fight another devastating war all on its own. This is a different kind of lunacy, far more likely and far more local. The Sinophile's nephew has been pulling the strings all along. He's a master puppeteer, manipulating the gullible Tysoe as well as the hypochondriac Stephen Paynter. He's in the background in every scene pushing, urging, coaxing his subjects to do what they want to do anyway.

You don't have to live in a villain's lair under the Swiss Alps to make events go your way. You just have to meet enough people who want whatever will help *your* plans along and then persuade them to follow the dictates of their own hearts.

Is it plausible that a character actor could manipulate the rich and famous? Any conman will tell you yes.

If you're willing to let yourself go and enjoy the ride, it's a fun film from start to finish. The opening funeral reunites Hastings, Japp, and a very much missed and sadly underused Miss Lemon. And her cat.

The scene where Abe Ryland, millionaire, playing chess with the Russian grandmaster perfectly encapsulates the rest of the film. It's gorgeously shot and wildly implausible. Would a pack of rich elites — wearing the finest of evening dress — watch a chess match, hoping to send a signal to the world that we should give peace a chance?

I doubt it. The chess was reasonably accurate, however. Grandmasters and duffers of that era opened with the Ruy Lopez. The third move places the white bishop in column b, row 5. Watching that nerve-biting scene reminded me of the Sheep to Shawl contest at the Pennsylvania Farm Show. For us fiber arts fans, watching the sheep being sheared, the fleece carded and spun by a team of spinsters, then dyed and woven into a shawl was riveting. Non-fans like Bill leapt for the exits, desperate for escape. Non-chess fans will understand the emotion.

Luckily, when grandmaster Savaranoff moves his bishop, he's electrocuted and the plot kicks into high gear. More victims stack up quickly: coshed, knifed, cooked on a heating grill, and then Poirot himself dies in a bomb blast. The millionaire disappears under suspicious circumstances as does the French lady scientist. They must have done it! In between the killings, we keep running into Flossie Monroe, aging ingenue with a mysterious admirer of her own.

It all ties together beautifully. I enjoyed it when I didn't think I would. I didn't think *The Big Four* was filmable. I was happily proved wrong.

General Information

Based on: *The Big Four* (novel, 1927)
Run time: 1 hr., 27 min. **Subtitles:** Yes

Writers: Ian Hallard, Mark Gatiss
Director: Peter Lydon

Cast

David Suchet as Hercule Poirot
Hugh Fraser as Captain Hastings
Pauline Moran as Miss Lemon
Philip Jackson as Asst. Commissioner Japp
Nicholas Burns as Inspector Meadows
David Yelland as George

Tom Brooke as Tysoe
James Carroll Jordan as Abe Ryland
Patricia Hodge as Madame Olivier
Sarah Parish as Flossie Monro
Steven Pacey as Stephen Paynter
Teresa Banham as Diana Paynter
Jack Farthing as Gerald Paynter
Simon Lowe as Dr. Quentin
Peter Symonds as Jonathan Whalley
Barbara Kirby as Mrs. Andrews
Alex Palmer as Robert Grant

Film Locations

Stone Buildings, Lincoln's Inn, London (Ingles' office exterior)
The Manor House, Buckingham, Buckinghamshire (Whalley home exterior)
Little Missenden, Buckinghamshire (Whalley home)
Hughenden Manor, Buckinghamshire (prison gate, Whalley home interior)
Kensal Green Cemetery, London (funeral)
Syon House, London (Ryland's home, Ingles' office stairs)
Nuffield Place, Oxfordshire (Paynter home)
Noël Coward Theatre, Westminster, London (Methuselah Theatre entrance)
Hackney Empire, London (#4 showdown)

Dead Man's Folly (2013)

Playing a murder game at a fête is serious business when the body of a child is found in the boathouse

The good point first: This adaptation is faithful to the text to the point of lifting entire chunks of Agatha's dialog. Except, of course, when it doesn't. Specifically, Amy Folliat didn't get to quote Edmund Spenser (1552/53-1599). Since she didn't and it describes her despair, I'll do it for her.

It's from Spenser's epic poem *The Faerie Queene*, Book One, Canto Nine, Stanza 40. I've updated the spelling and included the previous seven lines to set the stage for what she says (in italics):

> He there does now enjoy eternal rest
> And happy ease, which thou doest want and crave,
> And further from it daily wanderest:
> What if some little pain the passage have,
> That makes frail flesh to fear the bitter wave?
> Is not short pain well borne, that brings long ease,
> And lays the soul to sleep in quiet grave?
> *Sleep after toil, port after stormy seas,*
> *Ease after war, death after life does greatly please.*

Amy Folliat, despite being one of the grandest ladies in the county, endured many sorrows. Her husband was an alcoholic gambler, her dutiful older son went down with his ship, and her younger son was a greedy, cheating, lying wastrel. Three rounds of death duties left her bankrupt. She's reduced to living in penury, renting the lodge from social-climbing Sir George Stubbs, but allowed to haunt the gardens of the estate she once called home.

Fidelity to text

The usual compression of characters and changes in text, timing, and date you expect. The tacked-on Hollywood ending implied special people are above the law.

Quality of movie

This dragged. Celebrating Christie's Greenway led to interminable shots of Poirot walking pensively amidst the rhododendrons. Add intrusive music, remove action, and that elitist ending. Bleah.

After Amy Folliat quotes Spenser to Poirot, she tells him the world is full of wicked people. She should know. Younger son, James, was a shining example.

Poirot says repeatedly in the novel, not so much in this adaptation, that Amy Folliat is key to understanding the crime and its motive. That's why he returns to her, over and over. She knew what might happen when she introduced dim but gorgeous Hattie to Sir George and it did. Leopards don't change their spots.

Underlying all of Agatha's novels is a sharp understanding of human nature. Who is the most likely person to murder a wife? Her husband.

Agatha also liked to play with mistaken identity. Is someone who they claim to be? In *A Murder Is Announced*

Hattie Stubbs
(*Stephanie Leonidas*),
the dim wife

Sir George Stubbs
(*Sean Pertwee*),
the vulgar husband

Mrs. Amy Folliat
(*Sinéad Cusack*),
the last of the family

Etienne De Souza
(*Elliot Barnes-Worrell*),
the distant cousin

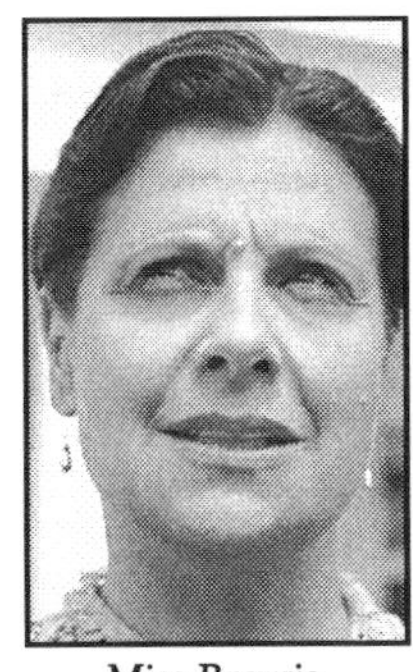

Miss Brewis
(*Rebecca Front*),
the clear-eyed staffer

Sally Legge
(*Emma Hamilton*),
the straying wife

(1950), Miss Marple observes that the disruptions of the war meant that when someone new moved into a village, you had to take it on faith they were who they claimed. If someone local vouches for them, that means immediate acceptance.

Thus, in *Dead Man's Folly* (1956), when Amy Folliat — the grandest lady in the district — accepts the parvenu Sir George Stubbs and his halfwit, foreign wife, so does everyone else. Amy Folliat may be a penniless widow, but she's still the lady of the manor.

Why does this woman who traces her ancestors back to Edmund Spenser's time accept Sir George so willingly? It isn't because he lets her live in his lodge and wander his gardens, pruning his rhododendrons. It's because, as old Merdell says, there will always be Folliats at Nasse. Sir George is her secret worthless son, James, wanted by the police in several countries, fled home to mom and seeking sanctuary.

The film gives a bit of verbal detail. Amy met James in Paris where she was chaperoning beautiful, dim, orphaned Hattie. Hattie, as Poirot later discovers, was not destitute as Amy claimed. Oh no. She was an heiress. Even better, she was a docile heiress who would sign anything if someone she trusted — like Amy Folliat — told her to. Amy thought Hattie should marry James, renamed Sir George Stubbs, and so she did.

Amy convinced herself — against all evidence — that with a new name, a new background, and a rich new wife, her worthless younger son would become a better man.

As if. The night after the couple arrive at Nasse (a dark and stormy night!), and before the locals get a close look at Hattie, he and his criminal Italian wife murder her. All the servants are new, it's been years since anyone in the village saw him, and Amy Folliat accepts him. Thus, James Folliat becomes Sir George Stubbs, using swindled real Hattie's money to buy Nasse.

A big mistake in the film was not having Sean Pertwee wear a beard. Sir George's beard was mentioned several times in the novel. A beard at the time was unusual but a beard disguises a man from villagers who might otherwise remember him. It was hard to believe no one other than Old Merdell recognized him. Any of the older residents could have.

The music was off-putting. While better orchestrated than a typical TV movie by far, it made sure you knew when something ominous was about to happen, when to jump, when to swoon, and when to worry. It was intrusive, unusual for a series that usually does the music quite well. The brass band at the fête was a nice touch.

On the plus side, the film looked great. Many of the outdoor scenes were shot at Greenway so you get a peek at Agatha's house.

Etienne De Souza has a gorgeous sailing yacht, and I wanted to see a lot more of it. I couldn't discover which vintage ship played that role but she's a beauty.

A tiny added bit of plot had Sir George framing De Souza. That was clever. A bigger, added plot point that didn't get cleverly exploited was having De Souza arrested for murder instead of sailing back to the Caribbean. While Poirot's investigating, De Souza's cooling his heels at Wandsworth awaiting trial. We don't see them speak and we should have.

The tacked-on ending was wrong, wrong, wrong. I understand Sir George needs to play the bereaved and grieving husband in public, but why is he sobbing in private? He got away with murder. He fooled everyone in England, thanks to his mother aiding and abetting him. The substitute Hattie vanished, letting him wait a decent interval, "meet" an Italian beauty, and marry her.

While he's weeping drunken crocodile tears, Poirot confronts Amy Folliat with her complicity. She demands and gets a private interview with Sir George. Although it happens offstage, it's clear a murder/suicide takes place, saving the Crown the cost of a public trial. And Poirot approves.

Wrong! Unacceptable! Three people died because Amy Folliat refused to see her son for what he was and Poirot let her take the easy way out. There's no justice for Marlene Tucker or Old Merdell. Maybe that's why the scriptwriter dropped the interview with the Tucker family. Aristocrats like the Folliats are above the law and peasants like the Tuckers don't deserve equal treatment.

This "rules for thee, but not for me" ending tipped my preference toward the Peter Ustinov version.

General Information

Based on: *Dead Man's Folly* (novel, 1956)
Run time: 1 hr., 29 min. **Subtitles:** Yes

Writer: Nick Dear **Director:** Tom Vaughan

Cast

David Suchet as Hercule Poirot
Zoë Wanamaker as Ariadne Oliver
Tom Ellis as Detective Inspector Bland
Nicholas Woodeson as D.S. Hoskins

Stephanie Leonidas as Hattie Stubbs
Sean Pertwee as Sir George Stubbs
Sinéad Cusack as Mrs. Amy Folliat
Elliot Barnes-Worrell as Etienne De Souza
Emma Hamilton as Sally Legge
Daniel Weyman as Alec Legge
James Anderson as Michael Weyman
Rebecca Front as Miss Brewis
Martin Jarvis as Captain Warburton
Rosalind Ayres as Mrs. Warburton
Sam Kelly as John Merdell
Ella Geraghty as Marlene Tucker
Angel Witney as Gertie Tucker
Chris Gordon as Bickford
Richard Dixon as Henden
Francesca Zoutewelle as Dutch Girl Hiker

Film Locations

Greenway, Galmpton, Devon (Nasse exteriors)
High Canons, Well End, Hertfordshire (Nasse interiors, garden-side exteriors)

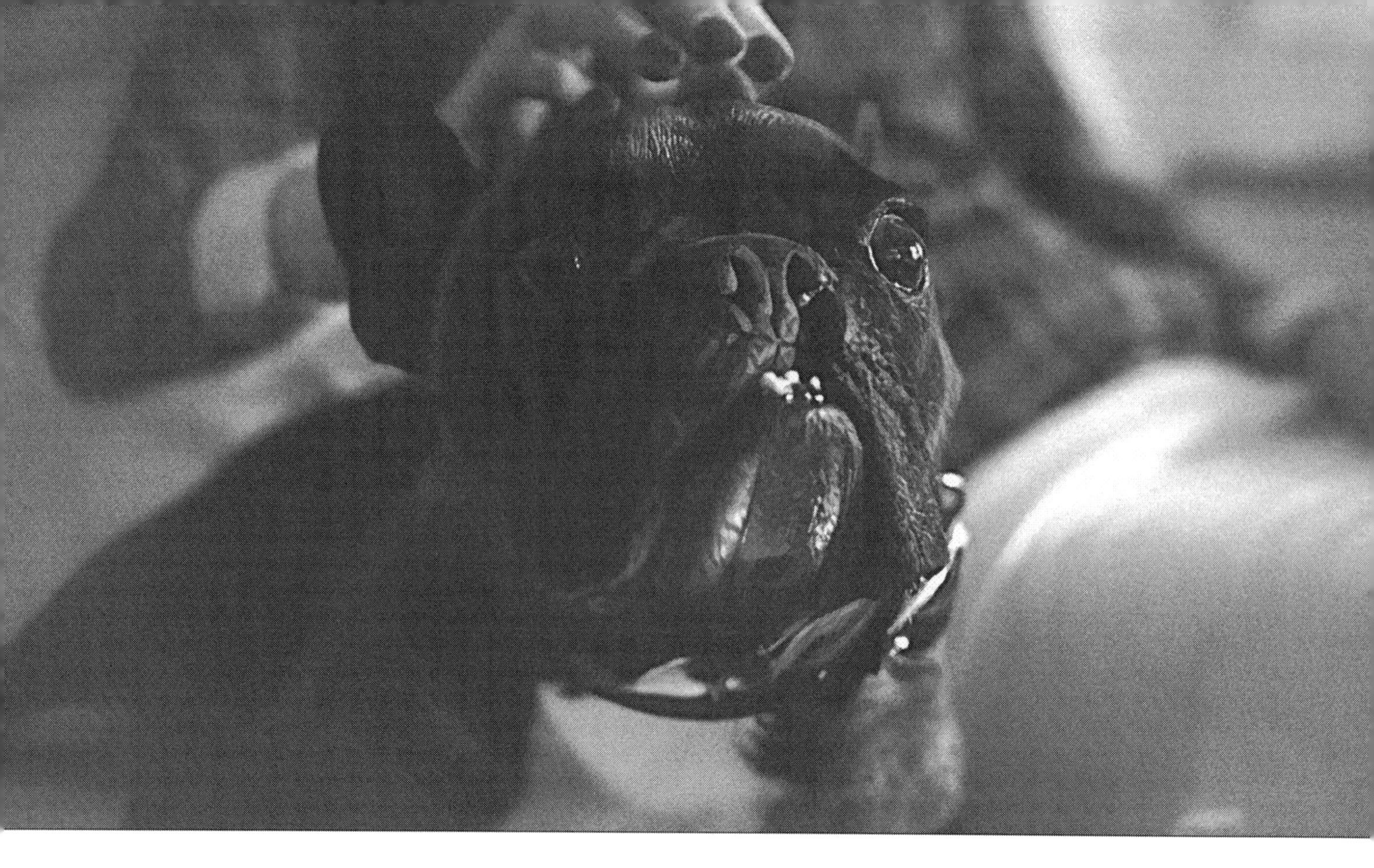

The Labours of Hercules (2013)

Successfully adapting a dozen tales into a great movie was a challenge worthy of Poirot's namesake

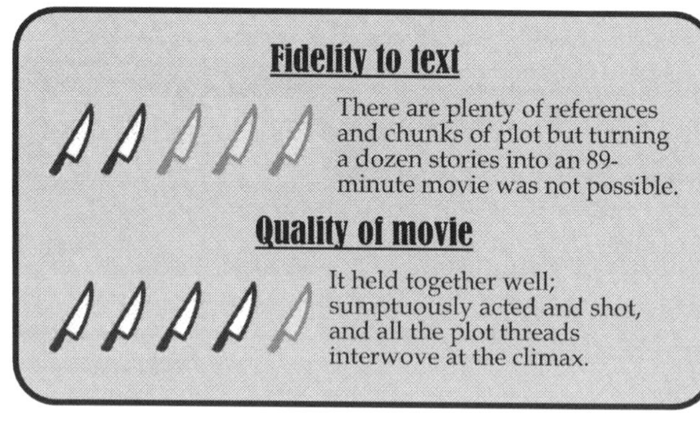

Over the years, all the short stories were filmed as one-hour episodes except for "The Lemesurier Inheritance" (criminal neglect) and the twelve stories in *The Labours of Hercules*. The novels became full-length films, many of them worthy of theatrical release instead of being mere made-for-TV movies.

If you (unlike me) started watching as soon as episodes began airing, you watched in fits and starts. A run of episodes would show off the short stories, followed by the occasional movie showcasing a novel. There'd be gaps between seasons, sometimes lasting for years. There'd be doubt if the producers would ever film each novel and all the short stories.

One by one, the stories were checked off, until *The Labours of Hercules* remained. These 12 stories are linked only by theme. Poirot, as a self-appointed task, looks for cases that remind him of his legendary namesake. They're fun and lighthearted but there's no story arc connecting one to the next. Hastings never appears, but Miss Lemon and Inspector Japp show up as needed.

The Labours would have been best served if each story had been filmed as an hour-long stand-alone, resulting in a single twelve-episode season. It would have fit in nicely with the early years, when Poirot was more lighthearted and fanciful. But after *Jewel Robbery at the Grand Metropolitan* (1993), no more short stories were filmed. The feature-length films took on a darker tone.

And so here we are, with twelve short stories that don't make a novel, being turned into a feature film, the last one before Poirot leaves the building in *Curtain*.

Thankfully, the producers managed to pull the rabbit out of the hat. The film is loaded with references to *Labours*. Sometimes, it's visual: the stolen painting is of Hercules killing the Hydra. Sometimes, it's almost a joke: the mountain hotel in the Alps is named Olympos.

Of the stories, "The Erymanthian Boar" became the core of the movie. It opens with Poirot setting a trap at a posh party to catch notorious thief and thrill-murderer Marrascaud. The house holds both the Hydra painting — the last in the series showing the twelve labors and the only one left unstolen — and a fabulous necklace made of diamonds the size of pigeon

Harold Waring
(*Rupert Evans*),
the innocent aide

Elsie Clayton
(*Morven Christie*),
the battered wife

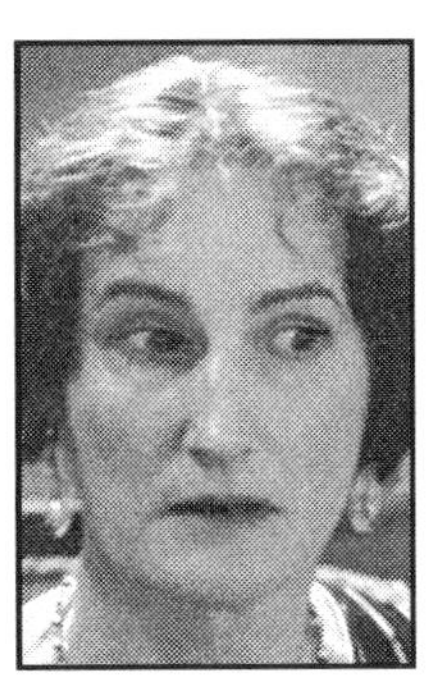
Mrs. Rice
(*Sandy McDade*),
the watchful mother

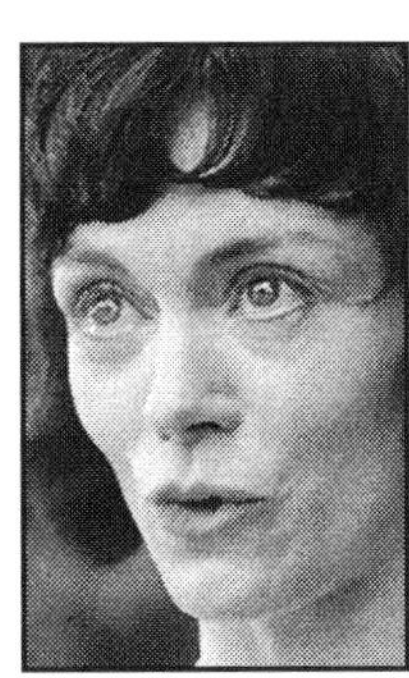
Katrina
(*Fiona O'Shaughnessy*),
the ailing ballerina

Alice Cunningham
(*Eleanor Tomlinson*),
the forensic expert

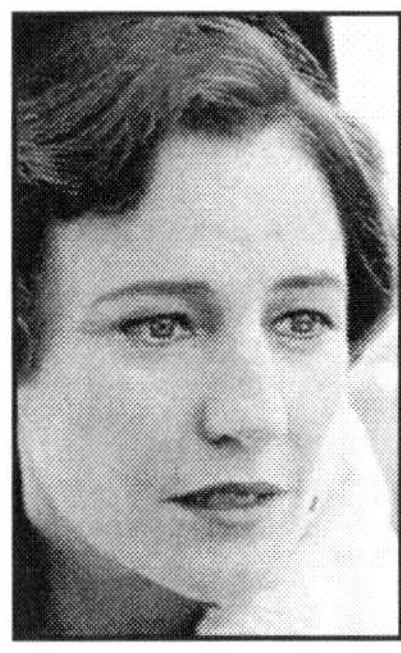
Countess Rossakoff
(*Orla Brady*),
the thief of love

eggs. Marrascaud stole the other paintings in the series; surely he won't resist going for this one.

Lucinda Le Mesurier (notice her last name) must wear the diamonds, painting a gigantic, neon target on her. She's reassured by Poirot that she's safe, even when she has to powder her nose. A disguised policewoman (lots of disguised police are floating around) will keep an eye on her, as will Poirot. He even teaches her a special recognition knock. But she's murdered anyway; the film implies she's been disemboweled which should have left the murderer drenched in blood. The policewoman gets killed as does at least one constable. Don't forget them even though the script does.

Poirot is devastated, falling into a deep depression. His doctor reminds him of how much he accomplished in his life and recommends taking on a new case. Poirot is dismissive until a challenge falls into his lap.

His chauffeur, taking him for a doctor-ordered drive, stops at a beautiful park and breaks down in tears. Poirot sees that he can, possibly, give someone happiness again and he takes on a meaningless-in-the-grand-scheme-of-things task of locating a ballerina's runaway lady's maid.

It's off to the Olympos hotel in the Swiss Alps and suddenly, Poirot discovers multiple cases, an old love whom he'd thought lost forever, and the trail of Marrascaud. On the funicular, he meets Harold Waring who was at the same posh party where Lucinda was slaughtered. Harold's in hiding from political scandal and a cascade of slanderous gossip (a sly nod to "The Augean Stables" and "The Lernean Hydra"). There's also Elsie Clayton and her mother, Mrs. Rice, on their way to meet Elsie's husband. Elsie casts longing glances at Harold. During the funicular ride, Poirot sees, heading back down, Countess Vera Rossakoff, his Irene Adler.

Cast your thoughts back to *The Double Clue* (1991) when we met the countess and Poirot let her escape theft charges and abscond to America. Then recall *Murder in Mesopotamia* (2002) where they were supposed to meet, but she stuck him with her hotel tab.

Since he's on his way up and she's on her way down, Poirot doesn't expect to see the countess but the next day she returns to the hotel. She introduces Poirot to her daughter, Alice. Alice is a criminologist. It was, the countess said, one of two possible futures for the girl. With a mother like her, daughter Alice would either be staunchly on the side of law and order or a far worse criminal than her mother.

General Information

Based on: *The Labours of Hercules*
(short story collection, 1947)
Run time: 1 hr., 29 min. **Subtitles:** Yes

Writer: Andy Wilson **Director:** Guy Andrews

Cast

David Suchet as Hercule Poirot
Stephen Frost as Chief Inspector
Nicholas McGaughey as Inspector Lementeuil
Isobel Middleton as Policewoman

Rupert Evans as Harold Waring
Morven Christie as Elsie Clayton
Sandy McDade as Mrs. Rice
Orla Brady as Countess Rossakoff
Eleanor Tomlinson as Alice Cunningham
Fiona O'Shaughnessy as Katrina
Simon Callow as Dr. Lutz
Tom Austen as Ted Williams
Tom Wlaschiha as Schwartz
Nigel Lindsay as Francesco
Richard Katz as Gustave
Patrick Ryecart as Sir Anthony Morgan
Lorna Nickson Brown as Lucinda Le Mesurier

Film Locations

Brocket Hall, Welwyn Garden City, Hertfordshire (party)
Syon House conservatory, London (Williams confesses romance)
Saint Hilaire du Touvet, France (funicular)
Dent de Crolles, Chartreuse Mountains, France
Halton House, Wendover, Buckinghamshire (Alpine hotel)

The action revs up, interweaving strands from "The Stymphalian Birds" (Harold, Elsie, her abusive husband, and Mrs. Rice), "The Arcadian Deer" (the ballerina's missing lady's maid), "The Girdle of Hippolyta" (the paintings hidden in plain sight), and "The Capture of Cerberus" (Binky, Alice's guard pug who barks when necessary and who could also be a sly nod to "The Nemean Lion"). There may be other bits I missed.

While these stories play out, Francesco, the corrupt concierge, keeps his hand open for bribes and tries to run the hotel with inept waiters.

There are plenty of deceptions and concealed identities, some of which are rather far-fetched. Dr. Lutz, who treats the ballerina Katrina, isn't just a quack but also is Marrascaud's fence? I guess his Viennese bedside manner and psychological patter fooled the ballerina, but it didn't fool Poirot.

That said, Poirot did make a mistake when he met Gustave, the inept waiter, and instantly assumed he was Lt. Druet, performing undercover surveillance for Inspector Lementeuil. Lt. Druet was someone else, someone Poirot overlooked.

It was also kind of far-fetched when, at the climax, multiple people pulled guns on each other, like the bar scene in *Deadpool* (2016) when villains walk in, threaten the bartender, and discover everyone in the joint is armed and dangerous.

I really liked Binky, Alice's pug. He provides important clues to Poirot because, like all dogs, he doesn't lie. Like the dog who didn't bark in the night, he knows who he knows.

The ending was mixed. It was sad for Poirot to see the life he might have had with Countess Vera. But when she asked him to spare her daughter as he'd spared her, he should've reminded her that theft wasn't the same as a psychotic's multiple murders. He didn't say anything, other than he was Poirot.

Curtain: Poirot's Last Case (2013)

What lengths will a dying Poirot go to stop a hidden multiple murderer who loves killing through suggestion?

What a fabulous sendoff this was to David Suchet, Hercule Poirot, and Agatha Christie. Beautifully cast, acted, and shot, with a haunting Chopin's "Raindrop" prelude (Opus 28, No. 15) as the leitmotif throughout the score. Listen to that melancholy piano music, the slow drip, drip, drip of tinkling notes, and try not to feel that an era has ended in sadness.

But every era ends! Get over it! This series had to end too, twenty-four years after *The Adventure of the Clapham Cook* in 1989 introduced us to Suchet's masterful portrayal of Poirot and Hugh Fraser as his faithful friend, sounding board, and sometime assistant, Capt. Arthur Hastings.

Adapting Poirot's swan song could have been dreadful. It could have been bathetic, awash in fake sentiment, trite, and worst of all, completely rewritten by some hack so Poirot lived to hunt murderers another day and the studio could continue raking in the bucks. But justice triumphed and Poirot went bravely into that good night, knowing he'd executed a man whom the law could never touch.

Remember, since Stephen Norton didn't commit the killings himself, merely worked upon the nerves of agitated, desperate, susceptible people, he's not guilty of murder. His false counsel was so sly and careful that even if his victim accused him in court, it's unprovable hearsay. An astute policeman could tie Stephen Norton to a series of unrelated murders, but only loosely. *His* hand never touches the gun, the poison bottle, the knife. He's just … unlucky in his choice of friends and acquaintances. His being on the scene is coincidence and can't be proved otherwise.

In the novel, Poirot states that he knows of at least five murders Norton was involved in and believes there were more. More accurately, just in the five murders Poirot knows about, there were ten victims. The murder victim (who in every case had it coming, which is why Norton succeeded) and the victim of Norton's lying advice who was executed by the Crown. Or committed suicide. Or had their life ruined by suspicion and ugly rumor. Add in the circle of family and friends who'll never be the same and you've got a lot of victims.

Poirot knew the risk he ran. He murdered Norton,

Judith Hastings (*Alice Orr-Ewing*), the true believer

Dr. Franklin (*Shaun Dingwall*), the devoted eugenicist

Barbara Franklin (*Anna Madeley*), the complaining wife

Major Allerton (*Matthew McNulty*), the amoral cad

Elizabeth Cole (*Helen Baxendale*), the grieving sister

Stephen Norton (*Aidan McArdle*), the genial birdwatcher

thereby breaking his own moral code and risking his soul to eternal damnation. What else could he do? He's not Batman, condemning thousands to millions of innocent victims to death at the Joker's hands because he's too damn dainty to shoot a rabid dog. There was also the risk that if he didn't pull it off, he'd be accused of murdering an innocent birdwatcher, something the Joker would cheerfully do.

He chooses to save innocent lives, accept death, and trust his soul to God's judgment.

There was so much to love in this episode. Styles was a shadow of its former glory; the walls bare of art and the rooms echoing because furniture was sold. That's not the only reason Styles didn't look like what you remembered. The producers used a different mansion than the one *The Mysterious Affair at Styles* took place in. The season is late autumn and cold, dreary winter is on her way. Color, life, and joy have drained away from Styles and its inhabitants.

Poirot isn't the only person at Styles with a problem. Hastings, called from Argentina to assist on their last hunt together, is mourning his wife. His daughter is there too. Judith is not his only child; the novel mentions three others. She's the youngest and the one he understands the least. He worries about her and he should.

Judith appears ready to have an affair with Major Allerton, a heartless cad. She has no desire to listen to her father suggest that perhaps a man who callously uses and abandons women is not the best prospect. It's easy to see why Hastings doesn't understand Judith. She's nothing like him. She's a eugenicist, stating publicly that useless and ailing people should be killed. Gently, because doing otherwise would be cruel, but she means it. I hope she never has a disabled child. According to her lights, they're unfit to live. Hastings considers human life to be sacred. If anything, the film softened Judith. She'd leave bodies piled high in her wake if she ran the world her way.

She carries a torch for Dr. Franklin, genius scientist with exactly the kind of ailing, invalid wife Judith believes should be put out of her misery, incidentally benefiting everyone else. They're two peas in a pod. In the novel, Dr. Franklin cheerfully says:

"Lots of people I'd like to kill. Don't believe my conscience would keep me awake at night afterwards. It's an idea of mine that about eighty percent of the human race ought to be eliminated. We'd get on much better without them."

I have to wonder who he expects to grow his food, keep his electricity and water flowing, and scrub his shining city upon the hill. Like it did with Judith, the film softens his character.

It's no surprise when Babs, his wife, is poisoned. The question is who did it. Poirot says suicide and the coroner and the inquest agree. Later, Dr. Franklin admits that Babs wasn't the suicidal type but he doesn't want to know the truth. Maybe because he suspects Judith murdered his unpleasant wife. With Babs gone, they're free to marry and head off to Africa. But they'd always have a cloud over their relationship, each wondering what the other did. Norton would triumph again.

The one flaw in this episode was removing the reconciliation between Toby and Daisy Luttrell. They're the elderly couple running Styles as a guesthouse. They're on the verge of penury, struggling to do something they were never trained for and snapping at each other. He thinks she's a bossy harridan, and she thinks he's an incompetent spendthrift. They're both right.

Norton plays Toby Luttrell like a harp, saying exactly the wrong thing in his hearing about spineless men being bullied and how real men would never let their wives use them as doormats. So it's no surprise when Toby shoots Daisy, mistaking her for a rabbit. Or so he says.

Afterwards, the film shows them at dinner at opposite ends of the table as if nothing happened. The novel goes into detail about Toby's distress over shooting Daisy. Poirot points out that Toby missed because he didn't want to kill his wife. He loved her and she loved him. He also points out Norton's power. He manipulates people in the heat of emotion to do something they'd never otherwise do.

Which is how Norton manipulates Hastings to murder.

Poirot ends his life and the series in triumph. He saves Hastings from his folly, removes an untouchable rabid dog, and ensures the innocent no longer suffer.

General Information

Based on: *Curtain* (novel, 1975)
Run time: 1 hr., 29 min. **Subtitles:** Yes

Writer: Kevin Elyot
Director: Hettie Macdonald

Cast

David Suchet as Hercule Poirot
Hugh Fraser as Captain Hastings
Adam Englander as Curtis
David Yelland as George

Aidan McArdle as Stephen Norton
Helen Baxendale as Elizabeth Cole
Alice Orr-Ewing as Judith Hastings
Shaun Dingwall as Dr. Franklin
Anna Madeley as Barbara Franklin
Claire Keelan as Nurse Craven
Philip Glenister as Sir William Boyd Carrington
Matthew McNulty as Major Allerton
John Standing as Col. Toby Luttrell
Anne Reid as Daisy Luttrell
Gregory Cox as Coroner

Film Locations

Shirburn Castle, Shirburn, Oxfordshire (Styles)
Eastbourne Pier, Grand Parade, Eastbourne (Hastings on beach with George)

Murder on the Orient Express (2017)

Sir Kenny plays with his train set and turns Poirot into an action hero with flexible ethics and a stiff corset

Fidelity to text

Did you know that Poirot is an acrobat, indulges himself in chases, wears a leather corset (in a thankfully deleted scene), and gets shot? I didn't either.

Quality of movie

It looks fabulous! Great acting, scenery, sets, train porn, musical score, and fancy camerawork. The budget's on the screen, other than the pittance paid to the scriptwriter.

Orson Welles called a movie studio the best toy a boy ever had, and Sir Kenneth Branagh would agree. That's why, after watching his *Orient Express* three times, to me he'll always be Sir Kenny.

The first time was in the theater. Bill and I spent the coin, because we wanted to send a signal to Hollywood that this is the kind of movie we'll pay to see.

We were wowed. This movie benefits from being seen on a huge screen, rather than a TV set.

When we borrowed *Orient Express* from the library and watched it again, we weren't quite as wowed. Its flaws began to show, such as Poirot's mustache which looked like wool roving fresh from the sheep rather than human hair.

Watching it a third time for this book, the spell was well and truly broken.

Part of the issue is that after watching 200+ movies and rereading the books, I'm much more familiar with Poirot. Sir Kenny is my eighth (!) Poirot to date. I've seen plenty of interpretations to compare to this fourth adaptation of *Orient Express*.

It's clear Sir Kenny wanted to put his own stamp on it. He played multiple roles as star, director, and producer, and the result is a cinematic extravaganza that's still not quite as extravagant as the 1974 version with Albert Finney.

The movie's infused with Branagh's ego. He gives himself the best lines. He shoots himself walking on top of the train only because it looks fantastic. His camera pans and swoops like a carnival ride.

But Kenny didn't think deeply about the script. He doesn't know Poirot.

Agatha's Poirot is a devout Catholic. He believes in order and method, justice, and following the law. He asks God for guidance. Her Poirot would not set up a priest, a rabbi, and an imam in front of a stone wall like firing squad targets and joke about it while an angry mob watches.

Poirot's scruples are why he's conflicted by his deduction at the climax. Should he permit twelve murderers to walk away or lie to the police that someone else dunnit? Poirot doesn't follow Ambrose Bierce's definition of the four types of murder: felonious, excusable, justifiable, and praiseworthy. They're all felonious to him. It shouldn't matter that Ratchett murdered Daisy Armstrong and indirectly

John Arbuthnot
(*Leslie Odom Jr.*),
the earnest doctor

Mary Debenham
(*Daisy Ridley*),
the lonely governess

Caroline Hubbard
(*Michelle Pfeiffer*),
the rude American

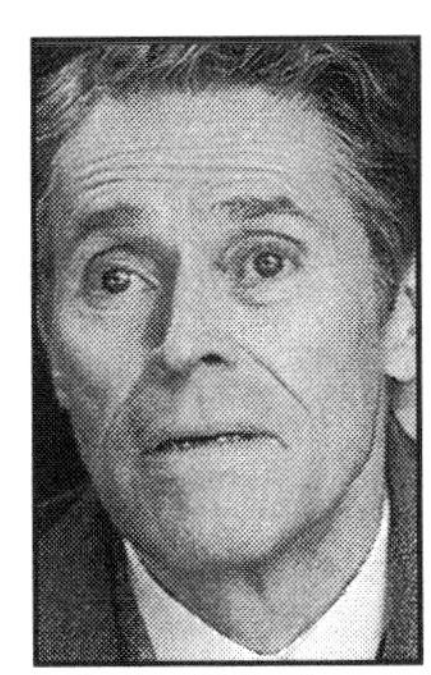

Gerhard Hardman
(*Willem Dafoe*),
the racist detective

Pilar Estravados
(*Penelope Cruz*),
the godly missionary

Princess Dragomiroff
(*Dame Judi Dench*),
the posh aristocrat

killed her baby sibling, mother, father, and maid. Poirot's religion teaches that only God can take a life; Ratchett should be given a chance to atone.

His decision matters to Ratchett's victims, especially when, in this version, Ratchett flees the country. The Armstrong clan were not granted the satisfaction of a trial, however fixed and corrupt it may have been. If the state can't try Ratchett, then who should? This is how you get vigilante justice. The family *must* take the law into their own hands because no one else will.

In addition to his moral scruples, Poirot's emotions are in turmoil because Ratchett asked for help and he refused. The guilt he feels is thick enough to spread on toast. If he'd been watching Ratchett's back, would the man still be alive?

Sir Kenny's Poirot cared about which solution he'd present to the Yugoslavian police only to the extent that it was neat and tidy and he didn't have to lie. Wrong again! Agatha's Poirot lies cheerfully whenever the need arises. Lying is a tool to reach the truth, like listening at keyholes, breaking into homes, and eavesdropping at open windows. He always pays close attention to his surroundings. That's his business. If a lie gets him to the truth, he'll lie.

Agatha's Poirot is never rude. Yet, in a busy Istanbul kitchen, Sir Kenny called M. Bouc's lady friend a prostitute to her face. There's no evidence onscreen. The judgment may be correct, but Poirot would never embarrass a woman in public.

Agatha's Poirot hates damp and cold. It must be freezing outside the snowbound train, yet there's Sir Kenny romping in the snow in his suit. Poirot would wear his muffler, heavy overcoat, gloves, and hat. Everyone else is bundled up in furs but not Sir Kenny. Maybe his absurd mustache keeps him warm.

Agatha's Poirot will search for clues, but he's not Action Boy. He uses his little gray cells. He listens to conversations. He asks probing questions. He observes carefully. He does not stride atop train cars in freezing cold weather! He does not indulge himself by chasing a suspect up and down the slippery, splintery, narrow passageways inside a railroad trestle bridge's underpinnings hundreds of feet over a chasm.

Nor does he put himself in a situation where he'll get shot by a suspect. Sir Kenny does. Poirot doesn't put other people in peril. So why is Sir Kenny interviewing Miss Debenham inside the baggage car, both doors wide open to the freezing cold with the drop on either side of the chasm just waiting for one of them to slip and plummet to their death? Because it gave him an opportunity to send the camera flying around the boxcar, like a boy playing with his marvelous toy.

Sir Kenny's lack of religious knowledge appears when he transformed Daisy's nursery maid (now missionary) from a Swede to a Spaniard. Good Catholic that he is, Poirot tries to decide the most just course of action by debating theology with the missionary. But if she's Spanish, she'll most likely be Catholic so there's not much to debate. If she's Swedish, there's plenty to debate about differing theologies. One of the hallmarks of Protestantism is it comes in a multitude of flavors, from Episcopalian (Catholic lite) to snake-handling Charismatic Pentecostals. There is no single head of the Church dispensing doctrine. They'd have *lots* to argue about so why did Sir Kenny make this unnecessary change? To cast Penélope Cruz, of course.

Putting Sir Kenny in complete charge allowed him to indulge his actor's ego. Some scenes were cut, so a theater audience didn't have to endure a shirtless Poirot adjusting his corset and trimming his nose hairs. We did have to watch Sir Kenny gaze longingly and repeatedly at a miniature of Katherine. Who? There is no Katherine in the canon. The closest Poirot has ever come to loving a woman is Vera Rossakoff. She's his Irene Adler, she rarely shows up, and that's probably not her real name. But Sir Kenny needed more dedicated screen time and so instead of advancing the story – like interviewing conductor Pierre Michel or learning why the Count is a dancing psycho – we get Poirot being maudlin.

Should you watch this? Let's use our gray cells like Poirot (Agatha's version). If you've never read the book or seen the other adaptations, yes. You won't notice the flaws, other than the extra time spent with Sir Kenny instead of the characters. Otherwise, it depends entirely on your tolerance of the boy in front of and behind the camera.

General Information

Based on: *Murder on the Orient Express* (novel, 1934)
Run time: 1 hr., 54 min. **Subtitles:** Yes

Writer: Michael Green
Director: Sir Kenneth Branagh

Cast

Sir Kenneth Branagh as Hercule Poirot
Tom Bateman as Bouc

Johnny Depp as Edward Ratchett
Josh Gad as Hector MacQueen
Sir Derek Jacobi as Edward Henry Masterman
Penélope Cruz as Pilar Estravados
Willem Dafoe as Gerhard Hardman
Dame Judi Dench as Princess Dragomiroff
Leslie Odom Jr. as Dr. John Arbuthnot
Daisy Ridley as Miss Mary Debenham
Michelle Pfeiffer as Caroline Hubbard
Olivia Colman as Hildegarde Schmidt
Sergei Polunin as Count Rudolph Andrenyi
Lucy Boynton as Countess Elena Andrenyi
Marwan Kenzari as Pierre Michel
Manuel Garcia-Rulfo as Biniamino Marquez
Miranda Raison as Sonia Armstrong

Film Locations

Valletta, Malta (harbor)
Department of Customs, Valletta, Malta
Fort St. Elmo, Valletta, Malta
Sirkeci Station, Istanbul, Turkey
Valle d'Aosta, Italy (snow exteriors)
Sursee, Switzerland (landscapes)
Sursee-Triengen Railway, Switzerland
Midland Line, New Zealand

The ABC Murders (2018)

Sarah Phelps stacks the deck against humanity in this grim, unceasing tirade starring a has-been Poirot

Fidelity to text

The murder plot remains. Everyone, including Poirot, desperately needs therapy for depression and assorted personality disorders.

Quality of movie

But only if you've never read the book and have a taste for unrelenting grim and dark. Otherwise, 2 ½ coshes.

Courtesy of the Agatha Christie movie marathon, I've read or reread the vast majority of her output, and I've watched over 200 film adaptations. The quality of films varies wildly, much more so than her writing. I like to think I know something about her, her literary themes, and her characters.

Keep that in mind when I say this version of the 1936 novel is not Agatha. Although the murder plot remains unchanged, everything else was altered and not necessarily for the better. Sarah Phelps, the writer, likes her characters and events worse. She does not have a sunny view of human nature.

Let's dispense with Hastings first. Our Captain, not normally the sharpest knife in the drawer, must have watched Phelps' previous adaptations and read the handwriting on the screen. In the novel, he assists Poirot and even (inadvertently) provides a vital clue. If he participated in this version, he'd probably have been made over into an adulterer *and* a child molester. Wisely, he remained safely in Argentina and avoided that fate.

Hastings had another reason to come to this conclusion: in Tony Randall's *The Alphabet Murders* (1965), he became a fat towel-clad buffoon.

No one else showed up to lift the angst. Virtually every character who was kind (Mary Drower, for example) got disappeared, died in obscurity (Inspector Japp), or aliens arrived and performed personality transplants between the individual and residents of the nearby prison or asylum.

Think I'm kidding? Rose Marbury, the indifferent but not ill-disposed landlady for A. B. Cust, becomes a drunken harridan who pimps out her daughter for a shilling a toss and screams she should have aborted Lily with a knitting needle.

Betty Barnard becomes not just a girl who wants to have fun but a full-fledged slut who steals her plain, fat, dowdy sister Megan's boyfriend and then cheats on him. Then she tells Megan that she should be grateful because she's revealing what a creep Donald Fraser is. I won't argue the point because this Donald Fraser *is* a creep with a very weird relationship with Betty and Megan's mother.

Thora Grey's gold-digger ways get placed front and center, to the point of making her stupid. No smart girl with an eye for his lordship's title and fortune would put the moves on a man sobbing over his much-loved

A.B. Cust
(*Eamon Farren*),
the shattered salesman

Rose Marbury
(*Shirley Henderson*),
the cynical landlady

Betty Barnard
(*Eve Austin*),
the good-time girl

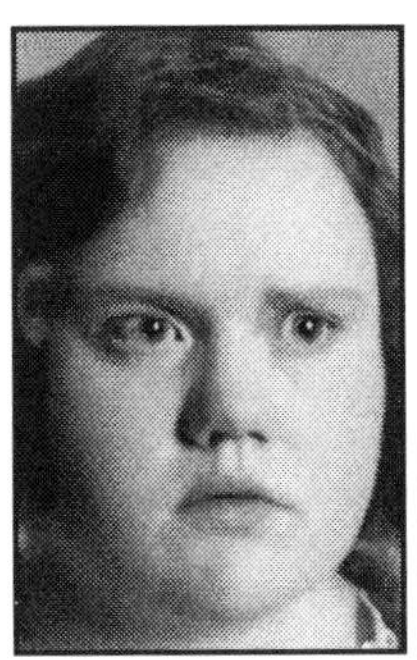

Megan Barnard
(*Bronwyn James*),
the jilted sister

Franklin Clarke
(*Andrew Buchan*),
the confident heir

Thora Grey
(*Freya Mavor*),
the loyal secretary

wife's imminent death. She'd bide her time, behave like a caring and conscientious secretary, and wait for months after the funeral. *Then* she'd move in for the ring, title, and riches.

Since Japp conveniently and gratefully dies of a heart attack, Inspector Crome takes center stage. If he looks familiar, he's Rupert Grint, all growed up with a mustache to make him look more adult and capable and less like Ron Weasley.

Poirot gets a radical rewrite. In the novel, he's at the height of his success as the most famous private detective in England, lauded wherever he goes. He's the natural choice for an aspiring serial killer to taunt, especially if the serial killer has an ulterior motive. All that's gone, other than A.B.C.'s letters. This Poirot is a forgotten, despised man. He fooled Japp into believing he was a Belgian policeman. Scotland Yard checked into his background and discovered there was no proof he had been a policeman or a detective. Or anything, for that matter. He appeared on that refugee train in 1914 or so, right after the Rape of Belgium, and when asked by the clerk what he was, lied and said "policeman."

Where this gets really stupid is that this Poirot, who's still the smartest man in the room, has to be told by Inspector Crome that he's been found out as a fraud. Poirot can read. He gets hate mail telling him to go back to France. Every newspaper in England would have run front-page stories about the celebrated celebrity detective conning Scotland Yard. Yet Poirot is supposed to not know this? Why didn't he know Japp had retired? They're longtime friends, yet Poirot never visited him and Japp said nothing in return?

It's only after three hours of teasing that this Poirot turns out to be a Catholic priest who lost his faith when the invading Germans burned his church to the ground, presumably with his screaming parishioners trapped inside. He flees to England, lies about his background, and, and, and, becomes a private detective? Because he's read lots of mysteries? No reason is ever given why he chose to become a detective, nor how he became a celebrity who hosts fancy murder mystery parties for the wealthy aristocracy.

Alexander Bonaparte Cust gets some changes. He plays backgammon instead of dominoes. He becomes far more attractive and younger than in the novel. He suffers from fits and fugues and blacks out frequently. He also indulges himself with Lily, his landlady's daughter, but he pays for a different service than sexual favors. No, he pays to be blindfolded and have Lily walk on his naked back, grinding her heels into his wounds, possibly as a way to punish himself as a monster who can't remember what he does during his fits.

It should be clear by now this is not *The A.B.C. Murders* you remember. It's not Agatha's story; it's Sarah Phelps'. It's gritty, grim, angsty, dark, filled with unsavory and unsympathetic characters to the extent that unless you like this sort of thing, you'll hate the movie. The script can be heavy-handed about how awful people are. It's also got a distinct vibe that the lower classes can't be trusted to listen to their betters.

Yet at the same time, if you like gritty and grim confirming your low opinion of humanity *and* you've never read anything Agatha wrote, this film may work for you. The story ties together, other than the aforementioned stupidity. It's beautifully filmed although those mean streets and dingy alleys are suspiciously clean. The color palette uses lots of reds and yellows, highlighting key images like blood and telephone boxes, yellow egg yolks and huge boils waiting to burst.

It can get tedious at times but we watched all three hours, one after the other. It was filmed to be shown at one-week intervals, meaning the audience had to be reminded of what happened previously.

It's also got John Malkovich as Poirot. He's too tall (think Peter Ustinov and Alfred Molina), he's rude (which Poirot never was), he's got a mustache and goatee he's forced to let go gray, he's bald, and his attempts at an accent are weird. If you're unfamiliar with the novel, he's a success as a con who's been found out, a forgotten man living on old dreams and good investments. He's a stranger in a strange land, unwanted until he's needed.

Agatha would have been horrified. It's Sarah Phelps' story so your reaction will depend on how you feel about *her* vision.

General Information

Based on: *The A.B.C. Murders* (novel, 1936)
Run time: 3 hrs. **Subtitles:** Yes

Writer: Sarah Phelps **Director:** Alex Gabassi

Cast

John Malkovich as Hercule Poirot
Rupert Grint as Inspector Crome
Michael Shaeffer as Sergeant Yelland
Shane Attwooll as Detective Bunce
Kevin McNally as Inspector Japp

Eamon Farren as A. B. Cust
Shirley Henderson as Rose Marbury
Anya Chalotra as Lily Marbury
Tamzin Griffin as Alice Asher
Eve Austin as Betty Barnard
Bronwyn James as Megan Barnard
Lizzy McInnerny as Jenny Barnard
Jack Farthing as Donald Fraser
Andrew Buchan as Franklin Clarke
Tara Fitzgerald as Lady Hermione Clarke
Christopher Villiers as Sir Carmichael Clarke
Freya Mavor as Thora Grey

Film Locations

Albert Court Kensington, London (Poirot's home)
Bradford City Hall, West Yorkshire (Scotland Yard)
Church of St. John the Baptist, Wakefield, West Yorkshire (Poirot's church)
Albert Terrace, Saltaire, West Yorkshire (Andover)
Ripon Spa Baths, North Yorkshire (Bexhill railway station)
City Varieties Music Hall, Leeds, West Yorkshire (*The Doncaster Empire*)

The Murder of Kuroido (J-2018)

(*Kuroido Goroshi*)

This faithful adaptation weakens the killer's motivation, but excels with distinctly Japanese touches

Fidelity to text

Allowing for necessary setting changes (Japan in the early 1950s), it's stunningly close.

Quality of movie

The one major change softened Dr. Sheppard and it didn't work. Otherwise, what a feast.

Like *And Then There Were None* or *Endless Night*, *The Murder of Roger Ackroyd* will always be a challenge to film. It's narrated in the first person by Dr. Sheppard, acting as Poirot's Watson during the murder investigation. Since he's telling the story *and Poirot trusts him*, we, the readers, believe every word Dr. Sheppard says.

As it turns out, Poirot stopped trusting Dr. Sheppard early on but he didn't inform the good doctor. And since we only know what Dr. Sheppard tells us, we don't know what Poirot thinks. We only know what Dr. Sheppard believes Poirot is thinking.

Dr. Sheppard is not merely an unreliable narrator on par with Hastings, who's not that bright, tends to miss the point, and misinterprets what he sees. Dr. Sheppard is a liar, a blackmailer, and a murderer. His fondest wish is to publish his explanation of the murder of Roger Ackroyd and title it *Poirot's Failure*.

As with other foreign language adaptations, I'm sticking with the familiar names that Agatha used.

The first time you read the novel (assuming no one spoiled the ending for you), Dr. Sheppard fools you completely. You can't read the novel twice as it becomes a radically different book. The second time through, you're searching the text for Agatha's carefully planted clues informing you what a liar he is.

What should a filmmaker do with an iconic story told by a liar who's in every scene *and* each scene is told from his point of view? They could devise something downright idiotic like ITV did with *Poirot*. Poor David Suchet. He did his best but he couldn't overcome the hack screenwriter.

Or, they could trust the audience, which is what the Fuji Television Network did.

They opened the film brilliantly. We meet Dr. Sheppard and Poirot. Dr. Sheppard hands over his diary — a manuscript detailing every incident of the murder investigation — to Poirot. Poirot accepts the manuscript but declines to read it at that moment. He wants to read in private, without Dr. Sheppard hovering over his shoulder.

The clock then spins backward in time to before the murder of Roger Ackroyd. We've already been primed to trust what Dr. Sheppard tells us because Poirot does.

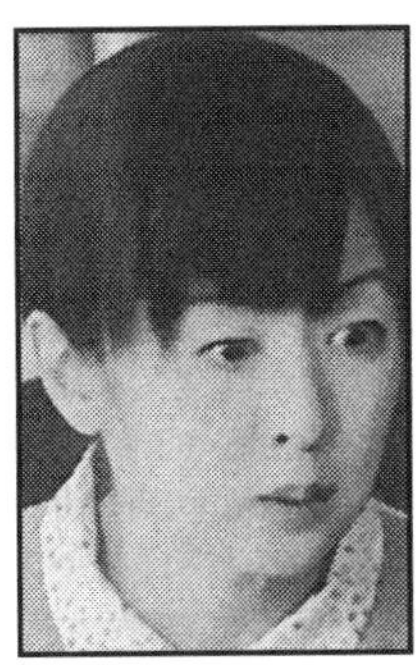

Shiba Kana
(*Yuki Saitô*),
the doctor's sister

Kuroido Rokusuke
(*Ken'ichi Endô*),
the wealthy man

Kuroido Hanako
(*Mayu Matsuoka*),
the obedient niece

Hyoudou Haruo
(*Osamu Mukai*),
the adopted son

Honda Asuka
(*Sayaka Akimoto*),
the parlormaid

Randou Gorou
(*Tomohiko Imai*),
the blocked writer

We learn about the tragic suicide of Mrs. Ferrars, the widow Roger Ackroyd loves. Dr. Sheppard confirms her death, then returns home, where his sister Caroline questions him closely. Caroline concludes Mrs. Ferrars committed suicide because she murdered her husband the year before.

Dr. Sheppard is taken aback by Caroline's nosiness and by how closely tied into village events she is. She makes it a point to know everyone and their business. She runs her brother's household and his life. It's obvious he can't hide a thing from Caroline.

Then Ackroyd invites Dr. Sheppard to dinner. Dr. Sheppard's been close to Ackroyd's household for years. He knows every member of the family well, including Ackroyd's ne'er-do-well stepson, Ralph Paton, who had been carousing in Tokyo but secretly returned to the village. It appears (a minor, amusing change) that Dr. Sheppard's also interested in Flora, Ackroyd's pretty niece.

After dinner, Ackroyd takes Dr. Shepherd into his office. He explains that shortly before Mrs. Ferrars' death, he had asked her to marry him. Her abusive, brutal husband's been dead over a year, so enough time has passed to satisfy the proprieties. But Mrs. Ferrars confessed she had a dreadful secret that prevented them marrying. She refuses to tell him, he leaves, and learns of her death.

While the men were talking, the butler gives Ackroyd the mail. He discovers Mrs. Ferrars' suicide note (love that blue stationery!), opens it, but can't read it with Dr. Sheppard hovering over his shoulder.

Dr. Sheppard leaves the office, telling the butler, Parker, that Ackroyd doesn't want to be disturbed.

Dr. Sheppard receives a late-night telephone call. To his horror, Parker tells him the master is dead, knifed to death in his office. He races off to the Ackroyd mansion, and we're off to the races.

The setup is perfect. You, the viewer, are primed to trust everything Dr. Sheppard sees and hears.

As the police investigate, Flora Ackroyd decides to ask the great detective, Poirot, to solve the murder. It's a very funny scene, particularly when Poirot shows off his square pumpkins, each with a mustache stamped on the side. You really can grow shaped fruit and vegetables in your home garden. There are specialty molds that you place around the baby fruit or vegetable (watermelons, pumpkins, squash, and cukes willingly conform) and it grows to fit the mold.

General Information

Based on: *The Murder of Roger Ackroyd* (novel, 1926)
Run time: 2 hr., 38 min. **Subtitles:** Yes

Writer: Kôki Mitani **Director:** Hidenori Jôhô

Cast

Mansai Nomura as Takeru Suguro (Hercule Poirot)
Oizumi Yo as Dr. Shiba Heisuke (James Sheppard)
Jirô Satô as Sodetake Koushirou (Inspector Raglan)

Yuki Saitô as Shiba Kana (Caroline Sheppard)
Ken'ichi Endô as Kuroido Rokusuke (Roger Ackroyd)
Osamu Mukai as Hyoudou Haruo (Ralph Paton)
Mayu Matsuoka as Kuroido Hanako (Flora Ackroyd)
Tamiyo Kusakari as Kuroido Mitsuru (Mrs. Cecil Ackroyd)
Tomohiko Imai as Randou Gorou (Hector Blunt)
Yasufumi Terawaki as Reizei Moichi (Geoffrey Raymond)
Sayaka Akimoto as Honda Asuka (Ursula Bourne)
Masato Wada as Chagawa Kenzo (Charles Kent)
Yô Yoshida as Karatsu Sanako (Mrs. Ferrers)

Meanwhile, Ralph Paton disappears. That's suspicious because he had the most to gain by his stepfather's death and the most to lose if Ackroyd lived. Ackroyd wanted Ralph and Flora to marry. Their opinions don't matter. Ralph's wasted his stepfather's money and time. Flora's on a tight financial leash, as is her mother, but she's not interested in Ralph or his potential riches.

As Poirot investigates, more secrets are revealed. The housekeeper has a drug-addicted son. The butler was dismissed from a previous post because of spying and attempted extortion. Writer Hector Blunt, Ackroyd's guest, is as interested in Flora as she is in him, despite Flora and Ralph being betrothed. Dr. Sheppard thinks Flora and Ralph want to marry but Ackroyd disapproved and is startled to learn it was the other way around. He's interested in Flora, possibly because marrying her would ingratiate him into the Ackroyd household still further and lead to a wealthier lifestyle.

The film takes its time unfolding, letting you feel how Dr. Sheppard and his sister live and how the community feels about Ackroyd. It doesn't feel English, despite most of the cast wearing Western dress and sitting on upholstered chairs. The main exception is Hector Blunt. His traditional kimono probably means something to a Japanese audience, a nuance lost on me.

The flaw came at the end. It's revealed that Dr. Sheppard had a good reason to blackmail Mrs. Ferrars, hounding her to suicide for more and more money. He murdered his friend, Ackroyd, to conceal his blackmail. Why did he do it? Not because he was speculating on the stock market as in the novel. No, his dear sister Caroline suffers from a brain tumor and he needs the money for an American brain specialist.

Um, no. First, if Dr. Sheppard and Ackroyd, the richest man around, are friends, why didn't Dr. Sheppard ask for a loan?

The other reason this doesn't work is that in the novel, Caroline functions as Dr. Sheppard's conscience. He must hide his sins from her and he speculates about what she knows or suspects. That's a much deeper portrait of them.

But don't let that stop you from watching this! It's great and makes ITV's version even more of a failure.

Promise of Death (J-2021)

(*Shi to no Yakusoku*)

Make an appointment with death to watch this faithful adaptation starring a comic Japanese Poirot

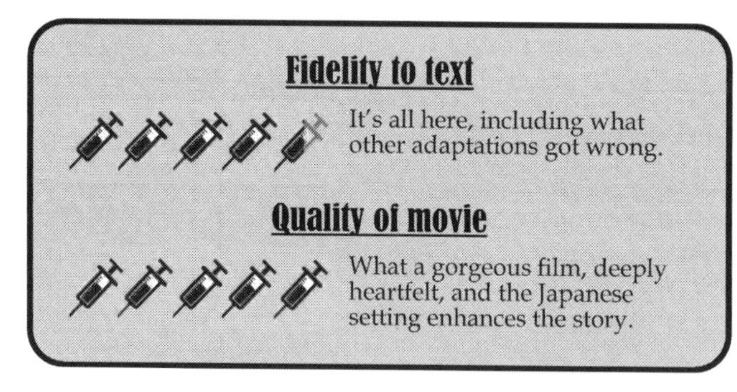

I never know what to expect watching an Agatha adaptation, and now that we're watching the foreign takes – which is to say not English or American – I discovered that I know even less. English-speaking cultures are not the be-all and end-all of how stories can be told. Human beings tend to want the same things the world over: a meaningful life, children and family, status, and a secure place in the world. How they express those desires varies from culture to culture. What one culture finds perfectly acceptable is anathema to another.

There's also the issue that even though many, many talented people make a film (it's art by committee!), it may still be bad. David Suchet's *Appointment with Death* is a prime example. Despite the experienced and talented cast and crew, that version was awful.

So how was the Japanese version? Amazingly good despite the poor quality of the film (Bill had trouble getting a clean copy) and having to rely solely on subtitles. Agatha's family dynamics translated beautifully. The transfer to 1955 Japan made Lady Westholme's crime even more understandable and tragic.

I'm sticking with the English names for the characters because I and you, dear reader, are more familiar with them.

Let's start with our new Poirot. This is Mansai Nomura's third outing as the character but our first look at him. I don't know why his three Agatha Christie films aren't readily available on DVD but they aren't. He's a very different Poirot, even comical at times. But he still wants order and method, and he's still the smartest person in the room. It's possible that his droll personality helps set him apart from the rest of the culture. I don't know. He's funny but there's no doubt that nearly everyone takes him very seriously.

Except Lady Westholme. That's the major change to the plot other than the new setting. When she appears onstage, it turns out she and Poirot know each other, but not because she's an important politician. No, a flashback makes clear they met when he arrested her sometime in the early 1930s. She was a skillful jewel thief in the Ginza and Poirot, a young policeman at the time, managed to catch her. She served her time and took full advantage of the chaos during and after the

Mrs. Hondo (*Keiko Matsuzaka*), the evil mother

Reiichiro Hondo (*Kôji Yamamoto*), the failure son

Nagiko Hondo (*Sylvia Grab*), the resentful nurse

Omomizu Hondo (*Hayato Ichihara*), the lovestruck son

Honami Uesugi (*Kyôka Suzuki*), the reformed pol

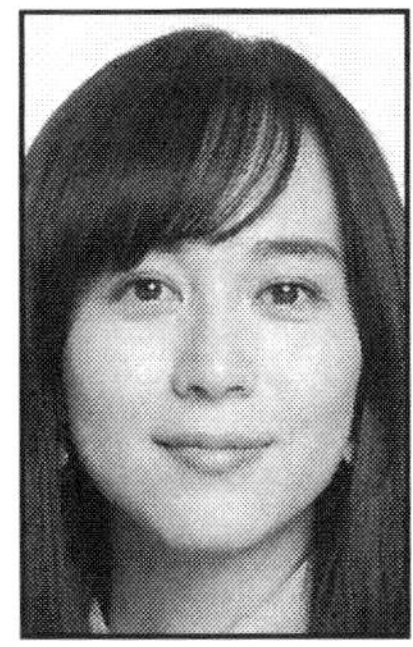
Kinuko Sara (*Manami Higa*), the lovestruck doctor

war to change her name, reinvent herself, and marry an up-and-coming politician. Lady Westholme's a widow, and she completely remade her life. She's a rising political star, and she left her past behind her.

General Information

Based on: *Appointment with Death* (novel, 1938)
Run time: 2 hr., 10 min. **Subtitles:** Yes

Writer: Kôki Mitani **Director:** Hidenori Jôhô

Cast

Mansai Nomura as Takeru Suguro
Kenji Anan as Daisaku Kawahari (Colonel Carbury)

Manami Higa as Kinuko Sara (Sarah King)
Keiko Matsuzaka as Mrs. Hondo (Mrs. Boynton)
Kôji Yamamoto as Reiichiro Hondo (Lennox Boynton)
Sylvia Grab as Nagiko Hondo (Nadine Boynton)
Hayato Ichihara as Omomizu Hondo (Raymond Boynton)
Mayu Hotta as Kyoko Hondo (Carol Boynton)
Nanoka Hara as Ayana Hondo (Ginevra Boynton)
Yoshiyuki Tsubokura as Kota Jumonji (Jefferson Cope)
Kyôka Suzuki as Honami Uesugi (Lady Westholme)
Satomi Nagano as Hana Asuka (Amabel Pierce)

Film Locations

Gamagori Classic Hotel, Gamagori, Aichi (hotel exterior)
Kumano Hongu Taisha Shrine
Warp Station Edo (replica town, flashback)
Hokoji Temple, Hamamatsu, Shizuoka (woodlands)

When Poirot asks Lady Westholme about what she's telling her ghostwriter (a great version of Amabel Pierce) helping write her autobiography, she responds she'll only admit what's necessary. She's forgotten her criminal past and expects Poirot to do the same.

Except the past never stays buried. Lady Westholme can't outrun her past when she meets the one person who not only knows who she was but who would revel in endlessly torturing her over it.

That's the great tragedy at the climax of *Promise of Death*. Lady Westholme remade herself into a better person and a champion of women in Japanese society but Mrs. Boynton didn't care. She craved a new victim. Mrs. Boynton wanted to humiliate Lady Westholme and she succeeded. Lady Westholme chose suicide rather than flee and reinvent herself again or be publicly and permanently dishonored.

If you think English culture is concerned with status, appearances, and saving face, they're toddlers playing in the sand compared to the Japanese.

But new life can be born out of tragedy and that's the other thing this film did so well. Mrs. Boynton is one of Agatha's great villains. She's an expert in psychological torture. She doesn't need to lay a hand on her unfortunate children and this film demonstrates her sadism well. It also shows the effect she had on her children. They look like adults (other than Ginevra), but they behave years younger. They're frightened mice in a way they weren't in the Ustinov version.

In particular, Nadine was handled perfectly. She's Lennox's wife. She loves him, but he's more dead than alive inside. He's given up hope and is waiting for either his mother to die or his own death. Nadine's good friends with Jefferson Cope but unlike the Ustinov version, and exactly as in the novel, they're friends. Only friends. They are not conducting an adulterous affair. This Jefferson Cope loves Nadine enough to want her happiness over his. When she chooses to stay with Lennox after Mrs. Boynton's death, it breaks his heart but he lets her go.

As Poirot interrogates the Boynton family, peeling back layer upon layer of deception, he proves to the children and Nadine that they love each other deeply and they are worthy of love. They all lie, but not to protect themselves. They lie and assume the blame for Mrs. Boynton's death to protect each other. In finding the truth, he sets them free.

There are some great, funny set pieces that circle back around into something more. Lady Westholme playfully pushes Poirot down a grassy slope. She pushes him again down a steeper, wooded hillside to buy herself time. Then she leaps to her own death, because Mrs. Boynton won.

There are also the tengu. They're a type of spirit and come in many forms, but the one you'll see here is more traditional, with a red, long-nosed face and garbed in white. Tengu might not harm you but then again, they might if they feel like it. Like European spirits, they're capricious. Seeing one means you should be wary.

During Poirot's summation of who could have killed Mrs. Boynton, you'll see each suspect attack her with a syringe while she tries to beat them off with her cane. And that includes the tengu Ginevra and Jefferson Cope saw. Was there a real tengu? Yes, there was.

Poirot's deductions demonstrated his brilliance. He saw Amabel Pierce was unreliable, parroting whatever the last person said to her. He recognized if a member of the Boynton family wanted to kill their mother, they'd do it at home where it could be easily disguised as a heart attack.

His most important deduction was seeing what no one else did: Mrs. Boynton did something wildly out of character. She took the family on vacation to give them false hope and make them more miserable than ever. But then she let her family off their leash so she could sit alone in front of a shrine while they enjoyed some freedom. Why did she do this? Poirot knew: She'd spotted a fresh victim. And he found her killer.

What a great, great movie. Don't miss it.

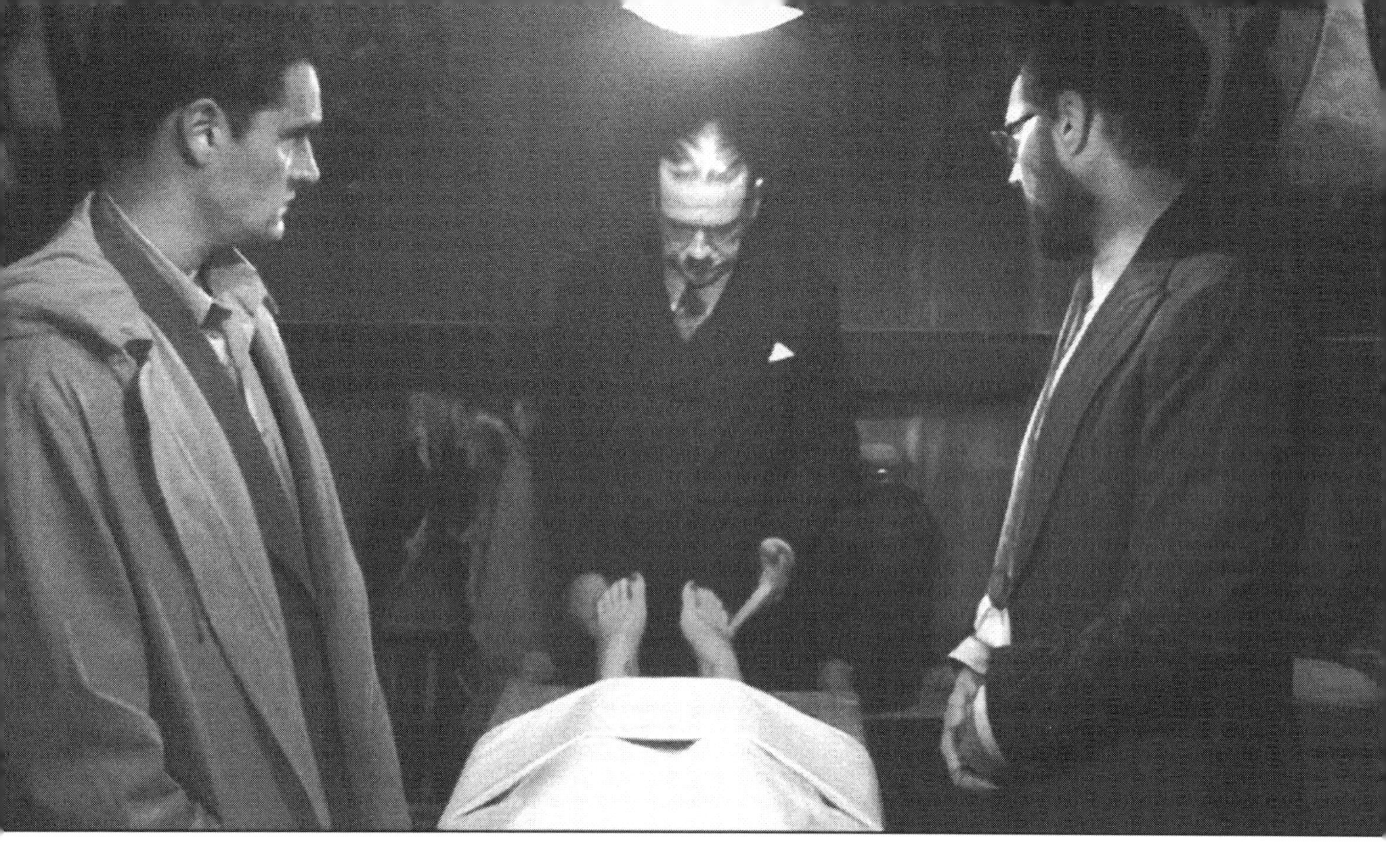

Death on the Nile (2022)

Branagh's river trip runs aground with lewd dancing, vanished crew, glacial pace, and too much CGI

Fidelity to text

Unneeded Poirot backstory, character consolidation, badly run ship, and the cast never went near Egypt.

Quality of movie

Gorgeous to watch, wonderful to hear, and tedious to sit through waiting for something to happen.

If you've read the novel or watched the previous two versions, you know that *Death on the Nile* largely takes place on board the paddle ship *Karnak* cruising up the river. It's right there in the title. Truth in advertising.

Not here.

That ship is fake.

It's a gorgeous fake — built on a sound stage in England — but it's not a real ship, subject to wind and Egyptian heat. The Ustinov film (1978) was filmed on board the paddle ship *Memnon*. The Suchet version (2004) was filmed on board the steamship *Sudan*. The closest this cast got to real water is a water park in the Cotswolds, riding '30s vintage wooden powerboats.

Unfortunately, Sir Kenneth Branagh, our director and star, wants total control. Like Orson Welles, he believes a film set is the best toy a boy could have, and he takes full advantage of the possibilities. It's his movie. It's his choice. But that doesn't mean I have to like it.

Faking the ship is on par with how he shot the movie. It's gorgeous, but virtually nothing you see is real other than wardrobe. All that scenery? Sound stages, CGI, and green screens. Any sweat on the cast was misted on by the film crew. If Sir Kenny had shot in Egypt, he would have encountered technical problems. It's doubtful the authorities in charge of those fabulous archeological sites would have permitted him to film as he chose, ranging all over like they did in 1978. Moreover, it would be much harder to make the Nile's banks look like they did in 1937, when the action takes place.

But when everything's CGI, it doesn't feel real. It was too perfect, too polished, too gleaming, too flawless. Each shot was beautifully composed to be symmetrical and when it was asymmetrical, it was still symmetrical. About the only unsymmetrical things were the fish and the crocodiles and they might have been fake too. Even the blood splatter on the bulkhead was painted on by some set designer, dot by dot.

The film's perfections and glacial pace made me look for imperfections and I found them. Take Salome Otterbourne (Sophie Okonedo). She morphed from a fading romance novelist into a black blues singer. That's not a problem. In fact, the movie came to life whenever she sauntered onscreen. Her character is based on Sister Rosetta Tharpe, who pioneered a gospel-infused, guitar-

Linnet Ridgeway (*Gal Gadot*), the entitled

Simon Doyle (*Armie Hammer*), the wayward

Jacqueline de Bellefort (*Emma Mackey*), the scorned

Salome Otterbourne (*Sophie Okonedo*), the troubadour

Rosalie Otterbourne (*Letitia Wright*), the manager

Dr. Windlesham (*Russell Brand*), the rejected

based music. That's Sister Rosetta's voice you hear. She played an electric guitar, but in 1937, she was 22 and electric guitars weren't widely available. There certainly weren't any with cords so long that Salome could strut through an entire nightclub.

The nightclub dancing scene was wrong. People have always enjoyed suggestive dancing (it's the most fun you can have standing up according to my sister, an accomplished ballroom dancer) but Simon and Jackie were dry-humping on that dance floor. Moves like that were reserved for whorehouses, not nightclubs. Then we're forced to watch Simon rub his face into Linnet's crotch during their getting-to-know-you dance. Taxi dancers show more restraint.

It felt just as forced and wrong watching Simon and Linnet dry-hump on the façade of Abu Simbel. (The Egyptian authorities would have denied access over this scene, another reason for a sound stage.) Perhaps the overt simulations of lust were supposed to compensate for their complete lack of chemistry.

It was not just wrong but insane for the crew to leave the ship every night and camp out on the shores of the Nile! No competent captain would leave the passengers — who expect luxury accommodations and on-call services at all hours — alone overnight, getting into mischief in the engine room or the bridge.

The crew abandoning ship every night led to the ridiculous scene where Poirot pursues the suspect, who slit Louise the maid's throat and shot Bouc, through the empty galley. To delay Poirot, the suspect pulls a pot of boiling water off the stove. A gunshot bursts a pipe filled with live steam. Who's boiling that water and running the engine? Ships don't run themselves.

To cap this absurdity, neither Poirot nor the suspect are sweating or even breathing hard after that mad dash up and down and all around.

And how did Simon warn his partner in the first place that Bouc was about to spill the beans about what he saw? He did that in previous adaptations; he should have done that here.

There was no set-up, none, to explain why Poirot took Euphemia Bouc's case to investigate her son's infatuation. It's canon that while Poirot likes matchmaking, he doesn't do what amounts to divorce work. Spying on Bouc's would-be wife? He should have said something to Bouc to explain why he accepted such an out-of-character case.

Then there's Euphemia Bouc's diatribe about the evils of love and marriage. Where did that come from? What's the relationship between her and her husband, Bouc's father? There's not one word of explanation for why Euphemia married Bouc's father, bore him a son, and then left. Nothing. That rant came out of the desert with less warning than a sandstorm.

The fatal change was revamping Linnet's character. I understand Sir Kenny's reasoning. He didn't want Gal Gadot playing the real Linnet. In the novel, she's a hyper-capable, self-absorbed, control-freak. She's completely unable to understand that other people have rights, including the right to make a mistake. To Linnet, people exist solely to fulfill her every wish.

Linnet is not a sympathetic character. Jackie's her only friend; the one person in the world who doesn't care about her money. So what does Linnet do when Jackie introduces her to her fiancé, Simon, and asks that Linnet give him a job? She steals her best, her *only* friend's man and then self-justifies her actions.

In the novel and the two previous films, this makes Linnet the villain. You understand why she's murdered. Poirot even warns Linnet of the danger she's courting. He tells her Nathan's parable to King David about the rich man craving the poor man's ewe lamb despite being richer than rich and having everything when the other man had nothing. As a good Catholic, Poirot knows the story. Sir Kenny didn't say a word, which was wrong.

Despite marrying Simon, Linnet tries to make up to Jackie by hoping they can still be friends. This is supposed to make her sympathetic, but I didn't believe it. If she's so empathetic, why did this nicer, kinder Linnet steal Jackie's man in the first place? Simon is a handsome lunk, no question. But Linnet can afford handsome lunks far more easily than she can afford losing friends. It didn't help that they had the magnetic allure of dry sand.

This is a beautiful, perfect, perfectly flawed film. Watch either of the other two versions to see real people. Everything here was computer generated, even the emotions.

General Information

Based on: *Death on the Nile* (novel, 1937)
Run time: 2 hr., 7 min. **Subtitles:** Yes

Writer: Michael Green
Director: Sir Kenneth Branagh

Cast

Sir Kenneth Branagh as Hercule Poirot
Tom Bateman as Bouc

Emma Mackey as Jacqueline de Bellefort
Armie Hammer as Simon Doyle
Gal Gadot as Linnet Ridgeway
Letitia Wright as Rosalie Otterbourne
Sophie Okonedo as Salome Otterbourne
Annette Bening as Euphemia Bouc
Rose Leslie as Louise Bourget
Russell Brand as Dr. Windlesham
Jennifer Saunders as Marie Van Schuyler
Dawn French as Bowers
Ali Fazal as Andrew Katchadourian
Susannah Fielding as Katherine
Rick Warden as Monsieur Blondin

Film Locations

Aswan, Egypt
Luxor, Egypt
Cairo, Egypt
Morocco
Cotswold Water Park, Cirencester
Clevedon Marine Lake, Clevedon
Surrey, England

III. Tommy & Tuppence

After *Styles*, Agatha wrote in a new genre: romantic spy thrillers. Not only was this a new way for her to tell a story, she made the protagonists personal. Tommy and Tuppence were young, adventurous, high-spirited, and itching to explore a world completely remade by World War I. In other words, Agatha and her husband Archie Christie.

Agatha was fond of them, but they appeared in only four novels and a short story collection that parodied noted mystery writers. They're different from her Marples and Poirots in two ways. Unlike them, Tommy and Tuppence aged in real time. Second, their stories are tied to current events, particularly in *The Secret Adversary* and *N or M?*

On screen, Francesca Annis and James Warwick are the iconic Tuppence and Tommy. But their run was limited. They filmed *Adversary* and most of the short stories in the collection but without the overall spy thriller arc. Nor did they get a crack at *N or M?*, *By the Pricking of My Thumb*, or *Postern of Fate*.

Alas, there are few other Tommy and Tuppence pairings. The German silent movie *Adventures, Inc.* is unsatisfactory for a host of reasons. A planned adaptation of the four novels starring David Walliams and Jessica Raine was dropped after two lackluster outings. But the French film is a delight and adding Miss Marple to *Pricking* worked surprisingly well. They deserve better.

The original Tommy and Tuppence: Eve Gray and Carlo Aldini from *Adventures, Inc.* (G-1929)

Anthony Andrews and Greta Scacchi (with a little help from Miss Marple) in *By the Pricking of My Thumbs* (2006)

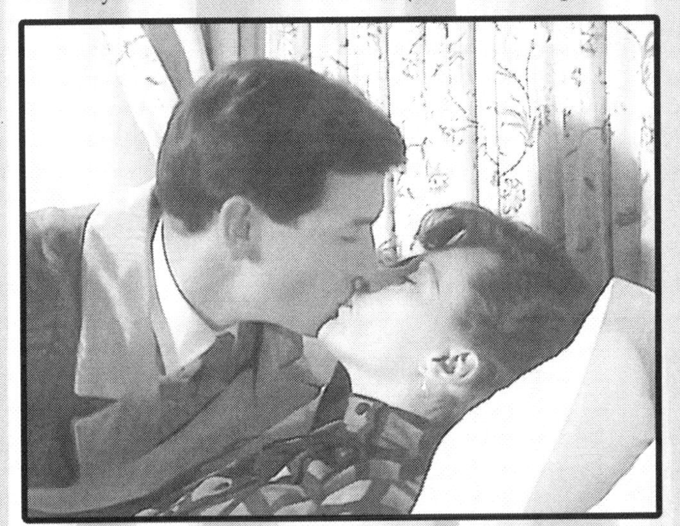

Francesca Annis and James Warwick in *The Sunnydale Mystery* (1983)

Jessica Raine and David Walliams in *N or M?* (2015)

Catherine Frot and André Dussollier as Prudence and Bélisaire Beresford in *My Little Finger Told Me* (F-2005)

No matter what trouble they found, Tommy and Tuppence remained passionately in love throughout their lives

Adventures, Inc. (G-1929)

(*Die Abenteurer G.m.b.H.*)

A Frenchified Tommy and Tuppence survive a shipwreck and discover adventure, kidnapping, and conspiracy

The basic story arc of *The Secret Adversary* (1922) is here. You get the missing damsel, secret papers, Tommy and Tuppence looking to support themselves, a wicked adventuress, spies, and a hidden villain. Beyond that, things change and shift.

Let's start with the physical film. The version we found on YouTube was in bad shape. If it weren't for the internet, *Die Abenteurer* wouldn't be available at all, except through some film institute's silent movie festival, so we should be grateful. It's better than nothing. The earliest silent adaptation, *The Passing of Mr. Quinn* (1928), no longer exists except through a few photographs and descriptions.

By the time *Die Abenteurer* was made — the German title translates to *Adventures Inc.* — silent movies were at their height. The industry knew how to handle acting, staging, set design, direction, camera tricks, stunts, title cards, and the all-important musical accompaniment, played by the theater's organist. Despite the contrary evidence in front of you when viewing this film, filmmakers knew how to tell a coherent story.

It's important to keep this in mind. This movie is so damaged that if you're a first-time viewer of a silent movie, you won't believe that filmmakers of the time were competent. The film stock is terrible, blurry and full of skips. There's also the problem of the missing soundtrack. A silent movie wasn't silent. They were designed with a piano or an organ score, to be played by the theater's house organist. The musical score — like a film score of today — supplied the mood, revved up when the action revved up, slowed down in quiet moments. Some scores even came with special effects like a sudden sharp blare to highlight explosions or gunshots.

The style of acting looks stagey and weird today. Silent movies depended on dramatic overacting, because there is no dialog. Emotion and speech have to be conveyed via charades. *Die Abenteurer* was also a contemporary for 1929. The makeup and clothing look wrong. The men's hairstyles in particular look odd, all spit curls and Brylcreem.

Silent movies did come with title cards, conveying

Fidelity to text

I think. It's hard to judge since at least two reels were missing: one near the climax, plus the ending. The film stock of this German silent movie was so deteriorated I couldn't always figure out what was happening.

Quality of movie

I think. No musical score, missing reels, degraded film stock, and the format make the movie difficult to enjoy. It will be even harder to enjoy if you're not familiar with silent movie conventions.

Pierre Lafitte
(*Carlo Aldini*),
the stoker-hero

Lucienne Fereoni
(*Eve Gray*),
the daring heroine

Jeanette Finné
(*Elfriede Borodin*),
the kidnap victim

Rita van den Meer
(*Hilda Bayley*),
the villainess

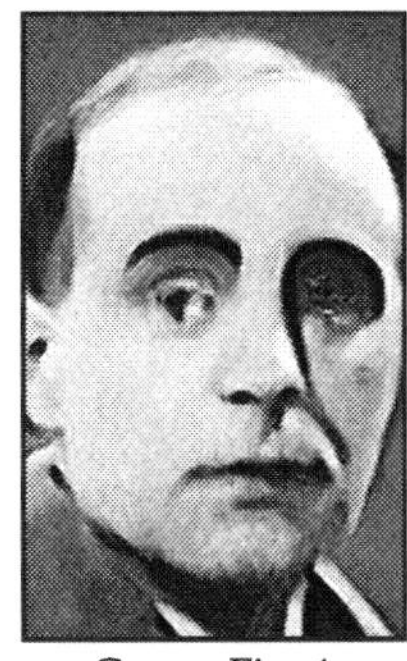

George Finné
(*Eberhard Leithoff*),
the spy brother

Marglin
(*Hans Mierendorff*),
the spymaster

dialog or other narration, but not many because they risk breaking the spell. Silent movies can be easily translated into foreign languages because gestures and facial expressions are so exaggerated that any audience should be able to understand. Swap out the few title cards and an English audience can easily enjoy and understand a German silent movie.

Part of the film is missing. Scenes stop and then restart somewhere else and it's obvious portions are missing. This is especially notable in two sections. Our hero, Tommy, is suddenly and abruptly walking a tightrope between buildings while carrying a ladder! We don't know how he found the tightrope or where he got the ladder.

The entire finale reel is missing. We get the climax when the villain is unmasked. Then the film stops without even a "The End" title card. A murder is left unexplained and the missing damsel, Jane Finn, still doesn't know who this mysterious man is who claims to be a relative.

So that's the chopped-up film that survived the vicissitudes of time.

What did scriptwriter Jane Bess (1891-1944), a prolific writer of German silent movies until 1933, do with Agatha's plot? She did what scriptwriters everywhere do: she hacked and slashed, using what she wanted of Agatha's storyline and discarding what she didn't. Jane Bess set the pattern: rewrite as you please, whether the source material needs it or not.

For starters, even though the movie is clearly *The Secret Adversary*, she Frenchified all the names: Tommy becomes Pierre, Tuppence becomes Lucienne, Jane Finn becomes Jeanette Finné and so on. The doomed ocean liner becomes the *Herculania* but that's more reasonable: a German production isn't going to start with the sinking of the *Lusitania* by German U-boats. We'll stick with Agatha's names, however, since that's what you'll do when you're watching the film. Nobody's talking.

We spend plenty of time on board the doomed ship with Jane Finn and her brother (!) and discover they're both secret agents! This is how Jane meets Rita, wicked adventuress. Jane's brother drowns but, weirdly, the script has a cousin showing up (like in the novel) but the cousin shares virtually the same name: Jane's brother is George while her mysterious cousin is named Georges. Because of the names' similarity, I was sure Jane's brother would reappear, but no.

Even more weirdly, we watch a hunky stoker on the same ship, amusing the child passengers after the sinking to keep them calm. The hunky stoker is none other than our Tommy. Yet he doesn't recognize Jane Finn later, despite being in the same lifeboat. He's also so clean, despite shoveling coal into a fiery furnace day in and day out, that he positively glows.

Then Jane gets kidnapped. Tommy meets Tuppence and somehow, it was decidedly unclear, Tuppence meets the villain and gets a wad of cash to buy her silence about Jane Finn. Except I couldn't tell how Tuppence knew about Jane Finn. Other people know about Jane Finn, including the spymaster, the minister, and the villains. As a stoker, Tommy wouldn't know Jane Finn, other than from the lifeboat. I'm not sure if footage was missing. The setting is often unclear. Despite Tommy and Tuppence's new French names, it didn't seem like any of the action took place in France. Or Germany, for that matter. The hotel remains the Savoy, in London, but nothing looked English.

There are fight scenes on staircases, Tommy inches his way up what looks like an airshaft, sprints across a tightrope with a ladder for no discernible reason, and performs primitively staged stunts. As you watch them, realize that it's all real. No CGI here, just clever camera work, and stuntmen risking life and limb with the help of offscreen mattresses.

I don't know how Rita gets murdered. I'm not sure of the relationship between Jane Finn and Georges, her mystery cousin. Those explanations must have been in last reel, along with Tommy and Tuppence's declaration of love and adventure.

Watching *Die Abenteurer* was a weird experience. Scriptwriter Jane Bess' attack on Agatha's prose set the stage for future Hollywood adaptations. Things got changed that didn't need changing at all (names), scenes were added that made no sense (Tommy as a ship's stoker entertaining kids), scenes were dropped (much-needed explanations), and characters who had reasonable motivations in the novel suddenly behave as if they were lobotomized because the new plot demanded they be stupid.

Should you watch *Die Abenteurer*? Maybe, if you want to ogle what is probably the most muscular Tommy ever (Carlo Aldini, a serious athlete as well as actor). Otherwise, probably not. The film isn't good enough to overcome its deficiencies.

General Information

Based on: *The Secret Adversary* (novel, 1922)
Run time: 1 hr., 16 min. **Subtitles:** Yes

Writer: Jane Bess **Director:** Fred Sauer

Cast

Carlo Aldini as Pierre Lafitte (Tommy Beresford)
Eve Gray as Lucienne Fereoni (Tuppence Beresford)

Shayle Gardner as Julius Vardier
Hans Mierendorff as Marglin
Eberhard Leithoff as George Finné
Elfriede Borodin as Jeanette Finné (Jane Finn)
Hilda Bayley as Rita van den Meer (Rita Vandemeyer)
John Mylong as Boris
Valy Arnheim as Wittington
Mikhail Rasumny as Georges Herward

The Secret Adversary (1983)

This lethargic conspiracy thriller boasted great sets and costumes, but needed a more active Tommy

Fidelity to text

This little wonder is the closest adaptation of the novel you'll find anywhere. Scene for scene, line for line, it's faithful to the point of being weighed down.

Quality of movie

Flat and lackluster when it should be racing along vroom, vroom, vroom. Tommy and Tuppence outings should be sparkling, frothy, light as air. This is flat seltzer water.

I've sat through three versions of *The Secret Adversary* and no filmmaker has yet to do justice to the novel.

This adaptation, with Francesca Annis as Tuppence and James Warwick as Tommy, is exceedingly faithful yet it didn't catch the spirit of the novel. They're young adventurers, footloose and fancy-free. Francesca as Tuppence does an admirable job. James Warwick is … stiff. He resists the hero's call that Tuppence leaps after like a trout spotting a well-tied fly, yet I don't recall him being so stodgy in the novel. Yes, he tries to rein in Tuppence, but he's excited too. He's having fun and showing off for the damsel.

In this film, it feels like Tommy's merely doing his duty to Tuppence and England. At least he's being a man about it. In his terrible version of *The Secret Adversary*, David Walliams portrayed Tommy as being less manly than Homer Simpson. I do sense, in this production, that Tommy fought bravely in the war and endured terrible things. Nonetheless, he's still young, male, fit, bursting with hormones, and that should be demonstrated.

It's the actor at fault, not the role. Tommy has many opportunities to play the stalwart action hero, quick with a quip, his fists, and a handy lantern. He doesn't even have to take his shirt off to provide the audience with gratuitous nudity and fan service. He rises to the occasion, but there's always this sense of distance as if Tommy wishes he were in his quiet garden deadheading roses, instead of doing what he must.

You'd almost believe Tommy was lying back, closing his eyes, and thinking of England.

Julius P. Hersheimmer is much livelier than Tommy despite Gavan O'Herlihy's dreadful Texas accent. Wikipedia and Internet Movie Database disagree on where he was born (Hollywood or Dublin but in either case, he's got Irish parents) so perhaps his accent issues arose naturally. Any problems Julius suffers in the script stem from Agatha's difficulty writing plausible Americans.

The big name in the film is Honor Blackman, one of the first Bond Girls. She plays (who else?) the aging femme fatale and adventuress Rita Vandemeyer. Having an actress on hand like Honor Blackman is reason enough to rewrite the source material so she can strut her stuff beyond what the text says. Where did Rita Vandemeyer come from? Why is she so desperate for

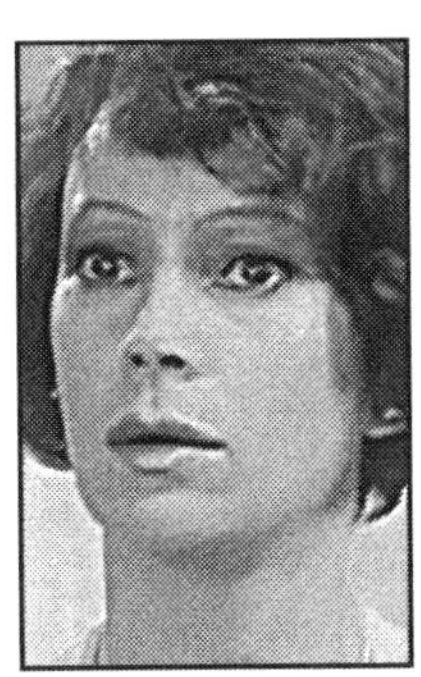
Tuppence Cowley
(*Francesca Annis*),
the adventure-seeker

Tommy Beresford
(*James Warwick*),
her partner in thrills

Julius P. Hersheimmer
(*Gavan O'Herlihy*),
the millionaire

Rita Vandemeyer
(*Honor Blackman*),
Mr. Brown's ally

James Peele Edgerton
(*Alec McCowen*),
the barrister

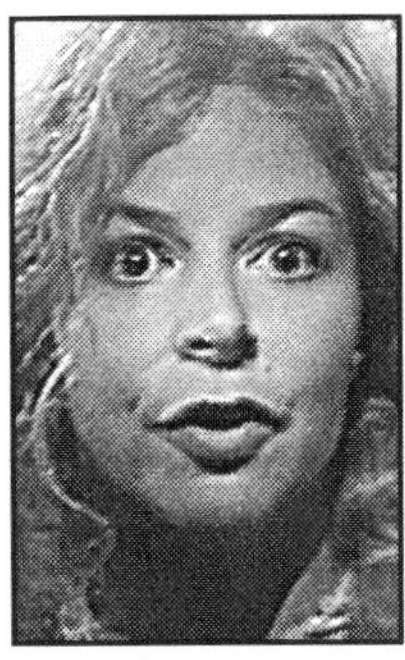
Annette
(*Toria Fuller*),
the French maid

money? How did she meet the mysterious Mr. Brown? Does she have any loyalties to anyone? All fascinating questions that must be answered by the fanfiction writers of the world since the producers didn't bother.

Well, they wouldn't, since they were staying true to the text.

If *The Secret Adversary* gets remade again, the producers should seize the opportunity and expand Ms. Vandemeyer's role. She's fascinating and enjoys the kind of louche life Tuppence craves if only her moral scruples didn't get in the way. Ms. Vandemeyer has no moral scruples. Sadly, age is catching up with Ms. Vandemeyer which is the only reason Tuppence got the drop on her. That must be the reason she entertains Tuppence's suggestion that she accept a huge payout and vanish to a quiet, anonymous life where she can grow old and safely deadhead her roses in peace.

Or not! For the likes of Rita Vandemeyer, dying in the saddle might be preferred to a long, slow decline.

There is a lot to like about this movie despite the lack of effervescence. The producers went all out on settings, accessories, clothes, and even a jaunty score. The cars are glorious vintage limousines, all Rolls-Royces, I assume. One scene after another at the Ritz making me wish I could time-travel to 1919 and stay there despite the lack of central heating. It would be worth it to sample those sumptuous meals complete with sparkling crystal, glittering chandeliers, and white-gloved waiters.

And the clothes. Oh my God, the clothes. Tuppence, despite her poverty, is a snappy dresser as is Rita Vandemeyer. So are Tommy, Julius, and everyone else. Even the background low-life thugs manage to look snazzy. Notice how Tommy, despite his stated poverty, still owns evening wear. He could have pawned his tuxedo, but he hasn't sunk that low. Not yet.

One point about the clothes. In 1919, flappers had yet to show up on the scene, which is why you don't see cloche hats, fringe, or shingled bobs. Most people, unless they were very rich, were making do with older clothes or altering them to fit the changing fashion. Clothes were changing radically compared to pre-war days, becoming lighter in weight, shorter, and less heavily ornamented. For ladies, that meant raising hemlines and removing excess fabric to stay in style. It's surprising how much a dress can be remade if you're skilled with a needle and willing to take the garment apart by ripping every single seam. Once you've done that, iron every scrap and then recut a new dress using only the least worn pieces of cloth. New clothing was costly so someone flat broke like Tuppence, despite the gorgeous wardrobe you see her wearing, would have done just that. Once you've made over a dress into the current fashion, the matching hat gets constructed from the scraps.

That's why I couldn't buy that scene where Tommy and Julius encounter the little girl on the beach wearing Tuppence's clothes. Virtually any child (other than a very wealthy one) would have known, coming across flotsam like an expensive, lace-trimmed dress and hat, to bring it home to mother. All that cloth and trim would have been worn again but only after it was carefully washed and remade. Mom or big sister would have gotten first dibs, not the kids' dress-up box. *Anyone* spotting Tuppence's clothes would have salvaged them and spent hours remaking them into a new outfit.

Notice also Tuppence's astonishing and openly worn cosmetics (those eyebrows!). Before the war, that kind of ostentatious makeup was the hallmark of prostitutes and actresses. A vicar's daughter like Tuppence would have never worn that sort of paint in public. Times changed.

Do you wonder how Tuppence, poor vicar's daughter but still a member of the gentry, could successfully impersonate a housemaid? Like most members of the gentry and higher up, she'd watched plenty of maids in action. She imitated what she saw when posing as Rita Vandemeyer's new maid. Rita bought Tuppence's story because it was true. Girls like Tuppence had to take whatever respectable work they could find after the war. Plenty of upper-class women accepted whatever story they were told simply to get a servant. Too many former housemaids had discovered the benefits of factory work where you got to go home at the end of the day.

All in all, *The Secret Adversary* is worth watching. It's a great period piece and easy on the eyes. But I wouldn't necessarily watch it a second time.

General Information

Based on: *The Secret Adversary* (novel, 1922)
Run time: 1 hr., 55 min. **Subtitles:** No

Writer: Pat Sandys **Director:** Tony Wharmby

Cast

James Warwick as Tommy Beresford
Francesca Annis as Tuppence Cowley

Gavan O'Herlihy as Julius P. Hersheimmer
Alec McCowen as Sir James Peele Edgerton
Honor Blackman as Rita Vandemeyer
Peter Barkworth as Mr. Carter
Toria Fuller as Jane Finn / Annette
John Fraser as Kramenin
George Baker as Whittington
Donald Houston as Boris
Joseph Brady as Dr. Hall
Wolf Kahler as The German
Reece Dinsdale as Albert
Peter Lovstrom as Henry
Matthew Scurfield as Conrad
Holly Watson as Child on Beach
Gabrielle Blunt as Annie
Norman Hartley as Florist
Roger Ostime as Ritz Hotel Receptionist
Nicholas Geake as Watson
Simon Watkins as Man at Astley Priors

Film Locations

The Bluebell Railway, Kent
The Ritz, Piccadilly, London

The Affair of the Pink Pearl (1983)

Tommy and Tuppence's first cases as fake heads of a detective agency channel the spirit of Sherlock Holmes

Fidelity to text

Text? Which text? The opening episode combines three stories into one, while ignoring the overall arc tying the short story collection together.

Quality of movie

A little Tuppence goes a long, long way. She's tiresome, and the episode is lackluster.

I like the book versions of Tommy and Tuppence. I haven't been thrilled with any of the filmed versions. They were indifferent at best.

The first filmed version of *The Secret Adversary* (the German-made *Die Abenteurer G.m.b.H.* in 1929) set the stage by rewriting Agatha's characters into something new and strange. The 1983 film of *The Secret Adversary* was so faithful to the text that it became stodgy. Well-done, beautifully-dressed stodge but still stodge. The less said about the 2015 version with David Walliams as Tommy, the better. Tommy and Tuppence were distorted almost beyond recognition.

I hoped the TV series of the *Partners in Crime* short stories (fifteen in all) would be better than those films. Short stories lend themselves to TV episodes because they get on with the action. They often benefit from being expanded, fleshing out sketchy details or answering unanswered questions.

Also, the 15 stories are pastiches of famous mystery writers of the 1910s and the first half of the 1920s. Agatha enjoyed making fun of famous writers and their famous detectives, including her own Hercule Poirot. The parody element could add another layer of enjoyment even though most of Agatha's targets are forgotten today.

Finally, *Partners in Crime* should be perfect for television as it has an overall arc involving Russian spies popping up every now and then, yet each individual episode can stand on its own. A viewer can watch the entire series and get a complete narrative or dip in now and then and still be satisfied with good television.

Based on the opening episode, I no longer have high hopes.

For starters, the producers omitted the entire Russian spy plot binding the stories into a cohesive whole. Those three stories ("The Sinister Stranger," "Blindman's Buff," "The Man Who Was No. 16") were not filmed. Instead, Inspector Marriot tells Tommy and Tuppence that the former owner of their new detective agency, Mr. Blunt, is a guest of his Majesty the King and, and, and … well, I don't know if anything will come of that setup where T&T have to keep an eye out for potential criminal

Col. Kingston Bruce (*Graham Crowden*), the host

Mrs. Kingston Bruce (*Noel Dyson*), the hostess

Beatrice Kingston Bruce (*Sussanah Morley*), the daughter

Lady Laura Barton (*Dulcie Gray*), the dipsomaniac

Hamilton Betts (*William Hootkins*), the millionaire

Phyllis Betts (*Lynda La Plante*), the pearl owner

General Information

Based on: "The Affair of the Pink Pearl" (short story, 1924)
Run time: 52 min. **Subtitles:** No

Writer: David Butler
Director: Tony Wharmby

Cast

Francesca Annis as Tuppence Beresford
James Warwick as Tommy Beresford
Reece Dinsdale as Albert
Arthur Cox as Inspector Marriott

Graham Crowden as Col. Kingston Bruce
Noel Dyson as Mrs. Kingston Bruce
Sussanah Morley as Beatrice Kingston Bruce
Charles Shaughnessy as John Rennie
Dulcie Gray as Lady Laura Barton
Ursula Mohan as Elise
William Hootkins as Hamilton Betts
Lynda La Plante as Phyllis Betts
Tim Woodward as Lawrence St. Vincent
Fleur Chandler as Janet Smith

accomplices of Mr. Blunt showing up at the office. We'll find out.

The first episode, *The Affair of the Pink Pearl*, combines three short stories into one episode. "The Fairy in the Flat" covers Tommy and Tuppence taking over Blunt's International Detective Agency but the Russian spies went back to Russia. Next comes "A Pot of Tea," a case engineered by Tuppence to get their detective agency publicity and to help a friend bring her young man to the altar. "The Affair of the Pink Pearl" is their first real case, brought by outsiders who need actual detecting done.

That's more than enough material for a 52-minute episode, yet there are scenes where you wait for something to happen and nothing does. You can sit through only so much mildly witty banter that doesn't advance the plot and rehashes well-established characters.

Our stars don't quite work either. As Tuppence, Francesca Annis is the headliner so she gets top billing over James Warwick as Tommy. If you've ever wondered what a manic pixie dream girl who's also a flapper would be like, look no further. Annis was 38 when she filmed this series and that's another issue. She's too old.

I appreciate it when Hollywood permits older women a starring role, especially as the heroine. No matter what Hollywood execs claim, they want their actresses young, younger, youngest even when the leading man is fifty years older than his costar. In *The First Wives Club* (1996), Goldie Hawn played an aging actress and she famously said there are three ages for women in Hollywood: babe, district attorney, and *Driving Miss Daisy* (1989). She's not wrong! But there's a point at which a woman should stop pretending she's an ingénue. She can be seductive and sophisticated but age-appropriate. Older women pretending to be their daughters is why we recognize the phrase "mutton dressed as lamb." That's what you'll see on the screen.

James Warwick is livelier than he was in *The Secret Adversary* but not by much. While at 36 he's too old to be playing a 25-year-old, his bigger issue is being upstaged by Annis. He made it easy for her; he's too laid back and gives off the distinct impression that he's depressed, tired, or both. Tommy's a veteran of the Great War and God only knows what he endured in the trenches in France but he's still young! Yet Warwick doesn't act like it. You'd think he's a man in late middle age.

As for the mystery, it's not bad. The "Pot of Tea" segment is "solved" when Tuppence reveals that she'd been hiding the missing hat-shop girl in their flat all along. The relieved Lawrence St. Vincent, minor peer and worried would-be fiancé, tells the Kingston Bruce household how wonderful their detective agency is. When a guest's pink pearl goes missing in their home, they hire the agency to find it.

This, by the way, was a missed opportunity for story enhancement. St. Vincent is visiting their home and the social-climbing couple are clearly angling to get him interested in their daughter, Beatrice, and not in some hat-shop girl. They're especially motivated because Beatrice in turn is enamored of a young, impoverished socialist.

The visiting American couple are amusing, even if they don't sound American. The wife, Phyllis Betts, (Lynda La Plante) amuses herself with Tommy, and their scenes are the episode's highlights. Her husband, Hamilton, is more concerned about his wife's stolen pink pearl than her virtue or faithfulness. It's obvious he gave up years ago. If Tommy is paying attention, he might see in their relationship his possible future with Tuppence.

The other plot thread that would have benefited from enhancing was Lady Laura Barton's. She's aging, living off her title since she's poor, and suspected of kleptomania. Her maid, Elise, fosters this rumor for reasons of her own. More should have been done with Lady Laura; a woman enduring genteel poverty is rife with dramatic possibilities. There's also the hint that Lady Laura would commit suicide if it's discovered she'd stolen the pink pearl because she doesn't remember stealing anything, even teaspoons. But a hint is all you get because too much time was wasted watching Tuppence behaving like Lucy Ricardo: in the office, in her and Tommy's shared flat, and while investigating the stolen pearl. Maybe her brain was damaged by those electric blue cocktails she chugged down.

I'd like to say the rest of the series can only go up from here. We'll find out! In the meantime, should you watch? It depends entirely on your tolerance for manic, madcap flappers and their long-suffering husbands.

Finessing the King (1983)

A newspaper banner holds the key to solving the Queen of Hearts' slaying in a seedy café's private room

Fidelity to text

Two short stories are combined, Bingo Hale shows up, as does an elderly waitress and a handgun.

Quality of movie

I didn't like it, but I didn't dislike it either. It looked great and, my goodness, but Tuppence can afford stylish clothes despite their detective agency not having any clients.

This episode has a strange backstory. Agatha wrote one short story that was published in two parts in *The Sketch* magazine. "Finessing the King" ended with the discovery of the body. The story arc concluded in "The Gentleman Dressed in Newspaper." Even though it was a single story, they kept the division when they were collected in *Partners in Crime*. That's why you see the story referenced under both names.

Agatha wrote each *Partners* story as a kinda sorta pastiche of a popular mystery author of the day. This time, it's now-forgotten American mystery writer, Isabel Ostrander (1883-1924). She used a pair of detectives, Tommy McCarty, ex-policeman, and Denis Riordan, fireman, to solve her cases. They were so obscure by 1982 that for the costume party scene, Tommy and Tuppence dress up as Watson and Holmes. Everyone still remembers those detectives.

Finessing the King opens with Tommy discussing how newspaper mastheads are coded to show newsstands and paperboys which is the current edition. This was common back when newspapers printed several editions per day. Tiny stars or spots were inserted into the masthead. The buying public never noticed, but the newsstand agent knew which stale papers to sell first.

Tommy uses this ploy to divert Tuppence's attention from going dancing. There's lots of witty banter, much of it lifted from the story. But without subtitles, I didn't get the jokes. For those with the same issue, Tuppence jokes about cooking Tommy dinner consisting of foods served at British boarding schools: kedgeree, rhubarb, junket, and nice gooey custard. He's not enthused.

Tuppence also complains about stay-at-home, boring husbands. She'd been brought up to believe that young husbands couldn't get out of the house fast enough, with or without their wives. As always, she prevails.

Their attention is drawn to a paragraph in the personals column (printed on the front page of the *Daily Leader*, something else newspapers no longer do):

> "I should go with three hearts. 12 tricks.
> Ace of Spades. Necessary to finesse the king."

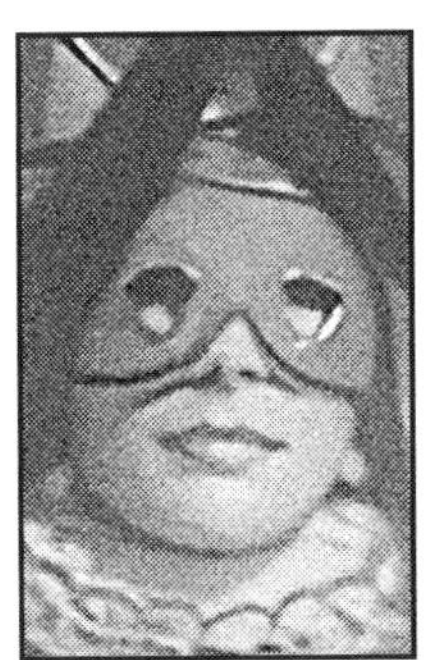
Lady Vere Merivale (*Annie Lambert*), the wealthy wife

Sir Arthur Merivale (*Benjamin Whitrow*), the loyal husband

Capt. Bingo Hale (*Peter Blythe*), the dedicated friend

Inspector Marriott (*Arthur Cox*), the police detective

Dr. Stoughton (*John Gillett*), the medical man

Widow (*Anna Turner*), the waitress

Tommy reads it as an expensive way of learning bridge, i.e., taking out newspaper adverts for each hand. Tuppence believes it's a secret message between illicit lovers.

Let's tackle the bridge reference first. I'm a non-bridge player. I *think* finessing a king is when you force your opponent (who holds a higher card in the suit than you do) to play it badly so you (with your lower cards) pick up more tricks and score points.

Tuppence deciphers the message as arranging a meeting at the Three Arts fancy dress charity ball, followed by a tryst at the Ace of Spades seedy café at midnight. Finessing the king means they're trying to fool her husband. Since it's a costume party, she and Tommy have to dress up and naturally, they should dress like fictional detectives, thus the Holmes and Watson outfits.

They have a lovely time at the fancy dress party, a time-honored British tradition that didn't seem to make it to the U.S. Among a horde of party-goers, they spot a lady dressed as the Queen of Hearts, a man as The Gentleman Dressed in Newspaper (from the Tenniel illustration from *Alice Through the Looking Glass* and a good, subtle match for the Queen of Hearts), and a devil in red satin.

Then it's off to the Ace of Spades where a chatty, elderly waitress (subtitles would have been so useful) implies that some drink orders are real and some are code for alcohol served in cups so when the bobbies raid the joint, the customers can claim they're sipping tea.

They watch the Queen of Hearts enter the curtained booth next to them, followed by the Gentleman Dressed in Newspaper (he's wearing the *Daily Leader*). After the man leaves hastily, Tuppence's intuition gets going, and she discovers the Queen of Hearts, stabbed through her heart. The Queen's barely alive but she moans, "Bingo did it."

Bingo Hale is the Queen of Heart's lover. His best friend, Sir Arthur, insists that a) Bingo and his wife, Lady Vere, would never canoodle, and b) Bingo would never murder Lady Vere. Sir Arthur's half right. Bingo himself is unsure about the murder because he was very drunk that night. He's arrested because it's his dagger sticking out of Lady Vere's heart, confirming Tuppence's evidence. But during their interview at Wandsworth Prison, he tells our dynamic duo that he loved Lady Vere and they would have married if they could.

General Information

Based on: "Finessing the King" (short story, 1924)
Run time: 51 min. **Subtitles:** No

Writer: Gerald Savory
Director: Christopher Hodson

Cast

Francesca Annis as Tuppence Beresford
James Warwick as Tommy Beresford
Reece Dinsdale as Albert
Arthur Cox as Inspector Marriott
Terry Cowling as Detective Sergeant Halliday

Benjamin Whitrow as Sir Arthur Merivale
Annie Lambert as Lady Vere Merivale
Peter Blythe as Capt. Bingo Hale
John Gillett as Dr. Stoughton
Anna Turner as Widow
Pat Gorman as Commissionaire
John Mangan as Pinocchio guest

The film picks up when Inspector Marriot, our friendly local policeman, brings Sir Arthur to meet Tommy and Tuppence. Watch the British class system in action when the inspector tries to question Sir Arthur and states unpleasant truths. Sir Arthur isn't having any of it and clearly wants pushy inspectors to remember their place at the bottom of the social register.

Inspector Marriot gets a chance to shine in this episode. He set up Tommy and Tuppence with the detective agency in the first episode. He's not only willing to think outside the box, he's a good enough policeman to recognize a lie when he hears one.

Let's go back to Lady Vere (the Queen of Hearts). Everyone knows — other than Sir Arthur — that she's been canoodling with Bingo. She's wealthy in her own right. Any policeman in the universe will tell you that when a rich, cheating woman is murdered, hubby is suspects number one through ninety-nine. It is that rare for her murderer to be someone else. Although we don't witness these scenes, it's clear from Inspector Marriot's dialog that he's been investigating Sir Arthur and he doesn't like what he's found.

Yet he can't ignore the facts. Lady Vere accused Bingo with her dying breath. She's clutching a piece of Bingo's newspaper costume in her hand. That's Bingo's dagger driven into her heart. There are rumors Bingo was seeing some American heiress but he tells Tommy and Tuppence it's not true. There are suggestions this rumor drove Lady Vere to suicide, making it look like Bingo murdered her as her revenge on him. But that doesn't pass the sniff test. Nor does Bingo murdering her feel right. If he's got any sense, he'd wait until *after* the wedding so he'd inherit the boodle.

So why does Inspector Marriot harass Tommy and Tuppence? Because they might spot the break in the case he *knows* is there, but he hasn't found. Which they do. And, as you may guess from the beginning, it all comes back to the Gentleman Dressed in Newspaper. One masked man looks very much like another if their build is similar and they're wearing identical costumes constructed from the *Daily Leader*.

This episode functioned. It was clever in spots, and there's that great costume ball. Overall, it's okay, like reading yesterday's newspaper when you haven't got anything better to do.

The House of Lurking Death (1983)

Something's fishy at the manor as Thurnly Grange's residents are dropping like poisoned flies

Fidelity to text

It's all there, with added plot to flesh out the characters and motivation, plus a school of red herrings.

Quality of movie

This should have been either longer or more tightly scripted. It dragged when it should have sprinted.

There's so much going on in the decaying mansion of Thurnly Grange that the short story should be expanded into a novel. Perhaps not one starring Tommy and Tuppence but like Agatha, who sometimes swapped detectives while revising her books, you can use someone else to solve the murder(s).

In this case, we've got an ideal candidate in Mary Chilcott, a suspicious guest at Thurnly Grange. Feel free to use the bare bones of this criminally underwritten story and flesh out your own Agatha Christie-style murder mystery. So get out your notebook as we examine the present and sink into the past, where old sins cast long shadows.

Our heroine, Lois Hargreaves, visits Tommy and Tuppence. She needs a poisoned box of chocolates investigated but she won't go to the police. She gives them some background about being orphaned and taken in by her aunt, Lady Lucy Radcliffe. Naturally, she doesn't give them all the details until it's too late.

Lady Radcliffe was an extremely wealthy widow. She's a lady because her husband was knighted, not because they were born into the aristocracy. After they bought Thurnly Grange from an impoverished peer, hubby died but Lady Radcliffe survived.

Lady Radcliffe had a companion her age, Miss Logan. Miss Logan's father was a famous doctor, a pioneer in the study of serum therapeutics. This was cutting-edge medicine in 1900, where blood from recovered patients was processed and used to prevent the same disease in other patients. It's similar to vaccines in that a small dose of antibodies prevents a larger, fatal disease like diphtheria. Serum therapeutics fell out of favor with the rise of antibiotics and vaccines, but they still work today.

Nobody becomes a companion to a rich, unpleasant old woman if they have other choices so why did Miss Logan? That question remains unanswered. Miss Logan must not have gotten a bequest from Lady Radcliffe's will (as companions normally do) so she's got no other place to go.

Lois also doesn't inform Tommy and Tuppence that Lady Radcliffe's death occurred under mysterious circumstances.

Got that in your notebook? Let's move on to the two adult non-servants in the Thurnly Grange household.

Dennis Radcliffe was Lady Radcliffe's nephew via

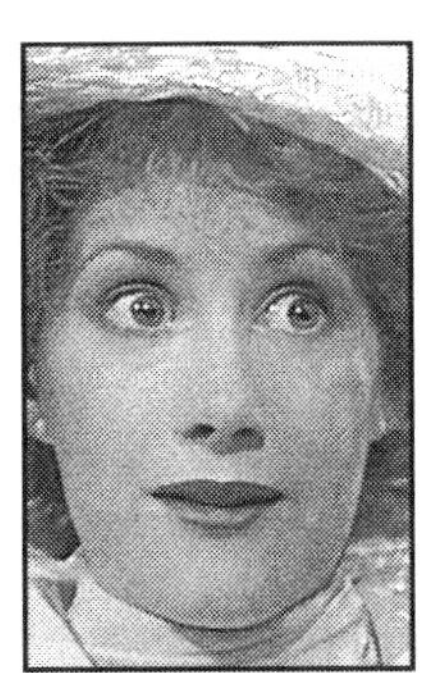

Lois Hargreaves (Lynsey Baxter), the naïve heiress

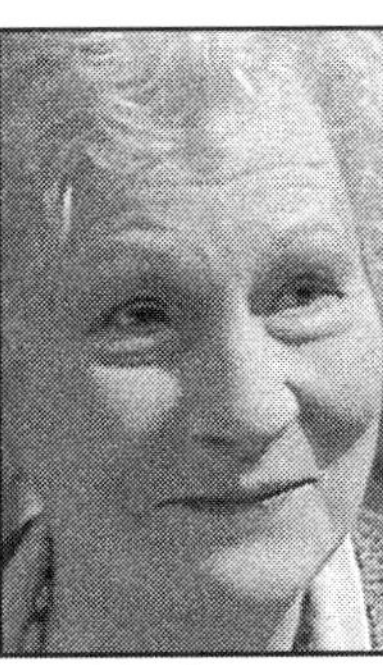

Miss Logan (*Joan Sanderson*), the ex-companion

Dennis Radcliffe (*Michael Cochrane*), the wastrel relative

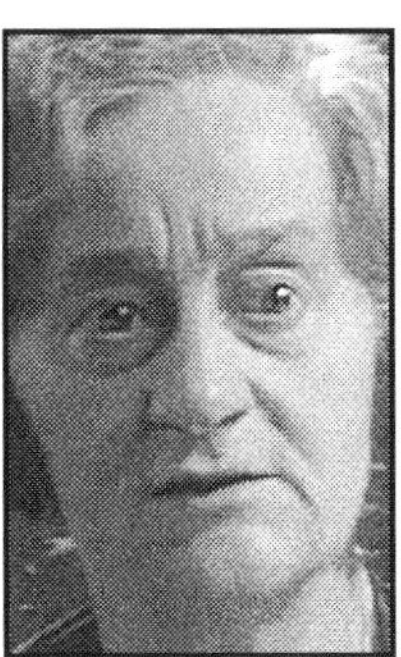

Hannah Macpherson (*Liz Smith*), the righteous maid

Mary Chilcott (*Louisa Rix*), the friend of Lois

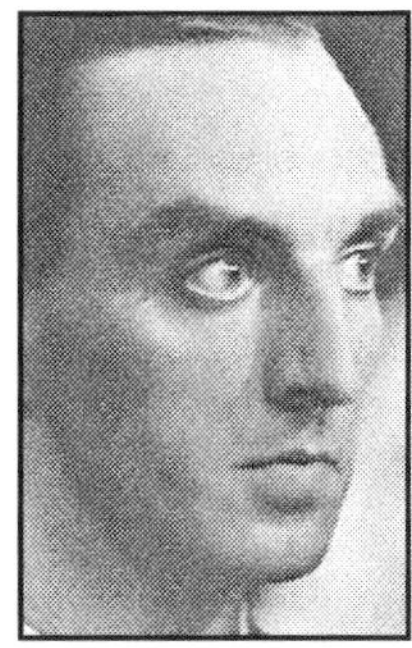

Dr. Burton (*Granville Saxton*), the devoted medico

her dead husband. Lois is not related to him although she does call him cousin. Dennis is a louche ne'er-do-well who drinks, comes in late, seduces parlormaids, gambles, and pursues Lois' friend. He was once Lady Radcliffe's heir but she disinherited him in favor of sweet, naïve Lois.

Dennis is unhappy and he has no other place to go. Lois loves Dennis, which he should encourage because rich wives aren't found at pubs. But he doesn't, which still works out because Lois feels so guilty about her windfall that she's leaving her huge inheritance to Dennis.

Finally, there's Mary Chilcott, Lois' best friend from school. They're the same age but Mary comes across as being much sharper than Lois, except where men are concerned. The question with Mary is why is she living at Thurnly Grange? Probably because she's got no family, no money, and no place to go. Dennis may not have coaxed her into bed, but he's trying.

The servants include Esther Quant, parlormaid. She fleshed out into a greedy, fast, painted girl who'd appreciate a fling with Dennis and is not above snacking on leftover tea sandwiches. Esther encourages Rose, the kitchen maid, to wear makeup and quit listening to her boring mother (the cook) and that elderly Jesus freak, Hannah.

Hannah, as old as Miss Logan, was Lady Radcliffe's devoted lady's maid. She quotes scripture at every occasion and recognizes painted whores of Babylon when she sees them. She's resentful, too, possibly because she didn't get a pension from Lady Radcliffe as she should have, allowing her to have a home of her own. Like everyone else at Thurnly Grange, she's trapped.

Dr. Burton got a makeover for the film, changing from an elderly doctor to a young one who's obviously got eyes for Lois and not just because she's a rich heiress. The incompetent village bobby is mentioned as are the other great houses in the district.

Dr. Burton argues with Lois because of another issue she glosses over and the film doesn't expand on: Lois' box of poisoned chocolates was not the first one! From the start, we know that two other households also received anonymous gifts of toxic chocolate, yet nobody's concerned when Lois gets one. They sample the chocolates and get sick.

Once is bad luck, twice is coincidence, three boxes of poisoned candy is someone's nefarious plan. Dr. Burton suspects socialists, I assume the local bobby knows and suspects village malcontents, but Lois is conflicted because she thinks the chocolates were sent from within the house.

Add to your plot the fact that the house is a crumbling pile with a rotting conservatory and no gardener to maintain it. Mary, looking for something to do that doesn't involve Dennis, has been tending the plants. One of the plants — Tuppence identifies it — is castor bean. Castor beans are a big, lovely, showy plant grown in hothouses in northern climes and outdoors in southern ones. In addition to the castor oil that can be distilled from the plant, you can use the seeds to make your own ricin, an immensely powerful neurotoxin.

There's also a big, menacing dog who doesn't seem to belong to the household but he's guarding it anyway.

Got all that? Ready to write that killer bestseller?

But hold up, because the plot thickens. After being consulted, Tommy and Tuppence discover in the morning's newspaper that Lois and Esther the maid are dead from eating poisoned fig paste sandwiches, Miss Logan is gravely ill, Dennis didn't come home for tea, and Mary? Oh, she's perfectly fine.

Except when Tommy and Tuppence arrive at Thurnly Grange, they discover that Dennis — who inherited a fortune the minute Lois bit into that fig paste sandwich — is also dead. Mary is healthy as ever as are the other servants.

What a great setup. All you have to do is figure out what comes next. What Agatha wrote may not be what you dream up. The scriptwriter stuck closely to her story so when the fiery climax arrives, that's Agatha raining down the fire of the Lord upon the murderer.

The ending is the weakest part of the episode and the short story. They both imply that Hannah knew Lady Radcliffe's death was suspicious. Hannah resents and dislikes the murderer but until now, she had no proof. Sadly, not enough detail was provided, nor do we know who inherits Thurnly Grange and the fortune.

It won't be Mary, who now has even fewer options on where to go.

Should you watch? There's a lot going on (even if it dragged in spots) so add it to your list, but only once.

General Information

Based on: "The House of Lurking Death" (short story, 1924)
Run time: 53 min. **Subtitles:** No

Writer: Jonathan Hales
Director: Christopher Hodson

Cast

Francesca Annis as Tuppence Beresford
James Warwick as Tommy Beresford
Reece Dinsdale as Albert

Joan Sanderson as Miss Logan
Liz Smith as Hannah Macpherson
Lynsey Baxter as Lois Hargreaves
Louisa Rix as Mary Chilcott
Michael Cochrane as Dennis Radcliffe
Anita Dobson as Esther Quant
Deddie Davies as Mrs. Holloway
Kim Clifford as Rose Holloway
Granville Saxton as Dr. Burton

Film Location

Nether Winchendon House, Aylesbury Buckinghamshire

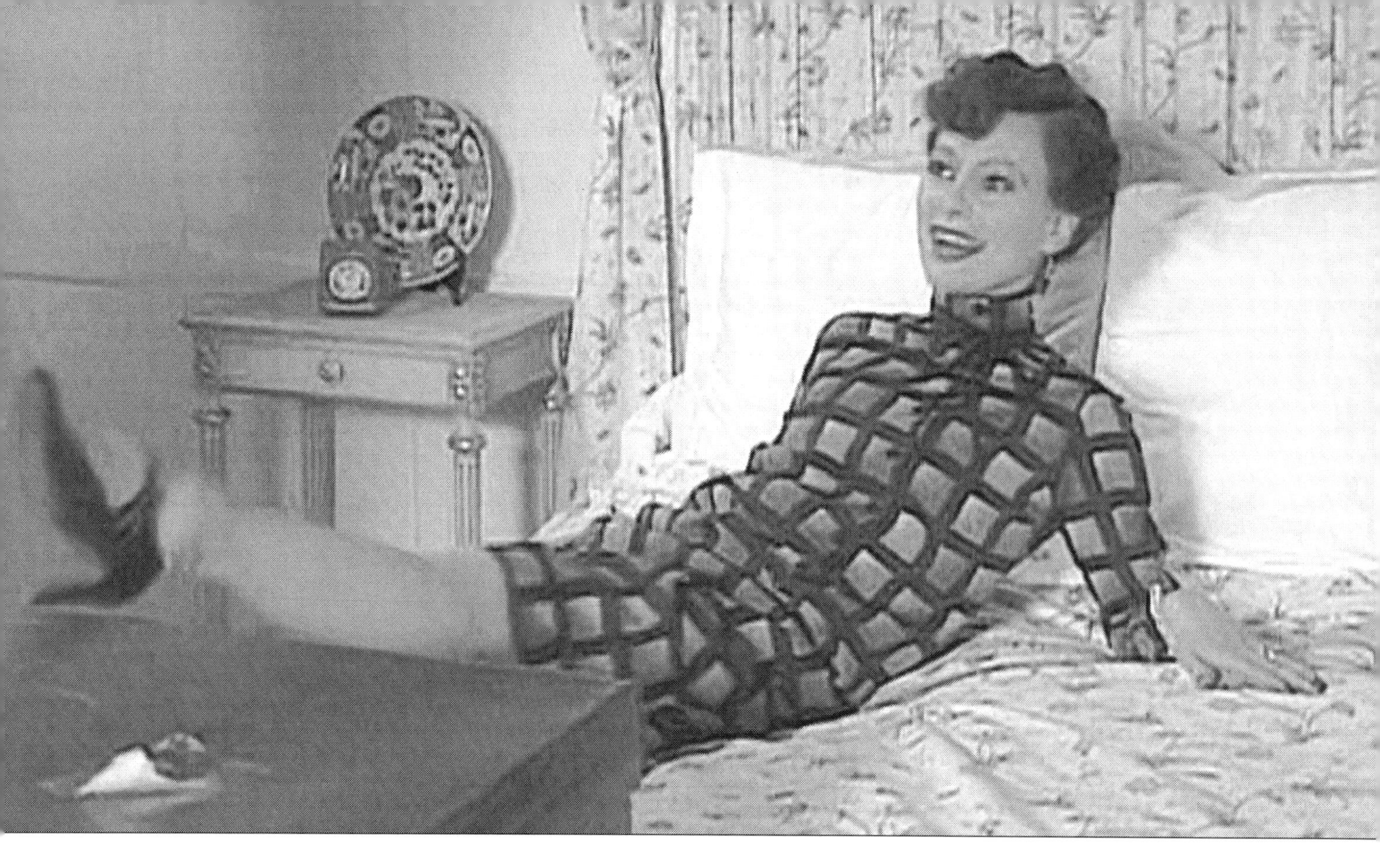

The Sunningdale Mystery (1983)

An impoverished typist lingers in jail as Tommy and Tuppence look into a case of cheating on the golf course

Fidelity to text

The short story consists solely of a conversation in a tea shop overheard by Inspector Marriot. Since that makes boring TV, expect added characters, scenes, motorcars, and horses.

Quality of movie

Adding new settings, fabulous clothes, motorcars, horses, and disgruntled staff helped but not enough.

When Agatha wrote the short stories for *Partners in Crime*, each one was a parody of a famous mystery novelist of the time. One century later, give or take, the vast majority of us have no idea who any of those authors were and their once name-checked detectives are even more obscure. Among others, she parodied G.K. Chesterton (whom you should have heard of but not necessarily for mysteries), Conan Doyle (whom you've heard of), and herself (whom you've definitely heard of or you wouldn't be watching the movie adaptations and reading my reviews). After that, it gets murky.

You *might* have heard of the author Agatha was toying with in "The Sunningdale Mystery" but not because of her mysteries. It's Emma Magdolna Rozália Mária Jozefa Borbála Orczy de Orci (1865-1947); Baroness Orczy to you and me and Emmuska to her family and friends. She's a blue blood aristocrat who emigrated with her parents to England in 1880 to escape peasant revolts in Austria-Hungary. She married an artist and they lived a poor but happy life.

Then, Baroness Emma got the idea from her landlady's daughter to write stories and earn some much-needed cash. She succeeded. Her most successful character was the Scarlet Pimpernel, the basis for every fop by day, superhero by night character you've ever heard of. Zorro, The Shadow, Batman, Superman; if the hero's got a dual identity you can thank the Baroness.

However, the Scarlet Pimpernel — despite being the paragon of derring-do when he's not pretending to be a waste of space — did not solve crimes. For that, the Baroness invented the Old Man in the Corner. She wrote a number of short stories about him and the lady journalist, Polly Burton, he chats up in the tea shop. The Old Man became the basis of every armchair detective you've ever heard of (Look! Nero Wolfe!) who solves crimes by applying his powerful intellect to the story he's told. The Old Man doesn't leave his chair, nor does he care about informing the police, collecting admissible evidence, having criminals arrested, or seeing justice done. He most definitely does not run about the countryside looking for clues.

Doris Evans
(*Emily Moore*),
the accused

Hollaby Junior
(*Denis Lill*),
the son

Hollaby Senior
(*Edwin Brown*),
the father

Major Barnard
(*Terence Conoley*),
the first golfer

Mr. Lecky
(*Denis Holmes*),
the second golfer

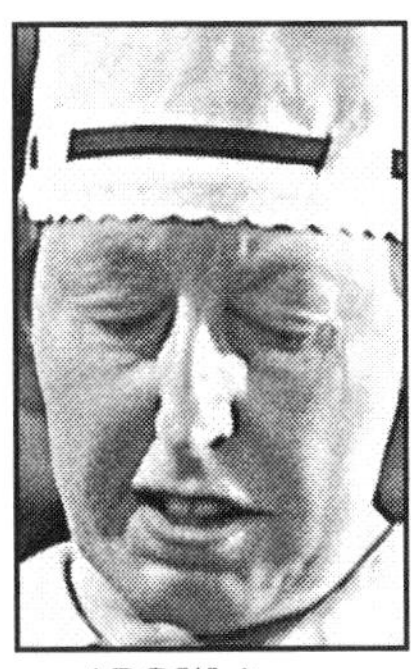

ABC Waitress
(*Dorothea Phillips*),
the audience

Crime, for him, is a puzzle to be solved. He's got some tics. He sits in the corner (keeping his back against the wall), drinks milk, and eats cheesecake. That's why in the tea shop, Tuppence sends back Tommy's order of steak, potatoes, peas, etc. The Old Man also habitually knots and unknots a string (think of a mouse-sized hangman's noose) as he listens to the story and then solves it. Tommy forgot to play with his string but he got the rest of the details correct, including having a charming lady hanging on his every word.

In Agatha's parody, Tommy and Tuppence — using lurid newspaper clippings — puzzle out a solution but who should they tell? They have no proof, just speculation. Lucky for them, Inspector Marriot is sitting at the next table listening in. Scotland Yard already has a suspect, it's not Doris Evans, and now they've got a plausible scenario to hang their investigation on.

That's not much to work with for a TV episode. It had to be enhanced with added characters, settings other than tea shops, searching for clues, and many flashbacks showing what happened instead of Tommy reading the newspaper story to Tuppence and the tea shop waitress.

Thus, we open with Albert pointedly showing his feckless employer where the scissors are located. Albert sets the tone for the rest of the servant class in the episode. The tea shop waitress disdains them, even more so when Tuppence countermands Tommy's order. The hotel manager is openly disbelieving about their name since the duo are feckless enough to not consider what name they'd use to register under. They could be indulging in an illicit tryst but the hotel manager has bills to pay so he checks them in anyway. When Tommy needs his golf clubs, the hotel porter pointedly shows his open, empty hand first.

Tuppence shows off her astonishing wardrobe. One wonders how she pays for it since Blunt's Brilliant Detectives doesn't have many cases and so earns very little. Don't miss her apricot negligee. Tommy perks right up. In fact, they enjoy several scenes bordering on salacious but still in the best of taste.

When not being abused by their inferiors, they drive through the countryside, ride down country lanes, and examine the golf course that Tommy fortuitously played in his youth.

General Information

Based on: "The Sunningdale Mystery" (short story, 1924)
Run time: 50 min. **Subtitles:** Yes

Writer: Jonathan Hales
Director: Tony Wharmby

Cast

Francesca Annis as Tuppence Beresford
James Warwick as Tommy Beresford
Reece Dinsdale as Albert

Denis Lill as Hollaby Junior
Edwin Brown as Hollaby Senior
Emily Moore as Doris Evans
Terence Conoley as Major Barnard
Denis Holmes as Mr. Lecky
Robin Parkinson as Landlord
Dorothea Phillips as ABC Waitress
Martin Rutledge as Cyril
Vivienne Ritchie as Girl
Jim Wiggins as Ticket Collector

Film Locations

The Bluebell Railway, East Grinstead, Kent
The Ravenswood, Sharpthorne, West Sussex (hotel)

In the meantime, poor Doris Evans waits in jail. She's young, pretty, a typist so she's poor, and accused of murder. True to The Old Man in the Corner format, Tommy and Tuppence never go near her. All her scenes are told in flashback. She's got good reason to be afraid as her story is ridiculous. She's shivering in that jail cell in the women's wing at Wandsworth and wishing she'd never taken that nice older man's offer of a walk home under his umbrella in the driving rain.

The mystery is clever, turning on one of Agatha's favorite tropes: Are you seeing what is real? Or are you being deceived? Everyone knows that's Captain Sessle on the golf course. His bright blue jacket is unmistakable. Why did his golf game deteriorate to that of a clumsy child's? It must be because of what the tall woman in brown (seen from a distance) said to him.

That last bit is where the short story does a better job. Tuppence works out how a man can wear a skirt over a set of plus-fours. Since the lower legs are stocking-clad and the shoes don't show, the silhouette reads as female. That wasn't spelled out in the film.

The hatpin murder weapon is clever. As Agatha and Tuppence both knew, a hatpin has always been seen as a woman's weapon. If you've never seen one, a lady's hatpin is essentially a steel knitting needle with a dagger-like point. They're six to ten inches long, with a fancy knob at one end. A lady might wear one, two, or even three to skewer her fashionably enormous hat to her towering hairdo. Edwardian ladies used them all the time. They were widely recommended as defense weapons as very few mashers cared to have one thrust into their flesh.

But as Tuppence made clear, ladies no longer used hatpins because they'd bobbed their hair and hats the size of turkey platters turned into snug-fitting cloches. She hadn't worn one in years. But a man, especially an older one, might not realize how much fashion had changed. Would the police catch on? Or would they think that since only women used hatpins, the murderer had to be female.

The reason to watch is Tuppence's fashion sense. It's divine, even if the episode needed more flair and flash and flirting.

The Clergyman's Daughter (1983)

Spirits haunting the Red House are driving away paying guests, so who ya gonna call? T & T!

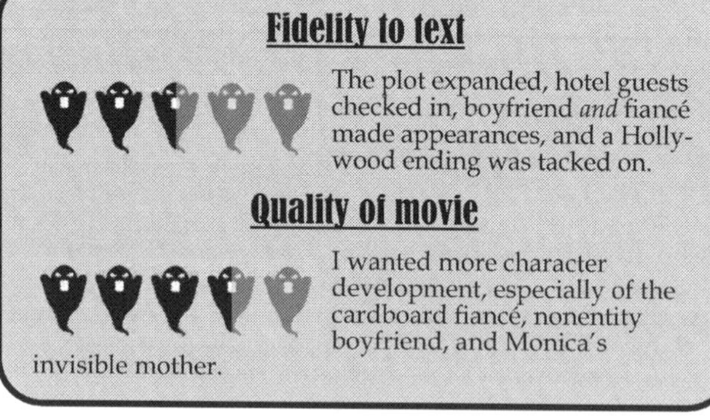

This episode combines two short stories "The Clergyman's Daughter" and "The Red House" into one episode because neither story has a complete arc. They were first published in 1923 in *The Grand* magazine as "The First Wish." It seems the story was split in two and gained new names when *Partners in Crime* was compiled in 1929.

Agatha liked teasing readers with the supernatural, but she often used it to show that what seems otherworldly is in reality good old-fashioned human avarice. Just because things go bump in the night doesn't mean a poltergeist is at work. Get out Occam's Razor and see if there's a simpler explanation.

This episode is the first in the series to explore the warmth and affection between Tommy and Tuppence. Previously, especially in the opening episode, Tuppence came across as a manic pixie dream girl, flapper division. It was tiresome to watch and God knows, she would be tiresome to live with.

This time, she's no longer as disdainful of Tommy's intellect or drive as she has been. They were charming to watch, especially when Tuppence channeled her inner medium in fancy hired clothes while Tommy played her long-suffering, bill-paying husband.

Another improvement was watching Albert do something other than play the office buffoon. He has a fixation about exciting cinema, and he put his movie-watching skills to use in the climax. He got to play the hero of his dreams.

Readers who remember the story will wonder: Albert the hero when he wasn't in either story? Well, yes. Such is the way of filmmakers when they adapt fiction, as he'd be the first to tell you.

Our story opens with Tuppence announcing — using her divination skills honed by years of guessing the future during Christmas Eve celebrations at the vicarage — that their next client would be a clergyman's daughter just like her.

In walks Monica Deane, an impoverished clergyman's daughter taking care of her invalid mother. That's a problem but not why she showed up at Blunt's Detective Agency. Neither is her inheriting a huge brick mansion that she can't afford to maintain. She solved that problem by taking in paying guests to

Monica Dean
(*Jane Booker*),
the scared homeowner

Norman Partridge
(*Geoffrey Drew*),
the boring fiancé

Gerald Rush
(*Alan Jones*),
the budding boyfriend

Crockett
(*Pam St. Clement*),
the expectant maid

O'Neill
(*David Delve*),
the hopeful nephew

Frank Mulberry
(*George Malpas*),
the garrulous gardener

make ends meet. It isn't even the mysterious events where unseen hands throw the crockery about, scaring away the newly arrived guests.

No, what has her spooked is that strangers are pressuring her to sell the mansion, and they all sport the same sinister gold tooth and oddly shaped ears. Why would they do this? Could it be that her late aunt, who was supposed to be wealthy yet left nothing but the house, had left something more behind?

The possibility exists. In the short story, Tommy charms the local bank manager by trading stories about silly elderly relatives who insisted on withdrawing all their money at the start of the Great War. In the film, Monica's fiancé Norman Partridge doesn't work for the bank, but passes along the information that the dear departed aunt had withdrawn all her money.

This is where the timing gets weird, because the Great War had been over for a few years when Tommy and Tuppence took over the Blunt Detective Agency and the dearly departed aunt had to have cash to pay the bills for her mansion. Yet very little cash made its way into Monica's hands. After she paid a few small legacies, the sole asset she had left was the house.

The film adds two couples who're chased from the Red House by beds falling apart in the middle of the night and clothes ripped to shreds by unseen hands and crockery thrown violently across the room by someone who's not there. Naturally, Monica must refund their money, putting her deeper into the hole.

That's why she's reassured when Tommy and Tuppence inform her that they only charge a fee when the job is successfully completed.

What I wanted to see was more scenes with Monica's fiancé, Norman Partridge, and wannabe boyfriend, Gerald Rush. Maybe it's the romance writer in me, but I wondered, what they were doing about Monica's peril? As far as I could see, nothing.

Fiancé Norman Partridge was some kind of financial adviser. He's rich and worthy, but Monica thinks he's dull. She'd be instantly better off by marrying him. He'd pay her bills and provide for her mother. Yet Monica's reluctant to commit.

But what does Norman see in a destitute clergyman's daughter with an invalid mother? As a well-off, socially secure member of the community, Norman doesn't have to hunt for a wife. Local mothers would be tossing bushels of daughters at him. Clearly, he wants Monica or he wouldn't be there. Yet we never get an explanation. Nor does Norman seem concerned about flying crockery and vandalism. That also didn't make any sense.

Boyfriend Gerald Rush is younger, handsomer, destitute, and an engineer so presumably he's good with his hands. Monica fancies him because who doesn't prefer poor and handsome to rich and ordinary? Gerald says virtually nothing, but stands around looking decorative. Like Norman, he doesn't seem to mind that Monica is being menaced by paranormal activity. He's not doing anything to investigate the situation either.

We never see Monica's mother, who should be even more concerned about poltergeists because if they wreck the hotel, she and Monica have nowhere to go.

Instead, we meet Crockett, the Mrs. Danvers-type housekeeper who came with the mansion. She might as well be wearing a sign saying "don't trust me." Crockett also has a mysterious, yet unseen nephew. If you're paying attention, you already know who the villains are and it isn't Norman or Gerald trying to take over the Red House for nefarious reasons of their own.

The other servant Monica inherits is Frank Mulberry, the elderly gardener. He's worked on the estate for years and knows exactly where he buried the potatoes. He cheerfully takes Tommy's money without telling Tommy what he wants to know.

The ending was completely rewritten in a manner that Albert would approve, with action, guns, digging up treasure in the middle of the night, hostages, and plucky office boys swinging to the rescue like Douglas Fairbanks Sr. in *The Black Pirate* (1926). Gerald assists badly and Norman assists not at all. Norman, in fact, disappears from the last half of the film as completely as a ghost in the noonday sun.

It's a light, fun episode but it really would have benefited from more time spent with Norman and Gerald, especially if they had to duel with poltergeists for Monica's favors.

General Information

Based on: "The Clergyman's Daughter" (short story, 1923)
Run time: 52 min. **Subtitles:** Yes

Writer: Paul Annett
Director: Paul Annett

Cast

Francesca Annis as Tuppence Beresford
James Warwick as Tommy Beresford
Reece Dinsdale as Albert

Jane Booker as Monica Deane
Alan Jones as Gerald Rush
Geoffrey Drew as Norman Partridge
Bill Dean as Mr. Hove
Elspeth MacNaughton as Mrs. Hove
Pam St. Clement as Crockett
David Delve as O'Neill
George Malpas as Frank Mulberry
Robbie Stevens as Mr. Cockwell
Janet Hampson as Mrs. Cockwell

Film Location

Horsted Place, Little Horsted, East Sussex

The Ambassador's Boots (1983)

Tuppence's friends come to her aid as they investigate mysterious doings aboard ship and in a chic nightclub

The original short story is short. Few characters show up and even fewer have speaking parts. Tommy and Tuppence, Albert the intrepid office boy, the ambassador, his valet Richards, Cicely Marsh, an unnamed Spanish-looking villain, and Inspector Grace (not Inspector Marriot) do the talking. The action is confined to the office, the embassy (where Tommy interviews Richards), and the beauty parlor. Nobody dies.

The film version is radically different.

We open with a lavish garden party at the American Embassy. What a fabulously well-dressed crowd of toffs swilling down elaborate cocktails and gorging on fancy canapes! Tommy and Tuppence — despite their cries of poverty in earlier episodes — fit right in. They both look spiffing. A Hungarian actress, Virma Le Strange, is effusively grateful to them for rescuing her in a previous (and unseen) case.

Like Sherlock Holmes, the *Partners In Crime* TV series loves referring to other investigations, unintentionally setting up plot possibilities for fanfiction writers everywhere. We'll assume no aluminum crutches or giant rats of Sumatra were involved in Miss La Strange's case.

Miss La Strange was so grateful that as a thank-you gift she got them invitations to the ambassador's garden soirée. She introduces them to the ambassador and then disappears back to wherever Hungarian actresses go.

Fidelity to text

While the basic plot remains, everything else from garden parties to bored society ladies was added.

Quality of movie

So much happens; gorgeous eye-candy and a happening nightclub full of flappers dancing up a storm.

The ambassador, Randolph Wilmot, is pleased to meet Tommy and Tuppence, because he experienced something that's been niggling at him and won't let go. It's unimportant, yet he can't stop thinking about it because it doesn't make any sense.

He and his valet, Richards, crossed the Atlantic on board the S.S. *Nomadic*. During the trip his suitcase containing, among other items, his boots was accidentally switched with Sen. Ralph Westerham's identical bag with identical initials. That's simple enough. What the ambassador can't understand is that when he later joshed Westerham about it, Westerham claimed the incident never happened.

Will Tommy and Tuppence take this minor, meaningless case? Naturally, because minor, meaningless cases are what they enjoy most.

The film greatly enhanced Richards, the valet. It's readily apparent he's got secrets he didn't have in the short story. His interview with Tommy is awkward

Randolph Wilmot (*T.P. McKenna*), the ambassador

Richards (*Clive Merrison*), the valet

Cicely March (*Jennie Linden*), the witness

Rodriguez (*Michael Carter*), the villain

Poppy St. Albans (*Tricia George*), the bored best friend

Gwen Forster (*Jo Ross*), the dapper best friend

and uncomfortable. He reveals a few minor details, including the odd story about rescuing a mysterious victim of seasickness. Later that night, he jumps off the bridge into the Thames and drowns.

The valet's suicide proves there's more going on than suitcase switching. Since a suicide doesn't add enough interest, Tuppence buys a flashy fuchsia beaded cocktail dress and goes nightclubbing with ambassador Wilmot to The Green Parrot.

She dances a very fine Charleston, Tuppence does, and the ambassador, despite being a good twenty years older, manages to keep up. He also flirts up a storm. I'd be very surprised if the ambassador hasn't enjoyed an affair or two while doing his duty at the embassy. It explains why his wife remains in Maine. Tuppence gracefully fends him off and they both enjoy The Green Parrot. It's a gorgeous nightclub, of the kind the ambassador doesn't get to enjoy in the U.S. There's alcohol, even more than there was at his garden soirée, where the cocktails flowed like English rain. There's also a hint of other social ills. One of the high-kicking dancers collapses but not, as Tuppence says, from drinking too much. It's something more sinister.

The Green Parrot didn't just have a fine dance band, jazzy cocktails, and a well-dressed clientele. It's got a fine black piano player who sings "It's a Long Way To Tipperary." Criminally, the performer isn't listed in either the show's credits nor at Internet Movie Database.

A few days later, in answer to Tommy's newspaper advert, a young woman shows up at the office with information about the mysterious victim of seasickness. Meanwhile, Tuppence, peeved that smug Tommy thought of the advert and she didn't, had already left to meet some old friends from their WWI days in the V.A.D (Voluntary Aid Detachment). That's a fascinating scene: four ladies reliving their life during wartime and now attempting to outrun boredom.

Tuppence is the most successful of the bunch, but don't miss Gwen Forster (Jo Ross). It's clear from her clothes that she's forging her own path in the world and the devil take the hindmost. Even today, her perfectly fitted and tailored man's suit, heavy makeup, and butch haircut would make her stand out, but back in 1926? Yet her friends don't give Gwen's appearance and lifestyle a second thought. Neither did the producers when they filmed this episode in 1983.

Meanwhile, Albert continues to suffer from watching too many detective movies. He practices his rope tricks and enlists his reluctant girlfriend for shadowing practice. Good thing that he did; when Tommy is interviewing Cicely Marsh about what she saw onboard the S.S. *Nomadic*, they're interrupted by a gun-wielding Spaniard who threatens Tommy and Cicely. Albert sneaks up and lassos him. Yes, Agatha wrote that scene, not some hack scriptwriter seeking to add excitement.

General Information

Based on: "The Ambassador's Boots" (short story, 1924)
Run time: 50 min. **Subtitles:** Yes

Writer and director Paul Annett

Cast

Francesca Annis as Tuppence Beresford
James Warwick as Tommy Beresford
Reece Dinsdale as Albert
Moira Brooker as Tilly
Arthur Cox as Inspector Marriott

T.P. McKenna as Randolph Wilmot
Clive Merrison as Richards
Jennie Linden as Cicely March
Michael Carter as Rodriguez
Tricia George as Poppy St. Albans
Norma West as Estelle Blaney
Jo Ross as Gwen Forster
Catherine Schell as Virma La Strange
Vera Jakob as Manners
Anna Sharkey as Madame Beatrice

Once Tommy's thrown the Spaniard down the office stairs and into the street, he escorts Cicely back to her beauty shop to pick up the mysterious paper she saw the seasick woman insert into the ambassador's boots. They take their time because Tommy fears Cicely will be kidnapped by suspicious taxi drivers. To throw them off track, they even stop for tea.

Finally, they arrive at Cicely's beauty salon, stylishly decorated in Art Deco glass and mirrors. She clearly uses the same decorator who designed The Green Parrot. Is that enough padding added to Agatha's barebones plot?

But wait! There's more! Tommy follows Cicely to the inner office, past ladies getting mudpack facials and a foreign widow demanding walk-in service. Once in the inner office, the truth is revealed.

It was Cicely all along. She was the mysterious dark-haired woman the valet let into the ambassador's stateroom in her hour of need. There was no message slipped into the ambassador's boots. Instead, as Tommy worked out, it wasn't the ambassador's misplaced boots that mattered. It was the *other* bag that was important; when switched, it wasn't inspected at customs because of diplomatic immunity.

The ending is suitably silly and dramatic. As Tommy struggles with Cicely and the Spaniard (Cicely's henchman), they're rushed by the foreign widow and the ladies getting facials. Who are they? Tuppence, of course, and her friends. They had infiltrated the beauty salon because Tommy left a note telling all to Albert and arranging the setup. That's the real reason why he spent so much time shaking Cicely's supposed tail; he needed time for the cavalry to arrive.

It's a well-done episode. It's amusing, sometimes very amusing. The clothes and settings are top-notch, particularly The Green Parrot. Watching Cicely be undone by a group of women in mudpacks was funny. And it's a reminder that, should you meet a seasick woman on board a ship, give her a bag and send her on her way.

The Unbreakable Alibi (1983)

Tommy and Tuppence are challenged to show how an adventurous woman can be witnessed in two places at once

Fidelity to text

Major character rewrites, a made-up-from-whole-canvas subplot, and sudden death when previously no one died.

Quality of movie

Everything tied together, including seemingly superfluous plot threads in the opening.

While watching this episode, you may wonder why Tommy and Tuppence are so concerned about railway timetables, hotel receipts, and chatting up waiters, concierges, and hotel chambermaids. In previous stories, they don't bother with the minutiae of police work. They rely on their intuition.

That's because this story parodies another once highly-regarded, now-forgotten mystery writer. Freeman Wills Crofts (1879-1957) was a railway engineer turned mystery writer. His carefully-plotted mysteries (Raymond Chandler was a fan) turned on meticulously planned crimes with equally meticulously planned alibis. His detective, Inspector French, methodically pursued every possible lead to its bitter end. To solve the crime, he spent a lot of time on trains, perusing his A.B.C. railway guide to verify schedules and matching them up with theater ticket stubs and hotel reservation guest books. He interviewed every single person who might have met the criminal, using his pocket lineup of photos to ensure he didn't misidentify someone.

The photo lineup is one trope the story included that the episode didn't. Tuppence collected an assortment of ladies' photographs not connected to the case to complement their picture of Una Drake. The additional photos are needed so when they quiz waiters and servants, they don't lead them to a false conclusion about which young lady they served.

Alibi-based police procedurals involving timetables were immensely popular in the Golden Age of mystery. Readers were familiar with how train travel worked, solving the crime along with the detective. They eventually fell out of favor but were still well enough known for *Monty Python's Flying Circus* to parody them on their sketch comedy show in the early 1970s.

Today's police procedurals don't rely as much on breaking alibis. They prefer cutting-edge forensics. Your alibi can be rock-solid, but if your DNA puts you on the scene, you'd better have a darn good lawyer.

A lawyer is something Una Drake turns out to need. She got a major personality transplant for the episode that turned her into a more interesting character. She's a sporting girl from Australia, working for an artist's magazine called *Pen and Palette*. When Mr.

Una Drake
(*Anna Nygh*),
the clever pursued

Montgomery Jones
(*Tim Meats*),
the dim pursuer

Peter le Marchant
(*Michael Jayes*),
the sleazy exporter

Hotel Receptionist
(*Gay Soper*),
the check-in witness

Head Waiter
(*Preston Lockwood*),
the server witness

Chambermaid
(*Elaine Wells*),
the tidying witness

Montgomery Jones meets her, he's smitten. He's not very bright but he's bright enough to know that if he wants her, he has to win a bet.

That's the quest she sets before him if he wants to win her heart. She claims she can be in two places at once. Can he figure out how she did it? If yes, he can claim what he wants: her hand in marriage. If no, she can claim what she wants: for him to quit pestering her.

There may be an underlying reason for her wager. In the short story, Una is game for anything. In the film, she's a compulsive gambler in serious hock to the bookies. Montgomery Jones isn't just addled with love over her. He's rich and probably stupid enough to give her money. She makes the bet believing that, even if he loses, he might still pay off a debt or two.

By the end of the show, it's a sure bet that if Montgomery Jones marries Una, he'll be trapped in a match made in hell. She'll despise him, and he'll end up bankrupt.

He's not very bright, but he's smart enough to ask Blunt's Brilliant Detective Agency for help. After they crack the case and he wins the bet, one wonders if he'll still want to marry Una. Probably, after he pays her legal fees and she finishes a stint at Wandsworth Prison.

The other major personality transplant is Peter le Marchant. He transforms from a pleasant, but innocuous man about town into a smarmy, sleazy import/export businessman with strong interests in art, money, and women. When Tommy (as Mr. Blunt) and Tuppence (as confidential secretary Miss Robinson) question him about his dinner at the Savoy with Una, he immediately attempts to seduce Tuppence. Tommy is not amused, although le Marchant doesn't know they're married. He's also being interviewed in what looks like his home office, with his bedroom conveniently in the next room, so why wait to start the seduction process?

Alas for Tommy and Tuppence, it's obvious that Una was in London with le Marchant. Too many people who know her saw her dine with him and are willing to swear to it.

So they head off to Torquay (Agatha's home!) and discover to their dismay that Una was there too. Too many people, including the railway dining car waiter and the hotel's staff saw her, spoke to her, and remembered her. How could they not? She made a point of being noticed, just like she did in London.

How could she be in two places at the same time? Here's where intuition comes into play, rescuing them from boring, plodding, methodical police work. The phrase "astral bodies" gives Tuppence an idea. She cables Australia to confirm her suspicion. In the meantime, Una digs her hole deeper.

Adding the subplot of art thieves was a nice touch. It turned a rather silly story into something more serious. It was subtle too. Peter le Marchant is in the import/export business. He likes art and it's obvious he has the morals of an alley cat. Una Drake works for an art magazine. She's got connections to galleries and art museums, and she's a compulsive gambler in hock up to her eyeballs. Could they be related to the stolen art that Tommy reads about in the newspaper?

They could indeed.

Una's no brighter than Montgomery Jones. She isn't just a gambler and a participant in art theft. She's in love with le Marchant, despite knowing what kind of man he is. So we see another reason behind the bet. Getting rid of pesky, always-around Montgomery Jones doesn't merely get him out of the way. She's preventing a possible witness from causing trouble later on.

Armed with her suspicions, Tuppence disguises herself as a reporter and interviews Una in her flat. Una, nerves completely gone to pieces, becomes suspicious of this nice lady. She confirms her suspicions, follows Tuppence, and confronts our duo in their office. She's armed, dangerous, and desperate. She no longer cares about her London alibi: It's fake! It's fake! She was in Torquay and everyone knows it!

It's at that point, as Una's waving the gun around, Montgomery Jones arrives with Una's twin sister, Vera. Vera confesses that she went to Torquay, while Una stayed in London. Simple, really. What's not simple is that Una also killed Peter le Marchant the night before. She claims it was an accident and perhaps it was. The best barrister Montgomery Jones' money can buy might save her from the gallows. Yep, the man Una dislikes might be the one who'll save her. But he still shouldn't marry her.

General Information

Based on: "The Unbreakable Alibi"
(short story, 1928)
Run time: 51 min. **Subtitles:** Yes

Writer: David Butler
Director: Christopher Hodson

Cast

Francesca Annis as Tuppence Beresford
James Warwick as Tommy Beresford
Reece Dinsdale as Albert

Anna Nygh as Una / Vera Drake
Tim Meats as Montgomery Jones
Michael Jayes as Peter le Marchant
Ellis Dale as Henri
Gay Soper as Hotel Receptionist
Elaine Wells as Chambermaid
Preston Lockwood as Head Waiter
Stephen Wale as Dining Car Attendant

The Man in the Mist (1983)

Pursued by a poet and a masher, an actress' search for her husband ends tragically in a tranquil village

Fidelity to text

A vastly improved ending, a police interrogation, and a total personality makeover for Bulger are just the start.

Quality of movie

There's plenty going on in this atmospheric and funny episode.

Envision the joke's setup: Tommy and Tuppence, failed detectives, lick their wounds and imbibe cocktails in the hotel bar in Adlington. They completely botched their last case. Priceless pearls went missing at the local lord's estate, and they chased after implausible but exciting suspects. The local constables pinned the crime on the second footman, well-known for his thieving background. He admitted it, too.

Keep in mind that nothing happens in Adlington. Everyone will tell you that.

Now, dress Tommy in a very traditional cassock and broad-brimmed hat, despite him not becoming a Roman Catholic priest. Tuppence remains stylish as always. Portraying a fallen woman who needs spiritual uplifting? She certainly doesn't dress like a devout churchgoer.

They discuss the case and drown their sorrows when into the bar walks Mervyn Estcourt (known to his friends as Bulger), a famous actress, and a fiery but pacifistic poet. The actress' future husband, the famous mountain-climbing Lord Leconbury, follows quickly afterwards, possibly to keep tabs on his famous, hot fiancée.

She's Gilda Glen, and she gets around.

Was she once Bulger's lover? Seems that way! How about the pacifist poet? Yep, him too. But lovers don't count in the marriage sweepstakes, not when she's got her eye on a rich peer. Too bad Gilda can't marry a title until after she gets rid of her inconvenient husband, with whom she eloped at age seventeen.

So what's Gilda Glen doing in Adlington where nothing ever happens? Tracking down her erstwhile husband whom she hasn't seen in twenty years but is still legally bound to, naturally. Who can help her? Why, perhaps that kind priest sitting at the bar with the fallen woman. He'll understand.

Gilda may be beautiful, but she's got the brains of a rabbit.

So does Bulger, who acquires (via the scriptwriter) a wife, a cement factory, and a roving eye, fully exposed when he hits on Tuppence. He knew Tommy back in the Great War. He didn't know Tommy became a priest ministering to fallen women because what else could that hot brunette be?

Tuppence fends him off gracefully and Bulger leaves, ostensibly to play golf before meeting his wife for dinner. She also gracefully handles the fiery but pacifistic poet ranting about strangling women while

Gilda Glen (*Linda Marlowe*), the lively actress

Mrs. Honeycott (*Anne Stallybrass*), the prim sister

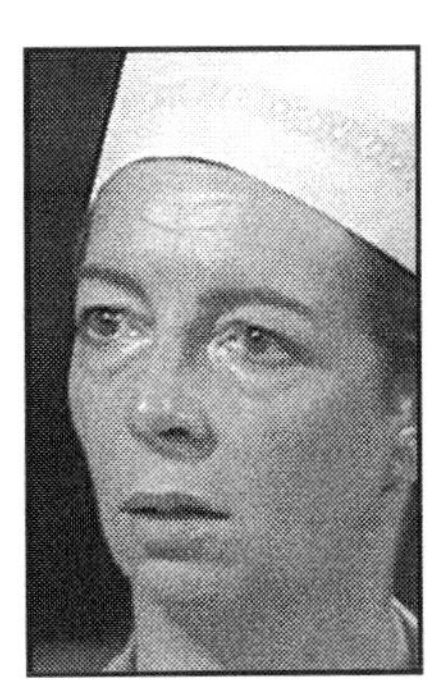
Ellen (*Valerie Lilley*), the housekeeper

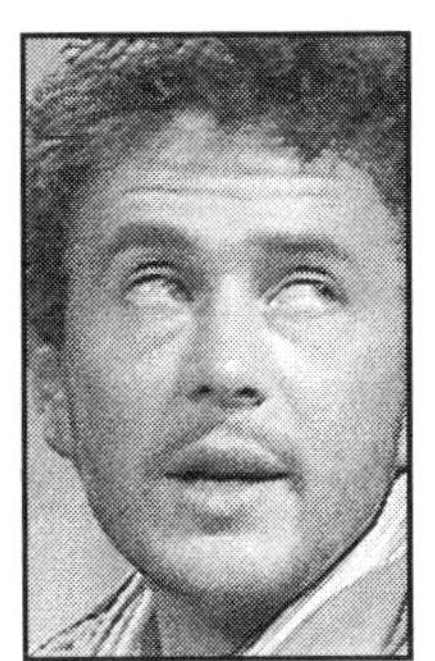
James Reilly (*Tim Brierley*), the fighting poet

Bulgar Estcourt (*Constantine Gregory*), the married lover

Police Constable (*Chris Johnston*), the local bobby

loving peace. Does James Reilly hate women in general, despite his peace-loving, poetical nature? Yes, but mainly Gilda Glen, because if he can't have her then no one can.

Then it's off to meet Gilda. According to her note, she needs Tommy's fatherly advice. She's staying with a local resident, Mrs. Honeycott, in a fog-shrouded house on mist-drenched Morgan's Avenue, next to the shadowy cemetery with a sinister reputation. According to Bulger, a constable who met a gruesome end still walks his ghostly beat down that misty lane. Do Tommy and Tuppence hear footsteps in the fog from some mysterious presence? Of course they do.

In front of them? Could be. In back of them? Sounds like it.

A constable — a live one! — looms out of the mist. Reilly races past them in a tearing hurry and vanishes into the house.

After the constable disappears into the mists, Tommy and Tuppence approach the house. They hear a scream, and Reilly charges out of the house and past them.

Inside, they meet Ellen the housemaid. She's right out of central casting and might share the same Irish county of origin as Reilly, ranting poet. She's upset because Reilly charged into the house and right back out. She's sure she heard a muffled scream.

Mrs. Honeycott arrives, but she's upset for other reasons. She's suddenly got a Roman Catholic priest and a fallen woman invading her home and, as the daughter of an Anglican minister, she doesn't hold with popery or harlots. She already has one in residence. Gilda Glen, actress with a past, is her much younger sister. Worse, not only has Gilda returned to Adlington, she wants her devout, churchgoing sister to help her get a divorce so she can marry again. If only her sister can remember hubby's last name.

Remember, nothing ever happens in Adlington.

Tommy and Tuppence sense danger, and they persuade Mrs. Honeycott to take them upstairs to Gilda. They discover she no longer needs to divorce her husband. She's dead, coshed in the head.

Who could have done it? Reilly the ranting poet is the obvious suspect. But wait! Bulger, Gilda's former lover, admits he had not gone golfing in the mist. He'd climbed up the drainpipe to the second-floor window to see Gilda and plead his case. Not marriage, naturally, as he already had a wife, two children, and a cement factory, but perhaps a fond farewell for old times' sake.

Reilly gets found, arrested, and grilled by the local bobbies. Bulger also ends up in the local jail and begs Tommy and Tuppence for help. His wife wouldn't understand. Actually, she probably understands all too well, but we don't meet her so we don't get her interpretation of the facts. The constable puts his own spin on events. He's doubtful that Tommy and Tuppence can shed light on the crime, considering how badly they muffed the jewel theft that brought them to Adlington in the first place.

The ending was vastly improved over the barebones text. Tommy spends some time discussing reality versus imagination. That is, what actually happens instead of what people interpret is happening because they don't witness it with their own eyes.

He arranges for most of the principals to reassemble at Mrs. Honeycott's house, other than Reilly and Bulger who are cooling their heels in jail. With Ellen and Mrs. Honeycott's able assistance, he restages what did happen. Certain sounds were heard. Footsteps on stairs. Pauses. Doors opening. Doors closing. Resetting late clocks. Pork chops for Monday's dinner instead of dodgy fish caught days ago.

Step by step, Tommy, just like Father Brown whom he's emulating, reenacts the scene of the crime, searching for what is real. He arrives at certain conclusions, one of them being that the scream, based on the timing, might not have been Gilda's. It might have been someone else. Perhaps someone who discovered her body. Someone who was so horrified at seeing — up-close and personal — a real woman's death with real blood and real brains splattered across the room, he screamed like a little girl.

Who could have murdered Gilda? Who would be the most likely suspect with evil in his heart, like all of us have? Not her sister. Despite disapproving of Gilda's immoral life choices, Mrs. Honeycott let her return to the family home. Bulger wasn't the type. Reilly had his stomach turned when faced with real violence as opposed to sanitary words on white paper.

Who was it? Why the most usual suspect of all, as Agatha and Father Brown would tell you. Gilda's long-ago husband.

Surprised? You shouldn't be, because sometimes, things happen in Adlington.

General Information

Based on: "The Man in the Mist" (short story, 1924)
Run time: 52 min. **Subtitles:** Yes

Writer: Gerald Savory
Director: Christopher Hodson

Cast

Francesca Annis as Tuppence Beresford
James Warwick as Tommy Beresford
Reece Dinsdale as Albert
Roger Kemp as Detective Inspector Jeavons
Chris Johnston as Police Constable

Linda Marlowe as Gilda Glen
Anne Stallybrass as Mrs. Honeycott
Constantine Gregory as Bulger Estcourt
Tim Brierley as James Reilly
Valerie Lilley as Ellen
Paddy Ward as Bartender
Patrick Marley as Lord Leconbury
Geoffrey Greenhill as Police Sergeant

The Case of the Missing Lady (1983)

A missing fiancée sends Tuppence undercover as a Russian ballerina dancing for her life at a creepy clinic

Fidelity to text

The plot's there, but hugely enhanced. Oddly, a Sherlock reference was removed, despite the story being a Sherlock parody.

Quality of movie

A bizarre tonal shift takes place near the end when a chase breaks out but fails on its own terms. Where's "Yakety Sax" when you need it?

Agatha read all the popular fiction of her time, something that's often forgotten today. She stands alone in the popular mind, surrounded by a force field shielding her from cultural contamination. Parodying famous (but now forgotten) mystery writers was a natural step as she worked out her own style. Think of all the authors who've gotten their start writing fanfiction.

"The Case of the Missing Lady" (1924) was her fourth Tommy and Tuppence outing, although it's placed later in the sequence in the *Partners in Crime* collection. Agatha parodies Arthur Conan Doyle's Sherlock Holmes. She layered in plenty of Sherlock references, not all of which made it into the film. In particular, Tommy plays a few notes of Mosgovskensky on the violin, making Gabriel Stavansson, experienced Arctic adventurer, flinch and Tuppence grind her teeth. The minute Stavansson's gone, Tuppence locks up the violin so Tommy can't torture anyone again.

Mosgovskensky is Tommy's attempt to make up a Russian composer. It may have been Agatha's inside joke in 1924. When rewriting this very slight story, the scriptwriter used the name for a Russian ballerina.

In addition to reworking the text, the scriptwriter added Sherlock references or made Agatha's choices more obvious. Tommy deduces who Stavansson is based on his appearance. He's right, but only because he and Tuppence read the newspapers and overheard Albert using his name. Stavansson is a Norwegian explorer, a disguise that Holmes used after he went over Reichenbach Falls with Moriarty. The creepy quack doctor uses armadillo gland extracts, a reference to "The Adventure of the Creeping Man" where extracts of languor monkey were used. Like Holmes, Tommy wears disguises, in this case an intrepid reporter and a tramp/gardener. We'll assume that Madame Mosgovskensky's driver (Tuppence's disguise) is Albert in disguise because Tommy's seen lurking in the shrubbery when they arrive. There's the quack doctor in general (Conan Doyle despised them) and villainous henchmen, male and female, always a Sherlock staple.

Another reference lies behind the reason why Stavansson arrived at their door. It's not murder, but it's serious. A woman has vanished. Tuppence even

Gabriel Stavansson (*Jonathan Newth*), the returning explorer

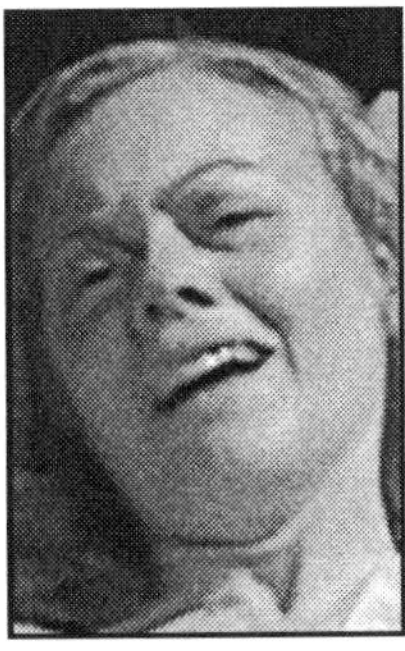

Mrs. Leigh Gordon (*Elisabeth Murray*), the missing fiancée

Lady Susan Clonray (*Elspeth March*), the supportive friend

Dr. Horriston (*Ewan Hooper*), the snake-oil seller

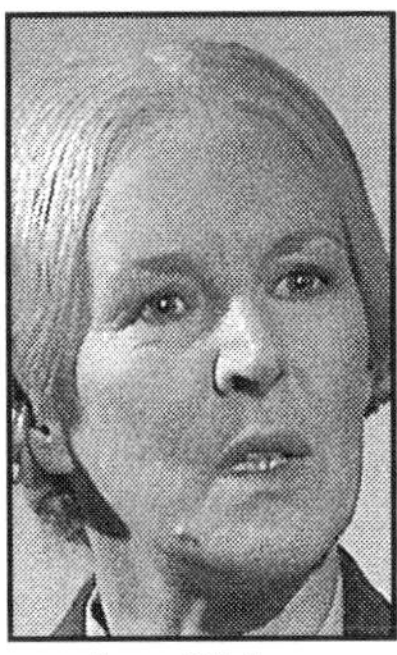

Irma Kleber (*Rowena Cooper*), the doctor's nurse

Muldoon (*Tim Pearce*), the sinister orderly

name-checks "The Disappearance of Lady Frances Carfax." Also, take a look at "The Adventure of the Copper Beeches" where a young lady is held captive by her evil father, with the help of a nefarious henchman.

Stavansson's fiancée, Mrs. Hermione Leigh-Gordon, could be the victim of foul play. Her cousin, Lady Susan, doesn't seem to know where she is and is reluctant to speak with Stavansson. Hermy's a widow, so it's possible she has a past Stavansson doesn't know.

Except we're given a clue to the ending at the beginning of the episode. Stavansson volunteers the information that he loathes fat women. Tuppence comments acidly about fashion agreeing with Stavansson but he doesn't notice. He shows off a picture of Hermy. Later, Tommy comments on how bony she is.

Then they're off to interview Lady Susan. Stavansson accompanies the dynamic duo who claim, to Lady Susan's suspicion, that they're also friends of the missing Hermy. Lady Susan may be fat and have a fat lapdog, but she's not stupid. As soon as the unwanted guests leave, she's on the telephone.

The next day, Tommy and Tuppence are told Lady Susan received a telegram from Hermy saying she's off to Monte Carlo. But they're not deceived. They track down the telegram's origin: Maldon, a tiny village in the middle of nowhere.

They find a mysterious doctor in residence at the Grange, operating a suspicious rest home. His henchman, Muldoon, is a goon from central casting.

Tommy investigates the home, disguised as an intrepid reporter. Not only is Dr. Horriston suspicious, so is the weird chemistry setup in his office. His assistant, nurse Irma Kleber, is even more dubious. Everything about her screams Ilse Koch, a German war criminal notorious for her vicious treatment of prisoners at Buchenwald and Majdanek. Tommy wouldn't know that in 1924, but when *Partners in Crime* was filmed in 1983, every sadistic nurse was a secret Nazi.

Tommy can't sneak inside to search for Hermy, so he disguises himself as a tramp gardener for hire. Meanwhile, Tuppence channels her inner diva and swans in, pretending to be the famous ballerina, Madame Mosgovskensky. She needs a rest before starting her own ballet company and charms Dr. Horriston into accepting her. That night, she hears dreadful moaning from one of the other rooms.

General Information

Based on: "The Case of the Missing Lady" (short story, 1924)
Run time: 51 min. **Subtitles:** Yes

Writer: Jonathan Hales
Director: Paul Annett

Cast

Francesca Annis as Tuppence Beresford
James Warwick as Tommy Beresford
Reece Dinsdale as Albert

Rowena Cooper as Irma Kleber
Ewan Hooper as Dr. Horriston
Elspeth March as Lady Susan Clonray
Elisabeth Murray as Mrs. Leigh Gordon
Jonathan Newth as Gabriel Stavansson
Tim Pearce as Muldoon
Mischa De La Motte as Manservant
Susie Fairfax as Girl in Shop

At this point, the tone of the episode flips from dark and creepy to surreal. Tommy and Tuppence fuel up with gin from a hip flask before exploring the house. Hermy must be rescued! They devise a plan. It does not involve calling Stavansson, who's used to danger and would probably enjoy rescuing his fiancée from certain death.

The next day, Tuppence insists on performing *Swan Lake* for Dr. Horriston, Nurse Irma, Muldoon, and the other rest home staff and patients, none of whom had appeared before. They must have been hiding in their rooms until Tuppence needed an audience. She swans out in ballet slippers and makeshift swan maiden costume, while Irma plays Tchaikovsky on the piano. But Tuppence can't dance ballet! So while Tommy is breaking in upstairs and sneaking around, she relates the story of *Swan Lake*. Except she's not clear on the details, so she makes it up. Eventually, everyone falls asleep. I found that hard to believe because rest home occupants and staff are always eager for a break in the routine.

In the meantime, Tommy locates Hermy and talks to her. He abandons her to her fate and looks for Tuppence. *They've* got to escape, he tells her, not Hermy. The episode devolves into a zany, madcap chase through the Grange and its extensive gardens. Tommy and Tuppence flee up and down the garden paths, pursued by Horriston, Irma, and Muldoon.

The episode flung itself into comedy, yet no orderlies show up. They should have! Everyone should have appeared, including Stavansson, Albert, Lady Susan, her ancient butler, and her dog! That chase scene should have been sped up, with orderlies and Stavansson popping in and out of the shrubbery. Lady Susan's lapdog should have been nipping at Tuppence's skirts. Or Irma's. Or ripping off Dr. Horriston's pants. The entire sequence should have been set to "Yakety Sax," Benny Hill's theme music.

When this episode was filmed, Benny Hill (1924-1992) had been riding high for decades on British TV. His show was syndicated worldwide. With an example like that, how could this chase scene be so lifeless? What a missed opportunity, and it would have tied up the loose ends of Stavansson's quest to save Hermy.

At least we got the ending, with Tommy and Tuppence speeding away, thankful that no one recognized them and promising never to speak of this again.

The Crackler (1983)

A nightclub's counterfeiting ring gives Tommy and Tuppence a way to combine investigating and dancing

Fidelity to text

The plot's expanded but everything you see was hinted at in the text.

Quality of movie

Silly and fast-paced, with surprisingly sharp observations about police work and the class system.

The final episode of *Partners In Crime* used (depending on how you're counting) the 8th or 10th story in the sequence. Since the short story collection had an overall story arc with an actual conclusion, I was hoping some of that ending would make its way into the final episode. It didn't.

In the book, after many adventures in the detective business, culminating with one last kidnapping as part of an international espionage case, Tuppence retires from the field. She's going to have a baby.

The TV series just ends. A pity, really, since some of the stories were excluded from the show. If *Partners in Crime* is ever filmed again, I hope they include all the stories, with the overall arc. Then we could enjoy how Agatha parodied herself.

In *The Crackler*, she parodied Edgar Wallace (1875-1932). He was a hugely popular, immensely prolific author. He wrote mysteries, thrillers, suspense, action-adventure, science fiction, and whatever else brought in money to feed his gambling habit. He wrote a variety of forms: nearly 200 novels, a thousand short stories, plays, and screenplays. Over 160 movies were based on his stories. The one everyone remembers today is *King Kong* (1933). He was able to write so fast because he dictated onto wax cylinders and teams of secretaries typed the manuscripts. One and done should have been his motto.

Another famous novel he wrote was *The Green Archer* (1923). A mysterious green-clad archer is involved, a la Robin Hood. It was filmed in 1925 and again in 1940. The second movie serial led directly to DC's Green Arrow. No Green Archer appears in this episode but you should know this trivia anyway.

The Crackler takes full advantage of Wallace's breakneck writing style and loosey-goosey plotting. The action never stops. It also showcases Inspector Marriott and how the aristocracy gets in the way of Scotland Yard's police work.

Marriott has a problem. Counterfeiters are flooding Britain with fake bank notes. He suspects they're being passed through the Python Club. He can't send constables to infiltrate the nightclub and secret gambling den. They'd be spotted instantly. He also can't raid the joint because the patrons are too high up the food chain. They'd rain down turmoil upon Scotland Yard because, after all, the higher the noble, the more the law doesn't apply. They're *special*, don't you know.

So Inspector Marriott again needs Tommy and

Hank Ryder
(*Shane Rimmer*),
the American tourist

Major Laidlaw
(*David Quilter*),
the hardcore gambler

Marguerite Laidlaw
(*Carolle Rousseau*),
the fascinating wife

Monsieur Heroulade
(*Lawrence Davidson*),
the suspect traveler

Jimmy Faulkener
(*Christopher Scoular*),
the young clubman

Harry the Bartender
(*Stan Pretty*),
the wise mixologist

Tuppence. They'll blend right in. Even better, one of Tommy's cousins, Jimmy Faulkener, is already a member of the club. Jimmy won't just get our dynamic duo through the front door. He'll make the introductions to the very people Inspector Marriott has his eyes on.

General Information

Based on: "The Crackler" (short story, 1924)
Run time: 51 min. **Subtitles:** Yes

Writer: Gerald Savory
Director: Christopher Hodson

Cast

Francesca Annis as Tuppence Beresford
James Warwick as Tommy Beresford
Reece Dinsdale as Albert
Arthur Cox as Inspector Marriott

Shane Rimmer as Hank Ryder
Carolle Rousseau as Marguerite Laidlaw
David Quilter as Major Laidlaw
Lawrence Davidson as Monsieur Heroulade
Christopher Scoular as Jimmy Faulkener
Peter Godfrey as Willie Maybrick
Stan Pretty as Harry the Bartender
Terence Hillyer as Chauffeur

They're Marguerite Laidlaw (she's French so she's automatically untrustworthy), her husband, Major Laidlaw, and Marguerite's father, Monsieur Heroulade. There are reasons to suspect them. They have no visible means of support. They're known gamblers. Major Laidlaw has an unsavory reputation in horse-racing circles. Counterfeit pound notes have been spread across the Channel in France as well as in London. M. Heroulade makes frequent trips between London and Paris and with his connections, is in the perfect position to move the money around.

The Python Club is everything you'd hope for. The dance band heats up the patrons, the cocktails cool them down, the women wear drop-dead gorgeous clothes, and the gambling den behind threatening tuxedo-clad gorilla doormen is slightly seedy without being tacky or low class. The gambling is very high-stakes, the sort that Edgar Wallace adored losing money at. There's a charming bartender too.

While Tuppence dances up a storm with Jimmy, Tommy flirts with Marguerite. Yet it's an American barfly who worms his way into Tommy's notice. Hank Ryder is eager to chat, drink, eat oysters, gamble, and drink some more. His liver must be made of iron. Hank's not very bright, taking Marguerite up on ridiculous bets until he finally piques Tommy's interest.

It seems Marguerite lured Hank into some kind of scavenger hunt in Whitechapel, where he found stacks of crispy, crackling pound notes. Tommy asks him if he can find the place again, and off they go.

Too late, Tommy discovers he'd been had.

This is all very Edgar Wallace; racing about from one plot point to the next with nary a word of explanation. For example, Tommy brings up Mrs. Barney and Madame Fahmy as examples of badly behaved aristocrats. Mrs. Barney is Natalie Clifford Barney (1876-1972). She was a wealthy, openly lesbian heiress, poet, literary lioness, violently opposed to monogamy, and all-around bon vivant. She was called "Mrs." because she signed a marriage contract with her aristocratic lesbian lover. She didn't kill anyone but, considering how she got around, it's surprising one of her army of exes didn't murder her.

The same could be said for Madame Fahmy (Marguerite Marie Alibert, 1890-1971). After a very checkered career including an affair with the Prince of Wales, she married an Egyptian aristocrat, Ali Kamel Fahmy Bey. They had a contentious relationship and in 1923, she shot him multiple times in their suite at the Savoy hotel. Madame Fahmy was acquitted in an English court. The Egyptian court — where she sued to get access to her dead husband's money — was less forgiving.

Another unexplained reference occurs when Tommy and Hank stumble down an alley. Hank points out one back gate among many, and Tommy wonders how he's so sure, like "the princess and the soldier." That's the Hans Christian Anderson story, "The Tinderbox." A soldier acquires a magic tinderbox, which he uses to kidnap a sleeping princess to admire her. An astute lady-in-waiting follows them and marks the doorstep with chalk, but the kidnapper marked all the other doorsteps with chalk so the princess couldn't be found.

Tommy runs into the same problem, but in true Edgar Wallace style, he pulls a solution out of his pocket. Alleys have alley cats and he likes being prepared so he carried with him a vial of tincture of valerian. Valerian is a potent drug for cats, right up there with catnip. When Tommy marks the doorstep with chalk, he also pours out the valerian.

It doesn't matter that the kidnapping counterfeiter marked all the other doorsteps in the alley with chalk crosses. Only this doorstep has a herd of dizzy, stoned cats meowing and rolling around and generally behaving like barflies at the end of the evening.

The constables rush in to save Tommy, as do Tuppence and Albert.

Albert! He had his adventures too! He followed Major Laidlaw and M. Heroulade through the English countryside on his motorcycle and was threatened by the chauffeur and then told a very different version of his adventures to Tuppence.

Partners in Crime could be uneven, but there's always something to like about each episode. It could be Tuppence's stupendous wardrobe, their unshakable thirst for cocktails, their chemistry, or even a genuine mystery. By combining everything, *The Crackler* made a nice ending to the series.

My Little Finger Told Me (F-2005)

(*Mon petit doigt m'a dit …*)

Tommy and Tuppence's love of life mixes with the French *joie de vivre* in this frothy story of child murders

Fidelity to text

Pretty darn close, with added unwanted visiting family and the French version of MI5.

Quality of movie

Light, frothy, funny, reasonably tight plot, and gorgeous scenery of the French Alps.

By the pricking of my thumbs,
Something wicked this way comes.
Open locks,
Whoever knocks.
Macbeth, Act 4, Scene 1

Along with the evil, something quite funny comes along for the ride. This was a surprisingly amusing film considering it's about the unsolved strangulations of between five and eight children (the novel is unclear and the film didn't bother spelling it out) and the poisonings of at least two old ladies in rest homes.

As usual, I'll stick with the names in the novel rather than the French versions.

This was Agatha's third Tommy and Tuppence novel, written near the end of her writing life. Published in 1968, she wrote it when she was 76. She wrote five more novels after this one, including the last Tommy and Tuppence novel, *Postern of Fate* (1973), which has never been filmed.

Pricking of My Thumbs is … interesting. You can tell Agatha's not the writer she was. Loose plot ends, like what Aunt Ada saw that got her killed, are never tied up. Like *Nemesis* (1971) and *Elephants Can Remember* (1972), it's an elegy on growing old and a meditation on change. Time makes fools of us all. The sly, witty, pretty girl (Aunt Ada) becomes a bad-tempered old crone. The young subaltern who loved her (Sir Josiah Penn) fades into a feeble, deaf old man. They're part of the tragedies of the novel, glossed over in both films (Don't miss the version starring Miss Marple!). Ada and Sir Josiah never married; not to each other nor to anyone else, and so they never built a life, together or apart.

It was a stroke of genius to cast Geneviève Bujold as Mrs. Lancaster. She's still recognizable — if you remember her — but she's no longer a luminous young beauty. Cruel time did that to her.

Mrs. Lancaster's life was also blighted by her decision when she was a young, free-spirited dancer. She aborted a baby because she didn't want to be hampered by a child. But later, she couldn't have children when she wanted them. Whether that sent her around the bend or she was predisposed that way we don't know, but she strangled children to give her dead daughter friends.

When her family discovered her macabre hobby, she

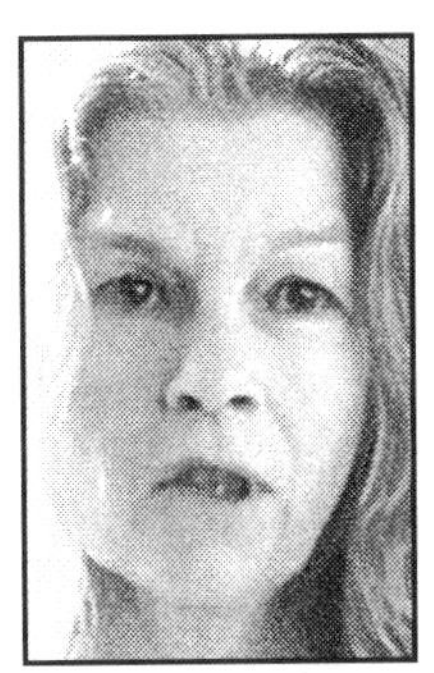

Rose Evangelista (*Geneviève Bujold*), the haunted mother

Maître Anet / Sévigné (*Laurent Terzieff*), the twin brothers

Françoise Blayes (*Valérie Kaprisky*), the village leader

Mme. Boscovan (*Alexandra Stewart*), the artist's wife

Alice Perry (*Anne Le Ny*), the rustic wife

Hélène Coupelay (*Valériane de Villeneuve*), the B&B owner

was hidden in rest homes, where she murdered old ladies who recognized her from her socially active, colorful, checkered past. They threatened her safety, and she, always, always came first.

Her husband, Sir Philip, and her brother-in-law, Mr. Eccles, concealed her crimes from the law since it was more important to keep her safe than to give any kind of justice to those murdered children and their families. What do a few peasants count for? Nothing. They loved her, so they covered up her sins. Her brother-in-law kills himself while in police custody as much to protect her as to conceal his own criminal activities.

The tragedies don't stop there. Her husband, Sir Philip, depends on his confidential secretary, Miss Bligh, to assist him in keeping Mrs. Lancaster hidden. She arranges Mrs. Lancaster's relocation when "something happens" and her wickedness might be revealed. She does it for love of Sir Philip, yet he never notices her adoration. She's a useful tool and nothing more.

There's another tragedy lurking under the froth and that's Tuppence's relationship with her own daughter. The daughter, son-in-law, and rambunctious twin boys moving into their château was a plot addition, giving Tuppence another reason to solve the mystery of the painting and what happened to Mrs. Lancaster. She didn't want to stay home and enjoy family time with a daughter she'd never been close to and a pair of noisy grandsons. We don't always feel the warmth at our own hearth. This could be read as the script's addition of a snippet of Agatha's own life. She was famously close to her mother. She did not enjoy that same closeness with her daughter.

All this lurks under the surface. If you aren't looking for tragedy, you won't see it. It's a very funny movie, loaded with sharp dialog and witty visual jokes (see the banner). If we spoke French and knew contemporary French culture, we'd probably have laughed even more. Subtitles don't convey a culture's subtle jokes. As an example, Tuppence's son-in-law tells a joke about Swiss farmers. You could substitute slow-witted yokels for "Swiss." So why Swiss and not, say, Austrian? It must be because it's funnier.

Frenchness abounds. Much of the scenery is pastoral and bucolic, but when Tommy's at MI5, the office looks like it was designed by Moebius. The scene with the gas masks for the important men making policy when the pert young women serving them wine didn't wear them was priceless. Watching him and the other senior staff attempt to solve major security issues for France does not inspire one with confidence, but it's all so stylish! Even the cafeteria is classy in the way an American one would never be. The attitudes, the insouciance, the great clothes worn with panache. This is not an American or an English movie.

The Sunny Ridge scenes just wouldn't be possible in an American rest home. The assisted living facility is a palatial château, surrounded by acres of manicured gardens. There's a staff of devoted, uniformed young women catering to the eccentric residents. Each resident has a luxurious suite. This being France, alcohol must flow freely. Pets abound, including monkeys on leashes. It looks like the poshest kind of residential hotel, not a warehouse for unwanted elderly relatives. Watch one of the ladies raise her chair to the ceiling, then later spin around in the chair, up in the air, and think about the last time you visited someone in a nursing home. They'd never get away with it. When Tuppence does something similar, riding a ceiling lamp like a trapeze artist after getting coshed in a churchyard, the doctor spouts wonderful psychobabble that was probably even sillier in French.

I wish the script had devoted more time to Mrs. Lancaster's past and how she enthralled men into insanity. I can understand why Sir Philip remained besotted with his wife. But his twin brother, the shady lawyer, Mr. Eccles? That was unclear. What was buried under the mystery grave that Tuppence was looking for because the vicar's knees were bad? How did the mysterious house tie in to the criminal gang's robberies? It was used to stash stolen goods as evidenced by Tuppence's discovery of a doll stuffed with diamonds stuffed up a chimney. But why stuff a doll up a chimney? And what did the Perrys have to do with the criminal gang? Or Sir Philip and Mrs. Lancaster?

When the answers aren't in the novel, that's the scriptwriter's chance to shine.

Still, this film's a diamond. Don't miss it.

General Information

Based on: *By the Pricking of My Thumbs* (novel, 1968)
Run time: 1 hr., 45 min. **Subtitles:** Yes

Writers: François Caviglioli, Nathalie Lafaurie
Director: Pascal Thomas

Cast

Catherine Frot as Prudence Beresford
André Dussollier as Col. Bélisaire Beresford
Bernard Verley as Le general (Sir Josiah Penn)
Pierre Lescure as Le commissaire Richard (Ivor Smith)

Geneviève Bujold as Rose Evangelista (Mrs. Lancaster)
Laurent Terzieff as Maître Anet / M. Sévigné (Mr. Eccles / Sir Phillip Stark)
Valérie Kaprisky as Françoise Blayes (Nellie Bligh)
Alexandra Stewart as Mme. Boscovan (Emma Boscovan)
Anne Le Ny as Alice Perry (Alice Perry)
Bernard Marcate as Amos Perry (Amos Perry)
Valériane de Villeneuve as Hélène Coupelay

Film Locations

Château de Chatillon, Chindrieux (Beresford home)
Château des Avenières, Cruseilles (rest home)
Château de Carron, Francin (house)
Le Châtelard, France (town)
Chemin du Revel (Prudence walking to church)
Lac du Bourget, Savoie, France (lake scenes)

The Secret Adversary (2015)

Updating Tommy and Tuppence to the Cold War era flounders on bumbling characters and silly plot

The BBC planned to film the four Tommy and Tuppence novels, including *Postern of Fate* (1973), which has never been filmed. They began with *The Secret Adversary* (1922), which introduces Tommy and Tuppence Beresford to each other and to us. It was an ambitious undertaking. Tommy and Tuppence start out as bright young moderns in 1919 and — unlike any of Agatha's other characters — age in real time. By *Postern of Fate*, they're grandparents in their 70s.

But the BBC filmed one season: *The Secret Adversary*, followed by *N or M?* The series was canceled after *N or M?* After enduring *The Secret Adversary*, I can see why.

So, what went wrong? The BBC is known for good adaptations. They spent money on costumes, sets, accessories, music, and cast. Everything, in fact, except the single most important component of any movie.

The script. It was dreadful.

This *Secret Adversary* doesn't work as an adaptation and it doesn't work as a movie for newcomers who've never heard of Tommy and Tuppence.

We'll begin at the beginning. In order to avoid having to age their cast 50 years, the BBC set all four episodes during the 1950s. Not in 1919, right after the demobilization of the Great War, when England was awash in returning soldiers who couldn't find jobs.

Agatha wrote her novel when memories of the war were still fresh and raw. England was moving from a war economy to a peacetime economy. There was massive social unrest. Bolsheviks lurked around every corner, if Sinn Fein or labor radicals weren't already there. Russia had endured a violent revolution, the tsar and his family murdered, the continent was soaked with blood, and political repercussions from the Great War abounded.

Fidelity to text

The names match. The secret adversary shows up. Virtually everything else was altered from a little to a lot.

Quality of movie

This could have been great but every time it reached for excellence, the plot fell apart.

In addition, England's social structure was under attack. The industrial revolution was revving up. Motorcars were showing up everywhere, women were finding a louder voice, and servants discovered that factory work paid better and was less demeaning.

Well, okay. You could make the same case for the early 1950s. England had just endured a traumatic war, the empire on which the sun never set was collapsing, Commies lurked under every bed, labor unions seethed, and women's voices kept getting louder and more insistent. This could work! Old wine in the golden age of espionage bottles, so to speak.

But they also changed Tommy and Tuppence, and a bad script made it worse.

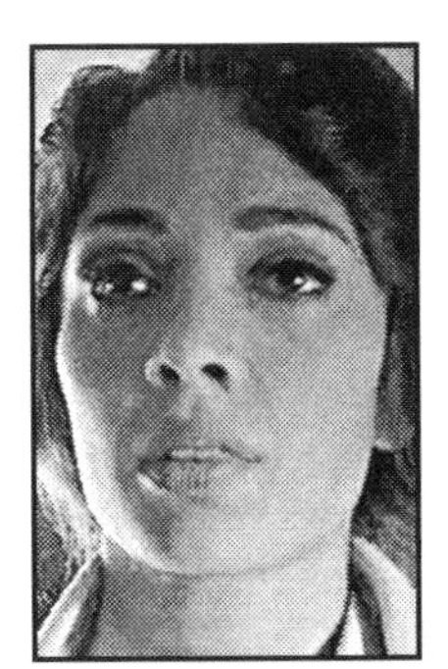

Jane Finn (*Camilla Marie Beeput*), the vanished link

Julius Hersheimmer (*Clarke Peters*), the worried rich man

Whittington (*Jonny Phillips*), the gang operative

Lucky (*Paul Brennen*), the gang muscle

Rita Vandemeyer (*Alice Krige*), the sinister singer

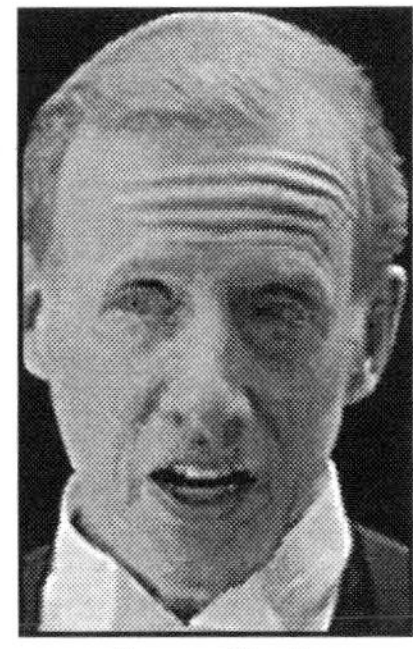

James Peel (*Andrew Havill*), the concerned K.C.

In the novel, Tommy and Tuppence are young and single. They meet by chance on the street. They're both broke and looking for work; any kind will do. They knew each other from years before, but this time, sparks fly and romance blooms.

Not here. Our heroes have been married for years and settled into staid middle-age. They have a son, George, a golden retriever, and a charming '50s cottage. I do not know how they afforded it, any more they afforded their very stylish wardrobes, because they're broke. That part remained. As the post-due bills stacked up, their youth fled and Tommy's waistline thickened.

Passion fled too, demonstrated by the twin beds they sleep in. I know vintage movies and TV pretended that sex didn't exist, but come on. Real married couples slept in double beds. The script made this choice to emphasize that Tommy and Tuppence are sexless and boring.

They shouldn't be this way. In the novels, they adore each other, they're hot for each other, and that doesn't change as they grow old. Agatha did something rare with Tommy and Tuppence. They married and stayed happy, despite life's usual traumas.

This Tommy and Tuppence are roommates. They have no chemistry together; not a spark of interest shows until Tuppence puts on a blonde wig. When Tommy shows he's attracted, she squashes him. They behave this way throughout. Tommy belittles Tuppence's intelligence, although she's obviously smarter and quicker than he is. She treats him like an overgrown 6-year-old. She even calls him (in public!) a child she's raising.

It makes you wonder why she married him, since he's been a failure his entire life. That's why they're broke. She wants him to get a job, and he's chasing get-rich-quick schemes.

This is not Tommy! In the novel, he's brave, stalwart, not given to flights of fancy, and not easily fooled. He's young and fit. He adores Tuppence even when she's being fanciful. Film Tommy is overweight, dopey, and so passive that he either resists investigating the mystery, or meekly goes along with whatever Tuppence (whom he resents) and the villains want him to do.

Novel Tommy does his homework. This Tommy is going to get rich raising bees and selling honey. Yet he hasn't read the beekeeping manual that came with the hives. His son (showing the respect Bart Simpson shows to Homer) rats Tommy out to mom. Just looking at the hives proved no one on the set consulted an actual beekeeper. A real beekeeper would never keep his expensive French queen (bought with what money?) inside a cloth-covered jam jar inside a closed box inside a shed for days. The queen would die.

Film Tommy and Tuppence don't demonstrate brains or consideration for anyone else. They reminded me of a mashup of two different married couples. Tuppence comes across as Lucy Ricardo, although more stylish. Tommy resembles Homer Simpson, but more buffoonish.

Yes, Tuppence doesn't have the common sense of Marge Simpson. Tommy isn't as smart or manly as Homer Simpson. Unlike Homer, Tommy has magical movie facial hair. No matter what happened or how long he'd been held captive, he was always freshly shaven. This proves his complete lack of testosterone.

Like T & T, every other character went through the plot-grinder, coming out radically different on the other side.

Julius Hersheimmer, an American millionaire from Texas, becomes an African-American millionaire who made his fortune by developing an artificial sweetener. Jane Finn is no longer his long-lost cousin. She's Julius' sugar cookie waiting for his divorce to be finalized.

Mr. Carter becomes Tommy's enabling and bumbling uncle, not the capable spy-master he was in the novel. Albert is no longer the cockney lift boy who Tommy and Tuppence meet and take under their wing. He morphs into a science teacher at a boys' school and emulates Q from the James Bond series.

The villains are still villains, but they're incompetent. They're dumb enough to buy Tommy's unbelievably passive act when he impersonates a moneyed gangster. Rita Vandemeyer becomes a fading opera star with a white Persian cat. She's supposed to be an adventuress who can hold her own in a man's world. No more.

At least the secret adversary remains, the only competent person in the film.

The ending was a hash of loose ends and ridiculous contrivances. A jar of honey figures prominently, shoehorned into the plot to justify Tommy's taste for get-rich-quick schemes that will leave his family in financial ruins and an unpleasant taste in yours.

General Information

Based on: *The Secret Adversary* (novel, 1922)
Run time: 2 hr., 42 min. **Subtitles:** Yes

Writer: Zinnie Harris **Director:** Edward Hall

Cast

David Walliams as Tommy Beresford
Jessica Raine as Tuppence Beresford
James Fleet as Maj. Anthony Carter
Matthew Steer as Albert Pemberton
Miles Roughley as George Beresford

Clarke Peters as Julius Hersheimmer
Alice Krige as Rita Vandemeyer
Paul Brennen as Lucky
Jonny Phillips as Whittington
Camilla Marie Beeput as Jane Finn
Madeline Appiah as Annette
Andrew Havill as James Peel
George Taylor as Dominic Villiers

Film Locations

Turville, Buckinghamshire (Beresford village)
Oak Hill Crescent, Surbiton, Surrey (Beresford home)
The Residence, Saunderton, Buckinghamshire
Kenilworth Court, London

N or M? (2015)

Numerous changes make a mess out of this novel's sole adaptation that's pretty but accidentally funny

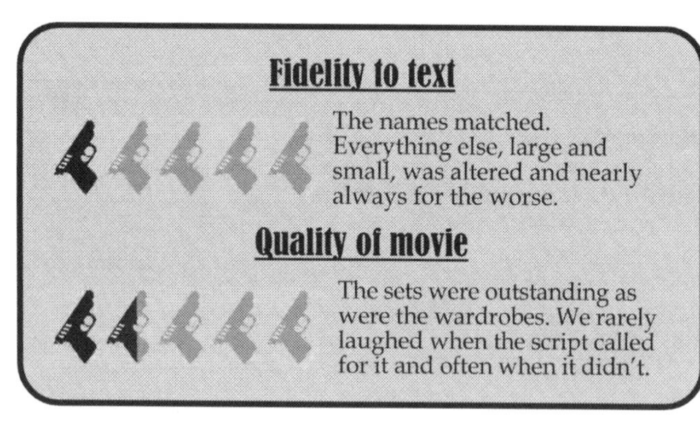

We first watched *N or M?* over two years ago, at the start of the Agatha project. We had to watch it again for book-related reasons. Time did not improve the film but it did clarify what might have been if only the BBC had paid for a decent script and hired leads who could hide their dislike of each other.

This was a terrible, inept adaptation of one of Agatha's more underrated novels with her underrated detectives, Tommy and Tuppence Beresford (hereafter nicknamed T & T). Rewatching it on the heels of rewatching *The Secret Adversary* (2015) gave the impression that the production company had an overall story arc planned, beginning in *Adversary*, continuing through *N or M?*, then the short story arc of *Partners in Crime*, followed by *By the Pricking of My Thumbs* and climaxing with *Postern of Fate*.

But because the first two films were so terrible, the follow-on movies weren't produced. Which is a pity, because this could have been wonderful. The T & T novels are spy capers, with a side trek into child murder and thieves' rings in *Thumbs*. Setting all five films during the Cold War was a genius move. The '50s were a golden age for espionage, with the Red Menace looming, Commies infiltrating institutions, double agents everywhere, and the Iron Curtain descending across Europe and imprisoning entire populations. British Intelligence had serious problems with Russian moles and traitors who wanted Great Britain to fall to the Communists. Look up Kim Philby and the Cambridge Five. They betrayed their country for ideological reasons and never doubted that they might be wrong.

If the five films had been made, we would have seen the unearthing of a major spy plot that would have forced Britain to her knees before the Russians. In *Adversary*, T & T become involved with MI5 and Mr. Brown's plans to destabilize England. But was he working alone? Mr. Brown told us he loathed what England had become and he threw himself off a building rather than reveal his secrets. There are already hints that Major Carter (Tommy's uncle) can't trust his coworkers on the Third Floor.

In *M or N?*, he knows he can't. The Third Floor has been infiltrated. Top-secret information is being leaked. Nuclear scientist Gilbert Worthing stole a nuclear bomb he was working on, and Tommy is sent

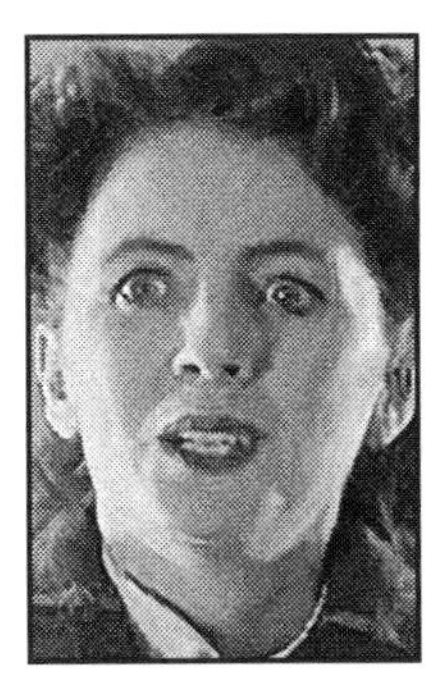
Sheila Perenna
(*Aoife McMahon*),
the wary innkeeper

Mrs. Sprot
(*Christina Cole*),
the charming widow

Mr. Minton
(*Robert Hands*),
the caring therapist

Mrs. Minton
(*Issy van Randwyck*),
the shrink's wife

Carl Denim
(*Ed Speleers*),
the secretive guest

Commander Haydock
(*Roy Marsden*),
the old sea dog

undercover as a birdwatcher to a coastal inn to look for it. A kept-in-the-dark Tuppence follows him, also in disguise. Despite their best efforts to fail they save the day and Carter's driver is unmasked as the mole. Major Carter rewards them with cash and the offer of a detective agency.

That launches *Partners in Crime*. They probably discover that the driver wasn't the evil genius behind the plot (after all, he would only know where his boss goes and not what he does). So T & T continue to hunt for the mole while investigating smaller crimes as a cover. They'd hide in plain sight while remaining off MI5's books.

Thumbs and *Postern* would follow, upping the stakes with each film, until T & T unmask the true secret adversary in *Postern* and save what's left of the British Empire. We'd even get an explanation for what was never answered in *N or M?* Why did atomic scientist Gilbert Worthing steal his nuclear bomb? How did he get that suspicious-looking shrouded object onto the flatbed truck by himself and then get it past security? Were those guards bribed? Part of the plot? Double agents were everywhere, at every level. Worthing must have had a compelling reason to risk himself, his family, and his country, but what was it? The answer must be part of the larger arc.

During the five films, we'd see Tommy grow into a capable man who's willing to listen to Tuppence's intuition. We'd see Tuppence fall back in love with a man she currently despises. Watch them hug when she discovers Tommy's still alive and tell me she loves her man. She doesn't. Tommy pulls her to him and Tuppence pulls back, stiff as a board. She doesn't melt into his arms or warm up to his kiss. She'd rather be anywhere else. Sheila and Carl Denim have more charisma and fire in their short scene than Tommy and Tuppence do in their six hours.

But instead of that wonderful concept, we got this mess.

Like *The Secret Adversary*, *N or M?* needed a good script. There were times when the movie genuinely came to life before collapsing back into rigor mortis. It's as though the production company despised Tommy so much, they were physically unable to deliver a movie that celebrated a capable man. Worse, they despised the notion of a long-married couple still enjoying each other's company. Recall that Hollywood has exactly two acceptable storylines for love: the exciting lead-up to the wedding and the traumatic lead-up to the divorce. Middle-aged people don't have hot sex lives with their spouses, only their partners in adultery.

The production company spent the money where it showed: fabulous sets and wardrobe. They didn't spend the money where it mattered: better direction, stars who liked each other, and a script that made sense. The script is vital, especially when your leads are ordinary people thrust into dangerously deep waters where their lives and everyone else's are at stake.

Exemplifying the script issues, a real head-scratcher took place inside the San Souci guest hotel. Tommy introduced himself as George Meadows, birdwatcher. Yet Mrs. Sprot calls him Mr. Beresford and Tommy never notices. Was this supposed to be a sign that Mrs. Sprot knew who he was? Or was it supposed to be a demonstration of Tommy's incompetence that he doesn't notice? Or say something to Carter at the finale? Similarly, Major Haydock calls him Tommy, when every other time they speak, the Major calls him Meadows. Again, Tommy doesn't notice nor is anything ever said. Was Major Haydock briefed by Mrs. Sprot? Who knows.

T & T bicker throughout like they're in junior high school. Who does each suspect? The person they're jealous of, instead of looking at facts. For Tommy, it has to be Carl Denim because Denim flirts with Tuppence. For Tuppence (although she turns out to be right) it's Mrs. Sprot. I'll let this slide only because Tommy is so obviously not a desirable male that it is suspicious that a merry divorcée like Mrs. Sprot would give him the time of day. He couldn't even be bothered to read a birdwatching guide while on the train, like he didn't bother reading the beekeeping manual in *Adversary*.

The script made T & T woefully unprepared, unwilling to learn or grow. They began *Adversary* as rank amateurs and they ended here as rank amateurs. They could not alter their behavior to do their job. Gilbert Worthing, traitorous scientist, called it right. He didn't believe Tommy was MI5. You won't either.

General Information

Based on: *N or M?* (novel, 1941)
Run time: 2 hr., 42 min. **Subtitles:** Yes

Writer: Claire Wilson **Director:** Edward Hall

Cast

Jessica Raine as Tuppence Beresford
David Walliams as Tommy Beresford
James Fleet as Major Carter
Matthew Steer as Albert Pemberton
Joanna Horton as Barbara Kemp

Danny Lee Wynter as Gilbert Worthing
Hannah Waddingham as Blonde Assassin
Aoife McMahon as Sheila Perenna
Issy van Randwyck as Mrs. Minton
Robert Hands as Mr. Minton
Ed Speleers as Carl Denim
Christina Cole as Mrs. Sprot
Roy Marsden as Commander Haydock
Alyy Khan as Major Khan
Pinar Ögün as Veronika Urbanowicz
Tam Williams as Harrison
Saffron Hocking as Teller
Trevor Cooper as Mr. Harrison
Susan Brown as Mrs. Harrison
Josh Cook as Dennis Harrison
Paul Cawley as Shopkeeper
David Moorst as Wilfred

Film Locations

Sheringham Station, Sheringham, Norfolk (train station)
Cromer, Norfolk (Sans Souci Hotel, seafront, pier)
Chatham Historic Dockyard, Chatham, Kent (London streets)

IV. And Then There Were None

And Then There Were None (1939) has what Hollywood would call a high-concept premise: ten sinners in an isolated locale are hunted down and slaughtered. Sound familiar? It's *Friday the 13th* without the gore.

There are two versions: one grim and one hopeful. Agatha radically revised the novel's ending for the play, turning Vera and Lombard, the two most selfish and evil of the murderers, into innocent heroes.

And Then There Were None explores the question of guilt and punishment. What's worse: killing an old lady, running over children, or abandoning natives to die? Operating while drunk, bearing false witness against a crook, or drowning a child that trusts you? When and how they die suggests what Agatha thought.

Shorn of its moral implications, Agatha's plot has been used ever since. Most are along the lines of *Mindhunters* (2004) with Val Kilmer or *Sabotage* (2014) with Arnold Schwarzenegger. The emphasis is on horrible deaths instead of the psychology of cruelty and despair in the face of the inevitable.

And Then There Were None is Agatha's most adapted story. Only *Murder on the Orient Express* (1934) comes close. More importantly, it's not just the bestselling mystery, it's one of the best-selling novels of all time. We found ten versions to review, and that's why it deserves a chapter of its own.

From top: figurines from *Ten Little Indians* (1965), *And Then There Were None* (1974), the Soviet *Ten Little Indians* (R-1987), *Ten Little Indians* (1989), and the French *They Were Ten* (F-2020).

Detective Ryuya Shôkokuji examine the figures from the Japanese version of *And Then There Were None* (2017).

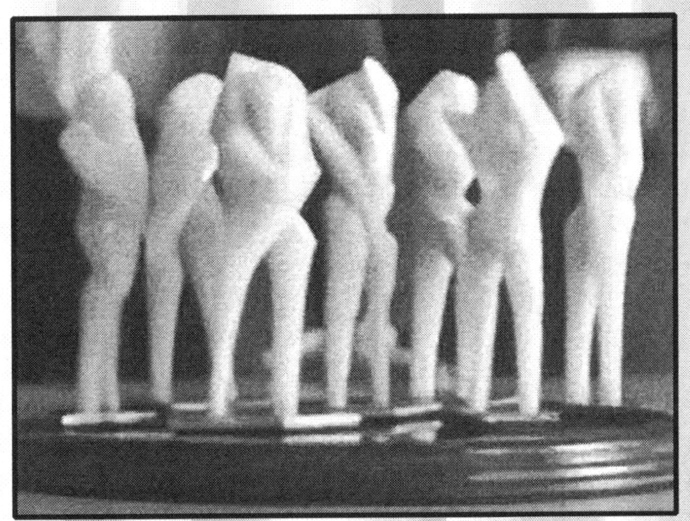

Art Deco-inspired figurines for *And Then There Were None* (2015).

No sculptures were used in the Indian *Unknown* (I-1965), so this is the closest we can find.

Indian centerpiece from *And Then There Were None* (1945)

Figures from the TV version of *Ten Little Indians* (1959)

Whether sculpted to look like indians, soldiers, or abstract figures, thę meaning is the same: doom for those they represent.

And Then There Were None (1945)

Mr. Owen's guests expected a quiet weekend at his island mansion, only to meet their judge, jury, & executioner

Fidelity to text

Compared to the play

Compared to the novel

If you've read the novel and wondered where the ending came from, the plot follows the play. Most film versions do, so don't be surprised when Vera's not guilty.

Quality of movie

It's terrific; alternately scary, atmospheric, tense, and funny. It's also surprisingly tidy and bloodless, since movies made in 1945 didn't revel in gore.

And Then There Were None is a very early "the murderer is in the house with you" film, a slasher flick with an A-list cast and none of the blood. Ten people are lured under false pretenses and trapped in an island mansion. Other than the Rogers — he's the butler and she's the cook — none of them know each other.

Right from the start, you'll get a feel for the characters. The boatman delivers eight strangers to Indian Island and during the journey, you can see how awkward and uncomfortable they are. You can also guess who'll be a cool customer later on. On their arrival, they are greeted by the butler, Rogers, and his wife. He tells them their host will be delayed. There's only a cat roaming the house and keeping an eye on things.

After a good dinner, everyone's relaxed and ready to be amused. Prince Nikita Starloff — he must be a professional party guest — sits at the piano and plays and sings the already-arranged sheet music "Ten Little Indians." It's a macabre little ditty, but no one suspects a sinister motive. They're on Indian Island, after all. There's even a circular arrangement of ten little Indian statues on the dining room table. Keep an ear out for the tune; you'll hear it several more times in the background.

Then the butler, obeying written instructions, cues up a record labeled "Swan Song" and the tension ratchets up. Instead of music, they hear a voice accusing everyone of murder, crimes they committed that couldn't be proved and prosecuted, and they all got away with it. Until now.

Does anyone feel guilty? Mrs. Rogers does. She screams and babbles, while her husband tries to shut her up. She faints. The exiled Russian prince cheerfully admits to running over two people while drunk; his complaint is that he lost his driver's license. Everyone else makes excuses, but they heard the record promising they'll be punished. As the guests die off, one by one, bits of the truth emerge. They're all guilty as charged. Or are they? Someone's acting as the executioner, so where is he or she?

This is a surprisingly funny movie considering the

Vera Claythorne (*June Duprez*), the secretary

Philip Lombard (*Louis Hayward*), the white hunter

Francis Quincannon (*Barry Fitzgerald*), the judge

Edward Armstrong (*Walter Huston*), the doctor

William Blore (*Roland Young*), the private eye

Thomas Rogers (*Richard Haydn*), the butler

General Information

Based on: *And Then There Were None* (novel, 1939)
Run time: 1 hr., 37 min. **Subtitles:** Yes

Writer: Dudley Nichols
Director: René Clair

Cast

June Duprez as Vera Claythorne
Louis Hayward as Philip Lombard
Roland Young as Detective William Henry Blore
Walter Huston as Dr. Edward G. Armstrong
Barry Fitzgerald as Judge Francis J. Quincannon
Judith Anderson as Emily Brent
Richard Haydn as Thomas Rogers
C. Aubrey Smith as Gen. Sir John Mandrake
Queenie Leonard as Ethel Rogers
Mischa Auer as Prince Nikita Starloff
Harry Thurston as Fred Narracott

body count. In one scene, four men spy on each other, some of them staring through keyholes. Rogers gets drunk and insubordinate. Seeing Rogers and his wife dead, Miss Brent's main concern is that there's no one who can find the breakfast marmalade. Miss Brent also speaks in quotes, possibly to prevent original thought from intruding. The private detective, Blore, always gets it wrong. The judge is sharp and witty. Dr. Armstrong is a secret lush. Lombard is a sardonic observer. The survivors argue over what they see, while completely missing the body lying at their feet.

Then there's the unnamed cat, who regularly provides comic relief. Kitty pops out of the woodpile when the characters nervously seek the source of a noise. Kitty soothes the judge as he does his Ernst Blofeld imitation. Kitty humanizes Miss Brent and leads the guests to her body. Don't miss the beautifully arranged yarn trail that almost — but not quite! — spells out who's the evil mastermind. It's a great touch when Kitty bats Miss Brent's yarn ball over the landing, and the ball dangles like a head in a noose.

Kitty is a dumb witness, seeing all and never telling. You could almost make the case that Kitty made the arrangements for her own amusement. What's more enjoyable for a cat than playing with mice until they die of fun?

If you're a cinema buff, you'll enjoy the mise en scène, the lighting, the carefully chosen camera angles. There are even special effects that permit the camera to pull through a keyhole. The director, René Clair, makes the most of his isolated location and even employs psychotropic weather to punctuate the action. He makes a visual joke about the hand of Mr. Owen and an aural joke with a well-timed sneeze. He breaks the cardinal rule forbidding characters to stare into the camera; they confess their sins to the audience, forcing us to see them as untrustworthy but scared people.

> *Very stupid to kill the only servant in the house. Now we don't even know where to find the marmalade.*
>
> EMILY BRENT

The vast majority of the novel moved directly to the screen, but not the ending. I understand why. Agatha rewrote the novel as a play in 1943, altering the ending to make it less grim and nihilistic. She didn't think audiences would pay to watch everyone die, especially during wartime. There's no redemption in the original novel but in the play, there is.

So that's the ending you get. The two most arguably evil characters in the novel, the last to die so they suffer the most, get retconned. A careful observer will see that Philip Lombard never says "I did it." He says "Lombard did it." Similarly, Lombard's monogrammed luggage has the wrong letters, but he has a ready explanation.

Likewise, Vera Claythorne never admits her guilt, but she doesn't deny it either. This time around, Vera didn't cause the death of the child she was responsible for. Instead, she took the blame for her crazy sister's murder of sister's fiancé, knowing that there wasn't enough evidence to convict her.

This retcon changes the ending where Vera and Lombard, as the two survivors, confront each other. In the novel, Vera shoots Lombard and, traumatized by terrible memories of her evil deed, hangs herself. She dies never knowing who masterminded her death. In the film, she and Lombard decide to trust each other and why not? He's the handsome hero, and she's the brave shield maiden so you know what's going to happen. But she still shoots Lombard. Then she finds out whodunnit, faces death by hanging, and foils the villain.

And it works, particularly since the original ending can't be filmed. (I was wrong about this, as you'll see with upcoming reviews.) In the novel, Scotland Yard detectives reconstruct the crime based on what they found on the island, but they can't reach a conclusion. They mention that Indian Island's owner, a man known to the police for many reasons, also died mysteriously. The final pages are devoted to printing a message found in a bottle, tossed into the sea by the mastermind, explaining what he did.

Even if they ended the movie implying that Vera hung herself after hearing the villain's confession, it would be deeply unsatisfying and depressing, especially to an audience in the middle of wartime.

Thus, the play gets filmed and it's one of the best Agatha adaptions I've seen to date. I'll watch it again to see a true mastermind (René Clair) film one of Agatha's finest novels.

Ten Little Indians (1959)

Compressing the story into an hour still succeeds in conveying the terror and suspense of the stage version

Fidelity to the play

This version is a mix of the novel and the stage play. Our hero and heroine still escape, but their back-story is much closer to the novel.

Quality of movie

The quality of the film is terrible. Blurry, out of focus, poor sound so you can't be sure what was just said. Otherwise, wow.

I didn't expect anything good from this production. The play soft-pedals the novel's ending but it's long enough to get some characterization in. Other filmed adaptations are 90 minutes or more. This kinescope version of *Ten Little Indians* is an hour long. That leaves darned little time to get to know ten people, each hiding a dirty secret. It's also live television so the actors had to get it right the first time. Which they did.

Since it's filmed on a set rather than a stage, the camera's free to move around a little more than it otherwise could. The relatively static location helps increase tension. The camera is as trapped as the unlucky recipients of U.N. Owen's invitation.

One hour long! Think about that. The stage presentation is probably two hours or more. I couldn't find any mention of how long a performance runs — probably because it varies depending on the speed of the actors — but I'm very sure it's longer than one hour.

Yet in this hour, the screenwriter worked in all ten victims plus the boatman. The action is compressed into a traumatic evening and terrified morning. The cast arrives, ferried to the island by the boatman, and discover what's in store for them. The script provides insight into most of the victims ranging from snapshot to documentary; their motivation, their struggle, their self-justification, and their comeuppance.

Mrs. Rogers, the cook married to the butler, gets the least air time of the ten but she's also the least culpable of the murderers. In the novel and stage versions, it's reasonably clear that she obeyed her husband and felt guilty ever since. That's why she dies so quickly and easily. She's given some mercy by U.N. Owen.

Frederick Marston, louche playboy, gets more time to suffer. He has a spat with Dr. Armstrong over his driving. Losing his driver's license for three years for killing some little kids didn't change him one bit. It was their fault for crossing the road without looking both ways and causing him petty legal troubles. He flirts with Vera, annoying her very much, annoys Philip Lombard, annoys everyone else, and gets what he deserves. All in less than ten minutes.

Rogers, the butler, goes next. Here, he's a cold, cold man, not the comic figure in the 1945 film. He's able to fully justify his actions, claiming that he tried to save

Vera Claythorne (*Nina Foch*), the governess

Philip Lombard (*Kenneth Haigh*), the mercenary

Lawrence Wargrave (*Barry Jones*), the judge

Edward Armstrong (*Romney Brent*), the doctor

William Blore (*James Berwick*), the detective

John Mackenzie (*Peter Bathurst*), the general

the mistress by racing out into the stormy night and failing. Do you think he cared about his wife's guilt? Not really, at least as long as she remained cowed.

Then it's General Mackenzie's turn. He's a daft, guilt-ridden old man searching for meaning and connection. He thinks he finds it with Philip Lombard but they've got — despite their mutual service to the Crown — little in common. His crime has eaten into him, ruining his life. It looks for a moment that U.N. Owen let him take the gentleman's way out, but no. It's a knife in the back to accompany the general's plaintive note.

Emily Brent is up next. She's self-righteous to a fare-thee-well, going so far as to tell Vera that she's inappropriately dressed. Vera wears a staid, black fitted dress with a white collar but from the way Emily Brent talks, you'd think Vera's dress was painted on with a neckline down to there. Detective Blore says it best (I'm paraphrasing because the sound quality was poor): Emily Brent could strut naked on board an Albanian freighter and the sailors would leave her alone.

As always, the star is Judge Wargrave. Vera Claythorne and Philip Lombard survive his machinations but they aren't the heart of novel, play, or film. It's the judge. He manipulates everyone like a master puppeteer. He pulls the strings from before the action starts. With each viewing of a version of *Ten Little Indians* (or *And Then There Were None* to use the alternative title), I'm impressed all over again by how well Agatha wrote this character. The judge is as self-justifying as they come but he's got a higher motive than mere gain. He wants to see justice done to murderers who escape justice. He enjoys being a hanging judge, but only if hanging is merited. But it's clear that he's a creepy man. Listen to him say he's always wanted to kill with his own hands but they were tied by the law.

His character is the most important in the success of the adaptation. If you can't believe Judge Wargrave, nothing else works. The only flaw in this film with Judge Wargrave is it was hard to believe he moved so fast without anyone noticing. Compressing the action to a single night and a morning didn't leave him much time to seduce Dr. Armstrong, lay false trails, sow fear and discontent, and in general panic and mislead the other victims without being detected. I'm still not sure how he offed Emily Brent and no one noticed. But that's a minor quibble.

General Information

Based on: *And Then There Were None* (novel, 1939)
Run time: 1 hr. **Subtitles:** No

Writer: Philip H. Reisman Jr.
Director: Paul Bogart

Cast

Nina Foch as Vera Claythorne
Kenneth Haigh as Philip Lombard
James Berwick as Det. William Henry Blore
Romney Brent as Dr. Edward Armstrong
Barry Jones as Mr. Justice Sir Lawrence Wargrave
Valerie French as Emily Brent
George Turner as Thomas Rogers
Peter Bathurst as Gen. John Gordon Mackenzie
Caroline Brenner as Ethel Rogers
Chandler Cowles as Frederick James Marston
Jeremiah Morris as Boatman

In this version, Dr. Armstrong, who should be a more dramatic character, fades in comparison to Judge Wargrave. He needed more time to fear, to panic, and to accept the lifeline tossed to him by the judge. Detective Blore, who got off many of the best lines, also needed more time but alas, there was none.

Vera Claythorne and Philip Lombard are the only characters noticeably different in the play, compared to the novel. Surprisingly, this version keeps their story much closer to the novel without making them actually guilty of murder. The scriptwriter did a very nice job of changing Agatha's explanation for why they ended up on the island while making it completely plausible. Vera is truly distraught, just like in the book. Her movie versions tend to be cooler because she knows she's not just innocent. Her sacrifice saved her sister from the hangman's noose.

This Vera is far more complex and anguished. She's attracted to Philip Lombard (no surprise) but she's also deeply conflicted because of her traumatic past.

Philip Lombard was better served in this version too. He's himself and not a disguised pal stepping in to see what's going on. Like Vera, two stories are floating around about him: the scurrilous false one and the sad true one. Which one did the gossips choose? You can guess the answer.

> *To the one universal virtue: nastiness!*
>
> FREDERICK JAMES MARSTON

The real flaw with this film was the film itself. Kinescope was a way of filming a live performance so it could be broadcast on television at another time. Television cameras were still used, but a film camera was trained on a television monitor to record it. It was never meant as a permanent record. It's blurry. The dialog is often unclear. You'll have to watch a scene twice or even three times to figure out what's being said. Luckily, that's no hardship.

Don't bypass this version of *And Then There Were None* because of the film stock. The script is so good, it should be remade just as it is.

Ten Little Indians (1965)

High on a Swiss mountaintop, ten people are gathered to face the ultimate justice they deserve

Fidelity to the play

The scriptwriter tossed much of the source material over Devil's Leap in a mad attempt to drag the play into the 1960s.

Quality of movie

Some of the changes work but not all. At the head of the list is a gratuitous and inane sex scene implying that blondes turn into round-heeled bimbos when faced with Hugh O'Brian.

This is the third theatrical adaptation of the stage play and it's not nearly as good as the 1945 version. The changes and updates were largely pointless considering how sluggish the pace is. It was nice to see more of the scenery surrounding the castle, showing how isolated the unlucky ten are.

That's not to say this version doesn't have its charms. There are some, starting with Hugh O'Brian as Hugh Lombard. Yes, all the names got "improved;" some for valid reasons but the rest only because the scriptwriter had to justify his salary.

Ten Little Indians starts rewriting Agatha from the first scene. We're not on a remote island, accessible only by boat with the boat back on the mainland. No, this time we're in an Austrian *schloss* in the dead of winter, accessible only by cable car. The *schloss* (Hohenwerfen Castle in real life) is impressive. It was built in the 1070s to be an inaccessible fortress although it couldn't have been as inaccessible as the movie implies because it got constructed. Someone dragged a million tons of stone up the mountain, followed by the furnishings.

In the movie, the roads to the *schloss* are gone, leaving only the cable car to carry guests and supplies and the Devil's Leap for desperate daredevils. I don't know if the villagers from down in the valley use the cable car (where do you think the housemaids come from?) but they aren't in the picture. The eight guests are not winter-savvy mountaineers so they didn't pack their parkas, pitons, crampons, and rope. They're trapped.

Even as recent hires, the servants, Herr and Frau Grohmann, are more resourceful than the guests. Once the fun starts and everyone's threatened with execution for their crimes, she attempts escape in the cable car. But it's Chekov's cable car, so the cable is cut and the car dramatically plummets down the valley. Herr Grohmann did pack his winter mountain-climbing gear, but his rope gets axed just like his wife's cable and he, too, plummets to his death. The parallel is ironically appropriate.

Another change is transforming Emily Brent, puritanical English spinster, into Ilona Bergen, hot German actress. This change did work. She got some witty dialog and was a sharp dresser: check out her pompoms! I've never seen a neckline like that before. The year 1965 did have some swinging fashions. In

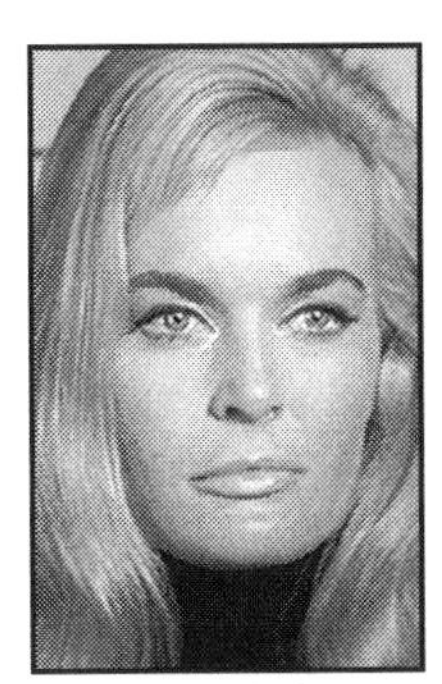
Ann Clyde (*Shirley Eaton*), the secretary

Hugh Lombard (*Hugh O'Brian*), the engineer

Judge Cannon (*Wilfrid Hyde-White*), the justice

Dr. Armstrong (*Dennis Price*), the surgeon

William Blore (Stanley Holloway), the detective

Mike Raven (*Fabian*), the pop star

another change, she knows General Mandrake. Sadly, that was an avenue the scriptwriter didn't spend enough time exploring, instead wasting time peeping on Ann Clyde as she undresses.

The playboy character gets updated, this time to an up-and-coming pop star. Fabian acquits himself well, even singing "Ten Little Indians" for his fans. He gets an amusing scene with Hugh O'Brian and the actress, demonstrating who is the boy and who is the man. After that, it's death by cyanide. At least this time, we don't get the doctor doing a fingertip drug analysis. Dr. Armstrong uses his nose to detect the telltale scent of bitter almonds.

After that, the main change is adding dramatics where none are needed. I suppose this was padding to compensate for the dragging last third, when the survivors are running around the *schloss* in a state of near-panic.

The film makes full use of our blonde heroine, renamed Ann Clyde. We get plenty of unnecessary shots of her in her underwear, dressing, undressing, and wrapping herself in a towel. I must be happy that she only does this behind a closed door and does not — as Hollywood insists today's actresses do — run around the *schloss* in her underwear while the gentlemen remain fully clothed.

She's also constantly overwhelmed by Hugh O'Brian's masculinity, to the point of doing whatever he tells her even when it's stupid and — you knew it was coming! — falling into bed with him at the first opportunity. I understand the attraction, but she doesn't know he's not a murderer. In reality, Ann Clyde would wait until after it's all over and then they'd go at it like rabbits. Not before.

Hugh O'Brian is our star, of course. He gets to be all manly, including engaging in fisticuffs with Herr Grohmann, the butler, over insults thrown about as everyone realizes what they're in for. He acquits himself well. We even get a flash of his manly chest, but not in that gratuitous "I'm easy" sex scene with Ann Clyde. Oh, no. For that, the film makes it clear that Hugh kept his pants on and merely unbuttoned his shirt. Sure. Whatever. If I was Ann Clyde, about to hand my virtue over to Hugh O'Brian, potential murderer, I'd have torn off his clothes. I'd make sure he had no weapons on him.

General Information

Based on: *And Then There Were None* (novel, 1939)
Run time: 1 hr., 31 min. **Subtitles:** Yes

Writers: Peter Yeldham and Harry Alan Towers
Director: George Pollock

Cast

Shirley Eaton as Ann Clyde
Hugh O'Brian as Hugh Lombard
Stanley Holloway as William Blore
Dennis Price as Dr. Armstrong
Wilfrid Hyde-White as Judge Cannon
Daliah Lavi as Ilona Bergen
Mario Adorf as Herr Grohmann
Leo Genn as General Mandrake
Marianne Hoppe as Frau Grohmann
Fabian as Mike Raven
Christopher Lee as U. N. Owen (voice)
Bill Mitchell as Narrator ("Whodunnit Break" voice)

Film Locations

Mayrhofen, Austria (village scenes)
Lindenbaumgruppe, Schwendau, Austria (monument sleigh passes)
Kenure House, Rush Co., Dublin (castle front porch and interiors)
Hohenwerfen Castle, Werfen, Austria (castle exteriors)

The real stars, however, are Wilfrid Hyde-White as Judge Cannon and Dennis Price as Dr. Armstrong. They're the heart of the novel, the center of the play, and the core of the film. They are the ones developing a deeply dysfunctional relationship but if you don't know the story, you don't know who is manipulating whom until too late. *Ten Little Indians* can only be watched once. The second time around, it's a different movie. Hyde-White and Price are fantastic, dancing their fatal *pas de deux*. Even if the rest of the movie stunk up the theater (which it doesn't), it would be worth watching for their performances.

I would be remiss if I did not mention the cat. There is a sleek gray kitty, astonishingly well-behaved with a pack of crazy strangers. Kitty shows up onscreen fairly often although not to the extent that the cat does in *And Then There Were None* (1945). Apart from luring General Mandrake to his death, there's no sense that Kitty planned the murders for her own amusement. She's just another pawn of U. N. Owen.

> *Did you ever hear of the two British gentlemen marooned on a desert island? They didn't speak to each other because no one had introduced them.*
>
> Ilona Bergen

The plot does have its holes, when you think about having to race around a huge *schloss* without being noticed, especially in the dark. That last act really drags. Some versions of the film have a two-minute "Whodunnit Break," where the audience has to suffer through a recap of murders and mayhem while they're supposed to confer with the guy in the next seat about the murderer's identity. It wasn't in the DVD version, but it's there in the special features section so you can appreciate what you were spared.

In the end, *Ten Little Indians* is still worth seeing. But only once. If you've only got time for one adaptation of the play, stick with *And Then There Were None* (1945). It's the gold standard of Christie adaptations.

Unknown (I-1965)

(*Gumnaam*)

All singing! All dancing! Bollywood takes on Agatha's darkest novel and turns it into a comic musical

Ten Little Indians (1939), later retitled *And Then There Were None*, was Agatha's seminal novel. At 100 million copies sold, it's the bestselling mystery in the world. It inspired countless imitations, starting with her stage play in 1943. You've seen it on stage (the ending's quite different), you've seen multiple filmed versions, you've seen films loosely based on the premise including slasher flicks like *Friday the 13th*, and you've read countless novels that use the same idea.

I guarantee you've never seen it performed like this.

The plot is simple: A pack of strangers are gathered in an isolated location and an unknown assassin picks them off one by one. As the story progresses, you learn that the strangers all earned their fate.

Now, consider India; a literate, cultured, wildly diverse country that's been strongly influenced by the British since the 1700s. Agatha's novels are wildly popular, in English and in translation. India also has a long history of filmmaking, frequently involving plenty of singing and dancing.

What could be more natural than Indian cinema making an Agatha Christie film and adding musical numbers? Which brings us to *Gumnaam*, which translates as *Unknown* or *Anonymous*, and is a very loose (and unlicensed) remake of *And Then There Were None*.

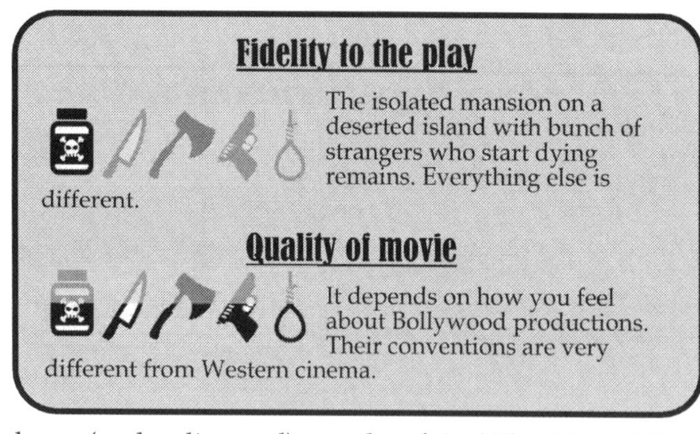

Fidelity to the play

The isolated mansion on a deserted island with bunch of strangers who start dying remains. Everything else is different.

Quality of movie

It depends on how you feel about Bollywood productions. Their conventions are very different from Western cinema.

None is no one's idea of a cozy, charming mystery. Everyone dies horribly because they deserved it. Even the stage play, softened considerably so the novel's two worst characters turn into our heroes, doesn't stint on the slashing and hacking and drowning and poisoning. It's hard to imagine any of the characters bursting into song, although it was done in 1945 by Mischa Auer, in 1965 by Fabian, and in 1974 by Charles Aznavour. Each played the first victim, sang their song, and promptly died from cyanide-laced cocktails.

Nobody danced. Certainly no one sang and danced in a huge Busby Berkeley-style spectacular with an ornate stage, statues with flashing, laser-beam eyes, and seemingly hundreds of gyrating, costumed backup dancers and singers. They didn't dance in happening nightclubs, backed by a combined orchestra / rock 'n' roll band, nor did they dance on the beach. They didn't

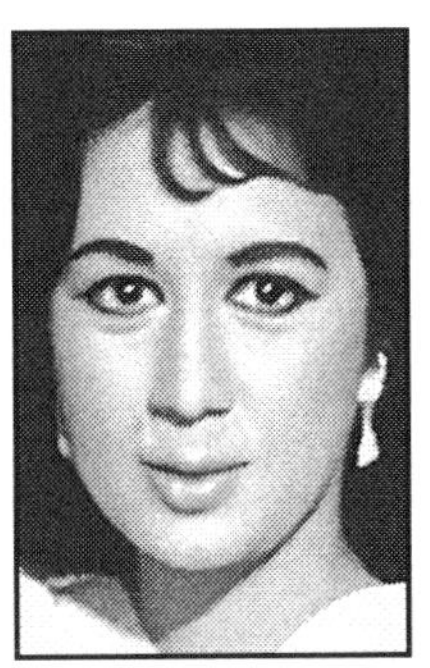

Asha
(*Nanda Karnataki*),
the secretary

Anand
(*Manoj Kumar*),
the air steward

Madhusudan Sharma
(*Tarun Bose*),
the judge

Rakesh Pran
(*Pran Sikand*),
the barrister

Miss Kitty
(*Helen*),
the dancer

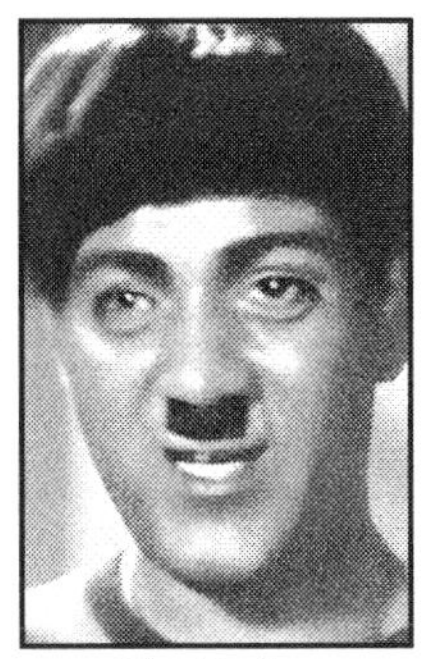

The Butler
(*Mehmood*),
the comic relief

sing and dance romantically in the rain. The castaways were too busy getting killed, or waiting to be killed.

But this is a Bollywood production, so you'll get all of that singing and dancing, performed by a star-studded cast who were the toast of Bollywood in 1965 and decades afterwards, although they're relatively unknown outside of India.

General Information

Based on: *And Then There Were None* (novel, 1939) (uncredited)
Run time: 2 hr., 31 min. **Subtitles:** Yes

Writers: Dhruva Chatterjee, Charandas Shokh
Director: Raja Nawathe

Cast

Nanda Karnataki as Asha
Manoj Kumar as Anand
Pran Sikand as Barrister Rakesh Pran
Helen as Miss Kitty
Mehmood as The Butler
Dhumal as Mister Dharamdas
Madan Puri as Dr. Acharya
Tarun Bose as Madhusudan Sharma
Manmohan as Mr. Kishan
Naina
Laxmi Chhaya as Masked Dancer
Baba Benjamin as Dancer
Herman Benjamin as Nightclub Bandleader
Hiralai as Khanna
Bazid Khan as Nightclub Announcer
Terence Lyons as Drummer
Surendra Rahi as Inspector
Ratna as Dancer

As you can imagine, I'm still not sure what I watched. I spent much of the film with my mouth hanging open. The only Bollywood films I've seen have been bits glimpsed on a TV in an Indian restaurant. I was completely unprepared for the experience.

The film opens with murky action shots depicting some kind of murderous conspiracy out of *The Godfather* (1972). It was hard to tell, which was truth in advertising of what was to come. I'm not sure we saw the entire film as released in 1965 in Mumbai. Some of the scene shifts were so choppy it felt like a reel was missing. Much of the film was so badly lit, the actors emoted in the dark. The subtitles were … adequate. They gave a sense of what was going on, but I'm positive I missed every nuance leading to a greater understanding of the film along with the humor that left audiences rolling in the aisles across India.

Still, what remained was surprisingly funny. Yes, the most nihilistic novel Agatha ever wrote has scenes played for laughs.

The opening number demonstrates how far away you are from the novel. After the murky conspiracy, we move to a happening nightclub where everyone is wearing a black domino: the audience, the staff, the dance band, the lead singer, the lead dancer in fringed gold lamé, her crew of backup dancers in pink fringe, and the army of boy dancers in black suits with silver piping and ruffled white shirts. The performers are strutting their stuff as if it's the last dance in the world. It's a high-energy mix of Indian music and '50s rock 'n' roll. Guitars, drums, horns, and sitars. Pay close attention because you'll never see any of those people again.

The performance over, the nightclub MC announces that a select group of seven people have won a fabulous two-week vacation at a luxury resort. They fly off, served by an air steward. The plane develops engine trouble, makes a forced landing in a pasture, the passengers and the steward exit with their luggage and the plane flies off, abandoning them.

After traipsing through the jungle, listening to a mysterious singer (the same lyrics heard during the opening credits and you'll hear them a lot), they find a palace. It's a decrepit ruin on the outside and opulent on the inside. God knows where the generator providing the electricity is hiding; maybe in the catacombs. It's surrounded by what looks like a convent's religious statue garden.

Inside, they encounter a sheet-draped body on the dining room table. As our eight castaways watch, it slowly rises to its feet as if pulled up by wires. The sheet slips away and reveals India's biggest comedian, Mehmood. Like Deadpool, he's aware he's being watched and not just by a crazed slasher who wants to murder the guests. Think of the other versions of *None* you've seen and replace the butler with Jerry Lewis or Jim Carrey. Mehmood's wildly out of place, almost in another movie, but it's Bollywood, so just go with it.

The castaways get to know each other but they're never directly accused of their crimes. They don't confess to each other or to the audience. Not until a very truncated, illogical ending do you learn there's no psychotic judge wanting to punish murderers who got away with it. No, it turns into a gangster revenge flick in the last fifteen minutes! The puppet master was angry because he'd been cheated in a smuggling deal and sent to prison.

Our innocent heroine's sole crime consisted of being a murdered crime boss' niece. The air steward turns out to be a policeman in disguise, on the track of our villain. No reason was given to explain why the villain went to all this trouble to remove five irritants and a niece, plus the butler and his sister. Yes, in the last five minutes, it's revealed the butler has a sister in red who's been following everyone around and singing the same song endlessly. Why? Don't know.

Gumnaam must have made much more sense in Hindi. It's wildly different from the other versions of *None*. It stands alone, sufficient unto itself, and that's why I gave it the rating I did. You, dear reader, should accept it on its own terms or dance away as fast as you can.

And Then There Were None (1974)

It's murder in the Middle East when strangers gather at a grand hotel to be slowly killed in unlikely ways

Fidelity to the play

Changes galore and all of them either bad or badly handled.

Quality of movie

This should have been good. Look at that international "A" cast and that gorgeous setting. But it dragged, it was blah, and the stars were wasted.

Other sources will tell you that this version of Agatha's novel and play reused the script from the 1965 version starring Hugh O'Brian as Hugh Lombard. Well, sort of.

The most obvious change was readjusting the action and dialog to reflect the new setting of a hotel in the middle of the desert in 1974. The hotel (the Abassi Hotel) is utterly gorgeous and one of the two reasons to watch the movie.

The other is the astonishing archeological ruins surrounding the hotel courtesy of movie magic. The real hotel is located in the center of the city of Isfahan, Iran. The ruins that appear to surround it – isolating the movie hotel in hundreds of square miles of barren sand – were filmed at the Temple of Debod, Persepolis, and Arg-e Bam. Gorgeous. Stunning. Amazing. Jaw-dropping.

Too bad the film didn't live up to the glorious sets.

Shifting the 1965 script to 1974 and the middle of the desert meant references to cable cars and rappelling down Devil's Leap in a blizzard went away. Their replacements were badly rewritten.

First, Mrs. Martino, the cook, flees the hotel and into the ruins. The rest of the cast follow her in hot pursuit, somehow missing her in the ruins. But U. N. Owen didn't. *He* managed to find her, strangle her against a pillar in the approved Persian fashion and return to the rest of the guests, his absence unnoticed despite the time it took to strangle a woman who's fighting back. Sure.

Worse, Martino, her butler-husband attempted to escape over 200 miles of open desert on foot with what appeared to be a single canteen of water and no hat or other equipment. I know the man was in a panic but really? One canteen?

And that led to a bigger logical flaw. How could U. N. Owen chase after him, find him in the trackless wastes, kill him, and make it back to the hotel without being detected? The alternative is that U. N. Owen sabotaged his canteen of water but how did U. N. Owen know that Martino would be this desperate? There's no scene showing someone poisoning the contents of the canteens.

There's also the change made to irresponsible playboy and drunk driver, Michel Raven. Instead of a callow boy hitting on the ladies and being firmly put in

Vera Clyde (*Elke Sommer*), the secretary

Hugh Lombard (*Oliver Reed*), the businessman

Arthur Cannon (*Richard Attenborough*), the justice

Edward Armstrong (*Herbert Lom*), the physician

Wilhelm Blore (*Gert Fröbe*), the detective

Gen. André Salvé (*Adolfo Celi*), the military man

his place by both women and alpha-male Hugh Lombard, we get Raven playing "Ten Little Indians" on the piano. Okay. But then Raven plays "In the Old-Fashioned Way" (the signature song of actor Charles Aznavour) and from somewhere, the instrumentation of an entire orchestra swells around him. That was consistent with the film's soundtrack, which varied between inappropriate and indifferent.

When I saw Hugh Lombard was played by Oliver Reed, I was looking forward to seeing this aggressive and sexy actor in action. I expected fireworks between him and hot blonde Elke Sommer, who portrayed Vera Clyde.

Nope. Not here. We also didn't get the gratuitous and ridiculous sex scene between Hugh and Vera like in the '65 version. Nor, also a plus, did we have to watch Vera prance around in her underwear like Hollywood so loves having hot blonde actresses do, whether it makes sense or not. It is hugely irritating to watch actresses strip for the camera for no discernible reason other than the director's perverse inclinations. Why can't directors have the actors emote in their skivvies? I'd watch Oliver Reed in his skivvies.

Oliver Reed, I'm sorry to say, phoned in his performance, leaving the reasons to watch him lost in the desert. There's also the fight scene with him and the butler. That got rewritten so much that it looks like he punches out the butler for no reason, unlike in the 1965 version. We slowed the DVD down and watched it frame by frame, and I still had a hard time seeing Martino throw the first punch and incite Hugh to punch back. It made me wonder how Hugh got those facial scars if he routinely sucker-punches outclassed opponents, while avoiding opponents who might successfully fight back. That's sure the vibe I got.

(The facial scarring, by the way, stems from Oliver Reed's 1963 bar fight when his opponent wielded a broken bottle. Oliver needed 63 stitches to sew his face back together. Not surprisingly, Reed, alongside Richard Burton, Peter O'Toole, and Richard Harris, was one of the great drunks of British cinema.)

The worst aspect of this version was Richard Attenborough, who played Judge Arthur Cannon. The judge is the heart and soul of novel, play, and film. If you, dear viewer, can't accept or believe Judge Cannon, you won't buy the story.

I know Richard Attenborough can act, but like Oliver Reed and Elke Sommer, he phoned in his performance. It didn't work for me, and his cane *really* didn't work for me. The cane showed he was handicapped. By definition, cane users have some mobility issues.

No worries there. I use one myself on occasion and it's pleasant to see a movie acknowledge that some of us cope with handicaps. But people who use canes do not zip around at top speed in vast hotels with numerous staircases or wildly uneven desert ruins loaded with tripping hazards, unnoticed by everyone including their victims until it is too late.

If Judge Cannon, cane user, was able to sprint up and down those staircases, handle poisonous snakes, and run around on those shifting sands, then there should have been a scene showing that his cane was window-dressing to make him appear disabled. If that had happened, I wouldn't have been quite as disbelieving of Judge Cannon, murderous mastermind. I could accept him concealing his physical abilities to better murder his victims. Anyone who's killing nine people without an Uzi needs to plan ahead, lay traps, and ensure he's underestimated.

Dr. Armstrong (Herbert Lom) is another key role. The judge seduces the doctor, playing on his intense fear of death and willingness to sacrifice everyone else if he gets to live. I bought the doctor, but not the judge. I really had trouble — again — with how the doctor sneaked out into the desert ruins with the judge (long distance over uneven footing at night) and get stabbed to death. Dr. Armstrong may have been a trusting drunk, but he could have fought off an elderly cripple.

There was just so much wrong with this film. It was slow, the performances were leaden, and the plot was riddled with logic holes. With the all-star cast and amazing setting, not to mention Agatha's great novel, it should have been better.

Watch it if you must, but as a travelogue with idiots getting in the way of the glorious scenery.

General Information

Based on: *And Then There Were None* (novel, 1939)
Run time: 1 hr., 38 min. **Subtitles:** No

Writer: Harry Alan Towers
Director: Peter Collinson

Cast

Elke Sommer as Vera Clyde
Oliver Reed as Hugh Lombard
Gert Fröbe as Wilhelm Blore
Herbert Lom as Dr. Edward Armstrong
Richard Attenborough as Judge Arthur Cannon
Stéphane Audran as Ilona Morgan
Alberto de Mendoza as Otto Martino
Adolfo Celi as Gen. André Salvé
Maria Rohm as Elsa Martino
Charles Aznavour as Michel Raven
Orson Welles as U. N. Owen (voice)

Film Locations

Persepolis, Iran (ruins next to the hotel)
Shah Mosque, aka Abbasi Mosque, Isfahan, Iran (hotel front door)
Shah Abbas Hotel, Isfahan, Iran (hotel interiors and courtyard)
Ali Qapu Palace, Esfahan, Iran (hotel balcony and hall)
Naqsh-i Jahan Square, Isfahan, Iran (hotel outdoors)

Ten Little Indians (R-1987)

(*Desyat Negrityat*)

Faithful version expands Blore's role, adds some hauntings, and suggests Vera was manipulated into murder

Fidelity to the novel

The epilogue's police investigation is dropped. Otherwise, unlike every other version, this follows the novel in setting, date, characters (including names), and fates.

Quality of movie

Fast paced, atmospheric, well-acted; this version has it all.

We didn't watch the Agatha films in the order they were released. We didn't originally plan to watch the foreign films, but eventually, we added them to the end of the list. And so, we finally reached the 1987 Soviet version of *And Then There Were None*. It's our tenth adaptation of the novel and it's a winner, albeit not for the unlucky victims. But they deserved their fate so it's okay.

I shouldn't be surprised that the Russian film industry would stick with the nihilistic novel, instead of the softer play. The Japanese version updated the novel to a very Japanese contemporary. The French version turned it into a contemporary slasher flick. Sarah Phelps stuck largely to the novel, but kept the play's confrontation between Vera and Justice Wargrave even though she still got her just desserts.

Stanislav Sergeyevich Govorukhin (Станислав Сергеевич Говорухин), the director and screenwriter, stuck to the novel. It's amazingly faithful, other than omitting some of the guilty remembrances and soul-searching along with the police investigation. But from the arrival on the island via a wonderful Russian ferry boat to Justice Wargrave's oral summation, it's all there. If you've read the novel, you'll recognize every one of these guilty people.

A fascinating part of the Agatha project is seeing different interpretations of the same novel. This version made Blore a larger, more dramatic man of action. It also provided new insight into Vera's backstory and character.

Of all the characters in the novel, William Henry Blore and Emily Brent get the most variation (apart from the play's wholesale rewrite of Vera and Lombard, turning those dastards into heroes).

Emily Brent's either a Bible-spouting, hypocritical spinster or a glamorous, murderous movie star. She's the nasty church lady here, the one who'd report Jesus to the authorities for daring to associate with people she disapproves of. Anyone who'd throw a pregnant young woman out onto the streets to starve and then dismiss her despairing suicide as proof she was rotten didn't get the message about Christian charity. Emily gets some screen time, especially when she has a vision

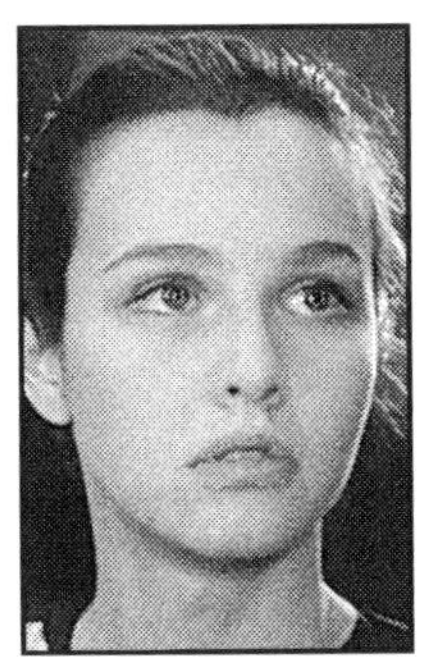
Vera Claythorne (*Tatyana Drubich*), the caregiver

Philip Lombard (*Aleksandr Kaydanovskiy*), the mercenary

Lawrence Wargrave (*Vladimir Zeldin*), the lawgiver

Edward Armstrong (*Anatoliy Romashin*), the lifegiver

William Blore (*Aleksey Zharkov*), the truth seeker

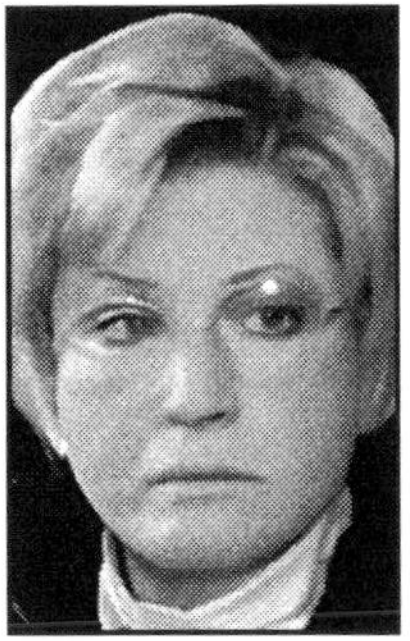
Emily Brent (*Lyudmila Maksakova*), the false Christian

of poor, drowned Beatrice Taylor, begging for sanctuary and being denied.

Blore, ex-police inspector turned private investigator, lied under oath for pay. His character in the adaptations range from almost nonexistent (the 1989 version mostly ignored him) to a comic and idiotic Keystone Kop who can be safely dismissed to an abusive cop who beats a suspect to death to a cop who perjures himself so the defendant (who's guilty of plenty of other stuff) is jailed so he can't finish beating his wife to death. Sometimes, the class divide is painfully obvious and he fails to cross it successfully as part of his undercover mission for U. N. Owen. In other films, no one notices that he's "not our kind, dear."

If he connects with anyone, it's Philip Lombard. Both are outside the social hierarchy. They're not servants (the Rogers and Vera). They're not gentry (Emily Brent or Anthony Marston). They're not socially respectable (Dr. Armstrong, General Maxwell, or Justice Wargrave).

Here, Blore's still guilty of perjury. He tells Lombard his only regret is that he didn't earn enough for lying in court. He's also a dynamic man of action, taking Lombard's usual role. This Lombard becomes a man in the shadows, watching and waiting to see what happens. They develop an interesting relationship. They're both predators and swiftly evaluated each other as the only capable men on the island. Rogers is a servant and quickly dies, the General is waiting for death, the doctor is pompous and old, the judge is even more pompous and old. They'll rescue themselves and, possibly, Vera, since she's young and pretty instead of old and shrewish like Emily Brent.

It was fascinating watching Blore evaluate Vera. It's almost as though he didn't buy her tragic story (it would have been in all the newspapers). That's why she went after Lombard. She knew Blore didn't believe her but Lombard didn't say anything. She took his hanging back as meaning she could manipulate him. She tried and succeeded, got his gun and shot him. Despite his experience, Lombard didn't recognize Vera as a threat the way Blore did.

Even more interesting was the flashback between Vera and Hugo. In ten films, this is the first where Hugo goes into detail about how, even though he loves his nephew, if Fate had been different and Cyril had been Cynthia, he'd be the peer with the title and the estate. He loves Vera but he's poor so they can't marry.

Hint, hint, hint.

General Information

Based on: *And Then There Were None* (novel, 1939)
Run time: 2 hr., 17 min. **Subtitles:** Yes

Writer and Director: Stanislav Govorukhin

Cast

Tatyana Drubich as Vera Claythorne
Aleksandr Kaydanovskiy as Capt. Philip Lombard
Aleksey Zharkov as William Blore
Anatoliy Romashin as Dr. Edward Armstrong
Vladimir Zeldin as Justice Lawrence Wargrave
Lyudmila Maksakova as Miss Emily Brent
Aleksey Zolotnitskiy as Thomas Rogers
Mikhail Gluzskiy as Gen. John Macarthur
Irina Tereshchenko as Ethel Rogers
Aleksandr Abdulov as Anthony James Marston
Fyodor Odinokov as Fred Narracott
Igor Yasulovich as U. N. Owen (voice)

Film Locations

Swallow's Nest, Crimea, Russia
Vorontsov Estate, Crimea, Russia

Hugo never says one word about how a tragic, completely accidental death for Cyril would be welcome. But that scene implies it, if Vera is that kind of a girl. Hugo doesn't misjudge her: *if* he wants the title and estate more than he loves his nephew. That's a big if. Yet that scene sticks in my mind. How badly does Vera want to marry a rich peer instead of a poor relation? If Hugo was hinting to Vera that he needed Cyril dead, he got what he wanted. And since it was a tragic, completely accidental death, no blame attaches to him, the next heir.

Which is also why Hugo — even if he wanted Vera to arrange Cyril's drowning — couldn't marry her. It wouldn't look right, for starters. Marrying the governess who drowned the boy who stood in the way? The gossips would have a field day. Hugo also sees clearly what kind of woman Vera is. She'd poison his coffee if he became a problem. Even if she never killed anyone again, Cyril's murder would always be a barrier between them; the lurking, ugly secret that would destroy any chance at happiness.

Like Vera, Hugo needed the inquest to state the drowning was accidental. If Vera claimed in court that it was Hugo's idea, he would naturally deny everything. After all, he never came out and said, "Drown that brat, and we'll be happy together." But he'd be forever tainted. He'd have the title, the loot, and the estate, but wherever he went, people would talk. An accidental death worked out great, for him. He wins and can marry a girl of his class with money of her own instead of a destitute governess.

Vera, who seems reasonably bright, wasn't bright enough to see the trap she walked into. Nor was she bright enough to understand that murdering a kid, even one she disliked (the novel makes it clear), would haunt her. She can't stop thinking about it. Anyone who knows her backs away, increasing her isolation.

This version is a don't-miss, and one of the four best: 1945 (for the play), 2015 (for the mashup), 2017 (for the contemporary), and this one. It's tragedy and the triumph of warped justice.

Ten Little Indians (1989)

Sly Stallone's brother was game, but this African safari version came down with sleeping sickness

Fidelity to the play

This is producer Harry Alan Tower's third try. You'd think by this time he'd get the story right. No such luck.

Quality of movie

What a wasted opportunity. Beautiful, exotic landscapes, dangerous animals, an intriguing setting, a mostly all-star cast, yet the movie flowed like treacle in January.

Movie producer Harry Alan Towers (1920-2009) knew a valuable property when he saw one. He acquired the rights to *And Then There Were None*, made the film (retitled *Ten Little Indians*) in 1965 and set it in an Austrian *schloss* in the dead of winter. He also hung onto the rights. He filmed it again in 1974, this time setting it at a grand hotel in the middle of the Iranian desert. And he retained the rights.

Towers should have gotten a good movie, considering he had Agatha's story, a mostly all-star cast, and the great idea of filming on location in South Africa. Yet he learned nothing from his two previous efforts.

We'll start with the script. The hacks writing it didn't waste time introducing us to the characters. Each of the ten people stranded in the safari camp had a different reason for being there, yet their confessions were either nonexistent or badly truncated. Did they assume we in the audience already knew the story? That's a terrible assumption because there's always a new generation who haven't watched any of the previous versions, seen the play, or read the book.

Marion Marshall (Brenda Vaccaro)'s makeover bugged me. Beginning with the 1965 version, Emily Brent, vindictively religious spinster, morphed into a famous actress. Okay. Movies update with the times. Except that in both the 1965 and the 1974 versions, the other nine targets of U.N. Owen recognized her.

If Marion Marshall is a famous actress, she'd have been mobbed. Instead, she's one of the crowd, until she makes her late-in-the-movie confession to Vera about murdering her lesbian lover to protect her budding Hollywood career.

There's also the little matter of Marion's wardrobe, hair, and makeup. She's a glamorous movie star. Except she didn't have enough luggage for the clothes I saw onscreen, nor did she have a lady's maid along to keep her glamorous and well-groomed at all times. Vera was almost as bad. She also lugged a (smaller) closet with her, as did Mrs. Rogers. Maybe they owned interdimensional luggage where one suitcase holds an entire department store, complete with jewelry counter, makeup bar, and beauty salon.

The setting was moved from a remote, isolated island to a remote, isolated camp in the bush. What a

Vera Claythorne (*Sarah Maur Thorp*), the secretary

Captain Lombard (*Frank Stallone*), the white hunter

Judge Wargrave (*Donald Pleasence*), the judge

Dr. Werner (*Yehuda Efroni*), the doctor

Mr. Blore (*Warren Berlinger*), the detective

Marion Marshall (*Brenda Vaccaro*), the actress

great idea! Cue Tarzan's yell! Yet the script didn't do a darned thing with it, other than a lone lioness and a monkey briefly showing up. Bugs were mentioned. That was it. Where were the animals? They hadn't been hunted to extinction in 1935. I expected monkeys, antelopes, prides of lions, elephants running through the camp. *George of the Jungle* (1997) did a better job depicting Africa than this.

Why didn't U.N. Owen lace the surrounding bush with working traps? Blore found a leg-trap by stepping on it, and then, a miracle! He pried its steel jaws open and *walked* away. No blood. No gaping tears in his trousers. No agonizing pain. Not even a limp! And he didn't tell anyone! That jungle should have been infested with Tarzan movie traps. Where was the quicksand? The venomous snakes? U.N. Owen could have executed his victims in far more interesting fashions *and* in ways that discouraged them from fleeing the camp. A Cape Town hotel would have been more dramatic.

The script ignored how the camp was run. Who kept those campfires and torches burning? Who kept the food laying around from being instantly overrun by flies and rodents? Who did the washing up? Who pumped the water for Vera's gratuitous shower scene? I will admit that we saw a lot less of Vera than I expected. The director showed astonishing self-discipline. Or lethargy, in keeping with how he directed the rest of the film.

The cast did their best but the script didn't give them anything to work with. Frank Stallone played Philip Lombard, great white hunter with a dark past. Previous movie adaptations waved aside Lombard's guilt by having his friend impersonate him after he committed suicide. We don't know if that's the case here, but whether he's the seasoned African hand or not, he had no charisma and no chemistry with Vera.

Worse, the script demanded that he vacillate between competence (fixing the radio and identifying a lioness by her paw prints) and incompetence (not recognizing blanks, unmanaged camp, and he didn't lead the survivors to freedom). He was so *passive*. If he was filling in for the late Philip Lombard, then we should have gotten scenes showing him out of his depth but gamely trying. Nothing. He was useless, and Vera was right to shoot him.

General Information

Based on: *And Then There Were None* (novel, 1939)
Run time: 1 hr., 40 min. **Subtitles:** Yes

Writers: Jackson Hunsicker & Gerry O'Hara
Director: Alan Birkinshaw

Cast

Sarah Maur Thorp as Vera Claythorne
Frank Stallone as Captain Lombard
Warren Berlinger as Mr. Blore
Yehuda Efroni as Dr. Werner
Donald Pleasence as Judge Wargrave
Brenda Vaccaro as Marion Marshall
Paul L. Smith as Elmo Rodgers
Herbert Lom as General Romensky
Neil McCarthy as Anthony Marston
Moira Lister as Ethel Mae Rodgers
Candice Hillebrand as Schoolgirl

Film Location

South Africa

The soul of the novel, play, and film versions is Justice Wargrave. Donald Pleasance played him, and he was ... adequate. The director didn't care so why should he? Dr. Werner (Yehuda Efroni), his dupe, is equally important. We should have seen Justice Wargrave seducing Dr. Werner, playing on his fear of death and desire to stay alive at all costs. But this Dr. Werner was a fatalist. A fatalist wouldn't have cooperated with Justice Wargrave's plans. He wouldn't have cared enough. Yet the script said he did and so that's what happened.

There's also Justice Wargrave's death scene. Vera, Lombard, Blore, and Dr. Werner find his body. He's been shot through the forehead and is hanging upside down from a tent roof (at last! A Tarzan-type scene.) His body lands on the ground. If you know the plot, you know where I'm going with this. How did Justice Wargrave, a sick old man, survive being unceremoniously dropped on his head from a height, slam down onto his back, and then swiftly and secretly recover to continue master-minding the panicked victims? How could he play dead so long and so publicly and no one notice?

Because the plot said so.

One nice touch showed up. When sophisticate Anthony Marston arrived, dropped off by a biplane, he had a teddy bear stuffed into the leg pocket of his flight suit. When he dressed for dinner (Marston also owned interdimensional luggage), the teddy bear disappeared. No one asked why he carried the bear around, another plot mistake because it would have given us a clue to his personality. It could have been a charm warding off death (ironic!), or he brought it at U.N. Owen's request (setup!). Anything! I wondered how Blore's murder would be finessed because there are no bears in Africa, and they are mentioned in the poem. Marston's teddy does the honors.

While there was no literal quicksand in the movie, there was plenty in the pacing. *Ten Little Indians* was slow and lethargic. No energy. No panic. The most interesting characters (Mrs. Rogers in particular who won a contest with her husband) went first. Clearly the director and the cast were bitten by tsetse flies and got sleeping sickness. By the end of the movie, you'll feel like you have it, too.

And Then There Were None (2015)

Sarah Phelps' three-hour adaptation of the novel gives plenty of space to delve into characters & their sins

Fidelity to the play/novel

The typical adaptation sticks with the play's happy ending. This is largely based on the novel: gruesome, paranoid, atmospheric, and horrifying.

Quality of movie

Gorgeously cast, scripted, shot, acted, and set designed. Well worth your three hours.

The film opens with a pan across jade soldier statues (designed by artist Isabel Riley). Because we're enlightened these days, we can't use Agatha's original title (look it up). We can't use the replacement title either because it's *also* becoming problematic. Thus, the default name for Agatha's seminal novel has become *And Then There Were None*. The poem at its center has morphed into "Ten Little Soldiers."

Each modernistic piece of glass represents one of U. N. Owen's ten deserving victims. They vary to match their corresponding character. Sadly, the camera pans over them so fast it's hard to grasp the symbolism. They all looked similar; amorphous, blocky, vaguely humanoid green glass. They could be Cubist alien ants.

The film was scripted, designed, cast, and shot to follow (mostly) Agatha's novel, while remaining — like the soldier statues — very much its own thing. No, scriptwriter Sarah Phelps did not use Agatha's dialog. Yes, she altered details to make the film more cinematic and less novelistic. She indulged in swearing, sexual innuendo, implied lesbianism, and a coke-fueled party near the end. She had three hours to give us backstory and humanize the island's visitors. She used every minute to create a close version of the novel.

This includes the nihilistic ending. Most adaptations follow the play's conclusion. It feels good to see our hero (Philip Lombard) and our heroine (Vera Claythorne) fall in love, escape with their lives, and learn they aren't murderers. It was someone else. They were innocent victims.

Not here.

Lombard got some rewriting. He still murdered at least 21 men but this time over diamonds rather than abandoning his African soldiers to die in the bush. He's honest enough to admit it. He's more action-oriented than in other adaptations. Smarter too. A born predator, he realizes almost immediately that they're being hunted. Unlike everyone else, he's suspicious of Justice Wargrave. He's attracted to Vera from the moment he spots a flash of her thigh on the train to the island. She's attracted too, not waiting for him to parade for her (and us) in a low-slung towel and a smile.

Vera's story (told via flashbacks) makes you believe she's an innocent victim of circumstance, still grieving over Cyril's drowning. In the novel, she disliked that snotty brat. Here, they're fond of each other. That makes the revelation of her true character all the more horrifying. She sent Cyril off to drown so her lover, his Uncle Hugo,

Vera Claythorne (*Maeve Dermody*), the governess

Philip Lombard (*Aidan Turner*), the mercenary

Lawrence Wargrave (*Charles Dance*), the judge

Dr. Edward Armstrong (*Toby Stephens*), the physician

William Blore (*Burn Gorman*), the detective

Emily Brent (*Miranda Richardson*), the spinster

would inherit. She'd marry Hugo and become the lady of the manor. But we learn near the end that Hugo figured out she lied. Justice Wargrave gives her a chance to beg for her life and she does, claiming she can get them both off because she's gotten away with murder before. But he pushes the chair away and Hugo and Cyril get justice.

One particular pleasure was seeing more of Emily Brent, spinster, than in previous adaptations. She's a hypocrite, a bully, and the worst kind of Christian. She'd happily burn Jesus at the stake for not meeting her standards or doing something she didn't approve, such as associating with prostitutes. She justifies her cruelty by claiming to be virtuous. Many adaptations change her into a glamorous movie star, softening her intolerant behavior and minimizing her crimes. That's a mistake because of what she represents.

The police detective, William Blore, has had numerous incarnations. Sometimes he's an idiot, almost comically inept. Other times, he's a cypher. Or he stays in the background and you never quite know why he's on the island in the first place.

Here, his murder becomes overt. Giving false testimony to send a man to the gallows is not as cinematic as beating a suspect to death in his jail cell. There should have been some dialog about how the police protect their own, explaining why he got away with murdering someone in custody. Phelps also created an interesting dynamic with Lombard as they hunt for Mr. Owen. Watch how Lombard taunts him and how Blore responds. You can tell who's top dog on this island.

This version emphasized the hypocrisy in British society. Consider U. N. Owen's choice of victims: Anthony Marston, young aristocrat; Gen. MacArthur, venerated military leader; Rogers, dedicated butler; Emily Brent, staunch churchgoer; Dr. Armstrong, respected surgeon; Justice Wargrave, admired judge; William Blore, responsible policeman; Vera Claythorne, governess of aristocratic children. The two outliers are Ethel Rogers and Lombard. She's an abused wife and is further abused by Emily Brent. Lombard is a soldier of fortune whose openly stated moral code is "what's in it for me."

The other eight are supposedly good, decent, respectable pillars of British society. Yet none of them care about anyone besides themselves and their desires. Examine their lives and you see nothing to respect or honor.

General Information

Based on: *And Then There Were None* (novel, 1939)
Run time: 2 hr., 54 min. **Subtitles:** Yes

Writer: Sarah Phelps **Director:** Craig Viveiros

Cast

Maeve Dermody as Vera Claythorne
Aidan Turner as Philip Lombard
Burn Gorman as D.S. William Blore
Toby Stephens as Dr. Edward Armstrong
Charles Dance as Judge Lawrence Wargrave
Miranda Richardson as Emily Brent
Noah Taylor as Thomas Rogers
Sam Neill as General John MacArthur
Anna Maxwell Martin as Ethel Rogers
Douglas Booth as Anthony Marston

Film Locations

Mullion Island, Cornwall (Soldier Island distant shots: CGI house added)
Newquay, Cornwall
Kynance Cove, Lizard, Cornwall (beach)
South Devon Railway, Buckfastleigh, Devon (railway)
Mullion Cove, Cornwall (harbor scene)
Holywell Bay, Cornwall
Waddesdon Manor, Waddesdon, Buckinghamshire (restaurant interior)
Wrotham Park, South Mimms, Hertfordshire (below stairs and kitchen)
Harefield Grove Farm, London (mansion)

Take Dr. Armstrong. Phelps gives him a backstory involving post-traumatic stress disorder dating back to his service as a surgeon in the trenches during the Great War. Armstrong's high-strung, easily upset, and a closet drunk. Plenty of men suffered during the Great War but they didn't murder their patients by operating drunk. Don't give him a pass because he's somehow special. Agatha didn't.

Notice how Agatha depicts the very people we're supposed to honor and respect as being better than the rest of us. In reality, they're worse.

This version did a wonderful job highlighting the class divide. Emily Brent, the oozer of Christian charity, was openly rude, even cruel to Vera. She's disdainful and sneering of Mrs. Rogers, who's on her knees helping her to dress. When Mrs. Rogers dies, Emily mouths the correct pieties, followed by a complaint to Mr. Rogers about her breakfast eggs. Remember, Emily threw her pregnant housemaid out into the street rather than show common human decency.

When Blore comes ashore, it's obvious he's not who he claims. He doesn't quite fit the image of a gentleman industrialist. I noticed at once he didn't say the right thing or respond correctly. Everyone else noticed too.

Ne'er-do-well Anthony Marston — who died early on — automatically assumes everyone at the house party is a member of his class. When Lombard opens his mouth, Marston asks about people they have in common. Marston can't imagine that anyone exists outside his charmed circle. That explains why, after he crushes two children with his car, his sole concern was losing his driver's license for six months.

Vera encounters her own class barriers. Despite being a secretary, she doesn't belong below-stairs. She doesn't belong upstairs either, with the grand company. They all know she works for her living. Lombard accepts her. Wargrave is subtly dismissive. Blore doesn't know how to respond. The others sneer.

I didn't think the novel could be filmed, a judgment confirmed after watching five other versions. But this version did *And Then There Were None* justice; a better one than the characters deserved.

And Then There Were None (J-2017)

(*Soshite daremo inakunatta*)

Miniseries stays true to the novel while expanding the police inquiry and adding contemporary technology

Fidelity to the novel

A police procedural bookends the film and the spinster becomes an actress in contemporary Japan.

Quality of movie

That's because our copy was terrible. Beautifully acted, paced, shot. Terror mounts on the island as the victims are picked off, one by one.

I really wish TV Asahi, who produced this film, would release their Agatha Christie adaptations to the wider world, either via streaming services or on DVD. They are that good. Agatha's fans deserve to see top-quality films of her novels. I can't imagine a business leaving money on the table, but here we are.

I'm sticking with the novel's character names to make it easier.

Like *The Great Actress Murder Case* (a.k.a. *The Mirror Crack'd*, 2018), this stars Ikki Sawamura as Detective Inspector Ryuya Shokokuji, head of Criminal Investigative Unit #1 in Tokyo. He gets the baffling cases.

The novel, in case you don't remember, ends with two epilogs. The first shows the assistant commissioner of Scotland Yard and Inspector Maine discussing the case. They're baffled by ten bodies, no motives, and no sign of the neat killer who tidied up the site. They've done background checks on the victims and discovered the recording was correct. Each victim had been involved with a suspicious death but got away with it. The man who'd made the arrangements for the island party, Mr. Morris, was well-known to the police for skirting the law. Conveniently dead of a sleeping pill overdose, he was unavailable for questioning. Diaries and journals let the police build up a timeline.

The second epilog was a message in a bottle, found by a fishing trawler. It was Justice Wargrave's confession and explanation.

Until Justice Wargrave's confession is revealed, the reader knows more details about the deaths and why the victims deserved it than the police, but only the most astute reader will realize whodunnit. The victims *never* learn who set them up until the moment of death and frequently, not even then.

The adaptations play around with this. Most of them are based on the stage play, so the audience sees the judge seduce the doctor into helping him find the murderer and then betray him. The audience also sees Vera discover the judge was the evil mastermind.

Not here. The judge, like in the novel, is one more victim and if you don't know the story, you'll be as shocked as anyone else when the truth is revealed. Vera shoots Philip Lombard several times (quadruple-

Shiramine Ryô (*Yukie Nakama*), the swim tutor

Ken Ishirugi (*Toshirô Yanagiba*), the military expert

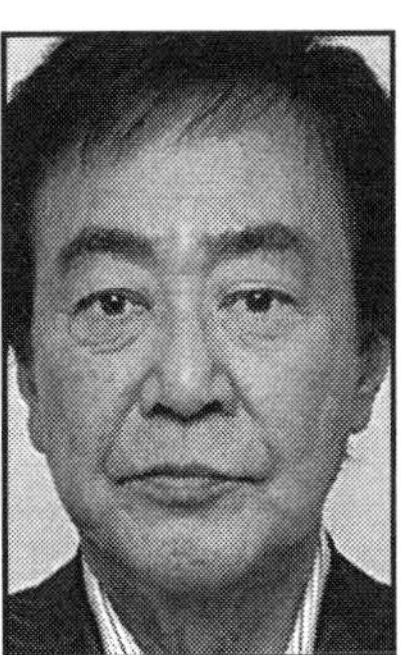

Iwamura Hyôgo (*Tsunehiko Watase*), the judge

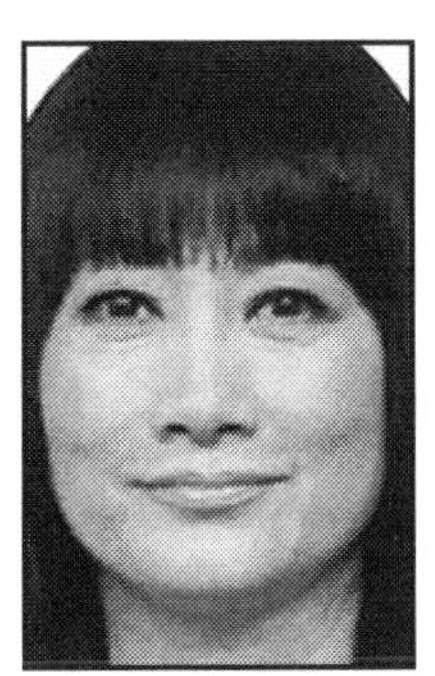

Dr. Kônami Erika (*Kimiko Yo*), the surgeon

Kumabe Kenkichi (*Jun Kunimura*), the detective

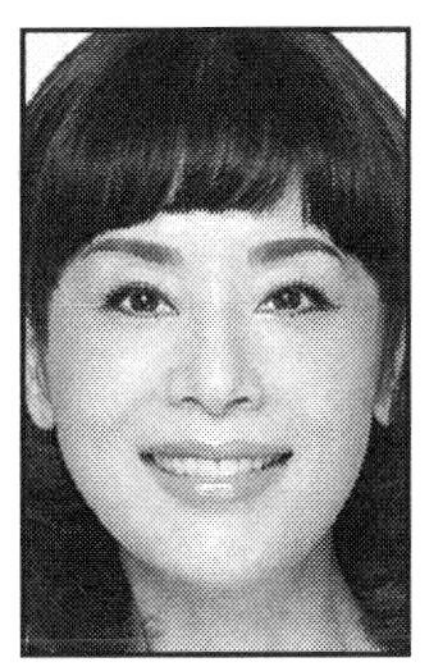

Hoshizura Ayako (*Mao Daichi*), the movie star

tap!), then staggers into the house, hallucinating all the way. She's remembering how she sent Cyril to his watery grave because she wanted her lover to inherit Cyril's money. Her guilt is overwhelming. In her room, the noose awaits. Just like in the novel, Vera hangs herself and kicks away the chair. Unlike every other version we've seen, there's no confrontation with the judge.

There are changes. Tony Marsden becomes an amateur boxer who, while drunk one night, intervenes in a mugging and accidentally murders someone. General Maxwell is now a senior member of the Japanese parliament. He sends his wife's lover into a terrorist attack he'd been told might happen. This makes him *more* guilty because other, innocent people died in that terrorist attack; people who could have been saved if he'd alerted the police. Spinster Emily Brent becomes a famous actress (which we've seen before). She forces her young, pretty housekeeper to have an abortion. There's a hint of something more in their relationship a la Brenda Vaccaro's 1989 performance, but only a hint. Dr. Armstrong becomes female, perfectly plausible in modern Japan. She also stopped drinking as a result of that patient dying and worked hard to redeem herself as a doctor. That didn't save her.

Blore, the detective, and Philip Lombard, the mercenary, have more interesting changes adding nuance to their crimes.

Blore lies in open court to the judge about a defendant's crimes. But it's not for monetary gain or to cover up his own criminal behavior. It's to get an abusive man in jail so he can't finish beating his wife to death.

Lombard is shown fighting with his men in a war zone. It's unclear how official they are so they could be mercenaries. During the fighting, his teenage daughter by a local woman (implying he's been there, on and off, for quite a while) drives up in a jeep to rescue dad from certain death. Save daughter? Die with his men? That's a more difficult choice than abandoning native troops in the jungle. He's also older than in other versions and no longer has any romantic interludes with Vera.

Vera's still Vera. Pretty and willing to murder a child to get what she wants.

The police procedural bookends the episodes and shows how Inspector Shokokuji, as brilliant and observant as Sherlock Holmes, sees clues everyone else misses. It's clear to him that the mastermind behind the crime is like masterminds everywhere. He wants to be recognized for his genius and applauded for his masterpiece. Except that murder is never art or a game.

He even invokes Sherlock Holmes! Bill, a longtime fan of Conan Doyle, spotted the trick and explained it to me. The judge shot himself and made it look like someone murdered him by using Mrs. Gibson's procedure from "The Problem of Thor Bridge." Similar to that story, the judge tied a weight to the gun and tossed the weight out of his room's second-story window. He sat down in his chair, the sheet attached to the ceiling primed to fall. When he shot himself, his hand dropped, allowing the weight to fall to the ground, taking the gun out the window with it. He used kelp for the string, knowing it would decay or be eaten. The weight was bricks, blending anonymously into the pile of bricks.

And, as a reward to the clever policeman who found it, one of the anonymous bricks contained a memory chip, like a message in a bottle tossed out at sea. The judge proves Inspector Shokokuji's point. He wants his masterpiece to be admired and written up in journals both scholarly and popular. Why else leave hidden cameras everywhere to record the murders, one by one? Why else include a taped confession and explanation?

You insects will remember my name forever! Bwah-ha-ha-ha-ha!

Something like that.

But Inspector Shokokuji is unimpressed. The judge still murdered ten people. Don't forget the shovel sticking out of his garden in his confession. That's where his accomplice is buried, similar to Justice Wargrave murdering Morris in the novel.

This is an amazing adaptation. Even Sarah Phelps' version in 2015 — otherwise very true to the text — wouldn't pass muster with the added gratuitous nudity and drug orgy. This one was marred only by the poor quality of the film. That could be easily fixed by TV Asahi making it available for streaming with English subtitles. Then a huge, new audience could enjoy this stellar version of *And Then There Were None*. Agatha would be pleased.

General Information

Based on: *And Then There Were None* (novel, 1939)
Run time: 3 hr., 33 min. **Subtitles:** Yes

Writer: Shûkei Nagasaka
Director: Akiyoshi Kimata

Cast

Ikki Sawamura as Ryuya Shôkokuji
YoshiYoshi Arakawa as Tatara Banpei

Yukie Nakama as Shiramine Ryô (Vera Claythorne)
Toshirô Yanagiba as Ken Ishirugi (Philip Lombard)
Jun Kunimura as Kumabe Kenkichi (William Blore)
Kimiko Yo as Dr. Kônami Erika (Dr. Edward Armstrong)
Tsunehiko Watase as Iwamura Hyôgo (Judge Lawrence Wargrave)
Mao Daichi as Miss Hoshizora Ayako (Emily Brent)
Isao Hashizume as Mr. Midorikawa (Thomas Rogers)
Masahiko Tsugawa as Monden Senmei (Gen. John Macarthur)
Mariko Fuji as Mrs. Midorikawa (Ethel Rogers)
Osamu Mukai as Gomyo Taku (Anthony Marston)
Zuimaro Awashima (voice, Ulick Norman Owen)

They Were Ten (F-2020)

(*Ils étaient dix*)

Ghosts and a black-shrouded avenger roam a decayed tropical island resort, adding slasher-flick vibes to dark tale

Like the 2017 Japanese version, the French version sticks to the novel. There's a police investigation and the ten unlucky guests have no idea who's pulling their strings. The closest any of the Paradise Hotel guests get is Kelly realizing she'd been tricked and Victoria finding the villain's lair by accident. Each guest slowly has his or her criminal past revealed.

But there are significant changes. They are so extensive that I can't use the novel's names because virtually every character other than Nina (Vera Claythorne) no longer has a direct correlation to the novel. Nina remains Vera, child murderess. But, in keeping with the increased nihilism of the script, Nina is even more villainous than Vera was!

How is this possible? Nina doesn't just actively encourage young Nathan to swim in the deep end. She watches him drown. And Nathan's not her single lover's nephew. Killing Nathan doesn't help her married lover Arnaud inherit wealth and a title. Killing Nathan hurts Arnaud and his wife, Barbara. Why did Nina drown their son? Because Barbara thoughtfully informed Nina that a) she's one in a string of bimbo coeds; b) Arnaud lied to them all and she's no different; c) Barbara pays the bills including for Nina's

Fidelity to the novel

Changed backstories, added police investigation, and more nihilism (if that's possible).

Quality of movie

Beautifully shot, paced, and acted. As long as you don't think too much about plausibility, it works.

"services"; d) Arnaud likes the rich lifestyle so he'll never leave; and e) Nina amuses Barbara with her naiveté. Killing Nathan was fueled by spite and revenge, pure and simple. Nina can't claim she made Arnaud's life better.

But let's go back to the beginning. We meet Nina on the French Caribbean island of Guadeloupe. She needs to get to the small, interisland airport to catch a flight. Her purse is snatched, so she meets Mathieu Le Goff and Léonie Baptista, the local law. They're helpful. Nina makes her flight, despite not having her passport or wallet. But she does have her cellphone. Thus, when Le Goff and Baptista find Nina's purse, they call her but she doesn't answer.

This sets off Le Goff's radar and, unbeknownst to the folks at the Paradise Hotel or the puppet master, he starts tracking Nina. Le Goff and Baptista discover that the pilot of the plane was poisoned and a critical page from his flight log was torn out. They get a phone call from the worried wife of one of the guests. The airfield is looking

Nina Goldberg (*Matilda Lutz*), the jilted student

Malik Alaoui (*Nassim Si Ahmed*), the penitent lawyer

Kelly Nesib (*Manon Azem*), the disloyal lover

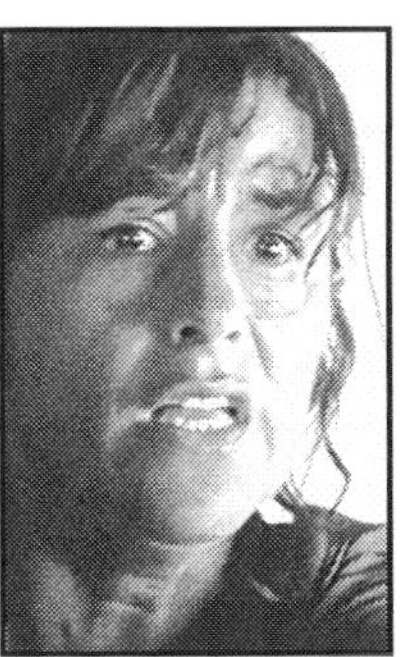
Victoria Deshotel (*Romane Bohringer*), the arrogant surgeon

Vincent Del Piero (*Patrick Mille*), the lecherous guru

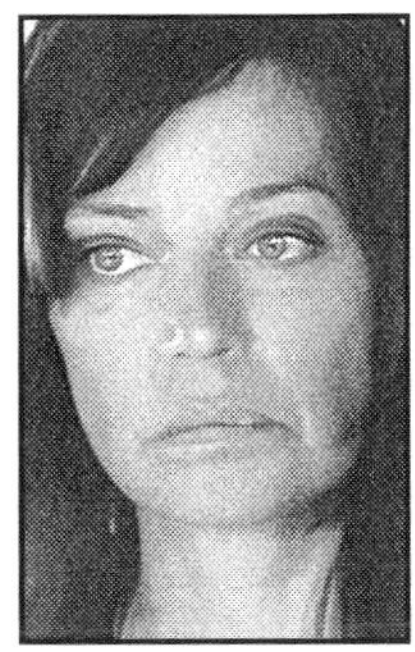
Eve Lombardi (*Marianne Denicourt*), the biased cop

for their expensive helicopter that particular guest rented.

Le Goff and Baptista's investigations bookend the five episodes, adding to the sense of urgency. They even raise the hope that they'll arrive in time to save someone. If Agatha wrote cozies, then they would, but she didn't.

Seven people arrive by plane at the island where cook/manager Myriam and handyman Eddy are waiting. Vincent the celebrity guru arrives in a helicopter he pilots himself. The eight guests are taken aback at the primitive facilities and that the people they expected to meet for business reasons aren't anywhere to be seen. The computer screen comes to life and we expect it to intone the familiar accusations.

Except it doesn't. The cryptic robotic voice gives no details about the guests' murderous pasts. This allows the ten to mostly avoid denying or confessing to each other or to the audience. Several never confess at all, although their crimes are shown in flashbacks. What you get instead are protests of innocence. Since each person has a guilty conscience, no one believes anyone else.

It's a varied bunch, too. Kelly is the dumb bimbo with the cute dog. She's convinced they're on a bizarre reality TV show. But when her dog dies from poisoned water, she heads straight into crazy town.

Victoria, the surgeon, is actively unpleasant and openly paranoid. She's not a good correlation to Dr. Armstrong. Like him, she kills a patient while operating but out of hubris, not drunkenness. She doesn't cooperate with the puppet master to find the true villain. She's too mistrustful of everyone but the guru for that.

The puppet master is Eve Lombardi, former policewoman. She's far more nihilistic than Justice Wargrave was. He killed his victims in order of culpability, saving the guiltiest for last. Eve just wants to kill them. She's not fussy about order or method. She's not patterning her murders on a nursery rhyme, although she does set up the scary altar with voodoo statuettes, removing them one by one as people die. But everyone on the island could have died quickly from drinking the poisoned water and she'd have been fine with that. Same with the deadfall and the poisonous viper leaping out of a trap that both missed their target.

General Information

Based on: *And Then There Were None* (novel, 1939)
Run time: 5 hr., 12 min. **Subtitles:** Yes

Writers: Bruno Dega, Jeanne Le Guillou
Director: Pascal Laugier

Cast

Mathieu Demy as Mathieu Le Goff
Wendy Nieto as Léonie Baptista

Matilda Anna Ingrid Lutz as Nina Goldberg
Nassim Si Ahmed as Malik Alaoui
Manon Azem as Kelly Nesib
Romane Bohringer as Victoria Deshotel
Patrick Mille as Vincent Del Piero
Marianne Denicourt as Eve Lombardi
Samuel Le Bihan as Xavier Troussaud
Guillaume de Tonquédec as Gilles Delfour
Samy Seghir as Eddy Hamraoui
Isabelle Candelier as Myriam Berto
Samuel Jouy as Arnaud
Samir Boitard as Jimmy
Virginie Ledoyen as Barbara
Jérôme Soufflet as Tom le Pilote
Fabien Baïardi as Aérodrome Manager
Julien Bodet as Julien Berto
Malick Laugier as Nathan
Mohand Mounsi as Ahmed
Richard Bohringer as Professeur Villemont
Murielle Hilaire as Sally
Jean-Christophe Brétignière as Distorted Voice

Film Location

Guadeloupe Island, France

Degree of guilt doesn't matter to *her*. Which is why she murders the innocent pilot without a qualm to conceal her tracks. Two of her victims — Eddy and Gilles — could even be construed as being poorly chosen. Eddy drove a truckload of illegal immigrants across France during a heatwave. They all died. Yet the flashbacks show that he stopped several times — despite being ordered not to — to provide water and relief from the heat. He didn't deliberately kill them. As a child, Gilles shoved a bully over a bridge in front of a train. They were both about twelve. Kids do amazingly stupid, impulsive things, and it was wrong. But it appears he remade his life.

Eve doesn't care. She's an Old Testament god where degree of guilt or extenuating circumstances don't matter. And why does she do this? Because her husband died of a heart attack on what looks like the courthouse steps in central Paris in broad daylight. Because he dressed and looked like a bum (his choice), no one rescued him. Or called an ambulance. Or called security so they could call the ambulance.

I know France is a secular country where they believe we're all just meat puppets, but I found that hard to believe. I also can't believe that's a good enough reason to execute 11 people: the nine on the island, her henchman Jimmy, and the pilot. And the dog. She's no better than anyone else on that island. She hurt so she wanted to hurt other people.

At the same time, Eve was very careful in her victim selection. She targeted people who wouldn't be looked for. Other than Vincent the guru and Gilles, no friend or family member came looking. No one. Vincent's wife called the Guadeloupe police. So did Gilles' boss. That's it.

I'll agree that they were all (except for Eddy and Gilles) guilty as sin. But so was she. I never thought I'd say Justice Wargrave was of sound mind, but he was compared to Eve. He was very careful in who he chose and how he killed them. Eve just wanted to watch people die.

Despite that, this is a great and fresh interpretation of a classic novel. Don't miss it.

V. The Rest of the Christies

Let's get one thing straight: Agatha Christie did not write cozies. She also wrote far more than mysteries. After *The Mysterious Affair at Styles* (1921), she experimented with a lighthearted espionage caper *The Secret Adversary* (1922). Then she wrote the conventional mystery *Murder on the Links* (1923), the romantic thriller *The Man in the Brown Suit* (1924), the Ruritanian romance / Wodehouse inspired *The Secret of Chimneys* (1925), and the novel that upended the conventions of the mystery genre *The Murder of Roger Ackroyd* (1926).

She also wrote nearly a dozen short stories a year, stretching her wings into new areas. She wrote mysteries, romance, thrillers, and paranormals with mystery and romance tropes. She liked strong elements of psychological horror, heading into the paranormal. The only consistent thread running through them is that people and events are not always as they seem.

This chapter is rich in stories from many genres. There's *Love From a Stranger* about marrying in haste and repenting at leisure. Tense courtroom drama in *Witness for the Prosecution*. A comedy about a very active dead body in *Spider's Web*. Murder by magic in *The Pale Horse*. There's young lovers-to-be investigating mysteries, charming women leading men into trouble, adventures on the high seas, and risque French versions of Agatha's stories.The versatility of her stories enable *The Man in the Brown Suit* to be filmed as a 1980s contemporary or *Sparkling Cyanide* as a 2003 police procedural that comments on the surveillance society. They can have their main detective removed entirely and the plot still works. Other cultures can film her novels and make them their own. Agatha's themes are universal.

From top: Many famous faces played killers, victims, and witnesses in the adaptations: Basil Rathbone, *Love from a Stranger* (1937); Britt Ekland, *Endless Night* (1972); Donald Sutherland and Faye Dunaway, *Ordeal by Innocence* (1984); Bill Bixby, *Murder Is Easy* (1982); Deborah Kerr, *Witness for the Prosecution* (1982); Kim Cattrall, *Witness for the Prosecution* (2016); Gillian Anderson and Christina Hendricks, *Crooked* House (2017); Emma Thompson and Hugh Laurie, *Why Didn't They Ask Evans?* (2022).

Marlene Dietrich in *Witness for the Prosecution* (1957)

Glenn Close in *Crooked House* (2017)

Antoine Dulery and Marius Colucci in *Family Murder Party* (F-2006)

There is no Poirot, Marple, or Tommy and Tuppence to rescue these people. This is Agatha at her darkest and most hopeful.

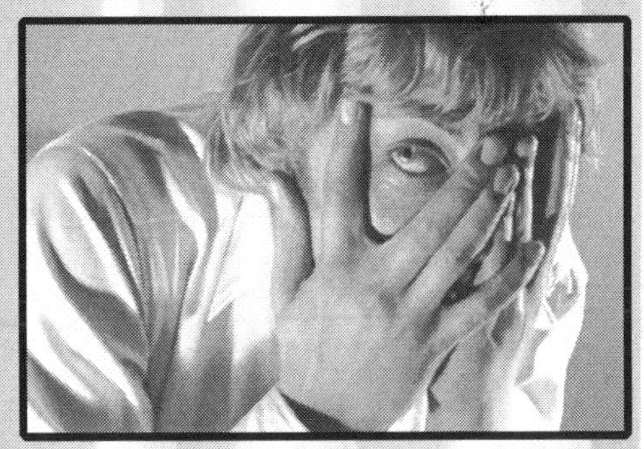
Hywel Bennett in *Endless Night* (1972)

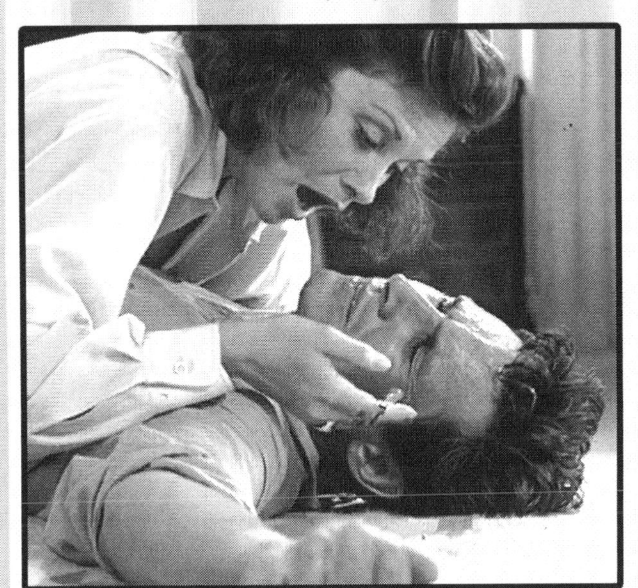
Stephanie Zimbalist and Simon Dutton in *The Man in the Brown Suit* (1989)

Rufus Sewell in *The Pale Horse* (2020)

Love from a Stranger (1937)

Carol's fiancé was unable to accept her wealth and need to see the world and pushed her into another's arms

Fidelity to text

The overall story arc remains. Plenty of name changes, additional characters, and scenes expand a very short story. How our heroine gets the money changes too: she hits big in the lottery.

Quality of movie

Pretty good, even allowing for the terrible video quality. Like it does in real life, the mood swings wildly between comedy and terror.

Love From a Stranger has a convoluted history. It began as the short story "Philomel Cottage" (1924). A couple of years later, when Agatha began writing plays, she adapted the short story and renamed it *The Stranger*. The play was never produced but it wasn't forgotten. "Philomel Cottage" was reprinted in the collection *The Listerdale Mystery* (1934), where it caught the attention of Frank Vosper.

Vosper (1899-1937) had his own dramatic life story, including his mysterious death at sea as part of a purported love triangle, but he was a talented writer and actor. He liked writing plays that he could strut his stuff in and "Philomel Cottage" fit the bill in spades. Vosper transformed the story into a play called *Love From a Stranger*. As scriptwriters do, he rewrote as he pleased, adding entire scenes made up of whole cloth. Agatha received a writing credit, possibly from reworking aspects of *The Stranger* into the new production.

The play was moderately successful and caught Hollywood's attention. It was reborn as *Love From a Stranger* with Basil Rathbone in the role that Frank Vosper wrote for himself: the dashing new lover with a hidden past.

The film's script underwent more changes so it isn't the stage version. But Agatha's original story remains: an unmarried woman who's barely keeping her head afloat financially and cannot marry her fiancé suddenly comes into money. The fiancé (expanded and dramatized in the film; in the short story he's a man with whom she has only an understanding) balks. Despite her good fortune, a wife with money of her own cuts his balls off. He can't stand it. In the movie, Ronnie the fiancé rants about how he's been slaving away in Sudan for years, waiting and saving, and finally landing a new job at home so he can finally afford to marry Cathy. But now that she's hit the lottery, he can't.

It isn't just that Cathy won big, thus making him less of a man. It's that she won at all because — *quelle horreur* — she played the French lottery. She gambled. How dare she. Now I'll agree that lotteries are an enormous money sink penalizing people who don't understand statistics. Nonetheless, someone does win in honestly run lotteries, you have to buy a ticket to

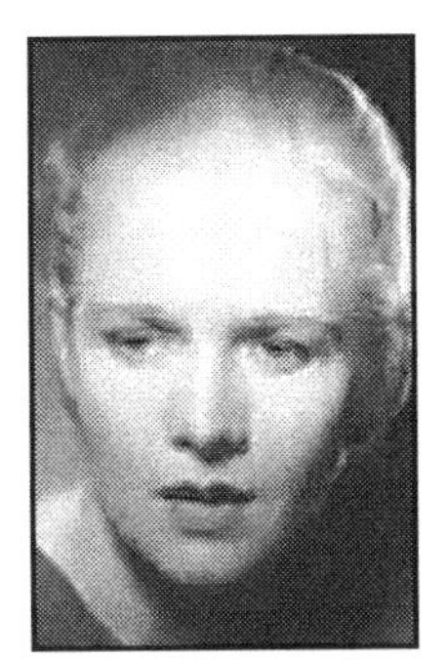

Carol Howard
(*Ann Harding*),
the unlucky winner

Gerald Lovell
(*Basil Rathbone*),
the romantic stranger

Ronald Bruce
(*Bruce Seton*),
the possessive fiancee

Kate Meadows
(*Binnie Hale*),
the close cousin

Aunt Lou
(*Jean Cadell*),
the sickly aunt

Emmy
(*Joan Hickson*),
the slightly dim maid

have a chance at all of winning, and a dollar spent now and then on a lottery ticket is a cheap way to indulge in hope and dreams.

There's probably an entire backstory for Ronnie the fiancé about why he loathes gambling and not just because the vast majority of gamblers lose everything. But we don't learn it. Instead, watching him rage at Cathy, we appreciate why she takes up with Basil Rathbone, who's caring and supportive and doesn't tell her she's an evil person for winning big in the lottery.

General Information

Based on: "Philomel Cottage" (short story, 1924)
Run time: 1 hr., 26 min. **Subtitles:** No

Writers: Frank Vosper, Frances Marion
Director: Rowland V. Lee

Cast

Ann Harding as Carol Howard
Bruce Seton as Ronald Bruce
Binnie Hale as Kate Meadows
Jean Cadell as Aunt Lou
Basil Rathbone as Gerald Lovell
Bryan Powley as Dr. Gribble
Joan Hickson as Emmy
Donald Calthrop as Hobson
Eugene Leahy as Mr. Tuttle
Ben Williams as Ship's Steward

Ronnie the fiancé did sacrifice for Cathy. He slaved for years in Sudan under what were probably awful conditions, but again, we are never shown what sacrifices he made. Instead, we watch Cathy cope with her officious boss, her live-in cousin who teaches piano, and their elderly, hypochondriac aunt who also lives with them. Cathy is poor and longs for nice things like fashionable hats. She wants to travel. To have adventures. To live. To do more than exist in a third-floor, cold-water walk-up that she shares with her cousin and her aunt. When she hits big, she sends her aunt to Brighton and sublets the apartment.

Ronnie can't get out of his own way enough to understand Cathy's dreams. He'd be an unpleasant husband, or at least it looks that way. This is a great rewrite of the short story, showing all the reasons Cathy was right to dump Ronnie.

Enter Basil Rathbone, a potential tenant to that third-floor walk-up. He's smooth, suave, sophisticated, and a gentleman of the world. Naturally, Cathy falls head over heels for him and they run off to Paris. She barely knows him. If you know your mystery tropes, Cathy, newly rich and still quite naïve, just pinned a target to herself.

Ronnie shows up in Paris along with the cousin and they discover that Cathy married Basil Rathbone. Ronnie is heartbroken, but he doesn't let that stop him from ranting at Cathy about what a fool she is. Does this make her reconsider her hasty marriage? As if.

That doesn't make Ronnie wrong. We all know the phrase "marry in haste, repent at leisure." Sometimes it works, if both partners are sane and don't expect the other to become their magical be-all and end-all soul mate who completes them.

In this case, Ronnie is dead right.

Once Cathy and Basil move off to the isolated charming cottage, everyone disappears from her life. She slowly begins to realize that charming Basil has odd and unpleasant quirks. Make sure you pay attention to the white scarf he winds about her neck. The servants let slip things about his plans that she knows nothing about. The doctor keeping tabs on Basil's heart leaves his copy of a true-crime book that includes a photograph of a notorious bigamist and wife-murderer. The picture looks awfully familiar, but will she see it in time?

Keep an eye out for Joan Hickson, the definitive Miss Marple, in one of her earliest film roles. She plays the dopey serving maid, Emmy. She's part of Philomel Cottage's staff along with her uncle, the gardener. It's decidedly odd to watch her perform in an Agatha Christie role predating Miss Marple by fifty years.

The ending slowly ratchets up the terror until Cathy discovers she's alone with a murderer. She must save herself, but she's not G.I. Jane or Wonder Woman. She's got to use her wits. She verbally spars with Basil in the manner of Scheherazade, telling one story after another, stalling for time while trying to escape. It's darned good acting and great to watch.

> *[Women are] born fools! And women's weakness is man's opportunity. … Did someone write that? Or did I think of it myself? If I did, it's good. It's very good.*
>
> Gerald Lovell

The only distraction I had was Cathy's coiffure. She has the worst hair ever in a movie. It might have been the crappy film stock but in many of her scenes, especially at the climax, she looked bald. She pulled all her hair out from the stress, I guess.

In the end, all is well again, and you could say she gets away with murder. Fully justified, naturally, because it was self-defense. Don't pass this adaptation up. It's worth searching for a better, cleaner copy. The studio let it fall out of copyright, so there are plenty of terrible versions out there. And if you should win the lottery, don't lose your head like Cathy nearly did.

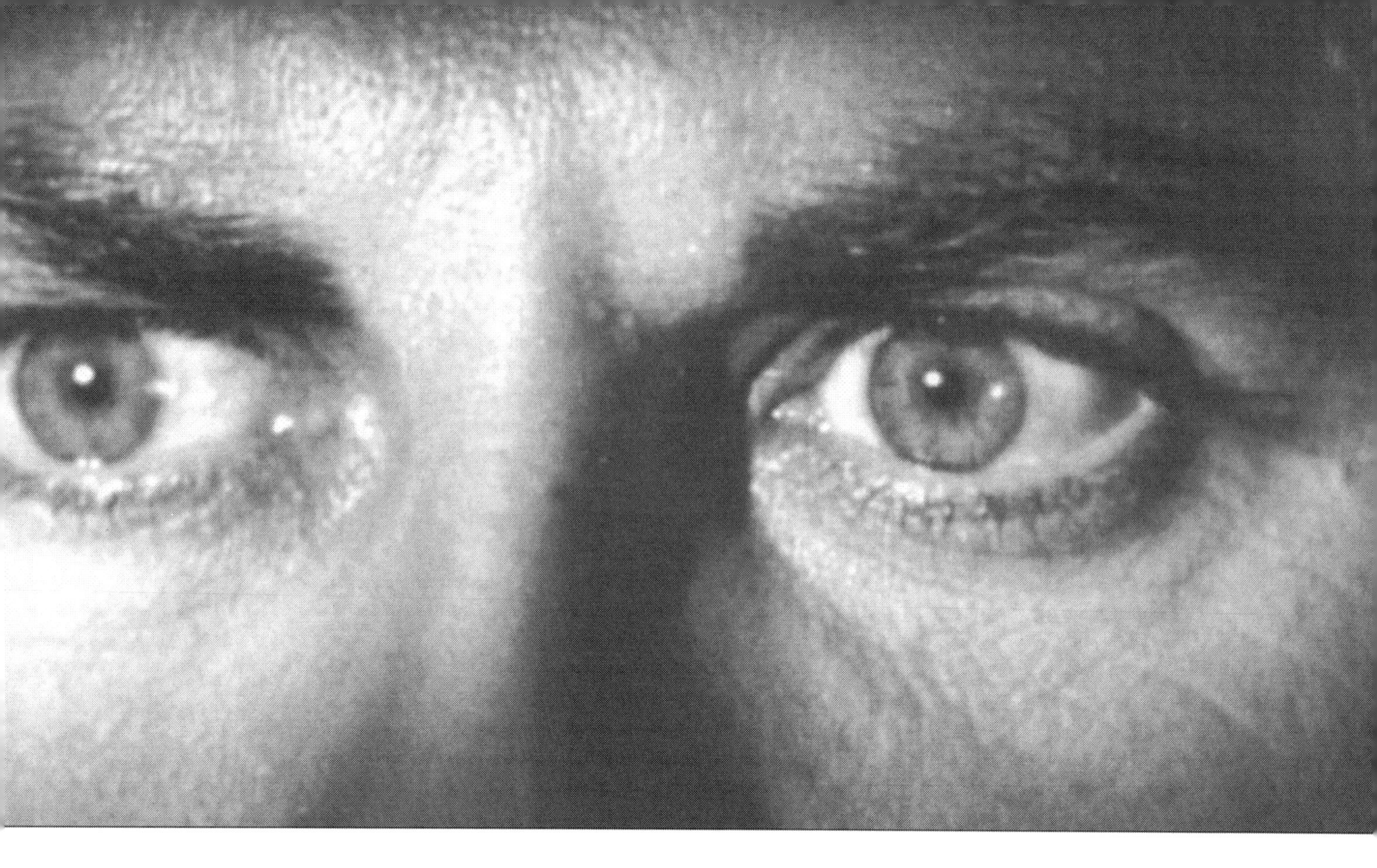

Love from a Stranger (1947)

He was tall, dark, and handsome, and Cecily couldn't resist his charms, but found danger instead of romance

Unlike the 1937 film, this version lets you know from the first moment that murder is lurking in the wings. Women are being strangled right and left in 1901 and policemen around the globe are baffled. A serial killer is on the loose; one who doesn't murder anonymous prostitutes. Instead, he chooses desperate, naïve, wealthy women who apparently have no other prospects. Murdering women with status definitely gets the police's interest.

I can see why women would want to marry Manuel Cortez (a very good John Hodiak). But I couldn't believe Cecily, our heroine, was that needy. She is obviously getting long in the tooth, but she's got a fiancé (Nigel Lawrence) slaving away overseas for years until they can marry. However, she doesn't care. Nor did it look reasonable that she had no other prospects until she hit big in the French lottery. Her flat, shared with her cousin and their aunt, was plush and crowded with furnishings, art, and knickknacks. They dressed well. They weren't one step away from the slum. She had a small income from a trust left by her father, enough to support them. That alone is a lure.

We don't watch any kind of backstory about her relationship with her cousin or aunt, or their supposed poverty. Instead, Cecily wakes up from a nightmare (a blatant signal of bad things to come) and is reassured by cousin Mavis that she won the French lottery. Since Cecily lived off the family trust instead of demeaning, dead-end jobs a la the 1937 version, we also don't understand why she's so desperate to gad about and travel. What was stopping her? Not dire poverty.

She's delighted with her winnings, and we assume that she's sharing with cousin and aunt, but this isn't spelled out. Instead, I got the distinct impression that Cecily was blowing money on herself. She gave them some financial assistance, but not as much as you would expect.

Cecily also got written up in the newspaper as a lottery winner, and the article attracts Manuel's attention. He's looking for a fresh victim and naïve, dopey Cecily is the perfect target. She's thrilled by his

Fidelity to text

Like the 1937 version, this film was freely adapted from Agatha's short story "Philomel Cottage" and Frank Vosper's stage play, *Love From a Stranger*. Names, behaviors, even the time setting got reworked and the opening is wildly different.

Quality of movie

It could have been better. A lot better. John Hodiak ably filled Basil Rathbone's shoes, but Sylvia Sidney was too old for the part of our naïve, lottery-winning heroine.

Cecily Harrington
(*Sylvia Sidney*),
the unlucky winner

Manuel Cortez
(*John Hodiak*),
the romantic stranger

Nigel Lawrence
(*John Howard*),
the nice fiancee

Mavis Wilson
(*Ann Richards*),
Cecily's cousin

Auntie Loo-Loo
(*Isobel Elsom*),
the worried relative

Dr. Horace Gribble
(*Philip Tonge*),
the true crime fan

attentions.

Then fiancé Nigel returns to England and Cecily. Unlike the 1937 version, we aren't given a reason to dislike him or approve of Cecily dumping him. He is a concerned and loving man. He doesn't rant and rave at Cecily for hitting big in the lottery. He doesn't tell her that they shouldn't travel. He's good-looking, he's hard-working, he doesn't demonstrate any bad habits. In short, he's a dream guy for 1901. But no. Again, this didn't make sense.

Nigel spots a rotter when he meets Manuel and investigates. Manuel's background is suspiciously clean, even for 1901 when it was easy to pick up stakes, change your name, and start over somewhere else. Nigel tries to warn Cecily, but she doesn't listen.

She was so dumb, so pliable. She did whatever Manuel told her. She showed no curiosity about his background, swallowing whatever story he told her. She didn't notice when Manuel gave her obvious hints about his past that any sensible woman should have noticed. The audience sure does, because the opening told us he's a Bluebeard without the beard. This kills any of the suspense, except for when Cecily will wake up and smell the coffee.

What made this really unbelievable was Cecily and Manuel had zero chemistry together. Without fireworks between them, why did she run off with him? Accept every word he says? They don't make you believe that they're crazy about each other.

Another flaw was the film's lethargic pacing. There was plenty of time to beef up Cecily's relationship with her cousin, aunt, and Nigel, as well as explain better why they couldn't marry. It felt like the scriptwriter didn't have an imagination and so Cecily was bland and dopey because the plot demanded it. Sylvia Sidney did the best she could with her part, but she wasn't given much to work with.

The film got better as it neared the end. Nigel kept investigating with cousin Mavis and he has the sense to involve Scotland Yard. They had more chemistry together than anyone else in the film. But of course, no one knows where Cecily and Manuel live because he told her not to tell anyone. Not so much as a postcard to her only living relatives, people with whom she lived for years, and of course, dopey Cecily agreed to live in isolation with a virtual stranger.

General Information

Based on: "Philomel Cottage" (short story, 1924)
Run time: 1 hr., 21 min. **Subtitles:** No

Writers: Philip MacDonald and Frank Vosper
Director: Richard Whorf

Cast

Sylvia Sidney as Cecily Harrington
John Hodiak as Manuel Cortez
Ann Richards as Mavis Wilson
John Howard as Nigel Lawrence
Isobel Elsom as Auntie Loo-Loo
Ernest Cossart as Billings
Philip Tonge as Dr. Horace Gribble
Anita Sharp-Bolster as Ethel
Frederick Worlock as Inspector Hobday
Phyllis Barry as Waitress
Billy Bevan as Taxi Driver
Colin Campbell as Bank Teller
David Cavendish as Policeman
Charles Coleman as Hotel Doorman
Bob Corey as Taxi Driver
Abe Dinovitch as Undetermined Secondary Role
Eddie Dunn as New York Police Detective
Eugene Eberle as Bellboy
John Goldsworthy as Clerk
Keith Hitchcock as Policeman
Donald Kerr as Undetermined Secondary Role
Nolan Leary as Man in Bar
Gerald Rogers as Postman
Brick Sullivan as Liverpool Bobby

At last, the penny drops and Cecily begins developing a brain. Too many questionable things happen, and she can't ignore them anymore. When Manuel is racing home to murder her, you'll be sure you know the ending. This was the movie's biggest surprise. Once Cecily and Manuel move to the isolated cliffside cottage, the film gives us numerous views of the ocean breaking on the rocky shore, the cliff looming overhead. You'll be positive this scenic deathtrap plays a critical role in the climax (Chekov's cliff in other words). You will also be wrong.

As expected, Nigel and the police show up in the nick of time, rescuing Cecily from her own foolishness. Manuel gets his just desserts, and it's gruesome for a 1947 film. And then it ends with Cecily and Nigel in a clinch without another word.

There are good things in this film. John Hodiak — whose career was cut short by a heart attack at age 41 — gave a flawless performance as the seductive serial killer. There are moments of comedy with railway station clerks. There are close calls where the suspense ramps up, only to vanish like sea spray in the air. The clothes are fantastic. No real person in 1901 ever enjoyed as fabulous a wardrobe as Cecily does. Even when she was supposedly poor, she was well-dressed. The costume designer was Michael Woulfe, largely forgotten today but he designed the most glamorous evening gowns for his stars. He did nightclub gowns too. Cecily, no matter what she's doing, looks great. Great nightgowns, great day dresses, spectacular evening dresses, and hats to die for. You'll have plenty of time to admire Michael Woulfe's artistry while waiting for something to happen.

So should you spare the time for this version of *Love From a Stranger*? For completeness' sake, yes. Otherwise, stick with the 1937 version. Uneven as it was, it was far better at explaining why the heroine chose to walk away from everyone she knew, abandon her faithful fiancé, and run off with a charismatic stranger. This one never bothered.

Witness for the Prosecution (1957)

Dietrich, Power, Laughton, Lanchester plus Billy Wilder's script and direction created a top-notch courtroom drama

Fidelity to the play

The film added flashbacks, meetings, fleshed out Sir Wilfred's character, and added Nurse Plimsoll, doing her darnedest to manage a cantankerous patient.

Quality of movie

What a stunner. It's beautifully shot, acted, paced, tightly scripted with snappy dialog, and features both comic relief and high courtroom drama.

If you've never seen the movie, go watch it now and come back for the review. This is one of those movies (like Audrey Hepburn and Cary Grant in *Charade* (1963)) that can only be viewed once. In all subsequent viewings, you are not watching the same movie since you know the surprise that's coming.

This doesn't dilute the pleasure: You'll hear every line of dialog differently; you'll interpret Christine's testimony differently, and most of all, you won't see Leonard Vole the same way. The movie will still be terrific, but the climax won't seize you by the throat and shake you like a terrier toying with a rat.

Witness For the Prosecution has a complex history. It began in 1925 as a short story, "Traitor's Hands." Agatha disliked her ending and decades later rewrote it as a play, expanding and updating it, and improving the ending.

The film follows Agatha's 1953 play, with added flashbacks setting up Leonard and Christine, as well as Leonard's meetings with Emily French. And of course, Sir Wilfred gets an entire backstory that didn't exist in the play. Sir Wilfred is recovering from a heart attack and watching him in the courtroom, you wonder if he's going to have another on the spot as he struggles to save his innocent client from his evil, conniving wife's testimony. Leonard Vole will hang for sure if he doesn't.

Although Marlene Dietrich's performance as Christine is what most people remember best from *Witness*, and she and Tyrone Power share top billing, it's really Charles Laughton's movie. He's in the majority of scenes as he tries to get justice done. Watch Laughton play with his monocle. He uses it to test clients of innocence or guilt, to distract attention from something else, and at the climax. He flashes it to draw attention to the murder weapon.

Watch him play with his pills during the trial, organizing them into neat grids to help him think. Chaotic alignments show when he's puzzled; when order returns, he's worked out a solution. Watch him put the prosecuting attorney in his place and force the police inspector to recall the scars he bears from their last meeting in court. Watch him spar with Nurse Plimsoll over his health, his schedule, his naps, his clothes, his bath, his cigars and brandy, and what cases are acceptable to take on. Miss Plimsoll comes around to his way of thinking right after the climax, encouraging

Christine Vole
(*Marlene Dietrich*),
the protective wife

Leonard Vole
(*Tyrone Power*),
the weak husband

Sir Wilfrid Roberts
(*Charles Laughton*),
the ailing barrister

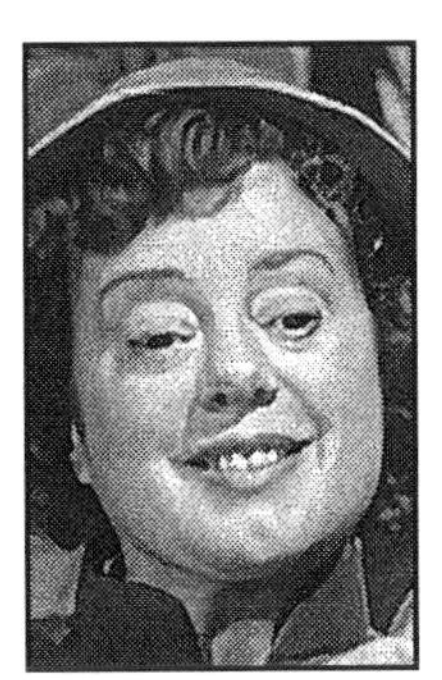

Miss Plimsoll
(*Elsa Lanchester*),
the firm nurse

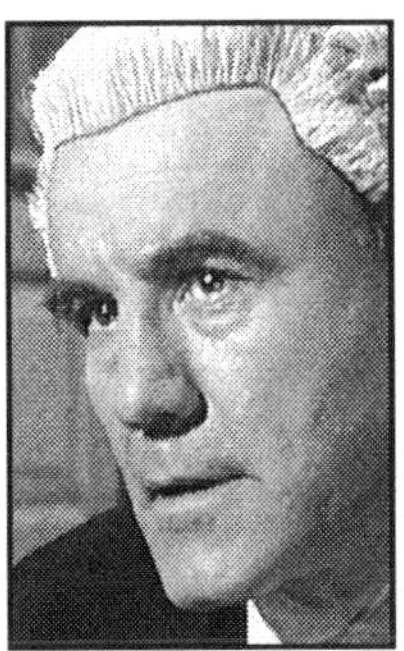

Mr. Myers
(*Torin Thatcher*),
the top prosecutor

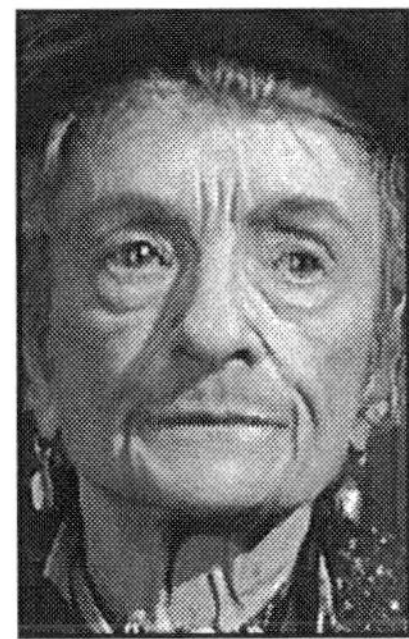

Janet MacKenzie
(*Una O'Connor*),
the observant servant

Sir Wilfred to take on the new case for the defense.

Miss Plimsoll is played by Elsa Lanchester, Laughton's real-life wife, and their relationship shows. Every scene between them is suffused with good-natured humor, even when he's being astoundingly rude. Miss Plimsoll is a very good nurse, and she's seen it all before. Or rather, she thought she had, until she gets the surprise of her life too.

By the way, her name "plimsoll" is a Britishism for Keds-type slip-on sneakers. The scriptwriters, Harry Kurnitz and Billy Wilder, came up with that name as a tiny, added amusement. Agatha, however, chose the name "Vole" for Leonard's last name. A vole is a small, furry rodent but it's also a slang term for winning all the tricks in some English card games. The name fits Leonard, a guy always looking for the main chance, who lives by his wits, who's always got an angle or a perfectly plausible explanation for why he's got his hand in the cookie jar. He would never do anything so mundane as get a real job and settle down. That would be boring and beneath him, unlike, say, living off a woman. Or several women.

However, a man can be a user and a cad without being a murderer. Tyrone Power plays Leonard and if you've only remembered him as a slab of pretty-boy beefcake in costume dramas, you'll be impressed. He was outstanding in this part, making you understand why Emily French was smitten even though she should have known better. Power was 43 when he made *Witness*; it was his final film as he died of a heart attack at age 44 in 1958.

While Emily French was a fool for Leonard, her housekeeper Janet MacKenzie knew better. She recognized Leonard right away as a deadbeat, untrustworthy loser getting by on charm. She has her own reasons for accusing Leonard of murder: 80,000 of them. She's got a great scene in the Old Bailey, sparring with both Sir Wilfred and the presiding judge. She gives them both as good as she gets, turning in another memorable performance.

Then there's Marlene Dietrich, playing Christine. Watch the flashback carefully where she meets Leonard. It sets up her character. She'll do just about anything to escape the ruins of Berlin. She's singing, playing the accordion, and showing off her legs to the soldiers in a basement dive when they meet. It wouldn't be a surprise if she did "private" performances for better-heeled clients to keep fed and safe. Keep an eye out for the poster advertising her talents. It might remind you of the role that made Marlene a star way back in 1930: *The Blue Angel*. Watch how she negotiates with Leonard over a spoonful of instant coffee and understand that a desperate, hungry woman will willingly do anything for food, safety, and warmth. When you see her in that rat-infested basement cabaret, keep in mind that she was 56 during filming.

The question you'll have from watching this flashback is: How much of what Christine says in court is real? This woman is carved from ice; remote and unemotional. Is there passion under that Teutonic exterior? Does she love her much-younger husband or is she merely grateful to him for getting her the heck out of Berlin? Now that he's no longer useful, will she discard him and move on? How does she really feel about Leonard's relationship with Emily French? Marlene Dietrich did not win an Oscar for this role but she should have. People simply couldn't believe that was her, all the way through the film.

This version of *Witness For the Prosecution* is one of the best Agatha Christie adaptations. Put it on your must-see list at once and for God's sake, don't read the Wikipedia summary before you watch it. You'll want to experience that amazing climax as it should be; fresh, raw, and unspoiled.

General Information

Based on: *Witness for the Prosecution* (play, 1953), from "Traitor's Hands" (short story, 1925)
Run time: 1 hr., 56 min. **Subtitles:** No

Writers: Billy Wilder, Harry Kurnitz
Director: Billy Wilder

Cast

Tyrone Power as Leonard Vole
Marlene Dietrich as Christine Vole
Charles Laughton as Sir Wilfrid Roberts
Elsa Lanchester as Miss Plimsoll
John Williams as Brogan-Moore
Henry Daniell as Mayhew
Ian Wolfe as Carter
Torin Thatcher as Mr. Myers
Norma Varden as Mrs. Emily Jane French
Una O'Connor as Janet MacKenzie
Francis Compton as Judge
Philip Tonge as Inspector Hearne
Ruta Lee as Diana

Sir Wilfrid: *Oh, pardon, Mrs. Vole. [Softly to Brogan-Moore] Handle her gently especially when you break the news of the arrest. Bear in mind, she's a foreigner. So be prepared for hysterics and even a fainting spell. Better have smelling salts ready, a box of tissues and a nip of brandy.*

Christine Vole: *[Enters] I do not think that will be necessary. I never faint because I'm not sure that I will fall gracefully and I never use smelling salts because they puff up the eyes.*

The Spider's Web (1960)

It's murder most fun as Clarissa and her friends play hide the body to save her stepdaughter and hubby

Fidelity to the play

It's a virtually line-for-line reenactment of the play, other than Pippa being nearly suffocated by the murderer.

Quality of movie

Funny, frothy, ridiculous, and as light as air. If you can accept the very stagy sets and the odd, often incongruous music, you'll enjoy this bit of murderous fluff.

The Spider's Web is a homicidal *I Love Lucy* episode. Glynis Johns portrays Lucy Ricardo, but since this is British, she's named Clarissa Hailsham-Brown. Long-suffering husband Ricky is renamed Henry Hailsham-Brown. The cartoon opening and closing credits with felonious flies and irritated spider policemen set the tone. The spritely, buoyant, sometimes jarringly unsuitable music adds to the skewed atmosphere. The very stagy backgrounds finish off the otherworldly sense of everything being off about 37 degrees. Some of the walls are obviously painted sets and not real walls with real paintings, like you expect in a movie. You'll keep thinking you entered a parallel dimension.

The stage design is probably offbeat because *Spider's Web* was originally a play Agatha wrote in 1954. It enjoyed several successful theatrical runs, and Charles Osborne novelized it in 2001.

If, dear reader, parts of the plot seem familiar, that's because they are. Agatha reworked four plot points from earlier properties:

* The first was lifted from the Poirot short story "The Adventure of the Cheap Flat" (1924). The Hailsham-Browns rent the fully furnished Copplestone Court for a song because they have the necessary last name.

* The treasure everyone is searching for but doesn't recognize as valuable is a rare postage stamp on an envelope containing other papers of interest. This plot point dates back to "A Case of the Buried Treasure" (1941), renamed "Strange Jest," a Miss Marple short story.

* Pippa believes she's guilty of murder via her voodoo experiments. That tidbit came from the Poirot novel, *Evil Under the Sun* (1941).

* Finally, the bridge game alibi dates back to the Poirot short story "The King of Clubs" (1923).

What's original is Clarissa Hailsham-Brown's vivid supposings and overactive imagination. Agatha does like using her repertory company of stock characters, putting them in various situations and making them jump on command, but she never wrote anyone else quite like Clarissa. Loopy, zany, sexy, adored by her amused husband, Clarissa doesn't live in the same universe as anyone around her. She is unique. Only Tuppence comes closest to her, other than Agatha herself. As the youngest

Clarissa Hailsham-Brown (*Glynis Johns*), the lady of the house

Inspector Lord (*Peter Butterworth*), the investigator

Sir Rowland Delahaye (*Jack Hulbert*), the guardian

Mildred Peake (*Cecily Courtneidge*), the gardener

Pippa Hailsham-Brown (*Wendy Turner*), the stepdaughter

Oliver Costello (*Ferdy Mayne*), the threat

by far of three children, she spent much of *her* play time "supposing" stories in her head.

In *Spider's Web* (the producers added "The" to the film's title for no discernible reason) Clarissa is faced with a classic sitcom situation. Her dear husband is bringing home — on very short notice — very important people for a high-level diplomatic meeting, and she has to have everything perfect. Meanwhile, there are house guests to amuse, her stepdaughter is practicing voodoo, it's the butler and cook's night out, and the gardener has been conducting open warfare with them. As an added irritation, the household has been receiving mysterious phone calls.

Could things get worse? Sure they could.

Henry's ex-wife's louche lover shows up, unannounced and unwanted. His evil ex-wife never appears but she's a real piece of work, making it understandable why Henry the diplomat married Clarissa the ditz. The ex-wife is vicious, self-centered, and utterly disinterested in their daughter, Pippa, unless she can be used to torture Henry and Clarissa or manipulate money out of them. Oliver Costello is exactly the type of lover an ex-wife like that would choose. He is suave, charming, and her drug-supplier. Pippa's afraid of him, and he's not above blackmailing Clarissa by threatening to take Pippa away.

Clarissa, fearing that Henry will show up at any moment with the VIPs, gets the gardener to show Oliver the door. With the house empty, she races around doing last-minute tidying and discovers Oliver's dead body behind the sofa.

What to do, what to do. As she's panicking, Pippa enters the room, sees the body, and announces that she murdered Oliver. Clarissa doesn't ask Pippa how she killed him. It seems clear enough: His head was bashed in. A teenaged girl could easily slam a fireplace poker into the back of the head of an unsuspecting man.

Clarissa summons the three men staying at the house, arranges the bridge game alibi, and talks them into moving the body into the secret passage to protect Pippa. The movie threatens to end early with them burying Oliver in the freshly dug sweet pea trench, but the police show up because somebody informed them that a dead body was lying around Copplestone Court.

The police inspector is not cowed by the houseguests, including Sir Rowland, the local justice of the peace. He handles the servants (who returned early and so are also underfoot) with aplomb. In Clarissa, however, he meets his match. He sees through the bridge game alibi (like Poirot, he discovers a card on the floor under the couch and knows that game was a fraud). The gardener, Miss Peake, reveals the existence of the secret passage. Over Clarissa's objections, the passage gets opened and Oliver Costello's body falls out. Considering he got his head bashed in, it's surprisingly bloodless.

Everyone leaves the room, the coroner is called in, and when the coroner arrives, the body has vanished. The coroner is suspicious about the police inspector's mental state. The police inspector is apoplectic.

It's left to Lucy — I mean Clarissa — to solve the murder, get the body out of the house, and clean everything up before Henry arrives with his diplomat guests. A lot of running around takes place, upstairs and down, and the body is found again, but this time, in Sir Rowland's bed. Add "who moved Oliver" to Clarissa's to-do list.

This is, I believe, the only time Agatha played with musical bodies. Other people have. Alfred Hitchcock did in *The Trouble with Harry* (1955). Donald Westlake did in *The Busy Body* (1966), filmed in 1967. There's also that cinematic classic *Weekend at Bernie's* (1989). But not Agatha. Yet here, in *Spider's Web*, she did.

That alone is reason enough to watch this little gem. It has its flaws. It's stagy. The cameraman must have believed he couldn't move the camera around and filmed the action as though he was sitting in row 5, seat 17 of the theater. The actors have to make up for the static camera with energy and timing and for the most part, they do. Glynis Johns is a wonder, and if you've only seen her as Mrs. Banks in *Mary Poppins* (1964), you're in for a treat. The musical score can only be described as weird. It highlights the action but as if everything happening on screen is a comic soufflé of a sitcom and not a murder mystery.

Like Clarissa, *The Spider's Web* is unique in the Agatha Christie canon.

General Information

Based on: *Spider's Web* (play, 1954)
Run time: 1 hr., 28 min. **Subtitles:** No

Writers: Eldon Howard and Albert G. Miller
Director: Godfrey Grayson

Cast

Glynis Johns as Clarissa Hailsham-Brown
John Justin as Henry Hailsham-Brown
Wendy Turner as Pippa Hailsham-Brown
Peter Butterworth as Inspector Lord
Anton Rodgers as Sgt. Jones
Jack Hulbert as Sir Rowland Delahaye
Basil Dignam as Hugo Birch
Ronald Howard as Jeremy Warrender
Cicely Courtneidge as Mildred Peake
David Nixon as Elgin
Joan Sterndale-Bennett as Mrs. Elgin
Ferdy Mayne as Oliver Costello
Robert Raglan as Dr. Berry

I wonder why it is that nobody ever believes me?

CLARISSA HAILSHAM-BROWN

Endless Night (1972)

Desire and lust burn brightly in this tragic tale of blighted love that ends in murder and madness

Endless Night (1967) is one of Agatha's best novels. However, it can only be read once. The second time around, it's a very different book. The same is true of the movie versions. There are two, this one and the wrong one with Miss Marple shoehorned in. Yes, you read that right. Miss Marple involved herself with Mike and Ellie Rogers. Watch that movie if you must for completeness. Watch this one to see the novel made flesh.

There's a fair amount of flesh in the movie, much more so than in the text. The novel's flesh is implied because Agatha wasn't that kind of a writer. Still, when Mike comes home to Gypsy's Acre to meet his true love, he describes it as being like a sailor coming home from the sea. Well. I was in the Navy. I know what sailors do as soon as they get home to their lover and close the door. The movie spells it out for you in a way the book does not.

The movie also gives you a much more dramatic final murder than the book does, including still more naked flesh. But it worked, with the added, strange feeling of being trapped in a supervillain's lair and a callback to the past. I can understand why Agatha was taken aback. It must have been jarring to watch what some hack screenwriter did to her beautifully written prose. But words are words and films are films and film is a visual medium. Mood and emotion must be conveyed visually.

There's a lot more hormones crashing about that were implied in the book and made flesh on film. Watch Mike meet Ellie, then meet her again and again. Each time you can see the waves of sex radiating off the two of them. He wants her, she wants him, and they both get what they want. When Mike's mother finds out, she's worried. When Ellie's family finds out, they're livid. They are concerned for very different reasons than Mike's mother, but their concerns are equally well-founded.

I'll say upfront this is an uneven movie with some jarring artistic choices. I've no idea why the film opens with crashing waves unless it's to imply that what follows is as impossible to stop as the raging tides. Watch Mike, looking very sharp, bidding on a gorgeous Renoir at Christie's auction house. He loses

Fidelity to text

Claudia and her murder disappear and annoying relatives show up more often. A veiled reference to sex in the novel gets fleshed out as does the last murder. Otherwise, it's spot-on.

Quality of movie

Haunting, elegiac, wistful, creepy, underrated; watch it and you'll understand why Ellie fell head-over-heels for dreamy ne'er-do-well Mike Rogers.

Michael Rogers (*Hywel Bennett*), the amoral rascal

Ellie Thomsen (*Hayley Mills*), the naïve heiress

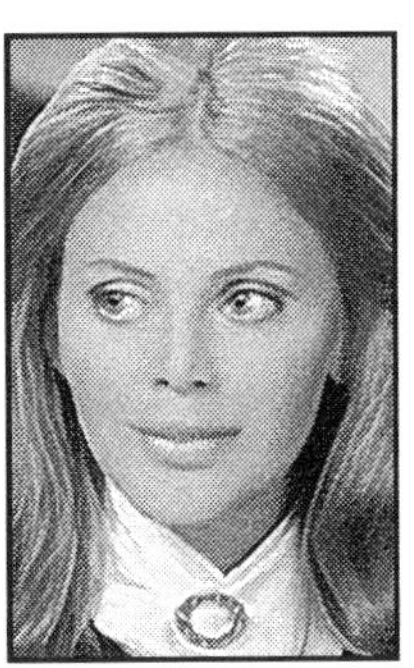

Greta (*Britt Ekland*), the irritating friend

Santonix (*Per Oscarsson*), the wary architect

Andrew Lippincott (*George Sanders*), the family attorney

Miss Townsend (*Patience Collier*), the threatening sibyl

the bid and you think "how sad." He wanted that painting. He loves beauty. Then you discover that despite driving a Rolls-Royce, he couldn't have afforded that painting. He's a hired chauffeur, that's not his car, and he's virtually penniless. Scene after scene, Mike demonstrates how much he appreciates, wants, and craves what he can't afford, what he can't have.

The house he drives clients to inspect in Italy is a good example. Mike meets the architect, Santonix, and they're kindred souls. Mike understands what Santonix can build in a way the crass clients never will. Could Santonix build Mike his dream house on his dream land? Sure, if the ailing Santonix lives long enough, and Mike can come up with a few million quid.

Then he meets Ellie on Gypsy's Acre, dancing across the meadow with the sea behind her like an elfin princess. He's smitten. He has no idea she's a fabulously wealthy heiress so he treats her like a normal girl, which she loves. But as they meet and meet again, there are … hints of oddness. Of strangeness. But they elope to Wales and then it's too late for Ellie's family to do anything about her marrying some working-class bloke with delusions of grandeur.

Ellie buys Gypsy's Acre despite the eerie warnings from Miss Townsend, the resident crazy gypsy, who walks Siamese cats on leashes. Ellie pays Santonix to build them their fabulous house despite more weird warnings and strange things happening.

They love the dream house. Personally, the house was a nightmare. That reverse roofline in England's climate? I guarantee the roof leaked within one week. It's a bizarrely automated house operated by remote-control, with magical windows, walls that rearrange themselves, retracting roofs, and a retracting floor with a pool underneath. Pay attention to the pool; you'll see it again when Mike's buried past rears up. The movie is worth watching just for the scenes of Santonix's interior design. If you think the '70s were all dirty hippies and muddy tie-dye, you're wrong. It was also a time for building houses suitable for a supervillain's lair.

Ellie provides Mike with everything he ever wanted, including his own, fully-subsidized antiques business where he's surrounded by beautiful objects. They're happy until Greta, Ellie's hot blonde companion, shows up. Ellie's relatives discover — at last! — they have something in common with Mike. They all loathe managing, bossy, controlling Greta. Ellie relies completely on Greta to a worrisome degree, something everyone disapproves of.

Then Ellie dies in a tragic riding accident as foretold by Miss Townsend. Mike is bereft and sleepwalks through the days and nights after her death. He really loved Ellie. He also loses Santonix, visiting the architect in the hospital as he dies. Santonix revives enough to ask Mike why he didn't "go the other way." It's a reminder that Santonix, like Mike's mother, knows him for what he truly is under his charming exterior.

Mike goes slowly crazy. He sees Ellie after her death but she doesn't see him. He realizes what he lost. He begins to understand the tragedy he set in motion because he wanted what he wanted and didn't care what he had to do to get it.

The tragic ending arrives inexorably as one lie after another is unveiled. True motivations are revealed, and lovers discover they don't want the same thing at all. Their goals are diametrically opposed, so one of them has to die. It's at the climax that you discover, as the reader discovers in the last two chapters of the novel, that what you thought you knew was wrong. All those red herrings, the ominous warnings about tragedy, the foreboding atmosphere; they concealed something else. A secret meeting is unearthed and a meticulously planned crime is revealed.

Endless Night is a tragedy, an elegy for what might have been, a wistful remembrance of wrong choices leading to a dreadful outcome. But the ending was inevitable because of Mike Rogers' character. Like Ellie was born to sweet delight, he was born to endless night.

This is a sadly undervalued movie. Watch it, then watch it again for a radically different experience. Like the tide, it's not the same twice.

General Information

Based on: *Endless Night* (novel, 1967)
Run time: 1 hr., 35 min. **Subtitles:** Yes

Writer: & Director: Sidney Gilliat

Cast

Hayley Mills as Ellie Thomsen
Hywel Bennett as Michael Rogers
Britt Ekland as Greta
Per Oscarsson as Santonix
George Sanders as Andrew Lippincott
Aubrey Richards as Dr. Philpott
Ann Way as Mrs. Philpott
Patience Collier as Miss Townsend
Peter Bowles as Reuben
Lois Maxwell as Cora
David Bauer as Uncle Frank
Helen Horton as Aunt Beth
Madge Ryan as Michael's Mother
Shirley Jones as Mills' singing voice
Windsor Davies as Sgt. Keene
Walter Gotell as Constantine
Geoffrey Chater as Coroner
David Healy as Jason
Bob Keegan as Innkeeper
Robert O'Neil as Broker
Mischa De La Motte as Maynard
Nicholas Courtney as Second Auctioneer
Leo Genn as Psychiatrist
Steven Wallen as Young Michael

Film Locations

St. James's, London (street scene)
Christie's Auction House, London (auction)
Albergo San Pietro, Salerno, Italy
Isle of Wight (home location)
Grim's Dyke House, Harrow Weald (asylum)

Mist (I-1973)

(*Dhund*)

Indian audiences take to obscure Christie play about spousal abuse, thwarted passion, and revenge

The Unexpected Guest (1958) is one of Agatha's lesser-known plays. Its working title was *Fog*. It did well in its inaugural run but seems to have been ignored afterwards. Charles Osborne novelized it in 1999, adding only enough connective tissue to make a script read like a novel.

In India, however, *The Unexpected Guest* took on a life of its own. Starting with this version, it's been filmed six times in various Indian languages and under different titles. We chose *Dhund* because it had subtitles *and* it set the stage for subsequent films.

The film made far more changes to the play than Osborne did. We experience Rani's misery (she's Thakur's unhappy wife), Thakur's brutality and craziness, and how it torments the household. Thakur's stepmother is miserable and trapped, but if *he* dies, her son, his half-brother, would inherit the estate. The son is about sixteen and has been driven insane by Thakur's cruelty.

The two servants (I guarantee there are more bustling about offscreen including whoever dresses, bathes, and toilets a man crippled from the waist down) get time too. Housemaid Radha is afraid of Thakur, but dutiful, obedient, and happy to cooperate with the police. Banke Lal is the equivalent of a butler.

Fidelity to text

Greatly fleshed-out characters, the butler gets a star turn, and Bollywood songs and dances!

Quality of movie

Involving and increasingly horrifying as Thakur's cruelty is revealed. Singing and dancing scenes integrate surprisingly well into the plot.

He runs the household but maintains a life of his own. He steals every scene from his first appearance watching a gyrating dancer in a "house of entertainment." The subtitles said brothel, but it didn't look like the dancer was a prostitute since she didn't go upstairs with any of her avid audience. It was the most chaste movie brothel I've ever seen.

Nor did the avid audience or musicians scatter when the police arrived. After all, the house's licensing fees were up to date as Banke points out to the police inspector.

Next, we learn all about Suresh Saxena; an unseen lover/motive in the play and fully fleshed out here. He's an up-and-coming, well-connected lawyer running for political office. In a flashback, we learn how they met, when he saved Rani from a despairing leap over a cliff to her death. Suresh becomes a regular visitor to the household, playing chess with Thakur and exchanging longing glances with Rani.

This being an Indian production and not a Hollywood

Thakur Singh
(*Danny Denzongpa*),
the angry husband

Rani Singh
(*Zeenat Aman*),
the fearful wife

Suresh Saxena
(*Sanjay Khan*),
the potential knight

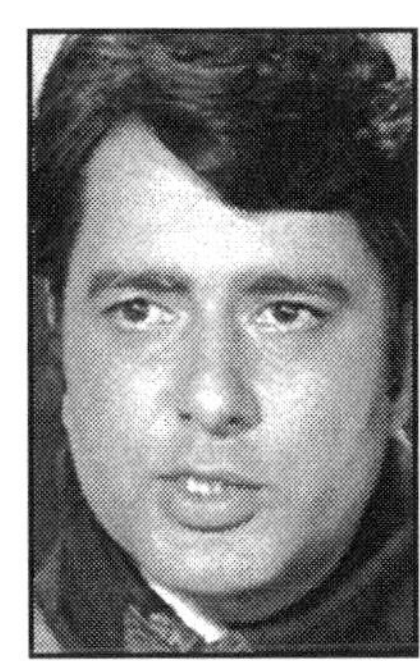

Chandra Shekha
(*Navin Nischol*),
the mystery stranger

Mrs. Singh
(*Urmila Bhatt*),
the vengeful mother

Banke Lal
(*Deven Verma*),
the comic servant

one, their affair is chaste: longing glances, conversations, and the occasional touch of hands. Similarly, there's a shower scene involving Rani (proving to the audience she couldn't have shot her husband) where you see the shower spray, her wet hair, and nothing below the top 1 inch of her shoulders. It was the most chaste shower I've ever seen.

Into the unhappy home sneaks Chandra Shekhar, the unexpected guest. He arrives in the middle of a foggy night, the victim of a car accident. Since the front door's unlocked, he walks in and discovers Thakur, asleep in his wheelchair. Except Thakur's dead and Rani is revealed standing next to him, holding a revolver.

Chandra leaps to the conclusion that Rani, despite her confession, is innocent of shooting her husband or at the very least, deserves to get away with murder. It must be her loveliness, especially when she reveals her sad story.

They concoct a plot about a robbery gone wrong to fool the servants and police and immediately, things go wrong. Inspector Joshi is no fool. When he questions the servants, they reveal that Rani had a suitor. Evidence is found linking Suresh to the scene of the crime, including the fact he lied about his whereabouts at the time of the shooting.

To Rani's horror, Suresh is arrested for murdering her husband. She's willing to take the blame. Suresh is equally sure Rani shot Thakur and he's ready to take the fall to save her.

The film adds a dramatic courtroom scene, where Suresh tests the theory that a lawyer who defends himself has a fool for a client. He doesn't do too badly. The courtroom scenes form an inadvertent documentary. The prosecutor and the judge say rather different things than you'd get in an American or a British courtroom.

At the high point of the trial, when it appears all hope for Suresh and Rani is lost, a surprise witness shows up. Chandra tells the real truth and you, dear reader, realize everything you saw was from the wrong point of view. In classic Agatha fashion, old sins have long shadows and the past is never dead. It's been biding its time, waiting for revenge.

Why was Chandra so eager to cover up the murder, absolving Rani of blame? Because he murdered Thakur, but only by accident. When he saw his nemesis, crippled and wheelchair-bound, he wanted him to live. Live, I tell you! Nothing could be more hateful to Thakur than living as half a man. Chandra didn't know how Thakur took his fury out on his family, his servants, even the unlucky neighbors who had to listen to his abuse and dodge the bullets he sent flying.

Thakur is a murder victim who had it coming. No one feels sorry for him. They're relieved he's dead. The wheels of karmic justice ground slowly but they eventually ground him into powder.

This being a Bollywood suspense thriller — and it is suspenseful — there's singing and dancing. Unlike *Gumnaam*, the musical interludes are much better integrated into the plot, starting with the opening and closing credits song. As best as I could tell from the subtitles, it sets up the film's theme of the power of fate on human lives.

Other performances reinforce the theme. Banke watches his lassie dance and sing in the "house of entertainment." Suresh sits through a different, lengthy entertainment of dancers, one in blue and one in fuchsia, giving their all to the customers. In both scenes, professional dancers, not the core characters, burst into song. Both song routines — assuming accurate subtitles — danced around the film's theme like a Greek chorus. For a Bollywood film, it was quite restrained.

There's so much to like about *Dhund*. It was filmed as a contemporary, leading to interesting views into Indian culture at that time. It's not just the mix of western and Indian dress or house decorations or even hearing English mixing with the Hindi. It's throwaway lines like Chandra telling the police he assumed that because the house he crashed nearby was large, they would have a telephone. That when Chandra's out on the golf course, with its jungle rough and red dirt greens, he's dressed to fit into the finest of English golf courses. That the hotel bar is in the open air, with charming tables and umbrellas sitting on dusty red clay instead of a paved terrace.

This is a very different, curry-flavored take on Agatha. It's still her, her plot, her motivations, and her characters. But it's also a dish of India.

General Information

Based on: *The Unexpected Guest* (play, 1942)
Run time: 2 hr., 10 min. **Subtitles:** Yes

Writer: Akhtar-Ul-Iman **Director:** B. R. Chopra

Cast

Madan Puri as Inspector Joshi
Jagdish Raj as Inspector Bakshi
Nana Palsikar as The Judge
Ashok Kumar as Public Prosecutor Mehta

Navin Nischol as Chandra Shekhar / Prakash (Michael Starkwedder)
Zeenat Aman as Rani Ranjit Singh (Laura Warwick)
Sanjay Khan as Advocate Suresh Saxena
Danny Denzongpa as Thakur Ranjit Singh (Richard Warwick)
Urmila Bhatt as Mrs. Singh
Deven Verma as Banke Lal
Uma Dhawan as Dancer
Padma Khanna as Brothel Dancer
Jayshree Talpade as Blue dressed dancer in "Jo Yahan Tha"

Film Location

Mahabaleshwar, Maharashtra, India

Songs

"Jo Yahan Tha" ("Who Was Here")
"Jubna Se Chunariya Khisak Gai Re" ("Chunariya slipped from Jubna")
"Uljhan Suljhe Na Rasta Sujhe Na" ("Do not solve the problem, do not find the way")
"Sansar Ki Har Shaye Ka Itna Hi Fasana Hai" ("Every bed in the world has the same fate")

Why Didn't They Ask Evans? (1980)

Bigger is not necessarily better. This three-hour epic replicates the novel, but forgets it's a movie

One of the oddities about this project is watching the Agatha Christie film oeuvre out of order. We saw the 2009 version of *Why Didn't They Ask Evans?* months ago and it was … bizarre. Throwing Miss Marple into the mix was just the beginning of a radical rewrite.

But I will say this: That movie zipped along. It moved so fast that entire chunks of the plot happened for no logical reason. The scriptwriter had to tie up all the loose ends and had run out of time to think it through, and so tossed everything on the screen and hoped it worked.

This version has the opposite problem. Virtually everything from the book is there: the dialog, setting, plot, and each and every character no matter how minor. Watch this film and you won't have to bother reading the novel. That's how complete it is. There's only one major change and it comes near the end. It replaces (for which I am grateful) a letter-reading scene. Instead, you watch a confrontation with the villain, a threat to Frankie, and her eventual rescue by Bobby. Actual dramatic action, what a concept.

I don't mean to be snarky, but this version is a reminder that film and books are different mediums. The book is an enjoyable leisurely read, spent with charming refugees from a P.G. Wodehouse novel. I liked it fine. However, move that same novel to the screen? If I'm looking at my watch, wondering when something's going to happen, then the movie isn't working.

Fidelity to text

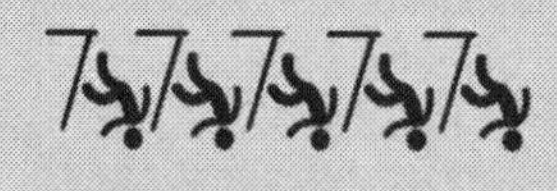

Practically everything in the book is in the novel, other than explaining how a suspect is identified and turning a boring letter into a dramatic ending.

Quality of movie

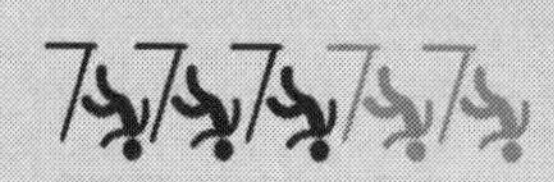

A leisurely book makes for a draggy movie. This film lasted three hours. A tight script removing the extraneous material would have made for a zippy two-hour movie with nothing lost.

There's plenty to like about this film. We'll start with the leads. Francesca Annis plays Frankie. She's 35, a little old to be playing a bright young thing, but she's lively and vibrant and you'll stop noticing. James Warwick, playing Bobby, is 33. He's also too old for his part, but again, you won't care. They displayed so much chemistry that they moved on from playing Frankie and Bobby to Tuppence and Tommy in *The Secret Adversary* (1983), followed by the series *Partners in Crime.*

Another very nice point about this version is it didn't castrate Bobby the way the 2009 version did. Here, you get the impression that Frankie and Bobby genuinely love each other even if they're too inhibited to say so. This Bobby is easygoing, but he's not going to be Frankie's doormat, nor is she a harridan in training.

Lady Frances Derwent (*Francesca Annis*), the plucky heroine

Bobby Jones (*James Warwick*), the reluctant hero

Sylvia Bassington-ffrench (*Connie Booth*), the concerned wife

Roger Bassington-ffrench (*Leigh Lawson*), the black sheep

Moira Nicholson (*Madeline Smith*), the crazy wife

Dr. Nicholson (*Eric Porter*), the mad doctor

John Gielgud plays Bobby's father, the vicar. Having just watched him play Lord Caterham in 1982's *The Seven Dials Mystery* was … odd, but acceptable. The roles are similar; a long-suffering father dealing with flighty offspring. He steals the scene every time he appears.

There's also Leigh Lawson playing Roger Bassington-ffrench. He was great, a wonderful Agatha villain. You can understand how she let him get away with murder. Multiple murders, no less! It's the charm. Yep, Roger escapes the gallows despite having earned himself three hangings. He even confesses to Frankie that he would have murdered his nephew (victim #4) but he would have made it quick because he liked the boy. The nephew stood in the way of inheriting Merroway Court and well, Roger didn't want to leave anything to chance.

The costume designer gives an observant viewer a clue early on about Roger's character. He's wearing spectator shoes, something no true gentleman wore during the 1930s. Lounge lizards wore spectator shoes, as did con men and car salesmen. Even social climbers wore them, but not the heir to the manor. But Roger's a second son and so has no expectations unless he makes them himself.

One problematic section revolved around the complicated murder plot. Why did Roger murder John Savage, a non-relative who did not stand in the way of him inheriting Merroway Court? Because John Savage had £700,000 pounds to leave to some lucky beneficiary. Roger arranged to fake the will to get the money needed to restore Merroway Court to its original magnificence after he murdered his brother and nephew to inherit it. It's a convoluted plot, the sort that works in a book when you can page back a few chapters and reread a section. In a movie? In pre-DVD days? Difficult to follow.

I suppose that's another reason to be agonizingly faithful to the text, just to make sure it's completely clear and understandable to the viewer.

General Information

Based on: *Why Didn't They Ask Evans?* (novel, 1934)
Run time: 3 hrs. **Subtitles:** No

Writer: Pat Sandys
Directors: John Davies, Tony Wharmby

Cast

Francesca Annis as Lady Frances Derwent
James Warwick as Bobby Jones

Leigh Lawson as Roger Bassington-ffrench
James Cossins as Henry Bassington-ffrench
Connie Booth as Sylvia Bassington-ffrench
Eirik Barclay as Tommy Bassington-ffrench
Eric Porter as Dr. Nicholson
Madeline Smith as Moira Nicholson
Robert Longden as Badger Beadon
John Gielgud as Reverend Jones
Mitzi Rogers as Mrs. Cayman
John Pennington as Mr. Cayman
Bernard Miles as Dr. Thomas
Doris Hare as Rose Pratt
Joan Hickson as Mrs. Rivington
Rowland Davies as Dr. George Arbuthnot
Frank Tregear as Mr. Roberts
Lynda La Plante as Mrs. Roberts
Deddie Davies as Postmistress
John Horsley as Mr. Spragg
Roy Boyd as Alan Carstairs

Film Locations

Bethany, Cuddington, Buckinghamshire (Wheeler & Owen office)
The Bernard Hall, Cuddington, Buckinghamshire (inquest)
St. Nicholas Church Cuddington, Aylesbury, Buckinghamshire (Rev. Jones' parish)
The Pitchings, Spurt Street, Cuddington, Buckinghamshire (tea room)
Hall Barn, Beaconsfield, Buckinghamshire (Bassington-ffrench home)
Wellfield House, Spurt Street, Cuddington, Buckinghamshire (hospital)
Tyringham Hall, Cuddington, Buckinghamshire (Frankie and Bobby keep watch)
Arley railway station, Arley, Worcestershire
Tibby's Cottage, Cuddington, Buckinghamshire (Rose Pratt's cottage)
Castle Ashby, Northamptonshire (Frankie's home)
Madoes, Long Crendon, Buckinghamshire (Swan Hotel)
St. Mary's Church, Long Crendon, Buckinghamshire (gardener's grave)

This production also marked Agatha's return to television. She'd watched too many terrible adaptations and had lost all enthusiasm for the medium. Theatrical adaptations were still being filmed, but no television until now. Her estate, controlled by daughter Rosalind, decided to offer her non-Poirot and non-Marple properties and *Evans* became a test case to see if it could be done. The production studio — London Weekend Television (LWT) — did it up right. They hired an all-star cast, fully utilized England's stately homes, and spent over £1 million to make everything on screen look perfect. They succeeded too! The film was so successful that it led to *The Agatha Christie Hour* in 1982 (using non-Poirot and non-Marple stories) and then *The Secret Adversary* in 1983. Christie was back on television.

While it was the style at the time to faithfully adapt classic novels for British television, there was another motivation in play. LWT did not want to piss off the estate. They weren't about to let some hack screenwriter mangle Agatha's text and thus lose access to all those novels, plays, and short stories. All that prestige! All that money! Just waiting for some lucky production company to cut the right deal with the estate. Which is why virtually the entire novel is onscreen to ensure future access to Agatha's estate.

Should you watch this version? Sure. It's slow compared to the 2009 and the 2022 versions, but it has the benefit of coherence and plausibility. It's fabulous eye-candy. The clothes, settings, cars, vintage aeroplanes, and all-star cast are fabulous. On top of that, you get a first-class tour of British buildings from charming cottages and garden follies to mansions big enough to house a hundred family members, guests, and the staff needed to run the place. It is an astonishing production. The pacing will give you plenty of time to gawk at the scenery and appreciate what a £1,000,000 would buy in 1980.

The Seven Dials Mystery (1981)

The death of a man surrounded by clocks leads Bundle and Battle into danger from a secret society

Fidelity to text

It's very close, other than John Gielgud coming across as more intelligent than Lord Caterham is supposed to be.

Quality of movie

Only if you're in on the genre joke. If you aren't, you won't enjoy the movie.

Agatha Christie didn't write her books in a cultural vacuum. She read widely, beginning with her family's collection of Victorian books and magazines. She was interested in all sorts and classes of people, and closely observed their behavior. She had — even more neglected now that she's turned into an institution — a sense of humor. You can tell what a person truly believes by what they're willing to make fun of. If you can make jokes about the silly asses of the aristocracy, then perhaps you don't see them as all-knowing gods who must be respected no matter how badly they behave.

Thus we come to *The Seven Dials Mystery*, published in 1929. It wasn't rapturously reviewed at the time and today, it's regarded as one of her least able efforts. It's ranked down there in the weeds along with *The Secret of Chimneys* (1925).

Seven Dials is a very loose sequel to *Chimneys*, using some of the same characters, such as Eileen "Bundle" Brent, Lord Caterham, Bill Eversleigh, George Lomax, Tredwell the butler, and Inspector Battle. The novel also begins at Chimneys, which Lord Caterham rented out and where the first murder takes place. Anthony Cade and Virginia Revel do not appear; presumably they're living happily ever after ruling his tiny Ruritanian-esque kingdom out in Mittel Europa. Likewise, there are no stolen, priceless diamonds floating around. However, there is a secret formula floating around, waiting to be stolen.

Seven Dials was another of Agatha's lighthearted thrillers, but it's more than that. It's a mashup between two very popular genres of the time: P.G Wodehouse's country house farces and John Buchan-style thrillers involving espionage, high stakes, secret societies, and governments at risk.

Yes, once again, Agatha Christie was at the cutting edge of genre writing. But, as a middle-aged, gentry-class married woman with a child, she wasn't seen in the same way as a leather-clad young literary Turk. No indeedy. And thus, *Seven Dials* isn't seen as being subversive despite her turning every standard convention of both genres on their heads.

The movie remains true to the novel both in storyline and in attitude. Watch those bright young things racing about the countryside in their motorcars, indulging in larks and practical jokes. Observe Jimmy Thesiger verbally sparring with his manservant over the purchase of handguns, remembering to wear shoes,

Superintendent Battle (*Harry Andrews*), the investigator

Eileen "Bundle" Brent (*Cheryl Campbell*), the amateur detective

Jimmy Thesiger (*James Warwick*), the man about town

Lorraine Wade (*Lucy Gutteridge*), the victim's sister

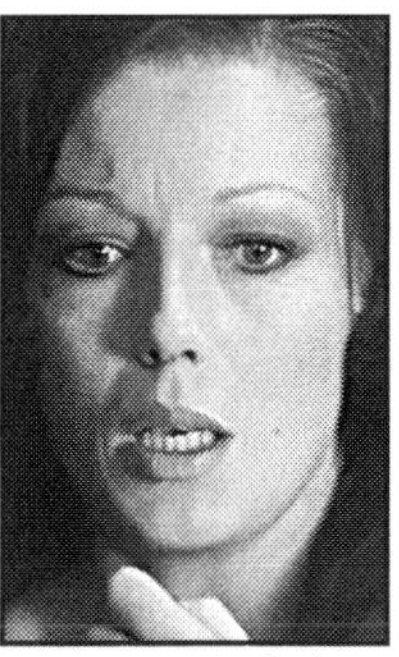

Countess Radzsky (*Rula Lenska*), the Hungarian

Bill Eversleigh (*Christopher Scoular*), the secretary

and not inviting ladies of dubious repute into his home. See Tredwell put Lady Coote in her place, reminding her that while he may be a mere butler, he knows how the aristocracy should behave while she will always remain a jumped-up social climber from some working-class household who got lucky. If you read Wodehouse, it's all familiar.

Similarly, if you know your Edwardian and Great War-era thrillers, you'll be familiar with the valuable formula that everyone wants (this time, it's one that will harden steel so airplanes can shed immense quantities of weight and become more lethal and cost-effective). You'll spot the unexpected murder of a total idiot as being more than it seems, particularly after the second, more dramatic murder. You'll look for the mysterious secret society bent on world domination, where all the members wear masks and only Number One knows who everyone is. Which all-important industrialist is Number One? Look! There's the dashing hero investigating the murders, trying to save the formula from evil foreigners, and unearthing the truth behind the Seven Dials.

These worlds collide when Lady Eileen "Bundle" Brent gets involved. (If you're wondering about her nickname, it's because she was a bundle of joy.) Eileen, Lord Caterham's daughter, is here because the first death occurred in her bed. Although it wasn't stated, I'm assuming the sheets got changed when Chimneys reverted back to the Caterham family.

As a bright, strong-willed young lady of the aristocracy to whom nothing bad could ever happen, she naturally investigates. Her investigation is aided by man-about-town Jimmy Thesiger, who's charming, helpful, not quite as stupid as he appears to be, and able to go everywhere.

Equally natural in both genres is the murder victim's half-sister, Lorraine, who — could she do anything else? — is desperate to discover who murdered her half-brother, the best brother a girl could ever have. Lorraine doesn't stand idly by when told to wait somewhere safe by Jimmy Thesiger. No, she plucks up her courage, arrives at Chimneys at 2 a.m., and has the packet containing the secret formula tossed out a window in front of her. She's shocked and horrified.

Jimmy, man-of-action, gets shot the same night during the struggle over the formula but he doesn't let that stop him from investigating. He's aided not just by Eileen and Lorraine, but by Bill Eversleigh, doofus in search of a Jeeves to run his life. Bill works for George Lomax in the Foreign Office so he's connected in various ways. He's the one who accidentally tells Eileen about the seedy nightclub called Seven Dials. She insists on going — could she do anything else? — and discovers that one of Chimney's footmen is now working there. Alfred the footman looks menacing but Lady Eileen soon puts him in his place. It's at Seven Dials that Eileen also realizes that Bill is a bad liar. He claimed no one went to Seven Dials but that is one happening nightclub.

Events proceed as you'd expect. Eileen infiltrates the secret society and from a closet watches the masked villains discuss their nefarious plans.

Soon thereafter, things fall apart and Agatha turns all your genre expectations on their heads. Don't miss an early precursor to a critical plot point in *Death on the Nile*.

We also learn that:

* Eileen isn't nearly as smart as she thinks she is. It's all book-smarts and not street-smarts.

* Bill Eversleigh isn't quite the doofus he seems, but he's still a doofus.

* Jimmy Thesiger isn't the hero he seems to be and how, exactly, does he pay for that lavish pied-à-terre?

* Lorraine might have a dead half-brother who needs avenging, but he's not the man she's focused on.

* Inspector Battle — dull, stolid, not very bright, overweight and decidedly unheroic — is proved to be something else entirely.

* The Seven Dials Secret Society is secretive but it's not what it seems to be either.

* About the only people who remain who we thought they were are Lady Coote, Lord Caterham, and George Lomax.

The movie could have been better paced. It dragged at times. Musical cues were sometimes overly obvious. The film stock was strange. Interior scenes were crisp and clear but when the characters went outside, the film turned fuzzy. It also desperately needed subtitles so you don't miss the witty lines. Most of all, if you can't handle the genre mashing, you'll wonder why you're wasting your time. But if you get Agatha's pastiche of typical thrillers of her day, you'll like *The Seven Dials Mystery*.

General Information

Based on: *The Seven Dials Mystery* (novel, 1929)
Run time: 2 hr., 12 min. **Subtitles:** No

Writer: Pat Sandys **Director:** Tony Wharmby

Cast

Harry Andrews as Superintendent Battle
Cheryl Campbell as Lady Eileen "Bundle" Brent
John Gielgud as Marquis of Caterhan
James Warwick as Jimmy Thesiger
Joyce Redman as Lady Coote
Leslie Sands as Sir Oswald Coote
Lucy Gutteridge as Lorraine Wade
Robert Longden as Gerry Wade
Terence Alexander as George Lomax
Christopher Scoular as Bill Eversleigh
Rula Lenska as Countess Radzsky
James Griffiths as Rupert "Pongo" Bateman
Brian Wilde as Tredwell
Hetty Baynes as Vera
John Vine as Ronny Devereux

Film Locations

Chenies Manor House, Buckinghamshire (Chimneys)
Glynde Place, Glynde, East Sussex (Wyvern Abbey)
Greenway, Galmpton, Devon (outdoor scenes)
Norman Shaw Buildings, Westminster, London (Scotland Yard)

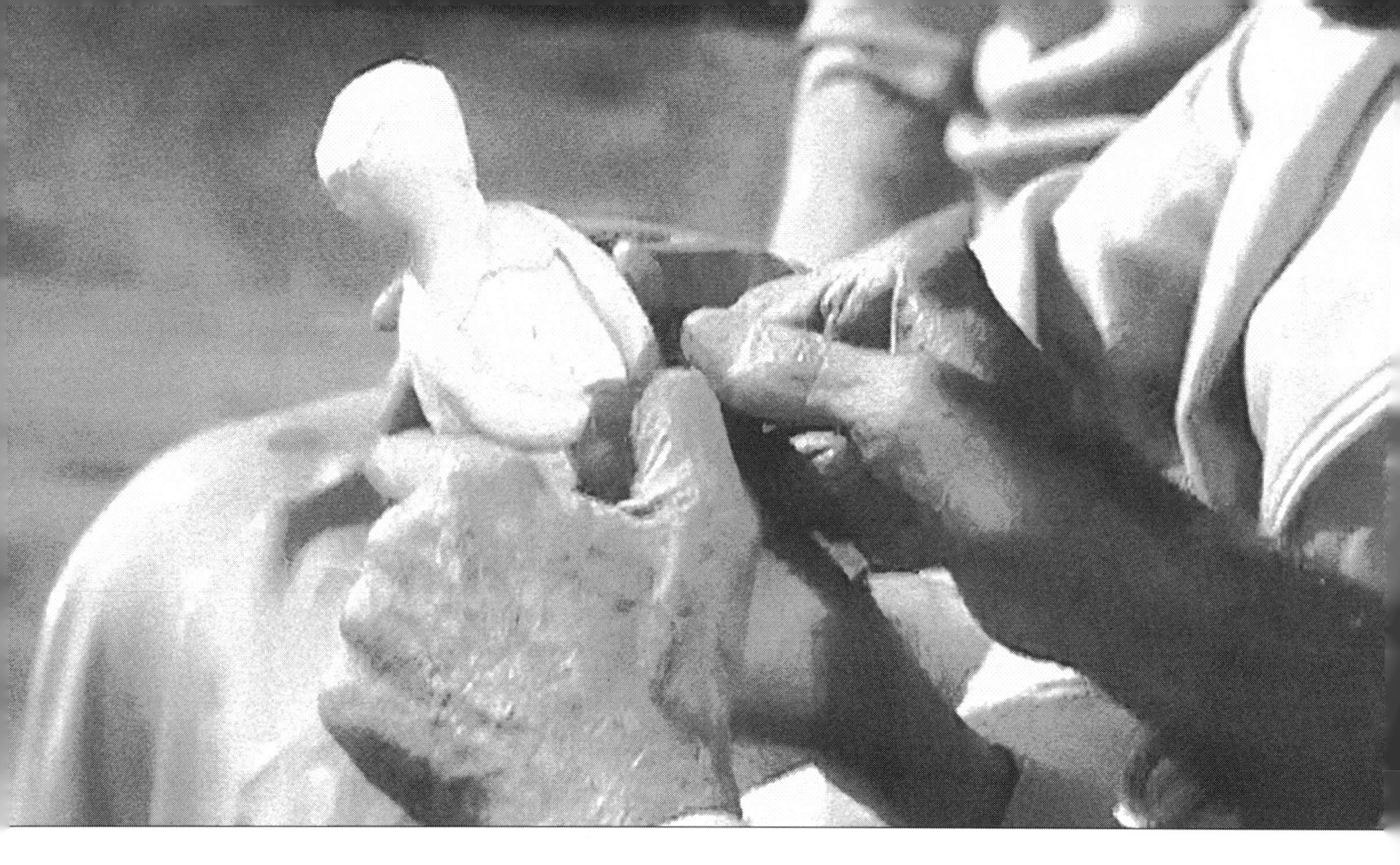

Spider's Web (1982)

Clarissa and her friends must find a treasure and a killer in this romp that uses Christie's theatrical script

Fidelity to the play

Agatha gets sole writing credit, so you know this is a line-for-line reading of the original play.

Quality of movie

This never came to life. Clarissa is supposed to be *the* effervescent, unbelievable, manic pixie dream girl. This Clarissa was more the charming lady of the manor.

Bill and I have slowly worked our way from 1929 (*Adventures, Inc.*) toward the present and here we are at 1982 and *Spider's Web*. I'd seen the 1960 version with the longer title of *The Spider's Web* starring Glynis Johns so I knew what to expect.

But first, a little backstory. By 1953, Agatha had written many plays. She'd developed a good understanding of what worked on stage and what didn't. As always, she liked changing things up and surprising her audience. So when film actress Margaret Lockwood asked for a comic mystery as a starring theatrical vehicle, Agatha used the opportunity to try something new. Lockwood didn't want to portray an evil femme fatale; she'd done enough of that in the movies. For her return to the stage, she wanted to be funny, frothy, effervescent, yet still involved in murder. The victim had to be someone for whom the phrase "justifiable homicide" was invented.

Agatha delivered in 1954 with *Spider's Web* and the character of Clarissa Hailsham-Brown. I assume Margaret Lockwood was suitably dazzling, ditzy, and off-kilter on stage. She played Clarissa in the BBC television adaptation in 1955 but it was not recorded. Which is a pity, because whatever Margaret Lockwood did, she set the tone for how Clarissa should be portrayed.

I envision Clarissa as a vivacious live wire who lives at 37° askew from the rest of us. She's the second wife of Henry Hailsham-Brown, a stuffy diplomat in the Foreign Service. We don't know why someone concerned about his career would fall head-over-heels in love with a wildly unsuitable woman, particularly when his first marriage ended dramatically in adultery, drug abuse, child abuse, and everything else you could think of.

None of that, by the way, was Henry's fault. It was his evil ex-wife, Miranda, who ran off with the aforementioned smarmy victim of justifiable homicide. You would think that Henry would choose to marry the most suitable of wives and not a British version of Lucy Ricardo. Yet he married Clarissa, making her his traumatized daughter's stepmother. Perhaps Agatha was implying that we never learn from our mistakes. Henry would always be attracted to unsuitable women.

But enough of Henry; he's in the play solely to set up the stakes and return at the end unaware that

Clarissa Hailsham-Brown (*Penelope Keith*), the lady of the house

Inspector Lord (*John Barcroft*), the investigator

Sir Rowland Delahaye (*Robert Flemyng*), the guardian

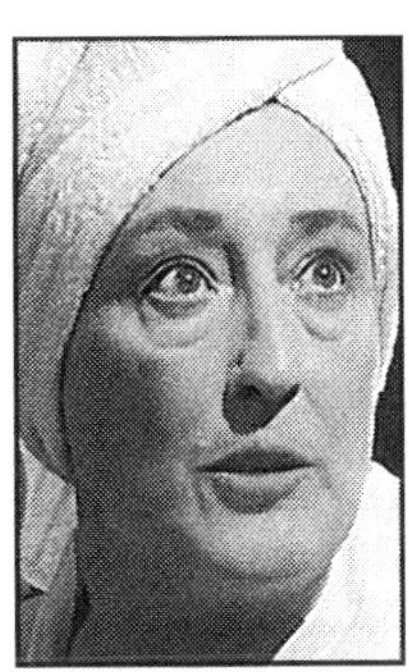

Mildred Peake (*Elizabeth Spriggs*), the gardener

Pippa Hailsham-Brown (*Holly Aird*), the daughter

Oliver Costello (*Brian Protheroe*), the threat

anything happened in his house in between. Clarissa is the center of *Spider's Web*. If you can't buy her as a manic pixie dream girl who everyone is convinced is lying when she's telling the truth and telling the truth when she's lying, the play doesn't sparkle. The actress playing Clarissa is vital. She makes the reactions of everyone else believable.

General Information

Based on: *Spider's Web* (play, 1954)
Run time: 1 hr., 45 min. **Subtitles:** Yes

Writer: Agatha Christie
Director: Basil Coleman

Cast

Penelope Keith as Clarissa Hailsham-Brown
Holly Aird as Pippa Hailsham-Brown
Jonathan Newth as Henry Hailsham-Brown
Robert Flemyng as Sir Rowland Delahaye
Thorley Walters as Hugo Birch
Elizabeth Spriggs as Mildred Peake
David Yelland as Jeremy Warrender
John Barcroft as Inspector Lord
Brian Protheroe as Oliver Costello
David Crosse as Elgin
Mark Draper as Constable Jones
Lee Fox as Doctor

Penelope Keith didn't work for me. Not the way Glynis Johns did. I could see why Henry would fall in love with either version although his reasons would be wildly different (sex appeal and fun versus well-bred competence). I could not, for one minute, buy Penelope as a ditz who lived in a world of her own. She came across as very capable, almost no-nonsense. Slightly prone to flights of fancy, yes, but mainly because the plot demanded it. She didn't radiate goofiness and *joie de vivre* the way Glynis Johns did. She was impeccably groomed, impeccably dressed, and moved like she'd spent her adolescence strapped to a backboard while learning how to walk without the book falling from her head.

With the center of the play not quite right, I had more time to notice what else did or didn't work. Remember, I've got the 1960 version for comparison.

The rest of the cast was fine, but I couldn't help wonder how this police inspector would have reacted to Glynis. It felt like he had to disbelieve a regal queen — because the plot demanded he do so — when he wanted to believe her. Inspector Lord had a much easier time dealing with the rest of the cast. They felt real. His refusal to believe the lady of the manor's story did not.

Spider's Web started life as a play, something both versions took into account during filming. Weirdly, they went in different directions. The 1960 version is obviously filmed on a stage set, right down to obviously painted backdrops instead of real furniture or bookshelves. The cameraman staked out his position and never moved again, making for a very static set.

Supposing I murdered someone, would you help me?

Clarissa Hailsham-Brown

Yet, at the same time, the 1960 version went *outside*. It went *upstairs* to find the body under the bolster. It had breakfast on the *veranda*. It even entered Miss Peake's *cottage* and checked out her double-dug trench. In other words, despite the house being a stage set, it was a stage set that expanded into the larger world.

The 1982 version confined itself — other than one short scene and an opening shot of the mansion — to the stage set. You get the library, the drawing room, the connecting hallway to the front door, and the secret passage. The camera moved with the cast through these real rooms, down to actual draperies at the windows instead of painted facsimiles. Yet it was a far more static set because you never saw anything other than those rooms.

The 1960 version had a bright, bouncy, jazzy score that was often wildly at odds with the action. But it was memorable, and if you wanted to emphasize that Clarissa was 37° askew from the rest of humanity, the musical score did its part. The 1982 version had music. I think. It was blandly appropriate and utterly forgettable and had nothing to do with Clarissa. Music can provide a subtle clue to the audience: this person is the hero, that person is the villain, that guy over there is the lucky, plucky sidekick. This next scene is going to be dramatic and scary so girls, hold on to your boyfriends! Not here.

Even the opening credits in 1960 were off-balance, with cartoon spider policemen coping with criminal flies, informing the audience that it was entering Clarissa's world. This version? The usual, as per the standard contract.

The entire point of the play and the subsequent films was to be amusing and frothy. This is a parody of classic English country house murders where nothing is taken too seriously because the victim had it coming. Will Clarissa suffer from coping with a dead body, peril to her husband's career, and the knowledge that her stepdaughter was experimenting with voodoo? Glynis Johns floats above it, unconcerned and unaffected. Penelope Keith copes, manages, and spends time in therapy and writing in her diary.

Should you watch this version? It depends on the Clarissa you want: manic pixie dream girl who will drive you crazy and make you laugh? Or someone sane and capable of flights of fancy only if the situation forces her to soar into the unknown.

The Case of the Middle-Aged Wife (1982)

Parker Pyne and a gigolo help an abandoned wife reunite with a husband wanting to feel young

I didn't know what to expect from the first episode of *The Agatha Christie Hour*. This was a television series developed to take advantage of her stories that did not use Hercule Poirot or Miss Marple. Agatha had died in 1976, so her daughter Rosalind controlled the estate and she did not want to see her mother's legacy further tarnished (i.e., another debacle like Tony Randall's outing as Poirot in *The Alphabet Murders*).

She took cautious steps into television, beginning with the mini-series *Why Didn't They Ask Evans?* in 1980. That was a very successful and faithful adaptation. It proved that when TV producers are reminded of their place via strict contracts and plenty of oversight, they are less likely to run amok. It also proved there was an immense television audience hungry for Agatha.

Fast-forward two years to the debut of *The Agatha Christie Hour*. It's ten episodes in all and uses lesser-known short stories, not all of them mysteries. These stories demonstrate Agatha's range and how skillfully she depicted the human heart. These stories also demonstrate that if you, dear reader, stick only to Poirot and Miss Marple, you're missing out on some good reading.

Are these mysteries? Not really, unless you consider humans to be mysteries at heart. Are they good stories that deserve to be reread? You bet. It makes me wonder why there's no complete collection of her short stories, other than one for Poirot and one for Miss Marple. Agatha wrote in genres other than mysteries. She liked a touch of the paranormal as well as some romance. Thus, when this show was developed, there was plenty of material to choose from and most of it was unknown to the audience.

Fidelity to text

Everything the text alludes to is onscreen with added characters to better dramatize the storyline.

Quality of movie

This had everything, including a big band with a crooner, and sly allusions to Archie Christie's affair with Nancy Neele.

The Case of the Middle-Aged Wife is a Parker Pyne story. He's a retired statistician who believes that there are five (and only five) kinds of unhappiness. He offers to make clients happy, based on his statistical analysis of the human condition and he's often right.

In this episode, we meet Maria Packington and her husband, George. He owns his business and they're well-enough off to afford a housemaid. Maria is dowdy and unhappy. She helped him build the business, and when they were successful, the status-conscious George didn't want his wife working anymore. Left with nothing to do, she stays home while George spends long evenings "entertaining clients."

Maria Packington (*Gwen Watford*), the unhappy wife

George Packington (*Peter Jones*), the obsessed husband

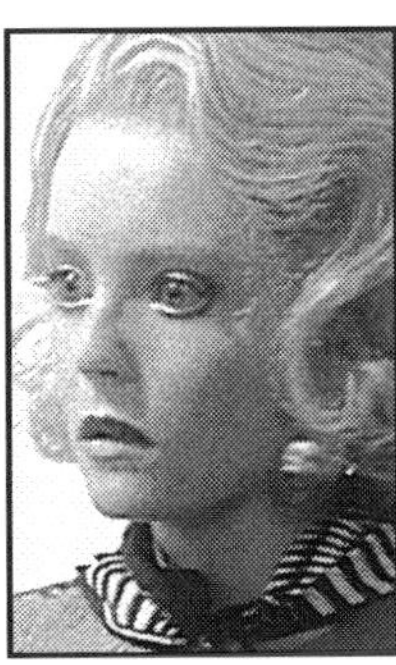

Nancy Purvis (*Kate Dorning*), the saucy secretary

Parker Pyne (*Maurice Denham*), the problem solver

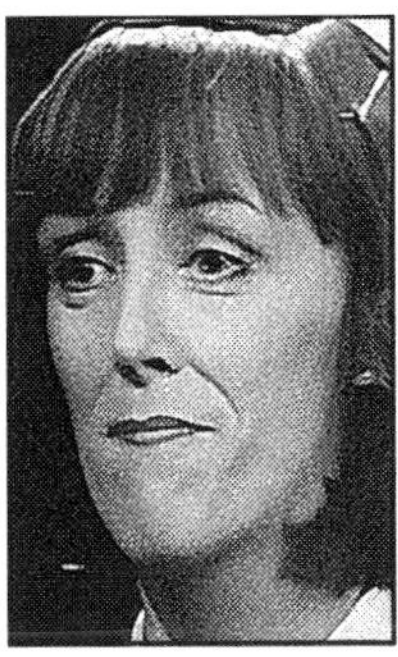

Miss Lemon (*Angela Easterling*), the efficient secretary

Claude Luttrell (*Rupert Frazer*), the expert gigolo

Maria knows who he's entertaining, and it's not businessmen. No, it's his cheap dyed-blonde tart of a secretary, Nancy Purvis. The short story doesn't give the secretary a name but the screenwriter did. Nancy. Nancy the secretary. Nancy the husband-poacher. Nancy, who's no better than she should be. If that rings a bell, recall Nancy Neele, the secretary for whom Archie left Agatha. While she didn't behave like Nancy Purvis, the connection is there if you want it.

Against Maria's accusations, George is defensive and angry. He's only helping out a poor but grateful girl who's too proud to ask for help. He has to coax her to accept money to fix her flat door (her worthless brother broke it) or to replace her tatty, thin coat (the poor girl must be freezing). Another added character is George's senior secretary, Miss Draper. Watch her face during her scenes. Like Edna, the housemaid, Miss Draper recognizes a man making a fool of himself. This is particularly true since George doesn't gets anything out of his relationship with Nancy other than feeling avuncular and generous.

In other words, Nancy isn't putting out. She doesn't have to. That leaves her more time for her own boyfriend, whom George knows nothing about. But I bet Miss Draper does.

Miserable Maria spots Parker Pyne's advert and consults with him. He persuades her to take a flier to the tune of two hundred guineas, up-front. Maria is bright enough to be wary and desperate enough to accept.

The first step is to make over Maria. The story notes Maria pays for the beauty treatments and new wardrobe.

Parker Pyne also introduces Maria to Claude Luttrell, a much younger man. He's handsome, charming, suave, and an excellent dancer. He's every woman's dream as long as you don't pay attention to the fact that, like Nancy, he's in it for the money. Parker Pyne employs Claude to romance lonely women, make them sparkle back to life, and show their husbands what they're ignoring in favor of cheap bottle-blonde tarts.

Maria goes dancing with Claude, lunches with Claude, and enjoys herself very much. She's no fool though. She knows he was hired to entertain her. She's smart, witty, perceptive, and then she does what Parker Pyne, statistician, never expected. She seduces Claude Luttrell's heart, cracking his lounge-lizard shell and touching the man inside. Maria does something that no other woman did with Claude. She genuinely enjoyed his company, she loved going places with him, she was honest and caring and grateful.

She upset Claude so much that he doesn't just refuse Maria's offer of a gold cigarette case. He tells Parker Pyne that he doesn't know if he can continue being a gigolo. Parker Pyne scoffs. The short story delves into Claude's flexible morals, but both story and film agree: Maria is a wonderful woman, and George should be grateful to have her.

There is so much to like about this episode. The scenes with Miss Lemon (before she went to work for Hercule Poirot) are amusing. The makeover is very well done. Plus, there's the Aphrodite nightclub with a big band and a crooner to enhance your dancing pleasure.

There's a surprisingly large amount of music crammed into the episode, which adds another layer of meaning. Nick Curtis plays the crooner. He's got a fabulous voice and manner. He sings twice in the nightclub and you hear him again on the radio, when George sits home alone and wonders where his life went wrong. You get two more jazz standards in the background, one during a restaurant scene and one for the big dance when George and Nancy meet Maria and Claude at the Aphrodite nightclub. Note how Claude looks happy with Maria but Nancy, when she's unobserved, looks bored with stuffy, middle-aged, paunchy George.

As I listened to that lovely, clever music, I wished for that kind of soundtrack in my own life. Classic jazz standards from the 1930s never get old.

Should you watch? There's no mystery. Yes, you should. It's a romance, something not normally associated with Agatha. This was a lovely, heart-warming opening episode and an introduction to Agatha's much larger body of work. Like Maria Packington, Agatha has unexpected depths worth exploring.

General Information

Based on: "The Case of the Middle-Aged Wife" (short story, 1932)
Run time: 52 min. **Subtitles:** Yes

Writer: Kevin Elyot
Director: Tom Shankland

Cast

Maurice Denham as Parker Pyne
Angela Easterling as Miss Lemon
Rupert Frazer as Claude Luttrell

Gwen Watford as Maria Packington
Peter Jones as George Packington
Kate Dorning as Nancy Purvis
Brenda Cowling as Miss Draper
Monica Grey as Beautician
Linda Robson as Edna
Nick Curtis as Crooner
Malcolm Hebden as Waiter
Nicholas Cooke as Eric

Songs

"The Very Thought of You" (1934), music and lyrics by Ray Noble (played in restaurant)
"Exactly Like You" (1930), music by Jimmy McHugh and lyrics by Dorothy Fields (sung in nightclub)
"I Surrender, Dear" (1931), music by Harry Barris and lyrics by Gordon Clifford (sung in nightclub)
"Nobody's Sweetheart Now" (1924), music by Billy Meyers and Elmer Schoebel and lyrics by Gus Kahn and Ernie Erdman (heard on radio)
"Try a Little Tenderness" (1932), composed by Jimmy Campbell, Reg Connelly, and Harry M. Woods. (played in nightclub)

In a Glass Darkly (1982)

A man struggles with war trauma as he's haunted by the vision of his wife's death by strangulation

Fidelity to text

The story got fleshed out, most significantly with what Agatha was very familiar with but didn't address directly: shell shock or as we call it, post-traumatic stress disorder (PTSD).

Quality of movie

Adding shell shock was a genius touch as a way of explaining Matthew's troubles. It fits the story, the mood, and the times.

The title of the second episode from *The Agatha Christie Hour* comes from chapter 13 of Paul's first letter to the Corinthians. Here it is from the King James Version so you can understand why Agatha used this verse.

> 9 For we know in part, and we prophesy in part.
> 10 But when that which is perfect is come, then that which is in part shall be done away.
> 11 When I was a child, I spake as a child, I understood as a child, I thought as a child: but when I became a man, I put away childish things.
> 12 For now we see through a glass, darkly; but then face to face: now I know in part; but then shall I know even as also I am known.
> 13 And abideth [what remains constant is] faith, hope, charity, these three; but the greatest of these is charity.

To translate into modern terms, we think we know but we don't and we should not deceive ourselves into believing otherwise. We can't know the future and must trust in God that all will be eventually made clear. The Bible teaches that charity is the highest form of love, signifying the reciprocal love between God and man. It's made manifest in unselfish love towards one's fellow humans.

When Matthew Armitage sees a vision in a mirror of a lovely young woman being strangled by a scarred man, he's badly shaken. When he's introduced to Sylvia Carslake, the sister of his best friend Neil, and recognizes her as the blonde in the mirror, he's worried. When he meets Sylvia's fiancé, Charles Crawley, and sees the scar on Crawley's neck, he's convinced he knows the truth.

Charles Crawley will murder Sylvia.

Matthew tells Sylvia of his vision but he doesn't tell her that he fell in love with her at first sight (a classic romance novel trope that sometimes happens in real life). He nobly heads off to war, sacrificing his happiness by not pursuing her. It wouldn't be fair to claim Charles Crawley is a strangler and then court Sylvia himself. His motives could be misconstrued.

While enduring the horrors of trench warfare (the producers did a decent job conveying the awfulness of the Great War on a limited budget) Matthew meets Neil

Matthew Armitage (*Nicholas Clay*), the husband

Sylvia Carslake (*Emma Piper*), the wife

Neil Carslake (*Shaun Scott*), the older brother

Alan Carslake (*Jonathon Morris*), the younger brother

Charles Crawley (*Brian Anthony*), the first fiancé

Derek Wainwright (*Nicholas Le Prevost*), the shrink

again. He hasn't seen him since Sylvia's fateful betrothal party. Neil tells Matthew that Sylvia broke the engagement to Charles Crawley shortly afterwards. Neil dies in the war, as so many young men did. Matthew returns home to break the news to Sylvia, the first time he's seen her since the betrothal party.

Later, Matthew is wounded. While he's recuperating in the hospital, Sylvia visits him. He's badly scarred but she's not repulsed. She tells him that Charles Crawley died fighting in the Somme. Then she confesses that she didn't marry Crawley because she fell in love with him at the betrothal party.

They marry, but there's trouble in paradise. Matthew's no longer worried that Charles Crawley will strangle Sylvia, but he can't leave the war behind. The film does a good job of showing his torment. He hears the guns going off in his head, sometimes louder, sometimes softer, but it never goes away completely. He gets flashbacks. It's shell shock, another horror that the Great War gave to the world.

Battles were vastly different prior to mechanization. They rarely lasted more than one day. There was a lot of down time, marching from one place to another. When the sun went down, it was pitch dark and the fighting stopped.

World War I was different. Larger armies could be organized and moved. That meant soldiers faced off in long lines. Artillery was more powerful, forcing them into trenches and dugouts. With multiple layers of trenches on each side, the war settled into a stalemate. The soldiers — on both sides — endured continuous bombardments, day and night. They fought on short notice or no notice, day or night. They endured mud that caused their feet to rot, diseases like dysentery, and the smell of rotting corpses and horses.

Many returning soldiers suffered terribly, as did their families. Agatha experienced it firsthand. During the war, she served in the hospital wards before she moved to the dispensary. She recalled in her autobiography throwing amputated limbs into the incinerator after they'd been hacked off some young man.

Keep that in mind when you dismiss her as a cozy mystery writer with a cozy, comfy life.

General Information

Based on: "In a Glass Darkly" (short story, 1934)
Run time: 54 min. **Subtitles:** Yes

Writer: William Corlett
Director: Desmond Davis

Cast

Nicholas Clay as Matthew Armitage
Emma Piper as Sylvia Carslake
Shaun Scott as Neil Carslake
Jonathon Morris as Alan Carslake
Paul Williamson as Mr. Carslake
Elspet Gray as Mrs. Carslake
Brian Anthony as Charles Crawley
Nicholas Le Prevost as Derek Wainwright
Marjorie Bland as Charlotte Hardy
David Cook as Captain Mountjoy
John Golightly as Commanding Officer
John Wheatley as Barton
Kenneth Midwood as Mr. Hobbs
Valerie Lush as Mrs. Hobbs
Eileen Davies as Nurse
Elizabeth Benson as Mrs. Armitage

Film Location

Kentwell Hall, Long Melford, Suffolk

Her husband, Archie, suffered too. He had flown planes — without wearing a parachute — that sometimes would break up in the air. He experienced long black moods where he didn't want anyone to help him or even be around him, including his wife.

By the time Agatha wrote "In a Glass, Darkly" in 1934, much of the trauma of the Great War had receded but it never vanished. She doesn't spell out shell shock as a contributing reason for Matthew Armitage's jealous rages and inability to cope with normal life, but she may not have felt she had to. Her audience knew all too well from coping with their own wounded fathers, brothers, uncles, cousins, husbands.

Another element the scriptwriter greatly enhanced was showing the passing of the Edwardian Age. Contrast the engagement party at Badgeworthy to the trenches or the hospital. Gone, all gone. The Victorian proprieties such as moral behavior were ridiculed. Parties and affairs were the fashionable thing, and it preyed on Matthew that perhaps his wife was bored with their rural life.

Giving Derek Wainwright a backstory fit in well too; psychiatry was a new medical discipline. A psychiatrist Derek Wainwright's age — old enough to serve and fight — would have more than professional reasons to treat shell shock.

The film almost ends up as a *Twilight Zone* episode. To his shock and horror, Matthew discovers who the strangler in the mirror truly is, and stops the crime in time.

As implied by the Biblical passage, Matthew Armitage thought he knew the future, but he did not. He thought he understood reality, but he was wrong. He changed the future, unknowingly, by telling Sylvia his vision without ever understanding who the man in the mirror was. Then, he learned what was true and how he had deceived himself in so many ways.

"In a Glass, Darkly" is a subtle story. It was made into a better, subtle, multi-layered film showing the passage of time and the loss of one era and the start of a another. It's well worth your time. Watch it twice and marvel at how it improves as you see more through your glass darkly.

ALAN CARSLAKE: *Infidelity is all the rage this year.*
MATTHEW ARMITAGE: *Not in Suffolk.*

The Girl in the Train (1982)

A feckless man discovers the knight inside him when a beautiful girl asks his help to escape a royal marriage

Watching *The Girl in the Train*, you'll get a tour of the docks in Portsmouth and appreciate Agatha's grasp of the romance genre. It's easy to forget how well read she was or that she had a sense of humor, because that's what her story was: a parody of romances found in ladies' magazines, then and now.

Well, not exactly now since ladies' magazines no longer publish short fiction. But they did and I remember reading this sort of story back in the 1970s. They were absurd, silly, frothy, and raced along at top speed to keep the reader turning pages, looking at ads, and planning to buy the next issue as soon as it hit the newsstand. Similar romances are still being written today. Visit any used book store (we recommend Cupboard Maker Books in Enola, Pa.) and look for category romance. You'll find similar stories by the shelf load. Or, go online and discover Kindle Unlimited. There's every possible permutation of damsels, heroic gentlemen, runaway marriages, secret identities, spies, undercover agents, princes and grand duchesses, annoying relatives, and Mittel-European kingdoms.

All those tropes appear in the eight pages of *The Girl in the Train*. They're all in the film too, along with acerbic cabbies, seen-it-all-before hoteliers, jaundiced executive secretaries, and overworked maids. If something isn't happening onscreen, wait thirty seconds and it will.

Fidelity to text

Significantly expanded over the slight short story, but the episode flubbed a big part of George's happy ending.

Quality of movie

Too much plot for 52 minutes, and it didn't sparkle as it should have.

Agatha, as a parodist, threw everything into the fictional blender and pressed frappé. The biggest change she made to this outrageously typical romance format is in the lead character. Romances are typically told from the viewpoint of the heroine — a damsel who may or may not be in distress — but whose point of view is always front and center. It's her story. She's the ingenue and the action revolves around what she's getting up to.

Not here. The ingenue is male.

He's George Rowland, gentleman, lover of fine tailoring, flower fancier, and man-about-town. He's young, he's good-looking, he's got prospects thanks to his wealthy uncle, and he's not very bright. He would fit in perfectly with Bertie Wooster's set. He'd be a member of the Drones Club and be nicknamed "Rowboat." I suspect Agatha read a lot of P.G. Wodehouse. She's written characters, particularly in

George Rowland
(*Osmund Bullock*),
the earnest fellow

Elizabeth
(*Sarah Berger*),
the conniving blonde

Jarrold
(*Ron Pember*),
the watcher

Karl
(*Glyn Baker*),
the prince

Sturm
(*Arthur Blake*),
the loyal flunky

Receptionist
(*Cherith Mellor*),
the world-weary clerk

The Seven Dials Mystery (1929), who could have stepped fully-formed from Wodehouse's pen.

George is very late to work one morning (a late night out on the town). He accepts a sprig of white heather from his favorite flower vendor — for luck — and discovers that his luck has run out with his uncle who owns the family firm. He's soon out on the street as a lazy good-for-nothing. He returns home and discusses his situation with Jeeves — I mean, Rogers, the butler. All prospects look dismal, and George realizes he doesn't want a job, he wants an adventure. He riffles through a railway guide and discovers there's a stop named Rowland Castle. It's perfect. That's his last name and the residents are sure to welcome him as a long-lost relation.

On the train, a hot blonde damsel wearing a red hat shoves her way into his first-class compartment and begs him to hide her. As a gentleman seeking adventure, he naturally obliges. Seconds later, a mysterious foreigner shows up hunting said damsel. George handles the situation, the foreigner is hauled off, and the damsel presses a package onto him and gives him instructions to follow a second man on the train who resembles King George V, who reigned from 1910 to 1936.

General Information

Based on: "The Girl in the Train" (short story, 1924)
Run time: 52 min. **Subtitles:** Yes

Writer: William Corlett
Director: Brian Farnham

Cast

Osmund Bullock as George Rowland
James Grout as William Rowland
Ernest Clark as Rogers
Sarah Berger as Elizabeth
Ron Pember as Jarrold
Roy Kinnear as Cabbie
David Neal as Prince Osric
Arthur Blake as Sturm
Glyn Baker as Karl
Cherith Mellor as Receptionist
Debbie Farrington as Maid
Matyelok Gibbs as Miss Garstang
Jo Warne as Flower Seller
Richard Bartlett as "The King"
Bill Treacher as Station Porter
Harry Fielder as Guard

Film Location

Portsmouth, England

The damsel, Elizabeth, then disappears.

George is overwhelmed. He can't disappoint this fascinating damsel! She needs him! Adventure awaits! Since he can't get off the train until the man who looks like King George V does, he ends up in Portsmouth and trails him to a second-rate hotel catering to commercial travelers on a budget. He has to be shown how to sign the hotel ledger by the lady hotelier. He chooses to sign in as "Lord Rowland."

More foreigners show up, the King George V look-alike explores the docks by night and leaves a mysterious message in the bathroom, George's room is broken into, and he rescues a suspicious stranger from a cupboard in George V's room.

All the while, he's got no idea what happened to Elizabeth.

Normally in a romance, we know what's happening to Elizabeth. She's the star, the main attraction, the center of the action. Not here. George is the innocent ingenue, in trouble over his head and gamely struggling. To further complicate his life (remember, if the action slows down, wait thirty seconds) the suspicious stranger is with Scotland Yard and he's hot on the heels of a suspected spy and his accomplice, Betty Bright-Eyes. Elizabeth. Betty. They couldn't be the same person, could they?

George is in a quandary. Could his gorgeous Elizabeth have been … using him? Yep, she sure could. She saw in George what everyone else saw: a genial idiot. As the cabbie says several times, there's one born every minute. Why, George is so dumb he doesn't recognize that the flower his favorite vendor gives him isn't white heather like she claimed. Everyone recognizes the sprig in his lapel as Cornish heath (*erica vagans*). I've no idea how the scriptwriter got the term "pale mauve" from that. Common flowers have loads of common names so perhaps that's the answer.

After discovering the true identity of Betty Bright-Eyes, George ends up back on the train to London. His newest shock is learning that the lovely Elizabeth was really a grand duchess who eloped with the second son of Lord so and so. She used him to run off with another man. Except she didn't because Elizabeth shows up (miraculously finding him on the correct train between Portsmouth and London) and reveals all. It was her brother who eloped with the grand duchess, and she helped them evade the grand duchess' wicked relatives.

There are two full novels' worth of activity going on behind George's adventures: the elopement and Balkan intrigue, plus spies infiltrating the naval defenses of Portsmouth and putting England at risk. Those events swirl around George, but he's barely aware of them. He never even makes it to Rowland Castle. But he's reunited with lovely, smart, conniving Elizabeth so he'll get his happy ever after.

Sadly, the film ran out of time and didn't circle back to George's financier uncle as the short story did. George is smart enough (in text) to realize that marrying Elizabeth, the daughter of Lord so-and-so, the sister-in-law to a grand duchess, the sister of the next Lord so-and-so, is exactly what his uncle would want and thus welcome him back to the firm.

The flaw in the film is it didn't sparkle. It's got everything needed for the romance of your dreams but needs the fizz of multiple bottles of champagne.

The Fourth Man (1982)

A French stranger on a train tells a tale about an orphan boy and girl and their beautiful tyrant ruler

Fidelity to text

There's a lot more backstory for the strange triangle of Annette, Félicie, and Raoul.

Quality of movie

It dragged. Worse, I couldn't understand why Félicie and Raoul were so entranced by Annette.

This story is a weirdy, one of Agatha's two dozen dives into the supernatural. Since she wrote long before shapeshifter romance came into vogue (or hot, sexy vampires), her paranormal world was based on what was popular at the time.

That meant ghosts. To be more precise, spirits. Spiritualism and the occult have a long and varied history in every culture going back millennia. In the 19th century, researchers were arguing if the soul was real. Where did it go after death? How much did it weigh? Can we communicate with those who have passed through the veil to the undiscovered country from which no man returns? Do we even want to?

You didn't learn any of this in school. Spiritualism, despite being openly practiced by millions of people, is even more disreputable in public school history text-books than religion. You'd think that wars were never fought over differences of belief; that we're all as rational as windup clockwork automatons. Sir Arthur Conan Doyle (1859-1930) would tell you differently. So would Sir Isaac Newton (1643-1727). He was a practicing alchemist but you didn't learn about *those* research activities in physics class.

Agatha wondered if — as children — we saw our bodies and our spirits as separate beings, "as though the body in which we have found our spirit lodged is at first strange to us." As a girl, her dreams were haunted by a spirit she called "the Gunman." This was an armed man who would show up at family gatherings, but only she could see him. He terrified her. She was also well aware of the currents of spiritualism oozing about her. A boyfriend introduced her to theosophy. She didn't think much of their belief system, but she learned the concepts.

Ghost stories were a natural subject as she explored fiction. People have told scary stories around the campfire since the dawn of time. Because spirits are noncorporeal and can travel where they want, we naturally arrive at asking who is riding around inside your meat body. Is it just you? Or has someone else come along for the ride? And might assume control of your healthy, fully-functional body?

She also understood, and this underlies *The Fourth Man*, that because a spirit isn't part of the Christian pantheon doesn't mean it is benign or friendly. There are plenty of malign beings drifting around on the astral plane. This is why you shouldn't ask "whoever is listening" to answer when you're experimenting with

Félicie Bault
(*Fiona Mathieson*),
the bullied girl

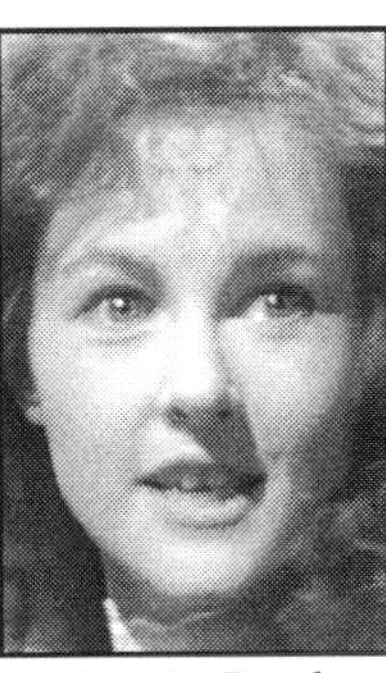

Annette Ravel
(*Prue Clarke*),
the doomed beauty

Raoul Letardau
(*John Nettles*),
the witness

Sir Campbell Clark
(*Alan MacNaughtan*),
the psychiatrist

Canon Parfitt
(*Geoffrey Chater*),
the clergyman

Sir George Durand
(*Michael Gough*),
the barrister

your Ouija board and planchette. You don't know who will answer or what you've just invited into your home.

That's the background behind *The Fourth Man*. Three men from the elite classes gather inside a first-class compartment on the night train north. They are a clergyman, Canon Parfitt; a barrister, Sir George Durand; and a doctor, Sir Campbell Clark. They know each other and are well-known to the public.

That includes Canon Parfitt, even though he lost some of his backstory in the adaptation. He was a trend-chasing vicar, one given to "scientific sermons." As he listens to the discussion of the Félicie Bault case, he comes up with sermon ideas that will draw him even more admiring attention. He still knows his Bible. When the doctor doubts the existence of spirits, he quotes John 4:24:

> *"God is a Spirit; and they that worship him must worship him in spirit and in truth." (King James version)*

The fourth man is Raoul Letardau, a French journalist working in London. He followed Sir Campbell Clark to the train station after hearing his lecture about Félicie Bault, a woman believed to have multiple personalities who strangled herself. He knew Félicie and another girl, Annette, when they were children in an orphanage. He knows the real story, not the one Sir Campbell Clark thinks he knows.

Imagine a campfire in the center of the compartment and you've got the picture. Raoul talks and the other three men are unwillingly hooked by his story until they, too, are forced to believe that humans might be more than rational meat puppets.

It's a wonderfully eerie setup, yet it didn't work. The trouble lay in the casting. The center of the story is the relationship between Annette, Félicie, and Raoul growing up in the orphanage in Brittany. Annette is lovely, vivacious, alive, eager to enjoy every moment under the sun. You can see why everyone adores her, until she opens her mouth.

Félicie is a dull, lumpy, sullen peasant girl. She's not pretty. She doesn't overcome her plainness with cleverness, charm, or industry. But Félicie has two things Annette lacks: strength and good health.

Félicie has something else Annette lacks and that's the rudiments of decency.

Annette is supposed to be bewitching; enslaving Raoul and Félicie and, I suppose, the other kids, although we never see them in the large seaside home that passes for an orphanage. All I saw was a selfish, bratty, spoiled mean girl. Annette was openly cruel to Félicie, to the point of hypnotizing her to eat a tallow candle and think it's the finest bread. She does this to torment Félicie, humiliate her in front of the other orphans, and show how much power she has over mind and body and yet make Félicie and Raoul still adore her. It takes a special actress to demonstrate this overpowering charisma. Prue Clarke doesn't have it.

General Information

Based on: "The Fourth Man" (short story, 1925)
Run time: 58 min. **Subtitles:** Yes

Writer: William Corlett
Director: Michael Simpson

Cast

John Nettles as Raoul Letardau
Michael Gough as Sir George Durand
Geoffrey Chater as Canon Parfitt
Alan MacNaughtan as Sir Campbell Clark
Prue Clarke as Annette Ravel
Fiona Mathieson as Félicie Bault
Roy Leighton as Young Raoul
Barbara Bolton as Mademoiselle
Frederick Jaeger as The Count
Eric Richard as Stage Manager
Christopher Wren as Annette's Attendant

Music

"C'è un sospiro per il si," inspired by John Keats' "O Blush Not So!" and written for the show

I could understand Raoul. Teenage boy, pretty girl, his brain shut down. But Félicie hated Annette and said so. She hung around, but it was obvious she did so because the script told her to, not because Annette was an enthralling goddess.

Eventually, the ghost story reaches its foreordained conclusion. Annette dies of consumption while Félicie remains alive and healthy. Except, someone moves into Félicie's body, causing the learned men to study her dual personalities. There are four in the short story, only two in the film. Yep, Agatha wrote a multiple personality short story in 1925. But since it's possession and not multiple personalities, Félicie rebels and seizes control of her body in the only way she can.

This should have been great! But it was flat.

Another aspect that could have been handled better was the song Annette sings several times in the episode. It was apparently written for the film. Unfortunately, she sings it in Italian and no translation via subtitle is provided. It seems to be roughly based on Keats' poem "O Blush not So!"

> *O Blush not So! O blush not so!*
> *Or I shall think you knowing;*
> *And if you smile, the blushing while,*
> *Then maidenheads are going.*
>
> *There's a blush for won't, and a blush for shan't,*
> *And a blush for having done it;*
> *There's a blush for thought, and a blush for nought,*
> *And a blush for just begun it.*

There are several more verses in the same vein. Understanding this would have shown what an unnerving child Annette was. Schools also don't teach you how racy John Keats (1795–1821) could be.

The Case of the Discontented Soldier (1982)

Life in a country village bores a retired major until he encounters romance and a quest for treasure

You never know what you'll get with a Parker Pyne story. He's a retired government statistician who uses his knowledge to stave off ennui and benefit mankind. As a "Detective of the Heart," he's all over the map in Agatha's 14 stories about him. He solves marital issues, boredom, existential despair, and the occasional odd crime.

He's got a staff, allowing Agatha to experiment with various supporting character types. He hires performers as needed to ensure total client satisfaction. He owns property for use in staging his scenarios.

His assistant is Miss Lemon. She's the ideal secretary, ultra-efficient and devoted to running the office. Hercule Poirot later hired her, and it's no wonder she works so well for him. She's used to an eccentric boss.

In *The Case of the Middle-Aged Wife*, we learned Parker Pyne has a lounge lizard on call, Claude Luttrell, to seduce the ladies as needed. In this episode, we're introduced to Claude's counterpart, the woman of mystery Madeline de Sera, who ascertains the workings of a gentleman's heart.

Pyne's adviser on dramatic yet believable scenarios is the famous novelist Ariadne Oliver. She doesn't appear until the dénouement, but she devised the plot involving treasure maps, kidnapping, near-death escapes, and rescuing damsels.

There's a lovely moment when Pyne asks that next time, she create a more original plot. No, she replies. People expect treasure maps, kidnappings and hair-breath escapes. Create something original, and they become confused and unhappy. This is how she's published 40 bestsellers translated into 20 languages.

Lally Bowers plays Ariadne and she's pitch-perfect. It's a shame *The Agatha Christie Hour* didn't film the other Parker Pyne stories featuring her, so we could watch Agatha developing her alter-ego.

As I said, the stories are all over the map as Agatha tested different genres and tropes and played with the question of "what is a detective." She was always cutting edge.

She also had a sense of humor, and thus we come to Major John Wilbraham. His problem is that his life is over. He retired from the Army and left Kenya, returning to a typical English village in the middle of nowhere. It's empty, blah, gray, and an eternity of boredom awaits.

Forever after her round-the-world cruise in 1922,

Maj. John Wilbraham (*William Gaunt*), the bored soldier

Freda Clegg (*Patricia Garwood*), the threatened woman

Madeleine de Sara (*Veronica Strong*), the mystery woman

Mrs. Benson (*Barbara New*), the watchful landlady

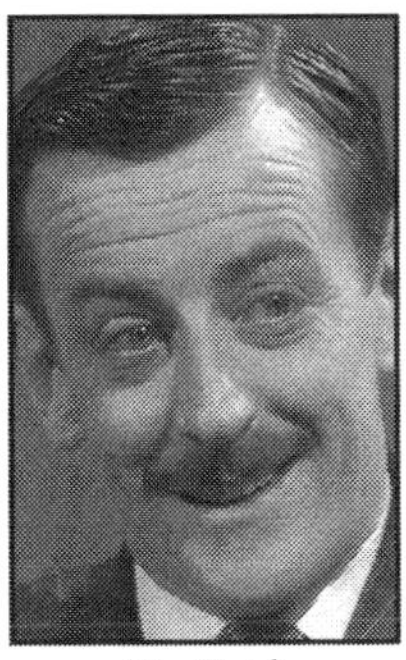
Mr. Reid (*Lewis Fiander*), the sinister solicitor

Charlie & Neville (*Jason Norman & Paul Dadson*), the sassy street urchins

Agatha remained fond of Africa. You can safely assume that if she portrays a retired officer positively, he served in Africa. If he's a pedantic bore who deserves to get murdered, that military man spent his time in India.

Major John (William Gaunt) is lonely, isolated, surrounded by strangers who either see him as husband number three, or as "that outsider." He's only got his noble dog at his side, and while Wally is a good listener, he doesn't keep up his end of the conversation. Wally, a handsome golden cocker spaniel, is portrayed by Walter Gaunt. Walter Gaunt is William Gaunt's dog, acting alongside his master in this and other roles. It explains why Wally is so attentive to Major John. He's not acting! The dog genuinely adores Major John.

Major John sees Parker Pyne's advert (*"Are You Happy?"*) and takes a chance. Pyne correctly diagnoses the problem. Retired empire builders get bored. They've lost their purpose in life. Ergo, adventure and a purpose must be found. It won't be found in that boring little village. A check for 50 guineas is handed over on the promise that Major John will be happy within six weeks or his money back.

Madeline de Sera enters and she interrogates Major John over lunch. She's a femme fatale, way out of his league, intimidatingly sultry, and not the kind of girl he pines for. Madeline, like Miss Lemon, is better at sizing up Major John's romantical aspirations than Parker Pyne is.

Then we meet Freda Clegg. She's a lonely young woman, making her way alone in the world, although she's not quite alone. She's got a nosy landlady and two street urchins who take an interest in her welfare.

She receives a visit from a strange solicitor from Australia about a mysterious legacy left by her sea-captain father. She hands over her father's papers, but can't imagine why. She knew nothing about that solicitor with a terrible Australian accent. Clearly, she needs a man to take charge of her life.

Fortunately, she's about to meet Major John. The solicitor sent her to a mysterious, abandoned house where she was set upon by thugs. (Not thugs from Africa as in the short story. These are London thugs). Major John overhears her cries for help and springs into action like ye knight of olde. The thugs flee, and Freda is overwhelmed, grateful, and very effusive.

General Information

Based on: "The Case of the Discontented Soldier" (short story, 1934)
Run time: 52 min. **Subtitles:** Yes

Writer: T.R. Bowen
Director: Michael Simpson

Cast

Maurice Denham as Parker Pyne
Angela Easterling as Miss Lemon
Veronica Strong as Madeleine de Sara
Lally Bowers as Mrs. Ariadne Oliver

William Gaunt as Maj. John Wilbraham
Walter Gaunt as Wally
Derek Smee as Head Waiter
Karen Mount as English Rose
Patricia Garwood as Freda Clegg
Jason Norman as Charlie
Paul Dadson as Neville
Barbara New as Mrs. Benson
Lewis Fiander as Mr. Reid
Peter Brayham as Thug 1
Terence Plummer as Thug 2
John Kearney as The Factor

Film Location

Turville, Buckinghamshire, Henley-on-Thames

Music

"If You Were The Only Girl (In The World)" (1916), written by Nat D. Ayer with lyrics by Clifford Grey, sung by George Robey and Violet Loraine

You can tell that Major John, while acting properly modest, is very pleased with himself and who wouldn't be? He rescued a damsel! Even better, exactly the kind of damsel he pines for.

Then, to add frosting to his cake, Freda still needs his help. They have a lovely lunch, they talk about her mysterious assailants, return to her flat, and discover that she's been robbed. Adventure! Life! Color! have returned to Major John's life. The sprinkles on his frosted cake arrive when he deduces that Freda still has what the solicitor wanted. They discover the map her father concealed inside a blown-out ostrich egg. And he can read it, because it's in Swahili, the language he learned in Kenya.

Could a man be happier? Well, sure. The hidden map is a treasure map, leading to a cache of ivory.

Freda and Major John separate for the evening, each back to their lonely lodgings.

Their plans for the next day are disturbed when they each receive a letter, supposedly from the other. Major John discovers Freda held captive in the rundown house where he rescued her from the thugs. He stops paying attention to his surroundings, gets coshed in the head, and awakens tied up in the cellar with Freda. The villainous solicitor tells them their fate, turns on the taps, and leaves them to drown. Major John rises to the occasion, burns the ropes tying his wrists together, and then, adding ice cream to his cake, he heroically rescues Freda again.

A month later, we see them in Kenya. There's no ivory cache. Nonetheless, champagne with cake and ice cream, Major John found the girl of his dreams, she's found her dream man, they're in Africa with Wally, and all ends happily. If only, Major John thinks, he hadn't wasted 50 guineas on Parker Pyne. But he is happy just like Pyne promised, so he magnanimously forgives him, even if the old man had nothing to do with it.

The episode works pretty well, although I would have liked more chemistry between our leads. I would have liked seeing much more of Ariadne Oliver. She steals the scene even more than Wally does.

Magnolia Blossom (1982)

A woman is caught between duty and passion when her husband attracts the notice of Scotland Yard

Fidelity to text

The plot remains. Other than the three leads, everyone else onscreen was added.

Quality of movie

When the other characters were added, the screenwriter neglected to make anyone compelling or provide understandable motivations.

Over her long career, Agatha wrote many stories that didn't involve Hercule Poirot or Miss Marple. There are so many that it's hard to grasp how much she wrote and in how many genres. She's reliably very good, but not always and "Magnolia Blossom," a very early story, is a case in point.

In the 1926 short story, you get three characters: the wealthy Theodora (her nickname, Theo, is the only interesting thing about her), Richard, her shady businessman husband, and Vincent, her would-be lover. No one else. The plot meanders, stranding plot points here and there, including the bombshell complication (ignored in the film) that Vincent is in London not because he's selling oranges for his South African farmers' association but because he was asked to investigate Richard's firm.

He was a bad investigator. When Theo asked him, he handed her the critical documents and the match to burn them with and got exactly zero in exchange. This is after Theo dumped him to run back to Richard in his hour of need.

Theo's not very bright either. She vacillates between glittering society hostess and lost damsel, swayed by the moment and inconsistent loyalties. She doesn't love her husband. After spending two weeks in Vincent's company, she was prepared to desert Richard and the mansion she owns and flee to South Africa with a stranger. Then, she reads an evening newspaper story about Richard being accused of fraud and flees back to him.

Why? Nothing changed, except she felt the bonds of loyalty or guilt. Loyalty or guilt that, mind you, meant nothing that morning when the maid packed her bags for South Africa.

The script tried to address Theo's vacillations with some guff about duty above all. We get words but nothing to show where she thought her duty lay. To the staff of her grand mansion? Bates, the butler, reminds her that he's served her family his entire life. I assume other servants have done so as well. Yet she was going to let them down, so that wasn't it. Was it duty to her family home and the garden she loves? Clearly, no loyalty there. Her family back in Devon? No, they don't exist. The memory of a beloved nanny exhorting young Theo about the importance of duty to

Theo Darrell
(*Ciaran Madden*),
the betrayed wife

Richard Darrell
(*Jeremy Clyde*),
the wronged husband

Vincent Easton
(*Ralph Bates*),
the other man

Bates
(*Brian Oulton*),
the loyal retainer

Clare Hamilton
(*Alexandra Bastedo*),
the saucy mistress

Colonel Jaggers
(*Jack May*),
the patsy partner

keep the world sane and chugging along? Nope. Is she concerned about what friends, relatives, or the press would say about her pouring salt on Richard's wounds by fleeing to South Africa with another man? Not that either.

Why is duty suddenly so important? Because the script says so.

Then there's her garden. Apparently, it wasn't just love at first sight between Theo and Vincent. They connected over her garden. Since Vincent is an orange farmer in South Africa, he might have wooed Theo while they stood in the conservatory, staring at the typical bleak, rainy, dreary, clammy, cold, gray English day, with tales of gorgeous sunny days on the veldt. No, we don't get a scene explaining the attraction between two dull, completely chemistry-free people.

What we get is the garden that's as fake as the romance. It looks like the set designer went to Hobby Lobby and bought bright, colorful fake flowers that were cheap, and paid no attention to whether or not a given flower comes in that color or if they bloom at the same time.

I couldn't stop myself from shouting at the TV. The other colors were bad enough but blue! Those vibrantly blue flowers never existed in nature, even in the minds of copywriters for plant catalogs who lie with gay abandon. Never believe a plant catalog when it tells you a flower is a true, rich, deep blue. It's a lie. They're purple. Or gray. Or greenish. If a flower isn't a bachelor's button or a Himalayan Blue Poppy, it's not blue no matter what the advert claims.

To compound the error, the magnolia blossoms the camera panned across not only looked like they were the cheapest polyester fakes glue-gunned to bare twigs, they were *blue*. Pale, icy blue. Magnolia flowers do not come in blue. They are white, creamy blush, delicate yellows, the palest pinks and the most flamboyant magentas. Not *blue*. Magnolias bloom in the spring but I'd lay odds that most of the flowers in Theo's garden were not spring-bloomers. No, they all came from Hobby Lobby where blooming seasons and verisimilitude in plant species color are unimportant.

This is particularly irritating because in England, gardening is a competitive sport! You cannot tell me that the set designer didn't know better. At least the flowering Clivia looked good. And real.

The other item that looked both good and real was Theo's dress at the climax. This was a gorgeous knockoff of a Callot Soeurs dress in true magnolia blossom colors: white, creamy blush, the palest of pinks. In the text, Agatha spells it Caillot but Callot Soeurs is probably who she was thinking of. Operated by the Callot sisters, they were one of the great haute couture houses in the 1910s and 1920s.

General Information

Based on: "Magnolia Blossom" (short story, 1926)
Run time: 51 min. **Subtitles:** Yes

Writer: John Bryden Rodgers
Director: John Frankau

Cast

Ciaran Madden as Theo Darrell
Jeremy Clyde as Richard Darrell
Ralph Bates as Vincent Easton
Brian Oulton as Bates
Alexandra Bastedo as Clare Hamilton
Jack May as Colonel Jaggers
Charles Hodgson as Cabinet Minister
Phillip Cade as Bobby Dorkins
Sarah-Jane Varley as Vanessa
Graham Seed as Charles Willerby
Jane Laurie as Imogen
Jennifer Croxton as Marlita
Keith Marsh as Ticket Inspector
Derek Fuke as Taxi Driver

At least raving about the flowers and Theo's dress took my mind off the script. In order for the story to work, it needed about six more passes. It also needed to be longer. I can't believe I'm saying this considering how tedious it was, but at 51 minutes, it felt padded with scenes of sparkling dinner parties crammed with sparkling conversation and fashionable evening wear. Those scenes did nothing to explain why Theo left Richard without a backward glance and then felt such an overpowering sense of duty that she had to return to him.

Those scenes could have set up a heartrending moment when Theo tells Vincent that their dinner guests would eviscerate Richard even more than Scotland Yard will when the fraud department arrives and so she must rush to his side. Those scenes implied that Richard was enjoying a torrid affair with a hot redhead but again, no follow-through other than Theo saying, "I know you cheated." But we didn't *watch* him carrying on with the redhead so there's the distinct possibility that Theo lies when it suits her.

There's also the problem of the elderly Colonel Jaggers. I needed to see either more of him or much less. He's another reason why Theo would have rushed back to Richard's side. She clearly liked the old man, but why? Had he helped raise her as a child to always put duty first? As a senior man in Richard's firm, he would be in deep trouble. Did he need Theo's aid to defend himself against charges of financial chicanery? She doesn't say and the script doesn't tell us. Like Bates, the butler, Colonel Jaggers' concerns are unimportant.

This could have been so much better if thought had been put into explaining why Theo behaved the way she did. Instead, you'll get fake flowers and irrational behavior. Skip it and watch something better.

The Mystery of the Blue Jar (1982)

A golfer hears a cry of 'murder' and with a French woman's help enlists a soul doctor to find the truth

Fidelity to text

Uncle George became far more prominent, the village suddenly gains residents, but most of all, the ending … shifted.

Quality of movie

Light and amusing, but not amusing enough. It needed to be more madcap.

Agatha knew her spiritualism. She could hardly avoid it as the culture around her was steeped in it. She had a boyfriend who introduced her to theosophy and the writings of the astonishing Madame Blavatsky (1831-1891). She used the supernatural frequently in her short stories. She even had Hercule Poirot comment on the power of superstition in "The Adventure of the Egyptian Tomb."

She used the supernatural as raw material for her stories, as any good writer does, but that doesn't mean she believed any of it. Recall that Larry Niven (b. 1938) said, "There is a technical, literary term for those who mistake the opinions and beliefs of characters in a novel for those of the author. The term is 'idiot'."

People regularly run face-first into this issue with Agatha's prose. They confuse her *characters* (venal, petty, bigoted, or small-minded) with her. She wasn't any of that. Similarly, she used the occult in her stories but don't you believe that she read her tarot cards every morning, studied her tea leaves every afternoon, and practiced automatic writing in the evening.

For her, the supernatural was interesting and made for a damn fine story. That went double if she could turn it on its head, something she loved doing.

"The Mystery of the Blue Jar," published in 1924, is a fine example. A young man, old enough to have served in the Great War, is studying law by day but he really wants to play golf. He spends every waking moment on the golf course when he's not studying. He even moved to a hotel next to a golf course so he can play daily at dawn and on weekends. An interesting tidbit buried in the story is that Jack Hartington is required to spend 5 and 1/2 days out of 7 imprisoned in the mahogany tomb of an office in the city. He doesn't get all of Saturday off! Only Sunday, which he spends entirely on the golf course, with no time for church.

The story opens when Jack, early-birding on the golf course, hears a woman screaming for help. She's being murdered. Startled rooks fly from the trees. While trying to find out who to rescue, he meets a damsel, who asks if he's suffering from shell shock.

The film greatly expands upon this set-up except the damsel doesn't ask about shell shock. That's a shame they left it out, because it provided another reason for Jack to fret over his sanity.

Otherwise, everything else was better in the film. We meet Jack and his Uncle George. We learn about their

Jack Hartington
(*Robin Kermode*),
the articles clerk

Uncle George
(*Derek Francis*),
the benign relative

Dr. Lavington
(*Michael Aldridge*),
the doctor of soul

Felise Marchaud
(*Isabelle Spade*),
the lady in distress

Mr. Dodds
(*Hugh Walters*),
the bookseller

Agnes
(*Glynis Brooks*),
the hotel servant

family, particularly Mad Harry, George's grandfather, and a wastrel and a gambler. We meet the local innkeeper, the local antiquarian bookseller, and the maid at the hotel where Jack lives. We also learn — an improvement on the story — that the hotel was once a grand mansion belonging to George's family until Mad Harry lost it gambling.

Uncle George is bluff and good-natured. He also primes Jack for his coming psychic adventure by discussing how things are not always as clear-cut as they seem. For example, he's not the least bit unhappy about losing the ancestral mansion and all the obligations that went with it. On the contrary; it's a huge benefit.

Sensible Uncle George, having done his duty by Jack, leaves to meet his wife in Italy. Jack continues to work hard, studying law by day and playing golf every other possible moment.

Then it happens. At 7:25 a.m., while on the course, he hears a woman's agonized screams. There's only one cottage in the woods near the golf course. The damsel in the cottage's garden hasn't heard a thing. Jack endures a few more mornings of being the only person who hears anything, at the same time each day, and worries increasingly that his hard work is affecting his sanity.

Luckily for Jack, Dr. Lavington, another guest at the hotel, comes to his aid. Uncle George had Dr. Lavington over for a drink and since he didn't say "beware of that quack" (despite calling Lavington "a doctor of the soul"), Jack decides the Doctor is respectable.

Jack consults Dr. Lavington, who takes his concerns seriously. He discusses the possibility that Jack has unusually keen senses; that one-in-a-thousand ability to detect something that's out of the ordinary. Something supernatural, in fact. He promises to investigate while Jack's in the city.

In a surprise turn, the damsel shows up at the hotel asking for Jack. She's Felise Marchaud, living in the cottage with her invalid father. She's tells him of her mysterious and frightening dreams involving a terrified woman and a big blue jar.

General Information

Based on: "The Mystery of the Blue Jar" (short story, 1924)
Run time: 51 min. **Subtitles:** Yes

Writer: T.R. Bowen
Director: Cyril Coke

Cast

Robin Kermode as Jack Hartington
Derek Francis as Uncle George
Michael Aldridge as Dr. Lavington
Isabelle Spade as Felise Marchaud
Philip Bird as Pierre Marchaud
Hugh Walters as Mr. Dodds
Glynis Brooks as Agnes
Ivor Roberts as Mr. Hubble
Robert Austin as Police Sergeant
Tara Ward as Portia

Film Location

The Square, Shere, Surrey

Dr. Lavington reports bad news to Jack. Mad Harry had a dreadful reputation, including admitting on his deathbed that he murdered his mistress. The mistress had lived in the cottage, and had come into money before vanishing. They meet Felise, and she tells them of her dreams about the blue jar.

Dr. Lavington asks Jack if he knows anything about it. Why yes, Uncle George has a big blue jar in his cottage he uses to hold umbrellas and walking sticks. Dr. Lavington decides they must hold a séance in the cottage. He arranges for Jack to bring the jar. The three of them commune over the jar in the dark, waiting for the spirits to speak.

And speak they do. Jack falls unconscious.

Did the spirits really speak? Not exactly! In one of Agatha's signature twists, Dr. Lavington is a fraud in league with the lovely Felise. Worse, her invalid father is another young man, a brother or lover perhaps. We aren't told.

Is all hope lost for Jack? No, in one of the improvements to the short story, Uncle George comes home early. He was seasick crossing the channel, recovered in Paris, and returned home. He sent Jack off to the séance, and while talking to the antiquarian bookseller, realizes that while people lie all the time, rooks don't. Jack heard the woman screaming yet the damsel claimed she didn't. Because the rooks fluttered into the sky in a fright, then the damsel lied. Rooks don't hear ghosts.

The ending was improved over the short story too. In keeping with Uncle George's personality makeover, he's not that concerned about losing a priceless piece of ancient Chinese porcelain as long as Jack is safe. He's got another big blue jar in the spare room! Plus, it's difficult to smuggle big pieces of porcelain out of the country so the first jar may come home.

My only complaint is the film should have sparkled more. This needed to be frothier. There are great moments, especially where Uncle George works out what happened with the bookseller who knows his village history. It's good entertainment but you probably won't watch it twice.

> *Here you are getting up at crack of dawn doing half a dozen holes before breakfast racing off to the City braving old Bierstowe before coffee dashing back here to finish up with Roman law … Plain as the nose on your face my boy, you're overdoing it!*
>
> UNCLE GEORGE

The Red Signal (1982)

Bad casting and an indifferent script reduces the power of a love triangle from a nuclear explosion to a squib

Fidelity to text

It's a virtually word for word remake of the short story, other than a few expanded scenes and that "improved" ending, which was terrible.

Quality of movie

Like the dry ice imitating London fog, it felt off and fake. It wasn't eerie enough.

The Red Signal demonstrates how people's poor communication skills lead to huge problems. Conversely, if any of the characters had been able to voice simple coherent sentences or ask for clarification, we wouldn't have had a plot. You'd think everyone got their exercise exclusively from jumping to conclusions.

One reason for Dermot, Claire, and Sir Alington's total inability to form complete sentences might be the intense shame surrounding mental illness at the time. Mental illness carried a far bigger stigma then than it does now. It was humiliating in every way, tainting the entire family as not just batty or dangerous, but even worse, socially unacceptable.

Patient confidentiality also clouds the issue. Sir Alington is scrupulous about not revealing what he knows about the Trent household. He also assumes that dear nephew Dermot understands who he is hinting about. Despite being a noted shrink, Sir Alington completely misunderstands what Dermot knows.

You don't expect better from Dermot, an ordinary young man of the period, but alienists are supposed to be better at reading people. You'd be wrong, leading you to suspect that Sir Alington isn't as good an alienist as he thinks he is. After all, he's diagnosing Jack Trent over a dinner party, followed perform a little more work than that to make a diagnosis, especially one that will lead to someone being locked up in an insane asylum.

There's also the issue of divorce. If Jack Trent is crazy and locked up in the loony bin, then Claire is stuck. She can't divorce him, not without an act of Parliament or some such extreme, very public action. She has to wait for him to die. Insanity as grounds for divorce didn't become legal until the late 1930s in the U.K. Divorce at the time of the episode (mid-1920s based on clothing and cars) was granted for adultery and abandonment. So people got divorced, but they went into court knowing at least one party was going to get dragged through the mud with private detectives discussing hotel room trysts involving third parties (the co-respondent). Divorce was never as casual as fiction would have you believe.

Claire Trent
(*Joanna David*),
the tortured wife

Jack Trent
(*Christopher Cazenove*),
the caring husband

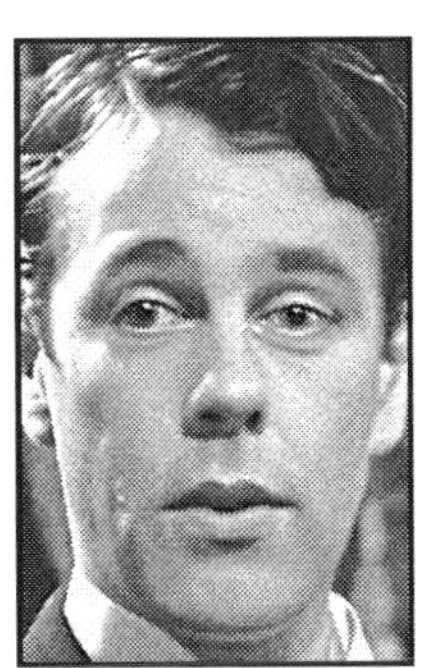
Dermot West
(*Richard Morant*),
the best friend to both

Sir Alington West
(*Alan Badel*),
the benevolent uncle

Violet Eversleigh
(*Carol Drinkwater*),
the vivacious guest

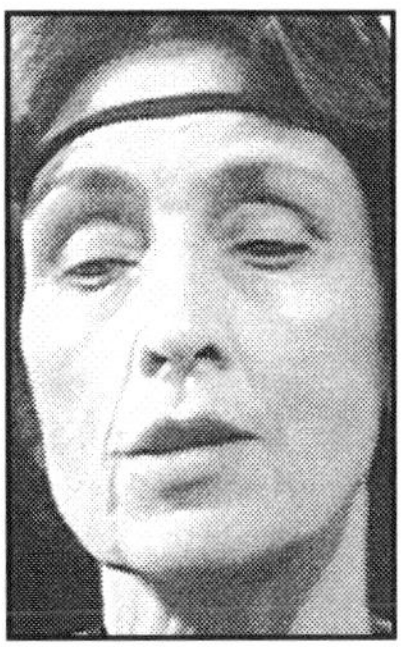
Mrs. Thompson
(*Rosalie Crutchley*),
the insightful medium

Divorcing your homicidal spouse was even harder as they were unlikely to cooperate with admitting adultery on the stand. Yes, Agatha and Archie endured this farce to get their divorce.

But that doesn't matter much in this story, because even with all that going on in the background, none of these educated, upper-class ladies and gentlemen were capable of clarity of speech and thought. I can't stand it when characters are willfully stupid because the plot depends on them not understanding or asking simple questions.

The warning red signal that Dermot receives for mysterious reasons was handled badly. No reason was given for *why* he gets the signal, other than (as in the short story) he just does. No rescue of a Bedouin shaman, no talisman picked up as a souvenir in the Great War, no history of the second sight in his family. No, he just does.

Worse, what the camera shows is a red and white drawing. When you think of all the tricks a good cameraman can do, it's pathetic. Why didn't a red haze descend over the camera, showing everything edged in fire? That would have been dramatic and then Dermot could have doubted his own sanity, making for a much more interesting film. Instead, the red signal is dull.

Claire, Jack's wife and Dermot's obsession, is even duller than the red signal. She's pretty enough but that's all. The actress didn't make me understand why Jack was ready to kill her and anyone who wanted her (the old trope of if I can't have you, no one can) nor why she fascinated Dermot. She was a hole in the screen.

If Carol Drinkwater had played Claire, it might be understandable. Instead, she portrayed auburn-haired Violet Eversleigh, live wire and life of the party. Most men and some women would be obsessed with *her*. Of course, Violet Eversleigh wouldn't have been as mealymouthed as Claire and that would have changed the plot completely. Our Violet has a husband somewhere offstage, probably at home working on his stamp collection while his wife works on her career as a co-respondent in divorce cases.

The ending was dreadful. Agatha's, I'm sorry to say, wasn't much better, but at least it was clear. Jack — who is a crack shot — shoots himself rather than get hauled off to jail for the murder of Sir Alington. There's still the question of who called Inspector Verrall and Constable Cawley. The reader must assume it was Claire, finally womaning up and demonstrating why she's such an object of fascination, but it's not spelled out.

General Information

Based on: "The Red Signal" (short story, 1924)
Run time: 51 min. **Subtitles:** Yes

Writer: William Corlett
Director: John Frankau

Cast

Joanna David as Claire Trent
Christopher Cazenove as Jack Trent
Richard Morant as Dermot West
Alan Badel as Sir Alington West
Carol Drinkwater as Violet Eversleigh
Rosalie Crutchley as Mrs. Thompson
Bob Keegan as Inspector Verrall
Andrew McCulloch as Constable Cawley
Michael Denison as Johnson
Hugh Sullivan as Milson
David Rolfe as Charlson
Ewan Roberts as McKern
Christopher Wren as Garry Benson
Michael Mellinger as Guido

I ranted to Bill during our nightly walk afterwards and worked out how the ending could have been so much better, redeeming the film.

When Dermot was on the run from the coppers, he could have hidden somewhere and overheard a conversation between strangers (a classic Agatha trope!) suggesting that he might have misinterpreted what Sir Alington said. That is, he'd hear one barfly say to the other, "I meant him, you dummy, not *her*."

"Well then, why didn't you say so?"

That would set up Dermot for his realization that he had no idea what was actually going on. The fog of confusion would begin to lift.

At the same time, there should have been an explanation for why Inspector Verrall and Constable Cawley, supposedly searching for Dermot, ended up in the Trent home. What should have happened was that Claire overheard Jack gloating over shooting Sir Alington and framing Dermot for the murder. Then, worse, (finally forcing spineless Claire to actually act instead of lounge around like a wan, pale, fainting flower) she'd hear him decide that tonight was the night to unite the knife with Claire.

Or she could already suspect Jack, because her maid told her about Sir Alington's murder. Or something like that. Anything! At that point, she summons Scotland Yard.

Thus, when Dermot finally realizes what a fool he'd been as Jack reveals his true nature, it wouldn't be a complete, utter, and wildly implausible surprise when Inspector Verrall, Constable Cawley, and Claire burst into the room. How did the Inspector know? Because Claire told him.

But there's not a hint of this onscreen. The Inspector and the Constable appear out of the fog because the plot demands they do so.

The reason to watch this mess, other than completeness' sake, is the séance scene. That was well done. Nothing else was.

Jane In Search of a Job (1982)

Wanted: Poor, hungry girl willing to impersonate Ostravia duchess. Well paying. Danger guaranteed.

Fidelity to text

The rescuing hero gets a name and a backstory. Other characters grow, and still more appear to flesh out Jane's world.

Quality of movie

Romantic escapades should be frothy, madcap, comic soufflés. This one didn't get its eggs beaten quite high enough.

Agatha was never one for pure, straight, undiluted genre writing and her non-mysteries were even more so. She wrote many short stories at the beginning of her career that were romances at heart, with criminal or supernatural trappings to enhance the story.

In "Jane In Search of a Job," every element of a typical lady's magazine romantic short is present. The ingenue is desperate for money. The long-suffering landlady is sympathetic but wants to get paid. The handsome young man across the hall is interested in her, and he's even more interested when he glimpses her in her pajamas (so shocking!).

Oh, wait, that last bit is from the film.

One of the many improvements over the short story was making our hero into a fully realized character. Instead of a stranger showing up in the nick of time, Jane has a neighbor in the boarding house. He's Nigel Guest; tall, blond, handsome, and on his way up the ladder as he'll attend Hendon College to become a police inspector. He's leapfrogging over regular lads who began their careers as beat constables in some quaint but minuscule village in the middle of nowhere. That fancy degree will move him up several rungs and he'll start his career in London at Scotland Yard.

Chief Inspector Japp would be impressed — not necessarily favorably — as *he* had to pound a beat while college boy skips those tedious steps. The local bobby in the quaint, minuscule village near Orion House (where the impersonation takes place) knows exactly how Japp would feel. He's nonplussed when Nigel bursts in demanding they swing into action, but his policing shows why Scotland Yard started Hendon College.

Jane *is* impressed by Nigel, but much more favorably. Still, she has her way to make in the world. She's a poor vicar's daughter and needs money. A dalliance isn't what she has in mind — even with tall, blond, and handsome — especially when tall and blond is rudely telling her what to do.

Fortunately for the future of their relationship, Nigel points out to her an unusual advert in the newspaper's agony column. It's asking for someone who looks like Jane. There's the lure of good money but for what?

Jane wolfs down her poached egg and heads out. She soon discovers she's competing against many tall, slim, fair young ladies in London. Ah, but she has a

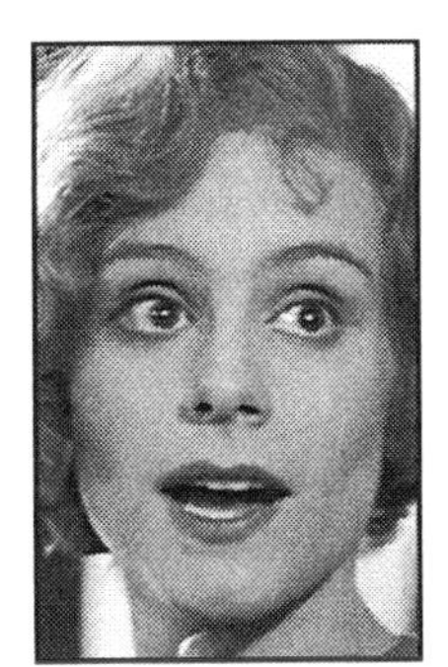
Jane Cleveland (*Elizabeth Garvie*), the desperate girl

Nigel Guest (*Andrew Bicknell*), the trainee bobby

Pauline (*Amanda Redman*), the grand duchess

Count Streptitch (*Tony Jay*), the duchess' courtier

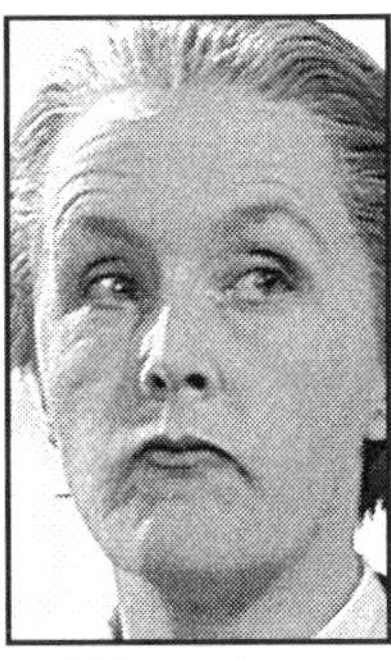
Princess Anna (*Stephanie Cole*), the lady in waiting

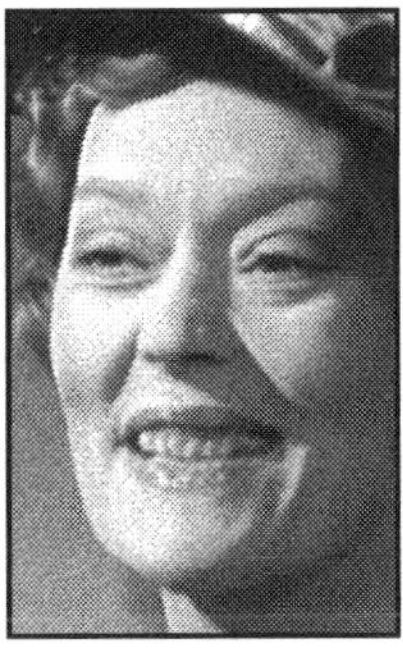
Lady Anchester (*Helen Lindsay*), the bazaar host

secret weapon. She speaks French fluently and demonstrates her skill to the mysterious Mittel European gentleman interviewing her. Then it's off to meet more mysterious Mittel Europeans, a count this time, and stern Princess Anna. Then the final step. Will the Grand Duchess of Ostravia, Pauline, approve?

She does! Jane has a job! She'll impersonate the Grand Duchess for £2,000 so that worthy lady can avoid Bolsheviks and vodka-swilling revolutionaries while raising money for the benefit of her poor, starving countrymen. Jane must endure the risks of kidnappers and bomb-throwers, so she asks for an additional £1,000. The Grand Duchess merrily agrees. Money is no object, she likes Jane, and she admits she has no head for business.

Royalty depends on good advisers for exactly those reasons. The count is less enthused about handing over sheafs of pound notes to Jane so she can outfit herself properly for the deception but Grand Duchess Pauline insists. The Ostravians behave exactly as Jane would expect minor Mittel Europa royalty to act.

Back in her boarding house room, Jane shows off her new red dress, bag, high-heeled shoes, sharp hat, and fox fur cape to Nigel. We'll assume she paid her back rent to the landlady before bounding up the stairs. She tells Nigel about her wonderful opportunity. Nigel, budding future police inspector and wet-blanket, throws cold water on Jane's job. He thinks something is wrong with the situation.

Jane discounts his suspicions and heads off to the fundraiser disguised as an American journalist. She'll interview Grand Duchess Pauline at Orion House, switch clothes with her, and then leave with Princess Anna, laying a false trail for the kidnappers. The Grand Duchess will pretend to be the red-clad American journalist and leave separately, safely anonymous, during the auction of the 100 donated pearls.

Meanwhile, Nigel demonstrates why he was accepted to Hendon College. He rides his motorcycle to Orion House, checks out suspicious back roads, discovers an even more suspicious abandoned racecar, and tries to figure out what's going on. Unlike red-clad lady journalists from America, he's not invited inside Orion House. He must spy from afar.

General Information

Based on: "Jane in Search of a Job" (short story, 1924)
Run time: 51 min. **Subtitles:** Yes

Writer: Gerald Savory
Director: Tom Shankland

Cast

Elizabeth Garvie as Jane Cleveland
Andrew Bicknell as Nigel Guest

Amanda Redman as Pauline, Grand Duchess of Ostravia
Stephanie Cole as Princess Anna
Tony Jay as Count Streptitch
Geoffrey Hinsliff as Colonel Kranin
Richard Tate as Manfred
Helen Lindsay as Lady Anchester
Roy Macready as Mr. Bissell
Neville Phillips as Delemain
Julia McCarthy as Miss Northwood
Robert McBain as Police Superintendent
George Waring as Station Sergeant
Martin Chamberlain as Police Sergeant
Hetty Baynes as Holly de Witt
Josie Kidd as Miss Thristle
Tex Fuller as Chauffeur
Mac Andrews as Footman

Film Location

Stowe House, Stowe, Buckinghamshire

As feared, Jane and Princess Anna are kidnapped by the chauffeur and driven to a ramshackle cottage in the middle of nowhere. The kidnappers are gracious enough to feed them and since Jane's starving, she eats the soup. Princess Anna does not and for a very good reason.

Then — you were expecting the twist, right? — the pearls to be auctioned off at Orion house are stolen by the red-clad lady journalist from America. Our Nigel's suspicions are realized. It had been a scam all along and poor, lovely, innocent Jane will be blamed. He must save her! He has to find her first, and along the way, notify the skeptical and slow local constable.

Jane wakes up and discovers she's back in her red dress, fur cape, and high-heeled shoes. Who changed her clothes while she was unconscious? Why is there a pistol in her hand? Could she have been ... used?

Yes, annoying but handsome Nigel was correct in his suspicions. However, he turns out to not have been as smart as he thought he was since Jane is also wearing Nigel's unconscious body stretched out over on top of hers. He found the house, found comatose Jane, and got his head coshed for his troubles.

The gang of thieves drive off. They meet a police roadblock and pass themselves off as French citizens. Since local bobbies aren't that bright, they're allowed to pass.

Or are they? Nigel may have been dumb enough to not watch his back, but before racing off to search for Jane, he was bright enough to call Scotland Yard. Good thing the thieves didn't murder her.

Back at Jane's boarding house, he tells Jane how he knew something was up. It was her shoes. The Grand Duchess wore low heels. Jane wore high heels. He knew there had been some kind of switch. Does Nigel have a foot fetish? No, he's the son of a boot manufacturer so he's not only going to be a police inspector, he's got family money.

All ends happily, even when eggs end up broken on the floor. Still, it should have been frothier. This is an amusing diversion, but you won't watch it twice.

The Manhood of Edward Robinson (1982)

A henpecked man turns a windfall into a sports car and discovers adventure, romance, and maturity

Fidelity to text

Greatly expanded, giving Edward a new best friend, Maud a character arc, and Noreen a more complex way of avoiding boredom.

Quality of movie

The changes made for a better, more sparkling story.

This is the last of *The Agatha Christie Hour* adaptations. To my surprise, the series held up very well overall, despite each episode being completely unrelated to the others in theme, characters, stories, directors, cast, or scriptwriters. That's quite an accomplishment! It's a reminder that Agatha wrote in many genres.

It's also a reminder there are loads of her stories waiting to be adapted into films. People get hung up on Hercule Poirot and Miss Marple, but she had other detectives (Parker Pyne in particular) and other genres besides straight mysteries.

Manhood is a good example. It's a light, fluffy, screwball romantic comedy. Hollywood used to excel at them, starting with *It Happened One Night* in 1934, when you watched bored madcap heiresses indulging themselves with ridiculous escapades, and connecting with some lucky gentleman from across the class divide. Yet Agatha published *Manhood* in 1924.

Another unusual aspect of *Manhood* is there are two equally important female leads but they're not the focus. It's Edward, the earnest young man who needs to stand up for himself and trust his judgment.

Even more unusual, the ladies (Maud the fiancée and Noreen the heiress) never meet. They don't know each other exists. They don't know they're competing for the same man's affections. By the end of the film, Edward knows them both well and must choose between them.

It's always interesting when main characters don't meet, and it's rarely done. The (filmed) example that springing to mind is the Bruce Willis sci-fi epic *The Fifth Element* (1997). Our hero Bruce crosses paths with the villain in an elevator and neither knows who the other is or why they're important so they run off to their respective plot threads.

Which means that, by the end, only Edward knows the whole story of what went on that momentous night. Will Edward ever admit to Maud that he met Lady Noreen, madcap heiress and part-time cat burglar? Probably not; Maud might not take it well.

I see I need to backtrack. The short story does a lot of telling, not showing, but movies need action. Thus, Edward gains a friend, Herbert. Herbert is, like Edward, a very junior stock clerk. He encourages Edward to live a little, to enter name-guessing

Edward Robinson
(*Nicholas Farrell*),
the diffident man

Maud Lithinglow
(*Ann Thornton*),
the firm fiancée

Mrs. Lithinglow
(*Margery Mason*),
the mother-in-law to be

Lady Noreen Elliot
(*Cherie Lunghi*),
the bored toff

Herbert
(*Tom Mannion*),
the advising friend

Jeremy
(*Nicholas Bell*),
the fearless pursuer

competitions in the newspaper, to consider that even though Maud is remarkably pretty, she can also be controlling. Do women turn into their mothers? If so, Edward can look forward to Maud becoming like her mother, who makes him sit and hold her yarn while she lectures him on his duty to her Maud.

Maud's mother is not the girl any man would want to marry unless he likes being a doormat, told what to do from his first waking moment to when he's finally asleep and oh, by the way, how whatever he's doing was wrong or could be improved.

Maud's heading in that direction, and she gets an actual story arc in the film, a huge improvement. In the short story, there's no reason for Maud to accept Edward's newfound self-confidence, but in the film, it's different. She lectures him on saving and scrimping because she's concerned about their future. She's genuinely trying to help and wants to be sure they're financially secure when they marry. But it comes across as nagging. The engagement ring is too expensive. The movie tickets (to a real movie called *Good Night, Vienna*, sometimes titled *Magic Night* (1932)) cost too much. They can't marry now but have to wait.

You can see why Edward might be having second thoughts, despite how well he and Maud dance together.

Then he wins the newspaper name-guessing contest and scores a quick £500. Should he be sensible like Maud and her mother would demand? Or should he blow the money on the car of his dreams? Edward buys the car, Herbert teaches him to drive it, and that means he sees less of Maud.

This was a very nice touch. His unexpected absences forced Maud to reevaluate her relationship with Edward. She wondered if her well-meaning treatment of him was driving him away. Why, she even complained about the cost of her engagement ring and refused to marry when he wanted! Maybe he doesn't want to marry her any more. Every scene between Maud and her mother amplified her doubts and fears.

The Christmas holidays arrive and Edward is faced with a decision. Run off and enjoy a magic night on his own with his fabulous new car? Or be a dutiful fiancé and spend it with Maud and her harridan mother? He lies to Maud and drives away in his new car.

General Information

Based on: "The Manhood of Edward Robinson" (short story, 1924)
Run time: 52 min. **Subtitles:** Yes

Writer: Gerald Savory
Director: Brian Farnham

Cast

Nicholas Farrell as Edward Robinson
Ann Thornton as Maud Lithinglow
Margery Mason as Mrs. Lithinglow
Cherie Lunghi as Lady Noreen Elliot
Tom Mannion as Herbert
Sallyanne Law as Millie
Patrick Newell as The Major
Bryan Coleman as Lord Melbury
Nicholas Bell as Jeremy
Rupert Everett as Guy
Fiona Hendley as Poppy
Simon Green as Sebastian
Georgina Coombs as Diana
Rio Fanning as Barman
Frank Duncan as Grosvenor
Julian Wadham as Gerald Champneys

Film Locations

Harpsden Court, Harpsden, Oxfordshire (Tantalus Hotel)
75 Victoria Road, London (Lady Noreen's home)

That's how Edward meets madcap, bored heiress Noreen. He nearly runs her over in the dark lane leading to the trendy hotel, parks his expensive new car next to the other expensive cars, enters and discovers a new world. This world is rich and titled, with gentlemen in tuxedos and ladies in evening gowns, all raucously drunk. When Edward — sadly out of place — leaves, he discovers he drove off in the wrong car.

Complications pile on complications. He discovers in a door pocket not his muffler (probably knitted by Maud) but a diamond necklace. The note with the necklace sends him to a rendezvous where he meets Lady Noreen. She thinks he's Gerald's brother, Edward. He takes a while to figure out who she is and decides to impersonate this Edward just so he could stay with her.

Their magic night together culminates in a tango in a very happening, exclusive nightclub where a crowd of bright young things right out of P. G. Wodehouse try to steal the necklace back from Noreen. While you're watching the action, keep an eye out for a very young Rupert Everett in one of his earliest roles.

Edward grows in self-confidence, tangos up a storm with Noreen, and defends her against all comers. They dance together well enough to clear the floor while everyone else watches. This does happen. I've watched my sister and her husband (dedicated ballroom dancers) provide the floor show at weddings. When they're dancing, no one else dares set foot on the dance floor and look like clodhoppers.

Edward and Noreen, despite being in a crowd of aristocrats, intimidate via their dancing. It must have been a wonderful feeling for Edward who was feeling sadly out of place.

Eventually, Edward must decide. Become the jewel thief Noreen thinks he is? Take her up on her offer of becoming partners in crime? Or gracefully decline, without revealing who he really is, a junior clerk slumming with the aristos (which would embarrass her dreadfully) and return to Maud.

It all turns out happily, as screwball comedies should. With tangos, fast cars, the class divide, stolen diamond necklaces, and the realization of true love, this was a charming episode and an excellent finish to the series.

Murder Is Easy (1982)

A series of fatal accidents plague a country village, but a statistician calculates the odds in favor of murder

This is a very odd movie. It was cutting-edge television in 1982 with exotic location shooting, stars, clothes, and hair. Bridget Conway's (Lesley-Anne Down) clothes are to die for; don't miss her teal jumpsuit lavishly adorned with silver zippers or her bright orange, bare-shouldered dress that made Bill perk up and take notice. You can tell it's 1982 because shoulder pads haven't arrived yet, nor is Bridget's hair fluffier than the gentlemen's.

Our hero, Luke Williams (Bill Bixby from *The Incredible Hulk*!) is no longer an expat policeman from Malaysia. Instead, he's an MIT computer scientist, mathematician, and probability expert on holiday in England. Despite his intelligence, he's still a bumbler; he misinterprets every clue, narrowly avoids getting the murderer's murderous attention, and arrives barely in time to save our heroine.

A bizarre scene at Oxford shows off bleeding-edge computers of the time. Luke takes Bridget there to use the college's mainframe to figure out whodunnit, so we see them in a large room with banks of computers, typing away at a plain-text terminal. The screenwriter had zero idea what programming them involved and the script made Bixby sound like an idiot. Even back then, viewers would have known better and today, it's like watching him do the time warp from a bad science-fiction film from the '50s. My Bill, who did computer programming in the '80s, was appalled.

Fidelity to text

There's some story compression (including vanishing the entire witchcraft subplot), character rewrites, and modernizing, but otherwise, you'll recognize the story.

Quality of movie

This should have been as poufy as Bill Bixby's hair but instead, it's flat.

Luke's friend, Jimmy Lorrimer, also gets a fairly substantial rewrite but his works. He performs the same function as in the novel and adds comic relief whenever he shows up. He's a member of the aristocracy and *expects* to get his own way, just like he *expects* to breathe. He has a wonderful scene with Luke, Bridget, and Lord Easterfield where he convinces his lordship to host this American stranger. He behaves impeccably while steamrollering his lordship until he drops the right bait to make him say yes.

Despite moving the story from 1939 to the Thatcher/Reagan era, this version is remarkably faithful to the text. Miss Marple does not show up (see ITV's unfortunate 2009 remake with Julia McKenzie), nor are entirely new subplots introduced to replace perfectly good existing ones. If anything, simplifying the plot made the movie more understandable. That's a must when you have to tell a complex story within 90

Luke Williams
(*Bill Bixby*),
the sleuth

Bridget Conway
(*Lesley-Anne Down*),
the secretary

Gordon Easterfield
(*Timothy West*),
the parvenu

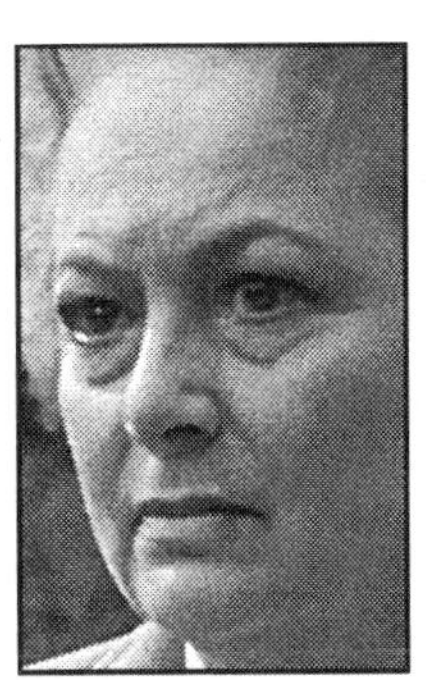

Honoria Waynflete
(*Olivia de Havilland*),
the curator

Constable Reed
(*Freddie Jones*),
the bobby

Lavinia Fullerton
(*Helen Hayes*),
the busybody

minutes involving seven murders — each committed differently! — and remain comprehensible.

Someday, we'll get the *good* version of *Murder Is Easy* we've been waiting for. I'd like to see the midnight rituals the antique dealer Mr. Ellsworthy conducts. I'd like to see Inspector Battle, who shows up at the end in the novel but not here.

Of the characters, Bridget Conway remains truest to the novel. Born into wealth, she's now a poor working girl. She's happy to marry Lord Easterfield despite his age and character. She doesn't want to be poor anymore, and she'd like to return to being the Lady of the Manor. Luke has issues with her practical mindset but then, he did in the novel.

Even better, this Bridget (unlike in the 2009 version) has an actual romance with Luke although I did *not* like her falling into bed with him within a day of their meeting. I can't stand how Hollywood forces actresses to behave like sluts. I especially can't stand it when the actresses play intelligent women. Do you really believe that Bridget Conway, shrewd gold-digger, would risk losing rich, easily managed Lord Easterfield over a one-night stand with any man, much less some out-of-towner? In Lord Easterfield's own mansion? Down the hall from Lord Easterfield's bedroom?

I don't. No one would. No, our Bridget would wait until *after* he put a ring on it. Then she'd conduct discreet affairs leading to sons that would bind them together permanently, keep the money flowing, and have her sons inherit the grand mansion and estate her family once owned.

Helen Hayes plays Lavinia Fullerton, the old lady who meets Luke on the train to London and pours out her improbable fears into his willing ears about the recent deaths in her village. He listens because nothing she says matches his probability theories but she's also interesting. She becomes even more interesting when he learns that she, after describing a serial killer in her quaint village, dies suddenly and horribly after being run over on her way to Scotland Yard. This is extremely improbable so off he goes to investigate. Helen Hayes doesn't get much screen time but she makes the most of it.

Sadly, she never shares a scene with the movie's other screen legend, Olivia de Havilland. She plays Honoria Waynflete, and she's magnificent. Clever, duplicitous and utterly believable no matter what she says or does. Along with Helen Hayes, she's the reason to watch this. You can tell who the pros are on this set. Bill Bixby is too much of a sitcom actor to fit easily into their exalted company. How good is Olivia, er, Honoria at covering up her crimes? Wonky Poo, Lavinia Fullerton's Himalayan cat, lets himself be cared for by her, never suspecting for a moment that she murdered his mistress.

There are strong hints of the class divide in the quaint village. Despite his status, Lord Easterfield is considered an upstart parvenu, awarded his title because of his newspaper empire. He's not that bright and more than one person in the village resents him taking over when Miss Waynflete and Miss Conway are higher than him on the social scale. Miss Waynflete didn't marry Lord Easterfield when they were young and his status as a tradesman's son might have been behind her decision. Or so people think. She says differently to Luke, but I'm sure it was there. It couldn't not have been.

The soundtrack was a problem. It indulged in all the worst aspects of TV music. It was nonexistent when background or mood music would have been appreciated, but when something happened, by God, that soundtrack let you know how to react in no uncertain terms. Were you supposed to laugh? The soundtrack told you three beats too soon. Should you gasp with fear? The soundtrack warned what was coming. Was a romantic scene coming up? The soundtrack lets you in on the secret. It was terrible and I say this knowing that I rarely pay attention to movie music. It's aural wallpaper. I only notice when it's exceptionally good or exceptionally bad. This was exceptionally bad, without the rationale of the music in *Spider's Web* (1960) which was as incongruous as the heroine.

Should you watch this film? It's much truer to the text than ITV's version which threw out most of Agatha's characters and subplots. But it lags when it should be energetic. But it's got Olivia de Havilland and Helen Hayes (who went on to play Miss Marple twice) so in the end the answer is: probably. Just don't expect anything spectacular like Bill Bixby turning into the Hulk.

General Information

Based on: *Murder Is Easy* (novel, 1939)
Run time: 1 hr., 30 min. **Subtitles:** Yes

Writer: Carmen Culver
Director: Claude Whatham

Cast

Bill Bixby as Luke Williams
Freddie Jones as Constable Reed
Timothy West as Lord Gordon Easterfield
Lesley-Anne Down as Bridget Conway
Olivia de Havilland as Honoria Waynflete
Helen Hayes as Lavinia Fullerton
Patrick Allen as Major Horton
Shane Briant as Dr. Thomas
Leigh Lawson as Jimmy Lorrimer
Jonathan Pryce as Mr. Ellsworthy
Ivor Roberts as Vicar
Trevor T. Smith as Rivers
Anthony Valentine as Abbot
Carol MacReady as Mrs. Pierce
Diana Goodman as Rose Humbleby

Film Locations

Marylebone Station, London
Hambleden village, Buckinghamshire
Church of St. Mary the Virgin and Hambleden War Memorial (Lavinia's funeral)
Binfield Manor, Binfield, Berkshire (Ashe Manor)
Radcliffe Camera, Oxford

The Witness for the Prosecution (1982)

A barrister's defense is complicated when a wife turns on her husband in the middle of his murder trial

One of the fascinations with the Agatha Christie Movie Project is seeing how different directors and stars handle the same storyline. A few changes here and there — they don't have to be wholesale rewrites like ITV's *Marple* (2004-2013) — can completely change the tenor of the film.

And so it proves here. Billy Wilder made an amazing movie, one of the very few that Agatha saw and liked. He collected stacks of award nominations, including the Oscar for best picture. That year's Academy Award didn't go to *Witness for the Prosecution*. Instead, *The Bridge Over the River Kwai* won. Perhaps the Academy made a mistake in judgment, perhaps not. Tastes vary. All of which is to say that remaking a landmark film is an exercise in peril.

I understand why they did this. Back in ye olden days, before DVD players and even further back, before VCRs, if you wanted to watch a movie you hoped it would show up on late-night cable or you traveled to some out-of-town film festival or revival house. By 1982, *Witness* was 25 years old. Memories fade and a new audience would judge a new production on its own merits.

The production company didn't take any chances. They reused (mostly) Billy Wilder's script and hired an all-star cast.

Did it work? Not really.

Fidelity to play

This remake is sometimes closer to the stage play than Billy Wilder's 1957 opus. Other times, it adds extraneous, unneeded material while cutting more important stuff.

Quality of movie

Stick to Billy Wilder directing Marlene Dietrich, Tyrone Power, and Charles Laughton. You won't miss a thing.

The script changes were good and bad. Sir Wilfred meets the mysterious Cockney woman in a dingy flat rather than at the noisy train station (bad). They kept Miss Plimsoll, the nurse clashing with crusty Sir Wilfrid (good). They added a scene showing the happy nurses, staff, and patients waving goodbye to Sir Wilfred when he leaves the hospital. He was an ornery patient and everyone, from the head doctor to the orderlies, were glad to see him go (okay, I guess). There's a very good prologue with the maid, Janet Mackenzie, walking anxiously back home to get a sewing pattern and hearing that cad with her mistress, followed by terrible sounds, and then discovering her body.

But this script skipped the entire backstory where Christine and Leonard Vole meet in the rubble of Berlin after the war. That scene was *important*: it showed how desperate Christine was *and* hinted at her acting skills. It showed how Leonard Vole got by on smarm, charm,

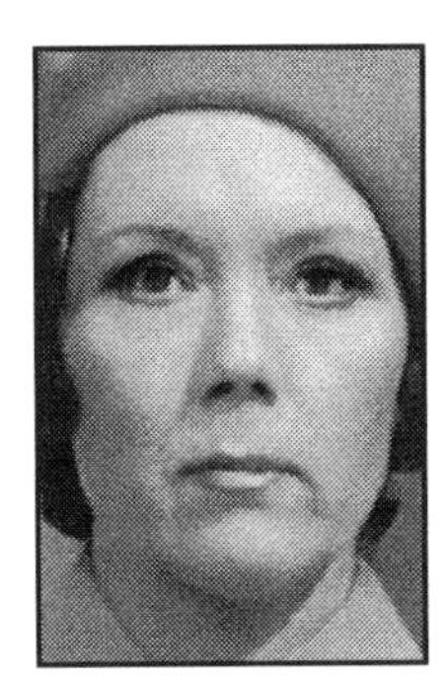
Christine (*Diana Rigg*), the loyal wife

Leonard Vole (*Beau Bridges*), the weak husband

Sir Wilfred Robarts (*Ralph Richardson*), the ailing barrister

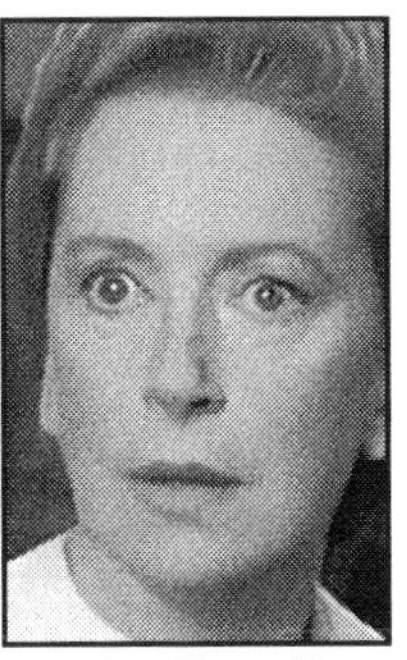
Miss Plimsoll (*Deborah Kerr*), the firm nurse

Mr. Myers (*Donald Pleasance*), the prosecutor

Janet Mackenzie (*Wendy Hiller*), the vengeful maid

and luck. He's not that smart and when he was young and handsome, his second-class skills didn't matter. As he got older, they did.

We also missed seeing Leonard demonstrate his magical egg-beater, the reason he chatted up Emily French. He needed money for his get-rich-quick invention and she had it. We didn't get scenes showing Leonard as a small-time grifter. They mattered because they made us dislike Leonard, making the prosecution witness' testimony all the more stunning.

Even shooting the film in color made a difference. Compare Sir Wilfred's monocle tests (much more extensive in 1957). They are far more effective in black and white than in color. Similarly, careful camera work in 1957 made you think you, like Sir Wilfred, were seeing far more of the mysterious Cockney woman than you were, which made revealing her ravaged face all the more shocking. In this version, she keeps twitching her scarecrow wig back and forth to hide her face. Despite the evocative rooming house, it didn't work. She behaved like she was pretending to suffer from the DTs. Sir Wilfred also didn't use his monocle at the climax, highlighting the knife on the evidence table.

The right cast can compensate for script weaknesses, but this cast was … not right.

Other than Sir Wilfred, the most important people onscreen are Leonard and Christine. You have to believe that Leonard is oily and smarmy, the kind of man who, when he says the sun rises in the east, you look out the window to check. Yet he also has to be charming to lonely, older ladies who crave a handsome man who flatters them, pays them attention, and makes them feel young and alive.

Tyrone Power was astonishingly good at portraying a man who shouldn't be trusted but you do anyway. Beau Bridges is a blank. He's a California boy, lost in London. We don't see him charming anyone, including Sir Wilfred. He doesn't bother. Because we don't see any scenes setting up his character, his murder of Emily French is all the stranger. Tyrone Power played Leonard as a man with no impulse control. He learned he'd inherit Emily's £80,000 and one week later, smashed her skull in so he didn't have to wait. No planning. No forethought. Beau Bridges was so lackadaisical he seemed to be sleepwalking through life. He would live off an old lady's affection, but he couldn't work up the energy to beat her to death.

Christine Vole is a German refugee, a woman who'd sell herself for a hot meal and coffee. She'd do anything to escape the ruins of Berlin. Despite her stardom and glamour, Marlene Dietrich was perfect for the part. Her accent — no surprise! — was spot-on. She conveyed the horrors she endured and what price she willingly paid for a better life. The scene in the Berlin nightclub where she met Leonard was crucial to show her desperation; more, it showed her gratitude. A grateful woman will put up with a lot from the man who rescues her.

I could not accept Diana Rigg as Christine Vole, who poured all her acting abilities into maintaining her accent. She was too polished. There should have been some roughness under the ice from the trauma she'd endured. But again, we didn't get to see anything of her beyond her meetings with Sir Wilfred and in the courtroom.

Christine's relations with Leonard was another area where Beau Bridges was miscast. Tyrone Power? Yes, any woman would put up with a lot from *him*. Bridges, however, was a handsome but charmless lump. As a couple, they were chemistry-free. Why would she stick with him, once she's safely in England? I couldn't see a reason other than gratitude.

Ralph Richardson as Sir Wilfred was acceptable, but he's no Charles Laughton. His monocle was largely removed from the script. His playing with his pills to indicate his thought processes during court scenes disappeared completely. He wasn't as acidic, nor was he as upset as Charles Laughton when he discovered how he'd been so completely fooled.

Another problem actress was Wendy Hiller as Janet Mackenzie. This is not because she can't act. It's because she made such a huge impression as the Princess Dragomiroff in *Murder on the Orient Express* (1974). Her voice is very distinctive, and I kept seeing a Russian princess and not a Scottish maid.

Should you watch this? For completeness' sake, sure. Otherwise, stick with Billy Wilder's wonderful, superlative film. It delivers. This doesn't.

General Information

Based on: *Witness for the Prosecution* (play, 1953), from "Traitor's Hands" (short story, 1925)
Run time: 1 hr., 37 min. **Subtitles:** No

Writers: John Gay, Billy Wilder, & Harry Kurnitz
Director: Alan Gibson

Cast

Ralph Richardson as Sir Wilfred Robarts
Deborah Kerr as Miss Plimsoll
Diana Rigg as Christine
Beau Bridges as Leonard Vole
Donald Pleasence as Mr. Myers
Wendy Hiller as Janet Mackenzie
David Langton as Mayhew
Richard Vernon as Brogan-Moore
Peter Sallis as Carter
Michael Gough as the Judge
Frank Mills as Chief Inspector Hearne
Patricia Leslie as Mrs. Emily French
Peter Copley as Dr. Harrison

Film Locations

South Black Lion Lane, London (Mackenzie walks to Mrs. French's house)
Walpole House, Chiswick Mall, London (exterior Mrs. French house)
Langley Park, Iver, Buckinghamshire (hospital)
Lincoln's Inn, London (car passes through gate)
5 Paper Buildings, Inner Temple, London (exterior Sir Wilfred's chambers)
Wormwood Scrubs Prison, London (exterior prison)
Central Criminal Courts, Old Bailey, London

Sparkling Cyanide (1983)

Under sunny Los Angeles skies, wealthy and powerful families are stalked by a cunning poisoner

In 1937, Agatha wrote a Poirot short story called "Yellow Iris." She later rewrote it; expanding the plot and making extensive changes to the murderer's identity, the motive, and swapped Colonel Race for Poirot as the detective and thus we have *Sparkling Cyanide*. Don't be concerned that you'll know whodunnit if you watch *Yellow Iris* (1993) before *Sparkling Cyanide*. You won't. You'll recognize a few plot elements and that's all.

It's fine when Agatha rewrites her stories. As a writer, I understand getting a better idea about an existing property and improving it to make that story more like the one I see in my head. What ends up on paper is never as good as what I imagine and I suppose Agatha had the same feeling. She rewrote more stories than just *Yellow Iris*. They're her stories and she knew what she was going for.

I can't say that about hack scriptwriters rewriting Agatha's prose, trying to improve it and regularly failing. There can be very good reasons for rewriting: a 90-minute movie doesn't provide much time for a complicated plot with a dozen important characters. Novels let us peek inside a character's mind and observe their innermost heart. Films need action, so internal soliloquies must be replaced with conversation. I expect stories to be compressed. I'm annoyed when perfectly good characters get renamed for no discernible reason.

Fidelity to text

Colonel Race disappears, the setting changes to contemporary Los Angeles, events get radically compressed, and a murder attempt while water skiing is added.

Quality of movie

It has its moments, but overall, it's as flat as stale champagne.

Hacks can inflict bigger changes on Agatha. In *Sparkling Cyanide*, the writing team changed the date to 1983 (forgivable although it turns the film into a celebration of '80s poufy hair and sequined dresses), moved the setting to Los Angeles (off-putting but tolerable), disappeared Colonel Race (his role was split among Tony Browne, Captain Kemp, and Eric Kidderminster which was understandable but undesirable), and worst of all, compressed the action from about a year to about two weeks.

That last change was unforgivable as it made the villain's behavior and motivation incomprehensible. No one, even in the movies, would behave that way. To compound the error, one of the three credited screenwriters for this indifferent film was Sue Grafton. You might remember her; she moved from scriptwriting to the Kinsey Millhone "Alphabet" series of best-selling detective novels, reaching *Y is for Yesterday* before dying in 2017.

Grafton also co-wrote *A Caribbean Mystery* (1983)

Iris Murdoch (*Deborah Raffin*), the good sister

Tony Browne (*Anthony Andrews*), the curious suitor

George Barton (*Josef Sommer*), the cuckolded hubby

Rosemary Barton (*Christine Belford*), the bad sister

Stephan Farraday (*David Huffman*), the ambitious pol

Ruth Lessing (*Pamela Bellwood*), the ambitious sec'y

starring Helen Hayes, meaning she's got two Agatha adaptations under her belt. After watching this one, I shudder to think what awaits me when Helen Hayes' Miss Marple films show up in the queue. (Reader, it worked.)

In the novel, the events took place over a year. Our villainess is Ruth Lessing (get it?), George Barton's secretary. She falls for Victor Drake and decides that while she wants the handsome, charming cad, she doesn't want to be poor. Victor's never going to work an honest day in his life so where should the money come from? Her secretary's salary? That won't do. But Victor is, in a roundabout way, an heir. If his wealthy cousin Rosemary dies, Rosemary's much younger, plainer, and far more personable sister, Iris, inherits. When Iris dies, Victor's mom, Lucilla Drake, inherits. Lucilla can't deny anything to Victor so he won't need to wait for her to die to get rich. Mom will give her darling baby boy as much cash as he wants if it will make him happy.

This makes sense, especially the timing. Ruth's too smart to murder heiresses suspiciously quickly. The passage of a year makes events look more natural.

In the film, Ruth (young, hot, and hyper-competent) adores George (old and balding) from afar. He's married so she can only pine for him while probably keeping tabs on his wife Rosemary's extracurricular activities. She's the classic secretary in love with her boss. I couldn't quite buy the attraction but whatever.

Then, during dinner in a restaurant, cheating, vindictive Rosemary dies after her champagne toast was laced with cyanide. Since the setting was shifted to 1980s Los Angeles, we're spared a fingertip drug analysis. The coroner tells Captain Kemp, LAPD, his opinion based on Rosemary's body, but it has to be confirmed at the autopsy. That's so much more plausible. Captain Kemp is competent so he's not willing to say murder or suicide because he doesn't have enough facts.

The family is in shock. Suicide seems unlikely but Rosemary was high-strung, high-maintenance, and depressed after her recent bout with flu. Sure. Whatever. Murder, on the other hand, might be unthinkable but plenty of people didn't like Rosemary. Her lover Stephen was dumping her in favor of his wife, Sandra. Sandra knew about the affair and loathed Rosemary. So who killed Rosemary?

Why Ruth, the adoring and efficient secretary did. While arranging Rosemary's funeral, she's also got to get Victor paid off on her boss' orders and hustled off to Buenos Aires and out of everyone's hair. That's when she discovers George doesn't love her and will never marry her, so Ruth immediately transfers her affections to Victor.

What? All in three days? I can't accept a capable woman suddenly falling for a ne'er-do-well when all she had to do was remain the competent, loyal, hot secretary to stodgy George Barton and wait. If she worked on him hard enough, he'd have come around and put a ring on it in six months.

Meanwhile, the late Rosemary's sister Iris flirts with Tony Browne, mysterious visiting British reporter. That's Anthony Andrews under what looks like caked-on bronzer. He wore more makeup than the ladies, which is saying something considering the multiple layers of mascara, eyeshadow, eyebrow pencil, lip gloss, and rouge they wore along with vast quantities of Aqua Net hairspray.

Ruth decides she's really been in love with Victor all along, so she masterminds the plot to murder Iris so Victor can inherit. Within one week. This all happens too fast and there's not enough build-up to make it convincing. I should be grateful that neither Ruth nor Iris fall into bed within one day of meeting their respective swains.

There were good moments, the best being when Tony Browne slowly works out how and why George Barton was murdered and tests his theory on Captain Kemp and Eric Kidderminster. We rarely get to see a detective's thought processes so well expressed on film. Another plus is the restaurant singer performing Cole Porter's "I Get a Kick Out of You." There's also the waterskiing scene, showcasing Lake Piru and powerful, low-to-the-water ski boats. The attempted murder plot looked improbable but the boats were top-notch.

This was an adequate film, adequately acted, and if you can ignore Ruth's implausible behavior, you might enjoy it. But really, Sue Grafton should have written a better, more plausible plot. She was adapting the best so it wasn't like *she* had to be brilliant. She just had to keep the sparkle.

General Information

Based on: *Sparkling Cyanide* (novel, 1945)
Run time: 1 hr., 40 min. **Subtitles:** Yes

Writers: Robert Malcolm Young, Sue Grafton, and Steve Humphrey
Director: Robert Michael Lewis

Cast

Deborah Raffin as Iris Murdoch
Anthony Andrews as Tony Browne
Harry Morgan as Captain Kemp

Josef Sommer as George Barton
Christine Belford as Rosemary Barton
Pamela Bellwood as Ruth Lessing
David Huffman as Stephan Farraday
June Chadwick as Sandra Farraday
Nancy Marchand as Lucilla Drake
Michael Woods as Victor Drake
Barrie Ingham as Eric Kidderminster
Anne Rogers as Viola Kidderminster
Shera Danese as Christine Shannon

Film Locations

Arden Villa, Pasadena, California (fundraiser)
Lake Piru, Ventura County, California (waterskiing scene)

Ordeal by Innocence (1984)

A nosy American seeks justice for an executed man and inflicts fresh wounds on a healing family

Hester gets youthened, Mary and Philip Durrant hate each other, Tina gets whitewashed, Maureen turns into an slut, and the changes keep on coming.

Quality of movie

Blurry, murky, shaky, poorly told, confusing, with loads of flashbacks, flash-sideways, and a truly dreadful soundtrack.

Let's start with the sole reason to watch this mess: The scenery is gorgeous. It's shot on location in Dartmouth in Devon. It's a town on the banks of the River Dart, a ria stretching far inland. The town clings to the steep hills lining the river. There are many, many boats gliding past in the background from small rowboats to ferries to sailing ships. The characters are constantly taking boats between Sunny Point and the town. There are plenty of scenes taking place on the docks so you'll get your boating fix.

After that, the all-star cast does the best they can with a murky script.

Faye Dunaway portrays family matriarch Rachel Argyle. It looked like she shot all her scenes in one day in her home office. She was murdered *before* the book opens so every time she appears, it's a flashback. To make sure you know you're seeing the past, the director filmed her in black and white, since, well, you know, the past was colorless.

Weirdly, Dunaway is only one year older than Sarah Miles, playing her daughter Mary Durrant. A non-similarity in appearance is to be expected since Rachel Argyle adopted all her children. However, it's extremely noticeable that the actresses look like contemporaries and not mother and daughter.

It's even more noticeable because Rachel Argyle's other adopted children (Jacko, Mickey, Tina, and Hester) resemble teenagers and young adults, rather than Rachel's fellow members of the Women's League.

There's also substantial differences in height. Donald Sutherland, 6 foot 4, (Arthur Calgary) towers over the rest of the cast and the camera angles make him look even taller. He's six inches taller than the next tallest cast members, the 5-feet-10 Christopher Plummer (Leo Argyle) and Michael Elphick (Inspector Huish). When he's standing next to Hester Argyle, he looks like a redwood waiting to crush her.

Hester's been youthened to a fourteen-year-old, so her love story with Arthur disappeared. She was transformed into not just a snotty teenager but one who sneaks out to watch X-rated movies. I found this unbelievable because Maureen Clegg, Jacko's widow, saw her regularly sneak into the films. She's the usher at the local cinema and one of her jobs is to keep nonpaying patrons out of the theater. She saw this and did nothing? I couldn't accept it because Maureen

Arthur Calgary (*Donald Sutherland*), the academic

Leo Argyle (*Christopher Plummer*), the father

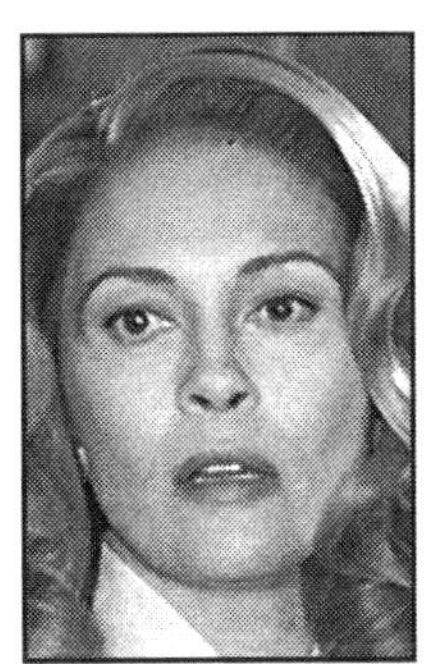

Rachel Argyle (*Faye Dunaway*), the late mother

Mary Durrant (*Sarah Miles*), the eldest adoptee

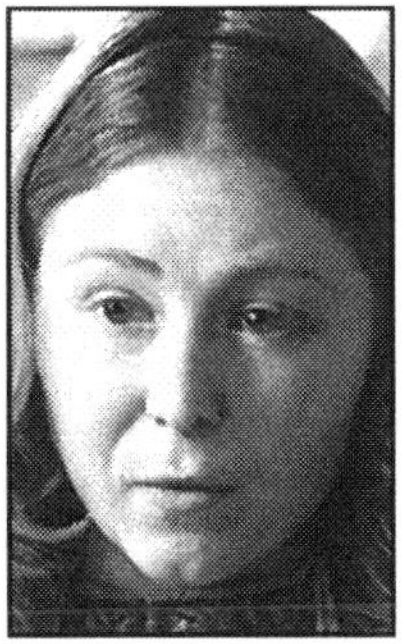

Hester Argyle (*Valerie Whittington*), the youngest adoptee

Kirsten Lindstrom (*Annette Crosbie*), the housekeeper

would lose her job.

Maureen also got turned into a slut. I cannot stand it when Hollywood decides that working-class women – by definition! — have loose morals. Maureen meets Calgary at the theater and drops hints about Jacko and the goings on at Sunny Point. When we next see her, she's nude and in his hotel bed! Ready to get it on with a complete stranger! Why did she do this? Because she's obviously no better than she should be and the director wanted to show some tits and he couldn't do it with the classier citizens. Gratuitous nudity: what Hollywood does best because it's easier than writing a decent script treating women as something other than brainless sex objects.

We first meet Tina Argyle in Mickey's bed. It's obvious she's naked but at least she owns a sheet. Why does she get to stay decent? Because, despite being adopted from poverty and her obvious lack of money, she's a *lady*. Tina also got whitewashed. In the novel, Tina is mixed-race from her Indian father and English mother. Here? That bit of complexity got erased. She also gets murdered; she survived the attempt in the novel.

Gwenda Vaughn, Leo's secretary, lost her plot. In a flashback, Rachel accuses her of having an affair with her boss. Gwenda — who was in love with Leo — was supposed to be on the verge of marrying him when Calgary shows up to see justice done. Not here; despite what Rachel says, you'll never see so much as a hint of impropriety in this boss/secretary relationship. Again, a weakening of the complexity of the Argyle household.

Inspector Huish becomes a typical dumb constable who refuses to see a miscarriage of justice. Yet he knows something that Calgary refuses to see: Jacko was guilty. Everyone in the family knew Jacko was guilty. They lived with his bad seed behavior and murder didn't surprise them. The movie disappeared Dr. McMaster, but in the novel, he explained to Calgary that Jacko might have been too cowardly to commit murder himself but he'd eagerly urge someone else to kill if it suited him.

Mary Durrant (Sarah Miles) got much older, turned into a lush, and cheated on her husband, Philip. Ian McShane (Philip) gets top billing for two scenes and gets murdered with no explanation given for why.

There were so many missed opportunities to explain what was going on. Why was Calgary pursued through the narrow streets of Dartmouth at night by a car with a clearly visible license plate? This plot thread goes nowhere. No one notices (the streets are suspiciously empty when needed for the plot), the fog miraculously clears so Calgary with his steel-trap memory can get the plate number, yet he never tells the police? No one goes looking for the car?

There's also the scene when Kirsten burns not one pair of gloves in the Aga but what looks to be four pairs. This is a dead giveaway as to whodunnit but why four pairs? Why show her face?

The movie wasn't just choppy. It was foggy. Really foggy. Like the director used every chunk of dry ice in England to up the atmospherics, except when Calgary needed to see something clearly and then not report it to the police.

There's also the irritating, jarring, jazzy soundtrack. Jazz musician Dave Brubeck and his quartet performed the music yet it wasn't written for the film. It seemed to belong to another movie entirely. The producers had a soundtrack, decided they didn't like it, and hired Dave. He didn't have time to write anything appropriate so they cobbled a soundtrack out of his other music and it shows. It's like Frankenstein music. It had nothing to do with the plot, didn't heighten action or emotion, and just … showed up as though jazz musicians were hiding in the fog. Sometimes an offbeat soundtrack works. In Glynis John's version of *Spider's Web*, the music was incongruous and offbeat but so was she.

I don't believe anyone in this version of *Ordeal* listened to jazz. No one had enough personality.

I can't recommend you watch this other than for completeness. ITV's 2007 production with Miss Marple (yes, they shoehorned in Miss Marple!) was so much better. Despite myriad changes, it beautifully captured the Shakespearean tragedy of a good man doing the right thing with fatal consequences. Stick with that version.

General Information

Based on: *Ordeal by Innocence* (novel, 1958)
Run time: 1 hr., 30 min. **Subtitles:** Yes

Writer: Alexander Stuart
Directors: Desmond Davis & Alan Birkinshaw

Cast

Donald Sutherland as Arthur Calgary
Christopher Plummer as Leo Argyle
Faye Dunaway as Rachel Argyle
Sarah Miles as Mary Argyle Durrant
Ian McShane as Philip Durrant
Phoebe Nicholls as Tina Argyle
Michael Maloney as Micky Argyle
Valerie Whittington as Hester Argyle
Billy McColl as Jacko Argyle
Annette Crosbie as Kirsten Lindstrom
Diana Quick as Gwenda Vaughan
Cassie Stuart as Maureen Clegg
Michael Elphick as Inspector Huish
George Innes as Archie Leach
Anita Carey as Martha Jessup
Ron Pember as Ferryman
Kevin Stoney as Solicitor
John Bardon as Night Porter
Brian Glover as Executioner
Rex Holdsworth as Police Doctor
Martyn Townsend as Detective
Doel Luscombe as Prison Governor
Alex Porwal as Young Policeman

Film Location

Dartmouth, Devon

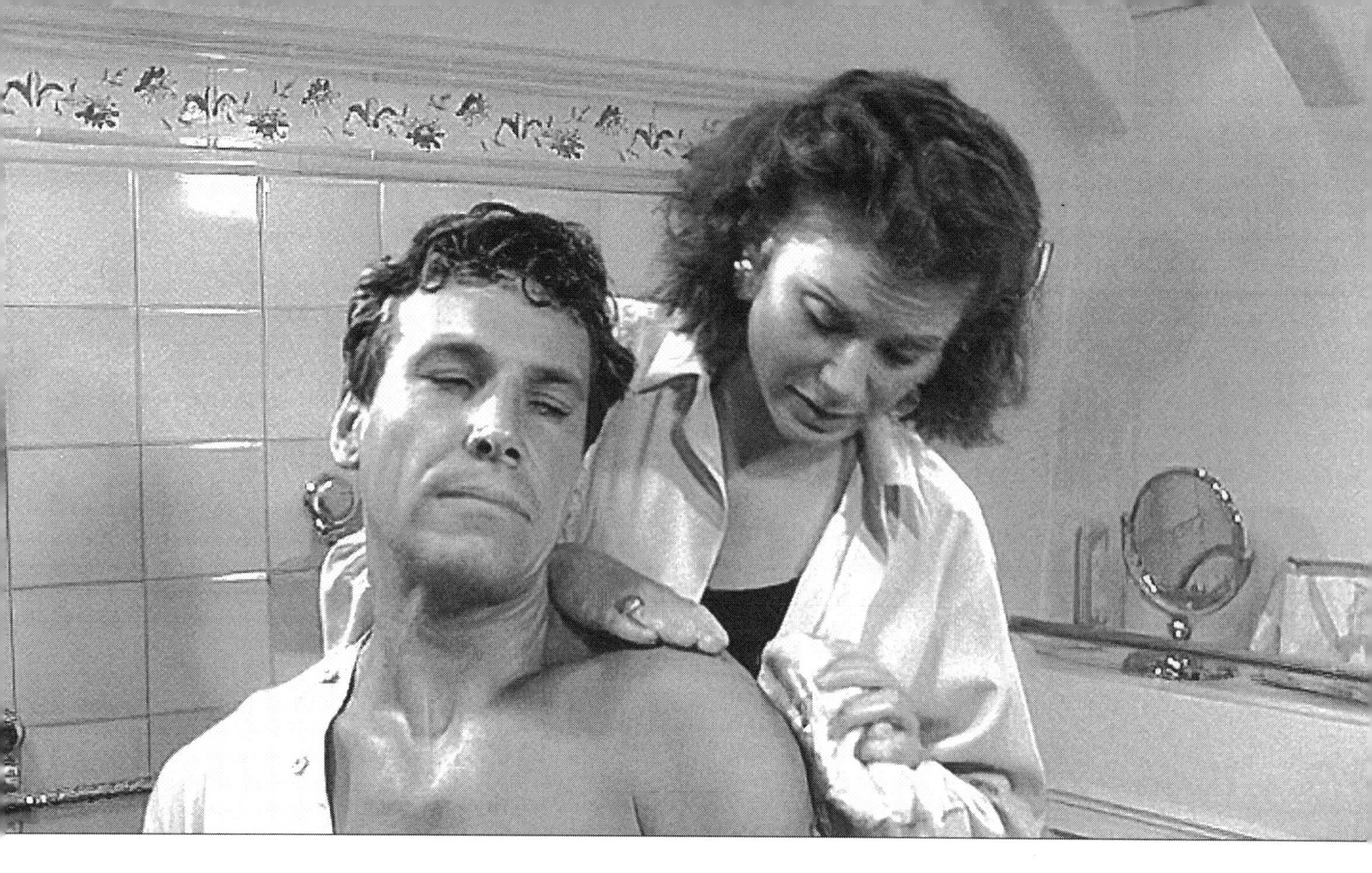

The Man in the Brown Suit (1989)

A young woman seeking adventure finds romance, peril, and stolen gems on a sea cruise and in southern Africa

Fidelity to text

It's amazingly close, other than date and setting. The film was shot in 1988, so what was then contemporary is now an '80s celebration of big hair, shoulder pads, and aerobics workout clothing.

Quality of movie

Don't believe what you read elsewhere; believe me instead! If you can relax and accept Rue McClanahan reprising Blanche Devereaux from *Golden Girls*, you'll have fun.

I didn't know anything other than the cast (the girl detective from *Remington Steele*, Blanche Devereaux, *The Equalizer*, *The White Shadow*, and Felix Unger) and the date change. I'm very familiar with the novel and was expecting a painful movie.

The Man in the Brown Suit is one of Agatha's forgotten books, yet it shouldn't be. It's a romantic thriller, involving murder, stolen diamonds, political intrigue, mistaken identity, and that's just for openers.

Anne Beddingfeld is alone in the world, highly romantic, and desperate for adventure. She's prone to lengthy internal monologues where she works out the troubles she's placed herself in. This works in a novel because the characters take up residence inside your skull. In the movies? Not so much. Movies don't handle internal monologues or narration well; they demand snappy dialog and action. Yet the scriptwriter (Carla Jean Wagner) managed to make it work.

Anne (Stephanie Zimbalist) talks to herself, letting the viewer know her thoughts. She talks to everyone else. She wears her heart on her sleeve. She wants excitement, not her boring, lonely job at Blockbuster Video (remember them?) in the mall in Buffalo. She's such a romantic wannabe adventuress that she gets her and her best friend, Valerie, stranded in the Cairo airport. Valerie flies back to Buffalo in a huff. She leaves Anne behind, trying to discover who just killed a stranger by frightening him enough to run out into traffic. She also meets, briefly, a man in a brown suit who captures her interest.

We're off to the races, yet it's oddly plausible. Anne gets into trouble with the Egyptian police and a representative from the American Embassy shows up to bail her out and put her on the next flight back to Buffalo. But when adventure calls, Anne cashes in her plane ticket and maxes out her credit cards to buy a ticket on the *Kilmorden Castle* in steerage. Well, not really. As the travel agent says (remember those?) it's called tourist class these days.

The *Kilmorden Castle* is a small cruise ship sailing from Cairo, down the Suez Canal, around the Horn of Africa to Mombasa and back. Not every cruise ship is designed to carry 2,000 passengers plus captain and

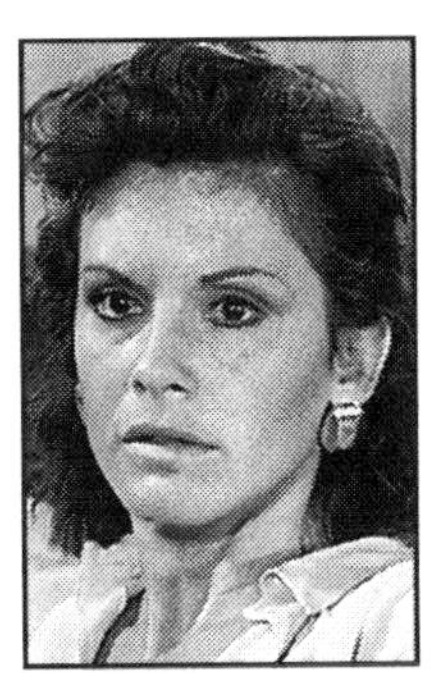

Anne Beddingfeld (*Stephanie Zimbalist*), the adventuress

Suzy Blair (*Rue McClanahan*), the wealthy friend

Harry Lucas (*Simon Dutton*), the man on the run

Sir Eustace Pedler (*Edward Woodward*), the mystery man

Gordon Race (*Ken Howard*), the American official

Edward Chichester (*Tony Randall*), the minister

crew. Many are considerably smaller to serve smaller routes, but they all have steerage, er, tourist class accommodations. Every ship has space below the waterline so why not rent out those berths?

While on board the *Kilmorden Castle*, Anne meets Blanche Devereaux, the guy from the American Embassy who tried to ship her off to Buffalo, Sir Eustace Pedler, and other, more suspicious passengers. She also meets the man in the brown suit when he crashes, wounded, into her cabin at night. Their encounter is right out of the novel as well as tens of thousands of torrid romance novels that followed in Agatha's footsteps. He's handsome, studly, escaping from danger, and flaunts his manly chest so Anne can treat his injuries.

Yes, folks, Agatha Christie developed a classic romance trope in 1924.

She didn't describe his manly chest. She didn't even state that Anne stripped off his shirt. But careful readers knew you couldn't bandage wounds over top of clothing. Those clothes must be stripped off. Agatha was a romantic at heart, seething with passion, and knew how compelling an unsuitable man can be. Your brain shuts off, the hormones take over, and you'll believe the most ridiculous story because, well, it's *him* telling you the absurd story and not your boring co-worker from Accounting.

This is why, gentlemen, you should lift weights. Then, when you strip off your shirt, you'll get noticed in a very positive manner. Ladies are attracted to a manly, chiseled chest and well-shaped biceps. This is an achievable goal, no plastic surgery needed; just time, effort, and push-ups.

But back to the ship. The film follows the novel closely, other than simplifying the plot and moving it to Africa's east coast. There's still the mysterious Colonel, a Moriarty of crime involved in gunrunning, drug-running, and gem smuggling. The novel's political stuff, economic fallout, and worker riots vanish. The scriptwriter didn't feel the need to replace plot in a storyline that's already stuffed full.

The mysterious Colonel has his henchmen. This gives Tony Randall the chance to appear as four characters, one of them in drag. Yes, folks, Agatha was once again cutting-edge in 1924. I agree that cruise ship passengers back in 1924 or even 1989 would be more likely to be fooled by a man in a dress than they would be today. Back then, if you spotted a tallish, ugly woman, that's what she was. There are a lot of us around. Tony Randall is 5 foot 8, so it worked. It wouldn't have worked if, say, Ken Howard (6 foot 6) tried to play the role. He plays Colonel Race instead.

Edward Woodward (the Equalizer) plays Sir Eustace Pedler and he's perfect. Think Bertie Wooster all growed up and in a position of authority. His secretary, Underhill, isn't Jeeves: he has a secret life and Jeeves had none. As in the novel, Underhill's intense respectability causes trouble for Sir Eustace.

A little backstory: Sir Eustace was based on a real person, Major E. A. Belcher, who sponsored Agatha and Archie's yearlong, round-the-world cruise in 1922 (read Christie's *The Grand Tour* for the details). That cruise inspired the novel *Brown Suit* as well as numerous short stories she wrote while at sea.

Equally good was Rue McClanahan, who did a marvelous job as Suzy Blair. She lights up the screen. In the novel, Suzy comes across as a woman who adores the company of men. Who better than Blanche Devereaux to portray her?

Yes, there are some slow spots. Anne can be annoying at times but she never magically transforms into Wonder Woman or G.I. Jane, capable of mowing down armies by herself. She's a real young woman using her wits and resources to rescue herself. You're also left unsure as to what happens to Sir Eustace (did he escape to Argentina? Let's hope so!).

I enjoyed this movie when I did not expect to. You may like it too. Before you watch, read our annotated version of the novel and recognize that Agatha developed an entire subgenre back in 1924. *The Man in the Brown Suit* was a romantic thriller before anyone knew what they were, complete with the meet cute, enemies to lovers, and dramatic and improbably well-timed rescues.

That way, you'll know that after Valerie flies back to Buffalo, the screenwriter didn't concoct any of the plot. It's all Agatha all the way.

General Information

Based on: *The Man in the Brown Suit* (novel, 1924)
Run time: 1 hr., 40 min. **Subtitles:** Yes

Writer: Carla Jean Wagner
Director: Alan Grint

Cast

Stephanie Zimbalist as Anne Beddingfeld
Rue McClanahan as Suzy Blair
Ken Howard as Gordon Race
Simon Dutton as Harry Lucas
Edward Woodward as Sir Eustace Pedler
Tony Randall as Rev. Edward Chichester
Nickolas Grace as Guy Underhill
María Casal as Anita Carton
Federico Luciano as Leo Carton
Rose McVeigh as Valerie
Bill Holden as John Eardsley

Film Location

Temple of Debod, Madrid, Spain

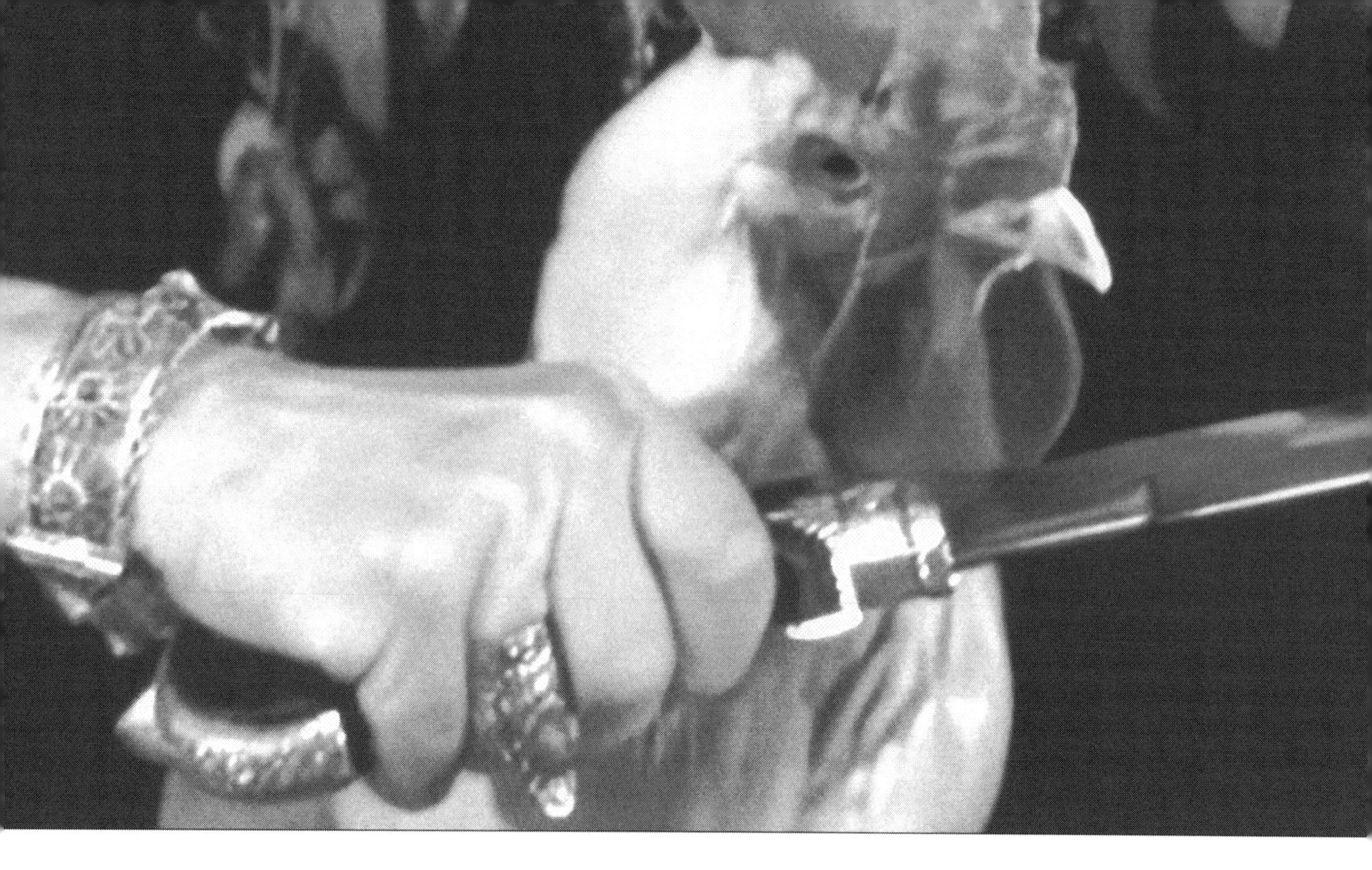

The Pale Horse (1997)

Blank the novel from your memory and you can enjoy this version with its transformed characters

Fidelity to text

Bad witches transformed the leads into near unrecognizability and removed Ariadne Oliver. A good witch left most of the plot in place.

Quality of movie

Choppy, uneven, murky, no subtitles so poor sound really mattered. But if you can live with that, the movie works on its own terms instead of Agatha's.

I don't know if Agatha's plot for *The Pale Horse* will ever be filmed. It's a weirdy; invoking characters from past novels (who are always written out of the films), yet being very much its own thing. Ariadne Oliver shows up now and again as does Mrs. Dane Calthrop. They both get Mark Easterbrook moving. Ariadne provides vital information near the climax. Sadly, both women are dispensed with here.

The Pale Horse also uses one of Agatha's favorite tropes which, by the way, she takes seriously although filmmakers can't seem to.

It's the supernatural. She wrote several short stories where the supernatural is real. In her detective fiction, the supernatural is always used as a distraction from the real, mundane crime. The practitioners are divided between those who are in it for the money and know what they're doing is fake (Thyrza Grey) and those who genuinely believe (Bella the hedge-witch). There's also a small, in-between contingent. They believe until their faith is tested and then either double-down or become apostates. Sybil the medium might fall into this category but we don't know. Agatha doesn't say and this script never shows the witches again after they're arrested.

Where Hollywood routinely fails — perhaps because they can't cope with non-atheists — is taking the serious people seriously. No matter what the practitioner secretly believes, the trappings of ritual look the same. The *intent* is different. How can that be shown? Only by what the script, director, and cinematographer show, which isn't easy. It's much easier to pan across murky jars, shrunken heads, and gyrating half-naked women than it is to show hours of prayer, purification rituals (including fasting), and more hours spent carefully chalking mystic symbols on the floor.

And so it proves here. We get the obligatory shots of mystic, badly lit objects and nothing of how Bella, the true believer, prays and purifies beforehand. We also get Mark's reaction. He's repelled by the theatricality.

Mark Easterbrook got a major rewrite. In print, he's a cultured, well-educated, well-connected scholar of India's Mughal Empire (1526-1857). That's one reason he has such a hard time buying Thyrza Grey and her witchy partners.

Here, he morphed into an ill-mannered, bad-boy sculptor in a leather jacket. He's rude to his rich,

Mark Easterbrook (*Colin Buchanan*), the rude sculptor

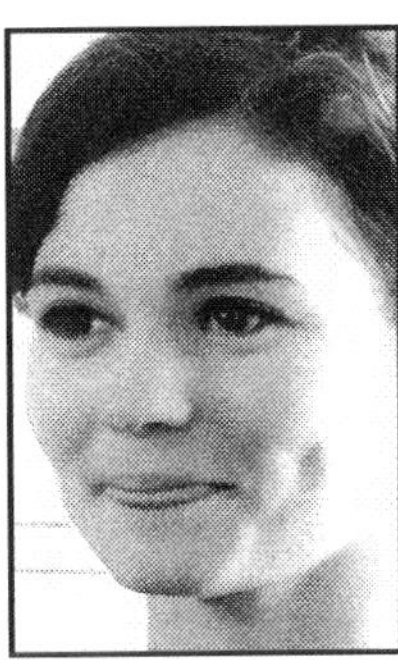
Kate Mercer (*Jayne Ashbourne*), the plucky girlfriend

Hermia Redcliffe (*Hermione Norris*), the wealthy girlfriend

Venables (*Michael Byrne*), the mysterious man

Thyrza Grey (*Jean Marsh*), the head witch

Dr. Osbourne (*Tim Potter*), the physician

upper-class date, Hermia, even after she bails him out of jail for suspected murder.

Wait. What? Yep, Mark is accused of murdering Father Gorman with a monkey wrench in the alley. The evidence is damning: It's his wrench, he's got blood on his hands, he wears a leather jacket, his hair is long, and he rides a motorcycle. He must be the villain or so says Detective-Inspector Lejeune.

Wait. What? Wasn't Detective-Inspector Lejeune a clever, imaginative copper working with Mark while performing all the plodding, behind-the-scenes, boring investigative work? Not here. This Lejeune is a caricature of PC Plod. Dull, slow, incapable of original thought, and instantly suspicious of long-haired, leather-clad, motorcycle-riding sculptors. It was painful watching the script badly mangle Lejeune's character when Agatha treated him with respect.

Fortunately, Sgt. Corrigan comes to Mark's rescue and takes his ridiculous story seriously. Why? Because he wants a promotion and if Lejeune fails, then so does he.

This is where *not* knowing the novel helps you enjoy the movie. It's set in 1964 (the novel was published in 1961) so an experienced detective-inspector would naturally be prejudiced against a bad-boy artist with blood on his hands and no good explanation for why. Mark doesn't make it easier, either, with his snotty attitude. But thanks to Hermia, who sticks by him for no reason that I could see, he makes bail and promptly dumps her in favor of a hot brunette.

Wait. What? Yep, Ginger, a fiery redhead, is magically whitewashed into a bland brunette named Kate. Thanks to Hollywood magic, movie Kate also doesn't lose all her hair to thallium poisoning as Ginger does in the novel.

Mr. Venables gains an elaborate backstory, along with a miraculous recovery from polio, making him much more of a viable suspect. He can't explain where the money came from to fill his mansion with fine art. He's also got a henchman whom Mark recognizes from the alley where Father Gorman got monkey-wrenched. Better editing and sound would have made these sections clearer.

Mr. Osborne got upgraded to a doctor for no discernible reason. A pharmacist always made more sense. Even into the 1960s, pharmacists did much of their own compounding and drug mixtures so it's plausible for a rogue chemist to make up poisonous mixtures. After all, the dose makes the poison.

This all sounds like I loathed this movie. It also sounds like the scriptwriter and the director tore the novel to shreds. I wouldn't say either of those things. They made something new out of Agatha's text that was internally consistent; not a given with book to film adaptations.

The movie works on its own terms. With better editing and subtitles, it would work even better. In fact, it could have been really interesting if the director and screenwriter had rewritten *more*. They could have devoted time to the culture clash between upper and lower class and traditional and modern thinking. They could have spent more time on the struggle between old-fashioned belief as demonstrated by the witches and cutting-edge belief in all things scientific and progressive.

Go back to the beginning with Mark and Hermia. They're watching a production of *Macbeth*. He's bored and underdressed for the theater. Why is Hermia with him in the first place? Must be his lower-class animal magnetism, which is why she agrees later to help him discover how the Pale Horse death program works. As a result, Hermia ends up with someone of her own class, a banker.

It makes perfect sense — in that era — for Lejeune to be suspicious of Mark. It also makes sense for Corrigan to go behind his superior's back to help Mark. Corrigan can see the future and wants to get in front of it.

Removing wealthy but slow-to-die relatives so you can inherit dates back to Hammurabi. An organization devoted to early inheritance using modern methods decked out in antiquated dress showed the clash between new and old. Even what the cast wore showed the struggle between the old and the new; Mark in his leather jacket, Kate in her minidress and tights from Mary Quant, and Hermia wearing Dior and making her mother proud.

Approach this *Pale Horse* by wiping the original and the other adaptations from your memory and you'll enjoy it much more.

General Information

Based on: *The Pale Horse* (novel, 1961)
Run time: 2 hrs. **Subtitles:** No

Writer: Alma Cullen **Director:** Charles Beeson

Cast

Colin Buchanan as Mark Easterbrook
Trevor Byfield as Detective-Inspector Lejeune
Andy Serkis as Sergeant Corrigan

Jayne Ashbourne as Kate Mercer
Hermione Norris as Hermia Redcliffe
Michael Byrne as Venables
Jean Marsh as Thyrza Grey
Ruth Madoc as Sybil Stamfordis
Maggie Shevlin as Bella
Leslie Phillips as Lincoln Bradley
Tim Potter as Dr. Osbourne
Louise Jameson as Florence Tuckerton
Catherine Holman as Poppy Tuckerton
Richard O'Callaghan as Donald

Film Locations

Brydges Place, London (Gorman murder)
Richmond Theatre, Richmond, Surrey (Macbeth performance)
Hall Barn, Beaconsfield, Buckinghamshire (Hermia's house)
St. Mary the Virgin Church, Hambleden, Buckinghamshire (Much Deeping church)
Hambleden Manor, Hambleden, Buckinghamshire (Venables' house)
Crossways Farm, Abinger Hammer, Surrey (witches house exterior)
Hambleden, Buckinghamshire (Much Deeping)
Wormwood Scrubs Prison, London (prison gate)
Raymond Burton House, London (exterior Bradley's office)
Market Place, St. Albans, Hertfordshire (Apex Gallery)

Sparkling Cyanide (2003)

This imaginative rewrite founders on dropped plot threads and turns into a celebration of Big Brother

Fidelity to text

A reverie from Iris' point of view became a modern police procedural starring doubles for Tommy and Tuppence.

Quality of movie

Decent acting, interesting set up, social commentary about the police state and social engineering, but the last fifteen minutes destroyed the movie.

This 1 hour, 34-minute movie gets terrible reviews. Yet, I was riveted until the one hour, 19-minute mark when the film snatched defeat from the jaws of victory. The setup was wonderful, but the script and director completely lost faith in their material at the climax.

This version made plenty of changes to Agatha's prose, starting with the focus. The novel is told mainly from Iris' point of view. It's a remembrance of things past as Iris figures out why her sister Rosemary would drink poisoned champagne. Colonel Race, Inspector Kemp, and Anthony Browne solve the mystery and rescue Iris. Anthony and Iris live happily ever after.

In this version, Colonel Race becomes sixtyish Col. Geoffrey Reece. Inspector Kemp transforms into his sixtyish wife, Catherine. Both work for a shadowy agency run by someone highly placed within the British government. Think MI5. They've got a charming, bantering, capable and fun Tommy and Tuppence vibe. Because the film's told from their point of view — as opposed to Iris' — *Sparkling Cyanide* becomes the one mystery genre Agatha didn't write: a police procedural.

We see plenty of Iris, Rosemary, George Barton, Ruth, and the Farradays, but they're no longer the center of the story. It's Tommy and Tuppence, I mean, Geoffrey and Catherine enjoying their adventure.

They're investigating Rosemary's death because Stephen Farraday (government minister with a promising future) and his well-connected wife, Amanda (Queen's Counsel) were at the table when Rosemary died. Not-MI5 springs into action. The Prime Minister needs to know if there's a scandal involving his cabinet minister. It's especially important Geoffrey and Catherine uncover the truth because the press won't ignore *this* sudden death. The hounds will bay and dig until they've unearthed every possible juicy, scandalous, newspaper-selling tidbit. Some of it might even be true.

That's because Rosemary's husband, George Barton, is no longer an anonymous, boring businessman. He's a crass, tough, scrap-metal millionaire who owns a soccer team. He's famous and his team's famous. That makes his wife famous and his wife's sister, Iris, moderately famous.

Most famous of all is George's new star, Carl "Fizz" Fitzgerald. That's who Anthony Browne morphs into: a

George Barton (*Kenneth Cranham*), the alpha tycoon

Ruth Lessing (*Lia Williams*), the lovelorn secretary

Iris Marle (*Chloe Howman*), the sad sister

Mark Drake (*Jonathan Firth*), the big brother

Stephen Farraday (*James Wilby*), the rising minister

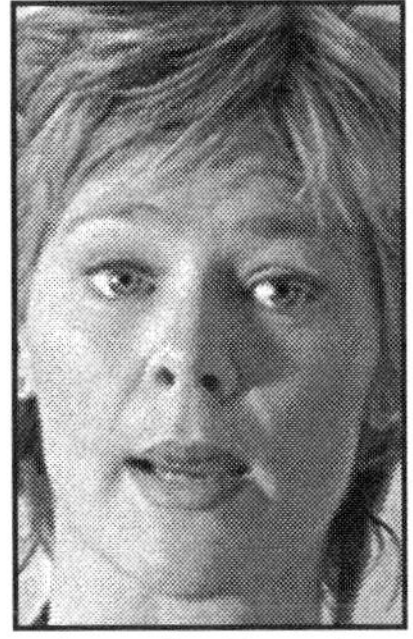
Alexandra Farraday (*Clare Holman*), the wounded wife

soccer star with a tremendous kick, capable of a hat trick. For you non-footy fans, that means our Fizz scored three goals all by himself in one game. This is very hard to do. Unfortunately, Fabulous Fizz doesn't get his chance to shine like he should have. The opening sets him up as energetic, talented, and volatile, and then gelds him.

Only George's secretary, Ruth Lessing, is not famous. Not even proximity to power can make some people shine.

They were seated at the same table that fateful night in the nightclub, when George delivered a champagne toast that ended in his wife's death.

So Geoffrey and Catherine spring into action. They enlist Catherine's pet hacker, Andy, to break into Stephen's credit card accounts, bank accounts, appointment schedules, and whatever else looks promising. He also checks into the Bartons, Iris, and anyone else connected to the case.

Mind, this is done without a single mention of search warrants, just cause, or due process of law. Andy the hacker discloses his concerns about prying into people's private lives without judicial oversight. Not that it stops him. He's just doing his job.

They discover Stephen had a torrid affair with Rosemary. Being revealed as an adulterer will harm his career and embarrass the party in power. Worse, Stephen is the cabinet minister for sport and recreation. He's being wooed by George Barton because George wants a knighthood. Who better to plead his case than the minister of sport? Stephen and Rosemary's illicit connection smacks of corruption. The Fleet Street headline writes itself:

"Barton Pimps Wife To Minister For Knighthood!"

While Andy's digging deep, Geoffrey and Catherine interview suspects and race about London. They discover that Rosemary was pregnant but had an abortion.

Meanwhile, to smoke out the murderer, George arranges another dinner party. This time, he drinks the cyanide-laced champagne and right in front of Geoffrey, Colonel, Catherine, and Andy. They watched it happen, yet never saw a thing.

Along the way, we're watching bits of Fizz, playing the supportive boyfriend to Iris. A boxing scene is supposed to show off his manliness. It looked like he couldn't box worth a darn so the scene was shot through a staircase railing. Fizz was poorly served by his actor and his script. He's supposed to be the kind of consummate athlete who's worth paying millions to play. Instead, he was blah.

That might be why – unlike in the novel – he didn't show up at the climax to rescue Iris! Her desperate calls to Fizz get routed to his voicemail. Yet during the tedious epilog, they're cuddling as though he'd been the hero.

CCTV cameras figured prominently, turning the movie's subtext into propaganda in favor of the surveillance society. Geoffrey and Catherine are constantly looking at footage, very little of it as blurry as it is in real life. Andy tells us the system's artificial intelligence is so good that it can identify a suspect even if a camera sees only a tiny bit of a person. Disguises such as beards, hats, and scarves won't fool his system; it always gets its man. The Chinese government would be deeply impressed since despite their best efforts, they're nowhere near that level of expertise. No one is, for which we should all be grateful.

We reach the climax and the movie falls apart. Instead of using their little gray cells, Geoffrey and Catherine use CCTV footage to spot the criminal mastermind. Meanwhile, Iris feels threatened and panics. She can't reach Fizz so she flees to her cousin, Mark Drake. She'll be safe with him, having not listened to a warning from Geoffrey and Catherine. But when she learns that he's behind the murders, she flees again. And who comes to her rescue? Geoffrey, Catherine, and a pack of bobbies.

It should have been Fizz. He's the love interest and a star soccer player. He should have tackled Mark Drake in that alley, and used his head like a soccer ball until the constables pulled him off.

But no. Fizz never shows up, and we never learn why.

We also never get an answer about why Rosemary had the abortion.

The worst loose end was the Farradays. They should have had their subplot wrapped up before the killer was revealed. That's when Stephen should have told Alexandra that his affair with Rosemary, which he ended, taught him who he really loved. It was her and he'd been too blind to see who was standing in front of him. That's what Agatha wrote but that's not what we got.

With a better climax and a fizzier Fizz,, this would have been a hat trick of a movie instead of an own goal.

General Information

Based on: *Sparkling Cyanide* (novel, 1945)
Run time: 1 hr., 34 min. **Subtitles:** Yes

Writer: Laura Lamson
Director: Tristram Powell

Cast

Oliver Ford Davies as Col. Geoffrey Reece
Pauline Collins as Dr. Catherine Kendall
Dominic Cooper as Andy Hoffman

Kenneth Cranham as George Barton
Rachel Shelley as Rosemary Barton
Chloe Howman as Iris Marle
Justin Pierre as Carl "Fizz" Fitzgerald
Susan Hampshire as Lucilla Drake
Jonathan Firth as Mark Drake
Lia Williams as Ruth Lessing
James Wilby as Stephen Farraday
Clare Holman as Alexandra Farraday
Ruth Platt as Rebecca Knight
Joseph Scatley as Sam Knight

Film Location

National Liberal Club, Westminster, London (Alexandra Farraday's legal chambers)

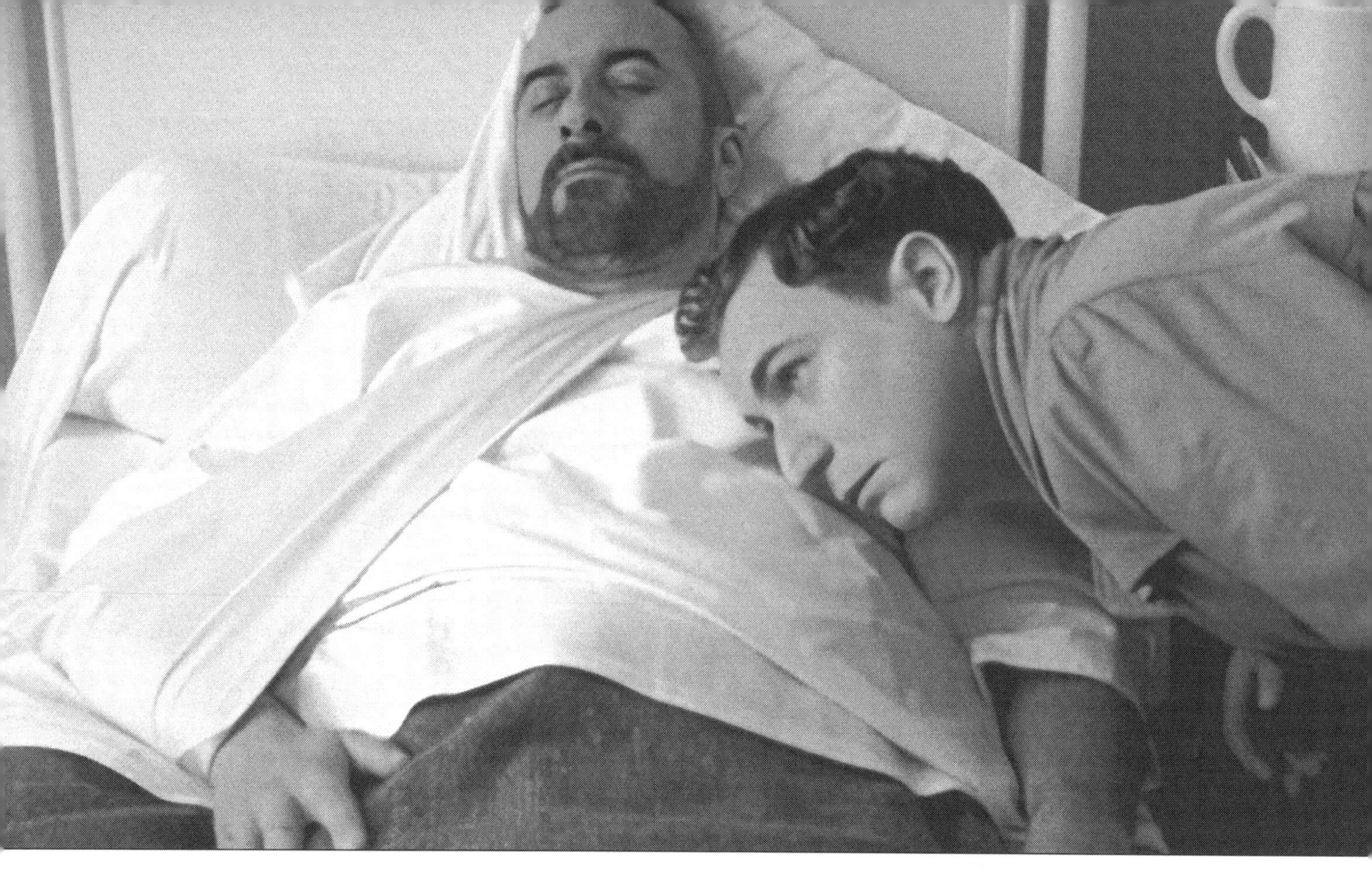

Family Murder Party (F-2006)

(*Petits Meurtres en Famille*)

Who slashed Simon? French TV spins a novel of family dysfunction into a six-hour-long soap opera

Fidelity to text

Poirot's gone, the plot's as soapy as can be, but motive and family ties remain.

Quality of movie

Well-paced, most of the loose ends tied up, but they skipped Inès' happy ending and that chirpy score! Bleah.

This long miniseries (6 hours, 20 minutes) is broken up into four 95-minute episodes. The script, casting, and direction all work together so you can keep the huge cast straight but I'd still recommend watching it as a marathon over two nights.

The film is based upon *Hercule Poirot's Christmas* and, despite removing Poirot and turning it into a police procedural set in Northern France near the Belgian border in 1939, everything you'd expect (and more!) is here.

Vicious, tyrannical, aging family patriarch? Check. Dysfunctional adult sons who don't get along? All but David are here. Their wives? Yep, for the most part. Illegitimate son from Africa? He's here (Éloi) but the parallel isn't exact. Long-estranged granddaughter who turns out to be an imposter? She's here. So is the police superintendent who's another unacknowledged, illegitimate son and loathes the old man. Château full of snoopy servants? Fifteen or more are keeping that pile up to standards.

And is the vicious old man, who's proud of making people hate him, slaughtered in a locked room mystery? Yes, he is.

The changes omit David the artist son, and add layer upon layer of soapy froth. It's like *Dynasty*, only despite everyone being rich and French, they aren't as spectacularly dressed and it's clear the château isn't as grand as it could be.

The lathering starts with the old man's son Édouard. He is married to Édith. He adores her, but she's got eyes only for Édouard's athletic, much younger brother, Victor. Victor's her age and, supposedly unbeknownst to Édouard, Victor's the father of their daughter, Alix.

Then there's brother Antonin, a widower who's been carrying on a ten-year long affair with head housekeeper, Louise. She's just discovered she's pregnant with his illegitimate baby. Like father, like son, yes? Antonin is a politician so he needs a wife but Louise is a domestic (*quelle horreur*!) and worse, a Jew. So Antonin, when summoned home for the old man's 70th birthday party, brings his fiancée, Madeline. She's a singer, actress, bombshell blonde. She starts out as high-maintenance and ends up in crazy town.

Victor's estranged from the family and has been since age 17 when he a) had the secret affair with older brother Édouard's wife and b) decided upon finding his mother's

Simon Le Tescou (*Robert Hossein*), the evil father

Édouard Le Tescou (*Bruno Todeschini*), the helpful son

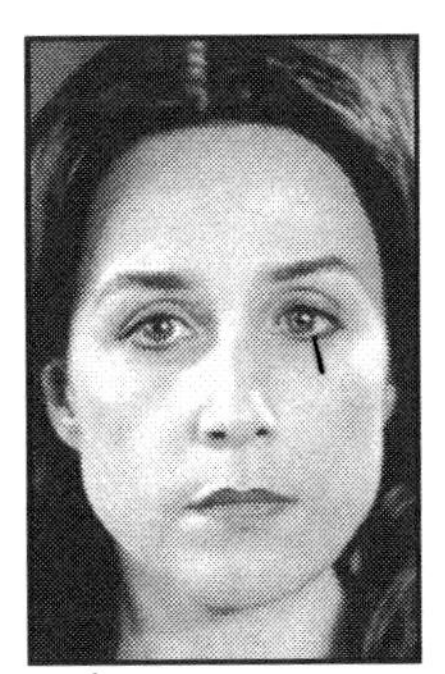

Édith Le Tescou (*Elsa Zylberstein*), the resentful wife

Victor Le Tescou (*Grégori Derangère*), the prodigal son

Antonin Le Tescou (*Mathias Mlekuz*), the corrupt son

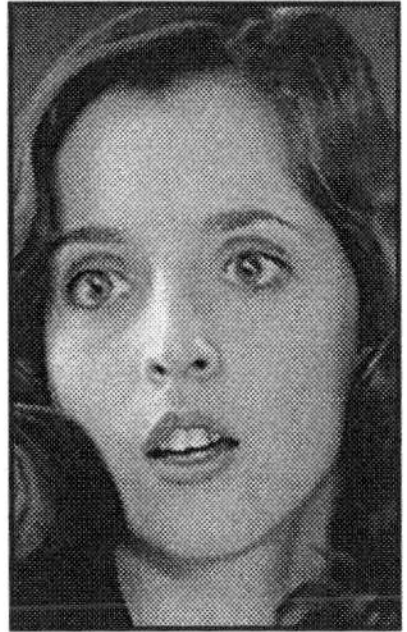

Inès Della Vega (*Leticia Dolera*), the fake granddaughter

crumpled body outside one of the château's third floor windows that papa killed her. Upon his return for the old man's 70th birthday party, Victor resumes his affair with Édith and confronts his father about maman's death.

Alix, Édouard and Édith's 16-year-old daughter overhears the truth about her parentage and rips into all three adults for their lies.

Inès, the Spanish granddaughter of Simon's estranged daughter is an impostor but that's not the soap. No, it's Diego, the real Inès' driver, the fake Inès' lover (until she learns what a vicious-tempered abusive jerk he is) who forces her to take the real Inès' place so they can rob the château. Diego is also a Spanish Republican, loyal to the Communists, and he can't go back to Franco's Spain. He and Richard blackmail Inès when it seems that she might be developing a conscience.

Head housekeeper Louise has been carrying a torch for Antonin for ten years. She's happy to be pregnant because, as we eventually learn, she's got another son by Antonin whom she gave up to a neighbor nine years ago.

Louise is being pursued, very discreetly from afar, by Mr. Paul, the butler. He's a widower with an estranged son (Richard) who's not just the château's dogsbody, but also a thief. Richard, it turns out, knows our eager young police inspector, Lampion.

Simon's not the only person who dies. So does Édouard (accidentally pushed over a cliff by his hated brother) and Madame Dupré, the château's chef of fifty years. She's poisoned and then shot so she can't tell what she knows.

Éloi, the young doctor from the Ivory Coast, is supposed to be the son of Simon's old friend but he turns out to be Simon's illegitimate son. He's unlike Simon or his half-brothers because he's rational, calm, and very capable. He falls madly in love with Inès but pushes her away, because it would be incest. She knows different.

The staff at the château have a close-up view of the goings-on. This is the first adaptation I've seen that makes it clear how much staff is needed to run a castle. The butler, the head housekeeper who's got four maids working for her, the chef with her four kitchen-maids, Simon's valet (we never see anyone else's valet or lady's maid but I assure you, they're there), Richard the dogsbody, at least one gardener, a stableman or two, and the gamekeeper with the dogs. At least fifteen servants sit for the servants' dinner before the family gets their fancier dinner.

General Information

Based on: *Hercule Poirot's Christmas* (novel, 1938)
Run time: 6 hr., 20 min. **Subtitles:** Yes

Writers: Anne Giafferi & Murielle Magellan
Director: Edwin Baily

Cast

Antoine Duléry as Larosière
Marius Colucci as Émile Lampion

Robert Hossein as Simon Le Tescou (Simeon Lee)
Michèle Moretti as Albertine Le Tescou
Bruno Todeschini as Édouard Le Tescou (Alfred Lee)
Elsa Zylberstein as Édith Le Tescou (Lydia Lee)
Liza Manili as Alix Le Tescou
Grégori Derangère as Victor Le Tescou (Harry Lee)
Mathias Mlekuz as Antonin Le Tescou (George Lee)
Leticia Dolera as Inès Della Vega (Pilar Estravados)
Grégoire Taulère as Diego
Disiz as Dr. Éloi (Stephen Farr)
Frédérique Bel as Madeleine (Magdalene Lee)
Jean-Marie Winling as Monsieur Paul (Edward Tressilian)
Marie Bunel as Louise

Film Location

Château de Beaumanoir, Le Leslay, Côtes-d'Armor, France

There's also Superintendent Larosière and his eager young assistant, Émile Lampion. Since Poirot's gone and the story's become a police procedural, they do everything that Poirot did.

But wait, you ask. Wasn't it a police superintendent who actually murdered the old man by cutting his throat and faking the locked room mystery?

Yes, it was, and it still is. Knowing the story made it fascinating to watch Larosière investigate while turning the clues the way he wanted them to go. Watch carefully and you'll see him distract Lampion whenever his young partner starts to see the truth. He chooses and discards patsies to blame and finally settles on Inès. She's not just foreign, she's an imposter so no one will come to her rescue.

Although this mini-series features Larosière and Lampion and is set on France's northern coast, like Season One of *Les Petits Meurtres d'Agatha Christie*, they are unrelated and not just because Larosière is the murderer. The miniseries is set in early 1939 instead of 1935 (Pope Pius XI's death pinpoints the date) so everyone is anxious about what's coming. Whether you're high or low status, Hitler is a topic of conversation.

What I did not like was how the mini-series summed up everyone's future but ignored Inès. She got plenty of screen time, from riding with the real Inès and worrying about the future as they escape Spain to meeting Éloi in town to waking up in the hospital after the car accident (not well scripted or shot) to Diego forcing her to take the real Inès' place in the family. And then being accused of murder and locked up!

Yet her and Éloi's ending consists of standing in the background under a black umbrella during the funeral. Everyone else, including minor servants, got their ending. Not her or Éloi. But that should be expected. They weren't French and so when the production company ran out of film shooting endless minutes of Alix riding on the beach, they got the chop.

Watch this one anyway and give Inès and Éloi their happy ending. They earned it.

The ABC Murders (F-2009)

(*Les meurtres ABC*)

Inspector Larosière battles a rival out for his job while being taunted by a killer leaving a string of bodies

Fidelity to text

Poirot and Hastings are replaced by French policemen in a police procedural. The murderer's different too!

Quality of movie

Surprisingly amusing while still being true to the text and the seriousness of murder.

We fell into the Agatha project and since that fateful day, we've never been terribly systematic about watching the adaptations. We watched the David Suchet Poirots in order, except when Peter Ustinov intruded. We watched the Joan Hicksons in order, except when the ITV Marple productions needed to be done based on what we could get on DVD at the library. If we needed to move a film up on the schedule because of one of the annotation projects, we did.

Eventually, we sort of watched them in the order in which they were released. Except when we didn't.

Which brings me to *Les Meurtres ABC*, the French adaptation of *The A.B.C. Murders*. It's part of the *Les Petits Meurtres d'Agatha Christie* series. We saw an episode (*Towards Zero*) from the second season because I hoped to watch a faithful adaptation of that classic novel. Alas, I was disappointed again. That experience made me decide to be more systematic. Bill and I went back to the first season of *Les Petits Meurtres* and watched this, the first episode.

At this point, dear reader, you'll need some explanation if you're going to watch French TV's take on Agatha. They filmed three seasons (to date). Unlike American TV, the seasons are of varying lengths and have nothing to do with the year. Each season — however long it is — has a different cast and takes place during a different era.

Thus, season 1 (2009-2012) has 11 episodes and takes place in the mid-1930s. Season 2 (2013-2019) has 27 episodes and takes place from 1959 to the early '60s. Season 3 (2021 to date) is airing in France and takes place during the mid-1970s.

The only thing the seasons have in common is the setting. It's northern France, along the English Channel, and up against the Belgian border. This probably means something in France, like setting an American TV cop show in North Dakota instead of New York or LA.

The other commonality is that each season has less to do with Agatha Christie than the previous one. Season one is relatively close to the text, other than turning them into police procedurals and removing whoever did the detecting. Season two plays fast and loose with the source material, preferring to focus on the detectives

André Custe
(*Denis Lavant*),
the proud salesman

Lili Daste
(*Chloé Stefani*),
the supportive servant

Bénédicte Calvez
(*Bérangère Bonvoisin*),
the sickly chatelaine

François Calvez
(*Pascal Demolon*),
the greedy heir

Dr. Granet
(*Jean-François Garreaud*),
the family physician

Yolande Bellec
(*Estelle Larrivaz*),
the judgmental sister

and assistants' sex lives and total lack of interest in police work other than for comic effect. Season three keeps the Christie name, tosses her out of the scripts completely and writes its own stories.

General Information

Based on: *The A.B.C. Murders* (novel, 1936)
Run time: 1 hr., 30 min. **Subtitles:** Yes

Writers: Sylvie Simon, Thierry Debroux
Director: Eric Woreth

Cast

Antoine Duléry as Larosière
Marius Colucci as Lampion
Nicolas Bridet as Duval
Dominique Daguier as Préfet de police

Denis Lavant as André Custe (A.B. Cust)
Bérangère Bonvoisin as Bénédicte Calvez (Lady Charlotte Clarke)
Pascal Demolon as François Calvez (Franklin Clarke)
Daniel Berlioux as Jean Calvez (Carmichael Clarke)
Jeanne Bournaud as Sophie (Thora Gray)
Jean-François Garreaud as Dr. Granet (Dr. Logan)
Anne Benoît as Mme. Daste (Mrs. Marbury)
Chloé Stefani as Lili Daste (Lily Marbury)
Célia Bernard as Aline Bellec (Betty Barnard)
Estelle Larrivaz as Yolande Bellec (Megan Barnard)
Alban Casterman as Yann Lebras (Donald Fraser)

Film Locations

Armentières, France
Blériot, France
Oxelaere, France
Cassel, France
Ambleteuse, France
Zuytpeene, France

So I went back to the beginning, where I should have started all along.

And it was pretty good!

The main changes (besides setting and becoming French) were removing Poirot and Hastings and changing the identity of the murderer and the motivation. Thus, we get Commissaire Jean Larosière. Think of what might have been if Poirot remained a Belgian policeman. He'd have moved up in the ranks, become a decorated and respected veteran, and the young Turks wanting to take his place would see him as a hidebound obstacle to modern police work. Like Poirot, Larosière is clever, a gourmand, and thinks differently. Unlike Poirot, he chases the ladies and frequently catches them.

Larosière's Hastings substitute is his hapless junior officer, Inspector Émile Lampion. Lampion isn't as dopey as Hastings. He's earnest, dogged, and loyal to his boss. Except when he's beguiled by one of the aforementioned young Turks.

That would be Commissaire Duval. Duval is much younger than Larosière and older than Lampion. He resents Larosière for many reasons, not the least of which is that Larosière refused to promote him because of his lack of police skills. Duval remedied some of that by taking extra instruction in policing in Stuttgart, Germany. He's a modern, ambitious man, not above pandering to higher-ups and the press if it means quicker advancement.

He's also not above seducing Lampion, introducing him to the joy of nude postcards of studly young men via that marvel of new technology, a stereoscope. Think of a vintage Viewmaster, with dirty pictures instead of scenic wonders. Lampion thinks he's found a kindred soul, although he feels guilty because of his disloyalty to Larosière. For his part, Duval enjoys using his younger subordinate but it doesn't mean a thing; not when he can use Lampion to get what he really wants.

In the end, Duval's ambition and showboating gets him killed by the ABC murderer and no one mourns him.

The ABC Murders still take place. There's still a series of taunting letters, mailed first to Larosière and then, when he's ousted for failing to solve the case, to Duval. Custe is still a hapless soul, struggling to overcome his permanent injuries from Verdun. His landlady's daughter, Lili, is still very kind to him.

If you're familiar with the novel, you'll assume you know where it's going until the rug's pulled out from under you. Duval arrests Megan because she must have murdered her hated fiancé-stealing sister. He waves away why she murdered a tramp by pouring gasoline over him and setting him afire as the product of a disturbed mind.

The Clarke family shows up on schedule and you're sure that Franklin, an oily wastrel, is who he is in the novel. He's a thief. He seduced his brother's secretary. When his brother's head is bashed in with a sledgehammer, he's not unhappy.

Custe is arrested. He's sure he's guilty, but he can't explain why or how he killed. Larosière, back on the case because Duval got his throat slashed, is suspicious because things don't add up. I'll assume police work went on in the background even though we didn't see it. He arranges with Lady Clarke to do the Poirot in her drawing room, and it's at that point the story takes an unexpected twist.

She did it! In cahoots with her lover, the doctor! Who's also Custe's doctor, Betty Barnard's doctor, and the tramp's doctor! Her doctor is the connective tissue between the victims. They did it because she's angry at her husband for stealing the credit for her scientific genius, pursuing hot, blonde secretaries, taking over her château and money, and in general being a bad husband.

Her lover, the doctor, committed the murders and very cruel, personal, and intimate they were too. Strangling, lighting someone on fire, bludgeoning, throat-cutting, setting up Custe as a patsy for the guillotine, and, when they're unmasked, he injects Lady Clarke with a killer dose of morphine to save her from the guillotine.

This adaptation fires on all cylinders, but as soon as we began discussing the film during our nightly walk, we saw the flaws. A lot of grim murders were committed to disguise killing Sir Carmichael Clarke, unwanted husband. But as Alfred Hitchcock observed: As long as the audience buys it in the theater and reality doesn't set in until after they've walked outside, the ending works.

The Cat and the Mice (F-2010)

(*Le chat et les souris*)

Men invade a posh boarding school for girls in the quest for stolen gems for which someone is willing to kill

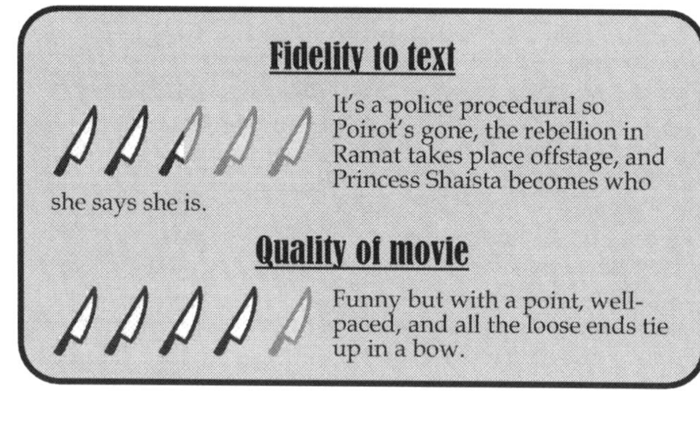

In *The Cat Among the Pigeons*, Agatha inserted Poirot almost as an afterthought to satisfy her readers and her publisher. He doesn't come onstage until late in chapter 17. Julia Upjohn, a budding Nancy Drew, works out where the diamonds must be hidden, knows who the great detective is (Maureen Summerhayes of *Mrs. McGinty's Dead* told her), and flees the posh girl's boarding school for London to seek his aid.

Between Julia, Detective Inspector Kelsey, and Miss Bulstrode, they could have solved the mystery on their own.

Since Poirot's off in London three-quarters of the time, it's easy to remove him completely and turn the book into a police procedural. Except what do you do with your stars? That would be Commissaire Jean Larosière (the Poirot substitute) and his sidekick, Inspector Émile Lampion (the Hastings substitute). They have to show up within the first few minutes no matter what the novel says.

As always with foreign adaptations, I'll stick with the novel's names for clarity when I can.

And so, the scriptwriter found a solution that appears to have nothing to do with subsequent events, yet proves to be significant. A little girl hunting mushrooms in the forest with her father discovers a woman's nude body, partially buried in the leaves. The location is critical because the mushroom-laced woods surround a former monastery which has been converted into a posh girls' boarding school.

Larosière and Lampion arrive on the scene, throwing Miss Bulstrode, the teachers, and the students into a tizzy. Men in the building! *Quelle horreur!* The only male allowed in Meadowbank is Victor the skeleton. The presence of a woman's body out in the woods is minor compared to the presence of male gendarmes roaming the hallways.

Larosière assigns the dead woman's case to Lampion. The question quickly becomes "who is she?" She's nude so there's no identification. The coroner (a very creepy guy) says she was knifed. He adds that her face was smashed in after her death, not before. It takes time for Lampion to work out why, but Larosière is very patient. He also cracks jokes, discomfiting Lampion.

This was a great moment and proof that season one of *The Little Murders of Agatha Christie* is far superior to

Armande Vaucher (*Brigitte Catillon*), the headmistress

Thérèse Baillon (*Marilyne Canto*), the heir apparent

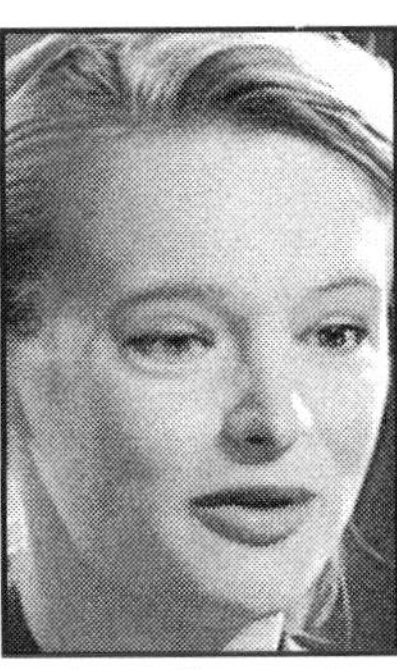

Anne Gampart (*Anouchka Vingtier*), the new secretary

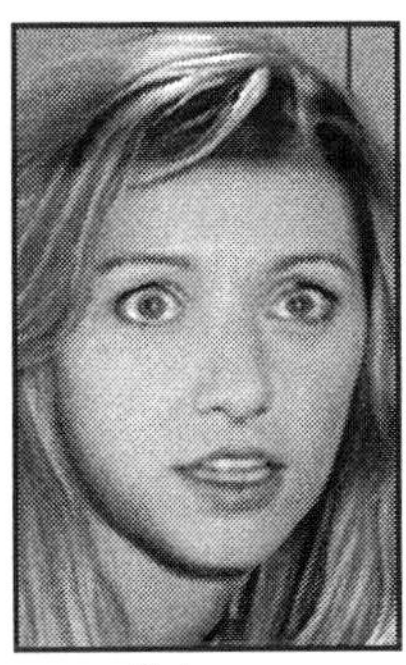

Solange (*Marion Monier*), the seductive student

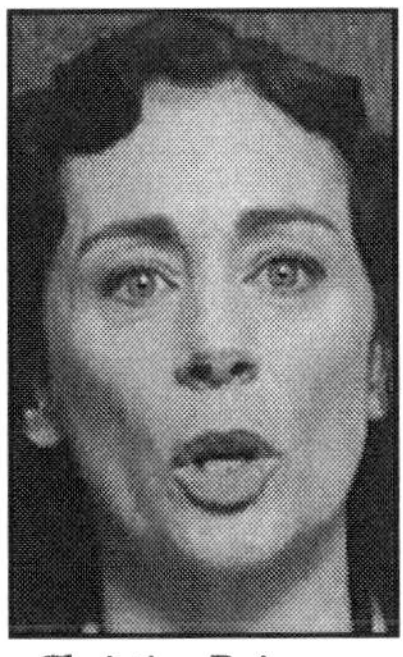

Christine Boisseau (*Isabelle Candelier*), the housekeeper

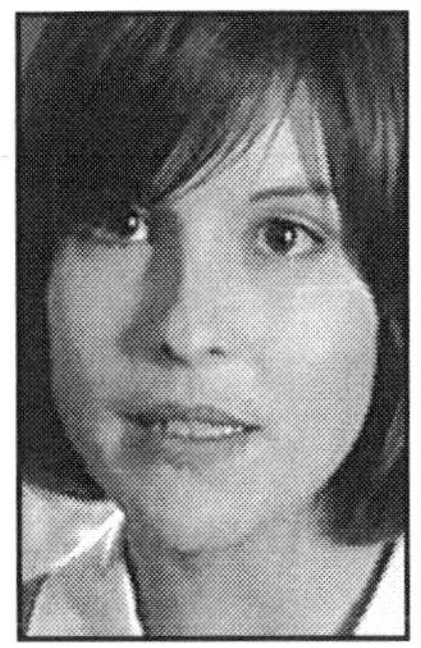

Juliette (*Flore Bonaventura*), the poor student

season two. Lampion is having a tough time with Larosière's gallows humor, but as Larosière tells him, they have a hard, often horrible job. If grim humor helps them cope, then it served their higher purpose which is getting justice for that woman and her family. Standing before the nude woman's body in the morgue, the coroner tells Lampion her body is trying to tell them who she is and what happened. Lampion mans up and takes pictures of a port wine stain. It's large, but it's also at the woman's waist so only a close family member will recognize it. He gets the local newspapers to print the pictures and, eventually, the letters come flooding in.

Most of them are fraudulent as Larosière predicted. But one of them isn't.

Meanwhile, Larosière interviews the teachers and encounters his past. The housekeeper, Christine Boisseau, (the film's highly altered version of Matron Johnson) knows him, oh very well indeed. She's unhappy to see him, and he doesn't understand why. She has an unhappy daughter, Juliette, who's being educated with the rich girls as a perk for mom cleaning up after them.

But nothing comes of the investigation and they leave, only to return a few days later when another woman is murdered. This time, they know precisely who got shot at close range in the locker room. It's the sadistic, prying, and annoying Miss Springer, games mistress. Unlike the body buried in the leaves, there's no question about her identity. The crimes seem unrelated but Miss Bulstrode is well-connected, her students even more so, so this murder must be solved at once.

Tensions at the school ramp up. We get wonderful scenes of the students avidly discussing the crimes whenever they're out of the teachers' earshot. The mean girls are led by Solange, an important government official's daughter. She's got a hate on for the housekeeper's daughter because why should the children of servants be educated? Juliette's going to spend her life on her knees, scrubbing Solange's floors. She doesn't need to read or write. Solange also goes after pudgy and plain Émilie. Luckily, Cassandra, who's got the second sight, foresees not just more murders. She "sees" Solange's comeuppance.

General Information

Based on: *Cat Among the Pigeons* (novel, 1959)
Run time: 1 hr., 38 min. **Subtitles:** Yes

Writers: Anne Giafferi & Murielle Magellan
Director: Eric Woreth

Cast

Antoine Duléry as Larosière
Marius Colucci as Lampion

Brigitte Catillon as Armande Vaucher (Honoria Bulstrode)
Marilyne Canto as Thérèse Baillon (Miss Chadwick)
Anouchka Vingtier as Anne Gampart (Ann Shapland)
Isabelle Candelier as Christine Boisseau
Caroline Ducey as Ève Mauger
Anna Cottis as Dorothy Davis (Angele Blanche)
Claire Magnin as Soeur Simone
Gaelle Hausermann as Gisèle Sandeau
Nailia Harzoune as Shaïna (Princess Shaista)
Marion Monier as Solange
Nastassja Girard as Cassandra
Stéphane Caillard as Annabelle de Lussac
Alexandra C. Hernandez as Émilie
Flore Bonaventura as Juliette
Thibaut Rottiers as Julien

Film Location

Chartreuse Notre-Dame-des-Prés, Neuville-sous-Montreuil (boarding school)

There's also Princess Shaista. Here, she's exactly who she says she is: the daughter of the recently murdered crown prince of Ramat. All the Ramat scenes take place offscreen and are alluded to in newspaper stories or dialog. Princess Shaista quickly makes friends with Annabelle, showing her the dagger she keeps in her luggage. Shaista is very clear. If she ever learns who murdered her father, she'll execute that person with her own hands. Shaista shows a bit of kindness to Juliette, giving her an unwanted tennis racket. It may have poor balance but it's better than anything Juliette and her mother can afford.

Meanwhile, the teachers are a seething stew of secrets. Miss Bulstrode suffers from a serious bone disease, needing a cane whenever no parents are around and regular morphine injections from Miss Chadwick. Miss Chadwick turns out to be having a lesbian relationship with Miss Mauger, the French teacher. Miss Davis, the English teacher (the film's version of Mlle. Blanche) is a nosy parker, eager to pass along gossip. Soeur Simone is the head nun and like Solange, doesn't believe in educating the children of servants. They'll get above their station in life and put on airs.

Events heat up, Soeur Simone is bashed in the head with a shovel, and the girls go wild, wilder, wildest. Solange attempts to seduce Lampion, then claims he tried to rape her when they're caught together. Larosière knows it's not true as girls are not Lampion's cup of tea. Nonetheless, it's a serious accusation and has to be faced or they'll both become traffic wardens if they keep their jobs at all.

Solange is knifed in the shower, a scene that might remind you a bit of *Psycho*. Lucky for her, Lampion walks into a tree, stumbles into the locker room shower to wash up his bloody nose, and rescues her before she bleeds out.

And that disfigured body in the leaves? Lampion learns who she is and why she had to have her face damaged. She was the real Ann Shapland, replacement secretary to Miss Bulstrode. She was killed by the woman impersonating her to steal the diamonds.

This isn't the novel, scene for scene. But it works beautifully, with the plot elements as tightly strung as a pro's tennis racket.

Game of Mirrors (F-2013)

(*Jeux de glaces*)

Everybody's incompetent, a loser, or a fool (including the police) at this rehab center for young crooks

Fidelity to text

Considerably simplified: Miss Marple vanishes, it's a police procedural, and Carrie Louise gets a personality transplant.

Quality of movie

An annoying soundtrack, women as stereotypes, and missed opportunities galore.

The first episode of the second season of *Little Murders* demonstrates truth in advertising. We watched one other episode of this season (*L'Heure Zéro* or *Towards Zero*) prior to this one. That film was #25 of 27 episodes. Everything I disliked in that film was on full display here, in the opening episode of the second season. If I'd watched the adaptations in order, I'd have been warned.

We open with comic animation showing how fun it is to knife or garrote people and how our detectives (Commissaire Swan Laurence, his secretary Marlène, and Alice Avril, girl reporter) attempt to solve the murders in a suitably madcap fashion because hey! Murder's a game and it should be treated as fun!

As always, I'll stick with the novel's names wherever I can. It's easier.

The film opens on a down-market Brigitte Bardot (her roots needed retouching very badly) wearing painted-on shorts and bikini top. She's shimmying to rock music (so hip and now!) while her hubby's working underneath a car and the inmates of her parents' criminal rehabilitation center ogle her and argue about ogling her. One of them gets his throat slashed, nearly taking his head off and spraying blood everywhere. Those madcap murderous youths!

The police are called. The superintendent reassures Carrie Louise and Lewis Serrocold that nosy reporters won't poke into their business. The murder, obviously committed by one of the brain-damaged inmates, will be hushed up. It's good to be powerful; you get the justice you demand.

But wait! Commissaire Laurence arrives at the scene of the crime in the nick of time, announces he's the new sheriff in this shithole town (although the superintendent outranks him), and that the murderer is not *this* brain-damaged convict but *that* left-handed one over there! He could tell from the knife slash across the throat — severing the carotid artery and the jugular vein — that the murderer couldn't be righthanded. He's arrogant, he's the smartest person around for miles, he doesn't want to be there, and he's already made his boss look like a fool.

Our Brigitte Bardot knockoff is instantly smitten, ignoring her boring American husband. Carrie Louise

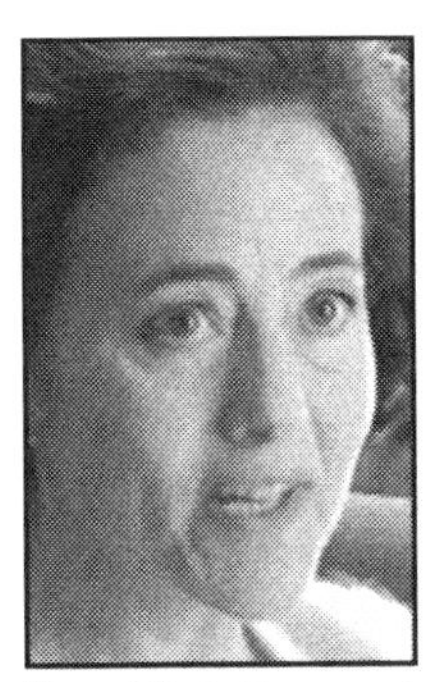

Rose-Marie Bousquet (*Catherine Mouchet*), the money

Etienne Bousquet (*Olivier Rabourdin*), the utopianist

Juliette White (*Stéphane Caillard*), the French temptress

Jimmy White (*Shane Woodward*), the American cuckold

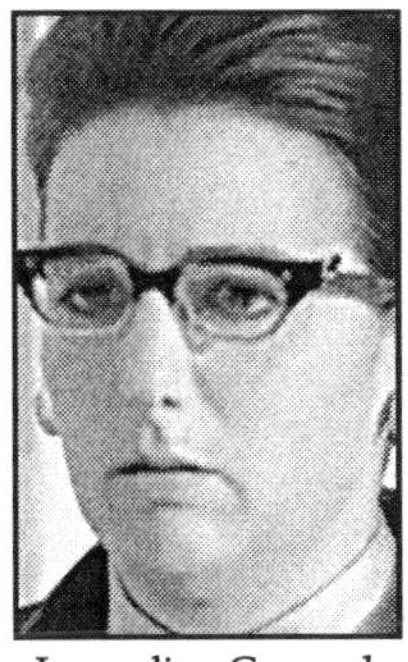

Jacqueline Cassard (*Solveig Maupu*), the good sister

Léonard Jandel (*Vincent Londez*), the co-conspirator

and Lewis are horrified. The publicity! People won't understand that these poor, violent souls need love and care in a bucolic setting, not being locked away in a grim prison. This murder, by the way, has nothing to do with the novel (typical of season two scripts) and is never referred to again (typical of season two's attention to detail).

Meanwhile, we meet Alice Avril, our red-haired Nancy Drew wannabe and girl reporter. She's currently writing the local paper's agony column. She hates her job. She wants better things, yet throughout this episode (and in *L'Heure Zéro*), she's incompetent. She doesn't see the clues in front of her, she ignores or conceals evidence, her relationship with Laurence quickly devolves into something out of junior high school where it's tit for tat insults. She's a morass of hurt feelings and doesn't grasp that murder is serious enough that emotions should be kept in check.

Laurence is a first-class jerk, no question, but he's serious about solving the crime. Alice is looking to score points off him and her ineptness is played for laughs. She can't remember her cover story about why Carrie Louise should hire her as a maid. When faced with a dead body — she's a reporter, remember — she collapses and then as soon as the body's out of sight, murder turns back into a fun game.

Then we meet Marlène, the Marilyn Monroe-lookalike secretary. We quickly learn Marlène's competence exists solely in looking good. She's barely capable of running an office and, later in *L'Heure Zéro*, she has no qualms about altering evidence for personal revenge. She works for the police and should know how to handle evidence. But it's played for laughs and hey, everyone agrees that no one needs to be serious about how citizens are unjustly accused or evidence is handled as long as it all turns out right in the end.

This season is set in the tail end of the 1950s and forges into the '60s. It goes to great pains to tell us that women want more than kitchen, church, and children. Yet they make no effort to show that the two female leads are competent or smart. Alice could be a clone of Lucy Ricardo in 1955, failing at one job after another. Marlène is right out of some '50s Mamie Van Doren or Jayne Mansfield flick, playing the dumb sex kitten.

General Information

Based on: *They Do It With Mirrors* (*Murder with Mirrors* in U.S.), 1952
Run time: 1 hr., 43 min. **Subtitles:** Yes

Writers: Sylvie Simon, Thierry Debroux
Director: Eric Woreth

Cast

Samuel Labarthe as Commissaire Laurence
Blandine Bellavoir as Alice Avril
Elodie Frenck as Marlène Leroy
Dominique Thomas as Ernest Tricard

Catherine Mouchet as Rose-Marie Bousquet (Carrie Louise Serrocold)
Olivier Rabourdin as Etienne Bousquet (Lewis Serrocold)
Stéphane Caillard as Juliette White (Gina Hudd)
Shane Woodward as Jimmy White (Walter Hudd)
Solveig Maupu as Jacqueline Cassard (Mildred Strete)
Guillaume Bienvenu as Antonin Lambert (Alexis Restarick)
Vincent Londez as Léonard Jandel (Edgar Lawson)
Gérard Pinteau as Pierre Montauban (Christian Gulbrandsen)
Christophe Piret as Robert Jourdeuil

Film Location

Chateau de Souverain-Moulin, Pittefaux, Pas de Calais (Bousquet home)

Except unlike them, she doesn't hide her intellect. She doesn't have one.

The other women get treated no better. Gina (our low-rent Brigitte Bardot) is a dumb slut. She openly cheats on her husband (or appears to do so), puts on a show for the violent inmates, tries to seduce Laurence, and carries on with her cousin, Alex Restarick.

Mildred, her sister, is everything a woman shouldn't be in France and gets even less respect than Gina does. She's plain, dowdy, prim, stuck-up, dumb, and bad at investing. We're told the other characters laugh at her behind her back because she's got nothing to offer. She's nothing like this in the novel, other than plain compared to Gina. Everyone's plain compared to Gina.

Carrie Louise gets a complete personality makeover, revealed in the climax. She's not the innocent naïf everyone believes she is. She fully backs hubby Lewis' plans to buy a tropical island and turn it into a utopia for their convicts. Those convicts will be fully redeemed as human beings once they're shielded from the evils of civilization. Well, maybe. When Lewis' embezzlement is revealed, the greater good is at stake. Carrie Louise is the mastermind behind Gulbrandsen's and Edgar's murders.

Edgar, by the way, is no longer Lewis' secret son. He's just another mental case to be used to build that shining city on the hill and then discarded when he's no longer useful.

Everything you won't like about season two is on display. Laurence is an arrogant jerk. Alice is annoying and incapable. Marlène isn't any better. The local police are the Keystone Kops, French division. Plot threads like the opening murder or who poisoned Carrie Louise's medicine or who injected arsenic into the chocolates are raised and then ignored. Every man is a sexist pig and every woman — who is supposed to be working for that brave new world when they'll be treated as fully-functioning human beings with brains — is either stupid, ditzy, or both. The soundtrack, something I rarely notice, is so annoying that I couldn't not notice it, demanding that I admire this clever plot twist or that witty repartee. Except the plot twists are not clever and the repartee is not so witty. Bleah. This soufflé was DOA.

The Witness For The Prosecution (2016)

In this version based on the original short story, forgiveness is impossible when love lies bleeding in your hand

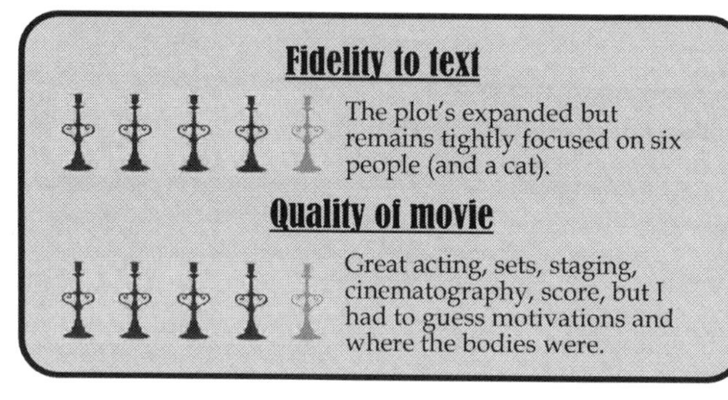

Did you notice "The" in the title? That's your clue this film is not the twice-filmed stage play *Witness for the Prosecution* (1957 and 1982). It's based on Agatha's original short story, initially titled "Traitor's Hands" (1925). She was unhappy with the ending because Leonard Vole got away with murder. When she rewrote the story into the play, Leonard got away with murder in court. Justice arrived moments later when his wife discovered what a lying, cheating dog he really was.

Don't expect that quasi-happy ending here, where murderers get their just desserts. This film is a tragedy for everyone. Well, except Leonard and Romaine, although their happy ending is not assured. They are still who they are. Leonard is a charming, shiftless ne'er-do-well and completely believable liar. As for Romaine, she gave up hope long ago and has no moral scruples left. Once she decides she's better off without him, he'll never wake up. If he decides he wants someone else, he'll murder her without hesitation and then, without her brains to save him, he'll hang for it. It'll work itself out.

The center of both story and film is John Mayhew, solicitor. He's not a barrister. As an American, the two classes of lawyers in Britain are confusing. Solicitors meet clients, provide legal advice, and do the dog's work of preparing cases. Barristers don the red gown and wig, take the material gathered by solicitors, and present the case before the bar. It's a class thing, demonstrated throughout the film. Observe Sir Charles, barrister, explain to Mayhew, solicitor, why Janet McIntyre behaves so possessively about Emily French. In his experience, lady's maids and valets are all like that. Mayhew's never met a lady's maid or valet.

Mayhew struggles at the bottom of the legal system. He's poor, wearing fusty, outdated suits. Clients don't seek him out by name. He solicits them by visiting the jail, going from cell to cell, and asking if anyone needs a representative. That's how he finds Leonard, arrested for the murder of Emily French. He takes on the case for a pittance.

Mayhew and Leonard quickly bond. With his lost, puppy dog eyes and air of naïve innocence, Leonard must remind Mayhew of his son, died in the war because he'd willingly lied about his son's age so they could enlist together to fight the Kaiser. The son died in a gas attack on his 17th birthday. His father survived with damaged lungs. His son's death saddles Mayhew

John Mayhew (*Toby Jones*), the doomed solicitor

Leonard Vole (*Billy Howle*), the accused husband

Romaine Heilger (*Andrea Riseborough*), the traitorous wife

Sir Charles Carter (*David Haig*), the hired gun

Emily French (*Kim Cattrall*), the wealthy siren

Janet McIntyre (*Monica Dolan*), the loyal maid

with endless guilt and grief. Saving Leonard, so obviously harmless, would be an act of redemption.

Enhancing his virtuous appearance, Leonard's sole concern is how his arrest will affect his common-law wife, Romaine. When Mayhew watches her sing a sentimental ballad on stage, perched on a silver crescent moon (you'll see the real crescent moon at the end of the film), he's overcome and sobs in his seat. When Romaine meets him, she immediately realizes what kind of man he is: a romantic fool. Romantics have a weakness. They can be unrealistic, believing what suits them. They avoid questions that would reveal unpleasant truths.

For example, ask yourself why Mayhew doesn't verify how Romaine became the show's headliner. He reasons she's notorious and can sing so that's why she's the star. Then he meets "Christine." *She* insists Romaine had permanently scarred her to steal her place in the spotlight. Mayhew believes her, yet doesn't verify her story either. Poirot or Miss Marple never believe what they're told; they always seek confirmation.

Another of Mayhew's weaknesses is his callousness towards women. After the trial's over, he doesn't return to Limehouse to pay "Christine" for giving him the letter proving Leonard's innocence. It was obvious she needed money desperately. Yes, Mayhew was in the hospital for several days, but that's no excuse. He had plenty of time to ensure that scarred, ailing woman was rewarded.

Another example occurs when he was in the hospital. Leonard visited and asked Mayhew if he should settle money on Janet McIntyre. Because Leonard was declared innocent, he inherited Emily French's entire estate and Janet — who in previous wills got a nice bequest — got nothing. Mayhew told Leonard he shouldn't give Janet a penny. What did he think Janet would live on? Leonard inherited £185,000 (in 1923 money!), plus the estate, stocks, bonds, antiques, art, and jewelry. Leonard was so rich that he told Mayhew to accept a 40% commission after selling Emily French's house. He could easily spare a few thousand pounds.

While Mayhew's readying the house for sale, he discovers what happened to Mimi, Emily French's cat. Mimi was drowned in the pond. Could the person who drowned the cat have been the murderer? Mayhew persuades Detective Inspector Breem to investigate and Janet ends up hanging for Emily's murder.

General Information

Based on: *Witness for the Prosecution* (play, 1953), from "Traitor's Hands" (short story, 1925)
Run time: 2 hr. **Subtitles:** Yes

Writer: Sarah Phelps **Director:** Julian Jarrold

Cast

Toby Jones as John Mayhew
Hayley Carmichael as Alice Mayhew
Dorian Lough as Detective Breem
David Haig as Sir Charles Carter

Billy Howle as Leonard Vole
Andrea Riseborough as Romaine Heilger
Kim Cattrall as Emily French
Monica Dolan as Janet McIntyre
Robert East as Justice Greville Parris
Tim McMullan as Sir Hugo Meredith
Miranda Nolan as Christine Moffat
Paul Ready as Tripp
Carla Langley as Dora
Ted Robbins as Bernie

Film Locations

Formby Beach, Southport, Merseyside (battlefield)
Abbey Square, Chester, Cheshire (French's home)
Liverpool Playhouse, Liverpool, Merseyside (exterior theatre)
Morecambe Winter Gardens, Lancashire (interior theatre, The Parisian Bar)
London Road Fire Station, Manchester (police station)
St. George's Hall, Liverpool (prison)
Liverpool Town Hall, Liverpool, Merseyside (French hotel, interiors)
Southport, Merseyside (beach)

I really liked how Sarah Phelps fleshed out Emily French. What kind of older woman pours out her interest, affection, and money on feckless but handsome young men? Emily enjoys keeping young men at her beck and call. Today, we'd call her a cougar.

Phelps also fleshed out Mayhew's wife, Alice. Alice has grieved their son's death for years. Mayhew, who claims he loves her, is so oblivious that, seated at the table across from her, he doesn't see her pierce her finger with a needle. She's trying to feel something, yet he doesn't notice. Nor does he notice that she never wears the beautiful scarf he gave her. As she tells him, he doesn't want love; he wants forgiveness. She'll never forgive him for killing her son.

Romaine got fleshed out too. She's been hardened by life and, even in a crowded theater, she's isolated. She's relegated to the chorus, another anonymous body in the back row. If she wants more, she'll have to fight for it.

I did not like how Leonard and Romaine met. She would have never been on the battlefield and where were the other soldiers? That field should have been littered with dead bodies, spent shells, destroyed vehicles, and debris. That battlefield was as pristine and empty as the tidal flats Mayhew walks across into the sea under the crescent moon. Leonard and Romaine would've met in some whorehouse behind the lines or a seedy bar, not in the trenches.

The film is moody and atmospheric. The buildings were Dickensian grim, the lighting hazy and dim. Even the air contributed. That choking yellow haze you see constantly exacerbating Mayhew's cough is the famous London smog. It's a mixture of coal and wood smoke from countless stoves and factories, mixed with industrial pollution.

There's plenty to like in this tragedy. The class differences, the backstage scenes, Janet's complex relationship with Emily French, Leonard and Romaine's lying self-justification, and Toby Jones' amazing performance as Mayhew.Just don't expect a happy ending for anyone and be prepared to see Mimi dragged from her watery grave.

Crooked House (2017)

One of Christie's favorite novels finally gets adapted in this well-cast, beautiful but sluggish noir tragedy

Fidelity to text

The usual character compressions and plot simplifications to squeeze a novel into a film. Charles gets gelded. The ending is vastly improved over Agatha's climax.

Quality of movie

Gorgeous to look at with a strong noir flavor. Sadly, our hero Charles has the charisma of a Ken doll and the pace often drags.

We began the Agatha project — watching all the movie and TV adaptations of her work — by accident. I brought *Crooked House* home from the library in July 2020, when the world was still largely shut-down by the Covid pandemic. We'd been annotating Agatha's out-of-copyright novels and it seemed interesting.

I liked *Crooked House* a lot. Up until this point, I'd read plenty of her books but had only seen one Agatha Christie movie (2017's *Murder on the Orient Express* in the theater). Now that I've sat through nearly 200 adaptations, I don't like it nearly as much.

What changed? Among other things, I learned a lot about pacing (this film drags) and detective work. I couldn't buy Charles as an investigator. He didn't ask many questions, he didn't seem to listen to the answers, and what he did hear didn't change the course of his investigation until the climax when he magically recalled that Lady Edith poisoned moles with cyanide when she wasn't blasting them with a shotgun a la Elmer Fudd hunting wabbits.

Charles' anemic detective work made me long for Poirot. Any Poirot would do, even Tony Randall's despite *his* movie being remarkably stupid. Max Irons plays Charles. He should have lit up the screen and radiated virility which would explain why a desperate Sophia, who shagged him in Cairo, begged him for help.

Charles and Sophia had zero chemistry. The script and the tepid direction didn't do either of them any favors. Even so, a more charismatic actor (like Aiden Turner who played Philip Lombard in 2015's *And Then There Were None*) could have overcome the bland writing. What did Sophia see in Charles? In Egypt, he treated her like a pretty girl, not an heiress. As a budding intelligence officer, Charles flunked his first test when he didn't investigate the holes in her story or ask relatives back home to tell him more about this pretty girl.

What made their love story worse was we were never given a convincing explanation for their breakup. MI5 asked him to spy on her and he refused. She was called home by grandpa to run the family business. So, Charles dumped her rather than spy on her but forced a big fight when she had to leave so he wouldn't have to admit what he'd been asked to do? The script was woefully unclear, other than Charles

Edith de Haviland (*Glenn Close*), the matriarch

Philip Leonides (*Julian Sands*), the acerbic writer

Magda Leonides (*Gillian Anderson*), the fading actress

Sophia Leonides (*Stefanie Martini*), the determined heiress

Brenda Leonides (*Christina Hendricks*), the Las Vegas widow

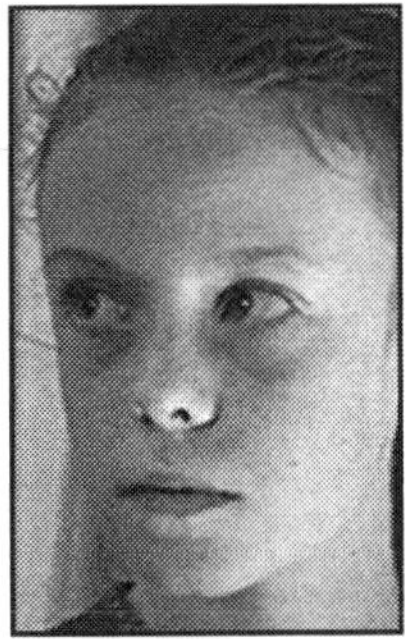

Josephine Leonides (*Honor Kneafsey*), the confident child

and Sophia couldn't communicate.

But the plot insisted she solve grandpa's murder discreetly so, instead of hiring someone competent like Poirot, she hired Charles despite whatever blowup they'd had in Egypt. Sure. Charles needed to radiate charisma and manliness demonstrating why Sophia still carried a torch for him. Instead, we got dull. If they marry (as they did in the novel), and that's a big if, she'll run roughshod over him, he'll kowtow to her every whim, and she'll despise him for it.

Despite the vacuous, central relationship, everything else is fun and well-worth watching.

Three Gables, the family mansion, is loaded with insight into the Leonides family. It isn't just sprawling. The fault lines run deep between family members and the house shows it. What you find behind closed doors can be wildly different from the suite next door. Thus, Brenda (Aristide's hot, much younger trophy wife) adorns a hot pink suite. Roger and Clemency live in an ultra-modern, space-age '50s extravaganza. Philip and Magda live surrounded by mementos of her theater career. Eustace has overlaid baronial splendor with rock'n'roll posters and a hi-fi system.

Glenn Close stars as Lady Edith, sister of Aristide Leonides' first wife. She's amazing. She's willing to make the hard choice and do the right thing yet still be concerned with the proprieties. Watch her face in Josephine's bedroom when she finds the notebook and opens it. She may have only suspected before but now, she knows. After she speaks with the cancer doctor, she knows she has little time left to act. When she and Josephine drive into the quarry and over the cliff, she's terrified of the terminal end but she doesn't let her own fear stop her.

Josephine is unusual among Agatha's murderers. She's twelve. Agatha was always cutting edge. With *Crooked House*, she was so cutting edge that her publisher asked her to change the ending and she refused. Even today, with bad seed kids a dime a dozen, it's a shock to read the novel for the first time and realize that annoying but helpful child murdered grandpa and Nanny. Honor Kneafsey played her perfectly, capturing a child who could still play with dolls, yet delusional enough to believe she's the smartest person around. Her Josephine is vain and self-important. Her dancing scene captures her personality: She's the only person in the room because other people, with their needs and wants, aren't real.

General Information

Based on: *Crooked House* (novel, 1949)
Run time: 1 hr., 55 min. **Subtitles:** Yes

Writers: Julian Fellowes, Tim Rose Price, and Gilles Paquet-Brenner
Director: Gilles Paquet-Brenner

Cast

Max Irons as Charles Hayward
Terence Stamp as Chief Inspector Taverner
David Kirkbride as Sergeant Glover

Glenn Close as Lady Edith de Haviland
Julian Sands as Philip Leonides
Gillian Anderson as Magda Leonides
Stefanie Martini as Sophia Leonides
Preston Nyman as Eustace Leonides
Honor Kneafsey as Josephine Leonides
Christian McKay as Roger Leonides
Amanda Abbington as Clemency Leonides
Christina Hendricks as Brenda Leonides
John Heffernan as Laurence Brown
Gino Picciano as Aristide Leonides
Jenny Galloway as Nanny

Film Locations

Hammersmith Apollo, Hammersmith, London (cinema and dance hall)
Minley Manor, Minley, Hampshire (Three Gables exteriors)
Tyntesfield, near Wraxall, Bristol (Three Gables interiors)
West Wycombe House, West Wycombe, Buckinghamshire (Three Gables interiors)
Hughenden Manor, Hughenden, Buckinghamshire (Three Gables interiors)
Dyrham Park, Dyrham, Gloucestershire
Hoxton Square, London (1950s Soho)
Lincoln's Inn Fields, Holborn, London
TUC Congress House courtyard, Bloomsbury, London (Associated Catering office)

Gillian Anderson as Magda channels every aging ingenue who never found the fame she was chasing. She's an alcoholic living on dreams. Philip, who writes learned tomes no one reads, has written her a screenplay that might let her find fame in the movies. Up till now, she demanded theatrical success but she never made it past provincial repertory companies. Suddenly, Hollywood doesn't seem as low-rent.

Trophy wife Brenda (Christina Hendricks) is way out her depth in the Leonides household. The family despises her and is eager to blame her for Aristide's death. It would be so convenient if that Las Vegas dancer and her Communist tutor lover were guilty instead of one of them. You really feel for Brenda. Josephine despises her enough, in her confessional notebook, to slam her handwriting as being that of a ten-year-old and thus easy to forge. Only Edith and Nanny feel any sympathy towards Brenda, and it's still tinged with contempt.

The climax is substantially improved over the novel. There, Edith and Josephine disappear and we discover that Edith drove them over a cliff into a quarry. Here, Edith is faced with horror. Her adored great-niece is a murderous psychopath. She doesn't want Josephine confined to an asylum nor does she want the family name dragged further into the mud. We watch her take Josephine for a drive for ice cream. They leave Three Gables, Edith supplying the police with a plausible explanation. As Josephine becomes wary, Edith gives her another explanation that's even more alluring: ballet lessons. Josephine is thrilled until she realizes that they're going to die horribly. She screams and struggles. But Edith doesn't stop.

The only weakness was adding the scene showing Edith at the doctor's office. In the novel, Edith didn't get the excuse of avoiding a lingering death by cancer. She chose murder/suicide because what else could she do?

Crooked House was one of Agatha's favorite novels. It's a pity this adaptation doesn't live up to it.

Ordeal by Innocence (2018)

The story of one of Christie's worst parents (and that's saying something) gets a Phelps makeover (& it works)

Fidelity to text

The plot remains but the characters are more complex. The murderer changes, but it worked.

Quality of movie

Sumptuous locations, great acting, a plot that tied together logically, and a red boat named *Anubis*!

Although the title card says "Agatha Christie's *Ordeal By Innocence*," Sarah Phelps wrote the script. You know what that means: she rewrote, replotted, added, subtracted, and by the time she finished, this film should have been titled "Sarah Phelps' *Ordeal By Innocence*." The new murderer works because other characters and their motivations changed enough to make it perfectly plausible.

After all, in Christie World, people murder their spouses all the time. Who is the most likely person to murder a woman? Her husband. And so it proves here, unlike the novel where it was Jacko, manipulating his lover, Kirsten, to murder his mother.

In Phelps' rewrite, Kirsten is Jack's mother. He lost the "o" to signal his character rewrite. Kirsten's still the overworked, downtrodden housekeeper and loving surrogate mother to the five adopted kids. Rachel knows the truth about Kirsten and Jack. So does Jack's father. He is, naturally, Leo Argyll. He raped Kirsten when she was a fifteen-year-old orphan, taken in by Rachel to help with baby Mary. Kirsten stayed, Leo apparently kept his hands off her after that, and Rachel adopted three more children.

Why did Leo stay, unable to acknowledge the son he sired? For the money, of course. I've read the book and watched three adaptations. Each time, Leo is less of a lion and more of a louse, a cad, a dilettante, and an unpublished author who'll never finish writing the darned book. He lives off Rachel because she's rich and he's not. That's her house.

In addition to his other character deficiencies, Leo cheats on Rachel. Everyone in the family knows. In a flashback, Rachel confronts Gwenda, the secretary, over her and Leo's affair. Gwenda wasn't Leo's first bit of sugar on the side and she won't be the last.

The real question, sadly not answered here despite plenty of time (three hours!) is why Rachel kept Leo around. Agatha didn't answer the question and neither did any of the screenwriters. Rachel is a complicated woman. She's rich, she's intelligent, she has status over and above her money, and she's a philanthropist. She wants children desperately but she's barren, so she adopted. Sadly, she's a bad mother. She's not evil like Mrs. Boynton in *Appointment With Death* (1938). But she's still the kind of mother whose kids end up in lifelong therapy and permanently estranged. She is one stone-cold fish.

Rachel Argyll
(*Anna Chancellor*),
the victim

Leo Argyll
(*Bill Nighy*),
the widower

Gwenda Vaughan
(*Alice Eve*),
the secretary

Jack Argyll
(*Anthony Boyle*),
the convicted

Kirsten Lindstrom
(*Morven Christie*),
the substitute

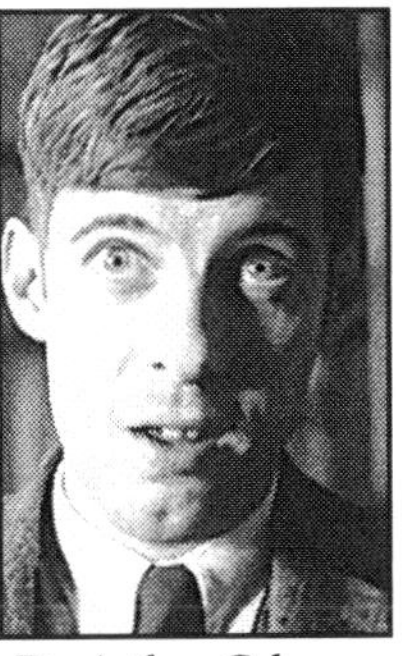

Dr. Arthur Calgary
(*Luke Treadaway*),
the witness

Lucky for Rachel, Kirsten stepped in and provided the love and affection the kids craved. She's the reason they're capable of empathy.

Rachel has managed to estrange every member of the family. Those who stay, do it because she controls the purse strings and they've got no other place to go. Mickey and Tina escaped. Mickey joined the army to fight in Korea and returned to open a garage. Tina got a bedsit in town and works as a librarian. Hester's escape attempt failed.

Mary and Philip might have managed to make their marriage work, but he's a bad husband. He's a losing gambler who broke his spine in a drunken car wreck, trapping him and Mary. When you watch Philip's bitterness, realize that he brought it on himself. He doesn't have to abuse Mary and the family but he's never controlled his appetites. With Leo around as an example, he's got no reason to improve his behavior. It's perfectly in keeping with Philip's character that he urges Arthur Calgary to raise a stink about Jack's alibi and innocence so Leo will pay for silence and they split the money. Money, by the way, he'd instantly lose gambling and drinking.

The revised plot beautifully sets up why Leo murdered Rachel and blamed Jack. Rachel's last day on earth consisted of her world collapsing around her:

* Jack confronted her with the truth of his birth, something she'd sworn to Kirsten she'd never reveal.

* Jack in anger told Rachel about Mickey and Tina's "incestuous" affair (they're not blood relatives but they were raised as brother and sister so I understand Rachel's disgust and fury).

* Mary brought Philip home from the hospital on a stretcher, permanently disabled because of his own stupidity.

* Rachel learned from a letter to Kirsten where Hester had been hiding for the last few months; she'd married some low-life in haste and was living in squalor. Rachel drugged Hester, got her to the hospital, and insisted on an obstetrics exam on her unconscious daughter followed by an immediate abortion of her first grandchild. Oh, and Rachel paid off Hester's squeeze. He, proving Rachel was right, took the £500 and abandoned his pregnant bride.

General Information

Based on: *Ordeal by Innocence* (novel, 1958)
Run time: 3 hr. **Subtitles:** Yes

Writer: Sarah Phelps
Director: Sandra Goldbacher

Cast

Luke Treadaway as Dr. Arthur Calgary

Bill Nighy as Leo Argyll
Anna Chancellor as Rachel Argyll
Morven Christie as Kirsten Lindstrom
Anthony Boyle as Jack Argyll
Christian Cooke as Mickey Argyll
Ella Purnell as Hester Argyll
Crystal Clarke as Tina Argyll
Eleanor Tomlinson as Mary Argyll Durrant
Matthew Goode as Philip Durrant
Alice Eve as Gwenda Vaughan
Brian McCardie as Bellamy Gould
Frances Grey as Lydia Gould
Luke Murray as Young Jack
Catriona McNicoll as Young Mary
Rhys Lambert as Young Mickey
Abigail Conteh as Young Tina
Hayden Robertson as Young Hester
Alexandra Finnie as Young Kirsten
Sandy Welch as Dr. Edwin Morsuch

Film Location

Ardgowan House, Inverclyde, Scotland
(Sunny Point House)

* To cap it off, her day ended when she caught Leo and Gwenda in the act.

Rachel confronted Leo. He said she wouldn't divorce him (the scandal!) and she said, "watch me." As a divorced man, Leo would be penniless. As a widower, he'd be rich. The choice was easy. He struck Rachel down and got Gwenda to help him cover up the truth (followed by marriage to seal the deal).

Why did Leo choose his hidden son, Jack, as his fall guy? Because Jack liked telling unpleasant truths, including the one about Bellamy Gould, Leo's friend, confidant, and chief constable. Gould agreed to frame Jack because he couldn't let his perverted secret be revealed *and* Jack had been screwing his wife.

In case you wonder why Gould, after attempting to run over Arthur Calgary and failing, committed suicide by auto, here's my answer. As chief constable, Gould faked evidence implicating Jack. If Arthur proves Jack's alibi, Gould will go to prison when his corruption comes to light. That's also why Jack — who delights in being difficult — got beaten to death in prison right after stupidly revealing to Leo what he knows.

Of the men in this story, only two show signs of character. Mickey, who genuinely wants to protect his sisters, and Arthur Calgary.

Phelps' take on Arthur was interesting. He's an unreliable witness because of his own sketchy past. This Arthur is a nuclear scientist who fell apart over guilt about helping to design Fat Man and Little Boy, the atomic bombs used to end WWII with Japan. He wasn't in the Arctic doing research. He was locked up in a nearby loony bin, escaped, and narrowly avoided running over Jack. Arthur must redeem himself by proving Jack's innocence.

The ending wraps around to the beginning and the bomb shelter Rachel had built under the mansion. Leo had Arthur hauled back to the asylum but afterwards, he's confronted by the kids. They know the truth and force Leo into the same fate he planned for Arthur: A lifetime in a cage.

This is not Agatha's novel. But if you take it on its own terms, Phelps' version works. Watch all three versions, and you'll see what I mean.

The Great Actress Murder Case (J-2018)

(*Daijoyuu Satsujin Jiken*)

Mirror Crack'd from Side to Side turns into a police procedural that disappears Miss Marple

Fidelity to text

A Miss Marple mystery becomes a Japanese police procedural! Yet everything important remains.

Quality of movie

The police procedural format works surprisingly well and Margot Bence finally gets some screen time.

This adaptation makes two radical changes to the novel. Miss Marple vanishes. No amateur sleuths, old lady division or any other kind, run loose in contemporary Tokyo. It's policemen all the way, at every level. That turns the novel into a police procedural, a format Agatha never wrote.

And it worked. It's old wine in shiny new, space-age saki bottles.

As with most of the foreign adaptations, I'll stick with the novel's names to make it easier for me and for you, dear reader.

The policeman in charge is Ryuya Shokokuji, the head of the First Criminal Investigation Division, Tokyo. Like Poirot and Miss Marple, he thinks very hard about what actually happened as opposed to what he's being told. He shares several characteristics with Sherlock Holmes. He's obsessive, detail-oriented, laser-focused, and interested in the truth rather than kowtowing to famous celebrities.

I'll use Shokokuji's name because he doesn't exist in Agatha's pantheon. I'm also following the Western custom of given name followed by family name.

His two assistants don't have parallels in Christie World either. The young lady is Fueko Misaki. She's devoted to Shokokuji but he doesn't notice her as a woman, at least not until she demonstrates her parkour skills to prove how someone could climb to the third-floor balcony to leave a threatening letter for Marina Gregg. Watch Shokokuji's face as he watches her climb. But this being Japanese television instead of Hollywood, they remain professionals instead of instantly falling into bed and declaring their passionate love for each other.

Shokokuji's other sidekick is Banpei Tatara, a newly assigned bumpkin from the provinces. Like Hastings and Watson, he's eager to help and his suggestions are always wrong.

Once you get over the shock of seeing Japanese policemen instead of Miss Marple, the plot hews pretty closely to the novel. It opens with a scene in a costume drama starring Marina. It's her comeback film after years spent in seclusion, and it's directed by her newest husband, Jason Rudd. Afterwards, they're hosting a gala party at their new mansion, bought from Heather

Madoka Irodori (*Hitomi Kuroki*), the star

Akira Kaido (*Ikkô Furuya*), the director

Sagiri Asakaze (*Naomi Zaizen*), the rival

Hiraomi Danbara (*Masahiko Tsugawa*), the producer

Kosame Taniguchi (*Haruna Kawaguchi*), the photographer

Matsumushi Matsuda (*Hayato Isomura*), the unwanted son

Badcock and her much older husband.

Be prepared for a weird and creepy added backstory revealed late in the film about Heather and her husband. After his wife died and according to the wishes of her family, he married his stepdaughter, Heather, when she came of age. And she, dutiful daughter, was okay with it.

Bill and I gawked over that one.

Anyway, back to the party. Heather fangirls all over Marina and soon afterwards, dies suddenly and shockingly after drinking Marina's cocktail. The police swoop in, using marvelous and unlikely *CSI*-style forensic techniques to analyze the fatal cocktail on the spot.

The investigation proceeds largely from Shokokuji's viewpoint. As it unfolds with interviews and detecting, each day is date-stamped and there's a location. Gradually, Shokokuji discovers that Marina received threatening letters and she's had arsenic added to her tea.

As Shokokuji uncovers the lies behind Marina's façade, two more people are murdered: Ella, Jason's secretary, and Guiseppe, the butler. Marina has enemies, notably Lola Brewster. She also had adopted three children. When she became pregnant with her own "real" baby, she got rid of those kids.

This is my fourth adaptation of *The Mirror Crack'd*. It's the first one to give Margot Bence *and her siblings* serious screen time. Finally, we see how they felt about being loved and wanted and then tossed aside as understudies in the dress rehearsal for the main performance. Shokokuji also uncovers the son of Marina's second hubby. His family was torn apart when dad abandoned mom and married Marina. Despite her stated wish for children, she wouldn't accept a stepchild. They had no relationship. It didn't look like Marina even recognized him. Why would she? He's an extra in the crowd and unworthy of notice.

Nor, true to form, did Marina recognize her daughter, Margot, or her brother when they were at the party or on the set. There's a scene late in the film where you see Marina sobbing as she watches her children being taken away from her. Don't be fooled by those crocodile tears. She made the arrangements herself. She's reveling in the emotion and not giving a damn about how those kids feel.

General Information

Based on: *The Mirror Crack'd from Side to Side* (novel, 1962)
Run time: 1 hr., 49 min. **Subtitles:** Yes

Writer: Hidekazu Nagasaka
Director: Izumi Isaji

Cast

Ikki Sawamura as Ryuya Shoukokuji
YoshiYoshi Arakawa as Tantara Banpei
Erena Mizusawa as Fueko Misaki

Hitomi Kuroki as Madoka Irodori (Marina Gregg)
Ikkô Furuya as Akira Kaido (Jason Rudd)
Naomi Zaizen as Sagiri Asakaze (Lola Brewster)
Masahiko Tsugawa as Hiraomi Danbara (Ardwyck Fenn)
Mari Nishio as Shimeko Akada (Ella Zielinsky)
Haruna Kawaguchi as Kosame Taniguchi (Margot Bence)
Hayato Isomura as Matsumushi Matsuda (Hailey Preston)
Narumi Fukuda as Hinata Hanakage (newscaster)
Kami Hiraiwa as Rin Kannokouji (Heather Badcock)
Takeo Nakahara as Koki Kannokouji (Mr. Badcock)

Film Locations

Seisen University main building (movie exterior, stairwell stabbing)
Wakeijuku dormitory, Tokyo (Kaminoyakata exterior)
Tokyo Metropolitan Police Headquarters (exterior)
APA Hotel Shinjuku Kabukicho (Kosame interview exterior)
Daiichi Hotel Tokyo Seafort (Sagiri interview exterior)

But then she miscarries. Her life falls apart, and she goes into seclusion. She does not reclaim her abandoned children, although she could have. Remember, they were props for her dress rehearsal as a mother.

Unfortunately, the script changed Margot and her brother. In the novel, Margot resented what Marina did to her and her sibs. She was angry when Marina didn't recognize them. But in the film, Margot and Matsumushi (her brother) give Marina a pass.

She's a famous movie star! She can't be judged by the standards that normal people are held to. Four versions of *The Mirror Crack'd* and not one hack scriptwriter or director bothered to read Agatha's own words about how Margot felt and what Marina's abandonment did to her and her sibs. Not one.

At least we got to see some of it and reach the true conclusion no one onscreen is willing to say: Marina Gregg is one selfish, self-centered, narcissistic bitch.

In fact, a new twist demonstrates the depths of Marina's narcissism. Why did she buy Heather's mansion? Because Heather had blogged about having a fever the day she met Marina at a recital around the time she miscarried. Marina had obsessively surfed the web, looking for mentions of her.self What you see is not a spur-of-the-moment murder fueled by rage. It's premeditated. Marina already suspected Heather of infecting her and her unborn baby. She needed to be sure but as soon as she was, she poisoned Heather for being foolish.

As for Shokokuji, he diligently follows every lead and reaches a logical conclusion. It's right out of *Sleeping Murder* as per Miss Marple herself: the culprit must be someone who was on the spot for each incident. The poisoned cocktail, the arsenic in the tea, the placement of the threatening letters, the butler's stabbing, the access to Ella's inhaler.

Only one person fits that description. Once Shokokuji works out the threatening letters were assembled from a single page in one newspaper where the date doesn't match what he's been told, he knows. It's Marina, who's far too special to adhere to normal human standards of behavior. Even in death, she's shielded from the consequences of her actions.

Zero Hour (F-2019)

(*L'Heure zéro*)

Ambition, lust, and murder star at a TV station, interrupted by high jinks by the police and press

Towards Zero is one of Agatha's best novels. It focuses on what Superintendent Battle calls "The Zero Hour." The murder is not the beginning of the story. It's the culmination of a long chain of events leading to one point: someone's death.

In the novel, the true murder is that of Audrey Strange. Her ex-husband, Neville, wants her dead but he wants her to suffer. So he murders Lady Tressilian and frames Audrey. That way, he can watch her twist in the wind as the Crown prosecutes and hangs her.

Along the way, Neville also murders Audrey's fiancé (an unprovable car accident) because if he can't have her, then nobody can, and Treves, a lawyer, who can identify Neville as having murdered a friend with a bow and arrow when they were both kids. It was an accident, mum! I swear it! Treves dies of a forced heart attack when he must climb the stairs (Neville hangs a warning sign claiming the lift is out of order). Again, unprovable.

Neville hates Audrey because she was so afraid of him, she left. Although the novel doesn't spell it out, he probably hit her as well as terrorized and gaslit her. To save face, he claimed he left her for the hotter, younger Kay. Audrey didn't argue, preferring safety to the truth.

There's a lot more, including unrequited love and a suicide survivor who returns to the scene just in time

Fidelity to text

Boil the plot down to "A man frames his hated ex-wife for murder," add a bloody glove, and you've got all the fidelity you're going to get.

Quality of movie

It depends on how you feel about an *I Love Lucy* sex farce mashed up with comic policemen and multiple murder.

to save Audrey.

The novel's been filmed a few times: a truly dreadful French version that the Agatha Christie estate disavowed (*Innocent Lies*, 1995). A version with Miss Marple (!) in place of Superintendent Battle that otherwise follows the text reasonably close for ITV Productions (*Towards Zero*, 2007). There's another French version (*L'Heure Zéro*, also in 2007) that reportedly follows the text. It's directed by Pascal Thomas who did the French Tommy and Tuppence films. It's not available with English subtitles so I can't see it for you.

And there's this version. It doesn't follow the text *at all* but it, unlike *Innocent Lies*, eschews an incest subplot and flirtations with the Nazis. There's plenty of sex, but it mostly takes place offscreen. It's alluded to constantly as the characters seem to do nothing but discuss their sex lives and the ramifications thereof but it's all in the name of *le sport*. You won't feel the need

Audrey Fontaine (*Barbara Schulz*), the icy star

Maxime Beaumont (*Nuno Lopes*), the libidinous chef

Claire Beaumont (*Alyzée Costes*), the ambitious upstart

Jean Devandière (*Christian Van Tomme*), the station manager

Marie Dupuis (*Annette Lowcay*), the loyal assistant

Ted Gautier (*Alban Casterman*), the careful producer

to take a shower afterwards.

I have no idea why a French television studio bought the rights to Agatha Christie stories and then didn't film them; instead rewriting them so completely that they bear little resemblance to the original properties.

General Information

Based on: *Towards Zero* (novel, 1944)
Run time: 1 hr., 34 min. **Subtitles:** Yes

Writers: Flore Kosinetz, Hélène Lombard
Director: Nicolas Picard-Dreyfuss

Cast

Samuel Labarthe as Swan Laurence
Marie Berto as Arlette Carmouille
Elodie Frenck as Marlène Leroy
Blandine Bellavoir as Alice Avril
Dominique Thomas as Ernest Tricard
Cyril Gueï as Tim Glissant

Barbara Schulz as Audrey Fontaine (Audrey Strange)
Nuno Lopes as Maxime Beaumont (Neville Strange)
Alyzée Costes as Claire Beaumont (Kay Strange)
Christian Van Tomme as Jean Devandière (Camilla Tressilian)
Annette Lowcay as Marie Dupuis (Mary Aldin)
Alban Casterman as Ted Gautier (Ted Latimer)

Film Locations

Lille, France
Tourcoing, Nord, France
Villeneuve-d'Ascq, Nord, France
Saint-Jans Capelle, France
Les Petit Bruxelles, Saints-Marie-Cappel (Maxime's restaurant)

Anyway.

I'm still unsure about what I watched.

It was silly when it wasn't infuriating. I've never seen such bad police work. It's supposed to be comic policemen but even so, that doesn't explain why they're so bad at their job. There are bodies. Shouldn't we at least see Commissaire Laurence interview suspects? Look for clues? He interviews Audrey, the main suspect, by trying to seduce her. And succeeds! And then he pouts when Audrey sends him 24 red roses to say once was enough. It's acceptable for him to dump his one-night-stands with roses but not for the lady to turn the tables.

Why didn't he interview the son of Roger Foucher when they found Roger's body? When someone dies under unusual circumstances (drowning while fishing), the family must be contacted and if they're suspicious, they'll say something! Yet Roger's son must come to the police station on his own — when the plot demanded it — to say dad was murdered.

Why was the TV station producer poisoned with strychnine and then knifed? Wasn't the strychnine enough? I guess the knife was there to implicate Chef Maxime and then he'd be found innocent despite only his fingerprints being found on the murder weapon. Because it was the strychnine that did the job? And he has an alibi of being dead drunk on his restaurant kitchen floor at the time?

Why would police secretary Marlène, presumably a professional who understands official procedures, especially if you want a successful trial to follow, fake a medical report? Marlène is convinced Chef Maxime is guilty of murder because he jilted her at the altar years ago, so she seduces the police surgeon, drugs him with Valium, steals the lab report, and alters the drug from strychnine to digitalin! And because in the end, she's proven correct, it's all swept under the rug? She behaved stupidly and irresponsibly because the plot demanded it. He jilted her at least fifteen years ago, he's a notorious womanizer, and she's still so hung up on him that she tampers with evidence?

When Laurence proves Chef Maxime murdered four people, does Marlène congratulate herself on her lucky escape? As if.

It was infuriating to watch Alice Avril, girl journalist, act as though her brain was between her legs. She knows Chef Maxime jilted her best friend, Marlène. She knows that he was married to Audrey. She knows that he's married to Claire. She knows he's a womanizing cheater. So what does she do? Practically fall into his arms while claiming she's fighting the attraction.

Um, no. It's perfectly possible to see a hot guy and not act on the attraction. That's what professional women do. So do professional men, for that matter. People who can't behave like professionals in mixed settings should stay home and let the rest of us get the job done.

Hollywood portrays women like this All. The. Time. It's maddening. That's how little they think of women. No matter what a Hollywood producer claims, we're bimbos with round heels.

I noticed the bright, poppy soundtrack because it was so annoying. It would have fit perfectly with an *I Love Lucy* episode.

At least the clothes were great and actually matched the characters wearing them. Audrey, the focused professional newscaster, wore Dior dresses and suits. Claire, her weather-girl rival, wore knock-offs of Yves Saint Laurent's Mondrian trapeze dresses. Marlène, the police inspector's secretary, wore good-quality department-store dresses. Alice, the up-and-coming girl journalist, wore student clothes because she hasn't yet figured out that people treat you based on your appearance.

These episodes also don't take place in Paris. Instead, the series is set in Lille, a city far to the north, on the Belgian border. Perhaps a French audience could see that the characters are provincials, explaining why they behave like Keystone Kops.

This was weird and very, very French. Give it your best Gallic shrug, take it on its own terms, and ignore Agatha's name above the credits. She had nothing to do with this.

The Pale Horse (2020)

A major rewrite darkens Mark's soul and heightens supernatural elements while retaining the novel's theme

Fidelity to text

This is true to the spirit but not to the text. What is real? What is smoke and mirrors? Who can you trust?

Quality of movie

Hypnotic and eerie, sunny horror juxtaposed with smart, upper-class Londoners discovering that the world is stranger than they imagined.

This is the third version of *The Pale Horse* (1961). Like the other two, the writer (Sarah Phelps) plays fast and loose with Agatha's text. Ariadne Oliver never shows up, nor does Mrs. Dane Calthrop. Someday, someone will film the novel, but that day has yet to arrive.

This version has undergone a radical transformation, even more extreme than inserting Miss Marple in the 2010 version. Mark Easterbrook, our lead, isn't just peripherally involved. Nor does he get involved by being accused of murder as in the 1997 version. This time, his name is on the list of people, some of whom died recently. He must figure out why he's on the list and why someone might want him dead.

There are other changes for Mark. He's well-connected with upper-class friends. He's a high-end antiques dealer with a perfect new second wife. He's got a sad past with a perfect dead first wife he's grieving over. He's carrying on an affair with an upper-class but rebellious girl who's a hostess in a seedy nightclub.

Yes, our hero is a cheating, lying dog. When he wakes up next to Thomasina Tuckerton's body, does he inform the police? Call her family? Call a doctor? Of course not. She's dead and he doesn't care.

He treats wife #2, Hermia, callously. It's unclear why Mark married her, other than wanting someone to run his household without paying for a housekeeper and a caterer. Wives work for free. As for Hermia, she's been in love with Mark for years. But that's changing as Mark slowly kills whatever feelings she had for him.

I felt very sorry for Hermia. She knows he's cheating, yet she's killing herself to be the perfect upper-crust housewife. She's making puff pastry cases for vol-au-vents, for God's sake, and piping in salmon mousse filling. Why? To entertain friends who don't appreciate the tedious hours it takes to master puff pastry. This being 1961, Hermia couldn't buy ready-made puff pastry from the supermarket freezer case. She had to make it herself with her own dainty hands.

Speaking of 1961, it's a pleasure watching people in Dior and serious jewelry dancing to Little Anthony and the Imperials. Like Hermia, they have no idea how the '60s tidal wave will overturn their lives.

But back to the story. Mark gets summoned into

Mark Easterbrook (*Rufus Sewell*), the antique dealer

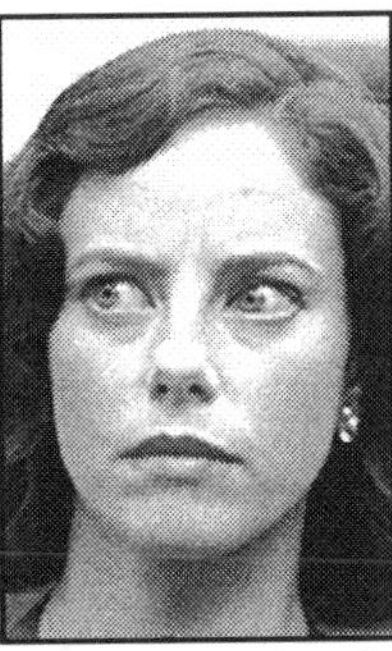

Hermia Easterbrook (*Kaya Scodelario*), the current wife

Delphine Easterbrook (*Georgina Campbell*), the late wife

David Ardingly (*Henry Lloyd-Hughes*), the impatient heir

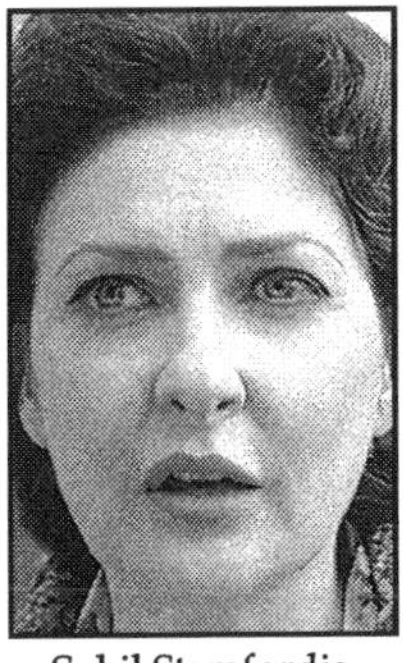

Sybil Stamfordis (*Kathy Kiera Clarke*), the witch

Zachariah Osborne (*Bertie Carvel*), the looney merchant

Inspector Lejeune's office about why his name is on the list. He's baffled. He doesn't admit he knows about Thomasina's death, despite her name being on the same list. At the police station, he meets Zachariah Osborne, small-time hardware store owner. Mark instantly dislikes him. Osborne has bad teeth and an annoying manner. He's clearly a working-class loon and can be safely ignored.

Except strange things keep happening. Mark endures creepy dreams about the tragic death of his first wife, Delphine. Corn dollies (ritually significant in harvest magic) materialize on his car. Osborne shows up at Mark's store claiming witches are killing the people on the list. Mark begins to suspect that he can't ignore this nutter.

While investigating why his name is on the list, Mark uncovers a connection between Delphine, a quaint village named Much Deeping, and the witchcraft Osborne ranted about. Delphine consulted a trio of village witches and died soon after. To learn more, Mark takes Hermia to the village's Lammas Festival. Lammas is the day midway between the Summer Solstice and the Autumnal Equinox. It's the first harvest of the year, followed by, hopefully, many more so the peasants and their lord won't starve during the winter. Every peasant culture has fertility rituals designed to encourage local gods to provide rain, sunshine, few pests, and bountiful harvests. As Christianity gradually overtook pagan England, it absorbed many of the older pagan rituals. They're still there if you look.

So instead of a familiar fête with coconut tosses and kiddie rides, Mark and Hermia encounter a parade of veiled girls in white dresses and villagers in bizarre masks. A corn king is sacrificed. And as you'd expect, the three witches are enjoying the festivities.

Later, we learn the witches suspect something is going on. They've noticed that a surprising number of their fortune-telling clients had close relatives die after the consultation. They've also noticed Jessie Davis seems to be connected to the deaths. I believe that's why when Jessie asked to speak to her dead mother, Sybil the witch channeled a hateful message telling Jessie how unhappy her mother was with what she was doing. They were warning her off.

General Information

Based on: *The Pale Horse* (novel, 1961)
Run time: 1 hr., 57 min. **Subtitles:** Yes

Writer: Sarah Phelps
Director: Leonora Lonsdale

Cast

Rufus Sewell as Mark Easterbrook
Sean Pertwee as D.I. Stanley Lejeune

Kaya Scodelario as Hermia Easterbrook
Georgina Campbell as Delphine Easterbrook
Sarah Woodward as Clemency Ardingly
Henry Lloyd-Hughes as David Ardingly
Ellen Robertson as Poppy Ardingly
Kathy Kiera Clarke as Sybil Stamfordis
Sheila Atim as Thyrza Grey
Rita Tushingham as Bella Webb
Bertie Carvel as Zachariah Osborne
Claire Skinner as Yvonne Tuckerton
Poppy Gilbert as Thomasina Tuckerton
Madeleine Bowyer as Jessie Davis
James Fleet as Oscar Venables
Kim Chapman as Rita
Martin Buchan as Vicar
Nicky Goldie as Mrs. Coppins

Film Locations

Bristol
Bisley, Gloucestershire (Much Deeping)
The Bear Inn, Bisley (Pale Horse pub)

Or perhaps Sybil really did channel that message from Jessie's mother.

This *Pale Horse* treated the occult with more care than usual. It opened with the usual pan across weird jars, but there was little of the usual smugness towards quaint rustic beliefs. The villagers conducting the Lammas Day parade were serious about it. The witches sensed when Mark was spying on them. They correctly foretold to Delphine that Mark would remarry within the year.

They have some power, but it's not Harry Potter-style magic. British occultist Dion Fortune (1890-1946) defined magic as the art and science of causing changes in consciousness in accordance with will. The witches willed Mark's thinking to change. He began to accept that reality was not as rational as he'd always insisted. He certainly didn't behave rationally. If he had, he would've listened to Delphine. He would've told the police the truth. He wouldn't have cheated on Hermia. But he did what he damned well pleased, justified his actions as being logical and wise, and the devil take the hindmost.

My understanding of the supernatural is why the ending did not confuse me. Mark accepts that his godson David had his Aunt Clemency (whom Mark loved!) murdered so he could inherit quicker. Inspired, he asks the witches to remove his obstacles — Hermia and Inspector Lejeune — like David did. Soon, Hermia's in the hospital in a drug-induced coma. While visiting, Mark witnesses Lejeune being rushed to the emergency ward with massive bleeding from his eyes, nose, mouth, and ears. When Mark confronts the statue of Jesus in a niche in the hall, he *dares* Christ to punish him.

Then it's off to meet Osborne and discover who'd been pulling the strings all along. Mark murders Osborne with a crowbar — are you surprised? — and instead of turning over a filing cabinet packed with evidence of dozens of murders to the police, he burns the lot to cover up his own sin.

So when you see Mark Easterbrook revisiting his murder of Delphine, over and over, he's getting the punishment he demanded. He didn't see what the witches knew: that the world is stranger than we know, and we defy God at our peril.

Checkmate (C-2022)

(*Min Guo Da Zhen Tan*)

Disgraced lawyer finds his Hastings on slow train from Peking in series set during the Republic of China era

Fidelity to text

Fewer suspects, cold northern China, and that's not Poirot or Hastings.

Quality of movie

Gorgeous to look at, and the surrounding story sets up our hero's isolation and need for justice.

IQiyi, a Chinese studio, licensed seven Poirot novels and one short story and made something fresh and new. In the 24-episode series *Checkmate*, they replaced Poirot with an idealistic young attorney gifted with Sherlock Holmes' attention to detail and added a big story arc tying the stories together.

This version of *Orient Express* made up the first 3½ episodes, so the story clocks in at about 2½ hours. As usual for the foreign adaptations, I'll use the novel's names when I can.

This is not the first time someone strung together her stories. In fact, Agatha was there first. Remember *The Big Four* (1927)? Stressed by her collapsed marriage to Archie and needing to meet her publisher's deadline, she and her brother-in-law, Campbell Christie, cobbled together a batch of Poirot short stories to create an arc involving a vast worldwide criminal conspiracy.

An attorney instead of a prosecutor, Si Tu Yan loves justice like Poirot. Luo Shao Chuan acts as Si Tu Yan's Hastings, but he's got a rich family.

Checkmate is set around 1920, during the era of the Republic of China (1912-1949). Ma Shi Ying (Samuel Ratchett) murders a local politician at the train station in front of hundreds of witnesses. In court, Si Tu is doing his summation, sure he'll convict Ratchett of murder.

Then, disaster. An unnamed official shows up and claims that Ratchett can't be convicted as he's no longer a Chinese citizen, but a Russian one and has immunity.

To Si Tu's horror, the judge agrees this obviously trumped-up argument overrides the entire case. When the camera pans across the agog courtroom spectators, pay attention. You'll recognize some of those faces later.

Si Tu resigns in disgust. He's then disgraced in newspapers across China, claiming it was his incompetence that led to the wrongful trial. He knows something's gone very, very wrong with the judicial system but he doesn't know, yet, that something bigger is happening.

During his last meal in Peking, Si Tu runs into Luo Shao at an outdoor noodle stand. Luo Shao has nothing but contempt for that worthless prosecutor, but he rethinks his assumption when his pistol is stolen and Si Tu solves the case. Not only does he keep Luo Shao from disgrace by arresting the wrong man, he displays his passion for justice.

They meet again at the train to Harbin. Si Tu is sitting

Qi Hong (*Liu Mei Ren*), the courtesan

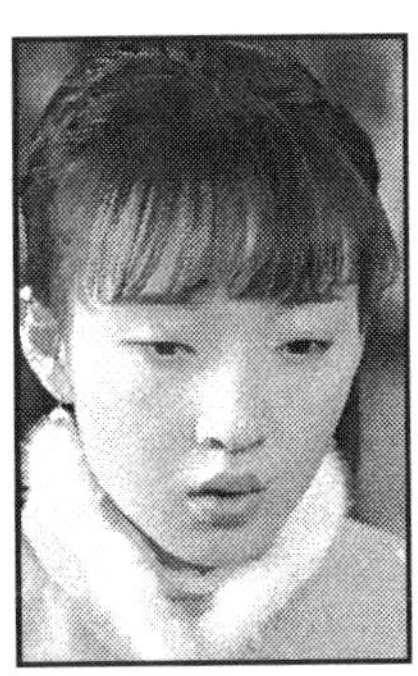
Bai Lu (*Li Ying Ying*), the former student

Princess Rong Xiang (*He Sai Fei*), the child's godmother

Wan Jixiang (*Qiao Jun Da*), the killer's secretary

George Brel (*Karl Dominik*), the U.S. consul

Liu Zijie (*Lin Peng*), the car's conductor

in third class with the rest of the rabble when Luo Shao rescues him and insists that he stay in first class. The conductor insists the car is full until Luo Shao points out whoever bought a ticket didn't show up.

General Information

Based on: *Murder on the Orient Express* (novel, 1934)
Run time: 2 hr., 30 min. **Subtitles:** Yes

Writer: Wu Yuan Bo **Director:** Zhang Wei Ke

Cast

Hu Yi Tian as Situ Yan
Zhang Yun Long as Luo Shaochuan
Zhang Xin Yu as Zhou Mowan / Fang Huaijin
Guo Zhen Yu as Xiao Liu

Sun Yan as Ma Shiying (Samuel Ratchett)
Qiao Jun Da as Wan Jixiang (Hector McQueen)
Lin Peng as Liu Zijie (Pierre-Paul Michel)
Li Ying Ying as Bai Lu (Mary Debenham)
Fang Xiao Li as Liao Yun, Yu Qin's mother
Liu Mei Ren as Qi Hong (Mrs. Hubbard)
Karl Dominik as George Brel (Count Andrenyi)
Pu Tao as Xu Fangting (Countess Andrenyi)
Yu Jian as Zong Yan (Col. Arbuthnot)
He Sai Fei as Princess Rong Xiang (Princess Dragomiroff)
Du He Qian as Shi Chunshan (Hildegarde Schmidt)
Zhang Jie as Xu Yu Qin
Shen Sheng Nan as Xu Yu Qin's daughter
Han Mo as Zhou Mowan (young)
Wang Zi Yi as Jin Qiming (young)
Zhu Ying Hua as Xu Fangting (young)

How can Luo Shao, who looks like he's military police, force the train's apprehensive conductor (Pierre-Paul Michel) to do this? Hard to say. The conductor refers to him as "Young Master." Perhaps his family owns the train? Clearly there's more to Luo Shao than meets the eye.

Si Tu accepts the first-class compartment because it allows Luo Shao to return a favor. It also helps that it's the most luxurious train on Earth. His pleasure, however, ends when he meets Samuel Ratchett in the same first-class car.

Gradually, we meet the rest of the passengers. There are nine of them, and they're a very mixed bag: Ratchett's secretary (Hector McQueen); a university student (Mary Debenham); a grieving older woman (the murder victim's mother who has no corollary in the novel); a flamboyant courtesan (Mrs. Hubbard); an American diplomat and his reclusive wife (Count and Countess Andrenyi); a former soldier (Col. Arbuthnot); a princess (Princess Dragomiroff); and her maid (Hildegarde Schmidt).

In the novel, Ratchett appeals to Poirot for protection from threats against his life. This Ratchett doesn't. He sneers at Si Tu. He got away with murder and he's glad. He doesn't need to ask some loser lawyer for help.

Things go bump in the night on the train, with lots of running up and down the passageway, and it's forced to stop because of damage to the rails. In the morning, the conductor and the secretary discover Ratchett's body. The window is open, letting in the freezing cold. There are clues scattered about. A doctor recruited from second-class says that Ratchett was stabbed nine times, almost at random.

Events proceed as you'd expect. Si Tu realizes someone's trying to fool him into thinking the murderer escaped the train into the snow. He works out the connections between the nine strangers and Ratchett. They were there because Ratchett had murdered Xu Yu Qin and her daughter. They were denied justice because Ratchett had connections and they did not.

It's at this point *Checkmate* diverges from the novel again. Ratchett's connections are far-reaching; they also saved him in Si Tu's courtroom. The other nine passengers were in the audience where Si Tu was the prosecuting attorney. They wanted to see justice done and were again denied.

Mary Debenham takes the blame. She was twelve when Ratchett murdered Xu and her daughter. She still blames herself because she told Ratchett there was no man in the house. *She* murdered Xu. *She* is willing to face trial because murderers deserve punishment. The others leap to her defense and Si Tu must choose: Does the spirit of the law matter more than the letter? It does. Justice denied is not justice and the Xu family has suffered enough.

The story unfolds over three episodes, with the climax occupying the first fifteen minutes of episode four. The story then moves onto the wintry city of Harbin, where Si Tu goes to the house of his mentor and discovers he died of a heart attack. He meets Luo Shao again. Luo Shao's father dies under more mysterious circumstances. He asks Si Tu to discover what happened and the next three episodes become a retelling of *The Murder of Roger Ackroyd*. But underneath is the season-wide arc.

As you watch the 24 episodes, you'll see reworkings of *Cat Among the Pigeons; One, Two, Buckle My Shoe; Five Little Pigs*; "The Kidnapped Prime Minister;" *Three Act Tragedy*; and *Curtain*. Si Tu will become a respected private detective in Harbin. He'll develop a team. Luo Shao will be his Hastings. The eager young reporter from the train will join them to solve the crimes, as will two young ladies with mysterious pasts. Eventually, Si Tu and Luo Shao will uncover a vast conspiracy stretching across China.

After the first three episodes, the story takes place in Harbin, known as the Ice City. This large city is far to the north, closer to Russia than to Shanghai or Beijing. It's a different China than what you normally see. Much of the filming was done during the winter so not all that snow is computer generated.

The Republic of China won't be what you expect either. They were fighting for their sovereignty; struggling with regional warlords tearing the country apart as well as interference from other countries like Russia.

Checkmate is a very different take on Agatha Christie's novels. Give it a try and see her in a whole new way.

Why Didn't They Ask Evans? (2022)

Director/author/actor Hugh Laurie creates a joyfully serious movie that respects the original material

Why Didn't They Ask Evans? is a convoluted novel. It contains hidden couples, faked identities, murders disguised as suicides, wills gone wrong, resentful younger sons, opium addiction, adventuresses disguised as ingenues, the class divide, feckless youth triumphant (they put off growing up for a few more glorious weeks), and at long last, requited childhood love. If you've never read it, hunt up an edition with a cast list; it'll help you keep everyone straight.

The complexity doesn't stop it from being fun. Published in 1934, it was one of Agatha's last "high-spirited young adventurers take on the world and have fun doing so." No grimdark here, with old sins casting long shadows. Bobby (our hero) doesn't know what to do with himself since leaving the Navy. But he needs to do something as every day, he gets older and his father the vicar despairs more. Frankie (our heroine) doesn't know what to do with herself either and the social whirl of gaiety is becoming forced and stale. Her parents probably fear she'll become a bluestocking spinster.

How do you adapt a sprawling novel? You can be so faithful to the text that you, dear audience, feel every moment crawling by (the 1982 version). You can throw the text onto a slow boat to China and go Gothic, weird, and extra-complicated (the 2009 version). Or, you can do what Hugh Laurie did here.

He's a multi-talented threat. He wrote the script, directed the film, produced the film, and acted in it as Dr. Nicholson, creepy headshrinker with a collection of mental health gizmos that got banned a long time ago because of how they traumatized the nutcases into catatonia. But in 1936, those gizmos were just fine to use. If the patients recovered, they paid well. If the patients died, their heirs paid double.

Laurie did that rare thing in an adaptation: He trusted Agatha's source material. He made his changes to simplify the story. He amplified characters so they all got time onscreen. He made updates to suit a modern audience's need for spectacle. Most of all, he played fair with the audience. He layered in clues so if you were paying attention, you knew something mattered. Those clues paid off at the end.

Most amazing of all, his version clocks in at 2 hours, 54 minutes and that time zips by like you're cruising down English lanes in your Lagonda. The 1982 version takes 3 hours and you'll feel every single minute crawl

Fidelity to text

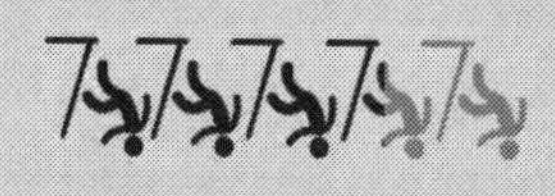

Bobby toughened up, Roger got softened up and caught, and the carnival came to town with roadies, drunken aristocrats, and scary goons.

Quality of movie

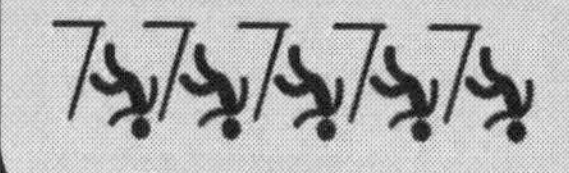

This doesn't just zip along, covering all the plot beats. It also plays fair, setting up clues for the audience's deductions.

Sylvia Bassington-ffrench (*Amy Nuttall*), the concerned wife

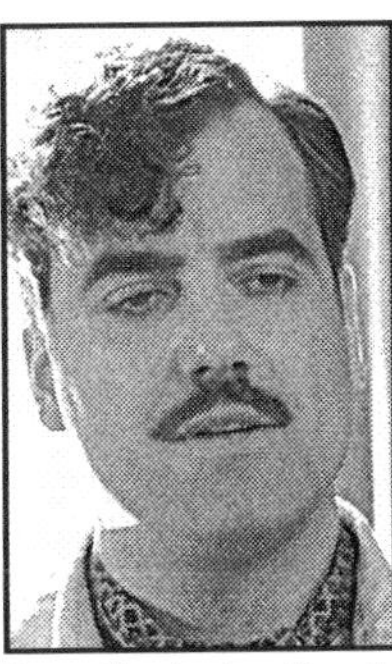
Roger Bassington-ffrench (*Daniel Ings*), the playboy brother

Dr. James Nicholson (*Hugh Laurie*), the serious shrink

Moira Nicholson (*Maeve Dermody*), the trapped spouse

Mr. Angel (*Nicholas Asbury*), the scary enforcer

Ralph "Knocker" Beadon (*Jonathan Jules*), the loyal friend

by. That version has its charms, but this one is better.

You'll note the subtle changes from the beginning. Bobby is out playing golf, but he's no duffer. He's Dr. Thomas' caddy, advising *him* how to play. He could become the local golf pro but that's not a suitable career field for a vicar's son and ex-naval officer. When he hears a scream, he doesn't dither or waste time. He climbs down to the missing man and hears the fateful dying words. Bobby checks the man's pockets and discovers the alluring photograph, along with an unusual keychain and a fancy fountain pen.

Moments later, Roger Bassington-ffrench shows up. He's concerned and helpful and blathers on about how he's in Marchbolt to look for a house and he'll stay with the body.

Since Bobbie's got to get back to the church to play the organ at the service, he accepts the kind stranger's offer.

He's late, but as he slides into his seat, Bobby spots Frankie in the pews. She's all grown up and she's a beauty. They played together as kids when the social divide didn't matter as much. Vicars' kids, because of dad's job ministering to the peasants and the local gentry alike, develop a wide range of friendships. They haven't seen each other in years but they recognize each other instantly.

Frankie reads the newspapers (unlike Bobby) and, eager for something to break up her boring routine, questions him closely about the body at the base of the cliff. They gradually become aware of larger undercurrents swirling around the dead man. That woman who claimed to be his sister? Mrs. Cayman didn't look like the fresh young damsel in the picture. Then Bobby is handed a poisoned beer. He's saved because he's running the traveling carnival's tilt-a-whirl and gets seasick enough to throw up most of the morphia.

Something is up.

He really knows something is up when Dr. Thomas proves the sudden and mysterious job offer from Argentina is a fraud. The plot thickens when Dr. Thomas commits suicide. It's both wildly unexpected *and* it's the exact method Dr. Thomas said he'd never use.

Meanwhile, Frankie goes sleuthing about Bassington-ffrench and discovers where he lives. A plan involving a car crash is concocted and rehearsed to get her inside Merroway Court where she can spy on Bassington-ffrench. The plan works, and she finds a dysfunctional household. The lord of the manor is a junkie, his wife is traumatized, they've got a son (the heir) watching the show, and Roger is the worthless brother on the couch.

Hugh Laurie toughened up Bobby; he's still calm and considered but he's no pushover. Yet he also softened Roger. In the novel, Roger isn't just a murderer in cahoots with Moira. He's the one who introduced his brother Henry to the joys of morphia when Henry suffered an injury. Need more villainy? Roger really, really, really wants to inherit Merroway but as long as his young nephew Tommy is alive, he's got no chance. Novel Roger arranges for a series of near-miss accidents for Tommy, setting him up as an accident-prone doofus. Then, when Tommy inherits after his father's death and dies soon thereafter, it won't look nearly as suspicious.

Novel Roger also gets away with his schemes. He writes the truth to Frankie while safely in Argentina, leaving Moira and probably the Caymans to face justice. This Roger shares adjoining jail cells with Moira. He won't get away with murder, and Tommy remains alive (if fatherless). Roger loses all around.

I'm not sure I agree with this choice. Why make a villain, even one as charming as Roger, less villainous? This Roger also isn't intent on inheriting Merroway Court, which was a motive totally in keeping with his character and how younger sons of the aristocracy feel. They're spares, kept on ice until needed, but otherwise ignored to find their own way in the world.

Still, this was a fun movie. Watching how Bobby, Frankie, Knocker, and Dr. Arbuthnot practice wrecking the car without wrecking Frankie was a pleasure all by itself. There's also the snake pit of a looney bin next door to Merroway Court. Brr. It will make you appreciate modern pharmaceuticals, just as you'll appreciate this version over the other two.

General Information

Based on: *Why Didn't They Ask Evans?* (novel, 1934)
Run time: 2 hr., 54 min. **Subtitles:** Yes

Writer: Hugh Laurie **Director:** Hugh Laurie

Cast

Will Poulter as Bobby Jones
Lucy Boynton as Frankie Derwent

Daniel Ings as Roger Bassington-ffrench
Miles Jupp as Henry Bassington-ffrench
Amy Nuttall as Sylvia Bassington-ffrench
Rufus Bateman as Tommy Bassington-ffrench
Hugh Laurie as Dr. James Nicholson
Maeve Dermody as Moira Nicholson
Jonathan Jules as Ralph "Knocker" Beadon
Alistair Petrie as Rev. Richard Jones
Nicholas Asbury as Mr. Angel
Morwenna Banks as Amelia Cayman
Richard Dixon as Leo Cayman
Christian Patterson as Sergeant Ellis
Nia Trussler Jones as Gladys Roberts
Benedict Wolf as Hari Singh
Paul Whitehouse as Askew
Patrick Barlow as Wilfred Bragge
Joshua James as Dr. George Arbuthnot
Leon Ockenden as Alex Pritchard
Nicholas Banks as "Thicko" Derwent-Broxley
Emma Thompson as Lady Marcham
Jim Broadbent as Lord Marcham

Film Locations

Pennard golf club, Gower, Wales (golf course)
Three Cliffs Bay, Gower Peninsula, Wales (Cliffs near golf course)
Guildford, Surrey (exterior street scenes)
Pennard Castle, Pennard, Gower Peninsula, Swansea, Wales (picnic scene)
Guildhall, High Street, Guildford, Surrey (Coroner's Court)
Polesden Lacey, Surrey (Frankie's home)
Adwell House, Adwell, Oxfordshire (B-F Home)
Tring Park School for the Performing Arts, Tring, Hertfordshire (The Grange)
Grange Cottage, Albury, Surrey (Pratt's home)
Middle Street, Shere, Surrey (Foot race at end)

VI. Agatha the Star

Agatha died in 1975, but not only do her books live on, but she has been reborn in fiction, both as a sleuth in novels and as a character on film.

The first foray was the Vanessa Redgrave/Dustin Hoffman "biopic" *Agatha* (1979). That film is a travesty made up from whole cloth. Distressed and overwhelmed by Archie dumping her for a secretary, Agatha would have never plotted to kill herself and frame the secretary for it. No wonder the family had kittens and sued to stop that film being released. *Agatha* is why we use hatchets for this chapter's symbol. That film was a hatchet job.

Her subsequent film appearances are more "true" to her life. Whether she's arguing with Poirot about killing him off in *Curtain* (1975), recalling her wartime service to reporters at a performance of *The Mousetrap*, or assisting a Time Lord in repelling a giant space wasp, she's intelligent, articulate, and very, very capable. They're certainly more respectful portrayals.

Meet Agatha as you've never envisioned her before, and know that her avatars don't begin to scratch the surface of everything she did.

From left: *Agatha and the Midnight Murders* (2020), *Murder By the Book* (1986), *Agatha and the Truth of Murder* (2018), *Agatha Christie: A Life In Pictures* (2004)

The Unicorn and the Wasp (2008)

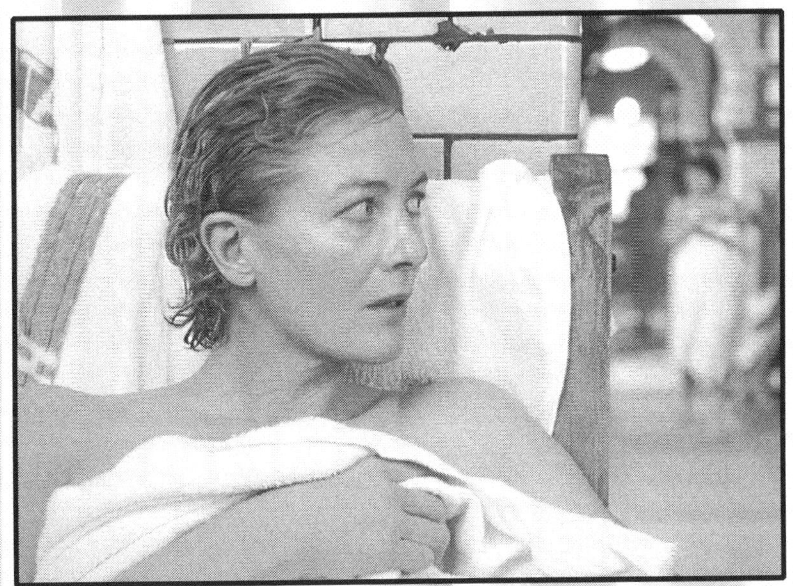

Agatha (1979)

Agatha Christie: A Life In Pictures (2004)

See How They Run (2022)

Agatha Christie and the Curse of Ishtar (2019)

Agatha as a fictional character. From top: battling aliens with Doctor Who; plotting to kill her husband's mistress; seeing her marriage to Archie Christie fall apart; serving tea during a home invasion, and risking her life with second husband Max Mallowan while investigating a relic theft ring.

Agatha (1979)

Christie's eleven-day disappearance inspires this revenge-plot romance that Ariadne Oliver would disdain

Fidelity to life

It is true Archie had an affair with Nancy Neele, Agatha disappeared in Harrogate for 11 days, the Christies divorced two years later, and Archie married Nancy afterwards. Everything else? Fiction.

Quality of movie

But only because the settings, costumes, and a period health spa are interesting.

This film was an hour and forty-five minutes long. As you endure each blah moment, you'll think longingly of big slabs of rhubarb pie. Why rhubarb? Because, as Garrison Keillor will tell you, nothing takes the taste of shame and humiliation out of your mouth like rhubarb pie.

This dreary hatchet job was inflicted on not just the audience, but upon the Christie family. Agatha was a famously private person. She would have been mortified seeing the most painful event of her life turned into entertainment. She would have been appalled by the badly scripted rewrite. She would have been horrified at how they turned what should have been intriguing into a slog across the wintry moors through knee-deep mud.

Folks, if you're going to rewrite someone's past to make a movie, make it interesting. Make it exciting. Make it plausible. Don't make it tedious or tiresome. Adding gratuitous nudity (including Agatha!) does not compensate for a bad script and cardboard actors. I know the setting was a health spa, but there would have been towels, slippers, and capacious robes. The story takes place in Yorkshire in December! England is not known for decent central heating, and it must have been freezing in 1926, yet the director ogles the flesh on display.

Not male flesh, by the way, but why do I expect any different? As long as I'm ranting about gratuitous nudity supposedly presented for artistic reasons, why were all the ladies on display young and firm? This is a health spa! Most of the ladies would have been old and sagging. That tells you right there how much the director wanted to leer at his actresses.

Our titular star is Vanessa Redgrave. Dorothy Parker (1893-1967) said Katharine Hepburn's acting ranged the gamut of human emotions from A to B. Vanessa Redgrave didn't make it to B. She popped her eyes and behaved like a woebegone sheep out on the moors. With each close-up, I was mesmerized by her blue eyeshadow, heavy mascara, and eyebrow pencil. I didn't know ladies in 1926 wore that much eye makeup at health spas, but okay. I couldn't understand why Archie married her in the first place.

I also couldn't understand why Archie was conducting a torrid affair with his secretary, Nancy

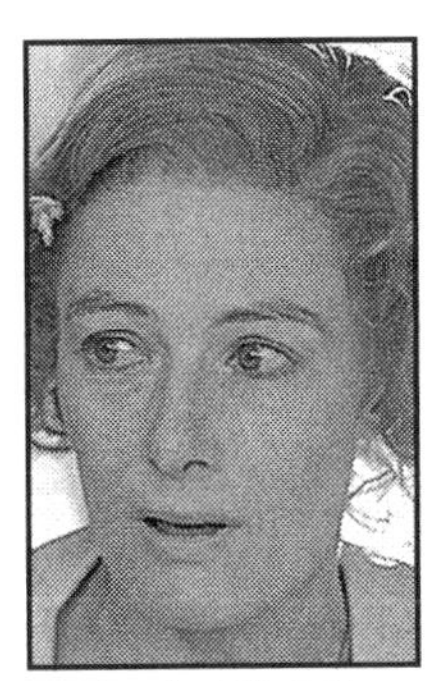
Agatha Christie (*Vanessa Redgrave*), the besieged wife

Wally Stanton (*Dustin Hoffman*), the suave columnist

Archie Christie (*Timothy Dalton*), the straying husband

Nancy Neele (*Celia Gregory*), the other woman

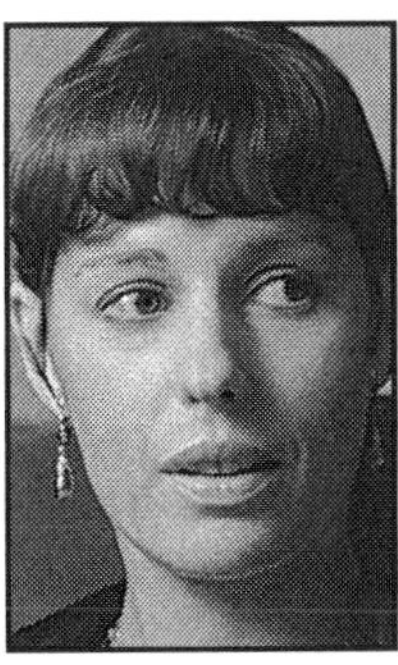
Evelyn Crawley (*Helen Morse*), the spa friend

John Foster (*Paul Brooke*), the local reporter

Neele, based on what we saw onscreen. Nancy was a cypher, with virtually no lines. Nancy was also, according to the dialog I could understand, fat. She had to visit the expensive health spa in Yorkshire to lose weight. The woman looked like a toothpick! If the script claims a woman needs to lose weight, don't cast an actress who needs to gain some to look normal.

I also don't grasp what a secretary's weight has to do with her secretarial duties, but the hack scriptwriters had to get Agatha and Nancy together at the health spa, away from prying eyes so they could take off their clothes.

A side note: I love subtitles. They keep me from missing clever dialog or plot points. Subtitles wouldn't have helped this movie. There were no clever lines and the plot points ranged from poorly thought-out to wildly implausible.

Our other star was Dustin Hoffman. He was stiff and uncomfortable, perfectly understandable considering his role. He played the smarmy American reporter who meets Agatha, falls in love with Agatha, rescues Agatha from certain death, and then nobly sails back across the Atlantic, never to reveal Agatha's secret plot to get Archie's secretary to murder her.

Did Agatha meet any American reporters in that health spa? She did not. Would any reporter worth his salary sit on the story of the century in exchange for a longing glance from her? As if. None of the reporters in this movie acted like reporters. Why look! There's Archie Christie, marching around all stiff and proper while police are dragging a pond looking for his wife's corpse. Do the baying hounds of the press notice him? They do not. They ignore the story right in front of them! There's Archie's friend, Lord Brackenbury, owner of the newspaper employing Dustin Hoffman's character. Lord Brackenbury — whose own paper is covering Agatha's disappearance as front-page news — tells Dustin not to pursue Agatha. No and I mean no newspaper owner ignores news that sends newsboys out into the street shouting "Extra! Extra!" because his friend might be embarrassed. Public embarrassment, shame, and humiliation sell newspapers!

Then there's the health spa. Agatha settles in, takes various weird but period health treatments, and writes in her journal. She notices the electric-chair-like gadgets. Remember, she's all weepy and mopey over Archie. Her archrival and nemesis, Nancy Neele, is also at the spa. Agatha takes copious notes and turns herself into an electrical engineer, rejiggering the components of the electric health chair so that she can seat herself in it and have Nancy turn on the juice and electrocute her!

Yes, according to this movie, Agatha tried to force Nancy Neele to murder her via electrocution. She'd die, Archie would be sad, his partner in adultery would be tried for murder, and the nice ladies at the health spa would be devastated, fired, and ruined for life. Every step of the way, movie Agatha did stupid things like leave unburnt evidence in the fireplace and devise super-convoluted plots when poison would have worked better.

Movie Agatha didn't have a daughter, didn't have friends other than her personal secretary, didn't have a mother who'd just died, and didn't have the brains that real Agatha did. Real Agatha was an expert in poisons thanks to her WWI experience working in a dispensary. Real Agatha knew perfectly well how to cover her tracks. She wrote mystery novels. She knew better than to leave evidence lying around.

Real Agatha would not have gotten down on her hands and knees to pack a reporter's perfectly ironed, over-starched, and squared-up shirts into his suitcase! Real Agatha grew up in a household where servants did that work. Even more, Real Agatha would not have slipped his incriminating story (which he had given her as a sign of his twu wuv) into his suitcase to be discovered later. Why did she do that? To tell him it was okay to publish the truth that she'd tried to get the Crown to murder Archie's cookie for her? No, no, no.

Agatha was badly written, badly plotted, played fast and loose with the facts even more than biopics normally do, and the worst crime of all, was tedious. Unless you've got a passionate interest in health spas of the 1920s, don't bother watching without a slab of rhubarb pie in front you. You'll need it to get the taste of this movie out of your mouth.

General Information

Based on: Original screenplay
Run time: 1 hr., 45 min. **Subtitles:** No

Writers: Kathleen Tynan and Arthur Hopcraft
Director: Michael Apted

Cast

Dustin Hoffman as Wally Stanton
Vanessa Redgrave as Agatha Christie
Timothy Dalton as Archie Christie
Helen Morse as Evelyn Crawley
Celia Gregory as Nancy Neele
Paul Brooke as John Foster
Carolyn Pickles as Charlotte Fisher
Timothy West as Kenward
Tony Britton as William Collins
Alan Badel as Lord Brackenbury
Robert Longden as Pettelson
Donald Nithsdale as Uncle Jones
Yvonne Gilan as Mrs. Braithwaite
Sandra Voe as Therapist
Barry Hart as Supt. MacDonald
David Hargreaves as Sergeant Jarvis
Tim Seely as Captain Rankin
Jill Summers as Nancy's Aunt
Christopher Fairbank as Luland
Liz Smith as Flora

Film Locations

Old Swan Hotel, Harrogate, North Yorkshire
Royal Baths, Harrogate, North Yorkshire
York Railway Station, York, North Yorkshire
Swan Street, Harrogate, North Yorkshire
Bath, Somerset (Harrogate)

Murder By the Book (1986)

Hercule Poirot's creator finds herself cast in her own murder mystery, but is she the victim or the killer?

Fidelity to life

This is pure imagination, but solidly based on Agatha's own writings and life.

Quality of movie

Our copy was terrible. Great acting and a clever script can't overcome serious technical difficulties.

While watching *Murder by the Book*, something Agatha said brought a variation of a meme to mind:

Agatha (to Poirot): "I wouldn't want you stranded in limbo, or worse still, a prey to writers who would exploit you — not look after you properly — like they did to poor James Bond. That would be so humiliating to you."

Sophie Hannah: "Hold my tea."

This is a very odd little film. It's short (45 minutes), yet packed full of incident. If you can locate a decent copy — it was released on laser-disk and videotape decades ago and we found our copy on YouTube — the picture and sound should be good enough quality that you can actually tell what's going on. I struggled. It didn't help there were no subtitles.

This is a pity because the writing was sharp, full of sly references to Agatha Christie's life and novels, and implied she rewrote parts of *Curtain* as a result of speaking with Hercule Poirot.

Wait. What? Agatha, a human writer, spoke with Poirot, her fictional creation?

Well, yeah. As a writer, I can tell you my characters regularly speak to me. They resent being forced to do stupid things for the sake of the plot. They have lives and thoughts outside of my words on the page. It really does work that way for me and I'm not the only one.

It's perfectly possible that Agatha wrote like Vladimir Nabokov (1899-1977). He famously said his characters were galley slaves and performed as they were told. They didn't run off with the narrative. He didn't allow them. Agatha wrote carefully constructed puzzle mysteries so she probably didn't let her characters run amok either. But she knew them well.

She knew Hercule Poirot well enough that she became heartily sick of him. She couldn't get rid of him; her publisher and agent would have had kittens. As a savvy businesswoman, she knew how much money he generated for all of them. She did get rid of Hastings. After *Murder on the Links* (1923), he only showed up on an as-need basis and then afterwards got deported to Argentina.

You see, Agatha didn't expect to write Poirot novels for the rest of her life. He started out as a sixty-something in *The Mysterious Affair at Styles* (1920). Her last novel with Poirot was *Elephants Can Remember*

Agatha Christie
(*Peggy Ashcroft*),
the creator

Hercule Poirot
(*Ian Holm*),
the created

Max Mallowan
(*Richard Wilson*),
the husband

Edmond Cork
(*Michael Aldridge*),
the agent

Sally
(*Dawn Archibald*),
the servant

Bingo
(*Chico*),
the pet

(1972). Fifty-two years! He was 112 by then. Or older. She got tired of him. His mannerisms became increasingly irritating. She didn't know much about Belgium or police work. Her alter-ego, Ariadne Oliver, voices similar frustrations about her fictional, Finnish, vegetarian detective, Sven Hjerson.

It's not a surprise that Agatha killed him off in *Curtain* (written in the early days of WWII but published in 1975). She purged herself and wrote a novel that would provide a nest egg for her family if she was killed during the war. Similarly, she wrote *Sleeping Murder* starring Miss Marple during the war but didn't publish until 1976. Agatha clearly liked her better, because Miss Marple doesn't die.

This brings us to *Murder by the Book*. Scriptwriter Nicholas Evans came up with a conceit familiar to every writer: What if your creation takes on a life of their own? He ties together Agatha's history, her intensely vivid dreams, and Poirot.

The opening scenes establish that she's elderly, in poor health, and living at Greenway with husband Max Mallowan. The lawn is infested with moles of the kind normally only seen in cartoons. The gardener is going to poison them which is why there's a bottle of poison in the kitchen.

Agatha's longtime agent, Edmond Cork, joins her, Max, and Bingo the dog for dinner. Assuming this takes place in 1974, *Postern of Fate* (1973) was in print. That was the last novel she ever wrote. What should she do next? Edmond brings the manuscript of Curtain with him, the novel she wrote near the peak of her writing powers.

Maybe it's time to publish it, he suggests. Agatha wants to read it first. While she's reading, the house empties out except for Bingo. That's when Poirot rings the doorbell to remonstrate with his creator. He doesn't want to die. He especially doesn't want to die of anything as mundane as a heart attack. Agatha insists she's trying to protect him, so he's not humiliated like James Bond.

For those of you who've forgotten, Ian Fleming (Bond's creator) died in 1964. Two final novels and a collection of short stories were published posthumously. Kingsley Amis wrote a James Bond follow-on, *Colonel Sun* (1968). It was … okay. Agatha would have known about it, just as she knew about the dreadful 1967 *Casino Royale* film that parodied Bond. It starred David Niven and Woody Allen, both of whom played 007. It wasn't any truer to James Bond than the Margaret Rutherford films were to Miss Marple.

She knew all about Sir Arthur Conan Doyle and how heartily sick he was of Sherlock Holmes. Conan Doyle tried to kill off Sherlock and had to bring him back to life. He lost control of Sherlock early on. Agatha never had to read stories in which Poirot sold linoleum or told ham radio enthusiasts how to use their equipment, but Conan Doyle did.

She didn't want that kind of fate for her creation. Good thing that Agatha didn't live long enough to see the amazing revolution in online fanfiction. There are loads of Poirot knockoffs (and Miss Marple too, and sometimes they work together!) but I'll let you discover them for yourself at Archive of Our Own.

She explains to Poirot why she's killing him, but he's not buying it. He steals part of the manuscript and locks himself into the one room where he won't be disturbed to read it. Agatha tries to serve him poisoned cocoa, with their cups on a rotating table top, but he's suspicious.

They end up stalking each other through the empty house. Poirot arms himself with Max's service revolver whereas Agatha chooses a striking, Middle-Eastern-style curved dagger.

Just when they find each other, Agatha wakes up. It's all been a vivid, detailed dream. But it gave her a great idea. The implication is that she'll use the spinning table idea when she revises *Curtain* for publication.

She gets what she wants. Poirot dies of a heart attack, saved from some hack writer who'll mistreat him. Poirot gets what he wants, going out with fireworks by doing something he'd never done in the previous 32 novels, two plays, or countless short stories.

Murder by the Book should be restored and released on DVD. It's a fascinating glimpse into not just Agatha's mind but the mind of every artist. What do you owe to your creation? And what do they owe to you, their creator?

General Information

Based on: Original screenplay
Run time: 45 min. **Subtitles:** No

Writer: Nick Evans
Director: Lawrence Gordon Clark

Cast

Peggy Ashcroft as Agatha Christie
Ian Holm as Hercule Poirot
Richard Wilson as Sir Max Mallowan
Michael Aldridge as Edmond Cork
John Atkinson as Gardener
Dawn Archibald as Sally
Chico as Bingo

EDMOND CORK: Plenty of great detectives outlive their creators. Why shouldn't Hercule Poirot?
AGATHA CHRISTIE: Over my dead body.

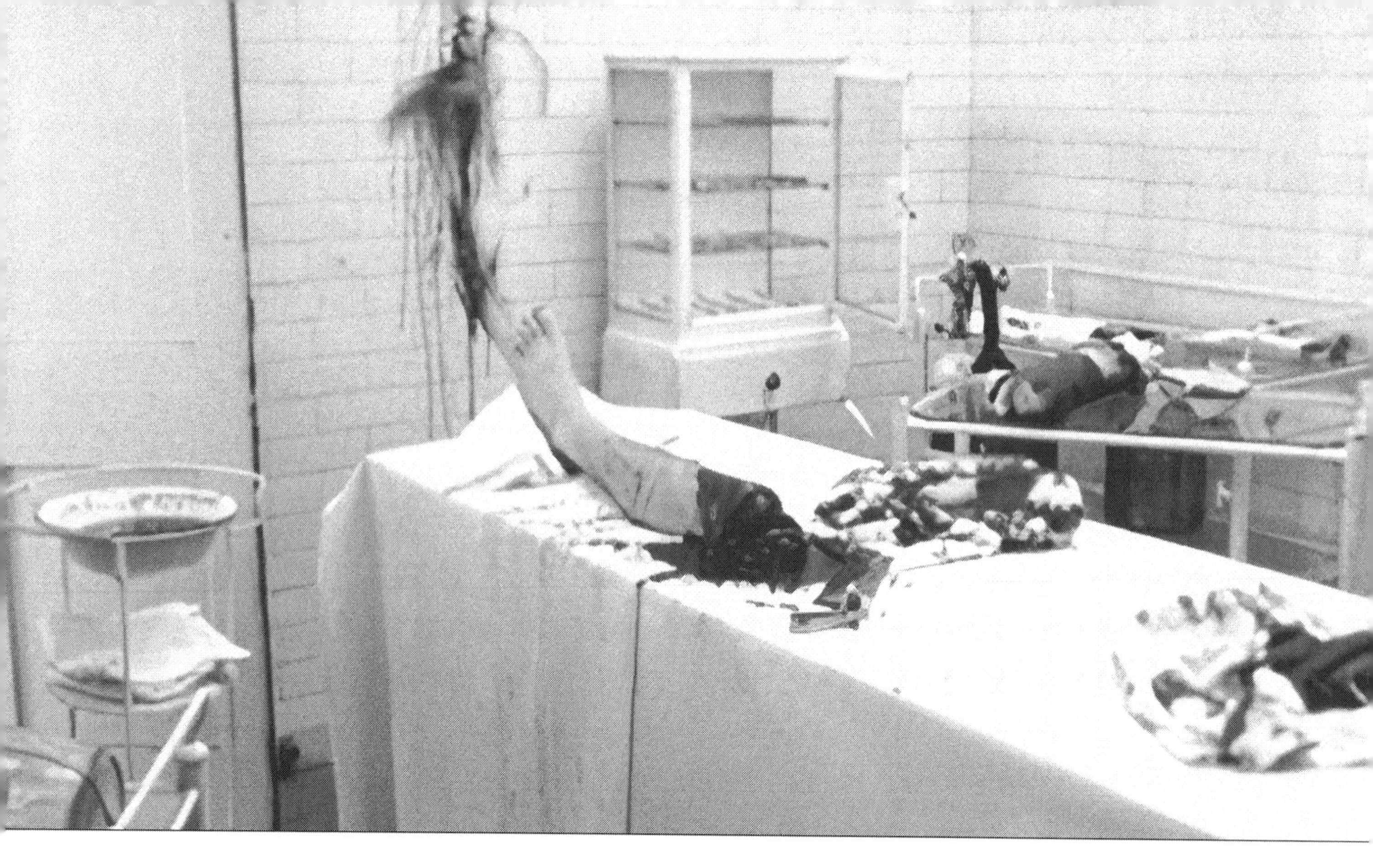

Agatha Christie: A Life in Pictures (2004)

Docudrama uses Christie's words to tell the story of her amazing life but leaves out inconvenient facts

Fidelity to life

It's reasonably accurate, particularly since every word comes from Agatha's memoirs or news reports. But it glossed over a *lot.*

Quality of movie

It should have been better since there's great story material: romance, death, cheating, fugue states, amnesia, divorce, and a second chance at love. Instead, it was confusing, and it dragged.

This is a reasonably accurate depiction of Agatha's early years, her eleven-day disappearance, Archie, Max Mallowan, and the tenth anniversary celebration of *The Mousetrap* in which Agatha sat for very rare interviews with reporters. All the dialog was taken from her autobiography, her very few interviews, and public reports. It's beautifully shot, with lovely period detail, and the acting works, other than Olivia Williams as Agatha with her brunette hair. The hair bothered me every time I saw it, because Agatha Christie was a redhead as a young woman, not a brunette.

If you're going to tell me something is true-to-life, then get the hair color correct. Wigs and dyes are cheap.

Do you see a problem here? If the film had been more involving and less confusing, I wouldn't focus on some hair stylist's choice of hair color. Seeing an obvious mistake like this made me wonder about the accuracy of the rest of the movie. If I'm paying attention to little nits like hair, then the movie failed. Do you think I noticed Agatha's hair color in the Vanessa Redgrave hatchet job? I did, but they got it right. The *Doctor Who* episode *The Unicorn and the Wasp* made Agatha a blonde, but it was close enough and the episode was so involving that I didn't care.

The audience should *never* pay attention to camera pyrotechnics, the wrong set decorations for a period piece, or that the time of year doesn't match the dialog. If the audience does, then the movie failed.

This film doesn't exactly fail, but it never gelled either. It was reverential to the point of dullness. I'd still choose it over the Vanessa Redgrave horror, but I'd choose virtually any Agatha Christie film over the Vanessa Redgrave horror.

Let's start with the structure. I can handle flashbacks. But flashbacks within flashbacks get confusing, especially when I'm having trouble understanding the dialog. We move forward in time to when Agatha was 72. She's at the tenth anniversary party for her play *The Mousetrap*. The opening scenes show the cake, with some very nice rolled fondant work in both mice and lettering. You see what I mean? I shouldn't be noticing skillful fondant work on a cake! If I'm noticing the cake, then there must not be any plot!

Agatha Christie (*Olivia Williams*), the young wife

Older Agatha (*Anna Massey*), the shy author

Archie Christie (*Raymond Coulthard*), the ruthless husband

Inspector Kenward (*Anthony O'Donnell*), the hunter

Psychiatrist (*Stephen Boxer*), the hypnotist

Kenyon (*Mark Gatiss*), the reporter

Anyway. Agatha agrees to a rare interview for the occasion. Reporters ask questions, and she reminisces. We swing back to her girlhood and young womanhood. Back and forth, back and forth, and occasionally sideways into the headshrinker's office. The shrink is trying to help Agatha recover her memory after ending up in a Harrogate spa. I kept noticing the goldfish in the bowl on the table and wondering why the goldfish stuck to the bottom of the bowl instead of swimming around more. Was the water that dirty?

Darn it. I lost track of the plot again.

We meet Agatha's feared nightmare figure from her childhood, the Gunman. He's a seedy man carrying a revolver. She wrote about him in her autobiography. The film never offers up an explanation of why this happened to her. Perhaps she was psychic? Picking up on bad vibes in the astral plane? No, I shouldn't be thinking about Agatha's possible clairvoyant tendencies. Must. Focus. On. Movie. Her ESP was bad, because if she'd been good, she wouldn't have married Archie Christie.

One thing this film did right was show how hot Archie was for Agatha. He wanted her and he got her. It was probably a very passionate relationship. *She* didn't want him to abandon her for Nancy Neele. I'm guessing — another missed plot area — that Archie cheated on Agatha with Nancy for months. Nancy was the secretary of Ernest Belcher, the British government official who took Archie and Agatha on the round-the-world cruise in 1922 to promote the Empire Exhibition. Nancy didn't come along on the ten-month-long cruise, so Archie didn't meet her until afterwards. But meet her, he did.

No details were given, other than Archie was a narcissist who didn't like being around anyone ill or unhappy. Agatha's adored mother died in 1926. Her death devastated Agatha. She moved into her childhood home to empty it of a lifetime of possessions and memories. She wasn't eating well, she wasn't sleeping, and Archie threw fuel on the fire by demanding a divorce because she wasn't paying him the attention he deserved, and he didn't want to be around a sad woman. No wonder she went crazy.

But as I said, the film's chronology was weird, jumping back and forth and sideways. While we're getting this story, we also get the story of Agatha nursing wounded soldiers in a Torquay hospital during World War I. Everyone talks about her time spent in the dispensary learning about poisons, but working the wards crammed with young men who'd endured the meat grinder of WWI must have been traumatic. Assisting in surgery? Cleaning up body parts? Nursing and scrubbing and bandaging young men missing limbs or horribly burned? No one ever talks about that part of her life, but it must have affected her.

It was at the dispensary that Agatha began working on Hercule Poirot and *The Mysterious Affair at Styles*. There's a wonderful scene where she and another nurse are treating two Belgian refugees for lice, combing them out of their hair and sprinkling them with lice powder. The ladies talk and the men sit quietly, not understanding a word. One of the refugees transforms into Hercule Poirot. One of the film's better tricks is having the same actor who played the Belgian refugee turned into Poirot also play police commissioner Kenward, who led the search after her disappearance.

There's also Mark Gatiss, playing a generic reporter named Kenyon. I'm not sure if he was a real person or the rare made-up character in a crowd of real people. I can't believe that a reporter in Harrogate during Agatha's disappearance would have been so low-key, so willing to take his time and investigate, when every reporter in England was baying for news. Agatha's disappearance made the front page of *The New York Times*. What English reporter would risk getting scooped by some Yank rag? Kenyon must be fake, to better smooth over documented discrepancies in what Agatha claimed happened and what did happen during her disappearance.

We also meet Max Mallowan, archeologist. That was a much happier relationship (second chance at love!). Agatha married him at 39, two years after her divorce from Archie. Very little film was wasted on Max, despite them being together for 46 happy years.

Should you watch this? Sure, why not. It's dull and muddled, but it's far more accurate than Vanessa Redgrave's travesty.

General Information

Based on: Original screenplay
Run time: 1 hr., 30 min. **Subtitles:** No

Writer & Director: Richard Curson Smith

Cast

Olivia Williams as Younger Agatha Christie
Anna Massey as Older Agatha
Raymond Coulthard as Archie Christie
Rosa Curson Smith as Rosalind Christie
Stephen Boxer as Psychiatrist
Anthony O'Donnell as Kenward / Hercule Poirot
Mark Gatiss as Kenyon
Richard Leaf as Gunman
Bonnie Wright as Young Agatha
Celia Montague as Clarisa Miller
Vicki Pepperdine as Carlo Fisher
Bertie Carvel as Max Mallowan
Olivia Darnley as Nurse
Edmund Kingsley as Soldier
Tim McMullan as Pharmacist
James Tucker as Reggie
Laura Maclaurie as Maid
Gregory Finnegan as Band Member
Cara Chase as Woman on Train

The Unicorn and the Wasp (2008)

The Doctor and his companion crash a country house party in 1926 in time for murder, secrets, and a vanishing

Obviously, Agatha Christie did not meet Doctor Who and Donna Noble at an English country house party. Nor did she meet a giant space wasp who murdered three people and tried to poison the Doctor. There was no high society jewel thief named the Unicorn. The space wasp didn't give Agatha amnesia. The space wasp's father didn't conduct a torrid affair with an English peeress in India, nor did he father her illegitimate, half-alien baby, later given up for adoption. Agatha also disappeared in December, and it's not December. Everyone's wearing summery clothes and they're out on the lawn enjoying afternoon cocktails so I'd vote for August.

Knowing all that, this is still a far more realistic, plausible, and faithful depiction of the events leading up to Agatha's 11-day disappearance than *Agatha* (1979), the dreadful, made-up-from-whole-cloth Vanessa Redgrave hatchet job.

That biopic was a travesty. It depicted Agatha as weepy, maudlin, suicidal, dopey, subservient, and incompetent. About the only thing it got right was that she'd recently discovered Archie was cheating on her. That film claimed that Agatha, while at the spa in Harrogate, maneuvered Archie Christie's new cookie into murdering her by electrocution so the Crown would hang said cookie and give Archie the sads.

What drivel.

Fidelity to life

Agatha disappeared for 11 days. That's a fact. She discussed it vaguely only once so Doctor Who delivers the answer! No, this didn't happen, but a murderous house party with an alien wasp is more realistic than that dreadful Vanessa Redgrave biopic.

Quality of movie

Give yourself license to laugh and let go of your preconceived notions about Agatha's disappearance. If you can't let go, don't watch. If you can, you'll love it.

Which leads me to investigate the accuracy of the *Doctor Who* episode, particularly since this show is not known for scientific or historical verisimilitude.

We meet Agatha when she's invited to a cocktail party, given by Lady Eddison. Lady Eddison is a major fan of her novels. Lady Eddison is fictional but it's true that everyone, high or low, liked Agatha's novels. She was well-regarded from her debut novel *The Mysterious Affair at Styles* (1920) and her reputation, popularity, and sales grew and grew with each short story and novel. Loads of highfalutin people would have been overjoyed to invite Agatha for a visit and have her accept. Lady Eddison was not unusual. We even see her poring over Agatha's latest book — one that took the world by storm — *The Murder of Roger Ackroyd.*

The Doctor (*David Tennant*), the 10th Doctor

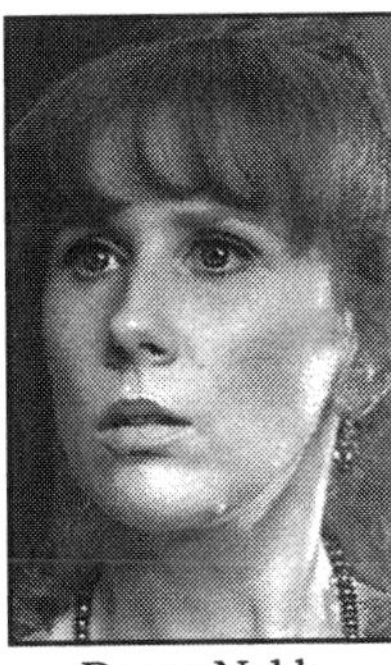

Donna Noble (*Catherine Tate*), the plucky sidekick

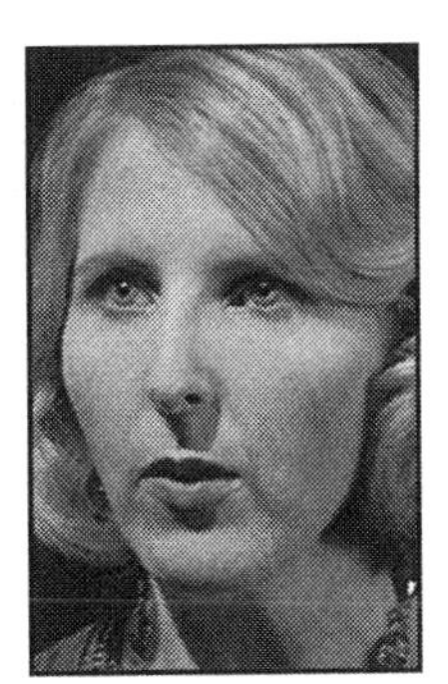

Agatha Christie (*Fenella Woolgar*), the doubting author

Lady Eddison (*Felicity Kendal*), the lady with a past

Reverend Golightly (*Tom Goodman-Hill*), the priest with secrets

Robina Redmond (*Felicity Jones*), the mysterious guest

Agatha is alone, because she's discovered Archie's affair. She — true to character — doesn't want to discuss it. It's embarrassing and uncomfortable to admit that her adored husband's a cheating dog. She was devastated and did not want to be the subject of gossip and pity. All very accurate. The film omits the trauma of her beloved mother's death, but that was another subject Agatha didn't like to talk about, so we'll concede this point.

Lady Eddison's house party looked like what I'd expect, with an assortment of interesting guests, including the local vicar. Since the Doctor uses his psychic paper to prove his bona fides and can talk his way into anywhere, he and Donna get invited in. Reasonably accurate.

The murders begin, which did not happen. Agatha works closely with the Doctor to solve them. She's observant, intelligent, a good judge of character, can think outside the box, and can put clues together. All very accurate since if she didn't have those skills, she wouldn't have been able to write 66 whodunnits, loads of short stories, and mystery plays that are still read and performed today. There's a reason why Agatha is the world's bestselling novelist.

Yet Agatha's self-confidence is shaky. She's unsure about the quality of her novels and wonders if anyone will read them after she's gone. Will she be forgotten and fade into the mists of time? I don't *know* if she felt insecure about her writing, but she was an author, so I'm sure she did. Every author wonders what the public sees in their works when the words on the page never measure up to the wonderful book in the mind.

Agatha is logical, sensible, forthright, and doesn't let the Doctor run roughshod over her. Why would she? He's behaving strangely, says strange things, and seems to be daft. Would Agatha do this? Probably. She knew her place in the world, and it wasn't jumping at the beck and call of some loon.

Would Agatha take responsibility for her novels deranging the mind of a giant killer space wasp? Possibly. She was a responsible person who fulfilled her obligations, which was another reason the worldwide interest in her disappearance mortified her. She was a private person and having everyone and their brother discuss her private life was humiliating. How responsible was she? Despite her life falling apart, she still fulfilled her book contract. She wrote *The Big Four*, followed by *The Mystery of the Blue Train* in 1928.

In her autobiography, Agatha mentions that it was while writing *Blue Train* that she knew she was a professional author. Because she needed the money, she delivered a book she had absolutely no interest in writing. She kept writing even after she divorced Archie and he married his cookie one week later. Agatha persevered.

In 1928, Agatha wrote the Poirot short story "Wasps' Nest." Wasps featured prominently. A few years later, Agatha wrote *Death in the Clouds* (1935). A wasp is found in the plane's compartment where no wasp should be, and the victim seems to have been stung to death. Are those stories coincidental? Perhaps not.

So there you have it. This *Doctor Who* episode is far more plausible in every way than the Vanessa Redgrave biopic. At 45 minutes, it zips along so you'll wish you got to spend more time with Agatha, the Doctor, and Donna Noble. That's very unlike Redgrave's opus where every minute drags itself past you, like slugs inching over your hostas and chewing them into lacy, slimy death.

You will need to watch this episode twice (at least!) in order to catch all the Agatha references worked into it. It's not just dialog either. Take a drink every time you spot a title, a technique (such as reflections in glass-fronted book cases), a murder weapon, a visual reference (yellow irises on the table), or a visual joke. I'll provide the first one: The Doctor is a mysterious man in a brown suit.

You can also spot the references to Clue (Cluedo for British readers). Professor Peach is obviously based on Professor Plum, and he's murdered in the library with a lead pipe. Miss Robina Redmond is Miss Scarlett. You can match up the rest.

Even if you're not a *Doctor Who* fan, don't miss this episode. It's fun, it's fast, and it provides the makings for an Agatha Christie trivia drinking game all in one.

General Information

Based on: Original script
Run time: 45 min. **Subtitles:** Yes

Writer: Gareth Roberts
Director: Graeme Harper

Cast

David Tennant as The Doctor
Catherine Tate as Donna Noble
Fenella Woolgar as Agatha Christie

Felicity Kendal as Lady Eddison
Tom Goodman-Hill as Rev. Golightly
Christopher Benjamin as Col. Hugh Curbishley
Adam Rayner as Roger Curbishley
Felicity Jones as Robina Redmond
David Quilter as Greeves
Daniel King as Davenport
Ian Barritt as Professor Peach
Leena Dhingra as Miss Chandrakala
Charlotte Eaton as Mrs. Hart
Damien Mantoulan as Christopher
Sandy McDonald as Footman

Film Locations

Cefn Mably Lakes, Cardiff, Wales (Agatha abandons car)
Hensol Castle, Cardiff, Wales (Harrogate Hotel)
Llansannor Court, Cowbridge, Wales (Eddison Manor, exterior and sitting room)
Tredegar House, Newport, Wales (Eddison Manor interiors)
St. Senwyn's Church, Llansannor, Wales (church)

Agatha and the Truth of Murder (2018)

Her marriage dying and creatively blocked, Agatha agrees to investigate a woman's murder in a railway car

Fidelity to life

A surprising amount of reality mixed into a Christie-esque murder mystery.

Quality of movie

Much better than it had any right to be and far, far better than what I was afraid of.

There's an amazing amount of reality mixed into this movie. Agatha did disappear for eleven days in December 1926 but she only discussed it publicly once, claiming she didn't remember.

Virtually the entire British police force mobilized to search England for her, tying up resources needed for local law enforcement. Newspapers around the world provided panting, inflammatory coverage.

Archie was conducting an affair with his secretary, Nancy Neele, and wanted a divorce. Agatha didn't like golf but she knew how to play. They did have one child, Rosalind, and Agatha's longtime secretary and friend was named Carlo Fisher. Beginning in 1930, Agatha wrote very personal non-mystery novels as Mary
, a pen name she hid behind for over twenty years.

While they probably never met, Arthur Conan Doyle really did hold a séance — using one of Agatha's gloves — seeking knowledge about her disappearance from the astral plane.

Most of all, Florence Nightingale Shore, Florence Nightingale's goddaughter, really was bludgeoned to death in a train compartment in 1920 and her murder was never solved. She really was a highly regarded, skilled nurse who devoted her life to her patients, including French-African soldiers during the war. She really did have a longtime dearest companion, Mabel Rogers, who strove mightily to find out who murdered Florence.

There really were newspaper headlines about a suspicious "Man in a Brown Suit" wanted for questioning in connection with Shore's murder. It was the biggest story of the day in 1920 and it's so forgotten today that Shore doesn't rate a Wikipedia page. Agatha would, naturally, have read all about it and probably had an opinion on whodunnit.

Agatha did not, however, get asked to solve Shore's murder nor did she disappear for eleven days to do so. Even so, this little gem of a movie is much closer to her real story and character than the dreadful Vanessa Redgrave/Dustin Hoffman hatchet job *Agatha* (1979).

Because of that film, I expected to hate this one; suffering through it for the sake of you, dear reader, so you don't have to. And, I'm astonished to say, it's a fun movie. It's respectful to Agatha, Conan Doyle, writers in general, and it's a functioning mystery.

I didn't expect that either.

So let's visit this parallel universe, much like our own. Although she's famous for her mystery novels, Agatha's struggling with her writing. Her marriage has

Wade Miller (*Dean Andrews*), the stern father

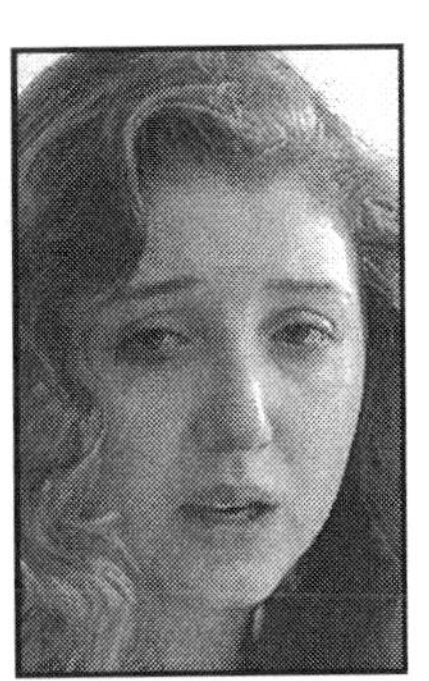
Daphne Miller (*Bebe Cave*), the sad daughter

Pamela Rose (*Samantha Spiro*), the loving mother

Franklin Rose (*Joshua Silver*), the loyal son

Randolph (*Tim McInnerny*), the deceased's cousin

Travis Pickford (*Blake Harrison*), the boxer and thief

collapsed, but she's holding out against Archie's wish for a divorce. Archie's so ready to divorce Agatha and marry Nancy the 24-year-old cookie that he's already introduced her to their young daughter Rosalind.

She visits Sir Arthur Conan Doyle for advice and they chat about writing, writer's block, and dealing with the public over golf. Sir Arthur suggests she design a golf course. It would stimulate her creativity without involving detectives or writing. Desperate, Agatha does some research, gets rebuffed by a well-known golf course designer (women couldn't possibly understand the complexity of golf courses), and designs one anyway. She builds a scale model in her office large enough to take up two dining room tables.

Archie admires the golf course model and instantly assumes Agatha designed it as a gift for him. Naturally, it needs his improvements and oh, by the way, let's call a truce even though he still wants a divorce so he can marry the cookie.

As Agatha's ready to pull her hair out, Nurse Mabel Rogers shows up and begs for help. It's been six years since Nurse Rogers' dearest friend (and lover) Florence Nightingale Shore was bludgeoned to death on the train. Scotland Yard is no closer to solving Florence's murder than when she was discovered, her head bashed in and clinging to life. Nurse Rogers is at the end of her rope.

Agatha looks over Nurse Rogers' folder and gets interested. She makes plans with Nurse Rogers and (offscreen) with Carlo, her faithful secretary. They invite the six main suspects to a remote country house to interrogate them and discover the truth as to which person bludgeoned Florence.

Why would six strangers show up at a remote country house? Because of a chance to inherit the mysterious Mr. Dower's enormous fortune. He had no living relatives so the lawyers handling his estate — represented by Agatha disguised as Mary Westmacott in a severe suit and prim hair and glasses — found them, brought them together, and is interviewing them to figure out degree of consanguinity to Mr. Dower and their moral fitness to inherit (a condition of the will to get them to talk).

Agatha and Nurse Rogers assumed correctly with their plot. It's amazing how people will cooperate if they think they'll inherit big money.

General Information

Based on: Original screenplay
Run time: 1 hr., 32 min. **Subtitles:** Yes

Writer: Tom Dalton **Director:** Terry Loane

Cast

Ruth Bradley as Agatha Christie
Pippa Haywood as Mabel Rogers
Ralph Ineson as Detective Inspector Dicks
Seamus O'Hara as PC Spencer

Dean Andrews as Wade Miller
Bebe Cave as Daphne Miller
Joshua Silver as Franklin Rose
Samantha Spiro as Pamela Rose
Blake Harrison as Travis Pickford
Tim McInnerny as Randolph
Luke Pierre as Zaki Hannachi
Liam McMahon as Archie Christie
Amelia Dell as Rosalind Christie
Clare McMahon as Carlo Fisher
Michael McElhatton as Sir Arthur Conan Doyle
Derek Halligan as Mr. Todd
Stacha Hicks as Florence Nightingale Shore
Brian McCardie as Sir Hugh Persimmion

Film Locations

Grey Abbey, Newtownards, Northern Ireland (country house)
The Downpatrick and County Down Railway, Northern Ireland (train, station)

Except they don't get six suspects. They get seven. Daphne Miller's father, Wade, comes along for the ride. He's a nasty piece of work, gets shot, and thrown out a second-story window. His murder — possibly related to Florence's? — means the police must be called in.

Neither Agatha or Nurse Rogers wanted this complication since there is no Mr. Dower or megabucks inheritance. Detective Inspector Dicks arrives, constable in tow, and complains vociferously about being shorthanded because virtually every policeman in England is searching for that bloody Christie woman.

Which Agatha, isolated in the country house interviewing suspicious heirs, did not know. But it very nicely sets up why DI Dicks is stuck in the isolated country house full of suspects when he would rather escort everyone down to the station house for interrogation.

There are some wonderful scenes where Agatha the writer learns that real-life murder is nothing like a book. It's not nearly as neat, tidy, or amusing. Unlike Sherlock Holmes, she reasons ahead of her data. The obvious suspect is often the guilty party (see the murder of Wade Miller). Unlike Agatha, DI Dicks saw through that one at once. Real murder involves plenty of blood, violence, and obsession.

You, dear reader, watching along, will be fooled along with Agatha. Any of the six people assembled could have murdered Florence. They all had motives. Yet only one murderer had the obvious brains to plan a crime that couldn't be easily solved *and* courtesy of a willing, equally motivated accomplice could be in two places at once *and* knew Florence's train schedule. DI Dicks grasps the answer very quickly when Agatha presents the data. It makes you wonder why Scotland Yard didn't, except that they never had this particular suspect on their radar.

Respectability makes wonderful camouflage.

Throughout, Agatha the detective grows in confidence. You can almost see her thinking about how she'd write future mysteries based on events around her. She'll be able to write a strangling scene with real conviction!

This was fun. The mystery played fair with viewers; every clue is there onscreen. It also played fair with Agatha, making her human instead of an icon on a plinth in a corner niche.

Agatha and the Curse of Ishtar (2019)

On an archaeological dig in Iran, Agatha finds a second chance at love and a scheme to steal rare artifacts

Fidelity to life

Max is real, the Woolleys are real, the timeline's close, and England had compelling reasons to exploit Middle Eastern oil reserves.

Quality of movie

So many failed opportunities and unanswered questions, yet surprisingly funny.

This is a weird movie. It can't decide if it wants to be a sex comedy, a second-chance-at-love romance, a mystery, or an examination of British *realpolitik* over vital resources. There's also sexism in the archeological biz and appropriation of native cultural goods being shipped off to British museums instead of remaining in the originating country's own museums.

That's a lot to pack into 95 minutes. Wait! There's also animal cruelty in the form of a hanged monkey so be forewarned. Although according to everyone *but* Katharine Woolley, Ella the monkey was a vicious, flea-ridden pest and good riddance to bad rubbish.

Plus, a touch of Grand Guignol.

Does this mashup work? Not really. The tone is wildly uneven and the bizarre, tinkling piano background music doesn't help.

Let's begin by examining what's real. Agatha's divorce from Archie became final in October 1928. Archie married Nancy Neele one week later. Agatha was struggling to rebuild her life, get back to writing, and had ideas for books other than mysteries. Those ideas eventually became her six Mary Westmacott novels, published between 1930 and 1956.

In late 1928, she rode the Orient Express to Istanbul where she was introduced to archaeologists Leonard and Katharine Woolley. They invited her to return and visit their dig in 1930. That's when she met Max Mallowan, 13 years her junior. He was instantly attracted to Agatha but she was more hesitant because of their age gap. But he was not investigating the theft of stolen relics, nor was he ever a target for murder.

The Woolleys did not have a noisy, red-hot, sheet-scorching sex life. Apparently, their marriage was never consummated due to Katharine's health problems (she may have had Androgen Insensitivity Syndrome, causing her to be born without a uterus). Katharine did have a reputation for being forthright, charming, difficult, dangerous, and manipulative. She's the model for "Lovely" Louise Leidner, the victim (because she had it coming) in *Murder In Mesopotamia* (1936).

The Woolleys did major excavations at Ur in Iraq. The British had a strong presence there, having essentially squeezed a number of disparate, smaller states into one, larger, restive country they administered. The British government knew there was oil under the sand. They wanted it to fuel British

Leonard Woolley
(*Jack Deam*),
the archaeologist

Katharine Woolley
(*Katharine Kingsley*),
the vixen

Sir Constance Bernard
(*Stanley Townsend*),
the Empire official

Lord Ponsonby
(*Rory Fleck Byrne*),
the wealthy backer

Pearl Theroux
(*Crystal Clarke*),
the thwarted scholar

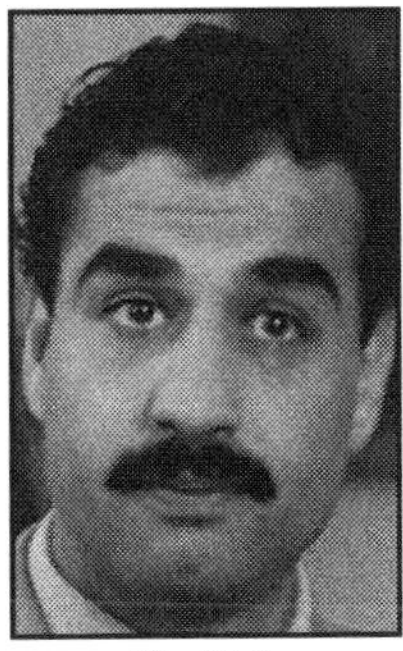

Ezekiel
(*Waj Ali*),
the Iraqi official

warships and industry. The British consulate was large and powerful, with fingers in many pies and deals operating within deals.

General Information

Based on: Original script
Run time: 1 hr., 35 min. **Subtitles:** Yes

Writer: Tom Dalton **Director:** Sam Yates

Cast

Lyndsey Marshal as Agatha Christie
Jonah Hauer-King as Max Mallowan

Jack Deam as Leonard Woolley
Katherine Kingsley as Katharine Woolley
Stanley Townsend as Sir Constance Bernard
Bronagh Waugh as Lucy Bernard
Rory Fleck Byrne as Marmaduke, Lord Ponsonby
Crystal Clarke as Pearl Theroux
Waj Ali as Ezekiel
Colin Farrell as Hutchins
Walles Hamonde as Ahkam
Waleed Elgadi as Dr. Al-Memar
Mark Lambert as Godfrey
Liran Nathan as Faisal
Daniel Gosling as Hugo
Sharif Dorani as Hadi
James Staddon as Patrick Mulholland
Emma Darlow as Claire

Film Location

Villa Bologna, Malta

The novel Agatha is reading is real. It's *Lady Into Fox* (1922) by David Garnett (1892-1981). An early fantasy novel, a young woman is transformed into a fox and tragedy ensues.

After that, everything was dredged up from the sand. Any accuracy is for a parallel universe about six or seven universes away from our own.

For example: Agatha might have enjoyed noisy, red-hot, scorched-sheet sex with Max but she would have *never* discussed it with anyone. As a well-bred Edwardian lady, she also wouldn't have jumped him within a few days of meeting and inside an underground tunnel, either.

During the Great War, she didn't work only in the hospital dispensary. She worked in the wards, tending wounded soldiers with all the intimate messes that entails. In her autobiography she recalls taking amputated limbs to the incinerator. You think she'd have the vapors over dissecting a monkey? And wouldn't know the difference between a kidney and a liver? Not a chance.

There are also problems with the core mystery. There aren't too many people involved. Obviously, Agatha, Max, and the Woolleys are not suspects. That leaves Lucy Bernard, her husband Sir Constance Bernard (the script gave him a poor first name), Marmaduke/Lord Ponsonby, Pearl Theroux, and Ezekial.

None of these people got enough screen time. Lucy's cheating on Sir Constance but with who? Since Max is our hero, he's off the list. Katharine's keeping Leonard busy. That leaves Marmaduke and Ezekial. In her spare time, Lucy is also stealing the dig finds for resale on the black market.

It's doubtful Lucy's sneaking around with Ezekial. He's both a native Iraqi and a representative of the native government, trying to keep an eye out for stolen antiquities. Marmaduke is the only man left. I'm assuming that's how Agatha worked it out but she never explains her reasoning. We never see a single scene where Lucy and Marmaduke even speak to each other, so how did she know?

And how did Marmaduke, an American, become Lord Ponsonby and the financier behind the dig? There should have been more explanation, maybe involving Lucy so we could accept they were having an affair and not just because of process of elimination.

Pearl Theroux — young, pretty, female, African — complains of being ill-used by Katharine. She's relegated to being the dogsbody, doing the most menial work or so she says. But we never see Katharine ordering her about, fetching tea or shawls. Like with Lucy and Marmaduke, Katharine and Pearl don't even speak to each other.

Then there's the case of the hanged monkey. Agatha's deduction that Ella was poisoned made sense. It'd be darned difficult to hang a monkey; the beast will bite and claw and fight and climb up the rope and throw its poo at its hangman. The only poison available was strychnine, but how did Ella get it? My first thought was *Indiana Jones and the Raiders of the Lost Ark* (1981). That monkey was poisoned because it ate poisoned dates. But we never see dates or any other toxic treat.

How did the dynamite get tossed into the tunnel where Agatha and Max were locked in passionate embrace? Who put it there? We never find out.

In fact, there seemed to be a lot of secret tunnels. At one point, Max and an Arab digger end up in a tunnel, the Arab identifies a relic as resembling one that had already been found and suddenly, they're surrounded by crated, stolen antiquities and there's Max's employer. He's dying, supposedly bitten by a poisonous snake. In a tunnel.

There's also the title. *The Curse of Ishtar* implies a supernatural element at work. Maybe an amulet or talisman of great power that will rain destruction on the unworthy. There's a big black piece of pottery that Max's employer's holding. Leonard reads the inscription to Agatha, and it doesn't seem to have anything to do with the plot at all, other than in the most metaphorical of senses.

Can the Curse of Ishtar be the black, poisonous fluid seeping from the earth? Is it oil? I guess that's what they meant. If the script wanted to make a point about money, greed, and oil combining into a toxic stew that poisons everything it touches, then it did it badly.

This should have been better. The material is there; second chance at love, naughty monkeys, imperial intrigue, adultery, and murder. The film looks good on paper but on celluloid it doesn't amount to a hill of sand.

Agatha and the Midnight Murders (2020)

While the Germans bomb London, Agatha travels to a seedy hotel to sell a Poirot manuscript to pay her taxes

Fidelity to life

Agatha was in London during the Blitz, she endured unending problems with Inland Revenue, and she needed money.

Quality of movie

This flick needs to be remade. There's a tight, tense, suspenseful, closed-circle mystery in there waiting to see the light of day. This isn't it.

Was there anything real here? Besides in some parallel universe where Agatha Christie changed faces every few years?

Glad you asked. Agatha really lived in London during the Blitz. Her hubby Max was in North Africa contributing to the war effort. She worked in the University College Hospital's pharmacy when she wasn't writing. It is possible Max cheated on her during their five-year separation.

She had major problems with Inland Revenue (British taxes) and the Internal Revenue Service (American taxes). Both agencies bedeviled her for decades, wanting her to pay taxes on her overseas royalties. The rules over how much changed depending on who she spoke to and how much money the Crown needed. In the 1960s, the Crown took 89 percent of her income beyond £15,000. She contemplated filing for bankruptcy and cut back on her writing to avoid taxation problems.

That wasn't the only government agency interested in Agatha. One of her books drew the attention of MI5. Her Tommy and Tuppence novel *N or M?* (1941), a spy thriller set in the early days of WWII, had a character named Major Bletchley. MI5 got involved because a top-secret, code-breaking operation took place at Bletchley Park and they needed to know if there was a leak. Agatha used the name because of an annoying wait while on a train outside Bletchley.

Because she feared dying in the Blitz and leaving her family without a source of income, she wrote two novels as insurance and a legacy. Since she lived, they weren't published until the end of her life: *Curtain* (1975) and *Sleeping Murder* (1976). She had a love/hate relationship with Hercule Poirot and killed him in *Curtain* so it would have been the last Poirot novel.

During the Blitz, the streets were patrolled by Air Raid Wardens. The sirens sounded, warning of incoming bombers. The wardens shooed everyone into underground shelters such as tube stations and cellars. There, the citizens waited until the all clear keeping their spirits up. Everyone knew the words to popular songs like "Hitler's only got one ball." About 40,000 civilians died during the Blitz, with tens of thousands more injured so most people didn't argue about seeking shelter.

By 1940, Agatha had fans worldwide. She'd been

Frankie Lei
(*Thomas Chaanhing*),
the buyer

Jun Yuhuan
(*Elizabeth Tan*),
the translator

Rocco Vella
(*Morgan Watkins*),
the bodyguard

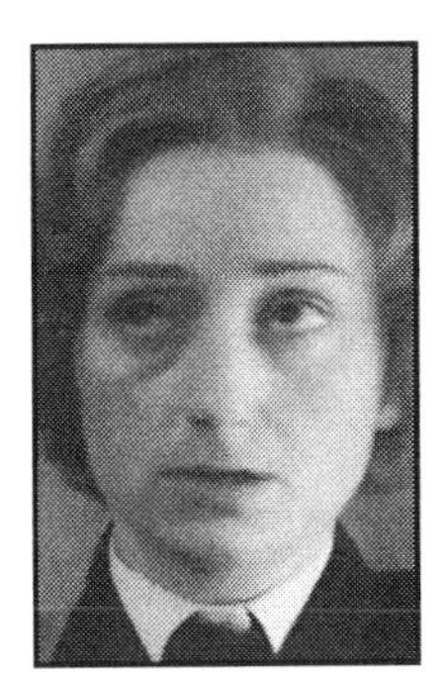

PC O'Hanauer
(*Jodie McNee*),
the air raid warden

Audrey Evans
(*Jacqueline Boatswain*),
the government official

Sir Malcolm Campbell
(*Alistair Petrie*),
the secret agent

translated into multiple languages. It's plausible she had Chinese fans. It's likely a major collector/fan with deep pockets would pay well for a new Poirot novel they could control.

It's very implausible that Agatha was so desperate for money she'd sell her unpublished manuscript of *Curtain* to some skeevy buyer under the table and pocket the cash. The idea of a deed to go with the manuscript, giving the owner publication rights, didn't make any sense. Deeds are for property, not unpublished books. If that was a genuine legal requirement, the script needed to spell it out better.

In fact, everything in the script needed to be spelled out better. There's a cracking good mystery buried under bad writing, static direction, and indifferent acting.

Too many scenes went nowhere, starting with the opening. An Air Raid Warden is searching the rubble (alone?) for victims. When one is found partially buried, the warden doesn't save the victim. No, he cuts off the victim's finger to steal a diamond ring. The warden then vanishes from the film! Why even have this scene?

It should have gone like this: Agatha reads the paper and learns that someone is robbing and mutilating Blitz victims. This gives her a compelling reason to hire Travis Pickford as her bodyguard when she visits a skeevy part of London to sell the manuscript.

Then later, that warden should reappear in the film. As it was, the maiming warden could have been PC O'Hanauer or Travis Pickford or someone else entirely. If the knife was supposed to be a clue, it didn't work.

Travis Pickford was another problem. If you recall *Agatha and the Truth of Murder* (2018), he was one of six suspects in the murder of Florence Nightingale Shore. He was innocent of that crime but he's not an innocent man. The police know him well. Why wasn't there a scene to help the audience remember him and understand why Agatha chose him as a bodyguard? Two full years passed between the airing of that movie and this one. Audiences forget.

How could Agatha sort of recognize the two American tourists, Audrey and Nell? She was wary of them but for no discernible reason. At the climax, it turns out they're from MI5 and not from Inland Revenue. They don't care about Agatha evading taxes but they do care about the Bletchley character in her spy novel. Yet Agatha doesn't tell them (or the audience) why she chose that name. Worse, if Agatha's afraid of being followed to the low-rent hotel where she's selling her manuscript for untaxable $$$, then we should have seen her looking over her shoulder at tea shops, on buses, and in the tube.

Audrey and Nell, MI5 agents in disguise, apparently knew Sir Malcolm Campbell. They exchange some very unclear banter implying … well, something about disloyalty, royalty, betrayal, and what good citizens do when England's under attack. If you're going to add a proto-James Bond to your cast, make full use of him! And why did he have the bimbo on his arm? What were they doing in that skeevy hotel in the first place?

Why was Eli, the mobster owner of the hotel, concerned about everyone going down into his cellar during the bombing raid? One of the characters said it must be because he stored black market goods down there. Yet when everyone trooped downstairs to avoid being blown to bits, the catacomb-like cellar stored old furniture and knickknacks.

How did Agatha find Frankie Lei, wealthy and unscrupulous superfan from Hong Kong in the first place? Why did she feel forced to meet him in a skeevy hotel when she could have just as easily handed him the manuscript and he hand her the envelope of cash while enjoying afternoon tea at the Ritz? We need a reason and there was none.

When Rocco (Frankie Lei's bodyguard) backhanded Clarence the bartender, he fell to the floor. Okay. But why, when his body was examined later, did his face look like it had been bashed in to silence him?

Why was Jun Yuhuan, Frankie Lei's translator, murdered? There was no reason. Similarly, there was no reason for Eli the mobster to get knifed in the eye. Did either of them know something about the connections between this assorted pack of strangers? If they did, the script didn't bother telling us.

In fact, the script didn't bother introducing us to any of the people in the hotel bar.

And why did they use yet another actress for Agatha? That made the least sense of all, making you wonder why this movie was ever made.

General Information

Based on: Original script
Run time: 1 hr., 31 min. **Subtitles:** Yes

Writer: Tom Dalton **Director:** Joe Stephenson

Cast

Helen Baxendale as Agatha Christie
Blake Harrison as Travis Pickford

Jodie McNee as PC O'Hanauer
Thomas Chaanhing as Frankie Lei
Elizabeth Tan as Jun Yuhuan
Morgan Watkins as Rocco Vella
Alistair Petrie as Sir Malcolm Campbell
Gina Bramhill as Grace Nicory
Jacqueline Boatswain as Audrey Evans
Vanessa Grasse as Nell Lewis
Daniel Caltagirone as Eli Schneider
Scott Chambers as Clarence Allen

Film Location

Corinthia Palace Hotel and Spa, Malta (hotel interiors)

Song

"Hitler Has Only Got One Ball," lyricist unknown, based on "Colonel Bogy March" by Lt. F. J. Ricketts

See How They Run (2022)

Someone wants to close *The Mousetrap* in this meta, self-aware farce stuffed with Easter eggs for Agatha fans

If you like this movie, you'll watch it several times to get all the in-jokes, the references to Agatha, and to appreciate how the film refers back to itself like a Mobius strip, where the climax duplicates what the seedy director storyboarded as being the correct climax to a mystery movie. It's arch and very much a film for people who love Golden Age mysteries, the theater, writers wrestling with Hollywood over their vision, and clever movies about the movies. If you don't belong to one of those categories, this movie will drive you mad.

Since the movie is set in the real world, how much is real? *The Mousetrap* opened on 6 October 1952 and was a hit from day one. It was loosely inspired by the tragic, systematic abuse and eventual murder of Dennis O'Neil, 12, on 9 January 1945, while in Britain's foster care system. His younger brothers survived. What happens to the surviving children who depended on adults to look out for them but fail them instead? Agatha ran with the idea.

The Rillington serial killer was real. In March of 1953, about when *The Mousetrap* would have hit its 100th performance, the strangled bodies of several women were discovered in a papered-over alcove in a dilapidated boarding house where John Reginald Halliday Christie (1899-1953) lived. This Christie, unrelated to Agatha, had a long history of offenses. More bodies were found around the property and in the back garden.

Fidelity to life

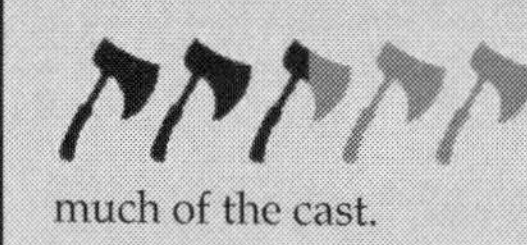

The Mousetrap, the clause in the movie production contract, the tragic child murders, and the serial killer are real. So are much of the cast.

Quality of movie

If you're familiar with Christie World and like meta, stagy, clever, self-referential movies, you'll love it. If you don't, you won't.

What's worse, Christie earlier was involved in a miscarriage of justice. In 1948, the bodies of Beryl Evans and her infant daughter, Geraldine, were found on the same property. Christie was the star witness for a criminally botched investigation including rampant police corruption, and a prosecution ending with Beryl's innocent husband, Timothy Evans, being hung in 1950.

This time around, the police were under immense pressure to get it right and not railroad some innocent man to the gallows because it was easy. That's why Inspector Stoppard, a functioning alcoholic who's not very good at his job, and a raw newbie constable got assigned what should have been a high-profile case involving Hollywood directors, big-name stars, and Agatha Christie, the biggest name of them all. Commissioner Harold Scott (a real person who ran the Metropolitan Police from 1945 to 1953) is under pressure from the Home Office to play nice with the theater people *and* solve the case while still focusing all

Leo Kopernick (*Adrien Brody*), the odious director

Mervyn Cocker-Norris (*David Oyelowo*), the flamboyant writer

Petula Spencer (*Ruth Wilson*), the sly impresario

Reece Shearsmith (*John Woolf*), the cheating producer

Dennis Corrigan (*Charlie Cooper*), the unnoticed usher

Agatha Christie (*Shirley Henderson*), the famous playwright

his efforts and manpower on finding the Rillington Place rapist and strangler.

Many of the people associated with *The Mousetrap* are real. Richard "Dickie" Attenborough and his wife, Sheila Sim, were the original stars. Petula Spencer was based on Peter Saunders, the theater impresario who drove the bargain with real producer, John Woolf, about filming rights. That clause in the contract about not beginning filming until after the play had been out of the West End theater for at least six months? That's real too. When Woolf signed that contract at the behest of Peter Saunders, he, like everyone else, didn't expect *The Mousetrap* to run forever. His second wife, Edana Romney, was real too. They divorced in 1955, and he married Ann Saville, who may or may not have been his personal assistant. Certainly the names match.

Agatha is real. So is her husband, Max Mallowan although he wasn't black. But in this parallel world, why not? Lucian Msamati made a much better Max Mallowan than Jonah Hauer-King in *Agatha and the Curse of Ishtar* (2019). Equally real is Agatha's distaste for public appearances so her sending a cake for the 100th performance would be in character.

The seedy director, Leo Kopernick, isn't real but he perfectly embodies countless Hollywood directors who understand that plays aren't movies and the point of a movie is to sell millions of tickets and boring movies won't do that. His storyboard of *his* vision proves his point.

The artsy writer, Mervyn Cocker-Norris, isn't real either, but he emulates countless writers with an artistic vision who get chewed up by Hollywood, leaving them drunken failures living on destroyed dreams. He's appalled by Leo's storyboard as it's exactly the sort of tawdry, clichéd ending he abhors.

The film is loaded with Easter eggs about Agatha and her world. Start with Inspector Stoppard, who was named for the playwright who wrote *The Real Inspector Hound*, a one-act play satirizing *The Mousetrap*. An especially nice one is near the climax, when the murderer invades Agatha's home and takes everyone hostage. Agatha, wanting to save the day, finds the rat poison and poisons one cup of tea out of the set of tea cups. This is how you know it's not the real Agatha. If *she* needed to poison a home invader without killing one of the guests, she'd have discreetly marked the cup (how the handle was oriented compared to the rest or an extra lump of sugar on the saucer or *something*). But this one didn't and the butler, Fellows (named after Julian Fellows of *Downton Abbey* fame) dies.

What the scene references is *Curtain* (1975), also played out in *Murder by the Book* (1986). In *Curtain*, Mrs. Franklin poisons a cup of coffee. She's entertaining her husband and some friends in their room. She sets out the coffee cups on a tray on a revolving bookcase/table, the critical cup arranged so her husband takes it. The group is momentarily distracted and Hastings innocently spins the table to retrieve a book from underneath. Since Mrs. Franklin didn't mark the poisoned cup, and didn't know the table was spun, she drinks the poisoned coffee instead of her husband. In *Murder by the Book*, Agatha and Poirot spar in a dream sequence and she, similarly, tries to poison his cocoa but not her own.

Agatha might have smacked a murderous home invader on the back of his head with a snow shovel, while trying to defend herself, her husband, and her guests. No matter what the provocation, I don't believe she'd have then tried to decapitate the home invader with the snow shovel.

It all works out in the end exactly as Leo storyboarded for converting *The Mousetrap* into a film. Inspector Stoppard and Constable Stalker separately work out that Dennis the usher is the murderer. They race, separately, to Agatha's home to confront Dennis and coincidentally, rescue the threatened, uninvited guests whom Dennis also wants to murder. Stoppard brings his military service revolver (because police in Britain are traditionally unarmed), Stalker her eagerness, and the climax plays out, complete with Molotov cocktails, last-minute leaps in front of a gunshot, and the detective cradling his injured partner.

The film was sometimes too clever and too subtle. It needed to be a little longer and a little less subtle so dumb viewers like me could have understood what was going on. But I'll rewatch it! That won't be a hardship.

General Information

Based on: Original screenplay
Run time: 1 hr., 38 min. **Subtitles:** Yes

Writer: Mark Chappell **Director:** Tom George

Cast

Sam Rockwell as Inspector Stoppard
Saoirse Ronan as Constable Stalker
Tim Key as Commissioner Harold Scott
Angus Wright as Sgt. Bakewell

Shirley Henderson as Agatha Christie
Lucian Msamati as Max Mallowan
Adrien Brody as Leo Kopernick
Harris Dickinson as Richard Attenborough
Pearl Chanda as Sheila Sim
David Oyelowo as Mervyn Cocker-Norris
Jacob Fortune-Lloyd as Gio
Charlie Cooper as Dennis Corrigan
Ruth Wilson as Petula Spencer
Ania Marson as Mother Spencer
Reece Shearsmith as John Woolf
Sian Clifford as Edana Romney
Pippa Bennett-Warner as Ann Saville
Paul Chahidi as Fellowes

Film Locations

St. Martin's Theatre, London (The Ambassadors Theatre, exteriors)
Dominion Theatre, Bloomsbury, London (The Ambassadors Theatre, foyer)
Savoy Hotel, London (hotel, exteriors)
Florin Court, Charterhouse Square, London (Mervyn and Gio's flat, exteriors)
Old Vic Theatre, Lambeth, London (audition)
Freemason's Hall, Covent Garden, London (The Ambassadors Theatre, bar)

Bibliography

Books

Aldridge, Mark. *Agatha Christie On Screen*. London: Palgrave Macmillan, 2016

Aldridge, Mark. *Agatha Christie's Poirot: The Greatest Detective in the World*. London: HarperCollins London, 2020.

Christie, Agatha. *Autobiography*. New York: Bantam, 1977

Christie, Agatha. *The Grand Tour*. HarperCollins, 2012.

Goddard, John. *Agatha Christie's Golden Age*. London: Stylish Eye Press, 2018.

Green, Julius. *Curtain Up: Agatha Christie: A Life in the Theatre*. New York: HarperCollins, 2015.

Haining, Peter. *Agatha Christie's Poirot: A Celebration of the Great Detective*. London: Boxtree Ltd., 1995

Hart, Anne. *The Life and Times of Miss Jane Marple: A Delightful Biography of Agatha Christie's Most Beloved Detective*. New York: Dodd, Mead & Company, 1985.

Hart, Anne. *The Life and Times of Hercule Poirot: A Lively, Fictionalized Biography of Agatha Christie's Most Famous Detective*. New York: G.P. Putnam's & Sons, 1990.

Palmer, Scott. *The Films of Agatha Christie*. London: B.T. Batsford Ltd., 1993

Riley, Dick and Pam McAllister, eds. *The Bedside, Bathtub, and Armchair Companion to Agatha Christie*. New York: Frederick Ungar Publishing Co., 1979

Riley, Dick and Pam McAllister, eds. *The New Bedside, Bathtub, and Armchair Companion to Agatha Christie*. New York: Frederick Ungar Publishing Co., 1986

Sanders, Dennis and Len Lovallo. *The Agatha Christie Companion: The Complete Guide to Agatha Christie's Life and Work*. New York: Avenel Books, 1984.

Sheeran, Peter. *Swigatha: A Re-Read of Agatha Christie*. 2021.

Suchet, David. *Poirot and Me*. London: Headline Books, 2013.

Wagstaff, Vanessa and Stephen Poole. *Agatha Christie: A Reader's Companion*. London: Aurum Press, Ltd., 2004.

Zemboy, James. *The Detective Novels of Agatha Christie: A Reader's Guide*. Jefferson, N.C., 2008.

Websites

Agatha Christie Ltd. (https://agathachristie.com/)

Agatha Christie Wiki (https://agathachristie.fandom.com/wiki/Main_Page)

Internet Movie Database (https://imdb.com/)

Investigating Agatha Christie's Poirot (https://investigatingpoirot.blogspot.com/)

Reelstreets (https://www.reelstreets.com/)

TV Locations U.K. (http://tvlocations.net/)

Wikipedia

Acknowledgments

Many people made this book possible besides the actors, actresses, writers, directors, set designers, costumers, makeup artists, and producers who brought Agatha to the screen.

Denise Philips of the Hershey Public Library was instrumental. As our interlibrary loan expert, she got the DVDs we needed. This book would have been far less complete without her.

Dimitri, Madeline, Lulu, and Sasha danced for their treats on Agatha movie nights. They ensured a bigger audience on social media than we would have gotten on our own.

Our kids put up with mom and dad hunting down and watching obscure films and were grateful we didn't insist they watch along with us.

Most of all, I want to thank my adored husband, Bill. It was his idea in the first place and his editing chops and mad layout skills made the book you see.

About the Author

Teresa Peschel never planned to become a writer, nor did she plan to become an expert on film versions of Agatha Christie stories. She always read mysteries but didn't seek out Agatha's writing. Then she got a laptop of her very own, and began writing to fill the website (peschelpress.com).

As a supportive wife, Teresa read and edited Bill's annotations to Agatha's first six novels. She got more and more interested and one thing led to another, resulting in this book in your hands.

At various times, Teresa has been a sales clerk, a college student, a naval officer, a housewife, and a mother. She gardens, sews, reads, writes, and is interested in sustainability, science fiction and fantasy, and answering in her own fiction (as Odessa Moon) the basic questions that so many sci-fi and fantasy authors skip. Who's taking care of those kids? Who's feeding the family? Do caregivers matter or have minds of their own? Is it possible to become more?

Agatha would tell you, yes. It's quite possible to reinvent yourself. Her books have been reinvented in film, many of them numerous times. The results haven't always been stellar, but they've always kept her in the public eye.

Teresa Dimitri Madeline Lulu Sasha

Index

This index lists films by their title. Foreign films are cross-referenced in their original language, the translated version, and the original novel. Also indexed are the actors and actresses who played Hercule Poirot, Miss Marple, Tommy and Tuppence, and Agatha Christie. As of 2023, all of Agatha's novels have been filmed except for *Death Comes as the End* (1945), *Destination Unknown* (1954), *Passenger to Frankfurt* (1970), and *Postern of Fate* (1973). *They Came to Baghdad* (1951) was filmed in 1952 for Westinghouse Studio One with Bea Arthur but that film is lost. No Mary Westmacott novels have been filmed.

Quality of Movie Ratings Index

5 Stars

4¾ Stars

4½ Stars

4 Stars

3½ Stars

3 Stars

2½ Stars

2 Stars

1½ Stars

1 Star

Unratable

Made in the USA
Monee, IL
21 July 2024

62361538R00240